Second Edition

The 8088 and 8086 Microprocessors
Programming, Interfacing, Software, Hardware, and Applications

Including the 80286, 80386, 80486, and Pentium™ Processors

WALTER A. TRIEBEL
Intel Corporation

AVTAR SINGH
San Jose State University

PRENTICE HALL
Upper Saddle River, New Jersey   Columbus, Ohio

To my daughter, Lindsey Triebel
—Walter A. Triebel

To my children: Jasbir, Harjeet, and Shara
—Avtar Singh

Library of Congress Cataloging-in-Publication Data

Triebel, Walter A.
   The 8088 and 8086 microprocessors : programming, interfacing,
software, hardware, and applications / Walter A. Triebel, Avtar
Singh. — 2nd ed.
     p.   cm.
   Includes bibliographical references and index.
   ISBN 0-13-367897-0
   1. Intel 8088 (Microprocessor)   2. Intel 8086 (Microprocessor)
I. Avtar Singh II. Title.
QA76.8.I292T77 1977
004.165—dc20   96-17896
                                         CIP

Cover photo: © Michael W. Davidson/Photo Researchers, Inc.
Acquisitions Editor: Charles E. Stewart, Jr.
Production Editor: Mary M. Irvin
Design Coordinator: Jill E. Bonar
Cover Designer: Brian Deep
Production Manager: Pamela A. Bennett
Editorial/Production Supervision: WordCrafters Editorial Services, Inc.

This book was set in Times Roman by Bi-Comp, Inc., and was printed and bound by Book
Press. The cover was printed by Phoenix Color Corp.

 © 1997, 1991 by Prentice-Hall, Inc.
Simon & Schuster/A Viacom Company
Upper Saddle River, New Jersey 07458

Printed in the United States of America
10 9 8 7 6 5 4 3 2

ISBN: 0-13-367897-0

Prentice-Hall International (UK) Limited, *London*
Prentice-Hall of Australia Pty. Limited, *Sydney*
Prentice-Hall of Canada, Inc., *Toronto*
Prentice-Hall Hispanoamericana, S. A., *Mexico*
Prentice-Hall of India Private Limited, *New Delhi*
Prentice-Hall of Japan, Inc., *Tokyo*
Simon & Schuster Asia Pte. Ltd., *Singapore*
Editora Prentice-Hall do Brasil, Ltda., *Rio de Janeiro*

Preface

Today Intel's 80x86 family of microprocessors is the most widely used architecture in modern microcomputer systems. The family includes both 16-bit microprocessors, such as the 8088, 8086, and 80286 processors, and 32-bit microprocessors, such as the 80386, 80486, and Pentium™ processors. The 8088, which is the 8-bit bus version of the 8086, is the microprocessor employed in the original IBM personal computer (PC). The 8088 and 8086 microprocessors were also used by many other manufacturers to make personal computers compatible with IBM's original PC. Moreover, IBM's original personal computer advanced technology (PCAT) was designed with the 80286 microprocessor. Like the PC, PCAT-compatible personal computers were made by many other manufacturers, and today they are built with 80486 and Pentium™-processor-based microcomputers. Intel's 80x86 family of microprocessors are also used in a wide variety of other electronic equipment.

The 8088 and 8086 Microprocessors: Programming, Interfacing, Software, Hardware, and Applications, 2nd edition, is a thorough study of the 8088 and 8086 microprocessors, their microcomputer system architectures, and the circuitry used in the design of the microcomputer of the original IBM PC. This new edition has been expanded to include extensive coverage of the 80286, 80386, 80486, and Pentium™ processors.

This book is written for use as a textbook in courses on microprocessors at vocational schools, colleges, and universities. The intended use is in a one-semester course in microprocessor technology that emphasizes both assembly language software and microcomputer circuit design. Individuals involved in the design of microprocessor-based electronic equipment need a systems-level understanding of the 80x86 microcomputer, that is, a thorough understanding of both their software and hardware. The first part of this book explores the software architecture of the 8088 and 8086 microprocessors and teaches the reader how to write, execute, and debug assembly language programs. In order to be successful at writing assembly language programs for the 8088/8086, one must learn:

1. *Software architecture*: the internal registers, flags, memory organization and stack, and how they are used from a software point of view.
2. *Software development tools*: how to use the commands of the program debugger (DEBUG) that is available in DOS to assemble, execute, and debug instructions and programs.
3. *Instruction set*: the function of each of the instructions in the instruction set, the permissible operand variations, and how to write statements using the instructions.
4. *Programming techniques*: basic techniques of programming, such as flowcharting, jumps, loops, strings, subroutines, and parameter passing.
5. *Applications.* The reader is led step by step through the process of writing programs for several practical applications. Examples are a block move routine, average calculating routine, and a data table sort routine.

All of this material is developed in detail in Chapters 2 through 6. In this new edition, many additions have been made to enhance coverage of the topic by making it more practical. For instance, examples are used to demonstrate practical concepts such as 32-bit addition and subtraction, masking of bits, and the use of branch and loop operations to implement IF-THEN-ELSE, REPEAT-UNTIL, and WHILE-DO program structures. In addition, the various steps of the assembly language program development cycle are explored.

The study of software architecture, instruction set, and assembly language programming is closely coupled with use of the DEBUG program on the PC. That is, the line-by-line assembler in DEBUG is used to assemble instructions and programs into the memory of the PC, while other DEBUG commands are used to execute and debug the programs. In this new edition, the use of a practical 80x86 assembler program, the Microsoft MASM Assembler, has been included. Using MASM and other PC-based software development tools, the student learns to create a source program; assemble the program; form a run module; and load, run, and debug a program.

The second part of the book examines the hardware architecture of microcomputers built with the 8088 and 8086 microprocessors. To understand the hardware design of an 8088- or 8086-based microcomputer system, the reader must begin by first understanding the function and operation of each of its hardware interfaces: memory, input/output, and interrupt. After this, the role of each of these subsystems can be explored relative to overall microcomputer system operation. It is this material that is presented in Chapters 7 through 11.

We begin in Chapter 7 by examining the architecture of the 8088 and 8086 microprocessors from a hardware point of view. Included is information such as pin layout, minimum and maximum mode signal interfaces, signal functions, and clock requirements. The latter part of Chapter 7 covers the memory interface of the 8088/8086. This material includes extensive coverage of memory bus cycles, address maps, memory interface circuits, program storage memory (ROM, PROM, and EPROM), and data storage memory (SRAM and DRAM). Practical bus interface circuit and memory subsystem design techniques are also examined.

This hardware introduction is followed by separate studies of the architectural characteristics, operation, and circuit designs for the input/output and interrupt interfaces of the 8088- and 8086-based microcomputer in Chapters 8 and 9, respectively. This material includes information such as the function of the signals at each of the interfaces, input/output and interrupt acknowledge bus cycle activity, and examples of typical interface circuit designs. Included in these chapters is detailed coverage of the VLSI peripheral ICs, such as the 8255A, 8253, 8237A, and 8259A.

The hardware design section continues in Chapter 10 with a study of the 8088-based microcomputer design used in the IBM PC. We present the circuitry used in the design of the memory subsystem, input/output interfaces, and interrupt interface on the system processor board of the PC. This chapter demonstrates a practical implementation of the material presented in the prior chapters on microcomputer interfacing techniques.

Much new material on hardware operation, design, and troubleshooting has been included in the second edition of the textbook. For example, in the input/output chapter, circuits and programs for polling switches, lighting LEDs, scanning displays and keyboards, and printing characters at a parallel printer port have been added. Also added is discussion of a number of additional peripheral IC devices; for instance, the 8250 UART and 8279 keyboard/display controller are studied. Finally, a complete chapter has been added covering PC bus interfacing and circuit construction, testing, and troubleshooting.

The third part of the textbook, which is new to the the second edition, provides detailed coverage of the other microprocessors of the 80x86 family: the 80286, 80386, 80486, and Pentium™ processors. Throughout these chapters, the focus is on how the processor's software and hardware architecture differs from that of the earlier family members. Advanced topics covered include real mode and protected mode operation, pipelining, virtual memory, cache memory, data and address parity, instruction set extensions, system control instructions, descriptors, paging, protection, multitasking, and virtual 8086 mode.

End-of-chapter Assignments provide questions to strengthen and reinforce students' understanding of the material presented in each chapter. Supplementary materials available from Prentice Hall are a solutions manual, transparencies, and a DOS-compatible diskette that contains the programs used in the book.

W.A.T.
A.S.

Contents

Contents   **vii**

Contents   ix

▲ 13   THE 80386, 80486, AND PENTIUM™ PROCESSOR FAMILIES: SOFTWARE ARCHITECTURE   740

▲ 14   THE 80386, 80486, AND PENTIUM™ PROCESSOR FAMILIES: HARDWARE ARCHITECTURE   818

Introduction to Microprocessors and Microcomputers

▲ 1.1 INTRODUCTION

In the past decade, most of the important advances in computer system technology have been closely related to the development of high-performance 16- and 32-bit microprocessor architectures and the microcomputer systems built with them. During this period, there had been a major change in the direction of businesses away from minicomputers to smaller, lower-cost microcomputers. The *IBM personal computer* (the PC, as it has become known), which was introduced in mid-1981, was one of the earliest microcomputers that used a 16-bit microprocessor, the 8088, as its central processing unit. A few years later it was followed by another IBM personal computer, the *PC/AT* (personal computer advanced technology). This new system was implemented using the more powerful 80286 microprocessor.

The PC and PC/AT quickly became cornerstones of the evolutionary process from minicomputer to microcomputer. In 1985 an even more powerful microprocessor, the 80386DX, was introduced. The 80386DX was Intel Corporation's first 32-bit member of the 8086 family of microprocessors. Availability of the 80386DX quickly lead to a new generation of very high performance PC/ATs. In the years that followed, Intel expanded its 32-bit architecture offering with the 80486 and Pentium™ processor families. These processors brought a new level of performance and capability to the personal computer marketplace. Today 80486 and Pentium™ processor based PC/AT microcomputers represent the industry standard computer platform.

Since the introduction of the IBM PC, the microprocessor market has matured significantly. Today, several complete families of 16- and 32-bit microprocessors are available. They all include support products such as *very large-scale integrated* (VLSI) peripheral devices, emulators, and high-level software languages. Over the same period of time, these higher-performance microprocessors have become more widely used in the design of new electronic equipment and computers. This book presents a detailed study of the software and hardware architectures of Intel Corporation's 8088 and 8086 microprocessors. An introduction to the 80286, 80386, 80486, and Pentium™ processors is also included.

In this chapter we begin our study with an introduction to microprocessors and microcomputers. The following topics are discussed:

1. The IBM and IBM-compatible personal computers: reprogrammable microcomputers
2. General architecture of a microcomputer system
3. Evolution of the Intel microprocessor architecture

▲ 1.2 THE IBM AND IBM-COMPATIBLE PERSONAL COMPUTERS: REPROGRAMMABLE MICROCOMPUTERS

The IBM personal computer (the PC), which is shown in Fig. 1.1, was IBM's first entry into the microcomputer market. After its introduction in mid-1981, market acceptance of the PC grew by leaps and bounds so that it quickly became the leading personal computer architecture. One of the important keys to its success is that an enormous amount of application software became available for the machine. Today, there are more than 50,000 off-the-shelf software packages available for use with the PC. They include business applications, software languages, educational programs, games, and even alternate operating systems.

Another reason for the IBM PC's success was the fact that it was an open system. By *open system*, we mean that the functionality of the PC can be expanded by simply adding boards into the system. Some examples of add-in hardware features are additional memory, a modem, serial communication interfaces, and a local area network interface. This system expansion is provided by the PC's expansion bus—five card slots in the original PC's chassis. IBM defined an 8-bit expansion bus standard known as the *I/O Channel*, and provided this information to other manufacturers so that they could build different types of add-in products for the PC. Just as for software, a wide variety of add-in boards quickly became available. The result was a very flexible system that could be easily adapted to a wide variety of applications. For instance, PCs can be enhanced with add-in hardware to permit their use as graphics terminals, to synthesize music, and even for the control of industrial equipment.

The success of the PC caused IBM to introduce additional family members. IBM's *PCXT* is shown in Fig. 1.2 and an 80286 based PC/AT is illustrated in Fig. 1.3. The PCXT employed the same system architecture as that of the original PC. It was also designed with the 8088 microprocessor, but had one of the floppy disk

Figure 1.1 Original IBM personal computer. (Courtesy of International Business Machines Corporation)

drives replaced with a 10M-byte hard disk drive. The original PC/AT was designed with a 6-MHz 80286 microprocessor and defined a new open system bus architecture that today is called the *industry standard architecture* (ISA). This architecture provides a 16-bit, higher-performance I/O expansion bus.

Today, 80486- and Pentium™ processor-based ISA PCs, not PCXTs, are the main stays of the personal computer marketplace. Figure 1.4 shows a popular Pentium™ processor-based PC/AT-compatible personal computer. Most of the

Figure 1.2 PCXT personal computer. (Courtesy of International Business Machines Corporation)

Figure 1.3 PC/AT personal computer. (Courtesy of International Business Machines Corporation)

systems that are implemented with the Pentium™ processor have either an ISA or *extended industry standard architecture* (EISA) bus and a second bus known as the *peripheral component interface* (PCI) *bus*. This new bus is a high speed I/O data bus intended for connection of high performance I/O interfaces, such as graphics, video, and high speed *local area network* (LAN). The PCI bus supports 32-bit and 64-bit data transfers and its data transfer rate is more than 10 times that of the ISA bus.

In 1987, IBM introduced a new family of personal computers called the *Personal System/2* which originally included five models: Model 30, Model 50, Model 60, Model 70, and Model 80. All but the Model 30 employ another new, high-performance bus architecture known as the *Micro Channel*. This bus architecture can be either 16- or 32-bits. Model 30 employs the older ISA expansion bus. Later

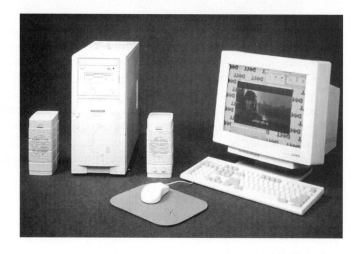

Figure 1.4 Dell Opti Plex GXMT 5133 Pentium™ processor-based PC/AT-compatible personal computer. (Courtesy of Dell Computer Corp.)

Figure 1.5 Personal System 2, Model 25. (Courtesy of International Business Machines Corporation)

the family was expanded with Models 25, 55, 65, 90, and 95. Figure 1.5 shows a Personal System/2 Model 25. This model uses an 8-MHz 8086 microprocessor and is implemented with an expansion bus that is compatible with the original PC's I/O Channel. These machines offer a wide variety of computing capabilities, range of performance, and software base for use in business and at home.

The IBM PC or a PC compatible is an example of a *reprogrammable microcomputer*. By reprogrammable microcomputer we mean that it is intended to run programs for a wide variety of applications. For example, one could use the PC with a standard application package for accounting or inventory control. In this type of application, the primary task of the microcomputer is to analyze and process a large amount of data, known as the *data base*. Another user could be running a word-processing software package. This is an example of a data input/output-intensive task. The user enters text information, which is reorganized by the microcomputer and then output to a diskette or printer. As a third example, a programmer uses a language, such as FORTRAN, to write programs for a scientific application. Here the primary function of the microcomputer is to solve complex mathematical problems. The personal computer used for each of these applications is the same; the difference is in the software application that the microcomputer is running. That is, the microcomputer is simply reprogrammed to run the new application.

Let us now look at what a microcomputer is and how it differs from the other classes of computers. Evolution of the computer marketplace over the last 25 years has taken us from very large *mainframe computers* to smaller *minicomputers*, and now to even smaller *microcomputers*. These three classes of computers did not originally replace each other. They all coexisted in the marketplace. Computer users had the opportunity to select the computer that best met their needs. The mainframe computer was used in an environment where it serviced a large number of users. For instance, a large university or institution would select a mainframe computer for its data-processing center. Here it would service hundreds of users. Mainframes are still widely used today to satisfy large computer requirements.

The minicomputer had been the primary computer solution for the small, multi-user business environment. In this environment, a range from several to a hundred users connect to the system with terminals. In this way, they all share the same computer system and many of these users may be actively working on the computer at the same time. An important characteristic of this computer system configuration is that all computational power resides at the minicomputer. The user terminals are what are known as *dumb terminals*; that is, they are not self-sufficient computers. If the minicomputer is not working, all users are down and cannot do any work at their terminals. Examples of a user community that would traditionally use a minicomputer are a department at a university or in business for a multiuser-dedicated need such as application software development.

Managers in a department may select a microcomputer, such as the PC/AT, for their personal needs, such as word processing and data-base management. The original IBM PC was called a personal computer because it was initially intended to be a single user system. That is, the user's personal computer. Several people could use the same computer, but only one at a time. Today, the microcomputer has taken over most of the traditional minicomputer user base. High-feature, high-performance PC/ATs have replaced the minicomputer as a *file server.* Many users have their personal computers attached to the file server through a *local area network*. However, in this more modern computer system architecture, all users also have local computational power in their own PC/ATs. The file server extends the computational power and system resources such as memory available to the user. If the file server is not operating, users can still do work by using their individual personal computers.

Along the evolutionary path from mainframes to microcomputers, the basic concepts of computer architecture have not changed. Just like the mainframe and minicomputer, the microcomputer is a general-purpose electronic data-processing system intended for use in a wide variety of applications. The key difference is that microcomputers, such as the IBM PC/AT, employ the newest VLSI circuit technology *microprocessing unit* (MPU) to implement the system. Microcomputers, such as a Pentium™ processor-based PC/AT, which are designed for the high-performance end of the microcomputer market, are physically smaller computer systems, outperform comparable minicomputer systems, and are available at a much lower cost.

▲ 1.3 GENERAL ARCHITECTURE OF A MICROCOMPUTER SYSTEM

The *hardware* of a microcomputer system can be divided into four functional sections: the *input unit, microprocessing unit, memory unit,* and *output unit.* The block diagram of Fig. 1.6 shows this general microcomputer architecture. Each of these units has a special function in terms of overall system operation. Next we will look at each of these sections in more detail.

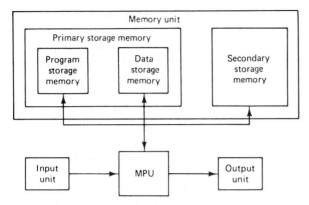

Figure 1.6 General architecture of a microcomputer system.

The heart of a microcomputer is its microprocessing unit (MPU). The MPU of a microcomputer is implemented with a VLSI device known as a *microprocessor*. A microprocessor is a general-purpose processing unit built into a single integrated circuit (IC). The microprocessor used in the original IBM PC is Intel Corporation's 8088, which is shown in Fig. 1.7.

Earlier we indicated that the 8088 is a 16-bit microprocessor. To be more accurate, it is the 8-bit external bus version in Intel's 8086 family of 16-bit microprocessors. Even though the 8088 has an 8-bit external bus, its internal architecture is 16 bits in length and it can directly process 16-bit-wide data. For this reason, we can consider the 8088 a 16-bit microprocessor.

The 8088 MPU is the part of the microcomputer that executes instructions of the program and processes data. It is responsible for performing all arithmetic operations and making the logical decisions initiated by the computer's program. In addition to arithmetic and logic functions, the MPU controls overall system operation.

The input and output units are the means by which the MPU communicates with the outside world. Input units, such as the *keyboard* on the IBM PC, allow

Figure 1.7 8088 microprocessor. (Courtesy of Intel Corporation)

the user to input information or commands to the MPU. For instance, a programmer could key in the lines of a BASIC program from the keyboard. Many other input devices are available for the PC, two examples being a *mouse*, for implementing a more user-friendly input interface, and a *joystick*, for use when playing video games.

The most widely used output devices of a PC are the *display* and the *printer*. The output unit in a microcomputer is used to give feedback to the user and for producing documented results. For example, key entries from the keyboard are echoed back to the display. By looking at the screen of the display, the user can confirm that the correct entry was made. Moreover, the results produced by the MPU's processing can be either displayed or printed. For our earlier example of a BASIC program, once it is entered and corrected a listing of the instructions could be printed. Alternate output devices are also available for the microcomputer; for instance, it can be equipped with a color video display instead of the monochrome video display.

The memory unit in a microcomputer is used to *store* information, such as number or character data. By store we mean that memory has the ability to hold this information for processing or for outputting at a later time. Programs that define how the computer is to operate and process data also reside in memory.

In the microcomputer system, memory can be divided into two different types, called *primary storage memory* and *secondary storage memory*. Secondary storage memory is used for long-term storage of information that is not currently being used. For example, it can hold programs, files of data, and files of information. In the original IBM PC, the *floppy disk drives* represented the secondary storage memory subsystems. It had two $5\frac{1}{4}$-inch drives that used double-sided, double-density *floppy-diskette* storage media that could each store up to 360K (360,000) bytes of data. This floppy diskette is an example of a removable media. That is, to use the diskette it is inserted into the drive and locked in place. If the diskette is either full or one with a different file or program is needed, the diskette is simply unlocked, removed, and another diskette installed.

The IBM PCXT also employed a second type of secondary storage device, called a *hard disk drive*. Typical hard disk sizes are 20MB (20 million), 40MB, 80MB, 420MB, and 1GB (1000 million) bytes. Earlier we pointed out that the original IBM PCXT was equipped with a 10MB hard disk drive; the hard disk drive of the original IBM PC/AT was 20MB. The hard disk drive differs from the floppy disk drive in that the media is fixed. This means that the media cannot be removed. However, being fixed is not a problem because the storage capacity of the media is so much larger.

Both the floppy diskette and hard disk are examples of read/write media. That is, a file of data can be read in from or written out to the storage media in the drive. Another secondary storage device that is becoming very popular in personal computers today is a CD drive. Here a removable *compact disk* (CD) is used as the storage media. This media has a very large storage capacity, more than 600K bytes, but is read-only. This means you cannot write information onto a CD for storage. For this reason, it is normally used for storage of large programs or files of data that are not to be changed.

Primary storage memory is normally smaller in size and used for temporary storage of active information, such as the operating system of the microcomputer, the program that is currently being run, and the data that it is processing. In Fig. 1.6 we see that primary storage memory is further subdivided into *program storage memory* and *data storage memory*. The program section of memory is used to store instructions of the operating system and application programs. The data section normally contains data that are to be processed by the programs as they are executed: for example, text files for a word-processor program or a data base for a data-base management program. However, programs can also be loaded into data memory for execution.

Typically, primary storage memory is implemented with both *read-only memory* (ROM) and *random-access read/write memory* (RAM) integrated circuits. The original IBM PC has 48K bytes of ROM and can be configured with 256K bytes of RAM without adding a memory expansion board. Modern PC/ATs made with 80486 and Pentium™ processors are typically equipped with 8MB of RAM.

Data, whether it represents numbers, characters, or instructions of a program, can be stored in either ROM or RAM. In the IBM PC a small part of the operating system and BASIC language are made resident to the computer by supplying them in ROM. By using ROM, this information is made *nonvolatile*—that is, the information is not lost if power is turned off. This type of memory can only be read from; it cannot be written into. On the other hand, data that are to be processed and information that frequently changes must be stored in a type of primary storage memory from which they can be read by the microprocessor, modified through processing, and written back for storage. This requires a type of memory that can be both read from and written into. For this reason, they are stored in RAM instead of ROM.

Earlier we pointed out that the instructions of a program can also be stored in RAM. In fact, the *DOS 5.0 operating system* for the PC is provided on diskettes, but to be used it must be loaded into the RAM of the microcomputer. Normally the operating system, supplied on floppy diskettes, is first read from the diskettes and written onto the hard disk. This is called *copying* of the operating system onto the hard disk. After this, the floppy-diskette version of the DOS may not be used again. The PC is set up so that when it is turned on the DOS program is automatically read from the hard disk, written into the RAM, and then run.

RAM is an example of a *volatile* memory. That is, when power is turned off, the data that it holds are lost. This is why the DOS program must be reloaded from the hard disk each time the PC is turned on.

▲ 1.4 EVOLUTION OF THE INTEL MICROPROCESSOR ARCHITECTURE

The principal way in which microprocessors and microcomputers are categorized is in terms of the maximum number of binary bits in the data they process, that is, their word length. Over time, five standard data widths have evolved for microprocessors and microcomputers: *4 bit*, *8 bit*, *16 bit*, *32 bit*, and *64 bit*.

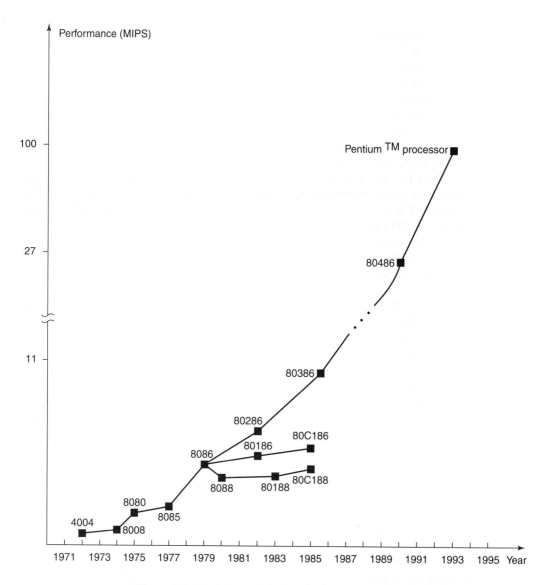

Figure 1.8 Evolution of the Intel microprocessor architecture.

Figure 1.8 illustrates the evolution of Intel's microprocessors since their introduction in 1972. The first microprocessor, the 4004, was designed to process data arranged as 4-bit words. This organization is also referred to as a *nibble* of data.

The 4004 implemented a very low-performance microcomputer by today's standards. This low performance and limited system capability restricted its use to simpler, special-purpose applications. A common use was in electronic calculators.

In 1974 a second generation of microprocessors began to be introduced. These devices, the 8008, 8080, and 8085, are 8-bit microprocessors. That is, they were all designed to process 8-bit (one-byte-wide) data instead of 4-bit data. The 8080, identified in Fig. 1.8, was introduced in 1975.

These newer 8-bit microprocessors were characterized by higher-performance operation, larger system capabilities, and greater ease of programming. They were able to provide the system requirements for many applications that could not be satisfied with the earlier 4-bit microprocessors. These extended capabilities led to widespread acceptance of multichip 8-bit microcomputers for special-purpose system designs. Examples of these dedicated applications are electronic instruments, cash registers, and printers.

Plans for development of third-generation 16-bit microprocessors were announced by many of the leading semiconductor manufacturers in the mid-1970s. Looking at Fig. 1.8, we see that Intel's first 16-bit microprocessor, the 8086, became available in 1979 and was followed the next year by its 8-bit bus version, the 8088. This was the birth of Intel's 8086 family architecture. Other family members, such as the 80286, 80186, and 80188, were introduced in the years that followed.

These 16-bit microprocessors provided higher performance and had the ability to satisfy a broad scope of special-purpose and general-purpose microcomputer applications. They all have the ability to handle 8-bit, 16-bit, and special-purpose data types. Moreover, their powerful instruction sets are more in line with those provided by a minicomputer.

In 1985, Intel Corporation introduced its first 32-bit microprocessor, the 80386DX. The 80386DX microprocessor brought true minicomputer-level performance to the microcomputer system. This device was followed by a 16-bit external bus version, the 80386SX in 1988. Intel's second generation of 32-bit microprocessors, called the 80486DX and 80486SX, became available in 1990 and 1991 respectively. They were followed by yet a higher-performance family, the Pentium™ processors, in 1993.

Microprocessor Performance—MIPS

In Fig. 1.8 the 8086 microprocessor families are illustrated relative to their performance. Here performance is measured in what are called *MIPS*; that is, how many million instructions they can execute per second. Today, the number of MIPS provided by a microprocessor is the standard most frequently used to compare performance. Notice that performance has been vastly increased with each new generation of microprocessor. For instance, the performance identified for the 80386DX corresponds to a device operating at 33 MHz and equals approximately 11 MIPS. With the introduction of the 33-MHz 80486DX, the level of performance capability of the architecture was raised to approximately 27 MIPS. This shows that performance of the 8086 architecture was more than doubled with the introduction of the 80486DX microprocessor.

The MIPS used in this chart are known as Drystone V1.1 MIPS. This means that they are measured by running a test program called the *Drystone program* and that the resulting performance measurements are normalized to those or a VAX 1.1 computer (VAX 1.1 was a minicomputer manufactured by Digital Equipment

Corporation). Therefore, we say that the 80486DX is capable of delivering up to 27 VAX MIPS of performance.

Transistor Density

The evolution of microprocessors is made possible by advances in semiconductor process technology. Semiconductor device geometry decreased from about five microns in the early 70s to submicron today. The smaller geometry permits integration of an order-of-magnitude more transistors into the same-size chip and at the same time has led to higher operating speeds. In Fig. 1.9 we see that the 4004 contained about 10,000 transistors. Transistor density was increased to about 30,000 with the development of the 8086 in 1979. With the introduction of the 80286, the transistor count was increased to approximately 140,000. The 275,000 transistors of

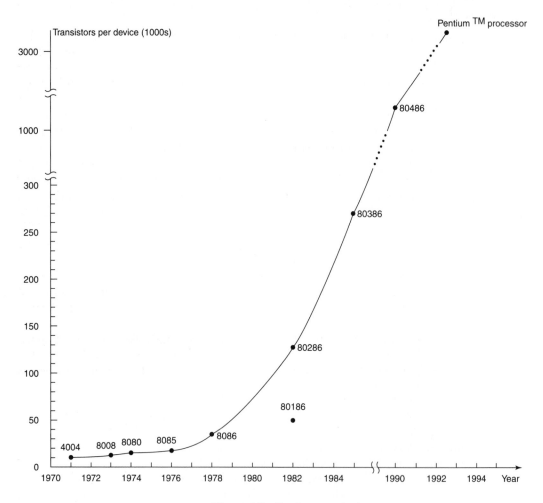

Figure 1.9 Device complexity.

the 80386DX almost doubled transistor density. The 80486DX is the first family member with a density above the one million transistor level (1,200,000 transistors). And with the Pentium™ complexity has risen to more than three million transistors.

Reprogrammable and Embedded Microprocessors

Microprocessors can be classified according to the type of application for which they have been designed. In Fig. 1.10 we have placed Intel microprocessors into two application-oriented categories: *reprogrammable microprocessors* and *embedded microprocessors and microcontrollers*. Initially devices such as the 8080 were most widely used as *special-purpose microcomputers*. By special-purpose microcomputer we mean a system that has been tailored to meet the needs of a specific application. These special-purpose microcomputers were used in *embedded control applications*, that is, an application in which the microcomputer performs a dedicated control function.

Embedded control applications are further divided into those that involve primarily *event control* and those that require *data control*. An example of an embedded control application that is primarily event control is a microcomputer used for industrial process control. Here the program of the microprocessor is used to initiate a timed sequence of events. On the other hand, an application that focuses more on data control than event control is a hard disk controller interface. In this case, a block of data that is to be processed, for example a file of data, must be quickly transferred from secondary storage memory to primary storage memory.

The spectrum of embedded control applications requires a wide variety of system features and performance levels. Devices developed specifically for the needs of this marketplace have stressed low cost and high integration. In Fig. 1.10 we see that the earlier multichip 8080 solutions were initially replaced by highly integrated 8-bit, single-chip microcomputer devices such as the 8048 and 8051. These devices were tailored to work best as event controllers. For instance, the 8051 offers one-order-of-magnitude-higher performance than the 8080, a more powerful instruction set, and special on-chip functions such as ROM, RAM, an interval/event timer, a universal asynchronous receiver/transmitter (UART), and programmable parallel I/O ports. Today these type of embedded control devices are called *microcontrollers*.

Later, devices such as the 80C186XL, 80C188XL, and 80386EX were designed to better meet the needs of data-control applications. They are also highly integrated but have additional features, such as string instructions and direct-memory access

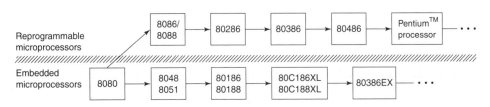

Figure 1.10   Embedded control and reprogrammable applications.

channels, which better handle the movement of data. They are known as embedded microprocessors.

The category of reprogrammable microprocessors represents the class of applications in which a microprocessor is used to implement a *general-purpose microcomputer*. Unlike a special-purpose microcomputer, a general-purpose microcomputer is intended to run a wide variety of applications; that is, while it is in use it can be easily reprogrammed to run a different application. Two examples of reprogrammable microcomputers are the personal computer and file server. In Fig. 1.10 we see that the 8086, 8088, 80286, 80386, 80486, and Pentium™ processor are the Intel microprocessors intended for use in this type of application.

Architectural compatibility is a critical need of microprocessors developed for use in reprogrammable applications. As shown in Fig. 1.11, each of the new members of the 8086/8088 family provides a superset of the earlier device's architecture. That is, the features offered by the 80386 microprocessor are a superset of the 80286 architecture and those of the 80286 are a superset of the original 8086/8088 architecture.

Actually the 80286, 80386, 80486, and Pentium™ processors can operate in either of two modes—the *real-address mode* or *protected-address mode*. When in the real mode, they operate like a high-performance 8086/8088. They can execute what is called the *base instruction set*, which is object code compatible with the 8086/8088. For this reason, operating systems and application programs written for the 8086 and 8088 run on the 80286, 80386, or 80486 architectures without modification. Further, a number of new instructions have been added in the instruction sets of the 80286, 80386, 80486, and Pentium™ processors to enhance their performance and functionality. We say that object code is *upward compatible* within the 8086 architecture. This means that 8086/8088 code will run on the 80286, 80386, 80486, and Pentium™ processors, but the reverse is not true if any of the new instructions are in use.

Microprocessors designed for implementing general-purpose microcomputers must offer more advanced system features than those of a microcontroller. For example, it needs to support and manage a large memory subsystem. The 80286 is capable of managing a one gigabyte (1GB) address space and the 80386 supports

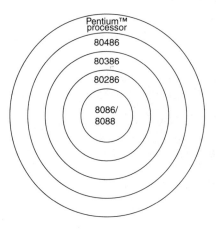

Figure 1.11 Code and system-level compatibility.

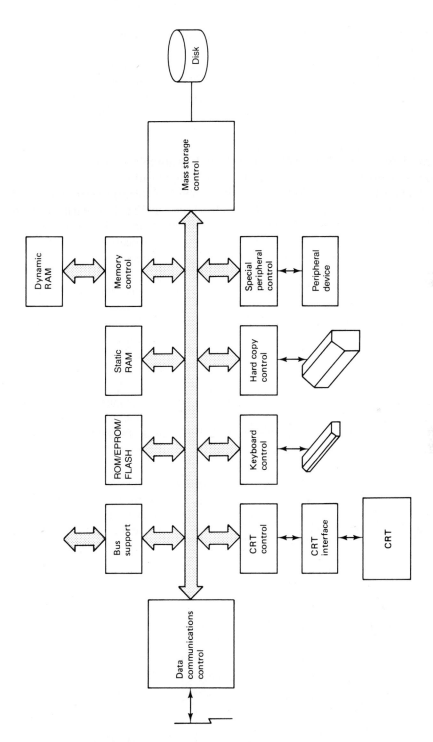

Figure 1.12 Peripheral support for the MPU.

64 terabyte (64T-byte) of memory. The architectures of the 80286, 80386, 80486DX, and Pentium™ processors have been enhanced with on-chip support for operating system functions such as *memory management*, *protection*, and *multitasking.* These new features become active only when the 80386 is operated in the protected mode. The 80386, 80486, and Pentium™ processors also have a special mode of operation known as *virtual 8086 mode* that permits 8086/8088 code to be run in the protected mode.

Reprogrammable microcomputers, such as those based on the 8086 family, require a wide variety of input/output resources. Figure 1.12 shows the kinds of interfaces that are frequently implemented in a personal computer or a minicomputer system. A large family of VLSI peripheral ICs are needed to support a reprogrammable microprocessor such as the 8086, 80286, 80386, 80486, and Pentium™ processors. Examples are floppy-disk controllers, hard-disk controllers, local-area-network controllers, and communication controllers. For this reason, the 8086, 8088, 80286, 80386, 80486, and Pentium™ processors are designed to implement a multichip microcomputer system. In this way a system can be easily configured with the appropriate set of I/O interfaces.

ASSIGNMENTS

Section 1.2

1. Which IBM personal computer employs the 8088 microprocessor?
2. What is meant by the term "open system"?
3. What is the I/O expansion bus of the original IBM PC called?
4. What does PC/AT stand for?
5. What does ISA stand for?
6. What bus architecture is used in the Model 80 Personal System/2?
7. What is a reprogrammable microcomputer?
8. Name the three classes of computers.
9. What are the main similarities and differences between the minicomputer and the microcomputer?
10. What does VLSI stand for?

Section 1.3

11. What are the four building blocks of a microcomputer system?
12. What is the heart of the microcomputer system called?
13. Is the 8088 an 8-bit or 16-bit microprocessor?
14. What is the primary input unit of the PC? Give two other examples of input units available for the PC.
15. What are the primary output devices of the PC?
16. Into what two sections is the memory of a PC partitioned?

17. What is the storage capacity of the standard $5\frac{1}{4}$-inch floppy diskette of the original PC? What is the storage capacity of the standard hard disk drive of the original PCXT?

18. What do ROM and RAM stand for?

19. How much ROM was provided in the original PC's processor board? What was the maximum amount of RAM that could be implemented on this processor board?

20. Why must DOS be reloaded from the hard disk each time power is turned on?

Section 1.4

21. What are the standard data word lengths for which microprocessors have been developed?

22. What was the first 4-bit microprocessor introduced by Intel Corporation? Eight-bit microprocessor? Sixteen-bit microprocessor? Thirty-two bit microprocessor?

23. Name five 16-bit members of the 8086 family architecture.

24. What does MIPS stand for?

25. Approximately how many MIPS are delivered by the 33 MHz 80486DX?

26. What is the name of the program that is used to run the MIPS measurement test for the data in Fig. 1.8?

27. Approximately how many transistors are used to implement the 8088 microprocessor? The 80286 microprocessor? The 80386DX microprocessor? The 80486DX microprocessor?

28. What is an embedded microcontroller?

29. Name the two groups into which embedded processors are categorized based on applications.

30. What is the difference between a multichip microcomputer and a single-chip microcomputer?

31. Name six 8086 family microprocessors intended for use in reprogrammable microcomputer applications.

32. Give the names for the 80386's two modes of operation.

33. What is meant by upward software compatibility relative to 8086 architecture microprocessors?

34. List three advanced architectural features provided by the 80386DX microprocessor.

35. Give three types of VLSI peripheral support devices needed in a reprogrammable microcomputer system.

Software Architecture of the 8088 and 8086 Microprocessors

▲ 2.1 INTRODUCTION

In this chapter we begin our study of the 8088 and 8086 microprocessor and assembly language programming. To program either the 8088 or 8086 using assembly language, we must understand how the microprocessor and its memory subsystem operate from a software point of view. For this reason, in this chapter, we will examine the *software architecture* of the 8088 and 8086 microprocessors. In the material that follows we will just refer to the 8088 microprocessor, but everything that is described for the 8088 also applies to the 8086. This is because the software architecture of the 8086 is identical to that of the 8088. The following topics are covered here:

1. Software—the microcomputer program
2. Internal architecture of the 8088/8086 microprocessor
3. Software model of the 8088/8086 microprocessor
4. Memory address space and data organization
5. Data types
6. Segment registers and memory segmentation
7. Dedicated and general use of memory
8. Instruction pointer
9. Data registers

10. Pointer and index registers

11. Status or flags register

12. Generating a memory address

13. The stack

14. Input/output address space

15. Addressing modes of the 8088/8086 microprocessor

▲ 2.2 SOFTWARE—THE MICROCOMPUTER PROGRAM

In this section, we begin our study of the 8088's software architecture with the topics of software and the microcomputer program. A microcomputer does not know how to process data. It must be told exactly what to do, where to get data, what to do with the data, and where to put the results when it is done. This is the job of *software* in a microcomputer system.

The sequence of commands that is used to tell a microcomputer what to do is called a *program*. Each command in the program is an *instruction*. A program may be simple and include just a few instructions, or very complex and contain more than 100,000 instructions. When the microcomputer is operating, it fetches and executes one instruction of the program after the other. In this way, the instructions of the program guide it step by step through the task that is to be performed.

Software refers to a wide variety of programs that can be run by a microcomputer. Examples are *languages*, *operating systems*, *application programs*, and *diagnostics*.

The native language of the IBM PC is the *machine language* of the 8088 microprocessor. Programs must always be coded in machine language before they can be run by the 8088. The 8088 microprocessor understands and performs operations for more than 100 instructions. A program written in machine language is often referred to as *machine code*. When expressed in machine code, instructions are encoded using 0s and 1s. A single machine language instruction can take anywhere from one to six bytes of code. Even though the 8088 only understands machine code, it is almost impossible to write programs directly in machine language. For this reason, programs are normally written in other languages, such as 8088 assembly language or a high-level language such as C.

In 8088 assembly language, each of the basic operations that can be performed by the 8088 microprocessor is described with alphanumeric symbols instead of with 0s and 1s. Each instruction is represented by a single *assembly language statement*. This statement must specify which operation is to be performed and what data are to be processed. For this reason, an instruction can be divided into two parts: its *operation code* (*opcode*) and its *operands*. The opcode is the part of the instruction that identifies the operation that is to be performed. For example, typical operations are add, subtract, and move. Each opcode is assigned a unique one- through five-letter combination. This letter combination is referred to as the *mnemonic* for the instruction. For example, the mnemonics for the earlier operations are ADD, SUB, and MOV. Operands describe the data that are to be processed as the microprocessor carries out the operation specified by the opcode. They identify whether the source and destination of the data are registers within the MPU or storage locations in data memory.

An example of an instruction written in 8088 assembly language is

```
ADD   AX,BX
```

This instruction says, "Add the contents of registers BX and AX together and put the sum in register AX." AX is called the *destination operand*, because it is the place where the result ends up, and BX is called the *source operand*.

An example of a complete assembly language statement is

```
START:   MOV AX,BX   ;Copy BX into AX
```

This statement begins with the word START:. START is an address identifier for the instruction MOV AX,BX. This type of identifier is known as a *label*. The instruction is followed by ;Copy BX into AX. This part of the statement is called a *comment*. Thus a general format for an assembly language statement is

```
LABEL:   INSTRUCTION   ;Comment
```

Programs written in assembly language are referred to as *source code*. An example of a short 8088 assembly language program is shown in Fig. 2.1(a). Notice that the program includes instruction statements with both a label and comment, instructions with a comment but no label, instructions without either a label or comment, and even statements that are just a comment. In fact, most statements do not have a label. An example of a statement without a label or comments is

```
MOV DS,AX
```

On the other hand, most statements have a comment. For instance, the statement

```
INC SI   ;Update pointers
```

has a comment, but no label. This type of documentation makes it easier for a program to be read, understood, and debugged. The comment part of the statement does not generate any machine code.

Assembly language programs cannot be directly executed by the 8088. They must still be converted to an equivalent machine language program for execution by the 8088. This conversion is done automatically by running the source program through what is called an *assembler*. Not all of the statements in the assembly language program of Fig. 2.1(a) are instruction statements. There are also statements that are used to control the translation process of the assembler. An example is the statement

$$DB \quad 64 \quad DUP(?)$$

This type of statement is known as a *pseudo-op statement* or *directive*. That is, it supplies directions to the assembler program. The machine language output produced by the assembler is called *object code*.

```
TITLE BLOCK-MOVE PROGRAM

        PAGE          ,132

COMMENT *This program moves a block of specified number of bytes
         from one place to another place*


;Define constants used in this program

        N=                  16        ;Bytes to be moved
        BLK1ADDR=           100H      ;Source block offset address
        BLK2ADDR=           120H      ;Destination block offset addr
        DATASEGADDR=        2000H     ;Data segment start address


STACK_SEG          SEGMENT           STACK 'STACK'
                   DB                64 DUP(?)
STACK_SEG          ENDS
CODE_SEG           SEGMENT           'CODE'
BLOCK              PROC        FAR
        ASSUME     CS:CODE_SEG,SS:STACK_SEG

;To return to DEBUG program put return address on the stack

                PUSH   DS
                MOV    AX, 0
                PUSH   AX

;Setup the data segment address

                MOV    AX, DATASEGADDR
                MOV    DS, AX

;Setup the source and destination offset adresses

                MOV    SI, BLK1ADDR
                MOV    DI, BLK2ADDR

;Setup the count of bytes to be moved

                MOV    CX, N

;Copy source block to destination block

NXTPT:          MOV    AH, [SI]       ;Move a byte
                MOV    [DI], AH
                INC    SI             ;Update pointers
                INC    DI
                DEC    CX             ;Update byte counter
                JNZ    NXTPT          ;Repeat for next byte
                RET                   ;Return to DEBUG program
BLOCK           ENDP
CODE_SEG        ENDS
        END         BLOCK             ;End of program
                (a)
```

Figure 2.1 (a) Example of an 8088 assembly language program. (b) Assembled version of the program.

```
 1
 2
 3                              TITLE BLOCK-MOVE PROGRAM
 4
 5                              PAGE        ,132
 6
 7                              COMMENT *This program moves a block of specified number of bytes
 8                                      from one place to another place*
 9
10
11                              ;Define constants used in this program
12
13 = 0010                          N=              16          ;Bytes to be moved
14 = 0100                          BLK1ADDR=       100H        ;Source block offset address
15 = 0120                          BLK2ADDR=       120H        ;Destination block offset addr
16 = 1020                          DATASEGADDR=1020H           ;Data segment start address
17
18
19 0000                             STACK_SEG       SEGMENT         STACK 'STACK'
20 0000  0040[                                      DB              64 DUP(?)
21       ??
22                      ]
23
24 0040                             STACK_SEG     ENDS
25
26
27 0000                             CODE_SEG      SEGMENT         'CODE'
28 0000                             BLOCK           PROC          FAR
29                                  ASSUME        CS:CODE_SEG,SS:STACK_SEG
30
31                              ;To return to DEBUG program put return address on the stack
32
33 0000  1E                         PUSH    DS
34 0001  B8 0000                    MOV     AX, 0
35 0004  50                         PUSH    AX
36
37                              ;Setup the data segment address
38
39 0005  B8 1020                    MOV     AX, DATASEGADDR
40 0008  8E D8                      MOV     DS, AX
41
42                              ;Setup the source and destination offset adresses
43
44 000A  BE 0100                    MOV     SI, BLK1ADDR
45 000D  BF 0120                    MOV     DI, BLK2ADDR
46
47                              ;Setup the count of bytes to be moved
48
49 0010  B9 0010                    MOV     CX, N
50
51                              ;Copy source block to destination block
52
53 0013  8A 24              NXTPT:  MOV     AH, [SI]              ;Move a byte
54 0015  88 25                      MOV     [DI], AH
55 0017  46                         INC     SI                   ;Update pointers
56 0018  47                         INC     DI
57 0019  49                         DEC     CX                   ;Update byte counter
```

Figure 2.1   (Continued)

```
58 001A   75 F7              JNZ      NXTPT        ;Repeat for next byte
59 001C   CB                 RET                   ;Return to DEBUG program
60 001D                      BLOCK    ENDP
61 001D                      CODE_SEG ENDS
62                           END      BLOCK        ;End of program
```

Segments and Groups:

N a m e	Length	Align	Combine	Class
CODE_SEG	001D	PARA	NONE	'CODE'
STACK_SEG	0040	PARA	STACK	'STACK'

Symbols:

N a m e	Type	Value	Attr	
BLK1ADDR	NUMBER	0100		
BLK2ADDR	NUMBER	0120		
BLOCK	F PROC	0000	CODE_SEG	Length = 001D
DATASEGADDR	NUMBER	1020		
N	NUMBER	0010		
NXTPT	L NEAR	0013	CODE_SEG	
@CPU	TEXT	0101h		
@FILENAME	TEXT	block		
@VERSION	TEXT	510		

```
    59 Source  Lines
    59 Total   Lines
    15 Symbols

47222 + 347542 Bytes symbol space free

     0 Warning Errors
     0 Severe  Errors
```

(b)

Figure 2.1   (Continued)

Figure 2.1(b) is the *listing* produced by assembling the assembly language source code in Fig. 2.1(a) with a macroassembler for the PC. Reading from left to right, this listing contains line numbers, addresses of memory locations, the machine language instructions, the original assembly language statements, and comments. For example, line 53, which is

```
0013 8A 24   NXTPT:  MOV AH,[SI]  ;Move a byte
```

shows that the assembly language instruction MOV AH,[SI] is encoded as 8A24 in machine language and that this 2-byte instruction is loaded into memory starting at address 0013_{16} and ending at address 0014_{16}. Note that for simplicity the machine language instructions are expressed in hexadecimal notation, not in binary form. Use of assembly language makes it much easier to write a program. But notice that there is still a one-to-one relationship between assembly and machine language instructions.

High-level languages make writing programs even easier. In a language such as BASIC, high-level commands such as FOR, NEXT, and GO are provided. These commands may no longer correspond to a single machine language statement. In fact, they may require many assembly language statements to be implemented. Again, the statements must be converted to machine code before it can be run on the 8088. The program that converts high-level-language statements to machine code instructions is called a *compiler*.

Some languages, for instance, BASIC, are not always compiled. Instead, *interpretive* versions of the language are available. When a program written in an interpretive form of BASIC is executed, each line of the program is interpreted just before it is executed and at that moment replaced with the corresponding machine language. It is the machine-code instructions that are executed by the 8088.

The question you may be asking yourself right now is: If it is so much easier to write programs with a high-level language, why is it important to know how to program the 8088 in its assembly language? Let us now answer this question.

We just pointed out that if a program is written in a high-level language, such as C, it must be compiled into machine code before it can be run on the 8088. The general nature with which compilers must be designed usually results in inefficient machine code. That is, the quality of the machine code that is produced for the program depends on the quality of the compiler program in use. What is found is that a compiled machine code implementation of a program that was written in a high-level language results in many more machine code instructions than an assembled version of an equivalent hand-written assembly language program. This leads us to the two key benefits derived from writing programs in assembly language: first, the machine code program that is produced will take up less memory space than the compiled version of the program; and second, it will execute faster.

Now we know the benefits attained by writing programs in assembly language, but we still do not know when these benefits are important. To be important, they must outweigh the additional effort that must be put into writing the program in assembly language instead of a high-level language. One of the major uses of assembly language programming is in *real-time applications*. By *real time* we mean that the task required by the application must be completed before any other input to the program can occur that will alter its operation. For example, the *device service routine* that controls the operation of the floppy-disk drive of the PC is a good example of the kind of program that is usually written in assembly language. This is because it is a segment of program that must closely control hardware of the microcomputer in real time. In this case, a program that is written in a high-level language probably could not respond quickly enough to control the hardware, and even if it could, operations performed with the disk subsystem would be much slower. Some other examples of hardware-related operations typically performed by routines written in assembly language are communication routines such as those that drive the display and printer in a personal computer and the I/O routines that scan the keyboard.

Assembly language is important not only for controlling hardware devices of the microcomputer system, but also when performing pure software operations. For instance, applications frequently require the microcomputer to search through a large table of data in memory looking for a special string of characters, say, a person's name. This type of operation can easily be performed by writing a program in a high-level language; however, for very large tables of data the search will take very long. By implementing the search routine through assembly language, the performance of the search operation is greatly improved. Other examples of software operations that may require implementation with high-performance routines derived with assembly language are *code translations*, such as from ASCII to EBCDIC, *table sort or search routines*, such as a bubble sort, and *mathematical routines*, such as those for floating-point arithmetic.

Not all parts of an application require real-time performance. For this reason, it is a common practice to mix, in the same program, routines developed using a high-level language and routines developed with assembly language. That is, assembly language is used to code those parts of the application that must perform real-time operations, and high-level language is used to write those parts that are not time critical. The machine code obtained by compiling or assembling the two types of program segments are linked together to form the final application program.

▲ 2.3 INTERNAL ARCHITECTURE OF THE 8088/8086 MICROPROCESSOR

The internal architectures of the 8088 and 8086 microprocessors are similar. They both employ what is called *parallel processing*; that is, they are implemented with simultaneously operating multiple processing units. Figure 2.2(a) illustrates the internal architecture of the 8088 and 8086 microprocessors. Here we find that they contain two processing units: the *bus interface unit* (BIU) and the *execution unit* (EU). Each unit has dedicated functions and they both operate at the same time. In essence, this parallel processing makes the fetch and execution of instructions independent operations. This results in efficient use of the system bus and higher performance for the 8088/8086 microcomputer system.

The bus interface unit is the 8088/8086's interface to the outside world; that is, it is responsible for performing all external bus operations. In general, the BIU performs bus operations, such as instruction fetching, reading and writing of data operands for memory, and inputting or outputting of data for input/output peripherals. These information transfers take place over the system bus. This bus includes an 8-bit bi-directional data bus for the 8088 (16 bits for the 8086) and a 20-bit address bus. The BIU is not just responsible for performing bus operations, it also performs other functions related to instruction and data acquisition. For instance, it is responsible for instruction queuing and address generation.

To implement these functions, the BIU contains the segment registers, the instruction pointer, address generation adder, bus control logic, and an instruction queue. Figure 2.2(b) shows the bus interface unit of the 8088/8086 in more detail. The BIU uses a mechanism known as an *instruction queue* to implement a pipelined architecture. This queue permits prefetch of up to four bytes (six bytes for the 8086) of instruction code. Whenever the queue is not full, the BIU is free to look ahead in the program by prefetching the next sequential instructions. These

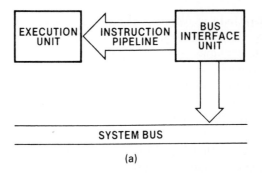

(a)

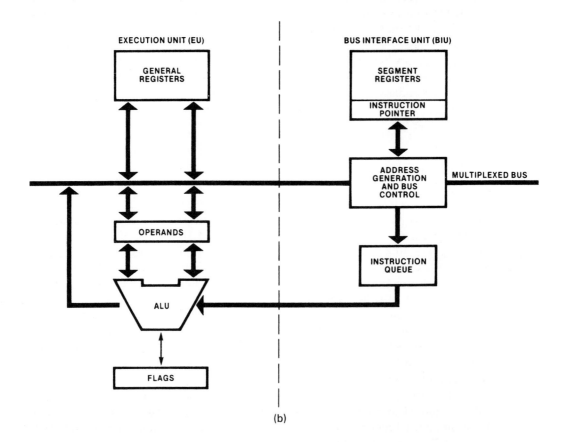

(b)

Figure 2.2 (a) Pipelined architecture of the 8088/8086 microprocessors. (Reprinted with permission of Intel Corp., © 1981) (b) Execution and bus interface units. (Reprinted with permission of Intel Corp., © 1981)

prefetched instructions are held in the first-in first-out (FIFO) queue. After a byte is loaded at the input end of the queue, it automatically shifts up through the FIFO to the empty location nearest the output. Here the code is held until the execution unit is ready to accept it. Since instructions are normally waiting in the queue, the time needed to fetch many instructions of the microcomputer's program is eliminated. If the queue is full and the EU is not requesting access to data operands in memory, the BIU does not perform any bus cycle.

The execution unit is responsible for decoding and executing instructions. Notice in Fig. 2.2(b) that it consists of the *arithmetic logic unit* (ALU), status and control flags, general-purpose registers, and temporary-operand registers. The EU accesses instructions from the output end of the instruction queue and data from the general-purpose registers or memory. It reads one instruction byte after the other from the output of the queue, decodes them, generates operand addresses if necessary, passes them to the BIU and requests it to perform the read or write cycle to memory or I/O, and performs the operation specified by the instruction on operands. During execution of the instruction, the EU may test the status and control flags and updates these flags based on the results of executing the instruction. If the queue is empty, the EU waits for the next instruction byte to be fetched and shifted to the top of the queue.

▲ 2.4 SOFTWARE MODEL OF THE 8088/8086 MICROPROCESSOR

The purpose of developing a *software model* is to aid the programmer in understanding the operation of the microcomputer system from a software point of view. To be able to program a microprocessor, one does not need to know all of its hardware architecture features. For instance, we do not necessarily need to know the function of the signals at its various pins, their electrical connections, or their electrical switching characteristics. The function, interconnection, and operation of the internal circuits of the microprocessor also need not normally be considered. What is important to the programmer is to know the various registers within the device and to understand their purposes, functions, operating capabilities, and limitations. Furthermore, it is essential to know how external memory is organized and how it is addressed to obtain instructions and data.

The software architecture of the 8088 microprocessor is illustrated with the software model shown in Fig. 2.3. Looking at this diagram, we see that it includes 13 16-bit internal registers: the *instruction pointer* (IP), four *data registers* (AX, BX, CX, and DX), two *pointer registers* (BP and SP), two *index registers* (SI and DI), and four *segment registers* (CS, DS, SS, and ES). In addition to these registers, there is another register called the *status register* (SR), with nine of its bits implemented for status and control flags.

Looking at the software model in Fig. 2.3, we see that the 8088 architecture implements independent memory and I/O address spaces. Notice that the memory address space is 1,048,576 (1MB) bytes in length and the I/O address space is 65,536 (64KB) bytes in length. Our concern here is what can be done with this architecture

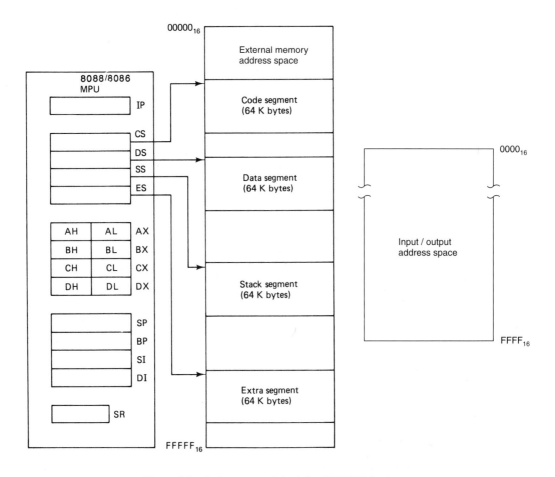

Figure 2.3 Software model of the 8088/8086 microprocessor.

and how to do it through software. For this purpose, we will now begin a detailed study of the elements of the model and their relationship to software.

▲ 2.5 MEMORY ADDRESS SPACE AND DATA ORGANIZATION

Now that we have introduced the idea of a software model, let us look at how information such as numbers, characters, and instructions are stored in memory. As shown in Fig. 2.4 the 8088 microcomputer supports 1MB of external memory. This memory space is organized from a software point of view as individual bytes of data stored at consecutive addresses over the address range 00000_{16} to $FFFFF_{16}$. In this way, we see that the memory in an 8088-based microcomputer is actually organized as 8-bit bytes, not as 16-bit words.

FFFFF
FFFFE
FFFFD
FFFFC

5
4
3
2
1
0

Figure 2.4 Memory address space of the 8088/8086 microprocessor.

The 8088 can access any two consecutive bytes as a *word* of data. In this case, the *lower-addressed byte* is the least significant byte of the word and the *higher-addressed byte* is its most significant byte. Figure 2.5(a) shows how a word of data is stored in memory. Notice that the storage location at the lower address, 00724_{16}, contains the value $00000010_2 = 02_{16}$. The contents of the next-higher-addressed storage location 00725_{16} are $01010101_2 = 55_{16}$. These two bytes represent the word $0101010100000010_2 = 5502_{16}$.

To permit efficient use of memory, words of data can be stored at even- or odd-address boundaries. The least significant bit of the address determines the type of *word boundary*. If this bit is 0, the word is said to be held at an *even-address boundary*. That is, a word at an even-address boundary corresponds to two consecutive bytes, with the least significant byte located at an even address. For example, the word in Fig. 2.5(a) has its least significant byte at address 00724_{16}. Therefore, it is stored at an even-address boundary.

A word of data stored at an even-address boundary, such as 00000_{16}, 00002_{16}, 00004_{16}, and so on, is said to be an *aligned word*. That is, all aligned words are located at an address that is a multiple of 2. On the other hand, a word of data that is stored at an odd-address boundary, 00001_{16}, 00003_{16}, or 00005_{16}, is called a *misaligned word*. Figure 2.6 shows some aligned and misaligned words of data. Here words 0, 2, 4, and 6 are examples of aligned-data words, while words 1 and 5 are misaligned words.

When expressing addresses and data in hexadecimal form, it is common to use the letter H to specify the base. For instance, the number $00AB_{16}$ can also be written as 00ABH.

EXAMPLE 2.1

What is the data word shown in Fig. 2.5(b)? Express the result in hexadecimal form. Is it stored at an even- or odd-address boundary? Is it an aligned or a misaligned word of data?

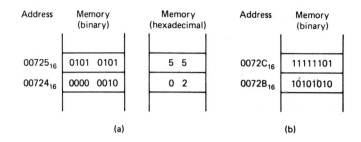

Figure 2.5 (a) Storing a word of data in memory. (b) An example.

Solution

The most significant byte of the word is stored at address $0072C_{16}$ and equals

$$11111101_2 = FD_{16} = FDH$$

Its least significant byte is stored at address $0072B_{16}$ and is

$$10101010_2 = AA_{16} = AAH$$

Together these two bytes give the word

$$1111110110101010_2 = FDAA_{16} = FDAAH$$

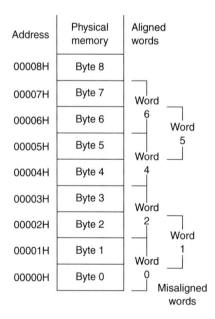

Figure 2.6 Examples of aligned and misaligned data words.

Expressing the address of the least significant byte in binary form gives

$$0072\text{BH} = 0072\text{B}_{16} = 0000000000111100101011_2$$

Since the right most bit (LSB) is logic 1, the word is stored at an odd-address boundary in memory; therefore, it is a misaligned word of data.

The *double word* is another data form that can be processed by the 8088 microcomputer. A double word corresponds to four consecutive bytes of data stored in memory. An example of double-word data is a *pointer*. A pointer is a two-word address element that is used to access data or code outside the current segment of memory. The word of this pointer that is stored at the higher address is called the *segment base address* and the word at the lower address is called the *offset value*.

Just like for words, a double word of data can be aligned or misaligned. An aligned double word is located at an address that is a multiple of 4, for instance, 00000_{16}, 00004_{16}, and 00008_{16}. A number of aligned and misaligned double words of data are shown in Fig. 2.7. Of these six examples, only double words 0 and 4 are aligned double words.

An example showing the storage of a pointer in memory is given in Fig. 2.8(a). Here we find that the higher-addressed word, which represents the segment base address, is stored starting at even-address boundary 00006_{16}. The most significant byte of this word is at address 00007_{16} and equals $00111011_2 = 3\text{B}_{16}$. Its least significant byte is at address 00006_{16} and equals $01001100_2 = 4\text{C}_{16}$. Combining these two

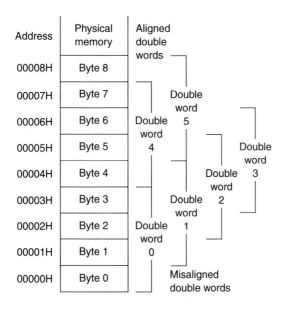

Figure 2.7 Examples of aligned and misaligned double words of data.

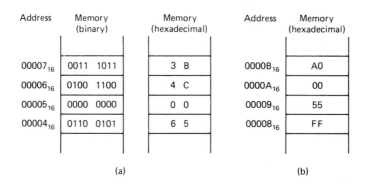

Address	Memory (binary)	Memory (hexadecimal)	Address	Memory (hexadecimal)
00007_{16}	0011 1011	3 B	$0000B_{16}$	A0
00006_{16}	0100 1100	4 C	$0000A_{16}$	00
00005_{16}	0000 0000	0 0	00009_{16}	55
00004_{16}	0110 0101	6 5	00008_{16}	FF
	(a)			(b)

Figure 2.8 (a) Storing a 32-bit pointer in memory. (b) An example.

values, we get the segment-base address, which equals $0011101101001100_2 = 3B4C_{16}$.

The offset part of the pointer is the lower-addressed word. Its least significant byte is stored at address 00004_{16}. This location contains $01100101_2 = 65_{16}$. The most significant byte is at address 00005_{16}, which contains $00000000_2 = 00_{16}$. The resulting offset is $0000000001100101_2 = 0065_{16}$. This is an example of an aligned double word of data.

EXAMPLE 2.2

How should the pointer with segment base address equal to $A000_{16}$ and offset address $55FF_{16}$ be stored at an even-address boundary starting at 00008_{16}? Is the double word aligned or misaligned?

Solution

Storage of the two-word pointer requires four consecutive byte locations in memory, starting at address 00008_{16}. The least significant byte of the offset is stored at address 00008_{16}. This value is shown as FF_{16} in Fig. 2.8(b). The most significant byte of the offset, which is 55_{16}, is stored at address 00009_{16}. These two bytes are followed by the least significant byte of the segment base address, 00_{16}, at address $0000A_{16}$, and its most significant byte, $A0_{16}$, at address $0000B_{16}$. Since the double word is stored in memory starting at address 00008_{16}, it is aligned.

▲ 2.6 DATA TYPES

In the last section we identified the fundamental data formats of the 8088 as the byte (8 bits), word (16 bits), or double word (32 bits). We also showed that these basic formats represent data elements that span one, two, or four consecutive bytes

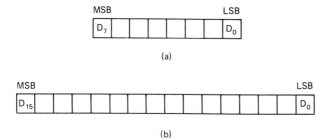

Figure 2.9 (a) Unsigned byte integer. (b) Unsigned word integer.

of memory, respectively. Here we will examine the types of data that can be coded into these formats for processing by the 8088 microprocessor.

The 8088 microprocessor can directly process data expressed in a number of different data types. Let us begin with the *integer data type*. The 8088 can process data as either *unsigned* or *signed* integer numbers; each type of integer can be either byte-wide or word-wide. Figure 2.9(a) represents an *unsigned byte* integer. This data type can be used to represent decimal numbers in the range 0 through 255. The *unsigned word* integer is shown in Fig. 2.9(b). It can be used to represent decimal numbers in the range 0 through 65,535.

EXAMPLE 2.3

What value does the unsigned word integer 1000_{16} represent?

Solution

First, the hexadecimal integer is converted to binary form:

$$1000_{16} = 0001000000000000_2$$

Next, we find the value for the binary number

$$0001000000000000_2 = 2^{12} = 2048$$

The *signed byte* integer and *signed word* integer of Figs 2.10(a) and (b) are similar to the unsigned-integer data types just introduced; however, here the most significant bit is a sign bit. A 0 in the MSB position identifies a positive number. For this reason, signed integers can represent byte and word decimal numbers in the ranges +127 to −128 and +32767 to −32768, respectively. For example, the number +3 expressed as a signed integer byte is $00000011_2 (03_{16})$. On the other hand, the 8088 always expresses negative numbers in 2s-complement notation. Therefore, −3 is coded as $11111101_2 (FD_{16})$.

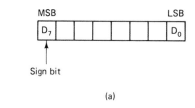

(a)

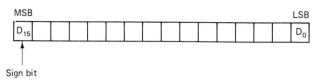

(b)

Figure 2.10 (a) Signed byte integer. (b) Signed word integer.

EXAMPLE 2.4

A signed word integer equals $FEFF_{16}$. What decimal number does it represent?

Solution

Expressing the hexadecimal number in binary form, we get

$$FEFF_{16} = 1111111011111111_2$$

Since the most significant bit is 1, the number is negative and is in 2s-complement form. Converting to its binary equivalent by subtracting 1 from the least significant bit and then complementing all bits gives

$$FEFF_{16} = -0000000100000001_2$$
$$= -257$$

The 8088 can also process data that is coded as *binary coded decimal* (BCD) *numbers*. Figure 2.11(a) lists the BCD values for decimal numbers 0 through 9. BCD data can be stored in either *unpacked* or *packed* form. For instance, the unpacked BCD byte in Fig. 2.11(b) shows that a single BCD digit is stored in the four least significant bits, and the upper four bits are set to 0. Figure 2.11(c) shows a byte with packed BCD digits. Here two BCD numbers are stored in a byte. The upper four bits represent the most significant digit of a two-digit BCD number.

Decimal	BCD
0	0000
1	0001
2	0010
3	0011
4	0100
5	0101
6	0110
7	0111
8	1000
9	1001

(a)

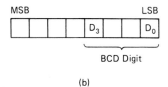

(b)

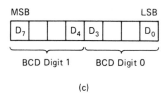

(c)

Figure 2.11 (a) BCD numbers. (b) An unpacked BCD digit. (c) Packed BCD digits.

EXAMPLE 2.5

The packed BCD data stored at byte address 01000_{16} equals 10010001_2. What is the two-digit decimal number?

Solution

Writing the value 10010001_2 as separate BCD digits gives

$$10010001_2 = 1001_{BCD}\ 0001_{BCD} = 91_{10}$$

Information expressed in *ASCII* (*American Standard Code for Information Interchange*) can also be directly processed by the 8088 microprocessor. Figure 2.12(a) shows how numbers, letters, and control characters are coded in ASCII. For instance, the number 5 is coded as

$$H_1H_0 = 00110101_2 = 35H$$

	b7	0	0	0	0	1	1	1	1
	b6	0	0	1	1	0	0	1	1
	b5	0	1	0	1	0	1	0	1
$b_4\ b_3\ b_2\ b_1$ \ H_1 / H_0		0	1	2	3	4	5	6	7
0 0 0 0	0	NUL	DLE	SP	0	@	P	'	p
0 0 0 1	1	SOH	DC1	!	1	A	Q	a	q
0 0 1 0	2	STX	DC2	"	2	B	R	b	r
0 0 1 1	3	ETX	DC3	#	3	C	S	c	s
0 1 0 0	4	EOT	DC4	$	4	D	T	d	t
0 1 0 1	5	ENQ	NAK	%	5	E	U	e	u
0 1 1 0	6	ACK	SYN	&	6	F	V	f	v
0 1 1 1	7	BEL	ETB	'	7	G	W	g	w
1 0 0 0	8	BS	CAN	(	8	H	X	h	x
1 0 0 1	9	HT	EM	)	9	I	Y	i	y
1 0 1 0	A	LF	SUB	*	:	J	Z	j	z
1 0 1 1	B	∨	ESC	+	;	K	[	k	}
1 1 0 0	C	FF	FS	,	<	L	\	l		
1 1 0 1	D	CR	GS	–	=	M	]	m	{
1 1 1 0	E	SO	RS	.	>	N	∧	n	~
1 1 1 1	F	SI	US	/	?	O	-	o	DEL

(a)

(b)

Figure 2.12   (a) ASCII table. (b) ASCII number.

where H denotes that the ASCII-coded number is in hexadecimal form. As shown in Fig. 2.12(b), ASCII data are stored as one character per byte.

EXAMPLE 2.6

Byte addresses 01100_{16} through 01104_{16} contain the ASCII data 01000001, 01010011, 01000011, 01001001, and 01001001, respectively. What do the data stand for?

Solution

Using the chart in Fig. 2.12(a), the data are converted to ASCII as follows:

$$(01100H) = 01000001_{ASCII} = A$$
$$(01101H) = 01010011_{ASCII} = S$$
$$(01102H) = 01000011_{ASCII} = C$$
$$(01103H) = 01001001_{ASCII} = I$$
$$(01104H) = 01001001_{ASCII} = I$$

▲ 2.7 SEGMENT REGISTERS AND MEMORY SEGMENTATION

Even though the 8088 has a 1MB address space, not all this memory can be active at one time. Actually, the 1MB of memory can be partitioned into 64KB (65,536 bytes) *segments*. A segment represents an independently addressable unit of memory consisting of 64K consecutive byte-wide storage locations. Each segment is assigned a *base address* that identifies its starting point, that is, its lowest-addressed byte storage location.

Only four of these 64KB segments can be active at a time. They are called the *code segment, stack segment, data segment,* and *extra segment*. The location of the segments of memory that are active, as shown in Fig. 2.13, are identified by the values of addresses held in the 8088's four internal segment registers: *CS* (code segment), *SS* (stack segment), *DS* (data segment), and *ES* (extra segment). Each of these registers contains a 16-bit base address that points to the lowest-addressed byte of the segment in memory. Four segments give a maximum of 256KB of active memory. Of this, 64KB are for code (*program storage*), 64KB are for a *stack*, and 128KB are for *data storage*.

The values held in these registers are usually referred to as the *current segment register values*. For example, the value in CS points to the first word-wide storage location in the current code segment. Code is always fetched as words, not as bytes.

Figure 2.14 illustrates the *segmentation of memory*. In this diagram, we have identified 64KB segments with letters such as A, B, and C. The data segment (DS) register contains the value B. Therefore, the second 64KB segment of memory from the top, which is labeled B, acts as the current data storage segment. This is one of the segments in which data that are to be processed by the microcomputer are stored. For this reason, this part of the microcomputer's memory address space must contain read/write storage locations that can be accessed by instructions as storage locations for source and destination operands. Segment E is selected for the code segment. It is this segment of memory from which instructions of the program are currently being fetched for execution. The stack segment (SS) register

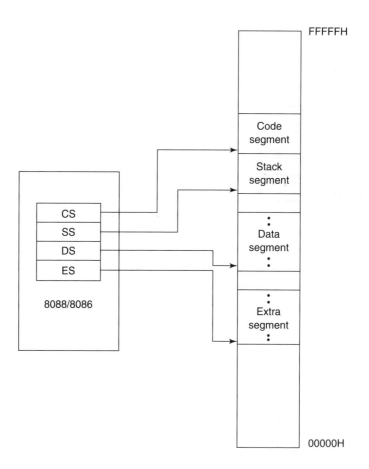

FFFFFH

Code
segment

Stack
segment

⋮
Data
segment
⋮

⋮
Extra
segment
⋮

00000H

CS
SS
DS
ES

8088/8086

Figure 2.13   Active segments of memory.

contains H, thereby selecting the 64KB segment labeled as H for use as a stack. Finally, the extra segment register ES is loaded with value J so that segment J of memory can function as a second 64KB data storage segment.

The segment registers are said to be *user accessible*. This means that the programmer can change the value they hold through software. Therefore, for a program to gain access to another part of memory, one just has to change the value of the appropriate register or registers. For instance, a new 128KB data space can be brought in by simply changing the values in DS and ES.

There is one restriction on the value that can be assigned to a segment as a base address: it must reside on a 16-byte address boundary. This is due to the fact

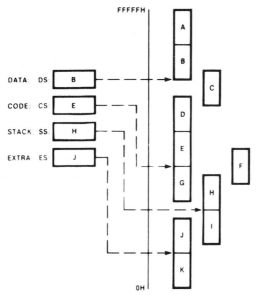

Figure 2.14 Contiguous, adjacent, disjointed, and overlapping segments. (Reprinted by permission of Intel Corp., © Intel Corp. 1979)

that increasing the 16-bit value in a segment register by 1 actually increases the corresponding physical address by 16. Valid examples are 00000_{16}, 00010_{16}, and 00020_{16}. Other than this restriction, segments can be set up to be *contiguous*, *adjacent*, *disjointed*, or even *overlapping*. For example, in Fig. 2.14, segments A and B are contiguous, whereas segments B and C are overlapping.

▲ 2.8 DEDICATED, RESERVED, AND GENERAL USE OF MEMORY

Any part of the 8088 microcomputer's 1MB address space can be implemented for user's access; however, some address locations have *dedicated functions*. These dedicated locations should not be used as general memory for storing data or instructions of a program. Let us now look at these reserved, dedicated use, and general-use parts of memory.

Figure 2.15 shows the *reserved*, *dedicated-use* and *general-use* parts of the 8088/8086's *address space*. Notice that storage locations from address 00000_{16} to 00013_{16} are dedicated and those from address 00014_{16} to $00007F_{16}$ are reserved. These 128 bytes of memory are used for storage of pointers to interrupt service routines. The dedicated part is used for storage of the pointers for the 8088's internal interrupts and exceptions. On the other hand, the reserved locations are saved for storage of pointers that are used by the user defined interrupts. As indicated earlier, each pointer requires four bytes of memory. Two bytes hold the 16-bit segment

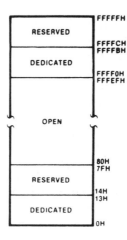

Figure 2.15 Dedicated, reserved, and general use memory. (Reprinted by permission of Intel Corp., © Intel Corp. 1979)

address and the other two hold the 16-bit offset. Therefore, this part of memory can contain up to 32 pointers.

At the high end of the memory address space is another reserved pointer area. It is located from address $FFFFC_{16}$ through $FFFFF_{16}$. These four memory locations are reserved for use with future products and should not be used. Intel Corporation, the manufacturer of the 8088, has identified the 12 storage locations from address $FFFF0_{16}$ through $FFFFB_{16}$ as dedicated for functions such as storage of the hardware reset jump instruction. For instance, physical address $FFFF0_{16}$ is where the 8088/8086 begins execution after receiving a reset.

▲ 2.9 INSTRUCTION POINTER

The next register from the 8088's software model of Fig. 2.3 that we will consider is the *instruction pointer* (IP). It is also 16 bits in length and identifies the location of the next word of instruction code to be fetched from the current code segment. The IP is similar to a conventional program counter; however, it contains the offset of the next word of instruction code instead of its actual address. This is because IP and CS are both 16 bits in length, but a 20-bit address is needed to access memory. Internal to the 8088, the offset in IP is combined with the current value in CS to generate the address of the instruction code. Therefore, the value of the address for the next code access is often denoted as CS:IP.

During normal operation, the 8088 fetches instruction code from the code segment of memory and stores them in its instruction queue. Every time an instruction is fetched from memory, the 8088 updates the value in IP such that it points to the first byte of the next word of code. In this way, it is always ready to fetch the next sequential instruction of the program. That is, IP is incremented by 2. Actually, the 8088 has an internal *code queue* and prefetches up to four bytes of instruction code and holds them internally waiting for execution.

After an instruction is read from the output of the instruction queue, it is decoded and, if necessary, operands are read from either the data segment of memory or internal registers. Next, the operation specified in the instruction is performed on the operands and the result is written back to either an internal register or a storage location in memory. The 8088 is now ready to execute the next instruction in the queue.

The active code segment can be changed by simply loading a new value into the CS register. For this reason, we can use any 64KB segment of memory for storage of instruction code.

▲ 2.10 DATA REGISTERS

As shown in Fig. 2.3, four *general-purpose data registers* are located within the 8088. During program execution, they are used for temporary storage of frequently used intermediate results. Their contents can be read, loaded, or modified through software. Any of the general-purpose data registers can be used as the source or destination of an operand during an arithmetic operation such as ADD or a logic operation such as AND. For instance, the values of two pieces of data, called A & B, could be moved from memory into separate data registers and operations such as addition, subtraction, and multiplication performed on them. The advantage of storing these data in internal registers instead of memory during processing is that they can be accessed much faster.

The data registers are shown in more detail in Fig. 2.16(a). Here we see that the four data registers are referred to as the *accumulator register* (A), the *base register* (B), the *count register* (C), and the *data register* (D). These names imply special functions that are meant to be performed by each register. Figure 2.16(b) summarizes the dedicated functions of the general-purpose data registers. Notice that the C register is used during string and loop operations. In the case of a string instruction, register C is used to store a count representing the number of bytes to be processed. This is the reason it is given the name count register. Another example of dedicated use of data registers is that all I/O operations require the data that

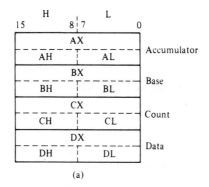

Register	Operations
AX	Word multiply, word divide, word I/O
AL	Byte multiply, byte divide, byte I/O, translate, decimal arithmetic
AH	Byte multiply, byte divide
BX	Translate
CX	String operations, loops
CL	Variable shift and rotate
DX	Word multiply, word divide, indirect I/O

(a)   (b)

Figure 2.16   (a) General-purpose data registers. (Reprinted by permission of Intel Corp., © Intel Corp. 1979) (b) Dedicated register functions. (Reprinted by permission of Intel Corp., Intel Corp. 1979)

are to be input or output to be in the A register, while register D holds the address of the I/O port.

Each of these registers can be accessed either as a whole 16 bits for word data operations or as two 8-bit registers for byte-wide data operations. References to a register as a word are identified by an X after the register letter. For instance, the 16-bit accumulator is referenced as AX. Similarly, the other three word registers are referred to as BX, CX, and DX.

On the other hand, when referencing one of these registers on a byte-wide basis, its high byte and low byte are identified by following the register name with the letter H or L, respectively. For the A register, the most significant byte is referred to as AH and the least significant byte as AL. The other byte-wide register pairs are BH and BL, CH and CL, and DH and DL.

▲ 2.11 POINTER AND INDEX REGISTERS

There are four other general-purpose registers shown in Fig. 2.3: two *pointer registers* and two *index registers*. They are used to store what are called *offset addresses*. An offset address represents the displacement of a storage location in memory from the segment base address in a segment register. That is, they are used as a pointer or index to select a specific storage location within a 64KB segment of memory. The values held in these registers can be read, loaded, or modified through software. Prior to executing an instruction that references one of these registers, the register is loaded with the offset address. In this way, to use the offset address in a register, the instruction simply specifies the register that contains the value of the offset address.

Figure 2.17 shows that the two pointer registers are the *stack pointer* (SP) and *base pointer* (BP). The contents of SP and BP are used as offsets from the current value of SS during the execution of instructions that involve the stack segment of memory. In this way, they permit easy access to locations in the stack part of memory. The value in SP always represents the offset of the next stack location that is to be accessed. That is, when SP is combined with the value in SS (SS:SP), it results in a 20-bit address that points to the *top of the stack*.

BP also represents an offset relative to the SS register. Its intended use is for access of data within the stack segment of memory. To do this, it is employed as the offset in an addressing mode called the based-addressing mode. This type of address will be described later in the chapter.

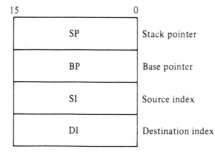

Figure 2.17 Pointer and index registers. (Reprinted by permission of Intel Corp., © Intel Corp. 1979)

One common use of BP is to reference parameters that were passed to a subroutine by way of the stack. In this case, instructions are included in the subroutine that use based addressing to read the values of parameters from the stack.

The index registers are used to hold offset addresses for instructions that access data stored in the data segment of memory. For this reason, they are combined with the value in the DS or ES register. In instructions that use indexed type of addressing, the *source index* (SI) register is used to store an offset address for a source operand, and the *destination index* (DI) register is used for storage of an offset that identifies the location of a destination operand. For example, a string instruction that requires an offset to the location of a source or destination operand would use these registers.

The index registers can also be used as source or destination registers in arithmetic and logical operations. Unlike the general-purpose registers, these registers must always be used for 16-bit operations and cannot be accessed as two separate bytes.

▲ 2.12 STATUS OR FLAGS REGISTER

The *status register*, which is also called the *flags register*, is another 16-bit register within the 8088. However, as shown in Fig. 2.18, just nine of its bits are implemented. Six of these bits represent *status flags*. They are the *carry flag* (CF), the *parity flag* (PF), the *auxiliary carry flag* (AF), the *zero flag* (ZF), the *sign flag* (SF), and the *overflow flag* (OF). The logic state of these status flags indicates conditions that are produced as the result of executing an instruction. That is, after executing an instruction, such as ADD, specific flag bits are reset (logic 0) or set (logic 1) based on the result that is produced.

Let us first summarize the operation of these flags:

1. The carry flag (CF): CF is set if there is a carry-out or a borrow-in for the most significant bit of the result during the execution of an arithmetic instruction. Otherwise, CF is reset.

2. The parity flag (PF): PF is set if the result produced by the instruction has even parity, that is, if it contains an even number of bits at the 1 logic level. If parity is odd, PF is reset.

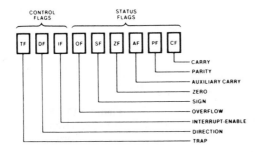

Figure 2.18 Status and control flags. (Reprinted by permission of Intel Corp., © Intel Corp. 1979)

3. The auxiliary carry flag (AF): AF is set if there is a carry-out from the low nibble into the high nibble or a borrow-in from the high nibble into the low nibble of the lower byte in a 16-bit word. Otherwise, AF is reset.

4. The zero flag (ZF): ZF is set if the result of an arithmetic or logic operation is zero. Otherwise, ZF is reset.

5. The sign flag (SF): The MSB of the result is copied into SF. Thus SF is set if the result is a negative number or reset if it is positive.

6. The overflow flag (OF): When OF is set, it indicates that the signed result is out of range. If the result is not out of range, OF remains reset.

For example, at the completion of execution of a byte-addition instruction, the carry flag (CF) could be set to indicate that the sum of the operands caused a carry-out condition. The auxiliary carry flag (AF) could also be set due to the execution of the instruction. This depends on whether or not a carry-out occurred from the least significant nibble to the most significant nibble when the byte operands are added. The sign flag (SF) is also affected and it will reflect the logic level of the MSB of the result. The overflow flag (OF) is set if there is a carry-out of the sign bit, but no carry into the sign bit (an indication of overflow).

The 8088 provides instructions within its instruction set that are able to use these flags to alter the sequence in which the program is executed. For instance, the condition ZF equal to logic 1 could be tested to initiate a jump to another part of the program. This operation is called *jump on zero*.

The other three implemented flag bits are *control flags*. They are the *direction flag* (DF), the *interrupt enable flag* (IF), and the *trap flag* (TF). These three flags are provided to control functions of the 8088 as follows:

1. The trap flag (TF): If TF is set, the 8088 goes into the *single-step mode*. When in the single-step mode, it executes an instruction and then jumps to a special service routine to determine the effect of executing the instruction. This type of operation is very useful for debugging programs.

2. The interrupt flag (IF): For the 8088 to recognize *maskable interrupt requests* at its INT input, the IF flag must be set. When IF is reset, requests at INT are ignored and the maskable interrupt interface is disabled.

3. The direction flag (DF): The logic level of DF determines the direction in which string operations will occur. When set, the string instruction automatically decrements the address. Therefore, the string data transfers proceed from high address to low address. On the other hand, resetting DF causes the string address to be incremented. In this way, data transfers proceed from low address to high address.

The instruction set of the 8088 includes instructions for saving, loading, or manipulating the flags. For instance, special instructions are provided to permit user software to set or reset CF, DF, and IF at any point in the program. For instance, just prior to the beginning of a string operation, DF could be reset so that the string address automatically increments.

A *logical address* in the 8088 system is described by a segment base and an offset. As shown in Fig. 2.19, both the segment base and offset are 16-bit quantities. This is because all registers and memory locations used in the address calculation are 16 bits long. However, the *physical addresses* that are used to access memory are 20 bits in length. The generation of the physical address involves combining a 16-bit offset value that is located in the instruction pointer, a base register, an index register, or a pointer register and a 16-bit segment base value that is located in one of the segment registers.

The source of the offset value depends on which type of memory reference is taking place. It can be the base pointer (BP) register, base (BX) register, source index (SI) register, destination index (DI) register, or instruction pointer (IP). An offset can even be formed from the contents of several of these registers. On the other hand, the segment base value always resides in one of the segment registers: CS, DS, SS, or ES.

For instance, when an instruction acquisition takes place, the source of the segment base value is always the code segment (CS) register and the source of the offset value is always the instruction pointer (IP). This physical address can be denoted as CS:IP. On the other hand, if the value of a variable is being written to memory during the execution of an instruction, typically, the segment base value will be specified by the data segment (DS) register and the offset value will be in the destination index (DI) register. That is, the physical address is given as DS:DI.

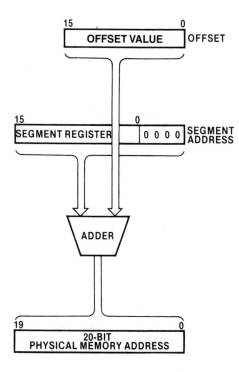

Figure 2.19 Generating a physical address. (Reprinted by permission of Intel Corp., © Intel 1981)

A provision in the processor called the *segment override prefix* can be used to change the segment from which the variable is accessed. For example, a prefix could be used to make a data access occur in which the segment base is in the ES register.

Another example is the stack address that is needed when pushing parameters onto the stack. This address is formed from the contents of the stack segment (SS) register and stack pointer (SP) and described as SS:SP.

Remember that the segment base address represents the starting location of the 64KB segment in memory, that is, the lowest-addressed byte in the segment. Figure 2.20 shows that the offset identifies the distance in bytes that the storage location of interest resides from this starting address. Therefore, the lowest-addressed byte in a segment has an offset of 0000_{16} and the highest-addressed byte has an offset of $FFFF_{16}$.

Figure 2.21 shows how a segment base value in a segment register and an offset value are combined to form a physical address. What happens is that the value in the segment register is shifted left by four bit positions, with its LSBs being filled with 0s. Then the offset value is added to the 16 LSBs of the shifted segment value, called the *segment address*. The result of this addition is the 20-bit physical address.

The example in Fig. 2.21 represents a segment base value of 1234_{16} and an offset value of 0022_{16}. First let us express the value of the segment base value in binary form. This gives

$$1234_{16} = 0001001000110100_2$$

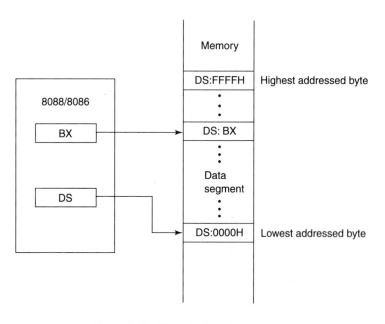

Figure 2.20 Boundaries of a segment.

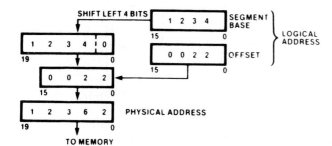

Figure 2.21 Physical address calculation example. (Reprinted by permission of Intel Corp., © Intel Corp. 1979)

Shifting left four times and filling with zeros results in the segment address as

$$00010010001101000000_2 = 12340_{16}$$

The offset in binary form is

$$0022_{16} = 0000000000100010_2$$

Adding the segment address and the offset, we get

$$00010010001101000000_2 + 0000000000100010_2 = 00010010001101100010_2$$

$$= 12362_{16}$$

$$= 12362H$$

This address calculation is done automatically by the 8088 microprocessor each time a memory access is initiated.

EXAMPLE 2.7

What would be the offset required to map to physical address location $002C3_{16}$ if the contents of the corresponding segment register are $002A_{16}$?

Solution

The offset value can be obtained by shifting the segment register contents left by four bit positions and then subtracting from the physical address. Shifting left gives

$$002A0_{16}$$

Now subtracting, we get the value of the offset:

$$002C3_{16} - 002A0_{16} = 0023_{16}$$

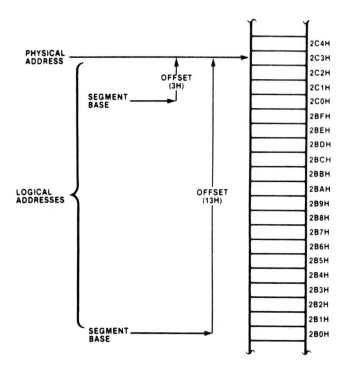

Figure 2.22 Relationship between logical and physical addresses. (Reprinted by permission of Intel Corp., © Intel Corp. 1979)

Actually, many different logical addresses can be mapped to the same physical address location in memory. This is done by simply changing the values of the segment base value in the segment register and its corresponding offset. The diagram in Fig. 2.22 demonstrates this idea. Notice that segment base $002B_{16}$ with offset 0013_{16} maps to physical address $002C3_{16}$ in memory. However, if the segment base is changed to $002C_{16}$ with a new offset of 0003_{16}, the physical address is still $002C3_{16}$. In this way, we see that physical address 002BH:0013H is equal to the physical address 002CH:0003H.

▲ 2.14 THE STACK

As indicated earlier, *stack* is implemented in the memory of the 8088 microcomputer. Stack is used for temporary storage of information such as data or addresses. For instance, when a *call* instruction is executed, the 8088 automatically pushes the current values in CS and IP onto the stack. As part of the subroutine, the contents of other registers can also be saved on the stack by executing *push* instructions. An example is the instruction PUSH SI. When executed, it causes the contents of SI to be pushed onto the stack. At the end of the subroutine, *pop* instructions can

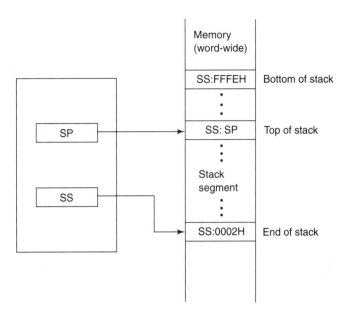

Figure 2.23 Stack segment of memory.

be included to pop values from the stack back into their corresponding internal registers. For example, POP SI causes the value at the top of the stack to be popped back into SI. At the end of the subroutine, a return instruction causes the values of CS and IP to be popped off the stack and put back into the internal register where they originally resided.

The stack is 64KB long and is organized from a software point of view as 32K words. Figure 2.23 shows that the lowest-addressed word in the current stack is pointed to by the segment base value in the SS register. The contents of the SP and BP registers are used as offsets into the stack segment of memory.

Looking at Fig. 2.23, we see that SP contains an offset value that points to a storage location in the current stack segment. The address obtained from the contents of SS and SP (SS:SP) is the physical address of the last storage location in the stack to which data were pushed. This memory address is known as the top of the stack. The value in the stack pointer is initialized to $FFFE_{16}$ upon start up of the microcomputer. Combining this value with the current value in SS gives the highest-addressed location in the stack (SS:FFFEH), that is, the *bottom of the stack*.

The 8088 pushes data and addresses to the stack one word at a time. Each time the contents of a register are to be pushed onto the top of the stack, the value in the stack pointer is first automatically decremented by two and then the contents of the register are written into the stack part of memory. In this way we see that the stack grows down in memory from the bottom of the stack, which corresponds to the physical address derived from SS:FFFEH, toward the *end of the stack*, which corresponds to the physical address obtained from SS and offset 0000_{16}.

When a value is popped from the top of the stack, the reverse of this sequence occurs. The physical address defined by SS and SP points to the location of the last value pushed onto the stack. Its contents are first popped off the stack and put into the specific register within the 8088; then SP is automatically incremented by two. The top of the stack now corresponds to the previous value pushed onto the stack.

An example that shows how the contents of a register are pushed onto the stack is shown in Fig. 2.24(a). Here we find the state of the stack prior to execution of the PUSH AX instruction. Notice that the stack segment register contains 105_{16}. As indicated, the bottom of the stack resides at the physical address derived from SS and offset $FFFE_{16}$. This gives the bottom of stack address A_{BOS} as

$$A_{BOS} = 1050_{16} + FFFE_{16}$$

$$= 1104E_{16}$$

Furthermore, the stack pointer, which represents the offset from the beginning of the stack specified by the contents of SS to the top of the stack, equals 0008_{16}. Therefore, the current top of the stack is at physical address A_{TOS}, which equals

$$A_{TOS} = 1050_{16} + 0008_{16}$$

$$= 1058_{16}$$

Addresses with higher values than that of the top of stack, 1058_{16}, contain valid stack data. Those with lower addresses do not yet contain valid stack data. Notice that the last value pushed to the stack in Fig. 2.24(a) was $BBAA_{16}$.

Figure 2.24(b) demonstrates what happens when the PUSH AX instruction is executed. Here we see that AX contains the number 1234_{16}. Notice that execution

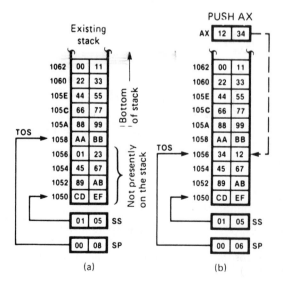

Figure 2.24 (a) Stack just prior to push operation. (Reprinted by permission of Intel Corp., © Intel Corp. 1979) (b) Stack after execution of the PUSH AX instruction. (Reprinted by permission of Intel Corp., © Intel Corp. 1979)

of the PUSH instruction causes the stack pointer to be decremented by two but does not affect the contents of the stack segment register. Therefore, the next location to be accessed in the stack corresponds to address 1056_{16}. It is to this location that the value in AX is pushed. Notice that the most significant byte of AX, which equals 12_{16}, now resides in memory address 1057_{16}, and the least significant byte of AX, which is 34_{16}, is held in memory address 1056_{16}.

Now let us look at an example in which stack data are popped from the stack back into the register from which they were pushed. Figure 2.25 illustrates this operation. In Fig. 2.25(a), the stack is shown to be in the state that resulted due to our prior PUSH AX example. That is, SP equals 0006_{16}, SS equals 0105_{16}, the address at the top of the stack equals 1056_{16}, and the word at the top of the stack equals 1234_{16}.

Looking at Fig. 2.25(b), we see what happens when the instructions POP AX and POP BX are executed in that order. Here we see that execution of the first instruction causes the 8088 to read the value from the top of the stack and put it

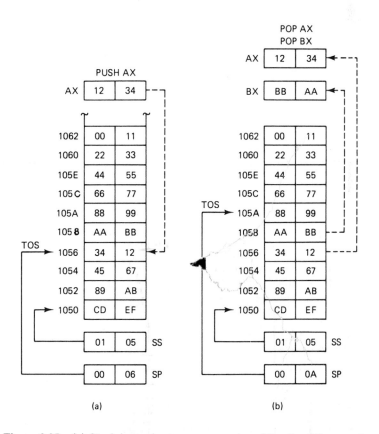

Figure 2.25 (a) Stack just prior to pop operation. (Reprinted by permission of Intel Corp., © Intel Corp. 1979) (b) Stack after execution of the POP AX and POP BX instructions. (Reprinted by permission of Intel Corp., © Intel Corp. 1979)

into the AX register as 1234_{16}. Next, SP is incremented to give 0008_{16} and another read cycle is initiated from the stack. This second read corresponds to the POP BX instruction, and it causes the value $BBAA_{16}$ to be loaded into the BX register. SP is incremented once more and now equals $000A_{16}$. Therefore, the new top of stack is at address $105A_{16}$.

From Fig. 2.25(b), we see that the values read out of 1056_{16} and 1058_{16} still remain at these addresses that now are above the top of the stack. Therefore, they no longer represent valid stack data. If new information are pushed to the stack, these values are written over.

Any number of stacks may exist in an 8088 microcomputer. A new stack can be brought in by simply changing the value in the SS register. For instance, executing the instruction MOV SS,DX loads a new value from DX into SS. Even though many stacks can exist, only one can be active at a time.

▲ 2.15 INPUT/OUTPUT ADDRESS SPACE

The 8088 has separate memory and input/output (I/O) address spaces. The *I/O address space* is the place where I/O interfaces, such as printer and terminal ports, are implemented. Figure 2.26 shows a map of the 8088's I/O address space. Notice that this address range is from 0000_{16} to $FFFF_{16}$. This represents just 64KB addresses; therefore, unlike memory, I/O addresses are just 16 bits long. Each I/O address corresponds to a byte-wide I/O port.

The part of the map from address 0000_{16} through $00FF_{16}$ is referred to as *page 0*. Some of the 8088's I/O instructions can only perform operations to I/O devices located in this part of the I/O address space. Other I/O instructions can input or output data from devices located anywhere in the I/O address space. Notice that the eight locations from address $00F8_{16}$ through $00FF_{16}$ are specified as reserved by Intel Corporation and should not be used.

▲ 2.16 ADDRESSING MODES OF THE 8088/8086

When the 8088 executes an instruction, it performs the specified function on data. These data, called operands, may be part of the instruction, may reside in one of the internal registers of the microprocessor, or may be stored at an address in memory. To access these different types of operands, the 8088 is provided with

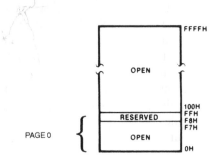

Figure 2.26 I/O address space. (Reprinted by permission of Intel Corp., © Intel Corp. 1979)

Register	Operand sizes	
	Byte (Reg 8)	Word (Reg 16)
Accumulator	AL, AH	AX
Base	BL, BH	BX
Count	CL, CH	CX
Data	DL, DH	DX
Stack pointer	—	SP
Base pointer	—	BP
Source index	—	SI
Destination index	—	DI
Code segment	—	CS
Data segment	—	DS
Stack segment	—	SS
Extra segment	—	ES

Figure 2.27 Direct addressing register and operand sizes.

various *addressing modes*. An addressing mode is a method of specifying an operand. The addressing modes are categorized into three types: *register operand addressing*, *immediate operand addressing*, and *memory operand addressing*. Let us now consider in detail the addressing modes in each of these categories.

Register Operand Addressing Mode

With the *register addressing mode*, the operand to be accessed is specified as residing in an internal register of the 8088. Figure 2.27 lists the internal registers that can be used as a source or destination operand. Notice that the data registers can be accessed as either a byte or word.

An example of an instruction that uses this addressing mode is

```
MOV AX,BX
```

This stands for move the contents of BX, the *source operand*, to AX, the *destination operand*. Both the source and destination operands have been specified as the contents of internal registers of the 8088.

Let us now look at the effect of executing the register addressing mode MOV instruction. In Fig. 2.28(a), we see the state of the 8088 just prior to fetching the instruction. Notice that the physical address formed from IP and CS (CS:IP) points to the MOV AX,BX instruction at address 01000_{16}. This instruction is fetched into the 8088's instruction queue, where it is held waiting to be executed.

Prior to execution of this instruction, the contents of BX are $ABCD_{16}$ and the contents of AX represent a don't-care state. The instruction is read from the output side of the queue, decoded, and executed. As shown in Fig. 2.28(b), the result produced by executing this instruction is that the value $ABCD_{16}$ is copied into AX.

Immediate Operand Addressing Mode

If an operand is part of the instruction instead of the contents of a register or memory location, it represents what is called an *immediate operand* and is accessed using the *immediate addressing mode*. Figure 2.29 shows that the operand, which can be 8 bits (Imm8) or 16 bits (Imm16) in length, is encoded as part of the instruction. Since the data are encoded directly into the instruction, immediate operands normally represent constant data. This addressing mode can only be used to specify a source operand.

In the instruction

MOV AL,15H

the source operand 15H (15_{16}) is an example of a byte-wide immediate source operand. The destination operand, which is the contents of AL, uses register ad-

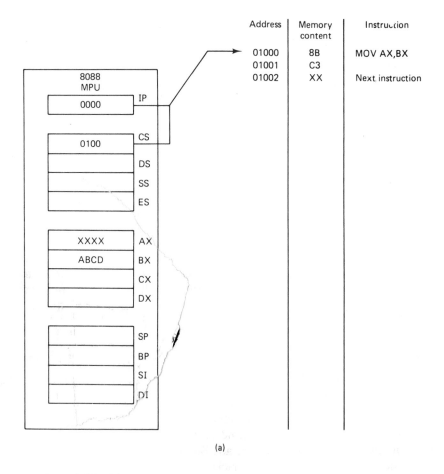

(a)

Figure 2.28 (a) Register addressing mode instruction before fetch and execution. (b) After execution.

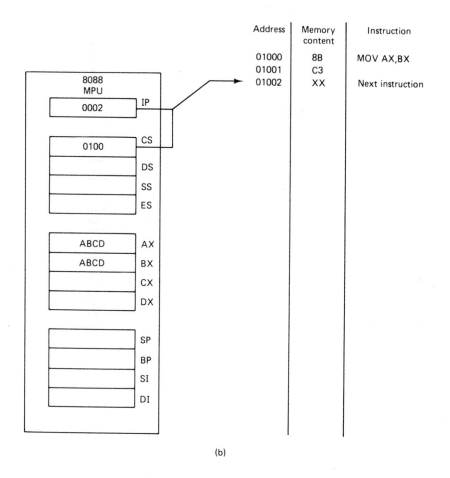

Address	Memory content	Instruction
01000	8B	MOV AX,BX
01001	C3	
01002	XX	Next instruction

8088 MPU

0002	IP	
0100	CS	
	DS	
	SS	
	ES	
ABCD	AX	
ABCD	BX	
	CX	
	DX	
	SP	
	BP	
	SI	
	DI	

(b)

Figure 2.28   (Continued)

dressing. Thus, this instruction employs both the immediate and register addressing modes.

Figure 2.30(a) and (b) illustrates the fetch and execution of this instruction. Here we find that the immediate operand 15_{16} is stored in the code segment of memory in the byte location immediately following the opcode of the instruction. This value is fetched, along with the opcode for MOV, into the instruction queue within the 8088. When it performs the move operation, the source operand is fetched from the queue, not from the memory, and no external memory operations are performed. Notice that the result produced by executing this instruction is that the immediate operand, which equals 15_{16}, is loaded into the lower-byte part of the accumulator (AL).

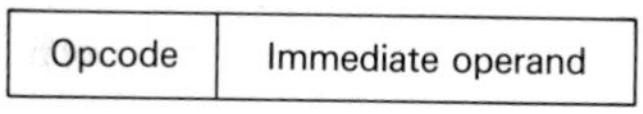

Opcode	Immediate operand

Figure 2.29   Instruction encoded with an immediate operand.

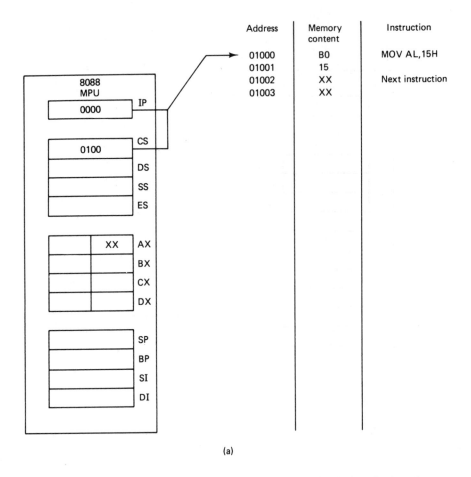

Address	Memory content	Instruction
01000	B0	MOV AL,15H
01001	15	
01002	XX	Next instruction
01003	XX	

8088
MPU

IP   0000

CS   0100

DS

SS

ES

AX   XX

BX

CX

DX

SP

BP

SI

DI

(a)

Figure 2.30 (a) Immediate addressing mode instruction before fetch and execution. (b) After execution.

Memory Addressing Modes

To reference an operand in memory, the 8088 must calculate the physical address (PA) of the operand and then initiate a read or write operation to this storage location. Looking at Fig. 2.31, we see that the physical address is formed from a *segment base address* (SBA) and an *effective address* (EA). SBA identifies the starting location of the segment in memory and EA represents the offset of the operand from the beginning of this segment of memory. Earlier we showed how SBA and EA are combined within the 8088 to form the physical address SBA:EA.

The value of the EA can be specified in a variety of ways. One way is to encode the effective address of the operand directly in the instruction. This represents the simplest type of memory addressing, known as the *direct addressing mode*. Figure 2.31 shows that an effective address can be made up from as many as three elements:

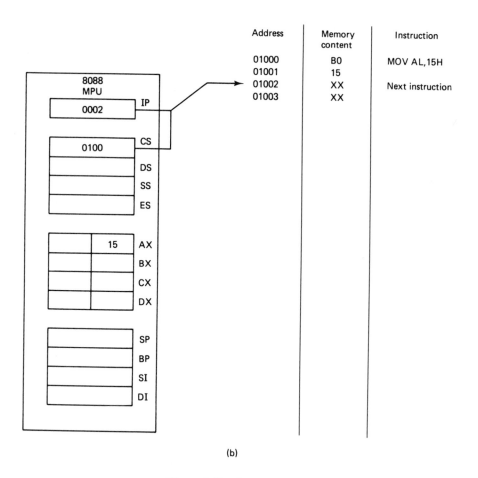

Address	Memory content	Instruction
01000	B0	MOV AL,15H
01001	15	
01002	XX	Next instruction
01003	XX	

(b)

Figure 2.30 (Continued)

the *base, index,* and *displacement.* Using these elements, the effective address calculation is made by the general formula

$$EA = Base + Index + Displacement$$

Figure 2.31 also identifies the registers that can be used to hold the values of the segment base, base, and index. For example, it tells us that any of the four segment registers can be the source of the segment base for the physical address calculation and that the value of base for the effective address can be in either the base register (BX) or base pointer register (BP). Also identified in Fig. 2.31 are the sizes permitted for the displacement.

Not all of these elements are always used in the effective address calculation. In fact, a number of memory addressing modes are defined by using various combinations of these elements. They are called *register indirect addressing, based ad-*

PA = SBA : EA

PA = Segment base : Base + Index + Displacement

$$PA = \begin{Bmatrix} CS \\ SS \\ DS \\ ES \end{Bmatrix} : \begin{Bmatrix} BX \\ BP \end{Bmatrix} + \begin{Bmatrix} SI \\ DI \end{Bmatrix} + \begin{Bmatrix} \text{8-bit displacement} \\ \text{16-bit displacement} \end{Bmatrix}$$

Figure 2.31 Physical and effective address computation for memory operands.

dressing, indexed addressing, and *based-indexed addressing.* For instance, using based addressing mode, the effective address calculation includes just a base. These addressing modes provide the programmer with different ways of computing the effective address of an operand in memory. Next, we will examine each of the memory operand addressing modes in detail.

Direct Addressing Mode. *Direct addressing mode* is similar to immediate addressing in that information is encoded directly into the instruction. However, in this case, the instruction opcode is followed by an effective address, instead of the data. As shown in Fig. 2.32, this effective address is used directly as the 16-bit offset of the storage location of the operand from the location specified by the current value in the segment register selected. The default segment register is DS. Therefore, the 20-bit physical address of the operand in memory is normally obtained as DS:EA. But, by using a *segment override prefix* (SEG) in the instruction, any of the four segment registers can be referenced.

An example of an instruction that uses direct addressing mode for its source operand is

```
MOV CX, [1234H]
```

This stands for "move the contents of the memory location with offset 1234_{16} in the current data segment into internal register CX." The offset is encoded as part of the instruction's machine code.

In Fig. 2.33(a), we find that the offset is stored in the two byte locations that follow the instruction's opcode. As the instruction is executed, the 8088 combines 1234_{16} with 0200_{16} to get the physical address of the source operand as follows:

$$PA = 02000_{16} + 1234_{16}$$
$$= 03234_{16}$$

Then it reads the word of data starting at this address, which is $BEED_{16}$, and loads it into the CX register. This result is illustrated in Fig. 2.33(b).

PA = Segment base: Direct address

$$PA = \begin{Bmatrix} CS \\ DS \\ SS \\ ES \end{Bmatrix} : \begin{Bmatrix} \text{Direct address} \end{Bmatrix}$$

Figure 2.32 Computation of a direct memory address.

Register Indirect Addressing Mode. *Register indirect addressing mode* is similar to the direct addressing we just described, in that an effective address is combined with the contents of DS to obtain a physical address. However, it differs in the way the offset is specified. Figure 2.34 shows that this time EA resides in either a base register or an index register within the 8088. The base register can be either base register BX or base pointer register BP, and the index register can be source index register SI or destination index register DI. Another segment register can be referenced by using a segment override prefix.

An example of an instruction that uses register indirect addressing for its source operand is

```
MOV AX,[SI]
```

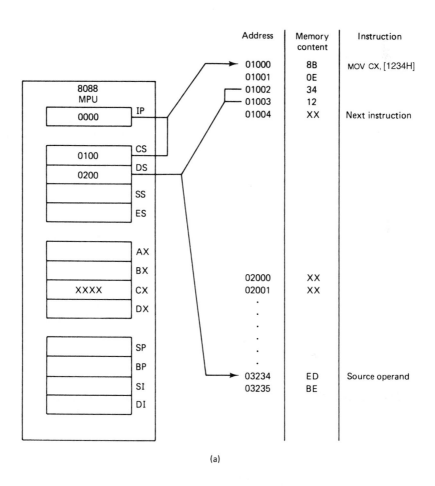

(a)

Figure 2.33 (a) Direct addressing mode instruction before fetch and execution. (b) After execution.

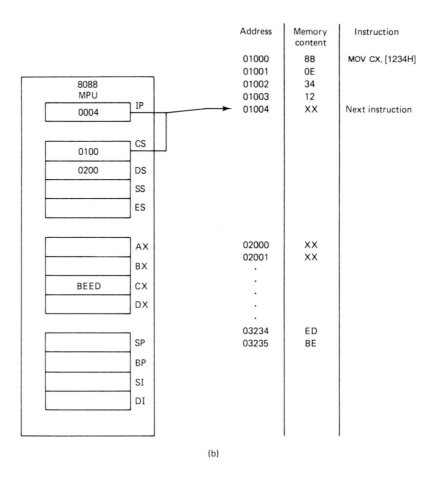

Address	Memory content	Instruction
01000	8B	MOV CX, [1234H]
01001	0E	
01002	34	
01003	12	
01004	XX	Next instruction
02000	XX	
02001	XX	
.		
.		
.		
.		
03234	ED	
03235	BE	

8088
MPU

IP 0004

CS 0100

DS 0200

SS

ES

AX

BX

CX BEED

DX

SP

BP

SI

DI

(b)

Figure 2.33 (Continued)

Execution of this instruction moves the contents of the memory location that is offset from the beginning of the current data segment by the value of EA in register SI into the AX register.

For instance, as shown in Fig. 2.35(a) and (b), if SI contains 1234_{16} and DS contains 0200_{16}, the result produced by executing the instruction is that the contents of memory location

$$PA = 02000_{16} + 1234_{16}$$

$$= 0323416$$

are moved to the AX register. Notice in Fig. 2.35(b) that this value is $BEED_{16}$. In this example, the value 1234_{16} that was found in the SI register must have been loaded with another instruction prior to executing the MOV instruction.

PA = Segment base: Indirect address

$$PA = \begin{Bmatrix} CS \\ DS \\ SS \\ ES \end{Bmatrix} : \begin{Bmatrix} BX \\ BP \\ SI \\ DI \end{Bmatrix}$$

Figure 2.34 Computation of an indirect memory address.

The result produced by executing this instruction and the example for the direct addressing mode are the same. However, they differ in the way in which the physical address was generated. The direct addressing method lends itself to applications where the value of EA is a constant. On the other hand, register indirect addressing can be used when the value of EA is calculated and stored, for example, in SI by a previous instruction. That is, EA is a variable. For instance, the instructions executed just before our example instruction could have incremented the value in SI by two.

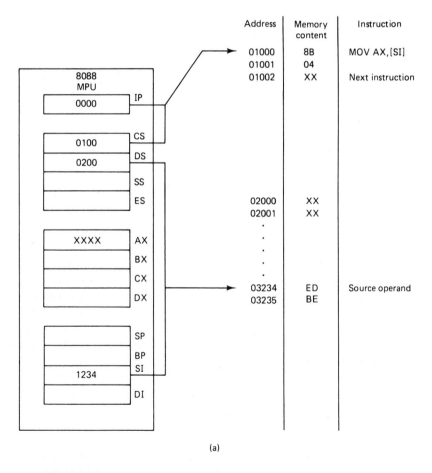

(a)

Figure 2.35 (a) Instruction using register indirect addressing mode before fetch and execution. (b) After execution.

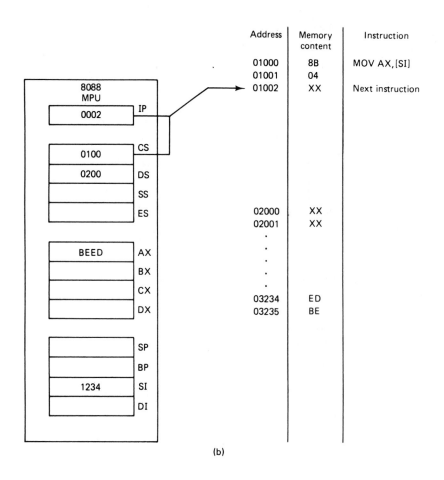

Address	Memory content	Instruction
01000	8B	MOV AX,[SI]
01001	04	
01002	XX	Next instruction
02000	XX	
02001	XX	
03234	ED	
03235	BE	

(b)

Figure 2.35 (Continued)

Based Addressing Mode. In the *based addressing mode*, the effective address of the operand is obtained by adding a direct or indirect displacement to the contents of either base register BX or base pointer register BP. The physical address calculation is shown in Fig. 2.36(a). Looking at Fig. 2.36(b), we see that the value in the base register defines the beginning of a data structure, such as a record, in memory and the displacement selects an element within this structure. To access a different element in the record, the programmer simply changes the value of the displacement. On the other hand, to access the same element in another similar record, the programmer can change the value in the base register so that it points to the beginning of the new record.

A MOV instruction that uses based addressing to specify the location of its destination operand is as follows:

```
MOV   [BX] + 1234H,AL
```

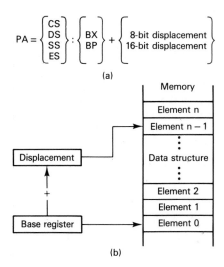

(a)

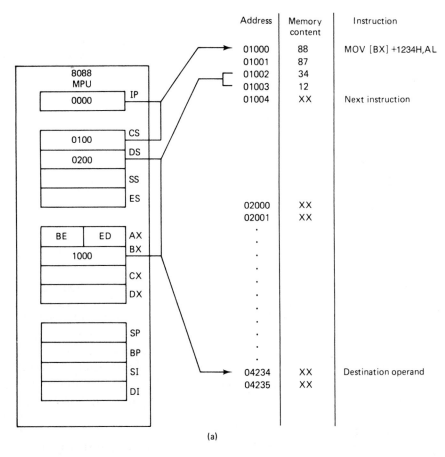

(b)

Figure 2.36 (a) Computation of a based address. (b) Based addressing of a structure of data.

(a)

Figure 2.37 (a) Instruction using direct base pointer addressing mode before fetch and execution. (b) After execution.

This instruction uses base register BX and direct displacement 1234_{16} to derive the EA of the destination operand. The based addressing mode is implemented by specifying the base register in brackets followed by a + sign and the direct displacement. The source operand in this example is located in byte accumulator AL.

As shown in Fig. 2.37(a) and (b), the fetch and execution of this instruction causes the 8088 to calculate the physical address of the destination operand from the contents of DS, BX, and the direct displacement. The result is

$$PA = 02000_{16} + 1000_{16} + 1234_{16}$$

$$= 04234_{16}$$

Then it writes the contents of source operand AL into the storage location at 04234_{16}. The result is that ED_{16} is written into the destination memory location. Again, the default segment register for this physical address calculation is DS, but can be changed to another segment register with the segment override prefix.

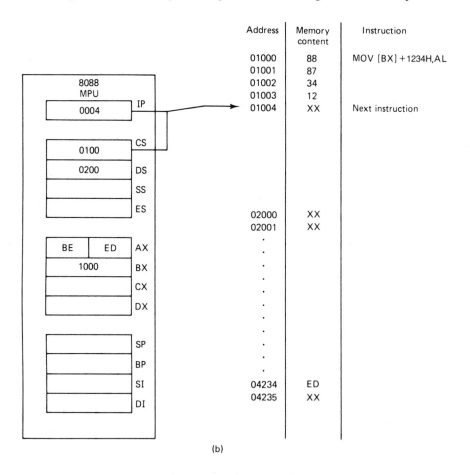

(b)

Figure 2.37 (Continued)

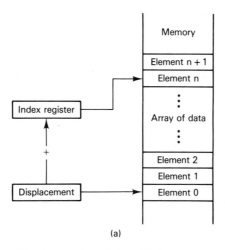

PA = Segment base: Index + Displacement

$$PA = \left\{ \begin{matrix} CS \\ DS \\ SS \\ ES \end{matrix} \right\} : \left\{ \begin{matrix} SI \\ DI \end{matrix} \right\} + \left\{ \begin{matrix} \text{8-bit displacement} \\ \text{16-bit displacement} \end{matrix} \right\}$$

(b)

Figure 2.38 (a) Indexed addressing of an array of data elements. (b) Computation of an indexed address.

If BP is used instead of BX, the calculation of the physical address is performed using the contents of the stack segment (SS) register instead of DS. This permits access to data in the stack segment of memory.

Indexed Addressing Mode. *Indexed addressing mode* works in a manner similar to that of the based addressing mode we just described. However, as shown in Fig. 2.38(a), indexed addressing mode uses the value of the displacement as a pointer to the starting point of an array of data in memory and the contents of the specified register as an index that selects the specific element in the array that is to be accessed. For instance, for the byte-size element array in Fig. 2.38(a), the index register holds the value n. In this way, it selects data element n in the array. Figure 2.38(b) shows how the physical address is obtained from the value in a segment register, an index in the SI or DI register, and a displacement.

Here is an example:

```
MOV  AL, [SI] + 2000H
```

The source operand has been specified using direct indexed addressing mode. Notice that the *direct displacement* is 2000H. Just like for the base register in based addressing, the index register, which is SI, is enclosed in brackets. The effective address is calculated as

$$EA = (SI) + 2000H$$

Sec. 2.16   Addressing Modes of the 8088/8086

65

and the physical address is obtained by combining the contents of DS with EA.

$$PA = DS:(SI) + 2000H$$

The example in Fig. 2.39(a) and (b) shows the result of executing the move instruction. First the physical address of the source operand is calculated from the contents of DS, SI, and the direct displacement.

$$PA = 02000_{16} + 2000_{16} + 1234_{16}$$

$$= 05234_{16}$$

Then the byte of data stored at this location, which is BE_{16}, is read into the lower byte (AL) of the accumulator register.

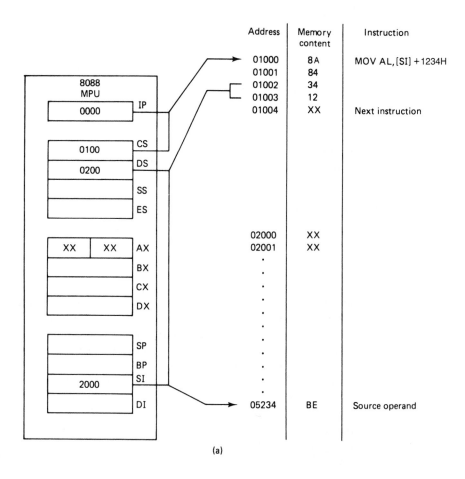

(a)

Figure 2.39 (a) Instruction using direct indexed addressing mode before fetch and execution. (b) After execution.

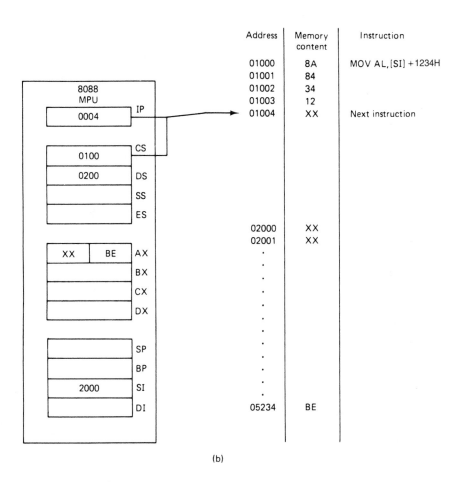

Address	Memory content	Instruction
01000	8A	MOV AL,[SI] +1234H
01001	84	
01002	34	
01003	12	
01004	XX	Next instruction
02000	XX	
02001	XX	
.		
.		
.		
.		
.		
.		
.		
.		
.		
05234	BE	

(b)

Figure 2.39 (Continued)

Based-Indexed Addressing Mode. Combining the based addressing mode and the indexed addressing modes together results in a new, more powerful mode known as *based-indexed addressing mode*. This addressing mode can be used to access complex data structures such as two-dimensional arrays. Figure 2.40(a) shows how it can be used to access elements in an $m \times n$ array of data. Notice that the displacement, which is a fixed value, locates the array in memory. The base register specifies the m coordinate of the array and the index register identifies the n coordinate. Any element in the array can be accessed simply by changing the values in the base and index registers. The registers permitted in the based-indexed physical address computation are shown in Fig. 2.40(b).

Let us consider an example of a move instruction using this type of addressing.

```
MOV   AH,[BX][SI] + 1234H
```

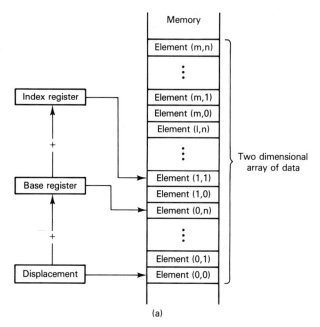

(a)

PA = Segment base: Base + Index + Displacement

$$PA = \begin{Bmatrix} CS \\ DS \\ SS \\ ES \end{Bmatrix} : \begin{Bmatrix} BX \\ BP \end{Bmatrix} + \begin{Bmatrix} SI \\ DI \end{Bmatrix} + \begin{Bmatrix} \text{8-bit displacement} \\ \text{16-bit displacement} \end{Bmatrix}$$

(b)

Figure 2.40 (a) Based-indexed addressing of a two-dimensional array of data. (b) Computation of a based-indexed address.

Notice that the source operand is accessed using based-indexed addressing mode. Therefore, the effective address of the source operand is obtained as

$$EA = (BX) + (SI) + 1234H$$

and the physical address of the operand is obtained from the current contents of DS and the calculated EA.

$$PA = DS:(BX) + (SI) + 1234H$$

An example of executing this instruction is illustrated in Fig. 2.41(a) and (b). Using the contents of the various registers in the example, the address of the source operand is calculated as

$$PA = 02000_{16} + 1000_{16} + 2000_{16} + 1234_{16}$$
$$= 6234_{16}$$

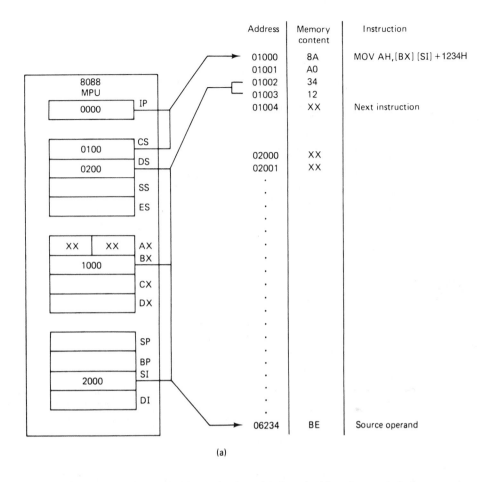

Address	Memory content	Instruction
01000	8A	MOV AH,[BX] [SI] +1234H
01001	A0	
01002	34	
01003	12	
01004	XX	Next instruction
02000	XX	
02001	XX	
06234	BE	Source operand

(a)

Figure 2.41   (a) Instruction using based-indexed addressing mode before fetch and execution. (b) After execution.

Execution of the instruction causes the value stored at this location to be read into AH.

ASSIGNMENTS

Section 2.2

1. What tells a computer what to do, where to get data, how to process the data, and where to put the results when done?
2. What is the name given to a sequence of instructions that is used to guide a computer through a task?
3. What is the native language of the 8088?

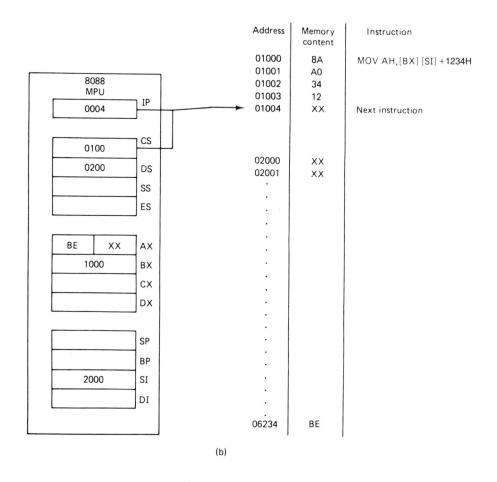

Address	Memory content	Instruction
01000	8A	MOV AH,[BX] [SI] +1234H
01001	A0	
01002	34	
01003	12	
01004	XX	Next instruction
02000	XX	
02001	XX	
06234	BE	

(b)

Figure 2.41   (Continued)

4. How does machine language differ from assembly language?

5. What does opcode stand for? Give two examples.

6. What is an operand? Give two types.

7. In the assembly language statement

```
START:   ADD  AX,BX   ;Add BX to AX
```

what is the label?

8. What is the function of an assembler? A compiler?

9. What is object code? What is source code?

10. Give two benefits derived from writing programs in assembly language instead of a high-level language.

11. What is meant by the phrase real-time application?

12. List two hardware-related applications that require use of assembly language programming. Name two software-related applications.

Section 2.3

13. Name the two internal processing units of the 8088.
14. Which processing unit of the 8088 is the interface to the outside world?
15. How large is the instruction queue of the 8088? The 8086?
16. List the elements of the execution unit.

Section 2.4

17. What is the purpose of a software model for a microprocessor?
18. What must an assembly-language programmer know about the registers within the 8088 microprocessor?
19. How many registers are located within the 8088?
20. How large is the 8088's memory address space?

Section 2.5

21. What is the highest address in the 8088's memory address space? Lowest address?
22. Is memory in the 8088 microcomputer organized as bytes, words, or double words?
23. The contents of memory location $B0000_{16}$ are FF_{16}, and those at $B0001_{16}$ are 00_{16}. What is the even-addressed data word stored at address $B0000_{16}$?
24. Show how the double word 12345678_{16} will be stored in memory starting at address $A001_{16}$.

Section 2.6

25. List five data types directly processed by the 8088.
26. Express each of the signed decimal integers that follow as either a byte- or word-hexadecimal number (use 2s-complement notation for negative numbers).
　(a) +127
　(b) −10
　(c) −128
　(d) +500
27. How would the integer in problem 26(d) be stored in memory starting at address $0A000_{16}$?
28. How would the decimal number −1000 be expressed for processing by the 8088?

29. Express the decimal numbers that follow as unpacked and packed BCD bytes.

(a) 29

(b) 88

30. How would the BCD number in problem 29(a) be stored in memory starting at address $0B000_{16}$? Assume that the least significant digit is stored at the lower address.

31. What is the statement that follows if it is coded in ASCII represented by the binary strings as

```
1001110
1000101
1011000
1010100
0100000
1001001
```

32. How would the decimal number 1234 be coded in ASCII and stored in memory starting at address $0C000_{16}$? Assume that the least significant digit is stored at the lower addressed memory location.

Section 2.7

33. How much memory can be active at a given time in the 8088 microcomputer?

34. Which of the 8088's internal registers are used for memory segmentation?

35. How much of the 8088's active memory is available as general-purpose data storage memory?

36. Which part of the 8088's memory address space is used to store instructions of a program?

Section 2.8

37. What is the dedicated use of the part of the 8088's address space from 00000_{16} through $0007F_{16}$?

38. What is stored at address $FFFF0_{16}$?

Section 2.9

39. What is the function of the instruction pointer register?

40. Give an overview of the fetch and the execution of an instruction as performed by the 8088.

41. What happens to the value in IP each time the 8088 fetches instruction code?

Section 2.10

42. Make a list of the general-purpose data registers of the 8088.

43. How is the word value of a data register labeled?

44. How are the upper and lower bytes of a data register denoted?

45. What dedicated operations are assigned to the CX register?

Section 2.11

46. What kind of information is stored in the pointer and index registers?

47. Name the two pointer registers.

48. For which segment register are the contents of the pointer registers used as an offset?

49. For which segment register are the contents of the index registers used as an offset?

50. What is the difference between SI and DI?

Section 2.12

51. Categorize each flag bit of the 8088 as either a control flag or a flag that monitors the status due to execution of an instruction.

52. Describe the function of each of the status flags.

53. How are the status flags used by software?

54. Which flag determines whether the address for a string operation is incremented or decremented?

55. Can the state of the flags be modified through software?

Section 2.13

56. What is the word length of the 8088's physical address?

57. What two address elements are combined to form a physical address?

58. Calculate the value of each of the physical addresses that follows. Assume all numbers as hexadecimal numbers.
  (a) 1000:1234
  (b) 0100:ABCD
  (c) A200:12CF
  (d) B2C0:FA12

59. Find the unknown value for each of the following physical addresses. Assume all numbers as hexadecimal numbers.
  (a) A000:? = A0123
  (b) ?:14DA = 235DA
  (c) D765:? = DABC0
  (d) ?:CD21 = 32D21

60. If the current values in the code segment register and the instruction pointer are 0200_{16} and $01AC_{16}$, respectively, what is the physical address of the next instruction?

61. A data segment is to be located from address $A0000_{16}$ to $AFFFF_{16}$; what value must be loaded into DS?

62. If the data segment register contains the value found in problem 61, what value must be loaded into DI if it is to point to a destination operand stored at address $A1234_{16}$ in memory?

Section 2.14

63. What is the function of the stack?

64. If the current values in the stack segment register and stack pointer are $C000_{16}$ and $FF00_{16}$, respectively, what is the address of the top of the stack?

65. For the base and offset addresses in problem 64, how many words of data are currently held in the stack?

66. Show how the value $EE11_{16}$ from register AX would be pushed onto the top of the stack as it exists in problem 64.

Section 2.15

67. For the 8088 microprocessor, are the input/output and memory address spaces common or separate?

68. How large is the 8088's I/O address space?

69. What is the name given to the part of the I/O address space from 0000_{16} through $00FF_{16}$?

Section 2.16

70. What is meant by an addressing mode?

71. Make a list of the addressing modes available on the 8088.

72. Identify the addressing modes used for the source and the destination operands in the instructions that follow.
   (a) MOV AL,BL
   (b) MOV AX,0FFH
   (c) MOV [DI],AX
   (d) MOV DI,[SI]
   (e) MOV [BX] + 0400H,CX
   (f) MOV [DI] + 0400H,AH
   (g) MOV [BX] [DI] + 0400H,AL

73. Compute the physical address for the specified operand in each of the following instructions from problem 72. The register contents and variables are as follows: $(CS) = 0A00_{16}$, $(DS) = 0B00_{16}$, $(SI) = 0100_{16}$, $(DI) = 0200_{16}$, and $(BX) = 0300_{16}$.

(a) Destination operand of the instruction in (c)
(b) Source operand of the instruction in (d)
(c) Destination operand of the instruction in (e)
(d) Destination operand of the instruction in (f)
(e) Destination operand of the instruction in (g)

Machine Language Coding and the DEBUG Software Development Program of the IBM PC

▲ 3.1 INTRODUCTION

In this chapter, we begin by exploring how the instructions for the 8088 microprocessor are encoded. This is followed by a study of the software development environment provided for this microprocessor with the IBM PC. Here we examine the DEBUG program. DEBUG is a program execution/debug tool that operates in the IBM PC's *disk operating system* (DOS) environment. First DEBUG's command set is thoroughly examined. Then we use these commands to load, assemble, execute, and debug programs. The topics discussed in this chapter are as follows:

1. Converting assembly language instructions to machine code
2. Encoding a complete program in machine code
3. The IBM PC and its DEBUG program
4. Examining and modifying the contents of memory
5. Input and output of data
6. Hexadecimal addition and subtraction
7. Loading, verifying, and saving machine code programs
8. Assembling instructions with the ASSEMBLE command
9. Executing instructions and programs with the TRACE and GO commands
10. Debugging a program

▲ 3.2 CONVERTING ASSEMBLY LANGUAGE INSTRUCTIONS TO MACHINE CODE

To convert an assembly language program to machine code, we must convert each assembly language instruction to its equivalent machine code instruction. In general, the machine code for an instruction specifies things like what operation is to be performed, what operand or operands are to be used, whether the operation is performed on byte or word data, whether the operation involves operands that are located in registers or a register and a storage location in memory, and if one of the operands is in memory, how its address is to be generated. All of this information is encoded into the bits of the machine code for the instruction.

The machine code instructions of the 8088 vary in the number of bytes used to encode them. Some instructions can be encoded with just one byte, others in two bytes, and many require even more. The maximum number of bytes an instruction might take is six. Single byte instructions generally specify a simpler operation with a register or a flag bit. For instance, *complement carry* (CMC) is an example of a single byte instruction. It is specified by the machine code byte 11110101_2, which equals $F5_{16}$. That is,

$$CMC = 11110101_2 = F5_{16}$$

The machine code for instructions can be obtained by following the formats that are used in encoding the instructions of the 8088 microprocessor. Most multibyte instructions use the *general instruction format* shown in Fig. 3.1. Exceptions to this format exist and will be considered later. For now, let us describe the functions of the various bits and fields (groups of bits) in each byte of this format.

Looking at Fig. 3.1, we see that byte 1 contains three kinds of information: the *operation code* (opcode), the *register direction bit* (D), and the *data size bit* (W). Let us summarize the function of each of these pieces of information.

1. Opcode field (6-bits)—specifies the operation, such as add, subtract, or move, that is to be performed.
2. Register direction bit (D bit)—specifies whether the register operand that is specified in byte 2 is the source or destination operand. A logic 1 at this bit position indicates that the register operand is a destination operand and a logic 0 indicates that it is a source operand.
3. Data size bit (W bit)—specifies whether the operation will be performed on 8-bit or 16-bit data. Logic 0 selects 8 bits and 1 selects 16 bits as the data size.

For instance, if a 16-bit value is to be added to register AX, the six most significant bits specify the add register operation. This opcode is 000000. The next bit, D, will be at logic 1 to specify that a register, AX in this case, holds the destination operand. Finally, the least significant bit, W, will be logic 1 to specify a 16-bit data operation.

The second byte in Fig. 3.1 has three fields. They are the *mode* (MOD) *field*, the *register* (REG) *field*, and the *register/memory* (R/M) *field*. These fields are used

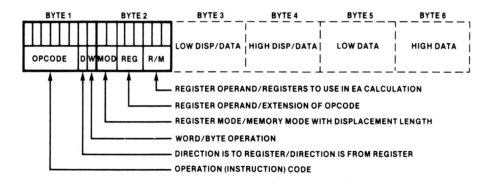

Figure 3.1 General instruction format. (Reprinted by permission of Intel Corp., © Intel Corp. 1979)

to specify which register is used for the first operand and where the second operand is stored. The second operand can be in either a register or a memory location.

The 3-bit REG field is used to identify the register for the first operand. This is the operand that was defined as the source or destination by the D bit in byte 1. The encoding for each of the 8088's registers is shown in Fig. 3.2. Here we find that the 16-bit register AX and the 8-bit register AL are specified by the same binary code. Notice that the decision whether to use AX or AL is made based on the setting of the operation size (W) bit in byte 1.

For instance, in our earlier example, we said that the first operand, which is the destination operand, is register AX. For this case, the REG field is set to 000.

The 2-bit MOD field and 3-bit R/M field together specify the second operand. Encoding for these two fields is shown in Figs. 3.3(a) and (b), respectively. MOD indicates whether the operand is in a register or memory. Notice that in the case of a second operand that is in a register, the MOD field is always 11. The R/M field along with the W bit from byte 1 selects the register.

For example, if the second operand, the source operand, in our earlier addition example is to be in BX, the MOD and R/M fields will be made 11 and 011, respectively.

REG	W = 0	W = 1
000	AL	AX
001	CL	CX
010	DL	DX
011	BL	BX
100	AH	SP
101	CH	BP
110	DH	SI
111	BH	DI

Figure 3.2 Register (REG) field encoding. (Reprinted by permission of Intel Corp., © Intel Corp. 1979)

CODE	EXPLANATION
00	Memory Mode, no displacement follows*
01	Memory Mode, 8-bit displacement follows
10	Memory Mode, 16-bit displacement follows
11	Register Mode (no displacement)

*Except when R/M = 110, then 16-bit displacement follows

(a)

MOD = 11			EFFECTIVE ADDRESS CALCULATION			
R/M	W = 0	W = 1	R/M	MOD = 00	MOD = 01	MOD = 10
000	AL	AX	000	(BX) + (SI)	(BX) + (SI) + D8	(BX) + (SI) + D16
001	CL	CX	001	(BX) + (DI)	(BX) + (DI) + D8	(BX) + (DI) + D16
010	DL	DX	010	(BP) + (SI)	(BP) + (SI) + D8	(BP) + (SI) + D16
011	BL	BX	011	(BP) + (DI)	(BP) + (DI) + D8	(BP) + (DI) + D16
100	AH	SP	100	(SI)	(SI) + D8	(SI) + D16
101	CH	BP	101	(DI)	(DI) + D8	(DI) + D16
110	DH	SI	110	DIRECT ADDRESS	(BP) + D8	(BP) + D16
111	BH	DI	111	(BX)	(BX) + D8	(BX) + D16

(b)

Figure 3.3 (a) Mode (MOD) field encoding. (Reprinted by permission of Intel Corp., © Intel Corp. 1979) (b) Register/memory (R/M) field encoding. (Reprinted by permission of Intel Corp., © Intel Corp. 1979)

EXAMPLE 3.1

The instruction

```
MOV BL,AL
```

stands for "move the byte contents from source register AL to destination register BL." Using the general format in Fig. 3.1, show how to encode the instruction in machine code. Assume that the 6-bit opcode for the move operation is 100010.

Solution

In byte 1 the first six bits specify the move operation and thus must be 100010.

$$OPCODE = 100010$$

The next bit, which is D, indicates whether the register that is specified by the REG part of byte 2 is a source or destination operand. Let us say that we will encode AL in the REG field of byte 2; therefore, D is set equal to 0 for source operand.

$$D = 0$$

The last bit (W) in byte 1 must specify a byte operation. For this reason, it is also set to 0.

$$W = 0$$

This leads to

$$BYTE\ 1 = 10001000_2 = 88_{16}$$

In byte 2 the source operand, which is specified by the REG field, is AL. The corresponding code from Fig. 3.2 is:

$$REG = 000$$

Since the second operand is also a register, the MOD field is made 11. The R/M field specifies that the destination register is BL for which the code from Fig. 3.3(b) is 011. This gives

$$MOD = 11$$
$$R/M = 011$$

Therefore, byte 2 is

$$BYTE\ 2 = 11000011_2 = C3_{16}$$

Thus the hexadecimal code for the instruction is given by

```
MOV BL,AL = 88C3H
```

For a second operand that is located in memory, there are a number of different ways its location can be specified. That is, any of the addressing modes supported by the 8088 microprocessor can be used to generate its address. The addressing mode is selected with the MOD and R/M fields.

Notice in Fig. 3.3(b) that the addressing mode for an operand in memory is indicated by one of the three values 00, 01, or 10 in the MOD field and an appropriate R/M code. The different ways in which the operand's address can be generated are shown in the effective address calculation part of the table in Fig. 3.3(b). These different address calculation expressions correspond to the addressing modes we introduced in Chapter 2. For instance, if the base register (BX) contains the memory address, this fact is encoded into the instruction by making MOD=00 and R/M=111.

EXAMPLE 3.2

The instruction

$$ADD\ AX, [SI]$$

stands for add the 16-bit contents of the memory location indirectly specified by SI to the contents of AX. Encode the instruction in machine code. The opcode for add is 000000.

Solution

To specify a 16-bit add operation with a register as the destination, the first byte of machine code will be

$$\text{BYTE } 1 = 00000011_2 = 03_{16}$$

The REG field bits in byte 2 are 000 to select AX as the destination register. The other operand is in memory and its address is specified by the contents of SI with no displacement. In Figs. 3.3(a) and (b), we find that for indirect addressing using SI with no displacement MOD equals 00 and R/M equals 100. That is,

$$\text{MOD} = 00$$

$$\text{R/M} = 100$$

This gives
$$\text{BYTE } 2 = 00000100_2 = 04_{16}$$

Thus the machine code for the instruction is

$$ADD\ AX, [SI] = 0304H$$

Some of the addressing modes of the 8088 need either data or an address displacement to be coded into the instruction. These types of information are encoded using additional bytes. For instance, looking at Fig. 3.1, we see that byte 3 is needed in the encoding of an instruction if it uses a byte size address displacement and both byte 3 and byte 4 are needed if the instruction uses a word size displacement.

The size of the displacement is encoded into the MOD field. For example, if the effective address is to be generated by the expression

$$(BX) + D8$$

where D8 stands for 8-bit displacement, MOD is set to 01 to specify memory mode with an 8-bit displacement and R/M is set to 111 to select BX.

Bytes 3 and 4 are also used to encode byte-wide immediate operands, word-wide immediate operands, and direct addresses. For example, in an instruction where direct addressing is used to identify the location of an operand in memory, the MOD field must be 00 and the R/M field 110. The actual value of the operand's address is coded into the bytes that follow.

If both a 16-bit displacement and a 16-bit immediate operand are used in the same instruction, the displacement is encoded into bytes 3 and 4 and the immediate operand into bytes 5 and 6.

EXAMPLE 3.3

What is the machine code for the instruction

$$XOR \ CL, \ [1234H]$$

This instruction stands for exclusive-OR the byte of data at memory address 1234_{16} with the byte contents of CL. The opcode for exclusive-OR is 001100.

Solution

Using 001100 as the opcode bits, 1 to denote the register as the destination operand, and 0 to denote byte data, we get

$$BYTE \ 1 = 00110010_2 = 32_{16}$$

The REG field has to specify CL which makes it equal to 001. In this case a direct address has been specified for operand 2. This requires MOD=00 and R/M=110. Thus

$$BYTE \ 2 = 00001110_2 = 0E_{16}$$

To specify the address 1234_{16}, we must use byte 3 and byte 4. The least significant byte of the address is encoded first followed by the most significant byte. This gives

$$BYTE \ 3 = 34_{16}$$

and

$$BYTE \ 4 = 12_{16}$$

Thus the machine code form of the instruction is given by

$$XOR \ CL, 1234H = 320E3412H$$

EXAMPLE 3.4

The instruction

```
ADD [BX][DI]+1234H,AX
```

means add the word contents of AX to the contents of the memory location specified by based-indexed addressing mode. The opcode for the add operation is 000000.

Solution

The add opcode, which is 000000, a 0 for source operand, and a 1 for word data gives

$$\text{BYTE } 1 = 00000001_2 = 01_{16}$$

The REG field in byte 2 is 000 to specify AX as the source register. Since there is a displacement and it needs 16 bits for encoding, the MOD field obtained from Fig. 3.3(a) is 10. The R/M field, which is also obtained from Fig. 3.3(b), is set to 001 for an effective address generated from DI and BX. This gives the second byte as

$$\text{BYTE } 2 = 10000001_2 = 81_{16}$$

The displacement 1234_{16} is encoded in the next two bytes, with the least significant byte first. Therefore, the machine code that results is

```
ADD [BX][DI]+1234H,AX = 01813412H
```

As we indicated earlier, the general format in Fig. 3.1 cannot be used to encode all of the instructions that can be executed by the 8088. There are minor modifications that must be made to this general format to encode a few instructions. In some instructions one or more additional single-bit fields need to be added. These one-bit fields and their functions are shown in Fig. 3.4.

For instance, the general format of the *repeat* (REP) instruction is

```
REP = 1111001Z
```

Here bit Z is 1 or 0 depending upon whether the repeat operation is to be done when the zero flag is set or when it is reset. Similarly the other two bits S and V in Fig. 3.4 are used to encode sign extension for arithmetic instructions and to specify the source of the count for shift or rotate instructions, respectively.

The formats for all of the instructions in the 8088's instruction set are shown in Fig. 3.5. This is the information that can be used to encode any 8088 instruction.

Instructions that involve a segment register need a two-bit field to encode which register is to be affected. This field is called the *SR field*. The four segment registers ES, CS, SS, and DS are encoded according to the table in Fig. 3.6.

Field	Value	Function
S	0 1	No sign extension Sign extend 8-bit immediate data to 16 bits if W=1
V	0 1	Shift/rotate count is one Shift/rotate count is specified in CL register
Z	0 1	Repeat/loop while zero flag is clear Repeat/loop while zero flag is set

Figure 3.4 Additional 1-bit fields and their functions. (Reprinted by permission of Intel Corp., © Intel Corp. 1979)

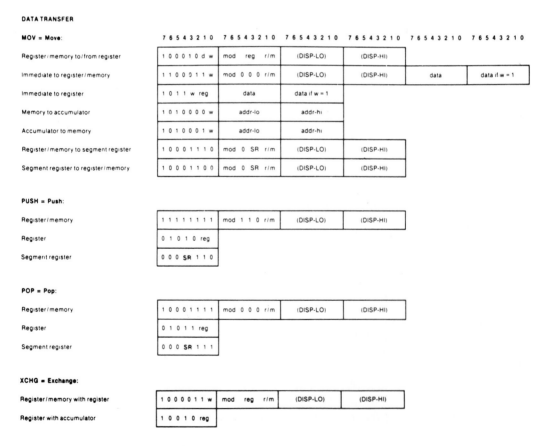

Figure 3.5 8088 instruction encoding tables. (Reprinted by permission of Intel Corp., © Intel Corp. 1979)

IN = Input from:

Fixed port

| 1 1 1 0 0 1 0 w | DATA-8 |

Variable port

| 1 1 1 0 1 1 0 w |

OUT = Output to:

Fixed port

| 1 1 1 0 0 1 1 w | DATA-8 |

Variable port

| 1 1 1 0 1 1 1 w |

XLAT = Translate byte to AL

| 1 1 0 1 0 1 1 1 |

LEA = Load EA to register

| 1 0 0 0 1 1 0 1 | mod   reg   r/m | (DISP-LO) | (DISP-HI) |

LDS = Load pointer to DS

| 1 1 0 0 0 1 0 1 | mod   reg   r/m | (DISP-LO) | (DISP-HI) |

LES = Load pointer to ES

| 1 1 0 0 0 1 0 0 | mod   reg   r/m | (DISP-LO) | (DISP-HI) |

LAHF = Load AH with flags

| 1 0 0 1 1 1 1 1 |

SAHF = Store AH into flags

| 1 0 0 1 1 1 1 0 |

PUSHF = Push flags

| 1 0 0 1 1 1 0 0 |

POPF = Pop flags

| 1 0 0 1 1 1 0 1 |

ARITHMETIC

ADD = Add:

7 6 5 4 3 2 1 0	7 6 5 4 3 2 1 0	7 6 5 4 3 2 1 0	7 6 5 4 3 2 1 0	7 6 5 4 3 2 1 0	7 6 5 4 3 2 1 0

Reg/memory with register to either

| 0 0 0 0 0 0 d w | mod   reg   r/m | (DISP-LO) | (DISP-HI) | | |

Immediate to register/memory

| 1 0 0 0 0 0 s w | mod 0 0 0 r/m | (DISP-LO) | (DISP-HI) | data | data if s: w=01 |

Immediate to accumulator

| 0 0 0 0 0 1 0 w | data | data if w=1 | | | |

ADC = Add with carry:

Reg/memory with register to either

| 0 0 0 1 0 0 d w | mod   reg   r/m | (DISP-LO) | (DISP-HI) | | |

Immediate to register/memory

| 1 0 0 0 0 0 s w | mod 0 1 0 r/m | (DISP-LO) | (DISP-HI) | data | data if s: w=01 |

Immediate to accumulator

| 0 0 0 1 0 1 0 w | data | data if w=1 | | | |

INC = Increment:

Register/memory

| 1 1 1 1 1 1 1 w | mod 0 0 0 r/m | (DISP-LO) | (DISP-HI) |

Register

| 0 1 0 0 0 reg |

AAA = ASCII adjust for add

| 0 0 1 1 0 1 1 1 |

DAA = Decimal adjust for add

| 0 0 1 0 0 1 1 1 |

SUB = Subtract:

Reg/memory and register to either

| 0 0 1 0 1 0 d w | mod   reg   r/m | (DISP-LO) | (DISP-HI) | | |

Immediate from register/memory

| 1 0 0 0 0 0 s w | mod 1 0 1 r/m | (DISP-LO) | (DISP-HI) | data | data if s: w=01 |

Immediate from accumulator

| 0 0 1 0 1 1 0 w | data | data if w=1 | | | |

Figure 3.5 (Continued)

SBB = Subtract with borrow:

	7 6 5 4 3 2 1 0	7 6 5 4 3 2 1 0	7 6 5 4 3 2 1 0	7 6 5 4 3 2 1 0	7 6 5 4 3 2 1 0	7 6 5 4 3 2 1 0
Reg/memory and register to either	0 0 0 1 1 0 d w	mod reg r/m	(DISP-LO)	(DISP-HI)		
Immediate from register/memory	1 0 0 0 0 0 s w	mod 0 1 1 r/m	(DISP-LO)	(DISP-HI)	data	data if s: w=01
Immediate from accumulator	0 0 0 1 1 1 0 w	data	data if w=1			

DEC Decrement:

Register/memory	1 1 1 1 1 1 1 w	mod 0 0 1 r/m	(DISP-LO)	(DISP-HI)
Register	0 1 0 0 1 reg			
NEG Change sign	1 1 1 1 0 1 1 w	mod 0 1 1 r/m	(DISP-LO)	(DISP-HI)

CMP = Compare:

Register/memory and register	0 0 1 1 1 0 d w	mod reg r/m	(DISP-LO)	(DISP-HI)		
Immediate with register/memory	1 0 0 0 0 0 s w	mod 1 1 1 r/m	(DISP-LO)	(DISP-HI)	data	data if s: w=1
Immediate with accumulator	0 0 1 1 1 1 0 w	data				
AAS ASCII adjust for subtract	0 0 1 1 1 1 1 1					
DAS Decimal adjust for subtract	0 0 1 0 1 1 1 1					
MUL Multiply (unsigned)	1 1 1 1 0 1 1 w	mod 1 0 0 r/m	(DISP-LO)	(DISP-HI)		

ARITHMETIC

	7 6 5 4 3 2 1 0	7 6 5 4 3 2 1 0	7 6 5 4 3 2 1 0	7 6 5 4 3 2 1 0	7 6 5 4 3 2 1 0	7 6 5 4 3 2 1 0
IMUL Integer multiply (signed)	1 1 1 1 0 1 1 w	mod 1 0 1 r/m	(DISP-LO)	(DISP-HI)		
AAM ASCII adjust for multiply	1 1 0 1 0 1 0 0	0 0 0 0 1 0 1 0	(DISP-LO)	(DISP-HI)		
DIV Divide (unsigned)	1 1 1 1 0 1 1 w	mod 1 1 0 r/m	(DISP-LO)	(DISP-HI)		
IDIV Integer divide (signed)	1 1 1 1 0 1 1 w	mod 1 1 1 r/m	(DISP-LO)	(DISP-HI)		
AAD ASCII adjust for divide	1 1 0 1 0 1 0 1	0 0 0 0 1 0 1 0	(DISP-LO)	(DISP-HI)		
CBW Convert byte to word	1 0 0 1 1 0 0 0					
CWD Convert word to double word	1 0 0 1 1 0 0 1					

LOGIC

NOT Invert	1 1 1 1 0 1 1 w	mod 0 1 0 r/m	(DISP-LO)	(DISP-HI)
SHL/SAL Shift logical/arithmetic left	1 1 0 1 0 0 v w	mod 1 0 0 r/m	(DISP-LO)	(DISP-HI)
SHR Shift logical right	1 1 0 1 0 0 v w	mod 1 0 1 r/m	(DISP-LO)	(DISP-HI)
SAR Shift arithmetic right	1 1 0 1 0 0 v w	mod 1 1 1 r/m	(DISP-LO)	(DISP-HI)
ROL Rotate left	1 1 0 1 0 0 v w	mod 0 0 0 r/m	(DISP-LO)	(DISP-HI)
ROR Rotate right	1 1 0 1 0 0 v w	mod 0 0 1 r/m	(DISP-LO)	(DISP-HI)
RCL Rotate through carry flag left	1 1 0 1 0 0 v w	mod 0 1 0 r/m	(DISP-LO)	(DISP-HI)
RCR Rotate through carry right	1 1 0 1 0 0 v w	mod 0 1 1 r/m	(DISP-LO)	(DISP-HI)

Figure 3.5 (Continued)

AND = And:

Reg/memory with register to either	0 0 1 0 0 0 d w	mod reg r/m	(DISP-LO)	(DISP-HI)		
Immediate to register/memory	1 0 0 0 0 0 0 w	mod 1 0 0 r/m	(DISP-LO)	(DISP-HI)	data	data if w=1
Immediate to accumulator	0 0 1 0 0 1 0 w	data	data if w=1			

TEST = And function to flags no result:

Register/memory and register	0 0 0 1 0 0 d w	mod reg r/m	(DISP-LO)	(DISP-HI)		
Immediate data and register/memory	1 1 1 1 0 1 1 w	mod 0 0 0 r/m	(DISP-LO)	(DISP-HI)	data	data if w=1
Immediate data and accumulator	1 0 1 0 1 0 0 w	data				

OR = Or:

Reg/memory and register to either	0 0 0 0 1 0 d w	mod reg r/m	(DISP-LO)	(DISP-HI)		
Immediate to register/memory	1 0 0 0 0 0 0 w	mod 0 0 1 r/m	(DISP-LO)	(DISP-HI)	data	data if w=1
Immediate to accumulator	0 0 0 0 1 1 0 w	data	data if w=1			

XOR = Exclusive or:

Reg/memory and register to either	0 0 1 1 0 0 d w	mod reg r/m	(DISP-LO)	(DISP-HI)		
Immediate to register/memory	0 0 1 1 0 1 0 w	data	(DISP-LO)	(DISP-HI)	data	data if w=1
Immediate to accumulator	0 0 1 1 0 1 0 w	data	data if w=1			

STRING MANIPULATION

7 6 5 4 3 2 1 0   7 6 5 4 3 2 1 0   7 6 5 4 3 2 1 0   7 6 5 4 3 2 1 0   7 6 5 4 3 2 1 0   7 6 5 4 3 2 1 0

REP = Repeat	1 1 1 1 0 0 1 z
MOVS = Move byte/word	1 0 1 0 0 1 0 w
CMPS = Compare byte/word	1 0 1 0 0 1 1 w
SCAS = Scan byte/word	1 0 1 0 1 1 1 w
LODS = Load byte/wd to AL/AX	1 0 1 0 1 1 0 w
STDS = Stor byte/wd from AL/A	1 0 1 0 1 0 1 w

CONTROL TRANS. ...

CALL = Call:

Direct within segment	1 1 1 0 1 0 0 0	IP-INC-LO	IP-INC-HI	
Indirect within segment	1 1 1 1 1 1 1 1	mod 0 1 0 r/m	(DISP-LO)	(DISP-HI)
Direct intersegment	1 0 0 1 1 0 1 0	IP-lo	IP-hi	
		CS-lo	CS-hi	
Indirect intersegment	1 1 1 1 1 1 1 1	mod 0 1 1 r/m	(DISP-LO)	(DISP-HI)

Figure 3.5 (Continued)

JMP = Unconditional Jump:

Direct within segment	1 1 1 0 1 0 0 1	IP-INC-LO	IP-INC-HI	
Direct within segment-short	1 1 1 0 1 0 1 1	IP-INC8		
Indirect within segment	1 1 1 1 1 1 1 1	mod 1 0 0 r/m	(DISP-LO)	(DISP-HI)
Direct intersegment	1 1 1 0 1 0 1 0	IP-lo	IP-hi	
		CS-lo	CS-hi	
Indirect intersegment	1 1 1 1 1 1 1 1	mod 1 0 1 r/m	(DISP-LO)	(DISP-HI)

RET = Return from CALL:

Within segment	1 1 0 0 0 0 1 1		
Within seg adding immed to SP	1 1 0 0 0 0 1 0	data-lo	data-hi
Intersegment	1 1 0 0 1 0 1 1		
Intersegment adding immediate to SP	1 1 0 0 1 0 1 0	data-lo	data-hi
JE/JZ = Jump on equal/zero	0 1 1 1 0 1 0 0	IP-INC8	
JL/JNGE = Jump on less/not greater or equal	0 1 1 1 1 1 0 0	IP-INC8	
JLE/JNG = Jump on less or equal/not greater	0 1 1 1 1 1 1 0	IP-INC8	
JB/JNAE = Jump on below/not above or equal	0 1 1 1 0 0 1 0	IP-INC8	
JBE/JNA = Jump on below or equal/not above	0 1 1 1 0 1 1 0	IP-INC8	
JP/JPE = Jump on parity/parity even	0 1 1 1 1 0 1 0	IP-INC8	
JO = Jump on overflow	0 1 1 1 0 0 0 0	IP-INC8	
JS = Jump on sign	0 1 1 1 1 0 0 0	IP-INC8	
JNE/JNZ = Jump on not equal/not zer0	0 1 1 1 0 1 0 1	IP-INC8	

CONTROL TRANSFER (Cont'd.)   7 6 5 4 3 2 1 0   7 6 5 4 3 2 1 0   7 6 5 4 3 2 1 0   7 6 5 4 3 2 1 0   7 6 5 4 3 2 1 0   7 6 5 4 3 2 1 0

JNL/JGE = Jump on not less/greater or equal	0 1 1 1 1 1 0 1	IP-INC8
JNLE/JG = Jump on not less or equal/greater	0 1 1 1 1 1 1 1	IP-INC8
JNB/JAE = Jump on not below/above or equal	0 1 1 1 0 0 1 1	IP-INC8
JNBE/JA = Jump on not below or equal/above	0 1 1 1 0 1 1 1	IP-INC8
JNP/JPO = Jump on not par/par odd	0 1 1 1 1 0 1 1	IP-INC8
JNO = Jump on not overflow	0 1 1 1 0 0 0 1	IP-INC8
JNS = Jump on not sign	0 1 1 1 1 0 0 1	IP-INC8
LOOP = Loop CX times	1 1 1 0 0 0 1 0	IP-INC8
LOOPZ/LOOPE = Loop while zero/equal	1 1 1 0 0 0 0 1	IP-INC8
LOOPNZ/LOOPNE = Loop while not zero/equal	1 1 1 0 0 0 0 0	IP-INC8
JCXZ = Jump on CX zero	1 1 1 0 0 0 1 1	IP-INC8

Figure 3.5   (Continued)

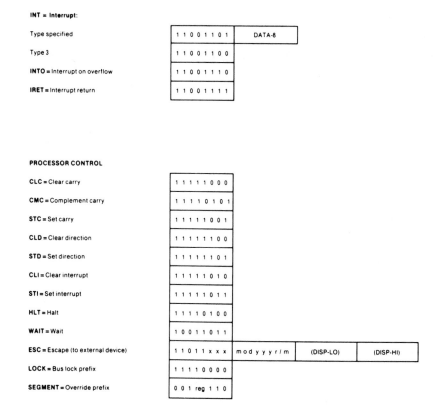

INT = Interrupt:

| Type specified | 1 1 0 0 1 1 0 1 | DATA-8 |

| Type 3 | 1 1 0 0 1 1 0 0 |

INTO = Interrupt on overflow | 1 1 0 0 1 1 1 0 |

IRET = Interrupt return | 1 1 0 0 1 1 1 1 |

PROCESSOR CONTROL

| **CLC** = Clear carry | 1 1 1 1 1 0 0 0 |

| **CMC** = Complement carry | 1 1 1 1 0 1 0 1 |

| **STC** = Set carry | 1 1 1 1 1 0 0 1 |

| **CLD** = Clear direction | 1 1 1 1 1 1 0 0 |

| **STD** = Set direction | 1 1 1 1 1 1 0 1 |

| **CLI** = Clear interrupt | 1 1 1 1 1 0 1 0 |

| **STI** = Set interrupt | 1 1 1 1 1 0 1 1 |

| **HLT** = Halt | 1 1 1 1 0 1 0 0 |

| **WAIT** = Wait | 1 0 0 1 1 0 1 1 |

| **ESC** = Escape (to external device) | 1 1 0 1 1 x x x | m o d y y y r / m | (DISP-LO) | (DISP-HI) |

| **LOCK** = Bus lock prefix | 1 1 1 1 0 0 0 0 |

| **SEGMENT** = Override prefix | 0 0 1 reg 1 1 0 |

Figure 3.5 (Continued)

EXAMPLE 3.5

The instruction

```
MOV WORD PTR [BP][DI]+1234H,0ABCDH
```

stands for "move the immediate data word $ABCD_{16}$ into the memory location specified by based-indexed addressing mode." Express the instruction in machine code.

Register	SR
ES	00
CS	01
SS	10
DS	11

Figure 3.6 Segment register codes.

Solution

Since this instruction does not involve one of the registers as an operand, it does not follow the general format that we have been using. From Fig. 3.5 we find that byte 1 in an immediate data to memory move is

$$1100011W$$

In our case, we are moving word-size data; therefore, W equals 1. This gives

$$\text{BYTE 1} = 11000111_2 = C7_{16}$$

Again from Fig. 3.5, we find that byte 2 has the form

$$\text{BYTE 2} = (\text{MOD})000(\text{R/M})$$

For a memory operand using a 16-bit displacement, Fig. 3.3(a) shows that MOD equals 10 and for based-indexed addressing using BP and DI with a 16-bit displacement, Fig. 3.3(b) shows that R/M equals 011. This gives

$$\text{BYTE 2} = 10000011_2 = 83_{16}$$

Byte 3 and 4 encode the displacement with its low byte first. Thus for a displacement of 1234_{16}, we get

$$\text{BYTE 3} = 34_{16}$$

and

$$\text{BYTE 4} = 12_{16}$$

Lastly, bytes 5 and 6 encode the immediate data also with the least significant byte first. For data word $ABCD_{16}$, we get

$$\text{BYTE 5} = CD_{16}$$

and

$$\text{BYTE 6} = AB_{16}$$

Thus the entire instruction in machine code is given by

```
MOV  WORD PTR [BP][DI]+1234H,ABCDH = C7833412CDABH
```

EXAMPLE 3.6 _____

The instruction

$$\text{MOV [BP][DI]+1234H,DS}$$

stands for "move the contents of the data segment register to the memory location specified by based-indexed addressing mode." Express the instruction in machine code.

Solution

From Fig. 3.5 we see that this instruction is encoded as

$$10001100(MOD)0(SR)(R/M)(DISP)$$

The MOD and R/M fields are the same as in Example 3.5. That is,

$$MOD = 10$$

and

$$R/M = 011$$

Moreover, the value of DISP is given as 1234_{16}. Finally from Fig. 3.6 we find that to specify DS, the SR field is

$$SR = 11$$

Therefore, the instruction is coded as

$$10001100100110110011010000010010_2 = 8C9B3412_{16}$$

▲ 3.3 ENCODING A COMPLETE PROGRAM IN MACHINE CODE

To encode a complete assembly language program in machine code, we must individually encode each of its instructions. This can be done by using the instruction formats shown in Fig. 3.5 and the information in the tables of Figs. 3.2, 3.3, 3.4, and 3.6. We first identify the general machine code format for the instruction in Fig. 3.5. After determining the format, the bit fields can be evaluated using the tables of Figs. 3.2, 3.3, 3.4, and 3.6. Finally, the binary-coded instruction can be expressed in hexadecimal form.

To execute a program on the PC, we must first store the machine code of the program in the code segment of memory. The bytes of machine code are stored in sequentially addressed locations in memory. The first byte of the program is stored at the lowest address and it is followed by the other bytes in the order in which they are encoded. That is, the address is incremented by one after storing each byte of machine code in memory.

EXAMPLE 3.7

Encode the "block move" program shown in Fig. 3.7(a) and show how it would be stored in memory starting at address 200_{16}.

Solution

To encode this program into its equivalent machine code, we will use the instruction set table in Fig. 3.5. The first instruction

```
MOV AX,2000H
```

is a "move immediate data to register" instruction. In Fig. 3.5, we find it has the form

$$1011(W)(REG)(DATA\ DATA\ IF\ W = 1)$$

Since the move is to register AX, Fig. 3.2 shows that the W bit is 1 and REG is 000. The immediate data 2000_{16} follows this byte with the least significant byte coded first. This gives the machine code for the instruction as

$$1011100000000000000100000_2 = B80020_{16}$$

The second instruction

```
MOV DS,AX
```

represents a "move register to segment register" operation. This instruction has the general format

$$10001110(MOD)0(SR)(R/M)$$

From Fig. 3.3(a) and (b), we find that for this instruction MOD = 11 and R/M is 000 for AX. Furthermore, from Fig. 3.6, we find that SR = 11 for data segment. This results in the code

$$1000111011011000_2 = 8ED8_{16}$$

for the second instruction.

```
        MOV AX,2000H    ;LOAD AX REGISTER
        MOV DS,AX       ;LOAD DATA SEGMENT ADDRESS
        MOV SI,100H     ;LOAD SOURCE BLOCK POINTER
        MOV DI,120H     ;LOAD DESTINATION BLOCK POINTER
        MOV CX,10H      ;LOAD REPEAT COUNTER
NXTPT:  MOV AH,[SI]     ;MOVE SOURCE BLOCK ELEMENT TO AH
        MOV [DI],AH     ;MOVE ELEMENT FROM AH TO DESTINATION BLOCK
        INC SI          ;INCREMENT SOURCE BLOCK POINTER
        INC DI          ;INCREMENT DESTINATION BLOCK POINTER
        DEC CX          ;DECREMENT REPEAT COUNTER
        JNZ NXTPT       ;JUMP TO NXTPT IF CX NOT EQUAL TO ZERO
        NOP             ;NO OPERATION
```

(a)

Instruction	Type of instruction	Machine code
MOV AX,2000H	Move immediate data to register	$1011100000000000000100000_2 = B80020_{16}$
MOV DS,AX	Move register to segment register	$1000111011011000_2 = 8ED8_{16}$
MOV SI,100H	Move immediate data to register	$1011111000000000000000001_2 = BE0001_{16}$
MOV DI,120H	Move immediate data to register	$1011111100100000000000001_2 = BF2001_{16}$
MOV CX,10H	Move immediate data to register	$1011100100010000000000000_2 = B91000_{16}$
MOV AH,[SI]	Move memory data to register	$1000101000100100_2 = 8A24_{16}$
MOV [DI],AH	Move register data to memory	$1000100000100101_2 = 8825_{16}$
INC SI	Increment register	$01000110_2 = 46_{16}$
INC DI	Increment register	$01000111_2 = 47_{16}$
DEC CX	Decrement register	$01001001_2 = 49_{16}$
JNZ NXTPT	Jump on not equal to zero	$0111010111110111_2 = 75F7_{16}$
NOP	No operation	$10010000_2 = 90_{16}$

(b)

Figure 3.7 (a) Block move program. (b) Machine coding of the block move program. (c) Storing the machine code in memory.

The next three instructions have the same format as the first instruction. In the third instruction, REG is 110 for SI and the data is 0100_{16}. This gives the instruction code as

$$10111110000000000000000001_2 = BE0001_{16}$$

The fourth instruction has REG coded as 111 (DI) and the data as 0120_{16}. This

Memory address	Contents	Instruction
200H	B8H	MOV AX,2000H
201H	00H	
202H	20H	
203H	8EH	MOV DS,AX
204H	D8H	
205H	BEH	MOV SI,100H
206H	00H	
207H	01H	
208H	BFH	MOV DI,120H
209H	20H	
20AH	01H	
20BH	B9H	MOV CX,10H
20CH	10H	
20DH	00H	
20EH	8AH	MOV AH,[SI]
20FH	24H	
210H	88H	MOV [DI],AH
211H	25H	
212H	46H	INC SI
213H	47H	INC DI
214H	49H	DEC CX
215H	75H	JNZ $-9
216H	F7H	
217H	90H	NOP

(c)

Figure 3.7 (Continued)

results in the code as

$$1011111100100000000000001_2 = BF2001_{16}$$

And in the fifth instruction REG is 001 for CX with 0010_{16} as the data. This gives its code as

$$101110010001000000000000_2 = B91000_{16}$$

Instruction six is a move of byte data from memory to a register. From Fig. 3.5, we find that its general format is

$$100010(D)(W)(MOD)(REG)(R/M)$$

Since AH is the destination and the instruction operates on bytes of data, the D and W bits are 1 and 0, respectively, and the REG field is 100. The contents of SI are used as a pointer to the source operand; therefore, MOD is 00 and R/M is 100. This gives the instruction code as

$$1000101000100100_2 = 8A24_{16}$$

The last MOV instruction has the same form as the last one. However, in this case, AH is the destination and DI is the address pointer. This makes D equal to 0 and R/M equal to 101. Therefore, we get

$$1000100000100101_2 = 8825_{16}$$

The next two instructions increment registers and have the general form

$$01000(REG)$$

For the first one, register SI is incremented. Therefore, REG equals 110. This results in the instruction code as

$$01000110_2 = 46_{16}$$

In the second, REG equals 111 to encode DI. This gives its code as

$$01000111_2 = 47_{16}$$

The two INC instructions are followed by a DEC instruction. Its general form is

$$01001(REG)$$

To encode CX, REG equals 001, which results in the instruction code as

$$01001001_2 = 49_{16}$$

The next instruction is a jump to the location NXTPT. Its form is

$$01110101(IP-INC8)$$

We will not yet complete this instruction because it will be easier to determine the number of bytes to be jumped after the data has been coded for storage in memory. The final instruction is NOP and it is coded as

$$10010000_2 = 90_{16}$$

The entire machine code program is shown in Fig. 3.7(b). As shown in Fig. 3.7(c), our encoded program will be stored in memory starting from memory address 200H. The choice of program beginning address establishes the address for the

NXTPT label. Notice that the MOV AH,[SI] instruction, which has this label, starts at address $20E_{16}$. This is nine bytes back from the value in IP after fetching the JNZ instruction. Therefore, the displacement (IP−INC8) in the JNZ instruction is −9, which is $F7_{16}$ as an 8-bit hexadecimal number. Thus the instruction is encoded as

$$0111010111110111_2 = 75F7_{16}$$

▲ 3.4 THE IBM PC AND ITS DEBUG PROGRAM

Now that we know how to convert an assembly language program to machine code and how this machine code is stored in memory, we are ready to enter it into the PC; execute it; examine the results that it produces; and, if necessary, debug any errors in its operation. It is the *DEBUG program*, which is part of the PC's disk operating system (DOS), that permits us to initiate these types of operations from the keyboard of the PC. In this section we will show how to load the DEBUG program from DOS, use it to examine or modify the contents of the MPU's internal registers, and how to return back to DOS from DEBUG.

Using DEBUG, the programmer can issue commands to the microcomputer in the PC. Assume that DOS has already been loaded and that a disk that contains the DEBUG program is in drive A, DEBUG is loaded by simply issuing the command

```
C:\DOS>a:debug (↵)
```

Actually, "DEBUG" can be typed in using either uppercase or lowercase characters. However, for simplicity, we will use all uppercase characters in this book.

EXAMPLE 3.8

Assuming that DOS has already been loaded and that the DEBUG program is in the DOS directory on drive C, initiate the DEBUG program from the keyboard of the PC. What prompt for command entry is displayed when in the debugger?

Solution

When the operating system has been loaded, DEBUG is brought up by entering

```
C:\DOS>DEBUG (↵)
```

Drive C is accessed to load the DEBUG program; DEBUG is then executed and its prompt, which is a "_", is displayed. DEBUG is now waiting to accept a command. Figure 3.8 shows what is displayed on the screen.

Figure 3.8 Loading the DEBUG program.

The keyboard is the input unit of the debugger and permits the user to enter commands to load data such as the machine code of a program; examine or modify the state of the MPU's internal registers; or execute a program. All we need to do is type in the command and then depress the enter (↵) key. These debug commands are the tools a programmer needs to use to enter, execute, and debug programs.

When the command entry sequence is completed, the DEBUG program decodes the entry to determine which operation is to be performed, verifies that it is a valid command, and if valid, passes control to a routine that performs the operation. At the completion of the operation, results are displayed on the screen and the DEBUG prompt (_) is redisplayed. The PC remains in this state until a new entry is made from the keyboard.

Six kinds of information are typically entered as part of a command: *a command letter*, *an address*, *a register name*, *a file name*, *a drive name*, and *data*. The entire command set of DEBUG is shown in Fig. 3.9. This table gives the name for each command, its function, and its general syntax. By *syntax*, we mean the order in which key entries must be made to initiate the command.

With the loading of DEBUG, the state of the microprocessor gets initialized. The *initial state* depends upon the DOS version and system configuration at the time the DEGUG command is issued. An example of the initial state is illustrated with the software model in Fig. 3.10. Notice that registers AX, BX, CX, DX, BP, SI, and DI are reset to zero; IP is initialized to 0100_{16}; CS, DS, SS, and ES are all loaded with 1342_{16}; and SP is loaded with $FFEE_{16}$. Finally, all of the flags except IF are reset to zero. We can use the register command to verify this initial state.

Let us now look at the syntax for the *REGISTER* (R) *command*. This is the debugger command that allows us to examine or modify the contents of internal registers of the MPU. Notice that the syntax for this command is given in Fig. 3.9 as

```
R [REGISTER NAME]
```

Here the command letter is R. It is followed by the register name. Figure 3.11 shows what must be entered as the register name for each of the 8088's registers.

An example of the command entry needed to examine or modify the value in register AX is

```
—R AX (↵)
```

Notice that brackets are not included around the register name. In Fig. 3.9, brackets are simply used to separate the various elements of the DEBUG commands. They are never entered as part of the command. Execution of this register command causes the current value in AX to be displayed as

```
AX 0000
:
```

Command	Syntax	Function
Register	R [REGISTER NAME]	Examine or modify the contents of an internal register
Quit	Q	End use of the DEBUG program
Dump	D [ADDRESS]	Dump the contents of memory to the display
Enter	E ADDRESS [LIST]	Examine or modify the contents of memory
Fill	F STARTING ADDRESS ENDING ADDRESS LIST	Fill a block in memory with the data in list
Move	M STARTING ADDRESS ENDING ADDRESS DESTINATION ADDRESS	Move a block of data from a source location in memory to a destination location
Compare	C STARTING ADDRESS ENDING ADDRESS DESTINATION ADDRESS	Compare two blocks of data in memory and display the locations that contain different data
Search	S STARTING ADDRESS ENDING ADDRESS LIST	Search through a block of data in memory and display all locations that match the data in list
Input	I ADDRESS	Read the input port
Output	O ADDRESS, BYTE	Write the byte to the output port
Hex Add/Subtract	H NUM1,NUM2	Generate hexadecimal sum and difference of the two numbers
Unassemble	U [STARTING ADDRESS ENDING ADDRESS]	Unassemble the machine code into its equivalent assembler instructions
Name	N FILE NAME	Assign the filename to the data to be written to the disk
Write	W [STARTING ADDRESS [DRIVE STARTING SECTOR NUMBER OF SECTORS]]	Save the contents of memory in a file on a diskette
Load	L [STARTING ADDRESS [DRIVE STARTING SECTOR NUMBER OF SECTORS]]	Load memory with the contents of a file on a diskette
Assemble	A [STARTING ADDRESS]	Assemble the instruction into machine code and store in memory
Trace	T [=ADDRESS] [NUMBER]	Trace the execution of the specified number of instructions
Go	G [=STARTING ADDRESS [BREAKPOINT ADDRESS....]]	Execute the instructions down through the breakpoint address

Figure 3.9 DEBUG program command set.

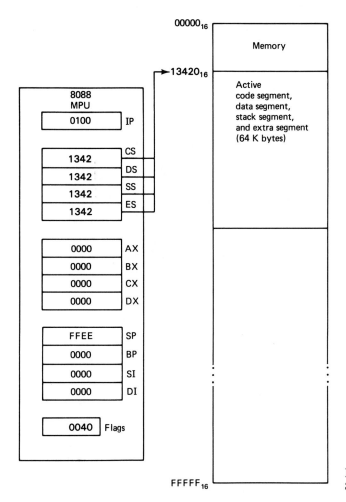

Figure 3.10 An initial state of the 8088 microprocessor.

Here we see that AX contains 0000_{16}. The examine register command is not yet complete. Note that a ":" followed by the cursor is displayed. We can now either depress ($\downarrow$) to complete the command, leaving the register contents unchanged, or enter a new value for AX following the colon and then depress ($\downarrow$). Let us load AX with a new value of $00FF_{16}$. This is done by the entry

$$:00FF \quad (\downarrow)$$

EXAMPLE 3.9 ─────────────────────

Verify the initialized state of the 8088 by examining the contents of its registers with the register command.

Symbol	Register
AX	Accumulator register
BX	Base register
CX	Count register
DX	Data register
SI	Source index register
DI	Destination index register
SP	Stack pointer register
BP	Base pointer register
CS	Code segment register
DS	Data segment register
SS	Stack segment register
ES	Extra segment register
F	Flag register
IP	Instruction pointer

Figure 3.11 Register mnemonics for the R command.

Solution

If we enter the register command without a specific register name, the debugger causes the state of all registers and flags to be displayed. That is, if we enter

$$-R \quad (\hookleftarrow)$$

the information displayed is that shown in Fig. 3.12. Looking at Fig. 3.12, we see that all registers were initialized as expected. To verify that all flags other than IF were reset, we can compare the flag settings that are listed to the right of the value for IP with the values in the table of Fig. 3.13. Note that all but IF correspond to the reset state. The last line displays the machine code and assembly language statement of the instruction pointed to by the current values in CS and IP (CS:IP).

```
-R
AX=0000  BX=0000  CX=0000  DX=0000  SP=FFEE  BP=0000  SI=0000  DI=0000
DS=1342  ES=1342  SS=1342  CS=1342  IP=0100   NV UP EI PL NZ NA PO NC
1342:0100 CD21              INT    21
-
```

Figure 3.12 Displaying the initialized state of the 8088 microprocessor.

EXAMPLE 3.10

Issue commands to the debugger on the PC that will cause the value in BX to be modified to $FF00_{16}$ and then verify that this new value is loaded into BX.

Flag	Meaning	Set	Reset
OF	Overflow	OV	NV
DF	Direction	DN	UP
IF	Interrupt	EI	DI
SF	Sign	NG	PL
ZF	Zero	ZR	NZ
AF	Auxiliary carry	AC	NA
PF	Parity	PE	PO
CF	Carry	CY	NC

Figure 3.13 Notations used for displaying the status flags.

Solution

To modify the value in BX, all we need to do is issue the register command with BX and then respond to the :_ by entering the value FF00$_{16}$. This is done with the command sequence

```
—R BX (↵)
BX 0000
:FF00 (↵)
—
```

We can verify that FF00$_{16}$ has been loaded into BX by issuing another register command as follows

```
—R BX (↵)
BX FF00
: (↵)
—
```

The displayed information for this command sequence is shown in Fig. 3.14.

```
-R BX
BX 0000
:FF00
-R BX
BX FF00
:-
-
```

Figure 3.14 Displayed information for Example 3.10.

The way in which the register command is used to modify flags is different from how it is used to modify the contents of a register. If we enter the command

```
—R F (↵)
```

the flag settings are displayed as

```
NV UP EI PL NZ NA PO NC—
```

To modify, just type in their new states (using the notations shown in Fig. 3.13) and depress the return key. For instance, to set the carry and zero flags, we enter

```
NV UP EI PL NZ NA PO NC— CY ZR (↵)
```

Note that the new flag states can be entered in any order.

EXAMPLE 3.11

Use the register command to set the parity flag to even parity. Verify that the flag has been changed.

Solution

To set PF for even parity, we can issue the register command for the flag register and then enter PE as the new flag data. This is done with the command sequence

```
—R F (↵)
NV UP EI PL NZ NA PO NC— PE (↵)
```

To verify that PF has been changed to its PE state, just enter another register command for the flag register as follows:

```
—R F   (↵)

NV UP EI PL NZ NA PE NC—  (↵)
```

Notice that the state of the parity flag has changed from PO to PE. Figure 3.15 shows these commands and the displayed flag status that results.

The REGISTER command is very important for debugging programs. For instance, it can be used to check the contents of a register or flag prior to and again just after execution of an instruction. In this way, we can tell whether or not the instruction correctly performed the required operation.

If the command that was entered is identified as being invalid, an *error message* is displayed. Let us look at an example of an invalid command entry. To do this, we will repeat our earlier example in which AX was loaded with $00FF_{16}$, but in the entry of $00FF_{16}$ the uppercase letter O is keyed in instead of zeros. The result produced by issuing this command is shown in Fig. 3.16. Here we see that a warning

```
-R F                              -R AX
NV UP EI PL NZ NA PO NC  -PE      AX 0000
-R F                              :00FF
NV UP EI PL NZ NA PE NC  -        ^ Error
-                                 -
```

Figure 3.15 Displayed information for Example 3.11.

Figure 3.16 Invalid entry.

"Error" is displayed and the symbol "^" is used to mark the starting location of the error in the command. To correct this error, the command is simply reentered.

We will examine one more command before going on. We now know how to invoke the DEBUG program from the DOS prompt, but we must also be able to return to DOS once in DEBUG. The debugger contains a command called *QUIT* (Q) to do this. Therefore, to return to the DOS we simply respond to the debug prompt with

Q (⏎)

▲ 3.5 EXAMINING AND MODIFYING THE CONTENTS OF MEMORY

In Section 3.4 we studied the command that permitted us to examine or modify the contents of the MPU's internal registers. Here we will continue our study of DEBUG's command set with those commands that are used to examine and modify the contents of memory. The ability to do this is essential for debugging programs. For instance, the contents at a memory address can be examined just before and just after execution of an instruction. In this way, we can verify that the instruction performs the operation correctly. Another use of this type of command is to load a program into the code segment of the microcomputer's memory. The complete command set of DEBUG was shown in Fig. 3.9. Six of these commands, DUMP, ENTER, FILL, MOVE, COMPARE, and SEARCH, are provided for use in examining or modifying the contents of storage locations in memory. Let us now look at the operations performed with each of these commands.

DUMP Command

The *DUMP* (D) *command* allows us to examine the contents of a memory location or a block of consecutive memory locations. Looking at Fig. 3.9, we see that the general syntax for DUMP is

D [ADDRESS]

If a segment register is not specified, the value of ADDRESS entered is automatically referenced to the current value in the data segment (DS) register.

DUMP can also be issued without ADDRESS. This gives the command

$$D \quad (\hookleftarrow)$$

Execution of this form of the command causes the 128 consecutive bytes starting at offset 0100_{16} from the current value in DS to be displayed. If DS is initialized with 1342_{16} when DEBUG is started, issuing this command gives the memory dump shown in Fig. 3.17.

Notice that 16 bytes of data are displayed per line and only the address of the first byte is shown at the left. From Fig. 3.17 we see that the address of the first location in the first line is denoted as 1342:0100. This corresponds to the physical address

$$13420_{16} + 0100_{16} = 13520_{16}$$

The second byte of data displayed in the first line corresponds to the memory address 1342:0101 or 13521_{16}, and the last byte on this line corresponds to the memory address 1342:010F or $1352F_{16}$. Note that the values of the eighth and ninth bytes are separated by a hyphen.

For all memory dumps, an ASCII version of the memory data is also displayed. It is displayed to the right of the hexadecimal data in Fig. 3.17. All bytes that result in an unprintable ASCII character are displayed as the "." symbol.

The results shown in Fig. 3.17 could be obtained with several other forms of the DUMP command. One way is to enter the current value of DS, which is 1342_{16}, and an offset of 0100_{16} in the address field. This results in the command

$$D \ 1342:100 \quad (\hookleftarrow)$$

Another way is to enter DS instead of its value with the offset. This gives

$$D \ DS:100 \quad (\hookleftarrow)$$

```
-D
1342:0100   75 07 05 00 00 00 B2 14-4C 00 2B 04 27 0C 06 74    u.......L.+.'..t
1342:0110   46 74 05 00 00 00 31 13-B2 14 99 00 31 13 31 13    Ft....1......1.1.
1342:0120   8A 40 8B 1E F2 39 9A 88-97 63 17 8B 1E F2 39 BA    .@...9...c....9.
1342:0130   61 46 E8 37 0B A0 5A 46-0A C0 74 2D 8B 1E AB 42    aF.7..ZF..t-...B
1342:0140   FE C8 75 0B 89 1E 5C 46-C6 06 5A 46 02 EB 1A 3B    ..u...\F..ZF...;
1342:0150   1E 5C 46 74 14 C6 06 5A-46 00 E8 17 01 75 03 E9    .\Ft...ZF....u..
1342:0160   FC 00 3C 59 75 03 E9 27-01 E8 97 01 8A C5 74 22    ..<Yu..'......t"
1342:0170   80 3E CE 09 00 75 10 80-F9 0D 75 0B E8 55 00 74    .>...u....u..U.t
-
```

Figure 3.17 Examining the contents of 128 consecutive bytes in memory.

In fact, the same results can be obtained by just issuing the command

$$D\ 100 \qquad (\leftarrow)$$

EXAMPLE 3.12

What is the physical address range of the bytes of data in the last line of data shown in Fig. 3.17?

Solution

In Fig. 3.17 we see that the first byte is at address 1342:0170. This is the physical address

$$13420_{16} + 0170_{16} = 13590_{16}$$

The last byte is at address 1342:017F and its physical address is

$$13420_{16} + 017F_{16} = 1359F_{16}$$

EXAMPLE 3.13

What happens if we repeat the entry D ($\leftarrow$) after obtaining the memory dump shown in Fig. 3.17?

Solution

The contents of the next 128 consecutive bytes of memory are dumped to the display. The displayed information is shown in Fig. 3.18.

```
-D
1342:0180  0B 72 0C 3C 0A 75 08 E8-4A 00 75 03 E9 D9 00 E9   .r.<.u..J.u.....
1342:0190  BF FE E8 23 40 75 02 EB-82 80 3E CE 09 00 75 15   ...#@u....>...u.
1342:01A0  80 F9 0D 75 10 E8 2C 00-74 E2 72 18 3C 0A 75 14   ...u..,.t.r.<.u.
1342:01B0  8A C5 E8 03 40 9A 49 C5-63 17 9A B3 B8 63 17 E8   ....@.I.c....c..
1342:01C0  9F 0A EB C3 9A 49 C5 63-17 9A B3 B8 63 17 E8 90   .....I.c....c...
1342:01D0  0A E9 7D FE E8 D1 01 74-66 89 2E D7 09 8A E8 24   ..}....tf......$
1342:01E0  7F 8A C8 3C 1B 74 07 3C-1D 75 3B EB 59 90 E8 B7   ...<.t.<.u;.Y...
1342:01F0  01 74 31 52 8A F0 E8 AF-01 74 38 3C 1C 75 0E C6   .t1R.....t8<.u..
-
```

Figure 3.18 Displayed information for repeat of 128-byte memory dump command.

Frequently, we do not want to examine such a large block of memory. Instead, we may want to look at just a few bytes or a specific-sized block. The dump command can also do this. This time we enter two addresses, the first address defines the

```
-D DS:200 201
1342:0200  06 CE
```

Figure 3.19 Displaying just two bytes of data.

starting point of the block and the second address identifies the end of the block. For instance, if we want to examine the two bytes of data that are at offsets equal to 200_{16} and 201_{16} in the current data segment, the command is

$$D \ DS:200 \ 201 \ (\hookleftarrow)$$

The result obtained by executing this command is given in Fig. 3.19.

EXAMPLE 3.14

Issue a dump command that will display the contents of the 32 bytes of memory that are located at offsets 0300_{16} through $031F_{16}$ in the current data segment.

Solution

The command needed to display the contents of this part of memory is

$$D \ 300 \ 31F \ (\hookleftarrow)$$

and the information that is displayed is shown in Fig. 3.20.

```
-D 300 31F
1342:0300  59 5F C3 E8 D0 3E 74 0A-E8 BF 3E E8 5C 3E 75 F3   Y_...>t...>.\>u.
1342:0310  0C 01 C3 80 3E 25 39 00-74 4A 53 52 FF 36 AB 42   ....>%9.tJSR.6.B
-
```

Figure 3.20 Displayed information for Example 3.14.

Up to now, all of the data displayed with the DUMP command was contained in the data segment of memory. It is also possible to examine data that are stored in the code segment, stack segment, or extra segment. To do this, we simply use the appropriate segment register name in the command. For instance, the command needed to dump the values in the first 16 bytes of the current code segment is

$$D \ CS:0 \ F \ (\hookleftarrow)$$

EXAMPLE 3.15

Use the DUMP command to examine the 16 bytes of memory just below the top of the stack.

Solution

The top of the stack is defined by the contents of the SS and SP registers (SS:SP). Earlier we found that SP was initialized to $FFEE_{16}$ when debug was loaded. There-

```
-D SS:FFEE FFFD
1342:FFE0                                                    00 00            ..
1342:FFF0  00 00 00 00 00 00 00 00-00 00 00 00 00 00          ..............
-
```

Figure 3.21 Displayed information for Example 3.15.

fore, the 16 bytes we are interested in reside at offset $FFEE_{16}$ through $FFFD_{16}$ from the current value in SS. This part of the stack is viewed with the command

$$D \;\; SS:FFEE \;\; FFFD \;\; (\downarrow)$$

The result displayed by executing this command is shown in Fig. 3.21.

ENTER Command

The DUMP command allowed us to examine the contents of memory, but we also need to be able to modify or enter the information in memory—for instance, to load a machine code program. It is for this purpose that the *ENTER* (E) *command* is provided in the DEBUG program.

In Fig. 3.9 we find that the syntax of the ENTER command is

$$E \;\; ADDRESS \;\; [LIST]$$

The address part of the E command is entered in the same way we just described for the DUMP command. If no segment name is included with the offset, the DS register is assumed. The list that follows the address is the data that gets loaded into memory.

As an example, let us write a command that will load five consecutive byte-wide memory locations that start at address DS:100 with the value FF_{16}. This is done with the command

$$E \;\; DS:100 \;\; FF \;\; FF \;\; FF \;\; FF \;\; FF \;\; (\downarrow)$$

To verify that the new values of data have been stored in memory, let us dump the contents of these locations to the display. To do this, we issue the command

$$D \;\; DS:100 \;\; 104 \;\; (\downarrow)$$

These commands and the displayed results are shown in Fig. 3.22. Notice that the byte storage locations from address DS:100 through DS:104 now all contain the value FF_{16}.

The ENTER command can also be used in a way in which it either examines or modifies the contents of memory. If we issue the command with an address but no data, what happens is that the contents of the addressed storage location are

```
-E DS:100 FF FF FF FF FF
-D DS:100 104
1342:0100  FF FF FF FF FF                              . . . . .
-
```

Figure 3.22 Modifying five consecutive bytes of memory and verifying the change of data.

displayed. For instance, the command

$$E \; DS:100 \; (\llcorner)$$

causes the value at this address to be displayed as follows:

$$1342:0100 \; FF.\_$$

Notice that the value at address 1342:0100 is FF_{16}.

At this point we have several options; for one, the return key can be depressed. This terminates the ENTER command without changing the contents of the displayed memory location and causes the debug prompt to be displayed. Two, rather than depressing return, we can depress the space bar. Again, the contents of the displayed memory location remain unchanged, but this time the command is not terminated. Instead, it causes the contents of the next consecutive memory address to be displayed. Let us assume that this was done. Then the display would read

$$1342:0100 \; FF. \; FF.\_$$

Here we see that the data stored at address 1342:0101 are also FF_{16}. A third type of entry that could be made is to enter a new value of data and then depress the space bar or return key. For example, we could enter 11_{16} and then depress space. This gives the display

$$1342:0100 \; FF. \; FF.11 \; FF.\_$$

The value pointed to by address 1342:101 has been changed to 11_{16} and the contents of address 1342:0102, which are FF_{16}, are displayed. Now depress the return key to finalize the data entry sequence.

EXAMPLE 3.16 ────────────────────────────────────

Start a data entry sequence by examining the contents of address DS:100 and then, without entering new data, depress the "−" key. What happens?

Solution

The data entry sequence is initiated as

$$E \; DS:100 \; (\llcorner)$$

$$1342:0100 \; FF.\_$$

```
-E DS:100
1342:0100   FF._
1342:00FF   FF._
-
```

Figure 3.23 Using the "−" key to examine the contents of the previous memory location.

Now entering "−" causes the address and data that follow to be displayed.

```
1342:00FF FF._
```

Notice that this is the address and contents of the storage location at the address equal to one less than DS:100. That is, the previous byte storage location. This result is shown in Fig. 3.23.

The ENTER command can also be used to enter ASCII data. This is done by simply enclosing the data entered in quotation marks. An example is the command

```
E DS:200 "ASCII" (↵)
```

This command causes the ASCII data for letters A, S, C, I, and I to be stored in memory at addresses DS:200, DS:201, DS:202, DS:203, and DS:204, respectively. This character data entry can be verified with the command

```
D DS:200 204 (↵)
```

Looking at the ASCII field of the data dump shown in Fig. 3.24, we see that the correct ASCII data were stored into memory. Actually, either single or double quote marks can be used. Therefore, the entry could also have been made as

```
E DS:200 'ASCII' (↵)
```

FILL Command

Frequently, we want to fill a block of consecutive memory locations all with the same data. For example, we may need to initialize storage locations in an area of memory with zeros. To do this by entering the data address by address with the ENTER command would be very time consuming. It is for this type of operation that the *FILL* (F) *command* is provided.

```
-E DS:200 "ASCII"
-D DS:200 204
1342:0200   41 53 43 49 49                          ASCII
-
```

Figure 3.24 Loading ASCII data into memory with the ENTER command.

```
-F 100 11F 22
-D 100 11F
1342:0100  22 22 22 22 22 22 22 22-22 22 22 22 22 22 22 22   """"""""""""""""""
1342:0110  22 22 22 22 22 22 22 22-22 22 22 22 22 22 22 22   """"""""""""""""""
-
```

Figure 3.25 Initializing a block of memory with the FILL command.

From Fig. 3.9, we see that the general form of the FILL command is

```
F   STARTING ADDRESS   ENDING ADDRESS   LIST
```

Here *starting address* and *ending address* specify the block of storage locations in memory. They are followed by a *list* of data. An example is the command

```
F 100 11F 22 (↵)
```

Execution of this command causes the 32 byte locations in the range 1342:100 through 1342:11F to be loaded with 22_{16}. The fact that this change in memory contents has happened can be verified with the command

```
D 100 11F (↵)
```

Figure 3.25 shows the result of executing these two commands.

EXAMPLE 3.17 _____

Initialize all storage locations in the block of memory from DS:120 through DS:13F with the value 33_{16} and the block of storage locations from DS:140 through DS:15F with the value 44_{16}. Verify that the contents of these ranges of memory are correctly modified.

Solution

The initialization operations can be done with the FILL commands that follow:

```
F 120 13F 33 (↵)
```

```
F 140 15F 44 (↵)
```

They are then verified with the DUMP command

```
D 120 15F (↵)
```

The information displayed by the command sequence is shown in Fig. 3.26.

```
-F 120 13F 33
-F 140 15F 44
-D 120 15F
1342:0120  33 33 33 33 33 33 33 33-33 33 33 33 33 33 33 33   3333333333333333
1342:0130  33 33 33 33 33 33 33 33-33 33 33 33 33 33 33 33   3333333333333333
1342:0140  44 44 44 44 44 44 44 44-44 44 44 44 44 44 44 44   DDDDDDDDDDDDDDDD
1342:0150  44 44 44 44 44 44 44 44-44 44 44 44 44 44 44 44   DDDDDDDDDDDDDDDD
-
```

Figure 3.26 Displayed information for Example 3.17.

MOVE Command

The *MOVE* (M) *command* allows us to copy a block of data from one part of memory to another part. For instance, using this command, a 32-byte block of data that resides in memory from address DS:100 to DS:11F can be copied to the address range DS:200 through DS:21F with a single operation.

The general form of the MOVE command is given in Fig. 3.9 as

```
M  STARTING ADDRESS  ENDING ADDRESS  DESTINATION ADDRESS
```

Notice that it is initiated by depressing the M key. After this, we must enter three addresses. The first two addresses are the *starting address* and *ending address* of the source block of data, that is, the block of data that is to be copied. The third address is the *destination starting address*, that is, the starting address of the section of memory to which the block of data is to be copied.

The command for our example, which copies a 32-byte block of data located at address DS:100 through DS:11F to the block of memory starting at address DS:200, is

M 100 11F 200 (⏎)

EXAMPLE 3.18

Fill each storage location in the block of memory from address DS:100 through DS:11F with the value 11_{16}. Then copy this block of data to a destination block starting at DS:160. Verify that the block move is correctly done.

Solution

First, we fill the source block with 11_{16} using the command

F 100 11F 11 (⏎)

Next it is copied to the destination with the command

M 100 11F 160 (⏎)

```
-F 100 11F 11
-M 100 11F 160
-D 100 17F
1342:0100  11 11 11 11 11 11 11 11-11 11 11 11 11 11 11 11   ................
1342:0110  11 11 11 11 11 11 11 11-11 11 11 11 11 11 11 11   ................
1342:0120  33 33 33 33 33 33 33 33-33 33 33 33 33 33 33 33   3333333333333333
1342:0130  33 33 33 33 33 33 33 33-33 33 33 33 33 33 33 33   3333333333333333
1342:0140  44 44 44 44 44 44 44 44-44 44 44 44 44 44 44 44   DDDDDDDDDDDDDDDD
1342:0150  44 44 44 44 44 44 44 44-44 44 44 44 44 44 44 44   DDDDDDDDDDDDDDDD
1342:0160  11 11 11 11 11 11 11 11-11 11 11 11 11 11 11 11   ................
1342:0170  11 11 11 11 11 11 11 11-11 11 11 11 11 11 11 11   ................
-
```

Figure 3.27 Displayed information for Example 3.18.

Finally, we dump the complete range from DS:100 to DS:17F by issuing the command

D 100 17F (↵)

The result of this memory dump is given in Fig. 3.27. It verifies that the block move is successfully performed.

COMPARE Command

Another type of memory operation we sometimes need to perform is to compare the contents of two blocks of data to determine if they are or are not the same. This operation can be done with the *COMPARE* (C) *command* of the DEBUG program. Figure 3.9 shows that the general form of this command is

C   STARTING ADDRESS   ENDING ADDRESS   DESTINATION ADDRESS

For example, to compare a block of data located from address DS:100 through DS:11F to an equal size block of data starting at address DS:160, we issue the command

C 100 10F 160 (↵)

This command causes the contents of corresponding address locations in each block to be compared to each other. That is, the contents of address DS:100 are compared to those at address DS:160, the contents at address DS:101 are compared to those at address DS:161, and so on. Each time unequal elements are found, the address and contents of that byte in both blocks are displayed.

Since both of these blocks contain the same information, no data are displayed. However, if this source block is next compared to the destination block starting at address DS:120 by entering the command

C 100 10F 120 (↵)

```
-C 100 10F 120
1342:0100  11  33  1342:0120
1342:0101  11  33  1342:0121
1342:0102  11  33  1342:0122
1342:0103  11  33  1342:0123
1342:0104  11  33  1342:0124
1342:0105  11  33  1342:0125
1342:0106  11  33  1342:0126
1342:0107  11  33  1342:0127
1342:0108  11  33  1342:0128
1342:0109  11  33  1342:0129
1342:010A  11  33  1342:012A
1342:010B  11  33  1342:012B
1342:010C  11  33  1342:012C
1342:010D  11  33  1342:012D
1342:010E  11  33  1342:012E
1342:010F  11  33  1342:012F
-
```

Figure 3.28 Results produced when unequal data are found with a COMPARE command.

all elements in both blocks are unequal; therefore, the information shown in Fig. 3.28 is displayed.

SEARCH Command

The *SEARCH* (S) *command* can be used to scan through a block of data in memory to determine whether or not it contains certain data. The general form of this command as given in Fig. 3.9 is

```
S  STARTING ADDRESS  ENDING ADDRESS  LIST
```

When the command is issued, the contents of each storage location in the block of memory between starting address and ending address are compared to the data in list. The address is displayed for each memory location where a match is found.

EXAMPLE 3.19

Perform a search of the block of data from address DS:100 through DS:17F to determine which memory locations contain 33_{16}.

Solution

The search command that must be issued is

```
S 100 17F 33 (↵)
```

Figure 3.29 shows that all addresses in the range 1342:120 through 1342:13F contain this value of data.

▲ 3.6 INPUT AND OUTPUT OF DATA

The commands studied in the last section allowed examination or modification of information in the memory of the microcomputer, but not in its input/output address

```
-S 100 17F 33
1342:0120
1342:0121
1342:0122
1342:0123
1342:0124
1342:0125
1342:0126
1342:0127
1342:0128
1342:0129
1342:012A
1342:012B
1342:012C
1342:012D
1342:012E
1342:012F
1342:0130
1342:0131
1342:0132
1342:0133
1342:0134
1342:0135
1342:0136
1342:0137
1342:0138
1342:0139
1342:013A
1342:013B
1342:013C
1342:013D
1342:013E
1342:013F
-
```

Figure 3.29 Displayed information for Example 3.19.

space. To access data at I/O ports, we use the *input* (I) and *output* (O) *commands*. These commands can be used to input or output data for any of the 64KB-wide ports in the 8088's I/O address space. Let us now look at how these two commands are used to read data at an input port or write data to an output port.

The general format of the input command as shown in Fig. 3.9 is

```
I   ADDRESS
```

Here ADDRESS identifies the byte wide I/O port that is to be accessed. When the command is executed, the data is read from the port and displayed. For instance, if the command

```
I 61   (↵)
```

is issued, and if the result displayed on the screen is

```
4D
```

This means that the contents of the port at I/O address 0061_{16} are $4D_{16}$.

EXAMPLE 3.20 ────────────────────────────────

Write a command that will display the byte contents of the input port at I/O address $00FE_{16}$.

Solution

To input the contents of the byte wide port at address FE_{16}, the command is

```
I FE  (↵)
```

Figure 3.9 gives the general format of the output command as

```
O  ADDRESS  BYTE
```

Here we see that both the address of the output port and the byte of data that is to be written to the port must be specified. An example of the command is

```
O 61 4F
```

This command causes the value $4F_{16}$ to be written into the byte-wide output port at address 0061_{16}.

▲ 3.7 HEXADECIMAL ADDITION AND SUBTRACTION

The DEBUG program also provides the ability to add and subtract hexadecimal numbers. Both operations are performed with a single command known as the *hexadecimal* (H) *command*. In Fig. 3.9, we see that the general format of the H command is

```
H  NUM1  NUM2
```

When executed, both the sum and difference of NUM1 and NUM2 are formed. These results are displayed as follows

```
NUM1+NUM2  NUM1-NUM2
```

Both numbers and the result are limited to four digits.

This hexadecimal arithmetic capability is useful when debugging programs. One example of a use of the H command is for the calculation of the physical address of an instruction or data in memory. For instance, if the current value in the code segment register is $0ABC_{16}$ and that in the instruction pointer is $0FFF_{16}$, the physical address is found with the command

```
H ABC0 0FFF  (↵)
```

```
BBBF 9BC1
```

Notice that the sum of these two hexadecimal numbers is $BBBF_{16}$ and their difference is $9BC1_{16}$. The sum $BBBF_{16}$ is the value of the physical address CS:IP.

The subtraction operation performed with the H command is also valuable in address calculations. For instance, a frequently used software operation is to jump a number of bytes of instruction code backwards in the code segment of memory. In this case, the physical address of the new location can be found by subtraction. Let us start with the physical address just found, $BBBF_{16}$, and assume that we want to jump to a new location 10_{10} bytes back in memory. First, 10_{10} is expressed in hexadecimal form as A_{16}. Then the new address is calculated as

$$H \ BBBF \ A \quad (\downarrow)$$

$$BBC9 \ BBB5$$

Therefore, the new physical address is $BBB5_{16}$. Because the hexadecimal numbers are limited to four digits, physical address calculations are limited to the address range 00000_{16} through $0FFFF_{16}$.

EXAMPLE 3.21

Use the H command to find the negative of the number 0009_{16}.

Solution

The negative of a hexadecimal number can be found by subtracting it from 0. Therefore, the difference produced by the command

$$H \ 0 \ 9 \ (\downarrow)$$

$$0009 \ FFF7$$

is $FFF7_{16}$, and is the negative of 9_{16} expressed in 2s-complement form.

EXAMPLE 3.22

If a byte of data is located at physical address $02A34_{16}$ and the data segment register contains 0150_{16}, what value must be loaded into the source index register such that DS:SI points to the byte storage location?

Solution

The offset required in SI can be found by subtracting the data segment base address from the physical address. Using the H command, we get

$$H \ 2A34 \ 1500 \ (\downarrow)$$

$$3F34 \ 1534$$

This shows that SI must be loaded with the value 1534_{16}.

▲ 3.8 LOADING, VERIFYING, AND SAVING MACHINE LANGUAGE PROGRAMS

Up to this point we learned how to use the register, memory, and I/O commands of DEBUG to examine or modify (1) the contents of the MPU's internal registers, (2) data stored in memory, or (3) information at an input or output port. Let us now look at how we can load machine code instructions and programs into the memory of the PC.

In Section 3.6 we found that the ENTER command can be used to load either a single or a group of memory locations with data, such as the machine code for instructions. As an example, let us load the machine code $88C3_{16}$ for the instruction MOV BL,AL. This instruction is loaded into memory starting at address CS:100 with the ENTER command

```
E CS:100 88 C3 (↵)
```

We can verify that it has been loaded correctly with the DUMP command

```
D CS:100 101 (↵)
```

This displays the data

```
1342:0100 88 C3
```

Let us now introduce another command that is important for debugging programs on the PC. It is the *UNASSEMBLE* (U) *command*. By *unassemble* we mean the process of converting machine code instructions to their equivalent assembly language source statements. The U command lets us specify a range in memory, and execution of the command causes the source statements for the memory data in this range to be displayed on the screen.

Looking at Fig. 3.9, we find that the syntax of the UNASSEMBLE command is

```
U [STARTING ADDRESS  ENDING ADDRESS]
```

We can use this command to verify that the machine code entered for an instruction is correct. To do this for our earlier example, the command that follows is issued

```
U CS:100 101 (↵)
```

This results in display of the starting address for the instruction followed by both the machine code and assembly forms of the instruction. This gives

```
1342:0100 88C3 MOV BL,AL
```

The entry sequence and displayed information for loading, verification, and unassembly of the instruction are shown in Fig. 3.30.

```
-E CS:100 88 C3
-D CS:100 101
1342:0100  88 C3
-U CS:100 101
1342:0100 88C3        MOV      BL,AL
-
```

Figure 3.30 Loading, verifying, and disassembly of an instruction.

EXAMPLE 3.23 ———————————————————

Use a sequence of commands to load, verify loading, and unassemble the machine code instruction 0304H. Load the instruction at address CS:200.

Solution

The machine code instruction is loaded into the code segment of the microcomputer's memory with the command

$$\text{E CS:200 03 04 (}\hookleftarrow\text{)}$$

Next, we can verify that it was loaded correctly with the command

$$\text{D CS:200 201 (}\hookleftarrow\text{)}$$

and finally unassemble the instruction with

$$\text{U CS:200 201 (}\hookleftarrow\text{)}$$

The results produced by this sequence of commands are shown in Fig. 3.31. Here we see that the instruction entered is

$$\text{ADD AX,[SI]}$$

```
-E CS:200 03 04
-D CS:200 201
1342:0200  03 04
-U CS:200 201
1342:0200 0304        ADD      AX,[SI]
-
```

Figure 3.31 Displayed information for Example 3.23.

Before going further we will cover two more commands that are useful for loading and saving programs. They are the *WRITE* (W) *command* and *LOAD* (L) *command*. These commands give the ability to save data stored in memory on a diskette and to reload memory from a diskette, respectively. We can load the machine code of a program into memory with the E command the first time we use it and then save it on a diskette. In this way, the next time the program is needed it can be simply reloaded from the diskette.

Figure 3.9 shows that the general forms of the W and L commands are

```
W [STARTING ADDRESS [DRIVE  STARTING SECTOR  NUMBER OF SECTORS]]

L [STARTING ADDRESS [DRIVE  STARTING SECTOR  NUMBER OF SECTORS]]
```

For instance, to save the ADD instruction we just loaded at address CS:200 in Example 3.23, we can issue the write command

```
W CS:200 1 10 1 (↵)
```

Notice that we have selected for the specification disk drive 1 (drive B), 10 as an arbitrary starting sector on the diskette, and an arbitrary length of 1 sector. Before the command is issued, a formatted data diskette must be inserted into drive B. Then issuing the command causes one sector of data starting at address CS:200 to be read from memory and written into sector 10 on the diskette in drive B. Unlike the earlier commands we have studied, the W command automatically references the CS register instead of the DS register. For this reason, the command

```
W 200 1 10 1 (↵)
```

will perform the same operation.

Let us digress for a moment to examine the file specification of the W command in more detail. The diskettes for an IBM PC that has double-sided, double-density drives are organized into 10,001 sectors that are assigned sector numbers over the range 0_{16} through $27F_{16}$. Each sector is capable of storing 512 bytes of data. With the file specification in a W command, we can select any one of these sectors as the starting sector. The value of the number of sectors should be specified based on the number of bytes of data that are to be saved. The specification that we made earlier for our example of a write command selected one sector (sector number 10_{16}) and for this reason could only save up to 512 bytes of data. The maximum value of sectors that can be specified with a write command is 80_{16}.

The LOAD command can be used to reload a file of data stored on a diskette anywhere in memory. As an example, let us load the instruction that we just saved on a diskette with a W command at a new address (CS:300). This is done with the L command

```
L 300 1 10 1 (↵)
```

The reloading of the instruction can be verified by issuing the U command

```
U CS:300 301 (↵)
```

This causes the display

```
1342:300 301  ADD AX,[SI]
```

EXAMPLE 3.24

Show the sequence of keyboard entries needed to enter the machine code program of Fig. 3.32 into memory of the PC. The program is to be loaded into memory

Machine code	Instruction
B8H	MOV AX,2000H
00H	
20H	
8EH	MOV DS,AX
D8H	
BEH	MOV SI,100H
00H	
01H	
BFH	MOV DI,120H
20H	
01H	
B9H	MOV CX,10H
10H	
00H	
8AH	MOV AH,[SI]
24H	
88H	MOV [DI],AH
25H	
46H	INC SI
47H	INC DI
49H	DEC CX
75H	JNZ $-9
F7H	
90H	NOP

Figure 3.32 Machine code and assembly language instructions of a block move program.

starting at address CS:100. Verify that the hexadecimal machine code was entered correctly and then unassemble the machine code to assure that it represents the source program. Save the program in sector 100 of a formatted data diskette.

Solution

We will use the ENTER command to load the program.

```
E CS:100 B8 00 20 8E D8 BE 0 01 BF 20 01 B9 10 0 8A 24 88 25 46

47 49 75 F7 90 (↵)
```

First, we verify that the machine code has been loaded correctly with the command

```
D CS:100 117 (↵)
```

Comparing the displayed source data in Fig. 3.33 to the machine code in Fig. 3.32, we see that it has been loaded correctly. Now the machine code can be unassembled

```
-E CS:100 B8 00 20 8E D8 BE 0 01 BF 20 01 B9 10 0 8A 24 88 25 46 47 49 75 F7 90
-D CS:100 117
1342:0100  B8 00 20 8E D8 BE 00 01-BF 20 01 B9 10 00 8A 24    . ....... .....$
1342:0110  88 25 46 47 49 75 F7 90                            .%FGIu..
-U CS:100 117
1342:0100 B80020      MOV     AX,2000
1342:0103 8ED8        MOV     DS,AX
1342:0105 BE0001      MOV     SI,0100
1342:0108 BF2001      MOV     DI,0120
1342:010B B91000      MOV     CX,0010
1342:010E 8A24        MOV     AH,[SI]
1342:0110 8825        MOV     [DI],AH
1342:0112 46          INC     SI
1342:0113 47          INC     DI
1342:0114 49          DEC     CX
1342:0115 75F7        JNZ     010E
1342:0117 90          NOP
-W CS:100 1 100 1
```

Figure 3.33 Displayed information for Example 3.24.

by the command

$$U \ CS:100 \ 117 \ (\lrcorner)$$

Comparing the displayed source program of Fig. 3.33 to that in Fig. 3.32, it again verifies correct entry. Finally, the program is saved on the data diskette with the command

$$W \ CS:100 \ 1 \ 100 \ 1 \ (\lrcorner)$$

At this time, it is important to mention that using the W command to save a program can be quite risky. For instance, if by mistake, the command is written with the wrong disk specifications, some other program or data on the diskette may be written over. Moreover, the diskette should not contain files that were created in any other way. This is because the locations of these files will not be known and may accidentally be written over by the selected file specification. Overwriting a file like this will ruin its contents. Even more important is to never issue the command to the hard disk (C:). This could destroy the installation of the disk operating system.

Another method of saving and loading programs is available in DEBUG and this alternate approach eliminates the overwrite problem. We will now look at how a program can be saved using a file name, instead of with a file specification.

By using the *name* (N) *command* along with the write command, a program can be saved on the diskette under a file name. In Fig. 3.9 we see that the N command is specified in general as

$$N \quad FILE \ NAME$$

FILE NAME has the form

$$NAME.EXT$$

Here the name of the file can be up to five characters, but must start with a letter. On the other hand, the extension (EXT) is from zero to three characters. Neither EXE or COM are valid extensions. Some examples of valid file names are BLOCK, TEMP.1, BLOCK1.ASM, and BLK_1.R1.

As part of the process of using the file name command, the BX and CX registers must be updated to identify the size of the program that is to be saved in the file. The size of the program in bytes is given as

$$(BX\ CX) = \text{number of bytes}$$

Together CX and BX specify an 8-digit hexadecimal number that identifies the number of bytes in the file. In general, the programs we will work with are small. For this reason, the upper four digits will always be zero. That is, the contents of BX will be 0000_{16}. Just using CX, permits a file to be up to 64KB long.

After the name command has been issued and the CX and BX registers initialized, the write command form

```
W [STARTING ADDRESS]
```

is used to save the program on the diskette. To reload the program into memory, we begin by naming the file and then simply issuing a load command with the address at which it is to start. This gives the sequence

```
N   FILE NAME
```

```
L [STARTING ADDRESS]
```

As an example let us look at how the name command is set up to save the machine program used in Example 3.24 in a file called BLK.1 on a diskette in drive A. First, the name command

```
N A:BLK.1  (↵)
```

is entered. Looking at Fig. 3.33, we see that the program is stored in memory from address CS:100 to CS:117. This gives a size of 18_{16} bytes. Therefore, CX and BX are initialized as follows:

```
R CX  (↵)
```

```
CX XXXX
```

```
:18  (↵)
```

```
R BX  (↵)
```

```
BX XXXX
```

```
:0  (↵)
```

Now the program is saved on the diskette with the command

```
W CS:100 (⏎)
```

To reload the program into memory, we simply perform the command sequence

```
N A:BLK.1 (⏎)
```

```
L CS:100 (⏎)
```

In fact, the program can be loaded starting at another address by just specifying that address in the load command.

Once saved on a diskette, the file extension can be changed to indicate an executable DOS file (that is a file with the extension .EXE) by using the rename (REN) command. To do this we must first return to the DOS with the command

```
Q (⏎)
```

and then issue the command

```
C:\DOS> REN A:BLK.1 BLK.EXE (⏎)
```

Programs that are in an executable file can be directly loaded when the DEBUG program is brought up. For our example, the program command is

```
C:\DOS> DEBUG A:BLK.EXE (⏎)
```

Execution of this command loads the program at address CS:100 and then displays the DEBUG prompt. The executable files can also be executed in DOS environment simply by entering the file name.

▲ 3.9 ASSEMBLING INSTRUCTIONS WITH THE ASSEMBLE COMMAND

All the instructions we have worked with up to this point have been hand assembled into machine code. The DEBUG program has a command that lets us automatically assemble the instructions of a program, one after the other, and store them in memory. It is called the *ASSEMBLE* (A) *command*.

The general syntax of ASSEMBLE is given in Fig. 3.9 as

```
A [STARTING ADDRESS]
```

Here "STARTING ADDRESS" is the address at which the machine code of the first instruction of the program is to be stored. For example, to assemble the instruction ADD [BX+SI+1234H],AX and store its machine code in memory starting at address CS:100, we start with the command entry

A CS:100 (↵)

The response to this command input is the display of the starting address in the form

1342:0100–

The instruction to be assembled is typed in following this address, and when the (↵) key is depressed, the instruction is assembled into machine code; it is stored in memory; and the starting address of the next instruction is displayed. As shown in Fig. 3.34, for our example, we have

1342:0100 ADD [BX+SI+1234],AX (↵)

1342:0104–

Now either the next instruction is entered or the (↵) key is depressed to terminate the ASSEMBLE command.

Assuming that the assemble operation just performed was terminated by entering (↵), we can view the machine code that was produced for the instruction by issuing a DUMP command. Notice that the address displayed as the starting point of the next instruction is 1342:0104. Therefore, the machine code for the ADD instruction took up 4 bytes of memory, CS:100, CS:101, CS:102, and CS:103. The command needed to display this machine code is

D CS:100 103 (↵)

In Fig. 3.34, we find that the machine code stored for the instruction is 01803412H.

At this point, the instruction can be executed or saved on a diskette. For instance, to save the machine code on a diskette in file INST.1, we issue the commands

N A:INST.1 (↵)

R CX   (↵)

:4   (↵)

R BX   (↵)

:0   (↵)

W CS:100   (↵)

Now that we have shown how to assemble an instruction, view its machine code, and save the machine code on a data diskette, let us look into how a complete

```
-A CS:100
1342:0100 ADD [BX+SI+1234],AX
1342:0104
-D CS:100 103
1342:0100   01 80 34 12                                    ..4.
-N A:INST.1
-R CX
:4
-R BX
:0
-W CS:100
-
```

Figure 3.34 Assembling the instruction ADD [BX+SI+1234H],AX.

program can be assembled with the A command. For this purpose, we will use the program shown in Fig. 3.35(a). The same program was entered as hand assembled machine code in Example 3.24.

We will begin by assuming that the program is to be stored in memory starting at address CS:200. For this reason, the *line-by-line assembler* is invoked with the command

A CS:200 (↵)

This gives the response

1342:0200—

Now we type in instructions of the program as follows:

1342:0200 MOV AX,2000 (↵)

1342:0203 MOV DS,AX   (↵)

1342:0205 MOV SI,100   (↵)

.   .   .   .

.   .   .   .

1342:0217 NOP   (↵)

1342:0218   (↵)

The details of the instruction entry sequence are shown in Fig. 3.35(b).

Now that the complete program has been entered, let us verify that it has been assembled correctly. This can be done with an UNASSEMBLE command. Notice in Fig. 3.35(b) that the program resides in memory over the address range CS:200 through CS:217. To unassemble the machine code in this part of memory,

```
MOV     AX,2000H                    -A CS:200
                                    1342:0200 MOV AX,2000
MOV     DS,AX                       1342:0203 MOV DS,AX
                                    1342:0205 MOV SI,100
MOV     SI,0100H                    1342:0208 MOV DI,120
                                    1342:020B MOV CX,10
MOV     DI,0120H                    1342:020E MOV AH,[SI]
                                    1342:0210 MOV [DI],AH
MOV     CX,010H                     1342:0212 INC SI
                                    1342:0213 INC DI
MOV     AH,[SI]                     1342:0214 DEC CX
                                    1342:0215 JNZ 20E
MOV     [DI],AH                     1342:0217 NOP
                                    1342:0218
INC     SI
                                    -
INC     DI

DEC     CX

JNZ     20EH                                    (b)

NOP

              (a)
```

```
-U CS:200 217
1342:0200 B80020       MOV     AX,2000
1342:0203 8ED8         MOV     DS,AX
1342:0205 BE0001       MOV     SI,0100
1342:0208 BF2001       MOV     DI,0120
1342:020B B91000       MOV     CX,0010
1342:020E 8A24         MOV     AH,[SI]
1342:0210 8825         MOV     [DI],AH
1342:0212 46           INC     SI
1342:0213 47           INC     DI
1342:0214 49           DEC     CX
1342:0215 75F7         JNZ     020E
1342:0217 90           NOP
-
          (c)
```

Figure 3.35 (a) Block move program. (b) Assembling the program. (c) Verifying the assembled program with the U command.

we issue the command

```
            U CS:200 217   (↵)
```

The results produced with this command are shown in Fig. 3.35(c). Comparing the instructions to those in Fig. 3.35(a) confirms that the program has been assembled correctly.

The ASSEMBLE command allows us to assemble instructions involving any of the various addressing modes. For instance, the instruction we used in our earlier example

```
            MOV AX,2000H
```

employs immediate addressing mode for the source operand. Instructions, such as

```
            MOV AX,[2000H]
```

which uses direct addressing mode for the source operand can also be assembled into memory.

ASSEMBLE also supports two pseudo-instructions that can be used to assemble data directly into memory. They are *data byte* (DB) and *data word* (DW). An example is

```
DB 1,2,3,'JASSI'
```

With this command, the byte size representation of numbers 1, 2, and 3 and the ASCII code for letters J, A, S, S, and I are assembled into memory.

▲ 3.10 EXECUTING INSTRUCTIONS AND PROGRAMS WITH THE TRACE AND GO COMMANDS

Once the program has been entered into the memory of the PC, it is ready to be executed. The DEBUG program allows us to execute the entire program with one *GO* (G) *command* or to execute the program in several segments of instructions by using *breakpoints* in the GO command. Moreover, by using the *TRACE* (T) *command*, the program can be stepped through by executing one or more instructions at a time.

Let us begin by examining the operation of the TRACE command in more detail. Trace provides the programmer with the ability to execute one instruction at a time. This mode of operation is also known as *single-stepping the program*; it is very useful during early phases of program debugging. This is because the contents of registers or memory can be viewed both before and after the execution of each instruction to determine whether or not the correct operation was performed.

The general form of the command as shown in Fig. 3.9 is

```
T [=STARTING ADDRESS] [NUMBER]
```

Notice that a *starting address* is specified as part of the command. This is the address of the instruction at which execution is to begin. It is followed by a *number* that tells how many instructions are to be executed. The use of the equal sign before the starting address is very important. If it is left out, the microcomputer usually hangs up and will have to be restarted with a power on reset.

If an instruction count is not specified in the command, just one instruction is executed. For instance, the command

```
T =CS:100 (↵)
```

causes the instruction starting at address CS:100 to be executed. At completion of the instruction's execution, the complete state of the MPU's internal registers is automatically displayed. At this point, other DEBUG commands can be issued, for instance, to display the contents of memory, or the next instruction can be executed.

This TRACE command can also be issued as

$$T \quad (\leftarrow)$$

In this case the instruction pointed to by the current values of CS and IP (CS:IP) is executed. This is the form of the TRACE command that is used to execute the next instruction.

If we want to step through several instructions, the TRACE command must include the number of instructions to be executed. This number is included after the address. For example, to trace through three instructions, the command is issued as

$$T \quad =CS:100 \quad 3 \quad (\leftarrow)$$

Again, the internal state of the MPU is displayed after each instruction is executed.

EXAMPLE 3.25

Load the instruction stored at file specification 1 10 1 at offset 100 of the current code segment. Unassemble the instruction. Then initialize AX with 1111H, SI with 1234H, and the word contents of memory address 1234_{16} to the value 2222_{16}. Next, display the internal state of the MPU and the contents of address 1234_{16} to verify their initialization. Finally, execute the instruction with the TRACE command. What operation is performed by the instruction?

Solution

First, the instruction is loaded at CS:100 from the diskette with the command

$$L \quad CS:100 \quad 1 \quad 10 \quad 1 \quad (\leftarrow)$$

Now the machine code is unassembled to verify that the instruction has loaded correctly.

$$U \quad 100 \quad 101 \quad (\leftarrow)$$

Looking at the displayed information in Fig. 3.36, we see that it is an ADD instruction. Next we initialize the internal registers and memory with the command sequence

```
R AX          (←)

AX 0000

:1111         (←)

R SI          (←)
```

```
-L CS:100 1 10 1
-U 100 101
1342:0100 0304          ADD     AX,[SI]
-R AX
AX 0000
:1111
-R SI
SI 0000
:1234
-E DS:1234 22 22
-R
AX=1111  BX=0000  CX=0000  DX=0000  SP=FFEE  BP=0000  SI=1234  DI=0000
DS=1342  ES=1342  SS=1342  CS=1342  IP=0100   NV UP EI PL NZ NA PO NC
1342:0100 0304          ADD     AX,[SI]
-D DS:1234 1235
1342:1230             22 22                                    " "
-T =CS:100

AX=3333  BX=0000  CX=0000  DX=0000  SP=FFEE  BP=0000  SI=1234  DI=0000
DS=1342  ES=1342  SS=1342  CS=1342  IP=0102   NV UP EI PL NZ NA PE NC
1342:0102 0000          ADD     [BX+SI],AL                     DS:1234=22

-
```

Figure 3.36 Displayed information for Example 3.25.

SI 0000

:1234   ($\hookleftarrow$)

E DS:1234 22 22   ($\hookleftarrow$)

Now the initialization is verified with the commands

R   ($\hookleftarrow$)

D DS:1234 1235   ($\hookleftarrow$)

In Fig. 3.36, we see that AX, SI, and the word contents of address 1234_{16} were correctly initialized. Therefore, we are ready to execute the instruction. This is done with the command

T =CS:100 ($\hookleftarrow$)

From the displayed trace information in Fig. 3.36, we find that the value 2222_{16} at address 1234_{16} was added to the value 1111_{16} held in AX. Therefore, the new contents of AX are 3333_{16}.

The GO command is typically used to run programs that are already working or to execute programs in the latter stages of debugging. For example, if the beginning part of a program is already operating correctly, a GO command can be used to execute this group of instructions and then stop execution at a point in the program where additional debugging is to begin.

The table in Fig. 3.9 shows that the general form of the GO command is

```
G =[STARTING ADDRESS [BREAKPOINT ADDRESS ....]]
```

The first address is the *starting address* of the segment of program that is to be executed, that is, the address of the instruction at which execution is to begin. The second address, the *breakpoint address*, is the address of the end of the program segment, that is, the address of the instruction at which execution is to stop. The breakpoint address that is specified must correspond to the first byte of an instruction. A list of up to 10 breakpoint addresses can be supplied with the command.

An example of the GO command is

```
G =CS:200 217 (↵)
```

This command loads the IP register with 0200_{16}, sets a breakpoint at address CS:217, and then begins program execution at address CS:200. Instruction execution proceeds until address CS:217 is accessed. When the breakpoint address is reached, program execution is terminated, the complete internal status of the MPU is displayed, and control is returned to DEBUG.

Sometimes we just want to execute a program without using a breakpoint. This can also be done with the GO command. For instance, to execute a program that starts at offset 100_{16} in the current CS, we can issue the GO command without a breakpoint address as follows

```
G =CS:100 (↵)
```

This command will cause the program to run to completion provided there are appropriate instructions in the program to initiate a normal termination, such as those needed to return to DEBUG. In the case of a program where CS and IP are already initialized with the correct values, we can just enter

```
G (↵)
```

However, it is recommended that the GO command always include a breakpoint address. If a GO is issued without a breakpoint address and the value of CS and IP are not already set up or the program is not correctly prepared for normal termination, the microcomputer can lock up. This is because the program execution may go beyond the end of the program into an area with data that represents invalid instructions.

EXAMPLE 3.26

In Section 3.8, we saved the block move program in file BLK.EXE on a data diskette in drive A. Load this program into memory starting at address CS:200. Then initialize the microcomputer by loading the DS register with 2000_{16}. Fill the block of memory from DS:100 through DS:10F with FF_{16}, and the block of memory from DS:120 through DS:12F with 00_{16}. Verify that the blocks of memory were initialized correctly. Load DS with 1342_{16}, and display the state of the MPU's registers. Display the assembly language version of the program from CS:200 through CS:217. Use a GO command to execute the program through address CS:20E. What changes have occurred in the contents of the registers? Now execute down through address CS:215. What changes are found in the blocks of data? Next execute the program down to address CS:217. What new changes are found in the blocks of data?

Solution

The commands needed to load the program are

$$N \ A:BLK.EXE \quad (\llcorner\!\lrcorner)$$

$$L \ CS:200 \quad (\llcorner\!\lrcorner)$$

Next we initialize the DS register and memory with the commands

$$R \ DS \quad (\llcorner\!\lrcorner)$$

$$DS \ 1342$$

$$:2000 \ (\llcorner\!\lrcorner)$$

$$F \ DS:100 \ 10F \ FF \quad (\llcorner\!\lrcorner)$$

$$F \ DS:120 \ 12F \ 00 \quad (\llcorner\!\lrcorner)$$

Now the blocks of data in memory are displayed using the commands

$$D \ DS:100 \ 10F \quad (\llcorner\!\lrcorner)$$

$$D \ DS:120 \ 12F \quad (\llcorner\!\lrcorner)$$

The displayed information is shown in Fig. 3.37. DS is restored with 1342_{16} using the command

$$R \ DS \ (\llcorner\!\lrcorner)$$

$$DS \ 2000$$

$$:1342 \ (\llcorner\!\lrcorner)$$

and the state of the MPU's registers is displayed with the command

$$R \quad (\llcorner\!\lrcorner)$$

```
-N A:BLK.EXE
-L CS:200
-R DS
DS 1342
:2000
-F DS:100 10F FF
-F DS:120 12F 00
-D DS:100 10F
2000:0100  FF FF FF FF FF FF FF FF-FF FF FF FF FF FF FF FF    ................
-D DS:120 12F
2000:0120  00 00 00 00 00 00 00 00-00 00 00 00 00 00 00 00    ................
-R DS
DS 2000
:1342
-R
AX=0000  BX=0000  CX=0020  DX=0000  SP=FFEE  BP=0000  SI=0000  DI=0000
DS=1342  ES=1342  SS=1342  CS=1342  IP=0100   NV UP EI PL NZ NA PO NC
1342:0100 0000          ADD     [BX+SI],AL                       DS:0000=CD
-U CS:200 217
1342:0200 B80020        MOV     AX,2000
1342:0203 8ED8          MOV     DS,AX
1342:0205 BE0001        MOV     SI,0100
1342:0208 BF2001        MOV     DI,0120
1342:020B B91000        MOV     CX,0010
1342:020E 8A24          MOV     AH,[SI]
1342:0210 8825          MOV     [DI],AH
1342:0212 46            INC     SI
1342:0213 47            INC     DI
1342:0214 49            DEC     CX
1342:0215 75F7          JNZ     020E
1342:0217 90            NOP
-G =CS:200 20E

AX=2000  BX=0000  CX=0010  DX=0000  SP=FFEE  BP=0000  SI=0100  DI=0120
DS=2000  ES=1342  SS=1342  CS=1342  IP=020E   NV UP EI PL NZ NA PO NC
1342:020E 8A24          MOV     AH,[SI]                          DS:0100=FF
-G =CS:20E 215

AX=FF00  BX=0000  CX=000F  DX=0000  SP=FFEE  BP=0000  SI=0101  DI=0121
DS=2000  ES=1342  SS=1342  CS=1342  IP=0215   NV UP EI PL NZ AC PE NC
1342:0215 75F7          JNZ     020E
-D DS:100 10F
2000:0100  FF FF FF FF FF FF FF FF-FF FF FF FF FF FF FF FF    ................
-D DS:120 12F
2000:0120  FF 00 00 00 00 00 00 00-00 00 00 00 00 00 00 00    ................
-G =CS:215 217

AX=FF00  BX=0000  CX=0000  DX=0000  SP=FFEE  BP=0000  SI=0110  DI=0130
DS=2000  ES=1342  SS=1342  CS=1342  IP=0217   NV UP EI PL ZR NA PE NC
1342:0217 90            NOP
-D DS:100 10F
2000:0100  FF FF FF FF FF FF FF FF-FF FF FF FF FF FF FF FF    ................
-D DS:120 12F
2000:0120  FF FF FF FF FF FF FF FF-FF FF FF FF FF FF FF FF    ................
-
```

Figure 3.37 Displayed information for Example 3.26.

Before beginning to execute the program, we will display the source code with the command

U CS:200 217   (↵)

The program that is displayed is shown in Fig. 3.37.
Now the first segment of program is executed with the command

G =CS:200 20E   (↵)

Looking at the displayed state of the MPU in Fig. 3.37, we see that DS was loaded with 2000_{16}, AX was loaded with 2000_{16}, SI was loaded with 0100_{16}, and CX was loaded with 0010_{16}.

Next, another GO command is used to execute the program down through address CS:215.

G =CS:20E 215   (↵)

We can check the state of the blocks of memory with the commands

D DS:100 10F   (↵)

D DS:120 12F   (↵)

From the displayed information in Fig. 3.37, we see that FF_{16} was copied from the first element of the source block to the first element of the destination block.
Now we execute through CS:217 with the command

G =CS:215 217   (↵)

and examine the blocks of data with the commands

D DS:100 10F   (↵)

D DS:120 12F   (↵)

We find that the complete source block has been copied to the destination block.

▲ 3.11 DEBUGGING A PROGRAM

In Sections 3.8, 3.9, and 3.10 we learned how to use DEBUG to load a machine code program into the memory of the PC, assemble a program, and execute the program. However, we did not determine if the program when run performed the operation for which it was written. It is common to have errors in programs and even a single error can render the program useless. For instance, if the address to which a "jump" instruction passes control is wrong, the program may get hung up. Errors in a program are also referred to as *bugs*; the process of removing them is called *debugging*.

The two types of errors that can be made by a programmer are the *syntax error* and the *execution error*. A syntax error is an error caused by not following the rules for coding or entering an instruction. These types of errors are typically identified by the microcomputer and signaled to the user with an error message. For this reason, they are usually easy to find and correct. For example, if a DUMP command was keyed in as

D DS:100120 (↵)

an error condition exists. This is because the space between the starting and ending address is left out. This incorrect entry is signaled by the warning "Error" in the display and the spot where the error begins, in this case, the 1 in 120, is marked with the symbol "^" to identify the position of the error.

An execution error is an error in the logic behind the development of the program. That is, the program is correctly coded and entered, but it still does not perform the operation for which it was written. This type of error can be identified by entering the program into the microcomputer and observing its operation. Even when an execution error has been identified, it is usually not easy to find the exact cause of the problem.

Our ability to debug execution errors in a program is aided by the commands of the DEBUG program. For instance, the TRACE command allows us to step through the program by executing just one instruction at a time. We can use the display of the internal register state produced by TRACE and the memory dump command to determine the state of the MPU and memory prior to execution of an instruction and again after its execution. This information will tell us whether the instruction has performed the operation planned for it. If an error is found, its cause can be identified and corrected.

To demonstrate the process of debugging a program, let us once again use the program that we stored in file A:BLK.EXE. We load it into the code segment at address CS:200 with the command

N A:BLK.EXE   (↵)

L 200   (↵)

Now the program resides in memory at addresses CS:200 through CS:217. The program is displayed with the command

U 200 217 (↵)

The program that is displayed is shown in Fig. 3.38. This program implements a block data transfer operation. The block of data to be moved starts at memory address DS:100 and is 16 bytes in length. It is to be moved to another block of

```
C:\DOS>DEBUG
-N A:BLK.EXE
-L 200
-U 200 217
1342:0200 B82010          MOV     AX,2000
1342:0203 8ED8            MOV     DS,AX
1342:0205 BE0001          MOV     SI,0100
1342:0208 BF2001          MOV     DI,0120
1342:020B B91000          MOV     CX,0010
1342:020E 8A24            MOV     AH,[SI]
1342:0210 8825            MOV     [DI],AH
1342:0212 46              INC     SI
1342:0213 47              INC     DI
1342:0214 49              DEC     CX
1342:0215 75F7            JNZ     020E
1342:0217 90              NOP
-F 2000:100 10F FF
-F 2000:120 12F 00
-T =CS:200 5

AX=2000  BX=0000  CX=0010  DX=0000  SP=FFEE  BP=0000  SI=0100  DI=0120
DS=1020  ES=1342  SS=1342  CS=1342  IP=0203   NV UP EI PL NZ NA PO NC
1342:0203 8ED8            MOV     DS,AX

AX=2000  BX=0000  CX=0010  DX=0000  SP=FFEE  BP=0000  SI=0100  DI=0120
DS=2000  ES=1342  SS=1342  CS=1342  IP=0205   NV UP EI PL NZ NA PO NC
1342:0205 BE0001          MOV     SI,0100

AX=2000  BX=0000  CX=0010  DX=0000  SP=FFEE  BP=0000  SI=0100  DI=0120
DS=2000  ES=1342  SS=1342  CS=1342  IP=0208   NV UP EI PL NZ NA PO NC
1342:0208 BF2001          MOV     DI,0120

AX=2000  BX=0000  CX=0010  DX=0000  SP=FFEE  BP=0000  SI=0100  DI=0120
DS=2000  ES=1342  SS=1342  CS=1342  IP=020B   NV UP EI PL NZ NA PO NC
1342:020B B91000          MOV     CX,0010

AX=2000  BX=0000  CX=0010  DX=0000  SP=FFEE  BP=0000  SI=0100  DI=0120
DS=2000  ES=1342  SS=1342  CS=1342  IP=020E   NV UP EI PL NZ NA PO NC
1342:020E 8A24            MOV     AH,[SI]                    DS:0100=FF
-D DS:120 12F
2000:0120  00 00 00 00 00 00 00 00-00 00 00 00 00 00 00 00    ................
-T 2

AX=FF00  BX=0000  CX=0010  DX=0000  SP=FFEE  BP=0000  SI=0100  DI=0120
DS=2000  ES=1342  SS=1342  CS=1342  IP=0210   NV UP EI PL NZ NA PO NC
1342:0210 8825            MOV     [DI],AH                    DS:0120=00

AX=FF00  BX=0000  CX=0010  DX=0000  SP=FFEE  BP=0000  SI=0100  DI=0120
DS=2000  ES=1342  SS=1342  CS=1342  IP=0212   NV UP EI PL NZ NA PO NC
1342:0212 46              INC     SI
-D DS:120 12F
2000:0120  FF 00 00 00 00 00 00 00-00 00 00 00 00 00 00 00    ................
-T 3

AX=FF00  BX=0000  CX=0010  DX=0000  SP=FFEE  BP=0000  SI=0101  DI=0120
DS=2000  ES=1342  SS=1342  CS=1342  IP=0213   NV UP EI PL NZ NA PO NC
1342:0213 47              INC     DI

AX=FF00  BX=0000  CX=0010  DX=0000  SP=FFEE  BP=0000  SI=0101  DI=0121
DS=2000  ES=1342  SS=1342  CS=1342  IP=0214   NV UP EI PL NZ NA PE NC
```

Figure 3.38 Program debugging demonstration.

```
1342:0214 49              DEC    CX

AX=FF00  BX=0000  CX=000F  DX=0000  SP=FFEE  BP=0000  SI=0101  DI=0121
DS=2000  ES=1342  SS=1342  CS=1342  IP=0215   NV UP EI PL NZ AC PE NC
1342:0215 75F7            JNZ    020E
-T

AX=FF00  BX=0000  CX=000F  DX=0000  SP=FFEE  BP=0000  SI=0101  DI=0121
DS=2000  ES=1342  SS=1342  CS=1342  IP=020E   NV UP EI PL NZ AC PE NC
1342:020E 8A24            MOV    AH,[SI]                        DS:0101=FF
-G =CS:20E 215

AX=FF00  BX=0000  CX=000E  DX=0000  SP=FFEE  BP=0000  SI=0102  DI=0122
DS=2000  ES=1342  SS=1342  CS=1342  IP=0215   NV UP EI PL NZ NA PO NC
1342:0215 75F7            JNZ    020E
-D DS:120 12F
2000:0120  FF FF 00 00 00 00 00 00-00 00 00 00 00 00 00 00   ................
-T

AX=FF00  BX=0000  CX=000E  DX=0000  SP=FFEE  BP=0000  SI=0102  DI=0122
DS=2000  ES=1342  SS=1342  CS=1342  IP=020E   NV UP EI PL NZ NA PO NC
1342:020E 8A24            MOV    AH,[SI]                        DS:0102=FF
-G =CS:20E 217

AX=FF00  BX=0000  CX=0000  DX=0000  SP=FFEE  BP=0000  SI=0110  DI=0130
DS=2000  ES=1342  SS=1342  CS=1342  IP=0217   NV UP EI PL ZR NA PE NC
1342:0217 90             NOP
-D DS:120 12F
2000:0120  FF FF FF FF FF FF FF FF-FF FF FF FF FF FF FF FF   ................
-
```

Figure 3.38 (Continued)

storage locations starting at address DS:120. DS equals 2000_{16}; therefore, it points to a data segment starting at physical address 20000_{16}.

Before executing the program, let us issue commands to initialize the source block of memory locations from address 100_{16} through $10F_{16}$ with FF_{16} and the bytes in the destination block starting at 120_{16} with 00_{16}. To do this, we issue the command sequence

$$F \ \ 2000:100 \ \ 10F \ \ FF \ \ (\leftarrow)$$

$$F \ \ 2000:120 \ \ 12F \ \ 00 \ \ (\leftarrow)$$

The first two instructions of the program in Fig. 3.38 are

MOV AX,2000H

and

MOV DS,AX

These two instructions, when executed, load the data segment register with the value 2000_{16}. In this way, they define a data segment starting at address 20000_{16}. The next three instructions are used to load the SI, DI, and CX registers with 100_{16}, 120_{16}, and 10_{16}, respectively. Let us now show how to execute these instructions and then determine if they perform the correct function. They are executed by issuing the command

```
T =CS:200 5   (⏎)
```

To determine if the instructions that were executed performed the correct operation, we just need to look at the trace display that they produce. This display trace is shown in Fig. 3.38. Here we see that the first instruction loads AX with 2000_{16} and the second moves this value into the DS register. Also notice in the last trace that is displayed for this command that SI contains 0100_{16}, DI contains 0120_{16}, and CX contains 0010_{16}.

The next two instructions copy the contents of memory location 100_{16} into the storage location at address 120_{16}. Let us first check the contents of the destination block with the D command

```
D DS:120 12F   (⏎)
```

Looking at the dump display in Fig. 3.38, we see that the original contents of these locations are 00_{16}. Now the two instructions are executed with the command

```
T 2   (⏎)
```

and the contents of address DS:120 are checked once again with the command

```
D DS:120 12F   (⏎)
```

The display dump in Fig. 3.38 shows that the first element of the source block was copied to the location of the first element of the destination block. Therefore, both address 100_{16} and address 120_{16} now contain the value FF_{16}.

The next three instructions are used to increment pointers SI and DI and decrement block counter CX. To execute them, we issue the command

```
T 3   (⏎)
```

Referring to the trace display in Fig. 3.38 to verify their operation, we find that the new values in SI and DI are 0101_{16} and 0121_{16}, respectively, and CX is now $000F_{16}$.

The jump instruction is next and it transfers control to the instruction eight bytes back if CX did not become zero. It is executed with the command

```
T   (⏎)
```

Notice that the result of executing this instruction is that the value in IP is changed to $020E_{16}$. This corresponds to the location of the instruction

```
MOV AH,[SI]
```

In this way we see that control has been returned to the part of the program that performs the data move operation.

The move operation performed by this part of the program was already checked; however, we must still determine if it runs to completion when the count in CX decrements to zero. Therefore, we will execute another complete loop with the GO command

$$G =CS:20E\ 215\quad (\lrcorner)$$

Correct operation is verified because the trace shows that CX has been decremented by one more and equals E. The fact that the second element has been moved can be verified by dumping the destination block with the command

$$D\ DS:120\ 12F\quad (\lrcorner)$$

Now we are again at address CS:215. To execute the jump instruction at this location, we can again use the T command

$$T\quad (\lrcorner)$$

This returns control to the instruction at CS:20E. The previous two commands can be repeated until the complete block is moved and CX equals 0_{16}. Or we can use the GO command to execute to the address CS:217, which is the end of the program.

$$G =CS:20E\ 217\quad (\lrcorner)$$

At completion, the overall operation of the program can be verified by examining the contents of the destination block with the command sequence

$$D\ DS:120\ 12F\quad (\lrcorner)$$

FF_{16} should be displayed as the data held in each storage location.

ASSIGNMENTS

Section 3.2

1. Encode the following instruction using the information in Figs. 3.1 through 3.4.

$$ADD\ AX,DX$$

Assume that the opcode for the add operation is 000000.

2. Encode the following instructions using the information in the tables of Figs. 3.2 through 3.6.
   (a) MOV [DI], DX

(b) MOV [BX][SI], BX

(c) MOV DL, [BX]+10H

3. Encode the instructions that follow using the tables in Figs. 3.2 through 3.6.

    (a) PUSH DS

    (b) ROL BL,CL

    (c) ADD AX, [1234H]

Section 3.3

4. How many bytes are required to encode the instruction MOV SI,0100H?

5. How many bytes of memory are required to store the machine code for the program in Fig. 3.7(a)?

Section 3.4

6. What purpose is served by the DEBUG program?

7. Can DEBUG be brought up by typing the command using lowercase letters?

8. If the DEBUG command R AXBX is entered to a PC, what happens?

9. Write the REGISTER command needed to change the value in CX to 10_{16}.

10. Write the command needed to change the state of the parity flag to PE.

11. Write a command that will dump the state of the MPU's internal registers.

Section 3.5

12. Write a DUMP command that will display the contents of the first 16 bytes of the current code segment.

13. Show an ENTER command that can be used to examine the contents of the same 16 bytes of memory that were displayed in problem 12.

14. Show the ENTER command needed to load five consecutive bytes of memory starting at address CS:100 of the current code segment with FF_{16}.

15. Show how an ENTER command can be used to initialize the first 32 bytes at the top of the stack to 00_{16}.

16. Write a sequence of commands that will fill the first six storage locations starting at address CS:100 with 11_{16}, the second six with 22_{16}, the third six with 33_{16}, the fourth six with 44_{16}, and the fifth six with 55_{16}; change the contents of storage locations CS:105 and CS:113 to FF_{16}; display the first 30 bytes of memory starting at CS:100; and then use a search command on this 30-byte block of memory to find those storage locations that contain FF_{16}.

Section 3.6

17. What DEBUG commands do I and O stand for?

18. What operation is performed by the command

I 123 (↵)

19. Write an output command that will load the byte-wide output port at I/O address 0124_{16} with the value $5A_{16}$.

Section 3.7

20. What two results are produced by the hexadecimal command?

21. How large can the numbers in an H command be?

22. The difference $FA_{16} - 5A_{16}$ is to be found. Write the H command.

Section 3.8

23. Show the sequence of commands needed to load the machine code instruction 320E3412H starting at address CS:100, unassemble it to verify that the correct instruction was loaded, and save it on a data diskette at file specification 1 50 1.

24. Write commands that will reload the instruction saved on the data diskette in problem 23 into memory at offset 400 in the current code segment and unassemble it to verify correct loading.

Section 3.9

25. Show how the instruction MOV [DI],DX can be assembled into memory at address CS:100.

26. Write a sequence of commands that will first assemble the instruction ROL BL,CL into memory starting at address CS:200 and then verify its entry by unassembling the instruction.

Section 3.10

27. Show a sequence of commands that will load the instruction saved on the data diskette in problem 23 at address CS:300; unassemble it to verify correct loading; initialize the contents of register CX to $000F_{16}$ and the contents of the word memory location starting at DS:1234 to $00FF_{16}$; execute the instruction with the TRACE command; and verify its operation by examining the contents of CX and the word of data stored starting at DS:1234 in memory.

28. Write a sequence to repeat Example 3.26; however, this time execute the complete program with one GO command.

Section 3.11

29. What is the difference between a syntax error and an execution error?

30. Write a sequence of commands to repeat the debug demonstration presented in Section 3.11, but this time use only GO commands to execute the program.

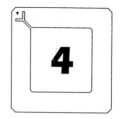

8088/8086 Microprocessor Programming 1

▲ 4.1 INTRODUCTION

Up to this point, we have studied the software architecture of the 8088 and 8086 microprocessors and the software development tools provided by the DEBUG program on the IBM PC. We found that the software architectures of the 8088 and 8086 microprocessors are identical and learned how to encode assembly language instructions in machine language and how to use the debugger to enter, execute, and debug programs.

In this chapter, we begin a detailed study of the instruction set of the 8088 and 8086 microprocessors. A large part of the instruction set is covered in this chapter. These instructions provide the ability to write simple programs. The rest of the instruction set and some more sophisticated programming concepts are covered in Chapter 5. The following topics are presented in this chapter:

1. The instruction set of the 8088/8086
2. Data transfer instructions
3. Arithmetic instructions
4. Logic instructions
5. Shift instructions
6. Rotate instructions

▲ 4.2 THE INSTRUCTION SET OF THE 8088/8086

The instruction set of a microprocessor defines the basic operations that a programmer can make the device perform. The 8088 and 8086 microprocessors have the same instruction set. This powerful instruction set contains 117 basic instructions. The wide range of operands and addressing modes permitted for use with these instructions further expands the instruction set into many more instructions executable at the machine code level. For instance, the basic MOV instruction expands into 28 different machine-level instructions.

For the purpose of discussion, the instruction set will be divided into a number of groups of functionally related instructions. In this chapter we consider the data transfer instructions, arithmetic instructions, the logic instructions, shift instructions, and rotate instructions. Advanced instructions such as those for program and processor control are covered in Chapter 5.

▲ 4.3 DATA TRANSFER INSTRUCTIONS

The 8088 microprocessor has a group of *data transfer instructions* that are provided to move data either between its internal registers or between an internal register and a storage location in memory. This group includes the *move byte or word* (MOV) instruction, *exchange byte or word* (XCHG) instruction, *translate byte* (XLAT) instruction, *load effective address* (LEA) instruction, *load data segment* (LDS) instruction, and *load extra segment* (LES) instruction. These instructions are discussed in this section.

The MOV Instruction

The MOV instruction shown in Fig. 4.1(a) is used to transfer a byte or a word of data from a source operand to a destination operand. These operands can be internal registers of the 8088 and storage locations in memory. Figure 4.1(b) shows the valid source and destination operand variations. This large choice of operands results in many different MOV instructions. Looking at this list of operands, we see that data can be moved between general-purpose registers, between a general-purpose register and a segment register, between a general-purpose register or segment register and memory, or between a memory location and the accumulator.

Notice that the MOV instruction cannot transfer data directly between a source and a destination that both reside in external memory. Instead, the data must first be moved from memory into an internal register, such as to the accumulator (AX), with one move instruction and then moved to the new location in memory with a second move instruction.

All transfers between general-purpose registers and memory can involve either a byte or word of data. The fact that the instruction corresponds to byte or word data is designated by the way in which its operands are specified. For instance, AL or AH would be used to specify a byte operand, and AX, a word operand. On the other hand, data moved between one of the general-purpose registers and a segment

Mnemonic	Meaning	Format	Operation	Flags affected
MOV	Move	MOV D,S	(S) → (D)	None

(a)

Destination	Source
Memory	Accumulator
Accumulator	Memory
Register	Register
Register	Memory
Memory	Register
Register	Immediate
Memory	Immediate
Seg-reg	Reg16
Seg-reg	Mem16
Reg16	Seg-reg
Memory	Seg-reg

(b)

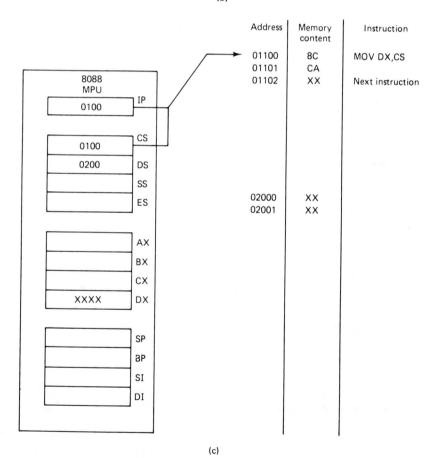

(c)

Figure 4.1 (a) MOV data transfer instruction. (b) Allowed operands. (c) MOV DX,CS instruction before execution. (d) After execution.

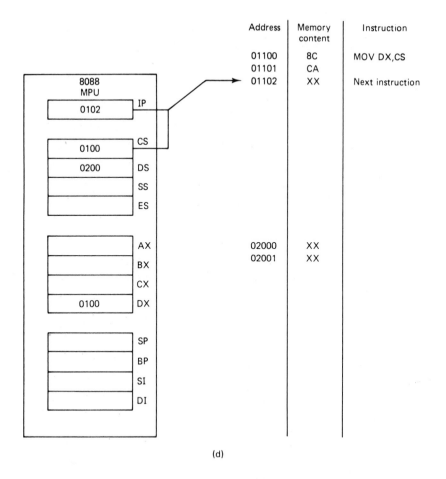

Address	Memory content	Instruction
01100	8C	MOV DX,CS
01101	CA	
01102	XX	Next instruction
02000	XX	
02001	XX	

8088
MPU

IP	0102
CS	0100
DS	0200
SS	
ES	

AX	
BX	
CX	
DX	0100

SP	
BP	
SI	
DI	

(d)

Figure 4.1 (Continued)

register or between a segment register and a memory location must always be word-wide.

In Fig. 4.1(a), we also find additional important information. For instance, flag bits within the 8088 are not modified by execution of a MOV instruction.

An example of a segment register to general-purpose register MOV instruction shown in Fig. 4.1(c) is

```
MOV DX,CS
```

In this instruction, the code segment register is the source operand and the data register is the destination. It stands for "move the contents of CS into DX." That is

$$(CS) \rightarrow (DX)$$

For example, if the contents of CS are 0100_{16}, execution of the instruction MOV DX,CS as shown in Fig. 4.1(d) makes

$$(DX) = (CS) = 0100_{16}$$

In all memory reference MOV instructions, the machine code for the instruction includes an offset address relative to the current data segment specified by the contents of the data segment register. An example of this type of instruction is

```
MOV [SUM],AX
```

In this instruction, the memory location identified by the variable SUM is specified using direct addressing. That is, the value of the offset SUM is encoded in the two byte locations that follow its opcode.

Let us assume that the contents of DS equals 0200_{16} and that SUM equals 1212_{16}. Then this instruction means "move the contents of accumulator AX to the memory location offset by 1212_{16} from the starting location of the current data segment." The physical address of this location is obtained as

$$PA = 02000_{16} + 1212_{16} = 03212_{16}$$

Thus the effect of the instruction is

$$(AL) \rightarrow (\text{Memory Location } 03212_{16})$$

and

$$(AH) \rightarrow (\text{Memory Location } 03213_{16})$$

EXAMPLE 4.1

What is the effect of executing the instruction

```
MOV CX,[SOURCE_MEM]
```

where SOURCE_MEM equal to 20_{16} is a memory location offset relative to the current data segment starting at address $1A000_{16}$?

Solution

Execution of this instruction results in the following:

$$((DS)0 + 20_{16}) \rightarrow (CL)$$
$$((DS)0 + 20_{16} + 1_{16}) \rightarrow (CH)$$

In other words, CL is loaded with the contents held at memory address

$$1A000_{16} + 20_{16} = 1A020_{16}$$

and CH is loaded with the contents of memory address

$$1A000_{16} + 20_{16} + 1_{16} = 1A021_{16}$$

EXAMPLE 4.2

Use the DEBUG program on the IBM PC to verify the operation of the instruction in Example 4.1. Initialize the word storage location pointed to by SOURCE_MEM to the value $AA55_{16}$ before executing the instruction.

Solution

First, the DEBUG program is invoked by entering the command

```
C:\DOS>DEBUG   (↵)
```

As shown in Fig. 4.2, this results in the display of the debugger's prompt

```
–
```

To determine the memory locations the debugger assigns for use in entering instructions and data, we can examine the state of the internal registers with the command

```
–R   (↵)
```

Looking at the displayed information for this command in Fig. 4.2, we find that the contents of CS and IP indicate that the starting address in the current code segment is 1342:0100 and the current data segment starts at address 1342:0000. Also note that the initial value in CX is 0000H.

To enter the instruction from Example 4.1 at location 1342:0100, we use the ASSEMBLE command

```
–A   (↵)
1342:0100 MOV CX,[20]   (↵)
1342:0104   (↵)
```

Note that we must enter the value of the offset address instead of the symbol SOURCE_MEM and that it must be enclosed in brackets to indicate that it is a direct address.

Let us now redefine the data segment so that it starts at $1A000_{16}$. This is done by loading the DS register with $1A00_{16}$ with the REGISTER command. As shown

```
C:\DOS>DEBUG
-R
AX=0000  BX=0000  CX=0000  DX=0000  SP=FFEE  BP=0000  SI=0000  DI=0000
DS=1342  ES=1342  SS=1342  CS=1342  IP=0100   NV UP EI PL NZ NA PO NC
1342:0100 0F            DB      0F
-A
1342:0100 MOV   CX,[20]
1342:0104
-R DS
DS 1342
:1A00
-E 20 55 AA
-T

AX=0000  BX=0000  CX=AA55  DX=0000  SP=FFEE  BP=0000  SI=0000  DI=0000
DS=1A00  ES=1342  SS=1342  CS=1342  IP=0104   NV UP EI PL NZ NA PO NC
1342:0104 FFF3          PUSH    BX
-Q

C:\DOS>
```

Figure 4.2   Display sequence for Example 4.2.

in Fig. 4.2, we do this with the entries

```
—R DS   (↵)
DS 1342
:1A00   (↵)
```

Now we initialize the memory locations at addresses 1A00:20 and 1A00:21 to 55_{16} and AA_{16}, respectively, with the ENTER command

```
—E 20 55 AA   (↵)
```

Notice that the bytes of the word of data must be entered in the reverse order. Finally, to execute the instruction, we issue the trace command

```
—T   (↵)
```

The result of executing the instruction is shown in Fig. 4.2. Note that CX has been loaded with $AA55_{16}$.

A use of the move instruction is to load initial address and data values into the registers of the MPU. This can be done by loading immediate data using instructions. For instance, the instruction sequence

```
MOV AX,2000H
MOV DS,AX
MOV ES,AX
MOV AX,3000H
MOV SS,AX
MOV AX,0H
```

```
MOV BX,AX
MOV CX,0AH
MOV DX,100H
MOV SI,200H
MOV DI,300H
```

uses immediate data to initialize the values in the segment, index, and data registers. In Fig. 4.1(b) we see that the immediate data cannot be directly loaded into a segment register. For this reason, the initial values of the segment base addresses for DS, ES, and SS are first loaded into AX and then copied into the appropriate segment registers. The result produced by executing the first five instructions in this sequence is to initialize the segment registers.

The next six instructions are used to initialize the data and index registers. First, the AX register is cleared to 0000_{16} and then BX is also cleared by copying this value from AX to BX. Finally, CX, DX, SI, and DI are loaded with the immediate values $000A_{16}$, 0100_{16}, 0200_{16}, and 0300_{16}, respectively.

The XCHG Instruction

In our study of the move instruction, we found that it could be used to copy the contents of a register or memory location into another register or contents of a register into a storage location in memory. In all of these cases, the original contents of the source location are preserved and the original contents of the destination are replaced. In some applications it is required to interchange the contents of two registers. For instance, we might want to exchange the data in the AX and BX registers. This could be done using multiple move instructions and storage of the data in a temporary register such as DX. However, to perform the exchange function more efficiently, a special instruction has been provided in the instruction set of the 8088. This is the exchange (XCHG) instruction. The forms of the XCHG instruction and its allowed operands are shown in Fig. 4.3(a) and (b). Here we see that it can be used to swap data between two general-purpose registers or between a general-purpose register and a storage location in memory. In particular, it allows for the exchange of words of data between one of the general-purpose registers, including the pointers and index registers, and the accumulator (AX), exchange of a byte or word of data between one of the general-purpose registers and a location in memory, or between two of the general-purpose registers.

Let us consider an example of an exchange between two internal registers. Here is an instruction.

```
XCHG AX,DX
```

Its execution by the 8088 swaps the contents of AX with that of DX. That is,

$$(AX \text{ original}) \rightarrow (DX)$$

$$(DX \text{ original}) \rightarrow (AX)$$

Mnemonic	Meaning	Format	Operation	Flags affected
XCHG	Exchange	XCHG D,S	(D) ↔ (S)	None

(a)

Destination	Source
Accumulator	Reg16
Memory	Register
Register	Register
Register	Memory

(b)

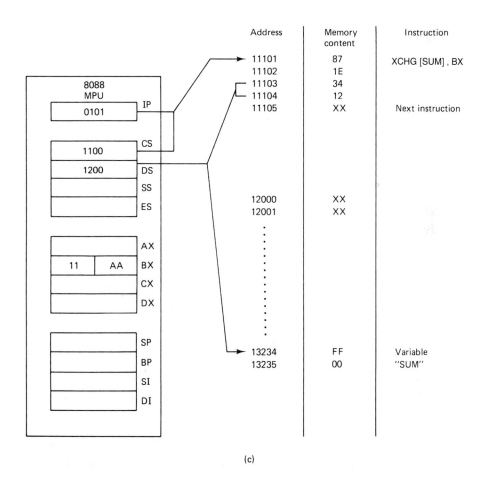

(c)

Figure 4.3 (a) Exchange data transfer instruction. (b) Allowed operands. (c) XCHG [SUM],BX instruction before fetch and execution. (d) After execution.

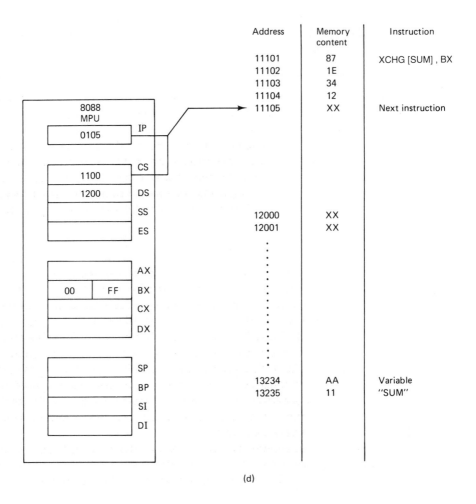

Address	Memory content	Instruction
11101	87	XCHG [SUM] , BX
11102	1E	
11103	34	
11104	12	
11105	XX	Next instruction
12000	XX	
12001	XX	
13234	AA	Variable
13235	11	"SUM"

8088 MPU

IP 0105

CS 1100
DS 1200
SS
ES

AX
BX 00 FF
CX
DX

SP
BP
SI
DI

(d)

Figure 4.3 (Continued)

or

$$(AX) \leftrightarrow (DX)$$

EXAMPLE 4.3

For the data shown in Fig. 4.3(c), what is the result of executing the following instruction?

    XCHG [SUM] , BX

Solution

Execution of this instruction performs the function

$$((DS)0 + SUM) \leftrightarrow (BX)$$

In Fig. 4.3(c), we see that $(DS) = 1200_{16}$ and the direct address SUM $= 1234_{16}$. Therefore, the corresponding physical address is

$$PA = 12000_{16} + 1234_{16} = 13234_{16}$$

Notice that this location contains FF_{16} and the address that follows contains 00_{16}. Moreover, note that BL contains AA_{16} and BH contains 11_{16}.

Execution of the instruction performs the following 16-bit swap.

$$(13234_{16}) \leftrightarrow (BL)$$

$$(13235_{16}) \leftrightarrow (BH)$$

As shown in Fig. 4.3(d), we get

$$(BX) = 00FF_{16}$$

$$(SUM) = 11AA_{16}$$

EXAMPLE 4.4

Use the IBM PC's DEBUG program to verify the operation of the instruction in Example 4.3.

Solution

The DEBUG commands needed to enter the instruction, enter the data, execute the instruction, and verify the result of its operation are shown in Fig. 4.4. Here we see that, after invoking DEBUG and displaying the initial state of the 8088's registers, the instruction is loaded into memory with the command

```
-A 1100:101   (↵)
1100:0101 XCHG   [1234],BX   (↵)
1100:0105   (↵)
-
```

Next, as shown in Fig. 4.4, R commands are used to initialize the contents of registers BX, DS, CS, and IP to $11AA_{16}$, 1200_{16}, 1100_{16}, and 0101_{16}, respectively, and then the updated register states are verified with another R command. Now memory locations DS:1234H and DS:1235H are loaded with the values FF_{16} and 00_{16}, respectively, with the E command

```
-E 1234 FF 00   (↵)
-
```

Before executing the instruction, its loading is verified with an unassemble command. Looking at Fig. 4.4, we see that it has been correctly loaded. Therefore,

```
C:\DOS>DEBUG
-R
AX=0000  BX=0000  CX=0000  DX=0000  SP=FFEE  BP=0000  SI=0000  DI=0000
DS=1342  ES=1342  SS=1342  CS=1342  IP=0100   NV UP EI PL NZ NA PO NC
1342:0100 0F            DB     0F
-A 1100:101
1100:0101 XCHG [1234],BX
1100:0105
-R BX
BX 0000
:11AA
-R DS
DS 1342
:1200
-R CS
CS 1342
:1100
-R IP
IP 0100
:101
-R
AX=0000  BX=11AA  CX=0000  DX=0000  SP=FFEE  BP=0000  SI=0000  DI=0000
DS=1200  ES=1342  SS=1342  CS=1100  IP=0101   NV UP EI PL NZ NA PO NC
1100:0101 871E3412       XCHG    BX,[1234]                      DS:1234=0000
-E 1234 FF 00
-U 101 104
1100:0101 871E3412       XCHG    BX,[1234]
-T

AX=0000  BX=00FF  CX=0000  DX=0000  SP=FFEE  BP=0000  SI=0000  DI=0000
DS=1200  ES=1342  SS=1342  CS=1100  IP=0105   NV UP EI PL NZ NA PO NC
1100:0105 8946FE         MOV     [BP-02],AX                     SS:FFFE=0000
-D 1234 1235
1200:1230            AA 11                                         ..
-Q

C:\DOS>
```

Figure 4.4   Display sequence for Example 4.4.

the instruction is executed by issuing the TRACE command

$$-T \quad (\hookleftarrow)$$

The displayed trace information in Fig. 4.4 shows that BX now contains $00FF_{16}$. To verify that the memory location was loaded with data from BX, we must display the data held at address DS:1234H and DS:1235H. This is done with the DUMP command

```
-D 1234 1235   (↵)
1200:1230              AA 11
```

In this way, we see that the word contents of memory location DS:1234H have been exchanged with the contents of the BX register.

The XLAT Instruction

The translate (XLAT) instruction has been provided in the instruction set of the 8088 to simplify implementation of the lookup table operation. This instruction is described in Fig. 4.5. When using XLAT, the contents of register BX represent

Mnemonic	Meaning	Format	Operation	Flags affected
XLAT	Translate	XLAT	$((AL)+(BX)+(DS)0) \rightarrow (AL)$	None

Figure 4.5 Translate data transfer instruction.

the offset of the starting address of the lookup table from the beginning of the current data segment. Also, the contents of AL represent the offset of the element to be accessed from the beginning of the lookup table. This 8-bit element address permits a table with up to 256 elements. The values in both of these registers must be initialized prior to execution of the XLAT instruction.

Execution of XLAT replaces the contents of AL by the contents of the accessed lookup table location. The physical address of this element in the table is derived as

$$PA = (DS)0 + (BX) + (AL)$$

An example of the use of this instruction is the software code conversions. For instance, an ASCII-to-EBCDIC conversion can be performed with the translate instruction. This requires an EBCDIC table in memory. The individual EBCDIC codes are located in the table at element displacements (AL) equal to their equivalent ASCII character values. That is, the EBCDIC code $C1_{16}$ for letter A would be positioned at displacement 41_{16}, which equals ASCII A, from the start of the table. The start of this ASCII-to-EBCDIC table in the current data segment is specified by the contents of BX.

As an illustration of XLAT, let us assume that $(DS) = 0300_{16}$, $(BX) = 0100_{16}$, and $(AL) = 0D_{16}$. Here $0D_{16}$ represents the ASCII character CR (carriage return). Execution of XLAT replaces the contents of AL by the contents of the memory location given by

$$PA = (DS)0 + (BX) + (AL)$$
$$= 03000_{16} + 0100_{16} + 0D_{16} = 0310D_{16}$$

Thus the execution can be described by

$$(0310D_{16}) \rightarrow (AL)$$

Assuming that this memory location contains 52_{16} (EBCDIC code for carriage return), this value is placed in AL. That is

$$(AL) = 52_{16}$$

The LEA, LDS, and LES Instructions

Another type of data transfer operation that is important is to load a segment and a general-purpose register with an address directly from memory. Special instructions are provided in the instruction set of the 8088 to give a programmer this capability. These instructions are described in Fig. 4.6. They are load register with effective address (LEA), load register and data segment register (LDS), and load register and extra segment register (LES).

Looking at Fig. 4.6(a), we see that these instructions provide the ability to manipulate memory addresses by loading a specific register with a 16-bit offset address or a 16-bit offset address together with a 16-bit segment address into either DS or ES.

The LEA instruction is used to load a specified register with a 16-bit offset address. An example of this instruction is

```
LEA SI, EA
```

When executed, it loads the SI register with an offset address value. The value of this offset is represented by the effective address EA. The value of EA can be specified by any valid addressing mode. For instance, if the value in DI equals 1000H and that in BS is 20H, then executing the instruction

```
LEA  SI, [DI + BX + 5H]
```

will load SI with the value

$$EA = 100H + 20H + 5H = 125H$$

That is,

$$(SI) = 0125H$$

The other two instructions, LDS and LES, are similar to LEA except that they load the specified register as well as the DS or ES segment register from memory. That is, they are able to load a complete address pointer that is stored in memory. In this way, a new data segment can be activated by executing a single instruction.

EXAMPLE 4.5 _____

Assuming that the 8088 is set up as shown in Fig. 4.6(b), what is the result of executing the following instruction:

```
LDS SI,[200H]
```

Mnemonic	Meaning	Format	Operation	Flags affected
LEA	Load effective address	LEA Reg16,EA	EA → (Reg16)	None
LDS	Load register and DS	LDS Reg16,Mem32	(Mem32) → (Reg16) (Mem32+2) → (DS)	None
LES	Load register and ES	LES Reg16,Mem32	(Mem32) → (Reg16) (Mem32+2) → (ES)	None

(a)

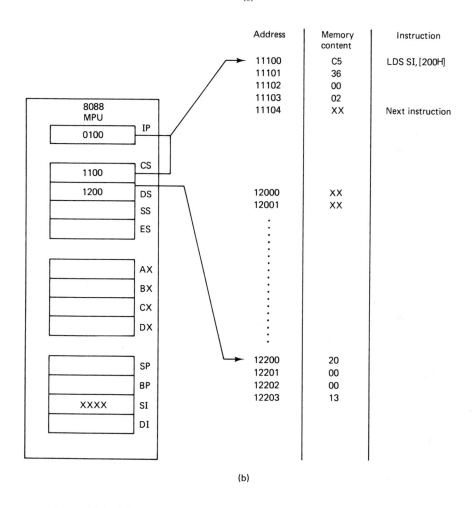

(b)

Figure 4.6 (a) LEA, LDS, and LES data transfer instructions. (b) LDS SI, [200] instruction before fetch and execution. (c) After execution.

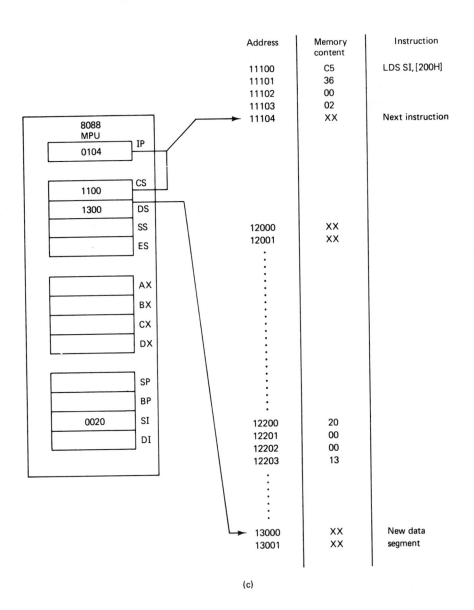

Address	Memory content	Instruction
11100	C5	LDS SI, [200H]
11101	36	
11102	00	
11103	02	
11104	XX	Next instruction
12000	XX	
12001	XX	
12200	20	
12201	00	
12202	00	
12203	13	
13000	XX	New data
13001	XX	segment

8088 MPU

IP 0104

CS 1100

DS 1300

SS

ES

AX

BX

CX

DX

SP

BP

SI 0020

DI

(c)

Figure 4.6 (Continued)

Solution

Execution of the instruction loads the SI register from the word location in memory whose offset address with respect to the current data segment is 200_{16}. Figure 4.6(b) shows that the contents of DS are 1200_{16}. This gives a physical address of

$$PA = 12000_{16} + 0200_{16} = 12200_{16}$$

It is the contents of this location and the one that follows that are loaded into SI. Therefore, in Fig. 4.6(c) we find that SI contains 0020_{16}. The next two bytes, that is, the contents of addresses 12202_{16} and 12203_{16}, are loaded into the DS register. As shown, this defines a new data segment address of 13000_{16}.

EXAMPLE 4.6 _____

Verify the execution of the instruction in Example 4.5 using DOS's debug program. The memory and register contents are to be those shown in Fig. 4.6(b).

Solution

As shown in Fig. 4.7, DEBUG is first brought up and then REGISTER commands are used to initialize registers IP, CS, DS, and SI with values 0100_{16}, 1100_{16}, 1200_{16}, and 0000_{16}, respectively. Next the instruction is assembled at address CS:100 with the command

```
                    —A CS:100              (↵)
                    1100:0100 LDS SI,[200]  (↵)
                    1100:0104              (↵)
```

```
C:\DOS>DEBUG
-R IP
IP 0100
:
-R CS
CS 1342
:1100
-R DS
DS 1342
:1200
-R SI
SI 0000
:
-A CS:100
1100:0100 LDS    SI,[200]
1100:0104
-E 200 20 00 00 13
-T

AX=0000  BX=0000  CX=0000  DX=0000  SP=FFEE  BP=0000  SI=0020  DI=0000
DS=1300  ES=1342  SS=1342  CS=1100  IP=0104    NV UP EI PL NZ NA PO NC
1100:0104 C0           DB       C0
-Q

C:\DOS>
```

Figure 4.7 Display sequence for Example 4.6.

Before executing the instruction, we need to initialize two words of data starting at location DS:200 in memory. As shown in Fig. 4.7, this is done with an E command.

```
—E 200 20 00 00 13        (⏎)
```

Then the instruction is executed with the TRACE command

```
—T                        (⏎)
```

Looking at the displayed register status in Fig. 4.7, we see that SI has been loaded with the value 0020_{16} and DS with the value 1300_{16}.

Earlier we showed how the segment registers, index registers, and data registers of the MPU can be initialized with immediate data. Another way of initializing them is from a table of data in memory. Using the LDS and LES instructions along with the MOV instruction provides an efficient method for performing register initialization from a data table. The sequence of instructions that follow will load the segment registers, index registers, and data registers of the MPU with initial addresses and data from a table located at starting address INIT_TABLE in the memory. The table is 18 bytes long and spans the address range INIT_TABLE through INIT_ TABLE+11H.

```
MOV AX,[INIT_TABLE]
MOV SS,AX
LDS SI,[INIT_TABLE+02H]
LES DI,[INIT_TABLE+06H]
MOV AX,[INIT_TABLE+0AH]
MOV BX,[INIT_TABLE+0CH]
MOV CX,[INIT_TABLE+0EH]
MOV DX,[INIT_TABLE+10H]
```

Looking at the source addresses in the instructions, we can determine the location of each of the addresses or data elements in the table. For example, the 16-bit base address for register SS is held in the table at addresses INIT_TABLE and INIT_TABLE+1 and the word of data for DX at addresses INIT_TABLE+10H and INIT_TABLE+11H. This table of information must be loaded into memory before the instruction sequence is executed.

In general, the base addresses or data values are fetched from the table in memory and loaded into the appropriate registers. The table location that is to be accessed is identified by the direct address specified for the source operand. For instance, the first instruction reads a base address, which is the word content of the memory location at address INIT_TABLE, into the AX register and then this value is copied into SS with a second MOV instruction. Notice that an LDS instruction is used to load the DI and DS registers, instead of MOV instructions. When this instruction is executed, the word of data for DI is loaded from table locations INIT_TABLE+2H and INIT_TABLE+3H, while the base address for DS is loaded from INIT_TABLE+4H and INIT_TABLE+5H.

▲ 4.4 ARITHMETIC INSTRUCTIONS

The instruction set of the 8088 microprocessor contains a variety of *arithmetic instructions*. They include instructions for the *addition*, *subtraction*, *multiplication*, and *division* operations. These operations can be performed on numbers expressed in a variety of numeric data formats. These formats include *unsigned* or *signed binary bytes* or *words*, *unpacked* or *packed decimal bytes*, or *ASCII numbers*. By *packed decimal* we mean that two BCD digits are packed into a byte-size register or a memory location. Unpacked decimal numbers are stored one BCD digit per byte. The BCD numbers are unsigned decimal numbers. ASCII numbers are expressed in ASCII code and stored one number per byte.

The status that results from the execution of an arithmetic instruction is recorded in the flags of the microprocessor. The flags that are affected by the arithmetic instructions are carry flag (CF), auxiliary flag (AF), sign flag (SF), zero flag (ZF), parity flag (PF), and overflow flag (OF). Each of these flags was discussed in Chapter 2.

For the purpose of discussion, we will divide the arithmetic instructions into the subgroups shown in Fig. 4.8.

Addition	
ADD	Add byte or word
ADC	Add byte or word with carry
INC	Increment byte or word by 1
AAA	ASCII adjust for addition
DAA	Decimal adjust for addition
Subtraction	
SUB	Subtract byte or word
SBB	Subtract byte or word with borrow
DEC	Decrement byte or word by 1
NEG	Negate byte or word
AAS	ASCII adjust for subtraction
DAS	Decimal adjust for subtraction
Multiplication	
MUL	Multiply byte or word unsigned
IMUL	Integer multiply byte or word
AAM	ASCII adjust for multiply
Division	
DIV	Divide byte or word unsigned
IDIV	Integer divide byte or word
AAD	ASCII adjust for division
CBW	Convert byte to word
CWD	Convert word to doubleword

Figure 4.8 Arithmetic instructions.

Mnemonic	Meaning	Format	Operation	Flags Affected
ADD	Addition	ADD D, S	$(S) + (D) \rightarrow (D)$ $Carry \rightarrow (CF)$	OF, SF, ZF, AF, PF, CF
ADC	Add with carry	ADC D, S	$(S) + (D) + (CF) \rightarrow (D)$ $Carry \rightarrow (CF)$	OF, SF, ZF, AF, PF, CF
INC	Increment by 1	INC D	$(D) + 1 \rightarrow (D)$	OF, SF, ZF, AF, PF
AAA	ASCII adjust for addition	AAA		AF, CF OF, SF, ZF, PF undefined
DAA	Decimal adjust for addition	DAA		SF, ZF, AF, PF, CF, OF, undefined

(a)

Destination	Source
Register	Register
Register	Memory
Memory	Register
Register	Immediate
Memory	Immediate
Accumulator	Immediate

(b)

Destination
Reg16
Reg8
Memory

(c)

Figure 4.9 (a) Addition arithmetic instructions. (b) Allowed operands for ADD and ADC instructions. (c) Allowed operands for INC instruction.

Addition Instructions: ADD, ADC, INC, AAA, and DAA

The form of each of the instructions in the *addition subgroup* is shown in Fig. 4.9(a); the allowed operand variations, for all but the INC instruction, are shown in Fig. 4.9(b). The allowed operands for the INC instruction are shown in Fig. 4.9(c). Let us begin by looking more closely at the *add* (ADD) instruction. Notice in Fig. 4.9(b) that it can be used to add an immediate operand to the contents of the accumulator, the contents of another register, or the contents of a storage location in memory. It also allows us to add the contents of two registers or the contents of a register and a memory location.

In general, the result of executing the instruction is expressed as

$$(S) + (D) \rightarrow (D)$$

That is, the contents of the source operand are added to those of the destination operand and the sum that results is put into the location of the destination operand.

EXAMPLE 4.7 ⎯⎯⎯⎯⎯⎯⎯⎯⎯⎯⎯⎯⎯⎯⎯⎯⎯⎯⎯⎯⎯⎯⎯

Assume that the AX and BX registers contain 1100_{16} and $0ABC_{16}$, respectively. What is the result of executing the instruction ADD AX,BX?

Solution

Execution of the ADD instruction causes the contents of source operand BX to be added to the contents of destination register AX. This gives

$$(BX) + (AX) = 0ABC_{16} + 1100_{16} = 1BBC_{16}$$

This sum ends up in destination register AX. That is,

$$(AX) = 1BBC_{16}$$

Execution of this instruction is illustrated in Fig. 4.10(a) and (b).

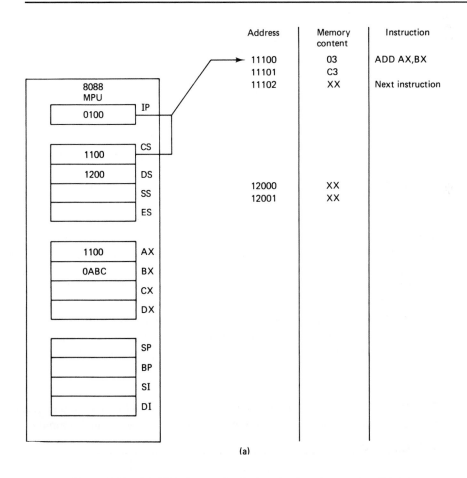

(a)

Figure 4.10 (a) ADD instruction before fetch and execution. (b) After execution.

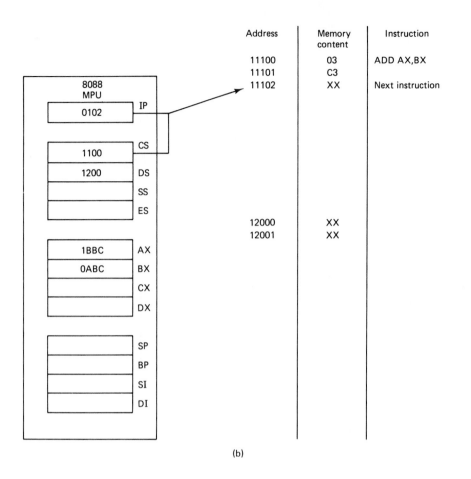

Address	Memory content	Instruction
11100	03	ADD AX,BX
11101	C3	
11102	XX	Next instruction
12000	XX	
12001	XX	

(b)

Figure 4.10 (Continued)

EXAMPLE 4.8

Use the debug program on the IBM PC to verify the execution of the instruction in Example 4.7. Assume that the registers are to be initialized with the values shown in Fig. 4.10(a).

Solution

The debug sequence for this is shown in Fig. 4.11. After the debug program is brought up, the instruction is assembled into memory with the command

```
-A 1100:0100           (↵)
1100:0100 ADD AX,BX    (↵)
1100:0102              (↵)
-
```

```
C:\DOS>DEBUG
-A 1100:0100
1100:0100 ADD AX,BX
1100:0102
-R AX
AX 0000
:1100
-R BX
BX 0000
:0ABC
-U 1100:100 100
1100:0100 01D8          ADD      AX,BX
-T =1100:100

AX=1BBC  BX=0ABC  CX=0000  DX=0000  SP=FFEE  BP=0000  SI=0000  DI=0000
DS=1342  ES=1342  SS=1342  CS=1100  IP=0102     NV UP EI PL NZ NA PO NC
1100:0102 0002          ADD      [BP+SI],AL                    SS:0000=CD
-Q

C:\DOS>
```

Figure 4.11 Display sequence for Example 4.8.

Next, as shown in Fig. 4.11, the AX and BX registers are loaded with the values 1100_{16} and $0ABC_{16}$, respectively, using R commands.

```
—R AX                   (↵)
AX 0000
:1100                   (↵)
—R BX                   (↵)
BX 0000
:0ABC                   (↵)
```

Next, the loading of the instruction is verified with the unassemble command

```
—U 1100:0100 0100     (↵)
```

and is shown in Fig. 4.11 to be correct.

We are now ready to execute the instruction with the TRACE command

```
—T =1100:0100           (↵)
```

From the trace dump in Fig. 4.11, we see that the sum of AX and BX, which equals $1BBC_{16}$, is now held in destination register AX. Also note that no carry (NC) has occurred.

The instruction *add with carry* (ADC) works similarly to ADD. But in this case, the content of the carry flag is also added; that is

$$(S) + (D) + (CF) \rightarrow (D)$$

The valid operand combinations are the same as those for the ADD instruction. ADC is primarily used for multiword add operation.

Sec. 4.4   *Arithmetic Instructions*   **163**

Another instruction that can be considered as part of the addition subgroup of arithmetic instructions is the *increment* (INC) instruction. As shown in Fig. 4.9(c), its operands can be the contents of a 16-bit internal register, an 8-bit internal register, or a storage location in memory. Execution of the INC instruction adds one to the specified operand. An example of an instruction that increments the high byte of AX is

```
INC AH
```

Looking at Fig. 4.9(a), we see how execution of these three instructions affects the earlier mentioned flags.

EXAMPLE 4.9

The original contents of AX, BL, word size memory location SUM, and carry flag (CF) are 1234_{16}, AB_{16}, $00CD_{16}$, and 0_{16}, respectively. Describe the results of executing the following sequence of instructions.

```
ADD AX,SUM
ADC BL,05H
INC WORD PTR SUM
```

Solution

By executing the first instruction, we add the word in the accumulator and the word in the memory location identified as SUM. The result is placed in the accumulator. That is,

$$(AX) \leftarrow (AX) + (SUM) = 1234_{16} + 00CD_{16} = 1301_{16}$$

The carry flag remains reset.

The second instruction adds to the lower byte of the base register (BL), the immediate operand 5_{16}, and the carry flag, which is 0_{16}. This gives

$$(BL) \leftarrow (BL) + IOP + (CF) = AB_{16} + 5_{16} + 0_{16} = B0_{16}$$

Since no carry is generated, CF stays reset.

The last instruction increments the contents of memory location SUM by one. That is,

$$(SUM) \leftarrow (SUM) + 1_{16} = 00CD_{16} + 1_{16} = 00CE_{16}$$

These results are summarized in Fig. 4.12.

Instruction	(AX)	(BL)	(SUM)	(CF)
Initial state	1234	AB	00CD	0
ADD AX,SUM	1301	AB	00CD	0
ADC BL,05H	1301	B0	00CD	0
INC WORD PTR SUM	1301	B0	00CE	0

Figure 4.12 Results due to execution of arithmetic instructions in Example 4.9.

EXAMPLE 4.10

Verify the operation of the instruction sequence in Example 4.9 by executing it with the debug program on the IBM PC. A source program that includes this sequence of instructions is shown in Fig. 4.13(a), and the source listing produced when the program is assembled is shown in Fig. 4.13(b). A run module that was produced by linking this program is stored in file EX410.EXE.

Solution

The DEBUG program is brought up and at the same time the run module from file EX410.EXE is loaded with the command

```
C:\DOS>DEBUG B:EX410.EXE  (↵)
```

```
TITLE    EXAMPLE 4.10
         PAGE    ,132
STACK_SEG          SEGMENT          STACK 'STACK'
                   DB               64 DUP(?)
STACK_SEG          ENDS

DATA_SEG           SEGMENT
SUM                DW               0CDH
DATA_SEG           ENDS

CODE_SEG           SEGMENT          'CODE'
EX410    PROC      FAR
         ASSUME    CS:CODE_SEG, SS:STACK_SEG, DS:DATA_SEG

;To return to DEBUG program put return address on the stack

         PUSH      DS
         MOV       AX, 0
         PUSH      AX

;Following code implements the Example 4.10

         MOV       AX, DATA_SEG     ;Establish data segment
         MOV       DS, AX

         ADD       AX, SUM
         ADC       BL, 05H
         INC       WORD PTR SUM

         RET                        ;Return to DEBUG program
EX410 ENDP

CODE_SEG           ENDS

         END       EX410
```

Figure 4.13(a) Source program for Example 4.10.

```
                    TITLE   EXAMPLE 4.10

                    PAGE        ,132

0000                            STACK_SEG       SEGMENT     STACK 'STACK'
0000      40 [                                  DB          64 DUP(?)
          ??
             ]

0040                            STACK_SEG       ENDS


0000                            DATA_SEG        SEGMENT
0000      00CD                  SUM             DW          0CDH
0002                            DATA_SEG        ENDS

0000                            CODE_SEG        SEGMENT     'CODE'
0000                            EX410   PROC    FAR
                                ASSUME  CS:CODE_SEG, SS:STACK_SEG, DS:DATA_SEG

                   ;To return to DEBUG program put return address on the stack

0000      1E                            PUSH    DS
0001      B8 0000                       MOV     AX, 0
0004      50                            PUSH    AX

                   ;Following code implements the Example 4.10

0005      B8  ---- R                    MOV     AX, DATA_SEG    ;Establish data segment
0008      8E D8                         MOV     DS, AX

000A      03 06 0000 R                  ADD     AX, SUM
000E      80 D3 05                      ADC     BL, 5H
0011      FF 06 0000 R                  INC     WORD PTR SUM

0015      CB                            RET                     ;Return to DEBUG program
0016                            EX410   ENDP

0016                            CODE_SEG        ENDS

                        END     EX410
```

Segments and groups:

N a m e	Size	align	combine	class
CODE_SEG	0016	PARA	NONE	'CODE'
DATA_SEG	0002	PARA	NONE	
STACK_SEG.	0040	PARA	STACK	'STACK'

Symbols:

N a m e	Type	Value	Attr	
EX410.	F PROC	0000	CODE_SEG	Length =0016
SUM.	L WORD	0000	DATA_SEG	

```
Warning Severe
Errors  Errors
0       0
```

Figure 4.13(b)   Source listing produced by assembler.

Next, we will verify the loading of the program by unassembling it with the command

$$-U \ 0 \ 12 \quad (\lrcorner)$$

Looking at the displayed instruction sequence in Fig. 4.13(c) and comparing it to the source listing in Fig. 4.13(b), we find that the program has loaded correctly.

```
C:DOS>DEBUG A:EX410.EXE
-U 0 12
0D03:0000 1E              PUSH    DS
0D03:0001 B80000          MOV     AX,0000
0D03:0004 50              PUSH    AX
0D03:0005 B8050D          MOV     AX,0D05
0D03:0008 8ED8            MOV     DS,AX
0D03:000A 03060000        ADD     AX,[0000]
0D03:000E 80D305          ADC     BL,05
0D03:0011 FF060000        INC     WORD PTR [0000]
-G A

AX=0D03  BX=0000  CX=0000  DX=0000  SP=003C  BP=0000  SI=0000  DI=0000
DS=0D05  ES=0CF3  SS=0D06  CS=0D03  IP=000A   NV UP EI PL NZ NA PO NC
0D03:000A 03060000        ADD     AX,[0000]                    DS:0000=00CD
-R AX
AX 0D05
:1234
-R BX
BX 0000
:AB
-R F
NV UP EI PL NZ NA PO NC  -
-E 0 CD 00
-D 0 1
0D05:0000  CD 00                                               ..
-T

AX=1301  BX=00AB  CX=0000  DX=0000  SP=003C  BP=0000  SI=0000  DI=0000
DS=0D05  ES=0CF3  SS=0D06  CS=0D03  IP=000E   NV UP EI PL NZ AC PO NC
0D03:000E 80D305          ADC     BL,05
-T

AX=1301  BX=00B0  CX=0000  DX=0000  SP=003C  BP=0000  SI=0000  DI=0000
DS=0D05  ES=0CF3  SS=0D06  CS=0D03  IP=0011   NV UP EI NG NZ AC PO NC
0D03:0011 FF060000        INC     WORD PTR [0000]              DS:0000=00CD
-T

AX=1301  BX=00B0  CX=0000  DX=0000  SP=003C  BP=0000  SI=0000  DI=0000
DS=0D05  ES=0CF3  SS=0D06  CS=0D03  IP=0015   NV UP EI PL NZ NA PO NC
0D03:0015 CB              RETF
-D 0 1
0D05:0000  CE 00
-G

Program terminated normally                                   ..
-Q

C:\DOS>
```

Figure 4.13(c) Debug session for execution of program.

Notice in Fig. 4.13(c) that the instructions for which we are interested in
verifying operation start at address 0D03:000A. For this reason, a GO command
will be used to execute down to this point in the program. This command is

$$\text{—G A} \quad (\downarrow)$$

Notice in the trace information displayed for this command that now CS contains
$0D03_{16}$ and IP contains $000A_{16}$; therefore, the next instruction to be executed is at
address 0D03:000A. This is the ADD instruction.

Now we need to initialize registers AX, BX, and the memory location pointed
to by SUM (WORD PTR [0000]). We must also ensure that the CF status flag is
set to NC (no carry). In Fig. 4.13(c), we find that these operations are done with

the following sequence of commands

```
-R AX        (↵)
AX 0D05
:1234        (↵)
-R BX        (↵)
BX 0000
:AB          (↵)
-R F         (↵)
NV UP EI PL NZ NA PO NC -    (↵)
-E 0 CD 00  (↵)
-D 0 1       (↵)
0DEB:0000 CD 00
```

Now we are ready to execute the ADD instruction. This is done by issuing the TRACE command

$$-T \quad (↵)$$

From the state information displayed for this command in Fig. 4.13(c), notice that the value CD_{16} has been added to the original value in AX, which was 1234_{16}, and the sum that results in AX is 1301_{16}.

Next the ADC instruction is executed with another T command.

$$-T \quad (↵)$$

It causes the immediate operand value 05_{16} to be added to the original contents of BL, which is AB_{16}, and the sum that is produced in BL is $B0_{16}$.

The last instruction is executed with one more T command, and it causes the SUM (WORD PTR [0000]) to be incremented by one. This can be verified by issuing the DUMP command

$$-D \ 0 \ 1 \quad (↵)$$

Notice that value of SUM is identified as a WORD PTR. This assembler directive means that the memory location for SUM is to be treated as a word-wide storage location. Similarly if a byte-wide storage location, say BYTE_LOC, is to be accessed, it would be identified as BYTE PTR [BYTE_LOC].

The addition instructions we just covered can also be used to add numbers expressed in ASCII code provided the binary result that is produced is converted back to its equivalent ASCII representation. This eliminates the need for doing a code conversion on ASCII data prior to processing it with addition operations. Whenever the 8088 does an addition on ASCII format data, an adjustment must be performed on the binary result to convert it to the equivalent decimal number.

It is specifically for this purpose that the *ASCII adjust for addition* (AAA) instruction is provided in the instruction set of the 8088. The AAA instruction should be executed immediately after the ADD instruction that adds ASCII data.

Assuming that AL contains the result produced by adding two ASCII coded numbers, execution of the AAA instruction causes the contents of AL to be replaced by its equivalent decimal value. If the sum is greater than nine, AL contains the LSD and AH is incremented by one. Otherwise, AL contains the sum and AH is unchanged. Both the AF and CF flags can be affected. Since AAA can only adjust data that are in AL, the destination register for ADD instructions that process ASCII numbers should be AL.

EXAMPLE 4.11

What is the result of executing the following instruction sequence?

```
ADD AL,BL
AAA
```

Assume that AL contains 32_{16}, which is the ASCII code for number 2, BL contains 34_{16}, which is the ASCII code for number 4, and AH has been cleared.

Solution

Executing the ADD instruction gives

$$(AL) \leftarrow (AL) + (BL) = 32_{16} + 34_{16} = 66_{16}$$

Next, the result is adjusted to give its equivalent decimal number. This is done by execution of the AAA instruction. The equivalent of adding 2 and 4 is decimal 6 with no carry. Therefore, the result after the AAA instruction is

$$(AL) = 06_{16}$$

$$(AH) = 00_{16}$$

and both AF and CF remain cleared.

The instruction set of the 8088 includes another instruction, called *decimal adjust for addition* (DAA). This instruction is used to perform an adjust operation similar to that performed by AAA but for the addition of packed BCD numbers instead of ASCII numbers. Information about this instruction is also provided in Fig. 4.9. Similar to AAA, DAA performs an adjustment on the value in AL. A typical instruction sequence is

```
ADD AL,BL
DAA
```

Remember that the contents of AL and BL must be packed BCD numbers, that is, two BCD digits packed into a byte. The adjusted result in AL is again a packed BCD byte.

As an example of the use of the instructions covered in this section, let us perform a 32-bit binary add operation on the contents of the processor's registers. We will implement the addition

$$(DX,CX) \leftarrow (DX,CX) + (BX,AX)$$

for the following data in the registers

$$(DX,CX) = FEDCBA98_{16}$$
$$(BX,AX) = 01234567_{16}$$

We first initialize the registers with the data using move instructions as follows:

```
MOV DX,0FEDCH
MOV CX,0BA98H
MOV BX,0123H
MOV AX,4567H
```

Next, the 16 least significant bits of the 32-bit number are added with the instruction.

```
ADD CX,AX
```

Note that the result from this part of the addition is in CX and the carry flag.

To add the most significant 16 bits, we must account for the possibility of a carry out from the addition of the lower 16 bits. For this reason, the ADC instruction must be used. Thus the last instruction is

```
ADC   DX,BX
```

Execution of this instruction produces the upper 16 bits of the 32-bit sum in register DX.

Subtraction Instructions: SUB, SBB, DEC, AAS, DAS, and NEG

The instruction set of the 8088 includes an extensive set of instructions provided for implementing subtraction. As shown in Fig. 4.14, the subtraction subgroup is similar to the addition subgroup. It includes instructions for subtracting a source and a destination operand, decrementing an operand, and adjusting the result of subtractions of ASCII and BCD data. An additional instruction in this subgroup is negate.

Mnemonic	Meaning	Format	Operation	Flags affected
SUB	Subtract	SUB D,S	$(D) - (S) \rightarrow (D)$ Borrow $\rightarrow$ (CF)	OF, SF, ZF, AF, PF, CF
SBB	Subtract with borrow	SBB D,S	$(D) - (S) - (CF) \rightarrow (D)$	OF, SF, ZF, AF, PF, CF
DEC	Decrement by 1	DEC D	$(D) - 1 \rightarrow (D)$	OF, SF, ZF, AF, PF
NEG	Negate	NEG D	$0 - (D) \rightarrow (D)$ $1 \rightarrow$ (CF)	OF, SF, ZF, AF, PF, CF
DAS	Decimal adjust for subtraction	DAS		SF, ZF, AF, PF, CF OF undefined
AAS	ASCII adjust for subtraction	AAS		AF, CF OF, SF, ZF, PF undefined

(a)

Destination	Source
Register	Register
Register	Memory
Memory	Register
Accumulator	Immediate
Register	Immediate
Memory	Immediate

(b)

Destination
Reg16
Reg8
Memory

(c)

Destination
Register
Memory

(d)

Figure 4.14 (a) Subtraction arithmetic instructions. (b) Allowed operands for SUB and SBB instructions. (c) Allowed operands for DEC instruction. (d) Allowed operands for NEG instruction.

The *subtract* (SUB) instruction is used to subtract the value of a source operand from a destination operand. The result of this operation in general is given as

$$(D) \leftarrow (D) - (S)$$

As shown in Fig. 4.14(b), it can employ the identical operand combinations similar to the ADD instruction.

The *subtract with borrow* (SBB) instruction is similar to SUB; however, it also subtracts the contents of the carry flag from the destination. That is,

$$(D) \leftarrow (D) - (S) - (CF)$$

EXAMPLE 4.12 _____

Assuming that the contents of registers BX and CX are 1234_{16} and 0123_{16}, respectively, and the carry flag is 0, what will be the result of executing the following instruction?

```
SBB BX,CX
```

Solution

Since the instruction implements the operation

$$(BX) - (CX) - (CF) \rightarrow (BX)$$

we get

$$(BX) = 1234_{16} - 0123_{16} - 0_{16}$$
$$= 1111_{16}$$

Since no borrow was needed, the carry flag will stay cleared.

EXAMPLE 4.13

Verify the operation of the subtract instruction in Example 4.12 by repeating the example using the debug program on the IBM PC.

Solution

As shown in Fig. 4.15, we first bring up the debug program and then dump the initial state of the 8088 with a REGISTER command. Next, we load registers BX, CX, and flag CF with the values 1234_{16}, 0123_{16}, and NC, respectively. Notice in Fig. 4.15 that this is done with three more R commands.

```
C:\DOS>DEBUG
-R
AX=0000  BX=0000  CX=0000  DX=0000  SP=FFEE  BP=0000  SI=0000  DI=0000
DS=1342  ES=1342  SS=1342  CS=1342  IP=0100   NV UP EI PL NZ NA PO NC
1342:0100 0F          DB      0F
-R BX
BX 0000
:1234
-R CX
CX 0000
:0123
-R F
NV UP EI PL NZ NA PO NC  -
-A
1342:0100 SBB BX,CX
1342:0102
-R
AX=0000  BX=1234  CX=0123  DX=0000  SP=FFEE  BP=0000  SI=0000  DI=0000
DS=1342  ES=1342  SS=1342  CS=1342  IP=0100   NV UP EI PL NZ NA PO NC
1342:0100 19CB        SBB     BX,CX
-U 100 101
1342:0100 19CB        SBB     BX,CX
-T

AX=0000  BX=1111  CX=0123  DX=0000  SP=FFEE  BP=0000  SI=0000  DI=0000
DS=1342  ES=1342  SS=1342  CS=1342  IP=0102   NV UP EI PL NZ NA PE NC
1342:0102 B98AFF      MOV     CX,FF8A
-Q

C:\DOS>
```

Figure 4.15 Display sequence for Example 4.13.

Now the instruction is assembled at address CS:100 with the command

```
—A              (↵)
1342:0100 SBB BX,CX (↵)
1342:0102       (↵)
—
```

Before executing the instruction, we can verify the initialization of the registers and the entry of the instruction by issuing the commands

```
        —R              (↵)
```

and

```
        —U 100 101    (↵)
```

Looking at Fig. 4.15, we find that the registers have been correctly initialized and that the instruction SBB BX,CX has been correctly entered.

Finally, the instruction is executed with a TRACE command. As shown in Fig. 4.15, the result of executing the instruction is that the contents of CX are subtracted from the contents of BX. The difference, which is 1111_{16}, resides in destination register BX.

___

Just as the INC instruction can be used to add one to an operand, the *decrement* (DEC) instruction can be used to subtract one from its operand. The allowed operands for DEC are shown in Fig. 4.14(c).

In Fig. 4.14(d), we see that the *negate* (NEG) instruction can operate on operands in a general-purpose register or a storage location in memory. Execution of this instruction causes the value of its operand to be replaced by its negative. The way this is actually done is through subtraction. That is, the contents of the specified operand are subtracted from zero and the result is returned to the operand location. The subtraction is actually performed by the processor hardware using 2s-complement arithmetic. To obtain the correct value of the carry flag that results from a NEG operation, the carry generated by the add operation used in the 2s-complement subtraction calculation must be complemented.

EXAMPLE 4.14

Assuming that register BX contains $003A_{16}$, what is the result of executing the following instruction?

```
                NEG BX
```

Solution

Executing the NEG instruction causes the 2s-complement subtraction that follows:

$$(BX) = 0000_{16} - (BX) = 0000_{16} + \text{2s-complement of } 003A_{16}$$
$$= 0000_{16} + FFC6_{16}$$
$$= FFC6_{16}$$

Since no carry is generated in this add operation, the carry flag is complemented to give

$$(CF) = 1$$

EXAMPLE 4.15

Verify the operation of the NEG instruction in Example 4.14 by executing it with the debugger on the IBM PC.

Solution

After loading the DEBUG program, we must initialize the contents of the BX register. This is done with the command

```
-R BX        (↵)
BX 0000
:3A          (↵)
-
```

Next the instruction is assembled with the command

```
-A                 (↵)
1342:0100 NEG BX   (↵)
1342:0102    (↵)
-
```

At this point, we can verify the initialization of BX by issuing the command

```
-R BX        (↵)
BX 003A
:            (↵)
-
```

To check the assembly of the instruction, we can unassemble it with the command

```
-U 100 101   (↵)
1342:0100 F7DB NEG BX
-
```

Now the instruction is executed with the command

$$-\text{T} \qquad\qquad (\leftarrow\rfloor)$$

The information that is dumped by issuing this command is shown in Fig. 4.16. Here the new contents in register BX are verified as $FFC6_{16}$, which is the negative of $003A_{16}$. Also note that the carry flag is set (CY).

In our study of the addition instruction subgroup, we found that the 8088 is capable of directly adding ASCII and BCD numbers. The SUB and SBB instructions can subtract numbers represented in these formats as well. Just as for addition, the results that are obtained must be adjusted to produce the corresponding decimal numbers. In the case of ASCII subtraction, we use the *ASCII adjust for subtraction* (AAS) instruction, and for packed BCD subtraction we use the *decimal adjust for subtract* (DAS) instruction.

An example of an instruction sequence for direct ASCII subtraction is

```
SUB AL,BL
AAS
```

ASCII numbers must be loaded into AL and BL before execution of the subtract instruction. Notice that the destination of the subtraction should be AL. After execution of AAS, AL contains the difference of the two numbers, and AH is unchanged if no borrow takes place or is decremented by one if a borrow occurs.

```
C:\DOS>DEBUG
-R BX
BX 0000
:3A
-A
1342:0100 NEG BX
1342:0102
-R BX
BX 003A
:
-U 100 101
1342:0100 F7DB          NEG     BX
-T

AX=0000  BX=FFC6  CX=0000  DX=0000  SP=FFEE  BP=0000  SI=0000  DI=0000
DS=1342  ES=1342  SS=1342  CS=1342  IP=0102   NV UP EI NG NZ AC PE CY
1342:0102 B98AFF         MOV     CX,FF8A
-Q

C:\DOS>
```

Figure 4.16 Display sequence for Example 4.15.

As an example, let us implement a 32-bit subtraction of two numbers X and Y that are stored in memory as

$$X = (DS:203H)(DS:202H)(DS:201H)(DS:200H)$$

MS byte of MS word	LS byte of MS word	MS byte of LS word	LS byte of LS word

$$Y = (DS:103H)(DS:102H)(DS:101H)(DS:100H)$$

The result of X − Y is to be saved in the place where X is stored in memory.

First, we subtract the least significant 16 bits of the 32-bit words using the instructions

```
MOV AX,[200H]
SUB AX,[100H]
MOV [200H],AX
```

Next, the most significant words of X and Y are subtracted. In this part of the 32-bit subtraction, we must use the borrow that might have been generated by the subtraction of the least significant words. Therefore, SBB must be used to perform the subtraction operation. The instructions to do this are

```
MOV AX,[202H]
SBB AX,[102H]
MOV [202H],AX
```

These instructions used direct addressing to access the data in memory. The 32-bit subtract operation can also be done with indirect addressing as follows:

```
MOV    SI,200H     ;Initialize pointer for X
MOV    DI,100H     ;Initialize pointer for Y
MOV    AX,[SI]     ;Subtract LS words
SUB    AX,[DI]
MOV    [SI],AX     ;Save the LS word of result
ADD    SI,2        ;Update pointer for X
ADD    DI,2        ;Update pointer for Y
MOV    AX,[SI]     ;Subtract MS words
SBB    AX,[DI]
MOV    [SI],AX     ;Save the MS word of result
```

Multiplication and Division Instructions: MUL, DIV, IMUL, IDIV, AAM, AAD, CBW, and CWD

The 8088 has instructions to support multiplication and division of binary and BCD numbers. Two basic types of multiplication and division instructions, for the processing of unsigned numbers and signed numbers, are available. To do these operations on unsigned numbers, the instructions are MUL and DIV. On the other hand, to multiply or divide 2s-complement signed numbers, the instructions are IMUL and IDIV.

Figure 4.17(a) describes these instructions. Notice in Fig. 4.17(b) that a single byte-wide or word-wide operand is specified in a multiplication instruction. It is the source operand. As shown in Fig. 4.17(a), the other operand, which is the destination, is assumed already to be in AL for 8-bit multiplication or in AX for 16-bit multiplication.

Mnemonic	Meaning	Format	Operation	Flags Affected
MUL	Multiply (unsigned)	MUL S	$(AL) \cdot (S8) \rightarrow (AX)$ $(AX) \cdot (S16) \rightarrow (DX),(AX)$	OF, CF SF, ZF, AF, PF undefined
DIV	Division (unsigned)	DIV S	(1) $Q((AX)/(S8)) \rightarrow (AL)$ $R((AX)/(S8)) \rightarrow (AH)$ (2) $Q((DX,AX)/(S16)) \rightarrow (AX)$ $R((DX,AX)/(S16)) \rightarrow (DX)$ If Q is FF_{16} in case (1) or $FFFF_{16}$ in case (2), then type 0 interrupt occurs	OF, SF, ZF, AF, PF, CF undefined
IMUL	Integer multiply (signed)	IMUL S	$(AL) \cdot (S8) \rightarrow (AX)$ $(AX) \cdot (S16) \rightarrow (DX),(AX)$	OF, CF SF, ZF, AF, PF undefined
IDIV	Integer divide (signed)	IDIV S	(1) $Q((AX)/(S8)) \rightarrow (AX)$ $R((AX)/(S8)) \rightarrow (AH)$ (2) $Q((DX,AX)/(S16)) \rightarrow (AX)$ $R((DX,AX)/(S16)) \rightarrow (DX)$ If Q is positive and exceeds $7FFF_{16}$ or if Q is negative and becomes less than 8001_{16}, then type 0 interrupt occurs	OF, SF, ZF, AF, PF, CF undefined
AAM	Adjust AL for multiplication	AAM	$Q((AL)/10) \rightarrow (AH)$ $R((AL)/10) \rightarrow (AL)$	SF, ZF, PF OF, AF, CF undefined
AAD	Adjust AX for division	AAD	$(AH) \cdot 10 + (AL) \rightarrow (AL)$ $00 \rightarrow (AH)$	SF, ZF, PF OF, AF, CF undefined
CBW	Convert byte to word	CBW	(MSB of AL) $\rightarrow$ (All bits of AH)	None
CWD	Convert word to double word	CWD	(MSB of AX) $\rightarrow$ (All bits of DX)	None

(a)

Source
Reg8
Reg16
Mem8
Mem16

(b)

Figure 4.17 (a) Multiplication and division instructions. (b) Allowed operands.

The result of executing a MUL or IMUL instruction on byte data can be represented as

$$(AX) \leftarrow (AL) \times (\text{8-bit operand})$$

That is, the resulting 16-bit product is produced in the AX register. On the other hand, for multiplication of data words, the 32-bit result is given by

$$(DX,AX) \leftarrow (AX) \times (\text{16-bit operand})$$

where AX contains the 16 LSBs and DX the 16 MSBs.

For the division operation, again just the source operand is specified. The other operand is either the contents of AX for 16-bit dividends or the contents of both DX and AX for 32-bit dividends. The result of a DIV or IDIV instruction for an 8-bit divisor is represented by

$$(AH),(AL) \leftarrow (AX)/(\text{8-bit operand})$$

where AH contains the remainder and AL the quotient. For 16-bit division, we have

$$(DX),(AX) \leftarrow (DX,AX)/(\text{16-bit operand})$$

Here AX contains the quotient and DX contains the remainder.

EXAMPLE 4.16

The 2s-complement signed data contents of AL equal -1 and the contents of CL are -2. What result will be produced in AX by executing the following instructions?

```
MUL CL
```

and

```
IMUL CL
```

Solution

As binary data, the contents of AL and CL are

$$(AL) = -1 \text{ (as 2's complement)} = 11111111_2 = FF_{16}$$
$$(CL) = -2 \text{ (as 2's complement)} = 11111110_2 = FE_{16}$$

Executing the MUL instruction gives

$$(AX) = 11111111_2 \times 11111110_2 = 1111110100000010_2$$
$$= FD02_{16}$$

The second instruction multiplies the same two numbers as signed numbers to generate the signed result. That is,

$$(AX) = -1_{16} \times -2_{16}$$

$$= 2_{16} = 0002H$$

EXAMPLE 4.17

Verify the operation of the MUL instruction in Example 4.16 by performing the same operation on the IBM PC with the debug program.

Solution

First the DEBUG program is loaded and then registers AX and CX are initialized with the values FF_{16} and FE_{16}, respectively. These registers are loaded as follows:

```
-R AX           (↵)
AX 0000
:FF             (↵)
-R CX           (↵)
CX 0000
:FE             (↵)
-
```

Next the instruction is loaded with the command

```
-A              (↵)
1342:0100 MUL CL
1342:0102       (↵)
-
```

Before executing the instruction, let us verify the loading of AX, CX, and the instruction. To do this, we use the commands as follows:

```
-R AX           (↵)
AX 00FF
:               (↵)
-R CX           (↵)
CX 00FE
:               (↵)
-U 100 101      (↵)
1342:0100 F6E1 MUL CL
-
```

To execute the instruction, we issue the T command.

```
        -T              (↵)
```

The displayed result in Fig. 4.18 shows that AX now contains $FD02_{16}$, which is the unsigned product of FF_{16} and FE_{16}.

```
C:\DOS>DEBUG
-R AX
AX 0000
:FF
-R CX
CX 0000
:FE
-A
1342:0100 MUL CL
1342:0102
-R AX
AX 00FF
:
-R CX
CX 00FE
:
-U 100 101
1342:0100 F6E1          MUL     CL
-T

AX=FD02  BX=0000  CX=00FE  DX=0000  SP=FFEE  BP=0000  SI=0000  DI=0000
DS=1342  ES=1342  SS=1342  CS=1342  IP=0102   OV UP EI NG NZ AC PE CY
1342:0102 B98AFF          MOV     CX,FF8A
-Q

C:\DOS>
```

Figure 4.18   Display sequence for Example 4.17.

As shown in Fig. 4.17(a), adjust instructions for BCD multiplication and division are also provided. They are *adjust AX for multiply* (AAM) and *adjust AX for divide* (AAD). The multiplication performed just before execution of the AAM instruction is assumed to have been performed on two unpacked BCD numbers with the product produced in AL. The AAD instruction converts the result in AH and AL to unpacked BCD numbers.

The division instructions can also be used to divide an 8-bit dividend in AL by an 8-bit divisor. However, to do this, the sign of the dividend must first be extended to fill the AX register. That is, AH is filled with zeros if the number in AL is positive or with ones if it is negative. This conversion is automatically done by executing the *convert byte to word* (CBW) instruction. Notice that the sign extension does not change the signed value for the data. It simply allows data to be represented using more bits.

In a similar way, the 32-bit by 16-bit division instructions can be used to divide a 16-bit dividend in AX by a 16-bit divisor. In this case, the sign bit of AX must be extended by 16 bits into the DX register. This can be done by another instruction, which is known as *convert word to double word* (CWD). These two sign extension instructions are also shown in Fig. 4.17(a).

EXAMPLE 4.18

What is the result of executing the following sequence of instructions?

```
MOV AL,0A1H
CBW
CWD
```

Solution

The first instruction loads AL with $A1_{16}$. This gives

$$(AL) = A1_{16} = 10100001_2$$

Executing the second instruction extends the most significant bit of AL, which is one, into all bits of AH. The result is

$$(AH) = 11111111_2 = FF_{16}$$

or

$$(AX) = 1111111110100001_2 = FFA1_{16}$$

This completes conversion of the byte in AL to a word in AX.

The last instruction loads each bit of DX with the most significant bit of AX. This bit is also one. Therefore, we get

$$(DX) = 1111111111111111_2 = FFFF_{16}$$

Now the word in AX has been extended to the double word. That is,

$$(AX) = FFA1_{16}$$
$$(DX) = FFFF_{16}$$

EXAMPLE 4.19

Use an assembled version of the program in Example 4.18 to verify the results obtained when it is executed.

Solution

The source program is shown in Fig. 4.19(a). Notice that this program differs from that described in Example 4.18 in that it includes the pseudo-op statements that are needed to assemble it and some additional instructions so that it can be executed using the debug program.

The source file is assembled with the macroassembler and then linked with the LINK program to give a run module stored in the file EX419.EXE. The source listing EX419.LST produced by assembling the source file EX419.ASM is shown in Fig. 4.19(b).

As shown in Fig. 4.19(c), the run module is loaded for execution as part of calling up the DEBUG program. This is done with the command

```
C:\DOS>DEBUG A:EX419.EXE    (↵)
```

The loading of the program can now be verified with the UNASSEMBLE command

$$-U \ 0 \ 9 \qquad (\lrcorner)$$

Looking at the instructions displayed in Fig. 4.19(c), we see that the program is correct.

From the unassembled version of the program in Fig. 4.19(c), we find that the instructions we are interested in start at address 0D03:0005. Thus we execute the instructions prior to the MOV AL,A1 instruction by issuing the command

$$-G \ 5 \qquad (\lrcorner)$$

The state information that is displayed in Fig. 4.19(c) shows that (AX) = 0000_{16} and (DX) = 0000_{16}. Moreover, (IP) = 0005_{16} and points to the first instruction that we are interested in. This instruction is executed with the command

$$-T \qquad (\lrcorner)$$

In the trace dump information of Fig. 4.19(c), we see that AL has been loaded with $A1_{16}$ and DX contains 0000_{16}.

Now the second instruction is executed with the command

$$-T \qquad (\lrcorner)$$

```
TITLE     EXAMPLE 4.19

        PAGE      ,132

STACK_SEG       SEGMENT         STACK 'STACK'
                DB              64 DUP(?)
STACK_SEG       ENDS


CODE_SEG        SEGMENT         'CODE'
EX419   PROC    FAR
        ASSUME  CS:CODE_SEG, SS:STACK_SEG

;To return to DEBUG program put return address on the stack

        PUSH    DS
        MOV     AX, 0
        PUSH    AX

;Following code implements Example 4.19

        MOV     AL, 0A1H
        CBW
        CWD

        RET                     ;Return to DEBUG program
EX419 ENDP

CODE_SEG        ENDS

        END     EX419
```

Figure 4.19(a) Source program for Example 4.19.

```
                            TITLE    EXAMPLE 4.19

                            PAGE     ,132

0000                                    STACK_SEG        SEGMENT          STACK 'STACK'
0000        40 [                        DB               64 DUP(?)
            ??
                    ]

0040                                    STACK_SEG        ENDS


0000                            CODE_SEG        SEGMENT          'CODE'
0000                            EX419    PROC    FAR
                            ASSUME   CS:CODE_SEG, SS:STACK_SEG

                    ;To return to DEBUG program put return address on the stack

0000    1E                              PUSH     DS
0001    B8 0000                         MOV      AX, 0
0004    50                              PUSH     AX

                    ;Following code implements Example 4.19

0005    B0 A1                           MOV      AL, 0A1H
0007    98                              CBW
0008    99                              CWD

0009    CB                              RET                          ;Return to DEBUG program
000A                            EX419    ENDP

000A                            CODE_SEG        ENDS

                            END     EX419
```

Segments and groups:

N a m e	Size	align	combine	class
CODE_SEG	000A	PARA	NONE	'CODE'
STACK_SEG.	0040	PARA	STACK	'STACK'

Symbols:

N a m e	Type	Value	Attr	
EX419.	F PROC	0000	CODE_SEG	Length =000A

Warning	Severe
Errors	Errors
0	0

Figure 4.19(b) Source listing produced by assembler.

Again looking at the trace information, we see that AX now contains the value $FFA1_{16}$ and DX still contains 0000_{16}. This shows that the byte in AL has been extended to a word in AX.

To execute the third instruction, the command is

$$-T \qquad (\lrcorner)$$

Then, looking at the trace information produced, we find that AX still contains $FFA1_{16}$ and the value in DX has changed to $FFFF_{16}$. This shows that the word in AX has been extended to a double word in DX and AX.

```
C:\DOS>DEBUG A:EX419.EXE
-U 0 9
0D03:0000 1E              PUSH    DS
0D03:0001 B80000          MOV     AX,0000
0D03:0004 50              PUSH    AX
0D03:0005 B0A1            MOV     AL,A1
0D03:0007 98              CBW
0D03:0008 99              CWD
0D03:0009 CB              RETF
-G 5

AX=0000  BX=0000  CX=0000  DX=0000  SP=003C  BP=0000  SI=0000 DI=0000
DS=0CF3  ES=0CF3  SS=0D04  CS=0D03  IP=0005  NV UP EI PL NZ NA PO NC
0D03:0005 B0A1            MOV     AL,A1
-T

AX=00A1  BX=0000  CX=0000  DX=0000  SP=003C  BP=0000  SI=0000 DI=0000
DS=0CF3  ES=0CF3  SS=0D04  CS=0D03  IP=0007  NV UP EI PL NZ NA PO NC
0D03:0007 98             CBW
-T

AX=FFA1  BX=0000  CX=0000  DX=0000  SP=003C  BP=0000  SI=0000 DI=0000
DS=0CF3  ES=0CF3  SS=0D04  CS=0D03  IP=0008  NV UP EI PL NZ NA PO NC
0D03:0008 99             CWD
-T

AX=FFA1  BX=0000  CX=0000  DX=FFFF  SP=003C  BP=0000  SI=0000 DI=0000
DS=0CF3  ES=0CF3  SS=0D04  CS=0D03  IP=0009  NV UP EI PL NZ NA PO NC
0D03:0009 CB             RETF
-G

Program terminated normally
-Q

C:\DOS>
```

Figure 4.19(c)   Debug session for execution of program.

To run the program to completion, enter the command

$$-G \qquad (\lrcorner)$$

This executes the remaining instructions, which cause control to be returned to the DEBUG program.

▲ 4.5 LOGIC INSTRUCTIONS

The 8088 has instructions for performing the logic operations *AND*, *OR*, *exclusive-OR*, and *NOT*. As shown in Fig. 4.20(a), the AND, OR, and XOR instructions perform their respective logic operations bit by bit on the specified source and destination operands, the result being represented by the final contents of the destination operand. Figure 4.20(b) shows the allowed operand combinations for the AND, OR, and XOR instructions.

For example, the instruction

$$\text{AND AX,BX}$$

causes the contents of BX to be ANDed with the contents of AX. The result is reflected by the new contents of AX. For instance, if AX contains 1234_{16} and BX contains $000F_{16}$, the result produced by the instruction is

$$1234_{16} \cdot 000F_{16} = 0001001000110100_2 \cdot 0000000000001111_2$$

$$= 0000000000000100_2$$

$$= 0004_{16}$$

This result is stored in the destination operand. This result is

$$(AX) = 0004_{16}$$

Notice that the 12 most significant bits are all zero. In this way we see how the AND instruction is used to mask the 12 most significant bits of the destination operand.

The NOT logic instruction differs from those for AND, OR, and exclusive-OR in that it operates on a single operand. Looking at Fig. 4.20(c), which shows

Mnemonic	Meaning	Format	Operation	Flags Affected
AND	Logical AND	AND D,S	$(S) \cdot (D) \rightarrow (D)$	OF, SF, ZF, PF, CF AF undefined
OR	Logical Inclusive-OR	OR D,S	$(S) + (D) \rightarrow (D)$	OF, SF, ZF, PF, CF AF undefined
XOR	Logical Exclusive-OR	XOR D,S	$(S) \oplus (D) \rightarrow (D)$	OF, SF, ZF, PF, CF AF undefined
NOT	Logical NOT	NOT D	$(\overline{D}) \rightarrow (D)$	None

(a)

Destination	Source
Register	Register
Register	Memory
Memory	Register
Register	Immediate
Memory	Immediate
Accumulator	Immediate

(b)

Destination
Register
Memory

(c)

Figure 4.20 (a) Logic instructions. (b) Allowed operands for the AND, OR, and XOR instructions. (c) Allowed operands for the NOT instruction.

the allowed operands for the NOT instruction, we see that this operand can be the contents of an internal register or a location in memory.

EXAMPLE 4.20

Describe the result of executing the following sequence of instructions.

```
MOV   AL,01010101B
AND   AL,00011111B
OR    AL,11000000B
XOR   AL,00001111B
NOT   AL
```

Here B is used to specify a binary number.

Solution

The first instruction moves the immediate operand 01010101_2 into the AL register. This loads the data that are to be manipulated with the logic instructions. The instruction performs a bit-by-bit AND operation of the contents of AL with immediate operand 00011111_2. This gives

$$01010101_2 \cdot 00011111_2 = 00010101_2$$

This result is placed in destination register AL.

$$(AL) = 00010101_2 = 15_{16}$$

Note that this operation has masked off the three most significant bits of AL.

The third instruction performs a bit-by-bit logical OR of the present contents of AL with immediate operand $C0_{16}$. This gives

$$00010101_2 + 11000000_2 = 11010101_2$$
$$(AL) = 11010101_2 = D5_{16}$$

This operation is equivalent to setting the two most significant bits of AL.

The fourth instruction is an exclusive-OR operation of the contents of AL with immediate operand 00001111_2. We get

$$11010101_2 \oplus 00001111_2 = 11011010_2$$
$$(AL) = 11011010_2 = DA_{16}$$

Note that this operation complements the logic state of those bits in AL that are ones in the immediate operand.

The last instruction, NOT AL, inverts each bit of AL. Therefore, the final contents of AL become

$$(AL) = \overline{11011010_2} = 00100101_2 = 25_{16}$$

These results are summarized in Fig. 4.21.

Instruction	(AL)
MOV AL,01010101B	01010101
AND AL,00011111B	00010101
OR AL,11000000B	11010101
XOR AL,00001111B	11011010
NOT AL	00100101

Figure 4.21 Results of example program using logic instructions.

EXAMPLE 4.21

Use the IBM PC's debug program to verify the operation of the program in Example 4.20.

Solution

After the debug program is brought up, the line-by-line assembler is used to enter the program as shown in Fig. 4.22. The first instruction is executed by issuing the T command

$$-\text{T} \qquad (\dashv)$$

The trace dump given in Fig. 4.22 shows that the value 55_{16} has been loaded into the AL register.

The second instruction is executed by issuing another T command.

$$-\text{T} \qquad (\dashv)$$

Execution of this instruction causes $1F_{16}$ to be ANDed with the value 55_{16} in AL. Looking at the trace information displayed in Fig. 4.22, we see that the three most significant bits of AL have been masked off to produce the result 15_{16}.

The third instruction is executed in the same way.

$$-\text{T} \qquad (\dashv)$$

It causes the value $C0_{16}$ to be ORed with the value $1F_{16}$ in AL. This gives the result $D5_{16}$ in AL.

```
C:\DOS>DEBUG
-A
1342:0100 MOV AL,55
1342:0102 AND AL,1F
1342:0104 OR AL,C0
1342:0106 XOR AL,0F
1342:0108 NOT AL
1342:010A
-T

AX=0055  BX=0000  CX=0000  DX=0000  SP=FFEE  BP=0000  SI=0000  DI=0000
DS=1342  ES=1342  SS=1342  CS=1342  IP=0102    NV UP EI PL NZ NA PO NC
1342:0102 241F            AND     AL,1F
-T

AX=0015  BX=0000  CX=0000  DX=0000  SP=FFEE  BP=0000  SI=0000  DI=0000
DS=1342  ES=1342  SS=1342  CS=1342  IP=0104    NV UP EI PL NZ NA PO NC
1342:0104 0CC0             OR      AL,C0
-T

AX=00D5  BX=0000  CX=0000  DX=0000  SP=FFEE  BP=0000  SI=0000  DI=0000
DS=1342  ES=1342  SS=1342  CS=1342  IP=0106    NV UP EI NG NZ NA PO NC
1342:0106 340F            XOR      AL,0F
-T

AX=00DA  BX=0000  CX=0000  DX=0000  SP=FFEE  BP=0000  SI=0000  DI=0000
DS=1342  ES=1342  SS=1342  CS=1342  IP=0108    NV UP EI NG NZ NA PO NC
1342:0108 F6D0             NOT     AL
-T

AX=0025  BX=0000  CX=0000  DX=0000  SP=FFEE  BP=0000  SI=0000  DI=0000
DS=1342  ES=1342  SS=1342  CS=1342  IP=010A    NV UP EI NG NZ NA PO NC
1342:010A 2B04             SUB     AX,[SI]                 DS:0000=20CD
-Q

C:\DOS>
```

Figure 4.22   Display sequence for Example 4.21.

A fourth T command is used to execute the XOR instruction.

$$-T \qquad (\lrcorner)$$

and the trace dump that results shows that the new value in AL is DA_{16}.

The last instruction is a NOT instruction and its execution with the command

$$-T \qquad (\lrcorner)$$

causes the bits of DA_{16} to be inverted. This produces 25_{16} as the final result in AL.

A common use of logic instructions is to mask a group of bits of a byte or word of data. By *mask*, we mean to clear the bit or bits to zero. Remember that when a bit is ANDed with another bit that is at logic 0, the result will always be 0. On the other hand, if a bit is ANDed with a bit that is at logic 1, its value will remain unchanged. Thus we see that the bits that are to be masked must be set to 0 in the mask, which is the source operand, and those that are to remain unchanged are set to 1. For instance, in the instruction

```
AND AX, 000FH
```

the mask equals $000F_{16}$; therefore, it would mask off the upper 12 bits of the word of data in AX. Let us assume that the original value in AX is $FFFF_{16}$. Then executing the instruction performs the operation

$$0000000000001111_2 \cdot 1111111111111111_2 = 0000000000001111_2$$

$$(AX) = 000F_{16}$$

This shows that just the lower four bits in AX remain intact.

The OR instruction can be used to set a bit or bits in a register or a storage location in memory to logic 1. If a bit is ORed with another bit that is 0, the value of the bit remains unchanged; however, if it is ORed with another bit that is 1, the bit will become 1. For instance, let us assume that we want to set bit 4 of the byte at the offset address CONTROL_FLAGS in the current data segment of memory to logic 1. This can be done with the following instruction sequence.

```
MOV    AL, [CONTROL_FLAGS]
OR     AL,10H
MOV    [CONTROL_FLAGS],AL
```

First the value of the flags are copied into AL and the logic operation

$$(AL) = XXXXXXXX_2 + 00010000_2 = XXXX1XXX_2$$

is performed. Finally, the new byte in AL, which has bit 4 set to 1, is written back to the memory location called CONTROL_FLAGS.

▲ 4.6 SHIFT INSTRUCTIONS

The four *shift instructions* of the 8088 can perform two basic types of shift operations. They are the *logical shift* and the *arithmetic shift*. Moreover, each of these operations can be performed to the right or to the left. The shift instructions are *shift logical left* (SHL), *shift arithmetic left* (SAL), *shift logical right* (SHR), and *shift arithmetic right* (SAR).

The logical shift instructions, SHL and SHR, are described in Fig. 4.23(a). Notice in Fig. 4.23(b) that the destination operand, the data whose bits are to be shifted, can be either the contents of an internal register or a storage location in memory. Moreover, the source operand can be specified in two ways. If it is assigned the value of 1, a 1-bit shift will take place. For instance, as illustrated in Fig. 4.24(a), executing

```
SHL AX,1
```

causes the 16-bit contents of the AX register to be shifted one bit position to the left. Here we see that the vacated LSB location is filled with zero and the bit shifted out of the MSB is saved in CF.

Mnemonic	Meaning	Format	Operation	Flags Affected
SAL/SHL	Shift arithmetic left/shift logical left	SAL/SHL D,Count	Shift the (D) left by the number of bit positions equal to Count and fill the vacated bits positions on the right with zeros	CF, PF, SF, ZF, OF AF undefined OF undefined if count ≠ 1
SHR	Shift logical right	SHR D,Count	Shift the (D) right by the number of bit positions equal to Count and fill the vacated bit positions on the left with zeros	CF, PF, SF, ZF, OF AF undefined OF undefined if count ≠ 1
SAR	Shift arithmetic right	SAR D,Count	Shift the (D) right by the number of bit positions equal to Count and fill the vacated bit positions on the left with the original most significant bit	OF, SF, ZF, PF, CF AF undefined

(a)

Destination	Count
Register	1
Register	CL
Memory	1
Memory	CL

(b)

Figure 4.23   (a) Shift instructions. (b) Allowed operands.

On the other hand, if the source operand is specified as CL instead of one, the count in this register represents the number of bit positions the contents of the operand are to be shifted. This permits the count to be defined under software control and allows a range of shifts from 1 to 255 bits.

An example of an instruction specified in this way is

```
SHR AX,CL
```

Assuming that CL contains the value 02_{16}, the logical shift right that occurs is as shown in Fig. 4.24(b). Notice that the two MSBs have been filled with zeros and the last bit shifted out at the LSB, which is zero, is placed in the carry flag.

In an arithmetic shift to the left, SAL operation, the vacated bits at the right of the operand are filled with zeros, whereas in an arithmetic shift to the right, SAR operation, the vacated bits at the left are filled with the value of the original MSB of the operand. Thus, in an arithmetic shift to the right, the original sign of the number is maintained. This operation is equivalent to division by powers of 2 as long as the bits shifted out of the LSB are zeros.

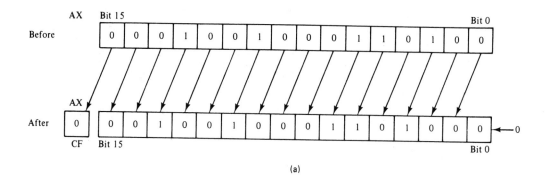

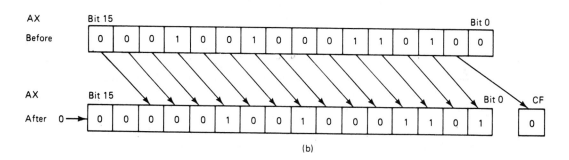

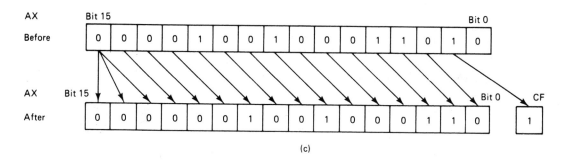

Figure 4.24 (a) Results of executing SHL AX,1. (b) Results of executing SHR AX,CL. (c) Results of executing SAR AX,CL.

EXAMPLE 4.22 _____

Assume that CL contains 02_{16} and AX contains $091A_{16}$. Determine the new contents of AX and the carry flag after the instruction

```
SAR AX,CL
```

is executed.

Solution

Figure 4.24(c) shows the effect of executing the instruction. Here we see that since CL contains 02_{16} a shift right by two bit locations takes place, and the original sign bit, which is logic 0, is extended to the two vacated bit positions. Moreover, the last bit shifted out from the LSB location is placed in CF. This makes CF equal to 1. Therefore, the results produced by execution of the instruction are

$$(AX) = 0246_{16}$$

and

$$(CF) = 1_2$$

EXAMPLE 4.23

Verify the operation of the SAR instruction in Example 4.22 by executing with the debug program on the IBM PC.

Solution

After invoking the debug program, we enter the instruction by assembling it with the command

```
-A              (↵)
1342:0100 SAR AX,CL     (↵)
1342:0102   (↵)
-
```

Next, registers AX and CL are loaded with data and the carry flag is reset. This is done with the command sequence

```
-R AX       (↵)
AX 0000
:091A       (↵)
-R CX       (↵)
CX 0000
:2          (↵)
-R F        (↵)
NV UP EI PL NZ NA PO NC - (↵)
-
```

Notice that the carry flag was already clear, so no status entry was made.
Now the instruction is executed with the T command

```
-T          (↵)
```

Note in Fig. 4.25 that the value in AX has become 0246_{16} and a carry (CY) has occurred. These results are identical to those obtained in Example 4.22.

```
C:\DOS>DEBUG
-A
1342:0100 SAR AX,CL
1342:0102
-R AX
AX 0000
:091A
-R CX
CX 0000
:2
-R F
NV UP EI PL NZ NA PO NC  -
-T

AX=0246  BX=0000  CX=0002  DX=0000  SP=FFEE  BP=0000  SI=0000  DI=0000
DS=1342  ES=1342  SS=1342  CS=1342  IP=0102   NV UP EI PL NZ AC PO CY
1342:0102 B98AFF        MOV     CX,FF8A
-Q

C:\DOS>
```

Figure 4.25 Display sequence for Example 4.23.

A frequent need in programming is to isolate the value in one bit of a word or byte of data by shifting it into the carry flag. The shift instructions can be used to perform this operation on data either in a register or a storage location in memory. The instructions that follow perform this type of operation on a byte of data stored in memory at address CONTROL_FLAGS.

```
MOV AL, [CONTROL_FLAGS]
MOV CL,04H
SHR AL, CL
```

The first instruction reads the value of the byte of data at address CONTROL_FLAGS into AL. Next a shift count of four is loaded into CL and then the value in AL is shifted to the right four bit positions. Since the MSBs of AL are reloaded with 0s as part of the shift operation, the results are

$$(AL) = 0000B_7B_6B_5B_4$$

and

$$(CF) = B_3$$

In this way, we see that bit B_3 of CONTROL_FLAGS has been isolated by placing it in CF.

▲ 4.7 ROTATE INSTRUCTIONS

Another group of instructions, known as the *rotate instructions*, are similar to the shift instructions we just introduced. This group, as shown in Fig. 4.26(a), includes the *rotate left* (ROL), *rotate right* (ROR), *rotate left through carry* (RCL), and *rotate right through carry* (RCR) instructions.

Mnemonic	Meaning	Format	Operation	Flags Affected
ROL	Rotate left	ROL D,Count	Rotate the (D) left by the number of bit positions equal to Count. Each bit shifted out from the leftmost bit goes back into the rightmost bit position.	CF OF undefined if count ≠ 1
ROR	Rotate right	ROR D,Count	Rotate the (D) right by the number of bit positions equal to Count. Each bit shifted out from the rightmost bit goes into the leftmost bit position.	CF OF undefined if count ≠ 1
RCL	Rotate left through carry	RCL D,Count	Same as ROL except carry is attached to (D) for rotation.	CF OF undefined if count ≠ 1
RCR	Rotate right through carry	RCR D,Count	Same as ROR except carry is attached to (D) for rotation.	CF OF undefined if count ≠ 1

Destination	Count
Register	1
Register	CL
Memory	1
Memory	CL

(b)

Figure 4.26 (a) Rotate instructions. (b) Allowed operands.

As shown in Fig. 4.26(b), the rotate instructions are similar to the shift instructions in several ways. They have the ability to rotate the contents of either an internal register or storage location in memory. Also, the rotation that takes place can be from 1 to 255 bit positions to the left or to the right. Moreover, in the case of a multibit rotate, the number of bit positions to be rotated is specified by the contents of CL. Their difference from the shift instructions lies in the fact that the bits moved out at either the MSB or LSB end are not lost; instead, they are reloaded at the other end.

As an example, let us look at the operation of the ROL instruction. Execution of ROL causes the contents of the selected operand to be rotated left the specified number of bit positions. Each bit shifted out at the MSB end is reloaded at the LSB end. Moreover, the content of CF reflects the state of the last bit that was shifted out. For instance, the instruction

```
ROL AX,1
```

causes a 1-bit rotation to the left. Figure 4.27(a) shows the result produced by executing this instruction. Notice that the original value of bit 15 is zero. This value has been rotated into CF and bit 0 of AX. All other bits have been rotated one bit position to the left.

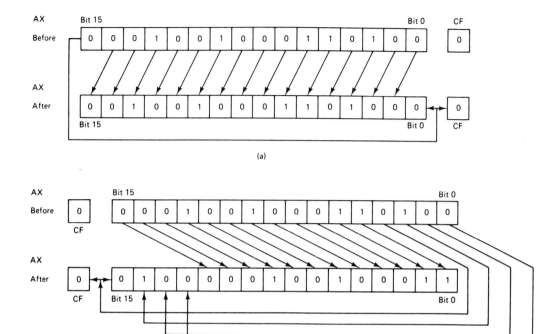

(a)

(b)

Figure 4.27 (a) Results of executing ROL AX,1. (b) Results of executing ROR AX,CL.

The ROR instruction operates the same way as ROL except that it causes data to be rotated to the right instead of to the left. For example, execution of

```
ROR AX,CL
```

causes the contents of AX to be rotated right by the number of bit positions specified in CL. The result for CL equal to four is illustrated in Fig. 4.27(b).

The other two rotate instructions, RCL and RCR, differ from ROL and ROR in that the bits are rotated through the carry flag. Figure 4.28 illustrates the rotation that takes place due to execution of the RCL instruction. Notice that the value returned to bit 0 is the prior content of CF and not bit 15. The value shifted out of bit 15 goes into the carry flag. Thus the bits rotate through carry.

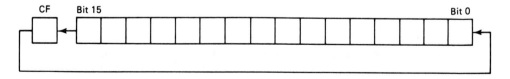

Figure 4.28 Rotation caused by execution of the RCL instruction.

EXAMPLE 4.24

What is the result in BX and CF after execution of the following instruction?

$$RCR \ BX,CL$$

Assume that, prior to execution of the instruction, $(CL) = 04_{16}$, $(BX) = 1234_{16}$, and $(CF) = 0$.

Solution

The original contents of BX are

$$(BX) = 0001001000110100_2 = 1234_{16}$$

Execution of the RCR instruction causes a 4-bit rotate right through carry to take place on the data in BX. The resulting contents of BX and CF are

$$(BX) = 1000000100100011_2 = 8123_{16}$$

$$(CF) = 0_2$$

In this way, we see that the original content of bit 3, which was zero, resides in carry flag and 1000_2 has been reloaded from the bit 15 end of BX.

EXAMPLE 4.25

Use the IBM PC's debug program to verify the operation of the RCR instruction in Example 4.24.

Solution

After loading DEBUG, the instruction is assembled into memory with the command

```
-A            (↵)
1342:0100 RCR BX,CL
1342:0102     (↵)
```

Next, BX and CX are loaded with data and CF is cleared by issuing the commands

```
-R BX         (↵)
BX 0000
:1234         (↵)
-R CX         (↵)
CX 0000
```

```
C:\DOS>DEBUG
-A
1342:0100 RCR BX,CL
1342:0102
-R BX
BX 0000
:1234
-R CX
CX 0000
:4
-R F
NV UP EI PL NZ NA PO NC   -
-T

AX=0000  BX=8123  CX=0004  DX=0000  SP=FFEE  BP=0000  SI=0000  DI=0000
DS=1342  ES=1342  SS=1342  CS=1342  IP=0102   OV UP EI PL NZ NA PO NC
1342:0102 B98AFF          MOV      CX,FF8A
-Q

C:\DOS>
```

Figure 4.29   Display sequence for Example 4.25.

```
:4                 (↵)
-R F               (↵)
NV UP EI PL NZ NA PO NC -     (↵)
-
```

Notice that CF is already cleared (NC); therefore, no entry is made for the flag register command.

Now we can execute the instruction with the command

$$-T \qquad (↵)$$

Looking at the trace information displayed in Fig. 4.29, we see that the new contents of BX are 8123_{16} and CF equals NC. These are the same results as obtained in Example 4.24.

The rotate instructions can be used to perform many of the same programming functions as the shift instructions. An example of a software operation that can be performed with the rotate instructions is the disassembly of the two hexadecimal digits in a byte of data in memory so that they can be added. The instructions

```
MOV AL,[HEX_DIGITS]
MOV BL,AL
MOV CL,04H
ROR BL,CL
AND AL,0FH
AND BL,0FH
ADD AL,BL
```

will perform this operation. First the byte containing the two hexadecimal digits is read into AL. Then a copy is made in BL. Next the four most significant bits in

BL are moved to the four least significant bit locations with a rotate operation. This repositions the most significant hexadecimal digit of the original byte into the least significant digit position in BL. Now the most significant hexadecimal digits in both AL and BL are masked off. This isolates one hexadecimal digit in the lower four bits of AL and the other in the lower four bits of BL. Finally, the two digits are added together in AL.

ASSIGNMENTS

Section 4.2

1. List five groups of instructions.

Section 4.3

2. Explain what operation is performed by each of the instructions that follows.
   (a) MOV AX,0110H
   (b) MOV DI,AX
   (c) MOV BL,AL
   (d) MOV [0100H],AX
   (e) MOV [BX+DI],AX
   (f) MOV [DI]+4,AX
   (g) MOV [BX][DI] +4,AX

3. Assume that registers AX, BX, and DI are all initialized to 0000_{16} and that all the data storage memory has been cleared. Determine the location and value of the destination operand as instructions (a) through (g) in problem 2 are executed as a sequence.

4. Write an instruction sequence that will initialize the ES register with the immediate value 1010_{16}.

5. Write an instruction that will save the contents of the ES register in memory at address DS:1000H.

6. Why will the instruction MOV CL,AX result in an error when it is assembled?

7. Describe the operation performed by each of the instructions that follows.
   (a) XCHG AX,BX
   (b) XCHG BX,DI
   (c) XCHG [DATA],AX
   (d) XCHG [BX+DI],AX

8. If register BX contains the value 0100_{16}, register DI contains 0010_{16}, and register DS contains 1075_{16}, what physical memory location is swapped with AX when the instruction in problem 7(d) is executed?

9. Assuming that (AL) = 0010_{16}, (BX) = 0100_{16}, and (DS) = 1000_{16}, what happens if the XLAT instruction is executed?

10. Write a single instruction that will load AX from address 0200_{16} and DS from address 0202_{16}.

11. Two code-conversion tables starting with offsets TABL1 and TABL2 in the current data segment are to be accessed. Write an instruction sequence that initializes the needed registers and then replaces the contents of memory locations MEM1 and MEM2 (offsets in the current data segment) by the equivalent converted codes from the respective code-conversion tables.

Section 4.4

12. What operation is performed by each of the following instructions?
 (a) ADD AX,00FFH
 (b) ADC SI,AX
 (c) INC   BYTE PTR [0100H]
 (d) SUB DL,BL
 (e) SBB DL,[0200H]
 (f) DEC BYTE PTR [DI+BX]
 (g) NEG BYTE PTR [DI]+0010H
 (h) MUL DX
 (i) IMUL BYTE PTR [BX+SI]
 (j) DIV   BYTE PTR [SI]+0030H
 (k) IDIV BYTE PTR [BX] [SI]+0030H

13. Assume that the state of 8088's registers and memory just prior to the execution of each instruction in problem 12 is as follows:

$$(AX) = 0010H$$
$$(BX) = 0020H$$
$$(CX) = 0030H$$
$$(DX) = 0040H$$
$$(SI) = 0100H$$
$$(DI) = 0200H$$
$$(CF) = 1$$
$$(DS:100H) = 10H$$
$$(DS:101H) = 00H$$
$$(DS:120H) = FFH$$
$$(DS:121H) = FFH$$
$$(DS:130H) = 08H$$
$$(DS:131H) = 00H$$
$$(DS:150H) = 02H$$
$$(DS:151H) = 00H$$
$$(DS:200H) = 30H$$
$$(DS:201H) = 00H$$

$$(DS:210H) = 40H$$
$$(DS:211H) = 00H$$
$$(DS:220H) = 30H$$
$$(DS:221H) = 00H$$

What is the result produced in the destination operand by executing instructions (a) through (k)?

14. Write an instruction that will add the immediate value $111F_{16}$ and the carry flag to the contents of the data register DX.

15. Write an instruction that will subtract the word contents of the storage location pointed to by the base register BX and the carry flag from the accumulator.

16. Two word-wide unsigned integers are stored at the physical memory addresses $00A00_{16}$ and $00A02_{16}$, respectively. Write an instruction sequence that computes and stores their sum, difference, product, and quotient. Store these results at consecutive memory locations starting at physical address $00A10_{16}$ in memory. To obtain the difference, subtract the integer at $00A02_{16}$ from the integer at $00A00_{16}$. For the division, divide the integer at $00A00_{16}$ by the integer at $00A02_{16}$. Use register indirect relative addressing mode to store the various results.

17. Assuming that $(AX) = 0123_{16}$ and $(BL) = 10_{16}$, what will be the new contents of AX after executing the instruction DIV BL?

18. What instruction is used to adjust the result of an addition that processed packed BCD numbers?

19. Which instruction is provided in the instruction set of the 8088 to adjust the result of a subtraction that involved ASCII coded numbers?

20. If AL contains $A0_{16}$, what happens when the instruction CBW is executed?

21. If the value in AX is $7FFF_{16}$, what happens when the instruction CWD is executed?

22. Two byte-sized BCD integers are stored at the symbolic offset addresses NUM1 and NUM2, respectively. Write an instruction sequence to generate their difference and store it at NUM3. The difference is to be formed by subtracting the value at NUM1 from that at NUM2. Assume that all storage locations are in the current data segment.

Section 4.5

23. Describe the operation performed by each of the following instructions.
    (a) AND BYTE PTR [0300H], 0FH
    (b) AND DX,[SI]
    (c) OR   [BX+DI],AX
    (d) OR   BYTE PTR [BX][DI]+10H,0F0H
    (e) XOR AX,[SI + BX]
    (f) NOT BYTE PTR [0300H]
    (g) NOT WORD PTR [BX+DI]

24. Assume that the state of 8088's registers and memory just prior to execution of each instruction in problem 23 is as follows:

$$(AX) = 5555H$$
$$(BX) = 0010H$$
$$(CX) = 0010H$$
$$(DX) = AAAAH$$
$$(SI) = 0100H$$
$$(DI) = 0200H$$
$$(DS:100H) = 0FH$$
$$(DS:101H) = F0H$$
$$(DS:110H) = 00H$$
$$(DS:111H) = FFH$$
$$(DS:200H) = 30H$$
$$(DS:201H) = 00H$$
$$(DS:210H) = AAH$$
$$(DS:211H) = AAH$$
$$(DS:220H) = 55H$$
$$(DS:221H) = 55H$$
$$(DS:300H) = AAH$$
$$(DS:301H) = 55H$$

What are the results produced in the destination operands by executing instructions (a) through (g)?

25. Write an instruction that when executed will mask off all but bit 7 of the contents of the data register.

26. Write an instruction that will mask off all but bit 7 of the word of data stored at address DS:0100H.

27. Specify the relation between the old and new contents of AX after executing the following sequence of instructions.

```
NOT    AX
ADD    AX,1
```

28. Write an instruction sequence that generates a byte size integer in the memory location defined as RESULT. The value of the integer is to be calculated from the logic equation:

$$(RESULT) = (AL \cdot NUM1) + ((\overline{NUM2} \cdot AL) + BL)$$

Assume that all parameters are byte sized. NUM1, NUM2, and RESULT are the offset addresses of memory locations in the current data segment.

29. Write an instruction sequence that will read the byte of control flags from the storage location at offset address CONTROL_FLAGS in the current data segment into register AL, mask off all but the most significant and least significant flag bits, and then save the result back in the original storage location.

30. Describe the operation that is performed by the following instruction sequence.

```
MOV BL,[CONTROL_FLAGS]
AND BL,08H
XOR BL,08H
MOV [CONTROL_FLAGS],BL
```

Section 4.6

31. Explain what operation is performed by each of the instructions that follow.
(a) SHL DX, CL
(b) SHL BYTE PTR [0400H],CL
(c) SHR BYTE PTR [DI],1
(d) SHR BYTE PTR [DI+BX],CL
(e) SAR WORD PTR [BX+DI],1
(f) SAR WORD PTR [BX][DI]+10H,CL

32. Assume that the state of 8088's registers and memory just prior to execution of each instruction in problem 31 is as follows:

$$(AX) = 0000H$$
$$(BX) = 0010H$$
$$(CX) = 0105H$$
$$(DX) = 1111H$$
$$(SI) = 0100H$$
$$(DI) = 0200H$$
$$(CF) = 0$$
$$(DS:100H) = 0FH$$
$$(DS:200H) = 22H$$
$$(DS:201H) = 44H$$
$$(DS:210H) = 55H$$
$$(DS:211H) = AAH$$
$$(DS:220H) = AAH$$
$$(DS:221H) = 55H$$
$$(DS:400H) = AAH$$
$$(DS:401H) = 55H$$

What are the results produced in the destination operands by executing instructions (a) through (f)?

33. Write an instruction that shifts the contents of the count register left by one bit position.

34. Write an instruction sequence that when executed shifts left by eight bit positions the contents of the word-wide memory location pointed to by the address in the destination index register.

35. Identify the condition under which the contents of AX would remain unchanged after executing of the instructions that follow.

```
MOV CL,4
SHL AX,CL
SHR AX,CL
```

36. Implement the following operation using shift and arithmetic instructions.

$$7(AX) - 5(BX) - (BX)/8 \rightarrow (AX)$$

Assume that all parameters are word sized.

37. Describe the operation performed by the instruction sequence that follows

```
MOV AL, [CONTROL_FLAGS]
AND AL,80H
SHL AL, 1
```

What is the result in AL after the shift is complete?

38. Write a routine that will read the word of data from the offset address ASCII_DATA in the current data segment of memory. Assume that this word storage location contains two ASCII coded characters. One character in the upper byte and the other in the lower byte. Disassemble the two bytes and save them as separate characters in the lower byte location of the word storage locations with offsets ASCII_CHAR_L and ASCII_CHAR_H in the current data segment. The upper eight bits in each of these character storage locations should be made zero. Use a SHR instruction to relocate the most significant bits.

Section 4.7

39. Describe what happens as each of the instructions that follows is executed by the 8088.
   (a) ROL DX, CL
   (b) RCL BYTE PTR [0400H],CL
   (c) ROR BYTE PTR [DI],1
   (d) ROR BYTE PTR [DI+BX],CL
   (e) RCR WORD PTR [BX+DI],1
   (f) RCR WORD PTR [BX] [DI]+10H,CL

40. Assume that the state of 8088's registers and memory just prior to execution of each of the instructions in problem 39 is as follows:

$$(AX) = 0000H$$
$$(BX) = 0010H$$
$$(CX) = 0105H$$
$$(DX) = 1111H$$
$$(SI) = 0100H$$
$$(DI) = 0200H$$
$$(CF) = 1$$
$$(DS:100H) = 0FH$$
$$(DS:200H) = 22H$$
$$(DS:201H) = 44H$$
$$(DS:210H) = 55H$$
$$(DS:211H) = AAH$$
$$(DS:220H) = AAH$$
$$(DS:221H) = 55H$$
$$(DS:400H) = AAH$$
$$(DS:401H) = 55H$$

What are the results produced in the destination operands by executing instructions (a) through (f)?

41. Write an instruction sequence that when executed rotates left through carry by one bit position the contents of the word-wide memory location pointed to by the address in the base register.

42. Write a program that saves the content of bit 5 in AL in BX as a word.

43. Repeat problem 38, but this time use a ROR instruction to perform the bit shifting operation.

8088/8086 Microprocessor Programming 2

▲ 5.1 INTRODUCTION

In Chapter 4 we discussed many of the instructions that can be executed by the 8088 and 8086 microprocessors. Furthermore, we used these instructions in simple programs. In this chapter, we introduce the rest of the instruction set and at the same time cover some more complicated programming techniques. The following topics are discussed in this chapter:

1. Flag control instructions
2. Compare instruction
3. Jump instructions
4. Subroutines and subroutine handling instructions
5. The loop and loop handling instructions
6. Strings and string handling instructions

▲ 5.2 FLAG CONTROL INSTRUCTIONS

The 8088 microprocessor has a set of flags that either monitor the status of executing instructions or control options available in its operation. These flags were described in detail in Chapter 2. The instruction set includes a group of instructions that when executed directly affects the state of the flags. These instructions, shown in Fig. 5.1, are *load AH from flags* (LAHF), *store AH into flags* (SAHF), *clear carry* (CLC), *set carry* (STC), *complement carry* (CMC), *clear interrupt* (CLI), and *set interrupt* (STI). A few more instructions exist that can directly affect the flags; however, we will not cover them until later in the chapter when we introduce the subroutine and string instructions.

Looking at Fig. 5.1, we see that the first two instructions, LAHF and SAHF, can be used either to read the flags or to change them, respectively. Notice that the data transfer that takes place is always between the AH register and the flag register. For instance, we may want to start an operation with certain flags set or reset. Assume that we want to preset all flags to logic 1. To do this, we can first load AH with FF_{16} and then execute the SAHF instruction.

EXAMPLE 5.1

Write an instruction sequence to save the current contents of the 8088's flags in the memory location at offset MEM1 of the current data segment and then reload the flags with the contents of the storage location at offset MEM2.

Solution

To save the current flags, we must first load them into the AH register and then move them to the location MEM1. The instructions that do this are

```
LAHF
MOV  [MEM1], AH
```

Similarly, to load the flags with the contents of MEM2, we must first copy the contents of MEM2 into AH and then store the contents of AH into the flags. The

Mnemonic	Meaning	Operation	Flags Affected
LAHF	Load AH from flags	(AH) ← (Flags)	None
SAHF	Store AH into flags	(Flags) ← (AH)	SF, ZF, AF, PF, CF
CLC	Clear carry flag	(CF) ← 0	CF
STC	Set carry flag	(CF) ← 1	CF
CMC	Complement carry flag	(CF) ← ($\overline{CF}$)	CF
CLI	Clear interrupt flag	(IF) ← 0	IF
STI	Set interrupt flag	(IF) ← 1	IF

Figure 5.1 Flag control instructions.

```
        LAHF
        MOV     [MEM1],AH
        MOV     AH,[MEM2]
        SAHF
```

Figure 5.2 Instruction sequence for saving the contents of the flag register and reloading it from memory.

instructions for this are

```
        MOV   AH,  [MEM2]
        SAHF
```

The entire instruction sequence is shown in Fig. 5.2.

EXAMPLE 5.2

Use the DEBUG program on the IBM PC to enter the instruction sequence in Example 5.1 starting at memory address 00110_{16}. Assign memory addresses 00150_{16} and 00151_{16} to symbols MEM1 and MEM2, respectively. Then initialize the contents of MEM1 and MEM2 to FF_{16} and 01_{16}, respectively. Verify the operation of the instructions by executing them one after the other with the TRACE command.

Solution

As shown in Fig. 5.3, the DEBUG program is called up with the DOS command

```
        C:\DOS>DEBUG              (↵)
```

Now we are ready to assemble the program into memory. This is done by using the ASSEMBLE command as follows

```
        -A 0:0110                      (↵)
        0000:0110 LAHF                 (↵)
        0000:0111 MOV [0150], AH       (↵)
        0000:0115 MOV AH, [0151]       (↵)
        0000:0119 SAHF                 (↵)
```

Now the contents of MEM1 and MEM2 are initialized with the ENTER command

```
        -E 0:0150 FF 01        (↵)
```

Next, the registers CS and IP must be initialized with the values 0000_{16} and 0110_{16} to provide access to the program. Also, The DS register must be initialized to

```
C:\DOS>DEBUG
-A 0:0110
0000:0110 LAHF
0000:0111 MOV      [0150],AH
0000:0115 MOV      AH,[0151]
0000:0119 SAHF
0000:011A
-E 0:150 FF 01
-R CS
CS 1342
:0
-R IP
IP 0100
:0110
-R DS
DS 1342
:0
-R
AX=0000  BX=0000  CX=0000  DX=0000  SP=FFEE  BP=0000  SI=0000  DI=0000
DS=0000  ES=1342  SS=1342  CS=0000  IP=0110   NV UP EI PL NZ NA PO NC
0000:0110 9F           LAHF
-T

AX=0200  BX=0000  CX=0000  DX=0000  SP=FFEE  BP=0000  SI=0000  DI=0000
DS=0000  ES=1342  SS=1342  CS=0000  IP=0111   NV UP EI PL NZ NA PO NC
0000:0111 88265001     MOV      [0150],AH                    DS:0150=FF
-T

AX=0200  BX=0000  CX=0000  DX=0000  SP=FFEE  BP=0000  SI=0000  DI=0000
DS=0000  ES=1342  SS=1342  CS=0000  IP=0115   NV UP EI PL NZ NA PO NC
0000:0115 8A265101     MOV      AH,[0151]                    DS:0151=01
-D 150 151
0000:0150   02 01
-T

AX=0100  BX=0000  CX=0000  DX=0000  SP=FFEE  BP=0000  SI=0000  DI=0000
DS=0000  ES=1342  SS=1342  CS=0000  IP=0119   NV UP EI PL NZ NA PO NC
0000:0119 9E           SAHF
-T

AX=0100  BX=0000  CX=0000  DX=0000  SP=FFEE  BP=0000  SI=0000  DI=0000
DS=0000  ES=1342  SS=1342  CS=0000  IP=011A   NV UP EI PL NZ NA PO CY
0000:011A 00F0         ADD      AL,DH
-Q

C:\DOS>
```

Figure 5.3 Display sequence for Example 5.2.

permit access to the data memory locations. This is done with the commands

```
—R CS               (↵)
CS 1342
:0
—R IP               (↵)
IP 0100
:0110               (↵)
—R DS               (↵)
DS 1342
:0                  (↵)
```

Before going further, let us verify the initialization of the internal registers. This is done by displaying their state with the R command

```
—R                  (↵)
```

Looking at the information displayed in Fig. 5.3, we see that all three registers have been correctly initialized.

Now we are ready to step through the execution of the program. The first instruction is executed with the command

−T   (↵)

Notice from the displayed trace information in Fig. 5.3 that the contents of the status register, which are 02_{16}, have been copied into the AH register.

The second instruction is executed by issuing another T command

−T   (↵)

This instruction causes the status, which is now in AH, to be saved in memory at address 0000:0150. The fact that this operation has occurred is verified with the D command

−D 150 151   (↵)

In Fig. 5.3, we see that the data held at address 0000:0150 is displayed by this command as 02_{16}. This verifies that status was saved at MEM1.

The third instruction is now executed with the command

−T   (↵)

Its function is to copy the new status from MEM2 (0000:0151) into the AH register. From the data displayed in the earlier D command, we see that this value is 01_{16}. Looking at the displayed information for the third instruction, we find that 01_{16} has been copied into AH.

The last instruction is executed with another T command and, as shown by its trace information in Fig. 5.3, it has caused the carry flag to set. That is, CF is displayed with the value CY.

The next three instructions, CLC, STC, and CMC, as shown in Fig. 5.1, are used to manipulate the carry flag. They permit CF to be cleared, set, or complemented, respectively. For example, if CF is 1 and the CMC instruction is executed, it becomes 0.

The last two instructions are used to manipulate the interrupt flag. Executing the clear interrupt (CLI) instruction sets IF to logic 0 and disables the interrupt interface. On the other hand, executing the STI instruction sets IF to 1, and the microprocessor is enabled to accept interrupts from that point on.

EXAMPLE 5.3 ───────────────

Of the three carry flag instructions, CLC, STC, and CMC, only one is really an independent instruction. That is, the operation that it provides cannot be performed by a series of the other two instructions. Determine which one of the carry instructions is the independent instruction.

Solution

Let us begin with the CLC instruction. The clear carry operation can be performed by an STC instruction followed by a CMC instruction. Therefore, CLC is not an independent instruction. The operation of the set carry (STC) instruction is equivalent to the operation performed by a CLC instruction, followed by a CMC instruction. Thus, STC is also not an independent instruction. On the other hand, the operation performed by the last instruction, complement carry (CMC), cannot be expressed in terms of the CLC and STC instructions. Therefore, it is the independent instruction.

EXAMPLE 5.4

Verify the operation of the following instructions that affect the carry flag,

```
CLC
STC
CMC
```

by executing them with the debug program of the IBM PC. Start with CF set to one (CY).

Solution

After bringing up the debug program, we enter the instructions with the ASSEMBLE command as

```
-A                        (↵)
1342:0100 CLC             (↵)
1342:0101 STC             (↵)
1342:0102 CMC             (↵)
1342:0103        (↵)
-
```

These inputs are shown in Fig. 5.4.
Next, the carry flag is initialized to CY with the R command

```
-R F                    (↵)
NV UP EI PL NZ NA PO NC -CY  (↵)
```

and in Fig. 5.4 the updated status is displayed with another R command to verify that CF is set to the CY state.

```
C:\DOS>DEBUG
-A
1342:0100 CLC
1342:0101 STC
1342:0102 CMC
1342:0103
-R F
NV UP EI PL NZ NA PO NC   -CY
-R F
NV UP EI PL NZ NA PO CY   -
-T

AX=0000  BX=0000  CX=0000  DX=0000  SP=FFEE  BP=0000  SI=0000  DI=0000
DS=1342  ES=1342  SS=1342  CS=1342  IP=0101    NV UP EI PL NZ NA PO NC
1342:0101 F9              STC
-T

AX=0000  BX=0000  CX=0000  DX=0000  SP=FFEE  BP=0000  SI=0000  DI=0000
DS=1342  ES=1342  SS=1342  CS=1342  IP=0102    NV UP EI PL NZ NA PO CY
1342:0102 F5              CMC
-T

AX=0000  BX=0000  CX=0000  DX=0000  SP=FFEE  BP=0000  SI=0000  DI=0000
DS=1342  ES=1342  SS=1342  CS=1342  IP=0103    NV UP EI PL NZ NA PO NC
1342:0103 8AFF            MOV     BH,BH
-Q

C:\DOS>
```

Figure 5.4 Display sequence for Example 5.4.

Now the first instruction is executed with the TRACE command

$$-T \qquad\qquad (\downarrow)$$

Looking at the displayed state information in Fig. 5.4, we see that CF has been cleared and its new state is NC.

The other two instructions are also executed with T commands and, as shown in Fig. 5.4, the STC instruction sets CF (CY in the state dump) and CMC inverts CF (NC in the state dump).

▲ 5.3 COMPARE INSTRUCTION

An instruction is included in the instruction set of the 8088 that can be used to compare two 8-bit or 16-bit numbers. It is the *compare* (CMP) instruction of Fig. 5.5(a). The compare operation enables us to determine the relationship between two numbers; that is whether they are equal or unequal, and when they are unequal, which one is larger. Figure 5.5(b) shows that the operands for this instruction can reside in a storage location in memory, a register within the MPU, or be part of the instruction. For instance, a byte-wide number in a register such as BL can be compared to a second byte-wide number that is supplied as immediate data.

The result of the comparison is reflected by changes in six of the status flags of the 8088. Notice in Fig. 5.5(a) that it affects the overflow flag, sign flag, zero flag, auxiliary carry flag, parity flag, and carry flag. The new logic state of these flags

Mnemonic	Meaning	Format	Operation	Flags Affected
CMP	Compare	CMP D,S	(D) − (S) is used in setting or resetting the flags	CF, AF, OF, PF, SF, ZF

(a)

Destination	Source
Register	Register
Register	Memory
Memory	Register
Register	Immediate
Memory	Immediate
Accumulator	Immediate

(b)

Figure 5.5 (a) Compare instruction. (b) Operand combinations.

can be used by the instructions that follow to make a decision whether or not to alter the sequence in which the program executes.

The process of comparison performed by the CMP instruction is basically a subtraction operation. The source operand is subtracted from the destination operand. However, the result of this subtraction is not saved. Instead, based on the result of the subtraction operation, the appropriate flags are set or reset. The importance of the flags lies in the fact that they lead us to an understanding of the relationship between the two numbers. For instance, if 5 is compared to 7 by subtracting 5 from 7, the ZF and CF both become logic 0. These conditions indicate that a smaller number was compared to a larger one. On the other hand, if 7 is compared to 5, we are comparing a large number to a smaller number. This comparison results in ZF and CF equal to 0 and 1, respectively. Finally, if two equal numbers, for instance, 5 and 5, are compared, ZF is set to 1 and CF cleared to 0 to indicate the equal to condition.

For example, let us assume that the destination operand equals 10011001_2 and that the source operand equals 00011011_2. Subtracting the source operand from the destination operand, we get

$$
\begin{array}{r}
10011001_2 \\
-00011011_2 \\
\hline
01111110_2
\end{array}
$$

In the process of the binary subtraction, we obtain the status that follows:

1. A borrow is needed from bit 4 to bit 3; therefore, the auxiliary carry flag AF is set.
2. There is no borrow to bit 7. Thus, carry flag CF is reset.

3. Even though there is no borrow to bit 7, there is a borrow from bit 7 to bit 6. This is an indication of the overflow condition. Therefore, the OF flag is set.

4. There are an even number of 1s; therefore, this sets the parity flag PF.

5. Bit 7 is zero and therefore the sign flag SF is reset.

6. The result that is produced is nonzero, which resets the zero flag ZF.

Notice that the result of binary subtraction is not correct if the numbers are considered as 8-bit signed numbers. This condition is indicated by the overflow flag having been set.

EXAMPLE 5.5

Describe what happens to the status flags as the sequence of instructions that follows is executed.

```
MOV AX, 1234H
MOV BX,0ABCDH
CMP AX,BX
```

Assume that flags ZF, SF, CF, AF, OF, and PF are all initially reset.

Solution

The first instruction loads AX with 1234_{16}. No status flags are affected by the execution of a MOV instruction.

The second instruction puts $ABCD_{16}$ into the BX register. Again, status is not affected. Thus, after execution of these two move instructions, the contents of AX and BX are

$$(AX) = 1234_{16} = 0001001000110100_2$$

and $$(BX) = ABCD_{16} = 1010101111001101_2$$

The third instruction is a 16-bit comparison with AX representing the destination and BX the source. Therefore, the contents of BX are subtracted from that of AX.

$$(AX) - (BX) = 0001001000110100_2 - 1010101111001101_2 = 0110011001100111_2$$

The flags are either set or reset based on the result of this subtraction. Notice that the result is nonzero and positive. This makes ZF and SF equal to zero. Moreover, the overflow condition has not occurred. Therefore, OF is also at logic 0. The carry and auxiliary carry conditions have occurred; therefore, CF and AF are 1. Finally, the result has odd parity; therefore, PF is 0. These results are summarized in Fig. 5.6.

Instruction	ZF	SF	CF	AF	OF	PF
Initial state	0	0	0	0	0	0
MOV AX,1234H	0	0	0	0	0	0
MOV BX,0ABCDH	0	0	0	0	0	0
CMP AX,BX	0	0	1	1	0	0

Figure 5.6 Effect on flags of executing instructions.

EXAMPLE 5.6

Verify the execution of the instruction sequence in Example 5.5 on the PC. Use DEBUG to load and run the instruction sequence, which is provided in run module EX56.EXE.

Solution

A source program written to implement a procedure that contains the instruction sequence executed in Example 5.5 is shown in Fig. 5.7(a). This program was assembled with MASM and linked with LINK to form a run module in file EX56.EXE. The source listing produced by the assembler is shown in Fig. 5.7(b).

To execute this program with DEBUG, we bring up the debug program and load the file from a data diskette in drive A with the DOS command

```
C:\DOS>DEBUG A:EX56:EXE   (⏎)
```

```
TITLE    EXAMPLE 5.6

        PAGE    ,132

STACK_SEG        SEGMENT         STACK 'STACK'
                 DB              64 DUP(?)
STACK_SEG        ENDS


CODE_SEG         SEGMENT         'CODE'
EX56    PROC     FAR
        ASSUME   CS:CODE_SEG, SS:STACK_SEG

;To return to DEBUG program put return address on the stack

        PUSH     DS
        MOV      AX, 0
        PUSH     AX

;Following code implements Example 5.6

        MOV      AX, 1234H
        MOV      BX, 0ABCDH
        CMP      AX, BX

        RET                      ;Return to DEBUG program
EX56    ENDP

CODE_SEG         ENDS

        END      EX56
```

Figure 5.7(a) Source program for Example 5.6.

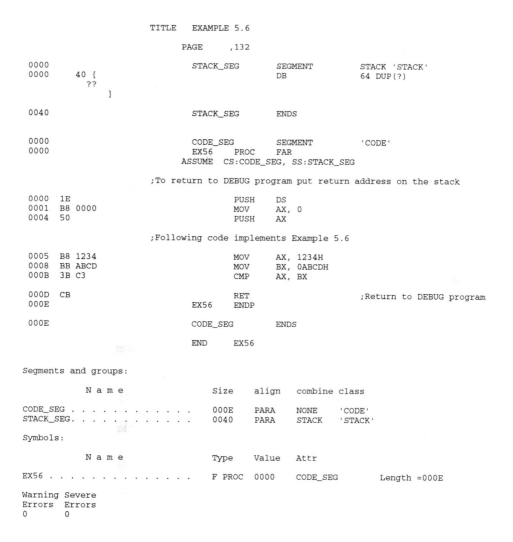

```
                     TITLE    EXAMPLE 5.6

                        PAGE      ,132

0000                               STACK_SEG       SEGMENT       STACK 'STACK'
0000      40 [                     DB              64 DUP(?)
          ??
             ]

0040                               STACK_SEG       ENDS


0000                               CODE_SEG        SEGMENT       'CODE'
0000                               EX56    PROC    FAR
                               ASSUME  CS:CODE_SEG, SS:STACK_SEG

              ;To return to DEBUG program put return address on the stack

0000      1E                               PUSH    DS
0001      B8 0000                          MOV     AX, 0
0004      50                               PUSH    AX

              ;Following code implements Example 5.6

0005      B8 1234                          MOV     AX, 1234H
0008      BB ABCD                          MOV     BX, 0ABCDH
000B      3B C3                            CMP     AX, BX

000D      CB                               RET                   ;Return to DEBUG program
000E                               EX56    ENDP

000E                               CODE_SEG        ENDS

                               END     EX56


Segments and groups:

              N a m e              Size    align    combine class

CODE_SEG . . . . . . . . . . . .   000E    PARA     NONE     'CODE'
STACK_SEG. . . . . . . . . . . .   0040    PARA     STACK    'STACK'

Symbols:

              N a m e              Type    Value    Attr

EX56 . . . . . . . . . . . . . .   F PROC  0000     CODE_SEG      Length =000E

Warning Severe
Errors  Errors
0       0
```

Figure 5.7(b) Source listing produced by assembler.

To verify its loading, the UNASSEMBLE command that follows can be used

$$-\text{U} \quad 0 \quad \text{D} \qquad (\hookleftarrow)$$

As shown in Fig. 5.7(c), the instructions of the source program are correctly displayed.

    First, we will execute the instructions up to the CMP instruction. This is done with the GO command

$$-\text{G} \quad \text{B} \qquad (\hookleftarrow)$$

```
C:\DOS>DEBUG A:EX56.EXE
-U 0 D
0F50:0000 1E              PUSH    DS
0F50:0001 B80000          MOV     AX,0000
0F50:0004 50              PUSH    AX
0F50:0005 B83412          MOV     AX,1234
0F50:0008 BBCDAB          MOV     BX,ABCD
0F50:000B 3BC3            CMP     AX,BX
0F50:000D CB              RETF
-G B

AX=1234  BX=ABCD  CX=000E  DX=0000  SP=003C  BP=0000  SI=0000  DI=0000
DS=0F40  ES=0F40  SS=0F51  CS=0F50  IP=000B  NV UP EI PL NZ NA PO NC
0F50:000B 3BC3            CMP     AX,BX
-T

AX=1234  BX=ABCD  CX=000E  DX=0000  SP=003C  BP=0000  SI=0000  DI=0000
DS=0F40  ES=0F40  SS=0F51  CS=0F50  IP=000D  NV UP EI PL NZ AC PO CY
0F50:000D CB              RETF
-G

Program terminated normally
-Q

C:\DOS>
```

Figure 5.7(c)   Execution of the program with DEBUG.

Note in Fig. 5.7(c) that AX has been loaded with 1234_{16} and BX with the value $ABCD_{16}$.

Next, the compare instruction is executed with the command

$$-T \qquad (\hookleftarrow)$$

By comparing the state information before and after execution of the CMP instruction, we find that auxiliary carry flag and carry flag are the only flags that have changed states and they have both been set. Their new states are identified as AC and CY, respectively. These results are identical to those found in Example 5.5.

▲ 5.4 JUMP INSTRUCTIONS

The purpose of a *jump* instruction is to alter the execution path of instructions in the program. In the 8088 microprocessor, the code segment register and instruction pointer keep track of the next instruction to be fetched for execution. Thus a jump instruction involves altering the contents of these registers. In this way, execution continues at an address other than that of the next sequential instruction. That is, a jump occurs to another part of the program. Typically, program execution is not intended to return to the next sequential instruction after the jump instruction. Therefore, no return linkage is saved when the jump takes place.

The Unconditional and Conditional Jump

The 8088 microprocessor allows two different types of jump instructions. They are the *unconditional jump* and the *conditional jump* instructions. In an unconditional jump, no status requirements are imposed for the jump to occur. That is, as the instruction is executed, the jump always takes place to change the execution sequence.

The unconditional jump concept is illustrated in Fig. 5.8(a). Notice that, when the instruction JMP AA in part I is executed, program control is passed to a point in part III identified by the label AA. Execution resumes with the instruction

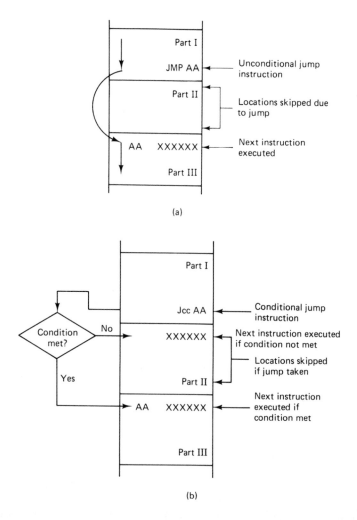

(a)

(b)

Figure 5.8 (a) Unconditional jump program sequence. (b) Conditional jump program sequence.

corresponding to AA. In this way, the instructions in part II of the program are bypassed; that is, they are jumped over.

On the other hand, for a conditional jump instruction, status conditions that exist at the time the jump instruction is executed decide whether or not the jump will occur. If this condition or conditions are met, the jump takes place; otherwise, execution continues with the next sequential instruction of the program. The conditions that can be referenced by a conditional jump instruction are status flags such as carry (CF), parity (PF), and overflow (OF) flags.

Looking at Fig. 5.8(b), we see that execution of the conditional jump instruction Jcc AA in part I causes a test to be initiated. If the conditions of the test are not met, the NO path is taken and execution continues with the next sequential instruction. This corresponds to the first instruction in part II. However, if the result of the conditional test is YES, a jump is initiated to the segment of program identified as part III and the instructions in part II are bypassed.

This type of software operation is referred to as making a *branch*. That is, a point in the program where a choice is made between two paths of execution. If the conditions specified by the jump instruction are met, program control is passed to the part of the program identified by the label. On the other hand, if it is not met, the next sequential instruction is executed.

The branch is a frequently used program structure and is sometime referred to as an *IF-THEN-ELSE* structure. By this, we mean that IF the conditions specified in the jump instruction are met, THEN program control is passed to the point identified by the label; ELSE the program continues with the instruction following the jump instruction.

Unconditional Jump Instruction

The unconditional jump instruction of the 8088 is shown in Fig. 5.9(a) together with its valid operand combinations in Fig. 5.9(b). There are two basic kinds of unconditional jumps. The first, called an *intrasegment jump*, is limited to addresses within the current code segment. This type of jump is achieved by just modifying the value in IP. The second kind of jump, the *intersegment jump*, permits jumps from one code segment to another. Implementation of this type of jump requires modification of the contents of both CS and IP.

Jump instructions specified with a *Short-label*, *Near-label*, *Memptr16*, or *Regptr16 operands* represent intrasegment jumps. The Short-label and Near-label operands specify the jump relative to the address of the jump instruction itself. For example, in a Short-label jump instruction an 8-bit number is coded as an immediate operand to specify the *signed displacement* of the next instruction to be executed from the location of the jump instruction. When the jump instruction is executed, IP is reloaded with a new value equal to the updated value in IP, which is (IP) + 2, plus the signed displacement. The new value of IP and current value in CS give the address of the next instruction to be fetched and executed. With an 8-bit displacement, the Short-label operand can only be used to initiate a jump in the range from -126 to $+129$ bytes from the location of the jump instruction.

Mnemonic	Meaning	Format	Operation	Affected flags
JMP	Unconditional jump	JMP Operand	Jump is initiated to the address specified by the operand	None

(a)

(b)

Figure 5.9 (a) Unconditional jump instruction. (b) Allowed operands.

On the other hand, the Near-label operand specifies a new value for IP with a 16-bit immediate operand. This size of offset corresponds to the complete range of the current code segment. The value of the offset is automatically added to IP upon execution of the instruction. In this way, program control is passed to the location identified by the new IP. Consider the following example of an unconditional jump instruction

```
JMP 1234H
```

It means jump to address 1234H. However, the value of the address encoded in the instruction is not 1234H, but the difference between the current (updated) value in IP and 1234_{16}. It is encoded as either an 8-bit constant (short label) or a 16-bit constant (near label) depending on the size of the difference.

The jump to address can also be specified indirectly by the contents of a memory location or the contents of a register. These two types correspond to the Memptr16 and Regptr16 operands, respectively. Just as for the Near-label operand, they both permit a jump to any address in the current code segment.

For example,

```
JMP BX
```

uses the contents of register BX for the offset in the current code segment. That is, the value in BX is copied into IP.

EXAMPLE 5.7

Verify the operation of the instruction JMP BX using the DEBUG program on the IBM PC. Let the contents of BX be 0010_{16}.

Solution

As shown in Fig. 5.10, DEBUG is invoked and then the line-by-line assembler is used to load the instruction with the command

```
— A                        (↵)
1342:0100 JMP BX  (↵)
1342:0102                  (↵)
```

Next, BX is initialized with the command

```
—R BX                      (↵)
BX 0000                    (↵)
:10                        (↵)
```

Let us check the value in IP before executing the JMP instruction. This is done with another R command as

```
—R           (↵)
```

Looking at the state information displayed in Fig. 5.10, we see that IP contains 0100_{16} and BX contains 0010_{16}.

Executing the instruction with the command

```
—T           (↵)
```

and then looking at Fig. 5.10, we see that the value in IP has become 10_{16}. Therefore, the address at which execution picks up is 1342:0010.

```
C:\DOS>DEBUG
-A
1342:0100 JMP BX
1342:0102
-R BX
BX 0000
:10
-R
AX=0000  BX=0010  CX=0000  DX=0000  SP=FFEE  BP=0000  SI=0000  DI=0000
DS=1342  ES=1342  SS=1342  CS=1342  IP=0100   NV UP EI PL NZ NA PO NC
1342:0100 FFE3         JMP     BX
-T

AX=0000  BX=0010  CX=0000  DX=0000  SP=FFEE  BP=0000  SI=0000  DI=0000
DS=1342  ES=1342  SS=1342  CS=1342  IP=0010   NV UP EI PL NZ NA PO NC
1342:0010 8B09         MOV     CX,[BX+DI]
DS:0010=098B
-Q

C:\DOS>
```

Figure 5.10   Display sequence for Example 5.7.

To specify an operand to be used as a pointer, the various addressing modes available with the 8088 can be used. For instance

```
JMP [BX]
```

uses the contents of BX as the address of the memory location that contains the offset address (Memptr16 operand). This offset is loaded into IP, where it is used together with the current contents of CS to compute the "jump to" address.

EXAMPLE 5.8

Use the DEBUG program to observe the operation of the instruction

```
JMP [BX]
```

Assume that the pointer held in BX is 1000_{16} and the value held at memory location DS: 1000 is 200_{16}. What is the address of the next instruction to be executed?

Solution

Figure 5.11 shows that first the debugger is brought up and then an ASSEMBLE command issued to load the instruction. This assemble command is

```
-A                              (↵)
1342:0100  JMP [BX]             (↵)
1342:0102                       (↵)
```

```
C:\DOS>DEBUG
-A
1342:0100 JMP [BX]
1342:0102
-R BX
BX 0000
:1000
-E 1000 00 02
-D 1000 1001
1342:1000  00 02                                              . .
-R
AX=0000  BX=1000  CX=0000  DX=0000  SP=FFEE  BP=0000  SI=0000  DI=0000
DS=1342  ES=1342  SS=1342  CS=1342  IP=0100  NV UP EI PL NZ NA PO NC
1342:0100 FF27          JMP     [BX]
DS:1000=0200
-T

AX=0000  BX=1000  CX=0000  DX=0000  SP=FFEE  BP=0000  SI=0000  DI=0000
DS=1342  ES=1342  SS=1342  CS=1342  IP=0200  NV UP EI PL NZ NA PO NC
1342:0200 4D            DEC     BP
-Q

C:\DOS>
```

Figure 5.11 Display sequence for Example 5.8.

Next BX is loaded with the pointer address using the R command

```
-R BX                    (↵)
BX 0000
:1000                    (↵)
```

and the memory location is initialized with the command

```
-E 1000 00 02            (↵)
```

As shown in Fig. 5.11, the loading of memory location DS: 1000 and the BX register are next verified with D and R commands, respectively.

Now the instruction is executed with the command

```
-T    (↵)
```

Notice from the state information displayed in Fig. 5.11 that the new value in IP is 0200_{16}. This value was loaded from memory location 1342:1000. Therefore, program execution continues with the instruction at address 1342:0200.

_____

The intersegment unconditional jump instructions correspond to the *Far-label* and *Memptr32 operands* that are shown in Fig. 5.9(b). Far-label uses a 32-bit immediate operand to specify the jump to address. The first 16 bits of this 32-bit pointer are loaded into IP and are an offset address relative to the contents of the code-segment register. The next 16 bits are loaded into the CS register and define the new code segment.

An indirect way to specify the offset and code-segment address for an intersegment jump is by using the Memptr32 operand. This time four consecutive memory bytes starting at the specified address contain the offset address and the new code segment address, respectively. Just like the Memptr16 operand, the Memptr32 operand may be specified using any one of the various addressing modes of the 8088.

An example is the instruction

```
JMP DWORD PTR [DI]
```

It uses the contents of DS and DI to calculate the address of the memory location that contains the first word of the pointer that identifies the location to which the jump will take place. The two-word pointer starting at this address is read into IP and CS to pass control to the new point in the program.

Conditional Jump Instruction

The second type of jump instruction is that which performs conditional jump operations. Figure 5.12(a) shows a general form of this instruction; Fig. 5.12(b) is a list of each of the conditional jump instructions in the 8088's instruction set.

Mnemonic	Meaning	Format	Operation	Flags affected
Jcc	Conditional jump	Jcc Operand	If the specified condition cc is true the jump to the address specified by the operand is initiated; otherwise the next instruction is executed.	None

(a)

Mnemonic	Meaning	Condition
JA	above	$CF = 0$ and $ZF = 0$
JAE	above or equal	$CF = 0$
JB	below	$CF = 1$
JBE	below or equal	$CF = 1$ or $ZF = 1$
JC	carry	$CF = 1$
JCXZ	CX register is zero	$(CF \text{ or } ZF) = 0$
JE	equal	$ZF = 1$
JG	greater	$ZF = 0$ and $SF = OF$
JGE	greater or equal	$SF = OF$
JL	less	$(SF \text{ xor } OF) = 1$
JLE	less or equal	$((SF \text{ xor } OF) \text{ or } ZF) = 1$
JNA	not above	$CF = 1$ or $ZF = 1$
JNAE	not above nor equal	$CF = 1$
JNB	not below	$CF = 0$
JNBE	not below nor equal	$CF = 0$ and $ZF = 0$
JNC	not carry	$CF = 0$
JNE	not equal	$ZF = 0$
JNG	not greater	$((SF \text{ xor } OF) \text{ or } ZF) = 1$
JNGE	not greater nor equal	$(SF \text{ xor } OF) = 1$
JNL	not less	$SF = OF$
JNLE	not less nor equal	$ZF = 0$ and $SF = OF$
JNO	not overflow	$OF = 0$
JNP	not parity	$PF = 0$
JNS	not sign	$SF = 0$
JNZ	not zero	$ZF = 0$
JO	overflow	$OF = 1$
JP	parity	$PF = 1$
JPE	parity even	$PF = 1$
JPO	parity odd	$PF = 0$
JS	sign	$SF = 1$
JZ	zero	$ZF = 1$

(b)

Figure 5.12 (a) Conditional jump instruction. (b) Types of conditional jump instructions.

Notice that each of these instructions tests for the presence or absence of certain status conditions.

For instance, the *jump on carry* (JC) instruction makes a test to determine if carry flag (CF) is set. Depending on the result of the test, the jump to the location specified by its operand either takes place or does not. If CF equals zero, the test fails and execution continues with the instruction at the address following the JC instruction. On the other hand, if CF equals one, the test condition is satisfied and the jump is performed.

Notice that for some of the instructions in Fig. 5.12(b) two different mnemonics can be used. This feature can be used to improve program readability. That is, for each occurrence of the instruction in the program, it can be identified with the mnemonic that best describes its function.

For instance, the instruction *jump on parity* (JP) or *jump on parity even* (JPE) can be used to test parity flag PF for logic 1. Since PF is set to one if the result from a computation has even parity, this instruction can initiate a jump based on the occurrence of even parity. The reverse instruction JNP/JPO is also provided. It can be used to initiate a jump based on the occurrence of a result with odd instead of even parity.

In a similar manner, the instructions *jump if equal* (JE) and *jump if zero* (JZ) have the same function. Either notation can be used in a program to determine if the result of a computation was zero.

All other conditional jump instructions work in a similar way except that they test different conditions to decide whether or not the jump is to take place. Examples of these conditions are: the contents of CX are zero, an overflow has occurred, or the result is negative.

To distinguish between comparisons of signed and unsigned numbers by jump instructions, two different names, which seem to imply the same, have been devised. They are *above* and *below*, for comparison of unsigned numbers and *less* and *greater* for comparison of signed numbers. For instance, the number $ABCD_{16}$ is above the number 1234_{16} if they are considered as unsigned numbers. On the other hand, if they are considered as signed numbers, $ABCD_{16}$ is negative and 1234_{16} is positive. Therefore, $ABCD_{16}$ is less than 1234_{16}.

The Branch Program Structure—IF-THEN-ELSE

Let us now look at some simple examples of how the conditional jump instruction can be used to implement the software branch program structure called IF-THEN-ELSE. One example would be a branch that is made based on the flag settings that result after the contents of two registers are compared to each other. That is,

```
CMP   AX, BX
JE    EQUAL
_     _           ; Next instruction if (AX) ≠ (BX)
      .
      .
```

```
EQUAL:        —    —              ; Next instruction if (AX) = (BX)
                       .
                     .
              —    —
```

First, the CMP instruction subtracts the value in BX from that in AX and adjusts the flags based on the result. Next the jump on equal instruction tests the zero flag to see if it is 1. If ZF is 1, it means that the contents of AX and BX are equal and a jump is made to the location in the program identified by the label EQUAL. Otherwise, if ZF is 0, which means that the contents of AX and BX are not equal, the instruction after the CMP instruction gets executed.

Similar instruction sequences can be used to initiate branch operations for other conditions. For instance, by using the instruction JG GREATER, the branch is taken if the value in BX is greater than that in AX.

Another common use of a conditional jump is to branch based on the setting of a specific bit in a register. When this is done, a logic operation is normally used to mask off the values of all of the other bits in the register. For example, we may want to mask off all bits of the value in AL other than bit 2 and then make a conditional jump if the unmasked bit is logic 1. This operation can be done with the instruction sequence

```
              AND   AL, 04H
              JNZ   BIT2_ONE
              —    —              ; Next instruction if B2 of AL = 0
                       .
                     .
              —    —
BIT2_ONE:     —    —              ; Next instruction if B2 of AL = 1
                       .
                     .
              —    —
```

First the contents of AL are ANDed with 04_{16} to give

$$(AL) = XXXXXXXX_2 \cdot 00000100_2 = 00000X00_2$$

Now the content of AL is zero if bit 2 is 0 and the resulting value in the ZF is 1. On the other hand, if bit 2 is 1, the content of AL is nonzero and ZF is 0. Remember we want to make the jump when bit 2 is 1. Therefore, a jump on not zero instruction is used to make the conditional test. When ZF is 1, the next instruction is executed, but if ZF is 0 the JNZ instruction passes control to the instruction identified by the label BIT2_ONE.

Let us look at how to perform this exact same branch operation in another way. Instead of masking off all of the bits in AL, we could shift bit 2 into the carry flag and then make a conditional jump if CF equals 1. This is done as follows:

Sec. 5.4   Jump Instructions   **225**

```
              MOV   CL,03H
              SHR   AL, CL
              JC    BIT2_ONE
              —     —              ; Next instruction if B2 of AL = 0
                    .
                    .
                    .
              —     —
BIT2_ONE:     —     —              ; Next instruction if B2 of AL = 1
                    .
                    .
                    .
              —     —
```

Notice that this implementation takes one extra instruction.

The Loop Program Structure—REPEAT-UNTIL and WHILE-DO

In many practical applications, we frequently need to repeat a part of the program many times. That is, a group of instructions may need to be executed over and over again until a condition is met. Before initiating the program sequence a parameter must be assigned to keep track of how many times the sequence of instructions has been repeated. This parameter is tested each time the sequence is performed to verify whether or not it is to be repeated again. For instance, to repeat a part of a program 10 times, we can begin by loading the count register CL with the value 10_{10}; execute the series of instructions; decrement the count in CL by 1; and after decrementing CL, test the zero flag to see if it has reached zero. If ZF is 0, which means that (CL) $\neq$ 0, program control is passed back to the first instruction of the sequence. This is repeated until CL becomes zero so that ZF tests as 1. This type of software structure is known as a *loop*.

Figure 5.13(a) shows a loop structure that is called *REPEAT-UNTIL*. Here we see that the sequence of instructions from label AGAIN to the conditional jump instruction Jcc represents the loop. Notice that the label for the instruction that is to be jumped to is located before the jump instruction that makes the conditional test. In this way, if the test result is false, program control returns to AGAIN and the segment of program repeats. This continues until the condition specified by "cc" is true. Before entering the loop the register that is to be used for the conditional test must be loaded with the appropriate count.

The instruction sequence in Fig. 5.13(b) implements a simple REPEAT-UN-TIL loop. Notice that first CL is initialized with the count value; therefore, the loop will repeat COUNT times. Then the operation performed by instructions 1 through n of the loop is performed. Next, the value in CL is decremented by 1 to indicate that the instructions in the loop are done and then ZF is tested with the JNZ instruction to determine if the value in CL has reached zero. If it has not, program control is returned to the instruction labeled AGAIN and the loop instruction sequence repeats. This continues until the value in CL reaches zero to identify that the loop is done. When this happens, the jump is not taken instead the instruction following JNZ AGAIN is executed.

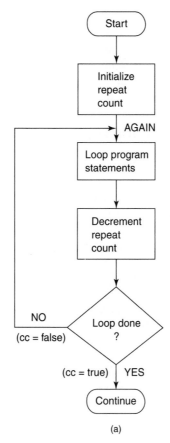

(a)

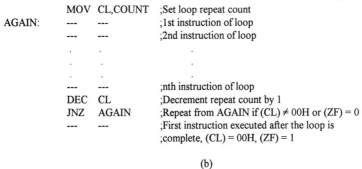

```
          MOV  CL,COUNT   ;Set loop repeat count
AGAIN:    ---  ---        ;1st instruction of loop
          ---  ---        ;2nd instruction of loop
           .    .              .
           .    .              .
           .    .              .
          ---  ---        ;nth instruction of loop
          DEC  CL         ;Decrement repeat count by 1
          JNZ  AGAIN      ;Repeat from AGAIN if (CL) ≠ 00H or (ZF) = 0
          ---  ---        ;First instruction executed after the loop is
                          ;complete, (CL) = 00H, (ZF) = 1
```

(b)

Figure 5.13 (a) REPEAT-UNTIL program sequence. (b) Typical REPEAT-UNTIL instruction sequence.

Another loop structure is shown in Fig. 5.14(a). It differs in that the conditional test that is used to decide whether or not the loop will repeat is made before entering the instruction sequence that is to be repeated. This sequence is known as a *WHILE-DO loop*. To implement this loop, we will need to use both a conditional and unconditional jump instruction. A typical WHILE-DO instruction sequence is shown in Fig. 5.14(b).

Applications Using the Loop and Branch Software Structures

As an application of the use of a conditional jump operation, let us write a program to move a block of N consecutive bytes of data starting at offset address BLK1ADDR to another block starting at offset address BLK2ADDR. We will assume that both blocks are in the same data segment, whose starting point is defined by the data segment value DATASEGADDR.

The steps to be implemented to solve this problem are outlined in the flowchart of Fig. 5.15(a). It has four basic operations. The first operation is initialization. Initialization involves establishing the initial address of the data segment. This is done by loading the DS register with the value DATASEGADDR. Furthermore, source index register SI and destination index register DI are initialized with offset addresses BLK1ADDR and BLK2ADDR, respectively. In this way, they point to the beginning of the source block and the beginning of the destination block, respectively. To keep track of the count, register CX is initialized with N, the number of bytes to be moved. This leads us to the following assembly language statements.

```
MOV   AX, DATASEGADDR
MOV   DS, AX
MOV   SI, BLK1ADDR
MOV   DI, BLK2ADDR
MOV   CX, N
```

Notice that DS cannot be directly loaded by immediate data with a MOV instruction. Therefore, the segment address was first loaded into AX and then moved to DS. SI, DI, and CX can be loaded directly with immediate data.

The next operation that must be performed is the actual movement of data from the source block of memory to the destination block. The offset addresses are already loaded into SI and DI; therefore, move instructions that employ indirect addressing can be used to accomplish the data transfer operation. Remember that the 8088 does not allow direct memory-to-memory moves. For this reason, AX will be used as an intermediate temporary storage location for data. The source byte is moved into AX with one instruction and then another instruction is needed to move it from AX to the destination location. Thus, the data move is accomplished by the following instructions.

```
NXTPT:    MOV  AH, [SI]
          MOV  [DI], AH
```

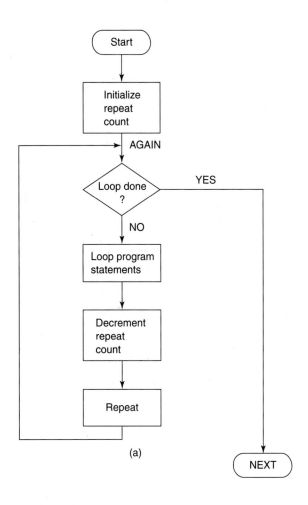

(a)

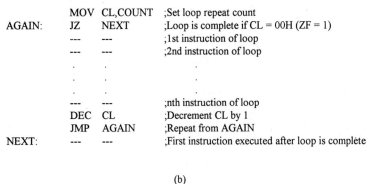

	MOV	CL,COUNT	;Set loop repeat count
AGAIN:	JZ	NEXT	;Loop is complete if CL = 00H (ZF = 1)
	---	---	;1st instruction of loop
	---	---	;2nd instruction of loop
	.	.	.
	.	.	.
	.	.	.
	---	---	;nth instruction of loop
	DEC	CL	;Decrement CL by 1
	JMP	AGAIN	;Repeat from AGAIN
NEXT:	---	---	;First instruction executed after loop is complete

(b)

Figure 5.14 (a) WHILE-DO program sequence. (b) Typical WHILE-DO instruction sequence.

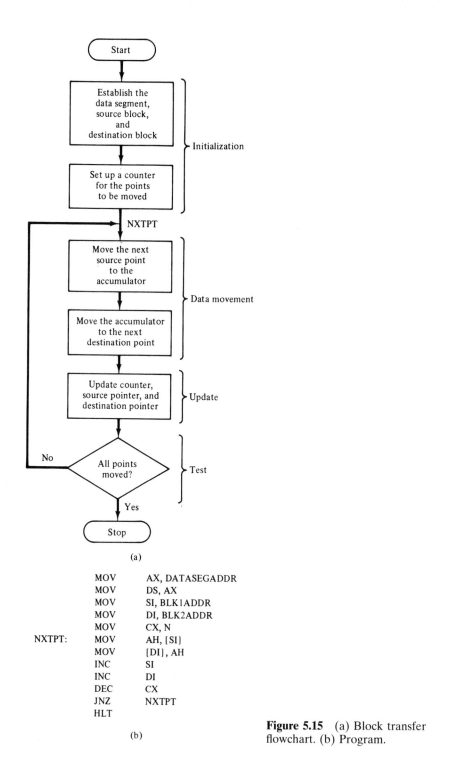

Figure 5.15 (a) Block transfer flowchart. (b) Program.

Notice that for a byte move only the higher eight bits of AX are used. Therefore, the operand is specified as AH instead of AX.

Now the pointers in SI and DI must be updated so that they are ready for the next byte move operation. Also, the counter must be decremented so that it corresponds to the number of bytes that remain to be moved. These updates can be done by the following sequence of instructions.

```
INC   SI
INC   DI
DEC   CX
```

The test operation involves determining whether or not all the data points have been moved. The contents of CX represent this condition. When its value is not 0, there still are points to be moved; whereas a value of 0 indicates that the block move is complete. This 0 condition is reflected by 1 in ZF. The instruction needed to perform this test is

```
JNZ   NXTPT
```

Here NXTPT is a label that corresponds to the first instruction in the data move operation. The last instruction in the program can be a *halt* (HLT) instruction to indicate the end of the block move operation. The entire program is shown in Fig. 5.15(b).

EXAMPLE 5.9

The following program

```
        CMP   AX, BX
        JC    DIFF2
DIFF1:  MOV   DX, AX
        SUB   DX, BX      ; (DX) = (AX) - (BX)
        JMP   DONE
DIFF2:  MOV   DX, BX
        SUB   DX, AX      ; (DX) = (BX) - (AX)
DONE:   —
```

implements an instruction sequence that calculates the absolute difference between the contents of AX and BX and places it in DX. Use the run module produced by assembling and linking the source program in Fig. 5.16(a) to verify the operation of the program for the two cases that follow:

(a) (AX) = 6, (BX) = 2

(b) (AX) = 2, (BX) = 6

Solution

The source program in Fig. 5.16(a) can be assembled with MASM and linked with LINK to produce a run module called EX59.EXE. The MASM and LINK programs will be discussed in Chapter 6. At this point, the only thing to note is that they are used to generate a run module that can be used in conjunction with the debug program. The source listing produced as part of the assembly process is shown in Fig. 5.16(b).

As shown in Fig. 5.16(c), the run module can be loaded as part of calling up the debug program by issuing the DOS command

```
C:\DOS> DEBUG A:EX59.EXE    (↵)
```

Next, the loading of the program is verified with the UNASSEMBLE command

```
-U 0 15   (↵)
```

Notice in Fig. 5.16(c) that the CMP instruction, which is the first instruction of the sequence that generates the absolute difference, is located at address 0D03:0005.

```
TITLE    EXAMPLE 5.9

         PAGE      ,132

STACK_SEG          SEGMENT          STACK 'STACK'
                   DB               64 DUP(?)
STACK_SEG          ENDS


CODE_SEG           SEGMENT          'CODE'
EX59     PROC      FAR
         ASSUME    CS:CODE_SEG, SS:STACK_SEG

;To return to DEBUG program put return address on the stack

         PUSH      DS
         MOV       AX, 0
         PUSH      AX

;Following code implements Example 5.9

         CMP       AX, BX
         JC        DIFF2
DIFF1:   MOV       DX, AX
         SUB       DX, BX          ; (DX) = (AX) - (BX)
         JMP       DONE
DIFF2:   MOV       DX, BX
         SUB       DX, AX          ; (DX) = (BX) - (AX)
DONE:    NOP

         RET                       ;Return to DEBUG program
EX59     ENDP

CODE_SEG           ENDS

         END       EX59
```

(a)

Figure 5.16(a) Source program for Example 5.9.

```
                    TITLE    EXAMPLE 5.9

                        PAGE       ,132

0000                              STACK_SEG       SEGMENT        STACK 'STACK'
0000     40 [                                     DB             64 DUP(?)
         ??
              ]

0040                              STACK_SEG       ENDS


0000                              CODE_SEG        SEGMENT        'CODE'
0000                              EX59    PROC    FAR
                                  ASSUME  CS:CODE_SEG, SS:STACK_SEG

              ;To return to DEBUG program put return address on the stack

0000     1E                               PUSH    DS
0001     B8 0000                          MOV     AX, 0
0004     50                               PUSH    AX

              ;Following code implements Example 5.9

0005     3B C3                            CMP     AX, BX
0007     72 07                            JC      DIFF2
0009     8B D0            DIFF1:          MOV     DX, AX
000B     2B D3                            SUB     DX, BX         ; (DX) = (AX) - (BX)
000D     EB 05 90                         JMP     DONE
0010     8B D3            DIFF2:          MOV     DX, BX
0012     2B D0                            SUB     DX, AX         ; (DX) = (BX) - (AX)
0014     90               DONE:           NOP

0015     CB                               RET                    ;Return to DEBUG program
0016                              EX59    ENDP

0016                              CODE_SEG        ENDS

                                  END     EX59
```

Segments and groups:

Name	Size	align	combine	class
CODE_SEG	0016	PARA	NONE	'CODE'
STACK_SEG.	0040	PARA	STACK	'STACK'

Symbols:

Name	Type	Value	Attr	
DIFF1.	L NEAR	0009	CODE_SEG	
DIFF2.	L NEAR	0010	CODE_SEG	
DONE	L NEAR	0014	CODE_SEG	
EX59	F PROC	0000	CODE_SEG	Length =0016

Warning Severe
Errors Errors
0   0

(b)

Figure 5.16(b)   Source listing produced by the assembler.

```
C:\DOS>DEBUG A:EX59.EXE
-U 0 15
0D03:0000 1E            PUSH    DS
0D03:0001 B80000        MOV     AX,0000
0D03:0004 50            PUSH    AX
0D03:0005 3BC3          CMP     AX,BX
0D03:0007 7207          JB      0010
0D03:0009 8BD0          MOV     DX,AX
0D03:000B 2BD3          SUB     DX,BX
0D03:000D EB05          JMP     0014
0D03:000F 90            NOP
0D03:0010 8BD3          MOV     DX,BX
0D03:0012 2BD0          SUB     DX,AX
0D03:0014 90            NOP
0D03:0015 CB            RETF
-G 5

AX=0000  BX=0000  CX=0016  DX=0000  SP=003C  BP=0000  SI=0000  DI=0000
DS=0DD6  ES=0DD6  SS=0DE8  CS=0D03  IP=0005   NV UP EI PL NZ NA PO NC
0D03:0005 3BC3          CMP     AX,BX
-R AX
AX 0000
:6
-R BX
BX 0000
:2
-T

AX=0006  BX=0002  CX=0016  DX=0000  SP=003C  BP=0000  SI=0000  DI=0000
DS=0DD6  ES=0DD6  SS=0DE8  CS=0D03  IP=0007   NV UP EI PL NZ NA PO NC
0D03:0007 7207          JB      0010
-G 14

AX=0006  BX=0002  CX=0016  DX=0004  SP=003C  BP=0000  SI=0000  DI=0000
DS=0DD6  ES=0DD6  SS=0DE8  CS=0D03  IP=0014   NV UP EI PL NZ NA PO NC
0D03:0014 90            NOP
-G

Program terminated normally
-R
AX=0006  BX=0002  CX=0016  DX=0004  SP=003C  BP=0000  SI=0000  DI=0000
DS=0DD6  ES=0DD6  SS=0DE8  CS=0D03  IP=0014   NV UP EI PL NZ NA PO NC
0D03:0014 90            NOP
-R IP
IP 0014
:0
-G 5

AX=0000  BX=0002  CX=0016  DX=0004  SP=0038  BP=0000  SI=0000  DI=0000
DS=0DD6  ES=0DD6  SS=0DE8  CS=0D03  IP=0005   NV UP EI PL NZ NA PO NC
0D03:0005 3BC3          CMP     AX,BX
-R AX
AX 0000
:2
-R BX
BX 0002
:6
-T

AX=0002  BX=0006  CX=0016  DX=0004  SP=0038  BP=0000  SI=0000  DI=0000
DS=0DD6  ES=0DD6  SS=0DE8  CS=0D03  IP=0007   NV UP EI NG NZ AC PE CY
```

Figure 5.16(c)   Executing the program with DEBUG.

```
0D03:0007 7207          JB      0010
-G 14

AX=0002  BX=0006  CX=0016  DX=0004  SP=0038  BP=0000  SI=0000  DI=0000
DS=0DD6  ES=0DD6  SS=0DE8  CS=0D03  IP=0014   NV UP EI PL NZ NA PO NC
0D03:0014 90            NOP
-G

Program terminated NORMALLY
-Q

C:\DOS>
```

Figure 5.16(c)   (Continued)

Let us execute down to this statement with the GO command

$$-G \ 5 \quad (\hookleftarrow)$$

Now we will load AX and BX with the case (a) data. This is done with the R commands

```
—R AX        (↵)
AX 0000
:6           (↵)
—R BX        (↵)
BX 0000
:2           (↵)
```

Next, we execute the compare instruction with the command

$$-T \quad (\hookleftarrow)$$

Note in the trace information display in Fig. 5.16(c) that the carry flag is reset (NC). Therefore, no jump will take place when the JB instruction is executed.

The rest of the program can be executed by inputting the command

$$-G \ 14 \quad (\hookleftarrow)$$

From Fig. 5.16(c), we find that DX contains 4. This result was produced by executing the SUB instruction at 0D03:000B. Before executing the program for the (b) set of data, the command

$$-G \quad (\hookleftarrow)$$

is issued. This command causes the program to terminate normally.

The R command shows that the value in IP must be reset and then we can execute down to the CMP instruction. This is done with the commands

```
-R IP       (↵)
IP 0014
:0          (↵)
```

and

```
-G 5        (↵)
```

Notice in Fig. 5.16(c) that IP again contains 0005_{16} and points to the CMP instruction. Next, the data for case (b) are loaded with R commands. This gives

```
-R AX       (↵)
AX 0000
:2          (↵)
-R BX       (↵)
BX 0002
:6          (↵)
```

Now a T command is used to execute the CMP instruction. Notice that CY is set this time. Therefore, control is passed to the instruction at 0D03:0010.

A GO command is now used to execute down to the instruction at 0D03:0014. This command is

```
-G 14   (↵)
```

Notice that DX again contains 4; however, this time it was calculated with the SUB instruction at 0D03:0012.

▲ 5.5 SUBROUTINES AND SUBROUTINE-HANDLING INSTRUCTIONS

A *subroutine* is a special segment of program that can be called for execution from any point in a program. Figure 5.17(a) illustrates the concept of a subroutine. Here we see a program structure where one part of the program is called the *main program*. In addition to this, we find a segment attached to the main program, known as a subroutine. The subroutine is written to provide a function that must be performed at various points in the main program. Instead of including this piece of code in the main program each time the function is needed, it is put into the program just once as a subroutine. A subroutine is also known as a *procedure*.

Wherever the function must be performed, a single instruction is inserted into the main body of the program to "call" the subroutine. Remember that the physical

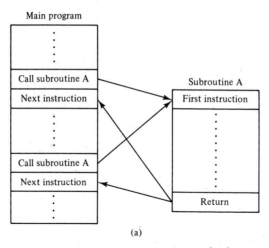

Main program

Call subroutine A

Next instruction

Call subroutine A

Next instruction

Subroutine A

First instruction

Return

(a)

Mnemonic	Meaning	Format	Operation	Flags Affected
CALL	Subroutine call	CALL operand	Execution continues from the address of the subroutine specified by the operand. Information required to return back to the main program such as IP and CS are saved on the stack.	None

(b)

Operand
Near-proc
Far-proc
Memptr16
Regptr16
Memptr32

(c)

Figure 5.17 (a) Subroutine concept. (b) Subroutine call instruction. (c) Allowed operands.

address CS:IP identifies the next instruction to be fetched for execution. Thus, to branch to a subroutine that starts elsewhere in memory, the value in either IP or CS and IP must be modified. After executing the subroutine, we want to return control to the instruction that follows the one that called the subroutine. In this way, program execution resumes in the main program at the point where it left off due to the subroutine call. A return instruction must be included at the end of the subroutine to initiate the *return sequence* to the main program environment.

The instructions provided to transfer control from the main program to a subroutine and return control back to the main program are called *subroutine-handling instructions*. Let us now examine the instructions provided for this purpose.

CALL and RET Instructions

There are two basic instructions in the instruction set of the 8088 for subroutine handling. They are the *call* (CALL) and *return* (RET) instructions. Together they provide the mechanism for calling a subroutine into operation and returning control back to the main program at its completion. We will first discuss these two instructions and later introduce other instructions that can be used in conjunction with subroutines.

Just like the JMP instruction, CALL allows implementation of two types of operations, the *intrasegment call* and the *intersegment call*. The CALL instruction is shown in Fig. 5.17(b), and its allowed operand variations are shown in Fig. 5.17(c).

It is the operand that initiates either an intersegment or an intrasegment call. The operands Near-proc, Memptr16, and Regptr16 all specify intrasegment calls to a subroutine. In all three cases, execution of the instruction causes the contents of IP to be saved on the stack. Then the stack pointer (SP) is decremented by two. This is the push operation that was introduced in the section covering the stack in Chapter 2. The saved values of IP is the offset address of the instruction that follows the CALL instruction. After saving this return address, a new 16-bit value, which is specified by the instruction's operand and corresponds to the storage location of the first instruction in the subroutine, is loaded into IP.

The types of operands represent different ways of specifying a new value of IP. Using a Near-proc operand, a subroutine located in the same code segment can be called. An example is

```
CALL 1234H
```

Here 1234H identifies the starting address of the subroutine. It is encoded as the difference between 1234H and the updated value of IP. That is, the IP for the instruction following the CALL instruction.

The Memptr16 and Regptr16 operands provide indirect subroutine addressing by specifying a memory location or an internal register, respectively, as the source of a new value for IP. The value specified is the actual offset that is loaded into IP. An example of a Regptr16 operand is

```
CALL BX
```

When this instruction is executed, the contents of BX are loaded into IP and execution continues with the subroutine starting at a physical address derived from the current CS and the new value of IP.

By using various addressing modes of the 8088, an operand that resides in memory can be used as the call to offset address. This represents a Memptr16 type of operand. For instance, the instruction

```
CALL [BX]
```

has its subroutine offset address at the memory location whose physical address is derived from the contents of DS and BX. The value stored at this memory location is loaded into IP. Again the current contents of CS and the new value in IP point to the first instruction of the subroutine.

Notice that in both intrasegment call examples the subroutine was located within the same code segment as the call instruction. The other type of CALL instruction, the intersegment call, permits the subroutine to reside in another code segment. It corresponds to the Far-proc and Memptr32 operands. These operands specify both a new offset address for IP and a new segment address for CS. In both cases, execution of the call instruction causes the contents of the CS and IP registers to be saved on the stack and then new values are loaded into IP and CS. The saved values of CS and IP permit return to the main program from a different code segment.

Far-proc represents a 32-bit immediate operand that is stored in the four bytes that follow the opcode of the call instruction in program memory. These two words are loaded directly from code segment memory into IP and CS with execution of the CALL instruction.

On the other hand, when the operand is Memptr32, the pointer for the subroutine is stored as four consecutive bytes in data memory. The location of the first byte of the pointer can be specified indirectly by one of the 8088's memory addressing modes. An example is

```
CALL DWORD PTR [DI]
```

Here the physical address of the first byte of the 4-byte pointer in memory is derived from the contents of DS and DI.

Every subroutine must end by executing an instruction that returns control to the main program. This is the return (RET) instruction. It is described in Fig. 5.18(a) and (b). Notice that its execution causes the value of IP or both the values of IP and CS that were saved on the stack to be returned back to their corresponding registers and the stack pointer to be adjusted appropriately. This is the pop operation that was discussed in Chapter 2. In general, an intrasegment return results from an intrasegment call and an intersegment return results from an intersegment call. In this way, program control is returned to the instruction that follows the call instruction in program memory.

There is an additional option with the return instruction. It is a 2-byte constant that can be included with the return instruction. This constant gets added to the stack pointer after restoring the return address. The purpose of this stack pointer displacement is to provide a simple means by which the *parameters* that were saved on the stack before the call to the subroutine was initiated can be discarded. For instance, the instruction

```
RET 2
```

when executed adds 2 to SP. This discards one word parameter as part of the return sequence.

Mnemonic	Meaning	Format	Operation	Flags Affected
RET	Return	RET or RET Operand	Return to the main program by restoring IP (and CS for fat-proc). If Operand is present, it is added to the contents of SP.	None

(a)

Operand
None
Disp16

(b)

Figure 5.18 (a) Return instruction. (b) Allowed operands.

EXAMPLE 5.10

The source program in Fig. 5.19(a) can be used to demonstrate the use of the call and return instructions to implement a subroutine. This program was assembled

```
TITLE    EXAMPLE 5.10

        PAGE      ,132

STACK_SEG         SEGMENT        STACK 'STACK'
                  DB             64 DUP(?)
STACK_SEG         ENDS


CODE_SEG          SEGMENT        'CODE'
EX510   PROC      FAR
        ASSUME    CS:CODE_SEG, SS:STACK_SEG

;To return to DEBUG program put return address on the stack

        PUSH      DS
        MOV       AX, 0
        PUSH      AX

;Following code implements Example 5.10

        CALL      SUM
        RET

SUM     PROC      NEAR
        MOV       DX, AX
        ADD       DX, BX         ; (DX) = (AX) + (BX)
        RET
SUM     ENDP

EX510 ENDP
CODE_SEG          ENDS

        END       EX510
```

Figure 5.19(a) Source program for Example 5.10.

```
                    TITLE   EXAMPLE 5.10

                      PAGE      ,132

  0000                          STACK_SEG      SEGMENT        STACK 'STACK'
  0000    40 [                                 DB             64 DUP(?)
            ??
                 ]

  0040                          STACK_SEG      ENDS


  0000                          CODE_SEG       SEGMENT        'CODE'
  0000                          EX510   PROC   FAR
                                  ASSUME  CS:CODE_SEG, SS:STACK_SEG

                      ;To return to DEBUG program put return address on the stack

  0000    1E                             PUSH    DS
  0001    B8 0000                        MOV     AX, 0
  0004    50                             PUSH    AX

                      ;Following code implements Example 5.10

  0005    E8 0009 R                      CALL    SUM
  0008    CB                             RET

  0009                          SUM      PROC    NEAR
  0009    8B D0                          MOV     DX, AX
  000B    03 D3                          ADD     DX, BX          ; (DX) = (AX) + (BX)
  000D    C3                             RET
  000E                          SUM      ENDP

  000E                          EX510    ENDP
  000E                          CODE_SEG       ENDS

                                   END    EX510

  Segments and groups:

              N a m e                 Size    align   combine class

  CODE_SEG . . . . . . . . . . . .    000E    PARA    NONE    'CODE'
  STACK_SEG. . . . . . . . . . . .    0040    PARA    STACK   'STACK'

  Symbols:

              N a m e                 Type    Value   Attr

  EX510. . . . . . . . . . . . . .    F PROC  0000    CODE_SEG    Length =000E
  SUM. . . . . . . . . . . . . . .    N PROC  0009    CODE_SEG    Length =0005

  Warning Severe
  Errors  Errors
  0       0
```

Figure 5.19(b)   Source listing produced by assembler.

and linked on the IBM PC to produce a run module in file EX510.EXE. Its source listing is provided for reference in Fig. 5.19(b). Trace the operation of the program by executing it with DEBUG for data (AX) = 2 and (BX) = 4.

Solution

We begin by calling up DEBUG and loading the program with the DOS command

C:\DOS>DEBUG A:EX510.EXE   (↵)

```
C:\DOS>DEBUG A:EX510.EXE
-U 0 D
0D03:0000 1E              PUSH     DS
0D03:0001 B80000          MOV      AX,0000
0D03:0004 50              PUSH     AX
0D03:0005 E80100          CALL     0009
0D03:0008 CB              RETF
0D03:0009 8BD0            MOV      DX,AX
0D03:000B 03D3            ADD      DX,BX
0D03:000D C3              RET
-G 5

AX=0000  BX=0000  CX=000E  DX=0000  SP=003C  BP=0000  SI=0000  DI=0000
DS=0F41  ES=0F41  SS=0F52  CS=0D03  IP=0005   NV UP EI PL NZ NA PO NC
0D03:0005 E80100          CALL     0009
-R AX
AX 0000
:2
-R BX
BX 0000
:4
-T

AX=0002  BX=0004  CX=000E  DX=0000  SP=003A  BP=0000  SI=0000  DI=0000
DS=0F41  ES=0F41  SS=0F52  CS=0D03  IP=0009   NV UP EI PL NZ NA PO NC
0D03:0009 8BD0            MOV      DX,AX
-D SS:3A 3B
0F52:0030                                   08 00                          . .
-T

AX=0002  BX=0004  CX=000E  DX=0002  SP=003A  BP=0000  SI=0000  DI=0000
DS=0F41  ES=0F41  SS=0F52  CS=0D03  IP=000B   NV UP EI PL NZ NA PO NC
0D03:000B 03D3            ADD      DX,BX
-T

AX=0002  BX=0004  CX=000E  DX=0006  SP=003A  BP=0000  SI=0000  DI=0000
DS=0F41  ES=0F41  SS=0F52  CS=0D03  IP=000D   NV UP EI PL NZ NA PE NC
0D03:000D C3              RET
-T

AX=0002  BX=0004  CX=000E  DX=0006  SP=003C  BP=0000  SI=0000  DI=0000
DS=0F41  ES=0F41  SS=0F52  CS=0D03  IP=0008   NV UP EI PL NZ NA PE NC
0D03:0008 CB              RETF
-G

Program terminated normally
-Q

C:\DOS>
```

Figure 5.19(c)   Executing the program with DEBUG.

The loading of the program is now verified with the UNASSEMBLE command

$$-U \quad 0 \quad D \quad (\downarrow)$$

Looking at Fig. 5.19(c), we see that the program was correctly loaded. Moreover, we find that the CALL instruction is located at offset 0005_{16} of the current code segment. The command

$$-G \quad 5 \quad (\downarrow)$$

executes the program down to the CALL instruction. The state information displayed in Fig. 5.19(c) shows that (CS) = $0D03_{16}$, (IP) = 0005_{16}, and (SP) = $003C_{16}$.

Now let us load the AX and BX registers with R commands.

```
                    −R AX        (↵)
                    AX 0000
                    :2           (↵)
                    −R BX        (↵)
                    BX 0000
                    :4           (↵)
```

Next, the CALL instruction is executed with the T command

$$−T \quad (↵)$$

and, looking at the displayed state information in Fig. 5.19(c), we find that CS still contains $0D03_{16}$, IP has been loaded with 0009_{16}, and SP has been decremented to $003A_{16}$. This information tells us that the next instruction to be executed is the move instruction at address 0D03:0009, and a word of data has been pushed to the stack.

Before executing another instruction, let us look at what got pushed onto the stack. This is done by issuing the memory dump command

$$−D \ SS:3A \ 3B \quad (↵)$$

Note from Fig. 5.19(c) that the value 0008_{16} has been pushed onto the stack. This is the address offset of the RETF instruction that follows the CALL instruction and is the address of the instruction to which control is to be returned at the completion of the subroutine.

Two more T commands are used to execute the move and add instructions of the subroutine. From the state information displayed in Fig. 5.19(c), we see that their execution causes the value 2_{16} in AX to be copied into DX and then the value 4_{16} in BX to be added to the value in DX. This results in the value 6_{16} in DX.

Now the RET instruction is executed by issuing another T command. In Fig. 5.19(c), we see that execution of this instruction causes the value 0008_{16} to be popped off the stack and put back into the IP register. Therefore, the next instruction to be executed is the one located at address 0D03:0008; this is the RETF instruction. Moreover, notice that, as the word is popped from the stack back into IP, the value in SP is incremented by two. After this, the program is run to completion by issuing a GO command.

PUSH and POP Instructions

After the context switch to a subroutine, we find that it is usually necessary to save the contents of certain registers or some other main program parameters. These values are saved by pushing them onto the stack. Typically, these data

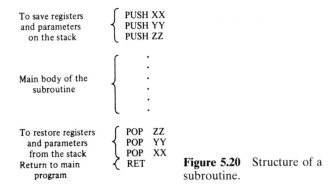

To save registers and parameters on the stack	{	PUSH XX PUSH YY PUSH ZZ
To restore registers and parameters from the stack	{	POP ZZ POP YY POP XX
Return to main program	{	RET

Figure 5.20 Structure of a subroutine.

correspond to registers and memory locations that are used by the subroutine. In this way, their original contents are kept intact in the stack segment of memory during the execution of the subroutine. Before a return to the main program takes place, the saved registers and main program parameters are restored. This is done by popping the saved values from the stack back into their original locations. Thus a typical structure of a subroutine is that shown in Fig. 5.20.

The instruction that is used to save parameters on the stack is the *push* (PUSH) instruction and that used to retrieve them back is the *pop* (POP) instruction. Notice in Fig. 5.21(a) and (b) that the standard PUSH and POP instructions can be written with a general-purpose register, a segment register (excluding CS), or a storage location in memory as their operand.

Execution of a PUSH instruction causes the data corresponding to the operand to be pushed onto the top of the stack. For instance, if the instruction is

PUSH AX

Mnemonic	Meaning	Format	Operation	Flags Affected
PUSH	Push word onto stack	PUSH S	$((SP)) \leftarrow (S)$ $(SP) \leftarrow (SP)-2$	None
POP	Pop word off stack	POP D	$(D) \leftarrow ((SP))$ $(SP) \leftarrow (SP)+2$	None

(a)

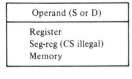

Operand (S or D)
Register Seg-reg (CS illegal) Memory

(b)

Figure 5.21 (a) PUSH and POP instructions. (b) Allowed operands.

the result is as follows:

$$((SP) - 1) \leftarrow (AH)$$
$$((SP) - 2) \leftarrow (AL)$$
$$(SP) \leftarrow (SP) - 2$$

This shows that the two bytes of AX are saved in the stack part of memory and the stack pointer is decremented by two so that it points to the new top of the stack.
On the other hand, if the instruction is

```
POP AX
```

its execution results in

$$(AL) \leftarrow ((SP))$$
$$(AH) \leftarrow ((SP)) + 1$$
$$(SP) \leftarrow (SP) + 2$$

In this manner, the saved contents of AX are restored back into the register.

EXAMPLE 5.11

Write a procedure named SQUARE that squares the contents of BL and places the result in BX. Assume that this procedure is called from another procedure in the same code segment.

Solution

The beginning of the procedure is defined with the pseudo-op statement

```
SQUARE PROC NEAR
```

To square the number in BL, we can use the 8-bit signed multiply instruction, IMUL. This instruction requires the use of register AX for its operation. Therefore, at entry of the procedure, we must save the value currently held in AX. This is done by pushing its contents to the stack with the instruction

```
PUSH AX
```

Now we load AX with the contents of BL using the instruction

```
MOV AL,BL
```

To square the contents of AL, we use the instruction

```
IMUL BL
```

which multiplies the contents of AL with the contents of BL and places the result in AX. The result is the square of the original contents of BL. To place the result in BX, we use the instruction

```
MOV BX,AX
```

This completes the square operation; but before we return to the main part of the program, the original contents of AX that were saved on the stack are restored with the pop instruction

```
POP AX
```

Then a return instruction is used to pass control back to the main program.

```
RET
```

The procedure must be terminated with the end procedure pseudo-op statement that follows:

```
SQUARE ENDP
```

The complete instruction sequence is shown in Fig. 5.22.

```
;Subroutine:   SQUARE
;Description:   (BX) = square of (BL)

SQUARE PROC   NEAR
       PUSH AX          ;Save the register to be used
       MOV  AL,BL       ;Place the number in AL
       IMUL BL          ;Multiply with itself
       MOV  BX,AX       ;Save the result
       POP   AX         ;Restore the register used
       RET
SQUARE ENDP
```

Figure 5.22 Program for Example 5.11.

EXAMPLE 5.12

A source program that can be used to demonstrate execution of the procedure written in Example 5.11 is shown in Fig. 5.23(a). The source listing produced when this program was assembled is given in Fig. 5.23(b), and the run module produced when it was linked is stored in file EX512.EXE. Use the DEBUG program to load this run module and verify its operation by executing it on the IBM PC.

```
TITLE    EXAMPLE 5.12

         PAGE    ,132

STACK_SEG        SEGMENT         STACK 'STACK'
                 DB              64 DUP(?)
STACK_SEG        ENDS


DATA_SEG         SEGMENT
TOTAL            DW              1234H
DATA_SEG         ENDS


CODE_SEG         SEGMENT         'CODE'
EX512   PROC     FAR
                 ASSUME  CS:CODE_SEG, SS:STACK_SEG, DS:DATA_SEG

;To return to DEBUG program put return address on the stack

         PUSH    DS
         MOV     AX, 0
         PUSH    AX

;Setup the data segment

         MOV     AX, DATA_SEG
         MOV     DS, AX

;Following code implements Example 5.12

         MOV     BL,12H          ;BL contents = the number to be squared
         CALL    SQUARE          ;Call the procedure to square BL contents
         RET                     ;Return to DEBUG program
EX512   ENDP

;Subroutine:     SQUARE
;Description:    (BX) = square of (BL)

SQUARE  PROC     NEAR
         PUSH    AX              ;Save the register to be used
         MOV     AL,BL           ;Place the number in AL
         IMUL    BL              ;Multiply with itself
         MOV     BX,AX           ;Save the result
         POP     AX              ;Restore the register used
         RET
SQUARE  ENDP

CODE_SEG         ENDS

         END     EX512
```

Figure 5.23(a)   Source program for Example 5.12.

Solution

The DEBUG program and run module can be loaded with the command

$$C:\DOS>DEBUG\ A:EX512.EXE\quad (\hookleftarrow)$$

After loading is completed, the instructions of the program are unassembled with the command

$$-U\ 0\ 18\quad (\hookleftarrow)$$

The displayed information in Fig. 5.23(c) shows that the program did load correctly.

```
                    TITLE    EXAMPLE 5.12

                        PAGE      ,132

0000                               STACK_SEG        SEGMENT        STACK 'STACK'
0000    0040[                      DB               64 DUP(?)
          ??
                      ]

0040                               STACK_SEG        ENDS


0000                               DATA_SEG         SEGMENT
0000    1234                       TOTAL            DW             1234H
0002                               DATA_SEG         ENDS


0000                               CODE_SEG         SEGMENT        'CODE'
0000                               EX512    PROC    FAR
                                       ASSUME  CS:CODE_SEG, SS:STACK_SEG, DS:DATA_SEG

                    ;To return to DEBUG program put return address on the stack

0000    1E                                  PUSH     DS
0001    B8 0000                             MOV      AX, 0
0004    50                                  PUSH     AX

                    ;Setup the data segment

0005    B8 ---- R                           MOV      AX, DATA_SEG
0008    8E D8                               MOV      DS, AX

                    ;Following code implements Example 5.12

000A    B3 12                               MOV      BL,12H            ;BL contents = the number
to be squared
000C    E8 0010 R                           CALL     SQUARE            ;Call the procedure to
square BL contents
000F    CB                                  RET                        ;Return to DEBUG program
0010                               EX512    ENDP

                    ;Subroutine:      SQUARE
                    ;Description:      (BX) = square of (BL)

0010                               SQUARE   PROC    NEAR
0010    50                                  PUSH     AX                ;Save the register to be
used
0011    8A C3                               MOV      AL,BL             ;Place the number in AL
0013    F6 EB                               IMUL     BL                ;Multiply with itself
0015    8B D8                               MOV      BX,AX             ;Save the result
0017    58                                  POP      AX                ;Restore the register used
0018    C3                                  RET
0019                               SQUARE   ENDP

0019                               CODE_SEG         ENDS


                        END      EX512
```

Figure 5.23(b) Source listing produced by the assembler.

From the instruction sequence in Fig. 5.23(c), we find that the part of the program whose operation we are interested in observing starts with the CALL instruction at address 0DEC:000C. Now we execute down to this point in the program with the GO command

$$-G \quad C \quad (\dashv)$$

Notice that BL contains the number 12H that will be squared by the subroutine.

```
Segments and Groups:

                N a m e                      Length   Align   Combine Class

CODE_SEG . . . . . . . . . . . . . .           0019    PARA    NONE    'CODE'
DATA_SEG . . . . . . . . . . . .               0002    PARA    NONE
STACK_SEG  . . . . . . . . . . .               0040    PARA    STACK   'STACK'

Symbols:

                N a m e                      Type    Value   Attr

EX512  . . . . . . . . . . . . .             F PROC  0000    CODE_SEG      Length = 0010
SQUARE . . . . . . . . . . . . .             N PROC  0010    CODE_SEG      Length = 0009

TOTAL  . . . . . . . . . . . . .             L WORD  0000    DATA_SEG

@CPU . . . . . . . . . . . . .               TEXT    0101h
@FILENAME  . . . . . . . . . . .             TEXT    EX512
@VERSION . . . . . . . . . . .               TEXT    510


    53 Source  Lines
    53 Total   Lines
    13 Symbols

 48016 + 440523 Bytes symbol space free

     0 Warning Errors
     0 Severe  Errors
```

Figure 5.23(b)   (Continued)

Now the call instruction is executed with the command

$$-\text{T}\quad(\hookleftarrow)$$

Notice from the displayed information for this command in Fig. 5.23(c) that the value held in IP has been changed to 0010_{16}. Therefore, control has been passed to address 0DEC:0010, which is the first instruction of procedure SQUARE. Moreover, note that stack pointer (SP) has been decremented to the value $003A_{16}$. The new top of the stack is at address 0DE7:003A. The word held at the top of the stack can be examined with the command

$$-\text{D SS:3A 3B}\quad(\hookleftarrow)$$

Notice in Fig. 5.23(c) that its value is $000F_{16}$. From the instruction sequence in Fig. 5.23(c), we see that this is the address of the RETF instruction. This is the instruction to which control is to be returned at the completion of the procedure.

Next, the PUSH AX instruction is executed with the command

$$-\text{T}\quad(\hookleftarrow)$$

and again, looking at the displayed state information, we find that SP has been decremented to the value 0038_{16}. Displaying the word at the top of the stack with

```
C:\DOS>DEBUG A:EX512.EXE
-U 0 18
0DEC:0000 1E          PUSH    DS
0DEC:0001 B80000      MOV     AX,0000
0DEC:0004 50          PUSH    AX
0DEC:0005 B8EB0D      MOV     AX,0DEB
0DEC:0008 8ED8        MOV     DS,AX
0DEC:000A B312        MOV     BL,12
0DEC:000C E80100      CALL    0010
0DEC:000F CB          RETF
0DEC:0010 50          PUSH    AX
0DEC:0011 8AC3        MOV     AL,BL
0DEC:0013 F6EB        IMUL    BL
0DEC:0015 8BD8        MOV     BX,AX
0DEC:0017 58          POP     AX
0DEC:0018 C3          RET
-G C

AX=0DEB  BX=0012  CX=0069  DX=0000  SP=003C  BP=0000  SI=0000  DI=0000
DS=0DEB  ES=0DD7  SS=0DE7  CS=0DEC  IP=000C   NV UP EI PL NZ NA PO NC
0DEC:000C E80100      CALL    0010
-T

AX=0DEB  BX=0012  CX=0069  DX=0000  SP=003A  BP=0000  SI=0000  DI=0000
DS=0DEB  ES=0DD7  SS=0DE7  CS=0DEC  IP=0010   NV UP EI PL NZ NA PO NC
0DEC:0010 50          PUSH    AX
-D SS:3A 3B
0DE7:0030                              0F 00                          ..
-T

AX=0DEB  BX=0012  CX=0069  DX=0000  SP=0038  BP=0000  SI=0000  DI=0000
DS=0DEB  ES=0DD7  SS=0DE7  CS=0DEC  IP=0011   NV UP EI PL NZ NA PO NC
0DEC:0011 8AC3        MOV     AL,BL
-D SS:38 39
0DE7:0030                           EB 0D                              ..
-G 17

AX=0144  BX=0144  CX=0069  DX=0000  SP=0038  BP=0000  SI=0000  DI=0000
DS=0DEB  ES=0DD7  SS=0DE7  CS=0DEC  IP=0017   OV UP EI PL NZ NA PE CY
0DEC:0017 58          POP     AX
-T

AX=0DEB  BX=0144  CX=0069  DX=0000  SP=003A  BP=0000  SI=0000  DI=0000
DS=0DEB  ES=0DD7  SS=0DE7  CS=0DEC  IP=0018   OV UP EI PL NZ NA PE CY
0DEC:0018 C3          RET
-T

AX=0DEB  BX=0144  CX=0069  DX=0000  SP=003C  BP=0000  SI=0000  DI=0000
DS=0DEB  ES=0DD7  SS=0DE7  CS=0DEC  IP=000F   OV UP EI PL NZ NA PE CY
0DEC:000F CB          RETF
-G

Program terminated normally
-Q

C:\DOS>
```

Figure 5.23(c)   Executing the program with DEBUG.

the command

$$-D \quad SS:38 \quad 39 \quad (\lrcorner)$$

we find that it is the same as the contents of AX. This confirms that the original contents of AX are saved on the stack.

Now we execute down to the POP AX instruction with the command

$$-G \quad 17 \quad (\lrcorner)$$

Looking at the displayed state information in Fig. 5.23(c), we find that the square of the contents of BL has been formed in BX.

Next, the pop instruction is executed with the command

$$-\text{T} \quad (\hookleftarrow)$$

and the displayed information shows that the original contents of AX have been popped off the stack and put back into AX. Moreover, the value in SP has been incremented to $003A_{16}$ so that once again the return address is at the top of the stack.

Finally, the RET instruction is executed with the command

$$-\text{T} \quad (\hookleftarrow)$$

As shown in Fig. 5.23(c), this causes the value 0010_{16} to be popped from the top of the stack back into IP. Therefore, IP now equals $000F_{16}$. In this way, we see that control has been returned to the instruction at address 0DEC:000F of the main program.

At times, we also want to save the contents of the flag register and if saved we will later have to restore them. These operations can be accomplished with *push flags* (PUSHF) and *pop flags* (POPF) instructions, respectively. These instructions are shown in Fig. 5.24. Notice that PUSHF saves the contents of the flag register on the top of the stack. On the other hand, POPF returns the flags from the top of the stack to the flag register.

▲ 5.6 THE LOOP AND THE LOOP-HANDLING INSTRUCTIONS

The 8088 microprocessor has three instructions specifically designed for implementing *loop operations*. These instructions can be used in place of certain conditional jump instructions and give the programmer a simpler way of writing loop sequences. The loop instructions are listed in Fig. 5.25.

The first instruction, *loop* (LOOP), works with respect to the contents of the CX register. CX must be preloaded with a count representing the number of times the loop is to be repeated. Whenever LOOP is executed, the contents of CX are first decremented by one and then checked to determine if they are equal to zero. If they are equal to zero, the loop is complete and the instruction following LOOP

Mnemonic	Meaning	Operation	Flags Affected
PUSHF	Push flags onto stack	((SP)) ← (Flags) (SP) ← (SP)-2	None
POPF	Pop flags from stack	(Flags) ← ((SP)) (SP) ← (SP)+2	OF, DF, IF, TF, SF, ZF, AF, PF, CF

Figure 5.24 Push flags and pop flags instructions.

Mnemonic	Meaning	Format	Operation
LOOP	Loop	LOOP Short-label	$(CX) \leftarrow (CX) - 1$ Jump is initiated to location defined by short-label if $(CX) \neq 0$; otherwise, execute next sequential instruction
LOOPE/LOOPZ	Loop while equal/ loop while zero	LOOPE/LOOPZ Short-label	$(CX) \leftarrow (CX) - 1$ Jump to location defined by short-label if $(CX) \neq 0$ and $(ZF) = 1$; otherwise, execute next sequential instruction
LOOPNE/ LOOPNZ	Loop while not equal/ loop while not zero	LOOPNE/LOOPNZ Short-label	$(CX) \leftarrow (CX) - 1$ Jump to location defined by short-label if $(CX) \neq 0$ and $(ZF) = 0$; otherwise, execute next sequential instruction

Figure 5.25 Loop instructions.

is executed; otherwise, control is returned to the instruction at the label specified in the loop instruction. In this way, we see that LOOP is a single instruction that functions the same as a decrement CX instruction followed by a JNZ instruction.

For example, the LOOP instruction sequence shown in Fig. 5.26(a) will cause the part of the program from the label NEXT through the instruction LOOP to be repeated a number of times equal to the value stored in CX. For example, if CX contains $000A_{16}$, the sequence of instructions included in the loop is executed 10 times.

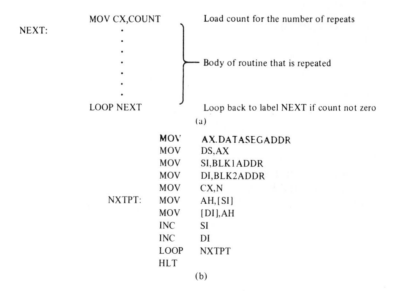

Figure 5.26 (a) Typical loop routine structure. (b) Block move program employing the LOOP instruction.

Figure 5.26(b) shows a practical implementation of a loop. Here we find the block move program that was developed in Section 5.4 is rewritten using the LOOP instruction. Comparing this program with the one in Fig. 5.15(b), we see that the instruction LOOP NXTPT has replaced both the DEC and JNZ instructions.

EXAMPLE 5.13

The source program in Fig. 5.27(a) demonstrates the use of the LOOP instruction to implement a software loop operation. This program was assembled by the macro-assembler on the IBM PC and linked to produce a run module called EX513.EXE. The source listing is shown in Fig. 5.27(b). Observe the operation of the loop by executing the program using DEBUG.

Solution

Looking at Fig. 5.27(c), we see that the run module is loaded with the DOS command

```
C:\DOS>DEBUG A:EX513.EXE   (⏎)
```

Now the loading of the program is verified by unassembling it with the command

```
–U 0 F   (⏎)
```

By comparing the instruction sequence displayed in Fig. 5.27(c) with the listing in Fig. 5.27(b), we find that the program has loaded correctly.

```
TITLE     EXAMPLE 5.13

        PAGE     ,132

STACK_SEG        SEGMENT        STACK 'STACK'
                 DB             64 DUP(?)
STACK_SEG        ENDS


CODE_SEG         SEGMENT        'CODE'
EX513   PROC     FAR
        ASSUME   CS:CODE_SEG, SS:STACK_SEG

;To return to DEBUG program put return address on the stack

        PUSH     DS
        MOV      AX, 0
        PUSH     AX

;Following code implements Example 5.13

        MOV      CX, 5H
        MOV      DX, 0H
AGAIN:  NOP
        INC      DX
        LOOP     AGAIN

        RET                      ;Return to DEBUG program
EX513   ENDP
CODE_SEG         ENDS

        END      EX513
```

Figure 5.27(a)   Source program for Example 5.13.

```
                              PAGE    ,132

0000                              STACK_SEG      SEGMENT         STACK 'STACK'
0000      40 [                                   DB              64 DUP(?)
          ??
             ]

0040                              STACK_SEG      ENDS


0000                              CODE_SEG       SEGMENT         'CODE'
0000          EX513    PROC       FAR
                                  ASSUME  CS:CODE_SEG, SS:STACK_SEG

              ;To return to DEBUG program put return address on the stack

0000  1E                          PUSH    DS
0001  B8 0000                     MOV     AX, 0
0004  50                          PUSH    AX

              ;Following code implements Example 5.13

0005  B9 0005                     MOV     CX, 5H
0008  BA 0000                     MOV     DX, 0H
000B  90               AGAIN:     NOP
000C  42                          INC     DX
000D  E2 FC                       LOOP    AGAIN

000F  CB                          RET                     ;Return to DEBUG program
0010          EX513    ENDP
0010          CODE_SEG            ENDS

                                  END     EX513
```

Segments and groups:

N a m e	Size	align	combine	class
CODE_SEG	0010	PARA	NONE	'CODE'
STACK_SEG.	0040	PARA	STACK	'STACK'

Symbols:

N a m e	Type	Value	Attr	
AGAIN.	L NEAR	000B	CODE_SEG	
EX513.	F PROC	0000	CODE_SEG	Length =0010

```
Warning  Severe
Errors   Errors
0        0
```

Figure 5.27(b) Source listing produced by the assembler.

Also we find from the instruction sequence in Fig. 5.27(c) that the loop whose operation we want to observe is located from address 0D03:000B through 0D03:000D. Therefore, we will begin by executing the instructions down to address 0D03:000B with the GO command

$$-G \quad B \quad (\hookleftarrow)$$

Again, looking at Fig. 5.27(c), we see that these instructions initialize the count in CX to 0005_{16} and the contents of DX to 0000_{16}.

```
C:\DOS>DEBUG A:EX513.EXE
-U 0 F
0D03:0000 1E           PUSH    DS
0D03:0001 B80000       MOV     AX,0000
0D03:0004 50           PUSH    AX
0D03:0005 B90500       MOV     CX,0005
0D03:0008 BA0000       MOV     DX,0000
0D03:000B 90           NOP
0D03:000C 42           INC     DX
0D03:000D E2FC         LOOP    000B
0D03:000F CB           RETF
-G B

AX=0000  BX=0000  CX=0005  DX=0000  SP=003C  BP=0000  SI=0000  DI=0000
DS=0DD7  ES=0DD7  SS=0DE8  CS=0D03  IP=000B   NV UP EI PL NZ NA PO NC
0D03:000B 90           NOP
-G D

AX=0000  BX=0000  CX=0005  DX=0001  SP=003C  BP=0000  SI=0000  DI=0000
DS=0DD7  ES=0DD7  SS=0DE8  CS=0D03  IP=000D   NV UP EI PL NZ NA PO NC
0D03:000D E2FC         LOOP    000B
-T

AX=0000  BX=0000  CX=0004  DX=0001  SP=003C  BP=0000  SI=0000  DI=0000
DS=0DD7  ES=0DD7  SS=0DE8  CS=0D03  IP=000B   NV UP EI PL NZ NA PO NC
0D03:000B 90           NOP
-G F

AX=0000  BX=0000  CX=0000  DX=0005  SP=003C  BP=0000  SI=0000  DI=0000
DS=0DD7  ES=0DD7  SS=0DE8  CS=0D03  IP=000F   NV UP EI PL NZ NA PE NC
0D03:000F CB           RETF
-G

Program terminated normally
-Q

C:\DOS>
```

Figure 5.27(c)   Executing the program with DEBUG.

Now we execute the loop down to address 0D03:000D with another GO command

$$-G \quad D \quad (\downarrow)$$

and, looking at the displayed information, we find that the pass count in DX has been incremented by one to indicate that the first pass through the loop is about to be completed.

Next the LOOP instruction is executed with the TRACE command

$$-T \quad (\downarrow)$$

From Fig. 5.27(c), we find that the loop count CX has decremented by one, meaning that the first pass through the loop is complete, and the value in IP has been changed to $000B_{16}$. Therefore, control has been returned to the NOP instruction that represents the beginning of the loop.

Now that we have observed the basic loop operation, let us execute the loop to completion with the command

$$-G \quad F \quad (\downarrow)$$

Sec. 5.6   The Loop and the Loop-Handling Instructions

The displayed information for this command in Fig. 5.27(c) shows us that at completion of the program the loop count in CX has been decremented to 0000_{16} and the pass count in DX has been incremented to 0005_{16}.

The other two loop instructions in Fig. 5.25 operate in a similar way except that they check for two conditions. For instance, the instruction *loop while equal* (LOOPE)/*loop while zero* (LOOPZ) checks the contents of both CX and the ZF flag. Each time the loop instruction is executed, CX decrements by one without affecting the flags, its contents are checked for 0, and the state of ZF that results from execution of the previous instruction is tested for 1. If CX is not equal to 0 and ZF equals 1, a jump is initiated to the location specified with the Short-label operand and the loop continues. If either CX or ZF is 0, the loop is complete and the instruction following the loop instruction is executed.

Instruction *loop while not equal* (LOOPNE)/*loop while not zero* (LOOPNZ) works in a similar way to the LOOPE/LOOPZ instruction. The difference is that it checks ZF and CX looking for ZF equal to 0 together with CX not equal to 0. If these conditions are met, the jump back to the location specified with the Short-label operand is performed and the loop continues.

EXAMPLE 5.14

Given the following sequence of instructions, explain what happens as they are executed.

```
             MOV      DL,05
             MOV      AX,0A00H
             MOV      DS, AX
             MOV      SI,0
             MOV      CX, 0FH
    AGAIN:   INC      SI
             CMP      [SI],DL
             LOOPNE   AGAIN
```

Solution

The first five instructions are for initializing internal registers. Data register DL is loaded with 05_{16}; data segment register DS is loaded via AX with the value $0A00_{16}$; source index register SI is loaded with 0000_{16}; and count register CX is loaded with $0F_{16}$ (15_{10}). After initialization, a data segment is set up at address $0A000_{16}$ and SI points to the memory location at address 0000_{16} in this data segment. DL contains the data 5_{10} and the CX register contains the loop count 15_{10}.

The part of the program that starts at the label AGAIN and ends with the LOOPNE instruction is a software loop. The first instruction in the loop increments SI by one. Therefore, the first time through the loop SI points to the memory address $A001_{16}$. The next instruction compares the contents of this memory location with the contents of DL, which are 5_{10}. If the data held at $A001_{16}$ are 5_{10}, the zero flag is set; otherwise, it is reset. The LOOPNE instruction then decrements CX (making it E_{16}) and then checks for CX = 0 or ZF = 1. If neither of these two conditions is satisfied, program control is returned to the instruction with the label AGAIN. This causes the comparison to be repeated for the examination of the contents of the next byte in memory. On the other hand, if either condition is satisfied, the loop is complete. In this way, we see that the loop is repeated until either a number 5_{10} is found or all locations in the address range $A001_{16}$ through $A00F_{16}$ have been tested and are found not to contain 5_{10}.

EXAMPLE 5.15

Figure 5.28(a) shows the source version of the program that is written in Example 5.14. This program was assembled by the macroassembler on the IBM PC and linked to produce run module EX515.EXE. The source listing that resulted from the assembly process is shown in Fig. 5.28(b). Verify the operation of the program by executing it with GO commands.

Solution

As shown in Fig. 5.28(a), the run module is loaded with the command

```
C:\DOS>DEBUG A:EX515.EXE   (↵)
```

```
TITLE    EXAMPLE 5.15

        PAGE      ,132

STACK_SEG        SEGMENT         STACK 'STACK'
                 DB              64 DUP(?)
STACK_SEG        ENDS


CODE_SEG         SEGMENT         'CODE'
EX515    PROC    FAR
        ASSUME   CS:CODE_SEG, SS:STACK_SEG

;To return to DEBUG program put return address on the stack

        PUSH     DS
        MOV      AX, 0
        PUSH     AX

;Following code implements Example 5.15

        MOV      DL, 5H
        MOV      AX, 0A00H
        MOV      DS, AX
        MOV      SI, 0H
        MOV      CX, 0FH
AGAIN:  INC      SI
        CMP      [SI], DL
        LOOPNE   AGAIN

        RET                         ;Return to DEBUG program
EX515    ENDP
CODE_SEG         ENDS

        END      EX515
```

Figure 5.28(a) Source program for Example 5.15.

```
                    TITLE    EXAMPLE 5.15

                         PAGE       ,132

    0000                               STACK_SEG        SEGMENT        STACK 'STACK'
    0000     40 [                                       DB             64 DUP(?)
             ??
                    ]

    0040                               STACK_SEG        ENDS


    0000                               CODE_SEG         SEGMENT        'CODE'
    0000                               EX515    PROC    FAR
                                                ASSUME  CS:CODE_SEG, SS:STACK_SEG

                    ;To return to DEBUG program put return address on the stack

    0000     1E                                 PUSH    DS
    0001     B8 0000                            MOV     AX, 0
    0004     50                                 PUSH    AX

                    ;Following code implements Example 5.15

    0005     B2 05                              MOV     DL, 5H
    0007     B8 0A00                            MOV     AX, 0A00H
    000A     8E D8                              MOV     DS, AX
    000C     BE 0000                            MOV     SI, 0H
    000F     B9 000F                            MOV     CX, 0FH
    0012     46                        AGAIN:   INC     SI
    0013     38 14                              CMP     [SI], DL
    0015     E0 FB                              LOOPNE  AGAIN

    0017     CB                                 RET                         ;Return to DEBUG program
    0018                               EX515    ENDP
    0018                               CODE_SEG         ENDS

                                      END      EX515

Segments and groups:

            N a m e                   Size    align   combine class

CODE_SEG . . . . . . . . . . .        0018    PARA    NONE    'CODE'
STACK_SEG. . . . . . . . . . .        0040    PARA    STACK   'STACK'

Symbols:

            N a m e                   Type    Value   Attr

AGAIN. . . . . . . . . . . . .        L NEAR  0012    CODE_SEG
EX515. . . . . . . . . . . . .        F PROC  0000    CODE_SEG        Length =0018

Warning Severe
Errors  Errors
0       0
```

Figure 5.28(b)   Source listing produced by assembler.

The program loaded is verified with the command

$$-U\ \ 0\ \ 17\ \ (\leftarrow)$$

Comparing the sequence of instructions displayed in Fig. 5.28(c) with those in the source listing of Fig. 5.28(b), we find that the program has loaded correctly.

Notice that the loop that performs the memory-compare operation starts at address 0D03:0012. Let us begin by executing down to this point with the GO

```
C:\DOS>DEBUG A:EX515.EXE
-U 0 17
0D03:0000 1E           PUSH    DS
0D03:0001 B80000       MOV     AX,0000
0D03:0004 50           PUSH    AX
0D03:0005 B205         MOV     DL,05
0D03:0007 B8000A       MOV     AX,0A00
0D03:000A 8ED8         MOV     DS,AX
0D03:000C BE0000       MOV     SI,0000
0D03:000F B90F00       MOV     CX,000F
0D03:0012 46           INC     SI
0D03:0013 3814         CMP     [SI],DL
0D03:0015 E0FB         LOOPNZ  0012
0D03:0017 CB           RETF
-G 12

AX=0A00  BX=0000  CX=000F  DX=0005  SP=003C  BP=0000  SI=0000  DI=0000
DS=0A00  ES=0DD7  SS=0DE9  CS=0D03  IP=0012   NV UP EI PL NZ NA PO NC
0D03:0012 46           INC     SI
-E A00:0 4,6,3,9,5,6,D,F,9
-D A00:0 F
0A00:0000  04 06 03 09 05 06 0D 0F-09 75 09 80 7C 02 54 75   .........u..|.Tu
-G 17

AX=0A00  BX=0000  CX=000B  DX=0005  SP=003C  BP=0000  SI=0004  DI=0000
DS=0A00  ES=0DD7  SS=0DE9  CS=0D03  IP=0017   NV UP EI PL ZR NA PE NC
0D03:0017 CB           RETF
-G

Program terminated normally
-Q

C:\DOS>
```

Figure 5.28(c)   Executing the program with DEBUG.

command

$$-G\ 12\quad (↵)$$

From the state information displayed in Fig. 5.28(c), we see that DL has been loaded with 05_{16}, AX with $0A00_{16}$, DS with $0A00_{16}$, SI with 0000_{16}, and CX with $000F_{16}$.
    Next, the table of data is loaded with the E command

$$-E\ A00:0\ 4,\ 6,\ 3,\ 9,\ 5,\ 6,\ D,\ F,\ 9\quad (↵)$$

The nine values in this list are loaded into consecutive bytes of memory over the range 0A00:0000 through 0A00:0008. The compare routine also checks the storage locations from 0A00:0009 through 0A00:000F. Let us dump the data held in this part of memory to verify that it has been initialized correctly. In Fig. 5.28(c), we see that this is done with the command

$$-D\ A00:0\ F\quad (↵)$$

and, looking at the displayed data, we find that it has loaded correctly.
    Now the loop is executed with the command

$$-G\ 17\quad (↵)$$

In the display dump for this command in Fig. 5.28(c), we find that SI has incremented to the value 0004_{16}; therefore, the loop was run only four times. The fourth time through the loop SI equals four and the memory location pointed to by SI, which is the address 0A00:0005, contains the value 5. This value is equal to the value in DL; therefore, the instruction CMP [SI],DL results in a difference of zero and the zero flag is set. Notice in Fig. 5.28(c) that this flag is identified as ZR in the display dump. For this reason, execution of the LOOPNZ instruction causes the loop to be terminated, and control is passed to the RETF instruction.

▲ 5.7 STRINGS AND STRING-HANDLING INSTRUCTIONS

The 8088 microprocessor is equipped with special instructions to handle *string operations*. By *string* we mean a series of data words (or bytes) that reside in consecutive memory locations. The string instructions of the 8088 permit a programmer to implement operations such as to move data from one block of memory to a block elsewhere in memory. A second type of operation that is easily performed is to scan a string of data elements stored in memory looking for a specific value. Other examples are to compare the elements of two strings in order to determine whether they are the same or different, and to initialize a set of consecutive memory locations. To implement complex operations such as these, typically several non-string instructions are required.

There are five basic string instructions in the instruction set of the 8088. These instructions, as listed in Fig. 5.29, are *move byte* or *word string* (MOVSB/ MOVSW),

Mnemonic	Meaning	Format	Operation	Flags Affected
MOVS	Move string	MOVSB/MOVSW	$((ES)0 + (DI)) \leftarrow ((DS)0 + (SI))$ $(SI) \leftarrow (SI) \pm 1$ or 2 $(DI) \leftarrow (DI) \pm 1$ or 2	None
CMPS	Compare string	CMPSB/CMPSW	Set flags as per $((DS)0 + (SI)) - ((ES)0 + (DI))$ $(SI) \leftarrow (SI) \pm 1$ or 2 $(DI) \leftarrow (DI) \pm 1$ or 2	CF, PF, AF, ZF, SF, OF
SCAS	Scan string	SCASB/SCASW	Set flags as per $(AL$ or $AX) - ((ES)0 + (DI))$ $(DI) \leftarrow (DI) \pm 1$ or 2	CF, PF, AF, ZF, SF, OF
LODS	Load string	LODSB/LODSW	$(AL$ or $AX) \leftarrow ((DS)0 + (SI))$ $(SI) \leftarrow (SI) \pm 1$ or 2	None
STOS	Store string	STOSB/STOSW	$((ES)0 + (DI)) \leftarrow (AL$ or $AX) \pm 1$ or 2 $(DI) \leftarrow (DI) \pm 1$ or 2	None

Figure 5.29 Basic string instructions.

compare string (CMPSB/CMPSW), *scan string* (SCASB/SCASW), *load string* (LODSB/LODSW), and *store string* (STOSB/STOSW). They are called the *basic string instructions* because each defines an operation for one element of a string. Thus these operations must be repeated to handle a string of more than one element. Let us first look at the operations performed by these instructions.

Move String—MOVSB, MOVSW

The instructions MOVSB and MOVSW perform the same basic operation. An element of the string specified by the source index (SI) register with respect to the current data segment (DS) register is moved to the location specified by the destination index (DI) register with respect to the current extra segment (ES) register. The move can be performed on a byte or a word of data. After the move is complete, the contents of both SI and DI are automatically incremented or decremented by one for a byte move and by two for a word move. The address pointers in SI and DI increment or decrement depending on how the direction flag DF is set.

For example, to move a byte the instruction

```
MOVSB
```

can be used.

An example of a program that uses MOVSB is shown in Fig. 5.30. This program is a modified version of the block move program of Fig. 5.28(b). Notice that the two MOV instructions that perform the data transfer and two INC instructions that update the pointer have been replaced with one move string byte instruction.

Compare String and Scan String—CMPSB/CMPSW and SCASB/SCASW

The compare strings instruction can be used to compare two elements in the same or different strings. It subtracts the destination operand from the source operand and adjusts the flags accordingly. The result of subtraction is not saved; therefore, the operation does not affect the operands in any way.

An example of a compare strings instruction for bytes of data is

```
          MOV     AX,DATASEGADDR
          MOV     DS,AX
          MOV     ES,AX
          MOV     SI,BLK1ADDR
          MOV     DI,BLK2ADDR
          MOV     CX,N
          CLD
NXTPT:    MOVSB
          LOOP    NXTPT
          HLT
```

Figure 5.30 Block move program using the move string instruction.

```
            MOV      AX,0
            MOV      DS,AX
            MOV      ES,AX
            MOV      AL,05
            MOV      DI,0A000H
            MOV      CX,0FH
            CLD
AGAIN:      SCASB
            LOOPNE   AGAIN
NEXT:
```

Figure 5.31 Block scan operation using the SCASB instruction.

```
            CMPSB
```

Again, the source element is pointed to by the address in SI with respect to the current value in DS and the destination element is specified by the contents of DI relative to the contents of ES. When executed, the operands are compared, the flags are adjusted, and both SI and DI are updated so that they point to the next elements in their respective strings.

The scan string instruction is similar to compare strings; however, it compares the byte or word element of the destination string at the physical address derived from DI and ES to the contents of AL or AX, respectively. The flags are adjusted based on this result and DI incremented or decremented.

A program using the SCASB instruction that implements a string scan operation similar to that described in Example 5.14 is shown in Fig. 5.31. Notice that we have made DS equal to ES.

Load and Store String—LODSB/LODSW and STOSB/STOSW

The last two instructions in Fig. 5.29, load string and store string, are specifically provided to move string elements between the accumulator and memory. LODSB loads a byte from a string in memory into AL. The address in SI is used relative to DS to determine the address of the memory location of the string element; SI is incremented by one after loading. Similarly the instruction LODSW indicates that the word-string element at the physical address derived from DS and SI is to be loaded into AX. Then the index in SI is automatically incremented by two.

```
            MOV      AX,0
            MOV      DS,AX
            MOV      ES,AX
            MOV      AL,05
            MOV      DI,0A000H
            MOV      CX,0FH
            CLD
AGAIN:      STOSB
            LOOP     AGAIN
```

Figure 5.32 Initializing a block of memory with a store string operation.

Prefix	Used with:	Meaning
REP	MOVS STOS	Repeat while not end of string $CX \neq 0$
REPE/REPZ	CMPS SCAS	Repeat while not end of string and strings are equal $CX \neq 0$ and $ZF = 1$
REPNE/REPNZ	CMPS SCAS	Repeat while not end of string and strings are not equal $CX \neq 0$ and $ZF = 0$

Figure 5.33 Prefixes for use with the basic string operations.

On the other hand, STOSB stores a byte from AL into a string location in memory. This time the contents of ES and DI are used to form the address of the storage location in memory. For example, the program in Fig. 5.32 will load the block of memory locations from $0A000_{16}$ through $0A00F_{16}$ with number 5.

Repeat String—REP

In most applications, the basic string operations must be repeated in order to process arrays of data. This is done by inserting a repeat prefix before the instruction that is to be repeated. The *repeat prefixes* of the 8088 are shown in Fig. 5.33.

The first prefix, REP, causes the basic string operation to be repeated until the contents of register CX become equal to zero. Each time the instruction is executed, it causes CX to be tested for 0. If CX is found not to be 0, it is decremented by one and the basic string operation is repeated. On the other hand, if it is 0, the repeat string operation is done and the next instruction in the program is executed. The repeat count must be loaded into CX prior to executing the repeat string instruction. Figure 5.34 is the memory load routine of Fig. 5.32 modified by using the REP prefix. As indicated in Fig. 5.33, the REP prefix is used with the MOVS and STOS instructions.

The prefixes REPE and REPZ stand for the same function. They are meant for use with the CMPS and SCAS instructions. With REPE/REPZ, the basic compare or scan operation can be repeated as long as both the contents of CX are not equal to 0 and the zero flag is 1. The first condition, CX not equal to 0, indicates that the end of the string has not yet been reached and the second condition, $ZF = 1$, indicates that the elements that were compared are equal.

The last prefix, REPNE/REPNZ, works similarly as the REPE/REPZ except that now the operation is repeated as long as CX is not equal to 0 and ZF is 0.

```
MOV     AX,0
MOV     DS,AX
MOV     ES,AX
MOV     AL,05
MOV     DI,0A000H
MOV     CX,0FH
CLD
REPSTOSB
```

Figure 5.34 Initializing a block of memory by repeating the STOSB instruction.

Mnemonic	Meaning	Format	Operation	Flags Affected
CLD	Clear DF	CLD	$(DF) \leftarrow 0$	DF
STD	Set DF	STD	$(DF) \leftarrow 1$	DF

Figure 5.35 Instructions for autoincrementing and autodecrementing in string instructions.

That is, the comparison or scanning is to be performed as long as the string elements are unequal and the end of the string is not yet found.

Autoindexing for String Instructions

Earlier we pointed out that during the execution of a string instruction the address indices in SI and DI are either automatically incremented or decremented. Moreover, we indicated that the decision to increment or decrement is made based on the setting of the direction flag DF. The 8088 provides two instructions, *clear direction flag* (CLD) and *set direction flag* (STD), to permit selection between *autoincrement* and *autodecrement mode* of operation. These instructions are shown in Fig. 5.35. When CLD is executed, DF is set to 0. This selects autoincrement mode and each time a string operation is performed SI and/or DI are incremented by one if byte data are processed and by two if word data are processed.

EXAMPLE 5.16 _____

Describe what happens as the following sequence of instructions is executed.

```
CLD
MOV AX,DATA_SEGMENT
MOV DS, AX
MOV AX, EXTRA_SEGMENT
MOV ES,AX
MOV CX,20H
MOV SI,OFFSET MASTER
MOV DI,OFFSET COPY
REPMOVSB
```

Solution

The first instruction clears the direction flag and selects autoincrement mode of operation for string addressing. The next two instructions initialize DS with the value DATA_SEGMENT. It is followed by two instructions that load ES with the value EXTRA_SEGMENT. Then the number of repeats, 20_{16}, is loaded into CX. The next two instructions load SI and DI with offset addresses MASTER and COPY that point to the beginning of the source and destination strings, respectively. Now we are ready to perform the string operation. Execution of REP MOVSB moves a block of 32 consecutive bytes from the block of memory locations starting at address MASTER in the current data segment (DS) to a block of locations starting at address COPY in the current extra segment (ES).

EXAMPLE 5.17

The source program in Fig. 5.36(a) implements the block move operation of Example 5.16. This program was assembled with the macroassembler on the IBM PC and linked to produce a run module called EX517.EXE. The source listing that was produced during the assembly process is shown in Fig. 5.36(b). Execute the program using DEBUG and verify its operation.

Solution

The program is loaded with the DEBUG command

$$C:\backslash DOS>DEBUG\ A:EX517.EXE\ \ (↵)$$

and verified by the UNASSEMBLE command

$$-U\ 0\ 18\ \ (↵)$$

```
TITLE    EXAMPLE 5.17

        PAGE     ,132

STACK_SEG        SEGMENT         STACK 'STACK'
                 DB              64 DUP(?)
STACK_SEG        ENDS


DATA_SEG         SEGMENT         'DATA'
MASTER           DB              32 DUP(?)
COPY             DB              32 DUP(?)
DATA_SEG         ENDS


CODE_SEG         SEGMENT         'CODE'
EX517    PROC    FAR
         ASSUME  CS:CODE_SEG, SS:STACK_SEG, DS:DATA_SEG, ES:DATA_SEG

;To return to DEBUG program put return address on the stack

        PUSH     DS
        MOV      AX, 0
        PUSH     AX

;Following code implements Example 5.17

        MOV      AX, DATA_SEG    ;Set up data segment
        MOV      DS, AX
        MOV      ES, AX          ;Set up extra segment

        CLD
        MOV      CX, 20H
        MOV      SI, OFFSET MASTER
        MOV      DI, OFFSET COPY
REP     MOVSB

        RET                      ;Return to DEBUG program
EX517 ENDP
CODE_SEG         ENDS

        END      EX517
```

(a)

Figure 5.36(a)   Source program for Example 5.17.

Sec. 5.7   *Strings and String-Handling Instructions*

265

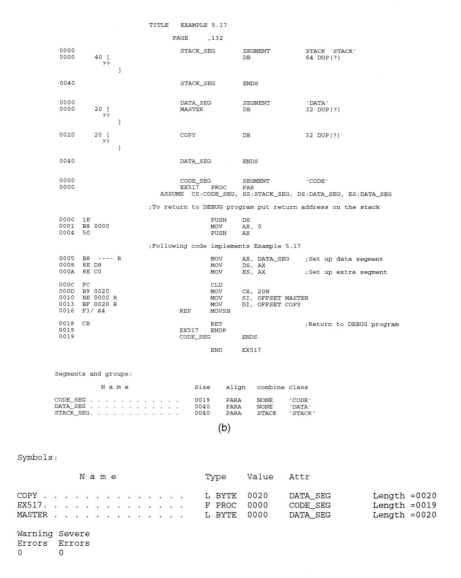

```
                    TITLE   EXAMPLE 5.17

                            PAGE    ,132

        0000                        STACK_SEG    SEGMENT      STACK 'STACK'
        0000    40 [                             DB           64 DUP(?)
                   ??
                        ]

        0040                        STACK_SEG    ENDS

        0000                        DATA_SEG     SEGMENT      'DATA'
        0000    20 [                MASTER       DB           32 DUP(?)
                   ??
                        ]

        0020    20 [                COPY         DB           32 DUP(?)
                   ??
                        ]

        0040                        DATA_SEG     ENDS

        0000                        CODE_SEG     SEGMENT      'CODE'
        0000                        EX517  PROC  FAR
                            ASSUME  CS:CODE_SEG, SS:STACK_SEG, DS:DATA_SEG, ES:DATA_SEG

                    ;To return to DEBUG program put return address on the stack

        0000    1E                           PUSH   DS
        0001    B8 0000                       MOV    AX, 0
        0004    50                            PUSH   AX

                    ;Following code implements Example 5.17

        0005    B8  ---- R                    MOV    AX, DATA_SEG   ;Set up data segment
        0008    8E D8                         MOV    DS, AX
        000A    8E C0                         MOV    ES, AX         ;Set up extra segment

        000C    FC                            CLD
        000D    B9 0020                       MOV    CX, 20H
        0010    BE 0000 R                     MOV    SI, OFFSET MASTER
        0013    BF 0020 R                     MOV    DI, OFFSET COPY
        0016    F3/ A4                 REP    MOVSB

        0018    CB                            RET                   ;Return to DEBUG program
        0019                          EX517   ENDP
        0019                          CODE_SEG ENDS

                                      END     EX517


        Segments and groups:

                        N a m e              Size    align   combine class

        CODE_SEG . . . . . . . . . . . .     0019    PARA    NONE    'CODE'
        DATA_SEG . . . . . . . . . . . .     0040    PARA    NONE    'DATA'
        STACK_SEG. . . . . . . . . . . .     0040    PARA    STACK   'STACK'
                                        (b)


        Symbols:

                        N a m e              Type    Value   Attr

        COPY . . . . . . . . . . . . . .     L BYTE  0020    DATA_SEG    Length =0020
        EX517. . . . . . . . . . . . . .     F PROC  0000    CODE_SEG    Length =0019
        MASTER . . . . . . . . . . . . .     L BYTE  0000    DATA_SEG    Length =0020

        Warning Severe
        Errors  Errors
        0       0
```

Figure 5.36(b)   Source listing produced by the assembler.

Comparing the displayed instruction sequence in Fig. 5.36(c) with the source listing in Fig. 5.36(b), we find that the program has loaded correctly.

First, we execute down to the REPZ instruction with the GO command

$$-G\ 16\quad (\llcorner\!\lrcorner)$$

and, looking at the state information displayed in Fig. 5.36(c), we see that CX has been loaded with 0020_{16}, SI with 0000_{16}, and DI with 0020_{16}.

Now the storage locations in the 32-byte source block that starts at address DS:0000 are loaded with the value FF_{16} using the FILL command

$$-F\ DS:0\ 1F\ FF\ \ \ (\hookleftarrow)$$

and each of the 32 bytes of the destination block, which starts at DS:0020, is loaded with the value 00_{16} with the FILL command

$$-F\ DS:20\ 3F\ 00\ \ \ (\hookleftarrow)$$

```
C:\DOS>DEBUG A:EX517.EXE
-U 0 18
0DE7:0000 1E            PUSH    DS
0DE7:0001 B80000        MOV     AX,0000
0DE7:0004 50            PUSH    AX
0DE7:0005 B8E90D        MOV     AX,0DE9
0DE7:0008 8ED8          MOV     DS,AX
0DE7:000A 8EC0          MOV     ES,AX
0DE7:000C FC            CLD
0DE7:000D B92000        MOV     CX,0020
0DE7:0010 BE0000        MOV     SI,0000
0DE7:0013 BF2000        MOV     DI,0020
0DE7:0016 F3            REPZ
0DE7:0017 A4            MOVSB
0DE7:0018 CB            RETF
-G 16

AX=0DE9  BX=0000  CX=0020  DX=0000  SP=003C  BP=0000  SI=0000  DI=0020
DS=0DE9  ES=0DE9  SS=0DED  CS=0DE7  IP=0016   NV UP EI PL NZ NA PO NC
0DE7:0016 F3            REPZ
0DE7:0017 A4            MOVSB
-F DS:0 1F FF
-F DS:20 3F 00
-D DS:0 3F
0DE9:0000  FF FF FF FF FF FF FF FF-FF FF FF FF FF FF FF FF    ................
0DE9:0010  FF FF FF FF FF FF FF FF-FF FF FF FF FF FF FF FF    ................
0DE9:0020  00 00 00 00 00 00 00 00-00 00 00 00 00 00 00 00    ................
0DE9:0030  00 00 00 00 00 00 00 00-00 00 00 00 00 00 00 00    ................
-G 18

AX=0DE9  BX=0000  CX=0000  DX=0000  SP=003C  BP=0000  SI=0020  DI=0040
DS=0DE9  ES=0DE9  SS=0DED  CS=0DE7  IP=0018   NV UP EI PL NZ NA PO NC
0DE7:0018 CB            RETF
-D DS:0 3F
0DE9:0000  FF FF FF FF FF FF FF FF-FF FF FF FF FF FF FF FF    ................
0DE9:0010  FF FF FF FF FF FF FF FF-FF FF FF FF FF FF FF FF    ................
0DE9:0020  FF FF FF FF FF FF FF FF-FF FF FF FF FF FF FF FF    ................
0DE9:0030  FF FF FF FF FF FF FF FF-FF FF FF FF FF FF FF FF    ................
-G

Program terminated normally
-Q

C:\DOS>
```

Figure 5.36(c) Executing the program with DEBUG.

Now a memory dump command is used to verify the initialization of memory

$$-\text{D DS:0 3F} \quad (\downarrow)$$

Looking at the displayed information in Fig. 5.36(c), we see that memory has been initialized correctly.

Now we execute the string move operation with the command

$$-\text{G 18} \quad (\downarrow)$$

Again looking at the display in Fig. 5.36(c), we see that the repeat count in CX has been decremented to zero and that the source and destination pointers have been incremented to $(SI) = 0020_{16}$ and $(DI) = 0040_{16}$. In this way, we see that the string move instruction was executed 32 times and that the source and destination addresses were correctly incremented to complete the block transfer. The block transfer operation is verified by repeating the DUMP command

$$-\text{D DS:0 3F} \quad (\downarrow)$$

Notice that both the source and destination blocks now contain FF_{16}.

ASSIGNMENTS

Section 5.2

1. Explain what happens when the instruction sequence

```
LAHF
MOV   [BX+DI], AH
```

is executed.

2. What operation is performed by the instruction sequence that follows?

```
MOV AH, [BX+SI]
SAHF
```

3. What instruction should be executed to ensure that the carry flag is in the set state? The reset state?

4. Which instruction when executed disables the interrupt interface?

5. Write an instruction sequence to configure the 8088 as follows: interrupts not accepted; save the original contents of flags SF, ZF, AF, PF, and CF at the address $A000_{16}$; and then clear CF.

Section 5.3

6. Describe the difference in operation and the effect on status flags due to the execution of the subtract words and compare words instructions.

7. Describe the operation performed by each of the instructions that follow.
   (a) CMP [0100H], AL
   (b) CMP AX, [SI]
   (c) CMP WORD PTR [DI], 1234H

8. What is the state of the 8088's flags after executing the instructions in problem 7 (a) through (c)? Assume that the following initial state exists before executing the instructions.

$$(AX) = 8001H$$
$$(SI) = 0200H$$
$$(DI) = 0300H$$
$$(DS:100H) = F0H$$
$$(DS:200H) = F0H$$
$$(DS:201H) = 01H$$
$$(DS:300H) = 34H$$
$$(DS:301H) = 12H$$

9. What happens to the ZF and CF status flags as the following sequence of instructions is executed? Assume that they are both initially cleared.

```
MOV BX,1111H
MOV AX,0BBBBH
CMP BX,AX
```

Section 5.4

10. What is the key difference between the unconditional jump instruction and conditional jump instruction?

11. Which registers have their contents changed during an intrasegment jump? Intersegment jump?

12. How large is a Short-label displacement? Near-label displacement? Memptr16 operand?

13. Is a Far-label used to initiate an intrasegment jump or an intersegment jump?

14. Identify the type of jump, the type of operand, and the operation performed by each of the instructions that follows.

(a) JMP 10H
(b) JMP 1000H
(c) JMP WORD PTR [SI]

15. If the state of the 8088 is as follows before executing each instruction in problem 14, to what address is program control passed?

$$(CS) = 1075H$$

$$(IP) = 0300H$$

$$(SI) = 0100H$$

$$(DS:100H) = 00H$$

$$(DS:101H) = 10H$$

16. Which flags are tested by the various conditional jump instructions?
17. What flag condition is tested for by the instruction JNS?
18. What flag conditions are tested for by the instruction JA?
19. Identify the type of jump, the type of operand, and the operation performed by each of the instructions that follows.
   (a) JNC 10H
   (b) JNP 1000H
   (c) JO DWORD PTR [BX]
20. What value must be loaded into BX such that execution of the instruction JMP BX transfers control to the memory location offset from the beginning of the current code segment by 256_{10}?
21. The program that follows implements what is known as a *delay loop*.

```
          MOV   CX,1000H
DLY:      DEC   CX
          JNZ   DLY
NXT:      —     —
```

   (a) How many times does the JNZ DLY instruction get executed?
   (b) Change the program so that JNZ DLY is executed just 17 times.
   (c) Change the program so that JNZ DLY is executed 2^{32} times.
22. Given a number N in the range $0 < N \le 5$, write a program that computes its factorial and saves the result in memory location FACT. (N! = 1*2*3*4*.....*N)
23. Write a program that compares the elements of two arrays, A(I) and B(I). Each array contains 100 16-bit signed numbers. The comparison is to be done by comparing the corresponding elements of the two arrays until either two elements are found to be unequal or all elements of the arrays have been compared and found to be equal. Assume that the arrays start in the current data segment at offset addresses $A000_{16}$ and $B000_{16}$, respectively. If

the two arrays are found to be unequal, save the address of the first unequal element of A(I) in memory location with offset address FOUND in the current data segment; otherwise, write all 0s into this location.

24. Given an array A(I) of 100 16-bit signed numbers that are stored in memory starting at address $A000_{16}$, write a program to generate two arrays from the given array such that one P(J) consists of all the positive numbers and the other N(K) contains all the negative numbers. Store the array of positive numbers in memory starting at address $B000_{16}$ and the array of negative numbers starting at address $C000_{16}$.

25. Given a 16-bit binary number in DX, write a program that converts it to its equivalent BCD number in DX. If the result is bigger than 16 bits, place all 1s in DX.

26. Given an array A(I) with 100 16-bit signed integer numbers, write a program to generate a new array B(I) as follows:

$$B(I) = A(I), \text{ for } I = 1, 2, 99, \text{ and } 100$$

and

$$B(I) = \text{median value of } A(I - 2), A(I - 1), A(I), A(I + 1),$$
$$\text{and } A(I + 2), \text{ for all other Is}$$

Section 5.5

27. Describe the difference between a jump and call instruction.

28. Why are intersegment and intrasegment call instructions provided in the 8088?

29. What is saved on the stack when a call instruction with a Memptr16 operand is executed? A Memptr32 operand?

30. Identify the type of call, the type of operand, and operation performed by each of the instructions that follows.
   (a) CALL 1000H
   (b) CALL WORD PTR [100H]
   (c) CALL DWORD PTR [BX+SI]

31. The state of the 8088 is as follows. To what address is program control passed after executing each instruction in problem 30?

$$(CS) = 1075H$$
$$(IP) = 0300H$$
$$(BX) = 0100H$$
$$(SI) = 0100H$$
$$(DS:100H) = 00H$$
$$(DS:101H) = 10H$$

$$(DS{:}200H) = 00H$$
$$(DS{:}201H) = 01H$$
$$(DS{:}202H) = 00H$$
$$(DS{:}203H) = 10H$$

32. What function is performed by the RET instruction?

33. Describe the operation performed by each of the instructions that follows.
   (a) PUSH DS
   (b) PUSH [SI]
   (c) POP DI
   (d) POP [BX + DI]
   (e) POPF

34. What operation is performed by the following sequence of instructions?

```
PUSH AX
PUSH BX
POP  AX
POP  BX
```

35. Write a subroutine that converts a given 16-bit BCD number to its equivalent binary number. The BCD number is in register DX. Replace it with the equivalent binary number.

36. When is it required to include PUSHF and POPF instructions in a subroutine?

37. Given an array A(I) of 100 16-bit signed integer numbers, write a program to generate a new array B(I) so that

$$B(I) = A(I), \text{ for } I = 1 \text{ and } 100$$

and

$$B(I) = 1/4 \left[A(I - 1) - 5A(I) + 9A(I + 1)\right], \text{ for all other Is}$$

For the calculation of B(I), the values of A(I − 1), A(I), and A(I + 1) are to be passed to a subroutine in registers AX, BX, and CX and the subroutine returns the result B(I) in register AX.

38. Write a segment of main program and show its subroutine structure to perform the following operations. The program is to check continuously the three most significant bits in register DX and, depending on their setting, execute one of three subroutines: SUBA, SUBB, or SUBC. The subroutines are selected as follows:
   (a) If bit 15 of DX is set, initiate SUBA.
   (b) If bit 14 of DX is set and bit 15 is not set, initiate SUBB.
   (c) If bit 13 of DX is set and bits 14 and 15 are not set, initiate SUBC.

If a subroutine is executed, the corresponding bit of DX is to be cleared and then control returned to the main program. After returning from the subroutine, the main program is repeated.

Section 5.6

39. Which flags are tested by the various conditional loop instructions?
40. What two conditions can terminate the operation performed by the instruction LOOPNE?
41. How large a jump can be employed in a loop instruction?
42. What is the maximum number of repeats that can be implemented with a loop instruction?
43. Using loop instructions, implement the program in problem 22.
44. Using loop instructions, implement the program in problem 23.

Section 5.7

45. What determines whether the SI and DI registers increment or decrement during a string operation?
46. Which segment register is used to form the destination address for a string instruction?
47. Write equivalent instruction sequences using string instructions for each of the following:

(a) MOV AL, [SI]   **(c)** MOV AL, [DI]
     MOV [DI], AL   CMP AL, [SI]
     INC SI   DEC SI
     INC DI   DEC DI

(b) MOV AX, [SI]
     INC SI
     INC SI

48. Use string instructions to implement the program in problem 23.
49. Write a program to convert a table of 100 ASCII characters that are stored starting at offset address ASCII_CHAR into their equivalent table of EBCDIC characters and store them at offset address EBCDIC_CHAR. The translation is to be done using an ASCII_TO_EBCDIC conversion table starting at offset address ASCII_TO_EBCDIC. Assume that all three tables are located in different segments of memory.

Assembly Language Program Development and the Microsoft MASM Assembler

▲ 6.1 INTRODUCTION

In chapter 3 we learned how to use the DEBUG program development tool that is available in the PC's disk operating system. We found that there is a line-by-line assembler included in the DEBUG program; however, this assembler is not practical to use when writing longer programs. In this chapter we will study in detail the steps involved in developing larger assembly language application programs for the PC. We will also learn how to use other assembly language development tools such as Microsoft's macroassembler (MASM) and the linker (LINK) programs. The topics covered in the chapter are as follows:

1. Assembly language program development on the IBM PC
2. Statement syntax for the source program
3. Pseudo operations
4. Generating a source file with an editor
5. Assembling a source program with the MASM program
6. Creating a run module with the LINK program
7. Loading and executing a run module

▲ 6.2 ASSEMBLY LANGUAGE PROGRAM DEVELOPMENT ON THE IBM PC

In this section we will look at the process by which problems are solved using software. An assembly language program is written to solve a specific problem. This problem is sometimes known as the *application*. To develop a program that implements an application, the programmer goes through a multi-step process. A chart that outlines the steps in the *program development cycle* is shown in Fig. 6.1. Let us next examine each step of the development cycle.

Describing the Problem

Looking at the development cycle sequence in Fig. 6.1, we see that the programmer begins by making a clear description of the problem to be solved and ends with a program that correctly performs this function. The first step in the program development process is to understand and describe the problem that is to be solved. A clear, concise, and accurate description of the problem is an essential part of the process of obtaining a correct and efficient software solution. This description may be provided in an informal way, such as a verbal description, or in a more formal way with a written document.

The program we used in Chapter 3, a *block-move program*, is an example of a simple application. Its function is to move a fixed length block of data, called the *source block*, from one location in memory to another location in memory called the *destination block*. For the block-move program, a verbal or a written list of events may be used to describe this problem to the programmer.

On the other hand, in most practical applications, the problem to be solved is quite complex. The programmer must know what the input data are, what operations must be performed on this information, whether or not these operations need to be performed in a special sequence, whether or not there are time constraints on performing some of the operations, if error conditions can occur during the process, and what results need to be output. For this reason, most applications are described with a written document called an *application specification*. This specification is studied by the programmers before they begin to define a software solution for the problem.

Planning the Solution

From Fig. 6.1, we find that the second step in the program development process is to plan a solution for the problem. This assumes that a complete and clear description of the problem to be solved has been provided. Once we have this description, it needs to be carefully analyzed by the programmer. Typically, the problem is broken down into a series of basic operations, which when performed

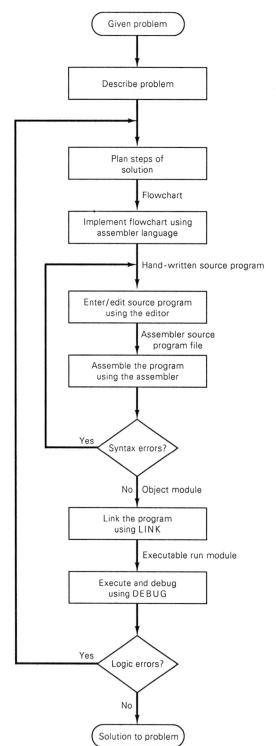

Figure 6.1 General program development cycle.

in a certain sequence will produce a solution to the problem. This solution plan is also known as the algorithm. Usually, the algorithm is described with another document called the *software specification*.

The proposed solution is normally presented in a pictorial form known as a *flowchart*. The flowchart is an outline that both documents the operations that must be performed by software to implement the planned solution and shows the sequence in which they are performed. Figure 6.2(a) is the flowchart for a block-move program.

The operations identified in the flowchart identify functions that can be implemented with assembly language instructions. For example, the first block indicates that operations must be performed to set up a data segment, initialize the starting pointers for the addresses of the source and destination blocks, and specify the count of the number of pieces of data that are to be moved. These types of operations can be achieved by moving either immediate data or data from a known memory location into appropriate registers.

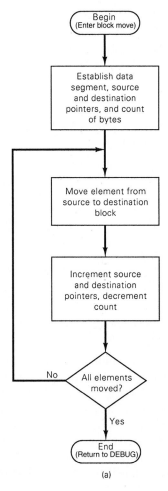

Figure 6.2 (a) Flowchart of a block move program. (b) Block-move source program.

```
TITLE BLOCK-MOVE PROGRAM

        PAGE        ,132

COMMENT *This program moves a block of specified number of bytes
            from one place to another place*


;Define constants used in this program

        N=                  16          ;Bytes to be moved
        BLK1ADDR=           100H        ;Source block offset address
        BLK2ADDR=           120H        ;Destination block offset addr
        DATASEGADDR=        2000H       ;Data segment start address


STACK_SEG           SEGMENT             STACK 'STACK'
                    DB                  64 DUP(?)
STACK_SEG           ENDS
CODE_SEG            SEGMENT             'CODE'
BLOCK               PROC        FAR
        ASSUME      CS:CODE_SEG,SS:STACK_SEG

;To return to DEBUG program put return address on the stack

                PUSH    DS
                MOV     AX, 0
                PUSH    AX

;Setup the data segment address

                MOV     AX, DATASEGADDR
                MOV     DS, AX

;Setup the source and destination offset adresses

                MOV     SI, BLK1ADDR
                MOV     DI, BLK2ADDR

;Setup the count of bytes to be moved

                MOV     CX, N

;Copy source block to destination block

NXTPT:          MOV     AH, [SI]        ;Move a byte
                MOV     [DI], AH
                INC     SI              ;Update pointers
                INC     DI
                DEC     CX              ;Update byte counter
                JNZ     NXTPT           ;Repeat for next byte
                RET                     ;Return to DEBUG program
BLOCK               ENDP
CODE_SEG            ENDS
        END         BLOCK               ;End of program

            (b)
```

Figure 6.2 (Continued)

A flowchart uses a set of symbols to identify both the operations required in
the solution and the sequence in which they are performed. Figure 6.3 lists the
most commonly used flow charting symbols. Notice that symbols are listed for
identifying the beginning or end of the flowchart, input or output of data, processing
functions, making a decision operation, connecting blocks within the flowchart, and
connections to other flowcharts. The operation to be performed is written inside
the symbol. The flowchart in Fig. 6.2(a) illustrates the use of some of these symbols.
Notice that a begin/end symbol, which contains the comment *Enter block-move*, is

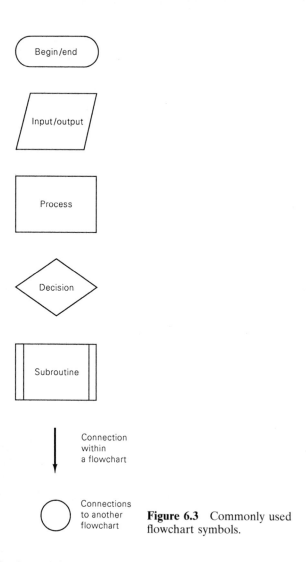

Figure 6.3 Commonly used flowchart symbols.

used to mark the beginning of the program and another that reads *Return to DEBUG* marks the end of the sequence. Process function boxes are used to identify each of the tasks (initialize registers, copy source element to destination, and increment source and destination address pointers and decrement data element count) that are performed as part of the block-move routine. Arrows are used to describe the sequence (flow) of these operations as the block-move operation is performed. Flowcharts and their descriptions are included as part of the software specification document.

The solution should be tested to verify that it correctly solves the stated problem. This can be done by specifying test cases with known inputs and outputs. Then, tracing through the operation sequence defined in the flowchart for these input conditions, the outputs are found and compared to the known test results. If the results are not the same, the cause of the error must be found, the algorithm is modified, and the tests are rerun. When the results match, the algorithm is assumed to be correct and the programmer is ready to move on to the next step in the development cycle.

The flowchart representation of the planned solution is a valuable aid to the programmer when coding the solution with the 8088 assembly language instructions. When a problem is very simple, the flowcharting step may be bypassed. A list of the tasks and the sequence in which they must be performed may be enough to describe the solution to the problem. However, for complex applications, a flowchart is an essential program development tool for obtaining an accurate and timely solution.

Coding the Solution with Assembly Language

The third step of the program development cycle, as shown in Fig. 6.1, is the translation of the flowchart solution into its equivalent assembly language program. This requires the programmer to implement the operations described in each symbol of the flowchart with a sequence of 8088 assembly language instructions. These instruction sequences are then combined together to form a handwritten assembly language program called the *source program*.

Two types of statements are used in the source program. First, there are the assembly language instructions. They are used to tell the microprocessor what operations are to be performed to implement the application.

The assembly language program in Fig. 6.2(b) implements the block-move operation flowchart of Fig. 6.2(a). Comparing the flowchart to the program, it is easy to see that the initialization block is implemented with the assembly language statements

```
MOV AX, DATASEGADDR
MOV DS, AX
MOV SI, BLK1ADDR
MOV DI, BLK2ADDR
MOV CX, N
```

The first two move instructions load a segment base address called DATASEG-ADDR into the data segment register. This defines the data segment in memory where the two blocks of data reside. Next, two more move instructions are used to load SI and DI with the starting offset address of the source block (BLK1ADDR) and destination block (BLK2ADDR), respectively. Finally, the count N of the number of bytes of data to be copied to the destination block is loaded into count register CX.

The source program also contains a second type of statement that is an instruction to the assembler program that is used to convert the assembly language program into machine code. Pseudo-op statements are examples of source program statements that are directed at the assembler program. We will discuss these statements later in the chapter. In Fig. 6.2(b), the statements

```
BLOCK    PROC    FAR
```

and

```
BLOCK    ENDP
```

are examples of modular programming pseudo-op statements. They mark the beginning and end, respectively, of the software procedure called BLOCK.

To do this step of the development cycle, the programmer must know the instruction set of the microprocessor, basic assembly language programming techniques, the assembler's instruction statement syntax, and the assembler's pseudo-operations. We will assume that the reader is familiar with the microprocessor's instructions and techniques of assembly language programming as these were the topics of Chapters 4 and 5. The next two sections in this chapter discuss instruction statement syntax and pseudo-operations, respectively, of the Microsoft program called *MASM*.

Creating the Source Program

The fourth step of program development as identified in Fig. 6.1 is the enter/edit source program. After having handwritten the assembly language program, we are ready to enter it into the computer. This is done with a program called an *editor*. We will use either the EDLIN or EDIT editors, which are available as part of the PC's DOS operating system. Using an editor, each of the statements of the program is typed into the computer. If errors are made as the statements are keyed in, the corrections can either be made at the time of entry or edited at a later time. The source program is saved by storing it in a file. The use of the DOS editors to create a *source file* is covered later in this chapter.

Assembling the Source Program into an Object Module

The fifth step in the flowchart of Fig. 6.1 is the point at which the assembly language source program is converted to its corresponding 8088 machine language program. To do this, we use a program called an *assembler*. The assembler program reads as its input the contents of the *assembler source file*; it converts this program statement by statement to machine code and produces a machine-code program as its output. This machine-code output is stored in a file called the *object module*.

If during the conversion operation syntax errors are found—that is, violations in the rules of writing 8088 assembly language instructions for the MASM assembler—they are automatically flagged by the assembler. As shown in the flowchart of Fig. 6.1, before going on, the cause of each error in the source program must be identified and then corrected. The corrections are made using the editor program. After the corrections are made, the source program must be reassembled. This edit-assemble sequence must be repeated until the program assembles with no error. We will discuss the use of the assembler later in this chapter.

Producing a Run Module

The object module produced by the assembler cannot be run directly on the 8088 microcomputer. As shown in Fig. 6.1, this module must be processed by the *LINK program* to produce an executable object module, which is known as a *run module*. The linker program converts the object module to a run module by making it address-compatible with the microcomputer on which it is to be run. For instance, if our system is implemented with memory at addresses $A000_{16}$ through $FFFF_{16}$, the executable machine-code output by the linker will also have addresses in this range.

There is another purpose for the use of a linker. This is that it is used to link together different object modules to generate a single executable object module. This allows program development to be done in modules, which are later combined to form the application program.

Verifying the Solution

Now the executable object module is ready to be run on the microcomputer. Once again, the PC's DOS operating system provides us with a program, which is called DEBUG, to perform this function. In Chapter 3 we found that DEBUG provides an environment in which we can run the program instruction by instruction or run a group of instructions at a time, look at intermediate results, display the contents of the registers within the microprocessor, and so on.

For instance, we could verify the operation of our earlier block-move program by running it for the data in the cases defined to test the algorithm. DEBUG is used to load the run module for block-move into the memory of the PC. After loading is completed and verified, other DEBUG commands are employed to run the program for the data in the test case. The debug program permits us to trace the operation as instructions are executed and observe each element of data as it is copied from the source to destination block. These results are recorded and compared to those provided with the test case. If the program is found to correctly perform the block-move operation, the program development process is complete.

On the other hand, Fig. 6.1 shows that if errors are discovered in the logic of the solution, the cause must be determined, corrections must be made to the algorithm, and then the assembly language source program must be corrected using the editor. The edited source file must be reassembled, relinked, and retested by running it with DEBUG. This loop must be repeated until it is verified that the program correctly performs the operation for which it was written.

Programs and Files Involved in the Program Development Cycle

The edit, assemble, link, and debug parts of the general program development cycle in Fig. 6.1 are performed directly on the IBM PC. Figure 6.4 shows the names

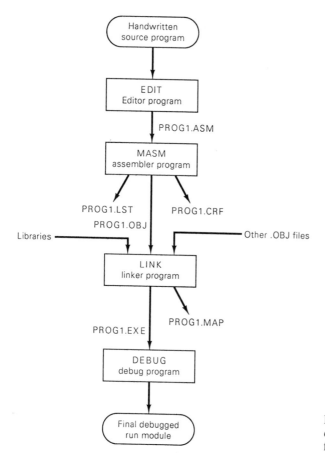

Figure 6.4 The DOS program development programs and user files.

of the programs and typical file names with extensions used as inputs and outputs during this process. For example, the *EDIT program* is an editor that is used to create and correct assembly language source files. The program that results is shown to have the name PROG1.ASM. This stands for program 1 assembly source code.

The program that can be used to assemble source files into object modules is called MASM, which stands for *macroassembler*. The assembler converts the contents of the source input file PROG1.ASM into three output files called PROG1.OBJ, PROG1.LST, and PROG1.CRF. The file PROG1.OBJ contains the object code module. The other two files provide additional information that is useful for debugging the application program.

Object module PROG1.OBJ can be linked to other object modules with the LINK program. For instance, programs that are available as object modules in a math library could be linked with another program to implement math operations. A library is a collection of prewritten, assembled, and tested programs. Notice that this program produces a run module in file PROG1.EXE and a map file called PROG1.MAP as outputs. The executable object module, PROG1.EXE, is run with the debugger program, which is called DEBUG. PROG1.MAP is supplied as support for the debugging operation by providing additional information such as where the program will be located when loaded into the microcomputer's memory.

▲ 6.3 STATEMENT SYNTAX FOR THE SOURCE PROGRAM

In the last section, we found that the source program is a series of assembly language and pseudo-operation statements that solve a specific problem. The assembly language statements tell the microprocessor the operations to be performed. On the other hand, the *pseudo-operation statements* direct the assembler program on how the program is to be assembled. Here we will study the rules that must be used when writing assembly language and pseudo-operation statements for the Microsoft MASM assembler.

Syntax of an Assembly Language Statement

A source program must be written using the syntax understood by the assembler program. By *syntax*, we mean the rules according to which statements must be written. The general format of an assembly language statement is

```
LABEL    OPCODE    OPERAND(S)    COMMENT(S)
```

Note that it contains four separate fields: the *label field*, *opcode field*, *operand field*, and *comment field*. An example is the instruction

```
START:   MOV  CX,10   ;Load a count of 10 into register CX
```

Here START is in the label field; MOV (for "move operation") is in the opcode field; the operands are CX and decimal number 10; and the comment field tells us that execution of the instruction loads a count of 10 into register CX. Note that the label field ends with a colon (:) and the comment field begins with a semicolon (;).

Not all of the fields may be present in an instruction. In fact, the only part of the format that is always required is the opcode. For instance, the instruction

```
MOV  CX,10   ;Initialize the count in CX
```

has nothing in the label field. Other instructions may not need anything in the operand field. The instruction

```
CLC   ;Clear the carry flag
```

is an example.

One rule that must be followed when writing assembly language statements is that the fields must be separated by at least one blank space, and if no label is used, the opcode field must be preceded by at least one space.

Let us now look at each field of an assembly language source statement in more detail. We will begin with the label field. It is used to give a *symbolic name* to an assembly language statement. When a symbolic name is given to an assembly language statement, other instructions in the program can reference the instruction by simply referring to this symbol instead of the actual memory address where the instruction is stored.

For example, it is common to use a jump instruction to pass control to an instruction elsewhere in the program. An example is the instruction sequence

```
        .
        .
        .
        JMP START
        .
        .
        .
START:  MOV CX,10 ; Initialize the count in CX
        .
        .
```

Execution of the jump instruction causes program execution to pass to the point in the program corresponding to label START—that is, the MOV instruction that is located further down in the program.

The label is an arbitrarily selected string of alphanumeric characters followed by a ":". Some examples of valid labels are: START, LOOPA, SUBROUTINE_A, and COUNT_ROUTINE. As in our earlier example, the names used for labels are typically selected to help document what is happening at that point of the program.

There are some limitations on the selection of labels. One limitation is that only the first 31 characters of the label are recognized by the assembler. Moreover, the first character of the label must be either a letter or the symbol ".". A period cannot be used at any other point in the label except as the first character.

Another restriction is that *reserved symbols*, such as those used to refer to the internal registers of the 8088 (AH, AL, AX, etc.), cannot be used. Still another restriction is that a label cannot include embedded blanks. This is the reason that the earlier example COUNT_ROUTINE has an underscore character (_) separating the two words. Use of the underscore makes the assembler view the character string as a single label.

Each of the basic operations that can be performed by the 8088 microprocessor is identified with a three-to six-letter *mnemonic*, which is called its *operation code* (opcode). For example, the mnemonics for the add, subtract, and move operations are ADD, SUB, and MOV, respectively. It is these mnemonics that are entered into the opcode field during the writing of the assembly language statements.

The entries in the operand field tell where the data that is to be processed is located and how it is to be accessed. An instruction may have zero, one, or two operands. For example, the move instruction

```
MOV   AX,BX
```

has two operands. Here the two operands are the accumulator (AX) register and the base (BX) register of the 8088. Note that the operands are separated by a comma. Furthermore, 8088 assembly language instructions are written with the destination operand first. Therefore, BX is the source operand (the "move from" location) and AX is the destination operand (the "move to" location). In this way, we see that the operation performed by the instruction is to move the value held in BX into AX. The notations used to identify the 8088's internal registers are shown in Fig. 6.5.

A large number of addressing modes are provided for the 8088 to help us in specifying the location of operands. Examples using each of the addressing modes are provided in Fig. 6.6. For example, the instruction that specifies an immediate data operand simply includes the value of the piece of data in the operand location. On the other hand, if the operand is a direct address it is specified using a label for the memory address.

The comment field can be used to describe the operation performed by the instruction. It is always preceded by ";". For instance, in the instruction

```
MOV   AX,BX   ;Copy BX into AX
```

the comment tells us that execution of the instruction causes the value in source register BX to be copied into destination register AX.

The assembler program ignores comments when it assembles a program into an object module. Comments are only produced in the source listing. This does

Symbol	Register
AX	Accumulator register
AH	Accumulator register high byte
AL	Accumulator register lower byte
BX	Base register
BH	Base register high byte
BL	Base register low byte
CX	Count register
CH	Count register high byte
CL	Count register low byte
DX	Data register
DH	Data register high byte
DL	Data register low byte
SI	Source index register
DI	Destination index register
SP	Stack pointer register
BP	Base pointer register
CS	Code segment register
DS	Data segment register
SS	Stack segment register
ES	Extra segment register

Figure 6.5 Symbols for specifying register operands.

Addressing mode	Operand	Example	Segment
Register	Destination	MOV AX,LABEL	—
Immediate	Source	MOV AL,15H	—
Direct	Destination	MOV LABEL,AX	Data
Register indirect	Source	MOV AX,[SI]	Data
		MOV AX,[BP]	Stack
		MOV AX,[DI]	Data
		MOV AX,[BX]	Data
Based	Destination	MOV [BX]+DISP,AL	Data
		MOV [BP]+DISP,AL	Stack
Indexed	Source	MOV AL,[SI]	Data
		MOV AL,[DI]	Data
Based indexed	Destination	MOV [BX][SI]+DISP,AH	Data
		MOV [BX][DI]+DISP,AH	Data
		MOV [BP][SI]+DISP,AH	Stack
		MOV [BP][DI]+DISP,AH	Stack

Figure 6.6 Examples using the various 8088 addressing modes.

not mean that comments are not important. In fact, they are very important. This is because they document the operation of the source program. If a program were picked up a long time after it was written—for instance, for a software update, the comments would permit the programmer to quickly understand its operation.

Syntax of a Pseudo-Operation Statement

The syntax used to write pseudo-operation statements is essentially the same as that for an assembly language statement. The general format is

```
LABEL    PSEUDO-OPCODE    OPERAND(S)    COMMENT(S)
```

Notice that the only difference is that the instruction opcode is replaced with a *pseudo-opcode*. It tells the assembler which type of operation is to be performed. For example, the pseudo-opcode DB stands for *define byte*, and if a statement is written as

```
DB  0FFH  ;Allocate a byte location initialized to FFH
```

it causes the next byte location in memory to be loaded with the value FF_{16}. This type of command can be used to initialize memory locations with data.

Another difference between the pseudo-operation statement and an assembly language statement is that pseudo-operations frequently have more than two operands. For instance, the statement

```
DB  0FFH,0FFH,0FFH,0FFH,0FFH
```

causes the assembler to load the next five consecutive bytes in memory with the value FF_{16}.

Constants in a Statement

Constants, such as an immediate value of data or an address, in an instruction or pseudo-operation can be expressed in any of five data types: *binary*, *decimal*, *hexadecimal*, *octal*, or *character*. The first four types of data are defined by including the letter B, D, H, or Q, respectively, after the number. For example, decimal number 9 is expressed in each of these four data forms as follows:

```
1001B
  9D
  9H
 11Q
```

One exception is that decimal numbers do not have to be followed by a D. Therefore, 9D can also be written simply as 9.

Another variation is that the first digit of a hexadecimal number must always be one of the numbers in the range 0 through 9. For this reason, hexadecimal A must be written as 0AH instead of AH.

Typically, data and addresses are expressed in hexadecimal form. On the other hand, it is more common to express the count for shift, rotate, and string instructions in decimal form.

EXAMPLE 6.1 ——————————————————————————————

The repeat count in CX for a string instruction is to be equal to decimal 255. Assume that the instruction that is to load the count has the form

```
MOV   CX,XX
```

where XX stands for the count, which is an immediate operand, that is to be loaded into CX. Show how the instruction would be written, first using decimal notation for the immediate operand and then using hexadecimal notation.

Solution

Using decimal notation, we get

```
MOV   CX,255D
```

or just

```
MOV   CX,255
```

In hexadecimal form, 255 is represented by FF_{16}. Therefore, the instruction becomes

```
MOV   CX,0FFH
```

The numbers used as operands in assembly language and pseudo-op statements can also be *signed* (positive or negative) *numbers*. For decimal numbers, this is simply done by preceding them with a + or − sign. For example, an immediate count of −10 that is to be loaded into the CX register with a MOV instruction can be written as

```
MOV   CX,-10
```

However, for negative numbers expressed in binary, hexadecimal, or octal form, the 2s-complement of the number must be entered.

EXAMPLE 6.2

The count in a MOV instruction that is to load CX is to be −10. Write the instruction and express the immediate operand in binary form.

Solution

The binary form of 10_{10} is 01010_2. Forming the 2s-complement, we get

$$
\begin{array}{r}
10101 \\
+1 \\
\hline
10110
\end{array}
$$

Therefore, the instruction is written as

```
MOV   CX,10110B
```

Character data can also be used as an operand. For instance, a string search operation may be used to search through a block of ASCII data in memory looking for a specific ASCII character, such as the letter A. When ASCII data are used as an operand, the character or string of characters must be enclosed by double quotes. For example, if the number 1 is to be expressed as character data, instead of numeric data, it is written as "1". In a string-compare operation, the data in memory are always compared to the contents of the AL register. Therefore, the character being searched for must be loaded into this register. For instance, to load the ASCII value of 1 into AL, we use the instruction

```
MOV   AL,  "1"
```

A second kind of operand specifies a storage location in memory. Such operands are written using the memory-addressing modes of the 8088, which are shown in Fig. 6.6. For instance, to specify that an operand is held in a storage location that is the tenth byte from the beginning of a source block of data located in the current data segment, we can use indirect addressing through source-index register SI. In this way, the location of the operand is specified as

$$10[SI] \quad or \quad [SI] + 10 \quad or \quad [SI + 10]$$

SI must be loaded with an offset that points to the beginning of the source-data block in memory.

Certain instructions require operands that are a memory address instead of data. Two examples are the *jump* (JMP) instruction and the *call* (CALL) instruction. Labels can be used to identify these addresses. For instance, in the instruction

```
JMP   LOOP
```

LOOP is a label that specifies the "jump to" address. *Attributes* may also be assigned to the label. An attribute specifies whether or not a given label is a *near, far, external,* or *internal label.*

Operand Expressions Using the Arithmetic, Relational, and Logical Operators

The operands we have used up to this point have all been either constants, variables, or labels. However, it is also possible to have an expression as an operand. For example, the instruction

```
MOV   AH,  A + 2
```

has an expression for its source operand. That is, the source operand is written as the sum of variable A and the number 2.

Figure 6.7 lists the *arithmetic, relational,* and *logical operators* that can be used to form operand expressions for use with the assembler. Expressions that are used for operands are evaluated as part of the assembly process. As the source program is assembled into an object module, the numeric values for the terms in the operand expressions are combined together based on the *precedence* of the operators in the expression, and then the expression is replaced with the resulting operand value in the final object code.

In Fig. 6.7 the operators are listed in the order of their precedence. By precedence we mean the order in which the assembler performs operations as it evaluates an expression. For instance, if the expression for an operand is

$$A + B * 2 / D$$

when the assembler evaluates the expression, the multiplication is performed first, the division second, and the addition third.

Type	Operator	Example	Function
Arithmetic	*	A * B	Multiplies A with B and makes the operand equal to the product
	/	A / B	Divides A by B and makes the operand equal to the quotient
	MOD	A MOD B	Divides A by B and assigns the remainder to the operand
	SHL	A SHL n	Shifts the value in A left by n bit positions and assigns this shifted value to the operand
	SHR	A SHR n	Shifts the value in A right by n bit positions and assigns this shifted value to the operand
	+	A + B	Adds A to B and makes the operand equal to the sum
	−	A − B	Subtracts B from A and makes the operand equal to the difference
Relational	EQ	A EQ B	Compares value of A to that of B. If A equals B, the operand is set to FFFFH and if they are not equal it is set to 0H
	NE	A NE B	Compares value of A to that of B. If A is not equal to B, the operand is set to FFFFH and if they are equal it is set to 0H
	LT	A LT B	Compares value of A to that of B. If A is less than B, the operand is set to FFFFH and if it is equal or greater than it is set to 0H
	GT	A GT B	Compares value of A to that of B. If A is greater than B, the operand is set to FFFFH and if it is equal or less than it is set to 0H
	LE	A LE B	Compares value of A to that of B. If A is less than or equal to B, the operand is set to FFFFH and if it is greater than it is set to 0H
	GE	A GE B	Compares value of A to that of B. If A is greater than or equal to B, the operand is set to FFFFH and if it is less than it is set to 0H
Logical	NOT	NOT A	Takes the logical NOT of A and makes the value that results equal to the operand
	AND	A AND B	A is ANDed with B and makes the value that results equal to the operand
	OR	A OR B	A is ORed with B and makes the value that results equal to the operand
	XOR	A XOR B	A is XORed with B and makes the value that results equal to the operand

Figure 6.7 Arithmetic, relational, and logical operators.

The order of precedence can be overcome by using parentheses. When parentheses are in use, whatever is enclosed within them is evaluated first. For example, if we modify the example we just used as follows:

$$(A + B * 2)/D$$

the multiplication still takes place first, but now it is followed by the addition and then the division. Use of the set of parentheses has changed the order of precedence.

In Fig. 6.7 we have shown a simple expression using each of the operators and described the function performed by the assembler for these expressions. For example, the operand expression

$$A \quad SHL \quad n$$

causes the assembler to shift the value of A to the left by "n" bits.

EXAMPLE 6.3

Find the value the assembler assigns to the source operand for the instruction

$$MOV \quad BH, (A * 4 - 2)/(B - 3)$$

for $A = 8$ and $B = 5$.

Solution

The expression is calculated as

$$(8 * 4 - 2)/(5 - 3) = (32 - 2)/(2)$$
$$= (30)/(2)$$
$$= 15$$

and using hexadecimal notation, we get the instruction

$$MOV \quad BH, 0EH$$

All the examples we have considered so far have used arithmetic operators. Let us now take an example of a relational operator. In Fig. 6.7, we find that there are six relational operators: *equal (EQ)*, *not equal (NE)*, *less than (LT)*, *greater than (GT)*, *less than or equal (LE)*, and *greater than or equal (GE)*. The example expression given for equal is

$$A \quad EQ \quad B$$

When the assembler evaluates this relational expression, it determines whether or not the value of A equals that of B. If they are equal to each other, the operand is made equal to $FFFF_{16}$; if they are unequal, the operand is made equal to 0_{16}.

This result is true for all relational operators. If by evaluating a relational expression we find that the conditions it specifies are satisfied, the operand expression is replaced with $FFFF_{16}$; if the conditions are not met, it is replaced by 0_{16}.

EXAMPLE 6.4

What value is used for the source operand in the expression

$$MOV \quad AX, A \quad LE \quad (B - C)$$

if $A = 234$, $B = 345$, and $C = 111$?

Solution

Substituting into the expression, we get

```
234 LE (345 - 111)
234 LE 234
```

Since the relational operator is satisfied, the instruction is equivalent to

```
MOV  AX,0FFFFH
```

The logical operators are similar to the arithmetic and relational operator; however, when they are used, the assembler performs the appropriate sequence of logic operations and then assigns the result that is produced to the operand.

The Value-Returning and Attribute Operators

Two other types of operators are available for use with operands; the *value-returning operators* and the *attribute operators*. The operators in each group, along with an example expression and description of their function, are given in Fig. 6.8.

The value-returning operators return the attribute (segment, offset, or type) value of a variable or label operand. For instance, assuming that the variable A is in a data segment, the instructions

```
MOV  AX,SEG A
MOV  SI,OFFSET A
MOV  CL,TYPE A
```

when assembled cause the 16-bit segment value for A to replace SEG A, the 16-bit offset value for variable A to replace OFFSET A, and the type number of the variable A to replace TYPE A, respectively. Assuming that A is a data byte, the value 1 will be assigned to TYPE A.

The attribute operators give the programmer the ability to change the attributes of an operand or label. For example, operands that use the BX, SI, or DI registers to hold the offset to their storage locations in memory are automatically referenced with respect to the contents of the DS register. An example is the instruction

```
MOV  AX,[SI]
```

We can use the *segment override* attribute operator to select another segment register. For instance, to select the extra segment register the instruction is written as

```
MOV  AX,ES:[SI]
```

Type	Operator	Example	Function
Value-returning	SEG	SEG A	Assigns the contents held in the segment register corresponding to the segment in which A resides to the operand
	OFFSET	OFFSET A	Assigns the offset of the location A in its corresponding segment to the operand
	TYPE	TYPE A	Returns to the operand a number representing the type of A; 1 for a byte variable and 2 for a word variable; NEAR or FAR for the label
	SIZE	SIZE A	Returns the byte count of variable A to the operand
	LENGTH	LENGTH A	Returns the number of units (as specified by TYPE) allocated for the variable A to the operand
Attribute	PTR	NEAR PTR A	Overrides the current type of label operand A and assigns a new pointer type: BYTE, WORD, NEAR, or FAR to A
	DS:,ES:,SS:	ES:A	Overrides the normal segment for operand A and assigns a new segment to A
	SHORT	JMP SHORT A	Assigns to operand A an attribute that indicates that it is within +127 or −128 bytes of the next instruction. This lets the instruction be encoded with the minimum number of bytes
	THIS	THIS BYTE A	Assigns to operand A a distance or type attribute: BYTE, WORD, NEAR, or FAR, and the corresponding segment attribute
	HIGH	HIGH A	Returns to the operand A the high byte of the word of A
	LOW	LOW A	Returns to the operand A the low byte of the word of A

Figure 6.8 Value-returning and attribute operators.

▲ 6.4 PSEUDO-OPERATIONS

The primary function of an assembler program is to convert the assembly language instructions of the source program to their corresponding machine instructions. However, practical assembly language source programs do not consist of assembly language statements only; they also contain what are called *pseudo-operation statements* (*pseudo-op statements* for short). In this section, we will look more closely at what a pseudo-op is and what pseudo-ops are available in MASM, as well as, how they are used as part of an assembly language source program.

The Pseudo-OP

In section 6.3 we introduced the syntax of the pseudo-op statements and found that they differ from assembly language instruction statements in that they are directions to tell the assembler how to assemble the source program instead of instructions to be processed by the microprocessor. That is, pseudo-ops are statements written in the source program but are meant only for use by the assembler program. The assembler program follows these *directives* (directions) during the assembling of the program, but does not produce any machine code for them.

A list of the pseudo-ops provided in MASM is shown in Fig. 6.9. Notice that the pseudo-ops are grouped into categories based on the type of operation they specify to the assembler. These categories are the *data pseudo-ops*, *conditional pseudo-ops*, *macro pseudo-ops*, and *listing pseudo-ops*. Notice that each category contains a number of different pseudo-ops. Here we will consider only a most frequently used subset of the pseudo-ops in these categories. For information on those pseudo-ops not covered here, the reader should consult the manual provided with Microsoft's MASM assembler.

Data Pseudo-Ops

The function of the pseudo-ops in the data group is to define values for constants, variables, and labels. Other functions that can be performed by these pseudo-ops are to assign a size to variables and to reserve storage locations for them in memory. The most commonly used pseudo-ops to handle these types of data operations are those listed in Fig. 6.10.

The first two data pseudo-ops in Fig. 6.10 are *equate* and *equal to*. Their pseudo-op-codes are EQU and =, respectively. Both of these pseudo-ops can be used to assign a constant value to a symbol. For example, the symbol AA can be

Type	Pseudo-ops		
Data	ASSUME	ENDS	NAME
	COMMENT	EQU	ORG
	DB	= (Equal	PROC
	DD	Sign)	PUBLIC
	DQ	EVEN	.RADIX
	DT	EXTRN	RECORD
	DW	GROUP	SEGMENT
	END	INCLUDE	STRUC
	ENDP	LABEL	
Conditional	ELSE	IFDEF	IFNB
	ENDIF	IFDIF	IFNDEF
	IF	IFE	IF1
	IFB	IFIDN	IF2
Macro	ENDM	IRPC	PURGE
	EXITM	LOCAL	REPT
	IRP	MACRO	
Listing	.CREF	PAGE	TITLE
	.LALL	.SALL	.XALL
	.LFCOND	.SFCOND	.XCREF
	.LIST	SUBTTL	.XLIST
	%OUT	.TFCOND	

Figure 6.9 Pseudo-ops of IBM's macroassembler.

Pseudo-op	Meaning	Function
EQU	Equate	Assign a permanent value to a symbol
=	Equal to	Set or redefine the value of a symbol
DB	Define byte	Define or initialize byte size variables or locations
DW	Define word	Define or initialize word size (2 byte) variables or locations
DD	Define double word	Define or initialize double word size (4 byte) variables or locations

Figure 6.10 Data pseudo-ops.

set equal to 0100_{16} with the equate statement

$$AA \quad EQU \quad 0100H$$

The value of the operand can also be assigned using the arithmetic, relational or logic expressions discussed in section 6.3. An example of the EQU pseudo-op, which uses an arithmetic expression to define an operand, is

$$BB \quad EQU \quad AA+5H$$

In this statement, the symbol BB is assigned the value of symbol AA plus 5. These two operations can also be done using the = pseudo-op. This gives the statements

$$AA = 0100H$$

$$BB = AA+5H$$

Once these values are assigned to AA and BB, they can be referenced elsewhere in the program by just using the symbol.

The difference between the EQU and = pseudo-ops lies in the fact that the value assigned to the symbol using EQU cannot be changed, whereas when = is used to define the symbol its value can be changed later in the program.

$$AA \quad EQU \quad 0100H$$
$$BB \quad EQU \quad AA+5H$$
$$\vdots$$
$$BB \quad EQU \quad AA+10H \quad ;This\ is\ illegal$$

Here AA is set equal to 0100_{16} and BB to 0105_{16}; the value of BB cannot be changed with the third EQU statement. On the other hand, if we use the = pseudo-ops as follows

$$AA = 0100H$$
$$BB = AA+5H$$
$$\vdots$$
$$BB = AA+10H \quad \text{;This is legal}$$

BB is assigned the new value of AA+10H as the third = pseudo-op is processed by the assembler.

The other three pseudo-ops given in Fig. 6.10 are *define byte* (DB), *define word* (DW), and *define double word* (DD). The function of these pseudo-ops is to define the size of variables as being byte, word, or double word in length, allocate space for them, and assign them initial values. If the initial value of a variable is not known, the DB, DW, or DD statement simply allocates a byte, word, or double word of memory to the variable name.

An example of the DB pseudo-op is

```
CC   DB   7
```

Here variable CC is defined as byte size and assigned the value 7. It is important to note that the value assigned with a DB, DW, or DD statement must not be larger than the maximum number that can be stored in the specified-size storage location. For instance, for a byte-size variable, the maximum decimal value is 255 for an unsigned number and +127 or −128 for a signed number.

Here is another example

```
EE   DB   ?
```

In this case, a byte of memory is allocated to the variable EE, but no value is assigned to it. Notice that use of a ? as the operand means that an initial value is not to be assigned.

Look at another example

```
MESSAGE   DB   "JASBIR"
```

Here each character in the string JASBIR is allocated a byte in memory, and these bytes are initialized with the ASCII values for the characters. This is the way ASCII data are assigned to a name.

If we need to initialize a large block of storage locations with the same value, the assembler provides a way of using the define byte, word, or double-word pseudo-op to repeat a value. An example is the statement

```
TABLE_A   DB   10 DUP(?),5 DUP(7)
```

This statement causes the assembler to allocate 15 bytes of memory for TABLE_A. The first ten bytes of this block of memory are left uninitialized and the next five bytes are all initialized with the value 7. Notice that use of *duplicate* (DUP) tells the assembler to duplicate the value enclosed in parentheses a number of times equal to the number that precedes DUP.

If each element of the table was to be initialized to a different value, the DB command would be written in a different way. For example, the command

```
TABLE_B   DB   0,1,2,3,4,5,6,7,8,9
```

sets up a table called TABLE_B and assigns to its ten storage locations the decimal values 0 through 9.

Segment Control Pseudo-Ops

Memory of the 8088-based microcomputer is partitioned into four kinds of segments: the code segment, data segment, extra segment, and stack segment. The code segment is where machine-code instructions are stored, the data and extra segments are for storage of data, and the stack segment is for a temporary storage location called the stack. Using the *segment control pseudo-ops* in Fig. 6.11, the statements of a source program written for the 8088 can be partitioned and assigned to a specific memory segment. These pseudo-ops can be used to specify the beginning and end of a segment in a source program and assign to them attributes such as a starting address boundary, the kind of segment, and how the segment is to be combined with other segments of the same name.

The beginning of a segment is identified by the *segment* (SEGMENT) pseudo-op and its end is marked by the *end of segment* (ENDS) pseudo-op. Here is an example of a segment definition

```
SEGA   SEGMENT   PARA PUBLIC 'CODE'
       MOV  AX,BX
         .
         .
         .
SEGA   ENDS
```

As shown, the information between the two pseudo-ops statements would be the instructions of the assembly language program.

Pseudo-op	Function
SEGMENT	Defines the beginning of a segment and specifies its kind, at what type of address boundary it is to be stored in memory, and how it is to be positioned with respect to other similar segments in memory
ENDS	Specifies the end of a segment
ASSUME	Specifies the segment address register for a given segment

Figure 6.11 Segment pseudo-ops.

Attribute	Function
PARA	Segment begins on a 16 byte address boundary in memory (4 LSBs of the address are equal to 0)
BYTE	Segment begins anywhere in memory
WORD	Segment begins on a word (2 byte) address boundary in memory (LSB of the address is 0)
PAGE	Segment begins on a 256 byte address boundary in memory (8 LSBs of the address are equal to 0)

Figure 6.12 Align-type attributes.

In this example, SEGA is the name given to the segment. The pseudo-op SEGMENT is followed by the operand PARA PUBLIC 'CODE'. Here PARA (*paragraph*) defines that this segment is to be aligned in memory on a 16-byte address boundary. This part of the operand is called the *align-type* attribute. There are other align-type attributes that can be used instead of PARA. They are given in Fig. 6.12 with brief descriptions of their functions.

PUBLIC, which follows PARA in the operand of the example SEGMENT pseudo-op, defines what is called a *combine-type* attribute. It specifies that this segment is to be concatenated with all other segments that are assigned the name SEGA to generate one physical segment called SEGA. Other combine-type attributes are given in Fig. 6.13.

The last part of the operand in the SEGMENT statement is 'CODE'; it specifies that the segment is a code segment. This entry is called a *class* attribute. All of the allowed segment classes are shown in Fig. 6.14.

At the end of the group of statements that are to be assigned to the code segment, there must be an ENDS pseudo-op. In Fig. 6.11, we find that this statement is used to mark the end of the segment. ENDS must also be preceded by the segment name, which is SEGA in our example.

The third pseudo-op in Fig. 6.11 is *assume* (ASSUME). It is used to assign the segment registers that hold the base addresses to the program segments. For instance, with the statement

ASSUME   CS:SEGA,DS:SEGB,SS:SEGC

Attribute	Function
PUBLIC	Concatenates segments with the same name
COMMON	Overlaps from the beginning segments with the same name
AT [expression]	Locates the segment at the 16-bit paragraph number evaluated from the expression
STACK	The segment is part of the run-time stack segment
MEMORY	Locates the segment at an address above all other segments

Figure 6.13 Combine-type attributes.

Attribute	Function
CODE	Specifies the code segment
DATA	Specifies the data segment
STACK	Specifies the stack segment
EXTRA	Specifies the extra segment

Figure 6.14 Class attributes.

we specify that register CS holds the base address for segment SEGA, register DS holds the base address for segment SEGB, and register SS holds the base address for segment SEGC. The ASSUME pseudo-op is written at the beginning of a code segment just after the SEGMENT pseudo-op.

Figure 6.15 shows the general structure of a code segment definition using the segment control pseudo-ops.

Modular Programming Pseudo-Ops

For the purpose of development, larger programs are broken down into smaller segments called *modules*. Typically, each module implements a specific function and has its own code segment and data segment. However, it is common that during the execution of a module a part of some other module may need to be called for execution or that data that resides in another module may need to be accessed for processing. To support capabilities such that a section of code in one module can be executed from another module or for data to be passed between modules, MASM provides *modular programming pseudo-ops*. The most frequently used modular programming pseudo-ops are listed in Fig. 6.16.

A section of a program that can be called for execution from other modules is called a *procedure*. Similar to the definition of a segment of a program, the beginning and end of a procedure must be marked with pseudo-statements. The beginning of the procedure is marked by the *procedure* (PROC) pseudo-op and its end by the *end of procedure* (ENDP) pseudo-op.

There are two kinds of procedures: a *near procedure* and a *far procedure*. Whenever a procedure is called, the return address has to be saved on the stack. After completing the code in the called procedure, this address is used to return execution back to the point of its initiation. When a near procedure is called into operation, only the code offset address (IP) is saved on the stack. Therefore, a near procedure can only be called from the same code segment. On the other hand, when a far procedure is called, both the contents of the code segment (CS) register

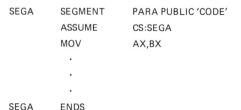

```
SEGA        SEGMENT     PARA PUBLIC 'CODE'
            ASSUME      CS:SEGA
            MOV         AX,BX
              .
              .
              .
SEGA        ENDS
```

Figure 6.15 Example using segment control pseudo-ops.

Pseudo-op	Function
proc-name PROC [NEAR]	Defines the beginning of a near-proc procedure
proc-name PROC FAR	Defines the beginning of a far-proc procedure
proc-name ENDP	Defines the end of a procedure
PUBLIC Symbol[. . . . . . .]	The defined symbols can be referenced from other modules
EXTRN name:type[. . . .]	The specified symbols are defined in other modules and are to be used in this module

Figure 6.16   Modular programming pseudo-ops.

and the code offset (IP) are saved on the stack. For this reason, a far procedure can be called from any code segment. Depending upon the kind of procedure, the *return* (RET) instruction at the end of the procedure restores either IP or both IP and CS from the stack.

If a procedure can be called from other modules, its name must be made *public* by using the PUBLIC pseudo-op. Typically this is done before entering the procedure. Thus, the structure for defining a procedure with name SUB_NEAR will be

```
              PUBLIC    SUB_NEAR
   SUB_NEAR   PROC
                 .
                 .
                 .
              RET
   SUB_NEAR   ENDP
```

In this example the PROC does not have either the NEAR or FAR attribute in its operand field. When no attribute is specified as an operand, NEAR is assumed as the default attribute by the assembler. In this way, we see that this procedure can only be called from other modules in the same code segment.

The structure of a far procedure that can be called from modules in other segments would be

```
              PUBLIC    SUB_FAR
   SUB_FAR    PROC      FAR
                 .
                 .
                 .
              RET
   SUB_FAR    ENDP
```

If a procedure in another module is to be called from the current module, its name must be declared external in the current procedure by using the *external reference* (EXTRN) pseudo-op. It is also important to know whether this call is to a module in the same code segment or in a different code segment. Depending upon the code segments, the name of the procedure must be assigned either a NEAR or FAR attribute as part of the EXTRN statement.

The example in Fig. 6.17 illustrates the use of the EXTRN pseudo-op. Here we see that an external call is made from module 2 to the procedure SUB that resides in module 1. Therefore, the procedure SUB is defined as PUBLIC in module 1. Notice that the two modules have different code segments, which are called CSEG1 and CSEG2. Thus the external call in module 2 is to a far procedure. Therefore, the PROC pseudo-op for SUB in module 1 and the external label definition of SUB in module 2 have the FAR attribute attached to them.

Pseudo-Op for Memory Usage Control

If the machine code generated by the assembler must reside in a specific part of the memory address space, an *origin* (ORG) pseudo-op can be used to specify the starting point of that memory area. In Fig. 6.18 we see that the operand in the ORG statement can be an expression. The value that results from this expression is the address at which the machine code is to begin loading. For example, the statement

```
ORG    100H
```

simply tells the assembler that the machine code for subsequent instructions is to be placed in memory starting at address 100_{16}. This pseudo-op statement is normally located at the beginning of the program.

```
              PUBLIC    SUB                           EXTRN     SUB:FAR
     CSEG1    SEGMENT                        CSEG2    SEGMENT
                 .                                       .
                 .                                       .
     SUB       PROC      FAR                           CALL      SUB
               MOV       AX,BX                           .
                 .                                       .
                 .                                       .
               RET                                       .
     SUB       ENDP                                      .
                 .                          CSEG2    ENDS
                 .
                 .
     CSEG1    ENDS

              Module 1                               Module 2
```

Figure 6.17 An example showing use of the EXTRN pseudo-op.

Pseudo-op	Function
ORG [expression]	Specifies the memory address starting from which the machine code must be placed
END [expression]	Specifies the end of the source program

Figure 6.18 ORG and END pseudo-ops.

If specific memory locations must be skipped—for example, because they are in a read-only area of memory—one can use ORG pseudo-ops as follows:

```
ORG   100H
ORG   $+200H
```

in which case memory locations 100_{16} to 300_{16} are skipped and the machine code of the program can start at address 301_{16}.

The End of Program Pseudo-Op

The *end* (END) pseudo-op, which is also described in Fig. 6.18, tells the assembler when to stop assembling. It must always be included at the end of the source program. Optionally, we can specify the starting point of the program with an expression in the operand field of the END statement. For instance, an END statement can be written as

```
END   PROG_BLOCK
```

where PROG_BLOCK identifies the beginning address of the program.

Pseudo-Ops for Program Listing Control

The last group of pseudo-ops we will consider is called the *listing control pseudo-ops.* The most widely used pseudo-ops in this group are shown in Fig. 6.19. The purpose of the listing control pseudo-ops is to give the programmer some options related to the way in which source program listings are produced by the assembler. For instance, we may want to set up the print output such that a certain number of lines are printed per page or we may want to title the pages of the listing with the name of the program.

The *page* (PAGE) pseudo-op lets us set the page width and length of the source listing produced as part of the assembly process. For example, if the PAGE pseudo-op

```
PAGE   50   100
```

is encountered at the beginning of a source program, then each printed page will have 50 lines and up to 100 characters in a line. The first operand, which specifies the number of lines per page, can be any number from 10 through 255. The second operand, which specifies the maximum number of characters per line, can range

Pseudo-op	Function
PAGE operand_1 operand_2	Selects the number of lines printed per page and the maximum number of characters printed per line in the listing
TITLE text	Prints 'text' on the second line of each page of the listing
SUBTTL text	Prints 'text' on the third line of each page of the listing

Figure 6.19   Listing control pseudo-ops.

from 60 to 132. The default values for these parameters are 66 lines per page and 80 characters per line. The default parameters are selected if no operand is included with the pseudo-op.

Chapter and page numbers are always printed at the top of each page in a source listing. They are in the form

```
[chapter number]-[page number]
```

As the source listing is produced by the assembler, the page number automatically increments each time a full page of listing information is generated. On the other hand, the chapter number does not change as the listing is generated. The only way to change the chapter number is by using the pseudo-op

```
PAGE +
```

When this form of the PAGE pseudo-op is processed by the assembler, it increments the chapter count and at the same time resets the page number to 1.

The second pseudo-op in Fig. 6.19 is *title* (TITLE). When this pseudo-op is included in a program, it causes the text in the operand field to be printed on the second line of each page of the source listing. Similarly, the third pseudo-op, *subtitle* (SUBTTL), prints the text included in the pseudo-op statement on the third line of each page.

An Example of a Source Program Using Pseudo-Ops

In order to have our first experience in using pseudo-ops in a source program, let us again look at the program in Fig. 6.2(b). This program is written to copy a given block of data from a location in memory known as the source block or another block location called the destination block. This program is similar to the one we used as an example in Chapter 3 [Fig. 3.7(a)]; however, here we have included pseudo-ops to prepare the program for assembly by MASM. In the sections that follow, we will use this program to learn various aspects of program development, such as creating a source file, assembling, linking, and debugging. For now we will just look at the pseudo-ops used in the program.

The program starts with a TITLE pseudo-op statement. The text "BLOCK_MOVE PROGRAM" that is included in this statement will be printed on the second line of each page of the source listing. This text should be limited to 60 characters. The second and third statements in the program are also pseudo-ops. The third statement is a *comment* pseudo-op and is used to place descriptive comments in the program. Note that it begins with the pseudo-opcode COMMENT and is followed by the comment enclosed within the delimiter "*". This comment gives a brief description of the function of the program.

There is another way of including comments in a program. This is by using ";" followed by the text of the comment. The next line in the program is an example of this type of comment. It indicates that the next part of the program is used to define variables that are used in the program. Four "equal to" ($=$) pseudo-op statements follow the comment. Notice that they equate N to the value 16_{10}, BLK1ADDR to the value 100_{16}, BLK2ADDR to the value 120_{16}, and DATASEG-ADDR to the value 2000_{16}.

There are two segments in the program: the stack segment and the code segment. The next three pseudo-op statements define the stack segment. They are

```
STACK_SEG   SEGMENT   STACK   'STACK'
            DB    64     DUP(?)
STACK_SEG   ENDS
```

In the first statement, the stack segment is assigned the name STACK_SEG; the second statement allocates a block of 64 bytes of memory for use as stack and leaves this area uninitialized. The third statement defines the end of the stack.

The code segment is defined between the statements

```
CODE_SEG    SEGMENT    'CODE'
```

and

```
CODE_SEG    ENDS
```

Here CODE_SEG is the name we have used for the code segment. At the beginning of the code segment an ASSUME pseudo-op is used to specify the base registers for the code and stack segments. Notice that CS is the base register for the code segment and SS the base register for the stack segment.

We also find at the end of the program an END pseudo-op. It identifies the end of the program, and BLOCK in this statement defines the starting address of the source program. Processing of this statement tells the assembler that the assembly is complete.

A PROC pseudo-op is included at the beginning of the source program and the ENDP pseudo-op is included at the end of the program. This makes the program segment a procedure that can be referenced as a module in a larger program.

▲ 6.5 CREATING A SOURCE FILE WITH AN EDITOR

Now that we have introduced assembly language syntax, the pseudo-ops, and an example of an assembly language program, let us continue by looking at how the source-program file is created on the IBM PC. Source program files are generated using a program called an *editor*. Basically, two types of editors are available: the *screen editor* and the *line editor*. They differ in that a screen editor allows one to work on a full screen of text at a time, while a line editor enables one to work on one text line at a time. Both types of editor program are provided in the IBM PC's DOS operating system. The line editor is called *EDLIN* and the screen editor is called *EDIT*. In this book we have assumed that the reader is already familiar with the commands of the DOS and the use of either the EDLIN or EDIT program. For this reason, we will just briefly describe the use of EDLIN and EDIT in creating a source-program file. If additional details are required, the DOS manual that is provided with the operating system software should be consulted.

Using the EDLIN Line-Editor

The diagram in Fig. 6.20(a) outlines the sequence of steps that take place during a typical editing session with EDLIN. We are interested in creating a source program in a file called BLOCK.SRC. This file will be stored on a diskette in drive A. We start by entering the following command to bring up the line-editor program

```
C:\DOS>EDLIN  A:BLOCK.SRC  (↵)
```

In response to this input, the EDLIN program is first loaded from the operating system and then executed. Once EDLIN is running, it checks to determine whether or not the file BLOCK.SRC already exists on the diskette in drive A. If it does exist, the file is loaded into memory and the response "End of input file" is displayed; on the next line the prompt "*_" is displayed. On the other hand, if the file does not exist, "New File" is displayed and it is followed by the prompt "*_".

Let us assume that BLOCK.SRC is a new file. Then the system will respond with the prompt

```
New file
*_
```

As shown in Fig. 6.20(a), the next input should be I followed by (↵). This is the *insert line* command; its entry causes line number 1:* to be displayed. We are now in the *line input mode* of editor operation. This is the mode used when creating new source-program files. Next the text for the first line of the program is keyed in following the line number; then the (↵) key is depressed. For instance, in Fig. 6.20(a) we entered the statement

```
1:*MOV  AX,DATASEGADDR  (↵)
```

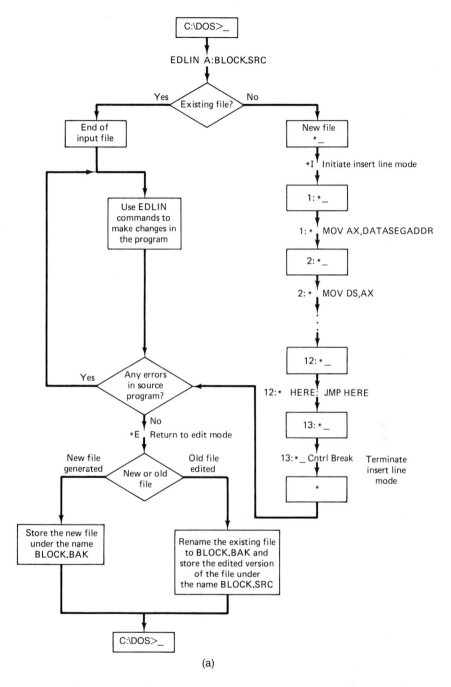

Figure 6.20 (a) Flowchart for creating and editing of source files with EDLIN. (b) Flowchart for creating and editing a source file with EDIT.

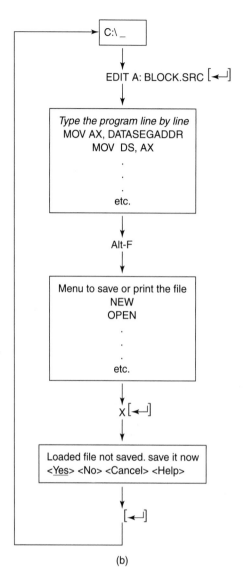

(b)   **Figure 6.20**   (Continued)

When ($\downarrow$) is depressed, the entry of line 1 is completed and line number 2:* is
displayed. Its text is now entered and ($\downarrow$) is depressed once more. For example, in
Fig. 6.20(a) we find

$$2:*MOV \quad DS,AX \qquad (\downarrow)$$

Repeating this sequence, the complete program is entered line by line. Here are
some additional line entries for the program

```
C:\DOS>EDLIN A:BLOCK.SRC
New file
*I
        1:*        MOV        AX,DATASEGADDR
        2:*        MOV        DS,AX
        3:*        MOV        SI,BLK1ADDR
        4:*        MOV        DI,BLK2ADDR
        5:*        MOV        CX,N
        6:*NXTPT:  MOV        AH,[SI]
        7:*        MOV        [DI],AH
        8:*        INC        SI
        9:*        INC        DI
       10:*        DEC        CX
       11:*        JNZ        NXTPT
       12:*^C

    *E
    C:\DOS
```

Figure 6.21 Entry of example program with the EDLIN editor.

```
        3:* MOV   SI,BLK1ADDR      (↵)
        4:* MOV   DI,BLK2ADDR      (↵)
                     .
                     .
       11:* JNZ   NXTPT            (↵)
```

After the last line of the program is entered, we must come out of the line input mode. This is done by depressing the "Ctrl" (control) and "Break" (break) keys together. On the keyboard of the PC the break key may be marked "Scroll Lock" on the top and "Break" on the front. Depression of these two keys together takes EDLIN out of the line input mode and puts it into the *edit mode*. Figure 6.21 shows the information displayed during the entry of this segment of program

Once we are in the edit mode, the program should be looked over closely for errors. If errors are found, they can be corrected using other editor commands. The commands provided in EDLIN and the syntax in which they must be entered are shown in Fig. 6.22. Notice that commands are provided that let us delete a line

Command	Format
Append Lines	[*n*] A
Copy Lines	[*line*] , [*line*] ,*line*, [*count*] C
Delete Lines	[*line*] [,*line*] D
Edit Line	[*line*]
End Edit	E
Insert Lines	[*line*] I
List Lines	[*line*] [,*line*] L
Quit Edit	Q
Move Lines	[*line*] , [*line*] ,*line*M
Page	[*line*] [,*line*] P
Replace Text	[*line*] [,*line*] [?] R [*string*] [<F6>*string*]
Search Text	[*line*] [,*line*] [?] S [*string*]
Transfer Lines	[*line*] T *filename* [.*ext*]
Write Lines	[*n*] W

Figure 6.22 EDLIN commands. (Courtesy of International Business Machines Corporation)

or lines, insert a new line or lines, list lines, delete or insert characters in a line, and replace or search for a string of characters. For instance, after loading a program from a diskette, the "List Lines" command can be used to display the lines of the program. The file created in our earlier example can be reloaded and displayed with the command sequence

```
C:\DOS>EDLIN A:BLOCK.SRC (↵)
* 1,11 L                  (↵)
```

The resulting display is shown in Fig. 6.23.

After all corrections have been made, the editing session is complete and it must be ended. The "End Edit" command is used for this purpose. Looking at Fig. 6.20(a), we see that it is entered as

```
*E    (↵)
```

The response of EDLIN to this entry depends on whether the current editing was done on an existing file or a new file that was just being created. In Fig. 6.20(a) we find that if it is a new file, such as in our earlier example, the edit mode is terminated and the lines of text that were entered are stored in a file called BLOCK.SRC and then the DOS prompt C:\DOS is displayed.

On the other hand, if we were editing an existing file called BLOCK.SRC, the original file (before editing) would be renamed using the original file name with the extension BAK. This file, BLOCK.BAK, is called the backup file. Next, the edited version of the program is saved in the file BLOCK.SRC. Then the DOS prompt C:\DOS is displayed. The creation of this *backup file* provides us with a way to get back to the original version of the program if necessary. It should be noted that a file with the extension BAK cannot be edited with EDLIN. However, this backup file can either be copied to another file or have its extension changed with a RENAME command, and then it can be edited.

Using the EDIT Screen Editor

A screen editor, such as EDIT, is easier to use than a line editor. When working on a document, such as an assembly language source program, the contents

```
C:\DOS>EDLIN A:BLOCK.SRC
End of input file
*1,11L
      1:*          MOV     AX,DATASEGADDR
      2:           MOV     DS,AX
      3:           MOV     SI,BLK1ADDR
      4:           MOV     DI,BLK2ADDR
      5:           MOV     CX,N
      6: NXTPT:    MOV     AH,[SI]
      7:           MOV     [DI],AH
      8:           INC     SI
      9:           INC     DI
     10:           DEC     CX
     11:           JNZ     NXTPT
*Q
Abort edit (Y/N)? Y
C:\DOS>
```

Figure 6.23 Listing of the example source program produced with the List Lines command.

of the file can be viewed on the screen during the edit session. This makes it possible to quickly read any part of the program and randomly make changes to its lines of code.

EDIT is *menu driven* text editor. That is, a simple key sequence is performed to display a *menu* of operations that can be performed. The desired operation is picked from the menu and then the return key depressed. At this point, a *dialog box* is displayed to assist in describing the operation that is to be performed. The dialog box is filled out with the appropriate information by typing it in at the keyboard. Then the return key is again depressed to initiate the defined operation.

Figure 6.20(b) shows the sequence of events that take place when a source program file is created with EDIT. For an example, we will simply repeat the creation of the block move program of Fig. 6.21, but this time we will save it as the file BLOCK.ASM. Again the sequence begins with a command to load and run the editor program. In this case, the command is

```
C:\DOS>EDIT A:BLOCK.ASM   (↵)
```

As with EDLIN, the EDIT program first checks to see if the file BLOCK.ASM already exists. If it does, the file is read from drive A, loaded into memory, and displayed on the screen. This would be the case if an existing source program is to be corrected or changed. At this point, we have already demonstrated one of the benefits of EDIT over EDLIN. That is, after loading, the complete source program is in view on the screen ready to be edited.

Looking at the flowchart, we see that the next step is to make the changes in the program. Then, the program would be carefully examined to verify that no additional errors were made during the edit process. The last step is to save the modified program in either the old file or as a file with a new name. Note that a backup file is not automatically made as part of the file save process of EDIT.

Let us assume that the file BLOCK.ASM does not already exist and go through the sequence of events that must take place to create a source program. In this case, the exact same command can be used to bring up the editor. However, when it comes up, no program can be loaded, so the screen remains blank. The lines of the assembly language program are simply typed in one after the other. The TAB key is used to make the appropriate indents in the instructions. For instance, to enter the first instruction of the program in Fig. 6.21, the TAB key is depressed once for a single indent and then MOV is keyed in. Another TAB is needed to indent again and then the operand AX,DATASEGADDR is entered. The first instruction is now complete and so the RETURN key is depressed to position the cursor for entry of the next instruction. This sequence is repeated until the whole block-move program has been entered. Notice that when entering the sixth instruction the label NXTPT: is entered at the left margin and then TAB is depressed to indent to the position for MOV.

The ease in which corrections can be made in the source file is another benefit of EDIT. If errors were made as the instructions of the block-move program were entered, the arrow keys can be used to simply reposition the cursor to the spot that needs to be changed. Next the DELETE key (for characters to the right of the cursor) or Backspace key (for characters to the left of the cursor) is used to remove the incorrect characters. Then, the correct characters are typed. Actually, the editing capability of EDIT is more versatile than just described. Commands are provided to move, copy, delete, find, or find and replace a character, string of characters, or block of text. For instance, we may need to change the name of an operand each time it occurs in a large program. Instead of having to go through the program instruction by instruction to find each occurrence of the operand, this operation can be done with a single find and replace command.

Assuming that all corrections have been made, we are now ready to save the program. At the top of the EDIT screen is a *menu bar* with four menus: *File*, *Edit*, *Search*, and *Options*. The save operations are located under the File menu. To select this menu, hold down the ALT key and depress the F key. This causes a *pop down menu* that lists the file commands to appear at the top of the screen. When the menu appears, the *New* command is highlighted. Use the down arrow (↓) key to move the highlighted area down to the *Save As* operation. Now depress the return (↵) key to initiate the file save operation. This displays the Save As dialog box. In the dialog box, A:BLOCK.ASM will automatically be filled in as the file name. If the file name is to remain the same, simply depress the return key to save the file. On the other hand, if the name is to be changed, type in the new drive designator and file name information before depressing (↵).

At this moment, the source program has been created, verified, and saved, but we are still in the EDIT program. We are ready to exit the EDIT program. *EXIT* is another operation that is in the File menu. To exit EDIT, depress ALT and then F to display the File pop-down menu. Use the (↓) key to select Exit (or type X) and then depress (↵). The EDIT program terminates and the DOS prompt reappears on the screen.

▲ 6.6 ASSEMBLING SOURCE PROGRAMS WITH MASM

Up to this point, we have studied the steps involved in writing a program, the assembly language syntax and pseudo-op statements provided in MASM, the structure of an assembly language program, and how to create a source program using the EDLIN and EDIT editors. Now is the time to learn how to bring up MASM, use it to assemble a source program file into an object-code module, and examine the outputs that are produced by the assembler.

Earlier we said that an assembler is the program used to convert a file that contains an assembly language source program to its equivalent object file of 8088 machine code. Figure 6.24 shows that the input to the assembler program is the assembly language source program. This is the program that is to be assembled. The source file is read by the assembler program from its file on the diskette and translated into three outputs. As shown in Fig. 6.24, these outputs are the *object module*, *the source listing*, and a *cross-reference table*.

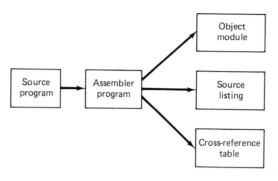

Figure 6.24 Assembling a source program.

Initiating the Assembly Process

To assemble a program, we must first change to the directory on drive C that contains the MASM program and then insert the diskette that contains the source file into drive A. The source file diskette should not be write protected. Now the assembler program is loaded by keying in

$$C:\backslash MASM>MASM \quad (\hookleftarrow)$$

In response to this entry, the following prompt is displayed.

$$Source\ filename[.ASM]:$$

Next we must enter the name of the source file with its extension and then depress ($\hookleftarrow$). Let us assume that we are assembling the source program that was shown in Fig. 6.2(b) and that its file was assigned the name BLOCK.SRC. Therefore, the input is

$$Source\ filename[.ASM]:A:BLOCK.SRC \quad (\hookleftarrow)$$

Next the assembler program displays a second prompt, which asks for entry of the file name (with extension) that is to be used to save the object-code module that it creates during the assembly process. This prompt is

$$Object\ filename[BLOCK.OBJ]:$$

Notice that the assembler automatically fills in the file name entered for the source file and appends this file name with the default extension OBJ. In our example, the file is to be created on the diskette in drive A. For this reason, we will reenter the name for the object file with drive A specified.

$$Object\ filename[BLOCK.OBJ]:A:BLOCK.OBJ \quad (\hookleftarrow)$$

Actually, the response can simply be

```
Object filename[BLOCK.OBJ]:A:    (⏎)
```

After this entry is made, a third prompt is displayed. This prompt is

```
Source listing[NUL.LST]:
```

Note that a file name of NUL.LST is automatically assigned for the source listing if the (⏎) key is depressed without entry of an alternate file name. This default file name causes suppression of a source listing, and none will be produced. If we want the assembler to create a source listing during the assembly process, we can enter a name for a listing file. Let us use a file BLOCK.LST to save our source listing. This is done by entering

```
Source listing[NUL.LST]:A:BLOCK.LST    (⏎)
```

Another way of issuing the source listing response lets us just print the listing instead of saving it in a file. This is done by simply entering LPT1 in place of a file name.

The last prompt displayed is for the name of a cross-reference table file. This prompt is

```
Cross reference[NUL.CRF]:
```

Again, depressing (⏎) without entering a file name causes creation of a cross-reference file to be suppressed. However, for our example, let us create one by assigning the name BLOCK.CRF to the file. This is done by making the entry

```
Cross reference[NUL.CRF]:A:BLOCK.CRF    (⏎)
```

This completes the inputs needed to assemble a source file.

As soon as the cross-reference file name entry is made, the assembly process begins and runs through to completion without any additional entries. First the contents of the source file are read from the file BLOCK.SRC on the diskette in drive A; it is translated and information for the listing and cross-reference table is produced; finally the object code, source listing, and cross-reference table are saved on the diskette in drive A in files BLOCK.OBJ, BLOCK.LST, and BLOCK.CRF, respectively. The contents of these files can be printed with the TYPE command of DOS. Displayed information for the start-up and execution of the assembler for our example program is shown in Fig. 6.25(a), the contents of the source-code file are shown in Fig. 6.25(b), and the source listing file is shown in Fig. 6.25(c).

The cross-reference-table file produced by MASM is not in the correct form to be printed. This is because it is not yet an ASCII file. To convert it to ASCII form, we can use the CREF program that is provided with MASM. For instance, to convert the cross-reference file for our example to an ASCII file, we issue the command

```
C:\DOS>CREF A.BLOCK.CRF A:BLOCK.REF     (↵)
```

This command reads the file BLOCK.CRF on the diskette in drive A as its input, converts it to an ASCII file, and outputs the ASCII file to a new file called BLOCK.REF, also on the diskette in drive A. Now the file BLOCK.REF can be displayed or printed with the TYPE command. Figure 6.25(d) shows the contents of the file.

In the assembly process, the default file extensions specified in the prompts can also be used. Assuming that the source file has the extension .ASM, the responses to the prompts would be

```
Source filename[.ASM]:A:BLOCK   (↵)
Object filename[BLOCK.OBJ]:A:   (↵)
Source listing[NUL.LST]:        (↵)
Cross reference[NUL.CRF]:        (↵)
```

Initiating the assembler with this sequence results in no source listing or cross-reference file. If the files reside in the MASM directory on drive C instead of a diskette in drive A, the responses to the prompts will be

```
Source filename[.ASM]:BLOCK   (↵)
Object filename[BLOCK.OBJ]:   (↵)
Source listing[NUL.LST]:LPT1(↵)
Cross reference[NUL.CRF]:      (↵)
```

In this example, we have elected to print the source listing to the printer connected at the LPT1 port of the PC instead of saving it in a file.

Once familiar with the use of the assembler, a command line entry sequence can be used to call it up. This is done by specifying the file names in the entry sequence that calls MASM from the DOS prompt. For our original example, the

```
C:\MASM>MASM
Microsoft (R) Macro Assembler Version 5.10
Copyright (C) Microsoft Corp 1981, 1988.  All rights reserved.

Source filename [.ASM]: A:BLOCK.SRC
Object filename [BLOCK.OBJ]: A:BLOCK.OBJ
Source listing  [NUL.LST]: A:BLOCK.LST
Cross-reference [NUL.CRF]: A:BLOCK.CRF

 47218 + 427466 Bytes symbol space free

    0 Warning Errors
    0 Severe  Errors
```

Figure 6.25(a)   Display sequence for assembly of a program.

```
TITLE BLOCK-MOVE PROGRAM

        PAGE       ,132

COMMENT *This program moves a block of specified number of bytes
        from one place to another place*


;Define constants used in this program

        N=                 16          ;Bytes to be moved
        BLK1ADDR=          100H        ;Source block offset address
        BLK2ADDR=          120H        ;Destination block offset addr
        DATASEGADDR=       2000H       ;Data segment start address

STACK_SEG          SEGMENT            STACK 'STACK'
                   DB                 64 DUP(?)
STACK_SEG          ENDS
CODE_SEG           SEGMENT            'CODE'
BLOCK              PROC       FAR
     ASSUME        CS:CODE_SEG,SS:STACK_SEG

;To return to DEBUG program put return address on the stack

        PUSH    DS
        MOV     AX, 0
        PUSH    AX

;Setup the data segment address

        MOV     AX, DATASEGADDR
        MOV     DS, AX

;Setup the source and destination offset adresses

        MOV     SI, BLK1ADDR
        MOV     DI, BLK2ADDR

;Setup the count of bytes to be moved

        MOV     CX, N

;Copy source block to destination block

NXTPT:    MOV    AH, [SI]       ;Move a byte
          MOV    [DI], AH
          INC    SI             ;Update pointers
          INC    DI
          DEC    CX             ;Update byte counter
          JNZ    NXTPT          ;Repeat for next byte
          RET                   ;Return to DEBUG program
BLOCK              ENDP
CODE_SEG           ENDS
     END           BLOCK                ;End of program
```

Figure 6.25(b)   Block-move source program.

command would be issued as

C:\MASM>MASM A:BLOCK.SRC,A:BLOCK.OBJ,A:BLOCK.LST,A:BLOCK.CRF (↵)

If any of the default names are to be used, simply enter a comma in place of a name.

Syntax Errors in an Assembled File

If the assembler program identifies *syntax errors* in the source file while it is being assembled, the locations of the errors are marked in the source listing file

```
 1
 2
 3                             TITLE BLOCK-MOVE PROGRAM
 4
 5                             PAGE          ,132
 6
 7                    COMMENT *This program moves a block of specified number of bytes
 8                             from one place to another place*
 9
10
11                             ;Define constants used in this program
12
13 = 0010                      N=            16        ;Bytes to be moved
14 = 0100                      BLK1ADDR=     100H      ;Source block offset address
15 = 0120                      BLK2ADDR=     120H      ;Destination block offset addr
16 = 2000                      DATASEGADDR=    2000H     ;Data segment start address
17
18
19 0000                        STACK_SEG     SEGMENT         STACK 'STACK'
20 0000  0040[                               DB        64 DUP(?)
21       ??
22              ]
23
24 0040                        STACK_SEG     ENDS
25
26
27 0000                        CODE_SEG      SEGMENT         'CODE'
28 0000                        BLOCK         PROC      FAR
29                             ASSUME        CS:CODE_SEG,SS:STACK_SEG
30
31                             ;To return to DEBUG program put return address on the stack
32
33 0000  1E                    PUSH   DS
34 0001  B8 0000               MOV    AX, 0
35 0004  50                    PUSH   AX
36
37                             ;Setup the data segment address
38
39 0005  B8 2000               MOV    AX, DATASEGADDR
40 0008  8E D8                 MOV    DS, AX
41
42                             ;Setup the source and destination offset adresses
43
44 000A  BE 0100               MOV    SI, BLK1ADDR
45 000D  BF 0120               MOV    DI, BLK2ADDR
46
47                             ;Setup the count of bytes to be moved
48
49 0010  B9 0010               MOV    CX, N
50
51                             ;Copy source block to destination block
52
53 0013  8A 24         NXTPT:  MOV    AH, [SI]                ;Move a byte
54 0015  88 25                 MOV    [DI], AH
55 0017  46                    INC    SI                      ;Update pointers
56 0018  47                    INC    DI
57 0019  49                    DEC    CX                      ;Update byte counter
```

Figure 6.25(c)   Source listing file.

with an *error number* and *error message*. Moreover, the total number of errors is displayed on the screen at the end of the assembly process. Looking at the displayed information for our assembly example in Fig. 6.25(a), we find that no errors occurred.

Figure 6.26(a) shows the response on the display when four syntax errors are found during the assembly process. The listing for the program, which is shown in Fig. 6.26(b), contains four syntax errors. Notice how the errors are marked in the

```
58 001A  75 F7          JNZ    NXTPT          ;Repeat for next byte
59 001C  CB             RET                   ;Return to DEBUG program
60 001D                 BLOCK      ENDP
61 001D                 CODE_SEG   ENDS
62                      END        BLOCK      ;End of program
```

Segments and Groups:

Name	Length	Align	Combine Class
CODE_SEG	001D	PARA	NONE 'CODE'
STACK_SEG	0040	PARA	STACK 'STACK'

Symbols:

Name	Type	Value	Attr
BLK1ADDR	NUMBER	0100	
BLK2ADDR	NUMBER	0120	
BLOCK	F PROC	0000	CODE_SEG Length = 001D
DATASEGADDR	NUMBER	2000	
N	NUMBER	0010	
NXTPT	L NEAR	0013	CODE_SEG
@CPU	TEXT	0101h	
@FILENAME	TEXT	block	
@VERSION	TEXT	510	

```
    59 Source  Lines
    59 Total   Lines
    15 Symbols

47222 + 347542 Bytes symbol space free

     0 Warning Errors
     0 Severe  Errors
```

Figure 6.25(c)   (Continued)

source listing. For instance, in Fig. 6.26(b) we find error number A2105 following the instruction DCR CX. Looking at Fig. 6.26(a), we find that this error message stands for a syntax error. The error that was made is that the mnemonic of the instruction is spelled wrong. It should read DEC CX. The source program must first be edited to correct this error and the other three errors, and then it must be reassembled.

EXAMPLE 6.5

What is the meaning of the error code at line 49 of the program source listing in Fig. 6.26(b)?

Solution

Looking at Fig. 6.26(b), we get the error number as A2009 and in Fig. 6.26(a) we see that it means that a symbol was not defined. The undefined symbol is N.

```
Microsoft Cross-Reference  Version 5.10      Sun May 17 18:17:20 1992
BLOCK-MOVE PROGRAM

   Symbol Cross-Reference          (# definition, + modification)  Cref-1

@CPU . . . . . . . . . . . . . .    1#
@VERSION . . . . . . . . . . . .    1#

BLK1ADDR . . . . . . . . . . . .   14#    44
BLK2ADDR . . . . . . . . . . . .   15#    45
BLOCK. . . . . . . . . . . . . .   28#    60     62

CODE . . . . . . . . . . . . . .   27
CODE_SEG . . . . . . . . . . . .   27#    29     61

DATASEGADDR. . . . . . . . . . .   16#    39

N. . . . . . . . . . . . . . . .   13#    49
NXTPT. . . . . . . . . . . . . .   53#    58

STACK. . . . . . . . . . . . . .   19
STACK_SEG. . . . . . . . . . . .   19#    24     29


   12 Symbols
```

Figure 6.25(d)   Cross-reference table file.

Object Module

The most important output produced by the assembler is the object-code file. The contents of this file are called the object module. The object module is a machine-language version of the program. Even through the object module is the machine code for the source program, it cannot be directly run on the microcomputer. It must first be processed by the linker to create an executable run module.

Source Listing

Let us now look more closely at the source listing in Fig. 6.25(c). Notice that the first column assigns a number to every statement line used when the source

```
C:\MASM>MASM
Microsoft (R) Macro Assembler Version 5.10
Copyright (C) Microsoft Corp 1981, 1988.  All rights reserved.

Source filename [.ASM]: A:EBLOCK.SRC
Object filename [EBLOCK.OBJ]: A:
Source listing  [NUL.LST]: A:EBLOCK
Cross-reference [NUL.CRF]: A:EBLOCK
A:EBLOCK.SRC(13): error A2105: Expected: instruction, directive, or label
A:EBLOCK.SRC(34): error A2105: Expected: instruction, directive, or label
A:EBLOCK.SRC(46): error A2009: Symbol not defined: N
A:EBLOCK.SRC(54): error A2105: Expected: instruction, directive, or label

  47200 + 427484 Bytes symbol space free

     0 Warning Errors
     4 Severe  Errors
```

Figure 6.26(a)   Displayed information for a source file with assembly syntax errors.

```
     1
     2
     3                           TITLE BLOCK-MOVE PROGRAM
     4
     5                           PAGE        ,132
     6
     7                           COMMENT *This program moves a block of specified number of bytes
     8                                   from one place to another place*
     9
    10
    11                           ;Define constants used in this program
    12
    13                                     N           16          ;Bytes to be moved
eblock.src(13): error A2105: Expected: instruction, directive, or label
    14 = 0100                              BLK1ADDR=   100H        ;Source block offset address
    15 = 0120                              BLK2ADDR=   120H        ;Destination block offset addr
    16 = 2000                              DATASEGADDR=2000H       ;Data segment start address
    17
    18
    19 0000                      STACK_SEG   SEGMENT            STACK 'STACK'
    20 0000   0040[                         DB                 64 DUP(?)
    21         ??                  ]
    22                      ]
    23
    24 0040                      STACK_SEG   ENDS
    25
    26
    27 0000                      CODE_SEG    SEGMENT            'CODE'
    28 0000                      BLOCK       PROC               FAR
    29                           ASSUME      CS:CODE_SEG,SS:STACK_SEG
    30
    31                           ;To return to DEBUG program put return address on the stack
    32
    33 0000  1E                  PUSH  DS
    34 0001  B8 0000             MOV   AX, 0
    35 0004  50                  PUSH  AX
    36
    37                           Setup the data segment address
eblock.src(34): error A2105: Expected: instruction, directive, or label
    38
    39 0005  B8 2000             MOV   AX, DATASEGADDR
    40 0008  8E D8               MOV   DS, AX
    41
    42                           ;Setup the source and destination offset adresses
    43
    44 000A  BE 0100             MOV   SI, BLK1ADDR
    45 000D  BF 0120             MOV   DI, BLK2ADDR
    46
    47                           ;Setup the count of bytes to be moved
    48
    49 0010  8B 0E 0000 U        MOV   CX, N
eblock.src(46): error A2009: Symbol not defined: N
    50
    51                           ;Copy source block to destination block
    52
    53 0014  8A 24       NXTPT:  MOV   AH, [SI]        ;Move a byte
    54 0016  88 25               MOV   [DI], AH
```

Figure 6.26(b)   Source listing for a file with syntax errors.

file for the program was created with the editor. The second column is the starting offset address of the machine-language instruction from the beginning of the current code segment. In the next column we find the bytes of machine code for the instructions. They are expressed in hexadecimal form. If an "R" is listed after a number, it means that an *external reference* exists and that the link operation may

```
    55 0018  46                    INC   SI              ;Update pointers
    56 0019  47                    INC   DI
    57                             DCR   CX              ;Update byte counter
eblock.src(54): error A2105: Expected: instruction, directive, or label
    58 001A  75 F8                 JNZ   NXTPT           ;Repeat for next byte
    59 001C  CB                    RET                   ;Return to DEBUG program
    60 001D                BLOCK       ENDP
    61 001D                CODE_SEG    ENDS
    62                     END         BLOCK             ;End of program
```

Segments and Groups:

N a m e	Length	Align	Combine Class
CODE_SEG	001D	PARA	NONE 'CODE'
STACK_SEG	0040	PARA	STACK 'STACK'

Symbols:

N a m e	Type	Value	Attr	
BLK1ADDR	NUMBER	0100		
BLK2ADDR	NUMBER	0120		
BLOCK	F PROC	0000	CODE_SEG	Length = 001D
DATASEGADDR	NUMBER	2000		
NXTPT	L NEAR	0014	CODE_SEG	
@CPU	TEXT	0101h		
@FILENAME	TEXT	eblock		
@VERSION	TEXT	510		

```
    59 Source  Lines
    59 Total   Lines
    14 Symbols

 47200 + 427052 Bytes symbol space free

     0 Warning Errors
     4 Severe  Errors
```

Figure 6.26(b)   (Continued)

modify this value. The machine-code instructions are followed by the original source-code instructions in the next column, and the comments in the last column.

For instance, at line number 39, the machine code for the assembly language instruction MOV AX,DATASEGADDR is found. This instruction is encoded with three bytes and is

```
     MOV  AX,DATASEGADDR = B80020H
```

A symbol table is also produced as part of the source listing. It is a list of all of the symbols defined in the program. The symbol table for our example program is shown at the bottom of the source listing in Fig. 6.25(c). Notice that the name of each symbol is listed along with its type (and length for data), value, and attribute. The types of symbols identified are *label*, *variable*, *number*, and *procedure*. For example, in Fig. 6.25(c) we find that the symbol BLK1ADDR is a number and its value is 0100_{16}. For this symbol, no attribute is indicated. On the other hand, for the symbol NXTPT, which is a near-label with value 00013_{16}, the attribute is CODE_SEG.

The source listing is a valuable aid in correcting errors in the program. For instance, earlier we found that syntax errors are marked in the source listing. Therefore, they can be easily found and corrected. Since both the source and corresponding machine code are provided in the source listing, it also serves as a valuable tool for identifying and correcting logical errors in the writing of the program.

EXAMPLE 6.6

What is the cause of the error A2105 that is located between lines 37 and 38 of the source listing in Fig. 6.26(b)?

Solution

In Fig. 6.26(b), we find that this error is in the comment and that the cause is a missing ";" at the start of the statement.

Cross-Reference Table

The cross-reference table is also useful when debugging programs that contain logical errors. The cross-reference table is a table that tells the number of the line in the source program at which each symbol is defined and the number of each line in which it is referenced. The line number followed by the symbol # is the location at which the symbol is defined. For instance, in the table of Fig. 6.25(d), we find that the label NXTPT is defined in line 53 and it is referenced in line 58.

Another use of the cross-reference table is when a program is to be modified in such a way that the name of a symbol must be changed. The cross-reference table can be used to find all of the locations where the symbol is used. In this way, the locations can be easily found and changed with the editor.

EXAMPLE 6.7

Use the cross-reference information in Fig. 6.25(d) to determine in which lines of the source listing in Fig. 6.25(c) the symbol BLK1ADDR is referenced.

Solution

The table in Fig. 6.25(d) shows that BLK1ADDR is referenced twice in the source program. These references are identified as lines 14 and 44 of the listing.

▲ 6.7 CREATING A RUN MODULE WITH THE LINK PROGRAM

In section 6.6 we indicated that the object module produced by the assembler is not yet an executable file. That is, in its current state it cannot be loaded with the DEBUG program and run on the 8088 microprocessor in the PC. To convert an object module to an executable machine-code file (run module), we must process it with the linker. The link operation for 8088 object code is performed by the LINK program, which is part of the DOS.

Modular Programming

At this point we may ask the question, "Why doesn't the assembler directly produce an executable run module?" To answer this question, let us look into an important idea behind the use of the LINK program and that is *modular programming*. The program we have been using as an example in this chapter is quite simple. For this reason, it can be easily contained in a single source file. However, most practical application programs are very large. For example, a source program may contain 2,000 assembly language statements. When assembled, this can result in as much as 4,000 to 8,000 bytes of machine code. For development purpose, programs of this size are frequently broken down into a number of parts called *modules* and the individual modules are worked on by different programmers. Each module is written independently and then all modules are combined together to form a single executable run module. This idea is illustrated in Fig. 6.27. Notice that the LINK program is the software tool that is used to combine the modules together. Its inputs are the object code for modules 1, 2, and 3. Execution of the linker combines these programs into a single run module.

The technique of writing larger programs as a series of modules has several benefits. First, since several programmers are working on the project in parallel, the program can be completed in a much shorter period of time. Another benefit is that the smaller sizes of the modules require less time to edit and assemble. For instance, if we were not using modular programming, to make a change in just one statement the complete program would have to be edited, reassembled, and re-

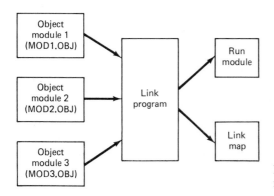

Figure 6.27 Linking object modules.

linked. On the other hand, when using modular programming, just that module containing the statement that needs to be changed can be edited and reassembled. Then the new object module is relinked with the rest of the old object modules to give a new run module.

A third benefit derived from modular programming is that it makes it easier to reuse old software. For instance, a new software design may need some functions for which modules have already been written as part of an old design. If these modules were integrated into a single large program, we would need to edit them out carefully and transfer them to the new source file. However, if these segments of program exist as separate modules, we may need to do no additional editing to integrate them into the new application.

Initiating the Link Program

Even though our example program has just one object module, we must still perform the link operation on it to obtain a run module. This is because the actual physical addresses to be used by the program when loaded on a PC need to be resolved. Let us now look at how this is done using the LINK program. First the MASM directory on the C drive must be entered and then the diskette that contains object file BLOCK.OBJ is put into drive A. Now we invoke the linker with the command

```
C:\MASM>LINK   (↵)
```

The linker program is loaded and starts to run. It begins by prompting for input of the object file name. This prompt is

```
Object Modules[.OBJ]:
```

In response to this prompt, we enter the names of all object modules that are to be linked together. The file names are listed, separated by the + sign. For example, to link the three object modules named MOD1.OBJ, MOD2.OBJ, and MOD3.OBJ the input would be

```
Object Modules[.OBJ]:A:MOD1.OBJ+A:MOD2.OBJ+A:MOD3.OBJ   (↵)
```

For our earlier example, we just have one object file, which is called BLOCK.OBJ. Therefore, the input is

```
Object Modules[.OBJ]:A:BLOCK   (↵)
```

Here, entry of the extension .OBJ is optional. That is, we could have entered just A:BLOCK followed by (↵).

Next, the linker program asks for input of the name of the file into which it is to save the run module. It does this with the prompt

```
Run file [BLOCK.EXE]:
```

Notice that it automatically creates a default file name by appending the .EXE extension to the first file name entered as part of the object module prompt. For this prompt, the file name can be changed, but the .EXE extension should be kept for compatibility with the DOS and DEBUG program. Let us use the default file name but assign it to drive A instead of C. To do this, the input entry is

```
Run File[BLOCK.EXE]:A:    (↵)
```

At the completion of this entry, a third prompt is displayed by the program. It is

```
List File[NUL.MAP]:
```

Selection of the default name NUL.MAP causes the linker to suppress formation of a link map file. For our example, we will request one to be generated and assign it the file name BLOCK.MAP. This is done by issuing the command

```
List File[NUL.MAP]:A:BLOCK.MAP    (↵)
```

The last prompt is

```
Libraries[.LIB]:
```

It asks us whether or not we want to include subroutines from a library in the link process. If so, just enter the name of the file that contains the libraries and depress (↵). Libraries are more widely used with high-level languages. For our example, we will not require use of a library; therefore, (↵) is simply depressed.

```
Libraries[.LIB]:    (↵)
```

This completes the start-up of the linker.

After the response to the library prompt, the linker program reads the object files, combines them, and resolves all external references. Moreover, it produces the information for the link map. Finally, it saves the run module on the diskette in drive A in file BLOCK.EXE and the link map information in BLOCK.MAP. The sequence of entries made to invoke the linker for our example is shown in Fig. 6.28(a) and the map file BLOCK.MAP is shown in Fig. 6.28(b).

The link map shows the start address, stop address, and length for each memory segment employed by the program that was linked. Looking at the link map for our program, which is shown in Fig. 6.28(b), we find that the code segment starts at address 00040_{16} and ends at address $0005C_{16}$. The program is $1D_{16}$ equals 30 bytes long.

EXAMPLE 6.8

From the link map in Fig. 6.28(b), find the range of addresses used for the stack segment. How many bytes are in use?

```
C:\MASM>LINK

Microsoft (R) Segmented-Executable Linker  Version 5.13
Copyright (C) Microsoft Corp 1984-1991.  All rights reserved.

Object Modules [.OBJ]: A:BLOCK
Run File [C:BLOCK.exe]: A:
List File [NUL.MAP]: A:BLOCK.MAP
Libraries [.LIB]:
Definitions File [NUL.DEF]:
```

(a)

```
Start  Stop   Length Name              Class
00000H 0003FH 00040H STACK_SEG         STACK
00040H 0005CH 0001DH CODE_SEG          CODE

Program entry point at 0004:0000
```

(b)

Figure 6.28 (a) Display sequence for initiating linking of object files. (b) Link map file.

Solution

The link map indicates that addresses from 00000_{16} to $0003F_{16}$ are used for storage of stack data. From the length we find that this represents 40H bytes.

▲ 6.8 LOADING AND EXECUTING A RUN MODULE

In Chapter 3 we learned how to bring up the DEBUG program; how to use its commands; and how to load, execute, and debug the operation of a program. At that time, we loaded the machine code for the program and data with memory-modify commands. Up to this point in this chapter, we have learned how to form a source program using assembly language and pseudo-op statements, how to assemble the program into an object module, and how to use the linker to produce a run module. Here we will load and execute the run module BLOCK.EXE that was produced in section 6.7 for the source program BLOCK.SRC.

When the DEBUG program was loaded in Chapter 3, we did not have a run module available. For this reason, we just brought up the debugger by typing in DEBUG and depressing (⏎). Now that we do have a run module, the debugger will be brought up in a different way and the run module will be loaded at the same time. This is done by issuing the command

C:\DOS>DEBUG A:BLOCK.EXE   (⏎)

In response to this command, both the DEBUG program and the run module BLOCK.EXE are loaded into the PC's memory. As shown in Fig. 6.29, after loading, the debug prompt "_" is displayed. Next the register status is dumped with an R command. Notice that DS is initialized with the value $11C6_{16}$.

```
C:\DOS>DEBUG A:BLOCK.EXE
-R
AX=0000  BX=0000  CX=005D  DX=0000  SP=0040  BP=0000  SI=0000  DI=0000
DS=11C5  ES=11C5  SS=11D5  CS=11D9  IP=0000   NV UP EI PL NZ NA PO NC
11D9:0000 1E            PUSH    DS
-U CS:0 1C
11D9:0000 1E            PUSH    DS
11D9:0001 B80000        MOV     AX,0000
11D9:0004 50            PUSH    AX
11D9:0005 B80020        MOV     AX,2000
11D9:0008 8ED8          MOV     DS,AX
11D9:000A BE0001        MOV     SI,0100
11D9:000D BF2001        MOV     DI,0120
11D9:0010 B91000        MOV     CX,0010
11D9:0013 8A24          MOV     AH,[SI]
11D9:0015 8825          MOV     [DI],AH
11D9:0017 46            INC     SI
11D9:0018 47            INC     DI
11D9:0019 49            DEC     CX
11D9:001A 75F7          JNZ     0013
11D9:001C CB            RETF
-G =CS:0 13

AX=2000  BX=0000  CX=0010  DX=0000  SP=003C  BP=0000  SI=0100  DI=0120
DS=2000  ES=11C5  SS=11D5  CS=11D9  IP=0013   NV UP EI PL NZ NA PO NC
11D9:0013 8A24          MOV     AH,[SI]                          DS:0100=50
-F DS:100 10F FF
-F DS:120 12F 00
= -G =CS:13 1A

AX=FF20  BX=0000  CX=000F  DX=0000  SP=003C  BP=0000  SI=0101  DI=0121
DS=2000  ES=11C5  SS=11D5  CS=11D9  IP=001A   NV UP EI PL NZ AC PE NC
11D9:001A 75F7          JNZ     0013
-D DS:100 10F
2000:0100  FF FF FF FF FF FF FF FF-FF FF FF FF FF FF FF FF   ................
-D DS:120 12F
2000:0120  FF 00 00 00 00 00 00 00-00 00 00 00 00 00 00 00   ................
-G

Program terminated normally
-D DS:100 10F
2000:0100  FF FF FF FF FF FF FF FF-FF FF FF FF FF FF FF FF   ................
-D DS:120 12F
2000:0120  FF FF FF FF FF FF FF FF-FF FF FF FF FF FF FF FF   ................
-Q

C:\DOS>
```

Figure 6.29   Loading and executing the run module BLOCK.EXE.

Let us now verify that the program has loaded correctly. This is done with the command

$$-\text{U CS:000 01C}\quad(\hookleftarrow)$$

Comparing the program displayed in Fig. 6.29 as a result of the command to the source program in Fig. 6.2(b), we see that they are essentially the same. Therefore, the program has been loaded correctly.

Now we will execute the first eight instructions of the program and verify the operation they perform. To do this, we issue the command

$$-\text{G =CS:000 013}\quad(\hookleftarrow)$$

The information displayed at the completion of this command is also shown in Fig. 6.29. Here we find that the registers have been initialized as follows: DS contains

2000_{16}, AX contains 2000_{16}, SI contains 0100_{16}, DI contains 0120_{16}, and CX contains 0010_{16}.

The FILL command is used to initialize the bytes of data in the source and destination blocks. The storage locations in the source block are loaded with FF_{16} with the command

```
—F DS:100 10F FF  (↵)
```

and the storage locations in the destination block are loaded with 00_{16} with the command

```
—F DS:120 12F 00  (↵)
```

Next we will execute down through the program to the JNZ instruction, address $01A_{16}$,

```
—G =CS:013 01A  (↵)
```

To check the state of the data blocks, we use the commands

```
—D DS:100 10F  (↵)
—D DS:120 12F  (↵)
```

Looking at the displayed blocks of data in Fig. 6.29, we see that the source block is unchanged and that FF_{16} has been copied into the first element of the destination block.

Finally, the program is run to completion with the command

```
—G  (↵)
```

By once more looking at the two blocks of data with the commands

```
—D DS:100 10F  (↵)
—D DS:120 12F  (↵)
```

we find that the contents of the source block have been copied into the destination block.

DEBUG is used to run a program when we must either debug the operation of the program or want to understand its execution step by step. If we just want to run a program, instead of observe its operation, another method can be used. The run module (.EXE file) can be executed at the DOS prompt by simply entering its name followed by (↵). This will cause the program to be loaded and then executed to completion. For instance, to execute the run module BLOCK.EXE that resides of a diskette in drive A, we enter

```
C:\DOS>A:BLOCK  (↵)
```

ASSIGNMENTS

Section 6.2

1. List the basic steps in the general development cycle for an assembly language program.
2. What document is produced as a result of the problem description step of the development cycle?
3. Give a name that is used to refer to the software solution planned for a problem. What is the name of the document that is used to describe this solution plan?
4. What is a flowchart?
5. Draw the flowchart symbol used to identify a subroutine.
6. What type of program is EDIT?
7. What type of program is used to produce an object module?
8. What does MASM stand for?
9. What type of program is used to produce a run module?
10. In which part of the development cycle is the EDIT program used? The MASM program? The LINK program? The DEBUG program?
11. Assuming that the file name is PROG_A, give typical names for the files that result from the use of the EDLIN program. The MASM program? The LINK program?

Section 6.3

12. What are the two types of statements in a source program?
13. What is the function of an assembly language instruction?
14. What is the function of a pseudo-operation?
15. What are the four elements of an assembly language statement?
16. What part of the instruction format is always required?
17. What are the two limitations on format when writing source statements for the MASM?
18. What is the function of a label?
19. What is the maximum number of characters of a label that will be recognized by the MASM?
20. What is the function of the opcode?
21. What is the function of operands?
22. In the instruction statement

```
SUB_A:   MOV  CL,0FFH
```

what are the source and destination operands?

23. What is the purpose of the comment field? How are comments processed by an assembler?

24. Give two differences between an assembly language statement and a pseudo-operation statement.

25. Write the instruction MOV AX,[32728D] with the source operand expressed both in binary and hexadecimal forms.

26. Rewrite the jump instruction JMP +25D with the operand expressed both in binary and hexadecimal forms.

27. Repeat Example 6.4 with the values A = 345, B = 234, and C = 111.

Section 6.4

28. Give another name for a pseudo-op.

29. List the names of the pseudo-op categories.

30. What is the function of the data pseudo-ops?

31. What happens when the statements

```
SRC_BLOCK = 0100H
DEST_BLOCK = SRC_BLOCK + 20H
```

are processed by the MASM assembler?

32. Describe the difference between the EQU and = pseudo-ops.

33. What does the statement

```
SEG_ADDR   DW   1234H
```

do when processed by the assembler?

34. What happens when the statement

```
BLOCK_1   DB   128 DUP(?)
```

is processed by the assembler?

35. Write a data pseudo-op statement to define INIT_COUNT as word size and assign it the value $F000_{16}$.

36. Write a data pseudo-op statement to allocate a block of 16 words in memory called SOURCE_BLOCK, but do not initialize them with data.

37. Write a pseudo-op statement that will initialize the block of memory storage locations allocated in problem 36 with the data values 0000H, 1000H, 2000H, 3000H, 4000H, 5000H, 6000H, 7000H, 8000H, 9000H, A000H, B000H, C000H, D000H, E000H, and F000H.

38. What does the statement

```
DATA_SEG   SEGMENT   BYTE MEMORY   'DATA'
```

mean?

39. Show how the segment-control pseudo-ops are used to define a segment called DATA_SEG that is aligned on a word-address boundary, overlaps other segments with the same name, and is a data segment.

40. What is the name of the smaller segments that modular programming techniques specify that programs should be developed in?

41. What is a procedure?

42. Show the general structure of a far procedure called BLOCK that is to be accessible from other modules.

43. What is the function of an ORG pseudo-op?

44. Write an origin statement that causes machine code to be loaded at offset 1000H of the current code segment.

45. Write a page statement that will set up the printout for 55 lines per page and 80 characters per line and a title statement that will title pages of the source listing with "BLOCK-MOVE PROGRAM".

Section 6.5

46. What type of editor is EDLIN? EDIT?

47. Write an EDLIN command that will initiate editing of line 20.

48. What operation would the EDLIN command 15,17D perform?

49. Describe the operation performed by the EDLIN command 10,12,15C.

50. List the basic editing operations that can be performed using EDIT.

51. What are the names of the four menus in the EDIT menu bar?

52. How could a backup copy of the program in file BLOCK.ASM be created from the file menu?

Section 6.6

53. What is the input to the assembler program?

54. What are the outputs of the assembler? Give a brief description of each.

55. What name does the command entry

```
C:\MASM>MASM A:BLOCK,  ,BLOCK.LST,BLOCK.CRF
```

assign to each of the input and output files of the assembler?

56. What is the cause of the first error statement in the source listing of Fig. 6.26(b)?

57. Use the cross-reference table for the program in Fig. 6.25(d) to find in which line a value is assigned to N and in which lines it is referenced.

Section 6.7

58. Can the output of the assembler be directly executed by the 8088 microprocessor in the IBM PC?

59. Give three benefits of modular programming.

60. What is the input to the LINK program?

61. What are the outputs of the LINK program? Give a brief description of each.

62. If three object modules called MAIN.OBJ, SUB1.OBJ, and SUB2.OBJ are to be combined with LINK, write the response that must be made to the linker's Object Modules[.OBJ]: prompt. Assume that all three files are on a diskette in drive A.

Section 6.8

63. Write a DOS command that will load run module LAB.EXE while bringing up the DEBUG program. Assume that the run module file is on a diskette in drive A.

Application Problems

64. Upgrade the programs written for the assignment problems 11, 16, 22, 28, 36, 38, 42, and 43 in Chapter 4 so that they can be assembled using the MASM and debugged using DEBUG.

65. Upgrade the programs written for the assignment problems 5, 22, 23, 24, 25, 26, 35, 37, 38, 43, 44, 48, and 49 in Chapter 5 so that they can be assembled using the MASM and debugged using DEBUG.

The 8088 and 8086 Microprocessors and Their Memory Interfaces

▲ 7.1 INTRODUCTION

Up to this point, we have studied the 8088 and 8086 microprocessors from a software point of view. We covered their software architecture, instruction set, writing programs in assembly language, and found that the 8088 and 8086 were identical from the software point of view. This is not true of the hardware architectures of the 8088 and 8086 microcomputer systems. Now we will begin to examine the 8088 and 8086 microcomputer from the hardware point of view. This chapter is devoted to signal interfaces, memory interfaces, memory devices, and external memory subsystems. The following topics are presented in this chapter:

1. The 8088 and 8086 microprocessors
2. Minimum-mode and maximum-mode systems
3. Minimum-mode interface
4. Maximum-mode interface
5. Electrical characteristics
6. System clock
7. Bus cycle
8. Hardware organization of the memory address space
9. Memory bus status codes
10. Memory control signals

333

11. Read and write bus cycles
12. Memory interface circuits
13. Programmable logic arrays
14. Program storage memory—ROM, PROM, and EPROM
15. Data storage memory—SRAM and DRAM
16. Program storage memory and data storage memory circuits

▲ 7.2 THE 8088 AND 8086 MICROPROCESSORS

The 8086, which was first announced as a product in 1978, was the first 16-bit microprocessor introduced by Intel Corporation. It was followed by a second member of the 8086 family, the 8088 microprocessor, in 1979. The 8088 is fully software compatible with its predecessor, the 8086. The difference between these two devices is in their hardware architecture. Just like the 8086, the 8088 is internally a 16-bit MPU. However, externally the 8086 has a 16-bit data bus and the 8088 has an 8-bit data bus. This is the key hardware difference. Both devices have the ability to address up to 1M byte of memory via their 20-bit address buses. Moreover, they can address up to 64K of byte-wide input/output ports.

The 8088 and 8086 are both manufactured using *high-performance metal-oxide semiconductor (HMOS) technology*, and the circuitry on their chips is equivalent to approximately 29,000 transistors. They are enclosed in 40-pin packages as shown in Fig. 7.1(a) and (b), respectively. Many of their pins have multiple functions. For example, in the pin layout diagram of the 8088 we see that address bus lines A_0 through A_7 and data bus lines D_0 through D_7 are multiplexed. For this reason, these leads are labeled AD_0 through AD_7. By *multiplexed* we mean that the same physical pin carries an address bit at one time and the data bit at another time.

▲ 7.3 MINIMUM-MODE AND MAXIMUM-MODE SYSTEMS

The 8088 and 8086 microprocessors can be configured to work in either of two modes. These modes are known as the *minimum mode* and the *maximum mode*. The minimum mode is selected by applying logic 1 to the $MN/\overline{MX}$ input lead. Minimum mode 8088/8086 systems are typically smaller and contain a single microprocessor. Connecting $MN/\overline{MX}$ to logic 0 selects the maximum mode of operation. This configures the 8088/8086 system for use in larger systems and with multiple processors. This mode-selection feature lets the 8088 or 8086 better meet the needs of a wide variety of system requirements.

Depending on the mode of operation selected, the assignments for a number of the pins on the microprocessor package are changed. As shown in Fig. 7.1(a), the pin functions of the 8088 specified in parentheses are those that pertain to a maximum-mode system.

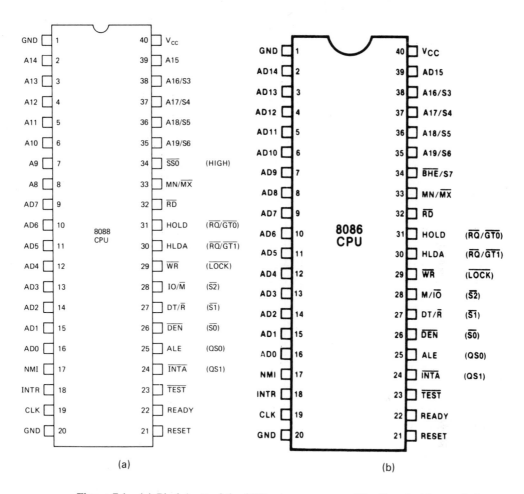

Figure 7.1 (a) Pin layout of the 8088 microprocessor. (Reprinted with permission of Intel Corporation, © 1981) (b) Pin layout of the 8086 microprocessor. (Reprinted with permission of Intel Corporation, © 1979)

The signals of the 8088 microprocessor that are common to both modes of operation, those unique to minimum mode and those unique to maximum mode, are listed in Fig. 7.2(a), (b), and (c), respectively. Here we find the name, function, and type for each signal. For example, the signal $\overline{RD}$ is in the common group. It functions as a read control output and is used to signal memory or I/O devices when the 8088's system bus is set up for input of data. Moreover, notice that the signals hold request (HOLD) and hold acknowledge (HLDA) are produced only in the minimum-mode system. If the 8088 is set up for maximum mode, they are replaced by the request/grant bus access control lines $\overline{RQ}/\overline{GT}_0$ and $\overline{RQ}/\overline{GT}_1$.

Common signals		
Name	Function	Type
AD7–AD0	Address/data bus	Bidirectional, 3-state
A15–A8	Address bus	Output, 3-state
A19/S6–A16/S3	Address/status	Output, 3-state
MN/$\overline{\text{MX}}$	Minimum/maximum Mode control	Input
$\overline{\text{RD}}$	Read control	Output, 3-state
$\overline{\text{TEST}}$	Wait on test control	Input
READY	Wait state control	Input
RESET	System reset	Input
NMI	Nonmaskable Interrupt request	Input
INTR	Interrupt request	Input
CLK	System clock	Input
V$_{\text{CC}}$	+5 V	Input
GND	Ground	

(a)

Minimum mode signals (MN/$\overline{\text{MX}}$ = V$_{\text{CC}}$)		
Name	Function	Type
HOLD	Hold request	Input
HLDA	Hold acknowledge	Output
$\overline{\text{WR}}$	Write control	Output, 3-state
IO/$\overline{\text{M}}$	IO/memory control	Output, 3-state
DT/$\overline{\text{R}}$	Data transmit/receive	Output, 3-state
$\overline{\text{DEN}}$	Data enable	Output, 3-state
$\overline{\text{SSO}}$	Status line	Output, 3-state
ALE	Address latch enable	Output
$\overline{\text{INTA}}$	Interrupt acknowledge	Output

(b)

Maximum mode signals (MN/$\overline{\text{MX}}$ = GND)		
Name	Function	Type
$\overline{\text{RQ}}/\overline{\text{GT}}$1, 0	Request/grant bus access control	Bidirectional
$\overline{\text{LOCK}}$	Bus priority lock control	Output, 3-state
$\overline{\text{S2}}$–$\overline{\text{S0}}$	Bus cycle status	Output, 3-state
QS1, QS0	Instruction queue status	Output

(c)

Figure 7.2 (a) Signals common to both minimum and maximum modes. (b) Unique minimum-mode signals. (c) Unique maximum-mode signals.

EXAMPLE 7.1

Which pins provide different signal function in the minimum-mode 8088 and minimum-mode 8086?

Solution

Comparing the pin layouts of the 8088 and 8086 in Fig. 7.1, we find the following:

(a) Pins 2 through 8 on the 8088 are address lines A_{14} through A_8, but on the 8086 they are address/data lines AD_{14} through AD_8.

(b) Pin 28 on the 8088 is IO/$\overline{\text{M}}$ and on the 8086 it is the M/$\overline{\text{IO}}$.

(c) Pin 34 of the 8088 is the $\overline{SSO}$ output and on the 8086 this pin supplies the $\overline{BHE}/S_7$ output.

▲ 7.4 MINIMUM-MODE INTERFACE

When the minimum mode of operation is selected, the 8088 or 8086 itself provides all the control signals needed to implement the memory and I/O interfaces. Figures 7.3(a) and (b) show block diagrams of a minimum-mode configuration of the 8088 and 8086 MPU, respectively. The minimum-mode signals can be divided into the following basic groups: address/data bus, status, control, interrupt, and DMA.

Address/Data Bus

Let us first look at the address/data bus. In an 8088-based microcomputer system these lines serve two functions. As an *address bus*, they are used to carry address information to the memory and I/O ports. The address bus is 20 bits long and consists of signal lines A_0 through A_{19}. Of these, A_{19} represents the MSB and A_0 the LSB. A 20-bit address gives the 8088 a 1M-byte memory address space. However, only address lines A_0 through A_{15} are used when accessing I/O. This gives the 8088 an independent I/O address space that is 64KB in length.

The eight *data bus* lines D_0 through D_7 are actually multiplexed with address lines A_0 through A_7, respectively. For this reason, they are denoted as AD_0 through AD_7. D_7 is the MSB in the byte of data and D_0 the LSB. When acting as a data bus, they carry read/write data for memory, input/output data for I/O devices, and interrupt-type codes from an interrupt controller.

Looking at Fig. 7.3(b), we see that the 8086 has 16 data bus lines instead of 8 as in the 8088. Data lines are multiplexed with address lines A_0 through A_{15} and are therefore denoted as AD_0 through AD_{15}.

Status Signals

The four most significant address lines, A_{19} through A_{16} of both the 8088 and 8086 are also multiplexed, but in this case with *status signals* S_6 through S_3. These status bits are output on the bus at the same time that data are transferred over the other bus lines. Bits S_4 and S_3 together form a 2-bit binary code that identifies which of the internal segment registers was used to generate the physical address that was output on the address bus during the current bus cycle. These four codes and the register they represent are shown in Fig. 7.4. Notice that the code $S_4S_3 = 00$ identifies a register known as the extra segment register as the source of the segment address.

Status line S_5 reflects the status of another internal characteristic of the MPU. It is the logic level of the internal interrupt enable flag. The status bit S_6 is always at the 0 logic level.

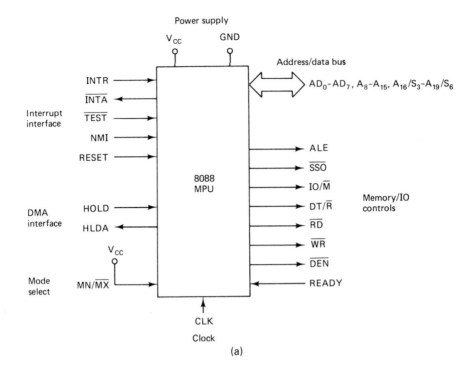

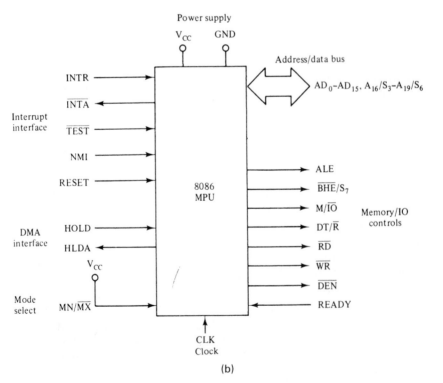

Figure 7.3 (a) Block diagram of the minimum-mode 8088 MPU. (b) Block diagram of a minimum-mode 8086 MPU.

S_4	S_3	Address Status
0	0	Alternate (relative to the ES segment)
0	1	Stack (relative to the SS segment)
1	0	Code/None (relative to the CS segment or a default of zero)
1	1	Data (relative to the DS segment)

Figure 7.4 Address bus status code. (Reprinted with permission of Intel Corporation, © 1979)

Control Signals

The *control signals* are provided to support the memory and I/O interfaces of the 8088 and 8086. They control functions such as when the bus carries a valid address, in which direction data are transferred over the bus, when valid write data are on the bus, and when to put read data on the system bus. For example, *address latch enable* (ALE) is a pulse to logic 1 that signals external circuitry when a valid address is on the bus. This address can be latched in external circuitry on the 1-to-0 edge of the pulse at ALE.

Using the IO/$\overline{\text{M}}$ (*IO/memory*) line, DT/$\overline{\text{R}}$ (*data transmit/receive*) line, and *status line* $\overline{\text{SSO}}$, the 8088 signals which type of bus cycle is in progress and in which direction data are to be transferred over the bus. The logic level of IO/$\overline{\text{M}}$ tells external circuitry whether a memory or I/O transfer is taking place over the bus. Logic 0 at this output signals a memory operation, and logic 1 an I/O operation. The direction of data transfer over the bus is signaled by the logic level output at DT/$\overline{\text{R}}$. When this line is logic 1 during the data transfer part of a bus cycle, the bus is in the transmit mode. Therefore, data are either written into memory or output to an I/O device. On the other hand, logic 0 at DT/$\overline{\text{R}}$ signals that the bus is in the receive mode. This corresponds to reading data from memory or input of data from an input port.

Comparing Fig. 7.3(a) and 7.3(b), we find two differences between the minimum-mode 8088 and 8086 microprocessors. First, the 8086's memory/IO control (M/$\overline{\text{IO}}$) signal is the complement of the equivalent signal of the 8088. Second, the 8088's $\overline{\text{SSO}}$ status signal is replaced by *bank high enable* ($\overline{\text{BHE}}$) on the 8086. Logic 0 on this line is used as a memory enable signal for the most significant byte half of the data bus, D_8 through D_{15}. This line also carries status bit S_7.

The signals *read* ($\overline{\text{RD}}$) and *write* ($\overline{\text{WR}}$), respectively, indicate that a read bus cycle or a write bus cycle is in progress. The MPU switches $\overline{\text{WR}}$ to logic 0 to signal external devices that valid write or output data are on the bus. On the other hand, $\overline{\text{RD}}$ indicates that the MPU is performing a read of data off the bus. During read operations, one other control signal is also supplied. This is $\overline{\text{DEN}}$ (*data enable*), and it signals external devices when they should put data on the bus.

There is one other control signal that is involved with the memory and I/O interface. This is the READY signal. It can be used to insert wait states into the bus cycle so that it is extended by a number of clock periods. This signal is provided by way of an external clock generator device and can be supplied by the memory or I/O subsystem to signal the MPU when it is ready to permit the data transfer to be completed.

Interrupt Signals

The key interrupt interface signals are *interrupt request* (INTR) and *interrupt acknowledge* ($\overline{\text{INTA}}$). INTR is an input to the 8088 and 8086 that can be used by an external device to signal that it needs to be serviced. This input is sampled during the final clock period of each *instruction acquisition cycle*. Logic 1 at INTR represents an active interrupt request. When an interrupt request is recognized by the MPU it indicates this fact to external circuits with pulses to logic 0 at the $\overline{\text{INTA}}$ output.

The $\overline{\text{TEST}}$ input is also related to the external interrupt interface. For example, execution of a WAIT instruction causes the 8088 or 8086 to check the logic level at the $\overline{\text{TEST}}$ input. If logic 1 is found, the MPU suspends operation and goes into what is known as the *idle state*. The MPU no longer executes instructions; instead, it repeatedly checks the logic level of the $\overline{\text{TEST}}$ input waiting for its transition back to logic 0. As $\overline{\text{TEST}}$ switches to 0, execution resumes with the next instruction in the program. This feature can be used to synchronize the operation of the MPU to an event in external hardware.

There are two more inputs in the interrupt interface: the *nonmaskable interrupt* (NMI) and the *reset interrupt* (RESET). On the 0-to-1 transition of NMI, control is passed to a nonmaskable interrupt service routine at completion of execution of the current instruction. NMI is the interrupt request with highest priority and cannot be masked by software. The RESET input is used to provide a hardware reset for the MPU. Switching RESET to logic 0 initializes the internal registers of the MPU and initiates a reset service routine.

DMA Interface Signals

The *direct memory access* (DMA) interface of the 8088/8086 minimum-mode microcomputer system consists of the HOLD and HLDA signals. When an external device wants to take control of the system bus, it signals this fact to the MPU by switching HOLD to the 1 logic level. For example, when the HOLD input of the 8088 becomes active, it enters the hold state at the completion of the current bus cycle. When in the hold state, signal lines AD_0 through AD_7, A_8 through A_{15}, A_{16}/S_3 through A_{19}/S_6, $\overline{\text{SSO}}$, IO/$\overline{\text{M}}$, DT/$\overline{\text{R}}$, $\overline{\text{RD}}$, $\overline{\text{WR}}$, $\overline{\text{DEN}}$, and INTR are all put into the high-Z state. The 8088 signals external devices that it is in this state by switching its HLDA output to the 1 logic level.

▲ 7.5 MAXIMUM-MODE INTERFACE

When the 8088 or 8086 microprocessor is set for the maximum-mode configuration, it produces signals for implementing a *multiprocessor/coprocessor system environment*. By *multiprocessor environment* we mean that more than one microprocessor exists in the system and that each processor executes its own program. Usually in this type of system environment, some system resources are common to all processors. They are called *global resources*. There are also other resources that are assigned to specific processors. These dedicated resources are known as *local* or *private resources*.

In the maximum-mode system, facilities are provided for implementing allocation of global resources and passing bus control to other microprocessors sharing the system bus.

8288 Bus Controller: Bus Commands and Control Signals

Looking at the maximum-mode block diagram in Fig. 7.5(a), we see that the 8088 does not directly provide all the signals that are required to control the memory, I/O, and interrupt interfaces. Specifically, the $\overline{WR}$, IO/$\overline{M}$, DT/$\overline{R}$, $\overline{DEN}$, ALE, and $\overline{INTA}$ signals are no longer produced by the 8088. Instead, it outputs status code

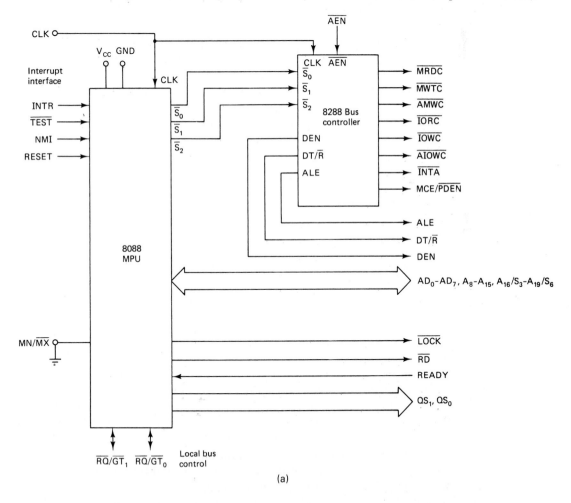

(a)

Figure 7.5 (a) 8088 maximum-mode block diagram. (b) 8086 maximum-mode block diagram.

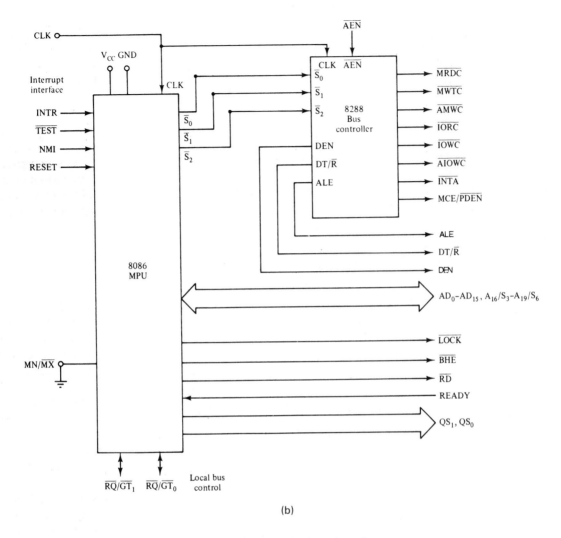

Figure 7.5 (Continued)

on three signal lines $\overline{S}_0$, $\overline{S}_1$, and $\overline{S}_2$ prior to the initiation of each bus cycle. This 3-bit *bus status code* identifies which type of bus cycle is to follow. $\overline{S}_2\overline{S}_1\overline{S}_0$ are input to the external *bus controller* device, the 8288, which decodes them to identify the type of MPU bus cycle. The block diagram and pin layout of the 8288 are shown in Fig. 7.6(a) and (b), respectively. In response, the bus controller generates the appropriately timed command and control signals.

Figure 7.7 shows the relationship between the bus status codes and the types of bus cycles. Also shown are the output signals that are generated to tell external circuitry which type of bus cycle is taking place. These output signals are *memory read command* ($\overline{\text{MRDC}}$), *memory write command* ($\overline{\text{MWTC}}$), *advanced memory write command* ($\overline{\text{AMWC}}$), *I/O read command* ($\overline{\text{IORC}}$), *I/O write command*

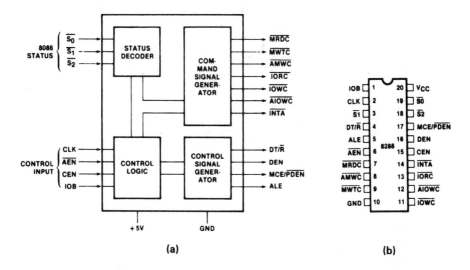

Figure 7.6 (a) Block diagram of the 8288. (Reprinted with permission of Intel Corporation, © 1979) (b) Pin layout. (Reprinted with permission of Intel Corporation, © 1979)

($\overline{\text{IORC}}$), *advanced I/O write command* ($\overline{\text{AIORC}}$), and *interrupt acknowledge* ($\overline{\text{INTA}}$).

The 8288 produces one or two of these seven command signals for each bus cycle. For instance, when the 8088 outputs the code $\overline{S}_2\overline{S}_1\overline{S}_0 = 001$, it indicates that an I/O read cycle is to be performed. In turn, the 8288 makes its $\overline{\text{IORC}}$ output switch to logic 0. On the other hand, if the code 111 is output by the 8088, it is signaling that no bus activity is to take place.

The other control outputs produced by the 8288 consist of DEN, DT/$\overline{\text{R}}$, and ALE. These three signals provide the same functions as those described for the minimum mode. Figure 7.5(b) shows that the 8288 bus controller connects to the

Status Inputs			CPU Cycle	8288 Command
$\overline{\text{S2}}$	$\overline{\text{S1}}$	$\overline{\text{S0}}$		
0	0	0	Interrupt Acknowledge	$\overline{\text{INTA}}$
0	0	1	Read I/O Port	$\overline{\text{IORC}}$
0	1	0	Write I/O Port	IOWC, AIOWC
0	1	1	Halt	None
1	0	0	Instruction Fetch	$\overline{\text{MRDC}}$
1	0	1	Read Memory	$\overline{\text{MRDC}}$
1	1	0	Write Memory	MWTC, AMWC
1	1	1	Passive	None

Figure 7.7 Bus status codes. (Reprinted with permission of Intel Corporation, © 1979)

8086 in the same way as it does to the 8088 and it also produces the same output signals.

Lock Signal

To implement a multiprocessor system, a signal called lock ($\overline{\text{LOCK}}$) is provided. This signal is meant to be output (logic 0) whenever the processor wants to lock out the other processors from using the bus. This would be the case when a shared resource is accessed. The $\overline{\text{LOCK}}$ signal is compatible with the *Multibus*, an industry standard for interfacing microprocessor systems in a multiprocessor environment.

Queue Status Signals

Two new signals that are produced by the 8088 and 8086 in the maximum-mode microcomputer system are queue status outputs QS_0 and QS_1. Together they form a 2-bit *queue status code*, QS_1QS_0. This code tells the external circuitry what type of information was removed from the queue during the previous clock cycle. Figure 7.8 shows the four different queue status codes. Notice that $QS_1QS_0 = 01$ indicates that the first byte of an instruction was taken off the queue. As shown, the next byte of the instruction is fetched is identified by the code 11. Whenever the queue is reset due to a transfer of control, the reinitialization code 10 is output.

Local Bus Control Signals: Request/Grant Signals

In a maximum-mode configuration, the minimum-mode HOLD and HLDA interface of the 8088/8086 is also changed. These two signals are replaced by *request/grant lines* $\overline{\text{RQ}}/\overline{\text{GT}}_0$ and $\overline{\text{RQ}}/\overline{\text{GT}}_1$. They provide a prioritized bus access mechanism for accessing the *local bus*.

QS1	QS0	Queue Status
0 (low)	0	No Operation. During the last clock cycle, nothing was taken from the queue.
0	1	First Byte. The byte taken from the queue was the first byte of the instruction.
1 (high)	0	Queue Empty. The queue has been reinitialized as a result of the execution of a transfer instruction.
1	1	Subsequent Byte. The byte taken from the queue was a subsequent byte of the instruction.

Figure 7.8 Queue status codes. (Reprinted with permission of Intel Corporation, © 1979)

▲ 7.6 ELECTRICAL CHARACTERISTICS

In the preceding sections, the pin layout and minimum- and maximum-mode interface signals of the 8088 and 8086 microprocessors were introduced. Here we will first look at power supply ratings of these processors and then their input and output electrical characteristics.

Looking at Fig. 7.1(a) we find that power is applied between pin 40 (V_{cc}) and pins 1(GND) and 20(GND). Pins 1 and 20 should be connected together. The nominal value of V_{cc} is specified as +5 V dc with a tolerance of ±10%. This means that the 8088 or 8086 will operate correctly as long as the difference in voltage between V_{cc} and GND is greater than 4.5 V dc and less than 5.5 V dc. At room temperature (25°C), both the 8088 and 8086 draw a maximum of 340 mA from the supply.

Let us now look at the dc I/O characteristics of the microprocessor, that is, its input and output logic levels. These ratings tell the minimum and maximum voltages for the 0 and 1 logic states for which the circuit will operate correctly. Different values are specified for the inputs and outputs.

The I/O voltage specifications for the 8088 are shown in Fig. 7.9. Notice that the minimum logic 1 (high-level) voltage at an output (V_{OH}) is 2.4 V. This voltage is specified for a test condition that identifies the amount of current being sourced by the output (I_{OH}) as −400 μA. All processors must be tested during manufacturing to ensure that under this test condition the voltages at all outputs will remain above the value of V_{OHmin}.

Input voltage levels are specified in a similar way. Except here the ratings identify the range of voltage that will be correctly identified as a logic 0 or a logic 1 at an input. For instance, voltages in the range V_{ILmin} = −0.5 V to V_{ILmax} = +0.8 V represent a valid logic 0 (lower level) at an input of the 8088.

The I/O voltage levels of the 8086 microprocessor are identical to those for the 8088 as shown in Fig. 7.9. However, there is one difference in the test conditions. For the 8086, V_{OL} is measured at 2.5 mA instead of 2.0 mA.

▲ 7.7 SYSTEM CLOCK

The time base for synchronization of the internal and external operations of the microprocessor in a microcomputer system is provided by the CLK input signal. At present, the 8088 is available in two different speeds. The standard part operates at 5 MHz and the 8088-2 operates at 8 MHz. On the other hand, the 8086 microprocessor is manufactured in three speeds. They are the 5-MHz 8086, the 8-MHz

Symbol	Meaning	Minimum	Maximum	Test condition
V_{IL}	Input low voltage	−0.5 V	+0.8 V	
V_{IH}	Input high voltage	+2.0 V	V_{cc} + 0.5 V	
V_{OL}	Output low voltage		+0.45 V	I_{OL} = 2.0mA
V_{OH}	Output high voltage	+2.4 V		I_{OH} = −400 uA

Figure 7.9 I/O voltage levels.

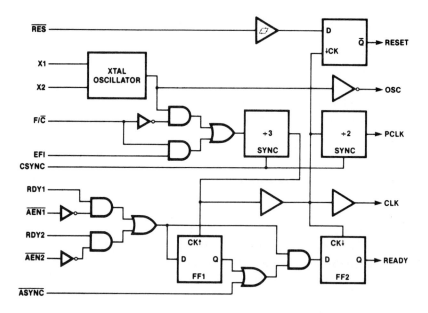

Figure 7.10 Block diagram of the 8284 clock generator. (Reprinted with permission of Intel Corporation, © 1979)

8086-2, and the 10-MHz 8086-1. CLK is externally generated by the 8284 clock generator and driver IC. Figure 7.10 is a block diagram of this device.

The standard way in which this clock chip is used with the 8088 is to connect either a 15- or 24-MHz crystal between its X_1 and X_2 inputs. This circuit connection is shown in Fig. 7.11. Notice that a series capacitor C_L is also required. Its typical value when used with the 15-MHz crystal is 12 pF. The *fundamental crystal frequency* is divided by 3 within the 8284 to give either a 5- or 8-MHz clock signal. This signal is internally buffered and output at CLK. The CLK output of the 8284 can be directly connected to the CLK input of the 8088. The 8284 connects to the 8086 in exactly the same way.

The waveform of CLK is shown in Fig. 7.12. Here we see that the signal is at Metal Oxide Semiconductor (MOS)-compatible voltage levels and not Transistor Transistor Logic (TTL) levels. Its minimum and maximum low logic levels are $V_{Lmin} = -0.5$ V and $V_{Lmax} = 0.6$ V, respectively. Moreover, the minimum and

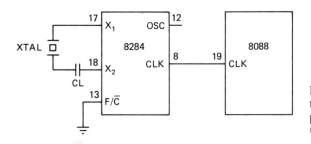

Figure 7.11 Connecting the 8284 to the 8088. (Reprinted with permission of Intel Corporation, © 1979)

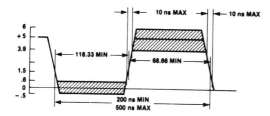

Figure 7.12 CLK voltage and timing characteristics for a 5 MHz processor. (Reprinted with permission of Intel Corporation, © 1979)

maximum high logic levels are $V_{Hmin} = 3.9$ V and $V_{Hmax} = V_{CC} + 1$ V, respectively. The *period* of the clock signal of the 8088 can range from a minimum of 200 ns to a maximum of 500 ns, and the maximum *rise* and *fall times* of its edges equal 10 ns.

In Fig. 7.10 we see that there are two more clock outputs on the 8284. They are the *peripheral clock* (PCLK) and *oscillator clock* (OSC). These signals are provided to drive peripheral ICs. The clock signal output at PCLK is half the frequency of CLK. For instance, if an 8088 is operated at 5 MHz, PCLK is 2.5 MHz. Also, it is at TTL-compatible levels rather than MOS levels. On the other hand, the OSC output is at the crystal frequency, which is three times that of CLK. These relationships are illustrated in Fig. 7.13.

The 8284 can also be driven from an external clock source. The external clock signal is applied to the external frequency input (EFI). Input F/$\overline{C}$ is provided for clock source selection. When it is strapped to the 0 logic level, the crystal between X_1 and X_2 is used. On the other hand, applying logic 1 to F/$\overline{C}$ selects EFI as the source of the clock. The clock sync (CSYNC) input can be used for external synchronization in systems that employ multiple clocks.

▲ 7.8 BUS CYCLE

A *bus cycle* defines the basic operation that a microprocessor performs to communicate with external devices. Examples of bus cycles are the memory read, memory write, input/output read, and input/output write. As shown in Fig. 7.14(a), a bus cycle corresponds to a sequence of events that start with an address being output on the system bus followed by a read or write data transfer. During these operations, a series of control signals are also produced by the MPU to control the direction and timing of the bus.

The bus cycle of the 8088 and 8086 microprocessors consists of at least four clock periods. These four time states are called T_1, T_2, T_3, and T_4. During T_1, the

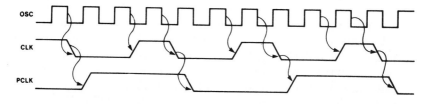

Figure 7.13 Relationship between CLK and PCLK. (Reprinted with permission of Intel Corporation, © 1979)

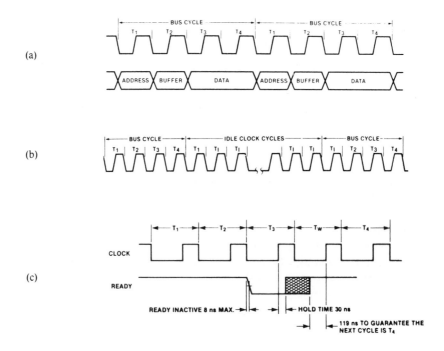

Figure 7.14 (a) Bus cycle clock periods. (Reprinted with permission of Intel Corporation, © 1979) (b) Bus cycle with idle states. (Reprinted with permission of Intel Corporation, © 1979) (c) Bus cycle with wait states. (Reprinted with permission of Intel Corporation, © 1979)

MPU puts an address on the bus. For a write memory cycle, data are put on the bus during state T_2 and maintained through T_3 and T_4. When a read cycle is to be performed, the bus is first put in the high-Z state during T_2 and then the data to be read must be available on the bus during T_3 and T_4. These four clock states give a *bus cycle duration* of 125 ns × 4 = 500 ns in an 8-MHz 8088 system.

If no bus cycles are required, the microprocessor performs what are known as *idle states*. During these states, no bus activity takes place. Each idle state is one clock period long, and any number of them can be inserted between bus cycles. Figure 7.14(b) shows two bus cycles separated by idle states. Idle states are performed if the instruction queue inside the microprocessor is full and it does not need to read or write operands from memory.

Wait states can also be inserted into a bus cycle. This is done in response to a request by an event in external hardware instead of an internal event such as a full queue. In fact, the READY input of the MPU is provided specifically for this purpose. Figure 7.14(c) shows that logic 0 at this input indicates that the current bus cycle should not be completed. As long as READY is held at the 0 level, wait states are inserted between states T_3 and T_4 of the current bus cycle, and the data that were on the bus during T_3 are maintained. The bus cycle is not completed until the external hardware returns READY back to the 1 logic level. This extends the duration of the bus cycle, thereby permitting the use of slower memory and I/O devices in the system.

EXAMPLE 7.2 _____

What is the duration of the bus cycle in the 8088-based microcomputer if the clock is 8 MHz and two wait states are inserted?

Solution

The duration of the bus cycle in an 8-MHz system is given in general by the expression

$$t_{cyc} = 500 \text{ ns} + N (125 \text{ ns})$$

In this expression N stands for the number of wait states. For a bus cycle with two wait states, we get

$$t_{cyc} = 500 \text{ ns} + 2(125 \text{ ns}) = 500 \text{ ns} + 250 \text{ ns}$$
$$= 750 \text{ ns}$$

▲ 7.9 HARDWARE ORGANIZATION OF THE MEMORY ADDRESS SPACE

From a hardware point of view, the memory address spaces of the 8088- and 8086-based microcomputers are organized differently. Figure 7.15(a) shows that the 8088's memory subsystem is implemented as a single $1M \times 8$ memory bank. Looking at the block diagram in Fig. 7.15(a), we see that these byte-wide storage locations are assigned to consecutive addresses over the range from 00000_{16} through $FFFFF_{16}$. During memory operations, a 20-bit address is applied to the memory bank over address lines A_0 through A_{19}. It is this address that selects the storage location that is to be accessed. Bytes of data are transferred between the 8088 and memory over data bus lines D_0 through D_7.

On the other hand, the 8086's memory address space as shown in Fig. 7.15(b) is implemented as two independent 512K-byte banks. They are called the *low* (*even*) *bank* and the *high* (*odd*) *bank*. Data bytes associated with an even address (00000_{16}, 00002_{16}, etc.) reside in the low bank and those with odd addresses (00001_{16}, 00003_{16}, etc.) reside in the high bank.

Looking at the circuit diagram in Fig. 7.15(b), we see that for the 8088 address bits A_1 through A_{19} select the storage location that is to be accessed. They are applied to both banks in parallel. A_0 and bank high enable ($\overline{BHE}$) are used as bank-select signals. Logic 0 at A_0 identifies an even-addressed byte of data and causes the low bank of memory to be enabled. On the other hand, $\overline{BHE}$ equal to

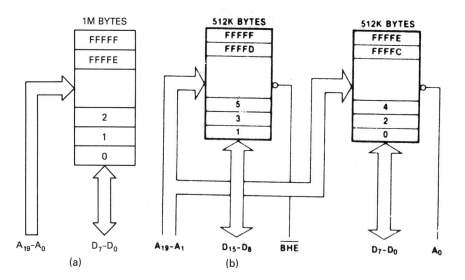

Figure 7.15 (a) 1M × 8 memory bank of the 8088. (b) High and low memory banks of the 8086. (Reprinted with permission of Intel Corporation, © 1979)

0 enables the high bank to access an odd-addressed byte of data. Each of the memory banks provides half of the 8086's 16-bit data bus. Notice that the lower bank transfers bytes of data over data lines D_0 through D_7, while data transfers for a high bank use D_8 through D_{15}.

We just saw that the memory subsystem of the 8088-based microcomputer system is actually organized as 8-bit bytes, not as 16-bit words. However, the contents of any two consecutive byte storage locations can be accessed as a word. The lower-addressed byte is the least significant byte of the word, and the higher-addressed byte is its most significant byte. Let us now look at how a byte and a word of data are read from memory.

Figure 7.16(a) shows how a byte-memory operation is performed to the storage location at address X. As shown in the diagram, the address is supplied to the memory bank over lines A_0 through A_{19}, and the bytes of data are written into or read from storage location X over lines D_0 through D_7. D_7 carries the MSB of the byte of data and D_0 carries the LSB. This shows that a byte of data is accessed by the 8088 in one bus cycle. A memory cycle for an 8088 running at 5 MHz with no wait states takes 800 ns.

When a word of data is to be transferred between the 8088 and memory, we must perform two accesses of memory, reading a byte in each access. Figure 7.16(b) illustrates how the word storage location starting at address X is accessed. Two bus cycles are required to access a word of data. During the first bus cycle, the least significant byte of the word, which is located at address X, is accessed. Again the address is applied to the memory bank over A_0 through A_{19}, and the byte of data is transferred to or from storage location X over D_0 through D_7.

Next, the 8088 automatically increments the address so that it now points to byte address X + 1. This address points to the next consecutive byte storage location

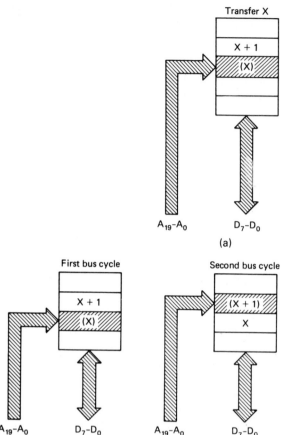

Transfer X

X + 1

(X)

$A_{19}-A_0$ D_7-D_0

(a)

First bus cycle

X + 1

(X)

$A_{19}-A_0$ D_7-D_0

Second bus cycle

(X + 1)

X

$A_{19}-A_0$ D_7-D_0

(b)

Figure 7.16 (a) Byte transfer by the 8088. (b) Word transfer by the 8088.

in memory, which corresponds to the most significant byte of the word of data at X. Now a second memory bus cycle is initiated. During this second cycle, data are written into or read from the storage location at address X + 1. Since word accesses of memory take two bus cycles instead of one, it takes 1.6 ms to access a word of data when the 8088 is operating at a 5-MHz clock rate with no wait states.

The 8086 microprocessor performs byte and word data transfers differently from the 8088. Let us next examine the data transfers that can take place in an 8086-based microcomputer.

Figure 7.17(a) shows that when a byte-memory operation is performed to address X, which is an even address, a storage location in the low bank is accessed. Therefore, A_0 is set to logic 0 to enable the low bank of memory and $\overline{BHE}$ to logic 1 to disable the high bank. As shown in the block diagram, data are transferred to or from the lower bank over data bus lines D_0 through D_7. D_7 carries the MSB of the byte and D_0 the LSB.

On the other hand, to access a byte of data at an odd address such as X + 1 in Fig. 7.17(b), A_0 is set to logic 1 and $\overline{BHE}$ to logic 0. This enables the high bank

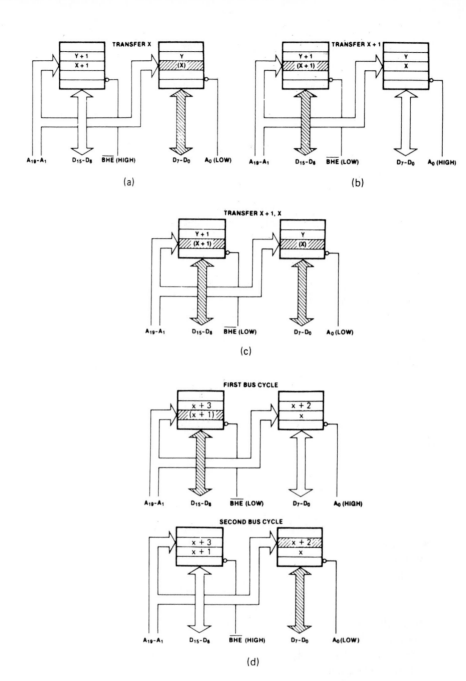

Figure 7.17 (a) Even-addressed byte transfer by the 8086. (Reprinted with permission of Intel Corporation, © 1979) (b) Odd-addressed byte transfer by the 8086. (Reprinted with permission of Intel Corporation, © 1979) (c) Even-addressed word transfer by the 8086. (Reprinted with permission of Intel Corporation, © 1979) (d) Odd-addressed word transfer by the 8086. (Reprinted with permission of Intel Corporation, © 1979)

of memory and disables the low bank. Data are transferred between the 8086 and the high bank over bus lines D_8 through D_{15}. Here D_{15} represents the MSB and D_8 the LSB.

Whenever an even-addressed word of data is accessed, both the high and low banks are accessed at the same time. Figure 7.17(c) illustrates how a word at even address X is accessed. Notice that both A_0 and $\overline{BHE}$ equal 0; therefore, both banks are enabled. In this case, two bytes of data are transferred from or to both banks at the same time. This 16-bit word is transferred over the complete data bus D_0 through D_{15}. The bytes of an even-addressed word are said to be aligned and can be transferred with a memory operation that takes just one bus cycle.

A word at an odd-addressed boundary is said to be unaligned. That is, the least significant byte is at the lower address location in the high memory bank. This is demonstrated in Fig. 7.17(d). Here we see that the odd byte of the word is located at address X + 1 and the even byte at address X + 2.

Two bus cycles are required to access this word. During the first bus cycle, the odd byte of the word, which is located at address X + 1 in the high bank, is accessed. This is accompanied by select signals $A_0 = 1$ and $\overline{BHE} = 0$ and a data transfer over D_8 through D_{15}. Even though the data transfer uses data lines D_8 through D_{15}, it is the low byte of the addressed data word to the processor.

Next the 8086 automatically increments the address so that $A_0 = 0$. This represents the next address in memory which is even. Then a second memory bus cycle is initiated. During this second cycle, the even byte located at X + 2 in the low bank is accessed. The data transfer takes place over bus lines D_0 through D_7. This transfer is accompanied by $A_0 = 0$ and $\overline{BHE} = 1$. To the processor, this is the high byte of the word of data.

▲ 7.10 MEMORY BUS STATUS CODES

Whenever a memory bus cycle is in progress, an address bus status code S_4S_3 is output by the processor. The status code is multiplexed with address bits A_{17} and A_{16}. This two-bit code is output at the same time the data are carried over the other data lines.

Bits S_4 and S_3 together form a 2-bit binary code that identifies which one of the four segment registers was used to generate the physical address that was output during the address period in the current bus cycle. The four *address bus status codes* are listed in Fig. 7.18. Here we find that code $S_4S_3 = 00$ identifies the extra segment register, 01 identifies the stack segment register, 10 identifies the code segment register, and 11 identifies the data segment register.

S_4	S_3	Segment register
0	0	Extra
0	1	Stack
1	0	Code/none
1	1	Data

Figure 7.18 Address bus status codes.

These status codes are output in both the minimum and the maximum modes. The codes can be examined by external circuitry. For example, they can be decoded with external circuitry to enable separate 1M-byte address spaces for ES, SS, CS, and DS. In this way, the memory address reach of the microprocessor can be expanded to 4M bytes.

▲ 7.11 MEMORY CONTROL SIGNALS

Earlier in the chapter we saw that similar control signals are produced in the maximum and minimum mode. Moreover, we found that in the minimum mode, the 8088 and 8086 microprocessors produce all the control signals. But in the maximum mode, they are produced by the 8288 bus controller. Here we will look more closely at each of these signals and their functions with respect to memory interface operation.

Minimum-Mode Memory Control Signals

In the 8088 microcomputer system of Fig. 7.19, which is configured for the minimum mode of operation, we find that the control signals provided to support the interface to the memory subsystem are ALE, IO/$\overline{\text{M}}$, DT/$\overline{\text{R}}$, $\overline{\text{RD}}$, $\overline{\text{WR}}$, and $\overline{\text{DEN}}$. These control signals are required to tell the memory subsystem when the bus is carrying a valid address, in which direction data are to be transferred over the bus, when valid write data are on the bus, and when to put read data on the bus. For example, *address latch enable* (ALE) signals external circuitry that a valid address is on the bus. It is a pulse to the 1 logic level and is used to latch the address in external circuitry.

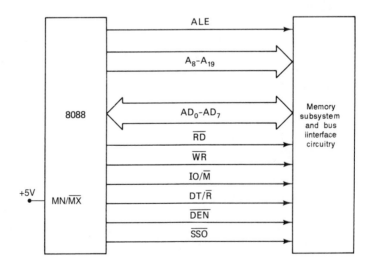

Figure 7.19 Minimum-mode 8088 memory interface.

The *input-output/memory* (IO/$\overline{\text{M}}$) and *data transmit/receive* (DT/$\overline{\text{R}}$) lines signal external circuitry whether a memory or I/O bus cycle is in progress and whether the 8088 will transmit or receive data over the bus. During all memory bus cycles, IO/$\overline{\text{M}}$ is held at the 0 logic level. The 8088 switches DT/$\overline{\text{R}}$ to logic 1 during the data transfer part of the bus cycle, the bus is in the transmit mode and data are written into memory. On the other hand, it sets DT/$\overline{\text{R}}$ to logic 0 to signal that the bus is in the receive mode, which corresponds to reading of memory.

The signals *read* ($\overline{\text{RD}}$) and *write* ($\overline{\text{WR}}$), respectively, identify that a read or write bus cycle is in progress. The 8088 switches $\overline{\text{WR}}$ to logic 0 to signal memory that a write cycle is taking place over the bus. On the other hand, $\overline{\text{RD}}$ is switched to logic 0 whenever a read cycle is in progress. During all memory operations, the 8088 produces one other control signal. It is *data enable* ($\overline{\text{DEN}}$). Logic 0 at this output is used to enable the data bus.

Status line ($\overline{\text{SSO}}$) is also part of the minimum-mode memory interface. The logic level that is output on this line during read bus cycles identifies whether a code or data access is in progress. $\overline{\text{SSO}}$ is set to logic 0 whenever instruction code is read from memory.

The control signals for the 8086's minimum-mode memory interface differ in three ways. First, the 8088's IO/$\overline{\text{M}}$ signal is replaced by memory/input-output (M/$\overline{\text{IO}}$) signal. Whenever a memory bus cycle is in progress, the M/$\overline{\text{IO}}$ output is switched to logic 1. Second, the signal $\overline{\text{SSO}}$ is removed from the interface. Third, a new signal, *bank high enable* ($\overline{\text{BHE}}$) has been added to the interface. $\overline{\text{BHE}}$ is used as a select input for the high bank of memory in the 8086's memory subsystem. That is, logic 0 is output on this line during the address part of all the bus cycles in which data in the high-bank part of memory is to be accessed.

Maximum Mode Memory Control Signals

When the 8088 is configured to work in the maximum mode, it does not directly provide all the control signals to support the memory interface. Instead, an external bus controller, the 8288, provides memory commands and control signals. Figure 7.20 shows an 8088 connected in this way.

Specifically, the $\overline{\text{WR}}$, IO/$\overline{\text{M}}$, DT/$\overline{\text{R}}$, $\overline{\text{DEN}}$, ALE, $\overline{\text{SSO}}$, and INTA signal lines on the 8088 are changed. They are replaced with a *multiprocessor lock signal* ($\overline{\text{LOCK}}$), a *bus status code* ($\overline{\text{S}}_2$ through $\overline{\text{S}}_0$), and a *queue status code* (QS$_1$QS$_0$). The 8088 still does produce the signal $\overline{\text{RD}}$, which provides the same function as it did in minimum mode.

The 3-bit bus status code $\overline{\text{S}}_2\overline{\text{S}}_1\overline{\text{S}}_0$ is output prior to the initiation of each bus cycle. It identifies which type of bus cycle is to follow. This code is input to the 8288 bus controller. Here it is decoded to identify which type of bus cycle command signals must be generated.

Figure 7.21 shows the relationship between the bus status codes and the types of bus cycles produced. Also shown in this chart are the names of the corresponding command signals that are generated at the outputs of the 8288. For instance, the input code $\overline{\text{S}}_2\overline{\text{S}}_1\overline{\text{S}}_0$ equal to 100 indicates that an instruction fetch bus cycle is to

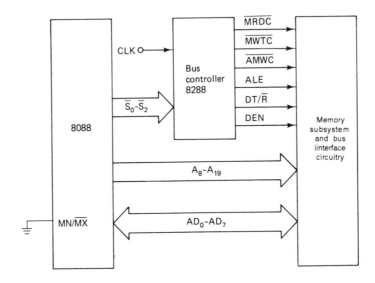

Figure 7.20 Maximum-mode 8088 memory interface.

take place. Since the instruction fetch is a memory read, the 8288 makes the *memory read command* ($\overline{\text{MRDC}}$) output switch to logic 0.

Another bus command that is provided for the memory subsystem is when $\overline{S}_2\overline{S}_1\overline{S}_0$ is 110. This represents a memory write cycle and it causes both the *memory write command* ($\overline{\text{MWTC}}$) and *advanced memory write command* ($\overline{\text{AMWC}}$) outputs to switch to the 0 logic level.

The other control outputs produced by the 8288 are DEN, DT/$\overline{\text{R}}$, and ALE. These signals provide the same functions as those produced by the corresponding pins on the 8088 in the minimum system mode.

The two status signals, QS_0 and QS_1, form an instruction queue code. This code tells the external circuitry what type of information was removed from the

Status Inputs			CPU Cycle	8288 Command
$\overline{S}_2$	$\overline{S}_1$	$\overline{S}_0$		
0	0	0	Interrupt acknowledge	$\overline{\text{INTA}}$
0	0	1	Read I/O port	$\overline{\text{IORC}}$
0	1	0	Write I/O port	$\overline{\text{IOWC}}$, $\overline{\text{AIOWC}}$
0	1	1	Halt	None
1	0	0	Instruction fetch	$\overline{\text{MRDC}}$
1	0	1	Read memory	$\overline{\text{MRDC}}$
1	1	0	Write memory	$\overline{\text{MWTC}}$, $\overline{\text{AMWC}}$
1	1	1	Passive	None

Figure 7.21 Memory bus cycle status codes produced in maximum mode. (Reprinted with permission of Intel Corporation, © 1979)

QS_1	QS_0	Queue status
0	0	No operation
0	1	First byte of an instruction
1	0	Queue empty
1	1	Subsequent byte of an instruction

Figure 7.22 Queue status code produced in maximum mode.

queue during the previous clock cycle. Figure 7.22 shows the four different queue statuses. Notice that $QS_1 QS_0 = 01$ indicates that the first byte of an instruction was taken from the queue. The next byte of the instruction that is fetched is identified by queue status code 11. Whenever the queue is reset, for instance, due to a transfer of control, the reinitialization code 10 is output. Moreover, if no queue operation occurred, status code 00 is output.

The last signal is the *bus priority lock* ($\overline{LOCK}$). This signal, as shown in the interface, can be used as an input to a bus arbiter together with bus status code $\overline{S}_0$ through $\overline{S}_2$ and CLK. The bus arbiter is used to lock other processors off the system bus during accesses of common system resources such as *global memory* in a multiprocessor system.

All of the memory control signals we just described for the 8088-based microcomputer system serve the same function in the maximum-mode 8086 microcomputer. However, there is one additional control signal in the 8086's memory interface. This is $\overline{BHE}$. $\overline{BHE}$ performs the same function as it did in the minimum-mode system. That is, it is used as an enable input to the high bank of memory.

▲ 7.12 READ AND WRITE BUS CYCLES

In the preceding section we introduced the status and control signals associated with the memory interface. Here we continue by studying the sequence in which they occur during the read and write bus cycles of memory.

Read Cycle

The memory interface signals of a minimum-mode 8088 system are shown in Fig. 7.23. Here their occurrence is illustrated relative to the four *time states* T_1, T_2, T_3, and T_4 of the 8088's bus cycle. Let us trace through the events that occur as data or instructions are read from memory.

The *read bus cycle* begins with state T_1. During this period, the 8088 outputs the 20-bit address of the memory location to be accessed on its multiplexed address/data bus AD_0 through AD_7, A_8 through A_{15}, and multiplexed lines A_{16}/S_3 through A_{19}/S_6. Notice that at the same time a pulse is also produced at ALE. The trailing edge or the high level of this pulse should be used to latch the address in external circuitry.

Also we see that at the start of T_1, signals $IO/\overline{M}$ and $DT/\overline{R}$ are set to the 1 and 0 logic levels, respectively. This indicates to circuitry in the memory subsystem that a memory cycle is in progress and that the 8088 is going to receive data from

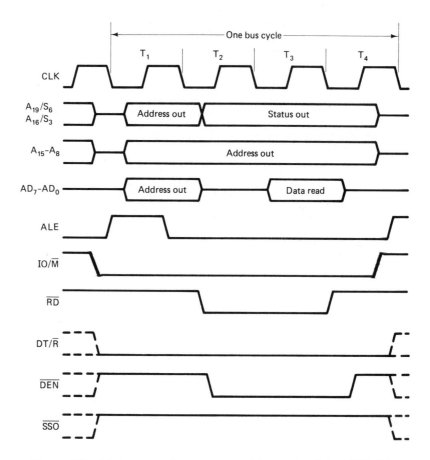

Figure 7.23 Minimum-mode memory read bus cycle of the 8088. (Reprinted with permission of Intel Corporation, © 1979)

the bus. Status $\overline{SSO}$ is also output at this time. Notice that all three of these signals are maintained at these logic levels throughout all four periods of the bus cycle.

Beginning with state T_2, status bits S_3 through S_6 are output on the upper four address bus lines A_{16} through A_{19}. Remember that bits S_3 and S_4 identify to external circuitry which segment register was used to generate the address just output. This status information is maintained through periods T_3 and T_4. The part of the address output on address bus lines A_8 through A_{15} is maintained through states T_2, T_3, and T_4. On the other hand, address/data bus lines AD_0 through AD_7 are put in the high-Z state during T_2.

Late in period T_2, $\overline{RD}$ is switched to logic 0. This indicates to the memory subsystem that a read cycle is in progress. $\overline{DEN}$ is switched to logic 0 to enable external circuitry to allow the data to move from memory onto the microprocessor's data bus.

As shown in the waveforms, input data are read by the 8088 during T_3. The memory must provide valid data during T_3 and maintain it until after the processor terminates the read operation. As shown in Fig. 7.23, it is in T_4 that the 8088 switches $\overline{RD}$ to the inactive 1 logic level to terminate the read operation. $\overline{DEN}$ returns to its inactive logic level late during T_4 to disable the external circuitry that allows data to move from memory to the processor. The read cycle is now complete.

A timing diagram for the 8086's memory read cycle is given in Fig. 7.24(a). Comparing these waveforms to those of the 8088 in Fig. 7.23, we find just four differences. They are that $\overline{BHE}$ is output along with the address during T_1; the data read by the 8086 during T_3 can be carried over all 16 data bus lines; M/$\overline{IO}$, which replaces IO/$\overline{M}$, is switched to logic 1 at the beginning of T_1 and is held at this level for the duration of the bus cycle; and the $\overline{SSO}$ status signal is not produced.

Figure 7.24(b) shows a read cycle of 8-bit data in a maximum-mode 8086-based microcomputer system. These waveforms are similar to those given for the minimum-mode read cycle in Fig. 7.24(a). Comparing these two timing diagrams, we see that the address and data transfers that take place are identical. In fact, the only difference found in the maximum-mode waveforms is that a bus cycle status code, $\overline{S}_2\overline{S}_1\overline{S}_0$, is output just prior to the beginning of the bus cycle. This status information is decoded by the 8288 to produce control signals ALE, $\overline{MRDC}$, DT/$\overline{R}$, and DEN.

Write Cycle

The *write bus cycle* timing of the 8088 in minimum mode is shown in Fig. 7.25(a). It is similar to that given for a read cycle in Fig. 7.23. Looking at the write

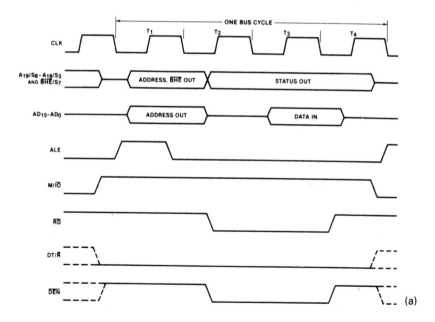

Figure 7.24 (a) Minimum-mode memory read bus cycle of the 8086. (Reprinted with permission of Intel Corporation, © 1979) (b) Maximum-mode memory read bus cycle of the 8086. (Reprinted with permission of Intel Corporation, © 1979)

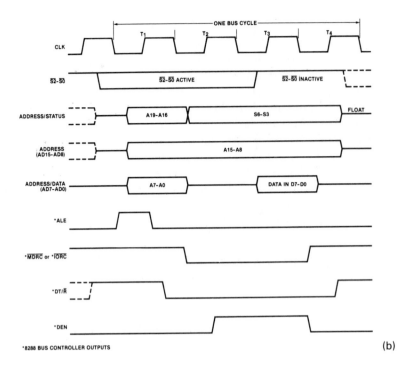

Figure 7.24 (Continued)

cycle waveforms, we find that during T_1 the address is output and latched with the ALE pulse. This is identical to the read cycle. Moreover, IO/$\overline{M}$ is set to logic 1 to indicate that a memory cycle is in progress and status information is output at $\overline{SSO}$. However, this time DT/$\overline{R}$ is switched to logic 1. This signals external circuits that the 8088 is going to transfer data over the bus.

As T_2 starts, the 8088 switches $\overline{WR}$ to logic 0. This tells the memory subsystem that a write operation is to follow over the bus. The 8088 puts the data on the bus late in T_2 and maintains the data valid through T_4. The writing of data into memory starts as $\overline{WR}$ becomes 0 and continues as it changes to 1 early in T_4. $\overline{DEN}$ enables the external circuitry to provide a path for data from the processor to the memory. This completes the write cycle.

Just as we described for the read bus cycle, the write cycle of the 8086 differs from that of the 8088 in four ways. Again, $\overline{SSO}$ is not produced; $\overline{BHE}$ is output along with the address; data are carried over all 16 data bus lines; and finally, M/$\overline{IO}$ is the complement of the 8088's IO/$\overline{M}$ signal. The waveforms in Fig. 7.25(b) illustrate a write cycle of word data in a maximum mode 8086 system.

▲ 7.13 MEMORY INTERFACE CIRCUITS

In this section, we will describe the memory interface circuits of an 8086-based microcomputer system. The 8086 system was selected instead of an 8088 microcom-

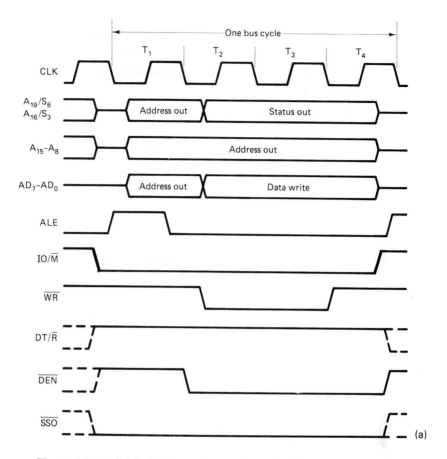

Figure 7.25 (a) Minimum-mode memory write bus cycle of the 8088. (Reprinted with permission of Intel Corporation, © 1979) (b) Maximum-mode memory write bus cycle of the 8086. (Reprinted with permission of Intel Corporation, © 1979)

puter because it is more complex. A memory interface diagram for a maximum-mode 8086-based microcomputer system is shown in Fig. 7.26. Here we find that the interface includes the 8288 bus controller, address bus latches and an address decoder, data bus transceiver/buffers, and bank write control logic. The 8088 micro-computer is simpler in that it does not require bank write control logic as its address space is organized as a single bank.

Looking at Fig. 7.26, we see that bus status code signals $\overline{S}_2$, $\overline{S}_1$, and $\overline{S}_0$, which are outputs of the 8086, are supplied directly to the 8288 bus controller. Here they are decoded to produce the command and control signals needed to control data transfers over the bus. In Fig. 7.21, the status codes that relate to the memory interface are highlighted. For example, the code $\overline{S}_2\overline{S}_1\overline{S}_0 = 101$ indicates that a data memory read bus cycle is in progress. This code makes the $\overline{MRDC}$ command output of the bus control logic to switch to logic 0. Notice in Fig. 7.26 that $\overline{MRDC}$ is applied directly to the $\overline{OE}$ input of the memory subsystem.

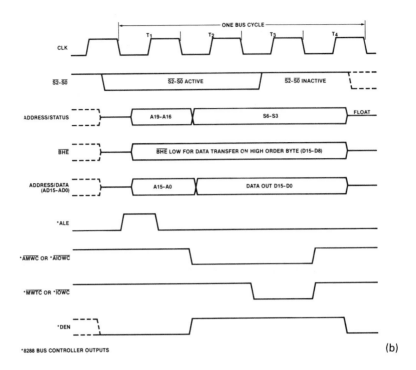

ONE BUS CYCLE

CLK

$\overline{S2}$-$\overline{S0}$ $\overline{S2}$-$\overline{S0}$ ACTIVE $\overline{S2}$-$\overline{S0}$ INACTIVE

ADDRESS/STATUS   A19-A16   S6-S3   FLOAT

$\overline{BHE}$ $\overline{BHE}$ LOW FOR DATA TRANSFER ON HIGH ORDER BYTE (D15-D8)

ADDRESS/DATA (AD15-AD0)   A15-A0   DATA OUT D15-D0

*ALE

*$\overline{AMWC}$ OR *$\overline{AIOWC}$

*$\overline{MWTC}$ OR *$\overline{IOWC}$

*DEN

*8288 BUS CONTROLLER OUTPUTS   **(b)**

Figure 7.25 (Continued)

Next let us look at how the address bus is latched, decoded, and buffered. Looking at Fig. 7.26, we see that address lines A_0 through A_{19} are latched along with and control signal $\overline{BHE}$ in the address bus latch. The latched address lines A_{17L} through A_{19L} are decoded to produce chip enable outputs $\overline{CE_0}$ through $\overline{CE_7}$. Notice that the 8288 bus controller produces the address latch enable (ALE) control signal from $\overline{S_2}\overline{S_1}\overline{S_0}$. ALE is applied to the CLK input of the latches and strobes the bits of the address and bank high enable signal into the address bus latches. These signals are buffered by the address latch devices. Latched address lines A_{0L} through A_{16L} and $\overline{CE_0}$ and $\overline{CE_7}$ are applied directly to the memory subsystem.

During read bus cycles, the $\overline{MRDC}$ output of the bus control logic enables the bytes of data at the outputs of the memory subsystem onto data bus lines D_0 through D_{15}. During read operations from memory, the bank read control logic determines whether the data are read from one of the two memory banks or from both. This depends on whether a byte- or word-data transfer is taking place over the bus.

Similarly during write bus cycles, the $\overline{MWTC}$ output of the bus control logic enables bytes of data from the data bus D_0 through D_{15} to be written into the memory. The bank write control logic determines to which memory bank the data is written.

Notice in Fig. 7.26 that in the bank write control logic the latched bank high enable signal $\overline{BHEL}$ and address line A_{0L} are gated with the memory write command

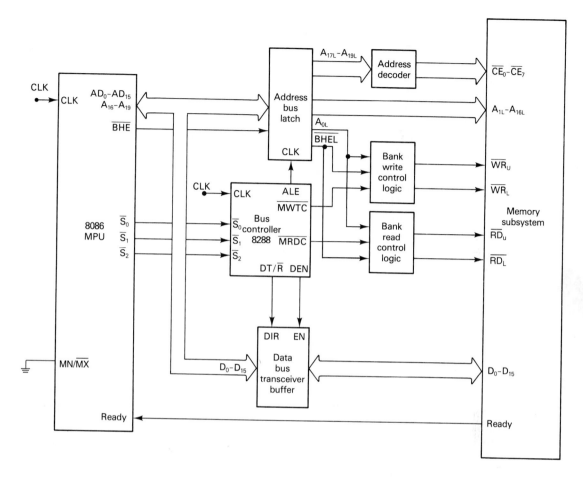

Figure 7.26 Memory interface block diagram.

signal $\overline{\text{MWTC}}$ to produce a separate write enable signal for each bank. These signals are denoted as $\overline{\text{WR}}_U$ through $\overline{\text{WR}}_L$. For example, if a word of data is to be written to memory over data bus lines D_0 through D_{15}, both $\overline{\text{WR}}_U$ and $\overline{\text{WR}}_L$ are switched to their active 0 logic level. Similarly $\overline{\text{MRDC}}$, A_{0L}, and $\overline{\text{BHEL}}$ are used by the memory read control logic to generate $\overline{\text{RD}}_U$ and $\overline{\text{RD}}_L$ signals for bank read control.

The bus transceivers control the direction of data transfer between the MPU and memory subsystem. In Fig. 7.26, we see that the operation of the transceivers is controlled by the DT/$\overline{\text{R}}$ and DEN outputs of the bus controller. DEN is applied to the EN input of the transceivers and enables them for operation. This happens during all read and write bus cycles. DT/$\overline{\text{R}}$ selects the direction of data transfer through the devices. Notice that it is supplied to the DIR input of the data bus transceivers. When a read cycle is in progress, DT/$\overline{\text{R}}$ is set to 0 and data are passed from the memory subsystem to the MPU. On the other hand, when a write cycle is taking place, DT/$\overline{\text{R}}$ is switched to logic 1 and data are carried from the MPU to the memory subsystem.

Address Latches and Buffers

The 74F373 is an example of an octal latch device that can be used to implement the *address latch* section of the 8086's memory interface circuit. A block diagram of this device is shown in Fig. 7.27(a) and its internal circuitry is shown in Fig. 7.27(b). Notice that it accepts eight inputs: 1D through 8D. As long as the clock (C) input is at logic 1, the outputs of the D-type flip-flops follow the logic level of the data applied to their corresponding inputs. When the clock is switched to logic 0, the current contents of the D-type flip-flops are latched. The latched information in the flip-flops is not output at data outputs 1Q through 8Q unless the output control ($\overline{OC}$) input is at logic 0. If $\overline{OC}$ is at logic 1, the outputs are in the high-impedance state. Figure 7.27(c) summarizes this operation.

In the 8086 microcomputer system, the 20 address lines (AD_0-AD_{15}, A_{16}-A_{19}) and the bank high enable signal $\overline{BHE}$ are normally latched in the address bus latch. The circuit configuration shown in Fig. 7.28 can be used to latch these signals. Notice that the latched outputs A_{0L} through A_{19L} and $\overline{BHEL}$ are permanently enabled by fixing $\overline{OC}$ at the 0 logic level. Moreover, the address information is latched at the outputs as the ALE signal from the bus controller returns to logic 0—that is, when the CLK input of all devices is switched from logic 1 to logic 0.

In general, it is important to minimize the propagation delay of the address signals as they go through the bus interface circuit. The switching property of the 74F373 latches that determine this delay for the circuit of Fig. 7.28 is called *enable-to-output propagation delay* and has a maximum value of 13 ns. By selecting fast latches, that is, latches with a shorter propagation delay time, a maximum amount of the 8086's bus cycle time is preserved for the access time of the memory devices. In this way slower, lower cost memory ICs can be used. These latches also provide buffering for the 8086's address lines. The outputs of the latch can sink a maximum of 24 mA.

The 74F374 is another IC that is frequently used as a latch in microcomputer systems. The circuit within this device is shown in Fig. 7.29(a). This circuit is similar to the 74F373 we just introduced in that it is an octal latch device. However, the flip-flops used to implement the latches are edge triggered instead of transparent. Notice in Fig. 7.29(b) that when $\overline{OC}$ is logic 0 the data outputs become equal to the value of the data inputs synchronous with a low to high transition at the CLK input.

In some applications, additional buffering is required on the latched address lines. For example, the diagram in Fig. 7.30(a) shows that some of the address lines may be buffered to provide an independent I/O address bus. In this case, a simple octal buffer/line driver device such as the 74F244 can be used as the I/O bus buffer. Figure 7.30(b) shows the buffer circuitry provided by the 74F244. The outputs of this device can sink a maximum of 64 mA.

Data Bus Transceivers

The *data bus transceiver* block of the bus interface circuit can be implemented with 74F245 octal bus transceivers ICs. Figure 7.31(a) shows a block diagram of

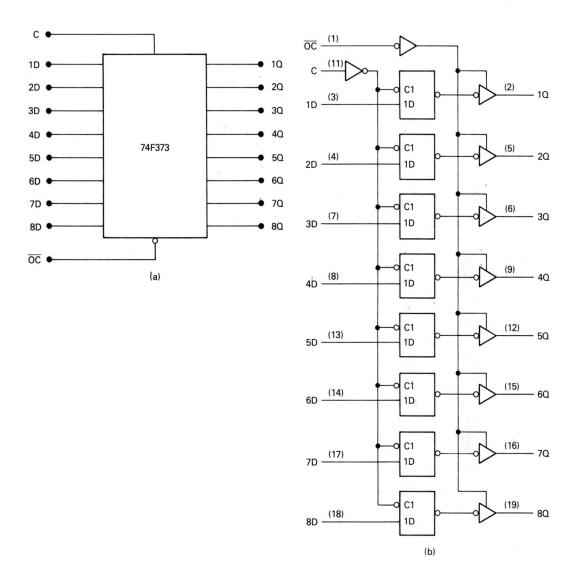

Figure 7.27 (a) Block diagram of an octal D-type latch. (b) Circuit diagram of the 74F373. (Courtesy of Texas Instruments Incorporated) (c) Operation of the 74F373. (Courtesy of Texas Instruments Incorporated)

Inputs			Output
$\overline{OC}$	Enable C	D	Q
L	H	H	H
L	H	L	L
L	L	X	Q_0
H	X	X	Z

(c)

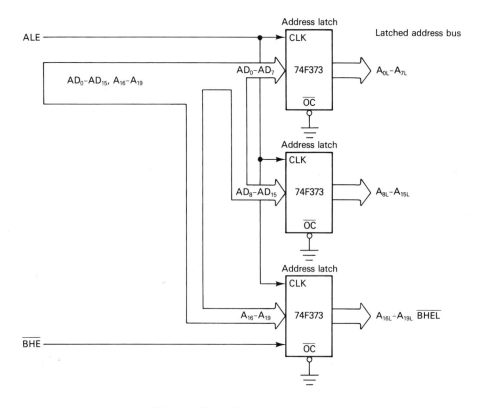

Figure 7.28 Address latch circuit.

this device. Notice that its bi-directional input/output lines are called A_1 through A_8 and B_1 through B_8. Looking at the circuit diagram in Fig. 7.31(b), we see that the $\overline{G}$ input is used to enable the buffer for operation. On the other hand, the logic level at the direction (DIR) input selects the direction in which data are transferred through the device. For instance, logic 0 at this input sets the transceiver to pass data from the B lines to the A lines. Switching DIR to logic 1 reverses the direction of data transfer.

Figure 7.32 shows a circuit that implements the data bus transceiver block of the bus interface circuit using the 74F245. For the 16-bit data bus of the 8086 microcomputer two devices are required. Here the DIR input is driven by the signal data transmit/receive ($DT/\overline{R}$), and $\overline{G}$ is supplied by data bus enable (DEN). These signals are outputs of the 8288 bus controller. Another key function of the data bus transceiver circuit is to buffer the data bus lines. This capability is defined by how much current the devices can sink at their outputs. This rating of the 74F245 is 64 mA.

The 74F646 device is an octal bus transceiver with registers. This device is more versatile than the 74F245 we just described. It can be configured to operate either as a simple bus transceiver or as a registered bus transceiver. Figure 7.33(a) shows the operations that can occur when used as a simple transceiver. Notice that

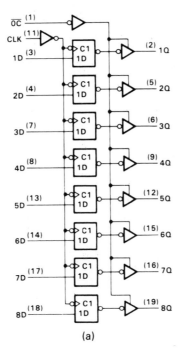

FUNCTION TABLE (EACH FLIP-FLOP)

INPUTS			OUTPUT
$\overline{OC}$	CLK	D	Q
L	↑	H	H
L	↑	L	L
L	L	X	Q_0
H	X	X	Z

(b)

(a)

Figure 7.29 (a) Circuit diagram of the 74F374. (Courtesy of Texas Instruments Incorporated) (b) Operation of the 74F374. (Courtesy of Texas Instruments Incorporated)

logic 0 at the SAB or SBA input selects the direction of data transfer through the device. The diagram in Fig. 7.33(b) shows that when configured for the registered mode of operation data do not directly transfer between the A and B buses. Instead, data are passed from the bus to an internal register with one control signal sequence and from the internal register to the other bus with another control signal. Notice that lines CAB and CBA control the storage of the data from the A or B bus into the register and SAB and SBA control the transfer of stored data from the registers to the A or B bus. The table in Fig. 7.33(c) summarizes all of the operations performed by the 74F646.

Address Decoders

As shown in Fig. 7.34, the *address decoder* in the 8086 microcomputer system is located at the output side of the address latch. A typical device that is used to perform this decode function is the 74F139 dual 2-line to 4-line decoder. Figure 7.35(a) and (b) show a block diagram and circuit diagram for this device, respectively. When the enable ($\overline{G}$) input is at its active 0 logic level, the output corresponding to the code at the BA inputs switches to the 0 logic level. For instance, when BA = 01, output Y_1 is logic 0. The operation of the 74F139 is summarized in the table of Fig. 7.35(c).

The circuit in Fig. 7.36 employs the address decoder configuration of Fig. 7.34. Notice that address lines A_{19L} and A_{18L} are applied to the B and A inputs of the

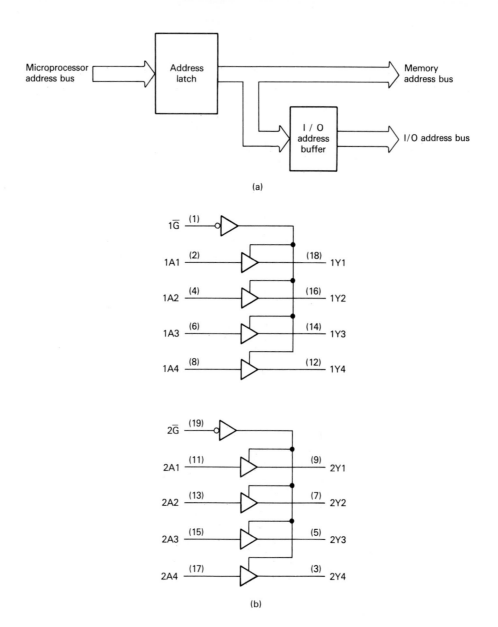

Figure 7.30 (a) Buffering the I/O address. (b) 74F244 circuit diagram. (Courtesy of Texas Instruments Incorporated)

74F139 decoder. Here they are decoded to produce chip enable outputs $\overline{CE}_0$ through $\overline{CE}_3$. Typically, independent decoders are used for memory and I/O. In this case, one of the decoders in the 74F139 can be used to produce four memory chip enables and the other decoder to provide four I/O device chip selects.

The block diagram of another commonly used decoder, the 74F138, is shown

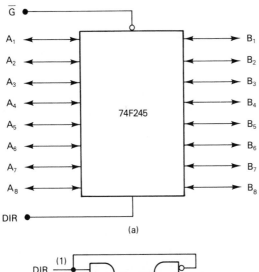

(a)

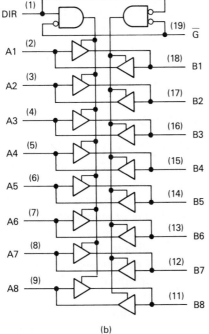

(b)

Figure 7.31 (a) Block diagram of the 74F245 octal bidirectional bus transceiver. (b) Circuit diagram of the 74F245. (Courtesy of Texas Instruments Incorporated)

in Fig. 7.37(a). The 74F138 is similar to the 74F139, except that it is a single 3-line to 8-line decoder. The circuit used in this device is shown in Fig. 7.37(b). Notice that it can be used to produce eight $\overline{CE}$ outputs. The operation of the 74F138 is described by the table in Fig. 7.37(c). Here we find that when enabled only the output that corresponds to the code at the CBA inputs switches to the active 0 logic level.

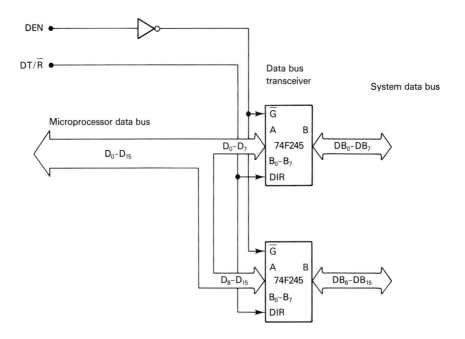

Figure 7.32 Data bus transceiver circuit.

▲ 7.14 PROGRAMMABLE LOGIC ARRAYS

In the last section we found that basic logic devices such as latches, transceivers, and decoders are required in the bus interface section of the 8086 microcomputer system. We showed that these functions were performed with standard logic devices such as the 74F373 octal transparent latch, 74F245 octal bus transceiver, and 74F139 2-line to 4-line decoder, respectively. Today *programmable logic array* (PLA) devices are becoming very important in the design of microcomputer systems. For example, address and control signal decoding in the memory interface in Fig. 7.26 can be implemented with PLAs, instead of with separate logic ICs. Unlike the earlier mentioned devices, PLAs do not implement a specific logic function. Instead, they are general-purpose logic devices that have the ability to perform a wide variety of specialized logic functions. PLA contains a general purpose AND-OR-NOT array of logic gate circuits. The user has the ability to interconnect the inputs to the AND gates of this array. The definition of these inputs determines the logic function that is implemented. The process used to connect or disconnect inputs of the AND gate array is known as *programming*.

Block Diagram of a PLA

The block diagram in Fig. 7.38 represents a typical PLA. Looking at this diagram, we see that it has 16 input leads, marked I_0 through I_{15}. There are eight

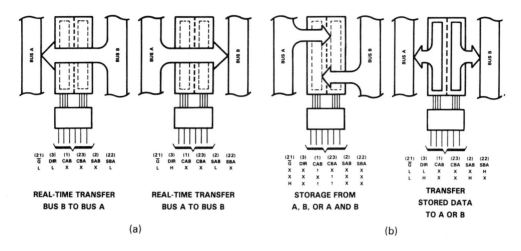

(21) $\overline{G}$	(3) DIR	(1) CAB	(23) CBA	(2) SAB	(22) SBA
L	L	X	X	X	L

REAL-TIME TRANSFER
BUS B TO BUS A

(21) $\overline{G}$	(3) DIR	(1) CAB	(23) CBA	(2) SAB	(22) SBA
L	H	X	X	L	X

REAL-TIME TRANSFER
BUS A TO BUS B

(a)

(21) $\overline{G}$	(3) DIR	(1) CAB	(23) CBA	(2) SAB	(22) SBA
X	X	↑	X	X	X
X	X	X	↑	X	X
H	X	↑	↑	X	X

STORAGE FROM
A, B, OR A AND B

(21) $\overline{G}$	(3) DIR	(1) CAB	(23) CBA	(2) SAB	(22) SBA
L	L	X	X	X	H
L	H	X	X	H	X

TRANSFER
STORED DATA
TO A OR B

(b)

INPUTS						DATA I/O*		OPERATION OR FUNCTION	
$\overline{G}$	DIR	CAB	CBA	SAB	SBA	A1 THRU A8	B1 THRU B8	'ALS646, 'ALS647 'AS646	'ALS648, 'ALS649 'AS648
X	X	↑	X	X	X	Input	Not specified	Store A, B unspecified	Store A, B unspecified
X	X	X	↑	X	X	Not specified	Input	Store B, A unspecified	Store B, A unspecified
H	X	↑	↑	X	X	Input	Input	Store A and B Data	Store A and B Data
H	X	H or L	H or L	X	X			Isolation, hold storage	Isolation, hold storage
L	L	X	X	X	L	Output	Input	Real-Time B Data to A Bus	Real-Time $\overline{B}$ Data to A Bus
L	L	X	X	X	H			Stored B Data to A Bus	Stored $\overline{B}$ Data to A Bus
L	H	X	X	L	X	Input	Output	Real-Time A Data to B Bus	Real-Time $\overline{A}$ Data to B Bus
L	H	X	X	H	X			Stored A Data to B Bus	Stored $\overline{A}$ Data to B Bus

(c)

Figure 7.33 (a) Transceiver mode data transfers of the 74F646. (Courtesy of Texas Instruments Incorporated) (b) Register mode data transfers. (Courtesy of Texas Instruments Incorporated) (c) Control signals and data transfer operations. (Courtesy of Texas Instruments Incorporated)

output leads. These leads are labeled F_0 through F_7. This PLA is equipped with three-state outputs. For this reason, it has a chip enable control lead. In the block diagram, this control input is marked $\overline{CE}$. The logic level of $\overline{CE}$ determines if the outputs are enabled or disabled.

When a PLA is used to implement random logic functions, the inputs represent Boolean variables, and the outputs are used to provide eight separate random logic functions. The internal AND-OR-NOT array is programmed to define a sum-of-product equation for each of these outputs in terms of the inputs and their complements. In this way, we see that the logic levels applied at inputs I_0 through I_{15} and the programming of the AND array determine what logic levels are produced at outputs F_0 through F_7. Therefore, the capacity of a PLA is measured by three properties—the number of inputs, the number of outputs, and the number of product terms (P-terms).

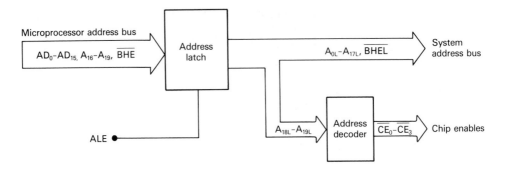

Figure 7.34 Address bus configuration with address decoding.

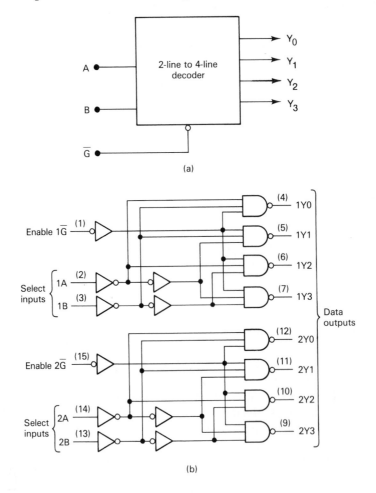

Figure 7.35 (a) Block diagram of the 74F139 2-line to 4-line decoder/demultiplexer. (b) Circuit diagram of the 74F139. (Courtesy of Texas Instruments Incorporated) (c) Operation of the 74F139 decoder. (Courtesy of Texas Instruments Incorporated)

INPUTS			OUTPUTS			
ENABLE	SELECT					
$\overline{G}$	B	A	Y0	Y1	Y2	Y3
H	X	X	H	H	H	H
L	L	L	L	H	H	H
L	L	H	H	L	H	H
L	H	L	H	H	L	H
L	H	H	H	H	H	L

(c)

Figure 7.35 (Continued)

Architecture of a PLA

We just pointed out that the circuitry of a PLA is a general purpose AND-OR-NOT array. Figure 7.39(a) shows this architecture. Here we see that the input buffers supply input signals A and B and their complements $\overline{A}$ and $\overline{B}$. Programmable connections in the AND array permit any combination of these inputs to be combined to form a product term (P-term). The product term outputs of the AND

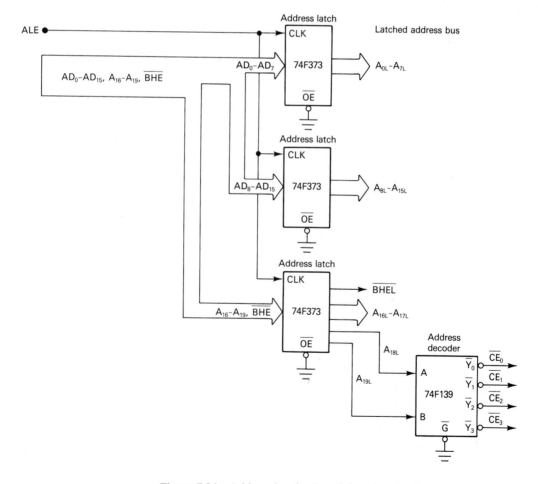

Figure 7.36 Address bus latch and decoder circuit.

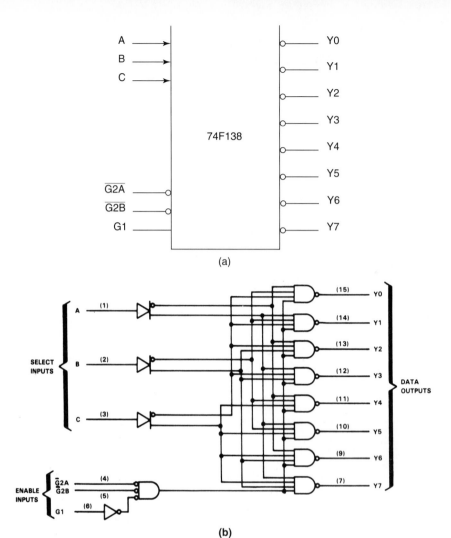

Figure 7.37 (a) Block diagram of 74F138 decoder. (b) 74F138s circuit diagram. (Courtesy of Texas Instruments Incorporated) (c) Operation of the 74F138 decoder. (Courtesy of Texas Instruments Incorporated)

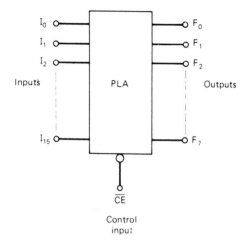

Figure 7.38 Block diagram of a PLA. (Walter A. Triebel and Alfred E. Chu, *Handbook of Semiconductor and Bubble Memories*, © 1982. Adapted with the permission of Prentice-Hall, Inc., Englewood Cliffs, N.J.)

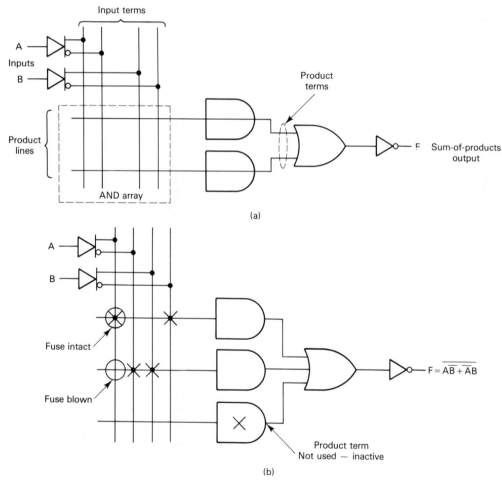

Figure 7.39 (a) Basic PLA architecture. (b) Implementing the logic function $F = \overline{A\overline{B} + \overline{A}B}$.

array are supplied to fixed inputs of the OR array. The output of the OR gate produces a sum-of-products function. Finally, the inverter complements this function.

The circuit of Fig. 7.39(b) shows how the function $F = \overline{(A\overline{B} + \overline{A}B)}$ is implemented with the AND-OR-NOT array. Notice that an X marked into the AND array means that the fuse is left intact, and no marking means that it has been blown to form an open circuit. For this reason, the upper AND gate is connected to A and $\overline{B}$ and produces the product term $A\overline{B}$. The second AND gate from the top connects to $\overline{A}$ and B to produce $\overline{A}B$. The bottom AND gate is marked with an X to indicate that it is not in use. Gates like this that are not to be active should have all of their input fuse links left intact.

In Fig. 7.40(a), we have shown the circuit structure that is most widely used in PLAs. It differs from the circuit shown in Fig. 7.39(a) in two ways. First, the inverter has a programmable three-state control and can be used to isolate the logic function from the output. Second, the buffered output is fed back to form another set of inputs to the AND array. This new output configuration permits the output pin to be programmed to work as a *standard output, standard input,* or *logic-controlled input/output.* For instance, if the upper AND gate, which is the control gate for the output buffer, is set up to permanently enable the inverter and the fuse links for its inputs that are fed back from the outputs are all blown open, the output functions as a standard output.

PLAs are also available in which the outputs are latched with registers. A circuit for this type of device is shown in Fig. 7.40(b). Here we see that the output of the OR gate is applied to the D input of a clocked D-type flip-flop. In this way, the logic level produced by the AND-OR array is not presented at the output until a pulse is first applied at the CLOCK input. Furthermore, the feedback input is produced from the complemented output of the flip-flop, not the output of the inverter. This configuration is known as a *PLA with registered outputs* and is designed to simplify implementation of *state machine* designs.

Standard PAL™ Devices

Now that we have introduced the block diagram of the PLA, types of PLAs, and internal architecture of the PLA, let us continue by examining a few of the widely used PAL devices. A PAL or a programmable array logic is a PLA in which OR array is fixed, only AND array is programmable.

The 16L8 is one of the more widely used PAL ICs. Its internal circuitry and pin numbering are shown in Fig. 7.41(a). This device is housed in a 20-pin package as shown in Fig. 7.41(b). Looking at this diagram, we see that it employs the PLA architecture that was illustrated in Fig. 7.40(a). Notice that it has ten dedicated input pins. All of these pins are labeled I. There are also two dedicated outputs, which are labeled with the letter O, and six programmable I/O lines, which are labeled I/O. Using the programmable I/O lines, the number of input lines can be expanded to as many as 16 inputs or the number of outputs can be increased to as many as 8 lines.

PAL is a trademark of Monolithic Memory Devices.

All of the 16L8's inputs are buffered and produce both the original form of the signal and its complement. The outputs of the buffers are applied to the inputs of the AND array. This array is capable of producing 64 product terms. Notice that the AND gates are arranged into eight groups of eight. The outputs of seven gates in each of these groups are used as inputs to an OR gate, and the eighth output is used to produce an enable signal for the corresponding three-state output buffer. In this way, we see that the 16L8 is capable of producing up to seven product terms for each output and each product term can be formed using any combination of the 16 inputs.

The 16L8 is manufactured with bipolar technology. It operates from a +5 V ±10% dc power supply and draws a maximum of 180 mA. Moreover, all of its inputs and outputs are at TTL compatible voltage levels. This device exhibits high-speed input-output propagation delays. In fact, the maximum I-to-O propagation delay is rated as 7 ns.

Another widely used PAL is the 20L8 device. Looking at the circuitry of this device in Fig. 7.42(a), we see that it is similar to that of the 16L8 just described. However, the 20L8 has a maximum of 20 inputs, 8 outputs, and 64 P-terms. The device's 24-pin package is shown in Fig. 7.42(b).

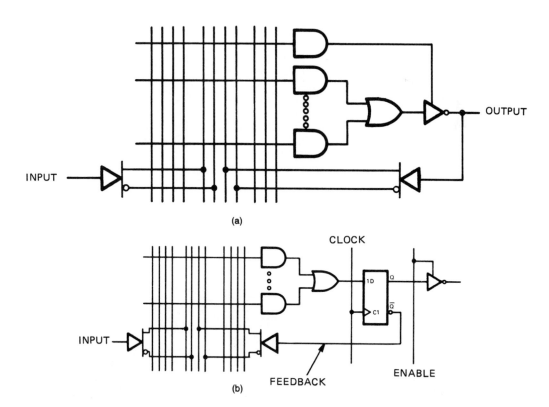

Figure 7.40 (a) Typical PLA architecture. (Courtesy of Texas Instruments Incorporated) (b) PLA with output latch. (Courtesy of Texas Instruments Incorporated)

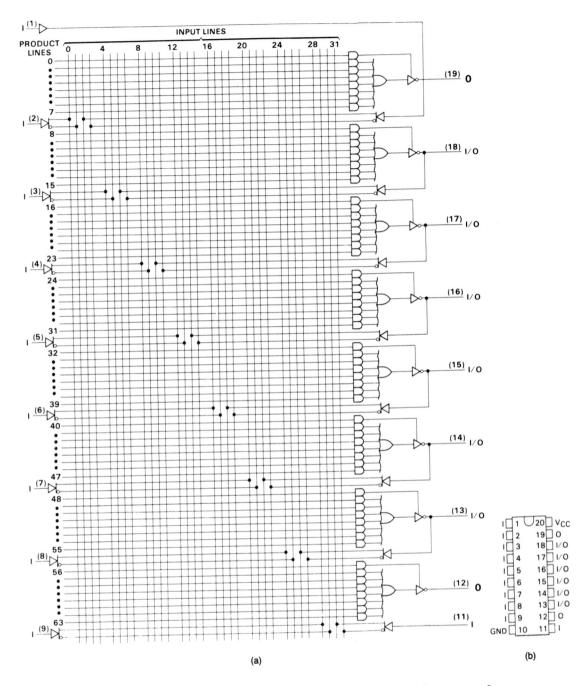

Figure 7.41 (a) 16L8 circuit diagram. (Courtesy of Texas Instruments Incorporated) (b) 16L8 pin layout. (Courtesy of Texas Instruments Incorporated)

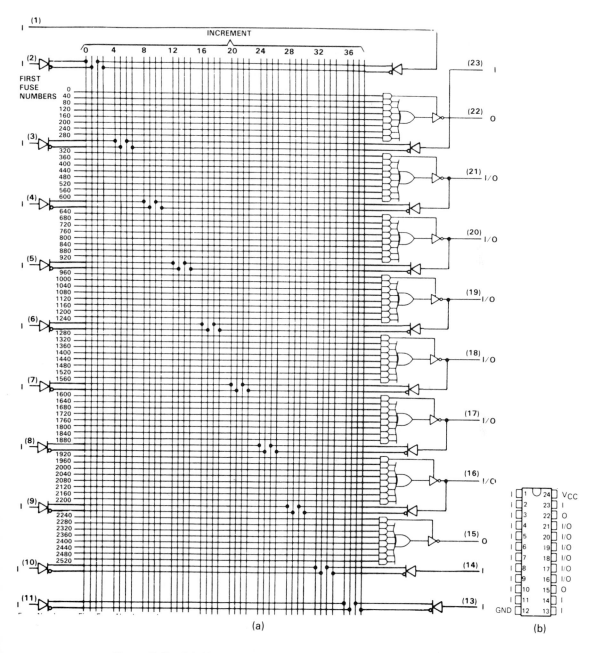

Figure 7.42 (a) 20L8 circuit diagram. (Courtesy of Texas Instruments Incorporated) (b) 20L8 pin layout. (Courtesy of Texas Instruments Incorporated)

The 16R8 is also a popular 20-pin PLA. The circuit diagram and pin layout for this device are shown in Fig. 7.43(a) and (b), respectively. From Fig. 7.43(a), we find that its eight fixed I inputs and AND-OR array are essentially the same as that of the 16L8. There is however one change—the outputs of eight AND gates, instead of seven, are supplied to the inputs of each OR gate.

A number of changes have been made at the output side of the 16R8. Notice that the outputs of the OR gates are first latched in D-type flip-flops with the CLK signal. They are then buffered and supplied to the eight Q outputs. Another change is that the enable signals for the output inverters are no longer programmable. Now all three-state outputs are enabled by the logic level of the $\overline{OE}$ control input.

The last change is in the part of the circuit that produces the feedback inputs. In the 16R8, these eight input signals are derived from the complementary outputs of the corresponding latches instead of the outputs of the buffers. For this reason, the output leads can no longer be programmed to work as direct inputs.

The 20R8 is the register output version of the 20L8 PAL. Its circuit diagram and pin layout are given in Fig. 7.44(a) and (b), respectively.

Expanding PLA Capacity

Some applications have requirements that exceed the capacity of a single PLA IC. For instance, a 16L8 device has the ability to supply a maximum of 16 inputs, 8 outputs, and 64 product terms. Capacity can be expanded by connecting several devices together. Let us now look at the way in which PLAs are interconnected to expand the number of inputs, outputs, and product terms.

If a single PLA does not have enough outputs, two or more devices can be connected together into the configuration of Fig. 7.45(a). Here we see that the inputs I_0 through I_{15} on the two devices are individually connected in parallel. This connection does not change the number of inputs.

On the other hand, the eight outputs of the two PLAs are separately used to form the upper and lower bytes of a 16-bit output word. The bits of this word are denoted as O_0 through O_{15}. So with this connection, we have doubled the number of outputs.

When data are applied to the inputs, PLA 1 outputs the eight least significant bits of data. At the same instant PLA 2 outputs the eight most significant bits. These outputs can be used to represent individual logic functions.

Another limitation on the application of PLAs is the number of inputs. The maximum number of inputs on a single 16L8 is 16. However, additional ICs can be connected to expand the capacity of inputs. Figure 7.45(b) shows how one additional input is added. This permits a 17-bit input denoted as I_0 through I_{16}. The new bit I_{16} is supplied through inverters to the $\overline{CE}$ inputs on the two PLAs. At the output side of the PLAs, outputs O_0 through O_7 of the two devices are individually connected in parallel. To use this connection, PLA devices with open-collector or three-state outputs must be used.

When I_{16} is logic 0, $\overline{CE}$ on PLA 1 is logic 0. This enables the device for operation, and the output functions coded for input I_0 through I_{15} are output at O_0 through O_7. At the same instant, $\overline{CE}$ on PLA 2 is logic 1 and it remains disabled.

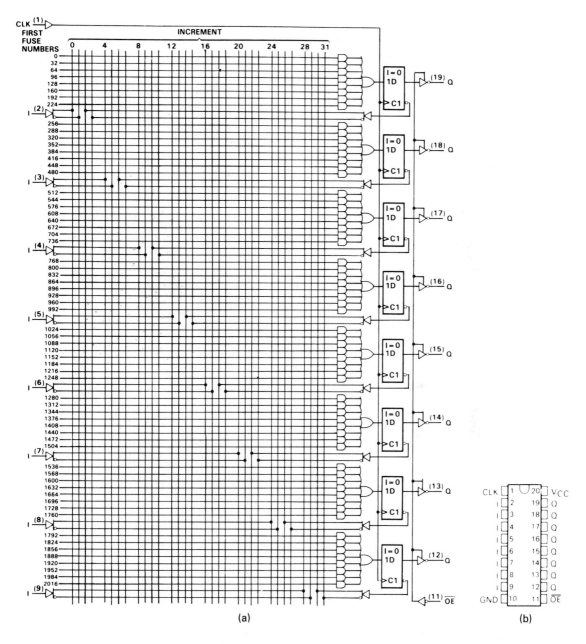

Figure 7.43 (a) 16R8 circuit diagram. (Courtesy of Texas Instruments Incorporated) (b) 16R8 pin layout. (Courtesy of Texas Instruments Incorporated)

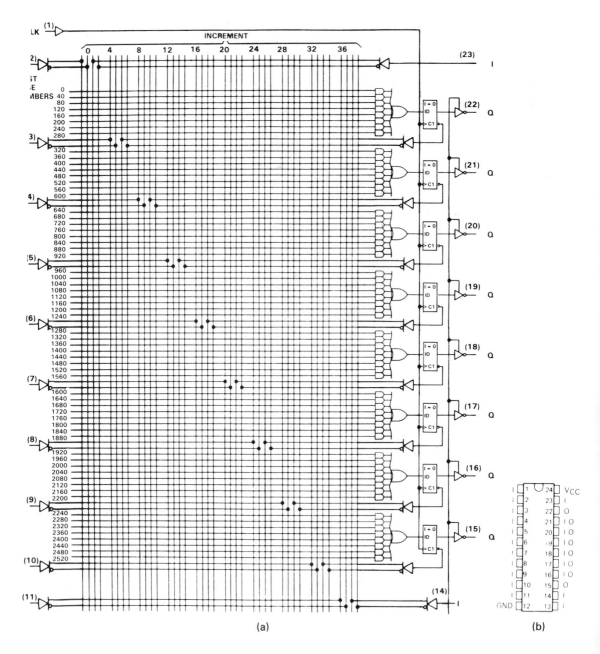

Figure 7.44 (a) 20R8 circuit diagram. (Courtesy of Texas Instruments Incorporated) (b) 20R8 pin layout. (Courtesy of Texas Instruments Incorporated)

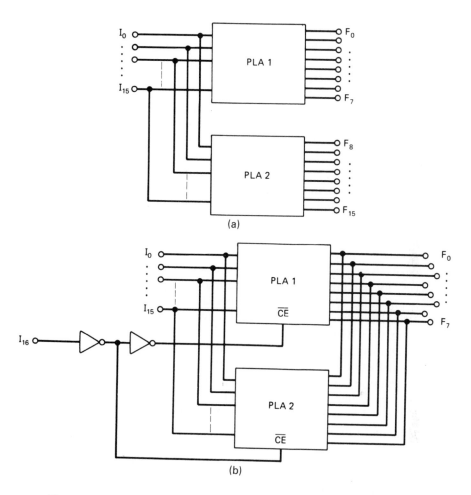

Figure 7.45 (a) Expanding output word length. (b) Expanding input word length. (Walter A. Triebel and Alfred E. Chu, *Handbook of Semiconductor and Bubble Memories*, © 1982. Adapted with the permission of Prentice-Hall, Inc., Englewood Cliffs, N.J.)

Making the logic level of I_{16} equal to 1 disables PLA 1 and enables PLA 2. Now the input at I_0 through I_{15} causes the output function defined by PLA 2 to be output at O_0 through O_7. Actually, this connection doubles the number of product terms as well as increases the number of inputs.

▲ 7.15 PROGRAM STORAGE MEMORY—ROM, PROM, AND EPROM

Read-only memory (ROM) is one type of semiconductor memory device. It is most widely used in microcomputer systems for storage of the program that determines overall system operation. The information stored within a ROM integrated circuit is permanent—or *nonvolatile*. This means that when the power supply of the device is turned off, the stored information is not lost.

ROM, PROM, and EPROM

For some ROM devices, information (the microcomputer program) must be built in during manufacturing and for others the data must be electrically entered. The process of entering data into a ROM is called *programming*. As the name ROM implies, once entered into the device this information can be read only. Three types of ROM devices exist. They are known as the *mask-programmable read-only memory* (ROM), the *one-time programmable read-only memory* (PROM), and the *erasable programmable read-only memory* (EPROM).

Let us continue by looking more closely into the first type of device, the mask-programmable read-only memory. This device has its data pattern programmed as part of the manufacturing process. This is known as *mask programming*. Once the device is programmed, its contents can never be changed. Because of this and the cost for making the programming masks, ROMs are used mainly in high-volume applications where the data will not change.

The other two types of read-only memories, the PROM and EPROM, differ from the ROM in that the data contents are electrically entered by the user. Programming is usually done with equipment called a *programmer*. Both the PROM and EPROM are programmed in the same way. Once a PROM is programmed, its contents cannot be changed. This is the reason they are sometimes called one-time programmable PROMs. On the other hand, the contents of an EPROM can be erased by exposing it to ultraviolet light. In this way, the device can be used over and over again simply by erasing and reprogramming. PROMs and EPROMs are most often used during the design of a product and for early production, when the code of the microcomputer may need to be changed frequently.

Block Diagram of a ROM

A block diagram of a typical ROM is shown in Fig. 7.46. Here we see that the device has three sets of signal lines: the address inputs, data outputs, and control inputs. This block diagram is valid for a ROM, PROM, or EPROM. Let us now look at the function of each of these sets of signal lines.

The address bus is used to input the signals that select between the data storage locations within the ROM device. In Fig. 7.46, we find that this bus consists of 11 address lines, A_0 through A_{10}. The bits in the address are arranged so that A_{10} is the MSB and A_0 is the LSB. With an 11-bit address, the memory device has $2^{11} = 2048$ unique data storage locations. The individual storage locations correspond to addresses over the range $00000000000_2 = 000_{16}$ through $11111111111_2 = 7FF_{16}$.

A bit of data is stored inside a ROM, PROM, or EPROM as either a binary 0 or binary 1. Actually, 8 bits of data are stored at every address. Therefore the total storage capacity of the device we are describing is $2048 \times 8 = 16,384$ bits; that is, the device we are describing is really a 16K-bit ROM. By applying the

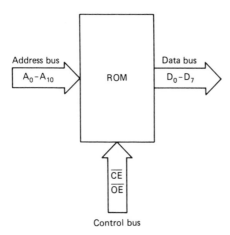

Figure 7.46 Block diagram of a ROM.

address of a storage location to the address inputs of the ROM, the byte of data held at the addressed location is read out onto the data lines. In the block diagram of Fig. 7.46, we see that the data bus consists of eight lines labeled as D_0 through D_7.

The control bus represents the control signals that are required to enable or disable the ROM, PROM, or the EPROM device. In the block diagram of Fig. 7.46, two control leads, output enable ($\overline{\text{OE}}$) and chip enable ($\overline{\text{CE}}$), are identified. For example, logic 0 at $\overline{\text{OE}}$ enables the three state outputs, D0 through D7, of the device. If $\overline{\text{OE}}$ is switched to the 1 logic level, these outputs are disabled (put in the high-Z state). Moreover, $\overline{\text{CE}}$ must be at logic 0 for the device to be active. Logic 1 at $\overline{\text{CE}}$ puts the device in a low-power standby mode. When in this state, the data outputs are in the high-Z state independent of the logic level of $\overline{\text{OE}}$.

Read Operation

For a microprocessor to read a byte of data from the device, it must apply a binary address to inputs A_0 through A_{10}. This address gets decoded inside the device to select the storage location of the byte of data that is to be read. Then the microprocessor must switch $\overline{\text{CE}}$ and $\overline{\text{OE}}$ to logic 0 to enable the device and outputs. Now the byte of data is available at D_0 through D_7 and the microprocessor can read the data over its data bus.

From our description of the read operation, it appears that after the inputs of the ROM are set up, the output appears immediately; however, in practice this is not true. A short delay exists between address inputs and data outputs. This leads us to three important timing properties defined for the read cycle of a ROM. They are called *access time* (t_{ACC}), *chip enable time*, (t_{CE}), and *chip deselect time* (t_{DF}).

Access time tells us how long it takes to access data stored in a ROM. Here we assume that both $\overline{\text{CE}}$ and $\overline{\text{OE}}$ are at their active 0 levels, and then an address is applied to the inputs of the ROM. In this case, the delay t_{ACC} occurs before the data stored at the addressed location are stable at the outputs. The microprocessor must wait at least this long before reading the data; otherwise, invalid results may be obtained.

Chip enable time is similar to access time. In fact, for most EPROMs they are equal in value. They differ in how the device is set up initially. This time the address is applied and $\overline{OE}$ is switched to 0, then the read operation is initiated by making $\overline{CE}$ active. Therefore, t_{CE} represents the chip enable to output delay instead of the address to output delay.

Chip deselect time is the opposite of access or chip enable time. It represents the amount of time the device takes for the data outputs to return to the high-Z state after $\overline{OE}$ becomes inactive—that is, the recovery time of the outputs.

Standard EPROM ICs

A large number of standard EPROM ICs are available today. Figure 7.47 lists the part numbers, bit densities, and byte capacities of the seven most popular devices. They range in size from the 16K-bit density (2K × 8) 2716 device, to the 1MB (128K × 8) 27010 device. Higher-density devices, such as the 27256 through 27010, are most popular for new system designs. In fact, some of the older devices, such as the 2716 and 2732, have already been discontinued by many manufacturers. Let us now look at some of these EPROMs in more detail.

The 27256 is an EPROM IC manufactured with the NMOS technology. Looking at Fig. 7.47, we find that it is a 256KB device and its storage array is organized as 32K × 8 bits. Figure 7.48 shows the pin layout of the 27256. Here we see that it has 15 address inputs, labeled A_0 through A_{14}, eight data outputs, identified as O_0 through O_7, and two control signals $\overline{CE}$ and $\overline{OE}$.

The 27256 is available in four access-time speed selections. In Fig. 7.49 we find that the speed of an EPROM is denoted by a dash and number at the end of its generic part number. For example, the standard 27256 is a 250 ns access-time device. On the other hand, the 27256-1 is faster; it has an access time of 170 ns.

In an erased EPROM, all storage cells hold logic 1. The device is put into the programming mode by switching on the V_{pp} power supply. Once in this mode, the address of the storage location that is to be programmed is applied to the address inputs, and the data that is to be loaded into this location is supplied to the data leads. Next the $\overline{CE}$ input is pulsed to load the data. Actually, a complex series of program and verify operations are performed to program each storage location in an EPROM. The two programming sequences in wide use today are

EPROM	Density (bits)	Capacity (bytes)
2716	16K	2K × 8
2732	32K	4K × 8
2764	64K	8K × 8
27128	128K	16K × 8
27256	256K	32K × 8
27512	512K	64K × 8
27010	1M	128K × 8

Figure 7.47 Standard EPROM devices.

Pin (27256)	2716	2732A	2764A / 27C64	27128A	27512
28 (V_{CC})	V_{CC}	V_{CC}	V_{CC}	V_{CC}	V_{CC}
27 (A_{14})	A_8	A_8	$\overline{PGM}$	$\overline{PGM}$	A_{14}
26 (A_{13})	A_9	A_9	N.C.	A_{13}	A_{13}
25 (A_8)	V_{PP}	A_{11}	A_8	A_8	A_8
24 (A_9)	$\overline{OE}$	$\overline{OE}/V_{PP}$	A_9	A_9	A_9
23 (A_{11})	A_{10}	A_{10}	A_{11}	A_{11}	A_{11}
22 ($\overline{OE}$)	$\overline{CE}$	$\overline{CE}$	$\overline{OE}$	$\overline{OE}$	$\overline{OE}/V_{PP}$
21 (A_{10})	O_7	O_7	A_{10}	A_{10}	A_{10}
20 ($\overline{CE}$)	O_6	O_6	$\overline{CE}$	$\overline{CE}$	$\overline{CE}$
19 (O_7)	O_5	O_5	O_7	O_7	O_7
18 (O_6)	O_4	O_4	O_6	O_6	O_6
17 (O_5)	O_3	O_3	O_5	O_5	O_5
16 (O_4)			O_4	O_4	O_4
15 (O_3)			O_3	O_3	O_3

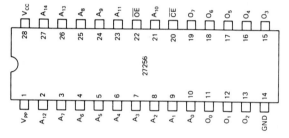

Figure 7.48 Pin layouts of standard EPROMs.

Pin (27256)	27512	27128A	2764A / 27C64	2732A	2716
1 (V_{PP})	A_{15}	V_{PP}	V_{PP}		
2 (A_{12})	A_{12}	A_{12}	A_{12}		
3 (A_7)	A_7	A_7	A_7	A_7	A_7
4 (A_6)	A_6	A_6	A_6	A_6	A_6
5 (A_5)	A_5	A_5	A_5	A_5	A_5
6 (A_4)	A_4	A_4	A_4	A_4	A_4
7 (A_3)	A_3	A_3	A_3	A_3	A_3
8 (A_2)	A_2	A_2	A_2	A_2	A_2
9 (A_1)	A_1	A_1	A_1	A_1	A_1
10 (A_0)	A_0	A_0	A_0	A_0	A_0
11 (O_0)	O_0	O_0	O_0	O_0	O_0
12 (O_1)	O_1	O_1	O_1	O_1	O_1
13 (O_2)	O_2	O_2	O_2	O_2	O_2
14 (GND)	Gnd	Gnd	Gnd	Gnd	Gnd

Part number	Access time
27256-3	300 ns
27256	250 ns
27256-2	200 ns
27256-1	170 ns

Figure 7.49 Speed selections for the 27256.

the *Quick-Pulse Programming Algorithm*™ and the *Intelligent Programming Algorithm*™. Flowcharts for these programming algorithms are given in Fig. 7.50(a) and (b), respectively.

Figure 7.48 also shows the pin layouts for the 2716 through 27512 EPROM devices. In this diagram, we find that both the 27256 and 27512 are available in a 28-pin package. A comparison of the pin configuration of the 27512 with that of the 27256 shows that the only differences between the two pinouts are that pin 1

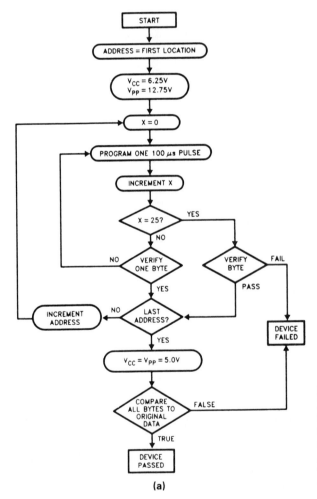

Figure 7.50 (a) Quick-Pulse Programming™ algorithm flowchart. (Reprinted with permission of Intel Corp., © Intel Corp, 1989) (b) Intelligent Programming™ algorithm flowchart. (Reprinted with permission of Intel Corp., © Intel Corp. 1989).

(a)

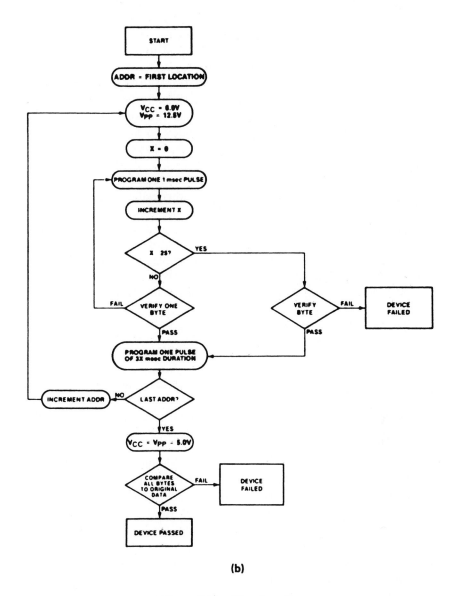

Figure 7.50 (Continued)

on the 27512 becomes the new address input A_{15}, and V_{pp}, which was at pin 1 on the 27256, becomes a second function performed by pin 22 on the 27512.

Expanding ROM Word Length and Word Capacity

In many applications, the microcomputer system requirements for ROM are greater than what is available in a single device. There are two basic reasons for expanding ROM capacity: first, the byte-wide length is not large enough; second, the total storage capacity is not enough bytes. Both of these expansion needs can be satisfied by interconnecting a number of ICs.

For example, the 8086 microprocessor has a 16-bit data bus. Therefore, its program memory subsystem needs to be implemented with two EPROMs connected as shown in Fig. 7.51(a). Notice that the individual address inputs, chip enable lines, and output enable lines on the two devices are connected in parallel. On the other hand, the eight data outputs of the two devices are each used to supply eight lines of the 16-bit data bus. This circuit configuration has a total storage capacity equal to 32K 16-bit words.

Figure 7.51(b) shows how two 27256s can be interconnected to expand the number of bytes of storage. Here the individual address inputs, data outputs, and output enable lines of the two devices are connected in parallel. However, the $\overline{CE}$ inputs of the individual devices remain independent and can be supplied by different outputs, identified as $\overline{CS_0}$ and $\overline{CS_1}$, of an address decoder circuit. In this way, only one of the two devices will be enabled at a time. This configuration results in a total storage capacity of 64K bytes. When several EPROMs are used in an 8088-based microcomputer, they are connected in this way.

▲ 7.16 DATA STORAGE MEMORY—SRAM AND DRAM

The memory section of a microcomputer system is normally formed from both read-only memories (ROM) and *random access read/write memories* (RAM). Earlier we pointed out that the ROM is used to store permanent information such as the microcomputer's hardware control program. RAM is different from ROM in two important ways. First, RAM can be used to save data by writing to it and later read it back for additional processing. Because of its read and write features, RAM finds wide use where data and programs need to be placed in memory only temporarily. For this reason, it is normally used to store data and programs for execution. The second difference is that RAM is volatile; that is, if power is removed from RAM all data is lost.

Static and Dynamic RAMs

There are two types of RAMs in use today, the *static RAM* (SRAM) and *dynamic RAM* (DRAM). For a static RAM, data, once entered, remains valid as long as the power supply is not turned off. On the other hand, to retain data in a DRAM, it is not sufficient just to maintain the power supply. For this type of device, we must both keep the power supply turned on and periodically restore the data in each storage location. This added requirement is necessary because the storage elements in a DRAM are capacitive nodes. If the storage nodes are not recharged at regular intervals of time, data would be lost. This recharging process is known as refreshing the DRAM.

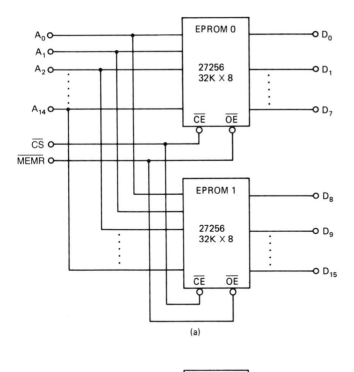

(a)

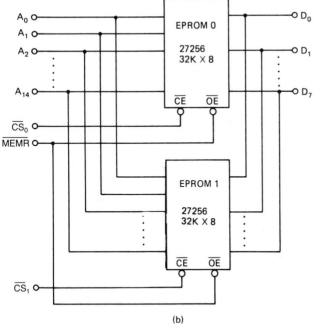

(b)

Figure 7.51 (a) Expanding word length. (b) Expanding word capacity.

Block Diagram of a Static RAM

A block diagram of a typical static RAM IC is shown in Fig. 7.52. By comparing this diagram with the one shown for a ROM in Fig. 7.46, we see that they are similar in many ways. For example, they both have address lines, data lines, and control lines. The data lines of the RAM, however, act as both inputs and outputs. For this reason, they are identified as a *bi-directional bus*.

A variety of static RAM ICs are currently available. They differ both in density and organization. The most commonly used densities in system designs are the 64K-bit and 256K-bit devices. The structure of the data bus determines the organization of the RAMs storage array. In Fig. 7.52, an 8-bit data bus is shown. This type of organization is known as a *byte-wide* RAM. Devices are also manufactured with by 1 and by 4 data I/O organizations. At the 64K-bit density, this results in three standard device organizations: $64K \times 1$, $16K \times 4$, and $8K \times 8$.

The address bus on the RAM in Fig. 7.52 consists of the lines labeled A_0 through A_{12}. This 13-bit address is what is needed to select between the 8K individual storage locations in an $8K \times 8$-bit RAM IC. The $16K \times 4$ and $64K \times 1$ devices require a 14-bit and 16-bit address, respectively.

To either read from or write to RAM, the device must first be chip enabled. Just like for a ROM, this is done by switching the $\overline{CE}$ input of the RAM to logic 0. Earlier we indicated that data lines D_0 through D_7 in Fig. 7.52 are bi-directional. This means that they will act as inputs when writing data into the RAM or as outputs when reading data from the RAM. The setting of the *write enable* ($\overline{WE}$) control input determines how the data lines operate. During all write operations to a storage location within the RAM, the $\overline{WE}$ input must be switched to the 0 logic level. This configures the data lines as inputs. On the other hand, if data are to be read from a storage location, $\overline{WE}$ is left at the 1 logic level. This input is normally activated by the $\overline{MEMW}$ control signal.

When reading data from the RAM, output enable ($\overline{OE}$) must be active. Applying the active memory signal at this input, enables the device's three-state outputs. Three-state data bus lines allow for the parallel busing needed to expand data memory by interconnecting multiple devices. For example, in Fig. 7.53 we see how four $8K \times 8$-bit RAMs are interconnected to form a $16K \times 16$-bit memory circuit. Here $\overline{CS}_0$ enables the bank 0 RAMs and $\overline{CS}_1$ the bank 1 RAMs.

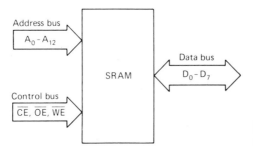

Figure 7.52 Block diagram of a static RAM.

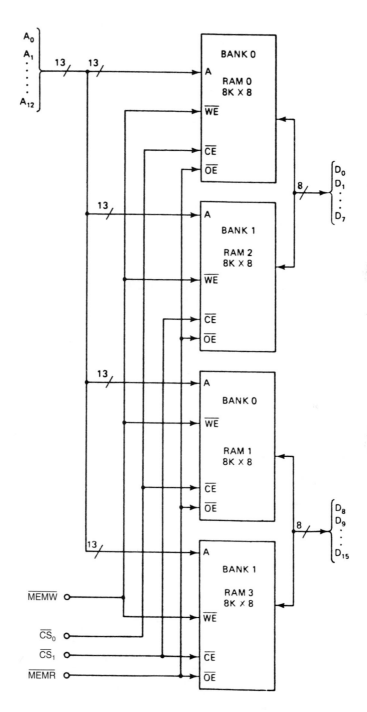

Figure 7.53 16K × 16-bit SRAM circuit.

SRAM	Density (bits)	Organization
4361	64K	64K × 1
4363	64K	16K × 4
4364	64K	8K × 8
43254	256K	64K × 4
43256A	256K	32K × 8

Figure 7.54 Standard SRAM devices.

Standard Static RAM ICs

Figure 7.54 is a list of a number of standard static RAM ICs. Here we find their part numbers, densities, and organizations. For example, the 4361, 4363, and 4364 are all 64K-bit density devices; however, they are each organized differently. The 4361 is a 64K × 1-bit device, the 4363 is a 16K × 4-bit device, and the 4364 is an 8K × 8-bit device.

The pin layouts of the 4364 and 43256A ICs are given in Fig. 7.55(a) and (b), respectively. Looking at the 4364 we see that it is almost identical to the block

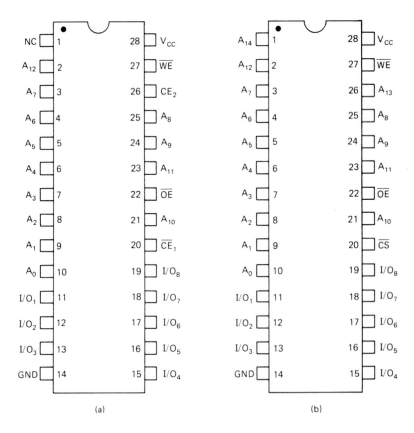

Figure 7.55 (a) 4364 pin layout. (b) 43256A pin layout.

Part number	Read/write cycle time
4364-10	100 ns
4364-12	120 ns
4364-15	150 ns
4364-20	200 ns

Figure 7.56 Speed selections for the 4364.

diagram shown in Fig. 7.52. The one difference is that it has two chip enable lines instead of one. They are labeled $\overline{CE}_1$ and CE_2. Notice that one is activated by logic 0 and the other by logic 1.

As shown in Fig. 7.56, the 4364 is available in four speeds. For example, the minimum read/write cycle time for the 4364-10 is 100 ns.

The waveforms for a typical write cycle are illustrated in Fig. 7.57. Let us trace the events that take place during the write cycle. Here we see that all critical timing is referenced to the point at which the address becomes valid. Notice that the minimum duration of the write cycle is identified as t_{WC}. This is the 100 ns *write cycle time* of the 4364-10. The address must remain stable for this complete interval of time.

Next $\overline{CE}_1$ and CE_2 become active and must remain active until the end of the write cycle. The durations of these pulses are identified as $\overline{CE}_1$ *to end of write* (t_{CW1}) *time* and CE_2 *to end of write* (t_{CW2}) *time*. As shown in the waveforms, we are assuming

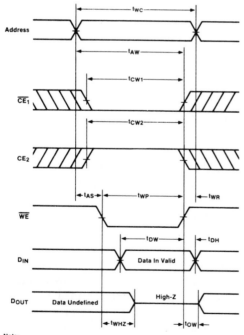

Note:
[1] A write occurs during the overlap of a low $\overline{CE}_1$ and a high CE_2 and a low $\overline{WE}$.
[2] $\overline{CE}_1$ or $\overline{WE}$ [or CE_2] must be high [low] during any address transition.
[3] If $\overline{OE}$ is high the I/O pins remain in a high impedance state.

Figure 7.57 Write-cycle timing diagram.

here that they begin at any time after the occurrence of the address but before the leading edge of $\overline{\text{WE}}$. The minimum value for both of these times is 80 ns. On the other hand, $\overline{\text{WE}}$ is shown to not occur until the interval t_{AS} elapses. This is the *address setup time* and represents the minimum amount of time the address inputs must be stable before $\overline{\text{WE}}$ can be switched to logic 0. For the 4364, however, this parameter is equal to 0 ns. The width of the write enable pulse is identified as t_{WP} and its minimum value equals 60 ns.

Data applied to the D_{IN} data inputs are written into the device synchronous with the trailing edge of $\overline{\text{WE}}$. Notice that the data must be valid for an interval equal to t_{DW} before this edge. This interval, which is called *data valid to end of write*, has a minimum value of 40 ns for the 4364-10. Moreover, it is shown to remain valid for an interval of time equal to t_{DH} after this edge. This *data hold time*, however, just like address setup time, equals 0 ns for the 4364. Finally, a short recovery period takes place after $\overline{\text{WE}}$ returns to logic 1 before the write cycle is complete. This interval is identified as t_{WR} in the waveforms, and its minimum value equals 5 ns.

The read cycle of a static RAM, such as the 4364, is similar to that of a ROM. Waveforms of a read operation are given in Fig. 7.58.

Standard Dynamic RAM ICs

Dynamic RAMs are available in higher densities than static RAMs. Currently, the most widely used DRAMs are the 64K-bit, 256K-bit, and 1M-bit devices. Figure 7.59 is a list of a number of popular DRAM ICs. Here we find the 2164B, which is organized as 64K × 1 bit, the 21256, which is organized as 256K × 1 bit, the 21464, which is organized as 64K × 4 bits, the 421000, which is organized as 1M × 1 bit, and the 424256, which is organized as 256K × 4 bits. Pin layouts for the 2164B, 21256, and 421000 are shown in Fig. 7.60(a), (b), and (c), respectively.

Some other benefits of using DRAMs over SRAMs are that they cost less, consume less power, and their 16- and 18-pin packages take up less space. For these reasons, DRAMs are normally used in applications that require a large amount of memory. For example, most systems that support at least 1M byte of data memory are designed using DRAMs.

The 2164B is one of the older NMOS DRAM devices. A block diagram of the device is shown in Fig. 7.61. Looking at the block diagram we find that it has eight address inputs, A_0 through A_7, a data input and data output marked D and Q, respectively, and three control inputs, *row address strobe* ($\overline{\text{RAS}}$), *column address strobe* ($\overline{\text{CAS}}$), and *read/write* ($\overline{\text{W}}$).

The storage array within the 2164B is capable of storing 65,536 (64K) individual bits of data. To address this many storage locations, we need a 16-bit address; however, this device's package has just 16 pins. For this reason, the 16-bit address is divided into two separate parts: an 8-bit *row address* and an 8-bit *column address*. These two parts are time-multiplexed into the device over a single set of address lines, A_0 through A_7. First the row address is applied to A_0 through A_7. Then $\overline{\text{RAS}}$ is pulsed to logic 0 to latch it into the device. Next, the column address is

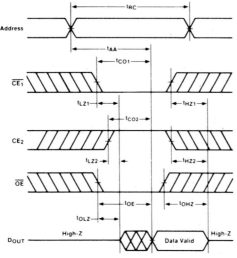

Note:
(1) $\overline{WE}$ is a high for a read cycle.
(2) The address inputs are valid prior to or coincident with the $\overline{CE}_1$ transition low and the CE_2 transition high.

Figure 7.58 Read-cycle timing diagram.

applied and $\overline{CAS}$ strobed to logic 0. This 16-bit address selects which one of the 64K storage locations is to be accessed.

Data are either written into or read from the addressed storage location in the DRAMs. Write data are applied to the D input and read data are output at Q. The logic levels of control signals $\overline{W}$, $\overline{RAS}$, and $\overline{CAS}$ tell the DRAM whether a read or write data transfer is taking place and control the three-state outputs. For example, during a write operation, the logic level at D is latched into the addressed storage location at the falling edge of either $\overline{CAS}$ or $\overline{W}$. If $\overline{W}$ is switched to logic 0 by an active $\overline{MEMW}$ signal before $\overline{CAS}$, an early write cycle is performed. During this type of write cycle, the outputs are maintained in the high-Z state throughout the complete bus cycle. The fact that the output is put in the high-Z state during the write operation allows the D input and Q output of the DRAM to be tied together. The Q output is also in the high-Z state whenever $\overline{CAS}$ is logic 1. This is the connection and mode of operation normally used when attaching DRAMs to the bi-directional data bus of a microprocessor. Figure 7.62 shows how 16 2164B devices are connected to make up a 64K × 16-bit DRAM array.

DRAM	Density (bits)	Organization
2164B	64K	64K × 1
21256	256K	256K × 1
21464	256K	64K × 4
421000	1M	1M × 1
424256	1M	256K × 4

Figure 7.59 Standard DRAM devices.

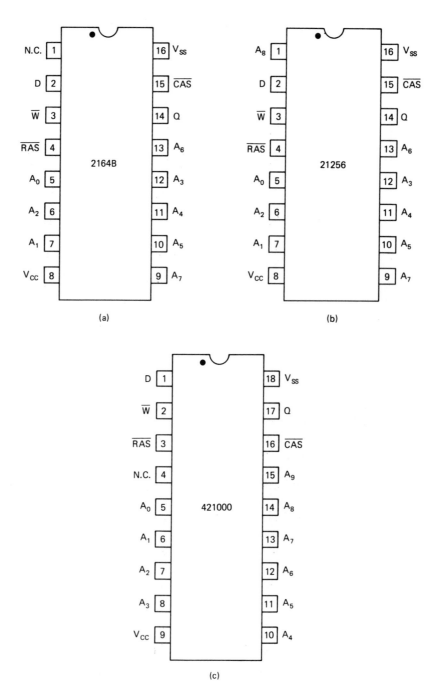

Figure 7.60 (a) 2164B pin layout. (b) 21256 pin layout. (c) 421000 pin layout.

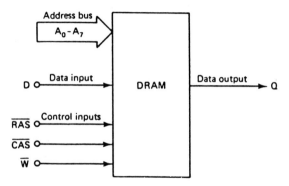

Figure 7.61 Block diagram of the 2164B DRAM.

The 2164B also has the ability to perform what are called *page mode* accesses. If $\overline{RAS}$ is left at logic 0 after the row address is latched inside the device, the address is maintained within the device. Then data cells along the selected row can be accessed by simply supplying successive column addresses. This permits faster access of memory by eliminating the time needed to set up and strobe additional row addresses.

Earlier we pointed out that the key difference between the DRAM and SRAM is that the storage cells in the DRAM need to be periodically refreshed; otherwise, they lose their data. To maintain the integrity of the data in a DRAM, each of the rows of the storage array must typically be refreshed periodically such as every 2 ms. All of the storage cells in an array are refreshed by simply cycling through the row addresses. As long as $\overline{CAS}$ is held at logic 1 during the refresh cycle, no data are output.

External circuitry is required to perform the address multiplexing, $\overline{RAS}$/ $\overline{CAS}$ generation, and refresh operations for a DRAM subsystem. *DRAM refresh controller* ICs are available to permit easy implementation of these functions. An example of such a device is the 82C08 DRAM refresh controller.

Parity, the Parity Bit, and Parity Checker/Generator Circuit

In microcomputer systems, the data exchanges that take place between the MPU and the memory must be done without error. However, problems such as noise, transient signals, or even bad memory bits can produce errors in the transfer of data and instructions. For instance, the storage location for one bit in a large DRAM array may be bad and stuck at the 0 logic level. This will not represent a problem if the logic level of the data written to the storage location is 0, but if it is 1 the value will always be read as 0. To improve the reliability of information transfer between the MPU and memory, a *parity bit* can be added to each byte of data. To implement data transfers with parity, a *parity checker/generator* circuit is required.

Figure 7.63 shows a parity checker/generator circuit added to the memory interface of a microcomputer system. Notice that the data passed between the MPU and memory subsystem is applied in parallel to the parity checker/generator circuit.

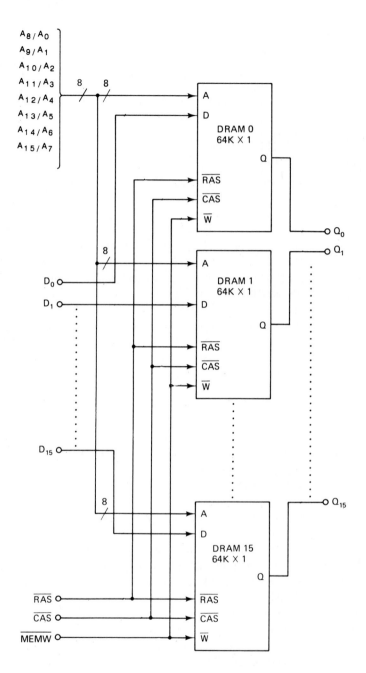

Figure 7.62 64K × 16-bit DRAM array.

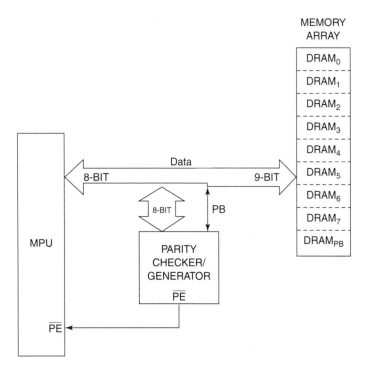

Figure 7.63 Data storage memory interface with parity checking/generation.

Assuming that the microprocessor has an 8-bit data bus, data words read from or written to memory by the MPU over the data bus are still byte-wide, but the data stored in memory is nine bits long. The data in memory consists of eight bits of data and one parity bit. Assuming that the memory array is constructed with 256K × 1-bit DRAMs, then, the memory array for a memory subsystem with parity would have nine DRAM ICs instead of eight. The extra DRAM is needed for storage of the parity bit for each byte of data stored in the other eight DRAM devices.

The parity checker/generator circuit can be set up to produce either *even parity* or *odd parity*. The 9-bit word of data stored in memory has even parity if it contains an even number of bits that are at the 1 logic level and odd parity if the number of bits at logic 1 is odd.

Let us assume that the circuit in Fig. 7.63 is used to generate and check for even parity. If the data written to memory over the 8088's data bus is FFH, the binary data word is 11111111_2. This word has 8 bits at logic 1; that is, it already has even parity. Therefore, the parity checker/generator circuit, which operates in the parity generate mode, outputs logic 0 on the parity bit line (PB) and the nine bits of data stored in memory is 011111111_2. On the other hand, if the word written to memory is 7FH, the binary word is 01111111_2. Since only seven bits are at logic 1, parity is odd. In this case, the parity checker/generator circuit makes the parity bit logic 1 and the nine bits of data saved in memory is 101111111_2. Notice that the data held in memory has even parity. In this way, we see that during all data memory write cycles, the parity checker/generator circuit simply checks the data word that is to be stored in memory and generates a parity bit. The parity bit is attached to the original 8-bits of data to make it nine bits. The 9-bits of data stored in memory have even parity.

The parity checker/generator works differently when data are read from memory. Now the circuit must perform its parity check function. Notice that the 8-bit data word from the addressed storage location in memory is sent directly to the MPU. However, at the same time, this word and the parity bit are applied to the inputs of the parity checker/generator circuit. This circuit checks to determine whether there are an even or odd number of logic 1s in the word with parity. Again we will assume that the circuit is set up to check for even parity. If the 9 bits of data read from memory are found to have an even number of bits at the 1 logic level, parity is correct. The parity checker/generator signals this fact to the MPU by making the parity error ($\overline{PE}$) output inactive logic 1. This signal is normally sent to the MPU to identify whether or not a memory *parity error* has occurred. If an odd number of bits are found to be logic 1, a parity error has been detected and $\overline{PE}$ is set to 0 to tell the MPU of the error condition. Once alerted to the error, the MPU can do any one of a number of things under software control to recover. For instance, it could simply repeat the memory read cycle to see if it takes place correctly the next time.

The 74AS280 device implements a parity checker/generator function similar to that we just described. In Fig. 7.64(a) we have shown a block diagram of the device. Notice that it has nine data input lines, which are labeled A through I. In the memory interface, lines A through H would be attached to data bus lines D_0 through D_7, respectively, and during a read operation the parity bit output of the memory array, D_{PB} would be applied to the I input.

The operation of the 74AS280 is described by the function table in Fig. 7.64(b). It shows how the Σ_{EVEN} and Σ_{ODD} outputs respond to an even or odd number of data inputs at logic 1. Notice that if there are 0, 2, 4, or 8 inputs at logic 1, the Σ_{EVEN} output switches to logic 1 and Σ_{ODD} to logic 0. This output response signals the even parity condition.

In practical applications, the Σ_{EVEN} and Σ_{ODD} outputs are used to produce the parity bit and parity error signal lines. Figure 7.64(c) is an even parity checker/generator configuration. Notice that Σ_{ODD} is used as the parity bit (D_{PB}) output that gets applied to the data input of the parity bit DRAM in the memory array. During a write operation $\overline{MEMR}$ is 0, which makes the I input 0, and therefore the parity of the byte depends only on data bits D_0 through D_7, which are applied to the A through H inputs of the 74AS280. As long as the input at A through H has an even number of bits at logic 1 during a memory write cycle, Σ_{ODD}, which is D_{PB}, is at logic 0 and the nine bits of data written to memory retains an even number of bits that are 1, that is, even parity. On the other hand, if the incoming byte at A through H has an odd number of bits that are logic 1, Σ_{ODD} switches to logic 1. The logic 1 at D_{PB} along with the odd number of 1s in the original byte again give the nine bits of data stored in memory an even parity.

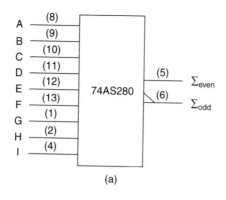

(a)

NUMBER OF INPUTS A	OUTPUTS	
THRU I THAT ARE HIGH	Σ EVEN	Σ ODD
0,2,4,6,8	H	L
1,3,5,7,9	L	H

(b)

(c)

Figure 7.64 (a) Block diagram of the 74AS280 (Texas Instruments Incorporated). (b) Function table (Texas Instruments Incorporated). (c) Even parity checker/generator connection.

Let us next look at what happens in the parity checker/generator circuit during a memory read cycle for the data storage memory subsystem. When the 8088 is reading a byte of data from memory, the 74AS280 performs the parity check operation. In response to the MPU's read request, nine bits of data are output by the memory array. They are applied to inputs A through I of the parity checker/generator circuit. The 74AS280 checks the parity and adjusts the logic levels of Σ_{EVEN} and Σ_{ODD} to represent this parity. If parity is even as expected, Σ_{EVEN}, which represents the parity error ($\overline{PE}$) signal, is at logic 1. This tells the MPU that a valid data transfer has taken place. However, if the data at A through I has an odd number of bits at logic 1, Σ_{EVEN} switches to logic 0 and informs the MPU that a parity error has occurred.

In a 16-bit microcomputer system, such as that built with the 8086 MPU, there are normally two 8-bit banks of DRAM ICs in the data storage memory array. In this case, a parity bit DRAM is added to each bank. Therefore, parity is implemented for each of the two bytes of a data word stored in memory. This is important because the 8086 can read either bytes or words of data from memory. For this reason, two parity checker/generator circuits are also required, one for the upper eight lines of the data bus and one for the lower eight lines. The parity error outputs of the two circuits are usually gated together and then applied to the parity error input of the MPU. In this way, the MPU is notified of a parity error if it occurs in an even-addressed byte data transfer, odd-addressed byte data transfer, or in either or both bytes of a 16-bit data transfer.

▲ 7.17 PROGRAM STORAGE MEMORY AND DATA STORAGE MEMORY CIRCUITS

In previous sections we studied the memory interface signals of the 8088 and 8086 microprocessors; we showed how the multiplexed bus is demultiplexed to give a system bus consisting of an independent 20-bit address bus and 8-bit or 16-bit data bus; we studied various interfacing devices and looked at the various types of memory devices. Here we will use the information we have gained to analyze the memory circuits of simple 8088- and 8086-based microcomputer systems.

Program Storage Memory

The program storage memory part of a microcomputer that is used to store fixed information such as instructions of the program or tables of data is typically implemented with ROM, PROM, or EPROM devices. EPROM devices, such as the 2716, 2764, and 27256, are organized with a byte-wide output; therefore, a single device is required to supply the 8-bit data bus of the 8088. They need to be arranged to provide a word-wide output when used in an 8086 system.

Figure 7.65(a) shows how a 2716 is connected to the demultiplexed system bus of a minimum-mode 8088-based microcomputer. This device supplies 2KB of program storage memory. To select one of the 2K of storage locations within the 2716, 11 bits of address are applied to address inputs A_0 through A_{10} of the EPROM. Assuming that bits A_0 through A_{10} of the 8088's address bus supply these inputs,

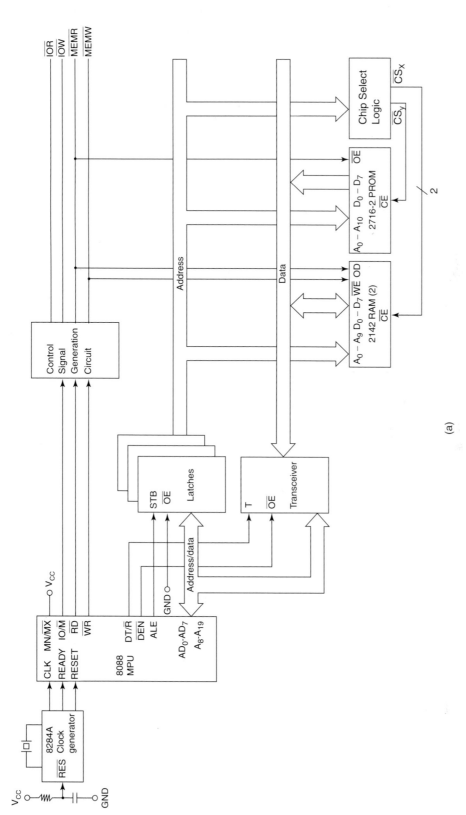

Figure 7.65 (a) Minimum-mode 8088 system memory interface. (Reprinted with permission of Intel Corp., © Intel Corp. 1981) (b) Minimum-mode 8086 system memory interface. (Reprinted with permission of Intel Corp., © Intel Corp. 1979) (c) Maximum-mode 8088 system memory interface. (Reprinted with permission of Intel Corp., © Intel Corp. 1981)

(a)

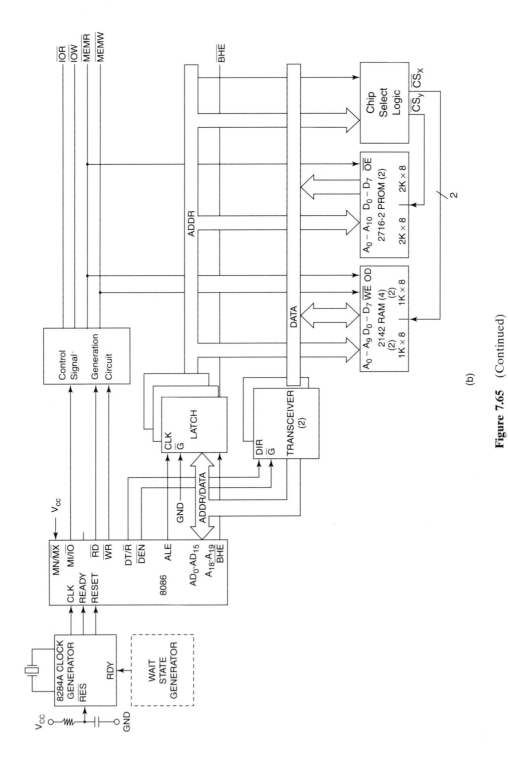

Figure 7.65 (Continued)

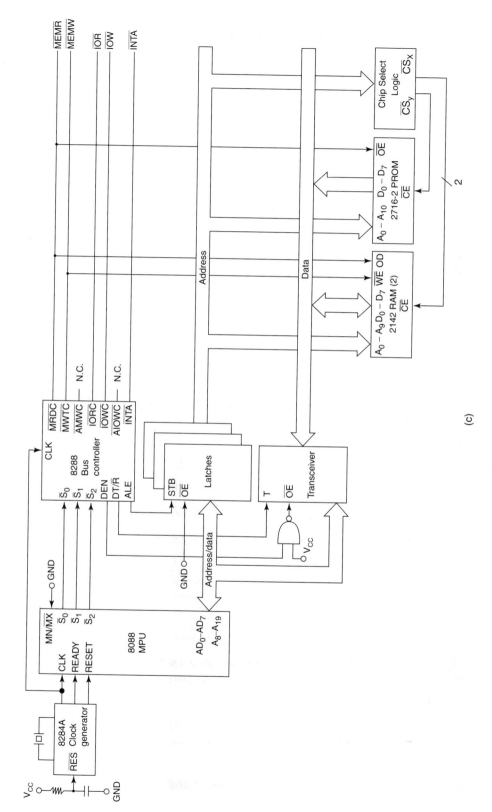

Figure 7.65 (Continued)

(c)

the address range corresponding to program memory is from

$$A_{10}A_9 \ldots A_0 = 00000000000_2 = 00000_{16}$$

to

$$A_{10}A_9 \ldots A_0 = 11111111111_2 = 007FF_{16}$$

assuming that $A_{19} - A^{11} = 0 \ldots 0$ generate the chip select signal $\overline{CS_x}$. Data outputs D_0 through D_7 of the EPROM are applied to data bus lines D_0 through D_7, respectively, of the 8088's system data bus. Data held at the addressed storage location are enabled onto the data bus by the control signal $\overline{MEMR}$ (memory read), which is applied to the $\overline{OE}$ (output enable) input of the EPROM.

In most applications, the capacity of program storage memory is expanded by attaching several EPROM devices to the system bus. In this case, additional high-order bits of the 8088's address are decoded to produce chip select signals. For instance, two address bits, A_{11} and A_{12}, can be decoded to provide four chip select signals. Each of these chip selects is applied to the $\overline{CE}$ (chip enable) input of one EPROM. When an address is on the bus, just one of the outputs of the decoder becomes active and enables the corresponding EPROM for operation. By using four 2716s, the program storage memory is increased to 8K bytes.

Now that we have explained how EPROMs are attached to the 8088's system bus, let us trace through the operation of the circuit for a bus cycle in which a byte of code is fetched from program storage memory. During an instruction acquisition bus cycle, the instruction fetch sequence of the 8088 causes the instruction to be read from memory byte by byte. The values in CS and IP are combined within the 8088 to give the address of a storage location in the address range of the program storage memory. This address is output on A_0 through A_{19} and latched into the address latches synchronously with the signal ALE. Bits A_0 through A_{10} of the system address bus are applied to the address inputs of the 2716. This part of the address selects the byte of code to be output. When the 8088 switches $\overline{RD}$ to logic 0 and IO/$\overline{M}$ to logic 0, the control signal generation circuit switches $\overline{MEMR}$ to logic 0. Logic 0 at $\overline{MEMR}$ enables the outputs of the 2716 and the byte of data at the addressed storage location is output onto system data bus lines D_0 through D_7. Early in the read bus cycle, the 8088 switches DT/$\overline{R}$ to logic 0 to signal the bus transceiver that data are to be input to the microprocessor, and later in the bus cycle $\overline{DEN}$ is switched to logic 0 to enable the transceiver for operation. Now the byte of data is passed from the system data bus onto the multiplexed address/data bus from which it is read by the MPU.

The circuit in Fig. 7.65(b) shows a similar circuit for a minimum-mode 8086 microcomputer system. Notice that because of the 16-bit data bus two octal transceivers and two EPROMs are required.

Figure 7.65(c) shows the program storage memory implementation for a maximum-mode 8088 microcomputer system. Let us look at how this circuit differs from the minimum-mode circuit of Fig. 7.65(a). The key difference in this circuit is that the 8288 bus controller is used to produce the control signals for the memory interface. Remember that in maximum mode the code output on status lines $\overline{S}_0$

through $\overline{S}_2$ identifies the type of bus cycle that is in progress. During all read operations of program memory, the 8088 outputs the instruction fetch memory bus status code, $\overline{S}_2\overline{S}_1\overline{S}_0 = 101$, to the 8288. In response to this input, the bus controller produces the memory read command ($\overline{MRDC}$) output. This output is used as the $\overline{OE}$ input of the 2716 EPROM and enables it for data output.

In the maximum-mode circuit, the 8288, rather than the 8088, produces the control signals for the address latches and data bus transceiver. Notice that three address latches are again used, but this time the ALE output of the 8288 is used to strobe the memory address into these latches. ALE is applied to the STB inputs of all three latch devices in parallel. The direction of data transfer through the data bus transceiver is set by the $DT/\overline{R}$ output of the bus controller and the DEN output is used to generate the $\overline{OE}$ input of the transceiver. Since DEN, not $\overline{DEN}$, is produced by the 8288, an inverter is constructed from the NAND gate that drives $\overline{OE}$ of the transceiver.

Data Storage Memory

Information that frequently changes is stored in the data storage part of the microcomputer's memory subsystem. Examples of information typically stored in data storage memory are application programs and data. This part of the memory subsystem is normally implemented with random access read/write memory (RAM). If the amount of memory required in the microcomputer is small, for instance, less than 32KB, the memory subsystem will usually be designed with static RAMs. On the other hand, systems that require a larger amount of data storage memory normally use dynamic RAMs (DRAMs) that provide larger storage capacity in the same size device. DRAMs require refresh support circuits. This additional circuitry is not warranted if storage requirements are small.

A 1K-byte random access read/write memory is also implemented in the minimum-mode 8088-based microcomputer circuit of Fig. 7.65(a). This part of the memory subsystem is implemented with two 2142 static RAM ICs. Each 2142 contains 1K, 4-bit storage locations; therefore, they both supply storage for just 4 bits of the byte. The storage location to be accessed is selected by a 10-bit address, which is applied to both RAMs in parallel over address lines A_0 through A_9. Data are read from or written into the selected storage location over data bus lines D_0 through D_7. Of course, through software, the 8088 can read data from memory either as bytes, words, or double words. The logic level of $\overline{MEMW}$ (memory write), which is applied to the write enable ($\overline{WE}$) input of both RAMs in parallel, signals whether a read or write bus cycle is in progress. $\overline{MEMR}$ is applied to the OD (output disable) input of both RAMs in parallel. When a write cycle is in progress, $\overline{RD}$ is at logic 1 which disables the outputs of the RAMs. Now the data lines act as inputs.

Just as for program storage memory, data storage memory can be expanded by simply attaching additional banks of static RAMs to the system bus. Once again, high-order address bits can be decoded to produce chip select signals. Each chip select output is applied to the chip enable input of both RAMs in a bank and, when active, it enables that bank of RAMs for operation.

Let us assume that the value of a byte-wide data operand is to be updated in memory. In this case, the 8088 must perform a write bus cycle to the address of the operand's storage location. First, the address of the operand is formed and output on the multiplexed address/data bus. When the address is stable, a pulse at ALE is used to latch it into the address latches. Bits A_0 through A_9 of the system address bus are applied to the address inputs of the 2142s. This part of the address selects the storage location into which the byte of data is to be written. Next the 8088 switches DT/$\overline{R}$ to logic 1 to signal the octal transceivers that data are to be output to memory. Later in the bus cycle, $\overline{DEN}$ is switched to logic 0 to enable the data bus transceiver for operation. Now the byte of data is output on the multiplexed address/data bus and passed through the transceiver to the system data bus and data inputs of the RAMs. Finally, the byte of data is written into the addressed storage location synchronously with the occurrence of the $\overline{MEMW}$ control signal.

The data storage memory circuitry of a minimum-mode 8086 system is also shown in Fig. 7.65(b). Here we see that two banks of RAM ICs are required.

The data storage memory circuit of a maximum-mode 8088 microcomputer is shown in Fig. 7.65(c). Just like in our description of the program storage memory part of this circuit, the difference between the maximum-mode and minimum-mode data storage memory circuits lies in the fact that the 8288 bus controller produces the control signals for the memory and bus interface logic devices. When the 8088 is accessing data storage memory, it outputs either the read memory (101) or write memory (110) bus status code. These codes are decoded by the 8288 to produce appropriate memory control signals. For instance, a status code of 110 (write memory) causes the memory write command ($\overline{MWTC}$) and advance memory write command ($\overline{AMWC}$) outputs to become active during all write bus cycles. In Fig. 7.65(c), we find that $\overline{MWTC}$ or $\overline{MEMW}$ is used to drive the $\overline{WE}$ input of the 2142 SRAMs. When $\overline{MWTC}$ is at its active 0 logic level, the input buffers of the SRAMs are enabled for operation. On the other hand, during read bus cycles, $\overline{MRDC}$ or $\overline{MEMR}$ is used to enable the outputs of the SRAMs.

EXAMPLE 7.3

Design a memory system consisting of 32K bytes of R/W memory and 32KB of ROM memory. Use SRAM devices to implement R/W memory and EPROM devices to implement ROM memory. The memory devices to be used are shown in Fig. 7.66(a). R/W memory address is to reside over the address range 00000_{16} = $07FFF_{16}$ and the address range of ROM memory is to be $F8000_{16}$ = $FFFFF_{16}$. Assume that the 8088 microprocessor system bus signals that follow are available for use: A_0 through A_{19}, D_0 through D_7, $\overline{MEMR}$, and $\overline{MEMW}$.

Solution

First let us determine the number of SRAM devices that are needed to implement the R/W memory. Since each device provides $2^{14} \times 4$ or 16K $\times$ 4 of storage, the

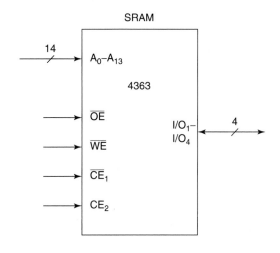

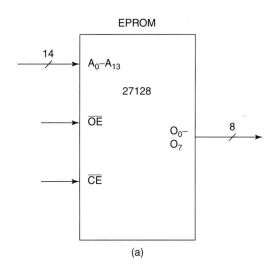

(a)

Figure 7.66 (a) Devices to be used in the system design of example 7.3. (b) Memory map of the system to be designed. (c) Memory organization for the system design. (d) Address range analysis for the design of chip select signals $\overline{CS_0}$, $\overline{CS_1}$, $\overline{CS_2}$, and $\overline{CS_3}$. (e) Chip select logic.

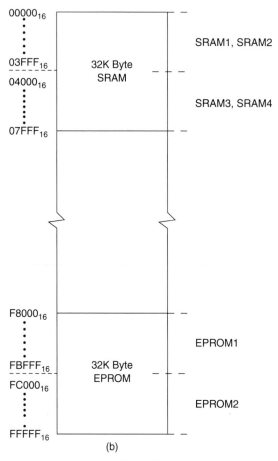

Figure 7.66(b) (Continued)

number of SRAM devices needed to implement 32KB of storage is

$$\text{No. of SRAM devices} = 32\text{KB}/(16\text{K} \times 4) = 4$$

To provide an 8-bit data bus, two SRAMs must be connected in parallel. Two pairs connected in this way are then placed in series to implement the R/W address range. Each pair implements 16K bytes. The first pair, SRAM_1 and SRAM_2, implement the address range $00000_{16} = 03\text{FFF}_{16}$ and the second pair, SRAM_3 and SRAM_4, implement addresses $04000_{16} = 07\text{FFF}_{16}$. The memory map in Fig. 7.66(b) shows the device allocation for this implementation.

Next let us determine the number of EPROM devices that are needed to implement the ROM memory. In this case, each device provides $2^{14} \times 8$ or 16KB of storage. To implement 32KB of storage, the number of EPROM devices needed is

$$\text{No. of EPROM devices} = 32\text{KB}/16\text{KB} = 2$$

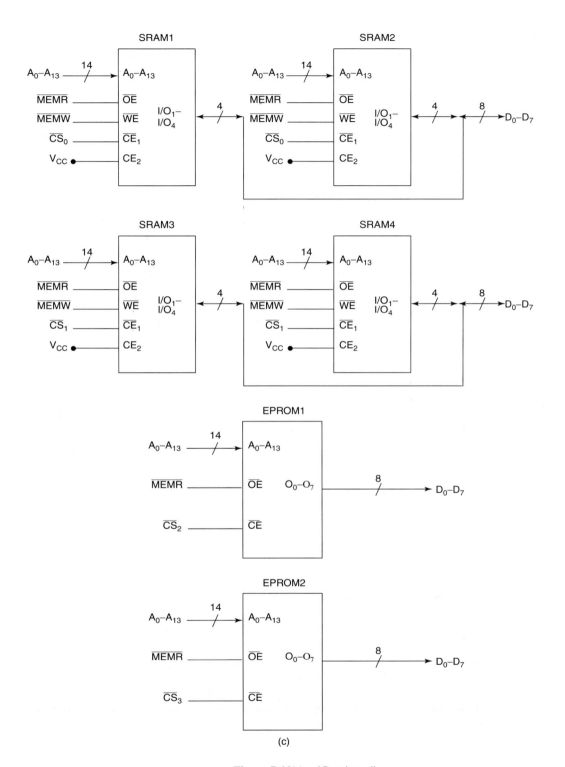

Figure 7.66(c) (Continued)

$$A_{19} \cdots \cdots \cdots \cdots A_0$$

$00000_{15} =$ 0000 0000 0000 0000 0000

$03FFF_{16} =$ $\underbrace{\text{0000 00}}$11 1111 1111 1111

$\overline{CS}_0$

$04000_{16} =$ 0000 0100 0000 0000 0000

$07FFF_{16} =$ $\underbrace{\text{0000 01}}$11 1111 1111 1111

$\overline{CS}_1$

$F8000_{16} =$ 1111 1000 0000 0000 0000

$FBFFF_{16} =$ $\underbrace{\text{1111 10}}$11 1111 1111 1111

$\overline{CS}_2$

$FC000_{16} =$ 1111 1100 0000 0000 0000

$FFFFF_{16} =$ $\underbrace{\text{1111 11}}$11 1111 1111 1111

$\overline{CS}_3$

(d)

Figure 7.66(d) (Continued)

These two devices must be connected in series to implement the ROM address range. Each device implements 16KB of storage. As shown in the memory map of Fig. 7.66(b), the first device, EPROM$_1$, implements the address range $F8000_{16} = FBFFF_{16}$. The second device, EPROM$_2$, implements the address range $FC000_{16} = FFFFF_{16}$.

The memory organization based on the above allocation of devices is shown in Fig. 7.66(c). Notice that we have used the various 8088 system bus signals (A_0-A_{19}, D_0-D_7, $\overline{\text{MEMR}}$, and $\overline{\text{MEMW}}$) to draw the circuit diagram. For example, the $\overline{\text{MEMW}}$ signal is applied to the $\overline{\text{WE}}$ input of all four SRAMs in parallel, but is not connected to the EPROMs.

The four chip select signals, $\overline{CS}_0$, $\overline{CS}_1$, $\overline{CS}_2$, and $\overline{CS}_3$, that are used in the circuit need to be produced for the appropriate address ranges. To design the circuit for generating the chip select signals, we first analyze the address ranges as shown in Fig. 7.66(d) to determine the address bits that should be used. For instance, to generate the range represented by SRAM$_1$ and SRAM$_2$, $\overline{CS}_0$ should be active for $A_{15}A_{14}A_{13}A_{12}A_{11}A_{10} = 000000_2$. Similarly the other address ranges tell us which address bits are needed to produce the other chip select signals. This information is used in Fig. 7.66(e) to design the chip select logic circuit with 74F138 3-line to 8-line decoders.

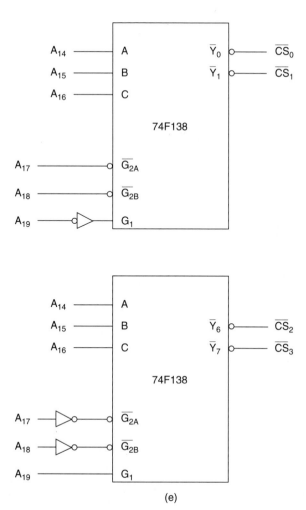

Figure 7.66(e) (Continued)

ASSIGNMENTS

Section 7.2

1. Name the technology used to fabricate the 8088 and 8086 microprocessors.
2. What is the transistor count of the 8088?
3. Which pin is used as the NMI input on the 8088?
4. Which pin provides the $\overline{BHE}/S_7$ output signals on the 8086?
5. How much memory can the 8088 and 8086 directly address?
6. How large is the I/O address space of the 8088 and 8086?

Section 7.3

7. How is minimum or maximum mode of operation selected?
8. Describe the difference between the minimum-mode 8088 system and maximum-mode 8088 system.
9. What output function is performed by pin 29 of the 8088 when in the minimum mode? Maximum mode?
10. Is the signal $M/\overline{IO}$ an input or output of the 8086?
11. Name one signal that is supplied by the 8088 but not by the 8086.
12. Are the signals QS_0 and QS_1 produced in the minimum mode or maximum mode?

Section 7.4

13. What are the word lengths of the 8088's address bus and data bus? The 8086's address bus and data bus?
14. Does the 8088 have a multiplexed address/data bus or independent address and data buses?
15. What mnemonic is used to identify the least significant bit of the 8088's address bus? The most significant bit of the 8088's data bus?
16. What does status code $S_4S_3 = 01$ mean in terms of the memory segment being accessed?
17. Which output is used to signal external circuitry that a byte of data is available on the upper half of the 8086's data bus?
18. What does the logic level on $M/\overline{IO}$ signal to external circuitry in an 8086 microcomputer?
19. Which output is used to signal external circuitry in an 8088-based microcomputer that valid data is on the bus during a write cycle?
20. What signal does a minimum-mode 8088 respond with when it acknowledges an active interrupt request?
21. Which signals implement the DMA interface in a minimum-mode 8088 or 8086 microcomputer system?
22. List the signals of the 8088 that are put in the high-Z state in response to a DMA request.

Section 7.5

23. Identify the signal lines of the 8088 that are different for the minimum-mode and maximum-mode interfaces.
24. What status outputs of the 8088 are input to the 8288?
25. What maximum-mode control signals are generated by the 8288?
26. What function is served by the $\overline{LOCK}$ signal in a maximum-mode 8088 microcomputer system?

27. What status code is output by the 8088 to the 8288 if a memory read bus cycle is taking place?

28. What command output becomes active if the status inputs of the 8288 are 100_2?

29. If the 8088 executes a jump instruction, what queue status code would be output?

30. What signals are provided for local bus control in a maximum-mode 8088 system?

Section 7.6

31. What is the range of power supply voltage over which the 8088 is guaranteed to work correctly?

32. What is the maximum value of voltage that is considered a valid logic 0 at bit D_0 of the 8088's data bus? Assume that the output is sinking 2 mA.

33. What is the minimum value of voltage that would represent a valid logic 1 at the INTR input of the 8088?

34. At what current value is V_{OLmax} measured on the 8086?

Section 7.7

35. What speed 8088s are generally available?

36. What frequency crystal must be connected between the X_1 and X_2 inputs of the clock generator if an 8088-2 is to run at full speed?

37. What clock outputs are produced by the 8284? What would be their frequencies if a 30-MHz crystal is used?

38. What are the logic levels of the clock waveforms applied to the 8088?

Section 7.8

39. How many clock states are in an 8088 bus cycle that has no wait states? How are these states denoted?

40. What is the duration of the bus cycle for a 5-MHz 8088 that is running at full speed and with no wait states?

41. What is an idle state?

42. What is a wait state?

43. If an 8086 running at 10 MHz performs bus cycles with two wait states, what is the duration of the bus cycle?

Section 7.9

44. How is the memory of an 8088 microcomputer organized from a hardware point of view? The memory of an 8086 microcomputer?

45. Give an overview of how a byte of data is read from memory address $B0003_{16}$ of an 8088-based microcomputer. List the memory control signals along with their active logic levels that occur during the memory read bus cycle.

46. Give an overview of how a word of data is written to memory starting at address $A0000_{16}$ of an 8088-based microcomputer. List the memory control signals together with their active logic levels that occur during the memory write cycle.

47. In which bank of memory in an 8086-based microcomputer are odd-addressed bytes of data stored? What bank select signal is used to enable this bank of memory?

48. Over which of the 8086's data bus lines are even-addressed bytes of data transferred and which bank select signal is active?

49. List the memory control signals together with their active logic levels that occur when a word of data is written to memory address $A0000_{16}$ in a minimum-mode 8086 microcomputer system.

50. List the memory control signals together with their active logic levels that occur when a byte of data is written to memory address $B0003_{16}$ in a minimum-mode 8086 microcomputer. Over which data lines is the byte of data transferred?

Section 7.10

51. In a maximum-mode 8088 microcomputer, what code is output on S_4S_3 when an instruction-fetch bus cycle is in progress?

52. What is the value of S_4S_3 if the operand of a pop instruction is being read from memory? The microcomputer employs the 8088 in the maximum mode.

Section 7.11

53. Which of the 8088's memory control signals is the complement of the corresponding signal on the 8086?

54. What memory control output of the 8088 is not provided on the 8086? What signal replaces it on the 8086?

55. In a maximum-mode 8088-based microcomputer, what memory bus status code is output when a word of instruction code is fetched from memory? Which memory control output(s) is(are) produced by the 8288?

56. In maximum mode, what memory bus status code is output when a destination operand is written to memory? Which memory control output(s) is (are) produced by the 8288?

57. When the instruction PUSH AX is executed, what address bus status code and memory bus cycle code are output by the 8088 in a maximum-mode microcomputer system? Which command signals are output by the 8288?

Section 7.12

58. How many clock states are in a read bus cycle that has no wait states? What would be the duration of this bus cycle if the 8086 is operating at 10 MHz?

59. What happens in the T_1 part of the 8088's memory read or write bus cycle?

60. Describe the bus activity that takes place as the 8088 in minimum mode writes a byte of data into memory address $B0010_{16}$.

61. Which two signals can be used to determine that the current bus cycle is a write cycle?

62. Which signal can be used to identify the start of a bus cycle?

Section 7.13

63. Give an overview of the function of each block in the memory interface diagram of Fig. 7.26.

64. When the instruction PUSH AX is executed, what bus status code is output by the 8086 in maximum mode, what are the logic levels of A_0 and $\overline{BHE}$, and what read/write control signals are produced by the bus controller?

65. What type of basic logic devices are provided by the 74F373 and 74F374 ICs?

66. What is the key difference between the 74F373 and 74F374?

67. Make a drawing to show how the address latch with I/O address buffer circuit in Fig. 7.30(a) can be constructed with 74F374 and 74F244 ICs. Assume that the latches and buffer circuits will be permanently enabled.

68. What logic devices are provided by the 74F245 IC?

69. In the circuit of Fig. 7.32, what logic levels must be applied to the $\overline{DEN}$ and $DT/\overline{R}$ inputs to cause data on the system data bus to be transferred to the microprocessor data bus?

70. Make a drawing like that in Fig. 7.32 to show the data bus transceiver circuit needed in an 8088-based microcomputer system.

71. What are the logic levels of the $\overline{G}$, DIR, CAB, CBA, SAB, and SBA inputs of the 74F646 when stored data in the A register is transferred to the B bus?

72. Name an IC that implements a 2-line to 4-line decoder logic function.

73. If the inputs to a 74F138 decoder are $G_1 = 1$, $\overline{G}_{2A} = 0$, $\overline{G}_{2B} = 0$, and CBA = 101, which output is active?

74. Make a drawing like that in Fig. 7.36 for an 8088-based microcomputer for which a 74F138 decoder is used to decode address line A_{17} through A_{19} into memory chip selects.

Section 7.14

75. What does PLA stand for?

76. List three properties that measure the capacity of a PLA.

77. What is the programming mechanism used in PAL called?

78. What does PAL stand for? Give the key difference between a PAL and a PLA.

79. Redraw the circuit in Fig. 7.39(b) to show how it can implement the logic function $F = (\overline{A}\overline{B} + AB)$.

80. How many dedicated inputs, dedicated outputs, programmable input/outputs, and product terms are supported on the 16L8 PAL?

81. What is the maximum number of inputs on a 20L8 PAL? The maximum number of outputs?

82. How do the outputs of the 16R8 differ from those of the 16L8?

83. Use a 16L8 to decode address lines A_{17L} through A_{19L} to generate $\overline{CE_0}$ through $\overline{CE_7}$.

Section 7.15

84. What is meant by the term *nonvolatile memory*?

85. What does PROM stand for? EPROM?

86. What must an EPROM be exposed to in order to erase its stored data?

87. If the block diagram of Fig. 7.46 has address lines A_0 through A_{16} and data lines D_0 through D_7, what is its byte capacity?

88. Summarize the read cycle of an EPROM. Assume that both $\overline{CE}$ and $\overline{OE}$ are active before the address is applied.

89. Which standard EPROM stores 64K 8-bit words?

90. What is the difference between a 2764A and a 2764A-1?

91. What are the values of V_{CC} and V_{pp} for the Intelligent Programming Algorithm™?

92. What is the duration of the programming pulses used for the Intelligent Programming Algorithm™?

Section 7.16

93. What do SRAM and DRAM stand for?

94. Are RAM ICs examples of nonvolatile or volatile memory devices?

95. What must be done to maintain the data in a DRAM valid?

96. Find the total storage capacity of the circuit similar to Fig. 7.53 if the memory devices are 43256As.

97. List the minimum values of each of the write cycle parameters that follow for the 4364-10 SRAM: t_{WC}, t_{CW1}, t_{CW2}, t_{WP}, t_{DW}, and t_{WR}.

98. Give two benefits of DRAMs over SRAMs.

99. Name the two parts of a DRAM address.

100. Show how the circuit in Fig. 7.62 can be expanded to 128K × 16 bits.

101. Give a disadvantage of the use of DRAMs in an application that does not require a large amount of memory.

102. If in Fig. 7.63, the data read from memory is 100100100_2, what is its parity? Repeat the same if the data is 011110000_2?

103. If the input to an 74AS280 parity checker/generator circuit that is set up for odd parity checking and generation is I H ... A = 111111111_2, what are its outputs?

104. What changes must be made in the circuit of Fig. 7.64(c) to convert it to an odd parity configuration?

105. Make a drawing similar to that shown in Fig 7.64(c) that can be used as the parity checker/generator in the data storage memory subsystem of an 8086 microcomputer system. Assume that the parity checking is performed independently for the upper and lower data bus lines and that the parity error outputs for the two banks are combined to form a single parity error signal.

Section 7.17

106. Make a diagram showing how four 2764 EPROMs can be connected to form a 16KB program storage memory subsystem. Also show a 16K-word program memory subsystem.

107. If we assume that the high-order address bits in the circuits formed in problem 102 are all logic 0, what is the address range of the program memory subsystems?

108. How many 2142 static RAMs would be needed in the memory array of the circuit in Fig. 7.65(a) if the capacity of data storage memory is to be expanded to 64KB?

109. How many 2716 EPROMs would be needed in the program memory array in the circuit of Fig. 7.65(a) to expand its capacity to 96K bits? If 2732s were used instead of 2716s, how many devices are needed to implement the 96K-bit program memory?

110. Repeat the design in Example 7.3 for the 8086 microprocessor system bus signals A_0-A_{19}, D_0-D_{15}, $\overline{\text{MEMR}}$, $\overline{\text{MEMW}}$, and $\overline{\text{BHE}}$. Use the same memory and device specifications.

8

Input/Output Interface of the 8088 and 8086 Microprocessors

In Chapter 7, we studied the memory interface of the 8088 and 8086 microprocessors. Here we will study another important interface of the 8088- and 8086-based micro-computer systems, the input/output (I/O) interface. The topics covered are types of I/O, the I/O interface, I/O data transfers, I/O instructions, I/O bus cycles, peripheral ICs that supply core I/O functions, such as the 8255A programmable peripheral interface, 8253 programmable interval timer, the 8237A direct memory access controllers, 8251 universal asynchronous receiver/transmitter, and special-purpose LSI peripheral ICs that are used to perform keyboard reading and display scanning functions. Following are the topics that are covered in this chapter.

1. Types of Input/Output
2. An isolated I/O interface
3. I/O data transfers
4. I/O instructions
5. I/O bus cycles
6. Byte-wide output ports using isolated I/O
7. Byte-wide input ports using isolated I/O
8. Input/output handshaking and a parallel printer interface
9. 8255A programmable peripheral interface

10. 8255A implementation of parallel I/O ports
11. Memory-mapped I/O ports
12. 8253 programmable interval timer
13. 8237A direct memory access controller
14. Serial communications interface
15. Special-purpose interface controllers

▲ 8.2 TYPES OF INPUT/OUTPUT

The 8088 and 8086 microcomputers can employ two different types of input/output (I/O). They are known as *isolated I/O* and *memory-mapped I/O*. These I/O methods differ in how I/O ports are mapped into the 8088/8086's address spaces. Practical microcomputer systems usually employ both kinds of I/O. That is, some peripheral ICs are treated as isolated I/O devices and others as memory-mapped I/O devices. Let us now look at each of these types of I/O.

When using isolated I/O in a microcomputer system, the I/O devices are treated separate from memory. This is achieved because the software and hardware architectures support separate memory and I/O address spaces. Figure 8.1 illustrates these memory and I/O address spaces. In our study of 8088/8086 software architecture in Chapter 2, we examined these address spaces from a software point of view. We found that information in memory or at I/O ports are organized as bytes of data; that the memory address space contains 1M consecutive byte addresses in the range 00000_{16} through $FFFFF_{16}$; and that the I/O address space contains 64K consecutive byte addresses in the range 0000_{16} through $FFFF_{16}$. Moreover, the contents of two consecutive memory or I/O addresses can be accessed as word-wide data. For instance, in Fig. 8.2(a), I/O addresses 0000_{16} and 0001_{16} can be treated as independent byte-wide I/O ports, port 0 and port 1, or they may be considered together as word-wide port 0.

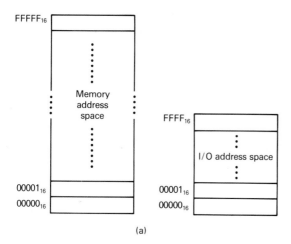

(a)

Figure 8.1 8088/8086 memory and I/O address spaces.

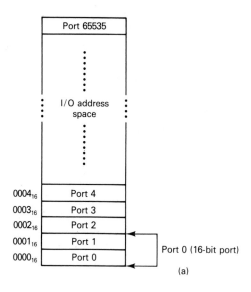

(a)

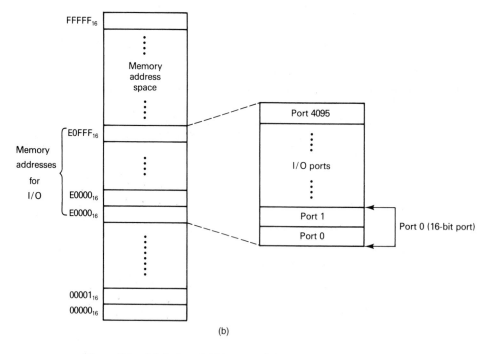

(b)

Figure 8.2 (a) Isolated I/O ports. (b) Memory-mapped I/O ports.

This isolated method of I/O offers some advantages. First, the complete 1MB memory address space is available for use with memory. Second, special instructions have been provided in the instruction set of the 8088/8086 to perform isolated I/O input and output operations. These instructions have been tailored to maximize I/O performance. A disadvantage of this type of I/O is that all input and output data transfers must take place between the AL or AX register and the I/O port.

I/O devices can be placed in the memory address space of the microcomputer, just as in the I/O address space. In this case, the MPU looks at the I/O port as though it is a memory location. For this reason, the method is known as *memory-mapped I/O*.

In a microcomputer system with memory-mapped I/O, some of the memory address space is dedicated to I/O ports. For example, in Fig. 8.2(b) the 4096 memory addresses in the range from $E0000_{16}$ through $E0FFF_{16}$ are assigned to I/O devices. Here the contents of address $E0000_{16}$ represent byte-wide port 0 and the contents of addresses $E0000_{16}$ and $E0001_{16}$ correspond to word-wide port 0.

When I/O is configured as memory-mapped, instructions that affect data in memory are used instead of the special input/output instructions. This is an advantage in that many more instructions and addressing modes are available to perform I/O operations. For instance, the contents of a memory-mapped I/O port can be directly ANDed with a value in an internal register. In addition, I/O transfers can now take place between an I/O port and an internal register other than just AL or AX. However, this also leads to a disadvantage. That is, the memory instructions tend to execute slower than those specifically designed for isolated I/O. Therefore, a memory-mapped I/O routine may take longer to execute than an equivalent program using the input/output instructions.

Another disadvantage of using this method is that part of the memory address space is lost. For instance, in Fig. 8.2(b) addresses in the range from $E0000_{16}$ through $E0FFF_{16}$, which are allocated to I/O, cannot be used to implement memory.

▲ 8.3 AN ISOLATED INPUT/OUTPUT INTERFACE

The isolated *input/output interface* of the 8088 and 8086 microcomputers permits them to communicate with the outside world. The way in which the MPU deals with input/output circuitry is similar to the way in which it interfaces with memory circuitry. That is, input/output data transfers also take place over the multiplexed address/data bus. This parallel bus permits easy interface to LSI peripherals such as parallel I/O expanders. Through this I/O interface, the MPU can input or output data in bit, byte, or word (for the 8086) formats.

Minimum-Mode Interface

Let us begin by looking at the isolated I/O interface for a minimum-mode 8088 system. Figure 8.3 shows this minimum-mode interface. Here we find the 8088, interface circuitry, and I/O ports for devices 0 through N. The circuits in the interface section must perform functions such as select the I/O port, latch output data, sample

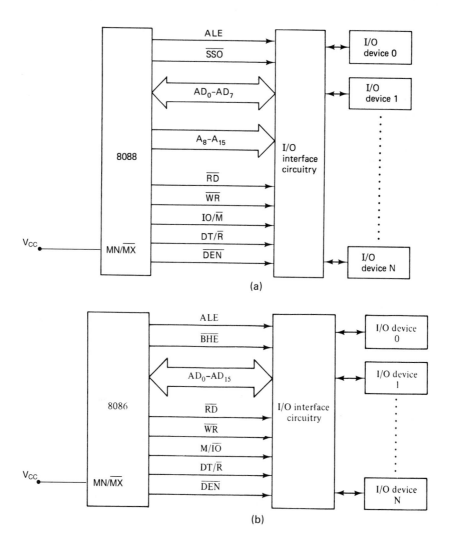

Figure 8.3 (a) Minimum-mode 8088 system I/O interface. (b) Minimum-mode 8086 system I/O interface.

input data, synchronize data transfers, and translate between TTL voltage levels and those required to operate the I/O devices.

The data path between the 8088 and I/O interface circuits is the multiplexed address/data bus. Unlike the memory interface, this time just the 16 least significant lines of the bus, AD_0 through AD_7 and A_8 through A_{15}, are in use. This interface also involves the control signals that we discussed as part of the memory interface. They are ALE, $\overline{SSO}$, $\overline{RD}$, $\overline{WR}$, IO/$\overline{M}$, DT/$\overline{R}$, and $\overline{DEN}$.

The isolated I/O interface of a minimum-mode 8086-based microcomputer system is shown in Fig. 8.3(b). Looking at this diagram, we find that the interface differs from that of the 8088 microcomputer in several ways. First, the complete

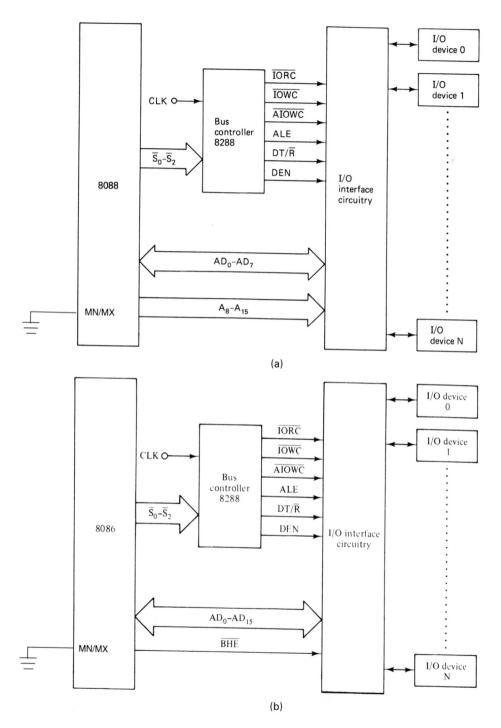

Figure 8.4 (a) Maximum-mode 8088 system I/O interface. (b) Maximum-mode 8086 system I/O interface.

data bus AD_0 through AD_{15} is used for input and output data transfers; second, the $M/\overline{IO}$ control signal is the complement of the equivalent signal $IO/\overline{M}$ in the 8088's interface; and third, status signal $\overline{SSO}$ is replaced by $\overline{BHE}$.

Maximum-Mode Interface

When the 8088 is strapped to operate in the maximum mode ($MN/\overline{MX}$ connected to ground), the interface to the I/O circuitry changes. Figure 8.4(a) illustrates this configuration.

As in the maximum-mode memory interface, the 8288 bus controller produces the control signals for the I/O subsystem. The 8288 decodes bus command status codes output by the 8088 at $\overline{S}_2\overline{S}_1\overline{S}_0$. These codes tell which type of bus cycle is in progress. If the code corresponds to an I/O read bus cycle, the 8288 generates the *I/O read command output* ($\overline{IORC}$) and for an I/O write cycle it generates *I/O write command outputs* ($\overline{IOWC}$) and ($\overline{AIOWC}$). The 8288 also produces the control signals ALE, DT/$\overline{R}$, and DEN. The address and data transfer path between 8088 and maximum-mode I/O interface remains address/data bus lines the AD_0 through AD_7 and A_8 through A_{15}.

Figure 8.4(b) shows the maximum-mode isolated I/O interface of an 8086 microprocessor system. There are only two differences between this interface diagram and that for the 8088 microprocessor. As in the minimum mode, the full 16-bit data bus is the path for data transfers, and the signal $\overline{BHE}$, which is not supplied by the 8088, is included in the interface.

The table in Fig. 8.5 shows the bus cycle status codes together with the command signals that they produce. Those for I/O bus cycles are highlighted. The MPU indicates that data are to be input (read I/O port) by code $\overline{S}_2\overline{S}_1\overline{S}_0 = 001$. This code causes the bus controller to produce control output I/O read command ($\overline{IORC}$). There is one other code that represents an output bus cycle. This is the write I/O port code $\overline{S}_2\overline{S}_1\overline{S}_0 = 010$. It produces two output command signals I/O write cycle ($\overline{IOWC}$) and advanced I/O write cycle ($\overline{AIOWC}$). These command signals are used to enable data from the I/O ports onto the system bus during an input operation and from the MPU to the I/O ports during an output operation.

▲ 8.4 INPUT/OUTPUT DATA TRANSFERS

Input/output ports in the 8088 and 8086 microcomputers can be either byte-wide or word-wide. The port that is accessed for input or output of data is selected by an *I/O address*. This address is specified as part of the instruction that performs the I/O operation.

I/O addresses are 16 bits in length and are output by the 8088 to the I/O interface over bus lines AD_0 through AD_7 and A_8 through A_{15}. AD_0 represents the LSB and A_{15} the MSB. The most significant address lines, A_{16} through A_{19}, are held at the 0 logic level during the address period (T_1) of all I/O bus cycles. Since 16 address lines are used to address I/O ports, the 8088's I/O address space consists of 64K byte-wide I/O ports.

Status inputs			CPU cycle	8288 command
$\overline{S}_2$	$\overline{S}_1$	$\overline{S}_0$		
0	0	0	Interrupt acknowledge	$\overline{INTA}$
0	0	1	Read I/O port	$\overline{IORC}$
0	1	0	Write I/O port	$\overline{IOWC}, \overline{AIOWC}$
0	1	1	Halt	None
1	0	0	Instruction fetch	$\overline{MRDC}$
1	0	1	Read memory	$\overline{MRDC}$
1	1	0	Write memory	$\overline{MWTC}, \overline{AMWC}$
1	1	1	Passive	None

Figure 8.5 I/O bus cycle status codes. (Reprinted with permission of Intel Corp., © Intel Corp. 1979)

The 8088 signals to external circuitry that the address on the bus is for an I/O port instead of a memory location by switching the IO/$\overline{M}$ control line to the 1 logic level. This signal is held at the 1 level during the complete input or output bus cycle. For this reason, it can be used to enable the address latch or address decoder in external I/O circuitry.

Data transfers between the 8088 and I/O devices are performed over the data bus. Data transfers to byte-wide I/O ports always require one bus cycle. Byte data transfers to a port are performed over bus lines D_0 through D_7. Word transfers also take place over the data bus, D_0 through D_7. However, this type of operation is performed as two consecutive byte-wide data transfers and takes two bus cycles.

For the 8086 microcomputer, I/O addresses are output on address/data bus lines AD_0 through AD_{15}. The logic levels of signals A_0 and $\overline{BHE}$ determine whether data are input/output for an odd-addressed byte-wide port, even-addressed byte-wide port, or a word-wide port. For example, if $A_0\overline{BHE} = 10$, an odd-addressed byte-wide I/O port is accessed. Byte data transfers to a port at an even address are performed over bus lines D_0 through D_7 and those to an odd-addressed port are performed over D_8 through D_{15}. Data transfers to byte-wide I/O ports always take place in one bus cycle.

Word data transfers between the 8086 and I/O devices are accompanied by the code $A_0\overline{BHE} = 00$ and are performed over the complete data bus, D_0 through D_{15}. A word transfer can require either one or two bus cycles. To ensure that just one bus cycle is required for the word data transfer, word-wide I/O ports should be aligned at even-address boundaries.

▲ 8.5 INPUT/OUTPUT INSTRUCTIONS

Input/output operations are performed by the 8088 and 8086 microprocessors that employ isolated I/O using the *in* (IN) and *out* (OUT) instructions. There are two types of IN and OUT instructions: the *direct I/O instructions* and *variable I/O*

Mnemonic	Meaning	Format	Operation	
IN	Input direct	IN Acc,Port	$(Acc) \leftarrow (Port)$	Acc = AL or AX
	Input indirect (variable)	IN Acc,DX	$(Acc) \leftarrow ((DX))$	
OUT	Output direct	OUT Port,Acc	$(Port) \leftarrow (Acc)$	
	Output indirect (variable)	OUT DX,Acc	$((DX)) \leftarrow (Acc)$	

Figure 8.6 Input/output instructions.

instructions. These instructions are listed in the table of Fig. 8.6. Their mnemonics and formats are provided together with a brief description of their operations.

Either of these two types of instructions can be used to transfer a byte or word of data. In the case of byte transfers, data are input/output over data bus lines D_0 through D_7. Word data are input or output as two consecutive byte transfers over the data bus D_0-D_7 or a single word transfer over D_0-D_{15} for an 8086 word-wide port that is aligned at an even-address boundary.

All data transfers take place between I/O devices and the MPU's AL or AX register. For this reason, this method of performing I/O is known as *accumulator I/O*. Byte transfers involve the AL register and word transfers the AX register. In fact, specifying AL as the source or destination register in an I/O instruction indicates that it is a byte transfer instead of a word transfer.

In a direct I/O instruction, the address of the I/O port is specified as part of the instruction. Eight bits are provided for this direct address. For this reason, its value is limited to the address range from $0_{10} = 00_{16}$ to $255_{10} = FF_{16}$. This range is referred to as page 0 in the I/O address space. An example is the instruction

```
IN AL,0FEH
```

Execution of this instruction causes the contents of the byte-wide I/O port at address FE_{16} of the I/O address space to be input to the AL register.

EXAMPLE 8.1

Write a sequence of instructions that will output the data FF_{16} to a byte-wide output port at address AB_{16} of the I/O address space.

Solution

First, the AL register is loaded with FF_{16} as an immediate operand in the instruction

```
MOV   AL,0FFH
```

Now the data in AL can be output to the byte-wide output port with the instruction

```
OUT   0ABH,AL
```

The difference between the direct and variable I/O instructions lies in the way in which the address of the I/O port is specified. We just saw that for direct

I/O instructions an 8-bit address is specified as part of the instruction. On the other hand, the variable I/O instructions use a 16-bit address that resides in the DX register within the MPU. The value in DX is not an offset. It is the actual address that is to be output on AD_0 through AD_7 and A_8 through A_{15} during the I/O bus cycle. Since this address is a full 16 bits in length, variable I/O instructions can access ports located anywhere in the 64KB I/O address space.

When using either type of I/O instruction, the data must be loaded into or removed from the AL or AX register before another input or output operation can be performed. In the case of a variable I/O instruction, the DX register must be loaded with an address. This requires execution of an additional instruction. For instance, the instruction sequence

```
MOV DX,0A000H
IN  AL,DX
```

inputs the contents of the byte-wide input port at $A000_{16}$ of the I/O address space.

EXAMPLE 8.2

Write a series of instructions that will output FF_{16} to an output port located at address $B000_{16}$ of the I/O address space.

Solution

The DX register must first be loaded with the address of the output port. This is done with the instruction

```
MOV  DX,0B000H
```

Next, the data that are to be output must be loaded into AL:

```
MOV  AL,0FFH
```

Finally, the data are output with the instruction

```
OUT  DX,AL
```

EXAMPLE 8.3

Data are to be read in from two byte-wide input ports at addresses AA_{16} and $A9_{16}$, respectively, and then output as a word to a word-wide output port at address $B000_{16}$. Write a sequence of instructions to perform this input/output operation.

Solution

We can first read in the byte from the port at address AA_{16} into AL and move it to AH. This is done with the instructions

```
IN   AL,0AAH
MOV  AH,AL
```

Now the other byte, which is at port $A9_{16}$, can be read into AL by the instruction

```
IN   AL,0A9H
```

To write out the word of data in AX, we can load DX with the address $B000_{16}$ and use a variable output instruction. This leads to the following

```
MOV   DX,0B000H
OUT   DX,AX
```

▲ 8.6 INPUT/OUTPUT BUS CYCLES

In Section 8.3, we found that the isolated I/O interface signals for the minimum-mode 8088 and 8086 microcomputer systems are essentially the same as those involved in the memory interface. In fact, the function, logic levels, and timing of all signals other than IO/$\overline{\text{M}}$ (M/$\overline{\text{IO}}$) are identical to those already described for the memory interface in Chapter 7.

Waveforms for the 8088's *I/O input (I/O read) bus cycle* and *I/O output (I/O write) bus cycle* are shown in Figs. 8.7 and 8.8, respectively. Looking at the input and output bus cycle waveforms, we see that the timing of IO/$\overline{\text{M}}$ does not change. The 8088 switches it to logic 1 to indicate that an I/O bus cycle is in progress. It is maintained at the 1 logic level for the duration of the I/O bus cycle. As in memory cycles, the address is output together with ALE during clock period T_1. For the input bus cycle, $\overline{\text{DEN}}$ is switched to logic 0 to signal the I/O interface circuitry when to put the data onto the bus and the 8088 reads data off the bus during period T_3.

On the other hand, for the output bus cycle in Fig. 8.6, the 8088 puts write data on the bus late in T_2 and maintains it during the rest of the bus cycle. This time $\overline{\text{WR}}$ switches to logic 0 to signal the I/O system that valid data are on the bus.

The waveforms of the 8086's input and output bus cycles are shown in Figs. 8.9 and 8.10, respectively. Let us just look at the differences between the input cycle of the 8086 and that of the 8088. Comparing the waveforms in Fig. 8.9 to those in Fig. 8.7, we see that the 8086 outputs the signal $\overline{\text{BHE}}$ along with the address in T-state T_1. Remember that for the 8086 microprocessor this signal is used along with A_0 to select the byte-wide or the word-wide port. Next, the 8086's data transfer path to the I/O interface is the 16-bit address/data bus, not eight bits as in the 8088 system. Therefore, data transfers, which take place during T_3, can take place over the lower 8 data bus lines, upper 8 data bus lines, or all 16 data bus lines. Third, the 8086 outputs logic 0 on the M/$\overline{\text{IO}}$ line, while the 8088 outputs logic 1 on the IO/$\overline{\text{M}}$ line. That is, the M/$\overline{\text{IO}}$ control signal of the 8086 is the complement of that of the 8088. Finally, the 8086 does not produce an $\overline{\text{SSO}}$ output signal like the one in the 8088.

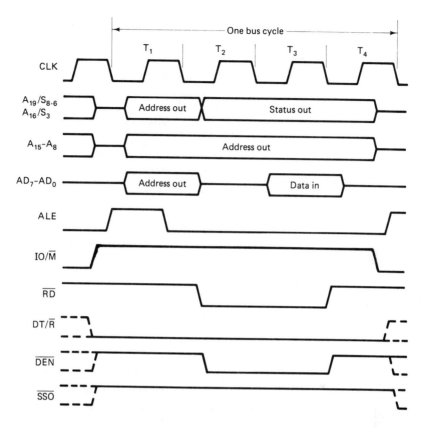

One bus cycle

| | T_1 | T_2 | T_3 | T_4 |

CLK

A_{19}/S_{8-6}
A_{16}/S_3 — Address out — Status out

$A_{15}-A_8$ — Address out

AD_7-AD_0 — Address out — Data in

ALE

IO/$\overline{M}$

$\overline{RD}$

DT/$\overline{R}$

$\overline{DEN}$

$\overline{SSO}$

Figure 8.7 Input bus cycle of the 8088.

▲ 8.7 BYTE-WIDE OUTPUT PORTS USING ISOLATED I/O

Up to this point, we have introduced the isolated I/O interface of the 8088 and 8086 microprocessors, the I/O instructions, and I/O bus cycles. Now we will show circuits that can be used to implement parallel output ports in a microcomputer system employing isolated I/O. Figure 8.11(a) is such a circuit for an 8088-based microcomputer. It provides 8-byte-wide output ports that are implemented using 74F374 octal latches. In this circuit, the ports are labeled port 0 through port 7. These eight ports give a total of 64 parallel output lines, which are labeled O_0 through O_{63}.

Looking at the circuit, we see that the 8088's address/data bus is demultiplexed just as was done for the memory interface. Notice that two 74F373 octal latches are used to form a 16-bit address latch. These devices latch the address A_0 through A_{15} synchronously with the ALE pulse. The latched address outputs are labeled A_{0L} through A_{15L}. Remember that address lines A_{16} through A_{19} are not involved in the I/O interface. For this reason, they are not shown in the circuit diagram.

Address/data bus lines AD_0 through AD_7 are also applied to one side of the 74F245 bus transceiver. At the other side of the transceiver, data bus lines D_0

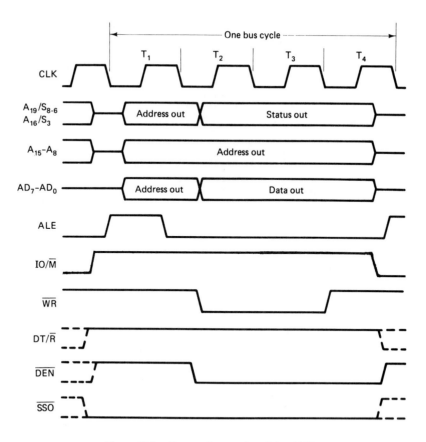

Figure 8.8 Output bus cycle of the 8088.

through D_7 are shown connecting to the output latches. It is over these lines that the 8088 writes data into the output ports.

Address lines A_{0L} and A_{15L} provide two of the three enable inputs of the 74F138 input/output address decoder. These signals are applied to enable inputs $\overline{G}_{2B}$ and G_1, respectively. The decoder requires one more enable signal at its $\overline{G}_{2A}$ input. It is supplied by the complement of IO/$\overline{M}$. These enable inputs must be $\overline{G}_{2B}\overline{G}_{2A}G_1 = 001$ to enable the decoder for operation. The condition $\overline{G}_{2B} = 0$ corresponds to an even address and $\overline{G}_{2A} = 0$ represents the fact that an I/O bus cycle is in progress. The third condition, $G_1 = 1$, is an additional requirement that A_{15L} be at logic 1 during all data transfers for this section of parallel output ports.

Notice that the three address lines $A_{3L}A_{2L}A_{1L}$ are applied to select inputs CBA of the 74F138 1-of-8 decoder. When the decoder is enabled, the P output corresponding to these select inputs switches to logic 0. Notice that logic 0 at this output enables the $\overline{WR}$ signal to the clock (CLK) input of the corresponding output latch. In this way, just one of the eight ports is selected for operation.

When valid output data are on D_0 through D_7, the 8088 switches $\overline{WR}$ to logic 0. This change in logic level causes the selected 74F374 device to latch in the data

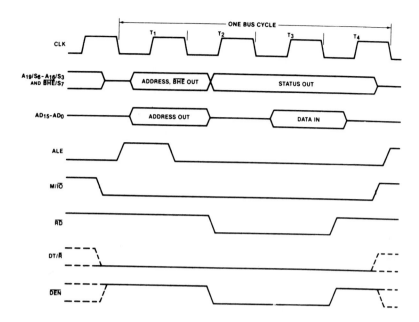

Figure 8.9 Input bus cycle of the 8086.

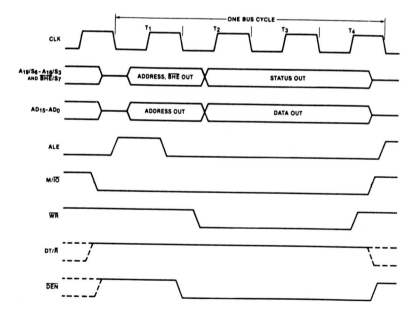

Figure 8.10 Output bus cycle of the 8086.

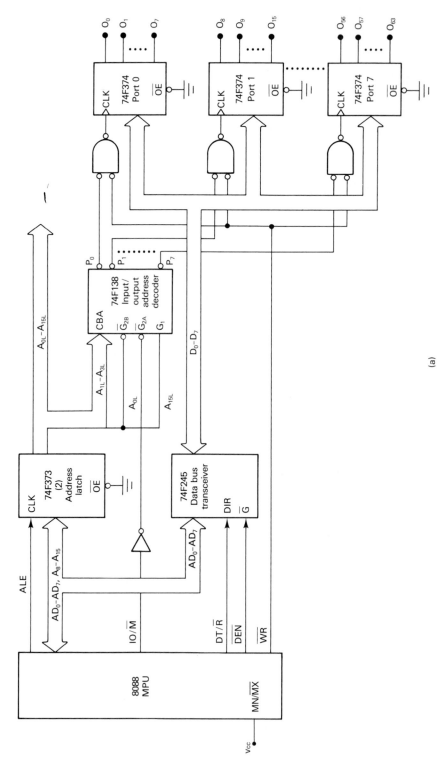

Figure 8.11 (a) Sixty-four-line parallel output circuit for an 8088-based microcomputer. (b) I/O address decoding for ports 0 through 7. (c) Sixty-four-line parallel output circuit for an 8086-based microcomputer.

(a)

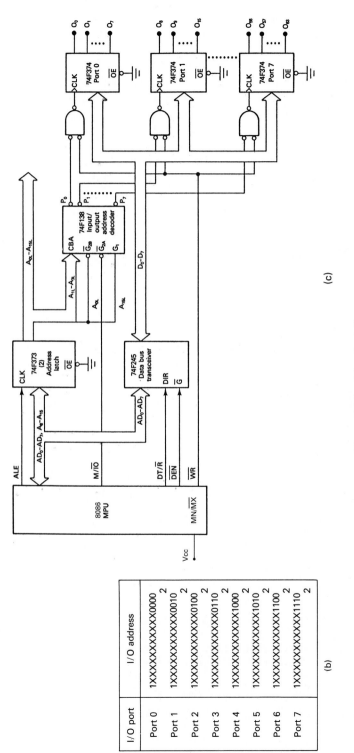

Figure 8.11 (Continued)

I/O port	I/O address
Port 0	$1XXXXXXXXXXXXX0000_2$
Port 1	$1XXXXXXXXXXXXX0010_2$
Port 2	$1XXXXXXXXXXXXX0100_2$
Port 3	$1XXXXXXXXXXXXX0110_2$
Port 4	$1XXXXXXXXXXXXX1000_2$
Port 5	$1XXXXXXXXXXXXX1010_2$
Port 6	$1XXXXXXXXXXXXX1100_2$
Port 7	$1XXXXXXXXXXXXX1110_2$

(b)

from the bus. The outputs of the latches are permanently enabled by the 0 logic level at their $\overline{\text{OE}}$ inputs. Therefore, the latched data appear at the appropriate port outputs.

The 74F245 in the circuit allows the data being output to pass from the 8088 to the output ports. This is accomplished by enabling the 74F245's DIR and $\overline{\text{G}}$ inputs with the DT/$\overline{\text{R}}$ and $\overline{\text{DEN}}$ signals, which are at logic 1 and 0, respectively.

Notice in Fig. 8.11(a) that not all address bits are used in the I/O address decoding. Here only latched address bits A_{0L}, A_{1L}, A_{2L}, A_{3L}, and A_{15L} are decoded. Figure 8.11(b) shows the addresses that select each of the I/O ports. Unused bits are shown as don't cares. By assigning various logic combinations to the unused bit, the same port can be selected by different addresses. In this way, we see that many addresses will decode to select each of the I/O ports. For instance, if all of the don't-care address bits are made 0, the address of port 0 is

$$1000000000000000_2 \ = \ 8000_{16}$$

However, if these bits are all made equal to 1 instead of 0, the address is

$$1111111111110000_2 \ = \ \text{FFF0}_{16}$$

and it still decodes to enable port 0. In fact, every I/O address in the range from 8000_{16} through FFF0_{16} that has its lower four bits equal to 0000_2 decodes to enable PORT 0.

EXAMPLE 8.4

To which output port in Fig. 8.11(a) are data written when the address put on the bus during an output bus cycle is 8002_{16}?

Solution

Expressing the address in binary form, we get

$$A_{15} \ldots A_0 = A_{15L} \ldots A_{0L} = 1000000000000010_2$$

The important address bits are

$$A_{15L} = 1$$

$$A_{0L} = 0$$

and

$$A_{3L}A_{2L}A_{1L} = 001$$

Moreover, whenever an output bus cycle is in progress, IO/$\overline{\text{M}}$ is logic 1. Therefore, the enable inputs of the 74F138 decoder are

$$\overline{\text{G}}_{2B} = A_{0L} = 0$$

$$\overline{\text{G}}_{2A} = \text{IO}/\overline{\text{M}} = 0$$

$$\text{G}_1 = A_{15L} = 1$$

These inputs enable the decoder for operation. At the same time, its select inputs are supplied with the code 001. This input causes output P_1 to switch to logic 0.

$$P_1 = 0$$

The gate at the CLK input of port 1 has as its inputs P_1 and $\overline{WR}$. When valid data are on the bus, $\overline{WR}$ switches to logic 0. Since P_1 is also 0, the CLK input of the 74F374 for port 1 switches to logic 0. At the end of the $\overline{WR}$ pulse, the clock switches from 0 to 1, a positive transition. This causes the data on D_0 through D_7 to be latched at output lines O_8 through O_{15} of port 1.

EXAMPLE 8.5

Write a series of instructions that will output the byte contents of the memory address DATA to output port 0 in the circuit of Fig. 8.11(a).

Solution

To write a byte to output port 0, the address that must be output on the 8088's address bus must be

$$A_{15}A_{14} \ldots A_0 = 1XXXXXXXXXXX0000_2$$

Assuming that the don't-care bits are all made logic 0, we get

$$A_{15}A_{14} \ldots A_0 = 1000000000000000_2$$
$$= 8000_{16}$$

Then the instruction sequence needed to output the contents of memory address DATA is

```
MOV   DX,8000H
MOV   AL,[DATA]
OUT   DX,AL
```

Figure 8.11(c) shows a similar output circuit for an 8086-based microcomputer system. Here again 64 output lines are implemented as eight byte-wide parallel ports, port 0 through port 7. Comparing this circuit to that for an 8088-based microcomputer in Fig. 8.11(a), we find just one difference. This is that the control signal $M/\overline{IO}$ is applied directly to the $\overline{G}_{2A}$ input of the 74F138 input/output address decoder. Since $M/\overline{IO}$ is the complement of the 8088's $IO/\overline{M}$ signal, it does not have to be inverted.

The Time Delay Loop and Blinking an LED at an Output

The circuit in Fig. 8.12 has an LED attached to output O_7 of parallel port 0. This circuit is identical to that shown in Fig. 8.11(a). Therefore, the port address as found in Example 8.5 is 8000H and the LED corresponds to bit 7 of the byte of data that is written to port 0. For the LED to turn on, O_7 must be switched to logic 0 and it will remain on until this output is switched back to 1. The 74374 is not an inverting latch; therefore, to make O_7 logic 0 we simply write 0 to that bit of the octal latch. To make the LED blink, we must write a program that first makes O_7 logic 0 to turn on the LED; delays for a short period of time; and then switches O_7 back to 1 to turn off the LED. This piece of program can run as a loop to make the LED continuously blink.

Let us begin by writing the sequence of instructions needed to initialize O_7 to logic 0. This is done as follows:

```
            MOV   DX,8000H   ;Initialize address of port 0
            MOV   AL,00H     ;Load data with bit 7 as logic 0
ON_OFF:     OUT   DX,AL      ;Output the data to port 0
```

After the out operation is performed, the LED will be turned on.

Next we must delay for a short period of time. This can be done with a software loop. The following instruction sequence produces such as delay.

```
            MOV  CX,0FFFFH   ;Load delay count of FFFFH
HERE:       LOOP HERE        ;Time delay loop
```

First the count register is loaded with $FFFF_{16}$. Then the loop instruction is repeatedly executed. With each occurrence of the loop, the count in CX is decremented by 1. After 65,335 repeats of the loop, the count in CX is 0000_{16} and the loop operation is complete. These executions perform no software function for the program other than to use time, which is the duration of the time delay. By using $FFFF_{16}$ as the count, the maximum delay is obtained. The duration of the delay can be shortened by simply loading a smaller number in CX.

Next the value in bit 7 of AL is complemented to 1 and then a jump performed to return to the output operation that writes the data to the output port.

```
            XOR   AL,80H     ;Complement bit 7 of AL
            JMP   ON_OFF     ;Return to output the new data
```

By performing an exclusive-OR operation on the value in AL with the value 80_{16}, the most significant bit is complemented to 1. The jump instruction returns control to the OUT instruction. Now the new value in AL, with MSB equal to 1, is output to port 0 and the LED turns off. After this, the time delay repeats; the value in AL is complemented back to 00_{16}; and the LED turns back on. In this way, we see that the LED blinks repeatedly with an equal period of on and off time that is set by the count in CX.

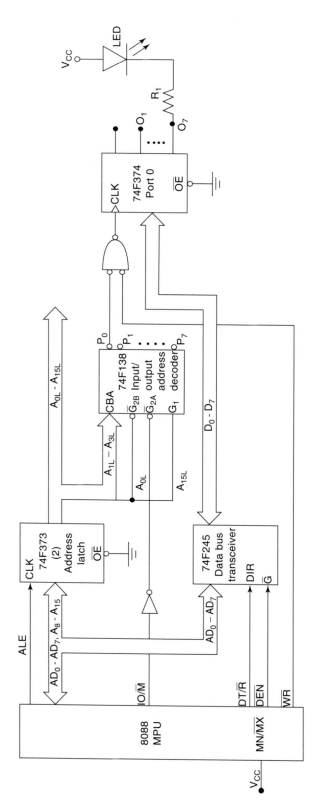

Figure 8.12 Driving an LED connected to an output port.

▲ 8.8 BYTE-WIDE INPUT PORTS USING ISOLATED I/O

In Section 8.7, we showed circuits that implemented eight byte-wide output ports for the 8088 and the 8086 microcomputer systems. These circuits used the 74F374 octal latch to provide the output ports. Here we will examine a similar circuit that implements input ports for the microcomputer system.

The circuit in Fig. 8.13 provides eight byte-wide input ports for an 8088-based microcomputer system employing isolated I/O. Just like in Fig. 8.11(a), the ports are labeled port 0 through port 7; however, this time the 64 parallel port lines are inputs, I_0 through I_{63}. Notice that eight 74F244 octal buffers are used to implement the ports. These buffers are equipped with three-state outputs.

When an input bus cycle is in progress, the I/O address is first latched into the 74F373 address latches. This address is accompanied by logic 1 on the $IO/\overline{M}$ control line. Notice that $IO/\overline{M}$ is inverted and applied to the $\overline{G}_{2A}$ input of the I/O address decoder. If during the bus cycle address bit $A_{0L} = 0$ and $A_{15L} = 1$, the address decoder is enabled for operation. Then the code $A_{3L}A_{2L}A_{1L}$ is decoded to produce an active logic level at one of the decoder's outputs. For instance, an input of $A_{3L}A_{2L}A_{1L} = 001$ switches the P_1 output to logic 0. P_1 is gated with $\overline{RD}$ to produce the $\overline{G}$ enable input for the port 1 buffer. If both $IO/\overline{M}$ and P_1 are logic 0, the $\overline{G}$ input for port 1 is switched to logic 0 and the outputs of the 74F244 are enabled. In this case, the logic levels at inputs I_8 through I_{15} are passed onto data bus lines D_0 through D_7, respectively. This byte of data is carried through the enabled data bus transceiver to the data bus of the 8088. As part of the input operation, the 8088 reads this byte of data into the AL register.

EXAMPLE 8.6 ⎯⎯⎯⎯⎯⎯⎯⎯⎯⎯⎯⎯⎯⎯⎯⎯⎯⎯⎯⎯⎯⎯⎯⎯⎯⎯

What is the I/O address of port 7 in the circuit of Fig. 8.13? Assume that all unused address bits are at logic 0.

Solution

For the I/O address decoder to be enabled, address bits A_{15} and A_0 must be

$$A_{15} = 1$$

and

$$A_0 = 0$$

Moreover, to select port 7, the address applied to CBA inputs of the decoder must be

$$A_{3L}A_{2L}A_{1L} = 111$$

Filling the unused bits with 0s gives the address

$$A_{15L} \dots A_{1L}A_{0L} = 1000000000001110_2$$

$$= 800E_{16}$$

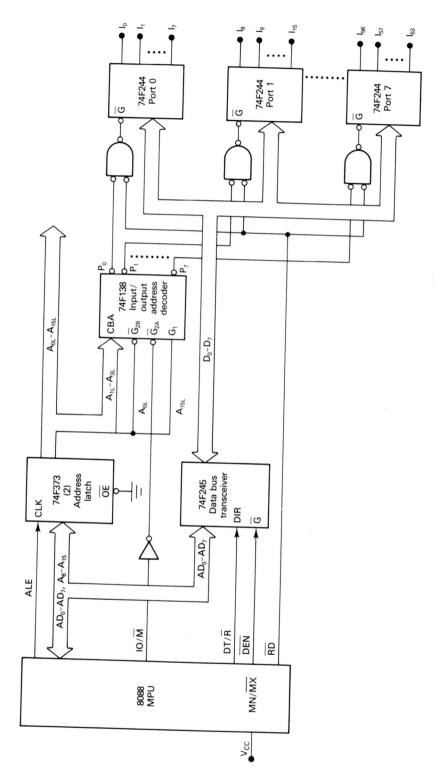

Figure 8.13 Sixty-four-line parallel input circuit for an 8088 microcomputer.

EXAMPLE 8.7 _____

For the circuit of Fig. 8.13, write an instruction sequence that will input the byte contents of input port 7 to the memory location DATA_7.

Solution

In Example 8.6 we found that the address of port 7 is $800E_{16}$. This address is loaded into the DX register with the instruction

```
MOV  DX,800EH
```

Now the contents of this port are input to the AL register by executing the instruction

```
IN  AL,DX
```

Finally, the byte of data is copied to memory location DATA_7 with the instruction

```
MOV  DATA_7,AL
```

_____

In practical applications, it is sometimes necessary within an I/O service routine to repeatedly read the logic level of an input line and test it for a specific logic level. For instance, input I_3 at port 0 in Fig. 8.13 can be checked to determine if it is at the 1 logic level. Normally, the I/O routine does not continue until the input under test switches to the appropriate logic level. This mode of operation is known as *polling* an input. The polling technique can be used to synchronize the execution of an I/O routine to an event in external hardware.

Let us now look at how a polling software routine is written. The first step in the polling operation is to read the contents of the input port. For instance, the instructions needed to read the contents of port 0 in the circuit of Fig. 8.13 are

```
              MOV  DX,8000H
POLL_I3:      IN   AL,DX
```

A label has been added to identify the beginning of the polling routine. After executing these instructions, the byte contents of port 0 are held in the AL register. Let us assume that input I_3 at this port is the line that is being polled. Therefore, all other bits in AL are masked off with the instruction

```
AND AL,08H
```

After this instruction is executed, the contents of AL will be either 00H or 08H. Moreover the zero flag is 1 if AL contains 00H, else it is 0. The state of the zero flag can be tested with a jump on zero instruction

```
JZ POLL_I3
```

If zero flag is 1, a jump is initiated to POLL_I3 and the sequence repeats. On the other hand, if it is 0, the jump is not made; instead, the instruction following the jump instruction is executed. That is, the polling loop repeats until input I_3 is tested and found to be logic 1.

Polling the Setting of a Switch

Figure 8.14 shows a switch connected to input 7 of an input port similar to that shown as port 0 of Fig. 8.13. Notice that when the switch is open input I_7 is pulled to +5V (logic 1) through pull-up resistor R_1. When the switch is closed, I_7 is connected to ground (logic 0). It is a common practice to poll a switch like this with software waiting for it to close.

The instruction sequence that follows will poll the switch at I_7.

```
                    MOV  DX, 8000H
        POLL_I7:    IN   AL,DX
                    SHL  AL,1
                    JC   POLL_I7
        CONTINUE:
```

First, DX is loaded with the address of port 0. Then the contents of port 0 are input to the AL register. Since the logic level at I_7 is in bit 7 of the byte of data in AL, a shift left by one bit position will put this logic level into CF. Now a jump on carry instruction is executed to test CF. If CF is 1, the switch is not yet closed. In this case, contol is returned to the IN instruction and the poll sequence repeats. On the other hand, if the switch is closed, bit 7 in AL is 0 and this value is shifted into CF. When the JC instruction detects this condition, the polling operation is complete and the instruction following JC is executed.

▲ 8.9 INPUT/OUTPUT HANDSHAKING AND A PARALLEL PRINTER INTERFACE

In some applications, the microcomputer must synchronize the input or output of information to a peripheral device. Two examples of interfaces that may require a synchronized data transfer are a serial communications interface and a parallel printer interface. Synchronization is achieved by implementing what is known as *handshaking* as part of the input/output interface.

Figure 8.15(a) shows a conceptual view of the interface between the *printer* and a *parallel printer port*. There are three general types of signals at the *printer interface*: data, control, and status. The data lines are the parallel paths used to transfer data to the printer. Transfers of data over this bus are synchronized with an appropriate sequence of control signals. However, data transfers can only take place if the printer is ready to accept data. Printer readiness is indicated through the parallel interface by a set of signals called status lines. This interface handshake sequence is summarized by the flowchart of Fig. 8.15(b).

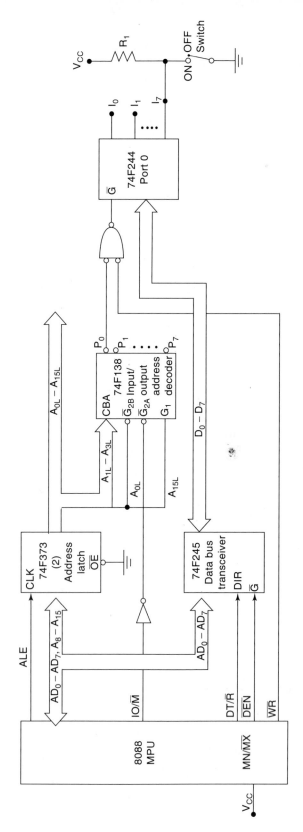

Figure 8.14 Reading the setting of a switch connected to an input port.

The printer is attached to the microcomputer system at a connector known as the parallel printer port. On the IBM PC, a 25-pin connector is used to attach the printer. The actual signals supplied at the pins of this connector are shown in Fig. 8.15(c). Notice that there are five status signals available at the interface and they are called Ack, Busy, Paper Empty, Select, and Error. In a particular implementation only some of these signals may be used. For instance, to send a character to the printer, the software may only test the Busy signal. If it is inactive, it may be a sufficient indication to proceed with the transfer.

A detailed block diagram of a simple parallel printer interface is shown in Fig. 8.16(a). Here we find eight data output lines D_0 through D_7, control signal strobe ($\overline{STB}$), and status signal busy (BUSY). The MPU outputs data representing the character to be printed through the parallel printer interface. Character data are latched at the outputs of the parallel interface and are carried to the data inputs of the printer over data lines D_0 through D_7. The $\overline{STB}$ output of the parallel printer interface is used to signal the printer that new character data is available. Whenever the printer is already busy printing a character, it signals this fact to the MPU with the BUSY input of the parallel printer interface. This handshake signal sequence is illustrated in Fig. 8.16(b).

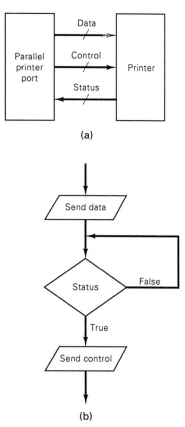

(a)

(b)

Figure 8.15 (a) Parallel printer interface. (b) Flowchart showing the data transfer in a parallel printer interface. (c) Parallel printer port pin assignments and types of interface signals.

Pin	Assignment
1	Strobe
2	Data 0
3	Data 1
4	Data 2
5	Data 3
6	Data 4
7	Data 5
8	Data 6
9	Data 7
10	Ack
11	Busy
12	Paper Empty
13	Select
14	Auto Foxt
15	Error
16	Initialize
17	Slctin
18	Ground
19	Ground
20	Ground
21	Ground
22	Ground
23	Ground
24	Ground
25	Ground

```
Data:              Data0, Data1, ........, Data7
Control:           Strobe
                   Auto Foxt
                   Initialize
                   Slctin
Status:            Ack
                   Busy
                   Paper Empty
                   Select
                   Error
```

(c)

Figure 8.15 (Continued)

Let us now look at the sequence of events that take place at the parallel printer interface when data are output to the printer. Figure 8.16(c) is a flowchart of a subroutine that performs a parallel printer interface character transfer operation. First the BUSY input of the parallel printer interface is tested. Notice that this is done with a polling operation. That is, the MPU tests the logic level of BUSY repeatedly until it is found to be at the not busy logic level. *Busy* means that the printer is currently printing a character. On the other hand, *not busy* signals that the printer is ready to receive another character for printing. After finding a not busy condition, a count of the number of characters in the printer buffer (microprocessor memory) is read; a byte of character data is read from the printer buffer; the character is output to the parallel interface; and then a pulse is produced at $\overline{\text{STB}}$. This pulse tells the printer to read the character off the data bus lines. The printer

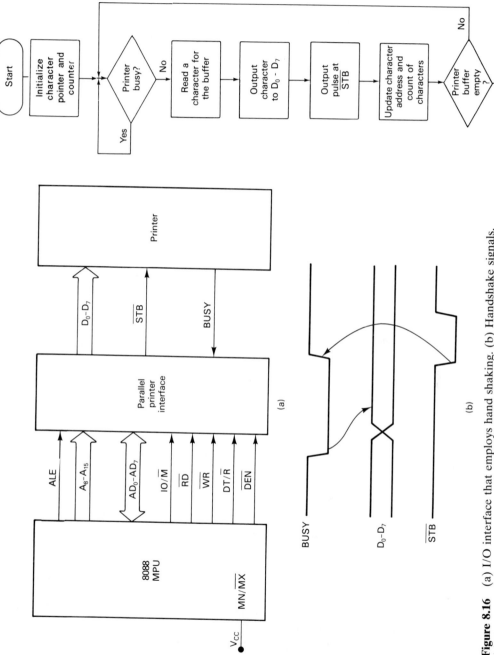

Figure 8.16 (a) I/O interface that employs hand shaking. (b) Handshake signals. (c) Handshake sequence flow chart. (d) Handshaking printer interface circuit.

449

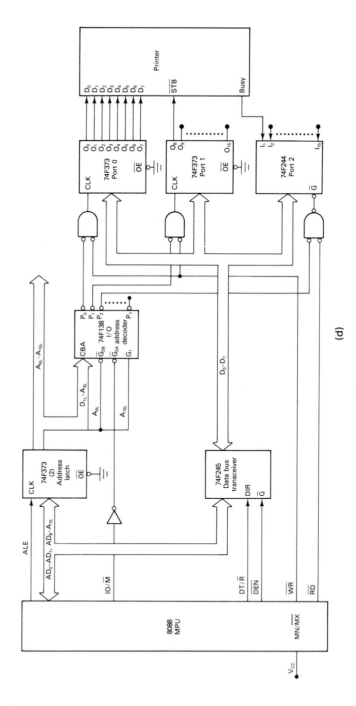

Figure 8.16 (Continued)

is again printing a character and signals this fact at BUSY. The handshake sequence is now complete. Now the count that represents the number of characters in the buffer is decremented and checked to see if the buffer is empty. If empty, the print operation is complete. Otherwise, the character transfer sequence is repeated for the next character.

The circuit in Fig. 8.16(d) implements the parallel printer interface of Fig. 8.16(a).

EXAMPLE 8.8

What are the addresses of the ports that provide the data lines, strobe output, and busy input in the circuit of Fig. 8.16(d)? Assume that all unused address bits are 0.

Solution

The I/O addresses that enable port 0 for the data lines, port 1 for the strobe output, and port 2 for the busy input are found as follows:

$$\text{Address of Port } 0 = 1000000000000000_2 = 8000_{16}$$

$$\text{Address of Port } 1 = 1000000000000010_2 = 8002_{16}$$

$$\text{Address of Port } 2 = 1000000000000100_2 = 8004_{16}$$

EXAMPLE 8.9

Write a program that will implement the sequence in Fig. 8.16(c) for the circuit in Fig. 8.16(d). Character data are held in memory starting at address PRNT_BUFF and the number of characters held in the buffer is identified by the count at address CHAR_COUNT. Use the port addresses from Example 8.8

Solution

First the character counter and the character pointer are set up with the instructions

```
MOV   CL, [CHAR_COUNT]
MOV   SI, PRNT_BUFF
```

Next the BUSY input is checked with the instructions

```
POLL_BUSY:    MOV   DX, 8004H
              IN    AL, DX
              AND   AL, 01H
              JNZ   POLL_BUSY
```

Next the character is copied into AL, and then it is output to port 0.

```
MOV   AL, [SI]
MOV   DX, 8000H
OUT   DX, AL
```

Now a strobe pulse is generated at port 1 with the instructions

```
          MOV   AL,00H      ;STB = 0
          MOV   DX,8002H
          OUT   DX,AL
          MOV   BX,0FH      ;Delay for STB duration
STROBE:   DEC   BX
          JNZ   STROBE
          MOV   AL,01H      ;STB = 1
          OUT   DX,AL
```

At this point, the value of PRNT_BUFF must be incremented and the value of CHAR_COUNT must be decremented. This is done with

```
          INC SI
          DEC CL
```

Finally, a check is made to see if the printer buffer is empty. If it is not empty, we need to repeat the prior instruction sequence. To do this, we execute the instruction

```
          JNZ POLL_BUSY
DONE:     —
```

The program comes to the DONE label after all characters are transferred to the printer.

▲ 8.10 8255A PROGRAMMABLE PERIPHERAL INTERFACE (PPI)

The 8255A is an LSI peripheral designed to permit easy implementation of *parallel I/O* in the 8088 and 8086 microcomputer systems. It provides a flexible parallel interface, which includes features such as single-bit, 4-bit, and byte-wide input and output ports; level-sensitive inputs; latched outputs; strobed inputs or outputs; and strobed bidirectional input/outputs. These features are selected under software control.

A block diagram of the 8255A is shown in Fig. 8.17(a) and its pin layout in Fig. 8.17(b). The left side of the block represents the *microprocessor's interface*. It includes an *8-bit bidirectional data bus* D_0 through D_7. Over these lines, commands, status information, and data are transferred between the MPU and 8255A. These data are transferred whenever the MPU performs an input or output bus cycle to an address of a register within the device. Timing of the data transfers to the 8255A is controlled by the *read/write control* ($\overline{RD}$ and $\overline{WR}$) signals.

The source or destination register within the 8255A is selected by a 2-bit *register select code*. The MPU must apply this code to the *register select inputs* A_0

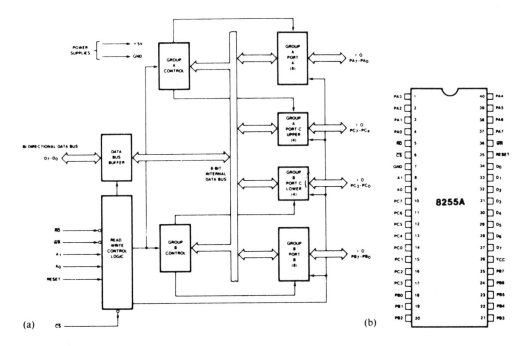

Figure 8.17 (a) Block diagram of the 8255A. (Reprinted by permission of Intel Corp., © Intel Corp. 1980) (b) Pin layout. (Reprinted by permission of Intel Corp., © Intel Corp. 1980)

and A_1 of the 8255A. The *port A*, *port B*, and *port C registers* correspond to codes $A_1A_0 = 00$, $A_1A_0 = 01$, and $A_1A_0 = 10$, respectively.

Two other signals are shown on the microprocessor interface side of the block diagram. They are the *reset* (RESET) and *chip select* ($\overline{CS}$) inputs. $\overline{CS}$ must be logic 0 during all read or write operations to the 8255A. It selects the 8255A's microprocessor interface circuitry for an input or output operation.

On the other hand, RESET is used to initialize the device. Switching it to logic 0 at power-up causes the internal registers of the 8255A to be cleared. *Initialization* configures all I/O ports for input mode of operation.

The right side of the block corresponds to three *byte-wide I/O ports*. They are called port A, port B, and port C and represent *I/O lines* PA0 through PA_7, PB_0 through PB_7, and PC_0 through PC_7, respectively. These ports can be configured for input or output operation. This gives us a total of 24 I/O lines.

We already mentioned that the operating characteristics of the 8255A can be configured under software control. It contains an 8-bit internal control register for this purpose. This register is represented by the *group A* and *group B control blocks* in Fig. 8.17(a). Logic 0 or 1 can be written to the bit positions in this register to configure the individual ports for input or output operation and to enable one of its three modes of operation. The control register is write only and its contents can be modified using microprocessor instructions. A write bus cycle to the 8255A with register select code $A_1A_0 = 11$ and an appropriate control word is used to modify the control registers.

The circuit in Fig. 8.18 is an example of how the 8255A can be interfaced to a microprocessor. Here we see that address lines A_0 and A_1 of the microprocessor are directly connected to the 8255A's register select inputs A_0 and A_1, respectively. The $\overline{CS}$ input of the 8255A is supplied from the output of the address decoder circuit whose inputs are address lines A_2 through A_{15} and $IO/\overline{M}$. To access either a port or the control register of the 8255A, $\overline{CS}$ must be active. Then the code A_1A_0 selects the port or control register to be accessed. The select codes are shown in Fig. 8.18.

For instance, to access port A, $A_1A_0 = 00$, $A_{15} = A_{14} = 1$, $A_{13} = A_{12} = \ldots = A_2 = 0$, which gives the port A address as

$$1100\ldots00_2 = C000_{16}$$

Similarly, it can be determined that the address of port B equals $C001_{16}$, that of port C is $C002_{16}$, and the address of the control registers is $C003_{16}$.

The bits of the control register and their control functions are shown in Fig. 8.19. Here we see that bits D_0 through D_2 correspond to the group B control block in the diagram of Fig. 8.17(a). Bit D_0 configures the lower four lines of port C for

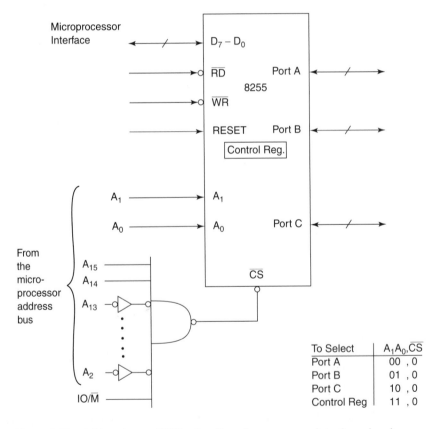

Figure 8.18 Addressing an 8255 using the microprocessor interface signals.

input or output operation. Notice that logic 1 at D_0 selects input operation, and logic 0 selects output operation. The next bit, D_1, configures port B as an 8-bit-wide input or output port. Again, logic 1 selects input operation and logic 0 selects output operation.

The D_2 bit is the mode select bit for port B and the lower four bits of port C. It permits selection of one of two different modes of operation called *mode 0* and *mode 1*. Logic 0 in bit D_2 selects mode 0, while logic 1 selects mode 1. These modes will be discussed in detail shortly.

The next four bits in the control register, D_3 through D_6, correspond to the group A control block in Fig. 8.17(a). Bits D_3 and D_4 of the control register are used to configure the operation of the upper half of port C and all of port A, respectively. These bits work in the same way as D_0 and D_1 to configure the lower half of port C and port B. However, there are now two mode select bits D_5 and D_6 instead of just one. They are used to select between three modes of operation known as *mode 0*, *mode 1*, and *mode 2*.

The last control register bit, D_7, is the *mode set flag*. It must be at logic 1 (active) whenever the mode of operation is to be changed.

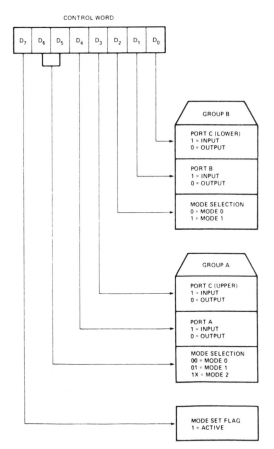

Figure 8.19 Control word bit functions. (Reprinted by permission of Intel Corp., © Intel Corp. 1980)

	MODE 0	
Pin	IN	OUT
PA$_0$	IN	OUT
PA$_1$	IN	OUT
PA$_2$	IN	OUT
PA$_3$	IN	OUT
PA$_4$	IN	OUT
PA$_5$	IN	OUT
PA$_6$	IN	OUT
PA$_7$	IN	OUT
PB$_0$	IN	OUT
PB$_1$	IN	OUT
PB$_2$	IN	OUT
PB$_3$	IN	OUT
PB$_4$	IN	OUT
PB$_5$	IN	OUT
PB$_6$	IN	OUT
PB$_7$	IN	OUT
PC$_0$	IN	OUT
PC$_1$	IN	OUT
PC$_2$	IN	OUT
PC$_3$	IN	OUT
PC$_4$	IN	OUT
PC$_5$	IN	OUT
PC$_6$	IN	OUT
PC$_7$	IN	OUT

Figure 8.20 Mode 0 port pin functions.

Mode 0 selects what is called *simple I/O operation*. By simple I/O, we mean that the lines of the port can be configured as level-sensitive inputs or latched outputs. To set all ports for this mode of operation, load bit D_7 of the control register with logic 1, bits $D_6D_5 = 00$, and $D_2 = 0$. Logic 1 at D_7 represents an active mode set flag. Now port A and port B can be configured as 8-bit input or output ports, and port C can be configured for operation as two independent 4-bit input or output ports. This is done by setting or resetting bits D_4, D_3, D_1, and D_0. Figure 8.20 summarizes the port pins and the functions they can perform in mode 0.

For example, if $80_{16} = 10000000_2$ is written to the control register, the 1 in D_7 activates the mode set flag. Mode 0 operation is selected for all three ports because bits D_6, D_5, and D_2 are logic 0. At the same time, the 0s in D_4, D_3, D_1, and D_0 set up all port lines to work as outputs. This configuration is illustrated in Fig. 8.21(a).

By writing different binary combinations into bit locations D_4, D_3, D_1, and D_0, any one of 16 different mode 0 I/O configurations can be obtained. The control words and I/O setups for the rest of these combinations are shown in Fig. 8.21(b) through (p).

EXAMPLE 8.10

What is the mode and I/O configuration for ports A, B, and C of an 8255A after its control register is loaded with 82_{16}?

Solution

Expressing the control register contents in binary form, we get

$$D_7D_6D_5D_4D_3D_2D_1D_0 = 10000010_2$$

Since D_7 is 1, the modes of operation of the ports are selected by the control word. The three least significant bits of the word configure port B and the lower four bits of port C. They give

$D_0 = 0$ Lower four bits of port C are outputs

$D_1 = 1$ Port B are inputs

$D_2 = 0$ Mode 0 operation for both port B and the lower four bits of port C

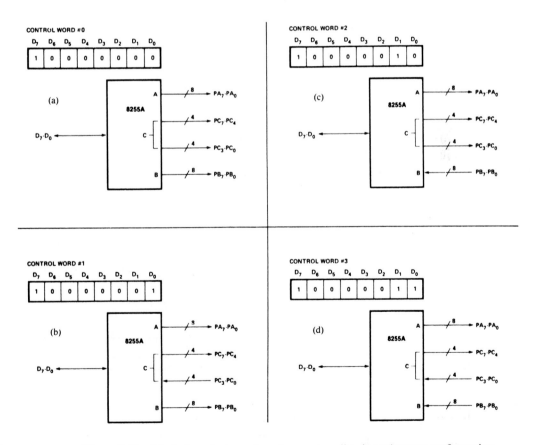

Figure 8.21 Mode 0 control words and corresponding input/output configuration. (Reprinted by permission of Intel Corp., © Intel Corp. 1980)

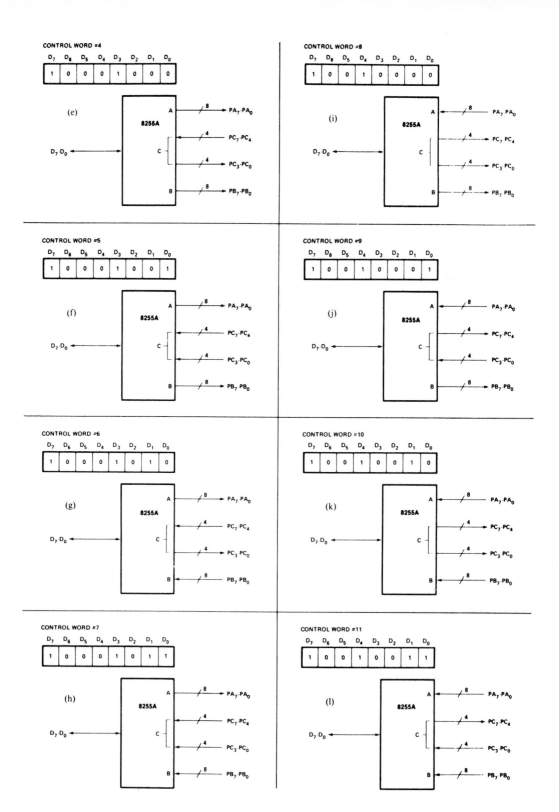

Figure 8.21 (Continued)

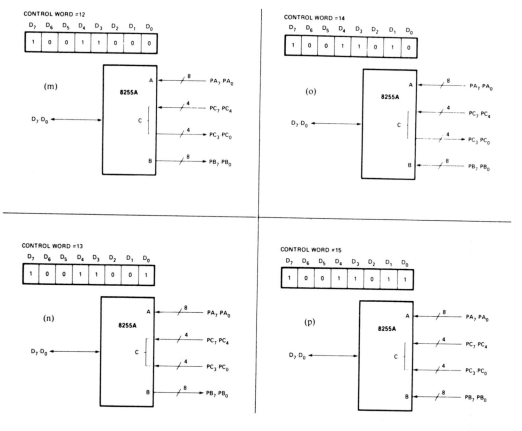

Figure 8.21 (Continued)

The next four bits configure the upper part of port C and port A.

$D_3 = 0$ Upper four bits of port C are outputs

$D_4 = 0$ Port A are outputs

$D_6D_5 = 00$ Mode 0 operation for both port A and the upper part of port C

This mode 0 I/O configuration is shown in Fig. 8.21(c).

Mode 1 operation represents what is known as *strobed I/O*. The ports of the 8255A are put into this mode of operation by setting $D_7 = 1$ to activate the mode set flag and setting $D_6D_5 = 01$ and $D_2 = 1$.

In this way, the A and B ports are configured as two independent *byte-wide I/O ports*, each of which has a *4-bit control/data port* associated with it. The control/

data ports are formed from the lower and upper nibbles of port C, respectively. Figure 8.22 lists the mode 1 functions of each pin at ports A, B, and C.

When configured in this way, data applied to an input port must be strobed in with a signal produced in external hardware. An output port in mode 1 is provided with handshake signals that indicate when new data are available at its outputs and when an external device has read these values.

As an example, let us assume for the moment that the control register of an 8255A is loaded with $D_7D_6D_5D_4D_3D_2D_1D_0 = 10111XXX$. This configures port A as a mode 1 input port. Figure 8.23(a) shows the function of the signal lines for this example. Notice that PA_7 through PA_0 form an 8-bit input port. On the other hand, the function of the upper port C leads are reconfigured to provide the port A control/data lines. The PC_4 line becomes *strobe input* $(\overline{STB}_A)$, which is used to strobe data at PA_7 through PA_0 into the input latch. Moreover, PC_5 becomes *input buffer full* (IBF_A). Logic 1 at this output indicates to external circuitry that a word has already been strobed into the latch.

The third control signal is at PC_3 and is labeled *interrupt request* ($INTR_A$). It switches to logic 1 when $\overline{STB}_A = 1$ making $IBF_A = 1$, and an internal signal *interrupt enable* ($INTE_A$) = 1. $INTE_A$ is set to logic 0 or 1 under software control by using the bit set/reset feature of the 8255A. This feature will be discussed later. Looking at Fig. 8.23(a), we see that logic 1 in $INTE_A$ enables the logic level of IBF_A to the

Pin	MODE 1 IN	MODE 1 OUT
PA_0	IN	OUT
PA_1	IN	OUT
PA_2	IN	OUT
PA_3	IN	OUT
PA_4	IN	OUT
PA_5	IN	OUT
PA_6	IN	OUT
PA_7	IN	OUT
PB_0	IN	OUT
PB_1	IN	OUT
PB_2	IN	OUT
PB_3	IN	OUT
PB_4	IN	OUT
PB_5	IN	OUT
PB_6	IN	OUT
PB_7	IN	OUT
PC_0	$INTR_B$	$INTR_B$
PC_1	IBF_B	$\overline{OBF}_B$
PC_2	$\overline{STB}_B$	$\overline{ACK}_B$
PC_3	$INTR_A$	$INTR_A$
PC_4	$\overline{STB}_A$	I/O
PC_5	IBF_A	I/O
PC_6	I/O	$\overline{ACK}_A$
PC_7	I/O	$\overline{OBF}_A$

Figure 8.22 Mode 1 port pin functions.

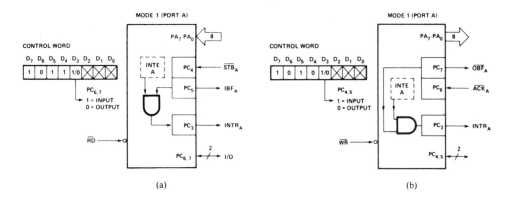

Figure 8.23 (a) Mode 1, port A input configuration. (Reprinted by permission of Intel Corp., © Intel Corp. 1980) (b) Mode 1, port A output configuration. (Reprinted by permission of Intel Corp., © Intel Corp. 1980)

INTR$_A$ output. This signal can be applied to an interrupt input of the MPU to signal it that new data are available at the input port. The corresponding interrupt service routine reads the data, which clears INTR$_A$ and IBF$_A$. The timing diagram in Fig. 8.24(a) summarizes these events for an input port configured in mode 1.

As another example, let us assume that the contents of the control register are changed to $D_7D_6D_5D_4D_3D_2D_1D_0 = 10100XXX$. This I/O configuration is shown in Fig. 8.23(b). Notice that port A is now configured for output operation instead of input operation. PA$_7$ through PA$_0$ are now an 8-bit output port. The control line at PC$_7$ is *output buffer full* ($\overline{OBF}_A$). When data have been written into the output port, $\overline{OBF}_A$ switches to the 0 logic level. In this way, it signals external circuitry that new data are available at the port outputs.

Signal line PC$_6$ becomes acknowledge ($\overline{ACK}_A$), which is an input. An external device reads the data and signals the 8255A that it has accepted the data provided at the output port by switching $\overline{ACK}_A$ to logic 0. When the $\overline{ACK}_A = 0$ is received by the 8255A, it in turn deactivates the $\overline{OBF}_A$ output. The last signal at the control port is output INTR$_A$, which is produced at the PC$_3$ lead. This output is switched to logic 1 when the $\overline{ACK}_A$ input becomes inactive. It is used to signal the MPU with an interrupt that indicates that an external device has accepted the data from the outputs. To produce the INTR$_A$, INTE$_A$ must equal 1. Again the interrupt enable (INTE$_A$) bit must be set to 1 using the bit set/reset feature. The timing diagram in Fig. 8.24(b) summarizes these events for an output port configured in mode 1.

EXAMPLE 8.11

Figure 8.25(a) and (b) show how port B can be configured for mode 1 operation. Describe what happens in Fig. 8.25(a) when the $\overline{STB}_B$ input is pulsed to logic 0. Assume that INTE$_B$ is already set to 1.

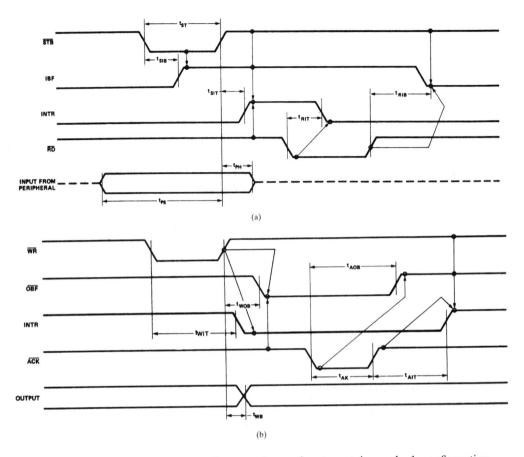

(a)

(b)

Figure 8.24 (a) Timing diagrams for an input port in mode 1 configuration. (b) Timing diagram for an output port in mode 1 configuration. (Reprinted by permission of Intel Corp., © Intel Corp. 1980)

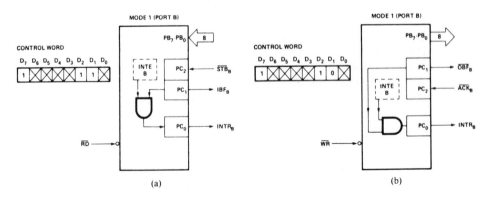

(a)   (b)

Figure 8.25 (a) Mode 1, port B input configuration. (Reprinted by permission of Intel Corp., © Intel Corp. (1980) (b) Mode 1, port B output configuration. (Reprinted by permission of Intel Corp., © Intel Corp. 1980)

Solution

As $\overline{STB}_B$ is pulsed, the byte of data at PB_7 through PB_0 is latched into the port B register. This causes the IBF_B output to switch to 1. Since $INTE_B$ is 1, $INTR_B$ switches to logic 1.

The last mode of operation, mode 2, represents what is known as *strobed bidirectional I/O*. The key difference is that now the port works as either input or output and control signals are provided for both functions. Only port A can be configured to work in this way. The I/O port and control signal pins are shown in Fig. 8.26.

To set up this mode, the control register is set to $D_7D_6D_5D_4D_3D_2D_1D_0 = 11XXXXXX$. The I/O configuration that results is shown in Fig. 8.27. Here we find that PA_7 through PA_0 operate as an *8-bit bidirectional port* instead of a unidirectional port. Its control signals are $\overline{OBF}_A$ at PC_7, $\overline{ACK}_A$ at PC_6, $\overline{STB}_A$ at PC_4, IBF_A at PC_5, and $INTR_A$ at PC_3. Their functions are similar to those already discussed for mode 1. One difference is that $INTR_A$ is produced by either gating $\overline{OBF}_A$ with $INTE_1$ or IBF_A with $INTE_2$.

In our discussion of mode 1, we mentioned that the *bit set/reset* feature could be used to set the INTE bit to logic 0 or 1. This feature also allows the individual

Pin	MODE 2 GROUP A ONLY
PA_0	$\leftrightarrow$
PA_1	$\leftrightarrow$
PA_2	$\leftrightarrow$
PA_3	$\leftrightarrow$
PA_4	$\leftrightarrow$
PA_5	$\leftrightarrow$
PA_6	$\leftrightarrow$
PA_7	$\leftrightarrow$
PB_0	—
PB_1	—
PB_2	—
PB_3	—
PB_4	—
PB_5	—
PB_6	—
PB_7	—
PC_0	I/O or $INTR_B$
PC_1	I/O or $\overline{ACK}_B$ or IBF_B
PC_2	I/O or OBF_B or $\overline{STB}_A$
PC_3	$INTR_A$
PC_4	$\overline{STB}_A$
PC_5	IBF_A
PC_6	$\overline{ACK}_A$
PC_7	$\overline{OBF}_A$

MODE 0 OR MODE 1 ONLY (bracket spanning PB_0–PB_7)

Figure 8.26 Mode 2 port pin functions.

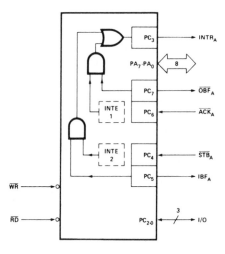

Figure 8.27 Mode 2 I/O configuration. (Reprinted by permission of Intel Corp., © Intel Corp. 1980)

bits of port C to be set or reset. To do this, we write logic 0 to bit D_7 of the control register. This resets the bit set/reset flag. The logic level that is to be latched at a port C line is included as bit D_0 of the control word. This value is latched at the I/O line of port C, which corresponds to the 3-bit code at $D_3D_2D_1$.

The relationship between the set/reset control word and input/output lines is illustrated in Fig. 8.28. For instance, writing $D_7D_6D_5D_4D_3D_2D_1D_0 = 00001111_2$ into the control register of the 8255A selects bit 7 and sets it to 1. Therefore, output PC_7 at port C is switched to the 1 logic level.

EXAMPLE 8.12

The interrupt control flag $INTE_A$ for output port A in mode 1 is controlled by PC_6. Using the set/reset feature of the 8255A, what command code must be written to the control register of the 8255A to set it to enable the control flag?

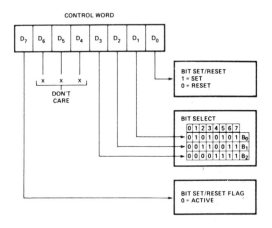

Figure 8.28 Bit set/reset format. (Reprinted by permission of Intel Corp., © Intel Corp. 1980).

Solution

To use the set/reset feature, D_7 must be logic 0. Moreover, $INTE_A$ is to be set; therefore, D_0 must be logic 1. Finally, to select PC_6, the code at bits $D_3 D_2 D_1$ must be 110. The rest of the bits are don't-care states. This gives us the control word as

$$D_7 D_6 D_5 D_4 D_3 D_2 D_1 D_0 = 0XXX1101_2$$

Replacing the don't-care states with the 0 logic level, we get

$$D_7 D_6 D_5 D_4 D_3 D_2 D_1 D_0 = 00001101_2 = 0D_{16}$$

We have just described and given examples of each of the modes of operation that can be assigned to the ports of the 8255A. It is also possible to configure the A and B ports with different modes. For example, Fig. 8.29(a) shows the control word and port configuration of an 8255A set up for bidirectional mode 2 operation of port A and input mode 0 operation of port B. It should also be noted that in all modes, the unused leads of port C can still be used as general purpose inputs or outputs.

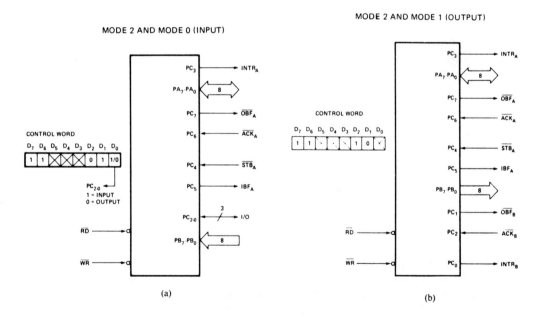

Figure 8.29 (a) Combined mode 2 and mode 0 (input) control word and I/O configuration. (Reprinted by permission of Intel Corp., © Intel Corp. 1980) (b) Combined mode 2 and mode 1 (output) control word and I/O configuration. (Reprinted by permission of Intel Corp., © Intel Corp. 1980)

EXAMPLE 8.13

What control word must be written into the control register of the 8255A so that port A is configured for bidirectional operation and port B is set up with mode 1 outputs?

Solution

To configure the mode of operation of the ports of the 8255A, D_7 must be 1.

$$D_7 = 1$$

Port A is set up for bidirectional operation by making D_6 logic 1. In this case, D_5 through D_3 are don't-care states.

$$D_6 = 1$$

$$D_5D_4D_3 = XXX$$

Mode 1 is selected for port B by logic 1 in bit D_2 and output operation by logic 0 in D_1. Since mode 1 operation has been selected, D_0 is a don't-care state.

$$D_2 = 1$$

$$D_1 = 0$$

$$D_0 = X$$

This gives the control word

$$D_7D_6D_5D_4D_3D_2D_1D_0 = 11XXX10X_2$$

Assuming logic 0 for the don't-care states, we get

$$D_7D_6D_5D_4D_3D_2D_1D_0 = 11000100_2 = C4_{16}$$

This configuration is shown in Figure 8.29(b).

EXAMPLE 8.14

Write the sequence of instructions needed to load the control register of an 8255A with the control word formed in Example 8.13. Assume that the control register resides at address $0F_{16}$ of the I/O address space.

Solution

First we must load AL with $C4_{16}$. This is the value of the control word that is to be written to the control register at address $0F_{16}$. The move instruction used to load AL is

MOV   AL,0C4H

These data are output to the control register with the OUT instruction

OUT   0FH,AL

In this case we have used direct I/O. This is because the I/O address of the control register is less than FF_{16}.

▲ 8.11 8255A IMPLEMENTATION OF PARALLEL INPUT/OUTPUT PORTS

In Section 8.7, we showed how parallel output ports can be implemented for the 8088 and 8086 microcomputer systems using 74F373 octal latches. Even through logic ICs can be used to implement parallel input and output ports, the 8255A PPI, which was introduced in Section 8.10, can be used to design a more versatile I/O interface. This is because its ports can be configured either as inputs or outputs under software control. Here we will show how the 8255A is used to design isolated parallel I/O interfaces for 8088- and 8086-based microcomputers.

The circuit in Fig. 8.30 shows how PPI devices can be connected to the bus of the 8088 to implement parallel input/output ports. This circuit configuration is for a minimum-mode 8088 microcomputer. Here we find a group of eight 8255A devices connected to the data bus. A 74F138 address decoder is used to select one of the devices at a time for input and output data transfers. The ports are located at even-address boundaries. Each of these PPI devices provides up to three byte-wide ports. In the circuit, they are labeled port A, port B, and port C. These ports can be individually configured as inputs or outputs through software. Therefore, this circuit is capable of implementing up to 192 I/O lines.

Let us look more closely at the connection of the 8255As. Starting with the inputs of the 74F138 address decoder, we see that its enable inputs are $\overline{G}_{2B} = A_0$ and $\overline{G}_{2A} = (IO/\overline{M})$. A_0 is logic 0 whenever the 8088 outputs an even address on the bus. Moreover, $IO/\overline{M}$ is switched to logic 1 whenever an I/O bus cycle is in progress. This logic level is inverted and applies logic 0 to the G_{2A} input. For this reason, the decoder is enabled for all I/O bus cycles to an even address.

When the 74F138 decoder is enabled, the code at its A_0 through A_2 inputs causes one of the eight 8255A PPIs to get enabled for operation. Bits A_5 through A_3 of the I/O address are applied to these inputs of the decoder. It responds by switching the output corresponding to this 3-bit code to the 0 logic level. Decoder outputs O_0 through O_7 are applied to the chip select ($\overline{CS}$) inputs of the PPIs. For instance, $A_5A_4A_3 = 000$ switches output O_0 to logic 0. This enables the first 8255A, which is numbered 0 in Fig. 8.30.

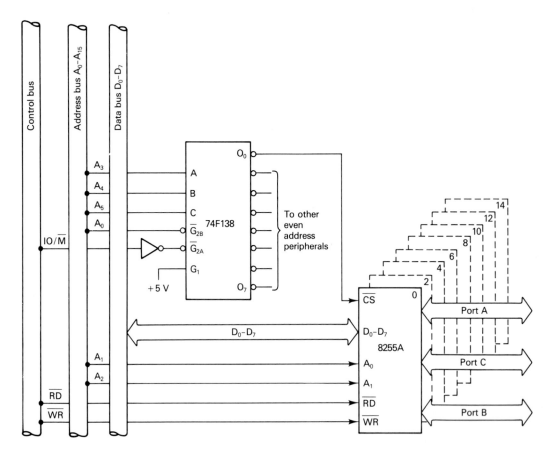

Figure 8.30 8255A parallel I/O ports in an 8088-based microcomputer.

At the same time that the PPI chip is selected, the 2-bit code A_2A_1 at inputs A_1A_0 of the 8255A selects the port for which data are input or output. For example, $A_2A_1 = 00$ indicates that port A is to be accessed. Input/output data transfers take place over data bus lines D_0 through D_7. The timing of these read/write transfers is controlled by signals $\overline{RD}$ and $\overline{WR}$.

EXAMPLE 8.15 ───

What must be the address bus inputs of the circuit in Fig. 8.30 if port C of PPI 14 is to be accessed?

Solution

To enable PPI 14, the 74F138 must be enabled for operation and its O_7 output switched to logic 0. This requires enable input $\overline{G}_{2B} = 0$ and chip select code CBA =

111. This in turn requires from the bus that

$$A_0 = 0 \text{ to enable 74F138}$$

and

$$A_5A_4A_3 = 111 \text{ to select PPI } 14$$

Port C of PPI 14 is selected with $A_1A_0 = 10$, which from the bus requires that

$$A_2A_1 = 10$$

The rest of the address bits are don't-care states.

EXAMPLE 8.16

Assume that in Fig. 8.30, PPI 14 is configured so that port A is an output port, both ports B and C are input ports, and all three ports are set up for mode 0 operation. Write a program that will input the data at ports B and C, find the difference $(C) - (B)$, and output this difference to port A.

Solution

From the circuit diagram in Fig. 8.30, we find that the addresses of the three I/O ports of PPI 14 are

$$\text{Port A address} = 00111000_2 = 38_{16}$$

$$\text{Port B address} = 00111010_2 = 3A_{16}$$

$$\text{Port C address} = 00111100_2 = 3C_{16}$$

The data at ports B and C can be input with the instruction sequence

```
IN    AL,3AH    ;Read port B
MOV   BL,AL     ;Save data from port B
IN    AL,3CH    ;Read port C
```

Now the data from port B are subtracted from the data at port C with the instruction

```
SUB   AL,BL     ;Subtract B from C
```

Finally, the difference is output to port A with the instruction

```
OUT   38H,AL    ;Write to port A
```

A similar circuit that implements parallel input/output ports for a minimum-mode 8086-based microcomputer system is given in Fig. 8.31. Let us now look at the differences between this circuit and the 8088 microcomputer circuit that is shown in Fig. 8.30. In Fig. 8.31, we find that the I/O circuit has two groups of eight 8255A devices, one connected to the lower eight data bus lines, and the other to the upper eight data bus lines. Each of these groups is capable of implementing up to 192 I/O lines to give a total I/O capability of 384 I/O lines.

Each of the groups of 8255As has its own 74F138 I/O address decoder. As in the 8088 microcomputer circuit, the address decoder is used to select one of the devices in a group at a time. The ports in the upper group are connected at odd-address boundaries and those in the lower group are at even-address boundaries. Let us first look more closely at the connection of the upper group of the 8255As. Starting with the inputs of the 74F138 decoder, we see that its $\overline{G_{2B}}$ input is driven by control signal $\overline{BHE}$, the $\overline{G_{2A}}$ input is supplied by control signal $M/\overline{IO}$, and the G_1 input is permanently enabled by fixing it at the 1 logic level. $\overline{BHE}$ is logic 0 whenever the 8086 outputs an odd address on the bus. Moreover, $M/\overline{IO}$ is switched to logic 0 whenever an I/O bus cycle is in progress. In this way, we see that the upper decoder is enabled for I/O bus cycles that access a byte of data at an odd I/O address. Actually, it is also enabled during all word-wide I/O data accesses.

The code on address lines A_3 through A_5 selects one of the eight 8255As for operation. When the upper 74F138 is enabled, the address code applied at the CBA inputs causes the corresponding output to switch to logic 0. This output is used as a chip select ($\overline{CS}$) input to one of the 8255As and enables it for input/output operation. The port that is accessed in the enabled PPI is selected by the code on lines A_1 and A_2 of the I/O address. Finally, the I/O data transfer takes place over data bus lines D_8 through D_{15}.

The connection of the lower group of PPIs in Fig. 8.31 is similar to that shown in Fig. 8.30. The only difference is that no inverter is required in the connection of the $M/\overline{IO}$ signal to the $\overline{G_{2A}}$ input of the 74F138 decoder. This bank is enabled for all byte-wide data accesses to an even address as well as for all word-wide data accesses.

▲ 8.12 MEMORY-MAPPED INPUT/OUTPUT

The *memory-mapped I/O interface* of a minimum-mode 8088 system is essentially the same as that employed in the accumulator I/O circuit of Fig. 8.30. Figure 8.32 shows the equivalent memory-mapped circuit. Ports are still selected by an address on the address bus and data are transferred between the 8088 and I/O device over the data bus. One difference is that now the full 20-bit address is available for addressing I/O. Therefore, memory-mapped I/O devices can reside anywhere in the 1M address space of the 8088.

Another difference is that during I/O operations memory read and write bus cycles are initiated instead of I/O bus cycles. This is because we are using memory instructions, not input/output instructions, to perform the data transfers. Furthermore, $IO/\overline{M}$ stays at the 0 logic level throughout the bus cycle. This indicates that a memory operation is in progress instead of an I/O operation.

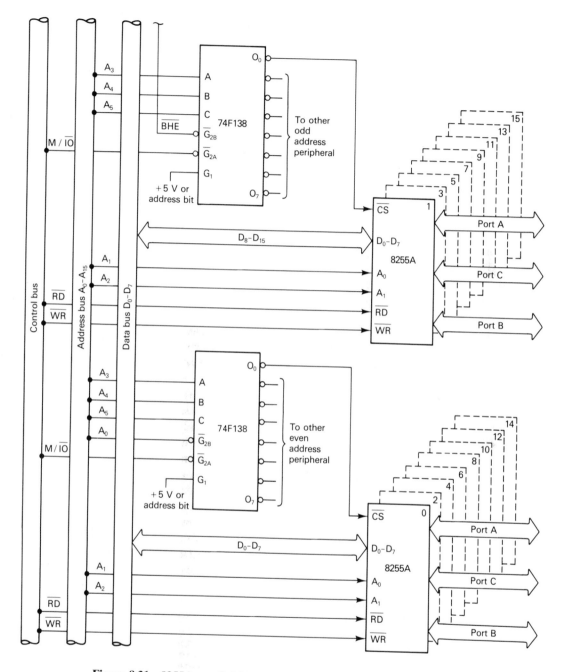

Figure 8.31 8255A parallel I/O ports at even- and odd-address boundaries in an 8086 based microcomputer.

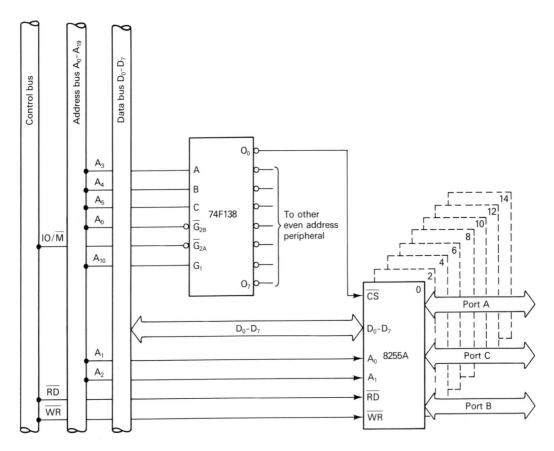

Figure 8.32 Memory-mapped 8255A I/O ports in an 8088 microcomputer.

Since memory-mapped I/O devices reside in the memory address space and are accessed with read and write cycles, additional I/O address latch, address buffer, data bus transceiver, and address decoder circuitry is not needed. The circuitry provided for the memory interface can be used to access memory-mapped ports.

The key difference between the circuits in Figs. 8.30 and 8.32 is that $IO/\overline{M}$ is no longer inverted. Instead, it is applied directly to the $\overline{G}_{2A}$ input of the decoder. Another difference is that the G_1 input of the decoder is not fixed at the 1 logic level; instead, it is supplied by address line A_{10}. The I/O circuits are accessed whenever $IO/\overline{M}$ is equal to logic 0, A_{10} is equal to logic 1, and A_0 equals 0.

EXAMPLE 8.17 ⎯⎯⎯⎯⎯⎯⎯⎯⎯⎯⎯⎯⎯⎯⎯⎯⎯⎯⎯⎯⎯⎯⎯⎯⎯⎯⎯

Which I/O port in Fig. 8.32 is selected for operation when the memory address output on the bus is 00402_{16}?

Solution

We begin by converting the address to binary form. This gives

$$A_{19} \ldots A_1 A_0 = 00000000010000000010_2$$

In this address, bits $A_{10} = 1$ and $A_0 = 0$. Therefore, the 74F138 address decoder is enabled whenever $IO/\overline{M} = 0$, which is the case during memory operations.

A memory-mapped I/O operation takes place at the port selected by $A_5 A_4 A_3 = 000$. This input code switches decoder output O_0 to logic 0 and chip selects PPI 0 for operation. That is

$$A_5 A_4 A_3 = 000$$

makes

$$O_0 = 0$$

and selects PPI 0.

The address bits applied to the port select inputs of the PPI are $A_2 A_1 = 01$. These inputs cause port B to be accessed. Thus the address 00402_{16} selects port B on PPI 0 for memory mapped I/O.

EXAMPLE 8.18

Write the sequence of instructions needed to initialize the control register of PPI 0 in the circuit of Fig. 8.32 so that port A is an output port, ports B and C are input ports, and all three ports are configured for mode 0 operation.

Solution

Referring to Fig. 8.19, we find that the control byte required to provide this configuration is

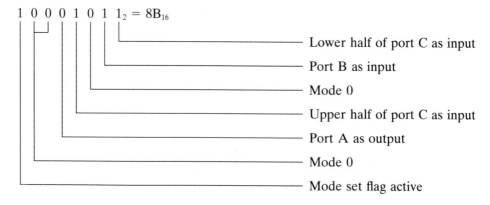

$$1 \; 0 \; 0 \; 0 \; 1 \; 0 \; 1 \; 1_2 = 8B_{16}$$

— Lower half of port C as input
— Port B as input
— Mode 0
— Upper half of port C as input
— Port A as output
— Mode 0
— Mode set flag active

From the circuit diagram, the memory address of the control register for PPI 0 is found to be $0000000010000000110_2 = 00406_{16}$. Since PPI 0 is memory mapped, the following move instructions can be used to initialize the control register.

```
MOV   AX,0        ;Create data segment at 00000₁₆
MOV   DS,AX
MOV   AL,08BH     ;Load AL with control byte
MOV   [406H],AL   ;Write control byte to PPI 0 control register
```

EXAMPLE 8.19

Assume that PPI 0 in Fig. 8.32 is configured as described in Example 8.18. Write a program that will input the contents of ports B and C, AND them together, and output the results to port A.

Solution

From the circuit diagram, we find that the addresses of the three I/O ports on PPI 0 are

$$\text{Port A address} = 00400_{16}$$

$$\text{Port B address} = 00402_{16}$$

$$\text{Port C address} = 00404_{16}$$

Now we set up a data segment at 00000_{16} and input the data from ports B and C.

```
MOV   AX,0        ;Create data segment at 00000₁₆
MOV   DS,AX
MOV   BL,[402H]   ;Read port B
MOV   AL,[404H]   ;Read port C
```

Next the contents of AL and BL must be ANDed and the result output to port A. This can be done with the instructions

```
AND   AL,BL       ;AND data at ports B and C
MOV   [400H],AL   ;Write to port A
```

Figure 8.33 shows a memory-mapped parallel I/O interface circuit for an 8086-based microcomputer system. Just like the accumulator-mapped circuit in Fig. 8.31, this circuit is capable of implementing up to 384 parallel I/O lines.

▲ 8.13 8253 PROGRAMMABLE INTERVAL TIMER

The 8253 is an LSI peripheral designed to permit easy implementation of *timer* and *counter functions* in a microcomputer system. It contains three independent 16-bit counters that can be programmed to operate in a variety of ways to implement

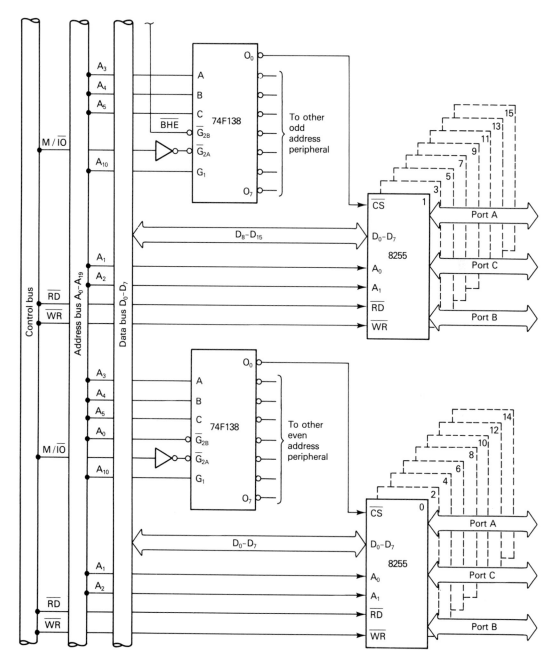

Figure 8.33 Memory-mapped 8255A I/O ports in an 8086 microcomputer.

timing functions. For instance, they can be set up to work as a one-shot pulse generator, square-wave generator, or a rate generator.

Block Diagram of the 8253

Let us begin our study of the 8253 by looking at the signal interfaces shown in its block diagram of Fig. 8.34(a). The actual pin location for each of these signals is given in Fig. 8.34(b). In a microcomputer system, the 8253 is treated as a peripheral device. Moreover, it can be memory mapped into the memory address space or

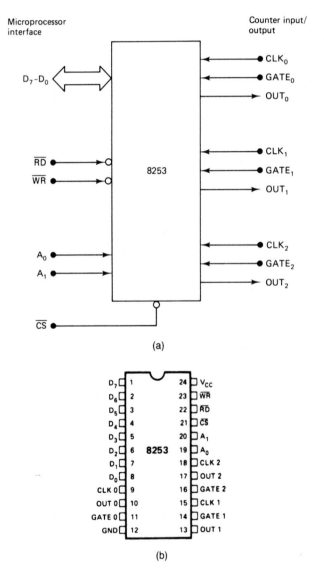

(a)

(b)

Figure 8.34 (a) Block diagram of the 8253 interval timer. (b) Pin layout. (Reprinted by permission of Intel Corp., © Intel Corp. 1987)

I/O mapped into the I/O address space. The microprocessor interface of the 8253 allows the MPU to read from or write to its internal registers. In this way, it can be configured in various modes of operation.

Now we will look at the signals of the microprocessor interface. The microprocessor interface includes an 8-bit bidirectional data bus, D_0 through D_7. It is over these lines that data are transferred between the MPU and 8253. Register address inputs A_0 and A_1 are used to select the register to be accessed, and control signals read ($\overline{RD}$) and write ($\overline{WR}$) indicate whether it is to be read from or written into, respectively. A chip select ($\overline{CS}$) input is also provided to enable the 8253's microprocessor interface. This input allows the designer to locate the device at a specific memory or I/O address.

At the other side of the block in Fig. 8.34(a), we find three signals for each counter. For instance, counter 0 has two inputs that are labeled CLK_0 and $GATE_0$. Pulses applied to the clock input are used to decrement counter 0. The gate input is used to enable or disable the counter. $GATE_0$ must be switched to logic 1 to enable counter 0 for operation. For example, in the square-wave mode of operation, the counter is to run continuously; therefore, $GATE_0$ is fixed at the 1 logic level and a continuous clock signal is applied to CLK_0. The 8253 is rated for a maximum clock frequency of 3 MHz. Counter 0 also has an output line that is labeled OUT_0. The counter produces either a clock or a pulse at OUT_0, depending on the mode of operation selected. For instance, when configured for the square-wave mode of operation, this output is a clock signal.

Architecture of the 8253

The internal architecture of the 8253 is shown in Fig. 8.35. Here we find the *data bus buffer, read/write logic, control word register,* and three *counters.* The data bus buffer and read/write control logic represent the microprocessor interface we just described.

The control word register section actually contains three 8-bit registers that are used to configure the operation of counters 0, 1, and 2. The format of a *control word* is shown in Fig. 8.36. Here we find that the two most significant bits are a code that assigns the control word to a counter. For instance, making these bits 01 selects counter 1. Bits D_1 through D_3 are a 3-bit mode select code, $M_2M_1M_0$, that selects one of six modes of counter operation. The least significant bit D_0 is labeled BCD and selects either binary or BCD mode of counting. For instance, if this bit is set to logic 0, the counter acts as a 16-bit binary counter. Finally, the 2-bit code RL_1RL_0 is used to set the sequence in which bytes are read from or loaded into the 16-bit count registers.

EXAMPLE 8.20

An 8253 receives the control word 10010000_2 over the bus. What configuration is set up for the timer?

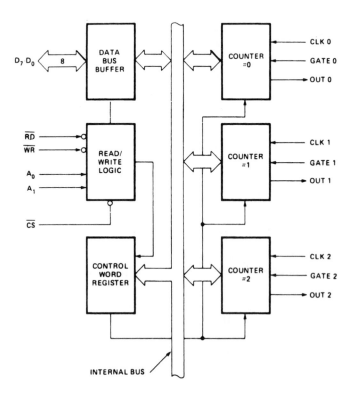

Figure 8.35 Internal architecture of the 8253. (Reprinted by permission of Intel Corp., © Intel Corp. 1987)

Solution

Since the SC bits are 10, the rest of the bits are for setting up the configuration of counter 2. Following the format in Fig. 8.36, we find that 01 in the RL bits sets counter 2 for the read/load sequence identified as the least significant byte only. This means that the next write operation performed to counter 2 will load the data into the least significant byte of its count register. Next the mode code is 000 and this selects mode 0 operation for this counter. The last bit, BCD, is also set to 0 and selects binary counting.

The three counters shown in Fig. 8.35 are each 16 bits in length and operate as *down counters*. That is, when enabled by an active gate input, the clock decrements the count. Each counter contains a 16-bit *count register* that must be loaded as part of the initialization cycle. The value held in the count register can be read at any time through software.

To read from or write to the counters of the 8253 or load its control word register, the microprocessor needs to execute instructions. Figure 8.37 shows the bus control information needed to access each register. For example, to write to

Control Word Format

D7	D6	D5	D4	D3	D2	D1	D0
SC1	SC0	RL1	RL0	M2	M1	M0	BCD

Definition Of Control

SC—SELECT COUNTER:

SC1	SC0	
0	0	Select Counter 0
0	1	Select Counter 1
1	0	Select Counter 2
1	1	Illegal

RL—READ/LOAD:

RL1	RL0	
0	0	Counter Latching operation (see READ/WRITE Procedure Section).
1	0	Read/Load most significant byte only.
0	1	Read/Load least significant byte only.
1	1	Read/Load least significant byte first, then most significant byte.

M—MODE:

M2	M1	M0	
0	0	0	Mode 0
0	0	1	Mode 1
X	1	0	Mode 2
X	1	1	Mode 3
1	0	0	Mode 4
1	0	1	Mode 5

BCD:

0	Binary Counter 16-Bits
1	Binary Coded Decimal (BCD) Counter (4 Decades)

Figure 8.36 Control word format for the 8253. (Reprinted by permission of Intel Corp., © Intel Corp. 1987)

$\overline{CS}$	$\overline{RD}$	$\overline{WR}$	A_1	A_0	
0	1	0	0	0	Load Counter No. 0
0	1	0	0	1	Load Counter No. 1
0	1	0	1	0	Load Counter No. 2
0	1	0	1	1	Write Mode Word
0	0	1	0	0	Read Counter No. 0
0	0	1	0	1	Read Counter No. 1
0	0	1	1	0	Read Counter No. 2
0	0	1	1	1	No-Operation 3-State
1	X	X	X	X	Disable 3-State
0	1	1	X	X	No-Operation 3-State

Figure 8.37 Accessing the registers of the 8253. (Reprinted by permission of Intel Corp., © Intel Corp. 1987)

the control register, the register address lines must be $A_1A_0 = 11$ and the control lines must be $\overline{WR} = 0$, $\overline{RD} = 1$, and $\overline{CS} = 0$.

EXAMPLE 8.21

Write an instruction sequence to set up the three counters of the 8253 in Fig. 8.38 as follows:

Counter 0: Binary counter operating in mode 0 with an initial value of 1234H.
Counter 1: BCD counter operating in mode 2 with an initial value of 100H.
Counter 2: Binary counter operating in mode 4 with initial value of 1FFFH.

Solution

First we need to determine the base address of the 8253. The base address, which is also the address of counter 0, is determined with A_1A_0 set to 00. In Fig. 8.38 we find that to select the 8253, $\overline{CS}$ must be logic 0. This requires that

$$A_{15}A_{14} \ldots A_7A_6A_5 \ldots A_2 = 00000000010000_2$$

Combining this part of the address with the 00 at A_1A_0, gives the base address as

$$0000000001000000_2 = 40H$$

Since the base address of the 8253 is 40H, and to select the mode register requires $A_1A_0 = 11$, therefore its address is 43H. Similarly, the three counters 0, 1, and 2 are at addresses 40H, 41H, and 42H, respectively. Let us first determine the mode words for the three counters. Following the bit definitions in Fig. 8.36, we get

$$\text{Mode word for counter } 0 = 00110000_2 = 30_{16}$$

$$\text{Mode word for counter } 1 = 01110101_2 = 55_{16}$$

$$\text{Mode word for counter } 2 = 10111000_2 = B8_{16}$$

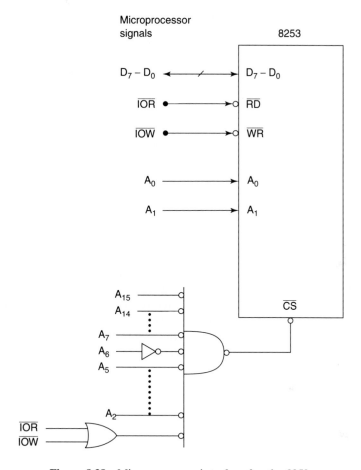

Microprocessor signals

8253

$D_7 - D_0$

$D_7 - D_0$

$\overline{IOR}$ $\overline{RD}$

$\overline{IOW}$ $\overline{WR}$

A_0 A_0

A_1 A_1

A_{15}

A_{14}

A_7

A_6

A_5

A_2

$\overline{CS}$

$\overline{IOR}$

$\overline{IOW}$

Figure 8.38 Microprocessor interface for the 8253.

The following instruction sequence can be used to set up the 8253 with the modes and counts:

```
MOV    AL,30H      ;Set up counter 0 mode
OUT    43H,AL
MOV    AL,55H      ;Set up counter 1 mode
OUT    43H,AL
MOV    AL,0B8H     ;Set up counter 2 mode
OUT    43H,AL
MOV    AL,34H      ;Load counter 0
OUT    40H,AL
MOV    AL,12H
OUT    40H,AL
MOV    AL,00H      ;Load counter 1
OUT    41,AL
MOV    AL,01H
OUT    41,AL
```

Sec. 8.13   8253 Programmable Interval Timer

481

```
MOV   AL,0FFH    ;Load counter 2
OUT   42,AL
MOV   AL,1FH
OUT   42,AL
```

Earlier we pointed out that the contents of a count register can be read at any time. Let us now look at how this is done in software. One approach is to simply read the contents of the corresponding register with an input instruction. In Fig. 8.37 we see that to read the contents of count register 0 the control inputs must be $\overline{CS} = 0$, $\overline{RD} = 0$, and $\overline{WR} = 1$, and the register address code must be $A_1A_0 = 00$. To ensure that a valid count is read out of count register 0, the counter must be inhibited before the read operation takes place. The easiest way to do this is to switch the $GATE_0$ input to logic 0 before performing the read operation. The count is read as two separate bytes, low byte first followed by the high byte.

The contents of the count registers can also be read without first inhibiting the counter. That is, the count can be read on the fly. To do this in software, a command must first be issued to the mode register to capture the current value of the counter into a temporary storage register. In Fig. 8.36, we find that setting bits D_5 and D_4 of the mode byte to 00 specifies the latch mode of operation. Once this mode byte has been written to the 8253, the contents of the temporary storage register for the counter can be read just as before.

EXAMPLE 8.22

Write an instruction sequence to read the contents of counter 2 on the fly. The count is to be loaded into the AX register. Assume that the 8253 is located at I/O address 40H.

Solution

First, we latch the contents of counter 2 and then this value is read from the temporary storage register. This is done with the following sequence of instructions:

```
MOV   AL,1000XXXXB   ;Latch counter 2,
                     ;XXXX must be as per the mode and counter type
OUT   43H,AL
IN    AL,42H         ;Read the low byte
MOV   BL,AL
IN    AL,42H         ;Read the high byte
MOV   AH,AL
MOV   AL,BL          ;(AX) = counter 2 value
```

Operating Modes of 8253 Counters

As indicated earlier, each of the 8253's counters can be configured to operate in one of six modes. Figure 8.39 shows waveforms that summarize operation for

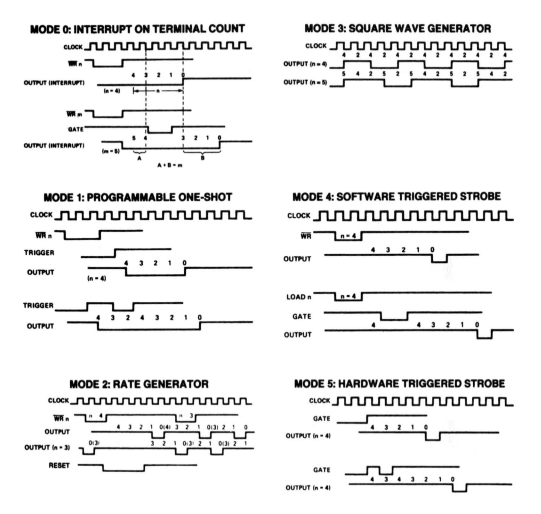

Figure 8.39 Operating modes of the 8253. (Reprinted by permission of Intel Corp., © Intel Corp. 1987)

each mode. Notice that mode 0 operation is known as interrupt on terminal count and mode 1 is called programmable one-shot. The GATE input of a counter takes on different functions, depending on which mode of operation is selected. The effect of the gate input is summarized in Fig. 8.40. For instance, in mode 0, GATE disables counting when set to logic 0 and enables counting when set to 1. Let us now discuss each of these modes of operation in more detail.

The *interrupt on terminal count* mode of operation is used to generate an interrupt to the microprocessor after a certain interval of time has elapsed. As shown in the waveforms for mode 0 operation in Fig. 8.39, a count of 4 is written into the count register synchronously with the pulse at $\overline{WR}$. After the write operation is complete, the count is decremeted by one for each clock pulse. When the count reaches 0, the terminal count, a 0-to-1 transition occurs at OUTPUT. This signal can be used as the interrupt input to the microprocessor.

Signal Status Modes	Low Or Going Low	Rising	High
0	Disables counting	—	Enables counting
1	—	1) Initiates counting 2) Resets output after next clock	—
2	1) Disables counting 2) Sets output immediately high	1) Reloads counter 2) Initiates counting	Enables counting
3	1) Disables counting 2) Sets output immediately high	1) Reloads counter 2) Initiates counting	Enables counting
4	Disables counting	—	Enables counting
5	—	Initiates counting	—

Figure 8.40 Effect of the GATE input for each mode. (Reprinted by permission of Intel Corp., © Intel Corp. 1987)

Earlier we found in Fig. 8.40 that GATE must be at logic 1 to enable the counter for interrupt on terminal count mode of operation. Figure 8.39 also shows waveforms for the case in which GATE is switched to logic 0. Here we see that the value of the count is 4 when GATE is switched to logic 0. It holds at this value until GATE returns to 1.

EXAMPLE 8.23

The counter of Fig. 8.41 is programmed to operate in mode 0. Assuming that the decimal value 100 is written into the counter, compute the time delay (T_D) that occurs until the positive transition takes place at the counter 0 output. Assume the relationship between the GATE and the CLK signal as shown in the figure.

Solution

Once loaded, counter 0 needs to decrement down for 100 pulses at the clock input. During this period, the counter is disabled by logic 0 at the GATE input for 2 clock periods. Therefore, the time delay is calculated as

$$T_D = (2 + 100)(T_{CLK0})$$
$$= (2 + 100)(1/1.19318) \ \mu s$$
$$= 85.5 \ \mu s$$

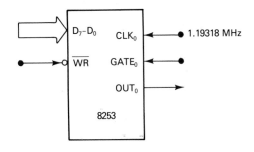

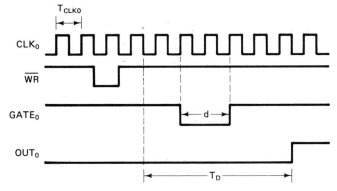

Figure 8.41 Mode 0 configuration.

Mode 1 operation implements what is known as a *programmable one-shot*. As shown in Fig. 8.39, when set for this mode of operation, the counter produces a single pulse at its output. The waveforms show that an initial count, which in this example is the number 4, is written into the counter synchronous with a pulse at $\overline{WR}$. When GATE, called TRIGGER in the waveshapes, switches from logic 0 to 1, OUTPUT switches to logic 0 on the next pulse at CLOCK and the count begins to decrement with each successive clock pulse. The pulse is completed as OUTPUT returns to logic 1 when the terminal count, which is zero, is reached. In this way, we see that the duration of the pulse is determined by the value loaded into the counter.

The pulse generator produced with an 8253 counter is what is called a *retriggerable one-shot*. By retriggerable we mean that, if after an output pulse has been started another rising edge is experienced at TRIGGER, the count is reloaded and the pulse width is extended by restarting the count operation. The lower one-shot waveform in Fig. 8.39 shows this type of operation. Notice that after the count is decremented to 2, a second rising edge occurs at TRIGGER. This edge reloads the value 4 into the counter to extend the pulse width to 7 clock cycles.

EXAMPLE 8.24

Counter 1 of an 8253 is programmed to operate in mode 1 and is loaded with the decimal value 10. The gate and clock inputs are as shown in Fig. 8.42. How long is the output pulse?

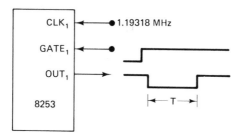

Figure 8.42 Mode 1 configuration.

Solution

The GATE input in Fig. 8.42 shows that the counter is operated as a nonretriggerable one-shot. Therefore, the pulse width is given by

$$T = (\text{counter contents}) \times (\text{clock period})$$

$$= 10 \, 1/1.19318 \, \text{MHz}$$

$$= 8.38 \, \mu s$$

When set for mode 2, *rate generator* operation, the counter within the 8253 is set to operate as a divide-by-N counter. Here N stands for the value of the count loaded into the counter. Figure 8.43 shows counter 1 of an 8253 set up in this way. Notice that the gate input is fixed at the 1 logic level. As shown in the table of Fig. 8.40, this enables counting operation. Looking at the waveforms for mode 2 operation in Fig. 8.39, we see that OUTPUT is at logic 1 until the count decrements to 1. Then the output switches to the active 0 logic level for just one clock pulse width. In this way, we see that there is one clock pulse at the output for every N clock pulses at the input. This is why it is called a divide-by-N counter.

EXAMPLE 8.25

Counter 1 of the 8253, as shown in Fig. 8.43, is programmed to operate in mode 2 and is loaded with the decimal number 18. Describe the signal produced at OUT_1.

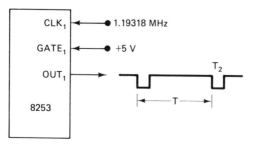

Figure 8.43 Mode 2 configuration.

Solution

In mode 2 the output goes low for one period of the input clock after the counter contents decrement to zero. Therefore,

$$T_2 = 1/1.19318 \text{ MHz} = 838 \text{ ns}$$

and

$$T = 18 \times T_2 = 15.094 \text{ } \mu s$$

Mode 3 sets the counter of the 8253 to operate as a *square-wave rate generator.* In this mode, the output of the counter is a square wave with 50% duty cycle whenever the counter is loaded with an even number. That is, the output is at the 1 logic level for exactly the same amount of time that it is at the 0 logic level. As shown in Fig. 8.39, all transitions of the output take place with respect to the negative edge of the input clock. The period of the symmetrical square wave at the output equals the number loaded into the counter multiplied by the period of the input clock.

If an odd number (N) is loaded into the counter instead of an even number, the time for which the output is high depends on $(N + 1)/2$, and the time for which the output is low depends on $(N - 1)/2$.

EXAMPLE 8.26

The counter in Fig. 8.44 is programmed to operate in mode 3 and is loaded with the decimal value 15. Determine the characteristics of the square wave at OUT_1.

Solution

$$T_{CLK1} = 1/1.19318 \text{ MHz} = 838 \text{ ns}$$

$$T_1 = T_{CLK1}(N + 1)/2 = 838 \text{ ns} \times [(15 + 1)/2]$$

$$= 6.704 \text{ } \mu s$$

$$T_2 = T_{CLK1}(N - 1)/2 = 838 \text{ ns} \times [(15 - 1)/2]$$

$$= 5.866 \text{ } \mu s$$

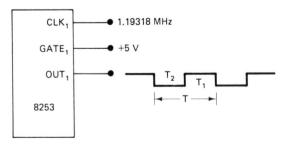

Figure 8.44 Mode 3 configuration.

$$T = T_1 + T_2 = 6.704 \ \mu s + 5.866 \ \mu s$$

$$= 12.57 \ \mu s$$

Selecting mode 4 operation for a counter configures the counter to work as a *software triggered strobed counter*. When in this mode, the counter automatically begins to decrement immediately upon loading with its initial value through software. Again, it decrements at a rate set by the clock input signal. The moment the terminal count is reached, the counter generates a single strobe pulse with duration equal to one clock pulse at its output. This pulse can be used to perform a timed operation. Figure 8.39 shows waveforms illustrating this mode of operation initiated by writing the value 4 into a counter. Moreover, in the table of Fig. 8.40, we find that the gate input needs to be at logic 1 for the counter to operate.

This mode of operation can be used to implement a long-duration interval timer or a free-running timer. In either application, the strobe at the output can be used as an interrupt input to a microprocessor. In response to this pulse, an interrupt service routine can be used to reload the timer and restart the timing cycle. Frequently, the service routine also counts the strobes as they come in by decrementing the contents of a register. Software can test the value in this register to determine if the timer has timed out a certain number of times, for instance, to determine if the contents of the register have decremented to zero. When it reaches zero, a specific operation, such as a jump or call, can be initiated. In this way, we see that software has been used to extend the interval of time at which a function occurs beyond the maximum duration of the 16-bit counter within the 8253.

EXAMPLE 8.27

Counter 1 of Fig. 8.45 is programmed to operate in mode 4. What value must be loaded into the counter to produce a strobe signal 10 μs after the counter is loaded?

Solution

The strobe pulse occurs after counting down the counter to zero. The number of input clock periods required for a period of 10 μs is given by

$$N = T/TCLK$$

$$= 10 \ \mu s/(1/1.19318 \ MHz)$$

$$= 12_{10} = C_{16} = 00001100_2$$

Thus the counter should be loaded with the number $0C_{16}$ to produce a strobe pulse 10 μs after loading.

The last mode of 8253 counter operation, mode 5, is called the *hardware triggered strobe*. This mode is similar to mode 4 except that now counting is initiated

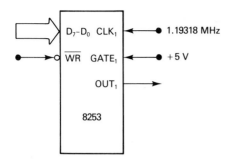

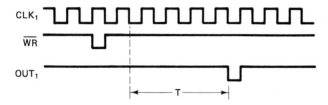

Figure 8.45 Mode 4 configuration.

by a signal at the gate input. That is, it is hardware triggered instead of software triggered. As shown in the waveforms of Fig. 8.39 and the table of Fig. 8.40, a rising edge at GATE starts the countdown process. Just as for software triggered strobed operation, the strobe pulse is output after the count decrements to zero.

▲ 8.14 8237A PROGRAMMABLE DIRECT MEMORY ACCESS CONTROLLER

The 8237A is the LSI controller IC that is widely used to implement the *direct memory access* (DMA) function in 8088- and 8086-based microcomputer systems. DMA capability permits devices, such as peripherals, to perform high-speed data transfers between either two sections of memory or between memory and an I/O device. In a microcomputer system, the memory or I/O bus cycles initiated as part of a DMA transfer are not performed by the MPU; instead, they are performed by a device known as a *DMA controller*, such as the 8237A. DMA mode of operation is frequently used when blocks or packets of data are to be transferred. For instance, disk controllers, local area network controllers, and communication controllers are devices that normally process data as blocks or packets. A single 8237A supports up to four peripheral devices for DMA operation.

Microprocessor Interface of the 8237A

A block diagram that shows the interface signals of the 8237A DMA controller is given in Fig. 8.46(a). The pin layout in Fig. 8.46(b) identifies the pins at which these signals are available. Let us now look briefly at the operation of the microprocessor interface of the 8237A.

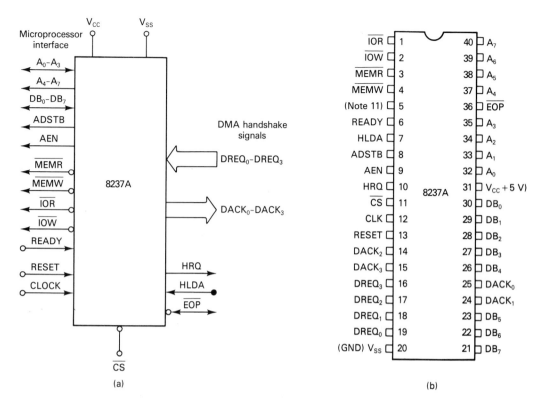

Figure 8.46 (a) Block diagram of the 8237A DMA controller. (b) Pin layout. (Reprinted by permission of Intel Corp., © Intel Corp. 1987)

In a microcomputer system, the 8237A acts as a peripheral controller device and its operation must be initialized through software. This is done by reading from or writing to the bits of its internal registers. These data transfers take place through its microprocessor interface. Figure 8.47 shows how the 8088 connects to the 8237A's microprocessor interface.

Whenever the 8237A is not in use by a peripheral device for DMA operation, it is in a state known as the *idle state*. When in this state, the microprocessor can issue commands to the DMA controller and read from or write to its internal registers. Data bus lines DB_0 through DB_7 are the path over which these data transfers take place. Which register is accessed is determined by a 4-bit register address that is applied to address inputs A_0 through A_3. As shown in Fig. 8.47 these inputs are directly supplied by address bits A_0 through A_3 of the microprocessor.

During the data transfer bus cycle, other bits of the address are decoded in external circuitry to produce a chip select ($\overline{CS}$) input for the 8237A. When in the idle state, the 8237A continuously samples this input, waiting for it to become active. Logic 0 at this input enables the microprocessor interface. The microprocessor tells the 8237A whether an input or output bus cycle is in progress with the signal

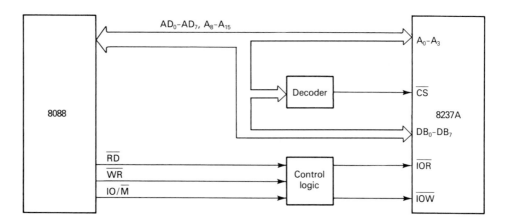

Figure 8.47 Microprocessor interface.

$\overline{\text{IOR}}$ or $\overline{\text{IOW}}$, respectively. In this way, we see that the 8237A is intended to be mapped into the I/O address space of the 8088 microcomputer.

DMA Interface of the 8237A

Now that we have described how a microprocessor talks to the registers of the 8237A, let us continue by looking at how peripheral devices initiate DMA service. The 8237A contains four independent DMA channels, channels 0 through 3. Typically, each of these channels is dedicated to a specific peripheral device. In Fig. 8.48, we see that the device has four DMA request inputs, denoted as DREQ_0 through DREQ_3. These DREQ inputs correspond to channels 0 through 3, respectively. In the idle state, the 8237A continuously tests these inputs to see if one is active. When a peripheral device wants to perform DMA operations, it makes a request for service at its DREQ input by switching it to its active state.

In response to the DMA request, the DMA controller switches the hold request (HRQ) output to logic 1. Normally, this output is supplied to the HOLD input of the 8088 and signals the microprocessor that the DMA controller needs to take control of the system bus. When the 8088 is ready to give up control of the bus, it puts its bus signals into the high-impedance state and signals this fact to the 8237A by switching the HLDA (hold acknowledge) output to logic 1. HLDA of the 8088 is applied to the HLDA input of the 8237A and signals that the system bus is now available for use by the DMA controller.

The 8237A tells the requesting peripheral device that it is ready by outputting a DMA acknowledge (DACK) signal. Notice in Fig. 8.45 that each of the four DMA request inputs, DREQ_0 through DREQ_3, has a corresponding DMA acknowledge output, DACK_0 through DACK_3. Once this DMA request/acknowledge handshake sequence is complete, the peripheral device gets direct access to the system bus and memory under control of the 8237A.

During DMA bus cycles, the system bus is driven by the DMA controller, not the MPU. The 8237A generates the address and all control signals needed to

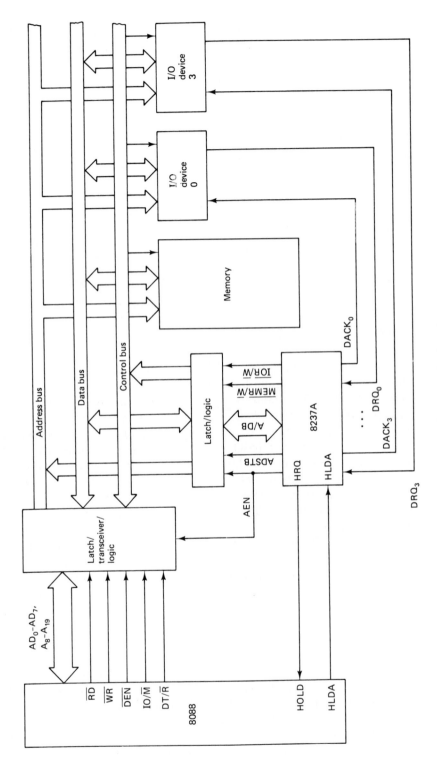

Figure 8.48 DMA interface.

perform the memory or I/O data transfers. At the beginning of all DMA bus cycles, a 16-bit address is output on lines A_0 through A_7 and DB_0 through DB_7. The upper eight bits of the address, which are available on the data bus lines, appear at the same time that address strobe (ADSTB) becomes active. Thus ADSTB is intended to be used to strobe the most significant byte of the address into an external address latch. This 16-bit address gives the 8237A the ability to directly address up to 64K bytes of storage locations. The address enable (AEN) output signal is active during the complete DMA bus cycle and can be used to both enable the address latch and disable other devices connected to the bus.

Let us assume for now that an I/O peripheral device is to transfer data to memory. That is, the I/O device wants to write data to memory. In this case, the 8237A uses the $\overline{\text{IOR}}$ output to signal the I/O device to put the data onto data bus lines DB_0 through DB_7. At the same time, it asserts $\overline{\text{MEMW}}$ to signal that the data available on the bus are to be written into memory. In this case, the data are transferred directly from the I/O device to memory and do not go through the 8237A.

In a similar way, DMA transfers of data can take place from memory to an I/O device. In this case, the I/O device reads data from memory and outputs it to the peripheral. For this data transfer, the 8237A activates the $\overline{\text{MEMR}}$ and $\overline{\text{IOW}}$ control signals.

The 8237A performs both the memory-to-I/O and I/O-to-memory DMA bus cycles in just four clock periods. The duration of these clock periods is determined by the frequency of the clock signal applied to the CLOCK input. For instance, at 5 MHz the clock period is 200 ns and the bus cycle takes 800 ns.

The 8237A is also capable of performing memory-to-memory DMA transfers. In such a data transfer, both the $\overline{\text{MEMR}}$ and $\overline{\text{MEMW}}$ signals are utilized. Unlike the I/O-to-memory operation, this memory-to-memory data transfer takes eight clock cycles. This is because it is actually performed as a separate four-clock read bus cycle from the source memory location to a temporary register within the 8237A and then another four-clock write bus cycle from the temporary register to the destination memory location. At 5 MHz, a memory-to-memory DMA cycle takes 1.6 μs.

The READY input is used to accommodate for the slow memory of I/O devices. READY must go active, logic 1, before the 8237A will complete a memory or I/O bus cycle. As long as READY is at logic 0, wait states are inserted to extend the duration of the current bus cycle.

Internal Architecture of the 8237A

Figure 8.49 is a block diagram of the internal architecture of the 8237A DMA controller. Here we find the following functional blocks: the timing and control, the priority encoder and rotating priority logic, the command control, and 12 different types of registers. Let us now look briefly at the functions performed by each of these sections of circuitry and registers.

The timing and control part of the 8237A generates the timing and control signals needed by the external bus interface. For instance, it accepts as inputs the

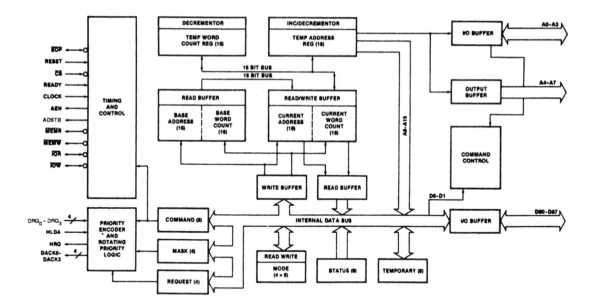

Figure 8.49 Internal architecture of the 8237A. (Reprinted by permission of Intel Corp., © Intel Corp. 1987)

READY and $\overline{\text{CS}}$ signals and produces as outputs signals such as ADSTB and AEN. These signals are synchronized to the clock signal that is input to the controller. The highest-speed version of the 8237A available today operates at a maximum clock rate of 5 MHz.

If multiple requests for DMA service are received by the 8237A, they are accepted on a priority basis. One of two priority schemes can be selected for the 8237A under software control. They are called *fixed priority* and *rotating priority*. The fixed-priority mode assigns priority to the channels in descending numeric order. That is, channel 0 has the highest priority and channel 3 the lowest priority. Rotating priority starts with the priority levels initially the same way as in fixed priority. However, after a DMA request for a specific level gets serviced, priority is rotated so that the previously active channel is reassigned to the lowest priority level. For instance, assuming that channel 1, which was initially at priority level 1, was just serviced, then $DREQ_2$ is now at the highest priority level and $DREQ_1$ rotates to the lowest level. The priority logic circuitry shown in Fig. 8.49 resolves priority for simultaneous DMA requests from peripheral devices based on the programmed priority scheme.

The command control circuit decodes the register commands applied to the 8237A through the microprocessor interface. In this way it determines which register is to be accessed and what type of operation is to be performed. Moreover, it is used to decode the programmed operating modes of the device during DMA operation.

Looking at the block diagram in Fig. 8.49, we find that the 8237A has 12 different types of internal registers. Some examples are the current address register, current count register, command register, mask register, and status register. The

Name	Size	Number
Base Address Registers	16 bits	4
Base Word Count Registers	16 bits	4
Current Address Registers	16 bits	4
Current Word Count Registers	16 bits	4
Temporary Address Register	16 bits	1
Temporary Word Count Register	16 bits	1
Status Register	8 bits	1
Command Register	8 bits	1
Temporary Register	8 bits	1
Mode Registers	6 bits	4
Mask Register	4 bits	1
Request Register	4 bits	1

Figure 8.50 Internal registers of the 8237A. (Reprinted by permission of Intel Corp., © Intel Corp. 1987)

names for all the internal registers are listed in Fig. 8.50, along with their sizes and how many are provided in the 8237A. Note that there are actually four current address registers and they are all 16 bits long. That is, there is one current address register for each of the four DMA channels. We will now describe the function served by each of these registers in terms of overall operation of the 8237A DMA controller. Addressing information for the internal registers is summarized in Fig. 8.51.

Each DMA channel has two address registers. They are called the *base address register* and the *current address register*. The base address register holds the starting address for the DMA operation, and the current address register contains the address of the next storage location to be accessed. Writing a value to the base address register automatically loads the same value into the current address register. In this way, we see that initially the current address register points to the starting I/O or memory address.

These registers must be loaded with appropriate values prior to initiating a DMA cycle. To load a new 16-bit address to the base register, we must write two separate bytes, one after the other, to the address of the register. The 8237A has an internal flip-flop called the *first/last flip-flop*. This flip-flop identifies which byte of the address is being written into the register. As shown in the table of Fig. 8.51, if the beginning state of the internal flip-flop (FF) is logic 0, then software must write the low byte of the address word to the register. On the other hand, if it is logic 1, the high byte must be written to the register. For example, to write the address 1234_{16} into the base address register and the current address register for channel 0 of a DMA controller located at base I/O address "DMA" (where DMA ≤ F0H and it is decided by how the $\overline{CS}$ for the 8237A is generated), the following instructions may be executed:

```
MOV   AL,34H      ;Write low byte
OUT   DMA+0,AL
MOV   AL,12H      ;Write high byte
OUT   DMA+0,AL
```

This routine assumes that the internal flip-flop was initially set to 0. Looking at Fig. 8.51, we find that a command can be issued to the 8237A to clear the internal flip-flop. This is done by initiating an output bus cycle to address DMA + C_{16}.

Channel(s)	Register	Operation	I/O address relative to the base	Internal FF	Data bus
0	Base and current address	Write	0_{16}	0 1	Low High
	Current address	Read	0_{16}	0 1	Low High
	Base and current count	Write	1_{16}	0 1	Low High
	Current count	Read	1_{16}	0 1	Low High
1	Base and current address	Write	2_{16}	0 1	Low High
	Current address	Read	2_{16}	0 1	Low High
	Base and current count	Write	3_{16}	0 1	Low High
	Current count	Read	3_{16}	0 1	Low High
2	Base and current address	Write	4_{16}	0 1	Low High
	Current address	Read	4_{16}	0 1	Low High
	Base and current count	Write	5_{16}	0 1	Low High
	Current count	Read	5_{16}	0 1	Low High
3	Base and current address	Write	6_{16}	0 1	Low High
	Current address	Read	6_{16}	0 1	Low High
	Base and current count	Write	7_{16}	0 1	Low High
	Current count	Read	7_{16}	0 1	Low High
All	Command register	Write	8_{16}	X	Low
All	Status register	Read	8_{16}	X	Low
All	Request register	Write	9_{16}	X	Low
All	Mask register	Write	A_{16}	X	Low
All	Mode register	Write	B_{16}	X	Low
All	Temporary register	Read	B_{16}	X	Low
All	Clear internal FF	Write	C_{16}	X	Low
All	Master clear	Write	D_{16}	X	Low
All	Clear mask register	Write	E_{16}	X	Low
All	Mask register	Write	F_{16}	X	Low

Figure 8.51 Accessing the registers of the 8237A.

If we read the contents of the register at address DMA$+0_{16}$, the value obtained is the contents of the current address register for channel 0. Once loaded, the value in the base address register cannot be read out of the device.

The 8237A also has two word count registers for each of its DMA channels. They are called the *base count register* and the *current count register*. In Fig. 8.50, we find that these registers are also 16 bits in length, and Fig. 8.51 identifies their address as 1_{16}, relative to the base address DMA for channel 0. The number of bytes of data that are to be transferred during a DMA operation is specified by the value in the base word count register. Actually, the number of bytes transferred is always one more than the value programmed into this register. This is because the end of a DMA cycle is detected by the rollover of the current word count from 0000_{16} to $FFFF_{16}$. At any time during the DMA cycle, the value in the current word count register tells how many bytes remain to be transferred.

The count registers are programmed in the same way as was just described for the address registers. For instance, to program a count of $0FFF_{16}$ into the base and current count registers for channel 1 of a DMA controller located at address "DMA," (where DMA $\leq$ F0H), the instructions that follow can be executed:

```
MOV   AL,0FFH    ;Write low byte
OUT   DMA+2,AL
MOV   AL,0FH     ;Write high byte
OUT   DMA+2,AL
```

Again we have assumed that the internal flip-flop was initially cleared.

In Fig. 8.50, we find that the 8237A has a single 8-bit command register. The bits in this register are used to control operating modes that apply to all channels of the DMA controller. Figure 8.52 identifies the function of each of its control

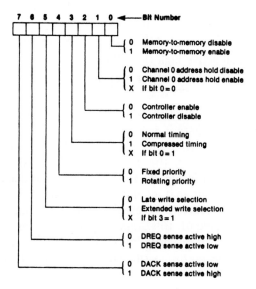

Figure 8.52 Command register format. (Reprinted by permission of Intel Corp., © Intel Corp. 1987)

bits. Notice that the settings of the bits are used to select or deselect operating features such as memory-to-memory, DMA transfer, and the priority scheme. For instance, when bit 0 is set to logic 1, the memory-to-memory mode of DMA transfer is enabled, and when it is logic 0, DMA transfers take place between I/O and memory. Moreover, setting bit 4 to logic 0 selects the fixed priority scheme for all four channels or logic 1 in this location selects rotating priority. Looking at Fig. 8.51, we see that the command register is loaded by outputting the command code to register at address 8_{16}, relative to the base address for the 8237A.

EXAMPLE 8.28

If the command register of an 8237A is loaded with 01_{16}, how does the controller operate?

Solution

Representing the command word as a binary number, we get

$$01_{16} = 00000001_2$$

Referring to Fig. 8.52, we find that the selected DMA operation can be described as follows:

> Bit 0 = 1 = Memory-to-memory transfers are disabled
> Bit 1 = 0 = Channel 0 address increments/decrements normally
> Bit 2 = 0 = 8237A is enabled
> Bit 3 = 0 = 8237A operates with normal timing
> Bit 4 = 0 = Channels have fixed priority, channel 0 having the highest priority and channel 3 the lowest priority
> Bit 5 = 0 = Write operation occurs late in the DMA bus cycle
> Bit 6 = 0 = DREQ is an active high (logic 1) signal
> Bit 7 = 0 = DACK is an active low (logic 0) signal

The *mode registers* are also used to configure operational features of the 8237A. In Fig. 8.50, we find that there is a separate mode register for each of the four DMA channels and that they are each 6 bits in length. Their bits are used to select various operational features for the individual DMA channels. A typical mode register command is shown in Fig. 8.53. As shown in the diagram, the two least significant bits are a 2-bit code that identifies the channel to which the mode command byte applies. For instance, in a mode register command written for channel 1, these bits must be made 01. Bits 2 and 3 specify whether the channel is to perform data write or data read or verify bus cycles. For example, if these bits are set to 01, the channel will only perform write data transfers (DMA data transfers from an I/O device to memory).

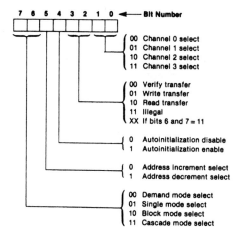

7 6 5 4 3 2 1 0 ◄— Bit Number

00 Channel 0 select
01 Channel 1 select
10 Channel 2 select
11 Channel 3 select

00 Verify transfer
01 Write transfer
10 Read transfer
11 Illegal
XX If bits 6 and 7 = 11

0 Autoinitialization disable
1 Autoinitialization enable

0 Address increment select
1 Address decrement select

00 Demand mode select
01 Single mode select
10 Block mode select
11 Cascade mode select

Figure 8.53 Mode register format. (Reprinted by permission of Intel Corp., © Intel Corp. 1987)

The next 2 bits of the mode register affect how the values in the current address and current count registers are updated at the end of a DMA cycle and DMA data transfer, respectively. Bit 4 enables or disables the autoinitialization function. When autoinitialization is enabled, the current address and current count registers are automatically reloaded from the base address and base count registers, respectively, at the end of a DMA operation. In this way, the channel is prepared for the next DMA operation to begin. The setting of bit 5 determines whether the value in the current address register is automatically incremented or decremented at completion of each DMA data transfer.

The two most significant bits of the mode register select one of four possible modes of DMA operation for the channel. The four modes are called *demand mode*, *single mode*, *block mode*, and *cascade mode*. These modes allow for either one byte of data to be transferred at a time or a block of bytes. For example, when in the demand transfer mode, once the DMA cycle is initiated, bytes are continuously transferred as long as the DREQ signal remains active and the terminal count (TC) is not reached. By reaching the terminal count, we mean that the value in the current word count register, which automatically decrements after each data transfer, rolls over from 0000_{16} to $FFFF_{16}$.

Block transfer mode is similar to demand transfer mode in that, once the DMA cycle is initiated, data are continuously transferred until the terminal count is reached. However, they differ in that, when in the demand mode, the return of DREQ to its inactive state halts the data transfer sequence. But, when in block transfer mode, DREQ can be released at any time after the DMA cycle begins, and the block transfer will still run to completion.

In the single transfer mode, the channel is set up such that it performs just one data transfer at a time. At the completion of the transfer, the current word count is decremented and the current address either incremented or decremented (based on the selected option). Moreover, an autoinitialization, if enabled, will not occur unless the terminal count has been reached at the completion of the current data transfer. If the DREQ input becomes inactive before the completion of the current data transfer, another data transfer will not take place until DREQ once more becomes active. On the other hand, if DREQ remains active during the complete data transfer cycle, the HRQ output of the 8237A is switched to its inactive 0 logic level to allow the microprocessor to gain control of the system bus for one bus cycle before another single transfer takes place. This mode of operation is typically used when it is necessary to not lock the microprocessor off the bus for the complete duration of the DMA operation.

EXAMPLE 8.29

Specify the mode byte for DMA channel 2 if it is to transfer data from an input peripheral device to a memory buffer starting at address $A000_{16}$ and ending at $AFFF_{16}$. Ensure that the microprocessor is not completely locked off the bus during the DMA cycle. Moreover, at the end of each DMA cycle, the channel is to be reinitialized so that the same buffer is to be filled when the next DMA operation is initiated.

Solution

For DMA channel 2, bit 1 and bit 0 must be loaded with 10_2.

$$B_1B_0 = 10$$

Transfer of data from an I/O device to memory represents a write bus cycle. Therefore, bit 3 and bit 2 must be set to 01.

$$B_3B_2 = 01$$

Selecting autoinitialization will set up the channel to automatically reset so that it points to the beginning of the memory buffer at completion of the current DMA cycle. This feature is enabled by making bit 4 equal to 1.

$$B_4 = 1$$

The address that points to the memory buffer must increment after each data transfer. Therefore, bit 5 must be set to 0.

$$B_5 = 0$$

Finally, to ensure that the 8088 is not locked off the bus during the complete DMA cycle, we will select the single transfer mode of operation. This is done by making bits B_7 and B_6 equal to 01.

$$B_7B_6 = 01$$

Thus the mode register byte is

$$B_7B_6B_5B_4B_3B_2B_1B_0 = 01010110_2 = 56_{16}.$$

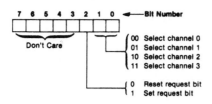

Figure 8.54 Request register format. (Reprinted by permission of Intel Corp., © Intel Corp. 1987)

Up to now, we have discussed how DMA cycles can be initiated by a hardware request at a DREQ input. However, the 8237A is also able to respond to software-initiated requests for DMA service. The *request register* has been provided for this purpose. Figure 8.50 shows that the request register has just four bits, one for each of the DMA channels. When the request bit for a channel is set, DMA operation is started, and when reset, the DMA cycle is stopped. Any channel used for software-initiated DMA must be programmed for block-transfer mode of operation.

The bits in the request register can be set or reset by issuing software commands to the 8237A. The format of a request register command is shown in Fig. 8.54. For instance, if a command is issued to the address of the request register with bits 0 and 1 equal to 01 and with bit 3 at logic 1, a block-mode DMA cycle is initiated for channel 1. In Fig. 8.51, we find that the request register is located at register address 9_{16}, relative to the base address for the 8237A.

A 4-bit *mask register* is also provided within the 8237A. One bit is provided in this register for each of the DMA channels. When a mask bit is set, the DREQ input for the corresponding channel is disabled. Therefore, hardware requests to the channel are ignored. That is, the channel is masked out. On the other hand, if

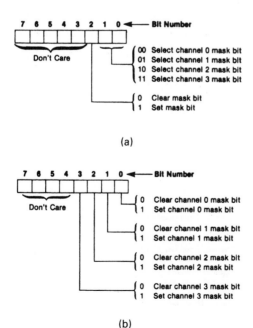

Figure 8.55 (a) Single channel mask register command format. (Reprinted by permission of Intel Corp., © Intel Corp. 1987) (b) Four channel mask register command format. (Reprinted by permission of Intel Corp., © Intel Corp. 1987)

the mask bit is cleared, the DREQ input is enabled and its channel can be activated by an external device.

The format of a software command that can be used to set or reset a single bit in the mask register is shown in Fig. 8.55(a). For example, to enable the DREQ input for channel 2, the command is issued with bits 1 and 0 set to 10 to select channel 2 and with bit 3 equal to 0 to clear the mask bit. Therefore, the software command byte would be 03_{16}. The table in Fig. 8.51 shows that this command byte must be issued to the 8237A with register address A_{16}, relative to the base address for the 8237A.

A second mask register command is shown in Fig. 8.55(b). This command can be used to load all four bits of the register at once. In Fig. 8.51, we find that this command is issued to relative register address F_{16} instead of A_{16}. For instance, to mask out channel 2 while enabling channels 0, 1, and 3, the command code is 04_{16}. Either of these two methods can be used to mask or enable the DREQ input for a channel.

At system initialization, it is a common practice to clear the mask register. Looking at Fig. 8.51, we see that a special command is provided to perform this operation. The mask register can be cleared by executing an output cycle to the register with relative address E_{16}.

The 8237A has a *status register* that contains information about the operating state of its four DMA channels. Figure 8.56 shows the bits of the status register and defines their functions. Here we find that the four least significant bits identify whether or not channels 0 through 3 have reached their terminal count. When the DMA cycle for a channel reaches the terminal count, this fact is recorded by setting the corresponding TC bit to the 1 logic level. The four most significant bits of the register tell if a request is pending for the corresponding channel. For instance, if a DMA request has been issued for channel 0 either through hardware or software, bit 4 is set to 1. The 8088 can read the contents of the status register through software. This is done by initiating an input bus cycle for register address 8_{16}, relative to the base address for the 8237A.

Earlier we pointed out that during memory-to-memory DMA transfers, the data read from the source address are held in a register known as the *temporary register*, and then a write cycle is initiated to write the data to the destination address. At the completion of the DMA cycle, this register contains the last byte that was transferred. The value in this register can be read by the microprocessor.

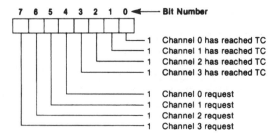

Figure 8.56 Status register. (Reprinted by permission of Intel Corp., © Intel Corp. 1987)

EXAMPLE 8.30 _____

Write an instruction sequence to issue a master clear to the 8237A and then enable all its DMA channels. Assume that the device is located at base I/O address 'DMA < F0H.'

Solution

In Fig. 8.48, we find that a special software command is provided to perform a master reset of the 8237A's registers. Since the contents of the data bus are a don't-care state when executing the master clear command, it is performed by simply writing to the register at relative address D_{16}. For instance, the instruction

```
OUT DMA+0DH,AL
```

can be used. To enable the DMA request inputs, all four bits of the mask register must be cleared. The clear mask register command is issued by performing a write to the register at relative address E_{16}. Again, the data put on the bus during the write cycle are a don't-care state. Therefore, the command can be performed with the instruction

```
OUT DMA+0EH,AL
```

DMA Interface for the 8088-Based Microcomputer Using the 8237A

Figure 8.57 shows how the 8237A is connected to the 8088 microprocessor to form a simplified DMA interface. Here we see that both the 8088 MPU and the 8237A DMA controller drive the same three system buses, address bus, data bus, and control bus. Let us now look at how each of these devices attaches to the system bus. The 8088's multiplexed address/data bus is demultiplexed using three 74F373 latches to form independent system address and data buses. The address bus is 20 bits in length and these lines are identified as A_0 through A_{19}. On the other hand, the data bus is byte-wide, with lines D_0 through D_7. Notice that the ALE output of the 8088 is used as the CLK input to the latches.

Looking at the 8237A, we find that the lower byte of its address, which is identified by A_0 through A_3 and A_4 through A_7, is supplied directly to the system address bus. On the other hand, the most significant byte of its address, A_8 through A_{15}, is demultiplexed from data bus lines DB_0 through DB_7 by another 74F373 latch. This latch is enabled by the AEN output of the DMA controller, and the address is loaded into the latch with the signal ADSTB. DB_0 through DB_7 are also directly attached to the system data bus.

Finally, let us look at how the system control bus signals are derived. The $IO/\overline{M}$, $\overline{RD}$, and $\overline{WR}$ control outputs of the microprocessor are gated together to produce the signals $\overline{MEMR}$, $\overline{MEMW}$, $\overline{IOR}$, and $\overline{IOW}$. These signals are combined

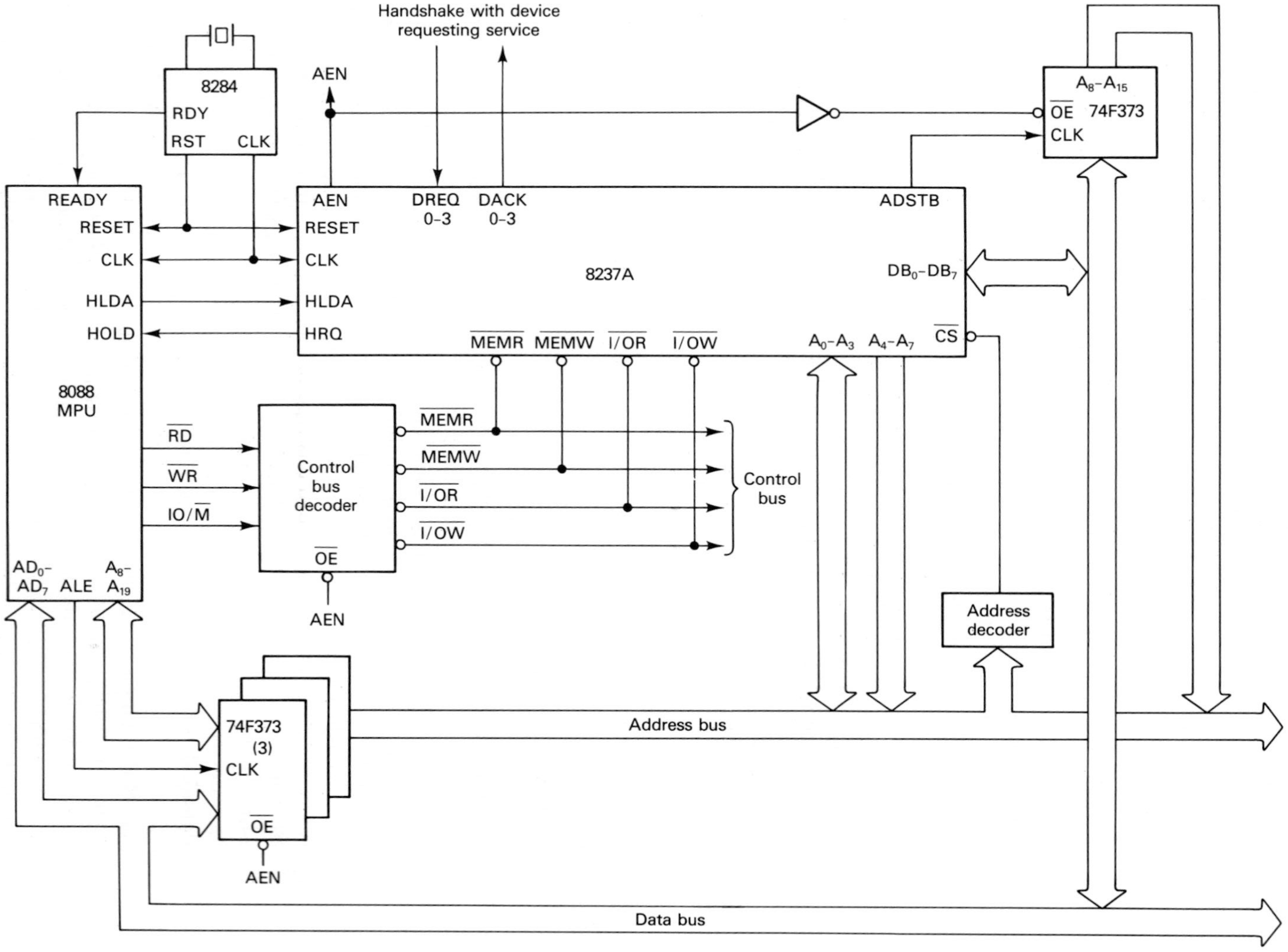

Figure 8.57 8088-based microcomputer with 8237A DMA interface.

to form the system control bus. Notice that these same four signals are generated as outputs of the 8237A and are also supplied to the control bus.

Now that we have shown how the independent address, data, and control signals of the 8088 and 8237A are combined to form the system address, data, and control buses, let us continue by looking at how the DMA request/acknowledge interface is implemented. I/O devices request DMA service by activating one of the 8237A's DMA request inputs, $DREQ_0$ through $DREQ_3$. When the 8237A receives a valid DMA request on one of these lines, it sends a hold request to the HOLD input of the 8088. It does this by setting the HRQ output to logic 1. After the 8088 gives up control of the system buses, it acknowledges this fact to the 8237A by switching its HLDA output to the 1 logic level. This signal is received by the DMA controller at its HLDA input and tells it that the system buses are available. The 8237A is now ready to take over control of the system buses, and it signals this fact to the device that is requesting service by activating its DMA acknowledge (DACK) line.

During the DMA operation, the 8237A generates all of the bus signals that are needed to access I/O devices and the memory. It also generates the AEN signals, which is used to disable the microprocessor's connection to the system bus. AEN does this by disabling the control bus decoder and the latches for the address bus. The microprocessor's connection to the data bus is also disabled in response to the hold request received on its HOLD input. Remember that logic 1 at HOLD puts the data bus lines in the high-Z state. Thus during a DMA operation, the 8237A is in complete control of the address bus, control bus, and data bus.

▲ 8.15 SERIAL COMMUNICATIONS INTERFACE

Another type of I/O interface that is widely used in microcomputer systems is known as a *serial communication port*. This is the type of interface that is commonly used to connect peripheral units, such as CRT terminals, modems, and printers, to a microcomputer. It permits data to be transferred between two units using just two data lines. One line is used for transmitting data and the other for receiving data. For instance, data input at the keyboard of a terminal are passed to the MPU part of the microcomputer through this type of interface. Let us now look into the two different types of serial interfaces that are implemented in microcomputer systems.

Synchronous and Asynchronous Data Communications

Two types of *serial data communications* are widely used in microcomputer systems. They are called *asynchronous communication* and *synchronous communications*. By synchronous, we mean that the receiver and transmitter sections of the two pieces of equipment that are communicating with each other must run synchronously. For this reason, as shown in Fig. 8.58(a), the interface includes a Clock line as well as Transmit data, Receive data, and Signal common lines. It is the clock signal that synchronizes both the transmission and reception of data.

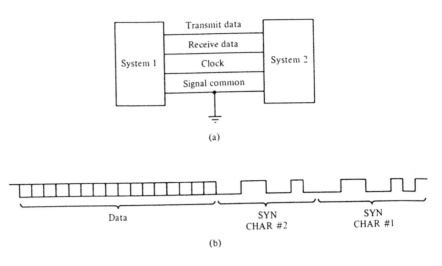

(a)

(b)

Figure 8.58 (a) Synchronous communications interface. (b) Synchronous data transmission format.

The format used for synchronous communication of data is shown in Fig. 8.58(b). To initiate synchronous transmission, the transmitter first sends out synchronization characters to the receiver. The receiver reads the synchronization bit pattern and compares it to a known sync pattern. Once they are identified as being the same, the receiver begins to read character data off the data line. Transfer of data continues until the complete block of data is received. If large blocks of data are being sent, the synchronization characters may be periodically resent to assure that synchronization is maintained. The synchronous type of communications is typically used in applications where high-speed data transfer is required.

The asynchronous method of communications eliminates the need for the Clock signal. As shown in Fig. 8.59(a), the simplest form of an asynchronous communication interface could consist of a Receive data, Transmit data, and Signal common communication lines. In this case, the data to be transmitted are sent out one character at a time and at the receiver end of the communication line synchronization is performed by examining synchronization bits that are included at the beginning and end of each character.

The format of a typical asynchronous character is shown in Fig. 8.59(b). Here we see that the synchronization bit at the beginning of the character is called the *start bit* and that at the end of the character the *stop bit*. Depending on the communications scheme, 1, 1½, or 2 stop bits can be used. The bits of the character are embedded between the start and stop bits. Notice that the start bit is either input or output first. It is followed in the serial bit stream by the LSB of the character, the rest of the character's bits, a parity bit, and the stop bits. For instance, 7-bit ASCII can be used and parity added as an eighth bit for higher reliability in transmission. The duration of each bit in the format is called a *bit time*.

The fact that a 0 or 1 logic level is being transferred over the communication line is identified by whether the voltage level on the line corresponds to that of a *mark* or a *space*. The start bit is always to the mark level. It synchronizes the

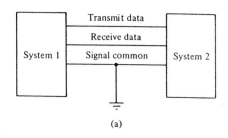

(a)

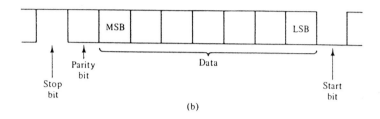

(b)

Figure 8.59 (a) Asynchronous communication interface. (b) Asynchronous data transmission format.

receiver to the transmitter and signals that the unit receiving data should start assembling the character. Stop bits are to the space level. The nontransmitting line is always at the space logic level. This scheme assures that the receiving unit sees a transition of logic level at the start bit of the next character.

Simplex, Half-Duplex, and Full-Duplex Communication Links

Applications require different types of asynchronous links to be implemented. For instance, the communication link needed to connect a printer to a microcomputer just needs to support communications in one direction. That is, the printer is an output-only device; therefore, the MPU only needs to transmit data to the printer. Data are not transmitted back. In this case, as shown in Fig. 8.60(a), a single unidirectional communication line can be used to connect the printer and microcomputer together. This type of connection is known as a simplex communication link.

Other devices, such as the CRT terminal with keyboard shown in Fig. 8.60(b), need to both transmit data to and receive data from the MPU. That is, they must both input and output data. This requirement can also be satisfied with a single communication line by setting up a half-duplex communication link. In a half-duplex link, data are transmitted and received over the same line; therefore, transmission and reception of data cannot take place at the same time.

If higher-performance communication is required, separate transmit and receive lines can be used to connect the peripheral and microcomputer. When this is done, data can be transferred in both directions at the same time. This type of link is illustrated in Fig. 8.60(c). It is called a full-duplex communication link.

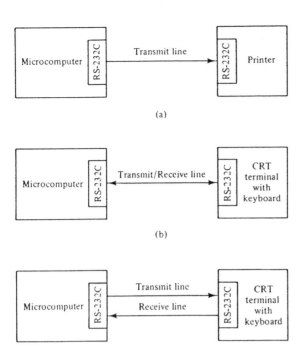

(a)

(b)

(c)

Figure 8.60 (a) Simplex communications link. (b) Half-duplex communications link. (c) Full-duplex communications link.

The USART and UART

Because serial communication interfaces are so widely used in modern electronic equipment, special LSI peripheral devices have been developed to permit easy implementation of these types of interfaces. Some of the names that these devices go by are UART (*universal asynchronous receiver/transmitter*) and USART (*universal synchronous/asynchronous receiver/transmitter*).

Both UARTs and USARTs have the ability to perform the parallel-to-serial conversions needed in the transmission of data and the serial-to-parallel conversions needed in the reception of data by a microprocessor. For data that are transmitted asynchronously, they also have the ability to frame the character automatically with a start bit, parity bit, and the appropriate stop bits.

For reception of data, UARTs and USARTs typically have the ability to check characters automatically as they are received for correct parity, and for two other errors, known as framing error and overrun error. A framing error means that after the detection of the beginning of a character with a start bit the appropriate number of stop bits were not detected. This means that the character that was transmitted was not received correctly and should be resent. An overrun error means that the prior character that was received was not read out of the USART's receive data register by the microprocessor before another character was received. Therefore, the first character was lost and should be retransmitted.

A block diagram of a UART is shown in Fig. 8.61. Here we see that it has four key signal interfaces: the microprocessor interface, the transmitter interface, the receiver interface, and the handshake control interface. Let us now look at each of these interfaces in more detail.

A UART cannot stand alone in a communication system. Its operation must typically be controlled by a microprocessor. The microprocessor interface is the interface that is used to connect the UART to an MPU. Looking at Fig. 8.61, we see that this interface consists of an 8-bit bidirectional data bus (D_0-D_7) and three control lines, $\overline{CS}$, $\overline{RD}$, and $\overline{WR}$.

All data transfers between the UART and MPU take place over the 8-bit data bus. Two uses of this bus are for the input of character data from the receiver of the UART and for the output of character data to its transmitter. Other types of information are also passed between the MPU and UART. Examples are mode control instructions, operation command instructions, and status.

LSI UARTs, just like the 8255A LSI peripheral we discussed earlier in the chapter, can be configured for various modes of operation through software. Mode control instructions are what must be issued to a UART to initialize its control registers for the desired mode of operation. For example, the format of the data frame used for transmitted or received data can be configured through software. Typical options are character length between five and eight bits; even, odd, or no parity; and 1, $1\frac{1}{2}$, or 2 stop bits.

Most UARTs have a status register that contains information related to its current state. For example, it may contain an Rx_{RDY} flag bit that represents the current state of receiver lines such as $\overline{RTS}$ and $\overline{DTR}$. This permits the MPU to examine the logic state of these lines through software and based on their settings take the necessary actions.

Besides information about transmission/receive status, the status register typically contains flag bits for error conditions such as parity error, overrun error, and framing error. After reception of a character, the MPU can first read these bits to

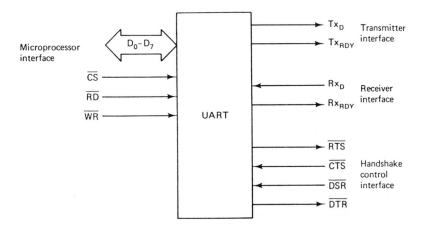

Figure 8.61 Block diagram of a UART.

assure that a valid character has been received. On finding a valid character status, the character can be read from the receive data register within the UART.

In the block in Fig. 8.61, we find the transmitter and receiver interfaces. The transmitter interface has two signal lines: transmit data (Tx_D) and transmitter ready (Tx_{RDY}). Tx_D is the line over which the transmitter section of the UART outputs serial data. This output line is connected to the receive data (Rx_D) input of the receiver section in the system at the other end of the communication line.

Usually, the transmitter section of an LSI UART can hold only one character at a time. This character data is held in the transmit data register within the UART. Since only one character can be held within the UART, it must signal the MPU when it has completed transmission of this character. The Tx_{RDY} line is provided for this purpose. As soon as transmission of the character is complete, the transmitter switches Tx_{RDY} to its active logic level. This signal can be returned to an interrupt input of the MPU. In this way, its occurrence can cause program control to be passed quickly to a service routine that will output another character to the transmitter data register and then reinitiate transmission.

The receiver section is similar to the transmitter we just described. However, here the receive data (Rx_D) line is the input that accepts bit-serial data that are transmitted from the other system's transmitter. The receive data input connects to the transmit data (Tx_D) output of the transmitter section in the system at the other end of the communications line. Here the receiver ready (Rx_{RDY}) output can be used as an interrupt to the MPU and it signals the MPU that a character has been received. The service routine that is initiated must first determine whether or not the character is valid, and if it is, it can read the character out of the UART's receive data register.

Using the handshake control signals $\overline{RTS}$, $\overline{DSR}$, $\overline{DTR}$, and $\overline{CTS}$, different types of asynchronous communication protocols can be implemented through the serial I/O interface. By protocol we mean a handshake sequence by which two systems signal their status to each other during communications.

An example of an asynchronous communication interface that uses these control lines is shown in Fig. 8.62. When the system 1 UART wants to send data to the UART of system 2, it issues a request at its request to sent ($\overline{RTS}$) output. $\overline{RTS}$ of the system 1 UART is applied to the data set ready ($\overline{DSR}$) input of the system 2 UART. In this way, it tells the UART of system 2 that the UART of system 1 wants to transmit data to it.

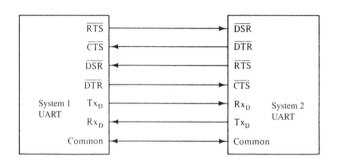

Figure 8.62 Asynchronous communications interface between two UARTs.

When the UART of system 2 is ready to receive data, it acknowledges this fact to system 1 by activating the data terminal ready ($\overline{\text{DTR}}$) output of its UART. This signal is returned to the clear to send ($\overline{\text{CTS}}$) input of system 1's UART and tells it to output data on Tx$_D$. At the same time, the receiver section of the UART within system 2 begins to read data from its Rx$_D$ input.

The implementation of this kind of interface using handshake signals requires programming of the UARTs and proper microprocessor interfaces to control the UARTs. In many practical cases, the handshake lines are not used in this way. Instead, the input lines on both UARTs are permanently connected to their enabled state by directly connecting them to logic 0 or 1. Moreover, the output handshake lines are simply ignored. This avoids the need for physical connections between the UARTs for handshake purpose.

Baud Rate and the Baud Rate Generator

The rate at which data transfers take place over the receive and transmit lines is known as the baud rate. By baud rate we mean the number of bits of data transferred per second. For instance, some of the common data transfer rates are 300 baud, 1200 baud, and 9600 baud. They correspond to 300 bits/second (bps), 1200 bps, and 9600 bps, respectively.

The baud rate at which data are transferred determines the bit time. That is, the amount of time each bit of data is on the communication line. At 300 baud, the bit time is found to be

$$t_{BT} = 1/300 \text{ bps} = 3.33 \text{ ms}$$

EXAMPLE 8.31

The data transfer across an asynchronous serial data communications line is observed and the bit time of a character is measured as .833 ms. What is the baud rate?

Solution

Baud rate is calculated from the bit time as

$$\text{Baud rate} = 1/t_{BT} = 1/.833\text{ms} = 1200 \text{ bps}$$

Baud rate is set by a part of the serial communication interface called the baud rate generator. This part of the interface generates the clock signal that is used to drive the receiver and transmitter parts of the UART. Some LSI UARTs have a built-in baud rate generator; others need an external circuit to provide this function.

The RS-232C Interface

The RS-232C interface is a standard hardware interface for implementing asynchronous serial data communication ports on devices such as printers, CRT terminals, keyboards, and modems. The pin definitions and electrical characteristics of this interface are defined by the Electronic Industries Association (EIA). The aim behind publishing standards, such as the RS-232C, is to assure compatibility between equipment made by different manufacturers.

Peripherals that connect to a microcomputer can be located anywhere from several feet to many feet from the system. For instance, in large systems it is common to have the microcomputer part of the system in a separate room from the terminals and printers. This leads us to the main advantage of using a serial interface to connect peripherals to a microcomputer, which is that as few as three signal lines can be used to connect the peripheral to the MPU: a receive data line, a transmit data line, and signal common. This results in a large savings in wiring costs and the small number of lines that need to be put in place also leads to higher reliability.

The RS-232C standard defines a 25-pin interface. Figure 8.63 lists each pin and its function. Note that the three signals that we mentioned earlier, transmit data, receive data, and signal ground, are located at pins 2, 3, and 7, respectively.

Pin	Signal
1	Protective Ground
2	Transmitted Data
3	Received Data
4	Request to Send
5	Clear to Send
6	Data Set Ready
7	Signal Ground (Common Return)
8	Received Line Signal Detector
9	Reserved for Data Set Testing
10	Reserved for Data Set Testing
11	Unassigned
12	Secondary Received Line Signal Detector
13	Secondary Clear to Send
14	Secondary Transmitted Data
15	Transmission Signal Element Timing
16	Secondary Received Data
17	Receiver Signal Element Timing
18	Unassigned
19	Secondary Request to Send
20	Data Terminal Ready
21	Signal Quality Detector
22	Ring Indicator
23	Data Signal Rate Selector
24	Transmit Signal Element Timing
25	Unassigned

Figure 8.63 RS-232C interface pins and functions.

Pins are also provided for additional control functions. For instance, pins 4 and 5 are the request to send and clear to send control signals.

The RS-232C interface is specified to operate correctly over a distance of up to 100 feet. To satisfy this distance specification, a bus driver is used on the transmit line and a bus receiver is used on the receive line. RS-232C drivers and receivers are available as standard ICs. These buffers do both the voltage-level translation needed to convert the TTL-compatible outputs of the UART to the mark (logic 1) and space (logic 0) voltage levels defined for the RS-232C interface. The voltage levels that are normally transmitted for a mark and a space are $+12$ V dc and -12 V dc, respectively. For the RS-232C interface, voltages from -3 V dc to -15 V dc are equal to a mark and all voltages from $+3$ V dc to $+15$ V dc are considered a space.

The RS-232C interface is specified to support baud rates of up to 20,000 bps. In general, the receive and transmit baud rates do not have to be the same; however, in most simpler systems they are set to the same value.

▲ 8.16 PROGRAMMABLE COMMUNICATION INTERFACE CONTROLLERS

The programmable communication interface controller is another important LSI peripheral for the 8088/8086 microcomputer system. It permits simple implementation of a serial data communications interface. For instance, it can be used to implement an RS-232C port. This is the type of interface that is used to connect a CRT terminal or a modem to a microcomputer. To support connection of these two peripheral devices, the microcomputer would need two independent RS-232C I/O ports. This function is normally implemented with a programmable communication controller known as a universal synchronous/asynchronous receiver transmitter (USART). As the name implies, a USART is capable of implementing either an asynchronous or synchronous communication interface. Here we will concentrate on its use in implementing an asynchronous communication interface.

The programmability of the USART provides for a very flexible asynchronous communication interface. Typically, they contain a full-duplex receiver and transmitter, which can be configured through software for communication of data using formats with character lengths between five and eight characters, with even or odd parity, and with 1, $1\frac{1}{2}$, or 2 stop bits. Moreover, they have the ability to detect automatically the occurrence of parity, framing, and overrun errors during data reception.

The 8251A USART

A block diagram showing the internal architecture of the 8251A is shown in Fig. 8.64(a) and its pin layout in Fig. 8.64(b). From this diagram we find that it includes four key sections: the bus interface section, which consists of the data bus buffer and read/write control logic blocks; the transmit section, which consists of the transmit buffer and transmit control blocks; the receive section, which consists

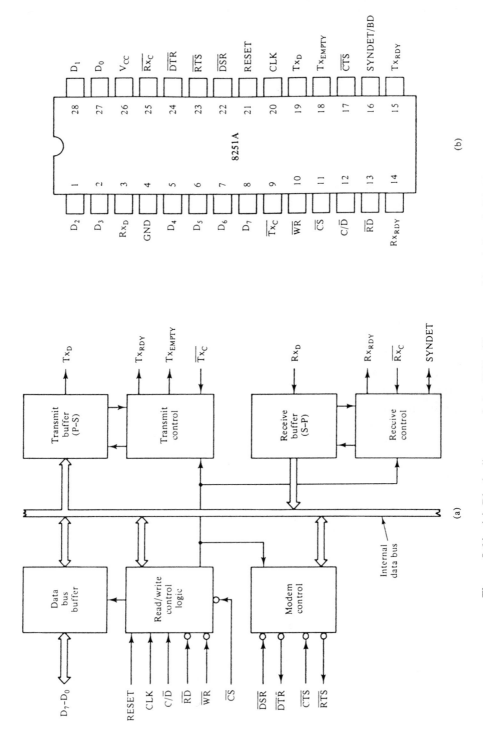

Figure 8.64 (a) Block diagram of the 8251. (Courtesy of Intel Corp.) (b) Pin layout. (Courtesy of Intel Corp.)

C/$\overline{\text{D}}$	$\overline{\text{RD}}$	$\overline{\text{WR}}$	$\overline{\text{CS}}$	Operation
0	0	1	0	8251A Data → Data bus
0	1	0	0	Data bus → 8251A Data
1	0	1	0	Status → Data bus
1	1	0	0	Data bus → Control
X	1	1	0	Data bus → 3-State
X	X	X	1	Data bus → 3-State

Figure 8.65 Read/write operations. (Courtesy of Intel Corp.)

of the receive buffer and receive control blocks; and the modem control section. Let us now look at each of these sections in more detail.

The bus interface section is used to connect the 8251A to a microprocessor such as the 8086. Notice that the interface includes an 8-bit bidirectional data bus D_0 through D_7 that is driven by the data bus buffer. It is over these lines that the microprocessor transfers commands to the 8251A, reads its status register, and inputs or outputs character data.

Data transfers over the bus are controlled by the signals C/$\overline{\text{D}}$ (control/data), $\overline{\text{RD}}$ (read), $\overline{\text{WR}}$ (write), and $\overline{\text{CS}}$ (chip select), which are all inputs to the read/write control logic section. Typically, the 8251A is located at a specific address in the microcomputer's I/O or memory address space. When the microprocessor is to access registers within the 8251A, it puts this address on the address bus. The address is decoded by external circuitry and must produce logic 0 at the $\overline{\text{CS}}$ input for a read or write bus cycle to take place to the 8251A.

The other three control signals, C/$\overline{\text{D}}$, $\overline{\text{RD}}$, and $\overline{\text{WR}}$, tell the 8251A what type of data transfer is to take place over the bus. Figure 8.65 shows the various types of read/write operations that can occur. For example, the first state in the table, C/$\overline{\text{D}}$ = 0, $\overline{\text{RD}}$ = 0, and $\overline{\text{WR}}$ = 1, corresponds to a character data transfer from the 8251A to the microprocessor. Notice that in general, $\overline{\text{RD}}$ = 0 signals that the microprocessor is reading data from the 8251A, $\overline{\text{WR}}$ = 0 indicates that data are being written into the 8251A, and the logic level of C/$\overline{\text{D}}$ indicates whether character data, control information, or status information is on the data bus.

EXAMPLE 8.32

What type of data transfer is taking place over the bus if the control signals are at $\overline{\text{CS}}$ = 0, C/$\overline{\text{D}}$ = 1, $\overline{\text{RD}}$ = 0, and $\overline{\text{WR}}$ = 1?

Solution

Looking at the table in Fig. 8.62, we see that $\overline{\text{CS}}$ = 0 means that the 8251A's data bus has been enabled for operation. Since C/$\overline{\text{D}}$ is 1 and $\overline{\text{RD}}$ is 0, status information is being read from the 8251A.

The receiver section is responsible for reading the serial bit stream of data at the Rx$_\text{D}$ (receive data) input and converting it to parallel form. When a mark voltage level is detected on this line indicating a start bit, the receiver enables a counter. As the counter increments to a value equal to one-half a bit time, the logic level at the Rx_D line is sampled again. If it is still at the mark level, a valid start pulse has been detected. Then Rx_D is examined every time the counter increments through another bit time. This continues until a complete character is assembled and the stop bit is read. After this, the complete character is transferred into the receive data register.

During reception of a character, the receiver automatically checks the character data for parity, framing, or overrun errors. If one of these conditions occurs, it is flagged by setting a bit in the status register. Then the Rx_{RDY} (receiver ready) output is switched to the 1 logic level. This signal is sent to the microprocessor to tell it that a character is available and should be read from the receive data register. Rx_{RDY} is automatically reset to logic 0 when the MPU reads the contents of the receive data register.

The 8251A does not have a built-in baud rate generator. For this reason, the clock signal that is used to set the baud rate must be externally generated and applied to the Rx_C input of the receiver. Through software the 8251A can be set up to internally divide the clock signal input at Rx_C by 1, 16, or 64 to obtain the desired baud rate.

The transmitter does the opposite of the receiver section. It receives parallel character data from the MPU over the data bus. The character is then automatically framed with the start bit, appropriate parity bit, and the correct number of stop bits and put into the transmit data buffer register. Finally, it is shifted out of this register to produce a bit-serial output on the Tx_D line. When the transmit data buffer register is empty, the Tx_{RDY} output switches to logic 1. This signal can be returned to the MPU to tell it that another character should be output to the transmitter section. When the MPU writes another character out to the transmitter buffer register, the Tx_{RDY} output resets.

Data are output on the transmit line at the baud rate set by the external transmitter clock signal that is input at Tx_C. In most applications, the transmitter and receiver operate at the same baud rate. Therefore, both Rx_C and Tx_C are supplied by the same baud rate generator. The circuit in Fig. 8.66 shows this type of system configuration.

The operation of the 8251A is controlled through the setting of bits in three internal control registers: the mode control register, command register, and the status register. For instance, the way in which the 8251A's receiver and transmitter operate is determined by the contents of the mode control register.

Figure 8.67 shows the organization of the mode control register and the function of each of its bits. Note that the two least significant bits B_1 and B_2 determine whether the device operates as an asynchronous or synchronous communication controller and in asynchronous mode how the external baud rate clock is divided within the 8251A. For example, if these two bits are 11, it is set for asynchronous operation with divide by 64 for the baud rate input. The two bits that follow these, L_1 and L_2, set the length of the character. For instance, when information is being transmitted and received as 7-bit ASCII characters, these bits should be loaded with 10.

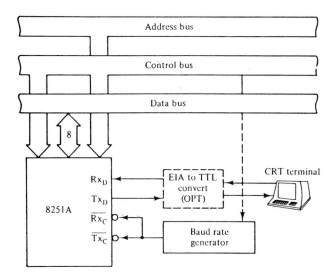

Figure 8.66 Receiver and transmitter driven at the same baud rate. (Courtesy of Intel Corp.)

The next two bits, PEN and EP, determine whether parity is in use and if so, whether it is even parity or odd parity. Looking at Fig. 8.67, we see that PEN enables or disables parity. To enable parity, it is set to 1. Furthermore, when parity is enabled, logic 0 in EP selects odd parity or logic 1 in this position selects even parity. To disable parity, all we need to do is reset PEN.

We will assume that the 8251A is working in the asynchronous mode; therefore, bits S_1 and S_2 determine the number of stop bits. Note that if 11 is loaded into these bit positions, the character is transmitted with 2 stop bits.

EXAMPLE 8.33

What value must be written into the mode control register in order to configure the 8251A such that it works as an asynchronous communications controller with

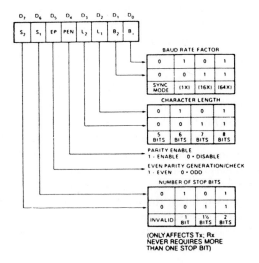

Figure 8.67 Mode instruction format. (Courtesy of Intel Corp.)

the baud rate clock internally divided by 16? Character size is to be 8 bits; parity is odd; and one stop bit is used.

Solution

From Fig. 8.67, we find that B_2B_1 must be set to 10 in order to select asynchronous operation with divide by 16 for the external baud clock input.

$$B_2B_1 = 10$$

To select a character length of 8 bits, the next two bits are both made logic 1. This gives

$$L_2L_1 = 11$$

To set up odd parity, EP and PEN must be made equal to 0 and 1, respectively.

$$EP\ PEN = 01$$

Finally, S_2S_1 are set to 01 for one stop bit.

$$S_2S_1 = 01$$

Therefore, the complete control word is

$$D_7D_6 \ldots \ldots D_0 = 01011110_2$$
$$= 5E_{16}$$

Once the configuration for asynchronous communications has been set up in the mode control register, the operation of the serial interface can be controlled by the microprocessor by issuing commands to the command register within the 8251A. The format of the command instruction byte and the function of each of its bits is shown in Fig. 8.68. Let us look at the function of just a few of its bits.

Tx_{EN} and Rx_{EN} are enable bits for the transmitter and receiver. Since both the receiver and transmitter can operate simultaneously, these two bits can both be set. Rx_{EN} is actually an enable signal to the Rx_{RDY} signal. It does not turn the receiver section on and off. The receiver runs at all times, but if Rx_{EN} is set to 0, the 8251A does not signal the MPU that a character has been received by switching Rx_{RDY} to logic 1. The same is true for Tx_{EN}. It enables the Tx_{RDY} signal.

The ER bit of the command register can be used to reset the error bits of the status register. The status register of the 8251A is shown in Fig. 8.69. Notice that bits PE, OE, and FE are error flags for the receiver. If the incoming character is found to have a parity error, the PE (parity error) bit gets set. On the other hand, if an overrun or framing error condition occurs, the OE (overrun error) or

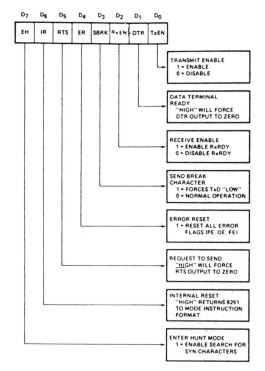

| D₇ | D₆ | D₅ | D₄ | D₃ | D₂ | D₁ | D₀ |

| EH | IR | RTS | ER | SBRK | RₓEN | DTR | TₓEN |

TRANSMIT ENABLE
1 = ENABLE
0 = DISABLE

DATA TERMINAL
READY
"HIGH" WILL FORCE
DTR OUTPUT TO ZERO

RECEIVE ENABLE
1 = ENABLE RₓRDY
0 = DISABLE RₓRDY

SEND BREAK
CHARACTER
1 = FORCES TₓD "LOW"
0 = NORMAL OPERATION

ERROR RESET
1 = RESET ALL ERROR
FLAGS (PE, OE, FE)

REQUEST TO SEND
"HIGH" WILL FORCE
RTS OUTPUT TO ZERO

INTERNAL RESET
"HIGH" RETURNS 8251
TO MODE INSTRUCTION
FORMAT

ENTER HUNT MODE
1 = ENABLE SEARCH FOR
SYN CHARACTERS

Figure 8.68 Command instruction format. (Courtesy of Intel Corp.)

FE (framing error) flag is set, respectively. The MPU should always examine these error bits before reading a character from the receive data register. If an error has occurred, a command can be issued to the command register to write a 1 into the ER bit. This causes all three of the error flags in the status register to be reset. Then a software routine can be initiated to cause the character to be retransmitted.

Let us look at just one more bit of the command register. The IR bit, which stands for internal reset, allows the 8251A to be initialized under software control. To initialize the device, the MPU simply writes a 1 into the IR bit.

Before the 8251A can be used to receive or transmit characters, its mode control and command registers must be initialized. The flowchart in Fig. 8.70 shows the sequence that must be followed when initializing the device. Let us just briefly trace through the sequence of events needed to set up the controller for asynchronous operation.

As the microcomputer powers up, it should issue a hardware reset to the 8251A. This is done by switching its RESET input to logic 1. After this, a load mode instruction must be issued to write the new configuration byte into the mode control register. Assuming that the 8251A is in the I/O address space of the 8088, the command byte formed in Example 8.32 can be written to the command register with the instruction sequence

```
MOV    DX,MODE_REG_ADDR
MOV    AL,5EH
OUT    DX,AL
```

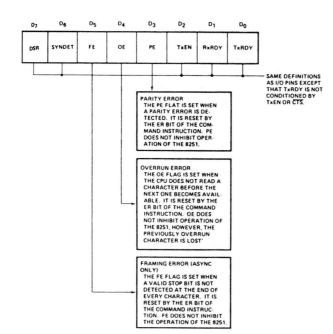

Figure 8.69 Status register. (Courtesy of Intel Corp.)

PARITY ERROR
THE PE FLAT IS SET WHEN A PARITY ERROR IS DETECTED. IT IS RESET BY THE ER BIT OF THE COMMAND INSTRUCTION. PE DOES NOT INHIBIT OPERATION OF THE 8251.

OVERRUN ERROR
THE OE FLAG IS SET WHEN THE CPU DOES NOT READ A CHARACTER BEFORE THE NEXT ONE BECOMES AVAILABLE. IT IS RESET BY THE ER BIT OF THE COMMAND INSTRUCTION. OE DOES NOT INHIBIT OPERATION OF THE 8251, HOWEVER, THE PREVIOUSLY OVERRUN CHARACTER IS LOST'

FRAMING ERROR (ASYNC ONLY)
THE FE FLAG IS SET WHEN A VALID STOP BIT IS NOT DETECTED AT THE END OF EVERY CHARACTER. IT IS RESET BY THE ER BIT OF THE COMMAND INSTRUCTION. FE DOES NOT INHIBIT THE OPERATION OF THE 8251.

SAME DEFINITIONS AS I/O PINS EXCEPT THAT TxRDY IS NOT CONDITIONED BY TxEN OR $\overline{CTS}$.

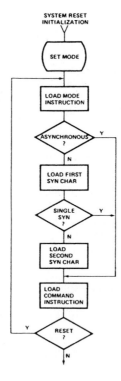

Figure 8.70 8251A initialization flowchart. (Courtesy of Intel Corp.)

where MODE_REG_ADDR is a variable equal to the address of the mode register of the 8251A.

Since bits B_2B_1 of this register are not 00, asynchronous mode of operation is selected. Therefore, we go down the branch in the flowchart to the load command instruction. Execution of another OUT instruction can load the command register with its initial value. For instance, this command could enable the transmitter and receiver by setting the Tx_{EN} and Rx_{EN} bits, respectively. During its operation the status register can be read by the microprocessor to determine if the device has received the next byte, if it is ready to send the next byte, or if any problem occurred in the transmission such as a parity error.

EXAMPLE 8.34

The circuit in Fig. 8.71(a) implements serial I/O for the 8088 microprocessor using an 8251A. It is to be used to continuously read serial characters from the RS-232C interface, complement the received characters with software, and send them back on the RS-232C interface. Each character is received and transmitted as an 8-bit character using two stop bits and no parity.

Solution

We must first determine the addresses for the registers in the 8251A that can be accessed from the microprocessor interface. Chip select ($\overline{CS}$) is enabled for I/O read or write operations to addresses for which

$$A_7A_6A_5A_4A_3A_2A_1 = 1000000$$

Bit A_0 of the address bus is used to select between the data and control (or status) registers. As shown in Fig. 8.71(b), the addresses for the data and the control (or status) register are XX80H and XX81H, respectively.

Next we must determine the mode word to select and 8-bit character with 2 stop bits and no parity. As shown in Fig. 8.71(c), it is EEH. Here we have used a baud rate factor of 16, which means that the baud rate is given as

$$\text{Baud rate} = \text{Baud rate clock}/16 = 19,200/16 = 1200 \text{ bps}$$

To enable the transmitter as well as receiver operation of the 8251A, the required command word as shown in Fig. 8.71(d) is equal to 15H. Notice that error reset has also been implemented by making the ER bit equal 1.

The flowchart of Fig. 8.71(e) shows how we can write software to implement initialization, the receive operation, and transmit operation. The program written to perform this sequence is shown in Fig. 8.71(f).

Initialization involves writing the mode word followed by the command word to the control register of the 8251A. It is important to note that this is done after the device has been reset. Since the control register's I/O address is 81H, the two words are output to this address using appropriate instructions.

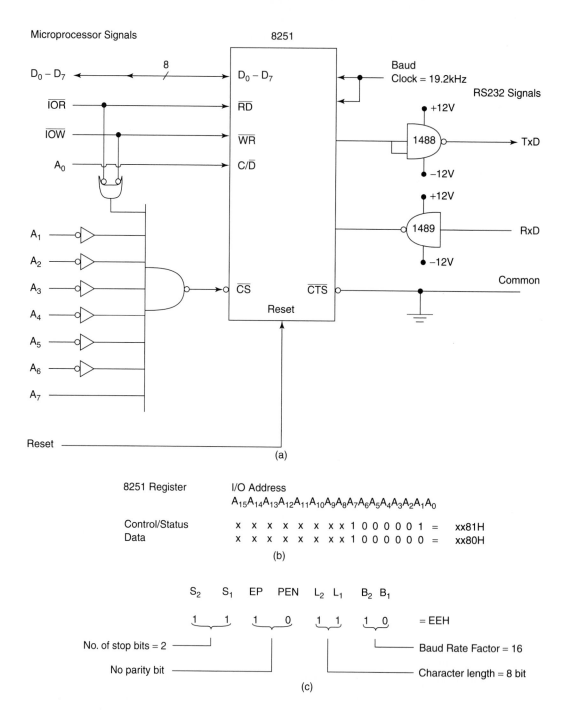

Figure 8.71 (a) Implementation of serial I/O using 8251. (b) Addresses for the 8251 registers. (c) Mode word. (d) Command word. (e) Flowchart for initialization, receive operation, and transmit operation. (f) Program for the implementation of initialization, receive operation, and transmit operation.

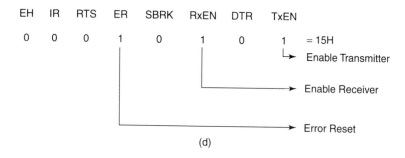

Figure 8.71 (Continued)

The receive operation starts by reading the contents of the status register at address 81H and checking if the LSB, which is Rx_{RDY} is at logic 1. If it is not 1, the routine keeps reading and checking till it does become 1. Next we read the data register at 80H for the receive data. The byte of data received is complemented and then saved for transmission.

The transmit operation also starts by reading the status register at address 81H and checking if bit 1, which is Tx_{RDY} is logic 1. If it is not, we again keep reading and checking until it becomes 1. Next the byte of data that was saved for transmission is written to the data register at address 81H. This causes it to be transmitted at the serial interface. The receive and transmit operations are repeated by jumping back to the point where the receive operation begins.

The 8250/16450 UART

The 8250 and 16450 are pin-for-pin and functionally equivalent universal asynchronous receiver transmitter ICs. These devices are newer than the 8251A USART and implement a more versatile serial I/O operation. For instance, they have a built-in programmable baud rate generator, double buffering on communication data registers, and enhanced status and interrupt signaling. The common pin layout for these devices is shown in Fig. 8.72(a).

The connection of the 8250/16450 to implement a simple RS-232C serial communications interface is shown in Fig. 8.72(b). Looking at the microprocessor interface, we find chip select inputs CS_0, CS_1, and $\overline{CS_2}$. To enable the interface, these inputs must be at logic 1, 1, and 0, respectively, at the same time that address strobe ($\overline{ADS}$) is logic 0. Therefore, the interface in Fig. 8.72(b) is enabled whenever logic 0 is applied to $\overline{CS_2}$ from the MPU's bus.

Let us next look at how data are read from or written into the registers of the 8250/16450. Data transfers between the MPU and communication controller take place over data bus lines D_0 through D_7. The MPU signals the peripheral whether a data input or output operation is to occur with the logic level at the data input strobe ($\overline{DISTR}$) and data output strobe ($\overline{DOSTR}$) inputs. Notice that when data are output during a memory write or output bus cycle, the MPU notifies the

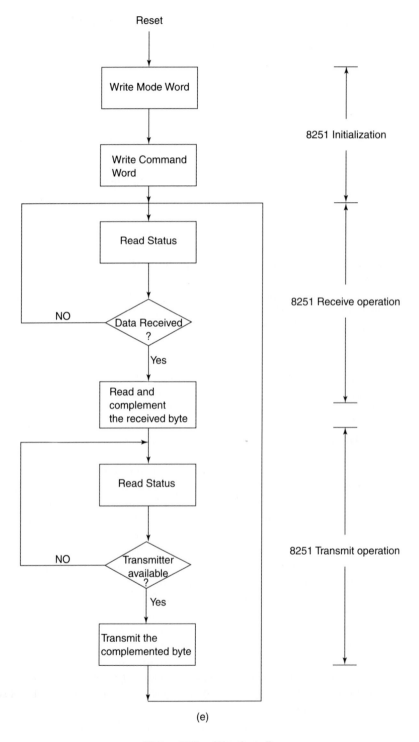

(e)

Figure 8.71 (Continued)

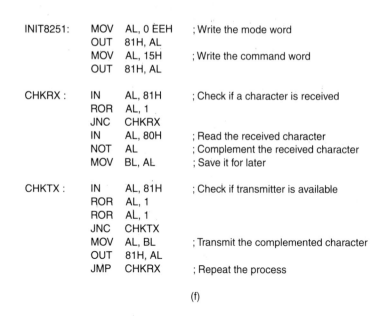

```
INIT8251:    MOV   AL, 0 EEH      ; Write the mode word
             OUT   81H, AL
             MOV   AL, 15H        ; Write the command word
             OUT   81H, AL

CHKRX :      IN    AL, 81H        ; Check if a character is received
             ROR   AL, 1
             JNC   CHKRX
             IN    AL, 80H        ; Read the received character
             NOT   AL             ; Complement the received character
             MOV   BL, AL         ; Save it for later

CHKTX :      IN    AL, 81H        ; Check if transmitter is available
             ROR   AL, 1
             ROR   AL, 1
             JNC   CHKTX
             MOV   AL, BL         ; Transmit the complemented character
             OUT   81H, AL
             JMP   CHKRX          ; Repeat the process
```

(f)

Figure 8.71 (Continued)

8250/16450 with logic 0 on the $\overline{\text{MEMW}}$ or $\overline{\text{I/OW}}$ signal line, which is applied to the $\overline{\text{DOSTR}}$ input.

During the read or write bus cycle, the register that is accessed is determined by the code at register select inputs A0, A1, and A2. In Fig. 8.68(b), we find that these inputs are attached to address lines A_0 through A_2, respectively. The registers selected by the various register select codes are shown in Fig. 8.73. Notice that the setting of the divisor latch bit (DLAB), which is in the line control register, is also involved in the selection of the register. For example, to write to the line control register the code at $A_2A_1A_0$ must be 011_2. Moreover, to read the receive buffer register the DLAB bit in the line control register must first be set to 0 and then a read performed with register select code $A_2A_1A_0$ equal to 000_2.

The function of the various bits of the 8250/16450's registers are summarized in the table of Fig. 8.74(a). Notice that the receive buffer register (RBR) and transmitter hold register (THR) correspond to the read and write functions of register 0. However, as mentioned earlier to perform these read or write operations the divisor latch bit (DLAB), which is bit 7 of the line control register (LCR), must have already been set to 0. From the table, we find that other bits of LCR are used to define the serial character data structure. For instance, Fig. 8.74(b) shows how the *word length select bits*, bit 0 (WLS$_0$) and bit 1 (WLS$_1$) of LCR select the number of bits in the serial character. Bit 2, *number of stop bits* (STB), selects the number of stop bits. If it is set to logic 0, one stop bit is generated for all transmitted data. On the other hand, if bit 2 is set to 1 one and a half stop bits are produced if character length is set to five bits and two stop bits are supplied if character length is six or more bits. The next two bits, bit 3 *parity enable* (PEN) and bit 4 *even parity*

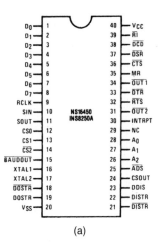

(a)

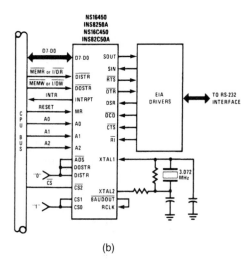

(b)

Figure 8.72 (a) Pin layout of the 8250/16450 UART (Courtesy of National Semiconductor Corporation). (b) 8250/16450 RS-232C interface. (Courtesy of National Semiconductor Corporation)

select (EPS), are used to select parity. First parity is enabled by making bit 3 logic 1 and then even or odd parity is selected by making bit 4 logic 1or 0, respectively. The LCR can be loaded with the appropriate configuration information under software control.

Looking at Fig. 8.72(b) we see that the baud rate generator is operated off a 3.072 MHz crystal. This crystal frequency can be divided within the 8250/16450 to produce a variety of data communication baud rates. The divisor values required

DLAB	A_2	A_1	A_0	Register
0	0	0	0	Receiver Buffer (read), Transmitter Holding Register (write)
0	0	0	1	Interrupt Enable
X	0	1	0	Interrupt Identification (read only)
X	0	1	1	Line Control
X	1	0	0	MODEM Control
X	1	0	1	Line Status
X	1	1	0	MODEM Status
X	1	1	1	Scratch
1	0	0	0	Divisor Latch (least significant byte)
1	0	0	1	Divisor Latch (most significant byte)

Figure 8.73 Register select codes. (Courtesy of National Semiconductor Corporation)

to produce standard baud rates are shown in Fig. 8.75. For example, to set the asynchronous data communication rate to 300 baud, a divisor equal to 640 must be used. The 16-bit divider must be loaded under software control into the divisor latch registers, DLL and DLM. Figure 8.74(a) shows that the eight least significant bits of the divisor are in DLL and the eight most significant bits in DLM.

EXAMPLE 8.35

What count must be loaded into the divisor latch registers to set the data communication rate to 2400 baud? What address code must be applied to the 8250/16450 when writing the bytes of the divider count into the DLL and DLM registers?

Solution

Looking at Fig. 8.75, we find that the divisor for 2400 baud is 80. When writing the byte into DLL, the address must make

$$A_2A_1A_0 = 000_2 \text{ with DLAB} = 1$$

and the value that is written is

$$DLL = 80 = 50H$$

For DLM the address must make

$$A_2A_1A_0 = 001_2 \text{ with DLAB} = 1$$

and the data is

$$DLM = 0 = 00H$$

	Register Address										
Bit No.	0 DLAB=0	0 DLAB=0	1 DLAB=0	2	3	4	5	6	7	0 DLAB=1	1 DLAB=1
	Receiver Buffer Register (Read Only)	Transmitter Holding Register (Write Only)	Interrupt Enable Register	Interrupt Ident. Register (Read Only)	Line Control Register	MODEM Control Register	Line Status Register	MODEM Status Register	Scratch Register	Divisor Latch (LS)	Latch (MS)
	RBR	THR	IER	IIR	LCR	MCR	LSR	MSR	SCR	DLL	DLM
0	Data Bit 0*	Data Bit 0	Enable Received Data Available Interrupt (ERBFI)	"0" if Interrupt Pending	Word Length Select Bit 0 (WLS0)	Data Terminal Ready (DTR)	Data Ready (DR)	Delta Clear to Send (DCTS)	Bit 0	Bit 0	Bit 8
1	Data Bit 1	Data Bit 1	Enable Transmitter Holding Register Empty Interrupt (ETBEI)	Interrupt ID Bit (0)	Word Length Select Bit 1 (WLS1)	Request to Send (RTS)	Overrun Error (OE)	Delta Data Set Ready (DDSR)	Bit 1	Bit 1	Bit 9
2	Data Bit 2	Data Bit 2	Enable Receiver Line Status Interrupt (ELSI)	Interrupt ID Bit (1)	Number of Stop Bits (STB)	Out 1	Parity Error (PE)	Trailing Edge Ring Indicator (TERI)	Bit 2	Bit 2	Bit 10
3	Data Bit 3	Data Bit 3	Enable MODEM Status Interrupt (EDSSI)	0	Parity Enable (PEN)	Out 2	Framing Error (FE)	Delta Data Carrier Detect (DDCD)	Bit 3	Bit 3	Bit 11
4	Data Bit 4	Data Bit 4	0	0	Even Parity Select (EPS)	Loop	Break Interrupt (BI)	Clear to Send (CTS)	Bit 4	Bit 4	Bit 12
5	Data Bit 5	Data Bit 5	0	0	Stick Parity	0	Transmitter Holding Register (THRE)	Data Set Ready (DSR)	Bit 5	Bit 5	Bit 13
6	Data Bit 6	Data Bit 6	0	0	Set Break	0	Transmitter Empty (TEMT)	Ring Indicator (RI)	Bit 6	Bit 6	Bit 14
7	Data Bit 7	Data Bit 7	0	0	Divisor Latch Access Bit (DLAB)	0	0	Data Carrier Detect (DCD)	Bit 7	Bit 7	Bit 15

*Bit 0 is the least significant bit. It is the first bit serially transmitted or received.

(a)

Bit 1	Bit 0	Word Length
0	0	5 Bits
0	1	6 Bits
1	0	7 Bits
1	1	8 Bits

(b)

Figure 8.74 (a) Register bit functions. (Courtesy of National Semiconductor Corporation) (b) Word length select bits. (Courtesy of National Semiconductor Corporation)

Desired Baud Rate	Divisor Used to Generate 16 x Clock	Percent Error Difference Between Desired and Actual
50	3840	—
75	2560	—
110	1745	0.026
134.5	1428	0.034
150	1280	—
300	640	—
600	320	—
1200	160	—
1800	107	0.312
2000	96	—
2400	80	—
3600	53	0.628
4800	40	—
7200	27	1.23
9600	20	—
19200	10	—
38400	5	—

Figure 8.75 Baud rates and corresponding divisors. (Courtesy of National Semiconductor Corporation)

Let us now turn our attention to the right side of the 8250/16450 in Fig. 8.72(b). Here the RS-232C serial communication interface is implemented. We find that the transmit data are output in serial for over the serial output (S_{OUT}) line and receive data are input over the serial input (S_{IN}) line. Handshaking for the asynchronous serial interface are implemented with the request to send ($\overline{RTS}$) and data terminal ready ($\overline{DTR}$) ouptuts and the data set ready ($\overline{DSR}$), data carrier detect ($\overline{DCD}$), clear to send ($\overline{CTS}$), and ring indicator (RI) inputs.

The serial interface input/output signals are buffered by EIA drivers for compatiblity with RS-232C voltage levels and drive currents. For example, a MC1488 driver IC can be used to buffer the output lines. It contains four TTL level to RS-232C drivers, each of which is actually a NAND gate. The MC1488 requires a +12V, −12V, and ground supply connections to provide the mark and space transmission voltage levels. The input lines of the interface can be buffered by the gates of a MC1489 RS-232C to TTL level driver. This IC contains four inverting buffers with tri-state outputs and operated from a single +5V supply. Figure 8.76 shows an RS-232C interface including the EIA driver circuitry.

▲ 8.17 SPECIAL-PURPOSE INTERFACE CONTROLLERS

Up to this point, we have introduced LSI controllers for some of the most widely used I/O interfaces. A large number of other LSI devices are available to simplify the implementation of other complex I/O interfaces. Some examples are keyboard/display controllers, CRT controllers, floppy disk controllers, hard disk controllers, and IEEE-488 bus controllers. Here we will introduce just one of these devices, the *8279 programmable keyboard/display interface*. However, before starting the 8279, let us briefly examine how the keyboard and display are typically serviced in a microcomputer system.

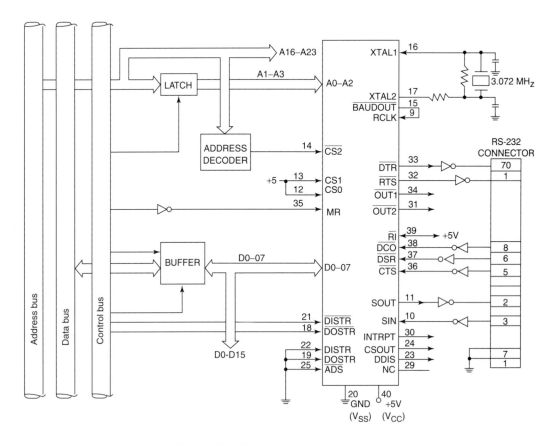

Figure 8.76 RS-232C interface with EIA drivers.

The Keyboard and Display Interfaces

A keyboard and display are important input and output devices in many digital electronic systems. For instance, all calculators and hand-held computers have both a keyboard and a display.

The circuit diagram in Fig. 8.77 shows how a keyboard is most frequently interfaced to a microcomputer. Note that the switches in the keyboard are arranged in an *array*. The size of the array is described in terms of the number of rows and the number of columns. In our example, the keyboard array has four rows, which are labeled R_0 through R_3, and four columns, which are labeled C_0 through C_3. The location of the switch for any key in the array is uniquely defined by a row and a column. For instance, the 0 key is located at the junction of R_0 and C_0, while the 1 key is located at R_0 and C_1.

Now that we know how the keys of the keyboard are arranged, let us look at how the microcomputer services them. In most applications, the microcomputer scans the keyboard array. That is, it strobes one row of the keyboard after the

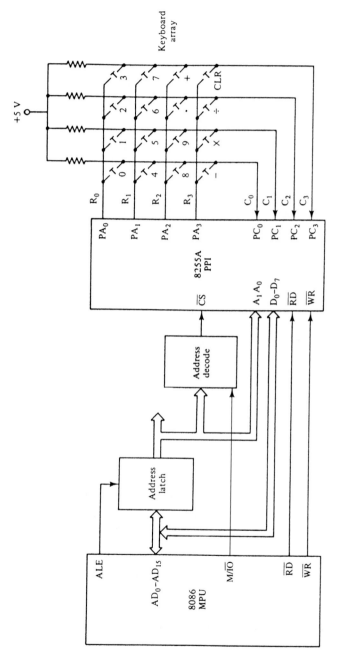

Figure 8.77 Keyboard interfaced to a microcomputer.

other by sending out a short-duration pulse, to the 0 logic level, on the row line. During each row strobe, all column lines are examined by reading them in parallel. Typically, the column lines are pulled up to the 1 logic level; therefore, if a switch is closed, a logic 0 will be read on the corresponding column line. If no switches are closed, all 1s will be read when the column lines are examined.

For instance, if the 2 key is depressed when the microcomputer is scanning R_0, the column code read back will be $C_3C_2C_1C_0 = 1011$. Since the microcomputer knows which row it is scanning (R_0) and which column the strobe was returned on (C_2), it can determine that the number 2 key was depressed. The microcomputer does not necessarily store the row and column codes in the form that we have shown. It is more common to just maintain the binary equivalent of the row or column. In our example, the microcomputer would internally store the row number as $R_0 = 00$ and the column number as $C_2 = 10$. This is a more compact representation of the row and column information.

Several other issues arise when designing keyboards for microcomputer systems. One is that when a key in the keyboard is depressed, its contacts bounce for a short period of time. Depending on the keyboard sampling method, this could result in incorrect reading of the keyboard input. This problem is overcome by a technique known as *keyboard debouncing*. Debouncing is achieved by resampling the column lines a second time, about 10 ms later, to assure that the same column line is at the 0 logic level. If so, it is then accepted as a valid input. This technique can be implemented either in hardware or software.

Another problem occurs in keyboard sampling when more than one key is depressed at a time. In this case, the column code read by the microcomputer would have more than 1 bit that is logic 0. For instance, if the 0 and 2 keys were depressed, the column code read back during the scan of R_0 would be $C_3C_2C_1C_0 = 1010$. Typically, two keys are not actually depressed at the same time. It is more common that the second key is depressed while the first one is still being held down and that the column code showing two key closures would show up in the second test which is made for debouncing.

Several different techniques are used to overcome this problem. One is called *two-key lockout*. With this method, the occurrence of a second key during the debounce scan causes both keys to be locked out and neither is accepted by the microcomputer. If the second key that was depressed is released before the first key is released, the first key entry is accepted and the second key is ignored. On the other hand, if the first key is released before the second key, only the second key is accepted.

A second method of solving this problem is that known as *N-key rollover*. In this case, more than one key can be depressed at a time and get accepted by the microcomputer. The microcomputer keeps track of the order in which they are depressed and as long as the switch closures are still present at another keyboard scan 10 ms later, they are accepted. That is, in the case of multiple key depressions, the key entries are accepted in the order in which their switches are closed.

The display interface used in most microcomputer systems is shown in Fig. 8.78. Here we are using a four-digit seven-segment numeric display. Notice that segment lines 'a' through 'g' of all digits of the display are driven in parallel by

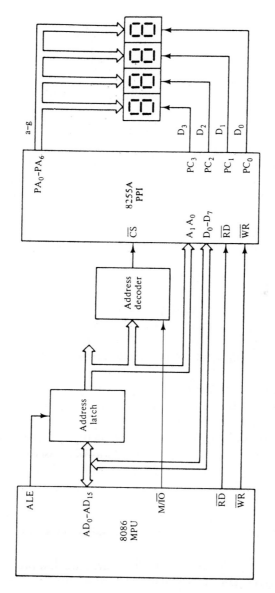

Figure 8.78 Display interfaced to a microcomputer.

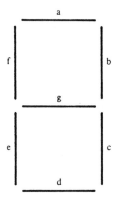

Figure 8.79 Seven-segment display labeling.

outputs of the microcomputer. It is over these lines that the microcomputer outputs signals to tell the display which segments are to be lighted to form the numbers in its digits. The way in which the segments of a seven-segment display digit are labeled is shown in Fig. 8.79. For instance, to form the number 1, a code is output to light just segments b and c.

The other set of lines in the display interface correspond to the digits of the display. These lines, which are labeled D_0 through D_3, correspond to digits 0, 1, 2, and 3, respectively. It is with these signals that the microcomputer indicates to the display which digit the number corresponding to the code on lines a through g should be displayed.

The way in which the display is driven by the microcomputer is said to be *multiplexed*. That is, data are not permanently displayed; instead, they are output to one digit after the other in time. This scanning sequence is repeated frequently such that the fact that the display is not permanently lighted cannot be recognized by the user.

The scanning of the digits of the display is similar to the scanning we have just described for the rows of the keyboard. A digit drive signal is output to one digit of the display after the other in time and during each digit drive pulse the seven-segment code for the number that is to be displayed in that digit is output on segment lines a through g. In fact, in most systems the digit drive signals for the display and row drive signals of the keyboard are supplied by the same set of outputs.

The 8279 Programmable Keyboard/Display Controller

The 8279 is an LSI device that is designed to make implementation of a keyboard/display interface similar to that which we have just described quite simple. This device can drive an 8 × 8 keyboard switch array and a 16-digit eight-segment display. Moreover, it can be configured through software to support key debouncing, two-key lockout, or N-key rollover modes of operation, and either left or right data entry to the display.

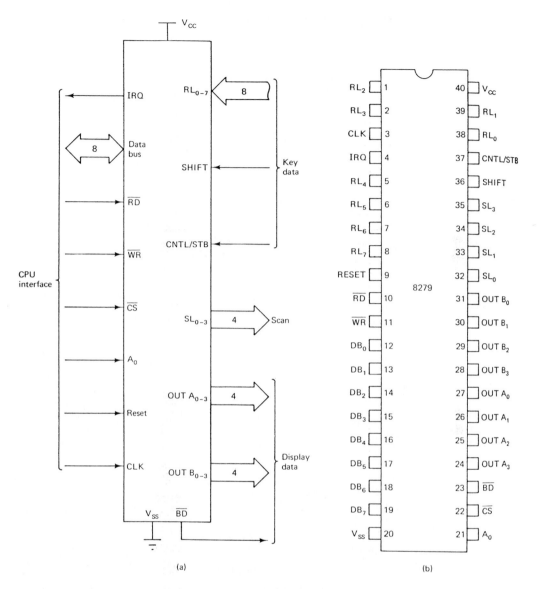

Figure 8.80 (a) Block diagram of the 8279. (Courtesy of Intel Corp.) (b) Pin layout. (Courtesy of Intel Corp.)

A block diagram of the device is shown in Fig. 8.80(a) and its pin layout in Fig. 8.80(b). From this diagram we see that there are four signal sections: The *MPU interface*, the *key data inputs*, the *display data outputs*, and the *scan lines* that are used by both the keyboard and display. Let us first look at the function of each of these interfaces.

The bus interface of the 8279 is similar to that found on the other peripherals that we have considered up to this point. It consists of the eight data bus lines DB_0

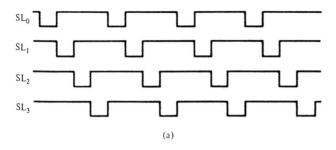

(a)

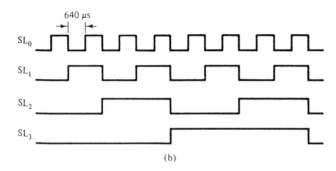

640 μs

(b)

Figure 8.81 (a) Decoded-mode scan line signals. (Courtesy of Intel Corp.) (b) Encoded-mode scan line signals. (Courtesy of Intel Corp.)

through DB_7. These are the lines over which the MPU outputs data to the display, inputs key codes, issues commands to the controller, and reads status information from the controller. Other signals found at the interface are the read ($\overline{RD}$), write ($\overline{WR}$), chip select ($\overline{CS}$), and address buffer (A_0) control signals. They are the signals that control the data bus transfers that take place between the microprocessor and 8279.

A new signal introduced with this interface is *interrupt request* (IRQ). This is an output that gets returned to an interrupt input of the 8088/8086 microcomputer. This signal is provided so that the 8279 can tell the MPU that it contains key codes that should be read.

The scan lines are used as row drive signals for the keyboard and digit drive signals for the display. There are just four of these lines, SL_0 through SL_3. However, they can be configured for two different modes of operation through software. In applications that require a small keyboard and display (four or less rows and digits), they can be used in what is known as the *decoded mode*. Scan output waveforms for this mode of operation are shown in Fig. 8.81(a). Notice that a pulse to the 0 logic level is produced at one output after the other in time.

The second mode of operation, which is called *encoded mode*, allows use of a keyboard matrix with up to eight rows and a display with up to 16 digits. When this mode of operation is enabled through software, the binary-coded waveforms shown in Fig. 8.77(b) are output on the SL lines. These signals must be decoded with an external decoder circuit to produce the digit and column drive signals.

Even though 16-digit drive signals are produced, only eight-row drive signals can be used for the keyboard. This is because the key code that is stored when a

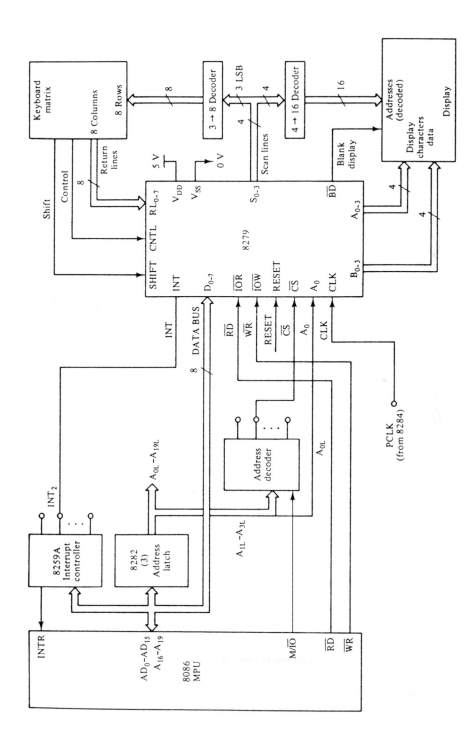

Figure 8.82   System configuration using the 8086 and 8279. (Courtesy of Intel Corp.)

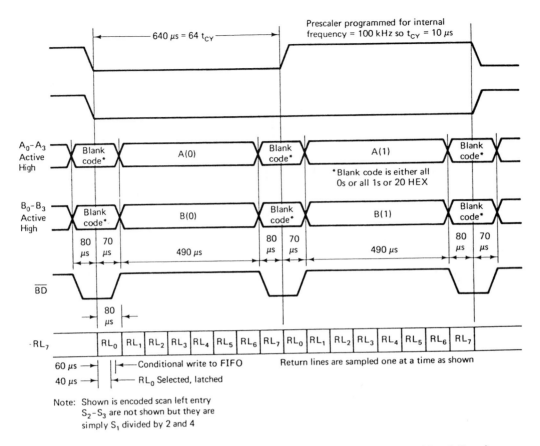

Figure 8.83 Keyboard and display signal timing. (Courtesy of Intel Corp.)

key depression has been sensed has just 3 bits allocated to identify the row. Figure 8.82 shows this kind of circuit configuration.

The key data lines include the eight return lines RL_0 through RL_7. These lines receive inputs from the column outputs of the keyboard array. They are not tested all at once as we described earlier. Looking at the waveforms in Fig. 8.83, we see that the RL lines are examined one after the other during each 640-μs row pulse.

If logic 0 is detected at a return line, the number of the column is coded as a 3-bit binary number and combined with the 3-bit row number to make a 6-bit key code. This key code input is first debounced and then loaded into an 8×8 key code FIFO within the 8279. Once the FIFO contains a key code, the IRQ output is set to logic 1. This signal can be used to tell the MPU that a keyboard input should be read from the 8279. There are two other signal inputs in this section. They are shift (SHIFT) and control/strobed (CNTL/STB). The logic levels at these two inputs are also stored as part of the key code when a switch closure is detected. The format of the complete key code byte that is stored in the FIFO is shown in Fig. 8.84.

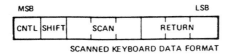

Figure 8.84 Key code byte format. (Courtesy of Intel Corp.)

A status register is provided within the 8279 that contains flags that indicate the status of the *key code FIFO*. The bits of the status register and their meanings are shown in Fig. 8.85. Notice that the three least significant bits, which are labeled NNN, identify the number of key codes that are currently held in the FIFO. The next bit, F, indicates whether or not the FIFO is full. The two bits that follow it, U and O, represent two FIFO error conditions. O, which stands for overrun, indicates that an attempt was made to enter another key code into the FIFO when it was already full. This condition could occur if the microprocessor does not respond quick enough to the IRQ signal by reading key codes out of the FIFO. The other error condition, underrun (U), means that the microprocessor attempted to read the contents of the FIFO when it was empty. The microprocessor can read the contents of the status register under software control.

The display data lines include two 4-bit output ports, OUT A_0 through OUT A_3 and OUT B_0 through OUT B_3, that are used as display segment drive lines. Segment data that are output on these lines are held in a dedicated display RAM area within the 8279. This RAM is organized 16×8 and must be loaded with segment data by the microprocessor. In Fig. 8.83 we see that during each 640-μs scan time the segment data for one of the digits are output at the OUT A and OUT B ports.

The operation of the 8279 must be configured through software. Eight command words are provided for this purpose. These control words are loaded into the device by performing write (output) operations to the device with buffer address bit A_0 set to logic 1. Let us now look briefly at the function of each of these control words.

The first command (*command word 0*) is used to set the mode of operation for the keyboard and display. The general format of this word is shown in Fig. 8.86(a). Here we see that the three most significant bits are always reset. These three bits are a code by which the 8279 identifies which command is being issued by the microprocessor. The next two bits, which are labeled DD, are used to set the mode of operation for the display. The table in Fig. 8.86(b) shows the options

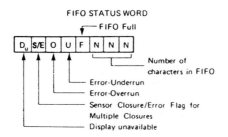

Figure 8.85 Status register. (Courtesy of Intel Corp.)

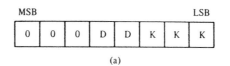

MSB   LSB

| 0 | 0 | 0 | D | D | K | K | K |

(a)

D	D	Display operation
0	0	8 8-bit character display – Left entry
0	1	16 8-bit character display – Left entry
1	0	8 8-bit character display – Right entry
1	1	16 8-bit character display -- Right entry

(b)

K	K	K	Keyboard operation
0	0	0	Encoded Scan Keyboard – 2-Key Lockout
0	0	1	Decoded Scan Keyboard – 2-Key Lockout
0	1	0	Encoded Scan Keyboard – N-Key Rollover
0	1	1	Decoded Scan Keyboard – N-Key Rollover
1	0	0	Encoded Scan Sensor Matrix
1	0	1	Decoded Scan Sensor Matrix
1	1	0	Strobed Input, Encoded Display Scan
1	1	1	Strobed Input, Decoded Display Scan

(c)

Figure 8.86 (a) Command word 0 format. (Courtesy of Intel Corp.) (b) Display mode select codes. (Courtesy of Intel Corp.) (c) Keyboard select codes. (Courtesy of Intel Corp.)

that are available. After power-up reset, these bits are set to 01. From the table we see that this configures the display for 16 digits with left entry. By left entry we mean that characters are entered into the display starting from the left.

The three least significant bits of the command word (KKK) set the mode of operation of the display. They are used to configure the operation of the keyboard according to the table in Fig. 8.86(c). The default code at power up is 000 and selects encoded scan operation with two-key lockout.

EXAMPLE 8.36

What should be the value of command word 0 if the display is to be set for eight eight-segment digits with right entry and the keyboard for decoded scan with N-key rollover?

Solution

The three MSBs of the command word are always 0. The next two bits, DD, must be set to 10 for eight eight-segment digits with right entry. Finally, the three LSBs are set to 011 for decoded keyboard scan with N-key rollover. This gives

$$\text{Command word } 0 = 000\text{DDKKK}$$
$$= 00010011_2$$
$$= 13_{16}$$

Command word 1 is used to set the frequency of operation of the 8279. It is designed to run at 100 kHz; however, in most applications a much higher frequency signal is available to supply its CLK input. For this reason, a *5-bit programmable prescaler* is provided within the 8279 to divide down the input frequency. The format of this command word is shown in Fig. 8.87.

For instance, in a 5-MHz 8086-based microcomputer system, the PCLK output of the 8284 clock driver IC can be used for the 8279's clock input. PCLK is one-half the frequency of the oscillator or 2.5 MHz. In this case the divider P must be

$$P = 2.5 \text{ MHz}/100 \text{ kHz} = 25$$

Twenty-five expressed as a 5-bit binary number is

$$P = 11001_2$$

Therefore, the value of command word 1 written to the 8279 is

$$\text{Command word } 1 = 001\text{PPPPP}_2$$
$$= 00111001_2$$
$$= 39_{16}$$

Let us skip now to *command word 6* because it is also used for initialization of the 8279. It can be used to initialize the complete display memory, the FIFO status, and the interrupt request output line. The format of this word is given in Fig. 8.88(a). The three C_D bits are used to control initialization of the display RAM. Figure 8.88(b) shows what values can be used in these locations. The C_F bit is provided for clearing the FIFO status and resetting the IRQ line. To perform the reset operation, a 1 must be written to C_F. The last bit, clear all (C_A), can be used to initiate both the C_D and C_F functions.

Figure 8.87 Command word 1 format. (Courtesy of Intel Corp.)

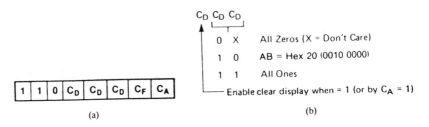

		0	X		All Zeros (X = Don't Care)
		1	0		AB = Hex 20 (0010 0000)
		1	1		All Ones

Figure 8.88 (a) Command word 6 format. (Courtesy of Intel Corp.) (b) C_D coding. (Courtesy of Intel Corp.)

EXAMPLE 8.37

What clear operations are performed if the value of command word 6 written to the 8279 is $D2_{16}$?

Solution

First we need to express the command word in binary form. This gives

$$\text{Command word } 6 = D2_{16} = 11010010_2$$

Note that the most significant C_D bit is set and the C_D bit that follows it is reset. This combination causes display memory to be cleared with all 0s. The C_F bit is also set and this causes the FIFO status and IRQ output to be reset.

As shown in Fig. 8.89, only one bit of *command word 7* is functional. This bit is labeled E and is an enable signal for what is called the special error mode. When this mode is enabled and the keyboard has N-key rollover selected, a multiple-key depression causes the S/E flag of the FIFO status register to be set. This flag can be read by the microprocessor through software.

The rest of the command codes are related to accessing the key code FIFO and display RAM. The key code FIFO is read only. However, before the microprocessor can access it, a read FIFO command must be issued to the 8279. This is *command word 2* and has the format shown in Fig. 8.90. When the 8279 is set up for keyboard scanning, the AI and AAA bits are don't-care states. Then all that needs to be done is issue the command $01000000_2 = 40_{16}$ to the 8279 and initiate read (input) cycles to the address of the 8279. For each read bus cycle, the key code at the top of the FIFO is read into the MPU.

The display RAM can be both read from or written into by the MPU. Just like for the FIFO, a command must be sent to the 8279 before reading or writing

| 1 | 1 | 1 | E | X | X | X | X | X = Don't care

Figure 8.89 Command word 7 format. (Courtesy of Intel Corp.)

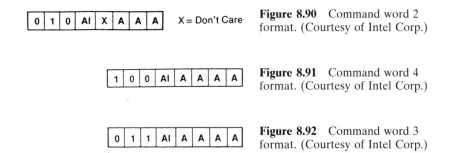

| 0 | 1 | 0 | AI | X | A | A | A | X = Don't Care

Figure 8.90 Command word 2 format. (Courtesy of Intel Corp.)

| 1 | 0 | 0 | AI | A | A | A | A |

Figure 8.91 Command word 4 format. (Courtesy of Intel Corp.)

| 0 | 1 | 1 | AI | A | A | A | A |

Figure 8.92 Command word 3 format. (Courtesy of Intel Corp.)

can be initiated. For instance, when the microprocessor wants to send new data to the display, it must first issue *command word 4*. This command has the format shown in Fig. 8.91. Here the AAAA in the four least significant bit locations is the address of the first location to be accessed. For instance, if 0000_2 is put into these bits of the command, the first write operation will be to the first location in display RAM. Moreover, if the AI bit is set in the command, autoincrement addressing is enabled. In this way, the display RAM address pointer is automatically incremented after the write operation is complete and a write cycle can be initiated to address 0001_2 of display RAM without first issuing another write command.

The MPU can also read the contents of the display RAM in a similar way. This requires that *command word 3* be issued to the 8279. Figure 8.92 shows the format of this read display RAM command.

ASSIGNMENTS

Section 8.2

1. Name the two types of input/output.
2. What type of I/O is in use when peripheral devices are mapped to the 8088's I/O address space?
3. Which type of I/O has the disadvantage that part of the address space must be given up to implement I/O ports?
4. Which type of I/O has the disadvantage that all I/O data transfers must take place through the AL or AX register?

Section 8.3

5. What are the functions of the 8088's address and data bus lines relative to an isolated I/O operation?
6. In a minimum-mode 8088 microcomputer, which signal indicates to external circuitry that the current bus cycle is for the I/O interface and not the memory interface?
7. List the differences between the 8088's minimum-mode I/O interface in Fig. 8.3(a) and that of the 8086 in Fig. 8.3(b).

8. What is the logic relationship between the signals $IO/\overline{M}$ and $M/\overline{IO}$?

9. In a maximum-mode system, which device produces the input (read), output (write), and bus control signals for the I/O interface?

10. Briefly describe the function of each block in the I/O interface circuit in Fig. 8.4(a).

11. In a maximum-mode 8086 microcomputer, what status code identifies an input bus cycle?

12. In the maximum-mode I/O interface of Fig. 8.4(a), what are the logic levels of $\overline{IORC}$, $\overline{IOWC}$, and $\overline{AIOWC}$ during an output bus cycle?

Section 8.4

13. How many bits are in the 8088's I/O address?

14. What is the range of byte addresses in the 8088's I/O address space?

15. What is the size of the 8086's I/O address space in terms of word-wide I/O ports?

16. In an 8086-based microcomputer system, what are the logic levels of A_0 and $\overline{BHE}$ when a byte of data is being written to I/O address $A000_{16}$? If a word of data is being written to address $A000_{16}$?

17. In an 8088 microcomputer system, how many bus cycles are required to output a word of data to I/O address $A000_{16}$? In an 8086 microcomputer system?

Section 8.5

18. Describe the operation performed by the instruction IN AX,1AH.

19. Write an instruction sequence to perform the same operation as that of the instruction in problem 18, but this time use variable or indirect I/O.

20. Describe the operation performed by the instruction OUT 2AH,AL.

21. Write an instruction sequence that will output the byte of data $0F_{16}$ to an output port at address 1000_{16}.

22. Write a sequence of instructions that will input the byte of data from input ports at I/O addresses $A000_{16}$ and $B000_{16}$, add these values together, and save the sum in memory location IO_SUM.

23. Write a sequence of instructions that will input the contents of the input port at I/O address $B0_{16}$ and jump to the beginning of a service routine identified by the label ACTIVE_INPUT if the least significant bit of the data is 1.

Section 8.6

24. In the 8088's input bus cycle, during which T state do the $IO/\overline{M}$, ALE, $\overline{RD}$, and $\overline{DEN}$ control signals become active?

25. During which T state in the 8088's input bus cycle is the address output on the bus? Are data read from the bus by the MPU?

26. If an 8088 is running at 5 MHz, what is the duration of the output bus operation performed by executing the instruction OUT 0C0H,AX?

27. If an 8086 running at 10 MHz inserts two wait states into all I/O bus cycles, what is the duration of a bus cycle in which a byte of data is being output?

28. If the 8086 in problem 27 was outputting a word of data to a word-wide port at I/O address $1A1_{16}$, what would be the duration of the bus cycle?

Section 8.7

29. What is the address of port 7 in the circuit of Fig. 8.11(a)?

30. What are the inputs of the I/O address decoder in Fig. 8.11(a) when the I/O address on the bus is $800A_{16}$? Which output is active? Which output port does this enable?

31. What operation does the instruction sequence

```
MOV   AL,0FFH
MOV   DX,8004H
OUT   DX,AL
```

perform to the circuit in Fig. 8.11(a)?

32. Write a sequence of instructions to output the word contents of the memory location called DATA to output ports 0 and 1 in the circuit of Fig. 8.11(a).

Section 8.8

33. Which input port in the circuit of Fig. 8.13 is selected for operation if the I/O address output on the bus is 8008_{16}?

34. What operation is performed to the circuit in Fig. 8.13 when the instruction sequence

```
MOV   DX,8000H
IN    AL,DX
AND   AL,0FH
MOV   [LOW_NIBBLE],AL
```

is executed?

35. Write a sequence of instructions to read in the contents of ports 1 and 2 in the circuit of Fig. 8.13 and save them at consecutive memory addresses $A0000_{16}$ and $A0001_{16}$ in memory.

36. Write an instruction sequence that will poll input I_{63} in the circuit of Fig. 8.13 checking for it to switch to logic 0.

Section 8.9

37. Name a method that can be used to synchronize the input or output of information to a peripheral device.

38. List the control signals in the parallel printer interface circuit of Fig. 8.16(a). Identify whether they are an input or output of the printer and briefly describe their functions.

39. Give an overview of what happens when a write bus cycle of byte-wide data is performed to I/O address 8000_{16} in Fig. 8.11(a).

40. Show what push and pop instructions are needed in the program written in Example 8.9 to preserve the contents of registers used by it so that it can be used as a subroutine.

Section 8.10

41. What kind of input/output interface is a PPI used to implement? How many I/O lines are available on the 8255A?

42. Figure 8.18 is modified so that A_1A_0 of the 8255A is supplied from A_3A_2 of the microprocessor. The $\overline{CS}$ is activated when $A_{15}A_{14}A_{13}A_{12} \ldots A_4 = 110000000000$. A_1 and A_0 are don't care states. List the addresses for port A, port B, port C, and the control register.

43. If the value $A4_{16}$ is written to the control register of an 8255A, what is the mode and I/O configuration of port A? Port B?

44. What function can be served by the port B lines of the 8255A when port A is configured for mode 2 operation?

45. Describe the mode 0, mode 1, and mode 2 I/O operations of the 8255A PPI.

46. What should be the control word if ports A, B, and C are to be configured for mode 0 operation? Moreover, ports A and B are to be used as inputs and C as an output.

47. Assume that the control register of an 8255A resides at memory address 00100_{16}. Write an instruction sequence to load it with the control word formed in problem 46.

48. If the value 03_{16} is written to the control register of an 8255A, what bit at port C is affected by the bit set/reset operation? Is it set to 1 or cleared to 0?

49. Assume that the control register of an 8255A is at I/O address 0100_{16}. Write an instruction sequence that will load it with the bit set/reset value given in problem 48.

Section 8.11

50. If I/O address $003E_{16}$ is applied to the circuit in Fig. 8.30 during a write cycle and the data output on the bus is 98_{16}, which 8255A is being accessed? Are data being written into port A, port B, port C, or the control register of this device?

51. If the instruction

```
IN  AL,08H
```

is executed to the I/O interface circuit in Fig. 8.30, what operation is performed?

52. What are the addresses of the A, B, and C ports of PPI 2 in the circuit of Fig. 8.31?

53. Assume that PPI 2 in Fig. 8.31 is configured as defined in problem 52. Write a program that will input the data at ports A and B, add these values together, and output the sum to port C.

Section 8.12

54. Distinguish between memory-mapped I/O and accumulator I/O.

55. What address inputs must be applied to the circuit in Fig. 8.32 in order to access port B of device 4? Assuming that all unused bits are 0, what would be the memory address?

56. Write an instruction that will load the control register of the port identified in problem 55 with the value 98_{16}.

57. Repeat problem 53 for the circuit in Fig. 8.33.

Section 8.13

58. What are the inputs and outputs of counter 2 of an 8253?

59. Write a control word for counter 1 that selects the following options: load least significant byte only, mode 5 of operation, and binary counting.

60. What are the logic levels of inputs $\overline{CS}$, $\overline{RD}$, $\overline{WR}$, A_1, and A_0 when the byte in problem 59 is written to an 8253?

61. Write an instruction sequence that will load the control word in problem 59 into an 8253 that is located starting at address 01000_{16} of the memory address space. A_1A_0 of the microprocessor are directly connected to A_1A_0 of the 8253.

62. Write an instruction sequence that will write the value 12_{16} into the least significant byte of the count register for counter 2 of an 8253 located starting at memory address 01000_{16}. A_1A_0 of the microprocessor are directly connected to A_1A_0 of the 8253.

63. Repeat Example 8.22 for the 8253 located at memory address 01000_{16}, but this time just read the least significant byte of the counter. A_1A_0 of the microprocessor are directly connected to A_1A_0 of the 8253.

64. What is the maximum time delay that can be generated with the timer in

Fig. 8.41? What will be the maximum time delay if the clock frequency is increased to 2 MHz?

65. What is the resolution of pulses generated with the 8253 in Fig. 8.41? What will be the resolution if the clock frequency is increased to 2 MHz?

66. Find the pulse width of the one-shot in Fig. 8.39 if the counter is loaded with the value 1000_{16}.

67. What count must be loaded into the square-wave generator of Fig. 8.44 to produce a 25-kHz output?

68. If the counter in Fig. 8.45 is loaded with the value 120_{16}, how long of a delay occurs before the strobe pulse is output?

Section 8.14

69. Are signal lines $\overline{\text{MEMR}}$ and $\overline{\text{MEMW}}$ of the 8237A used in the microprocessor interface?

70. Summarize the 8237A's DMA request/acknowledge handshake sequence.

71. What is the total number of user accessible registers in the 8237A?

72. Write an instruction sequence that will read the value of the address from the current address register for channel 0 into the AX register. Assume that the 8237A has the base I/O address 10H.

73. Assuming that an 8237A is located at I/O address 1000H, write an instruction sequence to perform a master clear operation.

74. Write an instruction sequence that will write the command word 00_{16} into the command register of an 8237A that is located at address 2000H in the I/O address space.

75. Write an instruction sequence that will load the mode register for channel 2 with the mode byte obtained in Example 8.29. Assume that the 8237A is located at I/O address F0H.

76. What must be output to the mask register in order to disable all the DREQ inputs?

77. Write an instruction sequence that will read the contents of the status register into the AL register. Assume that the 8237A is located at I/O address 5000H.

Section 8.15

78. Name a signal line that distinguishes an asynchronous communication interface from that of a synchronous communication interface.

79. Describe the sequence of signals that become active in Fig. 8.62 when system 2 transfers a character to system 1.

80. Define a simplex, a half-duplex, and a full-duplex communication link.

Section 8.16

81. To write a byte of data to the 8251A, what logic levels must the microprocessor apply to control inputs C/$\overline{\text{D}}$, $\overline{\text{RD}}$, $\overline{\text{WR}}$, and $\overline{\text{CS}}$?

82. The mode control register of an 8251A contains 11111111_2. What are the asynchronous character length, type of parity, and the number of stop bits?

83. Write an instruction sequence to write the control word given in problem 82 to a memory-mapped 8251A that is located at address MODE.

84. Describe the difference between a mode instruction and a command instruction used in 8251A initialization.

Section 8.17

85. Referring to Fig. 8.77 what is the maximum number of keys that can be supported using all 24 I/O lines of an appropriately configured 8255A?

86. Specify the mode of operation for the keyboard and display when an 8279 is configured with command word 0 equal to $3F_{16}$.

87. Determine the clock frequency applied to the input of an 8279 if it needs command word 1 equal to $1E_{16}$ to operate.

88. Summarize the function of each command word of the 8279.

Interrupt Interface of the 8088 and 8086 Microprocessors

▲ 9.1 INTRODUCTION

In Chapter 8 we covered the input/output interface of the 8088 and 8086 microcomputer systems. Here we continue with a special input interface, the *interrupt interface*. The following topics are presented in this chapter:

1. Types of interrupts
2. Interrupt address pointer table
3. Interrupt instructions
4. Enabling/disabling of interrupts
5. External hardware interrupt interface
6. External hardware interrupt sequence
7. 8259A programmable interrupt controller
8. 8259A interrupt interface circuits
9. Software interrupts
10. Nonmaskable interrupt
11. Reset
12. Internal interrupt functions

Interrupts provide a mechanism for changing program environment. Transfer of program control is initiated by either the occurrence of an event internal to the microprocessor or an event in its external hardware. For instance, when an interrupt signal occurs indicating that an external device, such as a printer, requires service, the MPU must suspend what it is doing in the main part of the program and pass control to a special routine that performs the function required by the device.

The section of program to which control is passed is called the *interrupt service routine*. When the MPU terminates execution in the main program, it remembers the location where it left off and then picks up execution with the first instruction in the service routine. After this routine has run to completion, program control is returned to the point where the MPU originally left the main body of the program.

The 8088 and 8086 microcomputers are capable of implementing any combination of up to 256 interrupts. These 256 interrupts are divided into four groups: *external hardware interrupts*, *software interrupts*, *internal interrupts*, and the *non-maskable interrupt*. The function of the external hardware, software, and nonmaskable interrupts can be defined by the user. On the other hand, the internal interrupts have dedicated system functions.

Hardware, software, and internal interrupts are serviced on a priority basis. *Priority* is achieved in two ways. First, the interrupt processing sequence implemented in the 8088/8086 tests for the occurrence of the various groups based on the hierarchy that follows: internal interrupt, nonmaskable interrupt, software interrupt, and external hardware interrupt. Thus we see that internal interrupts are the *highest-priority group* and the external hardware interrupts are the *lowest-priority group*. Second, each is given a different priority level by assigning it a *type number*. *Type 0* identifies the highest-priority interrupt and *type 255* identifies the lowest-priority interrupt. Actually, a few of the type numbers are not available for use with software or hardware interrupts. This is because they are reserved for special interrupt functions of the 8088/8086, such as internal interrupts. For instance, within the internal interrupt group an interrupt known as divide error is assigned to type number 0. Therefore, it has the highest priority of the internal interrupts. Another internal interrupt is called overflow and is assigned the type number 4. Overflow is the lowest-priority internal interrupt.

The importance of priority lies in the fact that, if an interrupt service routine has been initiated to perform a function at a specific priority level, only devices with higher priority can interrupt the active service routine. Lower-priority devices will have to wait until the routine is completed before their request for service can be acknowledged. For this reason, the user normally assigns tasks that must not be interrupted frequently to higher-priority levels and those that can be interrupted to lower-priority levels. An example of a high-priority service routine that should not be interrupted is that for a power failure.

We just pointed out that once an interrupt service routine is initiated, it can be interrupted only by a function that corresponds to a higher-priority level. For example, if a type 50 external hardware interrupt is in progress, it can be interrupted by any software interrupt, the nonmaskable interrupt, all internal interrupts, or any external interrupt with type number less than 50. That is, external hardware interrupts with priority levels equal to 50 or greater are *masked out*.

▲ 9.3 INTERRUPT ADDRESS POINTER TABLE

An *address pointer table* is used to link the interrupt type numbers to the locations of their service routines in the program storage memory. Figure 9.1 shows a map of the pointer table in the memory of the 8088 or 8086 microcomputer system. Looking at this table, we see that it contains *256 address pointers* (*vectors*). One pointer corresponds to each of the interrupt types 0 through 255. These address pointers identify the starting locations of their service routines in program memory.

Notice that the pointer table is located at the low-address end of the memory address space. It starts at address 00000_{16} and ends at $003FE_{16}$. This represents the first 1KB of memory.

Each of the 256 pointers requires two words (four bytes) of memory. These words are stored at even-address boundaries. The higher-addressed word of the two-word vector is called the *base address*. It identifies the program memory segment in which the service routine resides. For this reason, it is loaded into the code segment (CS) register within the MPU. The lower-addressed word of the vector is the *offset* of the first instruction of the service routine from the beginning of the

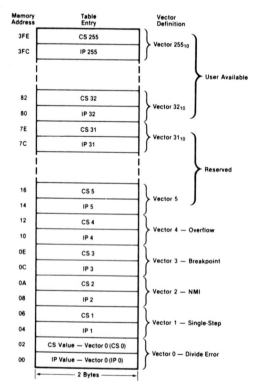

Figure 9.1 Interrupt vector table of the 8088/8086. (Reprinted by permission of Intel Corp., Intel Corp. © 1979)

code segment defined by the base address loaded into CS. This offset is loaded into the instruction pointer (IP) register. For example, the vector for type number 255 is stored at addresses from $003FC_{16}$ through $003FE_{16}$. IP_{255} is stored at address $003FC_{16}$ and CS_{255}, at $003FE_{16}$.

Looking more closely at the table in Fig. 9.1, we find that the first five pointers have dedicated functions. Pointers 0, 1, 3, and 4 are required for the 8088's and 8086's internal interrupts: *divide error*, *single step*, *breakpoint*, and *overflow*. Pointer 2 is used to identify the starting location of the nonmaskable interrupt's service routine. The next 27 pointers, 5 through 31, represent a reserved portion of the pointer table and should not be used. The rest of the table, the 224 pointers in the address range 00080_{16} through $003FF_{16}$, is available to the user for storage of interrupt vectors. These pointers correspond to type numbers 32 through 255 and can be employed by hardware or software interrupts. In the case of external hardware interrupts, the type number (priority level) is associated with an interrupt input level.

EXAMPLE 9.1

At what address should vector 50, CS_{50}, and IP_{50}, be stored in memory?

Solution

Each vector requires four consecutive bytes of memory for storage. Therefore, its address can be found by multiplying the type number by 4. Since CS_{50} and IP_{50} represent the words of the type 50 interrupt pointer, we get

$$\text{Address} = 4 \times 50 = 200$$

Converting to binary form gives

$$\text{Address} = 11001000_2$$

and expressing it as a hexadecimal number results in

$$\text{Address} = C8_{16}$$

Therefore, IP_{50} is stored at $000C8_{16}$ and CS_{50} at $000CA_{16}$.

▲ 9.4 INTERRUPT INSTRUCTIONS

A number of instructions are provided in the instruction set of the 8088 and 8086 microprocessors for use with interrupt processing. These instructions are listed with a brief description of their functions in Fig. 9.2.

For instance, the first two instructions, which are STI and CLI, permit manipulation of the interrupt flag through software. STI stands for *set interrupt enable*

Mnemonic	Meaning	Format	Operation	Flags Affected
CLI	Clear interrupt flag	CLI	$0 \rightarrow (IF)$	IF
STI	Set interrupt flag	STI	$1 \rightarrow (IF)$	IF
INT n	Type n software interrupt	INT n	$(Flags) \rightarrow ((SP) - 2)$ $0 \rightarrow TF, IF$ $(CS) \rightarrow ((SP) - 4)$ $(2 + 4 \cdot n) \rightarrow (CS)$ $(IP) \rightarrow ((SP) - 6)$ $(4 \cdot n) \rightarrow (IP)$	TF, IF
IRET	Interrupt return	IRET	$((SP)) \rightarrow (IP)$ $((SP) + 2) \rightarrow (CS)$ $((SP) + 4) \rightarrow (Flags)$ $(SP) + 6 \rightarrow (SP)$	All
INTO	Interrupt on overflow	INTO	INT 4 steps	TF, IF
HLT	Halt	HLT	Wait for an external interrupt or reset to occur	None
WAIT	Wait	WAIT	Wait for $\overline{TEST}$ input to go active	None

Figure 9.2 Interrupt instructions.

flag. Execution of this instruction enables the external interrupt input (INTR) for operation. That is, it sets interrupt flag (IF). On the other hand, execution of CLI (*clear interrupt enable flag*) disables the external interrupt input. It does this by resetting IF.

The next instruction listed in Fig. 9.2 is the *software interrupt* instruction INT n. It is used to initiate a software vector call of a subroutine. Executing the instruction causes the contents of the flags, CS, and IP to be saved on the stack and then program control is transferred to the subroutine pointed to by the vector for type number n specified in the instruction. This is done by loading the CS and IP registers with the contents of vector n from the interrupt vector table.

For example, execution of the instruction INT 50 initiates execution of a subroutine whose starting point is identified by vector 50 in the pointer table. That is, the MPU reads IP_{50} and CS_{50} from addresses $000C8_{16}$ and $000CA_{16}$, respectively, in memory, loads these values into IP and CS, uses them to calculate the physical address, and starts to fetch instructions from this new location in program memory.

An *interrupt return* (IRET) instruction must be included at the end of each interrupt service routine. It is required to pass control back to the point in the program where execution was terminated due to the occurrence of the interrupt. When executed, IRET causes the three words IP, CS, and flags to be popped from the stack back into the internal registers of the MPU. This restores the original program environment.

INTO is the *interrupt on overflow* instruction. This instruction must be included after arithmetic instructions that can generate an overflow condition, such as divide. It tests the overflow flag, and if the flag is found to be set, a type 4 internal interrupt is initiated. This causes program control to be passed to an overflow service routine that is located at the starting address identified by the vector IP_4 at 00010_{16} and CS_4 at 00012_{16} of the pointer table.

The last two instructions associated with the interrupt interface are *halt* (HLT) and *wait* (WAIT). They produce similar responses by the 8088/8086 and permit their operation to be synchronized to an event in external hardware. For instance, when HLT is executed, the MPU suspends operation and enters the idle state. It no longer executes instructions; instead, it remains idle waiting for the occurrence of an external hardware interrupt or reset interrupt. With the occurrence of either of these two events, the MPU resumes execution with the corresponding service routine.

If the WAIT instruction is used instead of the HLT instruction, the MPU checks the logic level of the $\overline{TEST}$ input prior to going into the idle state. Only if $\overline{TEST}$ is at logic 1 will the MPU go into the idle state. While in the idle state, the MPU continues to check the logic level at $\overline{TEST}$, looking for its transition to the 0 logic level. As $\overline{TEST}$ switches to 0, execution resumes with the next sequential instruction in the program.

▲ 9.5 ENABLING/DISABLING OF INTERRUPTS

An *interrupt enable flag* bit is provided within the 8088 and 8086 MPUs. Earlier we found that it is identified as IF. It affects only the external hardware interrupt interface, not the software or internal interrupts. The ability to initiate an external hardware interrupt at the INTR input is enabled by setting IF or masked out by resetting it. Through software, this can be done by executing the STI instruction or the CLI instruction, respectively.

During the initiation sequence of an interrupt service routine, the MPU automatically clears IF. This masks out the occurrence of any additional external hardware interrupt. If necessary, the interrupt flag bit can be set with an STI instruction at any time in the service routine to reenable the INTR input. At the end of the service routine, the external hardware interrupt interface is reenabled by the IRET instruction.

▲ 9.6 EXTERNAL HARDWARE INTERRUPT INTERFACE

Up to this point, we have introduced the interrupts of the 8088, its pointer table, interrupt instructions, and enabling/disabling interrupts. Let us now look at the *external hardware interrupt interface* of the 8088 and 8086 microcomputer systems.

Minimum Mode Interrupt Interface

We will begin with an 8088 microcomputer configured for the minimum system mode. The interrupt interface for this system is illustrated in Fig. 9.3(a). Here we see that it includes the multiplexed address/data bus and dedicated interrupt signal lines INTR and $\overline{INTA}$. We also see that external circuitry is required to interface

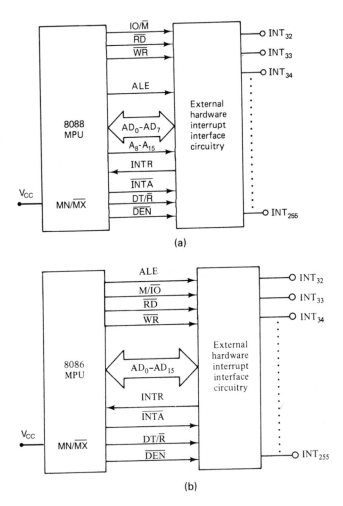

(a)

(b)

Figure 9.3 (a) Minimum-mode 8088 system external hardware interrupt interface. (b) Minimum-mode 8086 system external hardware interrupt interface.

the interrupt inputs, INT_{32} through INT_{255}, to the 8088's interrupt interface. This interface circuitry must identify which of the pending active interrupts has the highest priority and then pass its type number to the microprocessor.

In this circuit we see that the key interrupt interface signals are *interrupt request* (INTR) and *interrupt acknowledge* ($\overline{INTA}$). The input at the INTR line signals the 8088 that an external device is requesting service. The 8088 samples this input during the last clock period of each instruction execution cycle. Logic 1 represents an active interrupt request. INTR is *level triggered*; therefore, its active 1 level must be maintained until tested by the 8088. If it is not maintained, the request for service may not be recognized. Moreover, the logic 1 at INTR must be removed before the service routine runs to completion; otherwise, the same interrupt may get acknowledged a second time.

When an interrupt request has been recognized by the 8088, it signals this fact to external circuitry. It does this with pulses to logic 0 at its $\overline{INTA}$ output.

Actually, there are two pulses produced at $\overline{\text{INTA}}$ during the *interrupt acknowledge bus cycle*. The first pulse signals external circuitry that the interrupt request has been acknowledged and to prepare to send its type number to the 8088. The second pulse tells the external circuitry to put the type number on the data bus.

Notice that the lower eight lines of the address/data bus, AD_0 through AD_7, are also part of the interrupt interface. During the second cycle in the interrupt acknowledge bus cycle, external circuitry must put an 8-bit type number on bus lines AD_0 through AD_7. The 8088 reads this number off the bus to identify which external device is requesting service. It uses the type number to generate the address of the interrupt's vector in the pointer table and to read the new values of CS and IP into the corresponding internal registers. CS and IP values from the interrupt vector table are transferred to the 8088 over the data bus. Before loading CS and IP with new values, their old values and the values of the internal flags are automatically pushed to the stack part of memory.

Figure 9.3(b) shows the interrupt interface of a minimum-mode 8086 microcomputer system. Comparing this diagram to Fig. 9.3(a), we find that the only difference is that the data path between the MPU and interrupt interface is now 16 bits in length.

Maximum-Mode Interrupt Interface

The maximum-mode interrupt interface of the 8088 microcomputer is shown in Fig. 9.4(a). The primary difference between this interrupt interface and that shown for the minimum mode in Fig. 9.3(a) is that the 8288 bus controller has been added. In the maximum-mode system, it is the bus controller that produces the $\overline{\text{INTA}}$ and ALE signals. Whenever the 8088 outputs an interrupt acknowledge bus status code, the 8288 generates pulses at its $\overline{\text{INTA}}$ output to signal external circuitry that the 8088 has acknowledged an interrupt request. This interrupt acknowledge bus status code, $\overline{S_2 S_1 S_0} = 000$, is highlighted in Fig. 9.5.

A second change in Fig. 9.4(a) is that the 8088 provides a new signal for the interrupt interface. This output, which is labeled $\overline{\text{LOCK}}$, is called the *bus priority lock* signal. $\overline{\text{LOCK}}$ is applied as an input to a *bus arbiter*. In response to this signal, the arbitration logic ensures that no other device can take over control of the system bus until the interrupt acknowledge bus cycle is completed.

Figure 9.4(b) illustrates the interrupt interface of a maximum-mode 8086 microcomputer system. Again, the only difference between this circuit and that of the 8088 microcomputer is that the complete 16-bit data bus is used to transfer data between the MPU and interrupt interface circuits.

▲ 9.7 EXTERNAL HARDWARE INTERRUPT SEQUENCE

In the preceding section we showed the interrupt interfaces for the external hardware interrupts in minimum-mode and maximum-mode 8088 and 8086 microcomputer systems. We will continue by describing in detail the events that take place during the interrupt request, interrupt acknowledge bus cycle, and device service

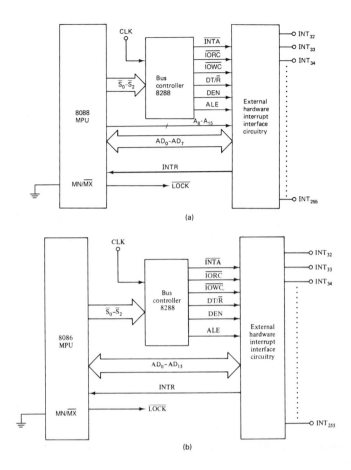

Figure 9.4 (a) Maximum-mode 8088 system external hardware interrupt interface. (b) Maximum-mode 8086 system external hardware interrupt interface.

routine. The events that take place in the external hardware interrupt service sequence are identical for an 8088-based or 8086-based microcomputer system. Here we will describe this sequence for the 8088 microcomputer.

The interrupt sequence begins when an external device requests service by activating one of the interrupt inputs, INT_{32} through INT_{255}, of the 8088's external interrupt interface circuit in Fig. 9.3. For example, if the INT_{50} input is switched to the 1 logic level, it signals the microprocessor that the device associated with priority level 50 wants to be serviced.

The external interface circuitry evaluates the priority of this input. If there is no interrupt already in progress or if this interrupt is of higher priority than the

Status inputs			CPU cycle	8288 command
$\overline{S}_2$	$\overline{S}_1$	$\overline{S}_0$		
0	0	0	Interrupt acknowledge	$\overline{INTA}$
0	0	1	Read I/O port	$\overline{IORC}$
0	1	0	Write I/O port	$\overline{IOWC}, \overline{AIOWC}$
0	1	1	Halt	None
1	0	0	Instruction fetch	$\overline{MRDC}$
1	0	1	Read memory	$\overline{MRDC}$
1	1	0	Write memory	$\overline{MWTC}, \overline{AMWC}$
1	1	1	Passive	None

Figure 9.5 Interrupt bus status code. (Reprinted by permission of Intel Corp., © Intel Corp. 1979)

one presently active, the external circuitry issues a request for service to the MPU.

Let us assume that INT_{50} is the only active interrupt request input. In this case, the external circuitry switches INTR to logic 1. This tells the 8088 that an interrupt is pending for service. To ensure that it is recognized, the external circuitry must maintain INTR active until an interrupt acknowledge pulse is issued by the 8088.

Figure 9.6 is a flow diagram that outlines the events that take place when the 8088 processes an interrupt. The 8088 tests for an active interrupt during the last T state of the current instruction. Note that it tests first for the occurrence of an internal interrupt, then the occurrence of the nonmaskable interrupt, and finally checks the logic level of INTR to determine if an external hardware interrupt has occurred.

If INTR is logic 1, a request for service is recognized. Before the 8088 initiates the interrupt acknowledge sequence, it checks the setting of IF (interrupt flag). If it is logic 0, external interrupts are masked out and the request is ignored. In this case, the next sequential instruction is executed. On the other hand, if IF is at logic 1, external hardware interrupts are enabled and the service routine is to be initiated.

Let us assume that IF is set to permit interrupts to occur when INTR is tested as 1. The 8088 responds by initiating the interrupt acknowledge bus cycles. This bus cycle is illustrated in Fig. 9.7. During T_1 of the first bus cycle, we see that a pulse is output on ALE along with putting the address/data bus in the high-Z state. The address/data bus stays in the high-Z state for the rest of the bus cycle. During periods T_2 and T_3, $\overline{INTA}$ is switched to logic 0. This signals external circuitry that the request for service has been granted. In response to this pulse, the logic 1 at INTR can be removed.

The signal identified as $\overline{LOCK}$ is produced only in maximum-mode systems. Notice that $\overline{LOCK}$ is switched to logic 0 during T_2 of the first INTA bus cycle and is maintained at this level until T_2 of the second INTA bus cycle. During this time,

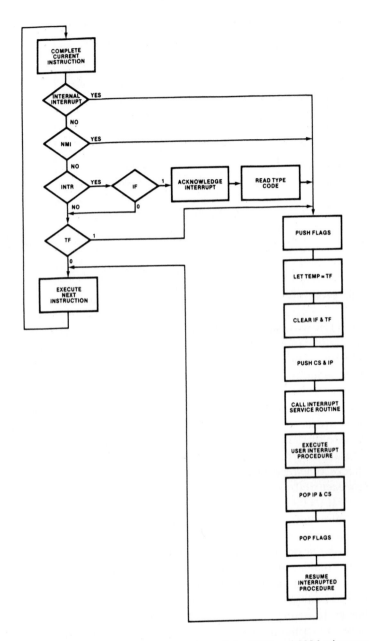

Figure 9.6 Interrupt processing sequence of the 8088 and 8086 microprocessors. (Reprinted by permission of Intel Corp., © Intel Corp. 1979)

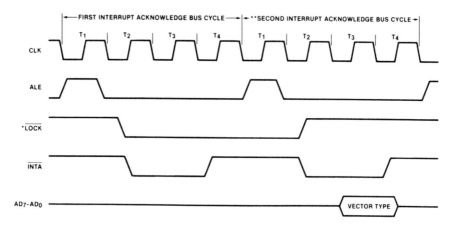

Figure 9.7 Interrupt acknowledge bus cycle. (Reprinted by permission of Intel Corp., © Intel Corp. 1979)

the 8088 is prevented from accepting any HOLD request. The $\overline{\text{LOCK}}$ output is used in external logic to lock other devices off the system bus, thereby ensuring that the interrupt acknowledge sequence continues through to completion without interruption.

During the second interrupt acknowledge bus cycle, a similar signal sequence occurs. However, this interrupt acknowledge pulse tells the external circuitry to put the type number of the active interrupt on the data bus. External circuitry gates one of the interrupt codes $32 = 20_{16}$ through $255 = \text{FF}_{16}$ onto data bus lines AD_0 through AD_7. This code must be valid during periods T_3 and T_4 of the second interrupt acknowledge bus cycle.

The 8088 sets up its bus control signals for an input data transfer to read the type number off the data bus. $\text{DT}/\overline{\text{R}}$ and $\overline{\text{DEN}}$ are set to logic 0 to enable the external data bus circuitry and set it for input of data. Also, $\text{IO}/\overline{\text{M}}$ is set to 1, indicating that data are to be input from the interrupt interface. During this input operation, the byte interrupt code is read off the data bus. For the case of INT_{50}, this code would be $00110010_2 = 32_{16}$. This completes the interrupt acknowledge part of the interrupt sequence.

Looking at Fig. 9.6, we see that the 8088 first saves the contents of the flag register by pushing it to the stack. This requires two write cycles and two bytes of stack. Then it clears IF. This further disables external interrupts from any other peripheral requesting service. Actually, the TF flag is also cleared. This disables the single-step mode of operation if it happens to be active. Next, the 8088 automatically pushes the contents of the CS and IP onto the stack. This requires four write bus cycles and four bytes of memory on the stack. The current value of the stack pointer is decremented by two as each of these values is placed onto the top of the stack.

Now the 8088 knows the type number associated with the external device that is requesting service. It must next call the service routine by fetching the interrupt vector that defines its starting point in the memory. The type number is internally multiplied by four, and this result is used as the address of the first word of the interrupt vector in the pointer table. Two-word read operations (four bus cycles) are performed to read the two-word vector from the memory. The first word, which is the lower-addressed word, is loaded into IP. The second, higher-addressed word, is loaded into CS. For instance, the vector for INT_{50} would be read from addresses $000C8_{16}$ and $000CA_{16}$.

The service routine is now initiated. That is, execution resumes with the first instruction of the service routine. It is located at the address generated from the new value in CS and IP. Figure 9.8 shows the structure of a typical interrupt service routine. The service routine must include PUSH instructions to save the contents of those internal registers that it will use. In this way, their original contents are saved in the stack during execution of the routine.

At the end of the service routine, the original program environment must be restored. This is done by first popping the contents of the appropriate registers from the stack by executing POP instructions. An IRET instruction must be executed as the last instruction of the service routine. This instruction causes the old contents of the flags, CS, and IP to be popped from the stack back into the internal registers of the 8088. The original program environment has now been completely restored, the interrupt interface has been reenabled, and execution resumes at the point in the program where it was interrupted.

Earlier we pointed out that the events that take place during the external hardware interrupt service sequence of the 8086 microcomputer are identical to those of the 8088 microcomputer. However, because the 8086 has a 16-bit data bus, slight changes are found in the external bus cycles that are produced as part of the program context switch sequence. For example, as the interrupt's program environment is initiated, three-word write cycles, instead of six-byte write cycles, are required to save the old values of the flags, instruction pointer register, and code-segment register on the stack. Moreover, when the new values of CS and IP are fetched from the address pointer table in memory, just two bus cycles take place. Because five instead of ten bus cycles take place, the new program environment is entered faster by the 8086 microcomputer.

The same is true when the original program environment is restored at the completion of the service routine. Remember that this is done by popping the old

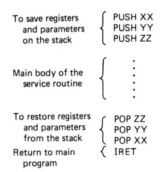

Figure 9.8 Structure of an interrupt service routine.

flags, old CS, and old IP from the stack back into the MPU with an IRET instruction. This operation is performed with three word read cycles by the 8086 and six-byte read cycles by the 8088.

EXAMPLE 9.2

The interrupting device in Fig. 9.9(a) interrupts the microprocessor each time the Interrupt Request input signal has a transition from 0 to 1. The corresponding interrupt type number generated by the 74LS244 in response to $\overline{\text{INTA}}$ is 60H.

    a. Describe the operation of the hardware for an active request at the Interrupt Request input.

    b. What is the value of the type number sent to the microprocessor?

    c. Assume that the original values in the segment registers are: (CS) = (DS) = 1000H and (SS) = 4000H; the main program is located at offsets of 200H from the beginning of the original code segment; the count is held at an offset of 100H from the beginning of the current data segment; the interrupt service routine starts at offset 1000H from the beginning of another code segment that begins at address 2000H:0000H; and the stack starts at an offset of 500H from the beginning of the current stack segment. Make a map showing the organization of the memory address space.

    d. Write the main program and the service routine for the circuit so that the positive transitions at INTR are counted as a decimal number.

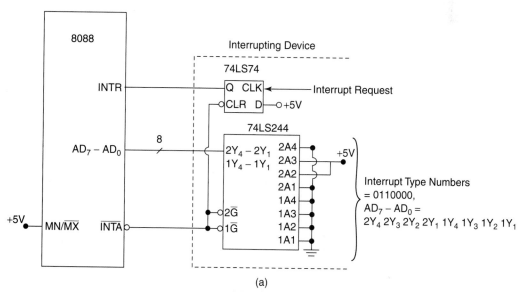

(a)

Figure 9.9 (a) Circuit for Example 9.2. (b) Memory organization. (c) Flowcharts for the main program and the service routine. (d) Main program and service routine.

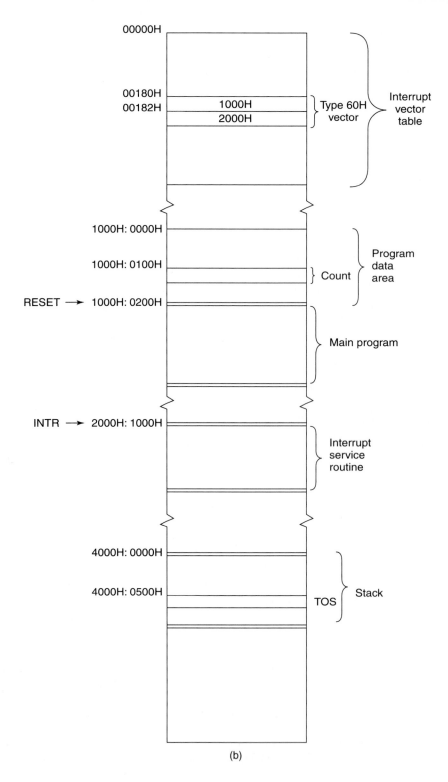

Figure 9.9 (Continued)

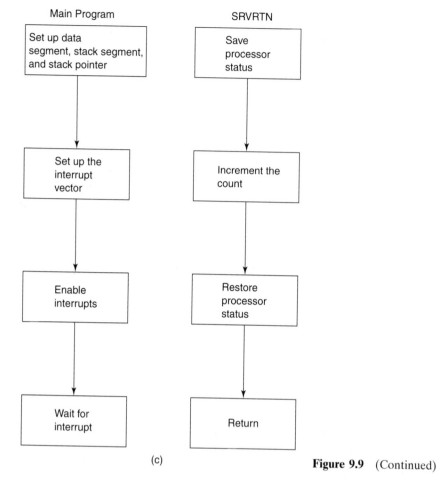

Main Program

| Set up data segment, stack segment, and stack pointer |
| Set up the interrupt vector |
| Enable interrupts |
| Wait for interrupt |

SRVRTN

| Save processor status |
| Increment the count |
| Restore processor status |
| Return |

(c)

Figure 9.9 (Continued)

Solution

a. Analysis of the circuit in Fig. 9.9(a) shows that a positive transition at the CLK input of the flip-flop (Interrupt Request) makes the Q output of the flip-flop logic 1 and presents a positive level signal at the INTR input of 8088. When the 8088 recognizes this as an interrupt request, it responds by generating the $\overline{\text{INTA}}$ signal. The logic 0 output on this line clears the flip-flop and enables the 74LS244 buffer to present the type number to the 8088. This number is read off the data bus by the 8088 and is used to initiate the interrupt service routine.

b. From the inputs and outputs of the 74LS244, we see that the type number is

$$\text{AD}_7 \ldots \text{AD}_1\text{AD}_0 = 2Y_42Y_32Y_22Y_11Y_41Y_31Y_21Y_1 = 01100000_2$$

$$\text{AD}_7 \ldots \text{AD}_1\text{AD}_0 = 60\text{H}$$

c. The memory organization in Fig. 9.9(b) shows where the various pieces of program and data are located. Here we see that the type 60H vector is located

;Main Program, START = 1000H:0200H

```
START:     MOV  AX,1000H           ;Setup data segment at 1000H:0000H
           MOV  DS,AX
           MOV  AX,4000H           ;Setup stack segment at 4000H:0000H
           MOV  SS,AX
           MOV  SP,0500H           ;TOS is at  4000H:0500H
           MOV  AX,0000H           ;Segment for interrupt vector table
           MOV  ES,AX
           MOV  AX,1000H           ;Service routine offset
           MOV  [ES:180H],AX
           MOV  AX,2000H           ;Service routine segment
           MOV  [ES:182H],AX
           STI                     ;Enable interrupts
HERE:      JMP  HERE               ;Wait for interrupt
```

; Interrupt Service Routine, SRVRTN = 2000H:1000H

```
SRVRTN:    PUSH AX                 ;Save register to be used
           MOV  AL,[0100H]         ;Get the count
           INC  AL                 ;Increment the count
           DAA                     ;Decimal asdjust the count
           MOV  [0100H],AL         ;Save the updated count
           POP  AX                 ;Restore the register used
(d)        IRET                    ;Return from the interrupt
```

Figure 9.9   (Continued)

in the interrupt vector table at address 60H × 4 = 180H. Notice that the byte-wide memory location used for Count is at address 1000H:0100H. This part of the memory address space is identified as the program data area in the memory map. The main part of the program, which is entered after reset, starts at address 2000H:1000H. On the other hand, the service routine is located at address 2000H:1000H in a separate code segment. For this reason, the vector held at 180H of the interrupt vector table is (CS) = 2000H and (IP) = 1000H. Finally, the stack begins at 4000H:0000H with the current top of the stack located at 4000H:0500H.

d. The flow charts in Fig. 9.9(c) show how the main program and interrupt service routines are to function. The corresponding software is given in Fig. 9.9(d).

▲ 9.8 8259A PROGRAMMABLE INTERRUPT CONTROLLER

The 8259A is an LSI peripheral IC that is designed to simplify the implementation of the interrupt interface in the 8088- and 8086-based microcomputer systems. This device is known as a *programmable interrupt controller* or *PIC*. It is manufactured using the NMOS technology.

The operation of the PIC is programmable under software control and it can be configured for a wide variety of applications. Some of its programmable features are the ability to accept level-sensitive or edge-triggered inputs, the ability to be

easily cascaded to expand from 8 to 64 interrupt inputs, and its ability to be configured to implement a wide variety of priority schemes.

Block Diagram of the 8259A

Let us begin our study of the PIC with its block diagram in Fig. 9.10(a). We
just mentioned that the 8259A is treated as a peripheral in the microcomputer.
Therefore, its operation must be initialized by the microprocessor. The *host processor interface* is provided for this purpose. This interface consists of eight *data bus
lines* D_0 through D_7 and control signals *read* ($\overline{RD}$), *write* ($\overline{WR}$), and *chip select*
($\overline{CS}$). The data bus is the path over which data are transferred between the MPU
and 8259A. These data can be command words, status information, or interrupt
type numbers. Control input $\overline{CS}$ must be at logic 0 to enable the host processor
interface. Moreover, $\overline{WR}$ and $\overline{RD}$ signal the 8259A whether data are to be written
into or read from its internal registers. They also control the timing of these data
transfers.

Two other signals, INT and $\overline{INTA}$, are identified as part of the host processor
interface. Together, these two signals provide the handshake mechanism by which
the 8259A can signal the MPU of a request for service and receive an acknowledg-
ment that the request has been accepted. INT is the interrupt request output of

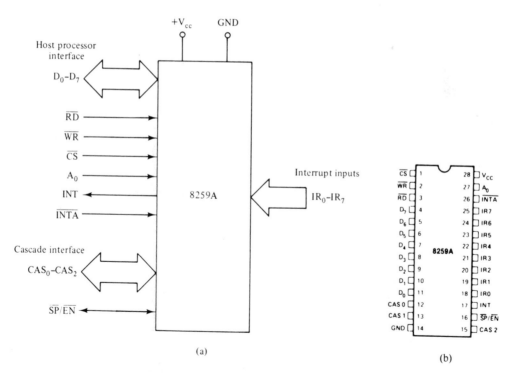

Figure 9.10 (a) Block diagram of the 8259A. (b) Pin layout. (Reprinted by permission of Intel Corp., © Intel Corp. 1979)

the 8259A. It is applied directly to the INTR input of the 8088 or 8086. Logic 1 is produced at this output whenever the 8259A receives a valid request from an interrupting device.

On the other hand, $\overline{\text{INTA}}$ is an input of the 8259A. It is connected to the $\overline{\text{INTA}}$ output of the 8088 or 8086. The MPU pulses this input of the 8259A to logic 0 twice during the interrupt acknowledge bus cycle, thereby signaling the 8259A that the interrupt request has been acknowledged and that it should output the type number of the highest-priority active interrupt on data bus lines D_0 through D_7 so that it can be read by the MPU. The last signal line involved in the host processor interface is the A_0 input. This input is normally supplied by an address line of the microprocessor such as A_0. The logic level at this input is involved in the selection of the internal register that is accessed during read and write operations.

At the other side of the block in Fig. 9.10(a), we find the eight *interrupt inputs* of the PIC. They are labeled IR_0 through IR_7. It is through these inputs that external devices issue a request for service. One of the software options of the 8259A permits these inputs to be configured for *level-sensitive* or *edge-triggered operation*. When configured for level-sensitive operation, logic 1 is the active level of the IR inputs. In this case, the request for service must be removed before the service routine runs to completion. Otherwise, the interrupt will be requested a second time and the service routine initiated again. Moreover, if the input returns to logic 0 before it is acknowledged by the MPU, the request for service will be missed.

Some external devices produce a short-duration pulse instead of a fixed logic level for use as an interrupt request signal. If the MPU is busy servicing a higher-priority interrupt when the pulse is produced, the request for service could be completely missed if the 8259A is in level-sensitive mode. To overcome this problem, the edge-triggered mode of operation is used.

Inputs of the 8259A that are set up for edge-triggered operation become active on the transition from the inactive 0 logic level to the active 1 logic level. This represents what is known as a *positive edge-triggered input*. The fact that this transition has occurred at an IR line is latched internal to the 8259A. If the IR input remains at the 1 logic level even after the service routine is completed, the interrupt is not reinitiated. Instead, it is locked out. To be recognized a second time, the input must first return to the 0 logic level and then be switched back to 1. The advantage of edge-triggered operation is that if the request at the IR input is removed before the MPU acknowledges service of the interrupt, its request is kept latched internal to the 8259A until it can be serviced.

The last group of signals on the PIC implement is known as the *cascade interface*. As shown in Fig. 9.10(a), it includes bidirectional *cascading bus lines* CAS_0 through CAS_2 and a multifunction control line labeled $\overline{\text{SP}/\text{EN}}$. The primary use of these signals is in cascaded systems where a number of 8259A ICs are interconnected in a *master/slave configuration* to expand the number of IR inputs from 8 to as high as 64.

In a cascaded system, the CAS lines of all 8259As are connected to provide a private bus between the master and slave devices. In response to the first $\overline{\text{INTA}}$ pulse during the interrupt acknowledge bus cycle, the master PIC outputs a 3-bit code on the CAS lines. This code identifies the highest-priority slave that is to be serviced. It is this device that is to be acknowledged for service. All slaves read this code off the *private cascading bus* and compare it to their internal ID code. A match condition at one slave tells the PIC that it has the highest-priority input. In response, it must put the type number of its highest-priority active input on the data bus during the second interrupt acknowledge bus cycle.

When the PIC is configured through software for the cascaded mode, the $\overline{SP}/\overline{EN}$ line is used as an input. This corresponds to its $\overline{SP}$ (*slave program*) function. The logic level applied at $\overline{SP}$ tells the device whether it is to operate as a master or slave. Logic 1 at this input designates master mode and logic 0 designates slave mode.

If the PIC is configured for single mode instead of cascade mode, $\overline{SP}/\overline{EN}$ takes on another function. In this case, it becomes an enable output that can be used to control the direction of data transfer through the bus transceiver that buffers the data bus.

A pin layout of the 8259A is given in Fig. 9.10(b).

Internal Architecture of the 8259A

Now that we have introduced the input/output signals of the 8259A, let us look at its internal architecture. Figure 9.11 is a block diagram of the PIC's internal circuitry. Here we find eight functional parts: the *data bus buffer*, *read/write logic*, *control logic*, *in-service register*, *interrupt request register*, *priority resolver*, *interrupt mask register*, and *cascade buffer/comparator*.

We will begin with the function of the data bus buffer and read/write logic sections. It is these parts of the 8259A that let the MPU have access to the internal registers. Moreover, they provide the path over which interrupt type numbers are passed to the microprocessor. The data bus buffer is an 8-bit bidirectional three-state buffer that interfaces the internal circuitry of the 8259A to the data bus of the MPU. The direction, timing, and source or destination for data transfers through the buffer are under control of the outputs of the read/write logic block. These outputs are generated in response to control inputs $\overline{RD}$, $\overline{WR}$, A_0, and $\overline{CS}$.

The interrupt request register, in-service register, priority resolver, and interrupt mask register are the key internal blocks of the 8259A. The interrupt mask register (IMR) can be used to enable or mask out individually the interrupt request inputs. It contains eight bits identified by M_0 through M_7. These bits correspond to interrupt request inputs IR_0 through IR_7, respectively. Logic 0 in a mask register bit position enables the corresponding interrupt input and logic 1 masks it out. The register can be read from or written into under software control.

On the other hand, the interrupt request register (IRR) stores the current status of the interrupt request inputs. It also contains one bit position for each of the IR inputs. The values in these bit positions reflect whether the interrupt inputs are active or inactive.

Which of the active interrupt inputs is identified as having the highest priority is determined by the priority resolver. This section can be configured to work using a number of different priority schemes through software. Following this scheme, it identifies the highest priority of the active interrupt inputs and signals the control

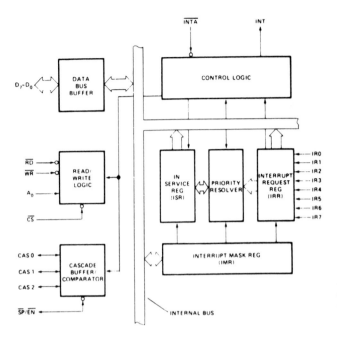

Figure 9.11 Internal architecture of the 8259A. (Reprinted by permission of Intel Corp., © Intel Corp. 1979)

logic that an interrupt is active. In response, the control logic causes the INT signal to be issued to the 8088 or 8086 microprocessor.

The in-service register differs in that it stores the interrupt level that is presently being serviced. During the first $\overline{\text{INTA}}$ pulse of an interrupt acknowledge bus cycle, the level of the highest active interrupt is strobed into ISR. Loading of ISR occurs in response to output signals of the control logic section. This register cannot be written into by the microprocessor; however, its contents may be read as status.

The cascade buffer/comparator section provides the interface between master and slave 8259As. As we mentioned earlier, this interface permits easy expansion of the interrupt interface using a master/slave configuration. Each slave has an *ID code* that is stored in this section.

Programming the 8259A

The way in which the 8259A operates is determined by how the device is programmed. Two types of command words are provided for this purpose. They are the *initialization command words* (ICW) and the *operational command words* (OCW). ICW commands are used to load the internal control registers of the 8259A to define the basic configuration or mode in which it is used. There are four such command words and they are identified as ICW_1, ICW_2, ICW_3, and ICW_4. On the other hand, the three OCW commands permit the 8088 or 8086 microprocessor to initiate variations in the basic operating modes defined by the ICW commands. These three commands are called OCW_1, OCW_2, and OCW_3.

Depending on whether the 8259A is I/O mapped or memory mapped, the MPU issues commands to the 8259A by initiating output or write cycles. This can be done by executing either the OUT instruction or MOV instruction, respectively. The address put on the system bus during the output bus cycle must be decoded with external circuitry to chip select the peripheral. When an address assigned to the 8259A is on the bus, the output of the decoder must produce logic 0 at the $\overline{CS}$ input. This signal enables the read/write logic within the PIC, and data applied at D_0 through D_7 are written into the command register within the control logic section synchronously with a write strobe at $\overline{WR}$.

The interrupt request input (INTR) of the 8088 or 8086 must be disabled whenever commands are being issued to the 8259A. This can be done by clearing the interrupt enable flag by executing the CLI (clear interrupt enable flag) instruction. After completion of the command sequence, the interrupt input must be reenabled. To do this, the microprocessor must execute the STI (set interrupt enable flag) instruction.

The flow diagram in Fig. 9.12 shows the sequence of events that must take place to initialize the 8259A with ICW commands. The cycle begins with the MPU outputting initialization command word ICW_1 to the address of the 8259A.

The moment that ICW_1 is written into the control logic section of the 8259A certain internal setup conditions automatically occur. First, the internal sequence logic is set up so that the 8259A will accept the remaining ICWs as designated by ICW_1. It turns out that if the least significant bit of ICW_1 is logic 1, command word ICW_4 is required in the initialization sequence. Moreover, if the next least significant bit of ICW_1 is logic 0, the command word ICW_3 is also required.

In addition to this, writing ICW_1 to the 8259A clears ISR and IMR. Also three operation command word bits, *special mask mode* (SMM) in OCW_3, *interrupt request register* (IRR) in OCW_3, and *end of interrupt* (EOI) in OCW_2, are cleared

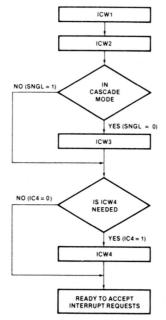

Figure 9.12 Initialization sequence of the 8259A. (Reprinted by permission of Intel Corp., © Intel Corp. 1979)

to logic 0. Furthermore, the *fully nested masked mode* of interrupt operation is entered with an initial priority assignment so that IR_0 is the highest-priority input and IR_7 the lowest-priority input. Finally, the edge-sensitive latches associated with the IR inputs are all cleared.

If the LSB of ICW_1 was initialized to logic 0, one additional event occurs. This is that all bits of the control register associated with ICW_4 are cleared.

In Fig. 9.12 we see that once the MPU starts initialization of the 8259A by writing ICW_1 into the control register, it must continue the sequence by writing ICW_2 and then optionally ICW_3 and ICW_4 in that order. Notice that it is not possible to modify just one of the initialization command registers. Instead, all words that are required to define the device's operating mode must be written into the 8259A once again.

We found that all four words need not always be used to initialize the 8259A. However, for its use in an 8088 or 8086 microcomputer system, words ICW_1, ICW_2, and ICW_4 are always required. ICW_3 is optional and is needed only if the 8259A is to function in the cascade mode.

Initialization Command Words

Now that we have introduced the initialization sequence of the 8259A, let us look more closely at the functions controlled by each of the initialization command words. We will begin with ICW_1. Its format and bit functions are identified in Fig. 9.13(a). Notice that address bit A_0 is included as a ninth bit and it must be logic 0. This corresponds to an even address for writing ICW_1.

Here we find that the logic level of the LSB D_0 of the initialization word indicates to the 8259A whether or not ICW_4 will be included in the programming sequence. As we mentioned earlier, logic 1 at D_0 (IC_4) specifies that it is needed. The next bit, D_2 (SNGL), selects between *single device* or *multidevice cascaded mode* of operation. When D_1 is set to logic 0, the internal circuitry of the 8259A is configured for cascaded mode. Selecting this state also sets up the initialization sequence such that ICW_3 must be issued as part of the initialization cycle. Bit D_2 has functions specified for it in Fig. 9.13(a); however, it can be ignored when the 8259A is being connected to the 8088/8086 and is a don't-care state. D_3, which is labeled LTIM, defines whether the eight IR inputs operate in the level-sensitive or edge-triggered mode. Logic 1 in D_3 selects level-triggered operation and logic 0 selects edge-triggered operation. Finally, bit D_4 is fixed at the 1 logic level and the three MSBs, D_5 through D_7, are not required in 8088- or 8086-based systems.

EXAMPLE 9.3 ———————————————————————

What value should be written into ICW_1 in order to configure the 8259A so that ICW_4 is needed in the initialization sequence, the system is going to use multiple 8259As, and its inputs are to be level-sensitive? Assume that all unused bits are to be logic 0. Give the result in both binary and hexadecimal form.

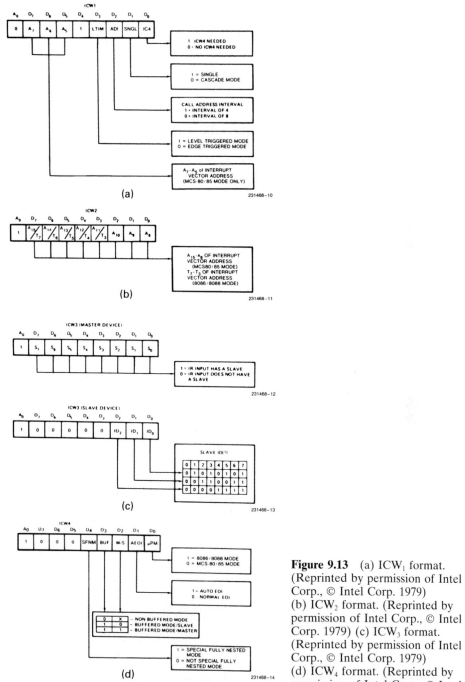

Figure 9.13 (a) ICW$_1$ format. (Reprinted by permission of Intel Corp., © Intel Corp. 1979) (b) ICW$_2$ format. (Reprinted by permission of Intel Corp., © Intel Corp. 1979) (c) ICW$_3$ format. (Reprinted by permission of Intel Corp., © Intel Corp. 1979) (d) ICW$_4$ format. (Reprinted by permission of Intel Corp., © Intel Corp. 1979)

NOTE:
Slave ID is equal to the corresponding master IR input.

Solution

Since ICW_4 is to be initialized, D_0 must be logic 1.

$$D_0 = 1$$

For cascaded mode of operation, D_1 must be 0.

$$D_1 = 0$$

And for level-sensitive inputs, D_3 must be 1.

$$D_3 = 1$$

Bits D_2 and D_5 through D_7 are don't-care states and are all made logic 0.

$$D_2 = D_5 = D_6 = D_7 = 0$$

Moreover, D_4 must be fixed at the 1 logic level.

$$D_4 = 1$$

This gives the complete command word

$$D_7D_6D_5D_4D_3D_2D_1D_0 = 00011001_2 = 19_{16}$$

The second initialization word, ICW_2, has a single function in the 8088 or 8086 microcomputer. As shown in Fig. 9.12(b), its five most significant bits D_7 through D_3 define a fixed binary code T_7 through T_3 that is used as the most significant bits of its type number. Whenever the 8259A puts the 3-bit interrupt type number corresponding to its active input onto the bus, it is automatically combined with the value T_7 through T_3 to form an 8-bit type number. The three least significant bits of ICW_2 are not used. Notice that logic 1 must be output on A_0 when this command word is put on the bus.

EXAMPLE 9.4

What should be programmed into register ICW_2 if the type numbers output on the bus by the device are to range from $F0_{16}$ through $F7_{16}$?

Solution

To set the 8259A up so that type numbers are in the range of $F0_{16}$ through $F7_{16}$, its device code bits must be

$$D_7D_6D_5D_4D_3 = 11110_2$$

The lower three bits are don't-care states and all can be 0s. This gives the command word

$$D_7D_6D_5D_4D_3D_2D_1D_0 = 11110000_2 = F0_{16}$$

The information of initialization word ICW_3 is required by only those 8259As that are configured for the cascaded mode of operation. Figure 9.13(c) shows its bits. Notice that ICW_3 is used for different functions depending on whether the device is a master or slave. In the case of a master, bits D_0 through D_7 of the word are labeled S_0 through S_7. These bits correspond to IR inputs IR_0 through IR_7, respectively. They identify whether or not the corresponding IR input is supplied by either the INT output of a slave or directly by an external device. Logic 1 loaded in an S position indicates that the corresponding IR input is supplied by a slave.

On the other hand, ICW_3 for a slave is used to load the device with a 3-bit identification code $ID_2ID_1ID_0$. This number must correspond to the IR input of the master to which the slave's INT output is wired. The ID code is required within the slave so that it can be compared to the cascading code output by the master on CAS_0 through CAS_2.

EXAMPLE 9.5

Assume that a master PIC is to be configured so that its IR_0 through IR_3 inputs are to accept inputs directly from external devices, but IR_4 through IR_7 are to be supplied by the INT outputs of slaves. What code should be used for the initialization command word ICW_3?

Solution

For IR_0 through IR_3 to be configured to allow direct inputs from external devices, bits D_0 through D_3 of ICW_3 must be logic 0.

$$D_3D_2D_1D_0 = 0000_2$$

The other IR inputs of the master are to be supplied by INT outputs of slaves. Therefore, their control bits must be all 1.

$$D_7D_6D_5D_4 = 1111_2$$

This gives the complete command word

$$D_7D_6D_5D_4D_3D_2D_1D_0 = 11110000_2 = F0_{16}$$

The fourth control word, ICW_4, which is shown in Fig. 9.13(d), is used to configure the PIC for use with the 8088 or 8086 and selects various features that are available in its operation. The LSB D_0, which is called microprocessor mode (μPM), must be set to logic 1 whenever the device is connected to the 8088. The next bit, D_1, is labeled AEOI for *automatic end of interrupt*. If this mode is enabled by writing logic 1 into the bit location, the EOI (*end of interrupt*) command does not have to be issued as part of the service routine.

Of the next two bits in ICW_4, BUF is used to specify whether or not the 8259A is to be used in a system where the data bus is buffered with a bidirectional bus transceiver. When buffered mode is selected, the $\overline{SP}/\overline{EN}$ line is configured as $\overline{EN}$. As indicated earlier, $\overline{EN}$ is a control output that can be used to control the direction of data transfer through the bus transceiver. It switches to logic 0 whenever data are transferred from the 8259A to the MPU.

If buffered mode is not selected, the $\overline{SP}/\overline{EN}$ line is configured to work as the master/slave mode select input. In this case, logic 1 at the $\overline{SP}$ input selects master mode operation and logic 0 selects slave mode.

Assume that the buffered mode was selected; then the $\overline{SP}$ input is no longer available to select between the master and slave modes of operation. Instead, the M/S bit of ICW_4 defines whether the 8259A is a master or slave device.

Bit D4 is used to enable or disable another operational option of the 8259A. This option is known as the *special fully nested mode*. This function is used only in conjunction with the cascaded mode. Moreover, it is enabled only for the master 8259A, not for the slaves. This is done by setting the SFNM bit to logic 1.

The 8259A is put into the fully nested mode of operation as command word ICW_1 is loaded. When an interrupt is initiated in a cascaded system that is configured in this way, the occurrence of another interrupt at the slave corresponding to the original interrupt is masked out even if it is of higher priority. This is because the bit in ISR of the master 8259A that corresponds to the slave is already set; therefore, the master 8259A ignores all interrupts of equal or lower priority.

This problem is overcome by enabling special fully nested mode of operation at the master. In this mode, the master will respond to those interrupts that are at lower or higher priority than the active level.

The last three bits of ICW_4, D_5 through D_7, must be logic 0.

Operational Command Words

Once the appropriate ICW commands have been issued to the 8259A, it is ready to operate in the fully nested mode. Three operational command words are also provided for controlling the operation of the 8259A. These commands permit further modifications to be made to the operation of the interrupt interface after it has been initialized. Unlike the initialization sequence, which requires that the ICWs be output in a special sequence after power-up, the OCWs can be issued under program control whenever needed and in any order.

The first operational command word, OCW_1, is used to access the contents of the interrupt mask register (IMR). A read operation can be performed to the register to determine the present setting of the mask. Moreover, write operations can be performed to set or reset its bits. This permits selective masking of the interrupt inputs. Notice in Fig. 9.14(a) that bits D_0 through D_7 of command word OCW_1 are identified as mask bits M_0 through M_7, respectively. In hardware, these bits correspond to interrupt inputs IR_0 through IR_7, respectively. Setting a bit to logic 1 masks out the associated interrupt input. On the other hand, clearing it to logic 0 enables the interrupt input.

For instance, writing $F0_{16} = 11110000_2$ into the register causes inputs IR_0 through IR_3 to be unmasked and IR_4 through IR_7 to be masked. Input A_0 must be logic 1 whenever the OCW_1 command is issued. In other words, the MPU address to access OCW_1 is an odd address.

EXAMPLE 9.6

What should be the OCW_1 code if interrupt inputs IR_0 through IR_3 are to be masked and IR_4 through IR_7 unmasked?

Solution

For IR_0 through IR_3 to be masked, their corresponding bits in the mask register must be made logic 1.

$$D_3D_2D_1D_0 = 1111_2$$

On the other hand, for IR_4 through IR_7 to be unmasked, D_4 through D_7 must be logic 0.

$$D_7D_6D_5D_4 = 0000_2$$

Therefore, the complete word for OCW_1 is

$$D_7D_6D_5D_4D_3D_2D_1D_0 = 00001111_2 = 0F_{16}$$

The second operational command word, OCW_2, selects the appropriate priority scheme and assigns an IR level for those schemes that require a specific interrupt level. The format of OCW_2 is given in Fig. 9.14(b). Here we see that the three LSBs define the interrupt level. For example, using $L_2L_1L_0 = 000_2$ in these locations specifies interrupt level 0, which corresponds to input IR_0.

The other three active bits of the word D_7, D_6, and D_5 are called *rotation* (R), *specific level* (SL), and *end of interrupt* (EOI), respectively. They are used to select a priority scheme according to the table in Fig. 9.14(b). For instance, if these bits are all logic 1, the priority scheme known as *rotate on specific EOI* command is enabled. Since this scheme requires a specific interrupt, its value must be included in $L_2L_1L_0$. A_0 must be logic 0 whenever this command is issued to the 8259A.

EXAMPLE 9.7

What OCW_2 must be issued to the 8259A if the priority scheme rotate on nonspecific EOI command is to be selected?

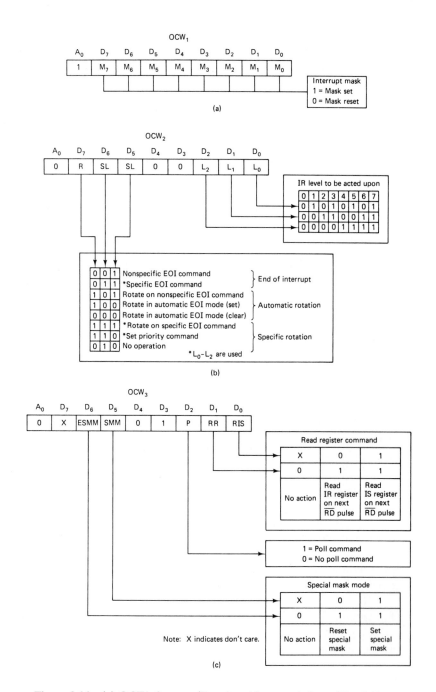

Figure 9.14 (a) OCW$_1$ format. (Reprinted by permission of Intel Corp., © Intel Corp. 1979) (b) OCW$_2$ format. (Reprinted by permission of Intel Corp., © Intel Corp. 1979) (c) OCW$_3$ format. (Reprinted by permission of Intel Corp., © Intel Corp. 1979)

Solution

To enable the rotate on nonspecific EOI command priority scheme, bits D_7 through D_5 must be set to 101. Since a specific level does not have to be specified, the rest of the bits in the command word can be 0. This gives OCW_2 as

$$D_7D_6D_5D_4D_3D_2D_1D_0 = 10100000_2 = A0_{16}$$

The last control word, OCW_3, which is shown in Fig. 9.14(c), permits reading of the contents of the ISR or IRR registers through software, issue of the poll command, and enable/disable of the special mask mode. Bit D_1, which is called *read register* (RR), is set to 1 to initiate reading of either the in-service register (ISR) or interrupt request register (IRR). At the same time, bit D_0, which is labeled RIS, selects between ISR and IRR. Logic 0 in RIS selects IRR and logic 1 selects IRS. In response to this command, the 8259A makes the contents of the selected register available so that they can be read by the MPU.

If the next bit, D_2, in OCW_3 is logic 1, a *poll command* is issued to the 8259A. The result of issuing a poll command is that the next $\overline{RD}$ pulse to the 8259A is interpreted as an interrupt acknowledge. In turn, the 8259A causes the ISR register to be loaded with the value of the highest-priority active interrupt. After this, a *poll word* is automatically put on the data bus. The MPU must read it off the bus.

Figure 9.15 illustrates the format of the poll word. Looking at this word, we see that the MSB is labeled I for interrupt. The logic level of this bit indicates to the MPU whether or not an interrupt input was active. Logic 1 indicates that an interrupt is active. The three LSBs $W_2W_1W_0$ identify the priority level of the highest-priority active interrupt input. This poll word can be decoded through software, and when an interrupt is found to be active, a branch is initiated to the starting point of its service routine. The poll command represents a software method of identifying whether or not an interrupt has occurred; therefore, the INTR input of the 8088 or 8086 should be disabled.

D_5 and D_6 are the remaining bits of OCW_3 for which functions are defined. They are used to enable or disable the special mask mode. ESMM (*enable special mask mode*) must be logic 1 to permit changing of the status of the special mask mode with the SMM (*special mask mode*) bit. Logic 1 at SMM enables the special mask mode of operation. If the 8259A is initially configured for the fully nested mode of operation, only interrupts of higher priority are allowed to interrupt an active service routine. However, by enabling the special mask mode, interrupts of higher or lower priority are enabled, but those of equal priority remain masked out.

Figure 9.15 Poll word format. (Reprinted by permission of Intel Corp., © Intel Corp. 1979)

EXAMPLE 9.8

Write a program that will initialize an 8259A with the initialization command words ICW_1, ICW_2, and ICW_3 derived in Examples 9.3, 9.4, and 9.5, respectively. Moreover, ICW_4 is to be equal to $1F_{16}$. Assume that the 8259A resides at address $A000_{16}$ in the memory address space.

Solution

Since the 8259A resides in the memory address space, we can use a series of move instructions to write the initialization command words into its registers. Notice that the memory address for an ICW is $A000_{16}$ if $A_0 = 0$ and it is $A001_{16}$ if $A_0 = 1$. However, before doing this, we must first disable interrupts. This is done with the instruction

```
        CLI             ;Disable interrupts
```

Next we will set up a data segment starting at address 00000_{16}.

```
        MOV AX,0                ;Create a data segment at 00000₁₆
        MOV DS,AX
```

Now we are ready to write the command words to the 8259A.

```
        MOV AL,19H              ;LOAD ICW1
        MOV 0A000H,AL           ;WRITE ICW1 TO 8259A
        MOV AL,0F0H             ;LOAD ICW2
        MOV 0A001H,AL           ;WRITE ICW2 TO 8259A
        MOV AL,0F0H             ;LOAD ICW3
        MOV 0A001H,AL           ;WRITE ICW3 TO 8259A
        MOV AL,1FH              ;LOAD ICW4
        MOV 0A001H,AL           ;WRITE ICW4 TO 8259A
```

Initialization is now complete and the interrupts can be enabled with the interrupt instruction

```
        STI             ;ENABLE INTERRUPTS
```

▲ 9.9 INTERRUPT INTERFACE CIRCUITS USING THE 8259A

Now that we have introduced the 8259A programmable interrupt controller, let us look at how it is used to implement the interrupt interface in 8088- and 8086-based microcomputer systems.

Figure 9.16(a) shows an interrupt interface circuit for a minimum-mode microcomputer system. Notice that data bus lines, D_0 through D_7, of the 8259A are connected directly to the 8088's multiplexed address/data bus. It is over these lines

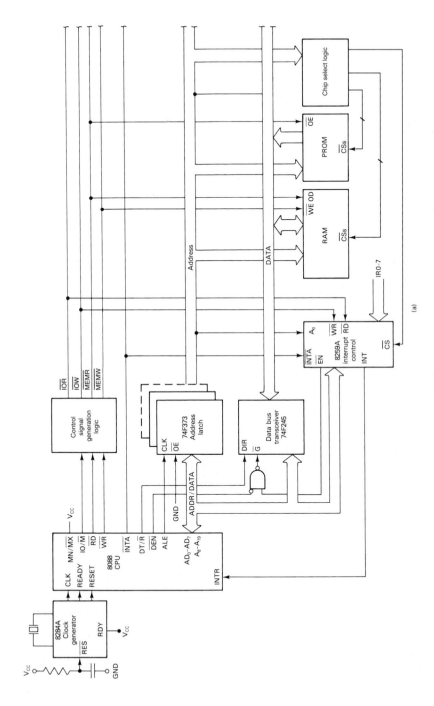

Figure 9.16 (a) Minimum-mode interrupt interface for the 8088 microcomputer using the 8259A. (Reprinted by permission of Intel Corp., © Intel Corp. 1979) (b) Minimum-mode interrupt interface for the 8086 microcomputer system using cascaded 8259As. (Reprinted by permission of Intel Corp., © Intel Corp. 1979) (c) Master/slave connection. (Reprinted by permission of Intel Corp., © Intel Corp. 1979)

581

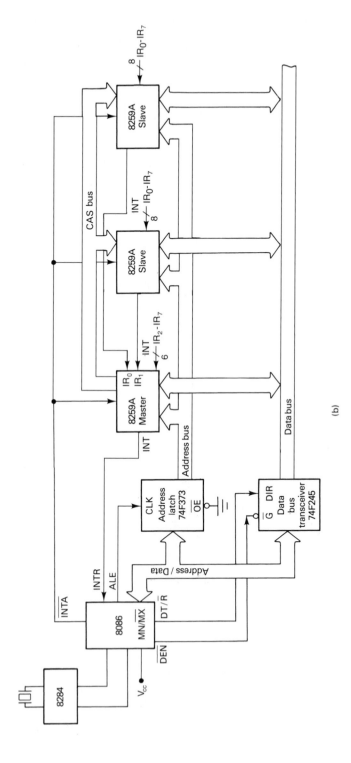

Figure 9.16 (Continued)

(b)

582

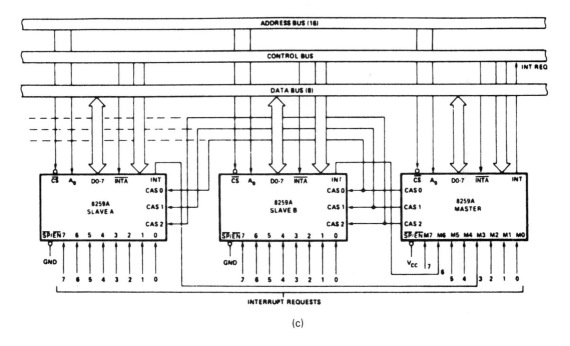

Figure 9.16 (Continued)

that the 8088 initializes the internal registers of the 8259A, reads the contents of these registers, and reads the type number of the active interrupt during the interrupt acknowledge bus cycle. In this circuit, the registers of the 8259A are assigned to unique I/O addresses. During input or output bus cycles to one of these addresses, bits of the demultiplexed address are decoded to generate the $\overline{CS}$ for the 8259A to enable the microprocessor interface. A specific register within the PIC is selected by the logic level of address bit A_0. The 8088's $\overline{RD}$, $\overline{WR}$, and IO/$\overline{M}$ control signals decoded to generate four control signals $\overline{IOR}$, $\overline{IOW}$, $\overline{MEMR}$, and $\overline{MEMW}$. $\overline{IOR}$ and $\overline{IOW}$ are supplied to the $\overline{RD}$ and $\overline{WR}$ inputs of the 8259A, respectively. These signals tell whether an input or output bus operation is taking place.

Let us trace the sequence of events that takes place as a device requests service through the interrupt interface circuit. The interrupt request inputs are identified as IR_0 through IR_7 in the circuit of Fig. 9.16(a). Whenever an interrupt input becomes active and either no other interrupts are active or the priority level of the new interrupt is higher than that of the already active interrupt, the 8259A switches its INT output to logic 1. This output is connected to the INTR input of the 8088, where it signals that an external device needs to be serviced. As long as the interrupt flag within the 8088 is set to 1, the interrupt interface is enabled, the interrupt request is accepted, and the interrupt acknowledge bus cycle is initiated. When the second pulse is output at $\overline{INTA}$, the 8259A is signaled to put the type number of its highest-priority active interrupt onto the data bus. The 8088 reads this number off the bus and then initiates a vectored transfer of control to the starting point of the corresponding service routine in program memory.

The circuit in Fig. 9.16(b) shows three 8259A devices connected in a *master/slave configuration* to construct an interrupt interface for a minimum-mode 8086 microcomputer system. If a request for interrupt service is initiated at an IR input of a slave, it causes the INT output of the corresponding slave to switch to logic 1. Looking at the circuit, we see that the INT outputs of the slave PICs are applied to separate interrupt inputs on the master PIC. The INT output of the master is supplied directly to the interrupt request input INTR of the 8086. Unlike the 8088 minimum-mode circuit in Fig. 9.16(a), this circuit has the three 8259As connected to the demultiplexed address and data bus lines. Each device must reside at unique addresses in the I/O or memory address space. In this way, during read or write bus cycles to the interrupt interface, the address output on the bus can be decoded to produce a chip enable signal to select the appropriate device.

The last group of signals in the interrupt interface is the CAS bus. Notice that these lines on all three PICs are connected in parallel. It is over these lines that the master signals the slaves whether or not the interrupt request has been acknowledged. A master/slave connection is shown in more detail in Fig. 9.16(c). Here we find that the rightmost device is identified as the master and the devices to the left as slave A and slave B. At the interrupt request side of the devices, we find that slaves A and B are cascaded to the master 8259A by attaching their INT outputs to the M_3 (IR_3) and M_6 (IR_6) inputs, respectively. This means that the identification code for slave A is 3 and that of slave B is 6. Moreover, the CAS lines on all three PICs are tied in parallel. Using the CAS lines, the master identifies the slaves whose interrupt request has been acknowledged.

Whenever an interrupt input is active at the master or at a slave and the priority is higher than that of an already active interrupt, the master controller switches INTR to logic 1, this signals the 8086 that an external device needs to be serviced. If the interrupt flag within the 8086 is set to 1, the interrupt interface is enabled and the interrupt request will be accepted. Therefore, the interrupt acknowledge bus cycle sequence is initiated. As the first pulse is output at interrupt acknowledge ($\overline{INTA}$), the master PIC is signaled to output the 3-bit cascade code of the device whose interrupt request is being acknowledged on the CAS bus. The slaves read this code and compare it to their internal code. In this way, the slave corresponding to the code is signaled to output the type number of its highest-priority active interrupt onto the data bus during the second interrupt acknowledge bus cycle. The 8086 reads this number off the bus and uses it to pass program control to the beginning of the corresponding service routine.

Figure 9.17 illustrates an interrupt interface implemented for a maximum-mode 8088 microcomputer system.

EXAMPLE 9.9

Analyze the circuit in Fig. 9.18(a) and write an appropriate main program and a service routine that counts as a decimal number the positive edges of the clock signal applied to IR_0 input of the 8259A.

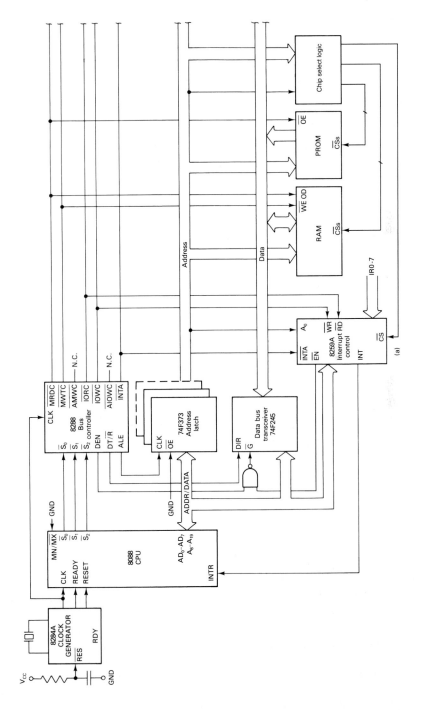

Figure 9.17 Maximum-mode interrupt interface for the 8088 MPU using the 8259A.

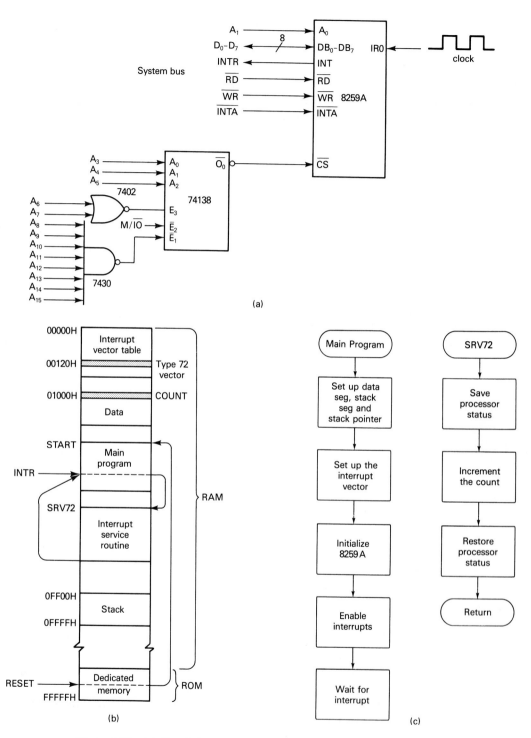

Figure 9.18 (a) Circuit for Example 9.9. (b) Software organizations. (c) Flowcharts for the main program and service routine.

586

Solution

The microprocessor addresses to which the 8259A in the circuit of Fig. 9.18(a) responds depend on how the $\overline{\text{CS}}$ signal for the 8259A is generated as well as the logic level of A_1 which is connected to its A_0. Notice that the A_0 of the microprocessor is not used in the circuit and therefore it is a don't-care address bit. Thus if A_0 is taken as 0 the 8259A responds to

$$A_{15} \ A_{14} \ A_{13} \ A_{12} \ A_{11}A_{10} \ A_9 \ A_8 \ A_7 \ A_6 \ A_5 \ A_4 \ A_3 \ A_2 \ A_1 \ A_0$$
$$= 1111111110000000_2 \text{ for } A_1 = 0, \text{M}/\overline{\text{IO}} = 0 \text{ and}$$
$$= 1111111110000010_2 \text{ for } A_1 = 1, \text{M}/\overline{\text{IO}} = 0.$$

These two are I/O addresses FF00H and FF02H respectively. The address FF00H is for the ICW_1 and FF02H is for the ICW_2, ICW_3, ICW_4, and OCW_1 command words. Let us now determine the ICWs and OCWs for the 8259A.

The fact that the M/$\overline{\text{IO}}$ signal is used in the circuit diagram tells us that the 8259A interfaces is for the 8086 microprocessor. Furthermore, we see that there is only one 8259A in the system and that the interrupt input is an edge. This information leads to the following ICW_1:

$$ICW_1 = 00010011_2 = 13\text{H}$$

Let us assume that we will use interrupt type 72 to service an interrupt generated by an edge presented to the IR_0. This leads to the following ICW_2:

$$ICW_2 = 01001000_2 = 48\text{H}$$

For a single 8259A ICW_3 is not needed. To determine ICW_4 let us assume that we will use auto EOI and nonbuffered mode of operation. This leads to the following ICW_4:

$$ICW_4 = 00000011_2 = 03\text{H}$$

For OCWs we will use only OCW_1 to mask all other interrupts but IR_0. This gives OCW_1 as

$$OCW_1 = 11111110_2 = \text{FEH}$$

Figure 9.18(b) shows the memory organization for the software. Let us understand the information presented in this memory organization. In the interrupt vector table we need to set up the type 72 vector. The type 72 vector is located at $4 \times 72 = 288 = 120\text{H}$. At address 120H we need to place the offset of the service routine and at address 122H the code segment value of the service routine.

In the data area we need a location to keep a decimal count of the edges of the input clock. Let us assume that it is location 01000H. The stack starts at 0FF00H and ends at 0FFFFH. The start address of the main program is denoted as START and that of the service routine as SRV72.

The flowcharts in Fig. 9.18(c) are for the main program and the service routine. The main program initializes the microprocessor and the 8259A. First of all we establish various segments for data and stack. This can be done using the following instructions:

```
;MAIN PROGRAM
          CLI                      ;Start with interrupts disabled
START:    MOV AX,0                 ;Extra segment at 00000H
          MOV ES,AX
          MOV AX,100H              ;Data segment at 01000H
          MOV DS,AX
          MOV AX,0FF0H             ;Stack segment at 0FF00H
          MOV SS,AX
          MOV SP,1000H             ;Stack end at 10000H
```

Next we can set up the IP and CS for the type 72 vector in the interrupt vector table. This can be accomplished using the following instructions:

```
          MOV AX,OFFSET SRV72      ;Get offset for the service routine
          MOV [ES:120H],AX         ;Setup the IP
          MOV AX,SEG SRV72         ;Get code seg for the service routine
          MOV [ES:122H],AX         ;Setup the CS
```

Having set up the interrupt type vector let us proceed now to initialize the 8259A. Using the analyzed information the following instructions can be executed to initialize the 8259A:

```
          MOV DX,0FF00H            ;ICW1 address
          MOV AL,13H               ;Edge trig input, single 8259
          OUT DX,AL
          MOV DX,0FF02H            ;ICW2,ICW4,OCW1 address
          MOV AL,48H               ;ICW2, type 72
          OUT DX,AL
          MOV AL,03H               ;ICW4, AEOI, non-buff mode
          OUT DX,AL
          MOV AL,0FEH              ;OCW1, mask all but IR0
          OUT DX,AL
          STI                      ;Enable the interrupts
```

Now the processor is ready to accept interrupts. We can write an endless loop to wait for the interrupt to occur. In a real situation we may be doing some other operation in which the interrupt will be received and serviced. For simplicity let us use the following instruction to wait for the interrupt

```
          HERE:    JMP HERE      ;Wait for interrupt
```

Figure 9.18(c) shows the flowchart for the interrupt service routine as well. The operations shown in the flowchart can be implemented using the following instructions:

```
SRV72:     PUSH AX            ;Save register to be used
           MOV AL,[COUNT]     ;Get the count
           INC AL             ;Increment the count
           DAA                ;Decimal adjust the count
           MOV [COUNT],AL     ;Save the new count
           POP AX             ;Restore the register used
           IRET               ;Return from interrupt
```

▲ 9.10 SOFTWARE INTERRUPTS

The 8088 and 8086 microcomputer systems are capable of implementing up to 256 software interrupts. They differ from the external hardware interrupts in that their service routines are initiated in response to the execution of a software interrupt instruction, not an event in external hardware.

The INT n instruction is used to initiate a software interrupt. Earlier in this chapter we indicated that n represents the type number associated with the service routine. The software interrupt service routines are vectored to, using pointers from the same memory locations as the corresponding external hardware interrupts. These locations are shown in the pointer table of Fig. 9.1. Our earlier example was INT 50. It has a type number of 50 and causes a vector in program control to the service routine whose starting address is defined by the values of IP and CS stored at addresses $00C8_{16}$ and $00CA_{16}$, respectively.

The mechanism by which a software interrupt is initiated is similar to that described for the external hardware interrupts. However, no external interrupt acknowledge bus cycles are initiated. Instead, control is passed to the start of the service routine immediately upon completion of execution of the interrupt instruction. As usual, the old flags, old CS, and old IP are automatically saved on the stack, and then IF and trap flag (TF) are cleared.

If necessary, the contents of other internal registers can be saved on the stack by including the appropriate PUSH instructions at the beginning of the service routine. Toward the end of the service routine, POP instructions must be included to restore these registers. Finally, IRET instruction is included to restore the original program environment.

Software interrupts are of higher priority than the external interrupts and are not masked out by IF. The software interrupts are actually *vectored subroutine calls*. A common use of these software routines is as *emulation routines* for more complex functions. For instance, INT 50 could define a *floating-point addition instruction* and INT 51 a *floating-point subtraction instruction*. These emulation routines are written using assembly language instructions, are assembled into machine code, and then are stored in the main memory of the 8088 microcomputer system. Other examples of their use are for *supervisor calls* from an operating system and for *testing* of external hardware interrupt service routines.

▲ 9.11 NONMASKABLE INTERRUPT

The nonmaskable interrupt (NMI) is another interrupt that is initiated from external hardware. However, it differs from the other external hardware interrupts in several ways. First, it cannot be masked out with the IF flag. Second, requests for service by this interrupt are signaled to the 8088 or 8086 microprocessor by applying logic 1 at the NMI input, not the INTR input. Third, the NMI input is positive edge triggered. Therefore, a request for service is latched internal to the MPU.

If the contents of the NMI latch are sampled as being active for two consecutive clock cycles, it is recognized and the nonmaskable interrupt sequence initiated. Initiation of NMI causes the current flags, current CS, and current IP to be pushed onto the stack. Moreover, the interrupt enable flag is cleared to disable all external hardware interrupts and the trap flag is cleared to disable the single-step mode of operation.

As shown in Fig. 9.1, NMI has a dedicated type number. It automatically vectors from the type 2 vector location in the pointer table. This vector is stored in memory at word addresses 0008_{16} and $000A_{16}$.

Typically, the NMI is assigned to hardware events that must be responded to immediately. Two examples are the detection of a power failure and detection of a memory read error.

▲ 9.12 RESET

The RESET input provides hardware means for initializing the 8088 or 8086 microcomputer. This is typically done at power-up to provide an orderly start-up of the system.

Figure 9.19(a) shows that the reset interface of the 8088 includes part of the 8284 clock generator device. The 8284 contains circuitry that makes it easy to implement the hardware reset function. Notice that the $\overline{\text{RES}}$ input (pin 11) of the clock generator is attached to an RC circuit. The signal at $\overline{\text{RES}}$ is applied to the input of an internal Schmitt trigger circuit. If the voltage across the capacitor is below the 1-logic-level threshold of the Schmitt trigger, the RESET output (pin 10) stays at logic 1. This output is supplied to the RESET input at pin 21 of the 8088. It can also be applied in parallel to reset inputs on LSI peripheral devices so that they are also initialized at power-on.

At power-on, $\overline{\text{RES}}$ of the 8284 is shorted to ground through the capacitor. This represents logic 0 at the input of the Schmitt trigger and RESET switches to logic 1. At the RESET input of the 8088, this signal is synchronized to the 0-to-1 edge of CLK. This is shown in the waveforms of Fig. 9.19(b). RESET must be held at logic 1 for a minimum of four clock cycles; otherwise, it will not be recognized.

The 8088 terminates operation on the 0-to-1 edge of the internal reset signal. Its bus is put in the high-Z state and the control signals are switched to their inactive states. These signal states are summarized in Fig. 9.20(a). Here we see that in a minimum-mode system, signals AD_0 through AD_7, A_8 through A_{15}, and $A_{16}/\overline{S}_3$ through $A_{19}/\overline{S}_6$, are immediately put in the high-Z state. On the other hand, signal

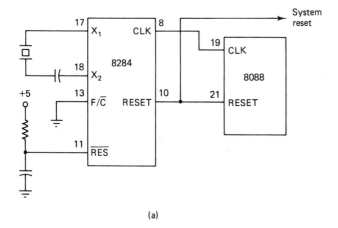

(a)

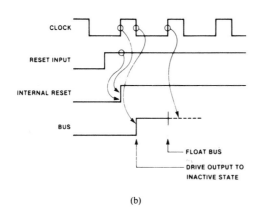

(b)

Figure 9.19 (a) Reset interface of the 8088. (Reprinted by permission of Intel Corp., © Intel Corp. 1979) (b) Reset timing sequence. (Reprinted by permission of Intel Corp., © Intel Corp. 1979)

lines $\overline{SSO}$, IO/$\overline{M}$, DT/$\overline{R}$, $\overline{DEN}$, $\overline{WR}$, $\overline{RD}$, and $\overline{INTA}$ are first forced to logic 1 for one clock interval and then they are put in the high-Z state synchronously with the positive edge of the next clock pulse. Moreover, signal lines ALE and HLDA are forced to their inactive 0 logic level. The 8088 remains in this state until the RESET input is returned to logic 0.

The hardware of the reset interface in an 8086 microcomputer system is identical to that just shown for the 8088 microprocessor. In fact, the reset and clock inputs, which are found at pins 21 and 19 of the 8088, respectively, in Fig. 9.19(a), are at these same pins on the 8086. Moreover, the waveforms given in Fig. 9.19(b) also describe the timing sequence that occurs when the reset input of the 8086 is activated. Remember that the 8086 produces some different signals than the 8088. For example, it has a $\overline{BHE}$ output instead of an $\overline{SSO}$ output. The state of the 8086's bus and control signals during reset is shown in Fig. 9.20(b).

In the maximum-mode system, the 8088 and 8086 respond in a similar way to an active reset request. However, this time the $\overline{S_2}\overline{S_1}\overline{S_0}$ outputs, which are inputs to the 8288 bus controller, are also forced to logic 1 and then put into the high-Z state. These inputs of the 8288 have internal pull-up resistors. Therefore, with the

Signals	Condition
AD_{7-0}	Three-state
A_{15-8}	Three-state
A_{19-16}/S_{6-3}	Three-state
$\overline{SSO}$	Driven to 1, then three-state
$\overline{S}_2/(IO/\overline{M})$	Driven to 1, then three-state
$\overline{S}_1/(DT/\overline{R})$	Driven to 1, then three-state
$\overline{S}_0/\overline{DEN}$	Driven to 1, then three-state
$\overline{LOCK}/\overline{WR}$	Driven to 1, then three-state
$\overline{RD}$	Driven to 1, then three-state
$\overline{INTA}$	Driven to 1, then three-state
ALE	0
HLDA	0
$\overline{RQ}/\overline{GT}_0$	1
$\overline{RQ}/\overline{GT}_1$	1
QS_0	0
QS_1	0

(a)

Signals	Condition
AD_{15-0}	Three-state
A_{19-16}/S_{6-3}	Three-state
BHE/S_7	Three-state
$\overline{S}_2/(M/\overline{IO})$	Driven to "1" then three-state
$\overline{S}_1/(DT/\overline{R})$	Driven to "1" then three-state
$\overline{S}_0/\overline{DEN}$	Driven to "1" then three-state
$\overline{LOCK}/\overline{WR}$	Driven to "1" then three-state
$\overline{RD}$	Driven to "1" then three-state
$\overline{INTA}$	Driven to "1" then three-state
ALE	0
HLDA	0
$\overline{RQ}/\overline{GT}_0$	1
$\overline{RQ}/\overline{GT}_1$	1
QS_0	0
QS_1	0

(b)

Figure 9.20 (a) Bus and control signal status of the 8088 during system reset. (b) Bus and control signal status of the 8086 during system reset. (Reprinted by permission of Intel Corp., © Intel Corp. 1979)

signal lines in the high-Z state, the input to the bus controller is $\overline{S}_2\overline{S}_1\overline{S}_0 = 111$. In response, its control outputs are set to ALE = 0, DEN = 0, DT/$\overline{R}$ = 1, and all its command outputs are switched to the 1 logic level. Moreover, outputs QS_0 and QS_1 of the MPU are both held at logic 0 and the $\overline{RQ}/\overline{GT}_0$ and $\overline{RQ}/\overline{GT}_1$, lines are held at logic 1.

CPU COMPONENT	CONTENT
Flags	Clear
Instruction Pointer	0000H
CS Register	FFFFH
DS Register	0000H
SS Register	0000H
ES Register	0000H
Queue	Empty

Figure 9.21 Internal state of the 8088/8086 after reset. (Reprinted by permission of Intel Corp., © Intel Corp. 1979)

When RESET returns to logic 0, the MPU initiates its internal initialization routine. The flags are all cleared; the instruction pointer is set to 0000_{16}; the CS register is set to $FFFF_{16}$; the DS register is set to 0000_{16}; the SS register is set to 0000_{16}; the ES register is set to 0000_{16}; and the instruction queue is emptied. The table in Fig. 9.21 summarizes this state.

Since the flags were all cleared as part of initialization, the external hardware interrupts are disabled. Moreover, the code segment register contains $FFFF_{16}$ and the instruction pointer contains 0000_{16}. Therefore, after reset execution begins at $FFFF0_{16}$. This location can contain an instruction that will cause a jump to the start-up program that is used to initialize the rest of the system's resources, such as I/O ports, the interrupt flag, and data memory. After system-level initialization is complete, another jump can be performed to the starting point of an application program.

▲ 9.13 INTERNAL INTERRUPT FUNCTIONS

Earlier we indicated that four of the 256 interrupts of the 8088 and 8086 are dedicated to the internal functions: divide error, overflow error, single step, and breakpoint. They are assigned unique type numbers, as shown in Fig. 9.22. Notice that they are the highest-priority type numbers. Moreover, in Fig. 9.6 we find that they are not masked out with the interrupt enable flag.

The occurrence of any one of these internal conditions is automatically detected by the MPU and causes an interrupt of program execution and a vectored transfer of control to the corresponding service routine. During the control transfer sequence, no external bus cycles are produced. Let us now look at each of these internal functions in more detail.

Divide Error

The *divide error* function represents an error condition that can occur in the execution of the division instructions. If the quotient that results from a DIV (divide) instruction or an IDIV (integer divide) instruction is larger than the specified destination, a divide error has occurred. This condition causes automatic initiation of a type 0 interrupt and passes control to a service routine whose starting point is defined by the values of IP_0 and CS_0 at addresses 00000_{16} and 00002_{16}, respectively, in the pointer table.

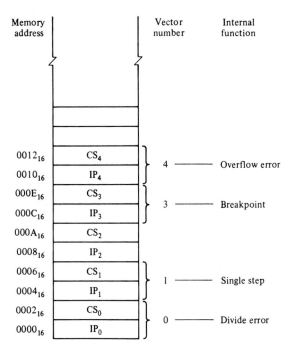

Memory address		Vector number	Internal function

0012_{16} — CS_4

0010_{16} — IP_4 — 4 ——— Overflow error

$000E_{16}$ — CS_3

$000C_{16}$ — IP_3 — 3 ——— Breakpoint

$000A_{16}$ — CS_2

0008_{16} — IP_2

0006_{16} — CS_1

0004_{16} — IP_1 — 1 ——— Single step

0002_{16} — CS_0

0000_{16} — IP_0 — 0 ——— Divide error

Figure 9.22 Internal interrupt vector locations.

Overflow Error

The *overflow error* is an error condition similar to that of divide error. However, it can result from the execution of any arithmetic instruction. Whenever an overflow occurs, the overflow flag gets set. In this case, the transfer of program control to a service routine is not automatic at occurrence of the overflow condition. Instead, the INTO (interrupt on overflow) instruction must be executed to test the overflow flag and determine if the overflow service routine should be initiated. If the overflow flag is found to be set, a type 4 interrupt service routine is initiated. Its vector consists of IP_4 and CS_4, which are stored at 00010_{16} and 00012_{16}, respectively, in memory. The routine pointed to by this vector can be written to service the overflow condition. For instance, it could cause a message to be displayed to specify that an overflow has occurred.

Single Step

The *single-step* function relates to an operating option of the 8088 or 8086. If the trap flag (TF) bit is set, the single-step mode of operation is enabled. This flag bit can be set or rest under software control.

When TF is set, the MPU initiates a type 1 interrupt to the service routine defined by IP_1 and CS_1 at 00004_{16} and 00006_{16}, respectively, at the completion of execution of every instruction of the user program. This permits implementation of the single-step mode of operation so that the program can be executed one instruction at a time. For instance, the service routine could include a WAIT instruction. In this way, a transition to logic 0 at the $\overline{\text{TEST}}$ input of the 8088 or 8086 could be used as the mechanism for stepping through a program one instruction at a time. This single-step operation can be used as a valuable software debugging tool.

Breakpoint Interrupt

The *breakpoint* function can also be used to implement a software diagnostic tool. A breakpoint interrupt is initiated by execution of the breakpoint instruction (*one-byte instruction with code* = $11001100_2 = CC_{16}$). This instruction can be inserted at strategic points in a program that is being debugged to cause execution to be stopped. This option can be used in a way similar to that of the single-step option. The service routine could again be put in the wait state, and resumption of execution down to the next breakpoint can be initiated by applying logic 0 to the $\overline{\text{TEST}}$ input.

ASSIGNMENTS

Section 9.2

1. What are the five groups of interrupts supported on the 8088 and 8086 MPUs?
2. What name is given to the special software routine to which control is passed when an interrupt occurs?
3. List in order the interrupt groups; start with the lowest priority and end with the highest priority.
4. What is the range of type numbers assigned to the interrupts in the 8088 and 8086 microcomputer systems?
5. Is the interrupt assigned to type 21 at a higher or lower priority than the interrupt assigned to type 35?

Section 9.3

6. Where are the interrupt pointers held?
7. How many bytes of memory does an interrupt vector take up?
8. What two elements make up an interrupt vector?
9. Which interrupt function's service routine is specified by $CS_4{:}IP_4$?
10. The breakpoint routine in an 8086 microcomputer system starts at address $AA000_{16}$ in the code segment located at address $A0000_{16}$. Specify how the breakpoint vector will be stored in the interrupt vector table.
11. At what addresses is the interrupt vector for type 40 stored in memory?

Section 9.4

12. What does STI stand for?
13. Which type of instruction does INTO normally follow? Which flag does it test?
14. What happens when the instruction HLT is executed?

Section 9.5

15. Explain how the CLI and STI instructions can be used to mask out external hardware interrupts during the execution of an uninterruptable subroutine.
16. How can the interrupt interface be reenabled during the execution of an interrupt service routine?

Section 9.6

17. Explain the function of the INTR and $\overline{\text{INTA}}$ signals in the circuit diagram of Fig. 9.4(a).
18. Which device produces $\overline{\text{INTA}}$ in a minimum-mode 8088 microcomputer system? In a maximum-mode 8088 microcomputer system?
19. Over which data bus lines does external circuitry send the type number of the active interrupt to the 8086?
20. What bus status code is assigned to interrupt acknowledge?

Section 9.7

21. Give an overview of the events in the order they take place during the interrupt request, interrupt acknowledge, and interrupt vector-fetch cycles of an 8088 microcomputer system.
22. If an 8086-based microcomputer is running at 10 MHz with two wait states, how long does it take to perform the interrupt acknowledge bus cycle sequence?
23. How long does it take the 8086 in problem 22 to push the values of the flags, CS, and IP to the stack? How much stack space do these values use?
24. How long does it take the 8086 in problem 22 to fetch its vector from memory?

Section 9.8

25. Specify the value of ICW1 needed to configure an 8259A as follows: ICW_4 not needed, single-device interface, and edge-triggered inputs.
26. Specify the value of ICW_2 if the type numbers produced by the 8259A are to be in the range 70_{16} through 77_{16}.
27. Specify the value of ICW_4 so that the 8259A is configured for use in an 8086

system, with normal EOI, buffered-mode master, and special fully nested mode disabled.

28. Write a program that will initialize an 8259A with the initialization command words derived in problems 25, 26, and 27. Assume that the 8259A resides at address $0A000_{16}$ in the memory address space.

29. Write an instruction that when executed will read the contents of OCW_1 and place it in the AL register. Assume that the 8259A has been configured by the software of problem 28.

30. What priority scheme is enabled if OCW_2 equals 67_{16}?

31. Write an instruction sequence that when executed will toggle the state of the read register bit in OCW_3. Assume that the 8259A is located at memory address $0A000_{16}$.

Section 9.9

32. How many interrupt inputs can be directly accepted by the circuit in Fig. 9.16(a)?

33. How many interrupt inputs can be directly accepted by the circuit in Fig. 9.16(b)?

34. Summarize the interrupt request/acknowledge handshake sequence for an interrupt initiated at an input to slave B in the circuit of Fig. 9.16(c).

Section 9.10

35. Give another name for a software interrupt.

36. If the instruction INT 80 is to pass control to a subroutine at address $A0100_{16}$ in the code segment starting at address $A0000_{16}$, what vector should be loaded into the interrupt vector table?

37. At what address would the vector for the instruction INT 80 be stored in memory?

Section 9.11

38. What type number and interrupt vector table addresses are assigned to NMI?

39. What are the key differences between NMI and the other external-hardware-initiated interrupts?

40. Give a common use of the NMI input.

Section 9.12

41. What device is normally used to generate the signal for the RESET input of the 8088?

42. List the states of the address/data bus lines and control signals $\overline{\text{BHE}}$, ALE, $\overline{\text{DEN}}$, DT/$\overline{\text{R}}$, $\overline{\text{RD}}$, and $\overline{\text{WR}}$ in a minimum-mode 8086 system when reset is at its active level.

43. What is the address from where the first instruction is fetched by the MPU after the reset has been applied?

44. Write a reset subroutine that initializes the block of memory locations from address $0A000_{16}$ to $0A0FF_{16}$ to zero. The initialization routine is at address 01000_{16}.

Section 9.13

45. List the internal interrupts serviced by the 8088.

46. Which vector numbers are allocated to internal interrupts?

47. What mode of operation is enabled with the trap flag? Which pointer holds the entry point for this service routine?

48. If the starting point of the service routine for problem 44 is defined by CS:IP = A000H: 0200H, at what addresses in memory are the values of CS and IP held? At what physical address does the service routine start?

10

IBM PC Microcomputer Hardware

▲ 10.1 INTRODUCTION

Having learned about the 8088 and 8086 microprocessors, their memory, input/output, and interrupt interfaces, we now turn our attention to a microcomputer system designed using this hardware. The microcomputer we will study in this chapter is the one found in the IBM PC, the original personal computer manufactured by IBM Corporation. The material covered in this chapter is organized as follows:

1. Architecture of the IBM PC system processor board
2. System processor circuitry
3. Wait state logic and NMI circuitry
4. I/O and memory chip select circuitry
5. Memory circuitry
6. Direct memory access circuitry
7. Timer circuitry
8. I/O circuitry
9. I/O channel interface

The IBM PC is a practical application of the 8088 microprocessor and its peripheral chip set as a general-purpose microcomputer. A block diagram of the system processor board (main circuit board) of the PC is shown in Fig. 10.1(a). This diagram identifies the major functional elements of the PC: MPU, PIC, DMA, PIT, PPI, ROM, and RAM. We will describe the circuitry used in each of these blocks in detail in the following sections of this chapter; however, for now let us begin here with an overview of the architecture of the PC's microcomputer system.

The heart of the PC's system processor board is the 8088 microprocessor unit (MPU). It is here that instructions of the program are fetched and executed. To interface to the peripherals and other circuitry such as memory, the 8088 microprocessor generates address, data, status, and control signals. Together these signals form what is called the *local bus* in Fig. 10.1(a). Notice that the local address and data bus lines are both buffered and demultiplexed to provide a separate 20-bit *system address bus* and 8-bit *system data bus*.

At the same time, the status and control lines of the local bus are decoded by the bus controller to generate the *system control bus*. This control bus consists of memory and I/O read and write control signals. The bus controller also produces the signals that control the direction of data transfer through the data bus buffers, that is, the signals needed to make the data bus lines work as inputs to the microprocessor during memory and I/O read operations and as outputs during write operations.

The operation of the microprocessor and other devices in a microcomputer system must be synchronized. The circuitry in the clock generator block of the PC in Fig. 10.1(a) generates clock signals for this purpose. The clock generator section also produces a power-on reset signal that is needed for initialization of the microprocessor and peripherals at power-up. Moreover, the clock generator section works in conjunction with the wait state logic to synchronize the MPU to slow peripheral devices. In Fig. 10.1(a), we see that the wait state logic circuitry monitors the system control bus signals and generates a wait signal for input to the clock generator. In turn, the clock generator synchronizes the wait input to the system clock to produce a ready signal at its output. This ready signal is input to the 8088 MPU and provides the ability to automatically extend bus cycles that are performed to slow devices by inserting wait states.

The memory subsystem of the PC system processor board we are studying in this chapter has 256KB of dynamic R/W memory (RAM) and 48KB of read-only memory (ROM). A memory map for the PC's memory is shown in Fig. 10.1(b). From the map, we find that the RAM address range is from 00000_{16} through $3FFFF_{16}$. This part of the memory subsystem can be implemented using $64K \times 1$-bit or $256K \times 1$-bit dynamic RAMs and is used to store operating system routines, application programs, and data that are to be processed. These programs and data are typically loaded into RAM from a mass storage device such as a diskette or hard disk.

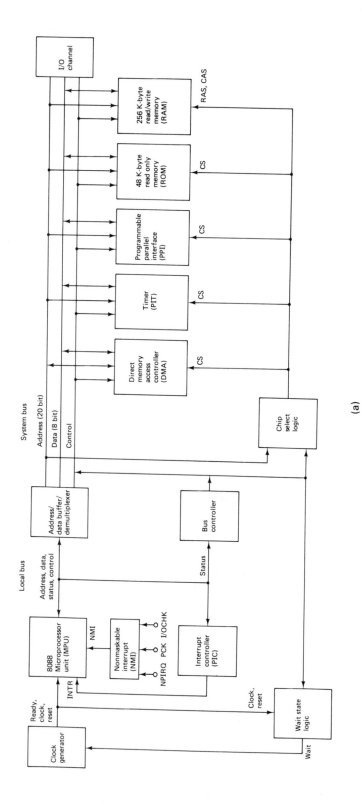

Figure 10.1 (a) IBM PC microcomputer block diagram. (b) Memory map. (c) PC system processor board peripheral addresses. (d) 8255A I/O map. (e) Interrupts. (Parts b, c, d, and e courtesy of International Business Machines Corporation)

(a)

Start Address		Function
Decimal	Hex	
0	00000	
16K	04000	
32K	08000	
48K	0C000	
64K	10000	
80K	14000	
96K	18000	
112K	1C000	64 to 256K Read/Write Memory
128K	20000	on System Board
144K	24000	
160K	28000	
176K	2C000	
192K	30000	
208K	34000	
224K	38000	
240K	3C000	
256K	40000	
272K	44000	
288K	48000	
304K	4C000	
320K	50000	
336K	54000	
352K	58000	
368K	5C000	
384K	60000	
400K	64000	
416K	68000	Up to 384K Read/Write
432K	6C000	Memory in I/O Channel
448K	70000	Up to 384K in I/O Channel
464K	74000	
480K	78000	
496K	7C000	
512K	80000	
528K	84000	
544K	88000	
560K	8C000	
576K	90000	
592K	94000	
608K	98000	
624K	9C000	

(b)

Figure 10.1   (Continued)

| Start Address | | Function |
Decimal	Hex	
640K	A0000	
656K	A4000	128K Reserved
672K	A8000	
688K	AC000	
704K	B0000	Monochrome
720K	B4000	
736K	B8000	Color/Graphics
752K	BC000	
768K	C0000	
784K	C4000	
800K	C8000	Fixed Disk Control
816K	CC000	
832K	D0000	
848K	D4000	192K Read Only Memory
864K	D8000	Expansion and Control
880K	DC000	
896K	E0000	
912K	E4000	
928K	E8000	
944K	EC000	
960K	F0000	Reserved
976K	F4000	
992K	F8000	48K Base System ROM
1008K	FC000	

(b)

Figure 10.1 (Continued)

Hex Range	Usage
000-00F	DMA Chip 8237A-5
020-021	Interrupt 8259A
040-043	Timer 8253-5
060-063	PPI 8255A-5
080-083	DMA Page Registers
0Ax*	NMI Mask Register
0Cx	Reserved
0Ex	Reserved
100-1FF	Not Usable
200-20F	Game Control
210-217	Expansion Unit
220-24F	Reserved
278-27F	Reserved
2F0-2F7	Reserved
2F8-2FF	Asynchronous Communications (Secondary)
300-31F	Prototype Card
320-32F	Fixed Disk
378-37F	Printer
380-38C**	SDLC Communications
380-389**	Binary Synchronous Communications (Secondary)
3A0-3A9	Binary Synchronous Communications (Primary)
3B0-3BF	IBM Monochrome Display/Printer
3C0-3CF	Reserved
3D0-3DF	Color/Graphics
3E0-3F7	Reserved
3F0-3F7	Diskette
3F8-3FF	Asynchronous Communications (Primary)

* At power-on time, the Non Mask Interrupt into the 8088 is masked off. This mask bit can be set and reset through system software as follows:

Set mask: Write hex 80 to I/O Address hex A0 (enable NMI)

Clear mask: Write hex 00 to I/O Address hex A0 (disable NMI)

** SDLC Communications and Secondary Binary Synchronous Communications cannot be used together because their hex addresses overlap.

(c)

Figure 10.1 (Continued)

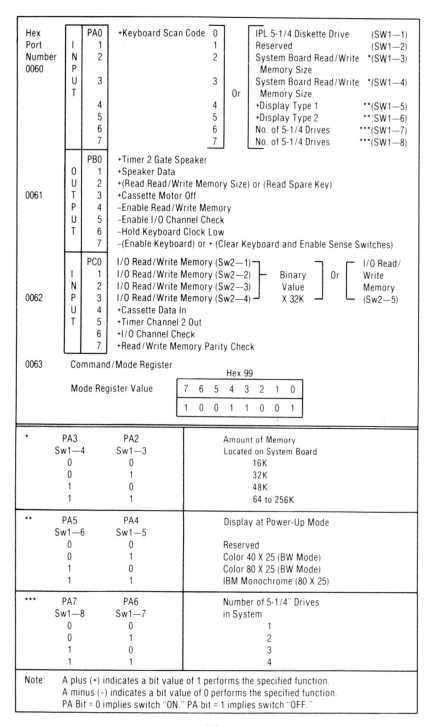

Hex Port Number 0060	INPUT	PA0	+Keyboard Scan Code 0		0	IPL 5-1/4 Diskette Drive (SW1—1)
		1	1		1	Reserved (SW1—2)
		2	2		2	System Board Read/Write *(SW1—3) Memory Size
		3	3	Or	3	System Board Read/Write *(SW1—4) Memory Size
		4	4		4	+Display Type 1 **(SW1—5)
		5	5		5	+Display Type 2 **(SW1—6)
		6	6		6	No. of 5-1/4 Drives ***(SW1—7)
		7	7		7	No. of 5-1/4 Drives ***(SW1—8)

0061	OUTPUT	PB0	+Timer 2 Gate Speaker
		1	+Speaker Data
		2	+(Read Read/Write Memory Size) or (Read Spare Key)
		3	+Cassette Motor Off
		4	−Enable Read/Write Memory
		5	−Enable I/O Channel Check
		6	−Hold Keyboard Clock Low
		7	−(Enable Keyboard) or + (Clear Keyboard and Enable Sense Switches)

0062	INPUT	PC0	I/O Read/Write Memory (Sw2—1) ⎤		⎤ I/O Read/
		1	I/O Read/Write Memory (Sw2—2) ├ Binary	Or	│ Write
		2	I/O Read/Write Memory (Sw2—3) │ Value		│ Memory
		3	I/O Read/Write Memory (Sw2—4) ⎦ X 32K		⎦ (Sw2—5)
		4	+Cassette Data In
		5	+Timer Channel 2 Out
		6	+I/O Channel Check
		7	+Read/Write Memory Parity Check

0063   Command/Mode Register

Hex 99

Mode Register Value

7	6	5	4	3	2	1	0
1	0	0	1	1	0	0	1

*	PA3 Sw1—4	PA2 Sw1—3	Amount of Memory Located on System Board
	0	0	16K
	0	1	32K
	1	0	48K
	1	1	64 to 256K

**	PA5 Sw1—6	PA4 Sw1—5	Display at Power-Up Mode
	0	0	Reserved
	0	1	Color 40 X 25 (BW Mode)
	1	0	Color 80 X 25 (BW Mode)
	1	1	IBM Monochrome (80 X 25)

***	PA7 Sw1—8	PA6 Sw1—7	Number of 5-1/4" Drives in System
	0	0	1
	0	1	2
	1	0	3
	1	1	4

Note: A plus (+) indicates a bit value of 1 performs the specified function.
A minus (−) indicates a bit value of 0 performs the specified function.
PA Bit = 0 implies switch "ON." PA bit = 1 implies switch "OFF."

(d)

Figure 10.1 (Continued)

Number	Usage
NMI	Parity
0	Timer
1	Keyboard
2	Reserved
3	Asynchronous Communications (Secondary)
	SDLC Communications
	BSC (Secondary)
4	Asynchronous Communications (Primary)
	SDLC Communications
	BSC (Primary)
5	Fixed Disk
6	Diskette
7	Printer

(e)

Figure 10.1 (Continued)

Furthermore, the memory map shows that ROM is located in the address range from $F4000_{16}$ to $FFFFF_{16}$. This part of the memory subsystem contains the basic system ROM of the PC. Included in these ROMs are fixed programs such as the *BASIC interpreter*, *power-on system procedures*, and *I/O device drivers*, or *BIOS* as it is better known.

The chip select logic section that is shown in the block diagram of Fig. 10.1(a) is used to select and enable the appropriate peripheral or memory devices whenever a bus cycle takes place over the system bus. To select a device in the I/O address space, such as the DMA controller, timer, or PPI, it decodes the address on the system bus to generate a chip select (CS) signal for the corresponding I/O device. This chip select signal is applied to the I/O device to enable it for operation. The memory chip selects are produced in a similar way by decoding the memory address on the system address bus.

The LSI peripherals included on the PC system processor board are the 8237A direct memory access (DMA) controller, 8253 programmable interval timer (PIT), 8255A programmable peripheral interface (PPI), and 8259A programmable interrupt controller (PIC). Note that each of these devices is identified with a separate block in Fig. 10.1(a). These peripherals are all located in the 8088's I/O address space, and their registers are accessed through software using the address ranges given in Fig. 10.1(c). For instance, the four registers within the PIT are located at addresses 0040_{16}, 0041_{16}, 0042_{16}, and 0043_{16}.

To support high-speed memory and I/O data transfers, the 8237A direct memory access controller is provided on the PC system board. This DMA chip contains four DMA channels, *DMA channel 0* through *DMA channel 3*. One channel, DMA 0, is used to refresh the dynamic R/W memory (RAM), and the other three channels are available for use with peripheral devices. For instance, DMA 2 is used to support floppy-disk-drive data transfers.

The 8253-based timer circuitry is used to generate time-related functions and signals in the PC. There are three 16-bit counters in the 8253, and they are driven by a 1.19-MHz clock signal. Timer 0 is used to generate an interrupt to the microprocessor approximately every 55 ms. This timing function is used by the system to keep track of time of the day. On the other hand, timer 1 is used to produce a DMA request every 15.12 μs to initiate refresh of the dynamic RAM. The last timer has multiple functions. It is used to generate programmable tones when driving the speaker and a record tone for use when sending data to the cassette for storage on tape.

The parallel I/O section of the PC's microcomputer, which is identified as PPI in Fig. 10.1(a), is implemented with the 8255A programmable peripheral interface controller. This device is configured through software to provide two 8-bit input ports and one 8-bit output port. The functions of the individual I/O lines of the PPI are given in Fig. 10.1(d). Here we see that these I/O lines are used to input data from the keyboard (keyboard scan code), output tones to the speaker (speaker data), and read in the state of memory and system configuration switches (SW1-1 through SW1-8). Through the PPI's ports, the microcomputer also controls the cassette motor and enables or disables I/O channel check. Note in Fig. 10.1(d) that switch inputs SW1-3 and SW1-4 are used to tell the MPU how much RAM is implemented on the system processor board. In the lower part of this table, we find that for a system with 64KB or 256KB they are both set to the 1 position.

The circuitry in the nonmaskable interrupt (NMI) logic block allows nonmaskable interrupt requests derived from three sources to be applied to the microprocessor. As shown in Fig. 10.1(a), these interrupt sources are the *numeric coprocessor interrupt request* (NPIRQ), *R/W memory parity check* (PCK), and *I/O channel check* (I/O CHK). If any of these inputs are active, the NMI logic outputs a request for service to the 8088 over the NMI signal line.

In addition to the nonmaskable interrupt interface, the PC architecture provides for requests for service to the MPU by interrupts at another interrupt input called *interrupt request* (INTR). Note in Fig. 10.1(a) that this signal is supplied to the 8088 by the output of the interrupt controller (PIC) block. The 8259A LSI interrupt controller that is used in the PC provides for eight additional prioritized interrupt inputs. The inputs of the interrupt controller are supplied by peripherals such as the timer, keyboard, diskette drive, printer, and communication devices. Interrupt priority assignments for these devices are given in Fig. 10.1(e). For example, the timer (actually just timer 2 of the 8253) is at priority level 0.

I/O channel, which is a collection of address, data, control, and power lines, is provided to support expansion of the PC system. The chassis of the PC has five 62-pin I/O channel card slots. In this way, the system configuration can be expanded by adding special function adapter cards, such as boards to control a monochrome or color display, floppy-disk drives, a hard disk drive, expanded memory, or to attach a printer. In Fig. 10.1(b), we see that I/O channel expanded

RAM resides in the part of the memory address space from 40000_{16} through $9FFFF_{16}$.

▲ 10.3 SYSTEM PROCESSOR CIRCUITRY

The system processor circuitry section of the IBM PC is shown in Fig. 10.2. It consists of the 8088 microprocessor, the 8284A clock generator, the 8288 bus controller, and the 8259A programmable interrupt controller. Here we will examine the operation of each of these sections of circuitry.

Clock Generator Circuitry

In Section 10.2, we pointed out that the clock generator circuitry serves three functions in terms of overall microcomputer system operation. They are *clock signal generation*, *reset signal generation*, and *ready signal generation*. Let us now explore the operation of the circuit for each of these functions in more depth.

The first function performed by the clock generator circuitry is the generation of the various clock signals that are needed to drive the 8088 microprocessor (U_3) and other circuits within the PC. As shown in Fig. 10.2, the 8284A clock generator/ driver (U_{11}) has a 14.31818-MHz crystal (Y_1) connected between its X_1 and X_2 pins. This crystal causes the oscillator circuitry within the 8284A to run and generate three clock output signals. They are oscillator clock (OSC), which is at 14.31818 MHz, TTL peripheral clock (PCLK), which is at 2.385 MHz, and 8088 microprocessor clock (CLK88), which is at 4.77 MHz. Note in Fig. 10.2 that the CLK88 output at pin 8 of the 8284A is connected to the CLK input of the 8088 at pin 19. In this way, we see that the 8088 in the IBM PC runs at 4.77 MHz.

The second purpose served by the clock generator circuitry is to generate a power-on reset signal for the system. When power is first turned on, the power supply section of the PC tells the clock generator that power is not yet stable by setting its power good (PWR GOOD) output to logic 0. Looking at Fig. 10.2, we find that this signal is applied to the $\overline{RES}$ input at pin 11 of the 8284A. Logic 0 at $\overline{RES}$ represents an active input to the power-on reset circuit within the 8284A; therefore, the RESET output at pin 10 switches to its active level, logic 1, to signal that a reset operation is to take place. Notice that the RESET output of the 8284A is applied directly to the RESET input at pin 21 of the 8088. When this input is at the 1 logic level, reset of the MPU is initiated.

As the voltage of the power supply builds up and becomes stable, the power supply switches PWR GOOD to logic 1. In response to this change in input, the RESET output of the 8284A returns to its inactive 0 logic level and the power-on reset is complete.

The last function served by the clock generator circuitry is to provide for synchronization of the 8088's bus operations with its memory and I/O peripherals. This synchronization is required to support the use of slow memory or peripheral devices on the system bus and is achieved by inserting wait states into the bus cycle

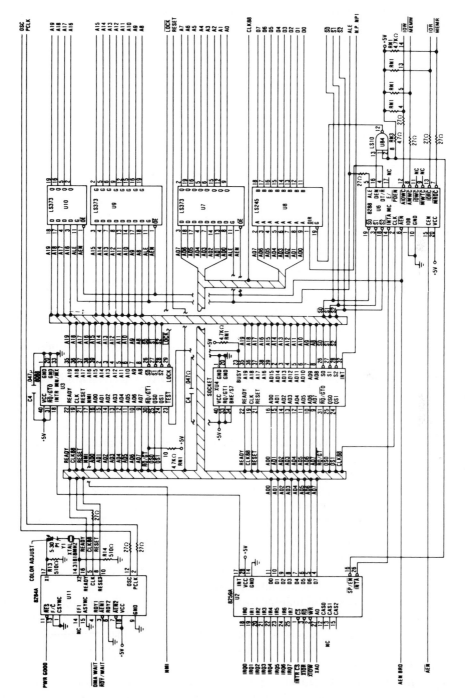

Figure 10.2 System processor circuitry. (Courtesy of International Business Machines Corporation)

to extend its duration. Let us now look at how and for what devices wait states are inserted into bus cycles of the microcomputer of the IBM PC.

The READY input at pin 22 of the 8088 is the signal that determines whether or not wait states are inserted into a bus cycle. If this input is at the 1 logic level when it is sampled by the processor, bus cycles are run to completion without inserting wait states. However, if its logic level is 0 when sampled, wait states are inserted into the current bus cycle until READY returns to 1. In Fig. 10.2, we see that the READY input of the 8088 is directly supplied by the READY output (pin 5) of the 8284A. The logic level of this output is determined by inputs $\overline{\text{DMA WAIT}}$ and $\overline{\text{RDY}}$/WAIT. Whenever input $\overline{\text{DMA WAIT}}$ is logic 0, the READY output is switched to logic 0. This means that wait states are automatically inserted whenever DMA transfer bus cycles are performed. On the other hand, logic 1 at the $\overline{\text{RDY}}$/WAIT input also causes READY to switch to logic 0. This signals that a slow memory or I/O device is being accessed and wait states are needed to extend the bus cycle. In the circuit under discussion, both I/O and DMA data transfers have one wait state inserted into each bus cycle.

Microprocessor, System Data Bus, and Bus Controller

The 8088 microprocessor (U_3) used in the PC is rated to operate at a maximum clock rate of 5 MHz. However, we just found that the CLK88 signal that is applied to its CLK input actually runs it at 4.77 MHz. At power up, the RESET input of the 8088 is activated by the 8284A to initiate a power-on reset of the MPU. This reset operation causes the status, DS, SS, ES, and IP registers within the 8088 to be cleared, the instruction queue to be emptied, and the code segment register to be initialized to FFFF$_{16}$. When RESET returns to its inactive level, the 8088 begins to fetch instructions from program memory starting at address FFFF0$_{16}$. The instruction at this location passes control to the PC's power-up program, which causes the rest of the system resources to be initialized, diagnostic tests to be run on the hardware, and the operating system loaded from diskette or hard disk. At this point, the microcomputer is up and running. Let us now look at how it accesses memory and I/O devices.

Earlier we pointed out that the microcomputer of the IBM PC is architected to have both a multiplexed local bus and a demultiplexed system bus. In general, memory and I/O peripherals are attached to the 8088 microprocessor at the system bus. However, there are some exceptions; both the 8259A interrupt controller and 8087 numeric coprocessor are attached directly to the local bus.

In Fig. 10.2, we find that the local bus includes the 8088's multiplexed address data bus lines AD_0 through AD_7, address lines A_8 through A_{19}, and maximum-mode status lines $\overline{S}_0$ through $\overline{S}_2$. Note that the local bus lines are connected to the 8259A programmable interrupt controller (U_2) and the socket for the 8087 numeric coprocessor (XU_4).

Let us now turn our attention to how the local bus lines are demultiplexed and decoded to form the system bus. Looking at Fig. 10.2, we see that the upper address lines are latched using 74LS373 devices U_9 and U_{10} to give system address bus lines A_8 through A_{19}. Another 74LS373 latch (U_7) is used to demultiplex low address signals A_0 through A_7 from the data signals to complete the system address bus. Finally, the separate system data bus lines, D_0 through D_7, are implemented with the 74LS245 bus transceiver U_8. These latches and transceivers also buffer the address and data bus lines to increase the drive capability at the system bus.

The 8288 bus controller U_5 monitors the codes output on the 8088's status lines $\overline{S}_0$ through $\overline{S}_2$. Based on these codes, it produces appropriate system bus control signals. For example, in Fig. 10.2 we see that the address latch enable (ALE) signal is output at pin 5 of the 8288 and supplied to the system bus. To ensure that address information is latched at the appropriate time when demultiplexing the local bus, ALE is also applied to the enable input (G) of all three 74LS373 latches. The 8288 also produces the DEN and DT/$\overline{R}$ signals that are used to control operation of the 74LS245 system data bus transceiver. Logic 1 at DEN (pin 16) signals when a data transfer can take place over the data bus; therefore, it is inverted and applied to the enable input ($\overline{G}$) of the transceiver. On the other hand, the logic level of DT/$\overline{R}$ (pin 4) identifies whether data are to be input or output over the system bus. For this reason, it is applied to the direction (DIR) input of the 74LS245.

The 8288 also produces I/O and memory read and write control signals. The outputs $\overline{IOR}$ and $\overline{IOW}$ are used to identify I/O read and write operations, respectively. Moreover, $\overline{MEMR}$ or $\overline{MEMW}$ is output to tell that a memory read or write operation is in progress, respectively. These signals are made available on the system bus.

Address enable inputs AEN BRD and $\overline{AEN}$ are active during all DMA cycles. These signals are applied to enable inputs $\overline{AEN}$ and CEN, respectively, of the 8288 and disable it when DMA transfers are to take place over the system bus. When disabled, the 8288 stops producing the I/O and memory read/write control signals. Signal AEN BRD is also used to disable the address latches and data transceiver so that the system address lines float when the 8237A DMA controller is to use the system bus.

Interrupt Controller

As shown in Fig. 10.2, an external hardware interrupt interface is implemented for the IBM PC with the 8259A programmable interrupt controller device U_2. It monitors the state of interrupt request lines IRQ_0 through IRQ_7 to determine if any external device is requesting service. In Fig. 10.1(c), the functions of the priority 0 through priority 7 interrupts are listed. For example, in this list we find that the IRQ_0 input is used to service the 8253 timer and IRQ_1 is dedicated to servicing the keyboard.

If an interrupt request input becomes active, the PIC switches its interrupt request (INT) output to the 1 logic level. Note in Fig. 10.2 that the INT output at pin 17 of the 8259A is supplied to the INTR input at pin 18 of the 8088. At completion of execution of the current instruction, the 8088 samples the logic level of its INTR input. Assuming that it is active, the 8088 responds to the request for service by outputting the interrupt acknowledge status code to the 8288 bus controller. In turn, the 8288 outputs logic 0 on interrupt acknowledge ($\overline{INTA}$), pin 14 of U_5. This signal is sent to the $\overline{INTA}$ input at pin 26 of the interrupt controller. Upon receiving this signal, the 8259A generates an active 0 level at $\overline{SP/EN}$, which, in conjunction with the data enable (DEN) output of the 8288, is used to float the system data bus lines. Now the interrupt controller outputs the type number of the active interrupt over the local data bus to the 8088. The MPU uses the type number to fetch the vector of the service routine for the interrupt from memory, loads it into CS and IP, and then executes the service routine.

The operating configuration of the 8259A needs to be initialized at power-on of the system. This initialization is achieved by writing to the 8259A's internal registers over the local bus. Earlier we pointed out that the peripherals in the PC are located in the I/O address space. For this reason, I/O instructions are used to access the registers of the PIC. This is why its read ($\overline{RD}$) and write ($\overline{WR}$) inputs are supplied by the I/O read ($\overline{XIOR}$) and I/O write ($\overline{XIOW}$) control signals, respectively. Moreover, when inputting data from or outputting data to the 8259A, the address of the register, which is either 20_{16} or 21_{16}, is output on the address bus. This address is decoded in the chip select logic circuit to produce chip select signal $\overline{INTR\,CS}$. This signal is applied to the $\overline{CS}$ input of the 8259A and enables its microprocessor interface.

In the sections of this chapter that follow, we will trace the operation of each of these segments of circuitry in detail.

▲ 10.4 WAIT STATE LOGIC AND NMI CIRCUITRY

The control logic circuitry shown in Fig. 10.3 provides several functions in terms of overall system operation. It consists of the wait state control circuit that is needed to extend memory and I/O bus cycles, the wait state and hold acknowledge logic that is used to grant the 8237A DMA controller access to the system bus, and the circuitry that generates the nonmaskable interrupt request.

Wait State Logic Circuitry

The wait state logic circuitry is used to insert one wait state into all I/O channel, I/O, and DMA bus cycles. Two wait state control signals, $\overline{RDY/WAIT}$ and $\overline{DMA\,WAIT}$, are produced by the circuit. $\overline{RDY/WAIT}$ is applied to the $\overline{AEN_1}$ input of the 8284A clock generator (see Fig. 10.2). Logic 1 at this input makes the READY output of the 8284A switch to logic 0. This output is applied to the READY input of the 8088 and initiates a wait state for the current bus cycle. On the other hand, signal $\overline{DMA\,WAIT}$ switches to logic 0 whenever a DMA bus cycle is initiated. It is applied to the RDY_1 input of the 8284A and, when at logic 0, it causes the READY output to switch to logic 0. In this way, it extends the DMA bus cycle by inserting wait states. Let us now examine just how the signal $\overline{RDY/WAIT}$ is produced.

I/O CH RDY (I/O channel ready) is one signal that can insert wait states into the processor's bus cycle. I/O CH RDY is used by cards located in the slots of the I/O channel interface. In Fig. 10.3, we find that this signal is applied to the preset (PR) input of the 74S74 flip-flop U_{82}. As long as I/O CH RDY is logic 0 the

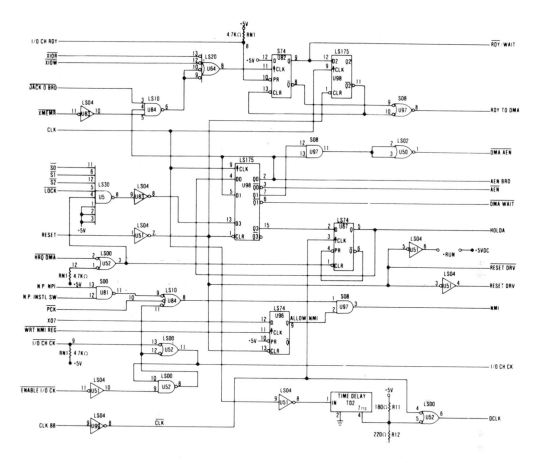

Figure 10.3 Wait state logic and NMI circuitry. (Courtesy of International Business Machines Corporation)

flip-flop is set and its Q output, which is the signal $\overline{RDY}/WAIT$, is held at logic 1, and wait states are inserted into the current bus cycle.

Let us now look at how $\overline{RDY}/WAIT$ is produced for an I/O read, I/O write, or memory refresh cycle. Note in Fig. 10.3 that the CLR input at pin 1 of D-type flip-flop U_{98} is tied to the RESET input through inverter U_{51}. This signal clears the flip-flop at power-up and initializes its Q_2 output to logic 1. As long as the I/O CH RDY input is logic 1, flip-flop U_{82} will set whenever a 0-to-1 transition occurs at its CLK input (pin 11). This causes its Q output to switch to logic 1 and its $\overline{Q}$ output to switch to logic 0. $\overline{RDY}/WAIT$ is now logic 1 and signals the 8088 that a wait state is to be inserted into the current bus cycle.

We will now look at what inputs cause an active transition at CLK. CLK is produced by the signals $\overline{XIOR}$ (I/O read), $\overline{XIOW}$ (I/O write), $\overline{DACK\ 0\ BRD}$ (DMA acknowledge channel 0), $\overline{XMEMR}$ (memory read), and AEN BRD (DMA cycle in progress) with a logic circuit formed from gates U_{83}, U_{84}, and U_{64}. If any input of NAND gate U_{64} switches to logic 0, a 0-to-1 transition is produced at CLK and flip-flop U_{82} sets. In this way, we see that if either an I/O read ($\overline{\text{XIOR}}$ = 0) or I/O write ($\overline{\text{XIOW}}$ = 0) cycle is initiated, a wait state is generated. Moreover, a wait state is initiated if a memory read ($\overline{\text{XMEMR}}$ = 0) occurs when a memory refresh is not in progress ($\overline{\text{DACK 0 BRD}}$ = 1) and a DMA cycle is in progress (AEN BRD = 1).

Now that we see how the wait state is inserted, let us look at how it is terminated so that just one wait state is inserted into the bus cycle. Since the logic 1 at $\overline{\text{RDY}}$/WAIT is also the data input (pin 12) of the 74LS175 flip-flop U_{98}, the next pulse at the CLK input (pin 9) causes its outputs to set. Therefore, output Q_2 switches to the 0 logic level. This logic 0 is returned to the CLR input at pin 13 of flip-flop U_{82} and causes it to reset. $\overline{\text{RDY}}$/WAIT returns to logic 0, signaling ready, and the bus cycle proceeds to completion after just one wait state.

Hold/Hold Acknowledge Circuitry

The 8088 in the PC is configured to operate in the maximum mode. When configured this way, there is no hold/hold acknowledge interface directly useable by the 8237A DMA controller. The $\overline{\text{DMA WAIT}}$ signal we mentioned earlier is coupled with a HOLDA signal produced in the control circuitry of Fig. 10.3 to implement a *simulated DMA interface* in the PC. Let us look at how DMA requests produce the $\overline{\text{DMA WAIT}}$ and HOLDA signals.

Peripheral devices issue a request for DMA service through the 8237A DMA controller. The 8237A signals the 8088 that it wants control of the system bus to perform DMA transfers by outputting the signal $\overline{\text{HRQ DMA}}$ (hold request DMA). In Fig. 10.3, we find that this signal is an input to NAND gate U_{52}. Whenever $\overline{\text{HRQ DMA}}$ is at its inactive 1 logic level, the output at pin 3 of U_{52} is logic 0. This signal is applied to the CLR input of the 74LS74 flip-flop U_{67} and holds it cleared. Therefore, HOLDA is at its inactive 0 logic level. The output at pin 3 of U_{52} is also applied to one input of NAND gate U_5. Here it is combined with status code $\overline{S_2}\overline{S_1}\overline{S_0}$. If the status output is 111_2 and $\overline{\text{LOCK}}$ = 1, the output of U_5 switches to 0 and signals that the 8088's bus is in the passive state and DMA is permitted to take over control of the bus. On the next pulse at the CLK input, flip-flop 3 in latch U_{98} sets, and its Q_3 output switches to the 1 level. Q_3 is applied to the data input of the 74LS74 flip-flop U_{67}, and on the next pulse at CLK88, its Q output, which is HOLDA, becomes active. This output remains latched at the 1 logic level until the DMA request is removed. HOLDA is sent to the HLDA input of the 8237A (see Fig. 10.8) and signals that the 8088 has given up control of the system bus.

At the same time, the logic 1 at HOLDA is returned to the Q_0 input (pin 4) of 74LS175 latch U_{98}. On the next pulse at CLK, signals AEN BRD and $\overline{\text{AEN}}$ become active and signal that a DMA cycle is in progress. These signals are used to disable and tristate the 8288 bus controller and system bus address latches (see Fig. 10.2), thereby isolating the 8088 microprocessor from the system bus. $\overline{\text{AEN}}$ also disables the decoder that generates peripheral chip selects for the I/O address space [see Fig. 10.4(a)]. AEN BRD is returned to the Q_1 input at pin 5 of latch U_{98}, and on the next pulse at CLK the $\overline{\text{DMA WAIT}}$ signal becomes active. The logic 0 at $\overline{\text{DMA WAIT}}$ is sent to the 8284A, where it deactivates the READY input

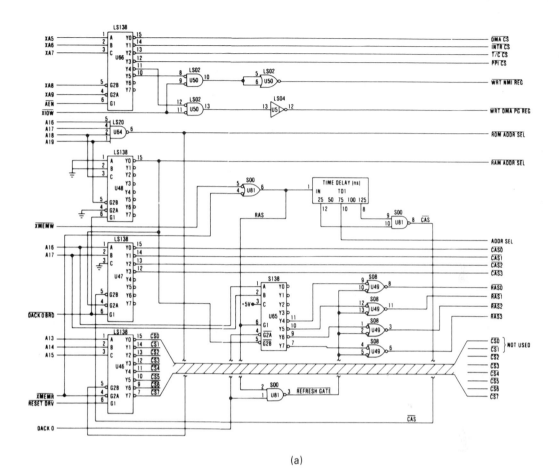

(a)

Address range	Signal	Function	Conditions
0–1F	$\overline{\text{DMA CS}}$	DMA controller	Non DMA bus cycle
20–3F	$\overline{\text{INTR CS}}$	Interrupt controller	Non DMA bus cycle
40–5F	$\overline{\text{T/C CS}}$	Interval timer	Non DMA bus cycle
60–7F	$\overline{\text{PPI CS}}$	Parallel peripheral interface	Non DMA bus cycle
80–9F	$\overline{\text{WRT DMA PG REG}}$	DMA page register	Non DMA bus cycle, XIOW active
A0–BF	$\overline{\text{WRT NMI REG}}$	NMI control register	Non DMA bus cycle, XIOW active

(b)

Figure 10.4 (a) Peripherals/memory chip select circuitry. (Courtesy of International Business Machines Corporation) (b) Peripheral address decoding. (c) ROM address decoding. (d) RAM address decoding.

Address range	Chip select
F0000-F1FFF	$\overline{CS}_0$
F2000-F3FFF	$\overline{CS}_1$
F4000-F5FFF	$\overline{CS}_2$
F6000-F7FFF	$\overline{CS}_3$
F8000-F9FFF	$\overline{CS}_4$
FA000-FCFFF	$\overline{CS}_5$
FC000-FDFFF	$\overline{CS}_6$
FE000-FFFFF	$\overline{CS}_7$

(c)

Address range	Active signal	Condition
00000-3FFFF	RAM ADDR SEL	Inactive DACK 0 BRD
00000-0FFFF	$\overline{RAS}_0$, $\overline{CAS}_0$	Active XMEMR or XMEMW
10000-1FFFF	$\overline{RAS}_1$, $\overline{CAS}_1$	Active XMEMR or XMEMW
20000-2FFFF	$\overline{RAS}_2$, $\overline{CAS}_2$	Active XMEMR or XMEMW
30000-3FFFF	$\overline{RAS}_3$, $\overline{CAS}_3$	Active XMEMR or XMEMW

Figure 10.4 (Continued)

(d)

to insert wait states. Finally, AEN BRD and the complement of $\overline{\text{DMA WAIT}}$ are gated together by the 74S08 AND gate U_{97} followed by a NOT to produce the signal $\overline{\text{DMA AEN}}$. In Fig. 10.8, this signal is used to enable the DMA address circuitry. In the DMA circuitry section, we will find that it is used to enable the 8237A to produce its own address and I/O or memory read/write control signals.

Nonmaskable Interrupt Circuitry

In Section 10.2, we indicated that there are three sources for applying a nonmaskable interrupt to the 8088 microprocessor. They are the 8087 numeric coprocessor, memory parity check, and I/O channel check. In Fig. 10.3, the signal mnemonics used to represent these three inputs are $\overline{\text{N P NPI}}$, PCK, and $\overline{\text{I/O CH CK}}$, respectively. These signals are combined in the NMI control logic circuitry to produce the nonmaskable interrupt request (NMI) signal. This output is applied directly to the NMI input at pin 17 of the 8088 (see Fig. 10.2). Let us now look at the operation of the NMI interrupt request control circuit.

The NMI control logic circuitry in Fig. 10.3 includes a *nonmaskable interrupt control register*. This register is implemented with the 74LS74 D-type flip-flop U_{96}. At reset of the PC, the NMI interface is automatically disabled. Note in Fig. 10.3 that the RESET signal is input to a 74LS04 inverter, and the output at pin 2 of this inverter is applied to the clear (CLR) input of the NMI control register flip-flop. Clearing the flip-flop causes its ALLOW NMI output to switch to logic 0. This output is used as the enable input of the 74S08 AND gate (U_{97}) that controls the

NMI output. As long as ALLOW NMI is logic 0, the NMI output is held at its inactive 0 logic level, and the NMI interface is disabled.

We now look at how the NMI interface gets turned on. Looking at Fig. 10.3, we find that the data input (pin 12) of the 74LS74 flip-flop is supplied by XD_7 of the data bus, and its clock input (CLK) at pin 11 is supplied by a chip select signal identified as $\overline{WR\ NMI\ REG}$ (write NMI register). As part of the initialization software of the PC, the NMI control register gets set by executing an instruction that writes a byte with its most significant bit (XD_7) set to logic 1 to any I/O address in the range $00A0_{16}$ through $00BF_{16}$. All these addresses decode to produce the chip select signal $\overline{WR\ NMI\ REG}$ at CLK; therefore, the 1 at XD_7 is loaded into the flip-flop and ALLOW NMI switches to logic 1. This supplies the enable input for the 74S08 AND gate to the NMI output. The NMI interface is now enabled and waiting for one of the NMI interrupt functions to occur.

Now that the NMI interface is enabled, let us look at how the numeric coprocessor, parity check, or I/O channel check interrupt requests are handled. Figure 10.3 shows that the inputs for each of these three functions are combined with the 74LS10 NAND gate U_{84}. If any combination of the NAND gate inputs is logic 0, the output at pin 8 switches to logic 1. This represents an active NMI request. As long as the NMI interface is enabled, this logic 1 is passed to the NMI output and on to the NMI input of the 8088.

Actually, each NMI interrupt input also has an enable signal that allows it to be individually enabled or disabled. For instance, in Fig. 10.3 we see that N P NPI is combined with the signal NP INSTL SW by the 74S00 NAND gate U_{81}. For the numeric coprocessor interrupt to be active, the N P INSTL SW input must be logic 1. N P INSTL SW stands for numerics processor install switch, which is the switch represented by the contacts marked 2-15 on SW1 in Fig. 10.10. Only when this switch is off (open) is the numeric coprocessor interrupt input enabled.

The parity check nonmaskable interrupt input can also be enabled or disabled; however, this part of the circuit is not shown in Fig. 10.3. To enable $\overline{PCK}$, a logic 0 must be written to bit 4 of output port PB of the 8255A U_{36} (see Fig. 10.10). This produces the signal $\overline{ENB\ RAM\ PCK}$ (enable RAM parity check), which is used to enable the parity check circuits that produce $\overline{PCK}$ in the RAM circuit (see Fig. 10.7).

Looking at Fig. 10.3, we see that to enable the NMI input for $\overline{I/O\ CH\ CK}$ (I/O channel check) logic 0 must be applied to the $\overline{ENABLE\ I/O\ CK}$ input. This signal is directly supplied by bit 5 of output port PB on the 8255A device U_{36} (see Fig. 10.10). This bit is set to logic 0 through software at power-up.

Up to this point, we have shown how the NMI input is enabled, disabled, or made active. However, since there are three possible sources for the NMI input, another question that must be answered is how does the 8088 know which of the three interrupt inputs has caused the request for service. It turns out that the signals PCK and I/O CH CK are returned to input ports on the 8255A device U_{36} (see Fig. 10.10). For instance, I/O CH CK is applied to input bit 6 on port PC of the 8255A. Therefore, the service routine for NMI can read these inputs through software, determine which has caused the request, and then branch to the part of the service routine that corresponds to the active input.

In the previous section, we found that the chip select signal $\overline{\text{WRT NMI REG}}$ was used as an enable input for the NMI control register. Besides the NMI control register chip select signal, chip selects are needed in the ROM, RAM, DMA, PPI, interval timer, and interrupt controller sections of the PC's system processor board circuitry. These chip selects are all generated by the I/O and memory chip select circuit that is shown in Fig. 10.4(a). Two types of chip select signals are produced, *I/O chip selects* and memory chip selects, and they are both generated by decoding of addresses. Let us now look at the operation of the circuits that produce these I/O and memory chip select outputs.

I/O Chip Selects

Earlier we found that in the architecture of the PC, LSI peripheral devices, such as the DMA controller, interrupt controller, programmable interval timer, and programmable peripheral interface controller, are located in the I/O address space of the 8088 microprocessor. I/O chip select decoding for these devices takes place in the circuit of Fig. 10.4(a) formed from devices U_{66}, U_{50}, and U_{51}. Let us begin by looking at the operation of this segment of circuitry in detail.

To access a register within one of the peripheral devices, an I/O instruction must be executed to read from or write to the register. The address output on address lines A_0 through A_9 during the I/O bus cycle is used to both chip select the peripheral device and select the appropriate register. Note in Fig. 10.4(a) that address bits XA_8 and XA_9 are applied to enable inputs G_{2B} and G_{2A}, respectively, of the 74LS138 three-line to eight-line decoder device (U_{66}). When these inputs are both at logic 0 and $\overline{\text{AEN}}$ is at logic 1, the decoder is enabled for operation. At the same time, address lines XA_5 through XA_7 apply a 3-bit code to the ABC inputs of the decoder. When U_{66} is enabled, the Y output corresponding to the code $XA_7XA_6XA_5$ is switched to its active 0 logic level. These Y signals produce I/O chip select outputs $\overline{\text{DMA CS}}$ (DMA chip select), $\overline{\text{INTR CS}}$ (interrupt request chip select), $\overline{\text{T/C CS}}$ (timer/counter chip select), $\overline{\text{PPI CS}}$ (parallel peripheral interface chip select), $\overline{\text{WRT NMI REG}}$ (NMI register chip select), and $\overline{\text{WRT DMA PG REG}}$ (DMA page register chip select).

For instance, if $XA_7XA_6XA_5 = 001$, output Y_1 switches to logic 0 and produces the chip select output $\overline{\text{INTR CS}}$ at pin 14. In Fig. 10.2, we find that this signal is applied to the $\overline{\text{CS}}$ input at pin 1 of the 8259A interrupt controller and enables its microprocessor interface for operation. At the same time, appropriate lower-order address bits are applied directly to the register select inputs of the peripherals to select the register that is to be accessed. For the 8259A in Fig. 10.2, we find that only one address bit XA_0 is used, and this signal is applied to register select input A_0 at pin 27.

To produce an I/O chip select signal, address bits XA_0 to XA_4 are not used and therefore, the individual I/O chip select signals produced actually correspond to a range of addresses. The address range for each chip select output is shown in

Fig. 10.4(b). For instance, any address in the range 0020_{16} through $003F_{16}$ decodes to produce the $\overline{\text{INTR CS}}$ chip select signal.

The signal $\overline{\text{AEN}}$ is at its active 0 logic level only during DMA bus cycles. When $\overline{\text{AEN}}$ is at logic 0, decoder U_{66} is disabled. Thus only the addresses output by the microprocessor will produce I/O chip select signals. This is identified as a condition required for the occurrence of all chip selects in Fig. 10.4(b). Looking at the circuit in Fig. 10.4(a), we also find that the NMI control register and DMA page register chip selects are gated with the I/O write control signal $\overline{\text{XIOW}}$ by NOR gates in IC U_{50}. Therefore, as shown in Fig. 10.4(b), for these two chip selects to take place, an additional condition must be satisfied; that is, they are only produced if an I/O write (output) bus cycle is taking place.

Since the upper address lines XA_{10} through XA_{15} are not used in the I/O chip select address decoder circuit, they represent don't-care states. Therefore, more than one range of addresses may be used to access each peripheral. For instance, any address in the ranges 0020_{16}-$FC20_{16}$, 0021_{16}-$FC21_{16}$, and 0022_{16}-$FC22_{16}$ will also decode to produce the signal $\overline{\text{INTR CS}}$.

Memory Chip Selects

The system processor board of the PC contains both read only memory (ROM) and random access read/write memory (RAM). The ROM part of memory is used to store embedded system software such as the BIOS, power-up diagnostics, and BASIC interpreter. On the other hand, programs that are typically loaded from disk, such as the operating system and application programs, are stored in the RAM. Here we will just look at the chip select signals that are produced for enabling the memory devices. These chip select signals are also generated in the I/O and memory chip select circuit of Fig. 10.4(a).

Let us begin by examining the circuitry that produces the chip selects needed by the ROM. The output signals produced for ROM in the circuit of Fig. 10.4(a) are ROM address select ($\overline{\text{ROM ADDR SEL}}$) and chip selects $\overline{\text{CS}}_0$ through $\overline{\text{CS}}_7$. Note that the signal $\overline{\text{ROM ADDR SEL}}$ is generated by combining the upper four address bits, A_{16} through A_{19}, with NAND gate U_{64}. If all three of these bits are at logic 1, the output at pin 6, which is $\overline{\text{ROM ADDR SEL}}$ switches to its active 0 logic level. This signal has two functions. First, it is used to enable the ROM chip select decoder U_{46} and, second, it is supplied to the *ROM array* (see Fig. 10.5) where it is used to control the direction of data transfer through the ROM data bus transceiver.

The chip select outputs for the EPROMs, which are labeled $\overline{\text{CS}}_0$ through $\overline{\text{CS}}_7$ in Fig. 10.4(a), are produced by the 74LS138 three-line to eight-line decoder U_{46}. Note that $\overline{\text{ROM ADDR SEL}}$ is applied to the G_{2B} chip enable input of the decoder. This enable signal ensures that the decoder decodes addresses in the range $F0000_{16}$ through $FFFFF_{16}$. Two other enable signals, $\overline{\text{XMEMR}}$ and $\overline{\text{RESET DRV}}$, are also applied to the decoder. $\overline{\text{XMEMR}}$ ensures that the decoder is enabled only during memory read operations.

Note that address lines A_{13} through A_{15} are applied to the ABC inputs of the decoder. This 3-bit code is decoded to generate the individual chip selects, $\overline{\text{CS}}_0$ through $\overline{\text{CS}}_7$. As shown in Fig. 10.4(a), chip selects $\overline{\text{CS}}_0$ and $\overline{\text{CS}}_1$ are not used.

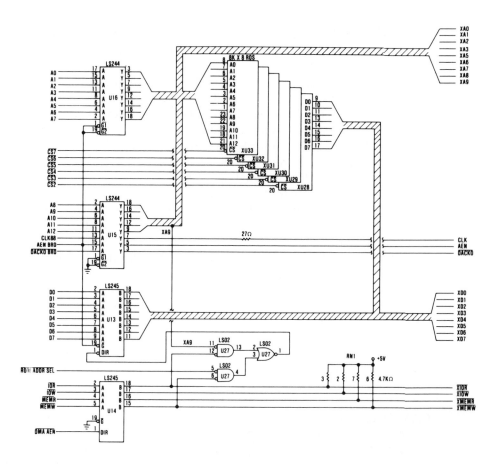

Figure 10.5 ROM circuitry. (Courtesy of International Business Machines Corporation)

However, the other six, $\overline{CS_2}$ through $\overline{CS_7}$, are each used to enable an individual EPROM device in the ROM array (see Fig. 10.5).

For example, if the input to the ROM address decoder is $A_{14}A_{13}A_{12} = 010$, chip select output $\overline{CS_2}$ is active, and a read operation is performed from one of the 8K-byte storage locations in the EPROM device that is located in the address range $F4000_{16}$ through $F5FFF_{16}$. The actual storage location in the EPROM device that is accessed is selected by the lower 13 address bits, which are applied directly to all the EPROM devices in parallel. The memory address range that corresponds to each of the ROM chip select outputs is given in Fig. 10.4(c). This chart shows that there are a total of 64K addresses decoded by the ROM address decoder circuitry.

We will now look at the circuitry used to produce the chip select, row address select, and column address select signals for the *RAM array* circuit. In Fig. 10.4(a), the chip select outputs that are used to control the operation of RAM are $\overline{RAM\,ADDR\,SEL}$ (RAM address select) and ADDR SEL (address select).

$\overline{\text{RAM ADDR SEL}}$ is produced by the 74LS138 decoder U_{48}. Looking at the circuit diagram, we find that if A_{19} is logic 0 and $\overline{\text{DACK 0 BRD}}$ is logic 1, the decoder is enabled for operation. Moreover, as long as address bit A_{18} is also logic 0, output Y_0 of the decoder, which is the same as $\overline{\text{RAM ADDR SEL}}$, switches to logic 0. In this way, we see that $\overline{\text{RAM ADDR SEL}}$ goes active whenever the 8088 outputs an address in the range 00000_{16} through $3FFFF_{16}$. This is the full address range of the RAM that resides on the system processor board. Note that this $\overline{\text{RAM ADDR SEL}}$ is applied to the G_{2A} input of the 74LS138 CAS decoder (U_{47}) and to input G_{2B} of the 74LS138 RAS decoder (U_{65}). It is also used in the RAM array circuit (see Fig. 10.6), where it controls the data bus transceiver.

The ADDR SEL signal is generated from $\overline{\text{XMEMW}}$ and $\overline{\text{XMEMR}}$ by NAND gate U_{81} and delay line TD_1. If either the memory read or write control input signal is at its active 0 logic level, the output at pin 6 of the NAND gate U_{81} switches to logic 1, and ADDR SEL becomes active after the time delay set by TD_1 elapses. ADDR SEL is supplied to the RAS/CAS address selector in the RAM array circuit (see Fig. 10.6), where it is used to select between the RAS and CAS parts of the address.

Note that the output at pin 6 of NAND gate U_{81}, which was used to produce ADDR SEL, is also the RAS (row address select) signal. RAS is applied to the G_1 enable input of the 74S138 RAS decoder (U_{65}). The other chip select inputs of this decoder are supplied by the signals $\overline{\text{RAM ADDR SEL}}$ and DACK 0 and must be logic 0 and logic 1, respectively, to enable the device for operation.

Now when U_{65} is enabled, the code at the ABC input is decoded to produce the corresponding RAS output. Note that the C input of the decoder is fixed at the 1 logic level and the other two inputs, A and B, are supplied by address bits A_{16} and A_{17}, respectively. For instance, if these two address bits are both logic 0, the input code is 100, and output Y_4 switches to the 0 logic level and generates the signal $\overline{\text{RAS}}_0$. After a short delay, which is set by TD_1, the $\overline{\text{CAS}}$ signal is output at pin 8 of U_{81}. This signal is applied to the G_{2B} input of the CAS decoder U_{47}. Here the other decoder enable inputs are supplied by $\overline{\text{RAM ADDR SEL}}$ and $\overline{\text{DACK 0 BRD}}$. When enabled, the address at the AB inputs causes the corresponding column address select output to occur. Assuming that A_{16} and A_{17} are still both 0, $\overline{\text{CAS}}_0$ switches to its active 0 logic level. In this way, we see that each RAS chip select is followed after a short delay by the corresponding CAS chip select. Figure 10.4(d) summarizes the address decoding for the RAM address chip selects.

During DRAM refresh, DACK_0 becomes active, which along with the RAS signal, is used to generate the $\overline{\text{RAS}}_0$, $\overline{\text{RAS}}_1$, $\overline{\text{RAS}}_2$, and $\overline{\text{RAS}}_3$ signals. These signals are generated independent of the RAS decoder outputs and are used to refresh the DRAM devices in the RAM array.

▲ 10.6 MEMORY CIRCUITRY

Earlier we found that the system processor board of the PC is equipped with 48KB of ROM and either 64KB or 256KB of RAM. The ROM array is implemented using EPROM devices and provides for nonvolatile storage of fixed information,

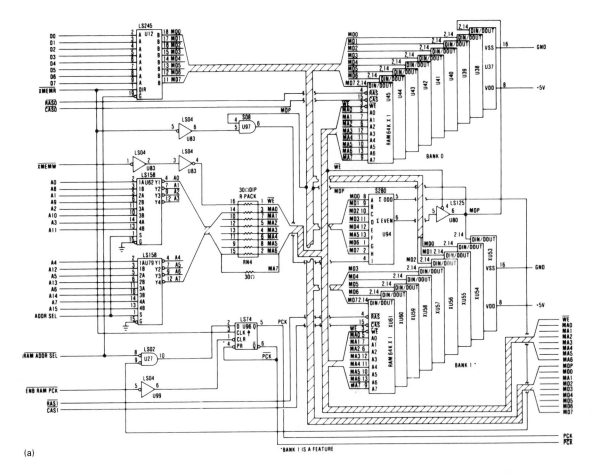

(a)

Figure 10.6 (a) RAM circuitry. (Courtesy of International Business Machines Corporation) (b) RAM banks 2 and 3. (Courtesy of International Business Machines Corporation)

such as the BIOS of the PC. On the other hand, RAM is volatile and is used for temporary storage of information such as application programs. This part of the memory subsystem can be implemented with either 64K-bit or 256K-bit dynamic RAM chips. In the previous section, we showed how the ROM and RAM chip select signals are generated. Here we will study how the EPROM devices are arranged to form the ROM array and how the DRAM devices are arranged to form the RAM array. We will also study how the memory arrays use the chip select signals and interface to the system bus.

ROM Array Circuitry

Let us begin by briefly examining the architecture of the ROM array of the PC. The circuitry of the ROM array is shown in Fig. 10.5. Looking at this circuit

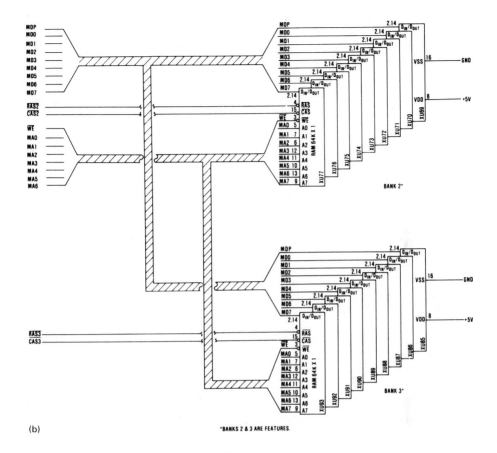

(b)

*BANKS 2 & 3 ARE FEATURES.

Figure 10.6 (Continued)

diagram, we find that it is implemented with six 8K × 8-bit EPROMs. These devices are labeled XU_{28} through XU_{33}. Note that each of these EPROMs is enabled by one of the ROM chip select signals, $\overline{CS}_2$ through $\overline{CS}_7$, that are generated by the ROM address decoder. For instance, EPROM XU_{28} is enabled by $\overline{CS}_2$. In Fig. 10.4(c), we find that this chip select output is at its active 0 logic level for all memory addresses in the range $F4000_{16}$ through $F5FFF_{16}$. Therefore, EPROM XU_{28} holds the information corresponding to these 8K addresses.

Now that we know how the individual EPROMs are selected, let us look at how a storage location within an EPROM is accessed and its data returned to the MPU. The address outputs on the lower 13 address lines of the system address bus, A_0 through A_{12}, are used to select the specific byte of data within an EPROM. These address inputs are first buffered with 74LS244 octal buffers U_{15} and U_{16} and then applied to the address inputs of all six EPROMs in parallel. Note that control signal AEN BRD must be at the 0 logic level for the address buffer to be enabled for operation.

The byte of code held at the addressed storage location in the chip selected EPROM is output on data lines D_0 through D_7 for return to the MPU. These data outputs are interfaced to the 8088's system data bus by the 74LS245 bus transceiver U_{13}. During a read bus cycle, data must be transferred from the outputs of the ROM array to the system data bus lines D_0 through D_7.

The direction of data transfer through the data bus transceiver is set by the logic level at its data direction (DIR) input. In Fig. 10.5, we find that the logic level at DIR is determined by the operation of the control logic formed from transceiver U_{14} and three NOR gates of IC U_{27}. The $\overline{IOR}$ and $\overline{MEMW}$ outputs of U_{14}, along with chip select signal $\overline{ROM\ ADDR\ SEL}$ and address bit XA_9, are inputs to the NOR gate circuit. In response to these inputs, the circuit switches DIR to logic 0 during all read bus cycles to storage locations in the address range of the ROM array and for all I/O read cycles from an address where XA_9 is logic 0. Logic 0 at DIR sets the direction of data transfer through U_{13} to be from memory to the 8088's system bus. That is, data are being read from the ROM array.

RAM Array Circuitry

The circuitry of the RAM array is shown in Fig. 10.6(a). This circuit shows just two of the four banks of RAM ICs that are provided for on the system processor board of the PC. These banks are identified as *bank 0* and *bank 1*. The circuitry for the other two banks, *bank 2* and *bank 3*, is shown in Fig. 10.6(b). In each bank, eight 64K × 1-bit dynamic RAMs (DRAMs) are used for data storage, and a ninth DRAM is included to hold parity bits for each of the 64K storage locations. In Fig. 10.6(a), we find that the DRAMs in bank 0 are labeled U_{37} through U_{45}. Device U_{37} is used to store the parity bit, and U_{38} through U_{45} store the bits of the byte of data. The data storage capacity of bank 0 is 64KB, and all four banks together give the system processor board a maximum storage capacity of 256KB.

Let us now examine how a byte of data is read from the DRAMs in bank 0. Address lines A_0 through A_{15} are applied to inputs of the 74LS158 data selectors U_{62} and U_{79}. These devices are used to multiplex the 16-bit memory address into a byte-wide row address and a byte-wide column address. The multiplexed address outputs of the data selectors are called MA_0 through MA_7 and are applied to address inputs A_0 through A_7 of all DRAMs in parallel. The select signal ADDR SEL, which is applied to the select (S) input of both data selectors, is used to select whether the RAS or CAS byte of the address is output on the MA lines.

We have assumed that the storage location to be accessed is located in bank 0. In this case, the RAS and CAS address bytes are output from the address multiplexer synchronously with the occurrence of the active $\overline{RAS}_0$ and $\overline{CAS}_0$ strobe signals, respectively. ADDR SEL initially sets the multiplexer to output the RAS address byte on the MA line. When RAS_0 switches to logic 0, it signals all DRAMs in bank 0 to accept the row address off of the MA lines. Next, ADDR SEL switches the logic level and causes the column address to be output from the multiplexer. It is accompanied by $\overline{CAS}_0$, which is applied to the $\overline{CAS}$ inputs of all DRAMs in bank 0. Logic 0 at $\overline{CAS}$ causes them to accept the column address from the MA lines. At this point, the complete address of the storage location that is to be accessed has been supplied to the RAM in bank 0.

We are also assuming that a read bus cycle is taking place. For this reason, the $\overline{XMEMW}$ input is logic 1 and signals all DRAMs that a read operation is to take place. Therefore, each device outputs a bit of data held in the storage location corresponding to the selected row and column address. The byte of data is passed over data lines MD_0 through MD_7 to the 74LS245 bus transceiver U_{12}. Here a 0 logic level at $\overline{XMEMR}$ sets the transceiver to pass data from the MA lines to system data bus lines D_0 through D_7 during all read cycles. Moreover, the signal $\overline{RAM\ ADDR\ SEL}$ enables the transceiver for operation during all bus cycles to the RAM array.

In our description of the read cycle, we did not consider the effect of the *parity generator/checker circuitry* that is included in the RAM array of the PC. *Parity* is a technique that is used to improve the reliability of data storage in a RAM subsystem. Whenever data are written into or read from the DRAMs in Fig. 10.6(a), the byte of data on lines MD_0 through MD_7 is also applied to inputs A through H of the 74S280 parity generator/checker device U_{94}. Therefore, including a ninth bit at logic 0 does not change the parity of the byte being written. The I input during a write operation is at logic 0 as it is inverse of $\overline{XMEMR}$, which is 1. Therefore, including a ninth bit at logic 0 does not change the parity of the byte being written. If the byte has *even parity* (contains an even number of bits at the 1 logic level), the Σ_{EVEN} output (pin 6) of U_{94} switches to logic 1. However, if parity is odd, Σ_{EVEN} switches to logic 0. During write bus cycles, this *parity bit* output is supplied to the DIN/DOUT pin of the *parity bit DRAM* over the MDP line and is stored in DRAM along with the byte of data.

On the other hand, during read operations, the parity bit that is read out of the parity bit DRAM on the MDP line is gated by AND gate U_{97} to the ninth input (I) of the 74S280 parity generator/checker. If the 9-bit word read from memory has *odd parity* (an extra 1 is added to even parity words as the parity bit), the Σ_{ODD} output (pin 5) of U_{94} switches to logic 1 to indicate that parity is correct. Σ_{ODD} is sent through NOR gate U_{27} to the data input at pin 2 of the 74LS74 parity check interrupt latch U_{96}. As long as no *parity error* has occurred, the $\overline{PCK}$ output of the latch remains at its inactive 1 logic level. However, if Σ_{ODD} signals that a parity error has been detected by switching to logic 0, the parity error interrupt latch sets, and the logic 0 that results at $\overline{PCK}$ issues a nonmaskable interrupt request to the MPU. The NMI service routine must test the logic level of PCK through the 8255A I/O interface to determine if the source of the NMI is PCK. Moreover, at completion of the parity error interrupt service routine, the parity error interrupt latch should be cleared by issuing the signal $\overline{ENB\ RAM\ PCK}$ through the 8255A I/O interface.

▲ 10.7 DIRECT MEMORY ACCESS CIRCUITRY

The 8088-based system processor board of the IBM PC supports the direct memory access (DMA) mode of operation for both its memory and I/O address spaces. This DMA capability permits high-speed data transfers to take place between two sections of memory or an I/O device and memory. The bus cycles initiated for these DMA transfers are not under control of the 8088 MPU; instead, they are performed by a special VLSI device known as a *DMA controller*. The DMA circuitry in the PC implements this function using the 8237A-5 DMA controller IC. Looking at the circuit drawing in Fig. 10.7, we find that the 8237A is labeled U_{35}. This device provides four independent DMA channels for the PC.

Even though the 8237A performs the actual DMA bus cycles by itself, the 8088 controls overall operation of the device. There are 16 registers within the 8237A that determine how and when the four DMA channels work. Since the microprocessor interface of the 8237A is I/O mapped, the 8088 communicates with these registers by executing I/O instructions. For instance, the 8237A must be configured with operating features such as autoinitialization, address increment or decrement, and fixed or rotating channel priority. These options are selected by loading the command and mode registers within the 8237A through a software initialization routine. Moreover, before a DMA transfer can be performed, the 8088 must send the 8237A information related to the operation that is to take place. This information could include a source base address, destination base address, count of the words of data to be moved, and an operating mode. The modes of DMA operation available with the 8237A are demand transfer mode, single transfer mode, block transfer mode, or cascade mode. Finally, the 8088 can obtain status information about the current DMA bus cycle by reading the contents of registers. For example, it can read the values in the current address register and current count register to determine which data have been transferred.

Let us now look briefly at the signals and operation of the microprocessor interface of the 8237A. In Fig. 10.7, we find that the microprocessor interface of the 8237A is enabled by the signal $\overline{\text{DMA CS}}$, which is applied to its $\overline{\text{CS}}$ input at pin 11. Figure 10.4(b) shows that $\overline{\text{DMA CS}}$ is active whenever an I/O address in the range 0000_{16} through $001F_{16}$ is output on the system address bus. The specific register to be accessed is selected using the four least significant address lines, XA_0 through XA_3. Data are read from or written into the selected register over system data bus lines XD_0 through XD_7. The 8088 signals the 8237A whether data are to be input or output over the bus with the control signal $\overline{\text{XIOR}}$ or $\overline{\text{XIOW}}$, respectively.

Earlier we pointed out that the four DMA channels of the PC are identified as DMA channels 0 through 3. Moreover, we found that channel 0 is dedicated to RAM refresh and that channel 2 is used by the floppy-disk subsystem. Use of a DMA channel is initiated by a request from hardware. In Fig. 10.7, the signals DRQ_0 through DRQ_3 are the hardware request inputs for DMA channels 0 through 3, respectively. DRQ_0 is generated by timer 1 of the 8253 programmable interval timer (see Fig. 10.8) and is used to initiate a DMA 0 refresh cycle for RAM every 15.12 μs. The other three DMA request lines are supplied from the I/O channel and are available for use by other I/O channel devices.

For a DMA request to be active, the corresponding DRQ input must be switched to the 1 logic level. Let us assume that a DRQ input has become active, the DMA request input for the active channel is not masked out within the 8237A, and a higher-priority channel is not already active. Then the response of the 8237A

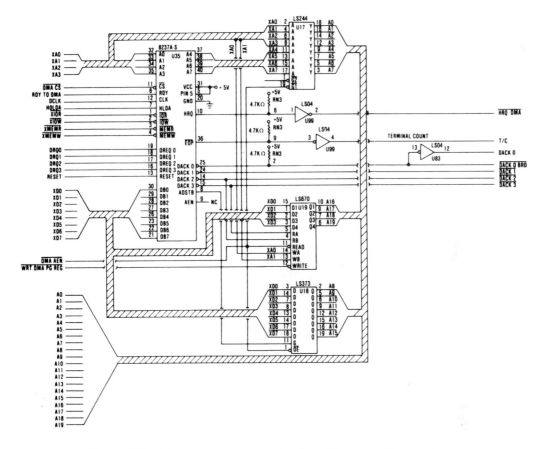

Figure 10.7 Direct memory access circuitry. (Courtesy of International Business Machines Corporation)

to the active DMA request is that it requests to take over control of the system bus by switching its hold request (HRQ) output to logic 1 and then waits in this state until the 8088 signals that it has given up the bus by returning a logic 1 on the hold acknowledge (HLDA) input of the 8237A.

The simulated hold/hold acknowledge handshake that takes place between the 8237A and 8088 is performed by the wait state control logic circuitry that is shown in Fig. 10.3. The HRQ signal that is output at pin 10 of the 8237A is applied to the $\overline{\text{HRQ DMA}}$ input of the wait state control logic circuit. The operation of this circuitry was described in detail in Section 10.3. For this reason, here we will just give an overview of the events that take place in the hold acknowledge handshake sequence.

In response to logic 0 at the $\overline{\text{HRQ DMA}}$ input, the circuit first waits until the 8088 signals that its bus is in the passive state (no bus activity is taking place) and then switches the HOLDA output to logic 1. This signal is returned to the HLDA input at pin 7 of the 8237A, where it signals that the 8088 has given up control of the system bus.

Next, the control logic switches signals AEN BRD and $\overline{\text{AEN}}$ to their active logic levels. These signals are used to tri-state the outputs of the 8288 bus controller, data bus transceiver, and system bus address latches. With these outputs floating, the MPU is isolated from devices connected to the system bus. Additionally these signals disable the decoder that produces chip selects for the peripherals located on the system processor board.

One clock later, the signal $\overline{\text{DMA WAIT}}$ becomes active. This signal is returned through the ready/wait logic of the 8284A to the READY input of the 8088 and ensures that the 8088 does not initiate a new bus cycle. The signal $\overline{\text{DMA AEN}}$ is now produced by the control logic and sent to the DMA address logic (see Fig. 10.7). Logic 0 at this input enables the address buffers for operation. $\overline{\text{DMA AEN}}$ is also applied to the DIR input of transceiver U_{14} (see Fig. 10.5) and isolates the I/O and memory read/write control signals from the system bus so that the DMA controller itself can provide them.

At this point, the 8237A is free to take control of the system bus; therefore, it outputs the DMA acknowledge ($\overline{\text{DACK}_0}$ to $\overline{\text{DACK}_3}$) signal corresponding to the device requesting DMA service. $\overline{\text{DACK}_0}$ is output as $\overline{\text{DACK 0 BRD}}$ to the refresh control circuitry. Logic 0 on this line signals the wait state circuit and RAM chip select decoder that DMA refresh bus cycles are to be initiated. The other three DACK outputs are supplied to the I/O channel.

Now that the 8237A has taken control of the system data bus, let us look at how a block of data is transferred from memory to a device in the I/O address space. To perform this operation, the DMA controller first outputs a 16-bit address on address lines A_0 through A_7 and data lines DB_0 through DB_7. Address bit A_8 through A_{15}, which are output on the data lines, are output in conjunction with a pulse on the address strobe (ADSTB) line at pin 8 of the 8237A. This pulse is used to latch the address into the 74LS373 latch, U_{18}. The four most significant bits of the 20-bit address are not produced by the 8237A; instead, they are generated by three DMA page registers within the 74LS670 register file device, U_{19}. The page registers are initialized by the processor at power on time. Once initialized, they provide the upper four bits of the address. The device contains four registers, only 3 of them are used for channels 1, 2, and 3. To access a page register I/O addresses 81_{16} to 83_{16} can be used for channels 1, 2, and 3, respectively. These addresses activate the required $\overline{\text{WRT DMA PG REG}}$ signal along with the two bits XA_1 and XA_0 to select the desired page register. The $DACK_2$ and $DACK_3$ signals are used to read the appropriate four bits from a page register and feed to the four upper address lines of the address bus.

A valid 20-bit source address is now available on system address bus lines A_0 through A_{19}. Next, the memory read ($\overline{\text{MEMR}}$) and I/O write ($\overline{\text{IOW}}$) control signals become active, and the data held at the addressed storage location are read over system data bus lines XD_0 through XD_7 to the I/O device. This completes the first data transfer.

We will assume that during the DMA bus cycle the source or destination address is automatically incremented by the 8237A. In this way, its current value points to the next data element that is to be read from memory or written to memory. Moreover, at completion of the DMA bus cycle, the count in the current word register is decremented by one. The new count stands for the number of data transfers that still remain to be performed.

This basic DMA transfer operation is automatically repeated by the 8237A until the current word register count rolls over from 0000_{16} to $FFFF_{16}$. At this moment, the DMA operation is complete and the end of process ($\overline{EOP}$) output is switched to logic 0. EOP is used to tell external circuitry that the DMA operation has run to completion. In Fig. 10.7, we see that $\overline{EOP}$ is inverted to produce the terminal count (T/C) signal for the I/O channel. In response to T/C, the requesting device removes its DMA request signal, and the 8237A responds by returning control of the system bus to the 8088.

▲ 10.8 TIMER CIRCUITRY

The timer circuitry of the IBM PC is shown in Fig. 10.8. This circuitry controls four basic system functions: *time-of-day clock*, *DRAM refresh*, *speaker*, and *cassette*. In the PC, the timers are implemented with the 8253-5 programmable interval timer IC. This device is labeled U_{34} in Fig. 10.8. The 8253 provides three independent, programmable, 16-bit counters for use in the microcomputer system. Here we will first look at how the 8253 is interfaced to the 8088 microprocessor and then at how it implements each of the four system functions.

Microprocessor Interface and Clock Inputs

The 8088 MPU communicates with the 8253's internal control registers through the microprocessor interface. In Fig. 10.1(c), we find that the control registers of the 8253 are located in the range 0040_{16} through 0043_{16} of the PC's I/O address space. Using I/O instructions, we can access the 8253's internal registers to configure the modes of operation for the timer and read or load its counters. For example, an input operation from I/O address 0040_{16} reads the current count in counter 0. On the other hand, an output operation to the same address loads an initial value into the count register for counter 0. The same type of operations can be performed to the registers for counters 1 and 2 by using address 0041_{16} or 0042_{16}, respectively. Moreover, the mode of operation for the counters is set up by writing a byte-wide control word to address 0043_{16}. However, the contents of the mode control register cannot be read through software.

Let us now look at how the 8088 performs data transfers to the 8253 over the system bus. The microprocessor interface of the 8253 is enabled by the signal T/C $\overline{CS}$, which is tied to its $\overline{CS}$ (chip select) input at pin 21. Figure 10.4(b) shows that this signal is at its 0 active logic level whenever an I/O address in the range 0040_{16} through $005F_{16}$ is output on the system address bus. The internal control register that is to be accessed is selected by a code that is applied to register select inputs A_0 and A_1 over system address bus lines XA_0 and XA_1. In Fig. 10.8, we see that system data bus lines XD_0 through XD_7 connect to the data lines D_0 through D_7 of the 8253. The 8088 tells the PIT whether data are to be read from or written

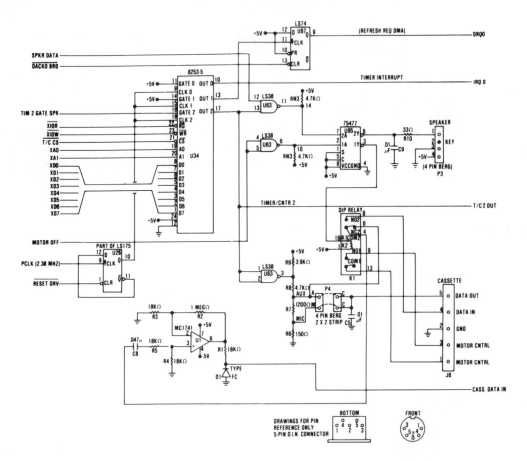

Figure 10.8 Timer circuitry. (Courtesy of International Business Machines Corporation)

into the selected register over these lines with logic 0 at $\overline{\text{XIOR}}$ (I/O read) or $\overline{\text{XIOW}}$ (I/O write), respectively.

The signal that is applied to the CLK inputs of the timers is derived from the 2.38-MHz PCLK (peripheral clock) signal. Note that PCLK is first divided by two using the 74LS175 D-type flip-flop U_{26}. This generates a 1.19-MHz clock for input to the timers. This signal drives clock inputs CLK_0, CLK_1, and CLK_2 in parallel. Note in Fig. 10.8 that the first two of these clock signals are permanently enabled to the counter by having +5 V connected directly to the $GATE_0$ and $GATE_1$ inputs, respectively. However, CLK_2 is enabled to the counter with signal TIM 2 GATE SPK. This signal must be switched to logic 1 (see Fig. 10.9) under software control to enable the clock input for counter 2.

Outputs of the PIT

In Fig. 10.8, the three outputs of the 8253 timer are labeled OUT_0, OUT_1, and OUT_2. OUT_0 is produced by timer 0 and is set up to occur at a regular time interval equal to 54.936 ms. This output is applied to the timer interrupt request input (IRQ_0) of the 8259A interrupt controller, where it represents the time-of-day interrupt.

Timer output OUT_1 is generated by timer 1 and also occurs at a regular interval, every 15.12 μs. In Fig. 10.8, we find that this signal is applied to the CLK input (pin 11) of the 74LS74 flip-flop U_{67} and causes the DRQ_0 output to set. Logic 1 at this output sends a request for service to the 8237A DMA controller and asks it to perform a refresh operation for the dynamic RAM subsystem. When the DMA controller has taken control of the system bus and is ready to perform the refresh cycle, it acknowledges this fact by outputting the refresh acknowledge ($\overline{\text{DACK 0 BRD}}$) signal. Logic 0 on this line clears flip-flop U_{67}, thereby removing the refresh request.

The output of the third timer, OUT_2, is used three ways in the PC. First, it is sent as the signal T/C2 OUT to input 5 on port C of the 8255A PIC (see Fig. 10.9). In this way, its logic level can be read through software. Second, it is used as an enable signal for speaker data in the speaker interface. When the speaker is to be used, the 8088 must write logic 1 to bit 0 of port B on the 8255A PIC (see Fig. 10.9). This produces the signal TIM 2 GATE SPK, which enables the clock for timer 2. Pulses are now produced at OUT_2. When a tone is to be produced by the speaker, the 8088 outputs the signal SPKR DATA at pin 1 of port B of the 8255A (see Fig. 10.9). Logic 1 at input SPKR DATA enables the pulses output at OUT_2 to the 75477 driver U_{95}. The driver output is supplied to the speaker. The frequency of the tone produced by the speaker can be changed by changing the count in timer 2.

The last use of counter 2 is to supply the record tone for the cassette interface. As shown in Fig. 10.8, the PC's cassette interface is through connector J_6. Data that are to be recorded on the tape are output on the DATA OUT line at pin 5 of J_6. In Fig. 10.8, we find that the data to be recorded on the cassette are output from the OUT_2 pin of the 8253 timer and are supplied through inverter U_{63} to a voltage divider. Jumper P_4 is used to select the voltage level for the DATA OUT signal. For instance, if a jumper is installed from A to C, DATA OUT is set for a 0.68-V high-signal level and 0 V as the low level.

Data played back from the cassette enter the microcomputer at the DATA IN input at pin 6 of connector J_6. DATA IN is passed through a set of contacts on DIP relay K_1 to the input of an amplifier made with the MC1741 device, U_1. Since it is a high-gain amplifier, the low-level signals read from the tape are saturated to produce a TTL-level signal at output CASS DATA IN. This signal is applied to input 4 at port B of the 8255A (see Fig. 10.9), where it can be read by the 8088 using IN instructions.

The motor of the cassette player is also turned on or off through circuitry shown in Fig. 10.8. When the MOTOR OFF input is switched to logic 0, DIP relay K_1 is activated. This connects the DATA IN signal to the input of the amplifier circuit formed from the MC1741 device U_1. At the same time, the motor control (MOTOR CNTRL) outputs at pins 1 and 3 of J_6 are connected through a relay contact and the motor turns on. MOTOR OFF is provided by output 3 at port B of the 8255A PIC (see Fig. 10.9).

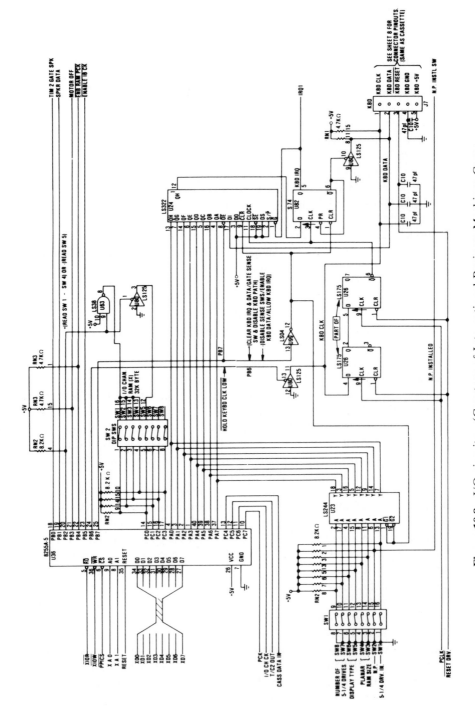

Figure 10.9 I/O circuitry. (Courtesy of International Business Machines Corporation)

Figure 10.9 shows the I/O circuitry of the IBM PC. Three basic types of functions are performed through this I/O interface. First, using this circuitry, the 8088 inputs data from the keyboard and outputs data to the cassette and speaker. Second, through this circuitry, the microprocessor reads the setting of DIP switches to determine system configuration information such as the size of the system memory, number of floppy-disk drives, type of monitor used on the system, and whether or not an 8087 numeric coprocessor is installed. Finally, certain I/O ports are used for special functions, such as clearing the parity check flip-flop and reading the state of the parity check flip-flop through software. The I/O circuitry of the PC system processor board is designed using the 8255A-5 programmable peripheral interface (PPI) IC. In this section, we will look at how the 8255A is interfaced to the 8088 MPU and at the different input/output operations that take place through its ports.

8255A Programmable Peripheral Interface

The 8255A PPI that implements the I/O circuitry is labeled U_{36} in Fig. 10.9. It has three 8-bit ports for implementing inputs or outputs. In the PC, ports PA and PC are configured to operate as inputs, and the lines of port PB are set up to work as outputs. In Fig. 10.1(d), we find that ports PA, PB, and PC reside at the I/O addresses 0060_{16}, 0061_{16}, and 0062_{16}, respectively.

Figure 10.1(d) also identifies the function of each pin at PA, PB, and PC. Here we find that input port PA is used to both read the configuration switches of SW1 and communicate with the keyboard. On the other hand, output port PB controls the cassette and speaker. It also supplies enable signals for RAM parity check, I/O channel check, and reading of the configuration switches or keyboard. Finally, we find that the input port PC is used to read the I/O channel RAM switches (SW2), parity check signal, I/O channel check signal, terminal count status from timer 2, and cassette data.

The operation of the ports of the 8255A are configurable under software control. This is done by writing a configuration byte to the command/mode control register within the device. In Fig. 10.1(d), we find that the command/mode register is located at address 0063_{16}. When configured by the initialization software of the PC, it is loaded with the value 99_{16}. This configuration code selects mode 0 operation for all three ports.

Loading of the control register, as well as inputting of data from ports PA and PC or outputting of data to port PB, is performed through the 8255A's microprocessor interface. In Fig. 10.9, we see that the microprocessor interface is activated by the $\overline{\text{PPICS}}$ (PPI chip select) signal, which is applied to the $\overline{\text{CS}}$ input at pin 6 of the 8255A. Figure 10.4(b) shows that this signal is at its active (logic 0) level whenever an I/O address in the range 0060_{16} through $007F_{16}$ is output on the system address bus. However, remember that just four of these addresses, 0060_{16} through 0063_{16}, are used by the 8255A interface. Note that the data bus inputs of the 8255A are tied to lines XD_0 through XD_7 of the system data bus. It is over these lines that the configuration information or input/output data are carried. The 8088 signals the PPI that data are to be read from or written into a register with signals $\overline{XIOR}$ and $\overline{XIOW}$, respectively, while the register to be accessed is determined by the register select code on address lines XA_0 and XA_1.

Inputting System Configuration DIP Switch Settings

Let us now look at how the settings of the system configuration DIP switches are input to the 8088 microprocessor. Looking at Fig. 10.9, we see that input port PA, which is at I/O address 0060_{16}, is connected to configuration switch SW1 through the 74LS244 buffer (U_{23}). To read the state of these switches, the keyboard data path must be disabled and the switch path enabled. This is done by writing a 1 to bit PB_7 of the output port. This output is inverted and then applied to the enable inputs of buffer U_{23}. Logic 0 at these inputs enables the buffer and causes the switch setting to pass through to port PA. Now the instruction

```
IN   AL,60H
```

can be used to read the contents of port PA. The byte of data read in can be decoded based on the table in Fig. 10.1(d) to determine the number of floppy-disk drives, type of display, presence or absence of an 8087, and size of the RAM on the system board.

EXAMPLE 10.1

The system configuration byte read from input port PA is $7D_{16}$. Describe the PC configuration for these switch settings.

Solution

Expressing the switch setting byte in binary form, we get

$$PA_7PA_6PA_5PA_4PA_3PA_2PA_1PA_0 = 7D_{16} = 01111101_2$$

Referring to the table in Fig. 10.1(d), we find that

$PA_0 = 1$	indicates that the system has floppy-disk drive(s)
$PA_1 = 0$	indicates that an 8087 is not installed
$PA_3PA_2 = 11$	indicates that the system processor board has 256K of memory
$PA_5PA_4 = 11$	indicates that the system has a monochrome monitor
$PA_7PA_6 = 01$	indicates that the system has two floppy drives

Scanning the Keyboard

The keyboard of the PC is also interfaced to the 8088 through port PA of the 8255A. In Fig. 10.9, we find that the keyboard attaches to the system processor board at connector KB_0. The keyboard interface circuit includes devices U_{82}, U_{26}, and U_{24}. At completion of the power-on reset service routine, output PB_7 of the 8255A is switched to logic 0. This disables reading of configuration switch SW1 and enables the keyboard data path and interrupt.

We will now examine how the 8088 determines that a key on the keyboard has been depressed. The keyboard of the PC generates a *keyscan code* whenever one of its keys is depressed. Bits of the keyscan code are input to the system processor board in serial form at the KBD DATA pin of the keyboard connector synchronously with pulses at KBD CLK. Note in Fig. 10.9 that KBD DATA is applied directly to the data input (DI) of the 74LS322 serial-in, parallel-out shift register (U_{24}). On the other hand, KBD CLK is input to the data input at pin 4 of one of the two D-type flip-flops in the 74LS175 device, U_{26}. This flip-flop circuit divides the clock by four before outputting it at pin 6. The clock produced at pin 6 of U_{26} is applied to the clock input of the 74S74 keyboard interrupt request flip-flop U_{82}, as well as the CLOCK input of the 74LS322 shift register. CLOCK is used by the shift register to clock in bits of the serial keyscan code from DI. When a byte of data has been received, the Q_H output at pin 12 of the shift register switches to logic 1. Q_H is returned to the data input of the 74S74 flip-flop U_{82}, and when logic 1 is clocked into the device, the keyboard interrupt request signal KBD IRQ becomes active. At the same moment that the interrupt signal is generated, the KBD DATA line is driven to logic 0 by the output at pin 8 of buffer U_{80} and the shift register is disabled.

In response to the IRQ_1 interrupt request, the 8088 initiates a keyscan-code service routine. This routine reads the keyscan code by inputting the contents of the shift register through port PA. After reading the code, it drives output PB_7 to logic 1 to clear the keyboard interrupt request flip-flop and keyscan shift register. Next, the service routine drives PB_7 back to logic 0. This reenables the keyboard interface to accept another character from the keyboard.

Port C Input and Output Functions

The switch configuration identified as SW2 in Fig. 10.9 represents what is called the *I/O channel RAM switches*. The five connected switches are used to identify the amount of read/write memory provided through the I/O channel. The settings of these switches are also read through the 8255A PPI. Once the settings are read from the switches, the total amount of memory can be determined by multiplying the binary value of the switch settings by 32KB.

Looking at the hardware in Fig. 10.9, we find that the settings of the five switches are returned to the 8088 over just four input lines, PC_0 through PC_3. To read the settings of switches SW2-1 through SW2-4, a logic 1 must first be written to output PB_2 and then input the contents of port PC. The four least significant bits of this byte are the switch settings. Logic 1 in a bit position indicates that the corresponding switch is in the OFF position (open circuit). Switch SW2-5 is read by switching PB_2 to logic 0 and once again reading the contents of port PC. In this byte, the content of the least significant bit represents the setting of SW2-5. These two bytes can be combined through software to give a single byte that contains all five switch settings.

The four most significant bit lines of port PC are supplied by signals generated elsewhere on the system processor board. PC_5 through PC_7 allow the 8088 to read the state of the RAM parity check (PCK), I/O channel check (I/O CH CK), and timer terminal count (T/C2 OUT) signals through software. On the other hand, CASS DATA IN, which is available at PC_4, is the data input line from the cassette interface.

▲ 10.10 INPUT/OUTPUT CHANNEL INTERFACE

The input/output channel is the system expansion bus of the PC. The chassis of the PC has five 62-pin I/O channel card slots. Earlier we pointed out that using these slots special function adapter cards, such as boards to control a monochrome or color display, floppy-disk drives, a hard disk drive, expanded memory, or a printer, can be added to the system to expand its configuration.

Figure 10.10(a) shows the electrical interface implemented with the I/O channel. In all, 62 signals are provided in each I/O channel slot. They include an 8-bit data bus, 20-bit address bus, six interrupts, memory and I/O read/write controls, clock and timing signals, a channel check signal, and power and ground pins.

The table in Fig. 10.10(b) lists the mnemonic and name for each of the I/O channel signals. For instance, here we see that the signal AEN stands for address enable. Also identified in this table is whether the signal is an input (I), output (O), or input/output (I/O). Notice that input/output channel ready (I/O CH RDY) is an input signal; input/output write command ($\overline{\text{IOW}}$) is an example of an output; and data bus lines D_0 through D_7 are the only signals that are capable of operating as inputs or outputs. In the next chapter we will learn how to interface to the system board using the I/O channel signals.

ASSIGNMENTS

Section 10.2

1. Name the three system buses of the PC.
2. What three functions are performed by the clock generator block in Fig. 10.1?
3. What I/O addresses are dedicated to the PPI?
4. What I/O addresses are assigned to the registers of the DMA controller? To the DMA page registers?
5. What functions are assigned to timer 0? Timer 1? Timer 2?

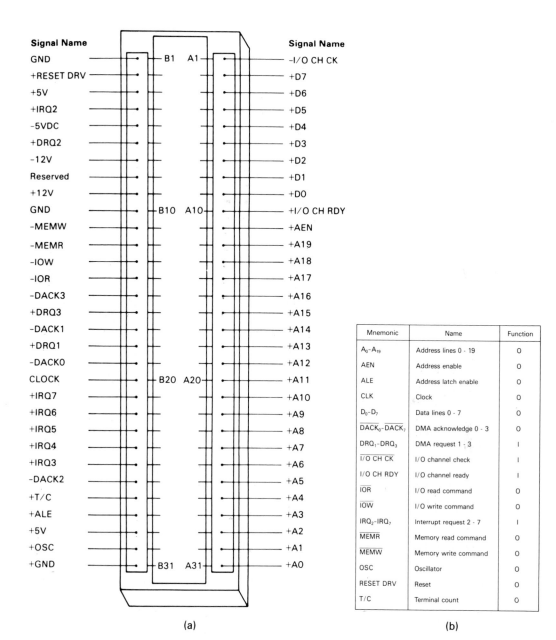

Signal Name			Signal Name
GND	B1	A1	-I/O CH CK
+RESET DRV			+D7
+5V			+D6
+IRQ2			+D5
-5VDC			+D4
+DRQ2			+D3
-12V			+D2
Reserved			+D1
+12V			+D0
GND	B10	A10	+I/O CH RDY
-MEMW			+AEN
-MEMR			+A19
-IOW			+A18
-IOR			+A17
-DACK3			+A16
+DRQ3			+A15
-DACK1			+A14
+DRQ1			+A13
-DACK0			+A12
CLOCK	B20	A20	+A11
+IRQ7			+A10
+IRQ6			+A9
+IRQ5			+A8
+IRQ4			+A7
+IRQ3			+A6
-DACK2			+A5
+T/C			+A4
+ALE			+A3
+5V			+A2
+OSC			+A1
+GND	B31	A31	+A0

(a)

Mnemonic	Name	Function
A_0-A_{19}	Address lines 0 - 19	O
AEN	Address enable	O
ALE	Address latch enable	O
CLK	Clock	O
D_0-D_7	Data lines 0 - 7	O
$\overline{DACK_0}$-$\overline{DACK_7}$	DMA acknowledge 0 - 3	O
DRQ_1-DRQ_3	DMA request 1 - 3	I
$\overline{I/O\ CH\ CK}$	I/O channel check	I
I/O CH RDY	I/O channel ready	I
$\overline{IOR}$	I/O read command	O
$\overline{IOW}$	I/O write command	O
IRQ_2-IRQ_7	Interrupt request 2 - 7	I
$\overline{MEMR}$	Memory read command	O
$\overline{MEMW}$	Memory write command	O
OSC	Oscillator	O
RESET DRV	Reset	O
T/C	Terminal count	O

(b)

Figure 10.10 (a) I/O channel interface. (Courtesy of International Business Machines Corporation) (b) Signal mnemonics, names, and functions.

6. Is port PA of the PPI configured for the input or output mode of operation? Port PB? Port PC?

7. Over which PPI lines are the state of the memory and system configuration switches input to the microprocessor?

8. Which output port of the PPI is used to turn ON/OFF the cassette motor?

9. Which output port of the PPI is used to output data to the speaker?

10. What are the three sources of the NMI signal?

11. What is assigned to the lowest-priority interrupt request?

12. What I/O device is assigned to priority level 5?

13. How much I/O channel expansion RAM is supported in the PC?

Section 10.3

14. What is the frequency of CLK88? PCLK?

15. At what frequency does the 8087 in the PC run?

16. What are the input and output signals of the 8284A's reset circuitry?

17. To what pin of the 8087 is RESET applied?

18. What are the input and output signals of the 8284A's wait state logic?

19. What does logic 0 at $\overline{\text{DMA WAIT}}$ mean? Logic 0 at $\overline{\text{RDY}}$/WAIT?

20. Which devices are attached to the local bus of the 8088?

21. What devices are used to demultiplex the local bus into the system address bus and system data bus?

22. What device is used to produce the system control bus signals?

23. At what pins of the 8288 are signals $\overline{\text{MEMW}}$ and $\overline{\text{MEMR}}$ output?

24. Give an overview of the interrupt request/acknowledge cycle that takes place between the 8259A and 8088.

Section 10.4

25. What is the source of the signal I/O CH RDY? To what logic level must it be switched to initiate a wait state?

26. What types of bus cycles cause the $\overline{\text{RDY}}$/WAIT output to switch to the 1 logic level? What input signal represents each of the bus cycles?

27. Give an overview of the operation of the hold/hold acknowledge circuitry.

28. Give an overview of how the NMI interface is enabled for operation.

29. Write an instruction sequence to disable NMI.

30. Can the parity check interrupt request be individually enabled/disabled? Explain.

31. How does the 8088 determine which of the NMI sources has initiated the request for service?

Section 10.5

32. Trace through the operation of the I/O chip select circuitry when an I/O write takes place to address $A0_{16}$.

33. Which I/O chip selects can occur during either an input or output bus cycle to an address in the range 0000_{16}-$007F_{16}$?

34. What are the outputs of the ROM chip select circuitry?

35. Trace through the operation of the ROM address decoder as address $FA000_{16}$ is applied to the input.

36. At what logic level must address bits A_{18} and A_{19} be for the $\overline{\text{RAM ADDR SEL}}$ output to switch to its active 0 logic level?

37. What $\overline{\text{RAS}}$ output is produced by U_{65} if the address input is 10100_{16}?

38. What $\overline{\text{CAS}}$ output is produced by U_{47} if the address input is 20200_{16}?

Section 10.6

39. Trace through the operation of the ROM circuitry in Fig. 10.5 as a read cycle is performed to address $F4000_{16}$.

40. Give an overview of the operation of the RAM circuitry in Fig. 10.6(a) as a byte of data is written to the DRAMs in bank 0.

Section 10.7

41. What are the sources of DMA requests for channels 1, 2, and 3?

42. Give an overview of the DMA request/acknowledge handshake sequence.

43. What must be loaded into the DMA page registers to implement DMA operation as follows: Channel 1 DMA memory address range $A0000_{16}$-$AFFFF_{16}$, Channel 2 DMA address range $B0000_{16}$-$BFFFF_{16}$, and channel 3 DMA address range $C0000_{16}$-$CFFFF_{16}$? Write an instruction sequence to initialize the 74LS670 device.

Section 10.8

44. What is the frequency of the timer interrupt produced by the 8253 timer? The refresh request signal?

45. What is the divisor loaded into counter 1?

46. Give an overview of how timer 2 is used to drive the speaker.

47. Draw the waveform of the signal applied to the speaker if the signal at OUT 2 is a square waveform of 3 KHz and SPKR DATA is a square waveform of 100 Hz.

Section 10.9

48. Write an instruction sequence to read SW1 through the 8255A in Fig. 10.9.

49. What is the function of signal KBD IRQ?

50. Write a simple keyboard interrupt service routine.

Section 10.10

51. What is the purpose of the I/O channel slots in the system processor board? How many are provided?

52. Which I/O channel connector pin is used to supply the signal I/O CH RDY to the system processor board? Is it active low or active high?

11

PC Bus Interfacing, Circuit Construction, Testing, and Troubleshooting

▲ 11.1 INTRODUCTION

In the last chapter we learned about the electronics of the original IBM PC's main processor board. Here we will continue our study of microcomputer electronics with circuits built using the PC's I/O channel signals. This includes the analysis, design, building, and testing of a variety of bus interface, input/output, and peripheral circuits. The following subjects are covered in this chapter:

1. PC bus-based interfacing
2. The PCμLAB laboratory test unit
3. Experimentation with the on-board circuitry of the PCμLAB
4. Building, testing, and troubleshooting circuits
5. Observing bus activity with a logic analyzer

▲ 11.2 PC BUS-BASED INTERFACING

In this section, we will examine some of the hardware that can be used to experiment with external circuitry in the PC bus-based laboratory environment. That is, we will now work with circuitry that is not already available as part of the PC's main processor board; instead, the circuits will be constructed external to the PC. This includes prebuilt circuits that are readily available on PC add-on boards, such as a serial communication interface, a parallel I/O expansion module, an analog-to-digital (A-to-D) converter, and a digital-to-analog (D-to-A) converter, or custom circuits that are hand-built on special prototyping boards. We call an experimental circuit that is built to test out a function a *prototype*.

The I/O channel expansion bus is where additional circuits are added into the microcomputer of the IBM PC. A variety of different methods can be used to implement these circuits. That is, a wide range of hardware is available for building experimental circuits. Figure 11.1 (a) and (b) show just two examples. These cards are known as *breadboards*; that is, a card meant for prototyping circuits. The breadboard card in Fig. 11.1(a) requires the circuit to be constructed on the board by inserting the leads of the devices through the holes and then the leads of the devices are soldered to permanently connect them together. Similar boards are available where the devices are interconnected by wire wrapping instead of with solder. On the other hand, the module shown in Fig. 11.1(b) is what is known as a *solderless breadboard*. Here the components are plugged in and interconnected with jumper wires. Therefore, it is more practical in that the breadboard can be reused many times.

These prototyping modules are intended to be plugged directly into the bus slots of the PC. However, this does not permit easy access to the circuits on the board for testing. One solution to this problem is the *board extender card* shown in Fig. 11.2. The board extender is plugged into the slot in the PC's main processor board and the card with the experimental circuitry is plugged into the top of the extender card. In this way, the circuitry to be tested becomes more accessible because it is located above the case of the PC.

The PC add-on prototyping cards we just discussed are widely used in industry; however, they require the cover of the PC to be left off and the testing of circuits

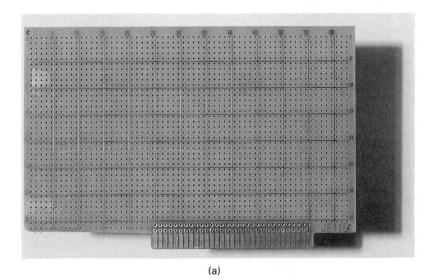

(a)

Figure 11.1 (a) Breadboard card. (b) Solderless breadboard card.

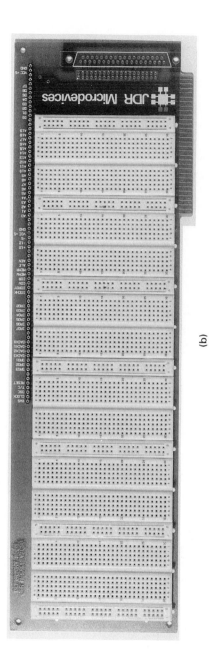

Figure 11.1 (Continued)

643

Figure 11.2 Extender card.

to take place in close contact to the other circuitry within the PC. In an educational environment, it is beneficial to have the complete experimental environment external to the PC. Moving the breadboard outside, permits easier access to the circuits for testing and modification, and limits the risk of damage to the PC.

The PCµLAB shown in Fig. 11.3 implements this type of laboratory environment. It is a bench top laboratory test unit. The illustration in Fig. 11.4 shows that the PCµLAB uses a bus interface module that is permanently left inside the PC. The interface board inside the PC buffers all the bus signals. Cables carry the signals of the I/O channel expansion bus over to the PCµLAB breadboard unit. This unit has a solderless breadboarding area for easy construction of circuits and connectors of a single I/O channel slot for using prebuilt add-on boards. This type of system offers a better solution for an educational microcomputer laboratory and will be used here for discussion.

▲ 11.3 THE PCµLAB LABORATORY TEST UNIT

In the last section we showed how the PCµLAB attaches to the personal computer. Here we will examine the features it offers for experimentation in the laboratory. Earlier we indicated that it has a breadboard area for building circuitry and an I/O channel slot for plugging in a prebuilt boards. It also has basic I/O devices such as *switches*, *LEDs*, a *speaker*, and some *internal I/O interface circuitry*. This

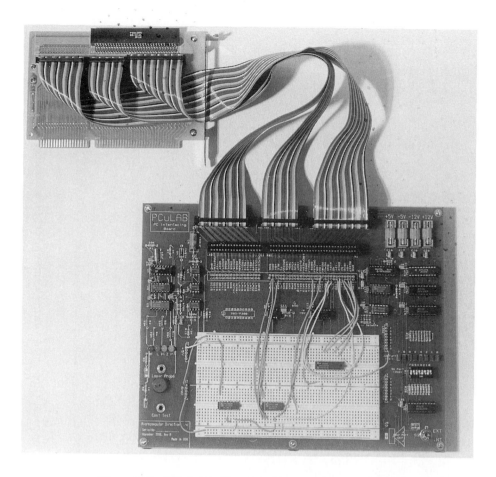

Figure 11.3 PCμLAB. (Reprinted with the permission of Microcomputer Directions, Inc.)

built-in I/O circuitry permits exploration of simple parallel I/O techniques, such as reading switches as inputs, lighting LEDs as outputs, polling a switch input, and generating tones at the speaker, without having to build any circuitry.

The layout of the top of the PCμLAB is shown in detail in Fig. 11.5. We will begin by identifying the input/output devices. On the right side we find both a block of eight switches, labeled 0 through 7, and a row of eight red LEDs, 0 through

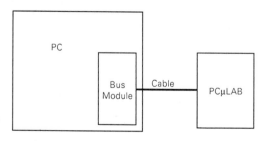

Figure 11.4 PCμLAB system configuration.

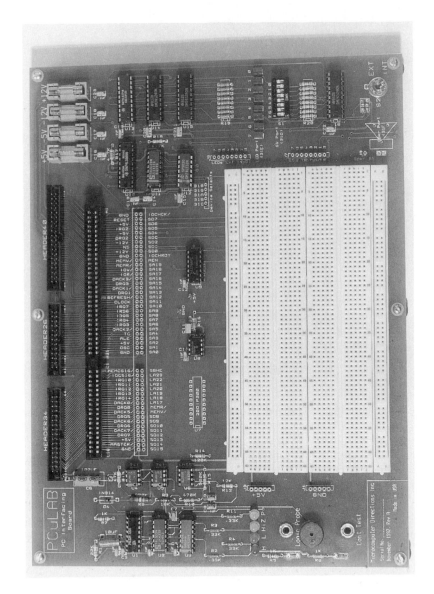

Figure 11.5 PCμLAB top panel. (Reprinted with the permission of Microcomputer Directions Inc.)

Figure 11.6 PCμLAB with add-on card. (Reprinted with the permission of Microcomputer Directions Inc.)

7. The switches can be used to supply inputs and the LEDs to produce outputs for either the built-in circuits or circuitry constructed on the breadboard area. The INT/EXT switch determines the use of these I/O devices. When it is in the INT (internal) position, they are connected directly to the on-board circuits. However, moving the switch to the EXT (external) position makes them available for connection to circuits implemented on the breadboard area.

All the signals of the PC's I/O channel expansion bus are made available at the connectors at the top of the front panel. Here we find that the signals are supplied at the PC slot and a receptacle connector. The slot is the connector into which pre-built boards are inserted. Figure 11.6 shows the PCμLAB with an add-on card inserted for testing. The receptacle connector is provided to permit connection of the bus signals to circuits built on the breadboard. For ease of use, mnemonics for all signals are labeled next to the connector. The table in Fig. 11.7 identifies the signal name for each of these mnemonics and whether it is an input or output.

Let us next look at the breadboarding area. This area permits the experimenter to build and test custom circuits. Figure 11.8 shows a circuit constructed on the breadboard area of the PCμLAB.

Looking at Fig. 11.5, we see that the breadboard area is implemented with two solderless breadboards. For this reason, it permits installation of two rows of ICs. A drawing of the electrical connection of the wire insertion clips is shown in the PCμLAB circuit layout master of Fig. 11.9. Notice that the column of five

Pin	Name	Type		Pin	Name	Type
A1	I/O CH CK	I		B1	GND	
A2	D7	I/O		B2	RESET DRV	O
A3	D6	I/O		B3	+5V	
A4	D5	I/O		B4	IRQ2	I
A5	D4	I/O		B5	–5V	
A6	D3	I/O		B6	DRQ2	I
A7	D2	I/O		B7	–12V	
A8	D1	I/O		B8	RESERVED	
A9	D0	I/O		B9	+12V	
A10	I/O CH RDY	I		B10	GND	
A11	AEN	O		B11	MEMW	O
A12	A19	O		B12	MEMR	O
A13	A18	O		B13	IOW	O
A14	A17	O		B14	IOR	O
A15	A16	O		B15	DACK3	O
A16	A15	O		B16	DRQ3	I
A17	A14	O		B17	DACK1	O
A18	A13	O		B18	DRQ1	I
A19	A12	O		B19	REFRESH	O
A20	A11	O		B20	CLOCK	O
A21	A10	O		B21	IRQ7	I
A22	A9	O		B22	IRQ6	I
A23	A8	O		B23	IRQ5	I
A24	A7	O		B24	IRQ4	I
A25	A6	O		B25	IRQ3	I
A26	A5	O		B26	DACK2	O
A27	A4	O		B27	T/C	O
A28	A3	O		B28	ALE	O
A29	A2	O		B29	+5V	
A30	A1	O		B30	OSC	O
A31	A0	O		B31	GND	

Figure 11.7 I/O channel interface signals.

vertical clips from a device pin are internally attached together. One is used up when the IC is inserted and the other four are for use in making jumper wire connections to other circuits. The jumpers must be made with wire that is rated 26 AWG (American wire gauge).

At both the top and bottom of the board, there are two horizontal rows of attached wire insertion clips. These four rows of clips are provided for power supply distribution. Two rows are intended to implement the +5 V power supply bus, and the other two are meant to be used as the common ground bus. The power supply for the circuit can be picked up with jumpers from the I/O channel connector or at the separate power supply terminal strip. Notice in Fig. 11.7 that +5 V is available at contacts B_3 and B_{29} of the I/O channel connector.

EXAMPLE 11.1

Which contacts of the I/O channel interface connector can be used as ground points?

Solution

Looking at Fig. 11.7, we see that ground (GND) is provided by contacts B_1, B_{10}, and B_{31} of the I/O interface connector.

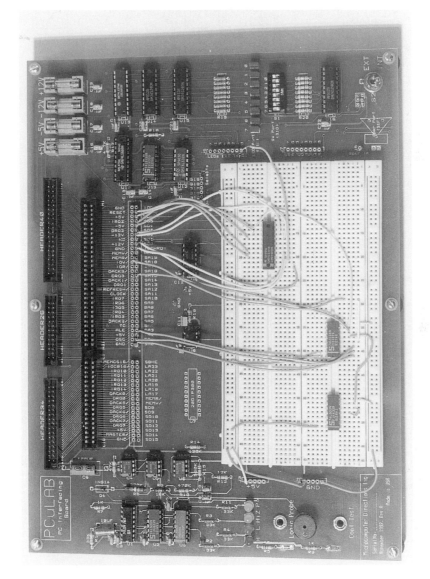

Figure 11.8 Breadboard circuit. (Reprinted with the permission of Microcomputer Directions, Inc.)

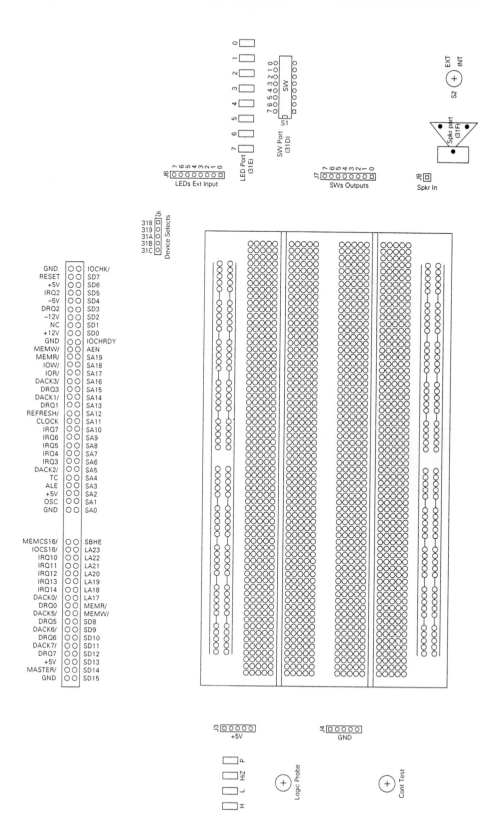

Figure 11.9 Circuit layout master. (Reprinted with the permission of Microcomputer Directions, Inc.)

Earlier we pointed out that the switches, LEDs, and speaker supply inputs and outputs for the on-board circuitry and can also be connected to circuits built on the breadboard. In both cases, I/O addresses are output over the address bus part of the I/O channel interface, A_0 through A_{15}, and data are input or output over the data bus lines D_0 through D_{15}.

EXAMPLE 11.2

At what contacts of the I/O channel connector are data bus lines D_0 through D_7 available?

Solution

In Fig. 11.7 we find that the data bus lines are supplied at contact A_2 through A_9 of the connector.

The PCμLAB also has built-in circuit test capability. It has both a continuity tester and a logic probe. Looking at Fig. 11.5, we see that the probes for the continuity tester get inserted into the female connectors identified as *CT*. The continuity tester is useful in debugging circuit connections. That is, it can be used to verify whether or not two points of a circuit are wired together. This is done by attaching one of the probes to the first point in the circuit and then touching the other probe to the second point. If they are connected together, the buzzer sounds. Care must be taken to assure that the power is not applied to the circuit under test while continuity tests are being made; otherwise, the tester circuits many be damaged.

The purpose of the logic probe is not to verify circuit connections; instead, it is used to determine the logic level of signals at various test points in a circuit. The probe that is used to input the signal from the circuit is inserted into the LP connector. Then, the probe is touched to the test point in the circuit. Based on the logic level of this signal, the red, green, or amber LED lights. Here red stands for logic 1, green for logic 0, and amber for high-Z state. The table in Fig. 11.10 shows the voltage levels corresponding to these three states. The second red LED, which is marked P, identifies that the signal at the test point is pulsing. By pulsing, we mean a signal, such as a square wave, that is repeatedly switching back and forth between the 0 and 1 logic levels.

Logic level	LED	Voltage
1	Red	$V > 2.4$ V
Hi–Z	Amber	0.4 V $< V < 2.4$ V
0	Green	$V < 0.4$ V

Figure 11.10 Logic state voltage levels.

The on-board circuitry of the PCμLAB implements simple parallel input/output interfaces. Having this circuitry built into the experimental board allows us to examine some basic I/O techniques without having to take the time to construct the circuitry. These interface circuits provide the ability to input the settings of the switches, light the LEDs, or sound a tone at the speaker. Earlier we pointed out that this circuitry becomes active when the INT/EXT switch is set to the INT position. In this section, we will describe the design and operation of the internal (on-board) circuits. The operation of these circuits is illustrated using several input and output examples.

I/O Address Decoding

Let us begin our study of the on-board circuitry with the address decoder circuit shown in Fig. 11.11(a). Here we find that a 74LS688 parity generator/checker IC (U_{10}), a 74LS138 3-line to 8-line decoder IC (U_{11}), and a 74LS32 quad-OR gate IC (U_{12}) perform the address decode function. They accept as inputs address bits A_0 through A_9 and the address enable (AEN) control signal. These inputs are directly picked up from the I/O channel expansion bus. As shown in Fig. 11.11(b), they correspond to the signals available at contacts A_{22} through A_{30} and A_{11} of the on-board I/O channel connector.

At the other side of the circuit, we find three I/O select outputs. They are labeled $\overline{\text{IORX31D}}$, $\overline{\text{IOWX31E}}$, and $\overline{\text{IOWX31F}}$ and stand for *I/O read address X31DH*, *I/O write address X31EH*, and *I/O write address X31FH*, respectively. These signals are used to select between the on-board I/O devices: switches, LEDs, or speaker. For instance, Fig. 11.11(c) shows that output $\overline{\text{IORX31D}}$ is used to enable input of the state of the switch settings.

In Fig. 11.11(b) we see that the address bits available at the I/O channel interface are A_0 through A_{19}. However, just the lower sixteen address lines A_0 through A_{15} are used in I/O addressing and many of these address bits are not used in the on-board address decoder circuit. For this reason, the unused address bits are considered don't care states. Therefore, the decoded address is

$$A_{15} \ldots A_0 = XXXXXXA_9A_8A_7A_6A_5A_4A_3A_2A_1A_0$$

Since many address bits are don't-care states, the outputs of the decoder do not correspond to unique addresses. Instead, a large number of I/O addresses decode to produce each chip select output.

Next we will look at how the higher-order address bits are decoded by the 74LS688 comparator. Looking at Fig. 11.11(a), we see that inputs P_0 through P_7 are supplied by address signals A_3 through A_9 and AEN. This gives

$$P_7P_6\ldots P_0 = AENA_9A_8A_7A_6A_5A_4A_3$$

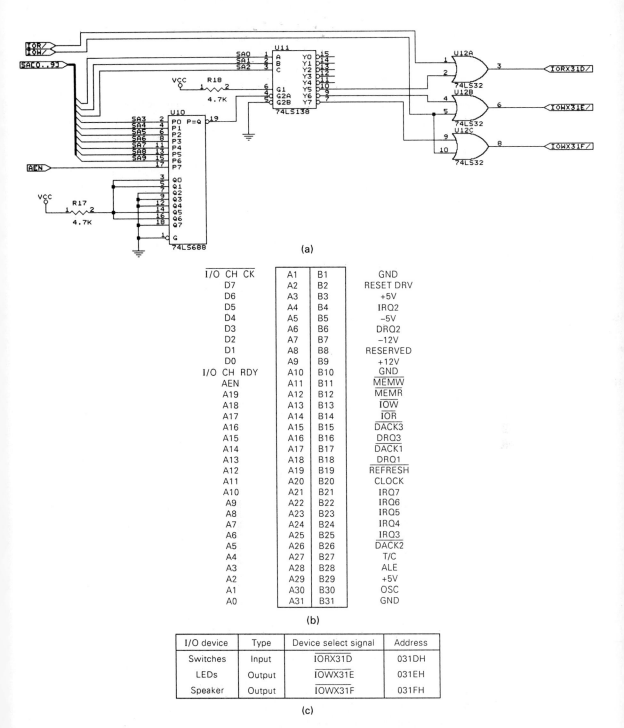

(a)

I/O CH CK	A1	B1	GND
D7	A2	B2	RESET DRV
D6	A3	B3	+5V
D5	A4	B4	IRQ2
D4	A5	B5	−5V
D3	A6	B6	DRQ2
D2	A7	B7	−12V
D1	A8	B8	RESERVED
D0	A9	B9	+12V
I/O CH RDY	A10	B10	GND
AEN	A11	B11	MEMW
A19	A12	B12	MEMR
A18	A13	B13	IOW
A17	A14	B14	IOR
A16	A15	B15	DACK3
A15	A16	B16	DRQ3
A14	A17	B17	DACK1
A13	A18	B18	DRQ1
A12	A19	B19	REFRESH
A11	A20	B20	CLOCK
A10	A21	B21	IRQ7
A9	A22	B22	IRQ6
A8	A23	B23	IRQ5
A7	A24	B24	IRQ4
A6	A25	B25	IRQ3
A5	A26	B26	DACK2
A4	A27	B27	T/C
A3	A28	B28	ALE
A2	A29	B29	+5V
A1	A30	B30	OSC
A0	A31	B31	GND

(b)

I/O device	Type	Device select signal	Address
Switches	Input	IORX31D	031DH
LEDs	Output	IOWX31E	031EH
Speaker	Output	IOWX31F	031FH

(c)

Figure 11.11 (a) Address decoder circuit. (Reprinted with the permission of Micro-computer Directions, Inc.). (b) Bus signals. (c) Output signals.

On the other hand, the Q inputs are set at fixed logic levels and represent

$$Q_7Q_6. \ldots Q_0 = 01100011_2$$

The circuit within the 74LS688 compares the address information at the P inputs to the fixed code at the Q inputs and if they are equal, it switches the P=Q output to logic 0. This means that the address on the bus corresponds to an on-board I/O device. This output is applied to the G_{2A} input of the 74LS138 decoder and enables it for operation. In this way, we see that all addresses with

$$A_{15} \ldots A_0 = XXXXXX1100011A_2A_1A_0 \text{ along with AEN} = 0$$

map to the PCμLAB's on-board I/O address space.

Once the 74LS138 decoder is enabled, the code on address lines A_0 through A_2 is used to produce the appropriate output. From the circuit diagram in Fig. 11.11(a), we find that the codes that produce the enable signals for the switches, LEDs, and speaker are

$$A_2A_1A_0 = 101_2 \text{ and active } \overline{IOR} \text{ produces } \overline{IORX31D}$$

$$A_2A_1A_0 = 110_2 \text{ and active } \overline{IOW} \text{ produces } \overline{IOWX31E}$$

$$A_2A_1A_0 = 111_2 \text{ and active } \overline{IOW} \text{ produces } \overline{IOWX31F}$$

This results in the device addresses as listed in Fig. 11.11(c). For example, reading of the switches is enabled by any address that is of the form

$$A_{15} \ldots A_0 = XXXXXX1100011101_2$$
provided AEN $= 0$.

Some examples of valid addresses are $031D_{16}$, $F31D_{16}$, $FF1D_{16}$, and $0F1D_{16}$. All of these addresses make the Y_5 output of the decoder circuit to switch to logic 0. Notice that this output is gated with the I/O channel expansion bus signal $\overline{IOR}$ by OR gate U_{12A}. In this way, the $\overline{IORX31D}$ output can only be active during input (I/O read) bus cycles.

EXAMPLE 11.3 ──────────────────────────────────────

Which output chip select does the I/O address $F71F_{16}$ produce when applied to the input of the circuit in Fig. 11.11(a)? What type of bus cycle must be in progress to produce this chip select output?

Solution

First the address expressed in binary form is

$$F71F_{16} = 1111011100011111_2$$

Considering the lower 10 bits, we get

$$A_9 \ldots A_0 = 1100011111_2 = 31F_{16}$$

Tracing the circuit, we find that this address bit combination makes the Y_7 output of U_{11} equal to logic 0. Y_7 is gated with bus signal $\overline{\text{IOW}}$ to produce the $\overline{\text{IOWX31F}}$ output. Therefore, $\overline{\text{IOWX31F}}$ is at its active 0 logic level as long as an output bus cycle is taking place.

Switch Input Circuit

The interface of switches S_0 through S_7 to the data bus is shown in Fig. 11.12. Notice that one contact from each of the eight switches is connected to ground (0 V). The other contact on each switch is supplied to one of the resistors in resistor pack R_{20} and the other end of each resistor is supplied by V_{cc} (+5 V). The connections between the resistors and the switch contacts are supplied as inputs to the data bus through the 74LS240 inverting buffers of IC U_{16}. For instance, S_0 is supplied from input A_4 of buffer U_{16A} to output Y_4 and onto data bus line D_0. Similarly, the state

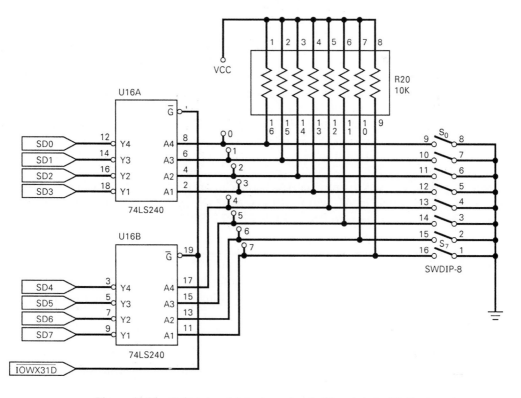

Figure 11.12 Switch input interface circuit. (Reprinted with the permission of Microcomputer Directions, Inc.)

of switch 7 is passed through the inverter at input A_1 of U_{16B} to data bus line D_7. Because inverting buffers are used in the circuit, logic 0 is applied to the data bus whenever a switch is open and logic 1 is put on the data bus if a switch is closed.

In the circuit diagram, we see that the switch input buffer gets enabled by the signal $\overline{\text{IORX31D}}$. Earlier we showed that this signal is at its active 0 logic level whenever an input bus cycle is performed to address $031D_{16}$. But, remember that the complete I/O address is not decoded; therefore, many other addresses also decode to enable this buffer.

The state of the switches can be read with an INPUT command. For instance, the DEBUG command

```
I 31D  (⏎)
```

causes the settings of all eight switches to be displayed as a hexadecimal byte. In this byte, the most significant bit represents the state of S_7 and the least significant bit that of S_0. Remember that a bit at logic 1 means a closed switch and logic 0 an open switch.

Let us now look at how to read the status of the switches into the accumulator of the MPU. This is done by simply executing an IN instruction. Therefore, after executing the instruction sequence

```
MOV DX,31DH
IN  AL,DX
```

the switch setting are held in AL.

In practical applications, it is common to want to determine the setting of a single switch. This can be done by additional processing of the byte in AL. For instance, to find the setting of S_7, we can use the instruction

```
AND AL,80H
```

Execution of this instruction ANDs the contents of AL with the value 80_{16}. Therefore, the result in AL will be 10000000_2 if switch 7 is closed or 00000000_2 if it is open. That is, the zero flag (ZF) will be 0 if SW_7 is open and 1 if it is closed.

EXAMPLE 11.4

Write a program that will poll S_0 waiting for it to be closed. Use a shift instruction to isolate and determine the setting of switch 0. Use a valid address other than $31D_{16}$ to read the setting of the switches.

Solution

The setting of the switches can be input to AL with the instructions

```
      MOV DX,0FF1DH
POLL: IN  AL,DX
```

Here we have used FF1D$_{16}$ as the I/O address for the switch port. Now the setting of switch 0, which is in the bit 0 position, is shifted into the carry flag (CF) with the instruction

```
SHR   AL,1
```

Finally, the setting of the switch is tested for 0 (open) by testing the carry flag with the instruction

```
JNC   POLL
```

If CF is 0, the switch is open and the poll loop is repeated. But if the switch is closed, CF is 1; the poll loop is complete; and the instruction following JNC is executed.

LED Output Circuit

Let us next look at the output circuit that drives the LEDs. Figure 11.13 shows the drive circuitry for LEDs 0 through 7. Here we see that the anode side of the individual LEDs are all connected in parallel and supplied by +5 V. On the other hand, the cathode sides of the LEDs are wired through separate resistors of resistor pack R_{19} to the outputs of the 74LS240 LED drive buffer (U_{14}). For example, the cathode of LED 0 connects through the uppermost 330Ω resistor to the Y_1 output of IC U_{14A}. The inputs to the inverting buffer are supplied by the outputs of the 74LS374 LED port latch (U_{13}).

To light an LED, an output bus cycle must be performed to load logic 1 into the corresponding bit of the LED port latch. As identified earlier, the I/O address accompanying this data and $\overline{\text{IOW}}$ must decode to produce logic 0 at $\overline{\text{IOWX31E}}$. Notice that this signal is used to clock the data on data bus lines D_0 through D_7 into the 74LS374 latch. The bits at the output of the latch are inverted by the 74LS240 buffer. Logic 0 at any output of the buffer provides a path to ground for the corresponding LED, and thus turns it on.

To try out the LEDs on the PCμLAB, we can turn them all on by issuing a single OUT command from DEBUG. This command is

```
O 31E FF   (↵)
```

They can be turned off with the command

```
O 31E 00   (↵)
```

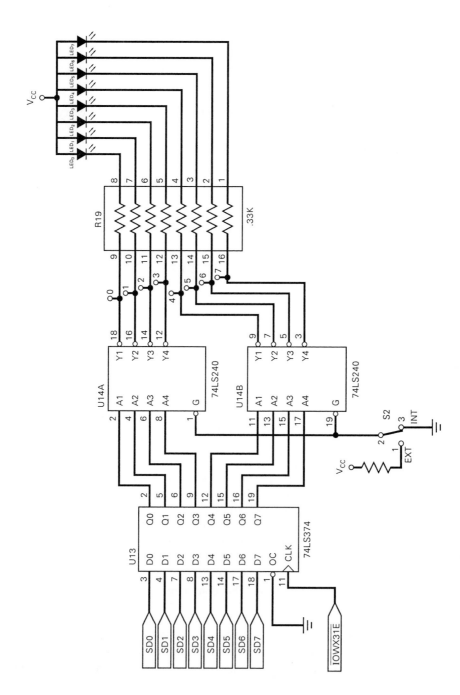

Figure 11.13 LED output interface circuit. (Reprinted with the permission of Microcomputer Directions, Inc.)

EXAMPLE 11.5 _____

Write a program that will blink LED 7.

Solution

To turn on LED 7, 80_{16} must be output to the LED port latch and it is turned off by outputting 00_{16}. Therefore, we begin with the instructions

```
              MOV DX,31EH
              MOV AL,80H
ON_OFF:   OUT DX,AL
```

Next we need to delay for a period of time before turning the LED off. To do this, a count is loaded into CX and a time delay is implemented using a LOOP instruction.

```
           MOV  CX,0FFFFH
HERE:   LOOP HERE
```

The duration of the time delay can be adjusted by simply changing the value loaded into CX.

After the time delay has elapsed, the value in bit 7 of AL is inverted with the instruction

```
XOR   AL,80H
```

The new contents of AL equal 00_{16}. This value will cause the LED 7 to turn off. Finally, a JMP instruction returns program control to ON_OFF.

```
JMP   ON_OFF
```

and the loop repeats. The complete program is shown in Fig. 11.14.

Speaker Drive Circuit

The speaker drive circuit of Fig. 11.15 is an output interface. It is implemented with 74LS74 data latch device (U_9) and the 75477 speaker driver (U_8). The tone to be sounded at the speaker can be generated under software control.

Let us begin by studying how a tone signal can be generated by the MPU and sent to the speaker. A tone is produced by applying a square wave to the speaker. This signal is output over data bus line D_0 to the D_1 input at pin 2 of U_{9A}. Looking at the circuit diagram, we find that the tone is passed from the Q_1 output at pin 5 of U_9 through the EXT/INT switch to the 2A input at pin 7 of U_8. It is

```
                MOV    DX,31EH

                MOV    AL,80H

    ON_OFF:     OUT    DX,AL

                MOV    CX,0FFFFH

    HERE:       LOOP   HERE

                XOR    AL,80H

                JMP    ON_OFF
```

Figure 11.14 LED blink program.

then output at pin 6 (2Y) of U_8 and sent through resistor R_{16} to the speaker. The other end of the speaker's coil is connected to $+V_{cc}$.

The square wave can be generated with a program similar to the one we used to blink LED 7. However, the data is output on data bus line D_0 rather than D_7, and it must be accompanied by address $31F_{16}$ instead of $31E_{16}$. This gives the program

```
                MOV    DX,31FH
                MOV    AL,01H
    ON_OFF:     OUT    DX,AL
                MOV    CX,0FFFFH
    HERE:       LOOP   HERE
                XOR    AL,01H
                JMP    ON_OFF
```

The pitch of the tone can be changed by varying the frequency of the square wave. This is done by adjusting the duration of the time delay; that is, changing the count that is loaded into CX. The lower the count, the higher the pitch.

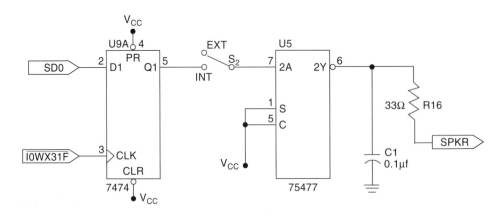

Figure 11.15 Speaker driver circuit. (Reprinted with the permission of Microcomputer Directions, Inc.)

▲ 11.5 BUILDING, TESTING, AND TROUBLESHOOTING CIRCUITS

In the last section, we examined the on-board circuits of the PCμLAB. Here we turn our attention to circuits that can be built on the breadboarding area of the PCμLAB. First, we will look at how circuits are constructed, then how their operation is tested, and finally, troubleshooting techniques that can be used if the circuit does not work.

Building a Circuit

Earlier we showed that the breadboard area is where custom circuits can be built and that it allows for mounting of two rows of ICs. Assuming that a schematic diagram of the circuit to be built is already available, the first step in the process of building the circuit is to make a layout diagram to show how the circuit will be constructed on the breadboard. This drawing can be made on a circuit layout master similar to the one shown in Fig. 11.9.

Figure 11.16(a) is the diagram for a circuit that implements a parallel output port to drive LED_0. This is the circuit we will use to illustrate the method used to

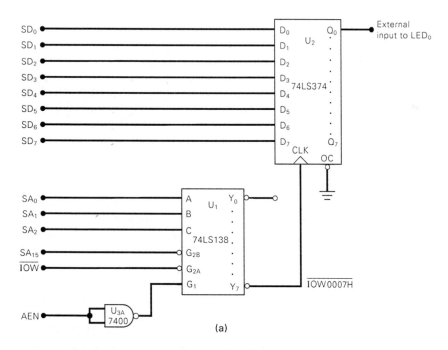

(a)

Figure 11.16 (a) LED drive circuit. (Reprinted with the permission of Microcomputer Directions, Inc.). (b) Schematic with pin numbers marked. (Reprinted with the permission of Microcomputer Directions, Inc.). (c) Completed layout master. (Reprinted with the permission of Microcomputer Directions, Inc.)

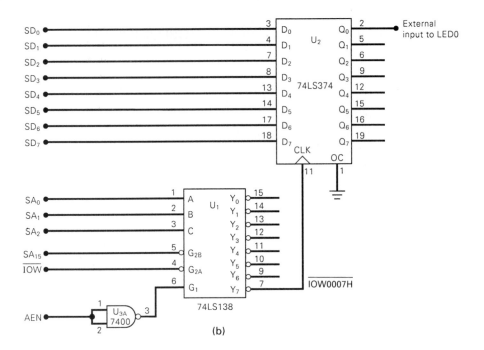

Figure 11.16 (Continued)

breadboard a circuit. Notice that the circuit uses a 74LS138 3-line to 8-line decoder, 7400 quad 2-input NAND gate, and a 74LS374 octal latch. The 74LS240 inverting buffer, 330Ω resistor, and LED_0 are supplied by the internal circuitry of the $PC\mu LAB$ by using input 0 of receptacle J_6. We begin by marking the IC pin numbers for each of the inputs and outputs into the circuit diagram. For instance, from the pin layout of the 74LS138 in Fig. 11.17, we find that its A, B, and C inputs are at pins 1, 2, and 3, respectively. Moreover, the Y_7 output is identified as pin 7. This is done for each IC to give the circuit shown in Fig. 11.16(b).

Now we are ready to make the layout drawing that shows how the circuits will be laid out on the $PC\mu LAB$'s breadboard area. To do this, we simply draw the ICs and pin connections onto one of the circuit layout masters. Figure 11.16 (c) shows the layout for our test circuit. Looking at this diagram, we see that +5 V is picked up by inserting a jumper between connector J_3 and one of the power bus lines of the breadboard. Ground is supplied in a similar way from connector J_4 to another power bus line. Then +5 V and GND can be jumpered from IC to IC. This completes the power distribution for the circuit.

Let us next look at how the inputs and outputs of the circuit are provided. At the output side, a jumper is used to connect the Q_0 output of the 74LS374 to the 0 input of connector J_6. The data input at pin 3 of the 74LS374 latch is picked up with a jumper to data bus line D_0 at pin A_9 of the I/O channel connector. The output of the 74LS138 decoder (pin 7) that supplies the clock to the latch is jumpered to pin 11 of the 74LS374 IC. Notice that the AEN input is inverted with a NAND

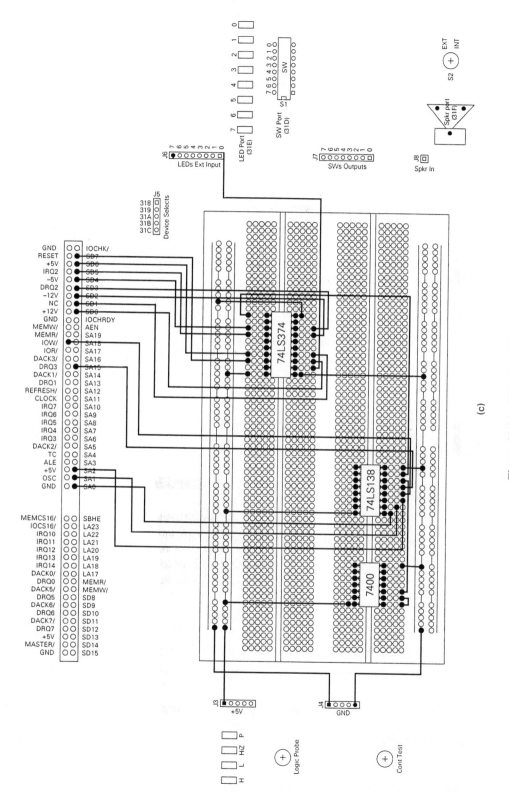

Figure 11.16 (Continued)

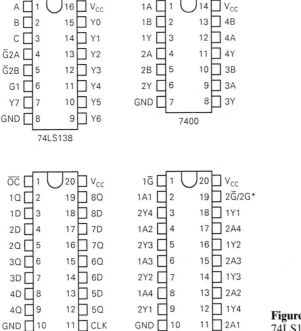

Figure 11.17 Pin layouts for 74LS138, 7400, 74LS374, and 74LS240.

gate. The inverter is formed by connecting pins 4 and 5 of the 7400 IC and then applying AEN to pin 4. The inverted output at pin 3 of the 7400 IC is supplied to the G_1 input at pin 6 of the 74LS138 decoder IC.

EXAMPLE 11.6

Use the circuit diagram layout in Fig. 11.16(c) to identify which pins of the I/O channel connector are used to supply the address signals to the A, B, and C inputs of the 74LS138 decoder.

Solution

In the circuit diagram, we find that the A, B, and C inputs of the decoder are attached to I/O channel address lines A_0, A_1, and A_2, respectively. These signals are picked up at pins A_{31}, A_{30}, and A_{29} of the I/O channel connector.

The layout drawing in Fig. 11.16(c) is our plan for constructing the circuit. This drawing and the schematic diagram marked with pin numbers serve as valuable tools when testing and troubleshooting circuits. Figure 11.8 shows the breadboard of this example circuit.

Testing the Operation of a Circuit

Now that the circuit has been constructed, we are ready to check out its operation. The process of checking out how an electronic circuit works is called *testing*. To test a circuit, we must first know the events that should take place when it is functioning correctly. Usually this means that it will produce certain outputs. These outputs may be a visual event like lighting an LED, audible event like sounding a tone, mechanical event like positioning a mechanism, or simply a signal waveshape that can be observed with an *instrument*. For instance, the function of our example circuit in Fig. 11.16(a) is to light an LED.

To test the operation of our example circuit we can simply turn on the LED or make it blink. However, to do this, the LED output interface must be driven with software. In this way, we see that to test microcomputer interface circuits they must be driven with software. In fact, they are normally driven by a special piece of software that is specifically written to exercise the interface. This segment of program is sometimes referred to as a *diagnostic program*.

The diagnostic routine does not have to be complex. For instance, to turn on LED_0 in our breadboard circuit we can simply execute the instructions

```
MOV   DX,0007H
MOV   AL,01H
OUT   DX,AL
```

Note that the I/O address 0007_{16} along with active $\overline{\text{IOW}}$ and inactive AEN produces an active low pulse at output Y_7 of the decoder. This pulse is used to clock the data into the octal latch to make the Q_0 output become logic 1. A software routine that will blink LED_0 is as follows

```
               MOV   DX,0007H
               MOV   AL,01H
ON_OFF:        OUT   DX,AL
               MOV   CX,0FFFFH
     HERE:     LOOP  HERE
               XOR   AL,01H
               JMP   ON_OFF
```

The operation of a circuit that produces an electrical output can be tested with instrumentation. For instance, if the circuit we just constructed did not include an LED at the output, we would need to observe the signal at the Q_0 output (pin 2) of the 74LS374 latch. Accessories, such as *IC test clips,* are available to provide easy attachment of instruments to the pins of an IC. Figure 11.18 shows some IC test clips. This type of clip is spring loaded and snaps tightly over the top of the IC. Instruments are connected to its pins instead of to those of the IC. For our example of the 74LS374 IC, a 20-pin IC test clip would be attached and then the probe of the instrument clipped onto pin 2 at the top of the test clip.

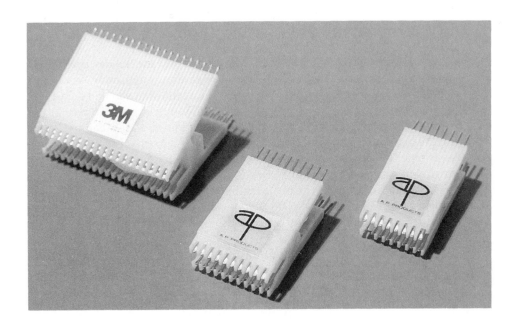

Figure 11.18 IC test clips.

Various instruments are available to test the electrical signals in a circuit. Figures 11.19(a), (b), and (c) show three examples, the *logic probe*, *multimeter*, and *oscilloscope*, respectively. The logic probe is a hand-held instrument that can be used to observe the logic level at a test point in a microcomputer circuit. As we pointed out earlier, a logic probe is built into the PCμLAB. This instrument has the ability to tell whether the signal tested is in the 0, 1, or high-Z logic state, or if it is pulsating. The probe is simply touched to the point in the circuit where the signal is to be observed and the logic level is signaled by one of the LEDs.

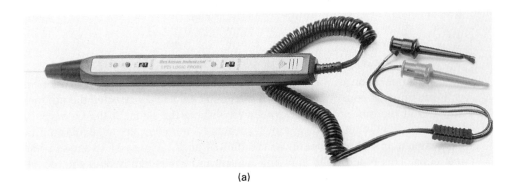

(a)

Figure 11.19 (a) Logic probe. (b) Digital multimeter. (c) Oscilloscope.

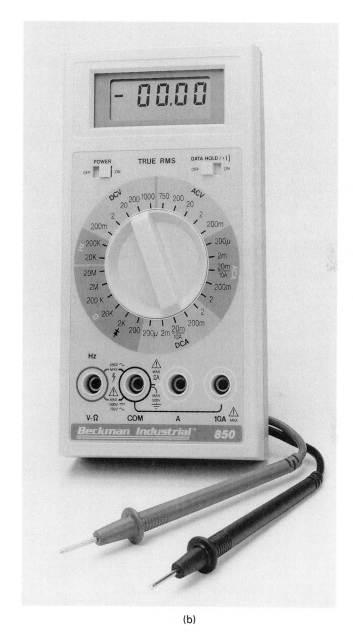

(b)

Figure 11.19   (Continued)

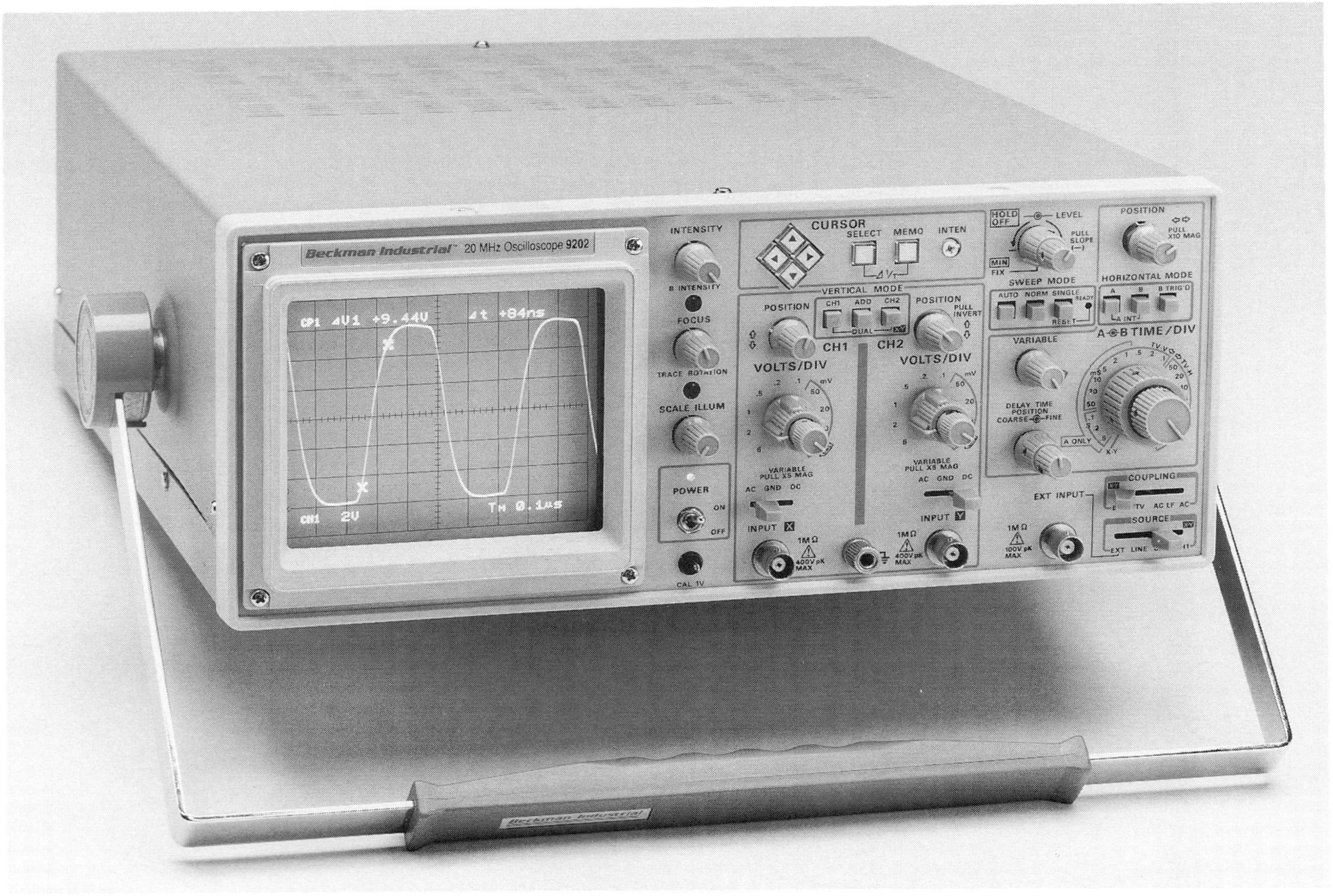

Figure 11.19 (Continued)

In microcomputer circuits, the multimeter is useful for measuring static voltage levels. For instance, it can be used to verify that +5 V is applied to each of the ICs. A multimeter can also be used to measure the logic levels at inputs and outputs, but they must be stable voltages, not pulsating signals. In this case, the meter displays the amount of voltage at the test point and from this value we can determine whether the signal is at logic 0, logic 1, or in the high-Z state.

Most multimeters also have the ability to measure resistance, AC voltage, AC and DC current. For instance, it could be used to find the amount of current the circuit draws from the V_{cc} supply.

We just mentioned that the logic probe can tell if the signal at a point under test is pulsating. However, in this case, a better instrument for observing the operation of the circuit is an oscilloscope (or *scope* as it is better known). The scope is the most widely used instrument for observing *periodic signals*. That is, signals, such as a square wave, that have a repeating pattern.

The scope displays the exact waveform of the pulsating signal on its screen. This type of representation gives us much more information. For instance, we can find the value of the high-voltage (logic 1), the value of the low-voltage (logic 0), how long the signal is at the 0 and 1 logic levels, and the shape of the signal as it transitions back and forth between 0 and 1. Figure 11.20(a) shows the shape of the signal produced at the Q_0 output at pin 2 of the 74LS374 when the diagnostic program that blinks LED_0 is running. The display of the waveform allows us to measure the period (T) of the square wave and calculate its frequency using

$$f = 1/T$$

Most scopes have the ability to display several signals on the screen at the same time. That is, they have several *signal channels.* The most common scope in use is the *dual-trace scope,* which has the ability to simultaneously display two signals. Figure 11.20(b) shows both the output square wave and clock input signals of our test circuit. In this example, the scope has been set up to synchronize the display of the square wave output, which is applied to channel 1, to the clock input at channel 2. For this reason, the waveforms represent their true relationship in time. Notice that a clock pulse is associated with the loading of each logic 0 and logic 1 into the Q_0 output of the latch. This mode of operation is known as using an *external sync.* That is, the sweep of the scope is initiated by an external signal, which in this case is the clock input.

Troubleshooting Microcomputer Interface Circuitry

In the testing of the operation of a circuit, we may find that it does not work. That is, it does not perform the function for which it was designed. In this case, we must identify what is the cause of the malfunction and then correct the problem. The process of finding the cause of a malfunction is called *troubleshooting* and the process of correcting the problem is known as *repair*. In this section we will look at some causes of malfunctions in circuits and then outline methods that can be used to troubleshoot microcomputer interface circuits.

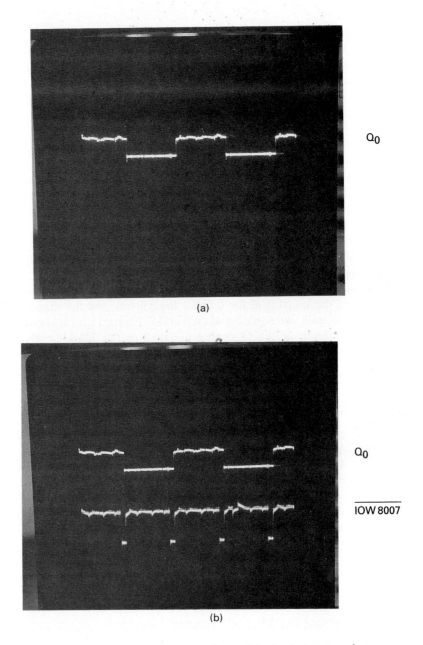

Figure 11.20 (a) Q_0 output waveform. (b) Clock input and square wave output.

The cause of problems found in malfunctioning circuits depends on the type of circuit being tested. In general electronic circuits fall into several categories. A first example is a breadboard of a new circuit design. In this case, the circuit may be working correctly, but not perform the function for which it was designed. That is, the malfunction may simply be due to the fact that a mistake was made in the design. This may be the most complicated type of failure to find and resolve.

The breadboard of a circuit we use in our laboratory exercises in this book is a second example. Here the circuit is known to operate correctly. For this reason, the most common causes for a circuit not to work are that a wiring mistake was made when the breadboard was built, or the software that was written to exercise the hardware has a bug.

A third example is a circuit in an existing electronic system, such as the IBM PC, that has failed. In this case, we know that the system had worked correctly in the past, but now malfunctions. Therefore, the cause of the problem may not be a mistake in the design, a wiring error, or incorrect software; instead, it is likely to be due to the failure of a component.

The final example is a circuit board, such as the main processor board of the IBM PC, that has just been built on a manufacturing line. Here a wide variety of malfunction causes exist. For instance, a lead of a component may not be correctly soldered; a lead of a device may be short circuited to a pin on another device with excess solder; the wrong component may have been inserted, or even a component may have been installed in reverse orientation.

Thus we have seen that there are many causes for a circuit to malfunction. In fact, most of the causes we just stated can affect any of the circuits. For instance, a short circuit could occur between the pins of two devices on the main processor board of the PC. This short may have been accidentally created when the system was opened to install an interface board, change the system configuration DIP switches, or replace another failing subsystem, such as a disk drive. As another example, it is also possible that a bad IC gets installed when building a breadboard of a circuit or even during the manufacturing of a printed circuit board. Finally, an open circuit may occur in a copper trace on the main processor circuit board of the PC even though the board had been working correctly for a long time. For instance, a crack may have been made by using too much force when inserting an interface board into the expansion bus connector.

Having looked at some of the causes of circuit failures, let us continue by exploring troubleshooting methods. We assume that the circuit is known to have worked previously. This would be the case in troubleshooting a circuit built for one of our laboratory exercises or when repairing an electronic system like a PC. We will begin with a general procedure that can be used to troubleshoot microcomputer interface circuits.

A general flowchart for testing and troubleshooting a microcomputer interface circuit is shown in Fig. 11.21. Here we will assume that a circuit breadboard and diagnostic software exist. Therefore, the first step is to test the operation of the interface. This is done by exercising the hardware by running the program and observing its operation visually or with instrumentation. If the hardware correctly performs its intended operation, the flowchart's Y path shows that we are done. On the other hand, if it does not work, the N path is taken. That is, we need to troubleshoot the circuit. It is important to remember that circuits may not work due to problems in either software or hardware or both software and hardware.

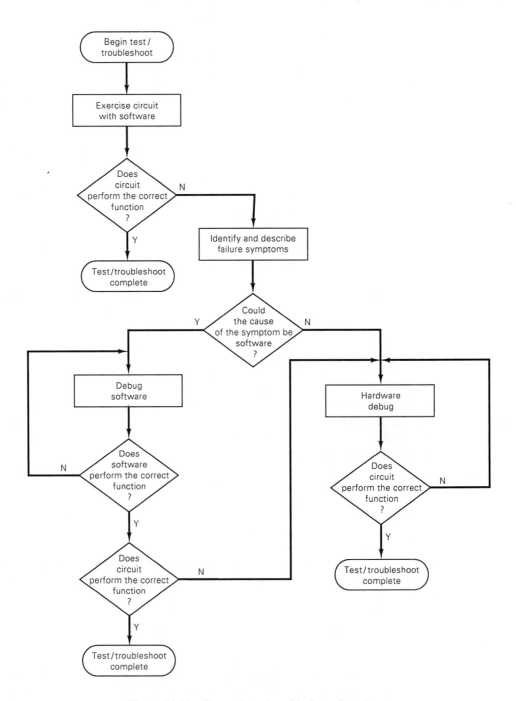

Figure 11.21 General test/troubleshoot flowchart.

Figure 11.21 shows that the first step in the troubleshooting part of the process is to identify and describe the symptoms of the failure. It is important to make a clear and concise description of the problem before beginning to examine the software or hardware. For example, in the case of the test circuit in Fig. 11.16(a), running the diagnostic program blinks LED 0. The failure symptom may be that the LED just remains off or it may turn on, but not blink.

Now we must decide whether or not software can be ruled out as a cause of the problem. For example, in a laboratory exercise where the program is given, software should not be the cause of the malfunction. Also, in the case of an application program running on a PC, which is known to have no bugs, software may be ruled out. In cases where correct software operation cannot be assumed, the operation of the program should be analyzed before testing the circuitry. That is, as shown in Fig. 11.21, software debug is the next step. If the program is found to be correct, the N path is followed in the flowchart and then hardware troubleshooting is begun.

When bugs are found in the program, they must be corrected and then the Y path is taken. Here we see that the interface circuit is retested to verify whether the software fixes make it work correctly. If the interface circuit does operate correctly, troubleshooting is complete.

Let us assume that the interface still does not function correctly. Then Fig. 11.21 shows that hardware troubleshooting must begin. After the hardware problems are identified and corrected, the interface circuit is once again tested.

Now that we have covered the general test and troubleshooting procedure, we will continue by looking more closely at the software debug part of the process. The steps in the software debug process are identified in the flowchart of Fig. 11.22. Notice that first the programming of any VLSI peripheral ICs in the circuit must be verified to be correct. If they are programmed as part of the program, the programming sequence and command values can be reviewed. In fact, software can be added to read back the contents of the registers (if possible) after programming to verify that they have been updated. In our example circuit of Fig. 11.16(a), there are no peripheral ICs. So this step is not required.

Next, the addresses corresponding to I/O devices or memory locations and data that are to be transferred over the bus must be checked. This will verify that the correct data is transferred and that it will go to the correct place in the circuit. In the square wave program we wrote earlier to blink LED_0, the address of the LED latch, which is 0007_{16}, is loaded into DX and the initial data that is to be output to the latch, 01_{16}, is loaded into AL. Both of these values are correct for the circuit under test.

Finally, the flowchart in Fig. 11.22 shows that the last step in the software debug process is to check the algorithm and its software implementation. This can be done by rechecking the flowchart to confirm that it provides a valid solution to the problem and then comparing the instruction sequence against the flowchart to assure that it implements this algorithm. The instructions of the program can also be traced through to verify correct operation for a known test case.

If software is not the cause of the problem, attention must be turned to the hardware. A general hardware troubleshooting procedure is outlined in Fig. 11.23.

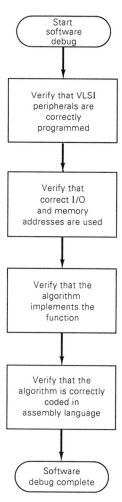

Figure 11.22 Software debug flowchart.

For now we will assume that the circuit undergoing troubleshooting is a breadboard built on the PCμLAB.

The first step identified in the flowchart is to make a thorough visual inspection of the circuit to assure that it is correctly constructed. This includes verifying that the correct IC pin numbers are marked into the schematic diagram; the circuit diagram layout does implement the circuit in the schematic; and that all jumper connections are consistent with those identified in the layout diagram. Second, the mechanical connections of the circuit should be checked to verify that they make good electrical connections. That is, the pins of the ICs are making good contact with the contacts of the solderless breadboard and that the wire connections provide good continuity between pins of the various ICs. The continuity tester of the PCμLAB can be used to check out these connections.

If the circuit connections are correct, the flowchart shows that the next step is to check out the power supply. That is, we should verify that +5 V is applied

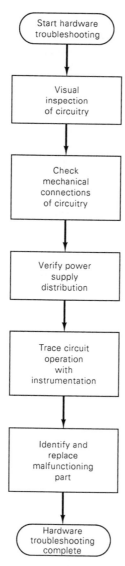

Figure 11.23 Hardware debug flowchart.

between the V_{cc} and GND pins of each IC. Here we are normally interested in knowing the exact amount of voltage. For this reason, the voltage measurements are usually taken with a multimeter. Since the $+V_{cc}$ supply of TTL ICs is rated at +5 V 5%, power supply measurements between +5.25 V and +4.75 V are satisfactory.

After the circuit connections and power supply have been ruled out as the cause of the malfunction, we are ready to begin checking the operation of the circuit. To be successful at this, we must understand the operation, signal flow through the circuit, and waveshapes expected at select test points. Typically, operation is traced by observing signals starting from the output and working back towards the input in an attempt to identify the point in the circuit up to which correct signals exist. For instance, in our breadboard circuit, we can begin by examining the waveform across the LED with an oscilloscope. This spot is identified as test point 1 (TP1) in the schematic of Fig. 11.24 and corresponds to pin 8 of resistor pack R_{19}. Assuming that a symmetrical square wave is not observed, the probe of the scope can be moved to pin 18 of the 74LS240 IC, test point 2 (TP2). If a square wave is not present there either, the next test point should be the input of the inverter at pin 2 of the 74LS240 (TP3). Assuming that the square wave signal is again not found, the output at pin 2 of the 74LS374 data latch, TP4, should be checked. This completes tracing of the data path from LED_0 to the data bus.

If a square wave is not observed at any test point in the data path from data bus line SD_0 to LED_0, the problem may be in the chip select decoder circuit. Earlier we found that this circuit produces the clock that loads the data into the 74LS374 latch. Notice that the clock is applied to pin 11 on U_2, which is identified as TP5. This signal is not a symmetrical square wave; instead, it is a repeating pulse that would appear as an asymmetrical square wave on the screen of a scope. Assuming that a pulse is not observed, this would be the reason that data is not being loaded from the data bus into the latch. In this case, the signal path of the latching

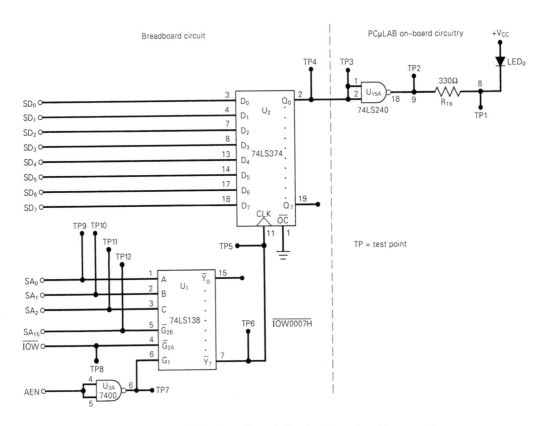

Figure 11.24 Breadboard circuit schematic with test points.

pulse must be traced back to pin 7 of the 74LS138, TP6, in an attempt to locate the pulse.

Let us assume that no clock pulse is observed at pin 7 of the 74LS138 IC. Then, we should continue by checking for signals $\overline{IOW}$ and $\overline{AEN}$ at inputs G_{2A} and G_1, respectively. There should be active low pulses on both $\overline{IOW}$ and $\overline{AEN}$. These points are identified as TP7 and TP8 in the circuit diagram of Fig. 11.24. If that is the case, the only signals that remain to be checked are address lines SA_0, SA_1, SA_2, and SA_{15} connected to A, B, C, and $\overline{G_{2B}}$, respectively. These signals are denoted as TP9, TP10, TP11, and TP12, respectively. To do this the sweep of the scope can be synchronized with $\overline{IOW}$ at $\overline{G_{2A}}$ and the logic levels that exist at inputs A, B, C, and $\overline{G_{2B}}$ observed during this pulse. Assuming that code CBA equals 110 and $\overline{G_{2A}} = 0$, output $\overline{Y_7}$ should be a pulse similar to that at $\overline{G_{2A}}$. Since no pulse was found at pin 7, we have found the source of the problem. The 74LS138 IC is bad and must be replaced.

After the bad IC is replaced, the operation is again observed. If LED_0 blinks, troubleshooting is complete. Otherwise, troubleshooting resumes by verifying that the clock pulse is produced at pin 7 of the 74LS138 and is passed to the clock input of 74LS374 data latch.

If an oscilloscope is not available, many of the test measurements during the troubleshooting process we just outlined can be made with the logic probe of the PCμLAB. For instance, the signals at the G_1, $\overline{G_{2A}}$ and $\overline{G_{2B}}$ enable inputs of the 74LS138 address decoder can be tested. However, the logic probe is not as versatile as the oscilloscope. For example, with the scope we could verify the logic level of the address inputs to the address decoder. This type of synchronous measurement at the time when $\overline{IOW}$ is 0 cannot be made with a logic probe.

Another instrument that is useful in troubleshooting microcomputer interface circuits is a *logic pulser*. The logic pulser can be set to output either a one-shot pulse or a square wave. This instrument can be used to inject a pulse or square wave into the input of a device in the circuit. Figure 11.25 shows a typical logic pulser.

Let us now look briefly at how a logic pulser can be used when troubleshooting the circuit in Fig. 11.24. The pulser would be set to pulse mode of operation and then the pulse injected at test point 2. As long as the connection through the resistor pack is good, the LED_0 should blink. Assuming that this part of the circuit works correctly, the pulser's probe can next be touched to test point 3. Again, the LED should blink. This verifies whether or not the 74LS240 inverter operates correctly. Just as with the oscilloscope, the logic pulser is used to check out the circuit step by step.

Hardware troubleshooting of circuit boards in a manufacturing environment can be quite different. Still a visual inspection is performed, but to look for different things. For instance, the quality of solder joints is checked. That is, whether they have enough solder, are of the correct shape, and that there are no solder shorts between pins of ICs and other components.

After a board has passed visual inspection, it is ready for circuit test. In this case the board is not tested with instruments circuit by circuit as we just described; instead, it is checked out with an automatic test system. The tester is programmed to perform a series of tests on the circuit board. The system provides information

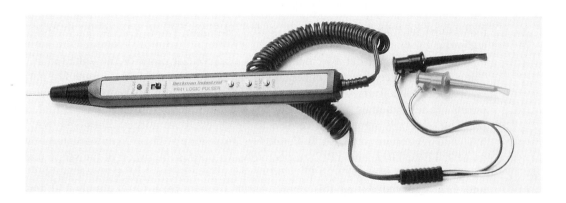

Figure 11.25 Logic pulser.

on tests that have passed and failed to guide the repair process. In this way, the board is tested and repaired step by step until it is completely functional.

Troubleshooting of an electronic system, such as a PC, that has been working is also different. In this case, we will assume that the symptoms of the problem have been identified; that the software is functional; and that we are investigating a hardware problem. Actually, servicing of a PC is normally a system level repair. That is, the failing subassembly (main processor board, add-on card, power supply, floppy-disk drive, keyboard, or monitor) is identified and replaced.

The hardware troubleshooting procedure outlined in Fig. 11.23 still applies to a system level repair. Therefore, the first step is a visual inspection; however, the inspection performed is different than that used when examining a breadboard or circuit board that just came off of the manufacturing line and includes a number of mechanical checks. For example, the system should be checked to verify that all cables are securely connected, the setting of the DIP switches and jumpers should be checked to assure that the system configuration is correct, and the surface of the circuit boards can be examined looking for overheated or burned components. An example of a mechanical check is to touch the components to see if any are abnormally hot, but be careful with this because some devices can get very hot. Moreover, to assure that the problem is not due to dirty connector contacts, the cables and add-on boards are removed, their contacts are cleaned, and then they are reseated into the connector.

Next we must begin to check the circuits and subassemblies. If the PC does not come up at all when the power switch is turned on, the first step should be to check the power supply voltages. However, if it boots up and loads the DOS operating system, diagnostic software, such as QAPlus™ by DiagSoft, Inc., can be used to analyze the function of the system. The diagnostic disk is inserted into the floppy-disk drive and the diagnostic program initiated from the keyboard. This program can exercise each of the PC's subassemblies and displays information indicating whether they have passed or failed the diagnostic tests.

Let us assume that the hard disk controller in a PC has failed the diagnostic test. The normal system level repair procedure is to replace the complete controller with another one to quickly get the system back up running. The bad board is usually returned to a circuit board repair location for IC level troubleshooting and repair. Some diagnostic programs permit IC level troubleshooting of the dynamic memory subsystem. In the case of a memory failure, the diagnostic program can identify the bad IC. Since many of the DRAMs in the PC are socket mounted, the repair may be made by replacing the failing device.

▲ 11.6 OBSERVING MICROCOMPUTER BUS ACTIVITY WITH A DIGITAL LOGIC ANALYZER

Up to this point, we observed signal waveforms in the microcomputer with an oscilloscope. However, this instrument only permits viewing of limited periodic signals at a time. The address, data, and control busses in a microcomputer have many lines. For instance, the data bus alone is eight bits wide in an 8088-based PC. When the microcomputer is running, the data bus could be returning read data or instruction code to the MPU, sending write data to memory, or be in the high-Z state if no bus activity is taking place. Moreover, the data being transferred is rarely the same; therefore, data bus activity is also not periodic.

To observe the operation of the data bus signals, we need to see the logic states of all eight data bits and some of the read/write control signals at the same time. This is not possible with a scope. It is for this type of measurement that an instrument known as a *digital logic analyzer* was developed. Let us now look briefly at what a logic analyzer is and what it is used for in testing microcomputer systems.

The logic analyzer is a modern digital test instrument that is very useful for testing and troubleshooting microcomputer systems. With it, nonperiodic signals, such as those of the address bus, data bus, and control bus can be measured and their waveforms viewed. Figure 11.26 shows a typical logic analyzer. Today, this type of instrument is available with 8, 16, or 32 channels. This means that they are capable of simultaneously sampling and displaying the waveshapes of up to 8, 16, or 32 signals. The probe is a pod that has clips for inputs to each channel. They are attached to the signals that are to be observed. For example, the data lines D_0 through D_7 and control signals, such as $\overline{RD}$, $\overline{WR}$, DT/$\overline{R}$, IO/$\overline{M}$, $\overline{DEN}$, READY, S_3, and S_4, can be sampled to monitor transfers over the data bus.

The logic analyzer operates differently than an oscilloscope. The oscilloscope immediately displays the voltage of the signal applied at its input. On the other hand, the logic analyzer samples the voltage at all inputs at a very high rate. This information is stored in memory as a logic 0 or logic 1, and not as a specific voltage level. The waveform of the signal can then be displayed on the screen using the stored data. The user of the instrument has the ability to start the sampling based on the occurrence of a specific event or events indicated by a combination of the logic values of the signal being monitored and continue until the trace buffer memory is full. Moreover, most logic analyzers permit the stored information to be displayed in a variety of ways.

Figure 11.26 Digital logic analyzer. (Hewlett-Packard Co.)

Sample waveforms taken from our test circuit in Fig. 11.16(a) are shown in Fig. 11.27(a). This display shows the address, data transfer, and address decoder output produced when the LED blink diagnostic routine runs. Here we see a timing diagram that clearly illustrates the relationship between the address, decoder output, and the data transfer to the latch. Notice that whenever address decoder output $\overline{\text{IOWX0007H}}$ switches from logic 0 to logic 1, the byte of data on the data bus, which is 00000001_2, is latched into the 74LS374 device and makes Q_0 switch to logic 1. Figure 4.27(b) shows the signals when the Q_0 output switches from logic 1 back to 0. Both transitions at Q_0 are shown with a single timing diagram in Fig. 4.27(c). Remember that the logic analyzer cannot display signals the way they really would look if observed with an oscilloscope. Since it just saves the logic level (0 or 1) of the signals in memory, waveshapes are shown with sharp transitions between these logic levels. When observed with a scope, the waveshapes may show rise and fall times between the 0 and 1 levels, and possibly *ringing*, *overshoots* and *undershoots* around the 0 and 1 logic levels.

A logic analyzer can also be set up to collect just code or data transfers over the data bus. Once this information is stored in memory, it can be *disassembled* into assembly language instructions and displayed on the screen. Figure 11.28 shows an example where a logic analyzer was used to disassemble a series of instructions. This capability permits us to monitor the execution of instructions by the MPU and compare the instruction execution sequence to events observed in the hardware.

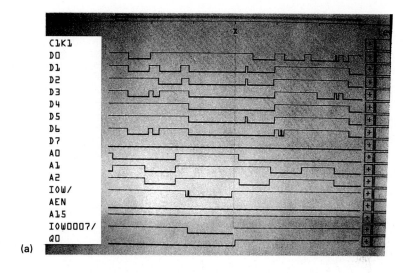

(a)

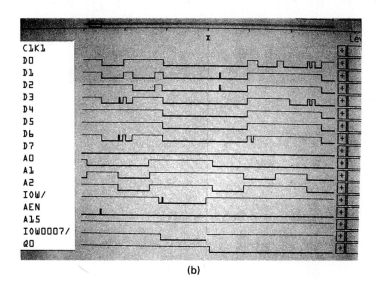

(b)

Figure 11.27 (a) Timing diagram for 0 to 1 transition at Q_0. (b) Timing diagram for 1 to 0 transition at Q_0. (c) Timing diagram showing both transitions at Q_0.

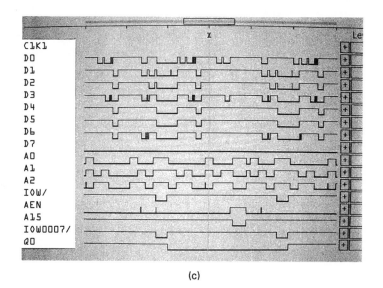

(c)

Figure 11.27 (Continued)

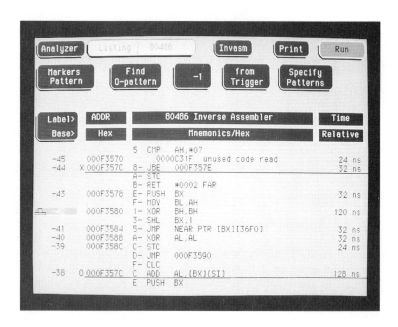

Figure 11.28 Disassembling code with a logic analyzer (Hewlett-Packard).

ASSIGNMENTS

Section 11.2

1. What is an experimental circuit board that is built to test an electronic function called?
2. What is a breadboard card?
3. What kind of breadboard does not require devices to be soldered in place; instead, they can be plugged in?
4. What is the purpose of an extender card?
5. List the parts of the PCμLAB.

Section 11.3

6. List three types of I/O devices that are built into the PCμLAB.
7. How are the on-board I/O devices set up for use with circuits built on the breadboard area?
8. How many I/O channel expansion slots are provided on the PCμLAB?
9. What size wire jumpers must be used to interconnect circuits on the breadboard area?
10. Which wire insertion clips are intended for use as the +5 V and GND for power distribution on the solderless breadboard?
11. At which contacts of the I/O channel connector are address lines A_0 through A_{19} available?
12. What is the purpose of the PCμLAB's continuity tester? How does it signal continuity?
13. Identify how the PCμLAB's logic probe signals the 0, 1, and high-Z logic states.
14. How does the logic probe identify that the signal at a test point is switching between the 0 and 1 logic levels?

Section 11.4

15. Which ICs are used in the I/O address decoder circuit of the PCμLAB?
16. Which output of the I/O address decoder circuit is used to enable data output to the LEDs?
17. Which I/O address bits are don't-care states?
18. Does the I/O address $771E_{16}$ activate an output of the I/O address decoder circuit? If so, which output signal is activated?
19. Why are the I/O select outputs of the I/O address decoder circuits produced only during I/O bus cycles?
20. If switches S_0 through S_3 are closed and switches S_4 through S_7 are open, what value will be transferred over the data bus when the switches are read with an IN instruction?

21. Will the command

$$\text{I FF1D } (\hookleftarrow)$$

read the state of the on-board switches?

22. Write an instruction sequence that will read the state of the switches, mask off all switch settings but S_0 and S_1, and if both switches are found to be closed, a jump is to be initiated to a service routine called SERVE_3.

23. What operation is performed by the instruction sequence that follows?

```
          MOV DX,31DH
POLL:     IN  AL,DX
          MOV CL,8
          SHR AL,CL
          JC  POLL
```

24. Which LED is driven with data from data bus line D_0? From D_7?

25. What will the command O FF1E 0F do?

26. Write a program that will scan the LEDs on the PCμLAB. That is, first light L_0 for a period of time, next turn off L_0 and turn on L_1, and so on until L_7 is lighted. The scan sequence should repeat continuously.

27. Describe the operation performed by the following instruction sequence

```
          MOV DX,31EH
          MOV AL,0H
BIN:      OUT DX,AL
          MOV CX,0FFFFH
DELAY:    DEC CX
          JNZ DELAY
          INC AL
          JMP BIN
```

28. What IC is used to drive the speaker?

29. Which instruction in the tone generation program given in the section on the speaker drive circuit needs to be changed to double the frequency of the tone? Write the new instruction.

Section 11.5

30. Write an instruction that reads the switch setting into AL in Fig. 11.29.

31. Mark the pin numbers into the circuit of Fig. 11.29 and then make a layout drawing on a circuit diagram master.

32. What is a program that is used to test the operation of a microcomputer circuit called?

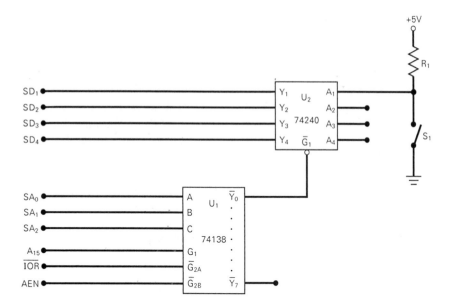

Figure 11.29 Switch input interface circuit.

33. What accessory is attached to the top of an IC to make it easier to connect the probe of an instrument?

34. Name three instruments that can be used to test the operation of a microcomputer interface circuit.

35. What information does a logic probe provide about the signal at a test point in a circuit?

36. When used to measure voltage, what information does a multimeter tell about the signal at a test point?

37. What information does an oscilloscope provide about the signal at a test point?

38. What is meant by *periodic signal*?

39. What is the process for determining the cause of a hardware malfunction in a circuit called?

40. If a breadboard of a circuit does not work when tested with a diagnostic program that was just written and never checked on working hardware, should hardware troubleshooting or software debug take place next?

41. Assume that a diagnostic program is available that has been checked out and verified to correctly test the interface. If a new PC interface module is tested and fails when checked out with this diagnostic program, what is the next step—software debug or hardware troubleshooting?

42. List three items that should be checked as part of the software debug process.

43. List three visual inspections that can be made as part of the hardware troubleshooting process used to determine why a circuit built on the breadboard area of the PCµLAB does not work.

44. During the hardware troubleshooting process of a breadboard circuit, what should be checked next if the circuit is found to be correctly constructed?

45. Assume that the circuit in Fig. 11.29 is being driven by a software routine that polls the state of switch 0 and that this program is known to operate correctly. What type of signal would you expect to see at test point 1 when the switch is closed and also when open? At test point 2? At test point 3?

46. If the results found at test points 1 and 2 of problem 45 when troubleshooting the circuit are:

Test point	Switch open	Switch closed
1	1	0
2	1	1

What do you think is the problem with the circuit?

Section 11.6

47. List three key groups of signals of the microcomputer system that are in general nonperiodic.

48. What instrument is usually used to observe nonperiodic signals in a microcomputer?

49. Compare an oscilloscope and a logic analyzer.

12

Real-Mode Software and Hardware Architecture of the 80286 Microprocessor

▲ 12.1 INTRODUCTION

The 80286 microprocessor is the MPU used to design IBM's original PCAT. This microprocessor can operate in either of two modes, the *real-address mode* (real mode) or the *protected-address mode* (protected mode). In the PCAT, it is used to implement a real mode microcomputer. This chapter focuses on just the real mode software and hardware architecture of the 80286. Here we will first examine the real-address mode software architecture and its extended instruction set. Then we study the hardware architecture of the 80286-based microcomputer system. In this chapter, we examine the signal interfaces of the 80286, its memory interface, I/O interface, and interrupts and exception processing. For this purpose, we discuss the following topics in the chapter.

1. The 80286 microprocessor
2. Internal architecture
3. Real-mode software model
4. Real-mode extended instruction set
5. Interfaces of the 80286
6. The 82288 bus controller
7. System clock
8. The bus cycle and bus states

9. Memory interface

10. I/O interface

11. Interrupt and exception processing

▲ 12.2 THE 80286 MICROPROCESSOR

The 80286, first announced in 1982, was the fifth member of Intel Corporation's 8086 microprocessor family. We already mentioned that the 80286 offers two modes of operation: real mode for compatibility with the existing 8086/8088 software base and protected mode, which offers enhanced system-level features such as memory management, multitasking, and protection. A number of changes have been made to both the software and hardware architecture of the 80286, primarily to improve its performance. For example, additional pipelining is provided within the 80286 to provide higher performance, the instruction set is enhanced with new instructions, the address and data buses are demultiplexed to simplify system design, and the bus is designed to support interleaved memory subsystems.

The original 80286 was manufactured using the high-performance metal-oxide-semiconductor III (HMOSIII) process, and its circuitry is equivalent to approximately 125,000 transistors. It is available in *plastic leaded chip carrier* (PLCC), *ceramic leadless chip carrier* (LCC), and *pin grid array* (PGA) packages. An 80286 in the LCC package is shown in Fig. 12.1. The PLCC is the lowest-cost package type and is the most widely used in commercial applications such as personal computers. The LCC and PGA are more rugged and are typically used in applications that require higher reliability.

Figure 12.1   80286 IC.
(Courtesy of Intel Corp.)

Each of these packages has 68 leads. The signal available on each lead is shown in Fig. 12.2. Notice that unlike in the earlier 8086 and 8088 devices, none of the signal lines of the 80286 is multiplexed with another signal. This is intended to simplify the microcomputer circuit design.

▲ 12.3 INTERNAL ARCHITECTURE

The internal architecture of the 80286 microprocessor is shown in Fig. 12.3. The 8086 and 8088 had just two processing units, the bus interface unit (BIU) and

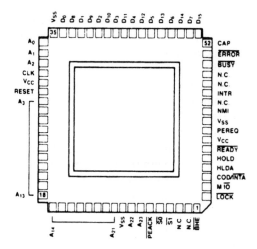

Figure 12.2 Pin layout of the 80286.
(Courtesy of Intel Corp.)

execution unit (EU). In Fig. 12.3 we find that the 80286 is internally partitioned into four independent processing units: the *bus unit* (BU), the *instruction unit* (IU), the *execution unit* (EU), and the *address unit* (AU). This additional parallel processing provides an important contribution to the higher level of performance achieved with the 80286 architecture.

The bus unit is the 80286's interface with the outside world. It provides a 16-bit data bus, 24-bit address bus, and the signals needed to control bus transfers. These buses are demultiplexed instead of multiplexed as in the 8086/8088 hardware architecture; that is, the 80286 has separate pins for its address and data lines. Demultiplexing of these buses improves the performance of the 80286's hardware architecture.

The bus unit is responsible for performing all external bus operations. In Fig. 12.3 we see that this processing unit contains the latches and drivers for the address bus, transceivers for the data bus, and control logic for generating the control signals needed to perform memory and I/O bus cycles.

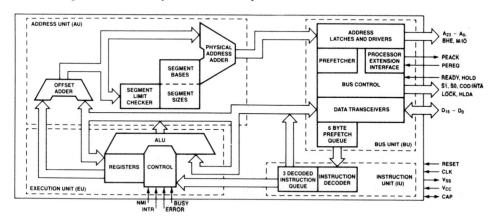

Figure 12.3 Internal architecture of the 80286. (Courtesy of Intel Corp.)

Sec. 12.3 Internal Architecture

Notice in Fig. 12.3 that the bus unit also contains elements called the *prefetcher* and *prefetch queue*. Together these elements implement a mechanism known as an *instruction stream queue*. This queue permits the 80286 to prefetch up to six bytes of instruction code. Whenever the queue is not full, that is, whenever it has room for at least two more bytes and, at the same time, the execution unit is not asking it to read or write operands from memory, the bus unit is free to look ahead in the program by fetching the next sequential instructions. These prefetched instructions are held in a first-in, first-out (FIFO) queue. With its 16-bit data bus, the 80286 fetches two instruction bytes in a single memory cycle. When a byte is loaded at the input end of the queue, all other bytes shift up through the FIFO to the empty locations nearer the output. In this way, the fetch time for most instructions is hidden.

The prefetcher that is provided in the 80286's bus unit has more intelligence than the one implemented in the 8086/8088 architecture. It has the ability to determine if an instruction that has been prefetched will cause a transfer in program control; for instance, a jump. When this type of instruction is detected, the queue is flushed and prefetch resumes at the point to which control is to be passed. The reset of the queue happens prior to the actual execution of the instruction. This feature results in an additional performance improvement for the 80286.

The address unit provides the memory management and protection services for the 80286. It off-loads the responsibility for address generation, translations, and checking from the bus unit and thereby further boosts the performance of the MPU. It contains dedicated hardware for performing high-speed address calculations, virtual-to-physical address translations, and limit and access rights attribute checks. For instance, in the real mode, the address unit calculates the address of the next instruction to be fetched. This is done by shifting the current contents of the code segment (CS) register left by four bit positions, filling the least significant bits with 0s, and adding the value in the instruction pointer (IP) register. This gives the 20-bit physical address that is output on the address bus. For protected mode, the address unit performs more functions. For instance, it performs the various address translations and protection checks needed when performing protected mode bus cycles.

Looking at Fig. 12.3 we see that the instruction unit accesses the output end of the prefetch queue. It reads one instruction byte after the other from the output of the queue and decodes them into the 69-bit instruction format used by the 80286's execution unit; that is, it off-loads the responsibility for instruction decoding from the execution unit. The instruction queue within the instruction unit permits three fully decoded instructions to be held waiting for the execution unit. Once again the result is improved performance for the MPU.

Notice in Fig. 12.3 that the execution unit includes the *arithmetic logic unit* (ALU), the 80286's registers, and a control ROM. The block labeled registers represents all the user-accessible registers, such as the general-purpose registers and segment registers. The control ROM contains the microcode sequences that define the operations performed by the 80286's instructions. The execution unit reads decoded instructions from the instruction queue and performs the operations that they specify. If necessary during the execution of an instruction, it requests that the address unit generate operand addresses and that the bus unit perform read or write bus cycles to access data in memory or at an I/O device.

▲ 12.4 REAL-MODE SOFTWARE MODEL

We will begin our study of the 80286 microprocessor by exploring its real-address mode software model and operation. Whenever the 80286 is powered on or reset, it comes up in the real mode. The 80286 will remain in the real mode unless it is switched to protected mode under software control. In fact, in many applications the 80286 is simply used in real mode.

In real mode, the 80286 operates like a high-performance 8086. For example, the standard 8-MHz 80286 provides more than five times higher performance than the standard 5-MHz 8086. Furthermore, the 10-MHz 80286 outperforms the 10-MHz 8086 by a factor of 7.

When in the real mode, the 80286 can be used to execute the base instruction set of the 8086/8088 architectures. The object code for the base instructions of the 80286 is identical to that of the 8086/8088. This means that operating systems and programs written for the 8086 and 8088 can be run on the 80286 without modification. An example is the disk operating system (DOS) of the original IBM PC. This operating system also runs on the 80286 in the original PCAT. For this reason, we can say that the 80286 is *object code compatible* with the 8086 and 8088 micro-processors.

A number of new instructions have been added in the instruction set of the 80286 to enhance performance and functionality. For example, instructions have been added to push or pop the complete register set, perform string I/O, and check the boundaries of data array accesses. We also say that object code is *upward compatible* within the 8086 architecture. By this, we mean that 8086/8088 object code will run on the 80286, but the reverse is not true if any of the new instructions are in use.

The real-mode software model of the 80286 is shown in Fig. 12.4. Here we see that it has 15 internal registers. Fourteen of them, the instruction pointer (IP), data registers (AX, BX, CX, and DX), pointer registers (BP and SP), index registers (SI and DI), segment registers (CS, DS, SS, and ES), and the flag register (F) are identical to the corresponding registers in the 8086's software model, and they serve the same functions. For instance, CS:IP points to the next instruction that is to be fetched.

A new register called the *machine status word register* (MSW) is added in the 80286 model. The only bit in MSW that is active in the real mode is the *protected-mode enable* (PE) bit. This is the bit that is used to switch the 80286 from real to protected mode.

Looking at Fig. 12.4, we find that the 80286 microcomputer's real-mode address space is also identical to that of the 8086 microcomputer. It is partitioned into a 1MB memory address space and a separate 64KB input/output address space. The memory address space resides in the range from address 00000_{16} to $FFFFF_{16}$. I/O addresses span 64KB of the range 0000_{16} to $FFFF_{16}$. Moreover, in the memory

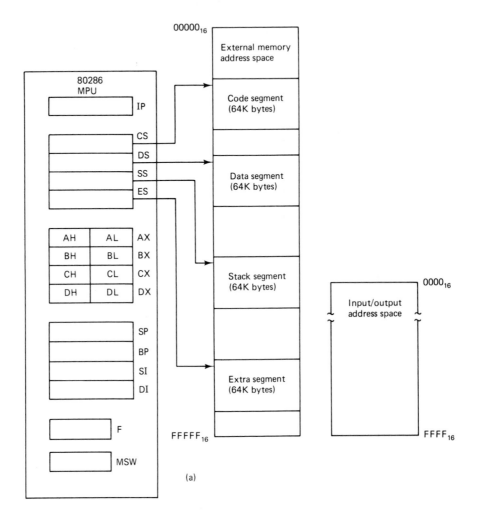

Figure 12.4 Real-mode software model of the 80286 microprocessor.

address space, just four 64KB segments are active at a time for a total of 256KB of active memory. Again, 64KB of the active memory are allocated for code storage, 64KB for stack, and 128KB for data storage.

Figures 12.5(a) and (b) show that the real-mode 80286 memory and I/O address spaces are partitioned into general-use and reserved areas in the same way as for the 8086. For instance, in Fig. 12.5(a) we find that the first 1KB of the memory address space, addresses 0_{16} through $3FF_{16}$, are reserved and are used for storage of the interrupt vector table. Figure 12.5(b) shows that the first 256-byte I/O addresses are identified as page 0. Page 0 are the I/O addresses that are directly accessible with an IN or OUT instruction.

Finally, the real-mode 80286 generates physical addresses in the same manner as the 8086. This address generation is illustrated in Fig. 12.6. Notice that the 16-

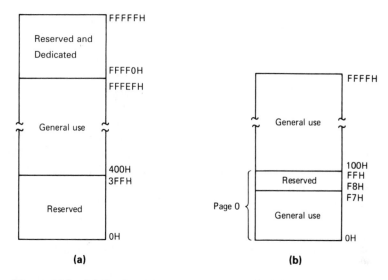

Figure 12.5 (a) Dedicated and general use of memory in real-mode. (Courtesy of Intel Corp.) (b) I/O address space. (Courtesy of Intel Corp.)

bit contents of a segment register, such as CS, are shifted left by four bit positions, the four least-significant bits are filled with 0s, and the result is added to a 16-bit logical address, such as the value in IP, to form the 20-bit physical memory address.

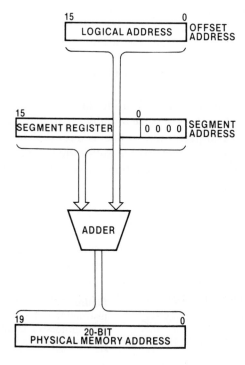

Figure 12.6 Real-address mode physical address generation. (Courtesy of Intel Corp.)

Figure 12.7 shows the evolution of the instruction set for the 8086 architecture. The instruction set of the 8086 and 8088 microprocessors, which is called the *base instruction set*, was enhanced in the 80286 microprocessor to implement what is called the *extended instruction set*. This extended instruction set includes several new instructions and implements additional addressing modes. For example, two instructions added as extensions to the basic instruction set are *push all* (PUSHA) and *pop all* (POPA). In Fig. 12.8, we see that the PUSH and IMUL instructions have been enhanced to permit the use of immediate operand addressing. In this way, we see that the 80286's real-mode instruction set is a superset of the basic instruction set. These instructions are all executable by the 80286 in the real mode. Let us now look at these and the other new instructions in more detail.

Push-All and Pop-All Instructions—PUSHA and POPA

When writing the compiler for a high-level language such as C, it is very common to push the contents of all of the general registers of the 80286 to the stack before calling a subroutine. If we use the PUSH instruction to perform this operation, many instructions are needed. To simplify this operation, special instructions are provided in the instruction set of the 80286. They are called push all (PUSHA) and pop all (POPA).

Looking at Fig. 12.8 we see that execution of PUSHA causes the values in AX, CX, DX, BX, SP, BP, SI, and DI to be pushed, in that order, onto the top of the stack. Figure 12.9 shows the state of the stack before and after execution of the instruction. As shown in Fig. 12.10, executing a POPA instruction at the end of the subroutine restores the old state of the 80286.

Stack Frame Instructions—ENTER and LEAVE

Before the main program calls a subroutine, quite often it is necessary for the calling program to pass the values of some *variables* (parameters) to the subroutine. It is a common practice to push these variables onto the stack before calling the routine. Then during the execution of the subroutine, they are accessed by reading from the stack and used in computations. Two instructions are provided

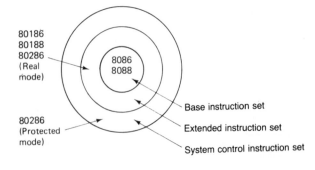

Figure 12.7 Evolution of the instruction set for the 8086 microprocessor family. (Courtesy of Intel Corp.)

Mnemonic	Meaning	Format	Operation
PUSH	Push	PUSH dw/db	Push the specified data word (dw) or sign extended data byte (db) onto the stack.
PUSHA	Push all	PUSHA	Push the contents of registers AX, CX, DX, BX, original SP, BP, SI, and DI onto the stack.
POPA	Pop all	POPA	Pop the stack contents into the registers DI, SI, BP, SP, BX, DX, CX, and AX.
IMUL	Integer multiply	IMUL rw, ew, dw/db	Perform the signed multiplication as follows: rw = ew*dw/db where rw is the word size register, ew is the effective word size operand, and the third operand is the immediate data word (dw) or a byte (db).
Logic instructions		Instruction db	Perform the logic instruction using the specified byte (db) as the count.
INS	Input string	INSB, INSW	Input the byte or the word size element of the string from the port specified by DX to the location ES:[DI].
OUTS	Output string	OUTSB, OUTSW	Output the byte or the word size element of the string from ES:[SI] to port specified by DX.
ENTER	Enter procedure	ENTER dw, 0/1/db	Make stack frame for procedure parameters.
LEAVE	Leave procedure	LEAVE	Release the stack space used by the procedure.
BOUND	Check array index against bounds	BOUND rw, md	Interrupt 5 occurs if the register word (rw) is not greater than or equal to the memory word at md and not less than or equal to the second memory word at md + 1.

Figure 12.8 Extended instruction set.

in the extended instruction set of the 80286 to allocate and de-allocate a data area called a *stack frame*. This data area, which is located in the stack part of memory, is used for local storage of parameters and other data used by the subroutine.

Normally, high-level languages allocate a stack frame for each procedure in a program. The stack frame provides a dynamically allocated local storage space for the procedure and contains data such as variables, pointers to the stack frames of the previous procedures from which the current procedure was called, and a return address for linkage to the stack frame of the calling procedure. This mechanism also permits access to the data in stack frames of the calling procedures.

The instructions used for allocation and de-allocation of stack frames are given in Fig. 12.8 as *enter* (ENTER) and *leave* (LEAVE). Execution of an ENTER instruction allocates a stack frame; it is de-allocated by executing the LEAVE instruction. For this reason, as shown in Fig. 12.11, the ENTER instruction is

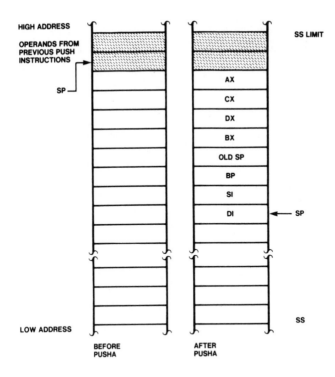

Figure 12.9 State of the stack before and after executing PUSHA. (Courtesy of Intel Corp.)

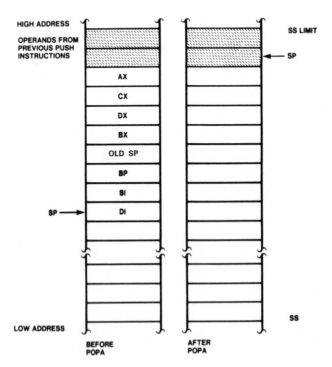

Figure 12.10 State of the stack before and after executing POPA. (Courtesy of Intel Corp.)

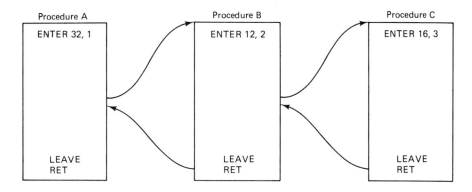

Figure 12.11 Enter/leave example.

used at the beginning of a subroutine, and LEAVE at the end, just before the return instruction.

Looking at Fig. 12.8, we find that the ENTER instruction has two operands. The first operand, identified as dw, is a word-size immediate operand. This operand specifies the number of bytes to be allocated on the stack for local data storage of the procedure. The second operand, which is a byte-size immediate operand, specifies what is called the *lexical nesting level* of the routine. This lexical level defines how many pointers to previous stack frames can be stored in the current stack frame. This list of previous stack frame pointers is called a *display*. The value of the lexical level byte must be limited to a maximum of 32 in 80286 programs.

An example of an ENTER instruction is

```
ENTER  12, 2
```

Execution of this instruction allocates 12 bytes of local storage on the stack for use as a stack frame. It does this by decrementing SP by 12. This defines a new top of stack at the address formed from the contents of SS and SP − 12. Also the *base pointer* (BP) that identifies the beginning of the previous stack frame is copied into the stack frame created by the ENTER instruction. This value is called the *dynamic link* and is held in the first storage location of the stack frame. The number of stack frame pointers that can be saved in a stack frame is equal to the value of the byte that specifies the lexical level of the procedure. Therefore, in our example, just two levels of nesting is specified.

The BP register is used as a pointer into the stack segment of memory. When a procedure is called, the value in BP points to the stack frame location that contains the previous stack frame pointer (dynamic link). Therefore, based-indexed addressing can be used to access variables in the stack frame by referencing the BP register.

The LEAVE instruction reverses the process of an ENTER instruction; that is, its execution deallocates the stack frame. This is done by first automatically loading SP from the BP register. This returns the storage locations of the current stack frame to the stack. Now SP points to the location where the dynamic link (pointer to the previous stack frame) is stored. Next, popping the contents of the stack into BP returns the pointer to the stack frame of the previous procedure.

To illustrate the operation of the stack frame instructions, let us consider the example of Fig. 12.11. Here we find three procedures. Procedure A is used to call procedure B, which in turn calls procedure C. It is assumed that the lexical levels for these procedures are 1, 2, and 3, respectively. The ENTER, LEAVE, and RET instructions for each procedure are shown in the diagram. Notice that the ENTER instructions specify the lexical levels for the procedures.

The stack frames created by executing the ENTER instructions in the three procedures are shown in Fig. 12.12. As the ENTER instruction in procedure A is executed, the old BP from the procedure that called procedure A is pushed onto the stack. BP is loaded from SP to point to the location of the old BP. Since the second operand is 1, only the current BP that is the BP for procedure A is pushed onto the stack. Finally, to allocate 32 bytes for the stack frame, 32 is subtracted from the current value in SP.

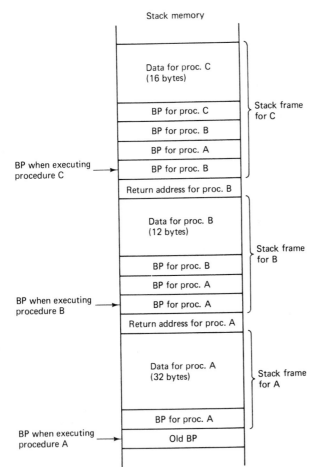

Figure 12.12 Stack after execution of enter instructions for procedures A, B, and C.

After entering procedure B, a second ENTER instruction is encountered. This time the lexical level is 2. Therefore, the instruction first pushes the old BP that is the BP for procedure A onto the stack, then pushes the BP previously stored on the stack frame for A to the stack, and lastly it pushes the current BP for procedure B to the stack. This mechanism provides access to the stack frame for procedure A from procedure B. Next, 12 bytes, as specified by the instruction, are allocated for local storage.

The ENTER instruction in procedure C has the lexical level of 3; therefore it pushes the BPs for the two previous procedures, that is, B and A, to the stack in addition to the BP for C and the BP for the calling procedure B.

Input String and Output String Instructions—INS and OUTS

In Fig. 12.8 we find that there are also input and output string instructions in the extended instruction set of the 80286. Using these string instructions, a programmer can either input data from an input port to a storage location directly in memory or output data from a memory location to an output port.

The first instruction, called *input string*, can be written in one of two ways, INSB or INSW. INSB stands for *input string byte* and INSW means *input string word*. Let us now look at the operation performed by the INSB instruction. INSB assumes that the address of the input port that is to be accessed is in the DX register. This value must be loaded prior to executing the string instruction. The address of the memory storage location into which the bytes of data are input is identified by the current values in ES and DI; that is, when executed, the input operation performed is

$$(ES:DI) \leftarrow ((DX))$$

Just as for the other byte string instructions, the value in DI is either incremented or decremented by 1 after the data transfer takes place.

$$(DI) \leftarrow (DI) \pm 1$$

In this way, it points to the next byte-wide storage location in memory to be accessed. Whether the value in DI is incremented or decremented depends on the setting of the DF flag. Notice in Fig. 12.8 that INSW performs the same data transfer operation except that since the word contents of the I/O port are input, the value in DI is incremented or decremented by 2.

The INSB instruction performs the operation we just described on one data element not on an array of elements. However, this basic operation can be repeated to handle a block input operation. Block operations are done by inserting a repeat (REP) prefix in front of the string instruction. For example, the instruction

```
REPINSW
```

will cause the contents of the word-wide port pointed to by the I/O address in DX to be input and saved in the memory location at the address specified by ES and DI. Then the value in DX is incremented by 2 (assuming that DF equals 0), the count in CX is decremented by 1, and the value in CX is tested to determine if it is 0. As long as the value in CX is not 0, the input operation is repeated. When CX equals 0, all elements of the array have been input, and the input string operation is complete. Remember that the count representing the number of times the string operation is to be repeated must be loaded into the CX register prior to executing the repeat input string instruction.

In Fig. 12.8 we also see that OUTSB and OUTSW are the two forms of the *output string* instruction. These instructions operate in a way similar to the input string instructions; however, they perform an output operation. For instance, executing OUTSW causes the operation that follows.

$$(ES:SI) \rightarrow ((DX))$$

$$(SI) \pm 2 \rightarrow (SI)$$

That is, the word of data held at the memory location pointed to by the address specified by ES and SI is output to the word-wide port pointed to by the I/O address in DX. After the output data transfer is complete, the value in SI is either incremented or decremented by 2.

An example of an output string instruction that can be used to output an array of data is

```
REPOUTSB
```

When executed this instruction causes the data elements of the array of byte-wide data pointed to by ES and SI to be output one after the other to the output port located at the I/O address specified by DX. Again, the count in CX defines the size of the array.

Check Array Index Against Bounds Instruction—BOUND

The *check array index against bounds* (BOUND) instruction, as its name implies, can determine if the contents of a register, known as the *array index*, lies within a set of minimum and maximum values, called the *upper and lower bounds*. This type of operation is important when accessing elements of an array of data in memory.

The format of the BOUND instruction is given in Fig. 12.8. An example is the instruction

```
BOUND  SI, [LIMITS]
```

Notice that the instruction contains two operands. The first operand represents the register whose word contents are to be tested to verify whether or not it lies within the boundaries. In our example, this is the source index register (SI). The second operand is the effective relative address of the first of two word-storage locations in memory that contain the values of the lower and upper boundaries. In the example, the word of data starting at address LIMITS is the value of the lower bound and that stored at address LIMITS+2 is the value of the upper bound.

When this BOUND instruction is executed, the contents of SI are compared with both the value of the lower bound at LIMITS and the upper bound at LIMITS+2. If it is found to be either less than the lower bound or more than the upper bound, an exception occurs and control is passed to a service routine through the vector for type 5. Otherwise, the next sequential instruction is executed.

▲ 12.6 INTERFACES OF THE 80286

Earlier we found that the 80286 microprocessor can be configured to work in either of two modes. These modes are known as the real-address mode and the protected-address mode. Let us now look at the signals produced at each of the 80286's interfaces when in these modes.

A block diagram of the 80286 microprocessor is shown in Fig. 12.13. Here we have grouped its signal lines into four interfaces: the *memory/IO interface, interrupt*

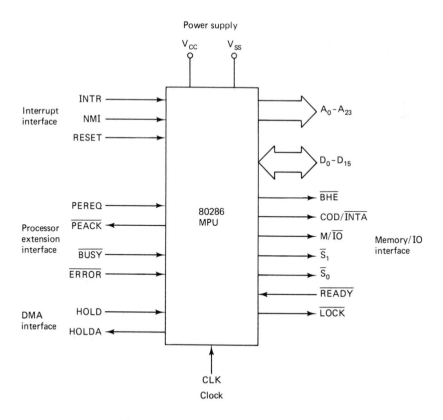

Figure 12.13 Block diagram of the 80286 MPU.

interface, DMA interface, and *processor extension interface.* Figure 12.14 lists each of the signals at the 80286's interfaces. Included in this table are a mnemonic, function, and type for each signal. For instance, the memory/IO control signal with the mnemonic M/$\overline{\text{IO}}$ stands for memory/IO select. This signal is an output produced by the 80286 that is used to signal external circuitry whether the current address available on the address bus is for memory or an I/O device. On the other hand, the signal INTR at the interrupt interface is the interrupt request input of the 80286. Using this input, external devices can signal the 80286 that they need to be serviced.

Memory/IO Interface

In a microcomputer system the address bus and data bus signal lines form the path over which the MPU talks with its memory and I/O subsystems. Unlike the older 8086 and 8088 microprocessors, the 80286 has a demultiplexed address/data bus. Notice in Fig. 12.2 that the address bus and data bus lines are located at different pins of the IC.

From an external hardware point of view, there is only one difference between an 80286 configured for the real-address mode or the protected-address mode. This difference is the size of the address bus. When in real mode, just the lower 20 address lines, A_0 through A_{19}, are active; in the protected mode all 24 lines, A_0 through A_{23}, are used. Of these, A_{23} is the most significant address bit and A_0 the least significant bit. As shown in Fig. 12.14 the address lines are outputs. They are

Mnemonic	Function	Type
CLK	System clock	I
D_{15}-D_0	Data bus	I/O
A_{23}-A_0	Address bus	O
$\overline{\text{BHE}}$	Bus high enable	O
$\overline{S}_1, \overline{S}_0$	Bus cycle status	O
M/$\overline{\text{IO}}$	Memory I/O select	O
COD/$\overline{\text{INTA}}$	Code/interrupt acknowledge	O
$\overline{\text{LOCK}}$	Bus lock	O
$\overline{\text{READY}}$	Bus ready	I
HOLD	Bus hold	I
HLDA	Hold acknowledge	O
INTR	Interrupt request	I
NMI	Nonmaskable interrupt request	I
PEREQ	Processor extension request	I
$\overline{\text{PEACK}}$	Processor extension acknowledge	O
$\overline{\text{BUSY}}$	Processor extension busy	I
$\overline{\text{ERROR}}$	Processor extension error	I
RESET	System reset	I
V_{SS}	System ground	I
V_{CC}	System power	I

Figure 12.14 Signal mnemonics, functions, and types.

used to carry address information from the 80286 to memory and I/O ports. In real-address mode, the 20-bit address gives the 80286 the ability to address a 1MB physical memory address space. On the other hand, in protected mode the extended 24-bit address results in a 16MB physical memory address space; however, in protected mode, virtual addressing is provided through software, and this results in a 1GB virtual memory address space.

In both the real and protected modes, the 80286 microcomputer has an independent I/O address space which is 64KB in length. Therefore, just address lines A_0 through A_{15} are used when addressing I/O devices.

Since the 80286 is a 16-bit microprocessor, its data bus is the 16 data lines D_0 through D_{15}. D_{15} is the MSB and D_0 the least significant bit. These lines are identified as bidirectional in Fig. 12.14. This is because they have the ability to carry data either in or out of the MPU. The kinds of data transferred over these lines are read/write data for memory, I/O data for I/O devices, and interrupt-type codes from an interrupt controller.

Control signals are required to support data transfers over the 80286's address/data bus. They are needed to signal when a valid address is on the address bus, in which direction data are to be transferred over the data bus, when valid write data are on the data bus, and when an external device can put read data on the data bus. The 80286 does not produce these signals directly. Instead, just like the 8086 in maximum mode, it outputs a 4-bit *bus status code* prior to the initiation of each bus cycle. This code identifies which type of bus cycle is to follow and must be decoded in external circuitry to produce the needed memory and I/O control signals.

In Fig. 12.15 we see that the bus status code is output on four of the 80286's signal lines: COD/$\overline{\text{INTA}}$, M/$\overline{\text{IO}}$, $\overline{S}_1$, and $\overline{S}_0$. The logic level of *code/interrupt acknowledge* (COD/$\overline{\text{INTA}}$) identifies whether the current bus cycle is for an instruction fetch or interrupt acknowledge operation. From the table we find that COD/$\overline{\text{INTA}}$ is logic 1 whenever an instruction fetch is taking place and logic 0 when an interrupt is being acknowledged. The next signal, *memory/IO* (M/$\overline{\text{IO}}$), tells whether a memory or I/O cycle is to take place over the bus. Logic 1 at this output signals

COD/$\overline{\text{INTA}}$	M/$\overline{\text{IO}}$	$\overline{S1}$	$\overline{S0}$	Bus Cycle Initiated
0 (LOW)	0	0	0	Interrupt acknowledge
0	0	0	1	Will not occur
0	0	1	0	Will not occur
0	0	1	1	None; not a status cycle
0	1	0	0	IF A1 = 1 then halt; else shutdown
0	1	0	1	Memory data read
0	1	1	0	Memory data write
0	1	1	1	None; not a status cycle
1 (HIGH)	0	0	0	Will not occur
1	0	0	1	I/O read
1	0	1	0	I/O write
1	0	1	1	None; not a status cycle
1	1	0	0	Will not occur
1	1	0	1	Memory instruction read
1	1	1	0	Will not occur
1	1	1	1	None; not a status cycle

Figure 12.15 Bus status codes. (Courtesy of Intel Corp.)

a memory operation, and logic 0 signals an I/O operation. Looking at the table in Fig. 12.15 more closely, we find that if the code on these two lines is 00 an interrupt is to be acknowledged, if it is 01 a data memory read or write is taking place, if it is 10 an I/O operation is in progress, and, finally, if it is 11 instruction code is being fetched.

The last two signals in Fig. 12.15 are called *status lines* and they identify the specific type of memory or I/O operation that will occur during a bus cycle. For example, when COD/$\overline{\text{INTA}}$ M/$\overline{\text{IO}}$ is 01, a status code of 01 indicates that data are to be read from memory. On the other hand, 10 at $\overline{S}_1\overline{S}_0$ indicates that data is being written into memory. As another example, we find that COD/$\overline{\text{INTA}}$ M/$\overline{\text{IO}}$ equals 11 and $\overline{S}_1\overline{S}_0$ equals 01 whenever the 80286 reads instruction code from memory.

EXAMPLE 12.1

What type of bus cycle is taking place if the bus status code COD/$\overline{\text{INTA}}$ M/$\overline{\text{IO}}$ $\overline{S}_1\overline{S}_0$ is 1001?

Solution

Looking at the table in Fig. 12.15 we see that the status code 1001 identifies an I/O read (input) bus cycle.

A bus control signal directly produced by the 80286 is *bus high enable* ($\overline{\text{BHE}}$). The logic levels of $\overline{\text{BHE}}$ and address bit A_0 identify whether a word or byte of data will be transferred during the current bus cycle. Moreover, if a byte transfer is to take place, the 2-bit code output at $\overline{\text{BHE}}$ A_0 tells whether the byte will be transferred over the upper or lower eight lines of the data bus. Figure 12.16 summarizes the state of these two signals for each type of data transfer. Notice that whenever a word of data is transferred over the bus both $\overline{\text{BHE}}$ and A_0 are set to logic 0.

$\overline{\text{BHE}}$	A0	Function
0	0	Word transfer
0	1	Byte transfer on upper half of data bus (D_{15}–D_8)
1	0	Byte transfer on lower half of data bus (D_{7-0})
1	1	Will never occur

Figure 12.16 $\overline{\text{BHE}}$ and A_0 encoding. (Courtesy of Intel Corp.)

EXAMPLE 12.2

If a byte of data is being written to memory over data bus lines D_0 through D_7, what code is output at $\overline{\text{BHE}}$ A_0?

Solution

In Fig. 12.16, we find that all transfers of byte data over the lower part of the address bus are accompanied by the code

$$\overline{BHE}\ A_0 = 10$$

The $\overline{READY}$ signal is used to insert wait states into the current bus cycle to extend it by a number of clock periods. This signal is an input to the 80286. Normally it is produced by the microcomputer's memory or I/O subsystem and supplied to the 80286 by way of the clock generator device. By signaling $\overline{READY}$, slow memory or I/O devices can tell the 80286 when they are ready to permit a data transfer to be completed.

One other control signal is supplied by the 80286 to support multiple-processor system architectures. This signal is the *bus lock* ($\overline{LOCK}$) output. In multi-processor systems that employ shared resources, such as global memory, this signal can be employed to assure that the 80286 can have control of the system bus to use the shared resource; that is, by switching the $\overline{LOCK}$ output to logic 0, an MPU can lock up the shared resource for its exclusive use.

Interrupt Interface

Looking at Fig. 12.13, we find that the key interrupt interface signals are *interrupt request* (INTR), *nonmaskable interrupt* (NMI), and *system reset* (RESET). INTR is an input to the 80286 that can be used by external devices to signal that they need to be serviced. This input is sampled at the beginning of each processor cycle. Logic 1 on INTR represents an active interrupt request. After an interrupt request has been recognized by the 80286, it initiates interrupt acknowledge bus cycles. In Fig. 12.15, we see that the occurrence of an interrupt acknowledge bus cycle is signaled to external circuitry with the bus status code COD/$\overline{INTA}$ M/$\overline{IO}$ $\overline{S_1}\overline{S_0}$ equal to 0000. This status code is decoded in external circuitry to produce an interrupt acknowledge signal.

The INTR input is maskable; that is, its operation can be enabled or disabled with the interrupt enable flag (IF) within the 80286's flag register. On the other hand, the NMI input, as its name implies, is a nonmaskable interrupt input. On the 0-to-1 transition of NMI, a request for service is latched within the 80286. Independent of the setting of the IF flag, control is passed to the beginning of the nonmaskable interrupt service routine at completion of execution of the current instruction.

Finally, the RESET input is used to provide a hardware reset to the 80286 microprocessor. Switching RESET to logic 1 initializes the internal registers of the 80286. When it is returned to logic 0, program control is automatically passed to a reset service routine.

DMA Interface

Now that we have examined the signals of the 80286's interrupt interface, let us turn to the *direct memory access* (DMA) interface. From Fig. 12.13 we find that the DMA interface is implemented with just two signals: *bus hold request* (HOLD) and *hold acknowledge* (HLDA). When an external device, such as a *DMA controller*, wants to take control of the system bus, it signals this fact to the 80286 by switching the HOLD input to logic 1. At completion of the current bus cycle, the 80286 enters the hold state. When in this state, the local bus signals are in the high-Z state. The 80286 signals external devices that it has given up control of the bus by switching its HLDA output to the 1 logic level. This completes the hold/hold acknowledge handshake.

Processor Extension Interface

A processor extension interface is provided on the 80286 microprocessor to permit it to easily interface with the 80287 *numeric coprocessor*. Whenever the 80287 needs the 80286 to read or write operands from memory, it signals this fact to the 80286. The 80287 does this by switching the *processor extension operand request* (PEREQ) input of the 80286 to logic 1. The processor extension handshake is completed when the 80286 signals the 80287 that it can have access to the bus. It signals this to the 80287 by switching the *processor extension acknowledge* ($\overline{\text{PEACK}}$) output to logic 0.

The other two signals included in the external coprocessor interface are $\overline{\text{BUSY}}$ and $\overline{\text{ERROR}}$. *Processor extension busy* ($\overline{\text{BUSY}}$) is an input to the 80286. Whenever the 80287 is executing a numeric instruction, it signals this fact to the 80286 by switching the $\overline{\text{BUSY}}$ input to logic 0. In this way, the 80286 knows not to request the numeric coprocessor to perform another calculation until $\overline{\text{BUSY}}$ returns to 1. If an error occurs in a calculation performed by the numeric coprocessor, it signals this condition to the 80286 by switching the *bus extension error* ($\overline{\text{ERROR}}$) input to the 0 logic level.

▲ 12.7 THE 82288 BUS CONTROLLER

In the previous section we pointed out that the 80286 does not directly produce all the signals that are required to control the memory, I/O, and interrupt interfaces. Instead, it outputs a status code prior to the initiation of each bus cycle that identifies which type of bus cycle is to follow. In an 80286-based microcomputer, three of these status lines, $\text{M}/\overline{\text{IO}}$, $\overline{\text{S}}_1$, and $\overline{\text{S}}_0$, are supplied as inputs to an external *bus controller* device, the 82288. Just as in a maximum-mode 8086 system, the bus controller decodes them to identify the type of MPU bus cycle and then generates appropriately timed command and control signals at its outputs.

Let us now look at how the 82288 interfaces with the 80286 MPU. A block diagram for the 82288 IC is shown in Fig. 12.17(a), and its pin layout is given in Fig. 12.17(b). Here we can find each of the signals that it accepts as inputs and produces as outputs. For instance, status inputs $\text{M}/\overline{\text{IO}}$, $\overline{\text{S}}_1$, and $\overline{\text{S}}_0$ are located at pins 18, 3, and 19, respectively.

The 82288 connects to the 80286 as shown in Fig. 12.18. Notice that the status outputs of the 80286 are simply connected directly to the corresponding input of

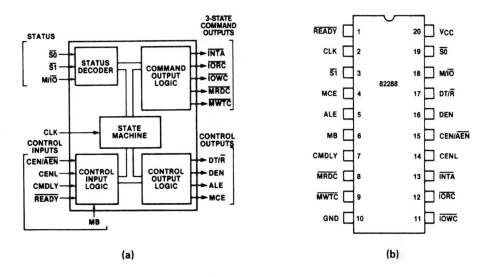

(a)   (b)

Figure 12.17   (a) Block diagram of the 82288. (Courtesy of Intel Corp.)
(b) Pin layout of the 82288. (Courtesy of Intel Corp.)

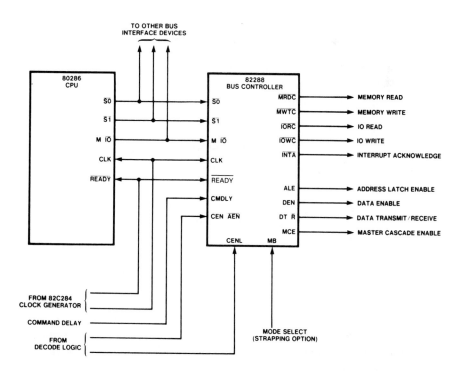

Figure 12.18   Decoding bus status with the 82288. (Courtesy of Intel Corp.)

Sec. 12.7   The 82288 Bus Controller   **707**

Type of Bus Cycle	M/$\overline{\text{IO}}$	$\overline{\text{S1}}$	$\overline{\text{S0}}$	Command Activated	DT/$\overline{\text{R}}$ State	ALE, DEN Issued?	MCE Issued?
Interrupt Acknowledge	0	0	0	$\overline{\text{INTA}}$	LOW	YES	YES
I/O Read	0	0	1	$\overline{\text{IORC}}$	LOW	YES	NO
I/O Write	0	1	0	$\overline{\text{IOWC}}$	HIGH	YES	NO
None; Idle	0	1	1	None	HIGH	NO	NO
Halt/Shutdown	1	0	0	None	HIGH	NO	NO
Memory Read	1	0	1	$\overline{\text{MRDC}}$	LOW	YES	NO
Memory Write	1	1	0	$\overline{\text{MWTC}}$	HIGH	YES	NO
None; Idle	1	1	1	None	HIGH	NO	NO

Figure 12.19 Control signals for each bus cycle. (Courtesy of Intel Corp.)

the 82288. Moreover, the clock (CLK) and ready ($\overline{\text{READY}}$) inputs of the 82288 are wired to the respective inputs of the 80286 and both are driven by outputs of the 82284 clock generator.

At the other side of the bus controller, we find the bus command and control signal outputs. The command outputs are: *memory read command* ($\overline{\text{MRDC}}$), *memory write command* ($\overline{\text{MWTC}}$), *I/O read command* ($\overline{\text{IORC}}$), *I/O write command* ($\overline{\text{IOWC}}$), and *interrupt acknowledge command* ($\overline{\text{INTA}}$). In Fig. 12.19 we see that just one of these command outputs becomes active for a given bus status code. For instance, when the 80286 outputs the code M/$\overline{\text{IO}}$ $\overline{S}_1\overline{S}_0$ equal to 001, it indicates that an I/O read cycle is to be performed. In turn, the 82288 makes its $\overline{\text{IORC}}$ output switch to logic 0. On the other hand, if the code 111 is output by the 80286, it is signaling the bus controller that no bus activity is to take place.

EXAMPLE 12.3

If the $\overline{\text{MRDC}}$ output of the 82288 has just switched to logic 0, what bus status code was output by the 80286?

Solution

Looking at Fig. 12.19 we find that the status code input to the 82288 that makes $\overline{\text{MRDC}}$ active is

$$\text{M/}\overline{\text{IO}}\ \overline{S}_1\overline{S}_0 = 101$$

The 82288 also produces the control signals *data transmit/receive* (DT/$\overline{\text{R}}$), *address latch enable* (ALE), *data enable* (DEN), and *master cascade enable* (MCE). Figure 12.19 shows the state of these control signals during each bus cycle. For example, during an I/O read cycle DT/$\overline{\text{R}}$ is set to logic 0, and both ALE and DEN are issued.

These command and control signals are needed to support memory and I/O data transfers over the address and data buses. Earlier we pointed out that they need to identify when the bus is carrying a valid address, in which direction data are to be transferred over the bus, when valid write data are on the bus, and when to put read data on the bus. For example, the ALE line signals external circuitry when a valid address word is on the bus. This address can be latched in external circuitry on the 0-to-1 edge of the pulse at ALE.

The direction in which data are to be transferred over the bus is signaled to external circuitry with the DT/$\overline{\text{R}}$ output. When this line is at logic 1 during the data transfer part of a bus cycle, the bus is in the transmit mode. Therefore, data are either written into memory or output to an I/O device. On the other hand, logic 0 at DT/$\overline{\text{R}}$ signals that the bus is in the receive mode. This corresponds to reading data from memory or input of data from an input device.

The signals $\overline{\text{MRDC}}$ and $\overline{\text{MWTC}}$, indicate a memory read bus cycle and a memory write bus cycle, respectively. The 82288 switches $\overline{\text{MWTC}}$ to logic 0 to signal external devices that valid write data are on the bus. On the other hand, a logic 0 on $\overline{\text{MRDC}}$ indicates that the 80286 is performing a read of data off the bus. During read operations, one other control signal is supplied. This is DEN, and it is the signal that is used to enable the data path buffers. Input and output bus cycles are performed in the same way; however, in this case $\overline{\text{IORC}}$ and $\overline{\text{IOWC}}$ are activated by the 82288 instead of $\overline{\text{MRDC}}$ and $\overline{\text{MWTC}}$.

The 82288 also has several control inputs. In Fig. 12.18 we find a *Multibus*™ *mode select* (MB) input. When the system is not using *Multibus*™ as the system bus, this input is connected to ground. Figure 12.17 includes three other signal lines that were not shown in the 80286/82288 interface circuit of Fig. 12.18. For instance, the *command enable/address enable* (CEN/$\overline{\text{AEN}}$) input can be used to enable or disable the command and DEN outputs of the 82288. To enable the 82288 for operation, this input must be at the 1 logic level. Designs which either use multiple 82288s or require the command output signals to be delayed are implemented by the last two inputs, CENL and CMDLY, respectively.

▲ 12.8 SYSTEM CLOCK

The time base for synchronization of the internal and external operations of the 80286 microprocessor is provided by the *clock* (CLK) input signal. The 80286 is available with three different clock speeds. The standard 80286 MPU operates at 8 MHz and its two faster versions, the 80286-10 and 80286-12, operate at 10 MHz and 12.5 MHz, respectively. CLK is generated externally by the 82C284 clock generator/driver IC. Figure 12.20(a) is a block diagram of this device, and Fig. 12.20(b) shows its pin layout.

The normal way in which the clock chip is used is to connect a crystal with twice the microprocessor clock frequency between the X_1 and X_2 inputs. This circuit connection is shown in Fig. 12.21. For instance, to run the 80286 at 8 MHz, a 16-MHz crystal is needed. Notice that loading capacitors C_1 and C_2 are required from X_1 and X_2, respectively, to ground. Typical capacitance values (device capacitance

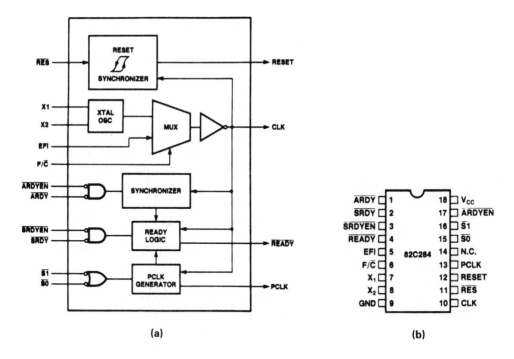

(a)

(b)

Figure 12.20 (a) Block diagram of the 82C284 clock generator. (Courtesy of Intel Corp.) (b) Pin layout. (Courtesy of Intel Corp.)

plus stray capacitance) for these capacitors are 25 pF and 15 pF, respectively. The fundamental crystal frequency produced by the oscillator within the 82C284 is divided by two to give the CLK output. As shown in Fig. 12.21, the CLK output of the 82C284 is applied directly to the CLK input of the 80286.

The waveform of the CLK input of the 80286 is given in Fig. 12.22. Here we see that the signal is specified at MOS-compatible voltage levels and not TTL levels. Its minimum and maximum low logic levels are $V_{Lmin} = -0.5$ V and $V_{Lmax} = 0.6$ V, respectively. Moreover, the minimum and maximum high logic levels are $V_{Hmin} = 3.8$ V and $V_{Hmax} = +5.5$ V, respectively. The period of the 8-MHz signal is a minimum of 62.5 ns, and the maximum rise and fall times of its edges are equal to 10 ns.

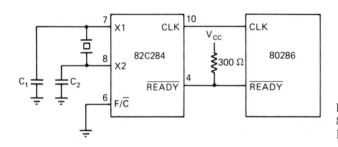

Figure 12.21 Connecting the 82C284 to the 80286. (Courtesy of Intel Corp.)

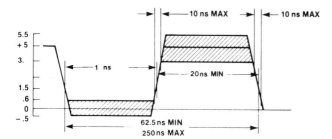

5.5
+5
3.

1.5
.6
0
−.5

←——10 ns MAX——→ ←— 10 ns MAX

←—1 ns—→

←--20ns MIN--→

←———62.5ns MIN———→
250ns MAX

Figure 12.22 CLK voltage and timing characteristics. (Courtesy of Intel Corp.)

In Fig. 12.20(a) we see that there is another clock output on the 82C284. This is the *processor clock* (PCLK) signal, which is provided to drive peripheral ICs. The clock produced at PCLK is half the frequency of CLK; that is, if the 80286 is to operate at 8 MHz, PCLK will be 4 MHz. This relationship is illustrated in Fig. 12.23. Also, it is at TTL-compatible voltage levels rather than at CMOS levels.

The 82C284 can also be driven from an external clock source. In this case, the external clock signal is applied to the *external frequency input* (EFI). Input F/$\overline{C}$ (*frequency/crystal select*) is provided for clock source selection. When it is strapped to the 0 logic level, as in Fig. 12.21, the crystal between X_1 and X_2 is used. On the other hand, applying logic 1 to F/$\overline{C}$ selects EFI as the source of the clock.

▲ 12.9 THE BUS CYCLE AND BUS STATES

A *bus cycle* is the activity performed whenever a microprocessor accesses information in program memory, data memory, or an I/O device. Figure 12.24 shows a traditional microprocessor bus cycle. It represents a sequence of events that start with an address, denoted as n, being output on the address bus during clock state T_1. Later in the bus cycle, while the address is still available on the address bus, a read or write data transfer takes place over the data bus. Notice that the data transfer for address n is shown to occur during clock state T_3. The interval denoted as *address access time* in Fig. 12.24 represents the amount of time that the address is stable prior to the actual read or write of data. During the bus cycle, a series of

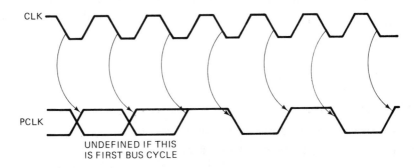

CLK

PCLK

UNDEFINED IF THIS
IS FIRST BUS CYCLE

Figure 12.23 Timing relationship between CLK and PCLK. (Courtesy of Intel Corp.)

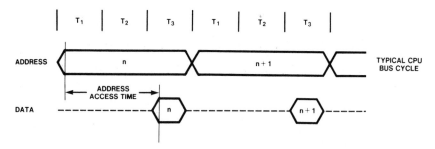

Figure 12.24 Traditional bus cycle. (Courtesy of Intel Corp.)

control signals is also produced by the MPU to control the direction and timing of the bus operation.

Before looking at the bus cycle of the 80286, let us examine the relationship between the timing of the 80286's CLK input and bus cycle states. In the last section we pointed out that the processor clock (PCLK) signal is at half the frequency of CLK. Therefore, as shown in Fig. 12.25, one processor clock cycle corresponds to two CLK cycles. These CLK cycles are labeled as *phase 1* (ϕ_1) and *phase 2* (ϕ_2). In an 8-MHz 80286 microcomputer system, each system clock cycle has a duration of 125 ns. Therefore, a processor clock cycle is 250 ns long.

In Fig. 12.25 we see that the two phases ($\phi_1 + \phi_2$) of a processor cycle are identified as one bus *T state*. Figure 12.26(a) shows a typical 80286 bus cycle. Notice that here the clock T states are labeled T_S and T_C. T_S stands for the *send-status state*. During this part of the bus cycle, the 80286 outputs a bus status code to the 82C288 bus controller, and in the case of a write cycle, write data are also output on the data bus. The second state, T_C, is called the *perform-command state*. It is during this part of the bus cycle that external devices are to accept write data from the bus, or in the case of a read cycle, put data on the bus. Also the address for the next bus cycle is output on the address bus during T_C. Since each bus cycle has a minimum of two T states, the minimum bus cycle duration in an 8-MHz system is 250 ns.

The bus cycle of the 80286 employs a technique known as *pipelining*. By pipelining we mean that addressing for the next bus cycle is overlapped with the data transfer of the prior bus cycle. In Figure 12.26(a) we see that address n becomes valid in the T_C state of the prior bus cycle and then the data transfer for address

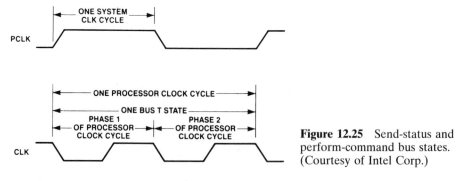

Figure 12.25 Send-status and perform-command bus states. (Courtesy of Intel Corp.)

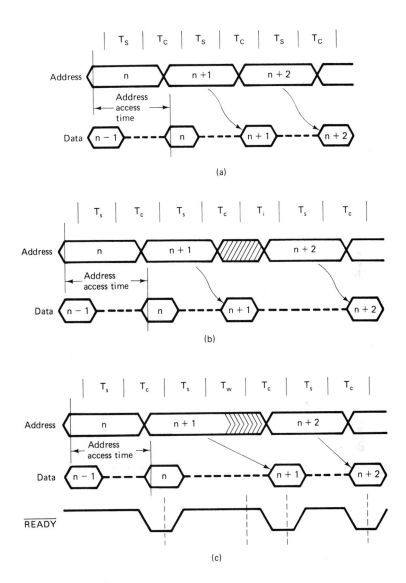

Figure 12.26 (a) Pipelined 80286 bus cycle. (Courtesy of Intel Corp.) (b) Bus cycle with idle states. (Courtesy of Intel Corp.) (c) Bus cycle with wait states. (Courtesy of Intel Corp.)

n takes place in the next T_C state. Moreover, notice that at the same time that data transfer n occurs address n + 1 is output on the address bus. In this way, we see that the 80286 begins addressing the next storage location that is to be accessed while it is still performing the read or write of data for the previously addressed storage location. Because of the address/data pipelining, the memory or I/O subsystem actually has five CLK periods to complete the data transfer even though the effective duration of every bus cycle is just four CLK periods.

Figure 12.26(a) shows that the effective address access time equals the duration of a complete bus cycle. This leads us to the benefit of the pipelined bus operation of the 80286 not found in the traditional bus operation shown in Fig. 12.24. This benefit is that for a fixed address access time (equal-speed memory design), the 80286 will have a shorter duration bus cycle than a processor that uses a nonpipelined bus cycle. This results in improved bus performance for the 80286. Another way of looking at this is to say that when using equal-speed memory designs, a pipelined microprocessor can be operated at a higher clock rate than a processor that executes a nonpipelined bus cycle. Once again the result is higher system performance. A pipelined memory subsystem design is much more complex and requires more hardware than that of a nonpipelined memory subsystem.

In Fig. 12.26(a) we see that at completion of the bus cycle for address n another bus cycle is initiated immediately for address n + 1. Sometimes another bus cycle will not be initiated immediately. For instance, if the 80286's prefetch queue is already full and the instruction that is currently being executed does not need to access operands in memory, no bus activity will take place. In this case, the bus goes into a mode of operation known as an *idle state* and no bus activity occurs. Figure 12.26(b) shows a sequence of bus activity in which several idle states exist between the bus cycles for addresses n and n + 1. The duration of a single idle state is equal to one processor cycle (two clock cycles).

Wait states can also be inserted into the 80286's bus cycle. This is done in response to a request by an event in external hardware instead of an internal event such as a full queue. In fact the $\overline{\text{READY}}$ input of the 80286 is provided specifically for this purpose. This input is sampled by the processor in the later part of the T_C state of every bus cycle to determine if the data transfer should be completed. Figure 12.26(c) shows that logic 1 at this input indicates that the current bus cycle should not be completed. As long as $\overline{\text{READY}}$ is held at the 1 level, the read or write data transfer does not take place and the current T_S state becomes a wait state (T_W) to extend the bus cycle. The bus cycle is not completed until external hardware returns $\overline{\text{READY}}$ back to logic 0. This ability to extend the duration of a bus cycle permits the use of slower memory or I/O devices in the microcomputer system.

▲ 12.10 MEMORY INTERFACE

In the preceding sections we studied the 80286 microprocessor, its internal architecture, the extended instruction set, the 82C288 bus controller, the 82C284 clock generator, and read/write bus cycles. Here we will continue by introducing its memory interface, hardware organization of the address space, data transfers through the memory interface, and the read and write bus cycles.

Memory Interface Circuit

A memory interface circuit diagram for a real-mode 80286-based microcomputer system is shown in Fig. 12.27. Here we find that the interface includes the

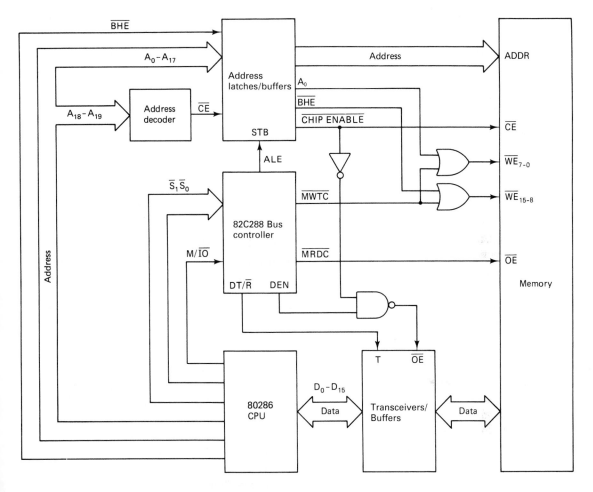

Figure 12.27   80286 system memory interface.

82C288 bus controller, an address decoder and address latches, data bus transceiver/ buffers, and bank select logic. Status signals, $M/\overline{IO}$, $\overline{S}_1$, and $\overline{S}_0$, which are output by the 80286, are supplied directly to the 82C288 bus controller. Here they are decoded to produce the command and control signals needed to control data transfers over the bus. In Fig. 12.28, the two status codes that relate to the memory interface are highlighted. The code $M/\overline{IO}$ $\overline{S}_1\overline{S}_0 = 101$ indicates that a memory read bus cycle is in progress. This code makes the $\overline{MRDC}$ output switch to logic 0. Notice in Fig. 12.27 that $\overline{MRDC}$ is applied to the output enable ($\overline{OE}$) input of the memory subsystem.

Next let us look at how the address bus is decoded, latched, and buffered. Address lines A_0 through A_{17} and $\overline{BHE}$ are sent directly to inputs of the address latches. On the other hand, bits A_{18} and A_{19} are first decoded and then passed on to the latch. Finally, the pulse at ALE is used to strobe address bits A_0 through A_{17}, $\overline{BHE}$, and the output of the decoder, which is chip enable ($\overline{CE}$), into the

M/$\overline{\text{IO}}$	$\overline{S}_1$	$\overline{S}_0$	Type of bus cycle
0	0	0	Interrupt acknowledge
0	0	1	I/O Read
0	1	0	I/O Write
0	1	1	None; idle
1	0	0	Halt or shutdown
1	0	1	Memory read
1	1	0	Memory write
1	1	1	None; idle

Figure 12.28 Memory bus status codes. (Courtesy of Intel Corp.)

latches. The address latches buffer the address lines, $\overline{\text{BHE}}$, and $\overline{\text{CE}}$ before passing them on to the memory subsystem.

This part of the memory interface demonstrates one of the benefits of the 80286's pipelined bus. Remember that the 80286 actually outputs the address in the T_C state of the prior bus cycle. Therefore, by putting the address decoder before the address latches instead of after, the code at address lines A_{18} and A_{19} can be fully decoded and stable prior to the occurrence of ALE in the T_S state of the current bus cycle; that is, since the address can be decoded prior to ALE, the decode propagation delay is transparent and does not decrease the overall access time of the memory subsystem.

The circuit in Fig. 12.27 allows just word reads from the memory, but either byte or word writes to the memory.

During read bus cycles, the $\overline{\text{MRDC}}$ output of the bus controller enables the data at the outputs of the memory subsystem onto data bus lines D_0 through D_{15}. On the other hand, during write operations to memory, control logic must determine whether data are written into the lower memory bank, the upper memory bank, or both banks. This depends on whether an even-byte, odd-byte, or word-data transfer is taking place over the bus. The bank-select logic performs this function. Notice in Fig. 12.27 that $\overline{\text{MWTC}}$ is gated with address bit A_0 to produce write enable $\overline{\text{WE}}_{7-0}$ for the low memory bank. For $\overline{\text{WE}}_{7-0}$ to be at its active logic 0 level, both A_0 and $\overline{\text{MWTC}}$ must be logic 0. This happens only when either an even addressed byte of data or a word of data is written to memory. Furthermore, $\overline{\text{MWTC}}$ is gated with $\overline{\text{BHE}}$ to produce the high memory bank write enable signal $\overline{\text{WE}}_{15-8}$. For this signal to switch to its active 0 logic level, $\overline{\text{BHE}}$ and $\overline{\text{MWTC}}$ must both be logic 0. This occurs when either an odd addressed byte of data or a word of data is written to memory.

The data bus transceiver/buffers control the direction of data transfers between the MPU and memory subsystem. The transceivers get enabled by switching their output enable ($\overline{\text{OE}}$) inputs to logic 0. Signals data bus enable (DEN) and chip enable ($\overline{\text{CE}}$) are combined with an inverter and NAND gate to produce $\overline{\text{OE}}$. When DEN is logic 1 and $\overline{\text{CE}}$ is logic 0, the output of the NAND gate switches to logic 0 and the transceivers are enabled. This happens during all read and write bus cycles to memory.

The direction in which data are passed through the transceiver/buffers is controlled by the bus controller. The bus controller sets its data transmit/receive

$(DT/\overline{R})$ output to logic 0 during all read cycles and logic 1 during all write cycles. This signal is applied to the DIR input of the transceiver to select the direction in which data are transferred.

Hardware Organization of the Memory Address Space

From a hardware point of view, the memory address space of the 80286 is implemented exactly the same as that of the 8086; that is, it is organized as two independent banks called the *low* (*even*) bank and the *high* (*odd*) bank. Data bytes associated with an even address $(000000_{16}, 000002_{16},$ etc.) reside in the low bank, and those with odd addresses $(000001_{16}, 000003_{16},$ etc.) reside in the high bank. When in the protected mode, these banks can each be as large as 8MB.

Looking at Fig. 12.29, we find that the 80286's real-mode physical address space is partitioned into a 512KB low bank and a 512KB high bank. In the real mode, address bits A_1 through A_{19} select the storage location that is to be accessed. Therefore, they are applied to both banks in parallel. Just as for the 8086, A_0 and bank high enable $(\overline{BHE})$ are used as bank-select signals. Logic 0 at A_0 identifies an even-addressed byte of data and causes the low bank of memory to be enabled. On the other hand, $\overline{BHE}$ equal to 0 enables the high bank for access of an odd-addressed byte of data. Each of the memory banks supplies half the 80286's 16-bit data bus. Notice that the lower bank transfers bytes of data over data lines D_0 through D_7; data transfers for the high bank use D_8 through D_{15}. Figures 12.30(a) through (d) show how an even-addressed byte of data, odd-addressed byte of data, even-addressed word of data, and odd-addressed word of data, respectively, are accessed. These accesses are the same as those in the 8086 based system described in an earlier chapter.

Read Cycle Timing

The memory interface signals that occur when the 80286 reads data from memory are shown in Fig. 12.31. Since the pipelined bus of the 80286 overlaps bus cycles, we have shown parts of three cycles in the timing diagram: the previous

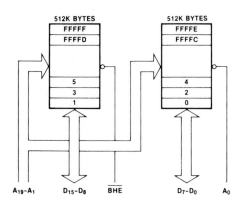

Figure 12.29 High and low memory banks. (Courtesy of Intel Corp.)

cycle, the current read cycle, and the next cycle. Let us now trace through the events that take place as data or instructions are read from memory.

The occurrence of all signals in the read bus cycle timing diagram are illustrated relative to the two timing states, T_S (send-status state) and T_C (perform-command state), of the 80286's bus cycle. The read cycle begins at phase 2 (ϕ_2) in the T_C state of the previous bus cycle. During this period, the 80286 outputs the 24-bit address of the memory location to be accessed on address bus lines A_0 through A_{23}. Also we see in Fig. 12.31 that at the start of ϕ_2, signal $M/\overline{IO}$ is set to logic 1 to indicate to the circuitry in the memory interface that a memory bus cycle is in progress, and $COD/\overline{INTA}$ is set to logic 1 if the bus cycle is being performed to fetch code data. In our description of the memory interface circuit of Fig. 12.27, we pointed out that these signals are stable during the T_C state of the previous bus cycle; therefore, the address decode logic circuitry can begin to decode them immediately. This will assure that a maximum amount of time will be available to access the memory subsystem. Notice that the status signals, $M/\overline{IO}$, and $COD/\overline{INTA}$ are maintained valid through ϕ_1 of state T_C of the read cycle. In ϕ_2 of T_C they are replaced with new values in preparation for the next bus cycle.

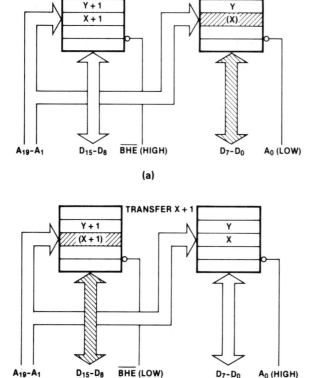

(a)

(b)

Figure 12.30 (a) Even-addressed byte transfer. (Courtesy of Intel Corp.) (b) Odd-addressed byte transfer. (Courtesy of Intel Corp.) (c) Even-addressed word transfer. (Courtesy of Intel Corp.) (d) Odd-addressed word transfer. (Courtesy of Intel Corp.)

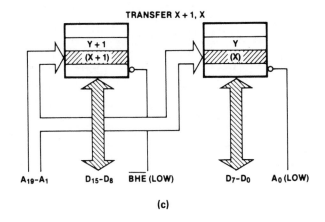

TRANSFER X + 1, X

(c)

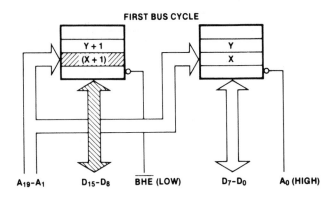

FIRST BUS CYCLE

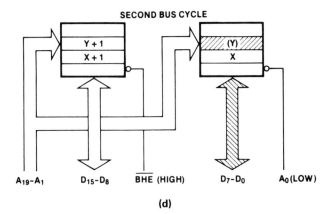

SECOND BUS CYCLE

(d)

Figure 12.30 (Continued)

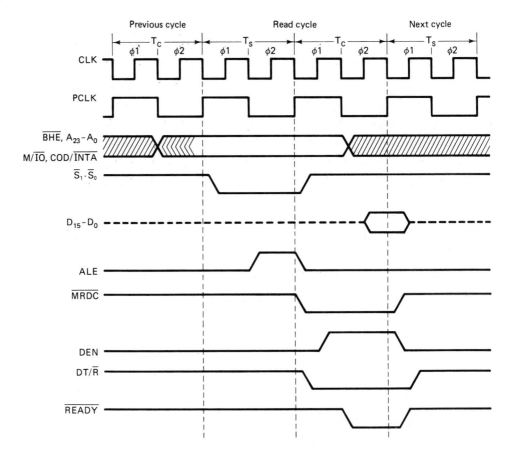

Figure 12.31 Memory read bus cycle timing diagram. (Courtesy of Intel Corp.)

At the beginning of ϕ_1 of the read cycle, the 80286 outputs status code $\overline{S}_1\overline{S}_0$ equal to 01 on the status bus. Remember that this code identifies that a read bus transfer is to take place. This status information is maintained through the T_S state. At the falling edge of CLK in the middle of T_S, the status lines are sampled by the 82C288 bus controller and the read cycle bus control sequence is started. At the same time the status information is output, $\overline{BHE}$ is also switched to logic 0 or 1, depending on whether or not the high memory bank is to be enabled during the read cycle.

With ϕ_2 of T_S, the bus controller takes over the timing control for the bus. It begins by producing a pulse to logic 1 at ALE during ϕ_2. The leading edge of this pulse can be used to latch the address and $\overline{BHE}$ into external circuitry.

At the start of the T_C state of the read cycle, the bus controller switches both DT/$\overline{R}$ and $\overline{MRDC}$ to logic 0. Logic 0 at DT/$\overline{R}$ is used to set the direction of the data bus transceivers so that they will pass data from the memory subsystem to the 80286. On the other hand, the logic 0 at $\overline{MRDC}$ enables the output buffers of the memory subsystem so that they output data to the inputs of the data bus transceivers. Later in ϕ_1, DEN is set to 1. This active logic level enables the data bus transceivers and lets the data available at its inputs pass through to the outputs, which are attached to the data bus of the 80286.

The 80286 and 82C288 sample the logic level of their $\overline{\text{READY}}$, inputs at the end of ϕ_2 in the T_C state of the read cycle. Assuming that $\overline{\text{READY}}$ is at its active 0 logic level, the MPU reads the data off the bus. The read cycle is now completed as the bus controller returns $\overline{\text{MRDC}}$, DEN, and DT/$\overline{\text{R}}$ to their inactive logic levels.

Write Cycle Timing

The write bus cycle timing diagram, shown in Fig. 12.32, is similar to that given for a read cycle in Fig. 12.31. Looking at the write cycle waveforms, we find that the address, M/$\overline{\text{IO}}$, and COD/$\overline{\text{INTA}}$ signals are output at the beginning of ϕ_2 of the T_C state of the previous bus cycle. All of these signals can be latched in

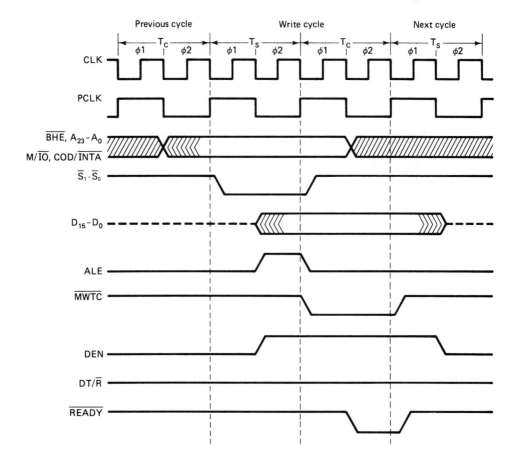

Figure 12.32 Memory write bus cycle timing diagram. (Courtesy of Intel Corp.)

external circuitry with the ALE pulse during ϕ_2 of the T_S state in the write cycle. Up to this point, the bus cycle is identical to that for the read cycle.

The $\overline{\text{BHE}}$ signal and status code $\overline{S}_1\overline{S}_0$ are output at the beginning of the T_S state of the write cycle. This also happened in the read cycle, but this time the status code is 10 instead of 01. This code is sampled by the 82C288 later in the T_S state to determine if it is a memory write cycle.

Let us now look at the control signal sequence produced by the bus controller for the write bus cycle. Notice that the 80286 outputs the data that is to be written to memory on the data bus at the beginning of ϕ_2 in the T_S state. After identifying the status code as that for a write cycle, the 82C288 switches DT/$\overline{R}$ (DT/$\overline{R}$ is normally in the 1 state) and DEN to logic 1. This sets the data bus transceivers to pass data from the MPU to the memory subsystem and enables it for operation. Finally, the memory write ($\overline{\text{MWTC}}$) output is switched to logic 0 at the beginning of the T_C state of the write cycle. $\overline{\text{MWTC}}$ signals the memory subsystem that valid write data are on the bus. Finally, late in the T_C state, the 80286 and 82C288 test

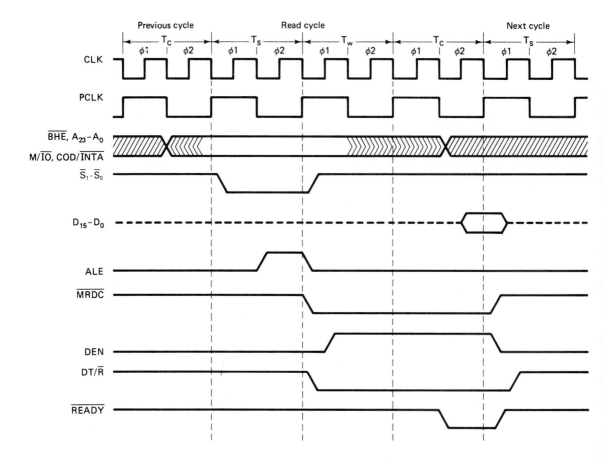

Figure 12.33 Read bus cycle with wait state. (Courtesy of Intel Corp.)

the logic level of $\overline{\text{READY}}$. If $\overline{\text{READY}}$ is logic 0, the write cycle is completed and the buses and control signals are prepared for the next read or write cycle.

Wait States in the Memory Bus Cycle

Wait states can be inserted to lengthen the memory bus cycle of the 80286. This is done with the $\overline{\text{READY}}$ input signal. Upon request from an event in external hardware, for instance, slow memory, the $\overline{\text{READY}}$ input is switched to logic 1. This signals the 80286 and the 82C288 that the current bus cycle should not be completed. Instead, it is extended by repeating the T_C state by a duration of one wait state (T_W), 125 ns for 8-MHz clock operation. Figure 12.33 shows a read cycle extended by one wait state. Notice that the control signals DT/$\overline{\text{R}}$, DEN, and $\overline{\text{MRDC}}$ are maintained throughout the wait-state period. In this way, the read cycle is not completed until $\overline{\text{READY}}$ switches to logic 0 in the T_C state that follows.

▲ 12.11 INPUT/OUTPUT INTERFACE

In section 12.10 we studied the memory interface of the 80286 microprocessor. Here we will examine another important interface of the 80286-based microcomputer system, the I/O interface.

The I/O Interface

The I/O interface of the 80286 microcomputer permits it to communicate with the outside world. The way in which the 80286 deals with I/O circuitry is similar to the way in which it interfaces with memory circuitry; that is, the transfer of I/O data also takes place over the data bus. The I/O interface allows easy interface to LSI peripheral devices such as parallel I/O expanders, interval timers, and serial communication controllers. Let us continue by looking at how the 80286 interfaces to its I/O subsystem.

Figure 12.34 shows a typical I/O interface. Here we see that the way in which the 80286 interfaces with I/O devices is identical to that of the maximum-mode 8086 microcomputer system. Notice that the interface includes the 82C288 bus controller, an address decoder, address latches/buffers, data bus transceiver/buffers, and I/O devices. An example of an I/O device is a programmable peripheral interface IC, such as the 8255A, that can be used to implement parallel I/O ports.

The I/O device that is accessed for input or output of data is selected by an *I/O address*. This address is specified as part of the instruction that performs the I/O operation. Just as for the 8086 architecture, the 80286's I/O address is 16 bits in length. As shown in Fig. 12.28, they are output to the I/O interface over address bus lines A_0 through A_{15}. The more significant address bits, A_{16} through A_{23}, are held at the 0 logic level during the address period of all I/O bus cycles.

In the circuit of Fig. 12.34, some of the address bits on address lines A_0 through A_{15} of the 80286 are decoded by the address decoder to produce I/O chip enable

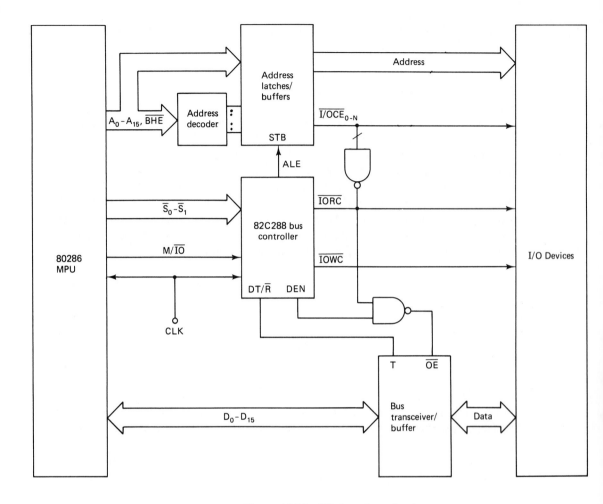

Figure 12.34 I/O interface circuit.

signals, $\overline{I/OCE}_0$ through $\overline{I/OCE}_N$, for the I/O devices. For instance, with three address bits, we can produce enough chip enable outputs to select up to eight I/O devices. The outputs of the address decoder are latched along with the rest of the address bits into the address latches. Latching of the address is achieved with the pulse output on the ALE line of the 82C288. The address bits that are sent directly to the I/O devices are typically used to select the register within the peripheral device that is to be accessed. For example, with four address lines, we can select one of 16 I/O device registers.

During I/O bus cycles, data are passed between the 80286 and the selected register within the enabled I/O device over data bus lines D_0 through D_{15}. The 80286 can input or output data in either byte-wide or word-wide format; however, most LSI peripherals used as I/O controllers in the 80286 microcomputer system are designed to interface with an 8-bit bus and are attached to either the upper or lower part of the bus. For this reason, I/O operations usually involve byte-wide data transfers.

Just as for the memory interface, the signals A_0 and $\overline{BHE}$ are used to signal whether an even- or odd-addressed byte of data is being transferred over the bus. Again logic 0 at A_0 and $\overline{BHE}$ equal to 1 identifies an even byte, and the byte of data is input or output over data bus lines D_0 through D_7. Moreover, logic 1 at A_0 and logic 0 at $\overline{BHE}$ identifies an odd byte, and the data transfer occurs over bus lines D_8 through D_{15}.

As in the memory interface, the 82C288 bus controller produces the control signals for the I/O interface in Fig. 12.34. The 82C288 decodes bus cycle status codes that are output by the 80286 on M/$\overline{IO}$, $\overline{S}_1$, and $\overline{S}_0$. The table in Fig. 12.35 shows the bus command status codes together with the type of bus cycle they produce. Those for I/O bus cycles have been highlighted. If the code corresponds to an I/O read bus cycle (M/$\overline{IO}$ $\overline{S}_1\overline{S}_0 = 001$), the 82C288 generates the *I/O read command output* ($\overline{IORC}$), and for I/O write bus cycles (M/$\overline{IO}$ $\overline{S}_1\overline{S}_0 = 010$), it generates the *I/O write command output* ($\overline{IOWC}$). Looking at Fig. 12.34, we see that $\overline{IORC}$ and $\overline{IOWC}$ are applied directly to the I/O devices and tell them whether data are to be input from or output to the enabled I/O device.

Notice in Fig. 12.34 that the 82C288 also produces control signals ALE, DT/$\overline{R}$, and DEN. These signals are used to set up the I/O interface circuitry for the input or output data transfer. The data bus transceiver/buffers control the direction of data transfers between the 80286 and I/O devices. The transceivers get enabled for operation whenever their output enable ($\overline{OE}$) inputs are switched to logic 0. Notice that the signals data bus enable DEN and $\overline{I/OCE}_{0-N}$ are combined with NAND gates to produce $\overline{OE}$. To enable the transceiver, DEN must be at logic 1 and at least one of the $\overline{I/OCE}_{0-N}$ lines must be at logic 0. These conditions occur during all I/O bus cycles.

The direction in which data are passed through the transceivers is determined by the logic level of the DIR input. This input is supplied by the DT/$\overline{R}$ output of the 82C288. During all input cycles, DT/$\overline{R}$ is logic 0, and the transceivers are set to pass data from the selected I/O device to the 80286. On the other hand, during output cycles, DT/$\overline{R}$ is switched to logic 1, and data passes from the 80286 to the I/O device.

M/$\overline{IO}$	$\overline{S}_1$	$\overline{S}_0$	Type of bus cycle
0	0	0	Interrupt acknowledge
0	0	1	I/O Read
0	1	0	I/O Write
0	1	1	None; idle
1	0	0	Halt or shutdown
1	0	1	Memory read
1	1	0	Memory write
1	1	1	None; idle

Figure 12.35 I/O bus cycle status codes. (Courtesy of Intel Corp.)

Input and Output Bus Cycle Timing

We just found that the I/O interface signals of the 80286 microcomputer are essentially the same as those involved in the memory interface. In fact, the function, logic levels, and timing of all signals other than the M/$\overline{\text{IO}}$ are identical to those already described for the memory interface in section 12.10.

Timing diagrams for the 80286's *input bus cycle* and *output bus cycle* are shown in Figs. 12.36 and 12.37, respectively. Looking at the input bus cycle waveforms, we see that address A_0 through A_{15} along with $\overline{\text{BHE}}$ and M/$\overline{\text{IO}}$ are output during the T_C state of the previous bus cycle. This time the 80286 switches M/$\overline{\text{IO}}$ to logic 0 to signal that an I/O bus cycle is to take place. At the beginning of T_S of the input cycle, $\overline{S_1}\overline{S_0}$ is set to 01 to signal that an input operation is in progress. This status information is input to the 82C288 and initiates an I/O read bus control sequence.

Let us continue with the sequence of events that takes place in external circuitry during the read bus cycle. First the 82C288 outputs a pulse to the 1 logic

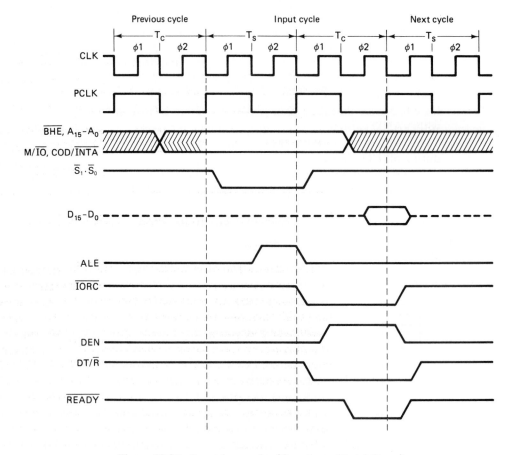

Figure 12.36 Input bus cycle. (Courtesy of Intel Corp.)

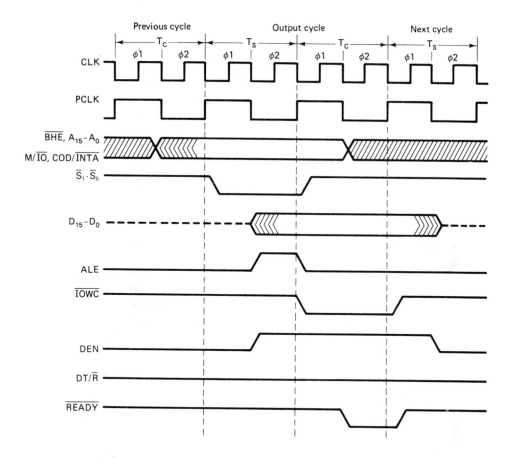

Figure 12.37 Output bus cycle. (Courtesy of Intel Corp.)

level on ALE. As shown in the circuit of Fig. 12.34, this pulse is used to latch the address information into the external address latch devices. At the beginning of T_C, $\overline{\text{IORC}}$ is switched to logic 0 to signal the enabled I/O device that data are to be input to the MPU, and DT/$\overline{\text{R}}$ is switched to logic 0 to set the data bus transceivers to the input direction. A short time later, the transceivers are enabled as DEN switches to logic 1, and the data from the I/O device are passed onto the 80286's data bus. As shown in Fig. 12.36 $\overline{\text{READY}}$ is at its active 0 logic level when sampled at the end of the T_C state; therefore, the data are read by the 80286. Finally, the 82C288 returns $\overline{\text{IORC}}$, DEN, and DT/$\overline{\text{R}}$ to their inactive logic level, and the input cycle is complete.

Looking at the output bus cycle timing diagram in Fig. 12.37, we see that the 80286 puts the data that is to be output onto the data bus at the beginning of ϕ_2 in the T_S state of the output cycle. At this same time, the 82C288 switches DEN to logic 1 and DT/$\overline{\text{R}}$ is maintained at the 1 level for transmit mode. From Fig. 12.34 we find that since DEN is logic 1, as soon as one of the I/O $\overline{\text{CE}}_{0\text{-N}}$ lines switches to logic 0, the data bus transceivers are enabled and set up to pass data from the

80286 to the I/O devices. Therefore, the data output on the bus is available on the data inputs of the enabled I/O device. Finally, the signal $\overline{\text{IOWC}}$ switches to logic 0 during the T_C state and tells the I/O device that valid output data is on the bus. Now the I/O device must read the data off the bus before the bus controller terminates the bus cycle. If the device cannot read data at this rate, it can hold $\overline{\text{READY}}$ at the 1 logic level to extend the bus cycle with wait states.

▲ 12.12 INTERRUPT AND EXCEPTION PROCESSING

In our study of the 8086 microprocessor, we found that interrupts provide a mechanism for quickly changing program environments. We also found that the transfer of program control to the interrupt service routine can be initiated by either an event internal to the microprocessor or an event in its external hardware.

Just as for the 8086-based microcomputer, the 80286 is capable of implementing up to 256 prioritized interrupts. They are divided into five groups: *external hardware interrupts, software interrupts, internal interrupts* and *exceptions, the non-maskable interrupt,* and *reset.* The functions of the external hardware, software, and nonmaskable interrupts are identical to those in the 8086 microcomputer and are again defined by the user. On the other hand, the internal interrupt and exception processing capability of the 80286 has been greatly enhanced. These internal interrupts and reset perform dedicated system functions in the 80286 system. The priority scheme by which the 80286 services interrupts and exceptions is identical to that described earlier for the 8086.

In the real mode, the 80286 processes interrupts in exactly the same way as the 8086; that is, the same events that were described in Chapter 9 take place during the interrupt request, interrupt acknowledge bus cycle, and device service routine.

Interrupt Vector and Interrupt Descriptor Tables

An address pointer table is used to link the interrupt type numbers to the locations of their service routines in program storage memory. In a real-mode 80286-based microcomputer system, this table is called the *interrupt vector table.* On the other hand, in a protected-mode system, the table is referred to as the *interrupt descriptor table.* Figure 12.38 shows a map of the interrupt vector table in the memory of a real-mode 80286 microcomputer. Looking at the table, we see that it is identical to the interrupt vector table of the 8086 microcomputer. It contains 256 address pointers (vectors), one for each of the interrupt type numbers 0 through 255. These address pointers identify the starting locations of their service routines in program memory. The content of this table is either held as firmware in EPROMs or loaded into RAM as part of the system initialization procedure.

Notice that in Fig. 12.38 the interrupt vector table is again located at the low-address end of the memory address space. It starts at address 00000_{16} and ends at word address $003FE_{16}$. Each of the 256 vectors requires two words (base address and offset) and is stored at an even-address boundary. Unlike the 8086, the interrupt

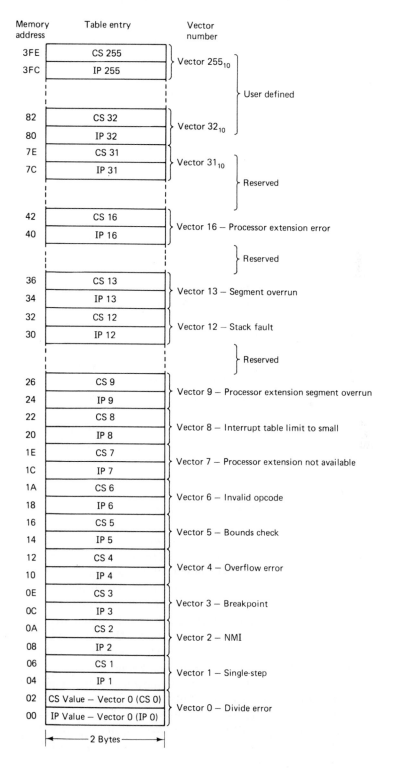

Figure 12.38 Real-mode interrupt vector table. (Courtesy of Intel Corp.)

vector table or interrupt descriptor table in an 80286-based microcomputer can be located anywhere in the memory address space. Its starting location and size are actually identified by the contents of a register within the 80286 called the *interrupt descriptor table register* (IDTR). When the 80286 is initialized at power-on, it comes up in the real mode with the bits of the base address in IDTR all equal to zero and the limit set to $03FF_{16}$. This positions the interrupt vector table as shown in Fig. 12.38. In the real mode, the value in IDTR should be left at this initial value to maintain compatibility with 8086/8088-based microcomputer software.

External Hardware Interrupt Interface

Up to this point in the section, we have introduced the types of interrupts supported by the 80286 and the real-mode interrupt vector table. Let us now look at the external hardware interrupt interface of the 80286 microcomputer.

A general interrupt interface for an 80286-based microcomputer system is illustrated in Fig. 12.39(a). Looking at this diagram, we see that it is similar to the interrupt interface of a maximum-mode 8086 microcomputer system. Notice that it includes the address and data buses, status signals $\overline{S}_0$, $\overline{S}_1$, and M/$\overline{IO}$, and dedicated interrupt signals INTR and $\overline{INTA}$. The external circuitry is required to interface interrupt inputs, INT_{32} through INT_{255}, to the 80286's interrupt interface. Just as in an 8086 system, this interface circuitry must identify which of the pending active interrupts has the highest priority, perform an interrupt request/acknowledge handshake, then pass a type number to the 80286.

In this circuit we see that the key interrupt interface signals are *interrupt request* (INTR) and *interrupt acknowledge* ($\overline{INTA}$). The logic level input at the INTR line signals the 80286 that an external device is requesting service. The 80286 samples this input during the last clock period of each instruction execution cycle—that is, at instruction boundaries. Logic 1 at INTR represents an active interrupt request. INTR is *level triggered*; therefore, its active level must be maintained until tested by the 80286. If it is not maintained, the request for service may not be recognized. For this reason, inputs INT_{32} through INT_{255} are normally latched. The 1 at INTR must be removed before the service routine runs to completion; otherwise, the same interrupt may be acknowledged a second time.

When an interrupt request has been recognized by the 80286, it signals this to external circuitry by outputting the interrupt acknowledge bus cycle status code on M/$\overline{IO}$ $\overline{S}_1\overline{S}_0$. This code, which equals 000, is highlighted in Fig. 12.40. Notice in Fig. 12.39(a) that this code is input to the 82C288 bus controller where it is decoded to produce a pulse to logic 0 at the $\overline{INTA}$ output. Actually, there are two pulses produced at $\overline{INTA}$ during the *interrupt acknowledge bus cycle*. The first pulse signals external circuitry that the interrupt request has been acknowledged and to prepare to send its type number to the 80286. The second pulse tells the external circuitry to put the interrupt type number on the data bus.

Notice that only the lower eight lines of the data bus, D_0 through D_7, are part of the interrupt interface. During the second cycle in the interrupt acknowledge bus sequence, external circuitry must put an 8-bit type number of the highest priority active interrupt request onto this part of the data bus. The 80286 reads this number off the bus to identify which external device is requesting service. Then, it uses the type number to generate the address of the interrupt's vector in the interrupt vector table or gate in the interrupt descriptor table.

Address lines A_0 through A_{23} are also shown in the interrupt interface circuit of Fig. 12.39(a). This is because LSI interrupt controller devices are typically used to implement most of the external circuitry. When a read or write bus cycle is performed to the controller, for example, to initialize its internal registers after system reset, some of the address bits are decoded to produce a chip select to enable the controller device, and other address bits are used to select the internal register that is to be accessed. Of course, the interrupt controller could be I/O mapped instead of memory mapped; in this case just address lines A_0 through A_{15} are used in the interface.

Figure 12.39(b) shows an interrupt interface circuit that uses a single 8259A programmable interrupt controller. This circuit implements eight interrupt request inputs. For applications that require more than eight interrupt request inputs, 8259A devices are cascaded into a master/slave configuration similar to the one for the 8088 microprocessor that was discussed in an earlier chapter.

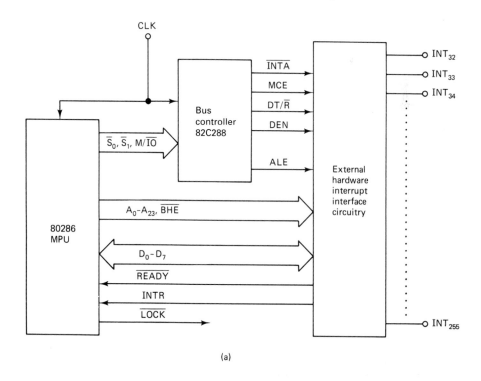

(a)

Figure 12.39 (a) 80286 microcomputer system external hardware interrupt interface.

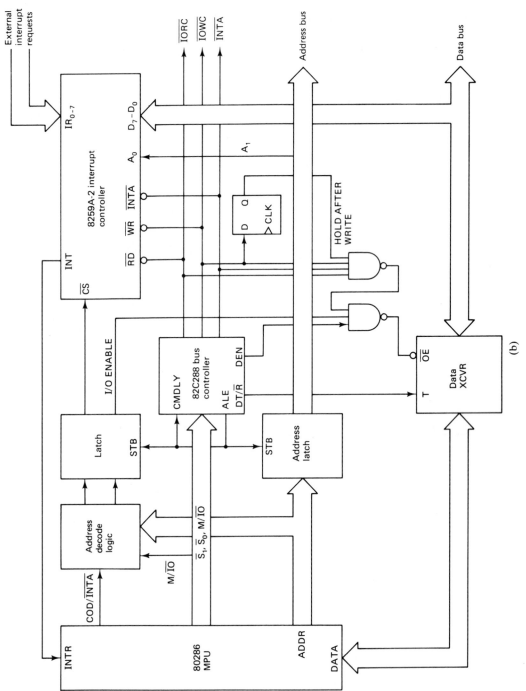

Figure 12.39 (b) Interrupt interface circuit using a 8259A. (Courtesy of Intel Corp.)

Internal Interrupt and Exception Functions

Earlier we indicated that some of the 256 interrupt vectors of the 80286 are dedicated to internal interrupt and exception functions. Internal interrupts and exceptions differ from external hardware interrupts in that they result from the execution of an instruction, not an event, that takes place in external hardware. That is, an internal interrupt or exception may be initiated because a fault condition was detected either during or after execution of an instruction. In this case, a routine is provided to service the internal condition.

Figure 12.41 identifies the internal interrupts and exceptions that are active in real mode. Here we find internal interrupts such as single step and breakpoint and exception functions such as divide error and overflow error that were also detected by the 8086; however, the 80286 also implements several new real-mode exceptions. For example, invalid opcode, bounds check, and processor-extension error are all new with the 80286. Let us now look at these new real-mode internal functions in more detail.

Bounds Check Exception. Earlier we pointed out that the BOUND (check array index against bounds) instruction can be used to test an operand, which is used as the index into an array, to verify that it is within a predefined range. If the index is less than the lower bound (minimum value) or greater than the upper bound (maximum value), a *bounds check exception* has occurred and control is passed to the exception handler pointed to by the values of CS_5 and IP_5.

Invalid Opcode Exception. The exception processing capability of the 80286 permits detection of undefined opcodes. This feature of the 80286 allows it to detect automatically whether or not the opcode to be executed as an instruction corresponds to one of the instructions in the instruction set. If it does not, execution is not attempted; instead, the opcode is identified as being undefined and the *invalid opcode exception* is initiated. In turn, control is passed to the exception handler identified by IP_6 and CS_6. This *undefined opcode detection* mechanism permits the 80286 to detect errors in its instruction stream.

M/$\overline{\text{IO}}$	$\overline{S}_1$	$\overline{S}_0$	Type of bus cycle
0	0	0	Interrupt acknowledge
0	0	1	I/O Read
0	1	0	I/O Write
0	1	1	None; idle
1	0	0	Halt or shutdown
1	0	1	Memory read
1	1	0	Memory write
1	1	1	None; idle

Figure 12.40 Interrupt bus status code. (Courtesy of Intel Corp.)

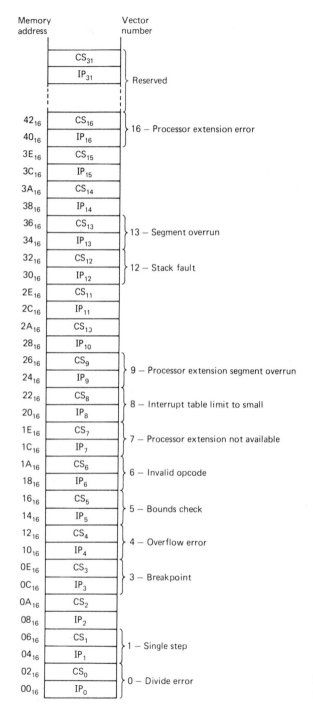

Figure 12.41 Real-mode internal exception vector locations.

Processor Extension Not Available Exception.   When the 80286 comes up in the real mode, both the EM (emulate) and MP (math present) bits of its machine status word are reset. This mode of operation corresponds to that of the 8088 or 8086 microprocessors. When set in this way, the *processor extension not available exception* cannot occur; however, if the EM bit has been set to 1 under software control (no math coprocessor is present) and the 80286 executes an ESC (escape) instruction for the 80287 math coprocessor, a processor extension not present exception is initiated through the vector specified by CS_7 and IP_7. This service routine could pass control to a software emulation routine for the floating-point arithmetic operation. If the MP (math present) bit and TS bit are both set (meaning that a math coprocessor is available in the system and a task is in progress) when the ESC or wait instruction is executed, an exception also takes place.

Interrupt Table Limit Too Small Exception.   Earlier we pointed out that the IDTR can be used to relocate the interrupt vector table in memory. If the location of the real-mode table has been changed such that the table extends beyond address $003FF_{16}$ and an interrupt is invoked that attempts to access a vector stored at an address higher than the limit, the *interrupt table limit too small exception* occurs. In this case, control is passed to the service routine by the vector $CS_8{:}IP_8$.

Processor Extension Segment Overrun Exception.   The *processor extension segment overrun exception* signals that the 80287 numeric coprocessor has overrun the limit of a segment while attempting to read or write its operand. This event is detected by the processor extension data channel within the 80286 and passes control to the service routine through interrupt vector 9. This exception handler can clear the exception, reset the 80287, determine the cause of the exception by examining the registers within the 80287, and then initiate a corrective action.

Stack Fault Exception.   In the real-mode, if the address of an operand access for the stack segment crosses the boundaries of the stack, a *stack fault exception* is produced. This causes control to be transferred to the service routine defined by CS_{12} and IP_{12}.

Segment Overrun Exception.   This exception occurs in the real mode if an instruction attempts to access an operand that extends beyond the end of a segment. For instance, if a word access is made to the address CS:FFFFH, DS:FFFFH, or ES:FFFFH, a *segment overrun exception* occurs.

Processor Extension Exception. As part of the handshake sequence between the 80286 microprocessor and 80287 math coprocessor, the 80286 checks the status of its $\overline{\text{ERROR}}$ input. If the 80287 encounters a problem performing a numeric operation, it signals this to the 80286 by switching its $\overline{\text{ERROR}}$ output to logic 0. This signal is normally applied directly to the $\overline{\text{ERROR}}$ input of the 80286. Logic 0 at this input signals that an error condition has occurred and causes a *processor extension exception* through vector 16.

ASSIGNMENTS

Section 12.2

1. Name the technology used to fabricate the 80286 microprocessor.

2. What is the approximate transistor count of the 80286?

3. In what three packages is the 80286 manufactured?

Section 12.3

4. Name the four internal processing units of the 80286.

5. What are the word lengths of the 80286's address bus and the data bus?

6. Does the 80286 have a multiplexed address/data bus or demultiplexed address and data buses?

7. How large is the 80286's instruction queue?

8. List three functions performed by the address unit.

9. What is the function of the instruction queue?

Section 12.4

10. How does the performance of an 8-MHz 80286 in real mode compare to that of a 5-MHz 8086?

11. What is meant when we say that the 80286 is object code compatible with the 8086?

12. What additional register has been provided in the 80286 operating in real mode as compared to the 8086?

Section 12.5

13. Describe the operation performed by the instruction PUSHA.

14. Which registers and in what order does the instruction POPA pop from the stack?

15. What is a stack frame?

16. How much stack does the instruction ENTER 20H,4 allocate for the stack frame? What is the lexical level?

17. If $(DS) = (ES) = 1075_{16}$, $(DI) = 100_{16}$, $(DF) = 0$, and $(DX) = 1000_{16}$, what happens when the instruction INSW is executed?

18. If $(DS) = (ES) = 1075_{16}$, $(SI) = 100_{16}$, $(DF) = 1$, $(CX) = F_{16}$, and $(DX) = 2000_{16}$, what happens when the instruction REPOUTSB is executed?

19. Explain the function of the bound instruction in the sequence

```
MOV    DI, VALUE
BOUND  DI, [LIMITS]
```

Assume that address LIMITS contains the value 0000_{16} and LIMITS $+ 2$ holds the value $00FF_{16}$.

Section 12.6

20. How large is the real-address mode address bus and physical address space? How large is the protected-address mode address bus and physical address space? How large is the protected-mode virtual address space?

21. What type of bus cycle is in progress when the bus status code COD/$\overline{\text{INTA}}$ M/$\overline{\text{IO}}$ $\bar{S}_1\bar{S}_0$ equals 1010?

22. If the code output as $\overline{\text{BHE}}$ A_0 equals 01, what type of data transfer is taking place over the bus?

23. Is the logic level output on COD/$\overline{\text{INTA}}$ intended to be directly used as the interrupt acknowledge signal to the external hardware interrupt interface circuitry?

24. Which signals implement the DMA interface?

25. What numeric processor can be attached to the processor extension interface?

Section 12.7

26. Which of the 80286's status outputs are input to the 82288?

27. If the input status code to the 82288 is 010, what command output is active?

28. What bus control signals are produced by the 82288?

29. To what logic level must CEN/$\overline{\text{AEN}}$ be set to enable the command outputs of the 82288?

Section 12.8

30. What speed 80286 ICs are available from Intel Corporation? How are these speeds denoted in the part number?

31. What frequency crystal must be connected between the X_1 and X_2 inputs of the 80C284-12 to run the device at full speed?

32. What clock outputs are produced by the 82C284? What would be their frequencies if a 20-MHz crystal is used?

Section 12.9

33. How many clock states are in an 80286 bus cycle that has no wait states? What would be the duration of this bus cycle for the 80286 operating at 10 MHz?

34. What does T_S stand for? What happens in this part of the processor cycle?

Assignments

35. What does T_C stand for? What happens in this part of the processor cycle?
36. Explain what is meant by pipelining of the 80286's bus.
37. What is an idle state?
38. What is a wait state? If an 80286 running at 10 MHz performs a bus cycle with two wait states, what is the duration of the bus cycle?

Section 12.10

39. Summarize the function of each of the blocks in the memory interface diagram of Fig. 12.27.
40. When the instruction PUSH AX is executed, what bus status code is output by the 80286 and what read/write control signal is produced by the 82C288?
41. What are the four types of data transfers that can take place over the data bus? How many bus cycles are required for each type of data transfer?
42. If an 80286 is running at 10 MHz and all memory accesses involve one wait state, how long will it take to fetch the word of data starting at address $0FF1A_{16}$? At address $0FF1D_{16}$?
43. During a bus cycle that involves an odd-addressed word transfer, which byte of data is transferred over the bus during the first bus cycle?
44. Describe the bus activity that takes place as the 80286 writes a byte of data into memory address $B0010_{16}$.
45. If the write cycle in Fig. 12.32 is for an 80286 running at 12.5 MHz, what is the duration of the bus cycle?
46. If the read cycle in Fig. 12.33 is for an 80286 running at 12.5 MHz, what is the duration of the bus cycle?

Section 12.11

47. Which signal indicates to the bus controller and external circuitry that the current bus cycle is for the I/O interface and not for the memory interface?
48. Which device produces the input (read), output (write), and bus control signals for the I/O interface?
49. Briefly describe the function of each block in the I/O interface circuit in Fig. 12.34.
50. If an 80286 running at 10 MHz inserts two wait states into all I/O bus cycles, what is the duration of a bus cycle in which a byte of data is being output?
51. If the 80286 in problem 50 was outputting a word of data to a word-wide port at I/O address $1A1_{16}$, what would be the duration of the bus cycle?
52. Summarize the sequence of events that take place at the I/O interface in Fig. 12.34 as a word of I/O data is output over data bus lines D_0 through D_{15} to a port at an even address.

Section 12.12

53. What are the five groups of interrupts supported by the 80286 MPU?

54. What is the range of type numbers assigned to the interrupts in the 80286 microcomputer system?

55. What is the real-mode interrupt address pointer table called? The protected-mode address pointer table?

56. What is the size of a real-mode interrupt vector?

57. The contents of which register determines the location of the interrupt address pointer table? To what value is this register initialized at reset?

58. The breakpoint routine in a real-mode 80286 microcomputer system starts at address $AA000_{16}$ in the code segment located at address $A0000_{16}$. Specify how the breakpoint vector will be stored in the interrupt vector table.

59. Explain the function of the INTR and $\overline{INTA}$ in the circuit diagram of Fig. 12.39(a).

60. How many interrupt inputs can be directly accepted by the circuit in Fig. 12.39(b)?

61. List the real-mode internal interrupts serviced by the 80286.

62. Which real-mode vector numbers are reserved for internal interrupts and exceptions?

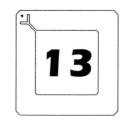

The 80386, 80486, and Pentium™ Processor Families: Software Architecture

▲ 13.1 INTRODUCTION

In this chapter, we study the software architecture of the *80386*, *80486*, and *Pentium™ processor* families. The chapter focuses on the 80386 family. The 80386 supports three modes of software operation called the *real-address mode* (real mode), the *protected-address mode* (protected mode), and *virtual 8086 mode*. We will explore each of these modes in the chapter. After first introducing the 80386 microprocessor, we examine its real-address-mode software architecture and assembly language instruction set. This is followed by a detailed study of the 80386's protected-address mode of operation and system control instruction set. The material on the 80386 completes with a description of the virtual 8086 mode. The chapter closes with sections that describe the differences between the software architecture of the 80386 and 80486 and Pentium™ processors families. The following topics are covered in the chapter.

1. The 80386 microprocessor family
2. Internal architecture of the 80386
3. Real-address-mode software model of the 80386
4. Real-address-mode instruction set of the 80386
5. Protected-address-mode software architecture of the 80386
6. Descriptor and page table entries of the 80386

740

7. Protected-mode system control instruction set of the 80386

8. Multitasking and protection

9. Virtual 8086 mode

10. The 80486 microprocessor family

11. The Pentium™ processor family

▲ 13.2 80386 MICROPROCESSOR FAMILY

The 80386 family of microprocessors, which were announced by Intel Corporation in 1985, represent the first 32-bit members of Intel's popular microprocessor architecture. The 80386DX MPU, the first entry in the 80386 family, was the sixth member of Intel Corporation's 8086 family of microprocessors. This device is the highest performance member of the 80386 family of MPUs. The 80386DX is a full 32-bit processor; that is, it has both 32-bit internal registers and a 32-bit external data bus. Several years later Intel brought the 80386SX microprocessor to market. This device, with its 32-bit internal registers and 16 bit data bus, provides a lower performance MPU for the 80386-based microcomputer system. In this chapter, we will primarily study the 80386DX MPU. However, both the 80386DX and 80386SX devices operate essentially the same way from a software point of view.

The chart in Fig. 13.1 is called the *iCOMP™ index*. A bar is used in this chart to represent a measure of the performance for each of Intel's MPUs. This index is provided by Intel Corporation so that the relative performance of their microprocessors can be compared. Notice that the members of the 80386 family offer low performance when compared to the newer 80486 and Pentium™ processor families. In fact, the slowest 80386SX MPU shown in Fig. 13.1, the -20, has a performance rating of 32, while the fastest 80386DX, the -33, is rated at 68. In this way, we see that by selecting between the various members of the 80386 family we can achieve a wide range of system performance levels.

We already have learned that from the software point of view the 80386DX offers several modes of operation: real-address mode, protected-address mode, and virtual 8086 mode. The real mode is for compatibility with the large existing 8086/8088 software base; protected mode offers an advanced software architecture with enhanced system-level features such as memory management, multitasking, and protection; and virtual 8086 mode provides 8086 real-mode compatibility while operating in the protected mode. Virtual 8086 mode was not supported by the protected mode of the 80286 microprocessor.

▲ 13.3 INTERNAL ARCHITECTURE OF THE 80386

The internal architecture of 8086 family of microprocessors has changed a lot as part of the evolutionary process from the original 8086 to the 80386. All members of the 8086 family employ what is called *parallel processing*. That is, they are implemented with simultaneously operating multiple processing units. Each unit

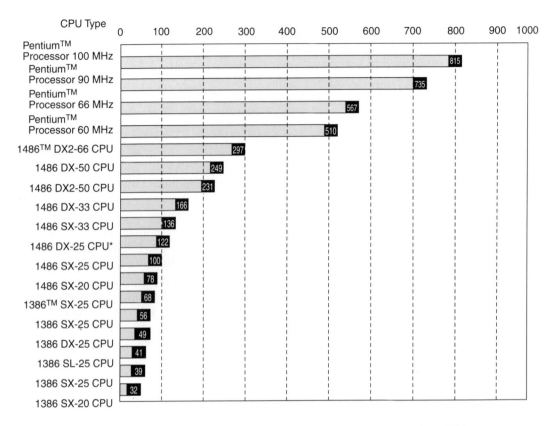

Figure 13.1 iCOMP™ index rating chart. (Reprinted by permission of Intel Corp., © Intel Corp. 1993)

has a dedicated function and they operate at the same time. The more the parallel processing, the higher the performance of the microprocessor.

In earlier chapters we examined the internal architecture of the 8086 and 80286 microprocessors. We found that the 8086 microprocessor contains just two processing units: the bus interface unit and execution unit. In the 80286 microprocessor, the internal architecture was further partitioned into four independent processing elements: the bus unit, the instruction unit, the execution unit, and the address unit. This additional parallel processing provided an important contribution to the higher level of performance achieved with the 80286 architecture.

The 80386DX's internal architecture is illustrated in Fig. 13.2. Here we see that to enhance the performance more parallel processing elements are provided. Notice that now there are six functional units: the *execution unit*, the *segment unit*, the *page unit*, the *bus unit*, the *prefetch unit*, and the *decode unit*. Let us now look more closely at each of the processing units of the 80386DX.

The bus unit is the 80386DX's interface to the outside world. By interface, we mean the path by which it connects to external devices. The bus interface provides a 32-bit data bus, 32-bit address bus, and the signals needed to control

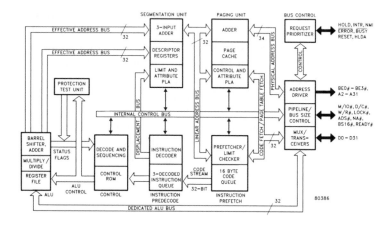

Figure 13.2 Internal architecture of the 80386DX MPU. (Reprinted by permission of Intel Corp., © Intel Corp. 1987)

transfers over the bus. In fact, 8-bit, 16-bit, and 32-bit data transfers are supported. These buses are demultiplexed like those of the 80286. That is, the 80386DX has separate pins for its address and data bus lines. This demultiplexing of address and data results in higher performance and easier hardware design. Expanding the data bus width to 32 bits further improves the performance of the 80386DX's hardware architecture as compared to that of either the 8086 or 80286.

The bus unit is responsible for performing all external bus operations. This processing unit contains the latches and drivers for the address bus, transceivers for the data bus, and control logic for signaling whether a memory, input/output, or interrupt acknowledge bus cycle is being performed. Looking at Fig. 13.2, we find that for data accesses the address of the storage location that is to be accessed is input from the paging unit, and for code accesses the address is provided by the prefetch unit.

The prefetch unit implements a mechanism known as an *instruction stream queue*. This queue permits the 80386DX to prefetch up to sixteen bytes of instruction code. Whenever the queue is not full, that is, it has room for at least four more bytes, and at the same time, the execution unit is not asking it to read or write operands from memory, the prefetch unit supplies addresses to the bus interface unit and signals it to look ahead in the program by fetching the next sequential instructions. Prefetched instructions are held in the FIFO queue for use by the instruction decoder. Whenever bytes are loaded at the input end of the queue, they are automatically shifted up through the FIFO to the empty locations near the output. With its 32-bit data bus, the 80386DX fetches four bytes of instruction code in a single memory cycle. Through this prefetch mechanism, the fetch time for most instructions is hidden.

If the queue in the prefetch unit is full and the execution unit is not requesting access to operands in memory, the bus interface unit does not need to perform any bus cycle. These intervals of no bus activity, which occur between bus cycles, are known as *idle states*.

The prefetch unit prioritizes bus activity. Highest priority is given to operand accesses for the execution unit. However, if the bus unit is already in the process of fetching instruction code when the execution unit requests it to read or write operands from memory or I/O, the current instruction fetch is first completed before the operand read/write cycle is initiated.

In Fig. 13.2, we see that the decode unit accesses the output end of the prefetch unit's instruction queue. It reads machine-code instructions from the output side of the prefetch queue and decodes them into the microcode instruction format used by the execution unit. That is, it off-loads the responsibility for instruction decoding from the execution unit. The *instruction queue* within the 80386DX's instruction unit permits three fully decoded instructions to be held waiting for use by the execution unit. Once again the result is improved performance for the MPU.

The execution unit includes the arithmetic/logic unit (ALU), the 80386DX's registers, special multiply, divide, and shift hardware, and a control ROM. By registers, we mean the 80386DX's general purpose registers, such as EAX, EBX, and ECX. The control ROM contains the microcode sequences that define the operation performed by each of the 80386DX's machine-code instructions. The execution unit reads decoded instructions from the instruction queue and performs the operations that they specify. It is the ALU that performs the arithmetic, logic, and shift operations required by an instruction. If necessary, during the execution of an instruction, it requests the segment and page units to generate operand addresses and the bus interface unit to perform read or write bus cycles to access data in memory or I/O devices. The extra hardware that is provided to perform multiply, divide, shift, and rotate operations improves the performance of instructions that employ these functions.

The segment and page units provide the memory management and protection services for the 80386DX. They off-load the responsibility for address generation, address translation, and segment checking from the bus interface unit; thereby further boosting the performance of the MPU. The segment unit implements the segmentation model of the 80386DX's memory management. That is, it contains dedicated hardware for performing high-speed address calculations, logical to linear address translation, and protection checks. For instance, when in the real mode, the execution unit requests the segment unit to obtain the address of the next instruction to be fetched by adding an appended version of the current contents of the code segment (CS) register with the value in the instruction pointer (IP) register to obtain the 20-bit physical address that is to be output on the address bus. This address is passed on to the bus unit.

For protected mode, the segment unit performs the logical to linear address translation and various protection checks needed when performing bus cycles. It contains the segment registers and the *6-word × 64-bit bit cache* that is used to hold the current descriptors within the 80386DX.

The page unit implements the protected mode paging model of the 80386DX's memory management. It contains the *translation lookaside buffer* that stores recently used page directory and page table entries. When paging is enabled, the linear address produced by the segment unit is used as the input of the page unit. Here the linear address is translated into the physical address of the memory or I/O location to be accessed. This physical memory or I/O address is output to the bus interface unit.

▲ 13.4 REAL-ADDRESS-MODE SOFTWARE MODEL OF THE 80386

Let us begin our study of the 80386DX microprocessor with its real-address-mode software model and operation. Just like the 80286 microprocessor, 80386DX comes up in the real mode after it is reset. The 80386DX will remain in this mode unless it is switched to protected mode by the software. In real mode, the 80386DX operates as a very high performance 8086. For instance, the original 16-MHz 80386DX provides more than 10 times higher performance than the standard 5-MHz 8086.

When in the real mode, the 80386DX can be used to execute the base instruction set of the 8086/8088 architecture. Similar to the 80286, object code for the base instructions of the 80386DX is identical to that of the 8086/8088. In this way, we see that object code compatibility is maintained between the 8086/8088 and 80386 family of microprocessors. This means that the operating systems and programs written for the 8086 and 8088 can be run directly on the 80386DX without modification.

As for the 80286, a number of new instructions have been added to the instruction set of the 80386DX to enhance its performance and functionality. In fact, the exact same instructions that were added to the 80286 to make the 80286's extended instruction set are also available in the 80386DX's instruction set. For instance, instructions have been added to push or pop the complete register set, perform string input/output, and check the boundaries of data array accesses. However, the real-mode instruction set has been further enhanced in the 80386DX. For example, it has a group of instructions that are provided to perform bit test and set operations. The object code of the 80386DX is also upward compatible within the 8086 architecture; that is, 8086/8088's object code will run on the real-mode 80386DX. But, the reverse is not true. For instance, if the bit test and set instructions are employed in the writing of a program, it will not run on the 8086 or the 8088 MPU.

The real-mode software model of the 80386DX is shown in Fig. 13.3. This register model is very different from those of the 8088, 8086, and 80286. Here we have highlighted the 17 internal registers that are used in real-mode application programming. Nine of them, the data registers (EAX, EBX, ECX, and EDX), pointer registers (EBP and ESP), index registers (ESI and EDI), and the flag register (EFLAGS) are identical to the corresponding registers in the 8086's software model except that they are now 32 bits in length. The segment registers (CS, DS, SS, and ES) and instruction pointer (IP) are identical to those of the 8086. Notice that they are still 16 bits long and they serve the same software functions. For instance, CS and IP together point to the next instruction that is to be fetched.

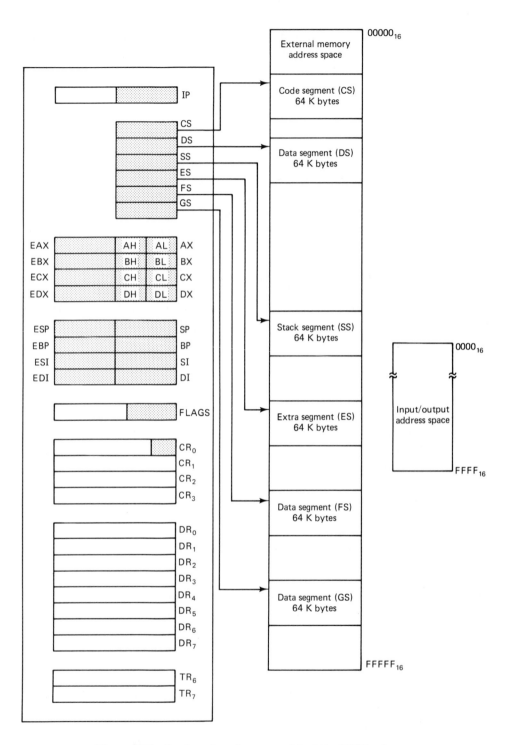

Figure 13.3 Real-mode software model of the 80386 microprocessor.

746

Several new registers are found in the real-mode 80386DX's software model. For instance, it has two more data segment registers, denoted as FS and GS. These registers are not implemented in the 8086 or the 80286 microprocessor. Another new register called *control register zero* (CR_0) is included in the model. This register is similar to the machine status word register of the 80286, but has some additional bits that are functional. The only bit in CR_0 that is active in the real mode is bit 0, which is the *protection enable* (PE) *bit*. PE is the bit that is used to switch the 80386DX from real to protected mode. At reset, PE is set to 0 and selects real-mode operation. The software model of the 80386SX is exactly the same as that shown in Fig. 13.3.

Looking at Fig. 13.3, we find that the 80386DX microcomputer's real-mode address space is identical to that of the 8086 and 80286 microcomputer. Again, it is partitioned into a 1MB memory address space and a separate 64KB input/output address space. The memory address space is from address 00000_{16} to $FFFFF_{16}$ and the I/O address space is from address 0000_{16} to $FFFF_{16}$. Since the 80386DX has six segment registers, not four as in 8086 and 80286, six 64KB segments of the memory address space are active at a time and give a maximum of 384KB of active memory. 64KB of the active memory are allocated for code, 64KB for stack, and 256KB for data storage. Figures 13.4(a) and (b) show that the real-mode 80386DX memory and I/O address spaces are partitioned into general-use and reserved areas in the same way as for the 8086 or 80286 microcomputer. Memory in an 80386SX based microcomputer system is organized in the same way from a software point of view.

Finally, the real-mode 80386DX generates physical addresses in the same manner as the 8086 or 80286. That is, the 16-bit contents of a segment register, such as CS, are shifted left by four bit positions, the four least significant bits are filled with 0s, and then it is added to a 16-bit offset, such as the value in IP, to form the 20-bit physical memory address. Notice that the IP register is shown to be larger than 16 bits in the software model, but just the lower 16 bits are active when the 80386DX is in real-mode.

▲ 13.5 REAL-ADDRESS-MODE INSTRUCTION SET OF THE 80386

Figure 13.5 illustrates the evolution of the instruction set for the 8086 architecture. The instruction set of the 8086 and 8088 microprocessors that is called the *base instruction set* is a subset of the 80386DX's real-address-mode instruction set. The instructions of the base instruction set were covered in detail in Chapters 4 and 5.

This base instruction set was enhanced in the 80286 microprocessor with a group of instructions known as the *extended instruction set*. All these instructions are also available in the real-mode instruction set of the 80386DX. We studied the operation of these instructions in Chapter 12.

The last group of instructions, identified in Fig. 13.5 as the *80386 specific instruction set*, were first implemented with the 80386DX microprocessor. In this way, we see that the 80386DX's real-mode instruction set is a superset of the 8086

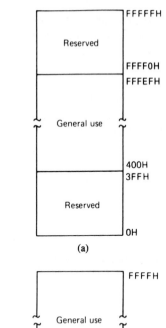

(a)

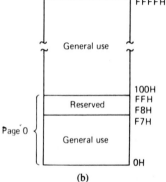

(b)

Figure 13.4 (a) Dedicated and general use of memory in the real mode. (Reprinted by permission of Intel Corp., © Intel Corp. 1979) (b) I/O address space. (Reprinted by permission of Intel Corp., © Intel Corp. 1979)

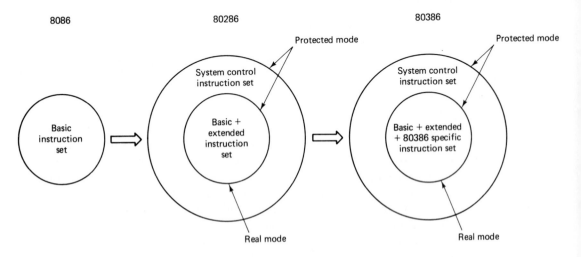

Figure 13.5 Evolution of the 8086 family instruction set.

and 80286 microprocessor instruction sets. The 80386SX microprocessor executes the exact same instruction set as the 80386DX. We will now continue by examining the instructions of the 80386 specific instruction set.

80386 Specific Instruction Set

The enhancements to the 80386DX's real-mode instruction set, which are highlighted in Fig. 13.6(a), represent the 80386 specific instruction set. For example, it includes instructions to directly load a pointer into the FS, GS, and SS registers. Moreover, it contains additional forms of existing instructions that have been added to perform the identical operations in a more general way, on special registers, or on a double word of data. First, we will look briefly at some of the instructions with expanded functions.

Figure 13.6(b) shows that the MOV instructions can be written with a control register (CR), debug register (DR), or test register (TR) as its source or destination operand. As an example, let us look at what function the instruction

$$\text{MOV} \quad \text{EAX}, \text{CR}_0$$

performs. Execution of this instruction causes the value of the flags in CR_0 to be copied into the EAX register. Looking at Fig. 13.6(b), we see that the string instructions have been expanded to support double-word (32-bit) operands. The instruction mnemonics for the double-word string operations are MOVSD, CMPSD, SCASD, LODSD, STOSD, INSD, and OUTSD. In all seven cases, the basic operation performed by the instruction is the same as described earlier for the 8088 processor; however, a double-word data transfer takes place. The same is true for the shift, convert, compare, jump, push, and pop instructions in Fig. 13.6(b). They simply perform their normal operation on double-word operands. One exception is that the 80386DX limits the count for shift instructions to a count of 32, instead of 256 as on the 8086 or 80286. Let us next look at the instructions that are implemented for the first time on the 80386DX MPU.

Sign-extend and Zero-extend Move Instructions: MOVSX and MOVZX

In Fig. 13.6(b), we find that a number of special-purpose move instructions have been added to the instruction set of the 80386DX. The first two instructions, *move with sign-extend* (MOVSX) and *move with zero-extend* (MOVZX), are used to sign extend or zero extend, respectively, a source operand as it is moved to the destination operand location. The source operand is either a byte or a word of data in a register or a storage location in memory, while the destination operand is either a 16- or 32-bit register.

For example, the instruction

$$\text{MOVSX} \quad \text{EBX}, \text{AX}$$

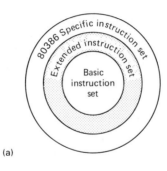

(a)

Mnemonic	Meaning	Format	Operation
PUSH	Push	PUSH dw/db	Push the specified data word (dw) or sign extended data byte (db) onto the stack.
PUSHA	Push all	PUSHA	Push the contents of registers AX, CX, DX, BX, original SP, BP, SI, and DI onto the stack.
POPA	Pop all	POPA	Pop the stack contents into the registers DI, SI, BP, SP, BX, DX, CX, and AX.
IMUL	Integer multiply	IMUL rw, ew, dw/db	Perform the signed multiplication as follows: rw = ew*dw/db where rw is the word size register, ew is the effective word size operand, and the third operand is the immediate data word (dw) or a byte (db).
Logic instructions		Instruction db	Perform the logic instruction using the specified byte (db) as the count.
INS	Input string	INSB, INSW	Input the byte or the word size element of the string from the port specified by DX to the location ES:[DI].
OUTS	Output string	OUTSB, OUTSW	Output the byte or the word size element of the string from ES:[SI] to port specified by DX.
ENTER	Enter procedure	ENTER dw, 0/1/db	Make stack frame for procedure parameters.
LEAVE	Leave procedure	LEAVE	Release the stack space used by the procedure.
BOUND	Check array index against bounds	BOUND rw, md	Interrupt 5 occurs if the register word (rw) is not greater than or equal to the memory word at md and not less than or equal to the second memory word at md + 1.

(b)

Figure 13.6 (a) 80386 specific instruction set. (b) Instructions of the 80386 specific instruction set.

750

is used to copy the 16-bit value in AX into EBX. As the copy is performed, the value in the sign bit, which is bit 15 of AX, is extended into the 16 higher-order bits of EBX. For example, if AX contains $FFFF_{16}$, the sign bit is logic 1. Therefore, after execution of the MOVSX instruction, the value that results in EBX is $FFFFFFFF_{16}$. The MOVZX instruction performs a similar function to the MOVSX instruction except that it extends the value moved to the destination operand location with zeros.

EXAMPLE 13.1

Explain the operation performed by the instruction

```
MOVZX   CX, BYTE PTR [DATA_BYTE]
```

if the value of data at memory address DATA_BYTE is FF_{16}.

Solution

When the MOVZX instruction is executed, the value FF_{16} is copied into the lower byte of CX and the upper eight bits are filled with 0s. This gives

$$(CX) = 00FF_{16}$$

Load Full Pointer Instructions: LSS, LFS, and LGS

The base instruction set of the 8086 includes two *load full pointer instructions*, LDS and LES. Three additional instructions of this type are performed by the 80386DX. Looking at Fig. 13.6(b), we find that they are: LSS, LFS, and LGS. Notice that executing the *load register and SS* (LSS) instruction causes both the register specified in the instruction and the stack segment register to be loaded from the source operand. For example, the instruction

```
LSS   ESP, [STACK_POINTER]
```

causes the first 32 bits starting at memory address STACK_POINTER to be loaded into the 32-bit register ESP and the next 16 bits into the SS register. The other two instructions, *load register and FS* (LFS) and *load register and GS* (LGS) perform a function similar to LSS. However, they load the specified register and the FS or GS register, respectively.

EXAMPLE 13.2

Write an instruction that will load the 48-bit pointer starting at memory address DATA_G_ADDRESS into the ESI and GS registers.

Solution

This operation is performed with the instruction

$$\text{LGS} \quad \text{ESI}, \quad [\text{DATA\_G\_ADDRESS}]$$

Bit Test and Bit Scan Instructions: BT, BTR, BTS, BTC, BSF, and BSR

The *bit test and bit scan instructions* of the 80386DX enable a programmer to test the logic value of a bit in either a register or a storage location in memory. Let us begin by examining the bit test instructions. They are used to test the state of a single bit in a register or memory location. When the instruction is executed, the value of the tested bit is saved in the carry flag. Instructions are provided that can also reset, set, or complement the contents of the tested bit during the execution of the instruction.

In Fig. 13.6(b), we see that the *bit test* (BT) instruction has two operands. The first operand identifies the register or memory location that contains the bit that is to be tested. The second operand contains an index that selects the bit that is to be tested. Notice that the index may be either an immediate operand or the value in register. When this instruction is executed, the state of the tested bit is simply copied into the carry flag.

Once the state of the bit is saved in CF, it can be tested through software. For instance, a conditional jump instruction could be used to test the value in CF, and if CF equals 1, program control could be passed to a service routine. On the other hand, if CF equals 0, the value of the index could be incremented, a jump performed back to the BT instruction, and the next bit in the operand tested.

Another example is the instruction

$$\text{BTR} \quad \text{EAX}, \text{EDI}$$

Execution of this instruction causes the bit in 32-bit register EAX that is selected by the index in EDI to be tested. The value of the tested bit is first saved in the carry flag and then it is reset in the register EAX.

EXAMPLE 13.3

Describe the operation that is performed by the instruction

$$\text{BTC BX}, 7$$

Assume that register BX contains the value $03F0_{16}$.

Solution

Let us first express the value in BX in binary form. This gives

$$(\text{BX}) = 0000001111110000_2$$

Execution of the *bit test and complement* instruction causes the value of bit 7 to be first tested and then complemented. Since this bit is logic 1, CF is set to 1. This gives

$$(CF) = 1$$

$$(BX) = 0000001101110000_2 = 0370_{16}$$

The *bit scan forward* (BSF) and *bit scan reverse* (BSR) instructions are used to scan through the bits of a register or storage location in memory to determine whether or not they are all 0. For example, by executing the instruction

```
BSF ESI, EDX
```

the bits of 32-bit register EDX are tested one after the other starting from bit 0. If all bits are found to be 0, the ZF is cleared. On the other hand, if the contents of EDX are not zero, ZF is set to 1 and the index value of the first bit tested as 1 is copied into ESI.

Byte Set On Condition: SETcc

The *byte set on condition* (SETcc) instruction can be used to test for various states of the flags. In Fig. 13.6(b), we see that the general form of the instruction is denoted as

```
SETcc S
```

Here the cc part of the mnemonic stands for a general-flag relationship and must be replaced with a specific relationship when writing the instruction. Figure 13.7 is a list of the mnemonics that can be used to replace cc and their corresponding flag relationships. For instance, replacing cc by A gives the mnemonic SETA. This stands for *set byte if above* and tests the flags to determine if

$$(CF) = 0 \text{ and } (ZF) = 0$$

If these conditions are satisfied, a byte of 1s is written to the register or memory location specified as the source operand. On the other hand, if the conditions are not valid, a byte of 0s is written to the source operand.

An example is the instruction

```
SETE AL
```

Looking at Fig. 13.7, we find that execution of this instruction causes the ZF to be tested. If ZF equals 1, 11111111_2 is written into AL; otherwise, it is loaded with 00000000_2.

Instruction	Meaning	Conditions code relationship
SETA r/m8	Set byte if above	CF = 0 · ZF = 0
SETAE r/m8	Set byte if above or equal	CF = 0
SETB r/m8	Set byte if below	CF = 1
SETBE r/m8	Set byte if below or equal	CF = 1 + ZF = 1
SETC r/m8	Set if carry	CF = 1
SETE r/m8	Set byte if equal	ZF = 1
SETG r/m8	Set byte if greater	ZF = 0 + SF = OF
SETGE r/m8	Set byte if greater	SF = OF
SETL r/m8	Set byte if less	SF <> OF
SETLE r/m8	Set byte if less or equal	ZF = 1 · SF <> OF
SETNA r/m8	Set byte if not above	CF = 1
SETNAE r/m8	Set byte if not above	CF = 1
SETNB r/m8	Set byte if not below	CF = 0
SETNBE r/m8	Set byte if not below	CF = 0 · ZF = 0
SETNC r/m8	Set byte if not carry	CF = 0
SETNE r/m8	Set byte if not equal	ZF = 0
SETNG r/m8	Set byte if not greater	ZF = 1 + SF <> OF
SETNGE r/m8	Set if not greater or equal	SF <> OF
SETNL r/m8	Set byte if not less	SF = OF
SETNLE r/m8	Set byte if not less or equal	ZF = 1 · SF <> OF
SETNO r/m8	Set byte if not overflow	OF = 0
SETNP r/m8	Set byte if not parity	PF = 0
SETNS r/m8	Set byte if not sign	SF = 0
SETNZ r/m8	Set byte if not zero	ZF = 0
SETO r/m8	Set byte if overflow	OF = 1
SETP r/m8	Set byte if parity	PF = 1
SETPE r/m8	Set byte if parity even	PF = 1
SETPO r/m8	Set byte if parity odd	PF = 0
SETS r/m8	Set byte if sign	SF = 1
SETZ r/m8	Set byte if zero	ZF = 1

Figure 13.7 SET instruction conditions.

EXAMPLE 13.4

Write an instruction that will load memory location EVEN_PARITY with the value FF_{16} if the result produced by the last instruction had even parity.

Solution

As shown in Fig. 13.7, the instruction that tests for (PF) = 1 and sets the byte to FF_{16} is

```
SETPE   [EVEN_PARITY]
```

▲ 13.6 PROTECTED-ADDRESS-MODE SOFTWARE ARCHITECTURE OF THE 80386

Having completed our study of the real-mode operation and instruction set of the 80386DX microprocessor, we are now ready to turn our attention to its protected-address-mode (protected mode) of operation. Earlier we indicated that whenever the 80386DX microprocessor is reset it comes up in real mode. Moreover, we indicated that the PE bit of control register zero (CR_0) can be used to switch the 80386DX into the protected mode under software control. When configured for protected mode, the 80386DX provides an advanced software architecture that supports memory management, virtual addressing, paging, protection, and multitasking. In this section we will examine the 80386DX's protected-mode register model, virtual memory address space, and memory management.

Protected-Mode Register Model

The protected-mode register set of the 80386DX microprocessor is shown in Fig. 13.8. Looking at this diagram, we see that its application register set is a superset of the real-mode register set shown in Fig. 13.3. Comparing these two diagrams, we find four new registers in the protected-mode model: the *global descriptor table register* (GDTR), *interrupt descriptor table register* (IDTR), *local descriptor table register* (LDTR), and *task register* (TR). Furthermore, the functions of a few registers have been extended. For example, the instruction pointer, which is now called EIP, is 32 bits in length; more bits of the flag register (EFLAGS) are active; and all four control registers, CR_0 through CR_3, are functional. Let us next discuss the purpose of each new and extended register, and how they are used in the segmented protected-mode operation of the microprocessor.

Global Descriptor Table Register. As shown in Fig. 13.9, the contents of the *global descriptor table register* define a table in the 80386DX's physical memory address space called the *global descriptor table* (GDT). This global descriptor table is one important element of the 80386DX's memory management system.

GDTR is a 48-bit register that is located inside the 80386DX. The lower two bytes of this register identified as LIMIT in Fig. 13.9, specify the size in bytes of the GDT. The value of LIMIT is one less than the actual size of the table. For instance, if LIMIT equals $00FF_{16}$, the table is 256 bytes in length. Since LIMIT has 16 bits, the GDT can be up to 65,536 bytes long. The upper four bytes of the GDTR, which are labeled BASE in Fig. 13.9, locate the beginning of the GDT in physical memory. This 32-bit base address allows the table to be positioned anywhere in the 80386DX's 4GB linear address space.

EXAMPLE 13.5 ———————————————————————————

If the limit and base in the global descriptor table register are $0FFF_{16}$ and 00100000_{16}, respectively, what is the beginning address of the descriptor table, size of the table in bytes, and ending address of the table?

Solution

The starting address of the global descriptor table in physical memory is given by the BASE. Therefore,

$$GDT_{START} = 00100000_{16}$$

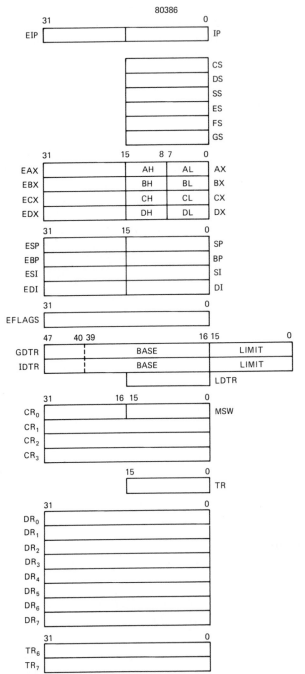

Figure 13.8 Protected-mode register model.

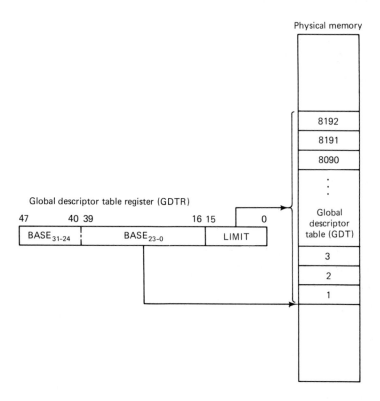

Figure 13.9 Global descriptor table mechanism.

The limit is the offset to the end of the table. This gives

$$GDT_{END} = 00100000_{16} + 0FFF_{16} = 00100FFF_{16}$$

Finally, the size of the table is equal to the value of LIMIT plus 1.

$$GDT_{SIZE} = FFF_{16} + 1_2 = 4096 \text{ bytes}$$

The GDT provides a mechanism for defining the characteristics of the 80386DX's *global memory* address space. Global memory is a general system resource that is shared by many or all software tasks. That is, storage locations in global memory are accessible by any task that runs on the microprocessor.

This table contains what are called *system segment descriptors*. These descriptors identify the characteristics of the segments of global memory. For instance, a segment descriptor provides information about the size, starting point, and access rights of a global memory segment. Each descriptor is eight bytes long; thus our earlier example of a 256-byte table provides storage space for just 32 descriptors. Remember that the size of the global descriptor table can be expanded by simply changing the value of LIMIT in the GDTR under software control. If the table is increased to its maximum size of 65,536 bytes, it can hold up to 8192 descriptors.

EXAMPLE 13.6

How many descriptors can be stored in the global descriptor table defined in Example 13.5?

Solution

Each descriptor takes up eight bytes; therefore, a 4096-byte table can hold

$$4096/8 = 512 \text{ descriptors}$$

The value of the BASE and LIMIT must be loaded into the GDTR before the 80386DX is switched from the real mode of operation to the protected mode. Special instructions are provided for this purpose in the system control instruction set of the 80386DX. These instructions will be introduced later in this chapter.

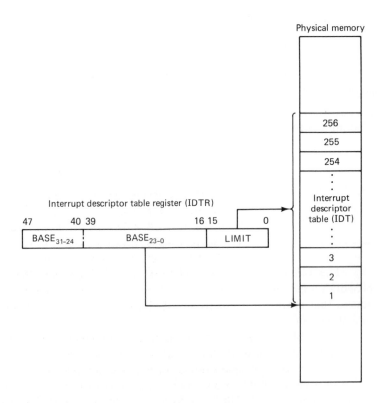

Figure 13.10 Interrupt descriptor table mechanism.

Once the 80386DX is in the protected mode, the location of the table is typically not changed.

Interrupt Descriptor Table Register. Just like the global descriptor table register, the *interrupt descriptor table register* (IDTR) defines a table in physical memory. However, this table contains what are called *interrupt descriptors*, not segment descriptors. For this reason, it is known as the *interrupt descriptor table* (IDT). This register and table of descriptors provide the mechanism by which the microprocessor passes program control to interrupt and exception service routines.

As shown in Fig. 13.10, just like the GDTR, the IDTR is 48 bits in length. Again, the lower two bytes of the register (LIMIT) define the table size. That is, the size of the table equals LIMIT+1 bytes. Since two bytes define the size, the IDT can also be up to 65,536 bytes long. But the 80386DX supports only up to 256 interrupts and exceptions; therefore, the size of the IDT should not be set to support more than 256 interrupts. The upper four bytes of IDTR (BASE) identify the starting address of the IDT in physical memory.

The types of descriptors used in the IDT are called *interrupt gates*. These gates provide a mean for passing program control to the beginning of an interrupt service routine. Each gate is eight bytes long and contains both attributes and a starting address for the service routine.

EXAMPLE 13.7 _____

What is the maximum value that should be assigned to LIMIT in the IDTR?

Solution

The maximum number of interrupt descriptors that can be used in an 80386DX microcomputer system is 256. Therefore, the maximum table size in bytes is

$$IDT_{SIZE} = 8_{10} \times 256 = 4096 \text{ bytes}$$

Thus

$$LIMIT = 0FFF_{16}$$

This table can also be located anywhere in the linear address space addressable with the 80386DX's 32-bit address. Just like the GDTR, the IDTR needs to be loaded before the 80386DX is switched from the real mode to protected mode. Special instructions are provided for loading and saving the contents of the IDTR. Once the location of the table is set, it is typically not changed after entering protected mode.

EXAMPLE 13.8 _____

What is the address range of the last descriptor in the interrupt descriptor table defined by base address 00011000_{16} and limit $01FF_{16}$?

Solution

From the values of the base and limit, we find that the table is located in the address range defined by

$$IDT_{START} = 00011000_{16}$$

and

$$IDT_{END} = 000111FF_{16}$$

The last descriptor in this table takes up the eight bytes of memory from address $000111F8_{16}$ through $000111FF_{16}$.

Local Descriptor Table Register. The *local descriptor table register* (LDTR) is also part of the 80386DX's memory management support mechanism. As shown in Fig. 13.11(a), each task can have access to its own private descriptor table in addition to the global descriptor table. This private table is called the *local descriptor table* (LDT) and defines a *local memory* address space for use by the task. The LDT holds segment descriptors that provide access to code and data in segments of memory that are reserved for the current task. Since each task can have its own segment of local memory, the protected-mode software system may contain many local descriptor tables. For this reason, we have identified LDT_0 through LDT_N in Fig. 13.11(a).

Figure 13.11(b) shows us that the 16-bit LDTR does not directly define the local descriptor table. Instead, it holds a selector that points to an *LDT descriptor* in the GDT. Notice that whenever a selector is loaded into the LDTR, the corresponding descriptor is transparently read from global memory and loaded into the *local descriptor table cache* within the 80386DX. It is this descriptor that defines the local descriptor table. As shown in Fig. 13.11(b), the 32-bit BASE identifies the starting point of the table in physical memory, and the value of the 16-bit LIMIT determines the size of the table. Loading of this descriptor into the cache creates the LDT for the current task. That is, everytime a selector is loaded into the LDTR, a local descriptor table descriptor is cached and a new LDT is activated.

Control Registers. The protected-mode model includes the four system control registers, identified as CR_0 through CR_3 in Fig. 13.8. Figure 13.12 shows these registers in more detail. Notice that the lower five bits of CR_0 are system control flags. These bits make up what is known as the *machine status word* (MSW). The most significant bit of CR_0 and registers CR_2 and CR_3 are used by the 80386DX's paging mechanism.

Let us continue by examining the machine status word bits of CR_0. They contain information about the 80386DX's protected-mode configuration and status. The 4 bits labeled PE, MP, EM, and R are control bits that define the protected-mode system configuration. The fifth bit, TS, is a status bit. These bits can be examined or modified through software.

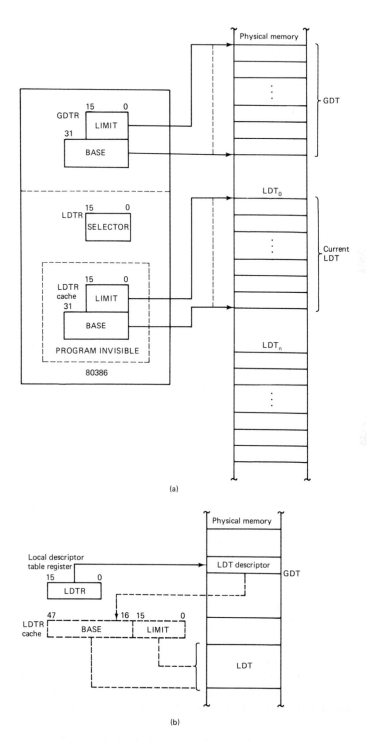

(a)

(b)

Figure 13.11 (a) Task with global and local descriptor tables. (b) Loading the local descriptor table register to define a local descriptor table.

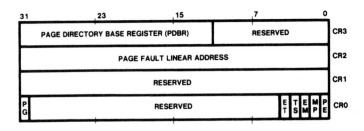

31	23	15	7	0	
PAGE DIRECTORY BASE REGISTER (PDBR)			RESERVED		CR3
PAGE FAULT LINEAR ADDRESS					CR2
RESERVED					CR1
P G	RESERVED			E T T S E M P M P E	CR0

Figure 13.12 Control registers. (Reprinted by permission of Intel Corp., © Intel Corp. 1986)

The *protected-mode enable* (PE) bit determines if the 80386DX is in the real or protected mode. At reset, PE is cleared. This enables real mode of operation. To enter protected mode, we simply switch PE to 1 through software. Once in protected mode, the 80386DX cannot be switched back to real mode under software control. The only way to return to real mode is by initiating a hardware reset.

The *math present* (MP) bit is set to 1 to indicate that a numeric coprocessor is present in the microcomputer system. On the other hand, if the system is to be configured so that a software emulator instead of a coprocessor is used to perform numeric operations, the *emulate* (EM) bit is set to 1. Only one of these two bits can be set at a time. Finally, the *extension-type* (R) bit is used to indicate whether an 80287 or 80387 numeric coprocessor is in use. Logic 1 in R indicates that an 80387 is installed. The last bit in the MSW, *task switch* (TS), automatically gets set whenever the 80386DX switches from one task to another. It can be cleared under software control.

The protected-mode software architecture of the 80386DX also supports paged memory operation. Paging is turned on by switching the PG bit in CR_0 to logic 1. Now addressing of physical memory is implemented with an address translation mechanism that consists of a page directory and page table that are both held in physical memory. Looking at Fig. 13.12, we see that CR_3 contains the *page directory base register* (PDBR). This register holds a 20-bit *page directory base address* that points to the beginning of the page directory. A page fault error occurs during the page translation process if the page is not present in memory. In this case, the 80386DX saves the address at which the page fault occurred in register CR_2. This address is denoted as *page fault linear address* in Fig. 13.12.

Task Register. The *task register* (TR) is a key element in the protected-mode task switching mechanism of the 80386DX microprocessor. This register holds a 16-bit index value called a *selector*. The initial selector must be loaded into TR under software control. This starts the initial task. After this is done, the selector is automatically changed whenever the 80386DX executes an instruction that performs a task switch.

As shown in Fig. 13.13, the selector in TR is used to locate a descriptor in the global descriptor table. Notice that when a selector is loaded into the TR the corresponding *task state segment* (TSS) *descriptor* automatically gets read from memory and loaded into the on-chip *task descriptor cache*. This descriptor defines a block of memory called the *task state segment* (TSS). It does this by providing the starting address (BASE) and the size (LIMIT) of the segment. Every task has its own TSS. The TSS holds the information needed to initiate the task, such as initial values for the user-accessible registers.

EXAMPLE 13.9

What is the maximum size of a TSS? Where can it be located in the linear address space?

Solution

Since the value of LIMIT is 16 bits in length, the TSS can be as long as 64K-bytes. Moreover, the base is 32 bits in length. Therefore, the TSS can be located anywhere in the 80386DX's 4G-byte address space.

EXAMPLE 13.10

Assume that the base address of the global descriptor table is 00011000_{16} and the selector in the task register is 2108_{16}. What is the address range where the TSS descriptor is stored?

Solution

The beginning address of the TSS descriptor is

$$\text{TSS\_DESCRIPTOR}_{\text{START}} = 00011000_{16} + 2108_{16}$$

$$= 00013108_{16}$$

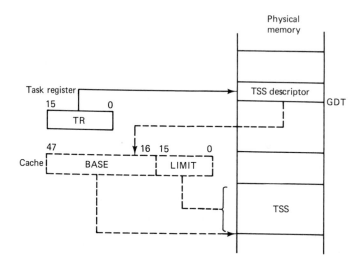

Figure 13.13 Task register and the task-switching mechanism.

Since the descriptor is eight bytes long, it ends at

$$TSS\_DESCRIPTOR_{END} = 001310F_{16}$$

Registers with Changed Functionality.   Earlier we pointed out that the function of a few of the registers that are common to both the real-mode and protected-mode register models changes as the 80386DX is switched into the protected mode of operation. For instance, the segment registers are now called the *segment selector registers*, and instead of holding a base address they are loaded with what is known as a *selector*. The selector does not directly specify a storage location in memory. Instead, it selects a descriptor that defines the size and characteristics of a segment of memory.

The format of a selector is shown in Fig. 13.14. Here we see that the two least significant bits are labeled RPL, which stands for *requested privilege level*. These bits contain either $00 = 0, 01 = 1, 10 = 2$, or $11 = 3$ and assign a request protection level to the selector. The next bit, which is identified as *table indicator* (TI) in Fig. 13.14, selects the table to be used when accessing a segment descriptor. Remember that in protected mode two descriptor tables are active at a time, the global descriptor table and a local descriptor table. Looking at Fig. 13.14, we find that if TI is 0 the selector corresponds to a descriptor in the global descriptor table. Finally, the 13 most significant bits contain an *index* that is used as a pointer to a specific descriptor entry in the table selected by the TI bit.

EXAMPLE 13.11

Assume that the base address of the LDT is 00120000_{16} and the GDT base address is 00100000_{16}. If the value of the selector loaded into the CS register is 1007_{16}, what is the request privilege level? Is the segment descriptor in the GDT or LDT? What is the address of the segment descriptor?

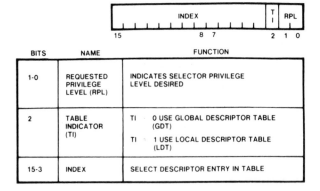

Figure 13.14   Selector format. (Reprinted by permission of Intel Corp., © Intel Corp. 1986)

Solution

Expressing the selector value in binary form, we get

$$(CS) = 0001000000000111_2$$

Since the two least significant bits are both 1,

$$RPL = 3$$

The next bit, bit 2, is also 1. This means that the segment descriptor is in the LDT. Finally, the value in the 13 most significant bits must be scaled by 8 to give the offset of the descriptor from the base address of the table. Therefore,

$$OFFSET = 0001000000000_2 \times 8 = 512 \times 8 = 4096$$
$$= 1000_{16}$$

and the address of the segment descriptor is

$$DESCRIPTOR_{ADDRESS} = 00120000_{16} + 1000_{16}$$
$$= 00121000_{16}$$

Another register whose function changes when the 80386DX is switched to protected mode is the flag register. As shown in Fig. 13.8, the flag register is now

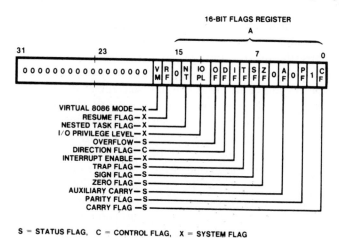

Figure 13.15 Protected-mode flag register. (Reprinted by permission of Intel Corp., © Intel Corp. 1986)

identified as EFLAGS and expands to 32 bits in length. The functions of the bits in EFLAGS are given in Fig. 13.15. Comparing this illustration to the 8086 flag register in Fig. 2.17, we see that five additional bits are implemented. These bits are only active when the 80386DX is in protected mode. They are the 2-bit *input/ output privilege level* (IOPL) code, the *nested task* (NT) flag, the *resume* (RF) flag, and the *virtual 8086 mode* (VM) flag.

Notice in Fig. 13.15 that each of these flags is identified as a system flag. That is, they represent protected-mode system operations. For example, the IOPL bits are used to assign a maximum privilege level to input/output. For instance, if 00 is loaded into IOPL, I/O can only be performed when the 80386DX is in the highest privilege level, which is called *level 0*. On the other hand, if IOPL is 11, I/O is assigned to the least privilege level, level 3.

The NT flag identifies whether or not the current task is a nested task, that is, if it was called from another task. This bit is automatically set whenever a nested task is initiated and can only be reset through software.

Protected-Mode Memory Management and Address Translation

Up to this point in the section, we have introduced the register set of the protected-mode software model for the 80386DX microprocessor. However, the software model of a microprocessor also includes its memory structure. Because of the memory management capability of the 80386DX, the organization of protected mode memory appears quite complex. Here we will examine how the *memory management unit* (MMU) of the 80386DX implements the address space and how it translates virtual (logical) addresses to physical addresses. We begin here with what is called the *segmented* and *paged models* of memory.

Virtual Address and Virtual Address Space. The protected-mode memory management unit employs memory pointers that are 48 bits in length and consist of two parts, the *selector* and the *offset*. This 48-bit memory pointer is called a *virtual address* and is used by the program to specify the memory locations of instructions or data. As shown in Fig. 13.16, the selector is 16 bits in length and the offset is 32 bits long. Earlier we pointed out that one source of selectors is the segment selector registers within the 80386DX. For instance, if code is being accessed in memory, the active segment selector will be the one held in CS. This part of the pointer selects a unique segment of the 80386DX's *virtual address space.*

The offset is held in one of the 80386DX's other user-accessible registers. For our example of a code access, the offset would be in the EIP register. This part of the pointer is the displacement of the memory location that is to be accessed within the selected segment of memory. In our example, it points to the first byte of the double word of instruction code that is to be fetched for execution. Since the offset

Figure 13.16 Protected-mode memory pointer.

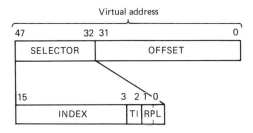

Virtual address

47   32 31   0

SELECTOR	OFFSET

15   3 2 1 0

INDEX	TI	RPL

Figure 13.17 Segment selector format.

is 32 bits in length, segment size can be as large as 4GB. We say as large as 4GB because segment size is actually variable and can be defined to be as small as 1 byte to as large as 4GB.

Figure 13.17 shows that the 16-bit selector breaks down into a *13-bit index, table select bit*, and two bits used for a *request privilege level*. The two RPL bits are not used in the selection of the memory segment. That is, just 14 of its 16 bits are employed in addressing memory. Therefore, the virtual address space can consist of 2^{14} (16,384 = 16K) unique segments of memory, each of which has a maximum size of 4GB. These segments are the basic elements into which the memory management unit of the 80386DX organizes the virtual address space.

Another way of looking at the size of the virtual address space is that, by combining the 14-bit segment selector with the 32-bit offset, we get a 46-bit virtual address. Therefore, the 80386DX's virtual address space can contain 2^{46} equals 64 terabytes (TB).

Segmented Partitioning of the Virtual Address Space. The memory management unit of the 80386DX implements both a segmented model and paged model of virtual memory. In the segmented model, the 80386DX's 64TB virtual address space is partitioned into a 32TB *global memory address space* and a 32TB *local memory address space*. This partitioning is illustrated in Fig. 13.18. The TI bit of the selector shown in Fig. 13.17 is used to select between the global or local descriptor tables that define the virtual address space. Within each of these address spaces, as many as 8192 segments of memory may exist. This assumes that every descriptor in both the global descriptor table and local descriptor table is in use and set for maximum size. These descriptors define the attributes of the corresponding segment. However, in practical system applications not all the descriptors are normally in use. Let us now look briefly at how global and local segments of memory are used by software.

In the multiprocessing software environment of the 80386DX, an application is expressed as a collection of tasks. By *task* we mean a group of program routines that together perform a specific function. When the 80386DX initiates a task, it can activate both global and local segments of memory. This idea is illustrated in Fig. 13.19. Notice that tasks 1, 2, and 3 each have a reserved segment of the local address space. This part of memory stores data or code that can only be accessed by the corresponding task. That is, task 2 cannot access any of the information in the local address space of task 1. On the other hand, all the tasks are shown to share the same segment of the global address space. This segment typically contains operating system resources and data that are to be shared by all or many tasks.

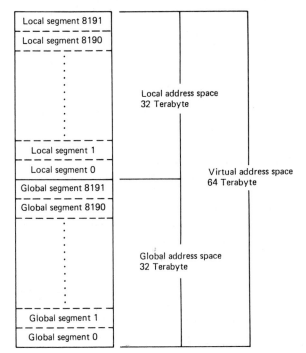

Local segment 8191
Local segment 8190

Local segment 1
Local segment 0
Global segment 8191
Global segment 8190

Global segment 1
Global segment 0

Local address space
32 Terabyte

Virtual address space
64 Terabyte

Global address space
32 Terabyte

Figure 13.18 Partitioning the virtual address space.

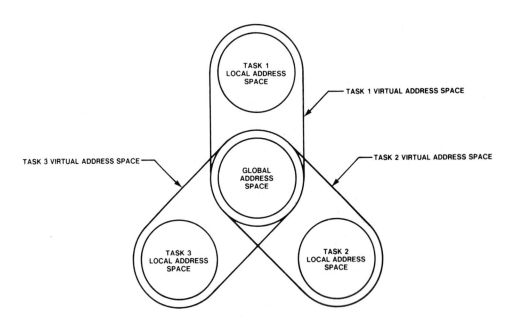

Figure 13.19 Global and local memory for a task. (Reprinted by permission of Intel Corp., © Intel Corp. 1987)

Physical Address Space and Virtual to Physical Address Translation. We have just found that the virtual address space available to the programmer is 64TB in length. However, the 32-bit protected-mode address bus of the 80386DX supports just a 4GB *physical address space*. Only a small amount of the information in virtual memory can reside in physical memory at a time.

If a segment of memory that is not present in physical memory is accessed by a program and space is available in physical memory, the segment is simply read from the hard disk and copied in physical memory. On the other hand, if the physical memory address space is full, another segment must first be sent out to the hard disk to make room for the new information. The memory manager part of the operating system controls the allocation and deallocation of physical memory and the swapping of data between the hard disk and physical memory of the computer. In this way, the memory address space of the computer appears much larger than the physical memory in the computer. For this reason, systems that employ a virtual address space that is larger than the implemented physical memory are equipped with a secondary storage device such as a hard disk. The segments that are not currently in use are stored on disk.

The segmentation and paging memory management units of the 80386DX provide the mechanism by which 48-bit virtual addresses are mapped into the 32-bit physical addresses needed by hardware. They employ a memory-based lookup table address translation process. This address translation is illustrated in Fig. 13.20. Notice that first a *segment translation* is performed on the virtual (logical) address.

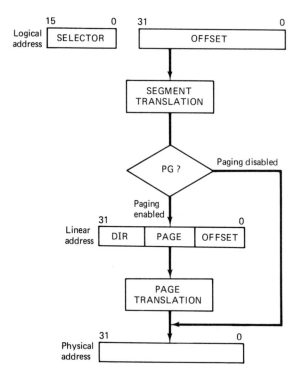

Figure 13.20 Virtual to physical address translation. (Reprinted by permission of Intel Corp., © Intel Corp. 1986)

Then, if paging is disabled, the *linear address* produced is equal to the physical address. However, if paging is enabled, the linear address goes through a second translation process, known as *page translation*, to produce the physical address.

As part of the translation process, the MMU determines whether or not the corresponding segment or page of the virtual address space currently exists in physical memory. If the segment or page is not present, it signals this condition as an error. Once this condition is identified, the memory manager software operating system can initiate loading of the segment or page from the external storage device to physical memory. This operation is called a *swap*. That is, an old segment or page gets swapped out to disk to make room in physical memory, and then the new segment is swapped into this space. Even though a swap has taken place, it appears to the program that all segments or pages are available in physical memory. Let us now look more closely at the address translation process.

We will begin by assuming that paging is turned off. In this case, the address translation sequence that takes place is the one highlighted in Fig. 13.21(a). Figure 13.21(b) describes the operations that take place during the segment translation process. Earlier we found that the 80386DX's segment selector registers, CS, DS, ES, FS, GS, and SS, provide the segment selectors that are used to index into either the global descriptor table or the local descriptor table. Whenever a selector value is loaded into a segment register, the descriptor pointed to by the index in the table selected by the TI bit is automatically fetched from memory and loaded into the corresponding *segment descriptor cache register*. It is the contents of this descriptor, not the selector, that defines the location, size, and characteristics of the segment of memory.

Notice in Fig. 13.22 that the 80386DX has one 64-bit internal segment descriptor cache register for each segment selector register. These cache registers are not accessible by the programmer. Instead, they are transparently loaded with a complete descriptor whenever an instruction is executed that loads a new selector into a segment register. For instance, if an operand is to be accessed from a new data segment, a local memory data segment selector would be first loaded into DS with the instruction

```
MOV   DS,AX
```

As this instruction is executed, the selector in AX is loaded into DS and then the corresponding descriptor in the local descriptor table is read from memory and loaded into the data segment descriptor cache register. The MMU looks at the information in the descriptor and performs checks to determine its validity.

In this way, we see that the segment descriptors held in the cache dynamically change as a task is performed. At any one time, the memory management unit permits just six segments of memory to be active. These segments correspond to the six segment selector registers, CS, DS, ES, FS, GS, and SS, and they reside in either local or global memory. Once the descriptors are cached, subsequent references to them are performed without any overhead for loading of the descriptor.

In Fig. 13.22, we find that this data segment descriptor has three parts, 12 bits of *access rights* information, a 32-bit *segment base address*, and a 20-bit *segment*

MOV DS, AX

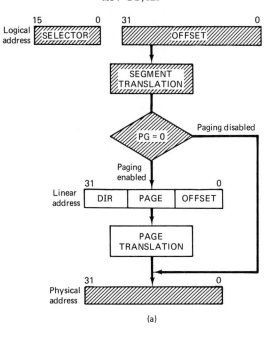

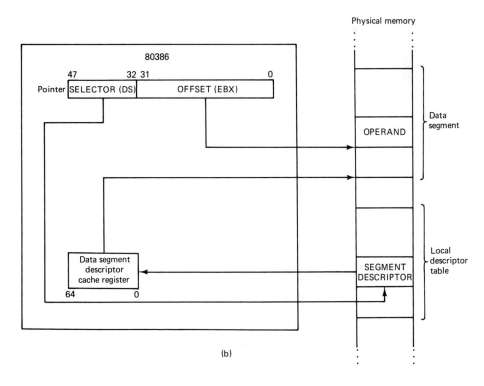

Figure 13.21 (a) Virtual to linear address translation. (Reprinted by permission of Intel Corp., © Intel Corp. 1986) (b) Translating a virtual address into a physical (linear) address.

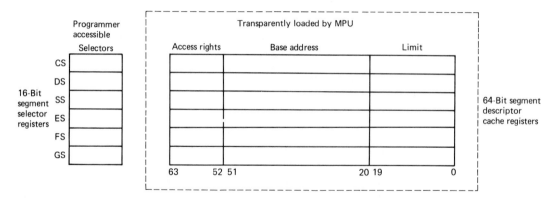

Figure 13.22 Segment selector registers and the segment descriptor cache registers.

limit. The value of the 32-bit base address identifies the beginning of the data segment that is to be accessed. The loading of the data segment descriptor cache completes the table lookup that maps the 16-bit selector to its equivalent 32-bit data segment base address.

The location of the operand in this data segment is determined by the offset part of the virtual address. For example, let us assume that the next instruction to be executed needs to access an operand in this data segment and that the instruction uses based-addressing mode to specify the operand. Then the EBX register holds the offset of the operand from the base address of the data segment. Figure 13.21(a) shows that the base address is directly added to the offset to produce the 32-bit physical address of the operand. This addition completes the translation of the 48-bit virtual address into the 32-bit linear address. As shown in Fig. 13.21(a), when paging is disabled, PG = 0, the linear address is the physical address of the storage location to be accessed in memory.

EXAMPLE 13.12

Assume that in Fig. 13.21(b) the virtual address is made up of a segment selector equal to 0100_{16} and offset equal to 00002000_{16} and that paging is disabled. If the segment base address read in from the descriptor is 00030000_{16}, what is the physical address of the operand?

Solution

The virtual address is given as

$$\text{Virtual address} = 0100{:}00002000_{16}$$

This virtual address translates to the physical address

$$\text{Linear address} = \text{Base address} + \text{Offset}$$
$$= 00030000_{16} + 00002000_{16}$$
$$= 00032000_{16}$$

The paging memory management unit works beneath the segmentation memory management unit and, when enabled it organizes the 80386DX's address space in a different way. Earlier we pointed out that when paging is not in use the 4GB physical address space is organized into segments that can be any size from 1 byte to 4GB. However, when paging is turned on, the paging unit arranges the physical address space into 1,048,496 pages that are each 4096 bytes long. Figure 13.23 shows the physical address space organized in this way. The fixed-size blocks of paged memory is a disadvantage in that 4K addresses are allocated by the memory manager even though it may not all be used. This creation of unused section of memory is called fragmentation. Fragmentation results in inefficient use of memory. However, paging greatly simplifies the implementation of the memory manager software. Let us continue by looking at what happens to the address translation process when paging is enabled.

In Fig. 13.24, we see that the linear address produced by the segment translation process is no longer used as the physical address. Instead, it undergoes a second translation called the *page translation*. Figure 13.25 shows the format of a linear address. Notice that it is composed of three elements, a 20-bit offset field, a 10-bit page field, and a 10-bit directory field.

The diagram in Fig. 13.26 illustrates how a linear address is translated into its equivalent physical address. Earlier we found that the location of the *page directory table* in memory is identified by the value in the page directory base register (PDBR) in CR_3. These twenty bits are actually the MSBs of the base address. The 12 lower bits are assumed to start at 000_{16} at the beginning of the directory and range to FFF_{16} for its end. Therefore, the page directory contains 4K byte memory locations and is organized as 1K, 32-bit addresses. These addresses

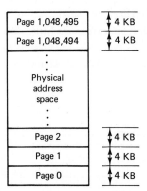

Figure 13.23 Paged organization of the physical address space.

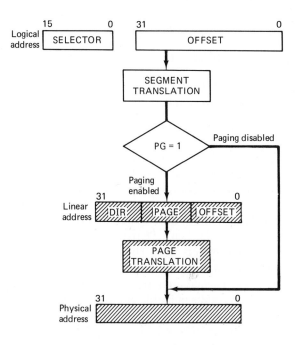

Figure 13.24 Paged translation of a linear address to a physical address. (Reprinted by permission of Intel Corp., © Intel Corp. 1986)

each point to a separate page table, which is also in physical memory. Notice that the 10-bit directory field of the linear address is the offset from the value in PDBR that selects one of the 1K 32-bit *page directory entries* in the page directory table. This pointer is cached inside the 80386DX in what is called the *translation lookaside buffer*. Its value is used as the base address of a *page table* in memory. As with the page directory, each page table is also 4K bytes long and contains 1K, 32-bit addresses. These addresses are called *page frame addresses*. Each page frame address points to a 4K frame of data storage locations in physical memory.

Next the 10-bit page field of the linear address selects one of the 1K, 32-bit *page table entries* from the page table. This table entry is also cached in the translation lookaside buffer. In Fig. 13.26 we see that it is another base address and selects a 4KB *page frame* in memory. This frame of memory locations is used for storage of data. The 12-bit offset part of the linear address identifies the location of the operand in the active page frame.

The 80386DX's translation lookaside buffer is actually capable of maintaining 32 sets of table entries. In this way, we see that 128KB of paged memory is always directly accessible. Operands in this part of memory can be accessed without first reading new entries from the page tables. If an operand to be accessed is not in

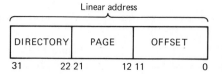

Figure 13.25 Linear address format.

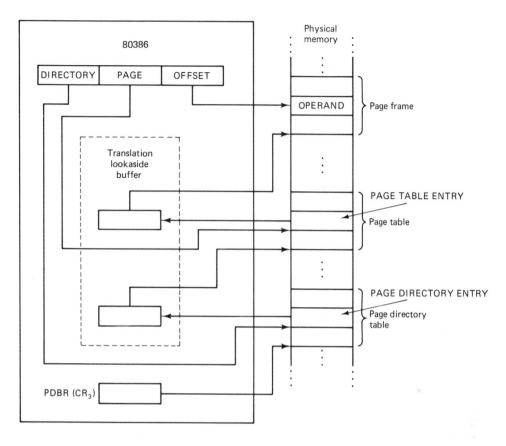

Figure 13.26 Translating a linear address to a physical address.

one of these pages, overhead is required to first read the page table entry into the translation lookaside buffer.

▲ 13.7 DESCRIPTOR AND PAGE TABLE ENTRIES OF THE 80386

In the previous section of this chapter we frequently used the terms *descriptor* and *page table entry*. We talked about the descriptor as an element of the global descriptor, local descriptor, and interrupt descriptor tables. Actually, there are several kinds of descriptors supported by the 80386DX, and they all serve different functions relative to overall system operation. Some examples are the *segment descriptor*, *system segment descriptor*, *local descriptor table descriptor*, *call gate descriptor*, *task state segment descriptor*, and *task gate descriptor*. We also discussed page table entries in our description of the 80386DX's page translation of virtual addresses. There are just two types of page table entries, the *page directory entry* and the *page table entry*. Let us now explore the structure of descriptors and page table entries.

Descriptors are the elements by which the on-chip memory manager manages the segmentation of the 80386DX's 64TB virtual memory address space. One descriptor exists for each segment of memory in the virtual address space. Descriptors are assigned to the local descriptor table, global descriptor table, task state segment, call gate, task gate, and interrupts. The contents of a descriptor provide mapping from virtual addresses to linear addresses for code, data, stack, and the task state segments and assign attributes to the segments.

Each descriptor is eight bytes long and contains three kinds of information. Earlier we identified the 20-bit *LIMIT* field and showed that its value defines the size of the segment or the table. Moreover, we found that the 32-bit *BASE* value provides the beginning address for the segment or the table in the 64GB linear address space. The third element of a descriptor, which is called the *access rights byte*, is different for each type of descriptor. Let us now look at the format of just two types of descriptors, the segment descriptor and system segment descriptor.

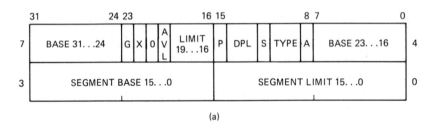

(a)

Bit Position	Name		Function	
7	Present (P)	P = 1	Segment is mapped into physical memory.	
		P = 0	No mapping to physical memory exists, base and limit are not used.	
6–5	Descriptor Privilege Level (DPL)		Segment privilege attribute used in privilege tests.	
4	Segment Descriptor (S)	S = 1	Code or Data (includes stacks) segment descriptor	
		S = 0	System Segment Descriptor or Gate Descriptor	
3	Executable (E)	E = 0	Data segment descriptor type is:	If Data Segment (S = 1, E = 0)
2	Expansion Direction (ED)	ED = 0	Expand up segment, offsets must be ≤ limit.	
		ED = 1	Expand down segment, offsets must be > limit.	
1	Writeable (W)	W = 0	Data segment may not be written into.	
		W = 1	Data segment may be written into.	
3	Executable (E)	E = 1	Code Segment Descriptor type is:	If Code Segment (S = 1, E = 1)
2	Conforming (C)	C = 1	Code segment may only be executed when CPL ≥ DPL and CPL remains unchanged.	
1	Readable (R)	R = 0	Code segment may not be read.	
		R = 1	Code segment may be read.	
0	Accessed (A)	A = 0	Segment has not been accessed.	
		A = 1	Segment selector has been loaded into segment register or used by selector test instructions.	

Type Field Definition

(b)

Figure 13.27 (a) Segment descriptor format. (b) Access byte bit definitions. (Reprinted by permission of Intel Corp., © Intel Corp. 1987)

The segment descriptor is the type of descriptor that is used to describe code, data, and stack segments. Figure 13.27(a) shows the general structure of a segment descriptor. Here we see that the two lowest addressed bytes, byte 0 and 1, hold the 16 least significant bits of the limit, the next three bytes contain the 24 least significant bits of the base address, byte 5 is the access rights byte, the lower four bits of byte 6 are the four most significant bits of the limit, the upper four bits include the *granularity* (G) and the *programmer available* (AVL) bits, and byte 7 is the eight most significant bits of the 32-bit base. Segment descriptors are only found in the local and global descriptor tables.

Figure 13.28 shows how a descriptor is loaded from the local descriptor table in global memory to define a code segment in local memory. Notice that the LDTR descriptor defines a local descriptor table between addresses 00900000_{16} and $0090FFFF_{16}$. The value 1005_{16}, which is held in the code segment selector register, causes the descriptor at offset 1000_{16} in the local descriptor table to be cached into the code segment descriptor cache. In this way, a 1MB code segment is activated starting at address 00600000_{16} in local memory.

The bits of the access rights byte define the operating characteristics of a segment. For example, they contain information about a segment such as whether the descriptor has been accessed, if it is a code or data segment descriptor, its privilege level, if it is readable or writeable, and if it is currently loaded into internal memory. Let us next look at the function of each of these bits in detail.

The function of each bit in the access rights byte is listed in Fig. 13.27(b). Notice that if bit 0 is logic 1 the descriptor has been accessed. A descriptor is marked this way to indicate that its value has been cached on the 80386DX. The memory manager software checks the information to find out if the segment is already in physical memory. Bit 4 identifies whether the descriptor represents a code/data segment or is a control descriptor. Let us assume that this bit is 1 to identify a segment descriptor. Then, the type bits, bits 1 through 3, determine whether the descriptor describes a code segment or a data segment. For instance, 000 means that it is a read/write data segment that grows upward from the base to the limit. The DPL bits, bits 5 and 6, assign a privilege level to the segment. For example, 00 selects the most privileged level, level 0. Finally, the present bit indicates whether or not the segment is currently loaded into physical memory. This bit can be tested by the operating system software to determine if the segment should be loaded from a secondary storage device such as a hard disk. For example, if the access rights byte has logic 1 in bit 7, the data segment is already available in physical memory and does not have to be loaded from an external device. Figure 13.29(a) shows the general form of a code segment descriptor and Fig. 13.29(b) a general data/stack segment descriptor.

EXAMPLE 13.13

The access rights byte of a segment descriptor contains FE_{16}. What type of segment descriptor does it describe and what are its characteristics?

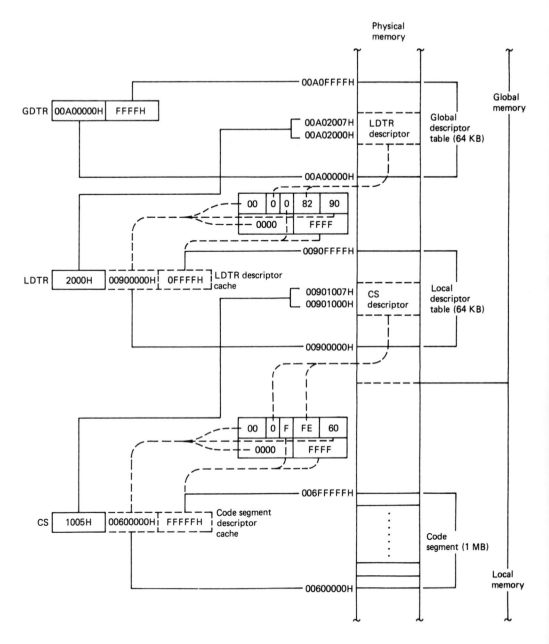

Figure 13.28   Creating a code segment.

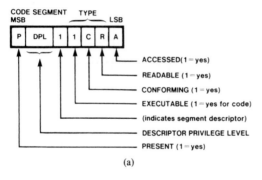

(a)

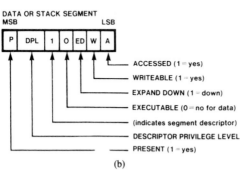

(b)

Figure 13.29 (a) Code segment descriptor access byte configuration. (Reprinted by permission of Intel Corp., © Intel Corp. 1987) (b) Data or stack segment access byte configuration. (Reprinted by permission of Intel Corp., © Intel Corp. 1987)

Solution

Expressing the access rights byte in binary form, we get

$$FE_{16} = 11111110_2$$

Since bit 4 is 1, the access rights byte is for a code/data segment descriptor. This segment has the characteristics that follow:

$$P = 1 = \text{segment is mapped into physical memory}$$
$$DPL = 11 = \text{privilege level 3}$$
$$E = 1 = \text{executable code segment}$$
$$C = 1 = \text{conforming code segment}$$
$$R = 1 = \text{readable code segment}$$
$$A = 0 = \text{segment has not been accessed}$$

An example of a system segment descriptor is the descriptor used to define the local descriptor table. This descriptor is located in the GDT. Looking at Fig. 13.30, we find that the format of a system segment descriptor is similar to the segment descriptor we just discussed. However, the type field of the access rights byte takes on new functions.

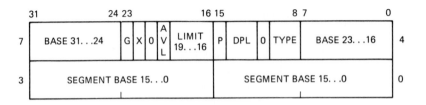

	31	24 23				16 15			8 7		0	
7	BASE 31...24	G	X	0	A V L	LIMIT 19...16	P	DPL	0 TYPE	BASE 23...16		4
3	SEGMENT BASE 15...0						SEGMENT BASE 15...0					0

Name	Value	Description
TYPE	0	Reserved by Intel
	1	Available 80286 TSS
	2	LDT
	3	Busy 80286 TSS
	4	Call gate
	5	Task gate
	6	80286 interrupt gate
	7	80286 trap gate
	8	Reserved by Intel
	9	Available 80386 TSS
	A	Reserved
	B	Busy 80386 TSS
	C	80386 call gate
	D	Reserved by Intel
	E	80386 interrupt gate
	F	80386 trap gate
P	0	Descriptor contents are not valid
	1	Descriptor contents are valid
DPL	0-3	Descriptor privilege level 0, 1, 2 or 3
BASE	32-bit number	Base address of special system data segment in memory
LIMIT	20-bit number	Offset of last byte in segment from the base

Figure 13.30 System segment descriptor format and field definitions.

EXAMPLE 13.14

If a system segment descriptor has an access rights byte equal to 82_{16}, what type of descriptor does it represent? What is its privilege level? Is the descriptor present?

Solution

First, we express the access rights byte in binary form. This gives

$$82_{16} = 10000010_2$$

Now we see that the bits that describe the type of the descriptor are given as

$$\text{TYPE} = 0010 = \text{local descriptor table descriptor}$$

The privilege level is given by

$$DPL = 00 = \text{privilege level } 0$$

and since

$$P = 1$$

the descriptor is present in physical memory.

Now that we have explained the format and use of descriptors, let us continue with page table entries. The format of either a page directory or page table entry is shown in Fig. 13.31. Here we see that the 20 most significant bits are either the base address of the page table if the entry is in the page directory table or the base address of the page frame if the entry is in the page table. Notice that only bits 12 through 31 of the base address are supplied by the entry. The 12 least significant bits are assumed to be equal to 0. In this way, we see that page tables and page frames are always located on a 4KB address boundary. In Fig. 13.26, we found that when accessed these entries are cached into the translation lookaside buffer.

The 12 lower bits of the entry supply protection characteristics or statistical information about the use of the page table or page frame. For example, the *user/supervisor* (U/S) and *read/write* (R/W) bits implement a two-level page protection mechanism. Setting U/S to 1 selects user-level protection. User is the low privilege level and is the same as protection level 3 of the segmentation model. That is, user is the protection level assigned to pages of memory that are accessible by application software. On the other hand, making U/S equal to 0 assigns supervisor-level protection to the table or frame. Supervisor corresponds to levels 0, 1, and 2 of the segmentation model and is the level assigned to operating system resources. The read/write (R/W) bit is used to make a user-level table or frame read-only or read/write. Logic 1 in R/W selects read-only operation. Figure 13.32 summarizes the access characteristics for each setting of U/S and R/W.

Protection characteristics assigned by a page directory entry are applied to all page frames defined by the entries in the page table. On the other hand, the attributes assigned to a page table entry only apply to the page frame that it defines. Since two sets of protection characteristics exist for all page frames, the page protection mechanism of the 80386DX is designed to always enforce the higher-privileged (more restricting) of the two protection rights.

Figure 13.31 Directory or page table entry format.

U/S	R/W	User	Supervisor
0	0	None	Read/write
0	1	None	Read/write
1	0	Read-only	Read/write
1	1	Read/write	Read/write

Figure 13.32 User- and supervisor-level access rights.

EXAMPLE 13.15

If the page directory entry for the active page frame is $F1000007_{16}$ and its page table entry is 010000005_{16}, is the frame assigned to the user or supervisor? What access is permitted to the frame from user mode and from supervisor mode?

Solution

First, the page directory entry is expressed in binary form. This gives

$$F10000003_{16} = 11110001000000000000000000000111_2$$

Therefore, the page protection bits are

$$U/S \ R/W = 11$$

This assigns user-mode and read/write accesses to the complete page frame. Next the page table entry for the frame is expressed in binary form as

$$01000005_{16} = 00000001000000000000000000000101_2$$

Here we find that

$$U/S \ R/W = 10$$

This defines the page frame as a user-mode, read-only page. Since the page frame attributes are the more restrictive, they apply. Looking at Fig. 13.32, we see that user software (application software) can only read data in this frame. On the other hand, supervisor software (operating system software) can either read data from or write data into the frame.

The other implemented bits in the directory and page table entry of Fig. 13.31 provide statistical information about the table or frame usage. For instance, the *present* (P) bit identifies whether or not the entry can be used for page address translation. P equal to logic 1 indicates that the entry is valid and is available for use in address translation. On the other hand, if P equals 0, the entry is either undefined or not present in physical memory. If an attempt is made to access a page table or page frame that has its P bit marked 0, a page fault results. This page fault needs to be serviced by the operating system.

The 80386DX also records the fact that a page table or page frame has been accessed. Just before a read or write is performed to any address in a table or frame, the *accessed* (A) bit of the entry is set to 1. This marks it as having been accessed. For page frame accesses, it also records whether the access was for a read or write operation. The *dirty* (D) bit is only defined for a page table entry, and it gets set if a write is performed to any address in the corresponding page frame. In a virtual demand paged memory system, the operating system can check the state of these bits to determine if a page in physical memory needs to be updated on the virtual storage device (hard disk) when a new page is swapped into its physical memory address space. The last three bits are labeled AVL and are available for use by the programmer.

▲ 13.8 PROTECTED-MODE SYSTEM CONTROL INSTRUCTION SET OF THE 80386

In Chapters 4 and 5, we studied the instruction set of the 8086/8088 microprocessor. The part of the instruction set introduced in these chapters represents the base instruction set of the 8086 architecture. In Sections 12.5 and 13.5, we introduced a number of new instructions that are available in the real-mode instruction set of the 80386 family. In protected mode, the 80386DX executes all the instructions that are available in the real mode. Moreover, it is enhanced with a number of additional instructions that either apply only to protected-mode operation or are used in the real mode to prepare the 80386DX for entry into the protected mode. As shown in Fig. 13.33, these instructions are known as the *system control instruction set*.

The instructions of the system control instruction set are listed in Fig. 13.34. Here we find the format of each instruction along with a description of its operation. Moreover, the mode or modes in which the instruction is available are identified. Let us now look at the operation of some of these instructions in detail.

Looking at Fig. 13.34, we see that the first six instructions can be executed in either the real or protected mode. They provide the ability to load (L) or store (S) the contents of the global descriptor table (GDT) register, interrupt descriptor table (IDT) register, and machine status word (MSW) part of CR_0. Notice that the instruction *load global descriptor table register* (LGDT) is used to load the GDTR from memory. Operand S specifies the location of the six bytes of memory that hold the limit and base to specify the size and beginning address of the GDT. The

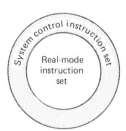

Figure 13.33 Protected-mode instruction set.

Instruction	Description	Mode
LGDT S	Load the global descriptor table register. S specifies the memory location that contains the first byte of the 6 bytes to be loaded into the GDTR.	Both
SGDT D	Store the global descriptor table register. D specifies the memory location that gets the first byte of the 6 bytes to be stored from the GDTR.	Both
LIDT S	Load the interrupt descriptor table register. S specifies the memory location that contains the first byte of the 6 bytes to be loaded into the IDTR.	Both
SIDT D	Store the interrupt descriptor table register. D specifies the memory location that gets the first byte of the 6 bytes to be stored from the IDTR.	Both
LMSW S	Load the machine status word. S is an operand to specify the word to be loaded into the MSW.	Both
SMSW D	Store the machine status word. D is an operand to specify the word location or register where the MSW is to be stored.	Both
LLDT S	Load the local descriptor table register. S specifies the operand to specify a word to be loaded into the LDTR.	Protected
SLDT D	Store the local descriptor table register. D is an operand to specify the word location where the LDTR is to be saved.	Protected
LTR S	Load the task register. S is an operand to specify a word to be loaded into the TR.	Protected
STR D	Store the task register. D is an operand to specify the word location where the TR is to be stored.	Protected
LAR D, S	Load access rights byte. S specifies the selector for the descriptor whose access byte is loaded into the upper byte of the D operand. The low byte specified by D is cleared. The zero flag is set if the loading completes successfully; otherwise it is cleared.	Protected
LSL R16, S	Load segment limit. S specifies the selector for the descriptor whose limit word is loaded into the word register operand R16. The zero flag is set if the loading completes successfully; otherwise it is cleared.	Protected
ARPL D, R16	Adjust RPL field of the selector. D specifies the selector whose RPL field is increased to match the PRL field in the register. The zero flag is set if successful; otherwise it is cleared.	Protected
VERR S	Verify read access. S specifies the selector for the segment to be verified for read operation. If successful the zero flag is set; otherwise it is reset.	Protected
VERW S	Verify write access. S specifies the selector for the segment to be verified for write operation. If successful the zero flag is set; otherwise it is reset.	Protected
CLTS	Clear task switched flag.	Protected

Figure 13.34 Protected-mode system control instruction set.

first word of memory contains the limit and the next four bytes contain the base. For instance, executing the instruction

```
LGDT    [INIT_GDTR]
```

loads the GDTR with the base and limit stored at address INIT_GDTR to create a global descriptor table in memory. This instruction is meant to be used during system initialization and before switching the 80386DX to the protected mode.

Once loaded, the current contents of the GDTR can be saved in memory by executing the *store global descriptor table* (SGDT) instruction. An example is the instruction

```
SGDT    [SAVE_GDTR]
```

The instructions LIDT and SIDT perform similar operations for the IDTR. The IDTR is also set up during initialization.

The instructions *load machine status word* (LMSW) and *store machine status word* (SMSW) are provided to load and store the contents of the machine status word (MSW), respectively. These are the instructions that are used to switch the 80386DX from real to protected mode. To do this, we must set the least significant bit in the MSW to 1. This can be done by first reading the contents of the machine status word, modifying the LSB (PE), and then writing the modified value back into the MSW part of CR_0. The instruction sequence that follows will switch an 80386DX operating in real mode to the protected mode:

```
SMSW    AX          ;Read from the MSW
OR      AX,1        ;Set the PE bit
LMSW    AX          ;Write to the MSW
```

The next four instructions in Fig. 13.34 are also used to initialize or save the contents of protected-mode registers. However, they can be used only when the 80386DX is in the protected mode. To load and to save the contents of the LDTR, we have the instructions LLDT and SLDT, respectively. Moreover, for loading and saving the contents of the TR, the equivalent instructions are LTR and STR.

The rest of the instructions in Fig. 13.34 are for accessing the contents of descriptors. For instance, to read a descriptor's access rights byte, the *load access rights byte* (LAR) instruction is executed. An example is the instruction

```
LAR  AX, [LDIS_1]
```

Execution of this instruction causes the access rights byte of the specified local descriptor to be loaded into AH. To read the segment limit of a descriptor, we use the *load segment limit* (LSL) instruction. For instance, to copy the segment limit for the specified local descriptor into register EBX, the instruction

```
LSL  EBX, [LDIS_1]
```

is executed. In both cases, ZF is set to 1 if the operation is performed correctly. The instruction *adjust RPL field of selector* (ARPL) can be used to increase the RPL field of a selector in memory or a register, destination (D), to match the protection level of the selector in a register, source (S). If an RPL-level increase takes place, ZF is set to 1. Finally, the instructions VERR and VERW are provided to test the accessibility of a segment for a read or write operation, respectively. If the descriptor permits the type of access tested for by executing the instruction, ZF is set to 1.

▲ 13.9 MULTITASKING AND PROTECTION

We say that the 80386DX microprocessor implements a *multitasking* software architecture. By this we mean that it contains on-chip hardware that both permits multiple tasks to exist in a software system and allows them to be scheduled for execution in a time-shared manner. That is, program control is switched from one task to another after a fixed interval of time elapses. For instance, the tasks can be executed in a round-robin fashion. This means that the most recently executed task is returned to the end of the list of tasks being executed. Even though the processes are executed in a time-shared fashion, an 80386DX microcomputer has the performance to make it appear to the user that they are all running simultaneously.

Earlier we defined a task as a collection of program routines that performs a specific function. This function is also called a *process*. Software systems typically need to perform many processes. In the protected-mode 80386DX-based microcomputer, each process is identified as an independent task. The 80386DX provides an efficient mechanism, called the *task switching mechanism*, for switching between tasks. For instance, an 80386DX running at 16 MHz can perform a task switch operation in just 19 μs.

We also indicated earlier that when a task is called into operation it can have both global and local memory resources. The local memory address space is divided between tasks. This means that each task normally has its own private segments of local memory. Segments in global memory can be shared by all tasks. Therefore, a task can have access to any of the segments in global memory. As shown in Fig. 13.35, task A has both a private address space and a global address space available for its use.

Protection and the Protection Model

Safeguards can be built into the protected-mode software system to deny unauthorized or incorrect accesses of a task's memory resources. The concept of safeguarding memory is known as *protection*. The 80386DX includes on-chip hardware that implements a *protection mechanism*. This mechanism is designed to put restrictions on the access of local and system resources by a task and to isolate tasks from each other in a multitasking environment.

Segmentation, paging, and descriptors are the key elements of the 80386DX's protection mechanism. We already identified that, when using a segmented memory model, a segment is the smallest element of the virtual memory address space that has unique protection attributes. These attributes are defined by the access rights information and limit fields in the segment's descriptor. As shown in Fig. 13.36(a), the on-chip protection hardware performs a number of checks during all memory accesses. Figure 13.36(b) is a list of the protection checks and restrictions imposed

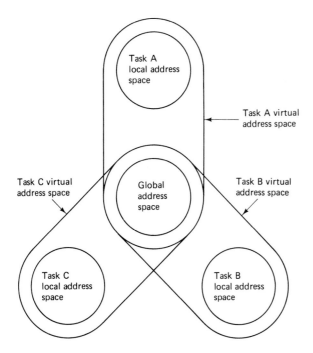

Task A
local address
space

Task A virtual
address space

Task C virtual
address space

Global
address
space

Task B virtual
address space

Task C
local address
space

Task B
local address
space

Figure 13.35 Virtual address space of a task. (Reprinted by permission of Intel Corp., © Intel Corp. 1987)

on software by the 80386DX. For example, when a data storage location in memory is written to, the type field in the access rights byte of the segment is tested to assure that its attributes are consistent with the register cache being loaded, and the offset is checked to verify that it is within the limit of the segment.

Let us just review the attributes that can be assigned to a segment with the access rights information in its descriptor. Figure 13.37 shows the format of a data segment descriptor and an executable (code) segment descriptor. The P bit defines whether a segment of memory is present in physical memory. Assuming that a segment is present, bit 4 of the type field makes it either a code segment or data segment. Notice that this bit is 0 if the descriptor is for a data segment and it is 1 for code segments. Segment attributes such as readable, writeable, conforming, expand up or down, and accessed are assigned by other bits in the type field. Finally, a privilege level is assigned with the DPL field.

Earlier we showed that whenever a segment is accessed, the base address and limit are cached inside the 80386DX. In Fig. 13.36(a), we find that the access rights information is also loaded into the cache register. However, before loading the descriptor the MMU verifies that the selected segment currently present in physical memory is at a privilege level that is accessible from the privilege level of the current program, that the type is consistent with the target segment selector register (CS = code segment, DS, ES, FS, GS, or SS = data segment), and that the reference into the segment does not exceed the address limit of the segment. If a violation is detected, an error condition is signaled. The memory manager software can determine the cause, correct the problem, and then reinitiate the operation.

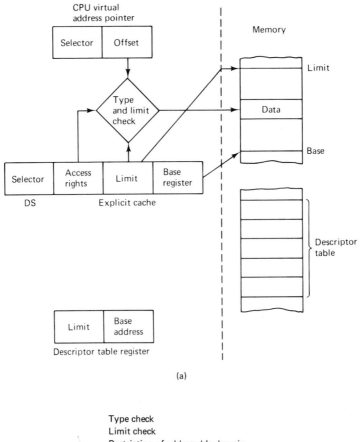

CPU virtual
address pointer

| Selector | Offset |

Type
and limit
check

Memory

Limit

Data

Base

| Selector | Access rights | Limit | Base register |

DS Explicit cache

Descriptor
table

| Limit | Base address |

Descriptor table register

(a)

Type check
Limit check
Restriction of addressable domain
Restriction of procedure entry point
Restriction of instruction set

(b)

Figure 13.36 (a) Testing the access rights of a descriptor. (Reprinted by permission of Intel Corp., © Intel Corp. 1982) (b) Protection checks and restrictions.

Let us now look at some examples of memory accesses that result in protection violations. For example, if the selector loaded into the CS register points to a descriptor that defines a data segment, the type check leads to a protection violation. Another example of an invalid memory access is an attempt to read an operand from a code segment that is not marked as readable. Finally, any attempt to access a byte of data at an offset greater than LIMIT, a word at an offset equal to or greater than LIMIT, or a double word at an offset equal to or greater than LIMIT − 2 extends beyond the end of the data segment and results in a protection violation.

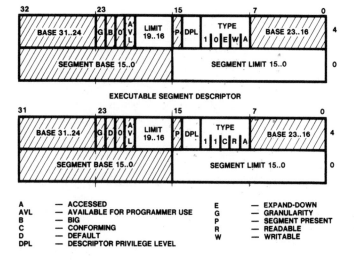

Figure 13.37 Data segment and executable (code) segment descriptors. (Reprinted by permission of Intel Corp., © Intel Corp. 1986)

The 80386DX's protection model provides four possible privilege levels for each task. They are called *levels 0, 1, 2,* and *3* and can be illustrated by concentric circles as in Fig. 13.38. Here level 0 is the most privileged and level 3 is the least privileged level.

System and application software are typically partitioned in the manner shown in Fig. 13.38. The kernel represents application-independent software that provides microprocessor oriented functions such as I/O control, task sequencing, and memory management. For this reason, it is kept at the most privileged level, level 0. Level 1 contains processes that provide system services such as file accessing. Level 2 is used to implement custom routines to support special-purpose system operations. Finally, the least privileged level, level 3, is the level at which user applications are run. This example also demonstrates how privilege levels are used to isolate system-level software (operating system software in levels 0 through 2) from the user's application software (level 3). Tasks at a level can use programs from the more privileged levels but cannot modify the contents of these routines in any way. In this way, applications are permitted to use system software routines from the three higher privilege levels without affecting their integrity.

Earlier we indicated that protection restrictions are put on the instruction set. One example of this is that the system control instructions can only be executed in a code segment that is at protection level 0. We also pointed out that each task is assigned its own local descriptor table. Therefore, as long as none of the descriptors in a task's local-descriptor-table references code or data is available to another task, it is isolated from all other tasks. That is, it has been assigned a unique part of the virtual address space. For instance, in Fig. 13.38 multiple applications running

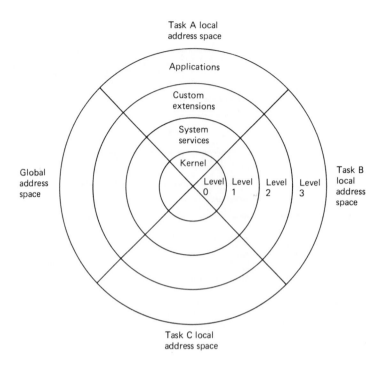

Figure 13.38 Protection model.

at level 3 are isolated from each other by assigning them different local resources. This shows that segments, privilege levels, and the local descriptor table provide protection for both code and data within a task. These types of protections result in improved software reliability because errors in one application will not affect the operating system or other applications.

Let us now look more closely at how the privilege level is assigned to a code or data segment. Remember that when a task is running it has access to both local and global code segments, local and global data segments, and stack segments. A privilege level is assigned to each of these segments through the access rights information in its descriptor. A segment may be assigned to any privilege level simply by entering the number for the level into the DPL bits.

To provide more flexibility, input/output has two levels of privilege. First, the I/O drivers, which are normally system resources, are assigned to a privilege level. For the software system of Fig. 13.38, we indicate that the I/O control routines are part of the kernel and are at level 0.

The IN, INS, OUT, OUTS, CLI, and STI instructions are what are called *trusted instructions*. This is because the protection model of the 80386DX puts additional restrictions on their use in protected mode. They can only be executed at a privilege level that is equal to or more privileged than the *input/output privilege level* (IOPL) code. IOPL supplies the second level of I/O privilege. Remember that the IOPL bits exist in the protected-mode flag register. These bits must be loaded with the value of the privilege level that is to be assigned to input/output instructions through software. The value of IOPL may change from task to task. Assigning the I/O instructions to a level higher than 3 restricts applications from directly performing I/O. Therefore, to perform an I/O operation, the application must request service by an I/O driver through the operating system.

Accessing Code and Data Through the Protection Model

During the running of a task, the 80386DX may need to either pass control to program routines at another privilege level or access data in a segment that is at a different privilege level. Accesses to code or data in segments at a different privilege level are governed by strict rules. These rules are designed to protect the code or data at the more privileged level from contamination by the less privileged routine.

Before looking at how accesses are made for routines or data at the same or different privilege levels, let us first look at some terminology used to identify privilege levels. We have already been using the terms descriptor privilege level (DPL) and I/O privilege level (IOPL). However, when discussing the protection mechanisms by which processes access data or code, two new terms come into play. They are *current privilege level* (CPL) and *requested privilege level* (RPL). CPL is defined as the privilege level of the code or data segment that is currently being accessed by a task. For example, the CPL of an executing task is the DPL of the access rights byte in the descriptor cache for the CS register. This value normally equals the DPL of the code segment. RPL is the privilege level of the new selector loaded into a segment register. For instance, in the case of code, it is the privilege level of the code segment that contains the routine that is being called. That is, RPL is the DPL of the code segment to which control is to be passed.

As a task in an application runs, it may require access to program routines that reside in segments at any of the four privilege levels. Therefore, the current privilege level of the task changes dynamically with the programs it executes. This is because the CPL of the task is normally switched to the DPL of the code segment currently being accessed.

The protection rules of the 80386DX determine what code or data can be accessed by a program. Before looking at how control is passed to code at different protection levels, let us first look at how data segments are accessed by code at the current privilege level. Figure 13.39 illustrates the protection level checks that are made for a data access. The general rule is that code can only access data that are at the same or a less privileged level. For instance, if the current privilege level of a task is 1, it can access operands that are in data segments with DPL equal to 1, 2, or 3. Whenever a new selector is loaded into the DS, ES, FS, or GS register, the DPL of the target data segment is checked to make sure that it is equal to or less privileged than the most privileged of either CPL or RPL. As long as DPL satisfies this condition, the descriptor is cached inside the 80386DX and the data access takes place.

One exception to this rule is when the SS register is loaded. In this case, the DPL must always equal the CPL. That is, the active stack (one is required for each privilege level) is always at the CPL.

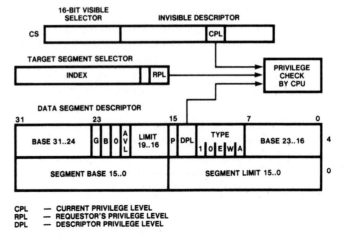

Figure 13.39 Privilege-level checks for a data access. (Reprinted by permission of Intel Corp., © Intel Corp. 1986)

EXAMPLE 13.16

Assuming that, in Fig. 13.39, DPL = 2, CPL = 0, and RPL = 2, will the data access take place?

Solution

DPL of the target segment is 2 and this value is less privileged than CPL = 0, which is the more privileged of CPL and RPL. Therefore, the protection criterion is satisfied and the access will take place.

Different rules apply as to how control is passed between code at the same privilege level and between code at different privilege levels. To transfer program control to another instruction in the same code segment, we can simply use a near jump or call instruction. In either case, just a limit check is made to ensure that the destination of the jump or call does not exceed the limit of the current code segment.

To pass control to code in another segment that is at the same or a different privilege level, a far jump or call instruction is used. For this transfer of program control, both type and limit checks are performed and privilege-level rules are applied. Figure 13.40 shows the privilege checks made by the 80386DX. There are two conditions under which the transfer in program control will take place. First, if CPL equals the DPL, the two segments are at the same protection level and the transfer occurs. Second, if the CPL represents a more privileged level than DPL, but the conforming code (C) bit in the type field of the new segment is set, the routine is executed at the CPL.

The general rule that applies when control is passed to code in a segment that is at a different privilege level is that the new code segment must be at a more

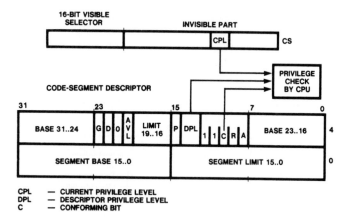

CPL — CURRENT PRIVILEGE LEVEL
DPL — DESCRIPTOR PRIVILEGE LEVEL
C — CONFORMING BIT

Figure 13.40 Privilege-level checks when directly passing program control to a program in another segment. (Reprinted by permission of Intel Corp., © Intel Corp. 1986)

privileged level. A special kind of descriptor called a *gate descriptor* comes into play to implement the change in privilege level. An attempt to transfer control to a routine in a code segment at a higher privilege level is still initiated with either a far call or far jump instruction. This time the instruction does not directly specify the location of the destination code; instead, it references a gate descriptor. In this case the 80386DX goes through a much more complex program control transfer mechanism.

The structure of a gate descriptor is shown in Fig. 13.41. Notice that there are four types of gate descriptors: the *call gate, task gate, interrupt gate,* and *trap gate*. The call gate implements an indirect transfer of control within a task from code at the CPL to code at a higher privilege level. It does this by defining a valid entry point into the more privileged segment. The contents of a call gate are the virtual address of the entry point: the *destination selector* and the *destination offset*. In Fig. 13.41, we see that the destination selector identifies the code segment that contains the program to which control is to be redirected. The destination offset points to the instruction in this segment where execution is to resume. Call gates can reside in either the GDT or a LDT.

The operation of the call gate mechanism is illustrated in Fig. 13.42. Here we see that the call instruction includes an offset and a selector. When the instruction is executed, this selector is loaded into CS and points to the call gate. In turn, the call gate causes its destination selector to be loaded into CS. This leads to the caching of the descriptor for the called code segment (executable segment descriptor). The executable segment descriptor provides the base address for the executable segment (code segment) of memory. Notice that the offset in the call gate descriptor locates the entry point of the procedure in the executable segment.

Whenever the task's current privilege level is changed, a new stack is activated. As part of the program context switching sequence, the old ESP and SS are saved

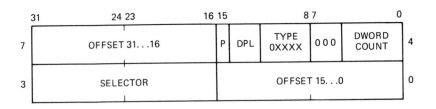

	31	24 23	16 15	8 7	0	
7	OFFSET 31...16		P	DPL	TYPE 0XXXX	0 0 0	DWORD COUNT	4
3	SELECTOR		OFFSET 15...0		0

Name	Value	Description
TYPE	4 5 6 7	— Call gate — Task gate — Interrupt gate — Trap gate
P	0 1	— Descriptor contents are not valid — Descriptor contents are valid
DPL	0–3	Descriptor privilege level
WORD COUNT	0–31	Number of double words to copy from callers stack to called procedures stack. Only used with call gate
DESTINATION SELECTOR	16-Bit selector	Selector to the target code segment (call interrupt or trap gate) Selector to the target task state segment (task gate)
DESTINATION OFFSET	32-Bit offset	Entry point within the target code segment

Figure 13.41 Gate descriptor format. (Reprinted by permission of Intel Corp., © Intel Corp. 1987)

on the new stack along with parameters and the old EIP and CS. This information is needed to preserve linkage for return to the old program environment.

Now the procedure at the higher privilege level begins to execute. At the end of the routine, a RET instruction must be included to return program control back to the calling program. Execution of RET causes the old values of EIP, CS, the parameters, ESP, and SS to be popped from the stack. This restores the original program environment. Now program execution resumes with the instruction following the call instruction in the lower privileged code segment. Figure 13.43 shows the privilege checks that are performed when program control transfer is initiated through a call gate. For the call to be successful, the DPL of the gate must be the same as the CPL and the RPL of the called code must be higher than the CPL.

Task Switching and the Task State Segment Table

Earlier we identified the task as the key program element of the 80386DX's multitasking software architecture and that another important feature of this archi-

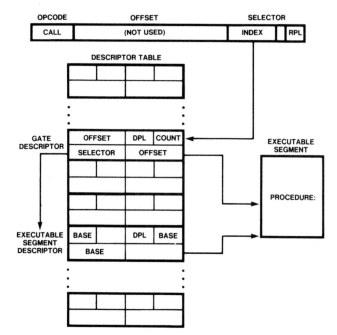

Figure 13.42 Call gate operation. (Reprinted by permission of Intel Corp., © Intel Corp. 1986)

tecture is the high-performance task switching mechanism. A task can be invoked either directly or indirectly. This is done by executing either the intersegment jump or intersegment call instruction. When a jump instruction is used to initiate a task switch, no return linkage to the prior task is supported. On the other hand, if a call is used to switch to the new task instead of a jump, back linkage information is automatically saved. This information permits a return to be performed to the instruction that follows the calling instruction in the old task at completion of the new task.

Each task that is to be performed by the 80386DX is assigned a unique selector called a *task state selector*. This selector is an index to a corresponding *task state segment descriptor* in the global descriptor table. The format of a task state segment descriptor is given in Fig. 13.44.

If a jump or call instruction has a task state selector as its operand, a direct entry is performed to the task. As shown in Fig. 13.45, when a call instruction is executed the selector is loaded into the 80386DX's task register (TR). Then the corresponding task state segment descriptor is read from the GDT and loaded into the task register cache. This only happens if the criteria specified by the access rights information of the descriptor are satisfied. That is, the descriptor is present (P = 1); the task is not busy (B = 0); and protection is not violated (CPL must be equal to DPL). Looking at Fig. 13.45, we see that, once loaded, the base address and limit specified in the descriptor define the starting point and size of the task's *task state segment* (TSS). This TSS contains all the information that is needed to either start or stop a task.

Before explaining the rest of the task switch sequence, let us first look more closely at what is contained in the task state segment. A typical TSS is shown in

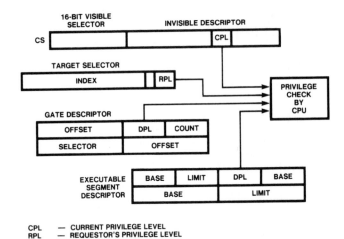

CPL — CURRENT PRIVILEGE LEVEL
RPL — REQUESTOR'S PRIVILEGE LEVEL
DPL — DESCRIPTOR PRIVILEGE LEVEL

Figure 13.43 Privilege-level checks for program control transfer with a call gate. (Reprinted by permission of Intel Corp., © Intel Corp. 1986)

Fig. 13.45. Its minimum size is 104 bytes. For this reason, the minimum limit that can be specified in a TSS descriptor is 00067_{16}. Notice that the segment contains information such as the state of the microprocessor (general registers, segment selectors, instruction pointer, and flags) needed to initiate the task, a back link selector to the TSS of the task that was active when this task was called, the local descriptor table register selector, a stack selector and pointer for privilege levels 0, 1, and 2, and an I/O permission bit map.

Now we will continue with the procedure by which a task is invoked. Let us assume that a task was already active when a new task was called. Then the new task is what is called a *nested task* and causes the NT bit of the flag word to be set to 1. In this case, the current task is first suspended and then the state of the 80386DX's user-accessible registers is saved in the old TSS. Next, the B bit in the new task's descriptor is marked busy; the TS bit in the machine status word is set to indicate that a task is active; the state information from the new task's TSS is loaded into the MPU; and the selector for the old TSS is saved as the back-link selector in the new task state segment. The task switch operation is now complete and execution resumes with the instruction identified by the new contents of the code segment selector (CS) and instruction pointer (EIP).

The old program context is preserved by saving the selector for the old TSS as the back-link selector in the new TSS. By executing return instruction at the

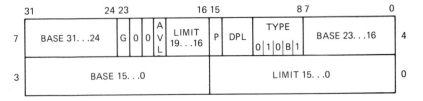

Figure 13.44 TSS descriptor format. (Reprinted by permission of Intel Corp., © Intel Corp. 1986)

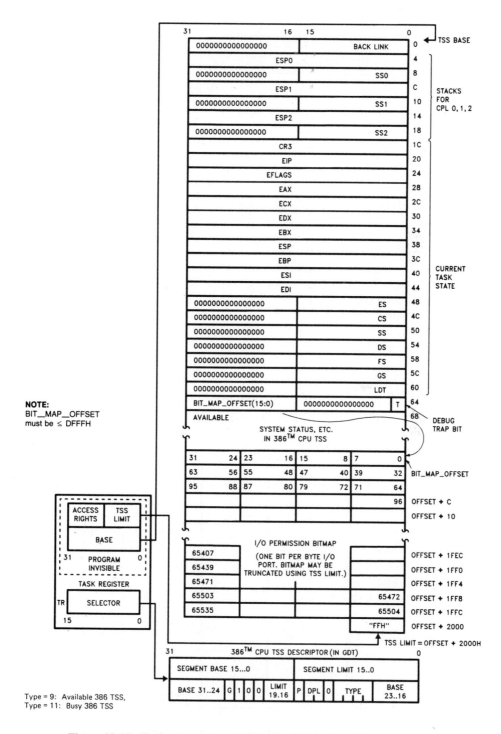

Figure 13.45 Task state segment table. (Reprinted by permission of Intel Corp., © Intel Corp. 1987)

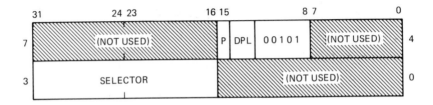

Figure 13.46 Task gate descriptor format. (Reprinted by permission of Intel Corp., © Intel Corp. 1986)

end of the new task, the back-link selector for the old TSS is automatically reloaded into TR. This activates the old TSS and restores the prior program environment. Now program execution resumes at the point where it left off in the old task.

The indirect method of invoking a task is by jumping to or calling a *task gate*. This is the method used to transfer control to a task at an RPL that is higher than the CPL. Figure 13.46 shows the format of a task gate. This time the instruction includes a selector that points to the task gate, which is in either the LDT or GDT, instead of a task state selector. The TSS selector held in this gate is loaded into TR to select the TSS and initiate the task. Figure 13.47 illustrates a task initiated through a task gate.

Let us consider an example to illustrate the principle of task switching. In Fig. 13.48, we have a table that contains TSS descriptors SELECT0 through SELECT3. These descriptors contain access rights and selectors for tasks 0 through 3, respectively. To invoke the task corresponding to selector SELECT2 in the

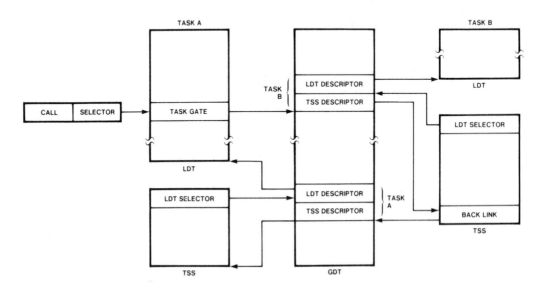

Figure 13.47 Task switch through a task gate. (Reprinted by permission of Intel Corp., © Intel Corp. 1987)

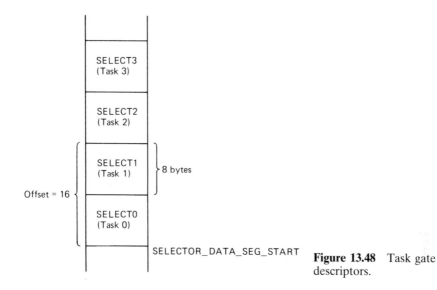

Figure 13.48 Task gate descriptors.

data segment where these selectors are stored, we can use the following procedure. First, the data segment register is loaded with the address SELECTOR_DATA_SEG_START to point to the segment that contains the selectors. This is done with the instructions

```
MOV  AX, SELECTOR_DATA_SEG_START
MOV  DS,AX
```

Since each selector is eight bytes long, SELECT2 is offset from the beginning of the segment by 16 bytes. Let us load the offset into register EBX.

```
MOV  EBX,0F
```

At this point we can use SELECT2 to implement an intersegment jump with the instruction

```
JMP  DWORD PTR [EBX]
```

Execution of this instruction switches program control to the task specified by the selector in descriptor SELECT2. In this case, no program linkage is preserved. On the other hand, by calling the task with the instruction

```
CALL  DWORD PTR [EBX]
```

the linkage is maintained.

▲ 13.10 VIRTUAL 8086 MODE

The 8086 and 8088 application programs, such as those written for the PC DOS operating system, can be directly run on the 80386DX in real mode. A protected-mode operating system, such as UNIX™, can also run DOS applications without change. This is done through what is called *virtual 8086 mode*. When in this mode, the 80386DX supports an 8086 microprocessor programming model and can directly run programs written for the 8086. That is, it creates a virtual 8086 machine for executing programs.

In this kind of application, the 80386DX is switched back and forth between protected mode and virtual 8086 mode. The UNIX operating system and UNIX applications are run in protected mode, and when the DOS operating system and a DOS application are to be run, the 80386DX is switched to the virtual 8086 mode. This mode switching is controlled by a program known as a *virtual 8086 monitor*.

Virtual 8086 mode of operation is selected by the bit called *virtual mode* (VM) in the extended flag register. VM must be switched to 1 to enable virtual 8086 mode of operation. Actually, the VM bit in EFLAGS is not directly switched to 1 by software. This is because virtual 8086 mode is normally entered as a protected-mode task. Therefore, the copy of EFLAGS in the TSS for the task would include VM equal 1. These EFLAGS are loaded as part of the task switching process. In turn, virtual 8086 mode of operation is initiated. The virtual 8086 program is run at privilege level 3. The virtual 8086 monitor is responsible for setting and resetting the VM bit in the task's copy of EFLAGS and permits both protected-mode tasks and virtual-8086-mode tasks to coexist in a multitasking program environment.

Another way of initiating virtual 8086 mode is through an interrupt return. In this case, the EFLAGS are reloaded from the stack. Again the copy of EFLAGS must have the VM bit set to 1 to enter the virtual 8086 mode of operation.

▲ 13.11 THE 80486 MICROPROCESSOR FAMILY

Intel's second generation of 32-bit microprocessors, the 80486 family, was introduced in 1989. The first product offered in this family was the *80486DX* MPU. This device is a full 32-bit microprocessor; that is, its internal registers and external data paths are both 32-bits wide. This device offers a number of advanced software and hardware architecture features as compared to the 80386DX. Two major changes that greatly improved performance were the addition of an on-chip *floating-point math coprocessor* and an on-chip *code and data cache memory*. The 80386 family supports both a math coprocessor and cache memory, but they needed to be implemented external to the device.

The 80486 family maintains real-mode and protected-mode software compatibility with the 80386 architecture. However, important changes have been made in the instruction set. First, and most important, is that the execution speed of most instructions of the instruction set has been improved for the 80486 family. This was done by changing the way in which they are performed by the MPU so that now most of the basic instructions are performed in just one clock cycle. For instance, the move, add, subtract, and logic operations can all be performed in a single clock cycle. With the 80386DX, these same operations took two or more clock cycles to be completed. Finally, a number of new instructions have been added to make the instruction set even more versatile. The result of these architectural changes was a more than 2× improvement in the overall performance for the 80486 family.

Similar to the 80386DX, the 80486DX was followed by an *80486SX* device. However, this time the SX version did not have a 16-bit external architecture. It also was a full 32-bit MPU, though it does not include the on-chip floating-point coprocessor unit. As we will see later, the 80486DX and 80486SX were followed by several new generations of 80486 MPUs which introduced additional architectural features that further enhance the performance of the family. Here we will focus on the 80486SX, not the 80486DX.

Let us next briefly compare the levels of performance offered by the 80386 family and 80486 family MPUs. Referring back to the iCOMP™ index chart in Fig. 13.1, we see that the 80486SX-20 has an iCOMP™ rating of 78 compared to a rating of 32 for the 80386SX-20. Moreover, the 80486DX-33 is rated at a level of 166, while the 80386DX-33 is at 68. In this way, we see that comparable 80486 family members do deliver more than twice the performance. Also, newer members of the 80486 family, such as the 80486DX2-66 (rated at 297 in the iCOMP™ chart), have widened this performance advantage to more than 4×.

Internal Architecture

We already mentioned that the internal architecture of the 80486 family is an improvement over that of the 80386 family. For instance, we said that a floating point coprocessor and cache memory are now on-chip. These are not the only changes that have been made to improve the performance of the 80486 family. Here we will explore the functional elements within the 80486DX microprocessor's architecture and how they have changed from that of the 80386DX.

A block diagram of the internal architecture of the 80486 family is shown in Fig. 13.49. Similar to the 80386 architecture, we find the execution unit, segmentation unit, paging unit, bus interface unit, prefetch unit, and decode unit. However, the function of many of these elements has been enhanced for the 80486 family. For instance, we already mentioned that the coding of instructions in the control ROM had been changed to permit instructions to be performed in less clock cycles. Some other changes are that the code queue in the prefetch unit has been doubled in size to 32 bytes. This permits more instructions to be held on chip ready for decode and execution. Also an improved algorithm is now used by the translation lookaside buffer in the paging unit. Finally, the bus interface unit has been modified to give the 80486 architecture a much faster and more versatile processor bus.

The 8086 family microprocessors available before the 80486DX are what are known as *complex instruction set computer* or *CISC* processors. That is, they have a large versatile instruction set that supports many complex addressing modes. In general, the instructions execute in two to many clock cycles. For instance, the 80386's register to register ADD instruction takes two clock cycles, but the same instruction when adding the content of a storage location in memory takes seven

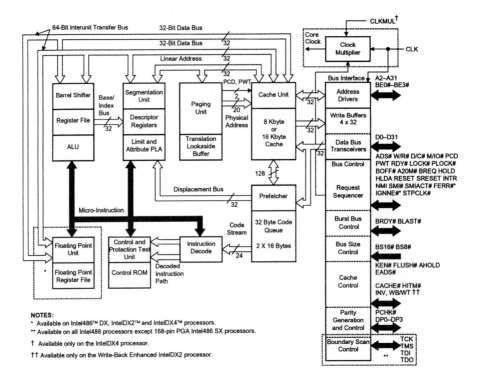

Figure 13.49 Internal architecture of the 80486DX MPU. (Reprinted by permission of Intel Corp., © Intel Corp. 1994)

clock cycles. Other instructions, for instance, the integer multiply (IMUL) and integer divide (IDIV) take even more clock cycles.

The 80486DX is the first member of this family with a high-performance *reduced instruction set computer* (RISC) integer core. A RISC processor is typically characterized as having a small instruction set, limited addressing modes, and single clock execution for instructions. The MPUs of the 80486 family are best described as *complex reduced instruction set computer* (CRISC). This is because a core group of instructions in the 80486's instruction set execute in a single clock cycle. For example, the register to register ADD is performed in a single cycle. At the same time, it retains the many complex instructions and addressing modes that make the instruction set more versatile. However, the number of clock cycles needed to execute many of these complex instructions have also been reduced in the 80486DX. For instance, the register to memory ADD is reduced from seven to three clock cycles.

Let us now look more closely at the new elements of the 80486DX's internal architecture. Traditionally, the *floating-point operations* of the microcomputer have been performed by an externally attached *floating-point coprocessor*. With the 80486DX, this function is integrated into the MPU. This *floating-point math unit* supports the processing of the 32-bit, 64-bit, and 80-bit number formats specified in the *IEEE 754 standard* for floating-point numbers. At the same time, it is upward software compatible with the older 8087, 80287, and 80387 numeric coprocessors. The result of this on-chip implementation function is higher-performance floating-point operation. Remember that this unit is not provided in the 80486SX MPU.

Addition of a high speed *cache memory* to a microcomputer system provides a way of improving overall system performance while permitting the use of low-cost, slow-speed memory devices in the main system memory. During system operation, the cache memory contains recently used instructions, data, or both. The objective is that the MPU accesses code and data in the cache most of the time, instead of from the main memory. Since less time is required to access the information from the cache memory, the result is a higher level of system performance. The internal *cache memory unit* of the 80486DX is 8KB in size and caches both code and data.

Real-Mode Software Model and Instruction Set of the 80486SX

At this point, we will turn our attention to the 80486SX MPU and its real-mode software model. The registers in the software model of the 80486SX are exactly the same as those shown for the 80386DX in Fig. 13.3. The organization and functionality of most of these registers are also the same. The one exception is the control register 0 (CR_0). In the 80386DX, this register has just one bit that is active in the real mode. For the 80486SX, two other bits, cache disable (CD) and not write-through (NW), are active. They are used to enable and configure the operation of the on-chip cache memory. Of course, the 80486DX has more registers in its real mode model. The new registers are needed to support the operation of the floating-point coprocessor.

The real-mode instruction set has been enhanced for the 80486 family. Figure 13.50(a) shows that the 80486SX's instruction set is simply a superset of that of the 80386DX. A group of new instructions called the *80486 specific instruction set* has been added. The instructions of the 80486 specific instruction set are summarized in Fig. 13.50(b). Since all of the earlier instructions are retained in all 80486 family processors and their object code is compatible with the 8086, 8088, 80286, and 80386

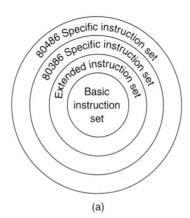

(a)

Figure 13.50 (a) 80486SX instruction set. (b) 80486 specific instruction set.

Mnemonic	Meaning	Format	Operation
BSWAP	Byte swap	BSWAP r32	Reverse the bye order of the 32-bit register.
XADD	Exchange and add	XADD D,S	(D) ↔ (S), (D) ← (S) + (D)
CMPXCHG	Compare and exchange	CMPXCHG D,S	if (ACC) = (D) (ZF) ← 1, (D) ← (S) Else (ZF) ← 0, (ACC) ← (D)

Figure 13.50 (Continued)

processors, upward software compatibility is maintained. Let us now look at the operation of each of the new instructions.

Byte Swap Instruction: BSWAP. When studying the 8086 microprocessor, we showed how the bytes of a double word of data were stored in memory. As shown in Fig. 13.51(a), the least significant byte is stored at the lowest value byte address, which is identified as address m. The next more significant bytes are held at address m + 1 and m + 2. Finally, the most significant byte is saved at the highest value byte address, m + 3. This method of storing information in memory is known as *little endian* organization.

Another method of double-word data organization, which is called *big endian*, is employed by other microprocessor architectures. For instance, Motorola's 68000 family of microprocessors store data in this way. Figure 13.51(b) shows how the bytes of a 32-bit word are arranged in big endian format. Notice that they are stored in the opposite order.

To make it easier for the 80486SX to process data which had been initially created in the big endian format, a special instruction was added to the real-mode instruction set. This *byte swap* (BSWAP) instruction is provided to convert the organization of the bytes of a double word of data between the big endian format and little endian formation. As shown in Fig. 13.50(b), the instruction has a single

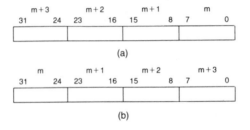

(a)

(b)

Figure 13.51 (a) Little endian memory format. (Reprinted by permission of Intel Corp., © Intel Corp. 1994) (b) Big endian memory format. (Reprinted by permission of Intel Corp., © Intel Corp. 1994)

32-bit register as its destination. Therefore, the double word that is to be converted must first be loaded into an internal register of the 80486SX.

An example is the instruction

```
BSWAP    EAX
```

Let us assume that the contents of EAX are in big endian format. Then, when this instruction is executed, the bytes of the double word of data in register EAX are rearranged into the little endian format. For instance, if the big endian contents of the register were

$$(EAX) = 1234H = 0001001000110010_2$$

the new contents of EAX after the byte swap has taken place will be

$$(EAX) = 4321H = 0100001100100001_2$$

Actually, BSWAP will convert the format of data either way. If the bytes of data in EAX are in little endian form when the instruction is executed, it will be changed to big endian form.

EXAMPLE 13.17

Write a program sequence that will read the double word contents of storage location DS:1000H in memory, rearrange the bytes from big endian to little endian organization, and then return the new value to the original storage location in memory.

Solution

The big endian format double word of data is read from memory with the instruction

```
MOV    EAX,[1000H]
```

Then, the double word is converted to little endian form by

```
BSWAP EAX
```

Finally, the double word is returned to memory with the instruction

```
MOV    [1000H],EAX
```

Exchange and Add Instruction: XADD. The second instruction added to the real mode instruction set of the 80486SX is the *exchange and add* (XADD) instruction. Looking at Fig. 13.50(b), we find that this instruction performs both an add and exchange operation on the contents of the source and destination operands. The source operand must be an internal register while the destination can be either another register or a storage location in memory.

For an example, let us determine the operation of the register to register exchange and add instruction

```
XADD   EAX,  EBX
```

We will assume that the contents of registers EAX and EBX are 1234_{16} and 1111_{16}, respectively. After the exchange and add operation takes place, the sum of these two values ends up in destination register EAX

$$(EAX) = 0001001000110100_2 + 0001000100010001_2 = 0010001101000101_2$$

$$= 2345_{16}$$

and the original contents of EAX is in EBX

$$(EBX) = 1234_{16}$$

Compare and Exchange Instruction: CMPXCHG.   The last of the new real-mode instructions is *compare and exchange* (CMPXCHG). This instruction performs a compare operation and an exchange operation that depends on the result of the compare. As shown in Fig. 13.50(b), the compare that takes place is not between the values of the source and destination operand. It is between the content of the accumulator register (AL,AX,EAX) and the corresponding size destination. If the accumulator and destination contain the same value, the zero flag is set to 1 and the content of the source register is loaded into the destination location. Otherwise, ZF is cleared to 0 and the content of the destination is loaded into the accumulator. The destination can be either a register or storage location in memory. The value in the accumulator must be loaded prior to execution of the CMPXCHG instruction.

As an example, let us consider the instruction

```
CMPXCHG   [2000H],  BL
```

and assume that register AL contains 11_{16}, register BL contains 22_{16}, and the byte memory location address 2000H contains 12_{16}. When the instruction is executed, the value in AL (11_{16}) is compared to that at address 2000H in memory (12_{16}). Since they are not equal, ZF is made logic 0 and the value 12_{16} is copied from memory into AL. Therefore, after execution of the instruction, the results are

$$(AL) = 12_{16}$$

$$(BL) = 22_{16}$$

$$(2000H) = 12_{16}$$

Protected Mode Software Architecture of the 80486SX

Now that we have examined the differences between the software architectures of the 80386DX and 80486SX in the real mode, let us turn our attention to protected-mode operation. The protected-mode operation of the 80486SX is essentially the same as that of the 80386DX. Enhancements have been made to the register set, system control instruction set, and the page tables. Here we will focus on the differences between the two MPUs.

Software Model. Similar to the real mode, the protected-mode software model of the 80486SX is essentially the same as that shown for 80386DX in Fig. 13.8. That is, the same set of registers exist in both processors; however, the 80486SX has some additional bits defined in the flag register and control registers. We will begin by examining these new register functions.

Figure 13.52 shows the protected-mode flags (EFLAGS) register of the 80486SX. In this illustration, the system control flags, bits that affect protected-mode operation, are identified. Comparing these bits to those of the 80386DX in Fig. 13.15, we find that just one new bit has been added. This is the *alignment check* (AC) flag, which is located in bit position 18. When this bit is set to 1, an alignment check is performed during all memory access operations that are performed at privilege level 3. A double word of data that is not stored at an address that is a multiple of four is said to be unaligned. If this double-word storage location is accessed, two memory bus cycles must be performed. The extra bus cycle that is introduced because the data is unaligned reduces overall system performance. The alignment check feature of the 80486SX can be used to identify when unaligned elements of data are accessed. If an unaligned access takes place, an alignment check exception, which is exception 17, occurs.

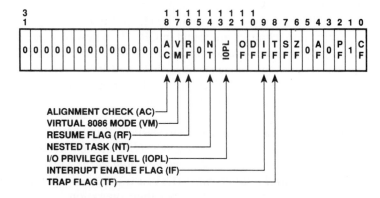

BIT POSITIONS SHOWN AS 0 OR 1 ARE INTEL RESERVED.
DO NOT USE. ALWAYS SET THEM TO THE VALUE PREVIOUSLY READ.

Figure 13.52 Protected mode flags register. (Reprinted by permission of Intel Corp., © Intel Corp. 1992)

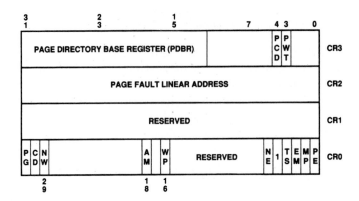

Figure 13.53 Control registers of the 80486SX. (Reprinted by permission of Intel Corp., © Intel Corp. 1992)

The 80486SX has four control registers just like the 80386DX; however, a number of new bits are now active. The control registers of the 80486SX are shown in Fig. 13.53 and those of the 80386DX in Fig. 13.12. Notice that five additional bits have been activated in CR_0 of the 80486SX. They are *alignment mask* (AM), *numeric error* (NE), *write protect* (WP), *cache disable* (CD), and *not write-through* (NW). Let us look at a few of these bits in detail.

We just said that the AC system control flag enabled memory data alignment checks. Actually it takes more than just setting AC to 1 to enable this mode of operation. The AM bit, which is bit 18 in CR_0, must also be set to 1. If AM is switched to 0, the alignment check operation is masked out.

Two other bits in CR_0, CD (bit 30) and NW (bit 29) are used to enable and control the operation of the on-chip cache memory. To enable the cache for operation, CD must be cleared to 0. The other bit enables write through and cache validation cycles to take place when it is set to 0. Therefore, to permit normal cache operation, both of these bits should be cleared to 0.

Some more changes are found in CR_3. Two new bits, *page-level cache disable* (PCD) and *page-level writes transparent* (PWT), have been defined. The state of these bits are output on signal lines PCD and PWT, respectively, during all bus cycles that are not paged. They are used as input signals to the control circuitry for an external cache memory subsystem.

System Control Instruction Set. The system control instruction set has been expanded by three instructions for the 80486SX microprocessor. They are *invalidate cache* (INVD), *write-back and invalidate data cache* (WBINVD), and *invalidate translation lookaside buffer entry* (INVLPG). Figure 13.54 shows the format of these instructions and briefly describes their operation.

The first two instructions, INVD and WBINVD support management of the on-chip and external cache memories. When an INVD instruction is executed the on-chip cache is flushed. That is, all of the data that it holds is made invalid. In addition to invalidating the content of the on-chip cache, execution of this instruction

Mnemonic	Meaning	Format	Operation
INVD	Invalidate cache	INVD	Flush internal cache and signal external cache to flush.
WBINVD	Write back and invalidate cache	WBINVD	Flush internal cache, signal external cache to write-back and flush.
INVLPG	Invalidate TLB entry	INVLPG	Invalidate the signal TLB entry.

Figure 13.54 80486 system control instruction set.

also initiates a special bus cycle known as a *flush bus cycle*. External circuitry must detect the occurrence of this cycle and initiate a flush of the data held in the external cache memory subsystem. WBINVD is similar to INVD in that it initiates a flush of the on-chip cache memory; however, it initiates a different special bus cycle, a *write back bus cycle*. External circuitry must again identify that a write back cycle has taken place and tell the external cache to write-back its content to the main memory.

The INVLPG instruction is used to invalidate a single entry in the 80486SX's internal translation lookaside table register. Notice that the instruction has an operand that identifies which entry is to be marked invalid.

Page Directory and Page Table Entries. The page directory and page tables of the 80486SX are the same size and serve the same function as they did in the 80386DX's protected-mode software architecture. However, a change has been made in the format of the page directory and page table entry. Two additional bits of the 32-bit entry are defined. Let us now look at the function of these two bits.

The format of a page directory/page table entry for the 80386DX is given in Fig. 13.31. Looking at the format of the 80486SX's entry in Fig. 13.55, we find that the two new bits are *page cache disable* (PCD) and *page write transparent* (PWT).

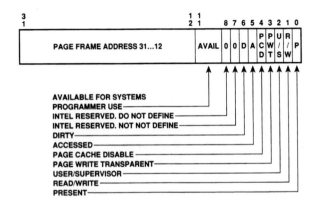

Figure 13.55 80486SX directory and page table entry format. (Reprinted by permission of Intel Corp., © Intel Corp. 1992)

These two bits are used for page-level control of the internal and external caches. To enable caching of a page, the PCD bit in the page table entry must be set to 0. Logic 1 in PWT selects page-level write through operation of the cache for the corresponding page.

When paging is in use, the logic levels of the PCD and PWT bits in the page table entry are output at the PCD and PWT pins of the MPU. This permits control of an external cache memory subsystem.

▲ 13.12 THE PENTIUM™ PROCESSOR FAMILY

The Pentium™ processor family, which was introduced in 1992, represents the high performance end of Intel's 8086 architecture. The Pentium™ processor is a 32-bit MPU, that is, it has a 32-bit register set and the instructions can process words as large as 32 bits in length. However, this 32-bit architecture is enhanced with a 64-bit external data bus and a variety of internal data paths that are 64-bits, 128-bits, or 256-bits wide. These large internal and external data paths result in an increased level of performance.

The MPUs of the Pentium™ processor family remain fully software compatible with the 80486 architecture. Just like the 80386 and 80486 MPUs, the Pentium™ processor comes up in real mode after reset and can be switched to the protected mode by executing a single instruction. Its real- and protected-mode software models and instruction sets are both supersets of those of the 80486DX. They have all of the same instructions, functional registers, and register bit definitions. However, just like for the 80486 MPU and 80386 MPU before that, a number of new instructions, flags, and control bits have been defined. For instance, two new real-mode instructions *compare and exchange 8 bytes* (CMPXCHG8B) and *CPU identification* (CPUID) and three new system control instructions *read and model specific register* (RDMSR), *write to model specific register* (WRMSR), and *resume from system management* (RSM) have been added to the instruction sets. Moreover, three additional flag bits, *ID flag* (ID), *virtual interrupt pending* (VIP), and *virtual interrupt flag* (VIF), have been activated in EFLAGS.

The Pentium™ processor also has a mode of operation known as *system management mode* (SMM). This mode of operation is also available on what are called *SL enhanced 80386 and 80486 MPUs*. This mode is primarily used to perform management of the system's power consumption. SMM is entered by an interrupt request from external hardware and return to real or protected mode is initiated by executing the RSM instruction.

A number of important advances are introduced with the internal architecture of the Pentium™ processor. Three of these are its *superscaler* pipelined architecture, independent code and data caches, and high performance floating-point unit. Let us next look briefly at each of these architectural features.

Intel uses the term superscaler to describe an architecture that has more than one execution unit. In the case of the Pentium™ processor, there are two execution units. These execution units, or *pipelines* as they are also known, process the instructions of the microcomputer program. Each of these execution units has its own ALU, address generation circuitry, and data cache interface.

Earlier we pointed out that the execution time of a core group of instructions were reduced to one clock cycle in the 80486 MPU family. With the Pentium™ processor's dual pipeline architecture, two instructions can be processed at the same time. Therefore, it has the capability of executing as many as two instructions per clock cycle. This pipelining makes a significant contribution to the higher level of performance achieved with the Pentium™ processor family.

The 80486 family of MPUs have an on-chip cache memory that is used to cache both code and data. With the Pentium™ processor, the on-chip cache memory subsystem has been further enhanced. Its cache memory has been expanded to 16KB and partitioned into a separate 8KB code and 8KB data caches. These independent caches result in more frequent use of the cache memory and leads to a higher level of performance for the Pentium™-processor-based microcomputer system.

All members of the Pentium™ processor family have a built-in floating point unit. This floating point math unit has been further enhanced from that used in the 80486 family. For instance, it employs faster hardwired, instead of microcoded, implementations of the floating-point add, multiply, and divide operations. The results are higher performance floating-point operation for the Pentium™ processor. In fact, it can execute floating-point instructions 5 to 10 times faster than the 80486DX-33 MPU.

Figure 13.1 shows the performance of the Pentium™ processor family relative to that of the 80386 and 80486 families. Notice that the iCOMP™ index of the entry level Pentium™ processor (60 MHz) MPU, which is 510, is more than twice that of the fastest 80486DX (50 MHz) MPU. With the introduction of faster family members, the Pentium™ processor's performance edge has increased. For instance, the 100 MHz device has an iCOMP™ rating of 815.

ASSIGNMENTS

Section 13.2

1. Name two MPUs in the 80386 family.
2. What size are the registers and the data bus of the 80386DX? The 80386SX?
3. What is the iCOMP™ rating of an 80386SX-25 MPU? An 80386DX-25 MPU?
4. List the three modes of software operation supported by the 80386DX.

Section 13.3

5. Name the six internal processing units of the 80386DX.
6. What are the word lengths of the 80386DX's address bus and data bus?

7. Does the 80386DX have a multiplexed address/data bus or separate address and data buses?
8. How large is the 80386DX's instruction stream queue?
9. In which unit is the instruction stream queue located?
10. How large is the descriptor cache?
11. Where are recently used page directory and page table entries stored?

Section 13.4

12. How does the performance of a 16-MHz 80386DX compare to that of a 5-MHz 8086?
13. What is meant when we say that the 80386DX is object code compatible with the 8086?
14. In the real mode, is the accumulator register 16 bits or 32 bits in length? The DS register?
15. What new registers are found in the 80386DX's real-mode software model?

Section 13.5

16. Describe the operation performed by the instruction PUSH 1234H.
17. Which registers and in what order does the instruction POPA pop from the stack?
18. What is a stack frame?
19. How much stack does the instruction ENTER 1FH,4 allocate for the stack frame? What is the lexical level?
20. If $(DS) = (ES) = 1075_{16}$, $(DI) = 100_{16}$, $(DF) = 0$, and $(DX) = 1000_{16}$, what happens when the instruction INSW is executed?
21. If $(DS) = (ES) = 1075_{16}$, $(SI) = 100_{16}$, $(DF) = 1$, $(CX) = 000F_{16}$, and $(DX) = 2000_{16}$, what happens when the instruction REPOUTSB is executed?
22. Explain the function serviced by the instruction

```
BOUND  DI,[LIMITS]
```

Assume that address LIMITS contains the value 0000_{16} and LIMITS + 2 holds the value $00FF_{16}$.
23. Write an instruction that will move the contents of control register 1 to the extended base register.
24. What instruction does the mnemonic SHLD stand for?
25. Describe the operation performed by the instruction MOVSX EAX,BL.
26. Write an instruction that will zero-extend the word of data at address DATA_WORD and copy it into register EAX.

27. What operation is performed when the instruction LFS EDI,DATA_F_ADDRESS is executed?

28. If the values in AX and CL are $F0F0_{16}$ and 04_{16}, what is the result in AX and CF after execution of each of the instructions that follow:
(a) BT AX,CL (b) BTR AX,CL (c) BTC AX,CL

29. What does the mnemonic SETNC stand for? What flag condition does it test for?

Section 13.6

30. List the protected-mode registers that are not part of the real-mode model.

31. What are the two parts of the GDTR called?

32. What function is served by the GDTR?

33. If the contents of the GDTR are $0021000001FF_{16}$, what are the starting and ending addresses of the table? How large is the table? How many descriptors can be stored in the table?

34. What is stored in the GDT?

35. What do IDTR and IDT stand for?

36. What is the maximum limit that should be used in the IDTR?

37. What is stored in the IDT?

38. What descriptor table defines the local memory address space?

39. What gets loaded into the LDTR? What happens when it gets loaded?

40. Which control register contains the MSW?

41. Which bit is used to switch the 80386DX from real-address mode to protected-address mode?

42. What MSW bit settings identify that floating-point operations are to be performed by an 80387 coprocessor?

43. What does TS stand for?

44. What must be done to turn on paging?

45. Where is the page directory base register located?

46. How large is the page directory?

47. What is held in the page table?

48. What gets loaded into TR? What is its function?

49. What is the function of the task descriptor cache?

50. What determines the location and size of a task state segment?

51. What is the name of the CS register in the protected mode? The DS register?

52. What are the names and sizes of the three fields in a selector?

53. What does TI equals 1 mean?

54. If the GDT register contains $0013000000FF_{16}$ and the selector loaded into

the LDTR is 0040_{16}, what is the starting address of the LDT descriptor that is to be loaded into the cache?

55. What does NT stand for? RF?

56. If the IOPL bits of the flag register contain 10, what is the privilege level of the I/O instructions?

57. What size is the 80386DX's virtual address?

58. What are the two parts of a virtual address called?

59. How large can a data segment be? How small?

60. How large is the 80386DX's virtual address space? What is the maximum number of segments that can exist in the virtual address space?

61. How large is the global memory address space? How many segments can it contain?

62. In Fig. 13.19, which segments of memory does task 3 have access to? Which segments does it not have access to?

63. What part of the 80386DX is used to translate virtual addresses to physical addresses?

64. What happens when the instruction sequence that follows is executed?

```
MOV   AX,[SI]
MOV   CS,AX
```

65. If the descriptor accessed in Problem 64 has the value $00200000FFFF_{16}$ and IP contains 0100_{16}, what is the physical address of the next instruction to be fetched?

66. Into how many pages is the 80386DX's address space mapped when paging is enabled? What is the size of a page?

67. What are the three elements of the linear address that is produced by page translation? Give the size of each element.

68. What is the purpose of the translation lookaside buffer?

69. How large is a page frame? What selects the specific storage location in the page frame?

Section 13.7

70. How many bytes are in a descriptor? Name each of its fields and give their sizes.

71. Which registers are segment descriptors associated with? System segment descriptors?

72. The selector 0224_{16} is loaded into the data segment register. This value points to a segment descriptor starting at address 00100220_{16} in the local descriptor table. If the words of the descriptor are

$$(00100220_{16}) = 0110_{16}$$
$$(00100222_{16}) = 0000_{16}$$
$$(00100224_{16}) = 1A20_{16}$$
$$(00100226_{16}) = 0000_{16}$$

what are the LIMIT and BASE?

73. Is the segment of memory identified by the descriptor in Problem 72 already loaded into physical memory? Is it a code segment or a data segment?

74. If the current value of EIP is 00000226_{16}, what is the physical address of the next instruction to be fetched from the code segment of Problem 72?

75. What do the 20 most significant bits of a page directory or page table entry stand for?

76. The page mode protection of a page frame is to provide no access from the user protection level and read/write operation at the supervisor protection level. What are the settings of R/W and U/S?

77. What happens when an attempt is made to access a page frame that has $P = 0$ in its page table entry?

78. What does the D bit in a page directory entry stand for?

Section 13.8

79. If the instruction LGDT [INIT_GDTR] is to load the limit $FFFF_{16}$ and base 00300000_{16}, show how the descriptor must be stored in memory.

80. Write an instruction sequence that can be used to clear the task-switched bit of the MSW.

81. Write an instruction sequence that will load the local descriptor table register with the selector $02F0_{16}$ from register BX.

Section 13.9

82. Define the term multitasking.

83. What is a task?

84. What two safeguards are implemented by the 80386DX's protection mechanism?

85. What happens if either the segment limit check or segment attributes check fails?

86. What is the highest privilege level of the 80386DX protection model called? Lowest level called?

87. At what protection level are applications run?

88. What is the protection mechanism used to isolate local and global resources?

89. What protection mechanism is used to isolate tasks?
90. What is the privilege level of the segment defined by the descriptor in Problem 72?
91. What does CPL stand for? RPL?
92. State the data access protection rule.
93. Which privilege-level data segments can be accessed by an application running at level 3?
94. Summarize the code access protection rules.
95. If an application is running at privilege level 3, what privilege-level operating system software is available to it?
96. What purpose does a call gate serve?
97. Explain what happens when the instruction CALL [NEW_ROUTINE] is executed within a task. Assume that NEW_ROUTINE is at a privilege level that is higher than the CPL.
98. What is the purpose of the task state descriptor?
99. What is the function of a task state segment?
100. Where is the state of the prior task saved? Where is the linkage to the prior task saved?
101. Into which register is the TSS selector loaded to initiate a task?
102. Give an overview of the task switch sequence illustrated in Fig. 13.47.

Section 13.10

103. Which bit position in EFLAGS is VM?
104. Is 80386DX protection active or inactive in virtual 8086 mode? If so, what is the privilege level of a virtual 8086 program?
105. Can both protected mode and virtual 8086 tasks coexist in an 80386DX multitasking environment?
106. Can multiple virtual 8086 tasks be active in an 80386DX multitasking environment?

Section 13.11

107. Give two on-chip additions of the 80486DX MPU that result in greater improvement in performance.
108. What is the key difference between the 80486DX and 80486SX MPUs?
109. What is the iCOMP™ rating of the 80486SX-33 MPU? The 80486DX-50 MPU?
110. What is the size of the 80486SX's instruction code queue?
111. What does CISC stand for? RISC? CRISC?
112. List three characteristics of a RISC processor.
113. Is the 80486SX best categorized as that of a CISC, RISC, or CRISC?

114. What are the new bits that are active in CR_0 of the real-mode 80486SX?

115. Does the 8086 architecture use little endian or big endian organization for data stored in memory?

116. If the contents of EAX are 0F0FH, what is the result in the register after executing the instruction SWAP EAX?

117. Write an instruction sequence that will read the big endian double-word elements of a table starting at address BIG_E_TABLE and converts them to little endian format in a table starting at address LIT_E_TABLE. Assume that the number of double-word elements in the table equals COUNT.

118. Write an instruction that will perform an exchange and add operation on the double-word storage location SUM and register EBX. If the original value in EAX is 01H and that in EBX is 00H, what is the result in SUM if the instruction is executed five times?

119. If the instruction CMPXCHG [DATA], BL is executed when the contents of AL is 11_{16}, BL is 22_{16}, and storage location SUM is 11_{16}, what results are produced?

120. What is the new flag that is active in the 80486SX's EFLAGS registers and in which bit position is it found?

121. Which bits in the protected mode CR_0 are used to control the operation of the on-chip cache memory?

122. What instruction should be executed to flush the on-chip cache and initiate a flush bus cycle?

123. What is the difference between the operations performed by the IND and WBINVD instructions?

124. Name the two new active bits in the 80486's page table entry.

Section 13.12

125. How wide is the Pentium™ processor's external data bus?

126. List two new real-mode instructions supported by the Pentium™ processor MPU.

127. Give the mnemonics for the three new flags activated in the Pentium™ processor's EFLAGS register.

128. What does the term "superscaler" mean?

129. How many pipelines are in a Pentium™ processor MPU?

130. What is the iCOMP™ rating of the 90-MHZ Pentium™ processor MPU?

The 80386, 80486, and Pentium™ Processor Families: Hardware Architecture

▲ 14.1 INTRODUCTION

In Chapter 13, we studied the software architecture of the 80386, 80486, and Pentium™ processor families. We covered their real- and protected-mode software architectures, the 80386 and 80486 specific instruction sets, and system control instruction set. Now we will turn our attention to the hardware architecture of the 80386, 80486, and Pentium™ processors. In this chapter, we examine the signal interface of the 80386DX MPU, its memory interface, input/output interface, and interrupts/exception processing. After completing this, we will introduce the 80486SX and Pentium™ processors. Here we will focus on the hardware architecture difference between these newer processors and the 80386DX. For this purpose, we have included the following topics in the chapter:

1. 80386 microprocessor family
2. Signal interfaces of the 80386DX
3. System clock of the 80386DX
4. 80386DX bus states and bus cycles
5. Memory interface of the 80386DX
6. Input/output interface of the 80386DX
7. Interrupt and exception processing of the 80386DX
8. The 80486 microprocessor family
9. The Pentium™ processor family

818

▲ 14.2 80386 MICROPROCESSOR FAMILY

Hardware compatibility of the 80386 family of microprocessors with either the 8086 or 80286 microprocessor is much less of a concern than software compatibility. In fact, a number of changes have been made to the hardware architecture of the 80386DX to improve both its versatility and performance. For example, additional pipelining has been provided within the 80386DX and the address and data buses have both been made 32 bits in length. These two changes in the hardware result in increased performance for 80386DX-based microcomputers. Another feature, *dynamic bus sizing* for the data bus, provides more versatility in system hardware design.

The original 80386DX was manufactured using Intel's complementary high-performance metal-oxide-semiconductor III (CHMOSIII) process. Its circuitry is equivalent to approximately 275,000 transistors, more than twice those used in the design of the 80286 MPU and almost 10 times that of the 8086.

The 80386DX is housed in a 132-pin ceramic *pin grid array* (PGA) package. An 80386DX in this package is shown in Fig. 14.1. This package can be either mounted into a socket that is soldered to the circuit board or have its leads inserted through the board and soldered. The signal at each lead of the package is shown in Fig. 14.2(a). Notice that all the 80386DX's signals are supplied at separate pins on the package. This is intended to simplify the microcomputer circuit design.

Looking at Fig. 14.2(a), we see that the rows of pins on the package are identified by row numbers 1 through 14 and the columns of pins are labeled A through P. Therefore, the location of the pin for each signal is uniquely defined by a column and row coordinate. For example, in Fig. 14.2(a) address line A_{31} is at

Figure 14.1 80386 IC. (Courtesy of Intel Corporation)

the junction of column N and row 2. That is, it is at pin N2. The pin locations for all of the 80386DX's signals are listed in Fig. 14.2(b).

EXAMPLE 14.1 ⎯⎯⎯⎯⎯⎯⎯⎯⎯⎯⎯⎯⎯⎯⎯⎯⎯⎯⎯⎯⎯⎯⎯⎯⎯⎯⎯⎯⎯

At what pin location is the signal D_0?

Solution

Looking at Fig. 14.2(a), we find the pin for D_0 is located in column H at row 12. Therefore, its pin is identified as H12 in Fig. 14.2(b).

The 80386SX MPU is not packaged in a PGA. It is available in a 100 lead *plastic quad flat package* (PQFP). A plastic package is used to permit lower cost

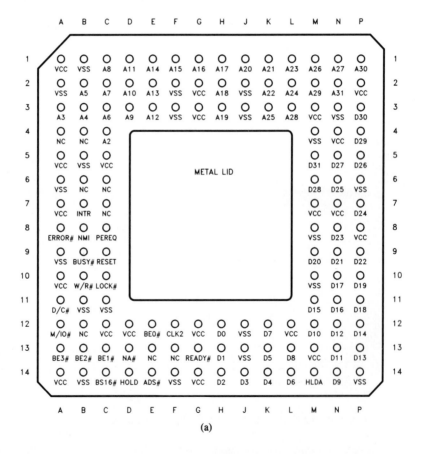

Figure 14.2 (a) Pin layout of the 80386. (Reprinted by permission of Intel Corp., © Intel Corp. 1987) (b) Signal pin numbering. (Reprinted by permission of Intel Corp., © Intel Corp. 1987)

Pin / Signal	Pin / Signal	Pin / Signal	Pin / Signal
N2 A31	M5 D31	A1 V_{CC}	A2 V_{SS}
P1 A30	P3 D30	A5 V_{CC}	A6 V_{SS}
M2 A29	P4 D29	A7 V_{CC}	A9 V_{SS}
L3 A28	M6 D28	A10 V_{CC}	B1 V_{SS}
N1 A27	N5 D27	A14 V_{CC}	B5 V_{SS}
M1 A26	P5 D26	C5 V_{CC}	B11 V_{SS}
K3 A25	N6 D25	C12 V_{CC}	B14 V_{SS}
L2 A24	P7 D24	D12 V_{CC}	C11 V_{SS}
L1 A23	N8 D23	G2 V_{CC}	F2 V_{SS}
K2 A22	P9 D22	G3 V_{CC}	F3 V_{SS}
K1 A21	N9 D21	G12 V_{CC}	F14 V_{SS}
J1 A20	M9 D20	G14 V_{CC}	J2 V_{SS}
H3 A19	P10 D19	L12 V_{CC}	J3 V_{SS}
H2 A18	P11 D18	M3 V_{CC}	J12 V_{SS}
H1 A17	N10 D17	M7 V_{CC}	J13 V_{SS}
G1 A16	N11 D16	M13 V_{CC}	M4 V_{SS}
F1 A15	M11 D15	N4 V_{CC}	M8 V_{SS}
E1 A14	P12 D14	N7 V_{CC}	M10 V_{SS}
E2 A13	P13 D13	P2 V_{CC}	N3 V_{SS}
E3 A12	N12 D12	P8 V_{CC}	P6 V_{SS}
D1 A11	N13 D11		P14 V_{SS}
D2 A10	M12 D10		
D3 A9	N14 D9	F12 CLK2	A4 N.C.
C1 A8	L13 D8		B4 N.C.
C2 A7	K12 D7	E14 ADS#	B6 N.C.
C3 A6	L14 D6		B12 N.C.
B2 A5	K13 D5	B10 W/R#	C6 N.C.
B3 A4	K14 D4	A11 D/C#	C7 N.C.
A3 A3	J14 D3	A12 M/IO#	E13 N.C.
C4 A2	H14 D2	C10 LOCK#	F13 N.C.
A13 BE3#	H13 D1		
B13 BE2#	H12 D0	D13 NA#	C8 PEREQ
C13 BE1#		C14 BS16#	B9 BUSY#
E12 BE0#		G13 READY#	A8 ERROR#
	D14 HOLD		
C9 RESET	M14 HLDA	B7 INTR	B8 NMI

(b)

Figure 14.2 (Continued)

for the device. This type of package is meant for *surface mount* installation. That is, its pins do not go through the board; instead, the device is laid on top of the circuit board and then soldered in place.

▲ 14.3 SIGNAL INTERFACES OF THE 80386DX

A block diagram of the 80386DX microprocessor is shown in Fig. 14.3. Here we have grouped its signal lines into four interfaces: the *memory/IO interface, interrupt interface, DMA interface,* and *coprocessor interface.* Figure 14.4 lists each of the

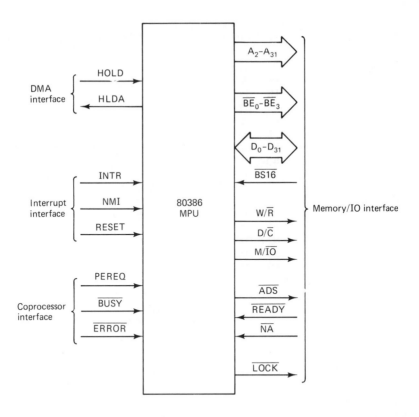

Figure 14.3 Block diagram of the 80386.

signals at the 80386DX's interfaces. Included in this table are a mnemonic, function, type, and active level for each signal. For instance, we find that the signal with the mnemonic M/$\overline{\text{IO}}$ stands for memory/IO indication. This signal is an output produced by the 80386DX that is used to tell external circuitry whether the current address available on the address bus is for memory or an I/O device. Its active level is listed as 1/0, which means that logic 1 on this line identifies a memory bus cycle and logic 0 an I/O bus cycle. On the other hand, the signal INTR at the interrupt interface is the maskable interrupt request input of the 80386DX. This input is active when at logic 1. By using this input, external devices can signal the 80386DX that they need to be serviced.

Memory/IO Interface

In a microcomputer system, the address bus and data bus signal lines form a parallel path over which the MPU talks with its memory and I/O subsystems. Like the 80286 microprocessor, but unlike the older 8086 and 8088, the 80386DX has a demultiplexed address/data bus. Notice in Fig. 14.2(b) that the address bus and data bus lines are located at different pins of the IC.

Name	Function	Type	Level
CLK2	System clock	I	–
A_{31}–A_2	Address bus	O	1
BE_3–BE_0	Byte enables	O	0
D_{31}–D_0	Data bus	I/O	1
$\overline{BS}_{16}$	Bus size 16	I	0
W/$\overline{R}$	Write/read indication	O	1/0
D/$\overline{C}$	Data/control indication	O	1/0
M/$\overline{IO}$	Memory I/O indication	O	1/0
$\overline{ADS}$	Address status	O	0
$\overline{READY}$	Transfer acknowledge	I	0
$\overline{NA}$	Next address request	I	0
$\overline{LOCK}$	Bus lock indication	O	0
INTR	Interrupt request	I	1
NMI	Nonmaskable interrupt request	I	1
RESET	System reset	I	1
HOLD	Bus hold request	I	1
HLDA	Bus hold acknowledge	O	1
PEREQ	Coprocessor request	I	1
$\overline{BUSY}$	Coprocessor busy	I	0
$\overline{ERROR}$	Coprocessor error	I	0

Figure 14.4 Signals of the 80386.

From a hardware point of view, there is only one difference between an 80386DX configured for the real-address mode or protected virtual-address mode. This difference is the size of the address bus. When in real mode, just the lower 18 address lines, A_2 through A_{19}, are active, while in the protected mode all 30 lines, A_2 through A_{31}, are functional. Of these, A_{19} and A_{31} are the most significant address bits, respectively. Actually, real-mode addresses are 20 bits long and protected-mode addresses are 32 bits long. The other two bits, A_0 and A_1 are decoded inside the 80386DX, along with information about the size of the data to be transferred, to produce *byte enable* outputs, $\overline{BE_0}$, $\overline{BE_1}$, $\overline{BE_2}$, and $\overline{BE_3}$.

As shown in Fig. 14.4, the address lines are outputs. They are used to carry address information from the 80386DX to memory and I/O ports. In real-address mode, the 20-bit address gives the 80386DX the ability to address a 1MB physical memory address space. On the other hand, in protected mode the extended 32-bit address results in a 4GB physical memory address space. Moreover, when in protected mode, virtual addressing is provided through software. This results in a 64TB virtual memory address space.

In both the real and protected modes, the 80386DX microcomputer has an independent I/O address space. This I/O address space is 64KB in length. Therefore, just address lines A_2 through A_{15} and the $\overline{BE}$ outputs are used when addressing I/O devices.

The 80386SX has the same number of active address lines as the 80386DX in the real mode, but less address lines in the protected mode. Its protected-mode address is just 25 bits long; therefore, the address space is limited to 16MB. This is the first key difference between the 80386SX and 80386DX MPUs. The 80386SX accesses the I/O address space in exactly the same way as the 80386DX.

Since the 80386DX is a 32-bit microprocessor, its data bus is formed from the 32 data lines D_0 through D_{31}. D_{31} is the most significant bit and D_0 the least significant bit. These lines are identified as bidirectional in Fig. 14.4. This is because they have the ability to either carry data in or out of the MPU. The kinds of data transferred over these lines are read/write data and instructions for memory, input/output data for I/O devices, and interrupt type codes from an interrupt controller.

The 80386SX has a 16-bit data bus instead of a 32-bit data bus. This is the second important difference between the 80386SX and 80386DX. This results in lower performance, but has the advantage of lower cost for the microcomputer system.

Earlier we indicated that the 80386DX supports dynamic bus sizing. Even though the 80386DX has 32 data lines, the size of the bus can be dynamically switched to 16 bits. This is done by simply switching the *bus size 16* ($\overline{BS\ 16}$) input to logic 0. When in this mode, 32-bit data transfers are performed as two successive 16-bit data transfers over bus lines D_0 through D_{15}. Since the 80386SX has a 16-bit data bus, it does not have this input.

Remember that the 80386DX supports byte, word, and double-word data transfers over its data bus during a single bus cycle. Therefore, it must signal external circuitry what type of data transfer is taking place and over which part of the data bus the data will be carried. The bus unit does this by activating the appropriate byte enable output signals.

Figure 14.5 lists each byte enable output signal and the part of the data bus it is intended to enable. For instance, here we see that an active $\overline{BE}_0$ corresponds to data bus lines D_0 through D_7. If a byte of data is being read from memory, just one of the byte enable outputs is made active. For instance, if the most significant byte of an aligned double word is read from memory, $\overline{BE}_3$ is switched to logic 0 and the data moves on data lines D_{24} through D_{31}. On the other hand, if a word of data is being read, two outputs become active. An example would be to read the most significant word of an aligned double word from memory. In this case, $\overline{BE}_2$ and $\overline{BE}_3$ are both switched to logic 0 and the data is carried by lines D_{16} through D_{31}. Finally, if an aligned double word read is taking place, all four $\overline{BE}$ outputs are made active and all data lines are used to transfer the data.

Byte Enable	Data Bus Lines
$\overline{BE}_0$	$D_0 - D_7$
$\overline{BE}_1$	$D_8 - D_{15}$
$\overline{BE}_2$	$D_{16} - D_{23}$
$\overline{BE}_3$	$D_{24} - D_{31}$

Figure 14.5 Byte enable outputs and data bus lines.

EXAMPLE 14.2

What code is output on the byte enable lines whenever the address on the bus is for an instruction acquisition bus cycle?

Solution

Since code is always fetched as 32-bit words (aligned double words), all the byte enable outputs are made active. Therefore,

$$\overline{BE_3}\overline{BE_2}\overline{BE_1}\overline{BE_0} = 0000_2$$

The byte enable lines work exactly the same way when write data transfers are performed over the bus. Figure 14.6(a) identifies what type of data transfer takes place for all the possible variations of the byte enable outputs. For instance, we find that $\overline{BE_3}\overline{BE_2}\overline{BE_1}\overline{BE_0} = 1110_2$ means that a byte of data is written over data bus lines D_0 through D_7.

EXAMPLE 14.3

What type of data transfer takes place and over which data bus lines are data transferred if the byte enable code output is

$$\overline{BE_3}\overline{BE_2}\overline{BE_1}\overline{BE_0} = 1100_2$$

Solution

Looking at the table in Fig. 14.6(a), we see that a word of data is transferred over data bus lines D_0 through D_{15}.

With its 16-bit data bus, the 80386SX can only transfer a byte or word of data over the bus during a single bus cycle. For this reason, the four byte enable signals of the 80386DX are replaced by just two signals, *byte high enable* ($\overline{BHE}$) and *byte low enable* ($\overline{BLE}$) on the 80386SX. Logic 0 at $\overline{BLE}$ tells that a byte of data is being transferred over data bus line D_0 through D_7 and logic 0 at $\overline{BHE}$ means a byte transfer is taking place over data bus lines D_8 through D_{15}. When a word of data is transferred, both of these signals are at their active 0 logic level.

The 80386DX performs what is called *data duplication* during certain types of write cycles. Data duplication is provided in the 80386DX to optimize the performance of the data bus when it is set for 16-bit mode. Notice that whenever a write cycle is performed in which data are only transferred over the upper part of the 32-bit data bus the data are duplicated on the corresponding lines of the lower part

$\overline{BE}_3$	$\overline{BE}_2$	$\overline{BE}_1$	$\overline{BE}_0$	$D_{31}-D_{24}$	$D_{23}-D_{16}$	$D_{15}-D_8$	D_7-D_0
1	1	1	0				XXXXXXXX
1	1	0	1			XXXXXXXX	
1	0	1	1		XXXXXXXX		
0	1	1	1	XXXXXXXX			
1	1	0	0			XXXXXXXX	XXXXXXXX
1	0	0	1		XXXXXXXX	XXXXXXXX	
0	0	1	1	XXXXXXXX	XXXXXXXX		
1	0	0	0		XXXXXXXX	XXXXXXXX	XXXXXXXX
0	0	0	1	XXXXXXXX	XXXXXXXX	XXXXXXXX	
0	0	0	0	XXXXXXXX	XXXXXXXX	XXXXXXXX	XXXXXXXX

(a)

$\overline{BE}_3$	$\overline{BE}_2$	$\overline{BE}_1$	$\overline{BE}_0$	$D_{31}-D_{24}$	$D_{23}-D_{16}$	$D_{15}-D_8$	D_7-D_0
1	1	1	0				XXXXXXXX
1	1	0	1			XXXXXXXX	
1	0	1	1		XXXXXXXX		DDDDDDDD
0	1	1	1	XXXXXXXX		DDDDDDDD	
1	1	0	0			XXXXXXXX	XXXXXXXX
1	0	0	1		XXXXXXXX	XXXXXXXX	
0	0	1	1	XXXXXXXX	XXXXXXXX	DDDDDDDD	DDDDDDDD
1	0	0	0		XXXXXXXX	XXXXXXXX	XXXXXXXX
0	0	0	1	XXXXXXXX	XXXXXXXX	XXXXXXXX	
0	0	0	0	XXXXXXXX	XXXXXXXX	XXXXXXXX	XXXXXXXX

(b)

Figure 14.6 (a) Types of data transfers for the various byte enable combinations. (b) Data transfers that include duplication.

of the bus. For example, looking at Fig. 14.6(b), we see that, when $\overline{BE}_3\overline{BE}_2\overline{BE}_1$ $\overline{BE}_0 = 1011_2$, data (denoted as XXXXXXXX) are actually being written over data bus lines D_{16} through D_{23}. However, at the same time, the data denoted as DDDDDDDD in Fig. 14.6(b) are automatically duplicated on data bus lines D_0 through D_7. In spite of the fact that the byte is available on the lower eight data bus lines, $\overline{BE}_0$ stays inactive. The same thing happens when a word of data is transferred over D_{16} through D_{31}. In this example, $\overline{BE}_3\overline{BE}_2\overline{BE}_1\overline{BE}_0 = 0011_2$, and Fig. 14.6(b) shows that the word is duplicated on data lines D_0 through D_{15}.

EXAMPLE 14.4

If a word of data that is being written to memory is accompanied by the byte enable code 1001_2, over which data bus lines are the data carried? Is data duplication performed for this data transfer?

Solution

In the tables of Fig. 14.6, we find that for the byte enable code 1001_2, the word of data is transferred over data bus lines D_8 through D_{23}. For this transfer, data duplication does not occur.

Control signals are required to support information transfers over the 80386DX's address and data buses. They are needed to signal when a valid address is on the address bus, in which direction data are to be transferred over the data bus, when valid write data are on the data bus, and when an external device can put read data on the data bus. The 80386DX does not directly produce signals for all these functions. Instead, it outputs bus cycle definition and control signals at the beginning of each bus cycle. These bus cycle indication signals must be decoded in external circuitry to produce the needed memory and I/O control signals.

Three signals are used to identify the type of 80386DX bus cycle that is in progress. In Figs. 14.3 and 14.4, they are labeled *write/read indication* $(W/\overline{R})$, *data/ control indication* $(D/\overline{C})$, and *memory/input-output indication* $(M/\overline{IO})$. The table in Fig. 14.7 lists all possible combinations of the bus cycle indication signals and the corresponding bus cycle types. Here we find that the logic level of memory/ input-output $(M/\overline{IO})$ tells whether a memory or I/O cycle is to take place over the bus. Logic 1 at this output signals a memory operation, and logic 0 signals an I/O operation. The next signal in Fig. 14.7, data/control indication $(D/\overline{C})$, identifies whether the current bus cycle is a data or control cycle. In the table, we see that it signals control cycle (logic 0) for instruction fetch, interrupt acknowledge, and halt/shut down operation and data cycle (logic 1) for memory and I/O data read and write operations. Looking more closely at the table in Fig. 14.7, we find that if the code on these two lines, $M/\overline{IO}$ $D/\overline{C}$, is 00 an interrupt is to be acknowledged; if it is 01, an input/output operation is in progress; if it is 10, instruction code is being fetched; and, finally, if it is 11, a data memory read or write is taking place.

The last signal identified in Fig. 14.7, write/read indication $(W/\overline{R})$, identifies the specific type of memory or input/output operation that will occur during a bus cycle. For example, when $W/\overline{R}$ is logic 0 during a bus cycle, data are to be read from memory or an I/O port. On the other hand, logic 1 at $W/\overline{R}$ says that data are to be written into memory or an I/O device. For example, all bus cycles that read instruction code from memory are accompanied by logic 0 on the $W/\overline{R}$ line.

$M/\overline{IO}$	$D/\overline{C}$	$W/\overline{R}$	Type of Bus Cycle
0	0	0	Interrupt acknowledge
0	0	1	Idle
0	1	0	I/O data read
0	1	1	I/O data write
1	0	0	Memory code read
1	0	1	Halt/shutdown
1	1	0	Memory data read
1	1	1	Memory data write

Figure 14.7 Bus cycle indication signals and types of bus cycles.

EXAMPLE 14.5 ——————————————————————————————————

What type of bus cycle is taking place if the bus cycle indication code
M/$\overline{\text{IO}}$ D/$\overline{\text{C}}$ W/$\overline{\text{R}}$ equals 010?

Solution

Looking at the table in Fig. 14.7, we see that bus cycle indication code 010 identifies
an I/O data read (input) bus cycle.

——

   Three bus cycle control signals are found at pins of the 80386DX. They are
identified in Figs. 14.3 and 14.4 as *address status* ($\overline{\text{ADS}}$), *transfer acknowledge*
($\overline{\text{READY}}$), and *next address request* ($\overline{\text{NA}}$). The $\overline{\text{ADS}}$ output is switched to logic 0
to indicate that the bus cycle indication code (M/$\overline{\text{IO}}$ D/$\overline{\text{C}}$ W/$\overline{\text{R}}$), byte enable code
($\overline{\text{BE}_3}\overline{\text{BE}_2}\overline{\text{BE}_1}\overline{\text{BE}_0}$), and address ($A_2$ through A_{31}) signals are all stable. Therefore,
it is normally applied to an input of the external bus control logic circuit and tells
it that a valid bus cycle indication code and address are available. In Fig. 14.7, the
bus cycle indication code M/$\overline{\text{IO}}$ D/$\overline{\text{C}}$ W/$\overline{\text{R}}$ = 001 is identified as *idle*. That is, it is
the code that is output whenever no bus cycle is being performed.
   $\overline{\text{READY}}$ can be used to insert wait states into the current bus cycle such that
it is extended by a number of clock periods. In Fig. 14.4, we find that this signal is
an input to the 80386DX. Normally, it is produced by the microcomputer's memory
or I/O subsystem and supplied to the 80386DX by way of external bus control logic
circuitry. By switching $\overline{\text{READY}}$ to logic 0, slow memory or I/O devices can tell
the 80386DX when they are ready to permit a data transfer to be completed.
   Earlier we pointed out that the 80386DX supports address pipelining at its
bus interface. By address pipelining, we mean that the address and bus cycle indication code for the next bus cycle is output before $\overline{\text{READY}}$ becomes active to signal
that the prior bus cycle can be completed. This mode of operation is optional. The
external bus control logic circuitry activates pipelining by switching the next address
request ($\overline{\text{NA}}$) input to logic 0. By using pipelining, delays introduced by the decode
logic can be made transparent and the address to data access time increased. In
this way, the same level of performance can be obtained with slower, lower-cost
memory devices.
   One other bus interface control output that is supplied by the 80386DX is
the *bus lock indication* ($\overline{\text{LOCK}}$). This signal is needed to support multiple-processor
architectures. In multiprocessor systems that employ shared resources, such as global
memory, this signal can be employed to assure that the 80386DX has uninterrupted
control of the system bus and the shared resources. That is, by switching its
$\overline{\text{LOCK}}$ output to logic 0, the MPU can lock up the shared resources for exclusive use.
   The 80386SX has the same bus cycle indication and control signals as the
80386DX. The signals that identify the type of bus cycle are write/read indication
(W/$\overline{\text{R}}$), data/control indication (D/$\overline{\text{C}}$), and memory/input-output indication (M/
$\overline{\text{IO}}$), while those that control the bus cycle are address status ($\overline{\text{ADS}}$), transfer
acknowledge ($\overline{\text{READY}}$), next address request ($\overline{\text{NA}}$) and bus lock indication

828   *The 80386, 80486, and Pentium™ Processor Families*   Chap. 14

($\overline{\text{LOCK}}$). Each of these signals serve the exact same function as they do for the 80386DX MPU.

Interrupt Interface

Looking at Figs. 14.3 and 14.4, we find that the key interrupt interface signals are *interrupt request* (INTR), *nonmaskable interrupt request* (NMI), and *system reset* (RESET). INTR is an input to the 80386DX that can be used by external devices to signal that they need to be serviced. The 80386DX samples this input at the beginning of each instruction. Logic 1 on INTR represents an active interrupt request.

When an active interrupt request has been recognized by the 80386DX, it signals this fact to external circuitry and initiates an interrupt acknowledge bus cycle sequence. In Fig. 14.7, we see that the occurrence of an interrupt acknowledge bus cycle is signaled to external circuitry with the bus cycle definition $M/\overline{IO}$ $D/\overline{C}$ $W/\overline{R}$ equal to 000. This bus cycle indication code can be decoded in the external bus control logic circuitry to produce an interrupt acknowledge signal. With this interrupt acknowledge signal, the 80386DX tells the external device that its request for service has been granted. This completes the interrupt request/acknowledge handshake. At this point, program control is passed to the interrupt's service routine.

The INTR input is maskable. That is, its operation can be enabled or disabled with the interrupt flag (IF) within the 80386DX's flag register. On the other hand, the NMI input, as its name implies, is a nonmaskable interrupt input. On any 0-to-1 transition of NMI, a request for service is latched within the 80386DX. Independent of the setting of the IF flag, control is passed to the beginning of the nonmaskable interrupt service routine at the completion of execution of the current instruction.

Finally, the RESET input is used to provide a hardware reset to the 80386DX microprocessor. Switching RESET to logic 1 initializes the internal registers of the 80386DX. When it is returned to logic 0, program control is passed to the beginning of a reset service routine. A diagnostic routine that tests the 80386DX microprocessor can also be initiated as part of the reset sequence.

The 80386SX's interrupt interface is exactly the same as that of the 80386DX. It is implemented with the same signals, interrupt request (INTR), nonmaskable interrupt request (NMI), and system reset (RESET), and identified to external circuitry with the same bus cycle code.

DMA Interface

Now that we have examined the signals of the 80386DX's interrupt interface, let us turn our attention to the *direct memory access* (DMA) interface. From Figs. 14.3 and 14.4, we find that the DMA interface is implemented with just two signals: *bus hold request* (HOLD) and *bus hold acknowledge* (HLDA). When an external device, such as a *DMA controller*, wants to take over control of the local address and data buses, it signals this fact to the 80386DX by switching the HOLD input to logic 1. At completion of the current bus cycle, the 80386DX enters the hold state. When in the hold state, its local bus signals are in the high-impedance state. Next, the 80386DX signals external devices that it has given up control of the bus by switching its HLDA output to the 1 logic level. This completes the hold/hold acknowledge handshake sequence. The 80386DX remains in this state until the hold request is removed. The 80386SX's DMA interface is exactly the same as that of the 80386DX.

Coprocessor Interface

In Fig. 14.3, we find that a coprocessor interface is provided on the 80386DX microprocessor to permit it to easily interface to either the *80287* or *80387 numeric coprocessor*. The 80387 cannot perform transfers over the data bus by itself. Whenever the 80387 needs to read or write operands from memory, it must signal the 80386DX to initiate the data transfers. The 80387 does this by switching the *coprocessor request* (PEREQ) input of the 80386DX to logic 1.

The other two signals included in the external coprocessor interface are $\overline{\text{BUSY}}$ and $\overline{\text{ERROR}}$. *Coprocessor busy* ($\overline{\text{BUSY}}$) is an input of the 80386DX. Whenever the 80387 is executing a numeric instruction, it signals this fact to the 80386DX by switching the $\overline{\text{BUSY}}$ input to logic 0. In this way, the 80386DX knows not to request the numeric coprocessor to perform another calculation until $\overline{\text{BUSY}}$ returns to 1. Moreover, if an error occurs in a calculation performed by the numeric coprocessor, this condition is signaled to the 80386DX by switching the *coprocessor error* ($\overline{\text{ERROR}}$) input to the 0 logic level. This interface is implemented the same way on the 80386SX MPU.

▲ 14.4 SYSTEM CLOCK OF THE 80386DX

The time base for synchronization of the internal and external operations of the 80386DX microprocessor is provided by the *clock* (CLK2) input signal. The 80386DX is available with four different clock speeds. The standard 80386DX-16 MPU operates at 16 MHz and its three faster versions, the 80386DX-20, 80386DX-25, and 80386DX-33, operate at 20, 25, and 33 MHz, respectively. The clock signal applied to the CLK2 input of the 80386DX is twice the frequency rating of the microprocessor. Therefore, CLK2 of an 80386DX-16 is driven by a 32-MHz signal. This signal must be generated in external circuitry.

The waveform of the CLK2 input of the 80386DX is shown in Fig. 14.8. This signal is specified at CMOS-compatible voltage levels and not TTL levels. Its minimum and maximum low logic levels are $V_{ILCmin} = -0.3$ V and $V_{ILCmax} = 0.8$ V, respectively. Moreover, the minimum and maximum high logic levels are $V_{IHCmin} = V_{CC} - 0.8$ V and $V_{IHCmax} = V_{CC} + 0.3$ V, respectively. The minimum period of the 16-MHz clock signal is $t_{cmin} = 31$ ns (measured at the 2.0 V level); its minimum high time t_{pmin} and low time t_{lmin} (measured at the 2.0 V level) are both equal to 9 ns; and the maximum rise time t_{rmax} and fall time t_{fmax} of its edges (measured between the $V_{CC} - 0.8$V and 0.8V levels) are both equal to 8 ns.

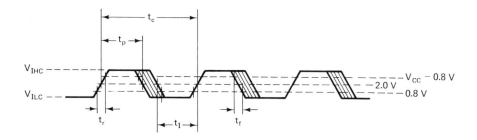

Figure 14.8 System clock (CLK2) waveform.

▲ 14.5 80386DX BUS STATES AND PIPELINED AND NONPIPELINED BUS CYCLES

Before looking at the bus cycles of the 80386DX, let us first examine the relationship between the timing of the 80386DX's CLK2 input and its bus cycle states. The *internal processor clock* (PCLK) signal is at half the frequency of the external clock input. Therefore, as shown in Fig. 14.9, one processor clock cycle corresponds to two CLK2 cycles. Notice that these CLK2 cycles are labeled as *phase 1* (ϕ_1) and *phase 2* (ϕ_2). In a 20-MHz 80386DX microprocessor, CLK2 equals 40 MHz and each clock cycle has a duration of 25 ns. In Fig. 14.9, we see that the two phases ($\phi_1 + \phi_2$) of a processor cycle are identified as one processor clock period. A processor clock period is also called a *T state*. Therefore, the minimum length of an internal processor clock cycle is 50 ns.

Nonpipelined and Pipelined Bus Cycles

A *bus cycle* is the activity performed whenever a microprocessor accesses information in program memory, data memory, or an I/O device. The 80386DX

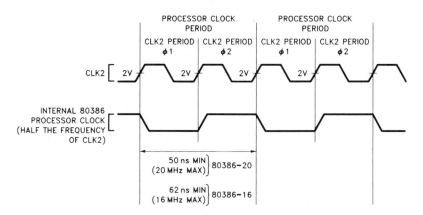

Figure 14.9 Processor clock cycles. (Reprinted by permission of Intel Corp., © Intel Corp. 1987)

can perform bus cycles with either of two types of timing: *nonpipelined* and *pipelined.* Here we will examine the difference between these two types of bus cycles.

Figure 14.10 shows a typical nonpipelined microprocessor bus cycle. Notice that the bus cycle contains two T states and that they are called T_1 and T_2. During the T_1 part of the bus cycle, the 80386DX outputs the address of the storage location that is to be accessed on the address bus, a bus cycle indication code, and control signals. In the case of a write cycle, write data are also output on the data bus during T_1. The second state, T_2, is the part of the bus cycle during which external devices are to accept write data from the data bus or, in the case of a read cycle, put data on the data bus.

For instance, in Fig. 14.10 we see that the sequence of events starts with an address, denoted as n, being output on the address bus in clock state T_1. Later in the bus cycle, while the address is still available on the address bus, a read or write data transfer takes place over the data bus. Notice that the data transfer for address n is shown to occur in clock state T_2. Since each bus cycle has a minimum of two T states (four CLK2 cycles), the minimum bus cycle duration for an 80386DX-20 is 100 ns.

Let us now look at a microprocessor bus cycle that employs *pipelining.* By pipelining we mean that addressing for the next bus cycle is overlapped with the data transfer of the prior bus cycle. When address pipelining is in use, the address, bus cycle indication code, and control signals for the next bus cycle are output during T_2 of the prior cycle, instead of the T_1 that follows.

In Fig. 14.11, we see that address n becomes valid in the T_2 state of the prior bus cycle, and then the data transfer for address n takes place in the next T_2 state. Moreover, notice that at the same time that data transfer n occurs, address n + 1 is output on the address bus. In this way, we see that the microprocessor begins addressing the next storage location that it is to access while it is still performing the read or write of data for the previously addressed storage location. Due to the address/data pipelining, the memory or I/O subsystem actually has five CLK2 cycles (125 ns for an 80386DX-20 running at full speed) to perform the data transfer, even though the duration of every bus cycle is just four CLK2 cycles (100 ns).

The interval of time denoted as *address access time* in Fig. 14.10 represents the amount of time that the address must be stable prior to the read or write of data actually taking place. Notice that this duration is less than the four CLK2 cycles in a nonpipelined bus cycle. Figure 14.11 shows that in a pipelined bus cycle

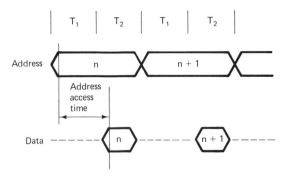

Figure 14.10 Typical read/write bus cycle.

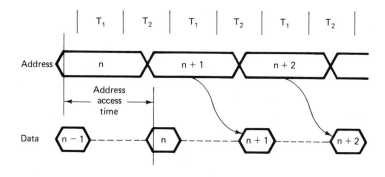

Figure 14.11 Pipelined bus cycle. (Reprinted by permission of Intel Corp., © Intel Corp. 1987)

the *effective address access time* equals the duration of a complete bus cycle. This leads us to the benefit of the 80386DX's pipelined mode of bus operation over the nonpipelined mode of operation. It is that, for a fixed address access time (equal speed memory design), the 80386DX pipelined bus cycle will have a shorter duration than its nonpipelined bus cycle. This results in improved bus performance.

In Fig. 14.11, we find that at completion of the bus cycle for address n another bus cycle is immediately initiated for address n + 1. Sometimes another bus cycle will not be immediately initiated. For instance, if the 80386DX's prefetch queue is already full and the instruction that is currently being executed does not need to access operands in memory, no bus activity will take place. In this case, the bus goes into a mode of operation known as an *idle state* and no bus activity occurs. Figure 14.12 shows a sequence of bus activity in which an idle state exists between the bus cycles for addresses n + 1 and n + 2. The duration of a single idle state is equal to two CLK2 cycles.

Wait states can be inserted to extend the duration of the 80386DX's bus cycle. This is done in response to a request by an event in external hardware instead of an internal event such as a full queue. In fact, the $\overline{\text{READY}}$ input of the 80386DX is provided specifically for this purpose. This input is sampled in the later part of the T$_2$ state of every bus cycle to determine if the data transfer should be completed.

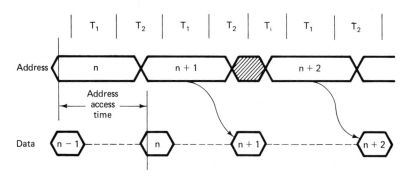

Figure 14.12 Idle states in bus activity.

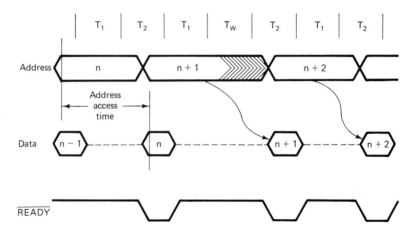

Figure 14.13 Bus cycle with wait states.

Figure 14.13 shows that logic 1 at this input indicates that the current bus cycle should not be completed. As long as $\overline{READY}$ is held at the 1 level, the read or write data transfer does not take place and the current T_2 state becomes a wait state (T_w) to extend the bus cycle. The bus cycle is not completed until external hardware returns $\overline{READY}$ back to logic 0. This ability to extend the duration of a bus cycle permits the use of slow memory or I/O devices in the microcomputer system.

Nonpipelined Read Cycle Timing

The memory interface signals that occur when the 80386DX reads data from memory are shown in Fig. 14.14. This diagram shows two separate nonpipelined read cycles. They are *cycle 1*, which is performed without wait states, and *cycle 2*, which includes one wait state. Let us now trace the events that take place in cycle 1 as data or instructions are read from memory.

The occurrence of all the signals in the read bus cycle timing diagram are illustrated relative to the two timing states, T_1 and T_2, of the 80386DX's bus cycle. The read operation starts at the beginning of phase 1 (ϕ_1) in the T_1 state of the bus cycle. At this moment, the 80386DX outputs the address of the double-word memory location to be accessed on address bus lines A_2 through A_{31}, the byte enable signals $\overline{BE}_0$ through $\overline{BE}_3$ that identify the bytes of the double word that are to be fetched, and switches address strobe ($\overline{ADS}$) to logic 0 to signal that a valid address is on the address bus. Looking at Fig. 14.14, we see that the address and cycle indication signals are maintained stable during the complete bus cycle; however, they must be latched into the external bus control logic circuitry synchronously with the pulse to logic 0 on $\overline{ADS}$. At the end of ϕ_2 of T_1, $\overline{ADS}$ is returned to its inactive logic 1 level.

Notice in Fig. 14.14 that the bus cycle indication signals, $M/\overline{IO}$, $D/\overline{C}$, and $W/\overline{R}$, are also made valid at the beginning of ϕ_1 of state T_1. The bus cycle indication

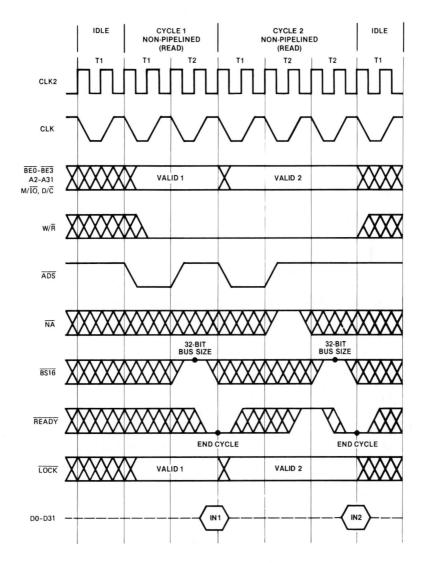

Figure 14.14 Nonpipelined read cycle timing. (Reprinted by permission of Intel Corp., © Intel Corp., 1987)

codes that apply to a memory read cycle are highlighted in Fig. 14.15. Here we see that, if code is being read from memory, M/$\overline{\text{IO}}$ D/$\overline{\text{C}}$ W/$\overline{\text{R}}$ equals 100. That is, signal M/$\overline{\text{IO}}$ is set to logic 1 to indicate to the circuitry in the memory interface that a memory bus cycle is in progress, D/$\overline{\text{C}}$ is set to 0 to indicate that code memory is to be accessed, and W/$\overline{\text{R}}$ is set to 0 to indicate that data are being read from memory.

At the beginning of ϕ_1 in T_2 of the read cycle, external circuitry must signal the 80386DX whether the bus is to operate in the 16- or 32-bit mode. In Fig. 14.14, we see that it does this with the BS $\overline{16}$ signal. The 80386DX samples this input in

M/$\overline{\text{IO}}$	D/$\overline{\text{C}}$	W/$\overline{\text{R}}$	Type of Bus Cycle
0	0	0	Interrupt acknowledge
0	0	1	Idle
0	1	0	I/O data read
0	1	1	I/O data write
1	0	0	Memory code read
1	0	1	Halt/shutdown
1	1	0	Memory data read
1	1	1	Memory data write

Figure 14.15 Memory read bus cycle indication codes.

the middle of the T_2 bus cycle state. The 1 logic level shown in the timing diagram indicates that a 32-bit data transfer is to take place.

Notice in Fig. 14.14 that at the end of T_2 the $\overline{\text{READY}}$ input is tested by the 80386DX. The logic level at this input signals whether the current bus cycle is to be completed or extended with wait states. The logic 0 shown at this input means that the bus cycle is to run to completion. For this reason, we see that data available on data bus lines D_0 through D_{31} are read into the 80386DX at the end of T_2.

Nonpipelined Write Cycle Timing

The nonpipelined write bus cycle timing diagram shown in Fig. 14.16 is similar to that given for a nonpipelined read cycle in Fig. 14.14. It includes waveforms for both a no wait state write operation (cycle 1) and a one wait state write operation (cycle 2). Looking at the write cycle waveforms, we find that the address, byte enable, and bus cycle indication signals are output at the beginning of ϕ_1 of the T_1 state. All these signals are to be latched in external circuitry with the pulse at $\overline{\text{ADS}}$. The one difference here is that W/$\overline{\text{R}}$ is at the 1 logic level instead of 0. In fact, as shown in Fig. 14.17, the bus cycle indication code for a memory data write is M/$\overline{\text{IO}}$ D/$\overline{\text{C}}$ W/$\overline{\text{R}}$ equals 111; therefore, M/$\overline{\text{IO}}$ and D/$\overline{\text{C}}$ are also at the logic 1 level.

Let us now look at what happens on the data bus during a write bus cycle. Notice in Fig. 14.16 that the 80386DX outputs the data that are to be written to memory onto the data bus at the beginning of ϕ_2 in the T_1 state. These data are maintained valid until the end of the bus cycle. In the middle of the T_2 state, the logic level of the BS $\overline{16}$ input is tested by the 80386DX and indicates that the bus is to be used in the 32-bit mode. Finally, at the end of T_2, $\overline{\text{READY}}$ is tested and found to be at its active 0 logic level. Since the memory subsystem has made $\overline{\text{READY}}$ logic 0, the write cycle is complete and the buses and control signal lines are prepared for the next write cycle.

Wait States in a Nonpipelined Memory Bus Cycle

Earlier we showed how wait states are used to lengthen the duration of the memory bus cycle of the 80386DX. Wait states are inserted with the $\overline{\text{READY}}$ input signal. Upon request from an event in external hardware, for instance slow memory, the $\overline{\text{READY}}$ input is switched to logic 1. This signals the 80386DX that the current

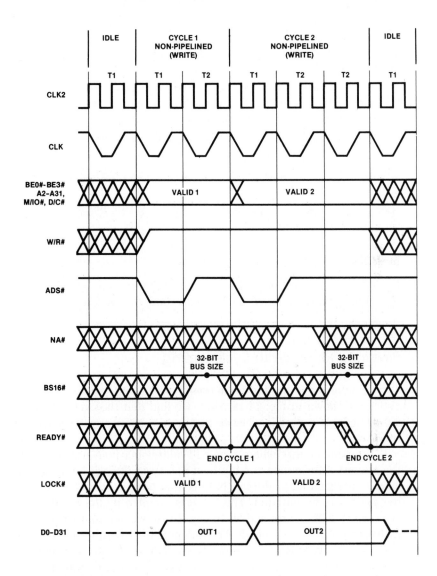

Figure 14.16 Nonpipelined write cycle timing. (Reprinted by permission of Intel Corp., © Intel Corp. 1987)

M/$\overline{\text{IO}}$	D/$\overline{\text{C}}$	W/$\overline{\text{R}}$	Type of Bus Cycle
0	0	0	Interrupt acknowledge
0	0	1	Idle
0	1	0	I/O data read
0	1	1	I/O data write
1	0	0	Memory code read
1	0	1	Halt/shutdown
1	1	0	Memory data read
1	1	1	Memory data write

Figure 14.17 Memory write bus cycle indication code.

bus cycle should not be completed. Instead, it is extended by repeating the T_2 state. Therefore, the duration of one wait state ($T_w = T_2$) equals 50 ns for 20-MHz clock operation.

Cycle 2 in Fig. 14.14 shows a read cycle extended by one wait state. Notice that the address, bank enable, and bus cycle indication signals are maintained throughout the wait-state period. In this way, the read cycle is not completed until $\overline{\text{READY}}$ is switched to logic 0 in the second T_2 state.

EXAMPLE 14.6 _____

If cycle 2 in Fig. 14.16 is for an 80386DX-20 running at full speed, what is the duration of the bus cycle?

Solution

Each T state in the bus cycle of an 80386DX running at 20 MHz is 50 ns. Since the write cycle is extended by one wait state, the write cycle takes 150 ns.

_____

Pipelined Read/Write Cycle Timing

Timing diagrams for both nonpipelined and pipelined read and write bus cycles are shown in Fig. 14.18. Here we find that the cycle identified as *cycle 3* is an example of a pipelined write bus cycle. Let us now look more closely at this bus cycle.

Remember that when pipelined addressing is in use, the 80386DX outputs the address information for the next bus cycle during the T_2 state of the current cycle. The signal next address ($\overline{\text{NA}}$) is used to signal the 80386DX that a pipelined bus cycle is to be initiated. This input is sampled by the 80386DX during any bus state when $\overline{\text{ADS}}$ is not active. In Fig. 14.18, we see that ($\overline{\text{NA}}$) is first tested as 0 (active) during T_2 of cycle 2. This nonpipelined read cycle is also extended with period T_{2P} because $\overline{\text{READY}}$ is not active. Notice that the address, byte enable, and bus cycle indication signals for cycle 3 become valid (identified as VALID 3 in Fig. 14.18) during this period and a pulse is produced at $\overline{\text{ADS}}$. This information is latched externally synchronous with $\overline{\text{ADS}}$ and decoded to produce bus enable and control signals. In this way, the memory access time for a zero wait state memory cycle has been increased.

Bus cycle 3 represents a pipelined write cycle. The data to be written to memory are output on D_0 through D_{31} at ϕ_2 of T_{1P} and remain valid for the rest of the cycle. Logic 0 on $\overline{\text{READY}}$ at the end of T_{2P} indicates that the write cycle is to be completed without wait states.

Looking at Fig. 14.18, we find that $\overline{\text{NA}}$ is also active during T_{1P} of cycle 3. This means that cycle 4 will also be performed with pipelined timing. Cycle 4 is an example of a zero wait state pipelined read cycle. In this case, the address information, bus cycle indication code, and address strobe are output during T_{2P} of cycle

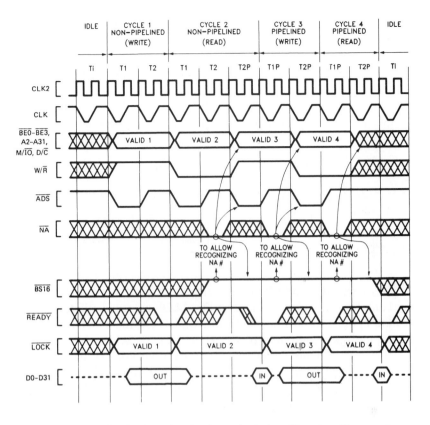

Figure 14.18 Pipelined read and write cycle timing. (Reprinted by permission of Intel Corp., © Intel Corp. 1987)

3 (the previous cycle), and memory data are read into the MPU at the end of T_{2P} of cycle 4.

▲ 14.6 MEMORY INTERFACE

Earlier we indicated that in protected mode the 32-bit address bus of the 80386DX results in a 4GB physical memory address space. As shown in Fig. 14.19, from a software point of view, this memory is organized as individual bytes over the address range from 00000000_{16} through $FFFFFFFF_{16}$. The 80386DX can also access data in this memory as words or double words.

Hardware Organization of the Memory Address Space

From a hardware point of view, the physical address space is implemented as four independent byte-wide banks, and each of these banks is 1GB in size. In Fig. 14.20, we find that the banks are identified as *bank 0, bank 1, bank 2*, and *bank 3*. Notice that these banks correspond to addresses that produce byte enable signals

FFFFFFFFH
FFFFFFFEH
FFFFFFFDH
⋮
4 GB Physical memory address space
⋮
00000002H
00000001H
00000000H

Figure 14.19 Physical address space.

$\overline{BE}_0$, $\overline{BE}_1$, $\overline{BE}_2$, and $\overline{BE}_3$, respectively. Logic 0 at a bank enable input selects the bank for operation. Looking at Fig. 14.20, we see that address bits A_2 through A_{31} are applied to all four banks in parallel. On the other hand, each memory bank supplies just eight lines of the 80386DX's 32-bit data bus. For example, byte data transfers for bank 0 take place over data bus lines D_0 through D_7, while byte data transfers for bank 3 are carried over data bus lines D_{24} through D_{31}.

When the 80386DX is operated in real mode, only the value on address lines A_2 through A_{19} and the $\overline{BE}$ signals are used to select the storage location that is to be accessed. For this reason, the physical address space is 1MB in length and

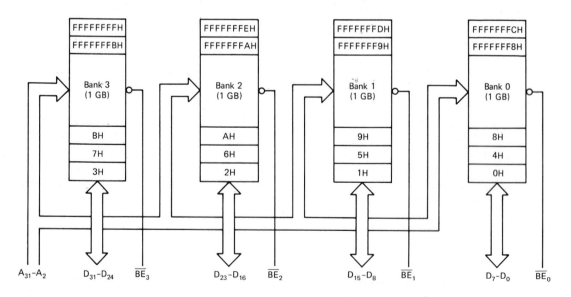

Figure 14.20 Hardware organization of the physical address space.

not 4GB. The memory subsystem is once again partitioned into four banks, as shown in Fig. 14.20 but this time each bank is 256KB in size.

Figure 14.20 shows that in hardware the memory address space is physically organized as a sequence of double words. The address on lines A_2 through A_{31} selects the double-word storage location. Therefore, each aligned double word starts at a physical address that is a multiple of four. For instance, in Fig. 14.20, we see that aligned double words start at addresses 00000000_{16}, 00000004_{16}, 00000008_{16}, up through $FFFFFFFC_{16}$.

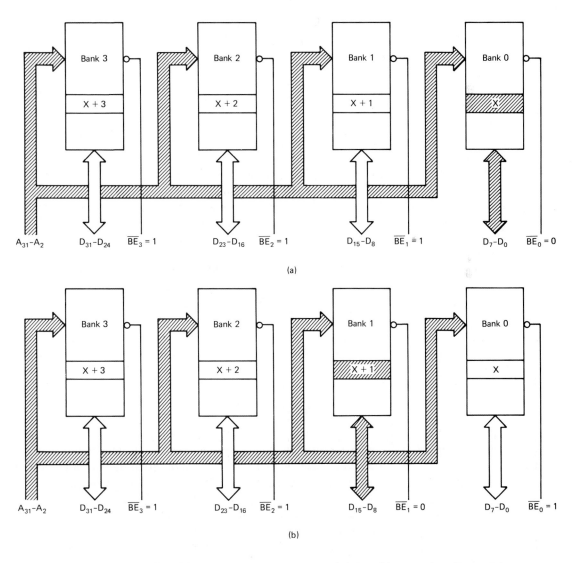

Figure 14.21 (a) Accessing a byte of data in bank 0. (b) Accessing a byte of data in bank 1. (c) Accessing a word of data in memory. (d) Accessing an aligned double word in memory.

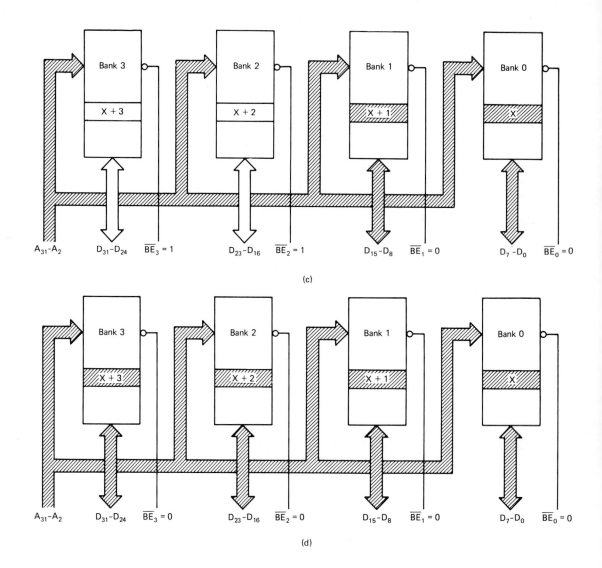

(c)

(d)

Figure 14.21 (Continued)

Each of the four bytes of a double word corresponds to one of the bank enable signals. For this reason, they are each stored in a different bank of memory. In Fig. 14.20, we have identified the range of byte addresses that corresponds to the storage locations in each bank of memory. For example, byte data accesses to addresses such as 00000000_{16}, 00000004_{16}, and 00000008_{16} all produce $\overline{BE}_0$, which enables memory bank 0, and the read or write data transfer takes place over data bus lines D_0 through D_7. Figure 14.21(a) illustrates how the byte at double-word aligned memory address X is accessed.

On the other hand, in Fig. 14.20 we see that byte addresses 00000001_{16}, 00000005_{16}, and 00000009_{16} correspond to data held in memory bank 1. Figure

14.21(b) shows how the byte of data at address X + 1 is accessed. Notice that $\overline{BE}_1$ is made active to enable bank 1 of memory.

Most memory accesses produce more than one bank enable signal. For instance, if the word of data beginning at aligned address X is read from memory, both $\overline{BE}_0$ and $\overline{BE}_1$ are generated. In this way, bank 0 and bank 1 of memory are enabled for operation. As shown in Fig. 14.21(c), the word of data is transferred to the MPU over data bus lines D_0 through D_{15}.

Let us now look at what happens when a double word of data is written to aligned double-word address X. As shown in Fig. 14.21(d), $\overline{BE}_0$, $\overline{BE}_1$, $\overline{BE}_2$, and $\overline{BE}_3$ are made 0 to enable all four banks of memory, and the MPU writes the data to memory over the complete data bus, D_0 through D_{31}.

All the data transfers we have described so far have been for what are called *double-word aligned data*. For each of these pieces of data all the bytes existed within the same double word, that is, a double word that is on an address boundary equal to a multiple of four. The diagram in Fig. 14.22 illustrates a number of aligned words and double words of data. Byte, aligned word, and aligned double-word data transfers are all performed by the 80386DX in a single bus cycle.

It is not always possible to have all words or double words of data aligned at double-word boundaries. Figure 14.23 shows some examples of misaligned words and double words of data that can be accessed by the 80386DX. Notice that word 3 consists of byte 3 that is in aligned double-word 0 and byte 4 that is in aligned double-word 4. Let us now look at how misaligned data are transferred over the bus.

The diagram in Fig. 14.24 illustrates a misaligned double-word data transfer. Here the double word of data starting at address X + 2 is to be accessed. However, this word consists of bytes X + 2 and X + 3 of the aligned double word at physical address X and bytes Y and Y + 1 of the aligned double word at physical address Y. Looking at the diagram, we see that $\overline{BE}_0$ and $\overline{BE}_1$ are active during the first bus

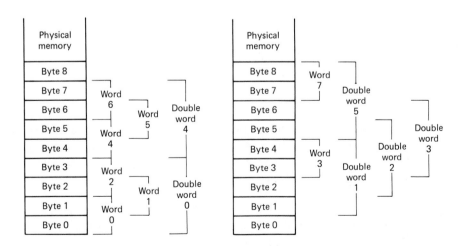

Figure 14.22 Examples of aligned data words and double words.

Figure 14.23 Examples of misaligned data words and double words.

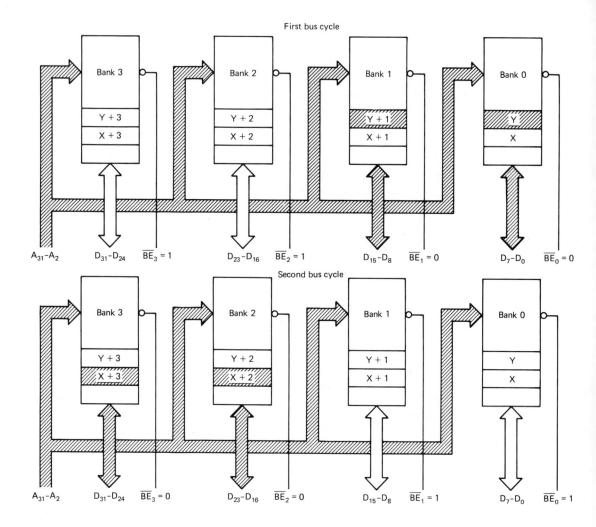

First bus cycle

Second bus cycle

Figure 14.24 Misaligned double-word data transfers.

cycle, and the word at address Y is transferred over D_0 through D_{15}. A second bus cycle automatically follows in which $\overline{BE}_3$ and $\overline{BE}_4$ are active, address X is put on the address bus, and the second word of data, X + 2 and X + 3, is carried over D_{16} through D_{31}. In this way, we see that data transfers of misaligned words or double words take two bus cycles.

EXAMPLE 14.7

Is the word at address $0000123F_{16}$ aligned or misaligned? How many bus cycles are required to read it from memory?

Solution

The first byte of the word is the fourth byte at aligned double-word address $0000123C_{16}$ and the second byte of the word is the first byte of the aligned double word at address 00001240_{16}. Therefore, the word is misaligned and requires two bus cycles to be read from memory.

Memory Interface Circuit

A memory interface diagram for a protected-mode, 80386DX-based microcomputer system is shown in Fig. 14.25. In Fig. 14.25, we find that the interface includes bus control logic, address bus latches and an address decoder, data bus transceiver/buffers, and bank write control logic. The bus cycle indication signals, M/$\overline{IO}$, D/$\overline{C}$, and W/$\overline{R}$, which are output by the 80386DX, are supplied directly to the bus control logic. Here they are decoded to produce the command and control signals needed to control data transfers over the bus. In Figs. 14.15 and 14.17, the status codes that relate to the memory interface are highlighted. For example, the code M/$\overline{IO}$ D/$\overline{C}$ W/$\overline{R}$ equal to 110 indicates that a data memory read bus cycle is in progress. This code switches the $\overline{MRDC}$ command output of the bus control logic to logic 0. Notice in Fig. 14.25 that $\overline{MRDC}$ is applied directly to the $\overline{OE}$ input of the memory subsystem.

Next let us look at how the address bus is decoded, buffered, and latched. Looking at Fig. 14.25, we see that address lines A_{29} through A_{31} are decoded to produce chip enable outputs $\overline{CE}_0$ through $\overline{CE}_7$. These chip enable signals are latched along with address bits A_2 through A_{28} and byte enable lines $\overline{BE}_0$ through $\overline{BE}_3$ into the address latches. Notice that the bus control logic receives $\overline{ADS}$ and the bus cycle indication code as inputs and produces the address latch enable (ALE), memory read command ($\overline{MRDC}$), and memory write command ($\overline{MWTC}$) control signals at its output. ALE is applied to the CLK input of the latches and strobes the bits of the address, byte enable, and chip enable signals into the address bus latches. These signals are buffered by the address latch devices and then output directly to the memory subsystem.

This part of the memory interface demonstrates one of the benefits of the 80386DX's pipelined bus mode. When working in the pipelined mode the 80386DX actually outputs the address in the T_2 state of the prior bus cycle. Therefore, by putting the address decoder before the address latches, instead of after, the code at address lines A_{28} through A_{31} can be fully decoded and stable prior to the T_1 state of the next bus cycle. In this way, the access time of the memory subsystem is reduced.

During read bus cycles, the $\overline{MRDC}$ output of the bus control logic enables the data at the outputs of the memory subsystem onto data bus lines D_0 through D_{31}. The 80386DX will read the appropriate byte, word, or double word of data. On the other hand, during write operations to memory, the bank write control logic determines into which of the four memory banks the data are to be written. This depends on whether a byte, word, or double-word data transfer is taking place over the bus.

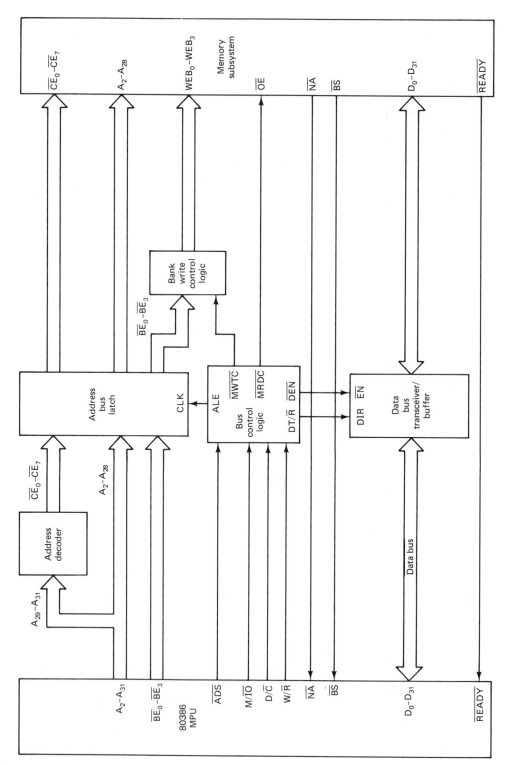

Figure 14.25 Memory interface block diagram.

Notice in Fig. 14.25 that the latched bank enable signals $\overline{BE}_0$ through $\overline{BE}_3$ are gated with the write command signal $\overline{MWTC}$ to produce a separate bank enable signal for each of the four banks of memory. These signals are denoted as $\overline{WEB}_0$ through $\overline{WEB}_3$ in Fig. 14.25. For example, if a word of data is to be written to memory over data bus lines D_0 through D_{15}, $\overline{WEB}_0$ and $\overline{WEB}_1$ are switched to their active 0 logic level.

The bus transceivers control the direction of data transfer between the MPU and memory subsystem. In Fig. 14.25, we see that the operation of the transceivers is controlled by the data transmit/receive (DT/$\overline{R}$) and data bus enable ($\overline{DEN}$) outputs of the bus control logic. $\overline{DEN}$ is applied to the enable ($\overline{EN}$) input of the transceivers and enables them for operation. This happens during all read and write bus cycles. DT/$\overline{R}$ selects the direction of data transfer through the transceivers. When a read cycle is in progress, DT/$\overline{R}$ is set to 0 and data are passed from the memory subsystem to the MPU. On the other hand, when a write cycle is taking place, DT/$\overline{R}$ is switched to logic 1 and data are carried from the MPU to the memory subsystem.

▲ 14.7 INPUT/OUTPUT INTERFACE

In Section 14.6 we studied the memory interface of the 80386DX microprocessor. Here we will examine another important interface of the 80386DX microcomputer system, the input/output interface.

Input/Output Interface and I/O Address Space

The input/output interface of the 80386DX microcomputer permits it to communicate with the outside world. The way in which the 80386DX deals with input/output (I/O) circuitry is similar to the way in which it interfaces with memory circuitry. That is, input/output data transfers also take place over the data bus. This parallel bus permits easy interface to LSI peripheral devices such as parallel I/O expanders, interval timers, and serial communication controllers. Let us continue by looking at how the 80386DX interfaces to its I/O subsystem.

A typical I/O interface circuit for an 80386DX-based microcomputer system is shown in Fig. 14.26. Notice that the interface includes the bus controller logic, an I/O address decoder, I/O address latches, I/O data bus transceiver/buffers, I/O bank write control logic, and the I/O subsystem. An example of a typical I/O device is a programmable peripheral interface (PPI) IC, such as the 8255A. This type of device is used to implement parallel input and output ports. Let us now look at the function of each of the blocks in this circuit more closely.

The I/O interface shown in Fig. 14.26 is designed to support 8-, 16-, and 32-bit I/O data transfers. Just as for the 8086 architecture, the 80386DX's I/O address is 16 bits in length and supports 64K independent byte-wide I/O ports. The part of the address on lines A_2 through A_{15} is used to specify the double-word I/O port that is to be accessed. When data are output to output ports, the logic levels of $\overline{BE}_0$ through $\overline{BE}_3$ determine which byte-wide port or ports are to be enabled for

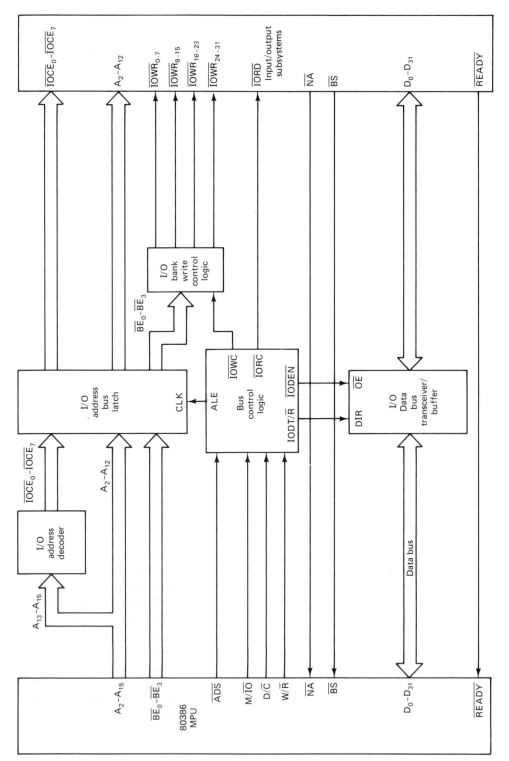

Figure 14.26 Byte, word, and double-word I/O interface block diagram.

operation. The more significant address bits, A_{16} through A_{31}, are held at the 0 logic level during the address period of all I/O bus cycles. The I/O address is specified as part of the instruction that performs the I/O operation. The 80386DX signals external circuitry that an I/O address is on the bus by switching its M/$\overline{IO}$ output to logic 0.

Notice in the circuit diagram that part of the I/O address that is output on address lines A_2 through A_{15} of the 80386DX is decoded by the I/O address decoder and then latched into the I/O address latches. Latching of the address is achieved with the pulse at the ALE output of the bus control logic. The bits of the address that are decoded produce I/O chip enable signals for the individual I/O devices. For instance, Fig. 14.26 shows that with three address bits, A_{13} through A_{15}, we produce enough chip enable outputs to select up to eight I/O devices. Notice that the outputs of the I/O address decoder are labeled $\overline{IOCE}_0$ through $\overline{IOCE}_7$. If a microcomputer employs a very simple I/O subsystem, it may be possible to eliminate the address decoder and simply use some of the latched high-order address bits as I/O enable signals.

In Fig 14.26 all the low-order address bits are shown to be latched and sent directly to the I/O devices. Typically, these address bits are used to select the register within the peripheral device that is to be accessed. For example, with just four of these address lines, we can select any one of 16 registers.

EXAMPLE 14.8

If address bits A_7 through A_{15} are directly used as chip enable signals and address lines A_6 through A_2 are used as register select inputs for the I/O devices, how many I/O devices can be used and what is the maximum number of registers that each device can contain?

Solution

The nine address lines when latched into the address latch produce the nine I/O chip enable signals, $\overline{IOCE}_0$ through $\overline{IOCE}_8$, for I/O devices 0 through 8. The lower five address bits are able to select one of 32 registers for each peripheral IC.

During input and output bus cycles, data are passed between the selected register in the enabled I/O device and the 80386DX over data bus lines D_0 through D_{31}. Earlier we pointed out that the 80386DX can input or output data in byte-wide, word-wide, or double-word format. Just as for the memory interface, the signals $\overline{BE}_0$ through $\overline{BE}_3$ are used to signal which byte or bytes of data are being transferred over the bus. Again logic 0 at $\overline{BE}_0$ identifies that a byte of data is input or output over data bus lines D_0 through D_7. On the other hand, logic 0 at $\overline{BE}_3$ means that a byte-data transfer is taking place over data bus lines D_{24} through D_{31}.

Many of the peripheral ICs that are used in the 80386DX microcomputer have a byte-wide data bus. For this reason, they are normally attached to the lower part of the data bus. That is, they are connected to data bus lines D_0 through D_7. If this is done in the circuit of Fig. 14.26, all I/O addresses must be scaled by four. This is because the first byte I/O address that corresponds to a byte transfer across the lower eight data bus lines is 0000_{16}, the next byte address that represents a byte transfer over D_0 through D_7 is 0004_{16}, the third I/O address is 00008_{16}, and so on. In fact, if only 8-bit peripherals are used in the 80386DX microcomputer system and they are all attached to I/O data bus lines D_0 through D_7, the bank enable signals are not needed in the I/O interface. In this case, address bit A_2 is used as the least significant bit of the I/O address and A_{15} the most significant bit. Therefore, from a hardware point of view, the I/O address space appears as 16K contiguous byte-wide storage locations over the address range from

$$A_{15} \ldots A_3 A_2 = 00000000000000_2$$

to

$$A_{15} \ldots A_3 A_2 = 11111111111111_2$$

In this case, the burden is put on software to assure that bytes of data are only input or output for addresses that are multiples of four and correspond to a data transfer over data bus lines D_0 through D_7.

As in the memory interface, bus control logic is needed to produce the control signals for the I/O interface. In Fig. 14.26 we see that the inputs to the bus control logic are the bus cycle indication signals $M/\overline{IO}$, $D/\overline{C}$, and $W/\overline{R}$. They are decoded to produce the I/O read command ($\overline{IORC}$) and I/O write command ($\overline{IOWC}$) outputs. $\overline{IORC}$ is applied directly to the input/output read ($\overline{IORD}$) input of the I/O devices and tells them when data are to be input. In this case, 32-bit data are always put on the data bus. However, the 80386DX only inputs the appropriate byte, word, or double word. On the other hand, $\overline{IOWC}$ is gated with the $\overline{BE}$ signals to produce a separate write enable signal for each byte of the data bus. They are labeled $\overline{IOWR}_{0-7}$, $\overline{IOWR}_{8-15}$, $\overline{IOWR}_{16-23}$, and $\overline{IOWR}_{24-31}$. These signals are needed to support writing of 8-, 16-, or 32-bit data through the interface.

The bus control logic section also produces the signals that are needed to latch the address and set up the data bus for an input or output data transfer. The data bus transceiver/buffers control the direction of data transfers between the 80386DX and I/O devices. They are enabled for operation when their output enable ($\overline{OE}$) input is switched to logic 0. Notice that the signal *I/O data bus enable* ($\overline{IODEN}$) is applied to the $\overline{OE}$ inputs.

The direction in which data are passed through the transceivers is determined by the logic level of the DIR input. This input is supplied by the *I/O data transmit/receive* ($IODT/\overline{R}$) output of the bus control logic. During all input cycles, $IODT/\overline{R}$ is logic 0 and the transceivers are set to pass data from the selected I/O device to the 80386DX. On the other hand, during output cycles, $IODT/\overline{R}$ is switched to logic 1 and data passes from the 80386DX to the I/O device.

Another input/output interface diagram is shown in Fig. 14.27. This circuit includes a bank select multiplexer in the data bus interface. This circuit is used to multiplex the 32-bit data bus of the 80386DX to an 8-bit I/O data bus for connection to 8-bit peripheral ICs. By using this circuit configuration, data can be input from or output to all 64K contiguous byte addresses in the I/O address space. In this case, hardware, instead of software, assures that byte data transfers to consecutive

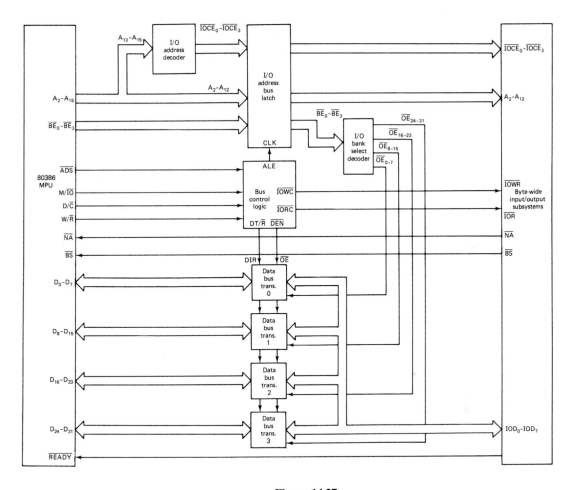

Figure 14.27

byte I/O addresses are performed to contiguous byte-wide I/O ports. The I/O bank select decoder circuit maps bytes of data from the 32-bit data bus to the 8-bit I/O data bus. It does this by assuring that only one bank enable ($\overline{BE}$) output of the 80386DX is active. That is, it checks to assure that a byte input or byte output operation is in progress. If more than one of the $\overline{BE}$ inputs of the decoder is active, none of the $\overline{OE}$ outputs of the decoder is produced and the data transfer does not take place. Now the I/O address 0000_{16} corresponds to a I/O cycle over data bus lines D_0 through D_7 to an 8-bit peripheral attached to I/O data bus lines IOD_0 through IOD_7; 0001_{16} corresponds to an input or output of a byte of data for the peripheral over lines D_8 through D_{15}; 0002_{16} represents a byte I/O transfer over D_{16} through D_{23}; and finally 0003_{16} accompanies a byte transfer over data bus lines D_{24} through D_{31}. That is, even though the byte of data for addresses 0000_{16} through 0003_{16} are output by the 80386DX on different parts of its data bus, they are all multiplexed in external hardware to the same 8-bit I/O data bus, IOD_0 through

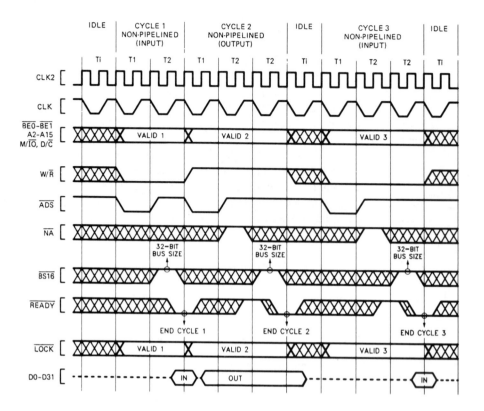

Figure 14.28 I/O read and I/O write bus cycles. (Reprinted by permission of Intel Corp., © Intel Corp. 1987)

IOD_7. In this way, the addresses of the peripheral's registers no longer need to be scaled by four in software.

Input and Output Bus Cycle Timing

We just found that the I/O interface signals of the 80386DX microcomputer are essentially the same as those involved in the memory interface. In fact, the function, logic levels, and timing of all signals other than the M/$\overline{\text{IO}}$ are identical to those already described for the memory interface in Section 14.6.

The timing diagram in Fig. 14.28 shows some *nonpipelined input* and *output bus cycles*. Looking at the waveforms for the first input/output bus cycle, which is called cycle 1, we see that it represents a zero wait state input bus cycle. Notice that the byte enable signals, $\overline{\text{BE}}_0$ through $\overline{\text{BE}}_3$; the address lines A_2 through A_{15}; the bus cycle indication signals M/$\overline{\text{IO}}$, D/$\overline{\text{C}}$, and W/$\overline{\text{R}}$; and address status ($\overline{\text{ADS}}$) signal are all output at the beginning of the T_1 state. This time the 80386DX switches M/$\overline{\text{IO}}$ to logic 0, D/$\overline{\text{C}}$ to 1, and W/$\overline{\text{R}}$ to logic 1 to signal external circuitry that an I/O data input bus cycle is in progress.

As shown in the block diagram of Fig. 14.27, the bus cycle indication code is input to the bus control logic and initiates an input bus control sequence. Let us continue with the sequence of events that takes place in external circuitry during the read cycle. First the bus control logic outputs a pulse to the 1 logic level on ALE. As shown in the circuit of Fig. 14.27, this pulse is used to latch the address information into the I/O address latch devices. The decoded part of the address, $\overline{IOCE_0}$ through $\overline{IOCE_7}$, selects the I/O device to be accessed, and the code on the lower address lines selects the register that is to be accessed. Later in the bus cycle, $\overline{IORC}$ is switched to logic 0 to signal the enabled I/O device that data are to be input to the MPU. In response to $\overline{IORC}$, the enabled input device puts the data from the addressed register onto the data bus. A short time later, IODT/$\overline{R}$ is switched to logic 0 to set the data bus transceivers to the input direction, and then the transceivers are enabled as $\overline{IODEN}$ is switched to logic 0. At this point, the data from the I/O device is available on the 80386DX's data bus.

In the waveforms of Fig. 14.28, we see that at the end of the T_2 state the 80386DX tests the logic level at its ready input to determine if the I/O bus cycle should be completed or extended with wait states. As shown in Fig. 14.28, $\overline{READY}$ is at its active 0 logic level when sampled. Therefore, the 80386DX inputs the data off the bus. Finally, the bus control logic returns $\overline{IORC}$, $\overline{IODEN}$, and IODT/$\overline{R}$ to their inactive logic levels, and the input bus cycle is complete.

Cycle 3 in Fig. 14.28 is also an input bus cycle. However, looking at the $\overline{READY}$ waveform, we find that this time it is not logic 0 at the end of the first T_2 state. Therefore, the input cycle is extended with a second T_2 state (wait state). Since some of the peripheral devices used with the 80386DX are older, slower devices, it is common to have several wait states in I/O bus cycles.

EXAMPLE 14.9

If the 80386DX that is executing cycle 3 in Fig. 14.28 is running at 20 MHz, what is the duration of this input cycle?

Solution

An 80386DX that is running at 20 MHz has a T state equal to 50 ns. Since the input cycle takes 3 T states, its duration is 150 ns.

Looking at the output bus cycle, cycle 2 in the timing diagram of Fig. 14.28, we see that the 80386DX puts the data that are to be output onto the data bus at the beginning of ϕ_2 in the T_1 state. This time the bus control logic switches $\overline{IODEN}$ to logic 0 and maintains IODT/$\overline{R}$ at the 1 level for transmit mode. From Fig. 14.26, we find that since $\overline{IODEN}$ is logic 0 and IODT/$\overline{R}$ is 1, the transceivers are enabled and set up to pass data from the 80386DX to the I/O devices. Therefore, the data output on the bus is available on the data inputs of the enabled I/O device. Finally, the signal $\overline{IOWC}$ is switched to logic 0. It is gated with $\overline{BE_0}$ through $\overline{BE_3}$ in the I/O bank write control logic to produce the needed bank write enable signals. These signals tell the I/O device that valid output data are on the bus. Now the

I/O device must read the data off the bus before the bus control logic terminates the bus cycle. If the device cannot read data at this rate, it can hold $\overline{\text{READY}}$ at the 1 logic level to extend the bus cycle.

EXAMPLE 14.10

If the output cycles performed to byte-wide ports by an 80386DX running at 20 MHz are to be completed in a minimum of 250 ns, how many wait states are needed?

Solution

Since each T state is 50 ns in duration, the bus cycle must last at least for the

$$\text{number of T states} = 250 \text{ ns}/50 \text{ ns} = 5$$

A zero wait state output cycle lasts just two T states; therefore, all output cycles must include a minimum of three wait states.

Similar to memory, the I/O bus cycle requirements exist for data transfers for aligned and unaligned I/O ports. That is, all word and double-word data transfers to aligned port addresses take place in just one bus cycle. However, two bus cycles are required to perform data transfers for unaligned 16- or 32-bit I/O ports.

Protected-Mode Input/Output

When the 80386DX is in the protected-address mode, the input/output instructions can only be executed if the current privilege level is greater than or equal to the I/O privilege level (IOPL). That is, CPL must have a numerical value that is lower than or equal to the numerical value of IOPL. Remember that IOPL is defined by the code in bits 12 and 13 of the flags register. If the current privilege level is less than IOPL, the instruction is not executed; instead, a general protection fault occurs. The general protection fault is an example of an 80386DX exception and will be examined in more detail in the next section.

In Chapter 13 we indicated that the task state segment (TSS) of a task includes a section known as the *I/O permission bit map*. This I/O permission bit map provides a second protection mechanism for the protected-mode I/O address space. Remember that the size of the TSS segment is variable. Its size is specified by the limit in the TSS descriptor. Figure 14.29 shows a typical task state segment. Here we see that the 16-bit *I/O map base* offset, which is held at word offset 66_{16} in the TSS, identifies the beginning of the I/O permission bit map. The upper end of the bit map is set by the limit field in the descriptor for the TSS. Let us now look at what the bits in the I/O permission bit map stand for.

Figure 14.30 shows a more detailed representation of the I/O permission bit map. Notice that it contains one bit position for each of the 65,536 byte-wide I/O ports in the 80386DX's I/O address space. In the bit map, we find that the bit position that corresponds to I/O port 0 (I/O address 0000_{16}) is the least significant

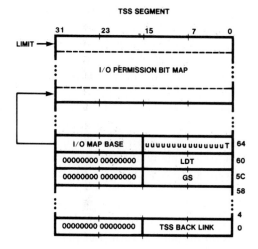

TSS SEGMENT

I/O PERMISSION BIT MAP

I/O MAP BASE   uuuuuuuuuuuuuuuT   64

00000000 00000000   LDT   60

00000000 00000000   GS   5C

58

4

00000000 00000000   TSS BACK LINK   0

Figure 14.29 Location of the I/O permission bit map in the TSS. (Reprinted by permission of Intel Corp., © Intell Corp. 1986)

bit at the address defined with the I/O bit map base offset. The rest of the bits in this first double word in the map represent I/O ports 1 through 31. Finally, the last bit in the table, which corresponds to port 65,535 and I/O address $FFFF_{16}$, is the most significant bit in the double word located at an offset of $1FFC_{16}$ from the I/O bit map base. In Fig. 14.30, we see that the byte address that follows the map must always contain FF_{16}. This is the least significant byte in the last double word of the TSS. The value of the I/O map base offset must be less than $DFFF_{16}$; otherwise, the complete map may not fit within the TSS.

Using this bit map, restrictions can be put on input/output operations to each of the 80386DX's 65,536 I/O port addresses. In protected mode, the bit for the I/O port in the I/O permission map is checked only if the CPL when the I/O instruction is executed is less privileged than the IOPL. If logic 0 is found in a bit

			FF	←TSS limit
65535			65504	←Base + $1FFC_{16}$
65503			65472	
65471			65440	
95 88	87 80	79 72	71 64	
63 56	55 48	47 40	39 32	
31 24	23 16	15 8	7 0	←Base

Figure 14.30 Contents of the I/O permission bit map.

position, it means that an I/O operation can be performed to the port address. On the other hand, logic 1 inhibits the I/O operation. Any attempt to input or output data for an I/O address marked with a 1 in the I/O permission bit map by code with a CPL that is less privileged than the IOPL results in a general protection exception. In this way, an operating system can detect attempts to access certain I/O devices and trap to special service routines for the devices through the general protection exception. In virtual 8086 mode, all I/O accesses reference the I/O permission bit map.

The I/O permission configuration defined by a bit map only applies to the task that uses the TSS. For this reason, many different I/O configurations can exist within a protected-mode software system. Actually, a different bit map could be defined for every task.

In practical applications, most tasks would use the same I/O permission bit map configuration. In fact, in some applications not all I/O addresses need to be protected with the I/O permission bit map. It turns out that any bit map position that is located beyond the limit of the TSS is interpreted as containing a 1. Therefore, all accesses to an address that corresponds to a bit position beyond the limit of the TSS will produce a general protection exception. For instance, a protected-mode I/O address space may be set up with a small block of I/O addresses to which access is permitted at the low end of the I/O address space and with access to the rest of the I/O address space restricted. A smaller table can be set up to specify this configuration. By setting the values of the bit map base and TSS limit such that the bit positions for all the restricted addresses fall beyond the end of the TSS segment, they are caused to result in an exception. On the other hand, the bit positions that are located within the table are all made 0 to permit I/O accesses to their corresponding ports. Moreover, if the complete I/O address space is to be restricted for a task, the I/O permission map base address can be simply set to a value greater than the TSS limit.

▲ 14.8 INTERRUPT AND EXCEPTION PROCESSING

In our study of the 8086 microprocessor, we found that interrupts provide a mechanism for quickly changing program environments. Moreover, we identified that the transfer of program control is initiated by either the occurrence of an event internal to the microprocessor or an event in its external hardware. Finally, we determined that the interrupts employ a well-defined context switching mechanism for changing the program environment.

Figure 14.31 illustrates the program context switching mechanism. Here we see that interrupt 32 occurs as instruction N of the main program is being executed. When the MPU terminates execution of the main program in response to interrupt 32, it first saves information that identifies the instruction following the one where the interrupt occurred, which is the instruction N + 1, and then picks up execution with the first instruction in the service routine. After this routine has run to completion, program control returns to the point where the MPU originally left the main program instruction N + 1, and then execution resumes.

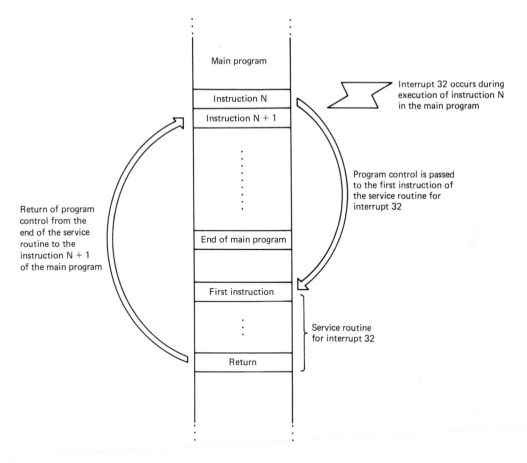

Figure 14.31 Interrupt program context switch mechanism.

The 80386DX's interrupt mechanism is essentially the same as that of the 8086. Just like the 8086-based microcomputer, the 80386DX is capable of implementing any combination of up to 256 interrupts. As shown in Fig. 14.32, they are divided into five groups: *external hardware interrupts, nonmaskable interrupts, software interrupts, internal interrupts and exceptions*, and *reset*. The functions of the external hardware, software, and nonmaskable interrupts are identical to those in the 8086 microcomputer and are defined by the user. On the other hand, the internal interrupt and exception processing capability of the 80386DX has been greatly enhanced. These internal interrupts and exceptions and reset perform dedicated system func-

Figure 14.32 Types of interrupts and their priority.

tions. The priority by which the 80386DX services interrupts and exceptions is identified in Fig. 14.32.

Interrupt Vector and Interrupt Descriptor Tables

An address pointer table is used to link an interrupt type number to the location of its service routine in program storage memory. In a real-mode, 80386DX-based microcomputer system, this table is called the *interrupt vector table*. On the other hand, in a protected-mode system, the table is referred to as the *interrupt descriptor table*. Figure 14.33 shows a map of the interrupt vector table in the memory of a real-mode 80386DX microcomputer. Looking at the table, we see that it contains 256 address pointers, which are identified as *Vector 0* through *Vector 255*. That is, one pointer corresponds to each interrupt type number, 0 through 255. As in the 8086 microcomputer system, these address pointers identify the starting locations of their service routines in program memory. The contents of these tables are either held as firmware in EPROMs or loaded into RAM as part of the system initialization routine.

Notice that in Fig. 14.33 the interrupt vector table is located at the low-address end of the memory address space. It starts at address 00000_{16} and ends at $003FE_{16}$. Unlike the 8086 microcomputer system, the interrupt vector table or interrupt descriptor table in an 80386DX microcomputer can be located anywhere in the memory address space. Its starting location and size are identified by the contents of a register within the 80386DX called the *interrupt descriptor table register* (IDTR). When the 80386DX is reset at power on, it comes up in the real mode with the bits of the base address in IDTR all equal to zero and the limit set to $03FF_{16}$. This positions the interrupt vector table as shown in Fig. 14.33. Moreover, when in the real mode, the value in IDTR is normally left at this initial value to maintain compatibility with 8086/8088-based microcomputer software.

The protected-mode interrupt descriptor table can reside anywhere in the 80386DX's physical address space. The location and size of this table are again defined by the contents of the IDTR. Figure 14.34 shows that the IDTR contains a 32-bit *base address* and a 16-bit *limit*. The base address identifies the starting point of the table in memory. On the other hand, the limit determines the number of bytes in the table.

The interrupt descriptor table contains gate descriptors, not vectors. In Fig. 14.34, we find that the table contains a maximum of 256 gate descriptors. These descriptors are identified as *Gate 0* through *Gate 255*. Each gate descriptor can be defined as a *trap gate, interrupt gate,* or *task gate*. Interrupt and trap gates permit control to be passed to a service routine that is located within the current task. On the other hand, the task gate permits program control to be passed to a different task.

Just like a real-mode interrupt vector, a protected-mode gate acts as a pointer that is used to direct program execution to the starting point of a service routine. However, unlike an interrupt vector, a gate descriptor takes up eight bytes of memory. For instance, in Fig. 14.34, we see that Gate 0 is located at addresses IDT + 0 through IDT + 7 and Gate 255 at addresses IDT + 7F8 through IDT + 7FF.

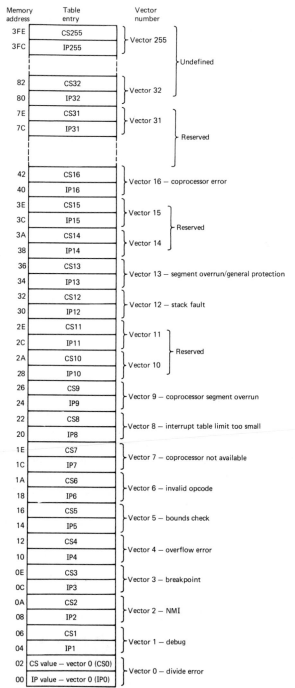

Memory address	Table entry	Vector number
3FE	CS255	Vector 255
3FC	IP255	
		Undefined
82	CS32	Vector 32
80	IP32	
7E	CS31	Vector 31
7C	IP31	Reserved
42	CS16	Vector 16 — coprocessor error
40	IP16	
3E	CS15	Vector 15
3C	IP15	Reserved
3A	CS14	Vector 14
38	IP14	
36	CS13	Vector 13 — segment overrun/general protection
34	IP13	
32	CS12	Vector 12 — stack fault
30	IP12	
2E	CS11	Vector 11
2C	IP11	Reserved
2A	CS10	Vector 10
28	IP10	
26	CS9	Vector 9 — coprocessor segment overrun
24	IP9	
22	CS8	Vector 8 — interrupt table limit too small
20	IP8	
1E	CS7	Vector 7 — coprocessor not available
1C	IP7	
1A	CS6	Vector 6 — invalid opcode
18	IP6	
16	CS5	Vector 5 — bounds check
14	IP5	
12	CS4	Vector 4 — overflow error
10	IP4	
0E	CS3	Vector 3 — breakpoint
0C	IP3	
0A	CS2	Vector 2 — NMI
08	IP2	
06	CS1	Vector 1 — debug
04	IP1	
02	CS value — vector 0 (CS0)	Vector 0 — divide error
00	IP value — vector 0 (IP0)	

Figure 14.33 Real-mode interrupt vector table.

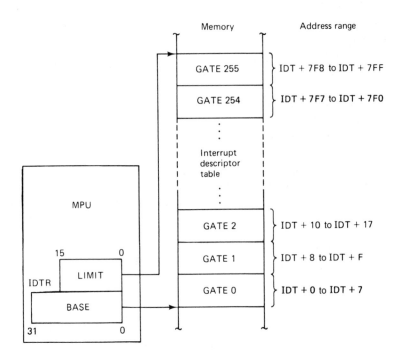

Figure 14.34 Accessing a gate in the protected-mode interrupt descriptor table.

If all 256 gates are not needed for an application, limit in the IDTR can be set to a value lower than 07FF$_{16}$ to minimize the amount of memory reserved for the table.

Figure 14.35 illustrates the format of a typical interrupt or trap gate descriptor. Here we see that the two lower-addressed words, 0 and 1, are the interrupt's *code offset 0 through 15* and *segment selector*, respectively. The highest-addressed word, word 3, is the interrupt's *code offset 16 through 31*. These three words identify the starting point of the service routine. The upper byte of word 2 of the descriptor is called the *access rights byte*. The settings of the bits in this byte identify whether or not this gate descriptor is valid, the privilege level of the service routine, and type of gate. For example, the *present bit* (P) needs to be set to logic 1 if the gate

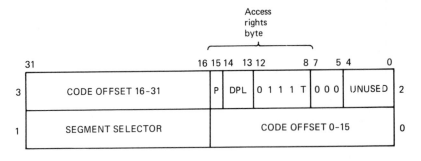

Figure 14.35 Format of a trap or interrupt gate descriptor.

descriptor is to be active. The next two bits, identified as DPL in Fig. 14.35, are used to assign a privilege level to the service routine. If these bits are made 00, level 0, which is the most privileged level, is assigned to the gate. Finally, the setting of the *type bit* (T) determines if the descriptor works as a trap gate or an interrupt gate. T equal to 0 selects the interrupt gate mode of operation. The only difference between the operation of these two types of gates is that, when a trap gate context switch is performed, IF is not cleared to disable external hardware interrupts.

Normally, external hardware interrupts are configured with interrupt gate descriptors. Once an interrupt request has been acknowledged for service, the external hardware interrupt interface is disabled with IF. In this way, additional external interrupts cannot be accepted unless the interface is reenabled under software control. On the other hand, internal interrupts, such as software interrupts, usually use trap gate descriptors. In this case, the hardware interrupt interface is not affected when the service routine for the software interrupt is initiated. Sometimes low-priority hardware interrupts are assigned trap gates instead of an interrupt gate. This will permit higher-priority external events to easily interrupt their service routine.

External Hardware Interrupt Interface

Up to this point in the section, we have introduced the types of interrupts supported by the 80386DX, its interrupt descriptor table, and interrupt descriptor format.

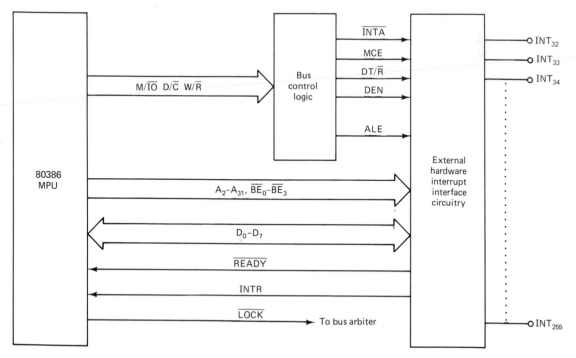

Figure 14.36 80386 microcomputer system external hardware interrupt interface.

Let us now look at the external hardware interrupt interface of the 80386DX microcomputer system.

A general interrupt interface for an 80386DX microprocessor is shown in Fig. 14.36. Here we see that it is similar to the interrupt interface of the maximum-mode 8086 microcomputer system. Notice that it includes the address and data buses, byte enable signals, bus cycle indication signals, lock output, and the ready and interrupt request inputs. Moreover, external circuitry is required to interface interrupt inputs, INT_{32} through INT_{255}, to the 80386DX's interrupt interface. This interface circuit must identify which of the pending active interrupts has the highest priority, perform an interrupt request/acknowledge handshake, and then set up the bus to pass an interrupt type number to the 80386DX.

In this circuit we see that the key interrupt interface signals are *interrupt request* (INTR) and *interrupt acknowledge* ($\overline{INTA}$). The logic level input at the INTR line signals the 80386DX that an external device is requesting service. The 80386DX samples this input at the beginning of each instruction execution cycle, that is, at instruction boundaries. Logic 1 at INTR represents an active interrupt request. INTR is *level triggered*; therefore, its active level must be maintained active by the external hardware until tested by the 80386DX. If it is not maintained, the request for service may not be recognized. For this reason, inputs INT_{32} through INT_{255} are normally latched. Moreover, the 1 at INTR must be removed before the service routine runs to completion; otherwise, the same interrupt may be acknowledged a second time.

When an interrupt request has been recognized by the 80386DX, it signals this fact to external circuitry by outputting the interrupt acknowledge bus cycle indication code on $M/\overline{IO}$ $C/\overline{D}$ $W/\overline{R}$. This code, which equals 000_2, is highlighted in Fig. 14.37. Notice in Fig. 14.36 that this code is input to the bus controller logic, where it is decoded to produce a pulse to logic 0 at the $\overline{INTA}$ output. Actually, two pulses are produced at $\overline{INTA}$ during the *interrupt acknowledge bus cycle sequence*. The first pulse, which is output during cycle 1, signals external circuitry that the interrupt request has been acknowledged and to prepare to send its type number to the 80386DX. The second pulse, which occurs during cycle 2, tells the external circuitry to put the type number on the data bus. The ready ($\overline{READY}$) input can be used to insert wait states into these bus cycles.

Notice that the lower eight lines of the data bus, D_0 through D_7, are also part of the interrupt interface. During the second cycle in the interrupt acknowledge bus cycle sequence, external circuitry puts the 8-bit type number of the highest-

$M/\overline{IO}$	$D/\overline{C}$	$W/\overline{R}$	Type of Bus Cycle
0	0	0	Interrupt acknowledge
0	0	1	Idle
0	1	0	I/O data read
0	1	1	I/O data write
1	0	0	Memory code read
1	0	1	Halt/shutdown
1	1	0	Memory data read
1	1	1	Memory data write

Figure 14.37 Interrupt acknowledge bus cycle indication code.

priority active interrupt request input onto this part of the data bus. The 80386DX reads the type number off the bus to identify which external device is requesting service. Then it uses the type number to generate the address of the interrupt's vector or gate in the interrupt vector or descriptor table, respectively.

Address lines A_2 through A_{31} and byte enable line $\overline{BE}_0$ through $\overline{BE}_3$ are also shown in the interrupt interface circuit of Fig. 14.36. This is because LSI interrupt controller devices are typically used to implement most of the external circuitry. When a read or write bus cycle is performed to the controller, for example, to initialize its internal registers after system reset, some of the address bits are decoded to produce a chip select to enable the controller device, and other address bits are used to select the internal register that is to be accessed. The interrupt controller could be I/O mapped, instead of memory mapped; in this case only address lines A_0 through A_{15} are used in the interface.

Another signal shown in the interrupt interface of Fig. 14.36 is the *bus lock indication* ($\overline{LOCK}$) output of the 80386DX. $\overline{LOCK}$ is used as an input to the bus arbiter circuit in multiprocessor systems. The 80386DX switches this output to its active 0 logic level and maintains it at this level throughout the complete interrupt acknowledge bus cycle. In response to this signal, the arbitration logic assures that no other device can take over control of the system bus until the interrupt acknowledge bus cycle sequence is completed.

External Hardware Interrupt Sequence

In the real mode, the 80386DX processes interrupts in exactly the same way as the 8086. That is, the same events that we described in Chapter 10 take place during the interrupt request, interrupt acknowledge bus cycle, and device service routine. On the other hand, in protected mode a more complex processing sequence is performed. When the 80386DX-based microcomputer is configured for the protected mode of operation, the interrupt request acknowledge handshake sequence appears to take place exactly the same way in the external hardware; however, a number of changes do occur in the internal processing sequence of the 80386DX. Let us now look at how the protected mode 80386DX reacts to an interrupt request.

When processing interrupts in protected mode, the general protection mechanism of the 80386DX comes into play. The general protection rules dictate that program control can only be directly passed to a service routine that is in a segment with equal or higher privilege; that is, a segment with an equal- or lower-numbered descriptor privilege level. Any attempt to transfer program control to a routine in a segment with lower privilege (higher-numbered descriptor privilege level) results in an exception unless the transition is made through a gate.

Typically, interrupt drivers are in code segments at a high privilege level, possibly level 0. Moreover, interrupts occur randomly; therefore, there is a good chance that the microprocessor will be executing application code that is at a low privilege level. In the case of interrupts, the current privilege level (CPL) is the privilege level assigned by the descriptor of the software that was executing when the interrupt occurred. This could be any of the 80386DX's valid privilege levels.

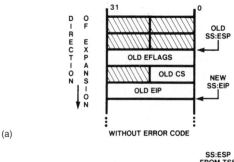

(a)

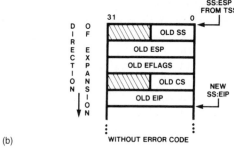

(b)

Figure 14.38 (a) Stack after context switch with no privilege-level transition. (Reprinted by permission of Intel Corp., © Intel Corp. 1986) (b) Stack after context switch with a privilege-level transition. (Reprinted by permission of Intel Corp., © Intel Corp. 1986)

The privilege level of the service routine is that defined in the interrupt or trap gate descriptor for the type number. That is, it is the descriptor privilege level (DPL).

When a service routine is initiated, the current privilege level may change. This depends on whether the software that was interrupted was in a code segment that was configured as *conforming* or *nonconforming*. If the interrupted code is in a conforming code segment, CPL does not change when the service routine is initiated. In this case, the contents of the stack after the context switch is as illustrated in Fig. 14.38(a). Since the privilege level does not change, the current stack (OLD SS: ESP) is used. Notice that as part of the interrupt initiation sequence the OLD EFLAGS, OLD CS, and OLD EIP are automatically saved on the stack. Actually, the *requested privilege level* (RPL) code is also saved on the stack. This is because it is part of OLD CS. RPL identifies the protection level of the interrupted routine.

However, if the segment is nonconforming, the value of DPL is assigned to CPL as long as the service routine is active. As shown in Fig. 14.38(b), this time the stack is changed to that for the new privilege level. The MPU is loaded with a new SS and new ESP from TSS, and the old stack pointer, OLD SS, and OLD

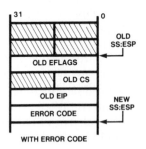

Figure 14.39 Stack contents after interrupt with an error. (Reprinted by permission of Intel Corp., © Intel Corp. 1986)

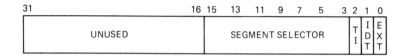

31	16	15	13	11	9	7	5	3	2	1	0
UNUSED		SEGMENT SELECTOR							T I	I D T	E X T

Figure 14.40 IDT error code format.

ESP, are saved on the stack followed by the OLD EFLAGS, OLD CS, and OLD EIP. Remember that for an interrupt gate IF is cleared as part of the context switch, but for a trap gate IF remains unchanged. In both cases, the TF flag is reset after the contents of the flag register are pushed to the stack.

Figure 14.39 shows the stack as it exists after an attempt to initiate an interrupt service routine that did not involve a privilege-level transition has failed. Notice that the context switch to the exception service routine caused an *error code* to be pushed onto the stack following the values of OLD EFLAGS, OLD CS, and OLD EIP.

One format of the error code is given in Fig. 14.40. Here we see that the least significant bit, which is labeled EXT, indicates whether the error was for an externally or internally initiated interrupt. For external interrupts, such as the hardware interrupts, the EXT bit is always set to logic 1. The next bit, which is labeled IDT, is set to 1 if the error is produced as a result of an interrupt. That is, it is the result of a reference to a descriptor in the IDT. If IDT is not set, the third bit indicates whether the descriptor is in the GDT (TI = 0) or the LDT (TI = 1). The next 14 bits contain the segment selector that produced the error condition. With this information available on the stack, the exception service routine can determine which interrupt attempt had failed and whether it was internally or externally initiated. A second format is used for errors that result from a protected-mode page fault. Figure 14.41 illustrates this error code and the function of its bits.

Just as in real mode, the IRET instruction is used to return from a protected-mode interrupt service routine. For service routines using an interrupt gate or trap gate, IRET is restricted to the return from a higher privilege level to a lower privilege level, for instance, from level 1 to level 3. Once the flags, OLD CS, and OLD EIP are returned to the 80386DX, the RPL bits of OLD CS are tested to see if they equal CPL. If RPL = CPL, an intralevel return is in progress. In this case the return is complete and program execution resumes at the point in the program where execution had stopped.

If RPL is greater than CPL, an interlevel return is taking place, not an intralevel return. During an interlevel return, checks are performed to determine if a protection violation will occur due to the protection-level transition. Assuming that no violation occurs, the OLD SS and OLD ESP are popped from the stack into the MPU and then program execution resumes.

Internal Interrupt and Exception Functions

Earlier we indicated that some of the 256 interrupt vectors of the 80386DX are dedicated to internal interrupt and exception functions. Internal interrupts and

Field	Value	Description
U/S	0	The access causing the fault originated when the processor was executing in supervisor mode.
	1	The access causing the fault originated when the processor was executing in user mode.
W/R	0	The access causing the fault was a read.
	1	The access causing the fault was a write.
P	0	The fault was caused by a not-present page.
	1	The fault was caused by a page-level protection violation.

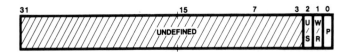

Figure 14.41 Page fault error code format and bit functions. (Reprinted by permission of Intel Corp., © Intel Corp. 1986)

exceptions differ from external hardware interrupts in that they occur due to the result of executing an instruction, not an event that takes place in external hardware. That is, an internal interrupt or exception is initiated because an error condition was detected before, during, or after execution of an instruction. In this case, a routine must be initiated to service the internal condition before resuming execution of the same or next instruction of the program.

Internal interrupts and exceptions are not masked out with the interrupt enable flag. For this reason, occurrence of any one of these internal conditions is automatically detected by the 80386DX and causes an interrupt of program execution and a vectored transfer of control to a corresponding service routine. During the control transfer sequence, no interrupt acknowledge bus cycles are produced.

Figure 14.42 identifies the internal interrupts and exceptions that are active in real mode. Here we find internal interrupts such as breakpoint and exception functions such as divide error and overflow error that were also detected by the 8086. However, the 80386DX also implements several new real-mode exceptions. Examples of exceptions that are not implemented on the 8086 are invalid opcode, bounds check, and interrupt table limit too small.

Internal interrupts and exceptions are further categorized as a *fault, trap*, or *abort* based on how the failing function is reported. In the case of an exception that causes a fault, the values of CS and IP saved on the stack point to the instruction that resulted in the fault. Therefore, after servicing the exception, the faulting instruction can be reexecuted. On the other hand, for those exceptions that result in a trap, the values of CS and IP pushed to the stack point to the next instruction that is to be executed, instead of the instruction that caused the trap. Therefore, upon completion of the service routine, program execution resumes with the instruc-

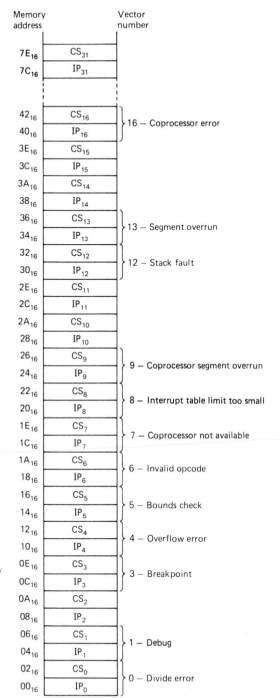

Figure 14.42 Real-mode internal interrupt and exception vector table.

tion that follows the instruction that produced the trap. Finally, exceptions that produce an abort do not preserve any information that identifies the location that caused the error. In this case the system may need to be restarted. Let us now look at the new 80386DX real-mode internal interrupts and exceptions in more detail.

Debug Exception. The *debug exception* relates to the debug mode of operation of the 80386DX. The 80386DX has a set of eight on-chip debug registers. Using these registers, the programmer can specify up to four breakpoint addresses and specify conditions under which they are to be active. For instance, the activating condition could be an instruction fetch from the address, a data write to the address, or either a data read or write for the address, but not an instruction fetch. Moreover, for data accesses the size of the data element can be specified as a byte, word, or double word. Finally, the individual addresses can be locally or globally enabled or disabled. If an access that matches any of these debug conditions is attempted, a debug exception occurs and control is passed to the service routine defined by IP_1 and CS_1 at word addresses 00004_{16} and 00006_{16}, respectively. The service routine could include a mechanism that allows the programmer to view the contents of the 80386DX's internal registers and its external memory.

If the trap flag (TF) bit in the flags register is set, the single-step mode of operation is enabled. This flag bit can be set or reset under software control. When TF is set, the 80386DX initiates a type 1 interrupt at the completion of execution of every instruction. This permits implementation of the single-step mode of operation that allows a program to be executed one instruction at a time.

Bounds Check Exception. Earlier we pointed out that the BOUND (check array index against bounds) instruction can be used to test an operand that is used as the index into an array to verify that it is within a predefined range. If the index is less than the lower bound (minimum value) or greater than the upper bound (maximum value), a *bound check exception* has occurred and control is passed to the exception handler pointed to by $CS_5:IP_5$. The exception produced by the BOUND instruction is an example of a fault. Therefore, the values of CS and IP pushed to the stack represent the address of the instruction that produced the exception.

Invalid Opcode Exception. The exception-processing capability of the 80386DX permits detection of undefined opcodes. This feature of the 80386DX allows it to detect automatically whether or not the opcode to be executed as an instruction corresponds to one of the instructions in the instruction set. If it does not, execution is not attempted; instead, the opcode is identified as being undefined and the *invalid opcode exception* is initiated. In turn, control is passed to the exception handler identified by IP_6 and CS_6. This *undefined opcode detection mechanism* permits the 80386DX to detect errors in its instruction stream. Invalid opcode is an example of an exception that produces a fault.

Coprocessor Extension Not Available Exception. When the 80386DX comes up in the real mode, both the EM (emulate coprocessor) and MP (math present) bits of its machine status word are reset. This mode of operation corresponds to that of the 8088 or 8086 microprocessor. When set in this way, the *coprocessor extension* *not available exception* cannot occur. However, if the EM bit has been set to 1 under software control (do not monitor coprocessor) and the 80386DX executes an ESC (escape) instruction for the math coprocessor, a processor extension not present exception is initiated through the vector at CS_7: IP_7. This service routine could pass control to a software emulation routine for the floating-point arithmetic operation. Moreover, if the MP and TS bits are set (meaning that a math coprocessor is available in the system and a task is in progress), when an ESC or WAIT instruction is executed, an exception also takes place.

Interrupt Table Limit Too Small Exception. Earlier we pointed out that the LIDT instruction can be used to relocate or change the limit of the interrupt vector table in memory. If the real-mode table has been changed, for example, its limit is set lower than address $003FF_{16}$ and an interrupt is invoked that attempts to access a vector stored at an address higher than the new limit, the *interrupt table limit too small exception* occurs. In this case, control is passed to the service routine by the vector CS_8 : IP_8. This exception is a fault; therefore, the address of the instruction that exceeded the limit is saved on the stack.

Coprocessor Segment Overrun Exception. The *coprocessor segment overrun exception* signals that the 80387 numeric coprocessor has overrun the limit of a segment while attempting to read or write its operand. This event is detected by the coprocessor data channel within the 80386DX and passes control to the service routine through interrupt vector 9. This exception handler can clear the exception, reset the 80387, determine the cause of the exception by examining the registers within the 80387, and then initiate a corrective action.

Stack Fault Exception. In the real mode, if the address of an operand access for the stack segment crosses the boundaries of the stack, a stack fault exception is produced. This causes control to be transferred to the service routine defined by CS_{12} and IP_{12}.

Segment Overrun Exception. This exception occurs in the real mode if an instruction attempts to access an operand that extends beyond the end of a segment. For instance, if a word access is made to the address CS:FFFFH, DS:FFFFH, or ES:FFFFH, a fault occurs to the *segment overrun exception* service routine.

Coprocessor Error Exception. As part of the handshake sequence between the 80386DX microprocessor and 80387 math coprocessor, the 80386DX checks the status of its $\overline{ERROR}$ input. If the 80387 encounters a problem performing a numeric operation, it signals this fact to the 80386DX by switching its $\overline{ERROR}$ output to logic 0. This signal is normally applied directly to the $\overline{ERROR}$ input of the 80386DX and signals that an error condition has occurred. Logic 0 at this input causes a *coprocessor error exception* through vector 16.

Protected-Mode Internal Interrupts And Exceptions. In protected mode, more internal conditions can initiate an internal interrupt or exception. Figure 14.43 identifies each of these functions and its corresponding type number.

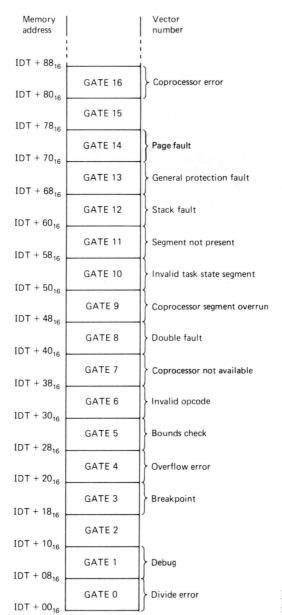

Figure 14.43 Protected-mode internal exception gate locations.

The figure shows memory addresses on the left and vector numbers on the right:

Memory address	Gate	Vector number
IDT + 88₁₆		
	GATE 16	Coprocessor error
IDT + 80₁₆		
	GATE 15	
IDT + 78₁₆		
	GATE 14	Page fault
IDT + 70₁₆		
	GATE 13	General protection fault
IDT + 68₁₆		
	GATE 12	Stack fault
IDT + 60₁₆		
	GATE 11	Segment not present
IDT + 58₁₆		
	GATE 10	Invalid task state segment
IDT + 50₁₆		
	GATE 9	Coprocessor segment overrun
IDT + 48₁₆		
	GATE 8	Double fault
IDT + 40₁₆		
	GATE 7	Coprocessor not available
IDT + 38₁₆		
	GATE 6	Invalid opcode
IDT + 30₁₆		
	GATE 5	Bounds check
IDT + 28₁₆		
	GATE 4	Overflow error
IDT + 20₁₆		
	GATE 3	Breakpoint
IDT + 18₁₆		
	GATE 2	
IDT + 10₁₆		
	GATE 1	Debug
IDT + 08₁₆		
	GATE 0	Divide error
IDT + 00₁₆		

▲ 14.9 THE 80486 MICROPROCESSOR FAMILY

In the last chapter we pointed out that the 80486 family of microprocessors is Intel Corporation's second generation of 32-bit processors. It brought a higher level of performance and more versatility to the 8086 architecture. Just like for the 80386 family, maintaining compatibility of the 80486 family's hardware architecture to

Figure 14.44 80486 IC. (Reprinted by permission of Intel Corp.)

earlier 8086 family MPUs was also less important. This does not mean that the signal interfaces were purposely changed. In fact, many of the 80486's interface signals are the same as those provided on the 80386DX. However, a number of enhancements have been made to the 80486 family that are directed at improving its performance and making the 80486-based microcomputer more versatile. Much of the focus of these enhancements was on the memory interface. For instance, it is now enabled to do dynamic bus sizing down to eight bits, high speed burst data transfers over the bus, and write operations are buffered. The addition of these new capabilities has expanded the number of interface signals.

A number of hardware elements that were normally implemented in external circuitry are for the first time added into the MPU with the 80486 family. Examples of these new on-chip hardware functions are parity generation/checking, code/data cache memory, and in the case of the 80486DX a floating-point mathematics unit. Addition of these capabilities called for further expansion of the number of interface signals.

The more advanced processes used to manufacture the 80486 family of MPUs permitted the integration of many more transistors into a single IC. The circuitry of the 80486DX is equivalent to approximately 1.2M transistors, four times more than the 80386DX. Actually, the 80486DX was the first IC made by Intel Corporation that contained more than one million transistors.

Originally the 80486DX and 80486SX were both manufactured in a 168-lead pin grid array package. Figure 14.44 shows a device in this package. The layout of the pins and signals on this package are shown in Fig. 14.45(a) and (b). For example, the pin located at the upper most left corner, which corresponds to row S and column 1, is address bit A_{27}. Another example is the data bus line D_{20}, which is located at the junction of row A and column 1. Later both devices were made available in a lower cost 196 lead plastic quad flat package.

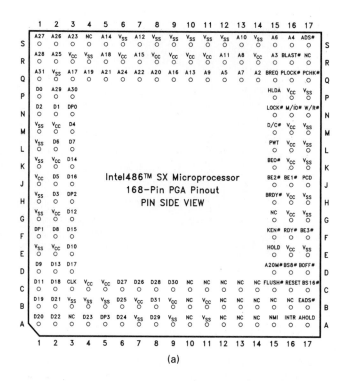

Figure 14.45 (a) Pin layout of the 80486SX PGA. (Reprinted by permission of Intel Corp., © Intel Corp. 1992) (b) Signal pin numbering. (Reprinted by permission of Intel Corp., © Intel Corp. 1992)

Signal Interfaces of the 80486SX MPU

Let us continue our study of the 80486 family of microprocessors by exploring its signal interfaces. Figure 14.46 is a block diagram showing the signal interfaces of the 80486SX MPU. Many of the 80486SX's interface signals are identical in name, mnemonic, and function to those on the 80386DX. For instance, we find that the 80486SX's 32 address bus lines are labeled A_2 through A_{31}, and its four byte enable signals, $\overline{BE_0}$ through $\overline{BE_3}$. However, most of the interfaces have some new signals that are provided to implement enhanced functions. In fact, the interrupt interface is the only interface that is completely unchanged. Here we will focus on the new signals at each of the 80486SX's interfaces.

Memory/IO Interface. Earlier we pointed out that many of the hardware enhancements of the 80486 family are in its memory interface. For this reason, most of the new signal lines of the 80486SX are located at this interface. Let us look at the function of these new signals.

The 80386DX MPU had the ability to configure the data bus as 16 bits instead of 32 bits by activating an input. The 80486SX also has this capability; however,

Address		Data		Control		N/C	V_CC	V_SS
A_2	Q14	D_0	P1	A20M#	D15	A3	B7	A7
A_3	R15	D_1	N2	ADS#	S17	A10	B9	A9
A_4	S16	D_2	N1	AHOLD	A17	A12	B11	A11
A_5	Q12	D_3	H2	BE0#	K15	A13	C4	B3
A_6	S15	D_4	M3	BE1#	J16	A14	C5	B4
A_7	Q13	D_5	J2	BE2#	J15	B10	E2	B5
A_8	R13	D_6	L2	BE3#	F17	B12	E16	E1
A_9	Q11	D_7	L3	BLAST#	R16	B13	G2	E17
A_{10}	S13	D_8	F2	BOFF#	D17	B14	G16	G1
A_{11}	R12	D_9	D1	BRDY#	H15	B15	H16	G17
A_{12}	S7	D_{10}	E3	BREQ	Q15	B16	J1	H1
A_{13}	Q10	D_{11}	C1	BS8#	D16	C10	K2	H17
A_{14}	S5	D_{12}	G3	BS16#	C17	C11	K16	K1
A_{15}	R7	D_{13}	D2	CLK	C3	C12	L16	K17
A_{16}	Q9	D_{14}	K3	D/C#	M15	C13	M2	L1
A_{17}	Q3	D_{15}	F3	DP0	N3	C14	M16	L17
A_{18}	R5	D_{16}	J3	DP1	F1	G15	P16	M1
A_{19}	Q4	D_{17}	D3	DP2	H3	R17	R3	M17
A_{20}	Q8	D_{18}	C2	DP3	A5	S4	R6	P17
A_{21}	Q5	D_{19}	B1	EADS#	B17		R8	Q2
A_{22}	Q7	D_{20}	A1	FLUSH#	C15		R9	R4
A_{23}	S3	D_{21}	B2	HLDA	P15		R10	S6
A_{24}	Q6	D_{22}	A2	HOLD	E15		R11	S8
A_{25}	R2	D_{23}	A4	INTR	A16		R14	S9
A_{26}	S2	D_{24}	A6	KEN#	F15			S10
A_{27}	S1	D_{25}	B6	LOCK#	N15			S11
A_{28}	R1	D_{26}	C7	M/IO#	N16			S12
A_{29}	P2	D_{27}	C6	NMI	A15			S14
A_{30}	P3	D_{28}	C8	PCD	J17			
A_{31}	Q1	D_{29}	A8	PCHK#	Q17			
		D_{30}	C9	PWT	L15			
		D_{31}	B8	PLOCK#	Q16			
				RDY#	F16			
				RESET	C16			
				W/R#	N17			

(b)

Figure 14.45 (Continued)

another input *bus size 8* ($\overline{BS8}$) also gives the ability to configure the data bus 8 bits wide. If BS $\overline{8}$ is at the active 0 logic level, data are transferred byte at a time over data bus lines D_0 through D_7.

The bus cycle indication signals M/$\overline{IO}$, D/$\overline{C}$, and W/$\overline{R}$ are the same on the 80486SX as on the 80386DX; however, a change has been made in the coding of the bus cycles. On the 80486SX, the halt/shutdown bus cycle is identified by the code 001_2, instead of 101_2. The code 101_2 is now reserved. The codes for all other types of bus cycles are unchanged.

An important difference between the memory interface of the 80386DX MPU and that of the 80486SX is that automatic *parity generation and checking* has been added. Parity has been added to each byte of the 80486SX's 32-bit data bus. An even parity bit is automatically generated for each byte of the data written to memory and on read operations each byte of data is checked for even parity. For this reason, four bidirectional *data parity* (DP_0 - DP_3) lines and a *parity status* ($\overline{PCHK}$) output have been added into the memory interface. The data parity lines are additional data bus lines that are used to carry parity data to and from memory. On the other hand, the parity status output is used to signal external circuitry whether or not a parity error has occurred on a read operation. Logic 0 at this output identifies a parity error condition.

The 80486SX also performs an operation known as address bit 20 mask auto-

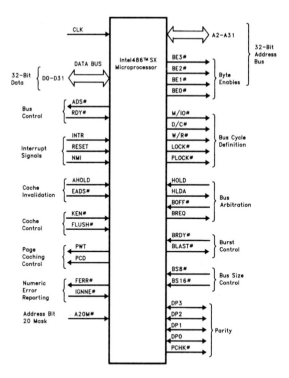

Figure 14.46 Block diagram of the 80486SX. (Reprinted by permission of Intel Corp., © Intel Corp. 1992)

matically. This is an operation that must be performed in all ISA bus compatible computers. In an 80386DX-based microcomputer, masking of A_{20} is accomplished with external circuitry. An extra input, *address bit 20 mask* ($\overline{A20M}$), has been added on the 80486SX to perform this function. Whenever $\overline{A20M}$ is logic 0, address bit A_{20} is masked out for bus cycles that access internal cache memory or external memory.

Another enhancement in the 80486 family of MPUs is the ability to perform what is known as *burst bus cycles*. A burst bus cycle is a special bus cycle that permits faster reads and writes of data. During a burst bus cycle, the transfer of the first element of data takes place in two clock cycles and further data elements are transferred in a single clock cycle. Non-burst bus cycles transfer one data element at a time and require a minimum of two clock cycles for each data transfer. Whenever the 80486SX requires data, it can perform the transfer with normal or burst bus cycles. If the external device can perform burst data transfers, it signals this fact to the MPU. This is done by switching the control signal *burst ready* ($\overline{BRDY}$), instead of $\overline{RDY}$, to logic 0.

During all memory bus cycles, the $\overline{BLAST}$ output signals when the last data transfer takes place. In the case of a normal bus cycle, only one data transfer takes place. This data transfer is marked by $\overline{BLAST}$ switching to logic 0. For burst cycle, multiple data transfers are performed, but $\overline{BLAST}$ is active only for the last one.

The 80486SX has a second type of lock signal. This signal, *pseudo-lock*

($\overline{PLOCK}$), differs from $\overline{LOCK}$ in that it locks out access to the bus by other devices for more than one bus cycle.

Cache Memory Control Interface.   A new group of interface signals are provided on the 80486 family MPUs to support internal and external cache memory subsystems. They include the *cache enable* ($\overline{KEN}$) input, *cache flush* ($\overline{FLUSH}$) input, the *page cache disable* (PCD) output, the *page write-through* ($\overline{PWT}$) output, the *address hold* (AHOLD) input, and the *valid external address* ($\overline{EADS}$) input. Let us next look briefly at the function of each of these signals.

The external memory subsystem has the ability to tell the 80486SX whether or not a bus cycle is cacheable. It does this by switching the $\overline{KEN}$ input to logic 0 or 1. Whenever $\overline{KEN}$ is set to logic 0 during a memory read bus cycle, the information carried over the bus is copied into the on-chip cache. If $\overline{KEN}$ remains at its inactive 1 logic level, a non-cacheable bus cycle takes place.

External circuitry also has the ability to invalidate all of the data in the on-chip cache memory of the 80486SX. This operation is known as a *cache flush*. To flush the on-chip cache, the $\overline{FLUSH}$ input is simply switched to its active 0 logic level for one clock cycle.

PCD and PWT are outputs of the MPU and are used to control external cache. Earlier we pointed out that the programmed logic levels of the page attribute bits in the page entry table, page directory table, or control register 3 are output on these lines when caching is enabled. The logic level of PCD signals the external cache memory subsystem whether or not the page of memory that is being accessed is configured as cacheable. Logic 1 at PWT indicates that write operations to the external cache are performed in a write-through fashion.

The last two signals, AHOLD and $\overline{EADS}$, are used to perform what is known as a *cache invalidate cycle*. This type of bus cycle is used to maintain consistency between data in the internal cache and external main memory. For instance, if another bus master device modifies data in main memory, a check must be immediately made to see if the contents of this storage location is currently held in the 80486SX's internal cache memory. If it is and the 80486SX would read the value at this address, the wrong value would be accessed from the cache. For this reason, the value in the cache must be invalidated.

The signal AHOLD is used to tri-state the address bus during a cache invalidate cycle. The first step in this cycle is for an external device to apply logic 1 to the AHOLD input of the 80486SX. In response to this input, the address lines are immediately put into the high-Z state. Next, the external device puts the address of the main memory storage location that was modified onto the 80486SX's address bus and then switches $\overline{EADS}$ to logic 1 to signal the MPU that a valid address is on the address bus. In this case, the address lines are inputs to the MPU. If the internal cache subsystem identifies that the contents of this memory location is stored in the cache, the value held in the cache is invalidated. Since the cache entry is no longer valid, consistency is restored between cache memory and main memory.

Bus Arbitration Interface.   The DMA interface of the 80386DX is expanded in the 80486SX MPU to make it into what is called the *bus arbitration interface*. Two new signals, *backoff input* ($\overline{\text{BOFF}}$) and *bus request output* (BREQ), have been added to the interface. Let us look at the function of each of these signals.

The BREQ output of the 80486SX signals whether or not the MPU is generating a request to use the external bus. When a bus cycle is to be performed, BREQ is switched to logic 0 and remains at this level until the bus cycle is completed. This device can be used by external circuitry to tell other bus masters that the MPU has a bus access pending.

$\overline{\text{BOFF}}$ is similar to the HOLD input of the MPU in that its active logic level tri-states the bus interface signals. However, there are two differences between the operation of $\overline{\text{BOFF}}$ and HOLD. First, a bus backoff operation is initiated at the completion of the current clock cycle, not at the end of the current bus cycle. Moreover, no hold acknowledge response is made to external circuitry. When $\overline{\text{BOFF}}$ returns to its inactive logic level, the interrupted bus cycle is restarted. This input can be used by external bus masters to quickly take over control of the system bus.

Non-Burst and Burst Bus Cycles

In our description of the memory interface signals, we found that the 80486SX's data bus can be dynamically configured for 8-bit, 16-bit, or 32-bit mode of operation. For each of these modes, the 80486SX can perform either of two bus cycles called a *non-burst bus cycle* or a *burst bus cycle*. Both of these cycles can be made cacheable or non-cacheable. Here we will look briefly at the bus activity for each of these bus cycles.

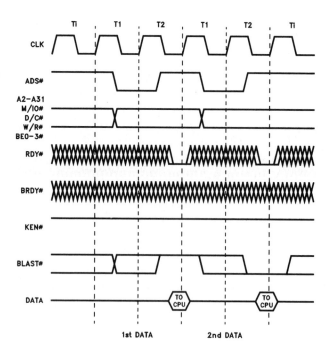

Figure 14.47 Non-burst, non-cacheable bus cycle. (Reprinted by permission of Intel Corp., © Intel Corp. 1992)

Non-Burst, Non-cacheable Bus Cycle. The timing diagram in Fig. 14.47 shows the sequence of bus activity that takes place as the 80486SX reads or writes data to memory or an I/O device with a *non-burst, non-cacheable bus cycle*. Notice that the minimum duration of a bus cycle takes two clock cycles. They are identified as T_1 and T_2 in the bus cycle timing diagram.

Looking at Fig. 14.47, we see that early in clock cycle T_1 the address (A_2 through A_{31}), byte enables ($\overline{BE_0}$ through $\overline{BE_3}$), and memory indication signals ($M/\overline{IO}$, $D/\overline{C}$, and $W/\overline{R}$) are made available and latched into external circuitry with the transition of $\overline{ADS}$. Assuming that the data transfer is to take place in a single bus cycle, $\overline{BLAST}$ is switched to the 0 logic level during clock cycle T_2. This tells the external circuitry that the data transfer is to be complete at the end of the current bus cycle. Therefore, at the end of T_2, external circuitry switches $\overline{RDY}$ to logic 0 to tell the MPU that the data transfer is to take place.

A bus cycle can be extended by any number of clock cycles by holding $\overline{RDY}$ at logic 1 during T_2.

Non-Burst, Cacheable Bus Cycle. Earlier we pointed out that the $\overline{KEN}$ input determines whether or not a bus cycle is cacheable. Figure 14.48 shows the 80486SX's *non-burst, cacheable bus cycle*. Here we see that the bus cycle starts the same way, but later in T_1 the external circuitry switches the $\overline{KEN}$ input to logic 0. This indicates that the cycle is a cacheable bus cycle. Only memory read bus cycles are cacheable; therefore, the MPU ignores $\overline{KEN}$ during all write and I/O bus cycles.

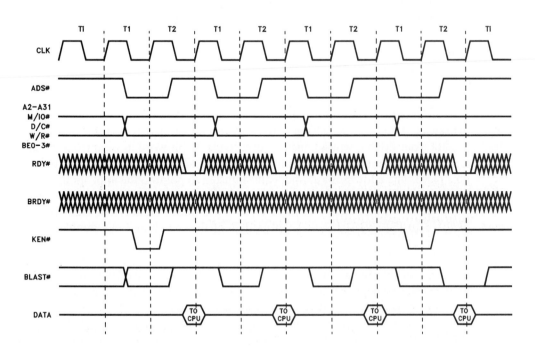

Figure 14.48 Non-burst, cacheable bus cycle. (Reprinted by permission of Intel Corp., © Intel Corp. 1992)

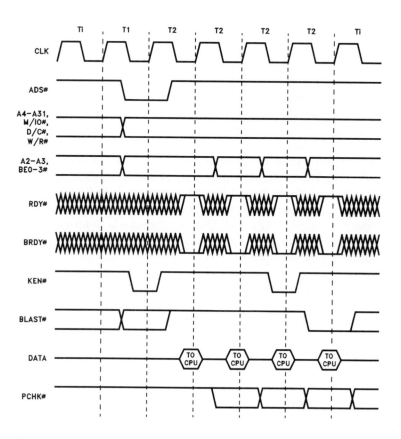

Figure 14.49 Burst, cacheable bus cycle. (Reprinted by permission of Intel Corp., © Intel Corp. 1992)

Information is stored in the internal cache memory as *lines*, which are 16 bytes wide. Whenever a cacheable read cycle is performed, a complete line of code or data (four double words), instead of a single 32-bit word, is read from memory. Looking at the timing diagram in Fig. 14.48, we see that four read data transfers take place. The address is automatically adjusted to point to the appropriate double word after each read operation and then $\overline{RDY}$ is made active. For this reason, the complete bus cycle takes a total of eight clock states. Notice that $\overline{BLAST}$ is not switched to the active 0 logic level until T_2 of the fourth and last double word of data is read.

Burst, Cacheable Bus Cycle. The *burst, cacheable bus cycle* of Fig. 14.49 is similar to the non-burst, cacheable bus cycle we just described in that four read operations are performed. One difference is that during a burst bus cycle external circuitry signals that burst data transfers are to take place by replying with logic 0 on $\overline{BRDY}$ instead of $\overline{RDY}$. A second and very important difference is that only the first data transfer takes two clock cycles. Notice that all four data transfers of the burst bus cycle are completed in just five clock states.

Cache Memory

When a microcomputer system employs a large main memory subsystem consisting of several megabytes, it is normally made with high capacity but relative slow-speed dynamic RAMs, EPROMs, and FLASH memory. Even though DRAM memories are available with access times as short as 60 ns and EPROMs as fast as 90 ns, these high-speed versions of the devices are expensive and still too slow to work in a microcomputer system that is running with zero wait states. For example, an 80486SX-25 microprocessor running at 25 MHz would require DRAMs with a better than 80 ns access time to implement a 0 wait state design. For this reason, wait states are introduced in all bus cycles to data and program memory. These waits states degrade the overall performance of the microcomputer system.

Addition of a cache memory subsystem to the microcomputer provides a means for improving overall system performance while still permitting the use of low-cost, slow-speed memory devices in main memory. In a microcomputer system with cache, a second smaller, but very fast memory section, is added between the MPU and main memory subsystem. Figure 14.50(a) illustrates this type of system architecture. This small, high-speed memory section is known as the *cache memory*. The cache is designed with fast, more expensive static RAMs and can be accessed without wait states. During system operation, the cache memory contains frequently used instructions and data. The objective is that the MPU accesses code and data in the cache most of the time, instead of from main memory. This results in close to 0-wait-state memory system operation even though accesses of the main memory require one or more wait states, thus resulting in higher performance for the micro-

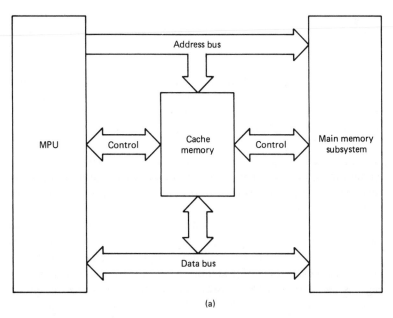

(a)

Figure 14.50 (a) Microcomputer system with cache memory. (b) Internal cache of the 80486SX.

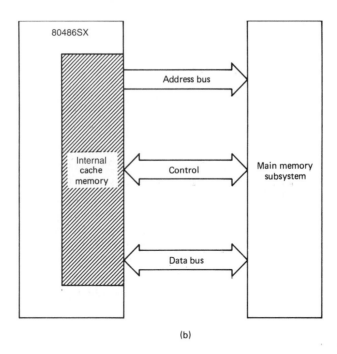

80486SX

Internal cache memory

Address bus

Control

Data bus

Main memory subsystem

(b)

Figure 14.50   (Continued)

computer. As shown in Fig. 14.50(b), the 80486SX's cache differs in that it is on-chip, that is, internal to the MPU.

External cache memories are widely used in high-performance 80486-based microcomputer systems today. Notice in Fig. 4.50(a) that on one side the external cache memory subsystem attaches to the local bus of the MPU and at the other side it drives the system bus of the microcomputer system. External caches typically range in size from 32KB to 512KB and can be used to cache both data and code. The 80486SX's internal cache also stores both code and data, but is smaller (8KB) in size. The internal cache of the 80486SX is called the *first level cache* and the external cache a *second level cache*.

Function of a Cache.   Let us continue our examination of cache for the microcomputer system by looking at how it affects the execution of a program. The first time the MPU executes a segment of program, one instruction after the other is fetched from main memory and executed. The most recently fetched instructions are automatically saved in the cache memory. That is, a copy of these instructions is held within the cache. For example, a segment of program that implements a loop operation could be fetched, executed, and placed in the cache. In this way, we see that the cache always holds some of the most recently executed instructions.

Now that we know what the cache holds, let us look at how the cached instructions are used during program execution. Many software operations involve repeated execution of the same sequence of instructions. A loop is a good example of this type of program structure. In Fig. 14.51, we find that the first execution of

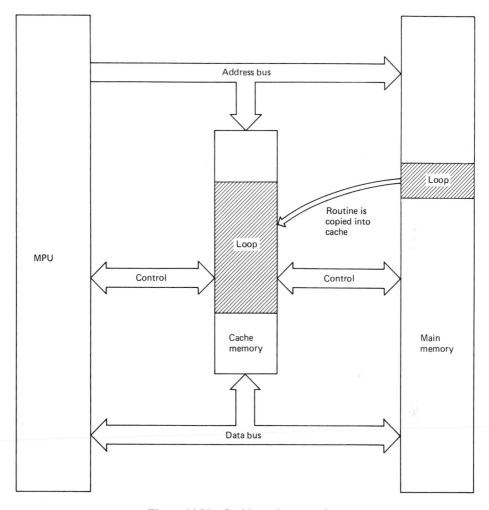

Figure 14.51 Caching a loop routine.

the loop references code held in the slow main program memory. During this access, the routine is copied into the internal cache of the MPU. When the instructions of the loop are repeated, the MPU reaccesses the routine by using the instructions held in the cache instead of refetching them from the main memory. Accesses to code in the internal cache are performed with no wait states, whereas those of code in main memory normally require wait states. In this way, we see that the use of cache reduces the number of accesses made from the slower main memory. The more frequently instructions held in the cache are used, the closer to 0-wait state operation is achieved, the more the overall execution time of the program is decreased, and the result is higher performance for the microcomputer system.

During execution of the loop routine, data operands that are accessed can also be cached in the internal cache of the 80486SX. If these operands are reaccessed during the repeated execution of the loop, they are also read from the cache instead of from main data memory. This further reduces execution time of the segment of program.

The Cache Hit, Cache Miss, and Hit Rate. We just found that the concept behind cache memory is that it stores recently used code and data and that if this information is to be reaccessed, it may be read from the cache with 0 wait state bus cycles rather than from main memory. When the address of a code or data storage location that is to be read is output on the local bus, the cache subsystem must determine whether or not the information to be accessed resides in both main memory and the cache memory. If it does, the memory cycle is considered a *hit* condition. In this case, a bus cycle is not initiated to the main memory subsystem; instead, the copy of the information in the cache is accessed.

On the other hand, if the address output on the local bus does not correspond to information that is already cached, the condition represents what is called a *miss*. This time the MPU reads the code or data from main memory and writes it into a corresponding location in cache.

Hit rate is a measure of how effective the cache subsystem operates. Hit rate is defined as the ratio of the number of cache hits to the total number of memory accesses, expressed as a percentage. That is, hit rate equals

$$\text{Hit rate} = \frac{\text{Number of hits}}{\text{Number of bus cycles}} \times 100\%$$

The higher the value of the hit rate, the better the cache memory design. For instance, a cache may have a hit rate of 85%. This means that the MPU reads code or data from the cache memory for 85 percent of its memory bus cycles. In other words, just 15 percent of the memory accesses are from the main memory subsystem. The hit rate is not a fixed value for a cache design. It depends on the code being executed and data used. That is, the hit rate may be one value for a specific application program and a totally different value for another.

A number of features of the cache design also affect the hit rate. For instance, the size, organization, and the update method of the cache memory subsystem all determine the maximum hit rate that may be achieved by a cache. Practical cache memories for microcomputer systems range in size from as small as 8KB to as large as 512KB. In general, the larger the size of the cache, the higher the hit rate. This is because the larger it is, the more data and code it holds, and the greater the chance that the information to be accessed resides in the cache. However, due to the fact that the improvement in hit rate decreases with increasing cache size and that the cost of the cache subsystem increases substantially with increasing size, most caches used today are 256KB.

Types of Cache Memory Organizations. The three most widely used cache memory organizations are those known as the *direct mapped cache*, *two-way set associative cache,* and *four-way set associative cache*. The direct mapped cache can also be called a *one-way set associative cache*. The organization of a 64KB direct-mapped cache memory is illustrated in Fig. 14.52. Notice that the cache memory array is

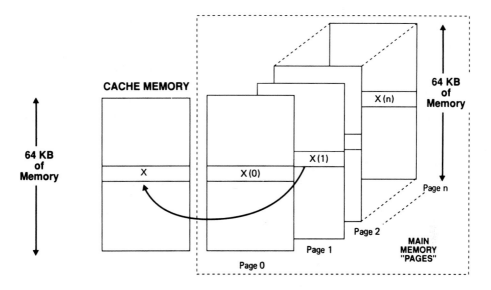

Figure 14.52 Organization of a direct-mapped memory subsystem. (Reprinted by permission of Intel Corp., © Intel Corp. 1990)

arranged as a single 64KB bank of memory, and the main memory is viewed as a series of 64KB pages, denoted as page 0 through page n. Notice that the data storage location at the same offset in all pages of main memory, which are identified as X(0) through X(n) in Fig. 14.52, map to a single storage location, marked X, in the cache memory array. That is, each location in a 64KB page of main memory maps to a different location in the cache memory array.

On the other hand, the 64KB memory array of a two-way set associative cache memory is organized into two 32KB banks. That is, the cache array is divided two ways, *BANK A* and *BANK B*. This cache memory subsystem configuration is shown in Fig. 14.53. Again main memory is mapped into pages equal to the size of a bank in the cache array. But, because a bank is now 32KB, there are twice as many main memory pages as compared to the direct-mapped organization. In this case, the storage location at a specific offset in every page of main memory can map to the same storage location in either the A or B bank. For example, the contents of storage location X(0) can be cached into either X_A or X_B. The two-way set associative organization results in higher hit rate operation.

The 80486SX's internal 8KB cache memory uses a 4-way set associative memory. Therefore, its configuration is similar to that shown in Fig. 14.52 except that it is arranged into four 2KB banks.

One example of a memory update method that affects hit rate is the data replacement algorithm. The method is based on the fact that there is a higher chance that more recently used information will be reused. For instance, the two-way set associative cache organization permits the use of a *least recently used* (LRU) replacement algorithm. In this method, the cache subsystem hardware keeps track of whether information X(A) in the BANK A storage location or X(B) in BANK

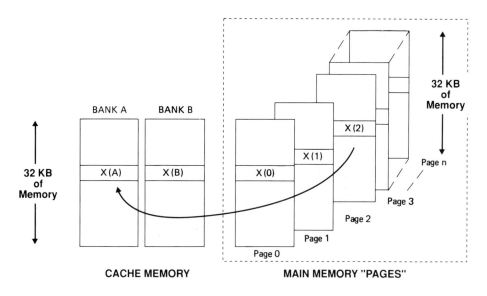

Figure 14.53 Organization of a two-way set associative memory subsystem. (Reprinted by permission of Intel Corp., © Intel Corp. 1990)

B is most recently used. For example, let us assume that the value at storage location X(A) in BANK A of Fig. 14.53 is X_0 from page 0 and that it was just loaded into the cache. On the other hand, X(B) in BANK B is from page 1 and has not been accessed for a long time. In this case, the value of X(B) in BANK B is tagged as the least recently used information. When a new value of code or data, for instance, from offset X(3) in page 3 is accessed, it must replace the value of X(A) in BANK A or X_B in BANK B. Therefore, the cache replacement algorithm automatically selects the cache storage location corresponding to the least recently accessed bank for storage of X_3. For our example, this would be storage location X(B) in BANK B. In this way, we see that the replacement algorithm maintains more recently used information in the cache memory array. The 4-way set associative cache memory of the 80486SX MPU uses the LRU replacement algorithm. This results in a higher maximum hit rate for the internal cache and a higher level of performance for the microcomputer system.

We found earlier that use of a cache reduced the number of accesses of main memory over the system bus. In our example of a loop routine, we saw that repeated accesses of the instructions that perform the loop operation were made from the internal cache, not from main memory. Therefore, fewer code and data accesses are performed across the system bus. That is, availability of the bus has been increased for external devices. This is another advantage of using cache in a microcomputer system. The freed-up bus bandwidth is available to other bus masters, such as DMA controllers or other processors in a multiple-processor system.

Organization and Operation of the 80486SX's Internal Cache. Let us next examine the organization and operation of the 80486SX's internal 8KB four-way set associa-

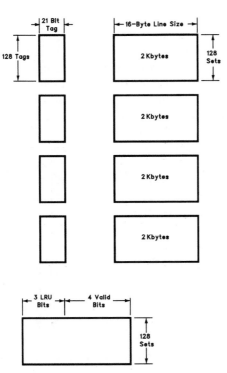

Figure 14.54 Organization of the on-chip cache of the 80486SX. (Reprinted by permission of Intel Corp., © Intel Corp. 1992)

tive cache memory. We will begin by determining how data is stored in the cache memory array.

Since the internal cache uses a four-way set associative organization, the data storage area is partitioned into four separate 2KB areas. Figure 14.54 illustrates how this memory is organized. We will refer to these areas of memory as *SET 0* through *SET 3*. Data are loaded, stored, validated, and invalidated in 16 byte-wide elements, which are called a *line of data*. The 80486SX's cache does not support filling of partial lines. Therefore, if a single double word of data is to be read from memory and copied into the cache, the MPU must fetch the complete line in which this double word is contained from memory. This is the reason that cacheable read bus cycles initiate four double-word data transfers. That is, they always access code or data a line (16 bytes) at a time so that a complete line of the cache gets filled. In this way, we see that the contents of each 2KB bank in the cache's storage array is further arranged into 128 lines of data.

Associated with each data storage set is a separate tag directory. The tag directory contains 128 21-bit tag entries, one corresponds to each line of data in the set. Each tag entry includes bits of information about the use of the line and whether or not it currently holds valid information.

When a read operation is initiated by the MPU and the information that is to be accessed is already in the internal cache, the information is obtained without performing external bus cycles. Instead, the information is simply read from the cache memory. However, if a cache miss occurs, a line of code or data must be read from main memory and copied into the cache. The on-chip cache circuitry must determine if there is room in the cache and if not, which of the current valid lines of information is to be replaced. It does this by checking the information in the tag directory. If the cache is found to contain invalid lines of data or code, one of them can be simply replaced with the new information. On the other hand, if there are no vacant line storage locations, the least recently used mechanism of the cache automatically checks the use information in the tag to determine which valid line of information will be replaced.

Next let us look at what happens when a data write operation is performed. Whenever a new value of data is to be written to a storage location in memory, the internal cache circuitry must first be checked to confirm whether or not the contents of this storage location also exist within the cache. If it does, the value must be either invalidated or updated as part of the write operation. Otherwise, a cache data consistency problem will be created.

The 80486SX's on-chip cache is implemented with a write update method that is known as *write-through*. With this method, all write bus cycles that result in a cache hit automatically update both the corresponding storage location in the internal cache and external memory. That is, write operations to main memory can be viewed as going through the cache. On the other hand, for a cache miss, the data is only written to main memory. Remember that cache write-through operation can be enabled or disabled with the no write-through (NW) bit of CR_0. However, write-through would not be disabled during normal operation.

Enabling and Disabling Internal Caching. The 80486SX's internal cache is equipped with a variety of methods of controlling the operation of the cache. For instance, the complete cache memory can be turned on or off, the memory address space can be mapped with cacheable and non-cacheable areas, and external circuitry can define any bus cycle as cacheable or non-cacheable. Let us briefly review how each of these cache memory controls are implemented on the 80486SX.

Remember that the operation of the cache memory can be enabled or disabled under software control. Logic 1 in the cache fill disable (CD) bit of control register CR_0 can be used to turn off filling of the cache. However, this does not completely disable the cache; it just stops it from being refilled. To completely disable the cache, the no write-through (NW) bit in CR_0 must also be set to 1 and then the cache must be flushed. The flush operation is needed to remove the stale data that was left in the cache when cache fill was turned off.

Mapping of parts of the memory address space as cacheable or non-cacheable can be achieved either through software or hardware. Under software control, each page of the memory address space can be configured as cacheable or non-cacheable with the page-level cache disable (PCD) bit in its page table entry. For instance, to make a page of memory non-cacheable the PCD bit is made 0. The memory address space can be mapped cacheable or non-cacheable on a byte wide basis by external circuitry. The *cache enable* ($\overline{KEN}$) input can be used to indicate whether or not the data for the current bus cycle should be cached. By decoding addresses in external circuitry and returning logic 1 at $\overline{KEN}$, a part of the address can be designated as non-cacheable.

Flushing the Cache. When the internal cache is flushed all of the line valid bits in the tag directory are invalidated. Therefore, after a *flush* occurs the cache is empty and will need to be refilled. The cache is flushed whenever the MPU is reset; it can be flushed under software control by executing the invalidate cache (INVD) instruction; or with external circuitry by activating the $\overline{\text{FLUSH}}$ input.

Cache Line Invalidations. We just described how the complete contents of the cache can be invalidated with a flush operation. It is also possible to invalidate individual lines of information within the cache. This is known as a *cache line invalidation* and is normally done to make the contents of the internal cache consistent with that of external memory.

If an external device changes the contents of a storage location in external memory and the value of this storage location is currently held in the 80486SX's internal cache memory, a cache consistency problem can occur. That is, they no longer contain the same value and the value in cache is no longer valid. If the 80486SX was to read this storage location, the incorrect value in the cache would be accessed and if this data was processed and written back to memory, the results in external memory would now be wrong.

To protect against inconsistency problems between the contents of the internal cache and external memory, external circuitry needs to initiate a cache line invalidation operation each time an external device modifies the content of a storage location in external memory. This is done by initiating an invalidate bus cycle. The first step in this process is to switch *address hold* (AHOLD) to logic 1. This puts the address bus lines into the high-Z state. Next, the external circuitry puts the address of the external memory storage location whose contents were changed onto the address lines and signals the 80486SX that a valid external address is available by switching $\overline{\text{EADS}}$ (*external address*) to logic 0. Now the address lines of the MPU act as inputs, instead of outputs. If this address corresponds to an element of data that is currently held in cache, the corresponding cache entry is invalidated. In this way, cache consistency is restored.

Internal Exceptions

Earlier we indicated that the external hardware interrupt interface of the 80486SX MPU is exactly the same as that of the 80386DX processors. In fact, the only difference between the interrupt/exception processing capability of the 80486SX and 80386DX is that one additional internal exception function is defined for the 80486SX and one that was performed by the 80386DX is no longer supported on the 80486SX. Here we will just look briefly at these two changes in exception processing.

The new exception that is activated for the first time in 80486 family MPUs is called *alignment check exception*. In our description of the software model of the 80486SX in Chapter 13, we identified two new control bits, the alignment check (AC) flag in EFLAGS and alignment mask (AM) control bit in CR_0, that are used to enable address alignment checking for memory access operations. At that time, we indicated that this function gives the 80386SX the ability to detect an attempt to access an unaligned double word of data. This exception is only detected for memory accesses initiated while in protected mode and executing user code privilege level 3. When this option is enabled, any attempt by the program to access an unaligned operand in memory results in an alignment check exception through exception gate 17.

The 80386DX exception function that is not supported by 80486 family MPUs is exception 9, coprocessor segment overrun.

▲ 14.10 THE PENTIUM™ PROCESSOR FAMILY

Many enhancements have been made to the hardware architecture of the MPUs in the Pentium™ processor family. Some examples of important improvements are that the data bus has been expanded to 64 bits, parity provided for the address bus, the on-chip cache memory is partitioned into separate code and data caches, the internal caches support either the write-through or write-back cache update methods, and pipelined bus cycles have been implemented. These hardware changes play a key role in giving the Pentium™ processor its higher level of performance and simplify the design of Pentium™ processor-based multiprocessor microcomputer systems.

We have seen that continued advances in process technology have enabled Intel Corporation to integrate more and more transistors into their MPUs. The Pentium™ family of microprocessors were originally built on a .6 micron manufacturing process, but since then has been moved to an even smaller geometry process. The reduction in transistor size achieved with these more advanced processes has permitted the integration of more than three million transistors into the Pentium™ processor.

(a)

Figure 14.55 (a) Pentium™ processor IC. (Reprinted by permission of Intel Corp., © Intel Corp. 1995) (b) Pin layout of the Pentium™ processor. (Reprinted by permission of Intel Corp., © Intel Corp. 1995)

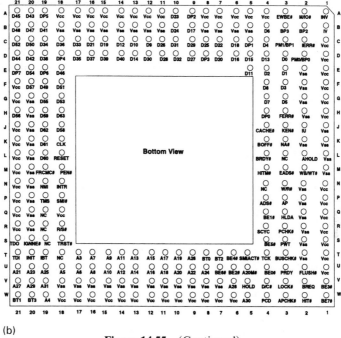

(b)

Figure 14.55 (Continued)

The Pentium™ processor and its pin layout are shown in Figs. 14.55(a) and (b), respectively. Here we see that it is housed in a 296-pin staggered pin grid array (SPGA) package.

In this section, we will examine some of the architectural advancements that are first introduced in the Pentium™ processor family.

Signal Interfaces of the Pentium™ Processor

A block diagram of the Pentium™ processor is shown in Fig. 14.56. Though a lot of changes have been made in the hardware architecture of the Pentium™ processor, many of the interface signals are the same as those used on 80386 and 80486 family MPUs. For example, similar to the 80386DX and 80486SX, the type of bus cycle is defined by the code $M/\overline{IO}$ $D/\overline{C}$ $W/\overline{R}$ and the interrupt interface consists of INTR, NMI, and RESET. Most of the interface signals first introduced on the 80486 family of MPUs are also provided on Pentium™ processors. For instance, the signal lines $\overline{A20M}$, $\overline{BOFF}$, $\overline{BRDY}$, $\overline{FLUSH}$, $\overline{KEN}$, PWT, and PCD are all part of the Pentium™ processor's memory/IO and cache memory interfaces. Here we will just examine some of the new signals of the memory/IO interface.

Earlier we pointed out that the memory/IO interface has been improved by making the data bus 64 bits wide and by adding parity on the address bus. The data bus now consists of bidirectional data lines D_0 through D_{63}. Because of the larger data bus, the number of byte enable and data parity lines has been

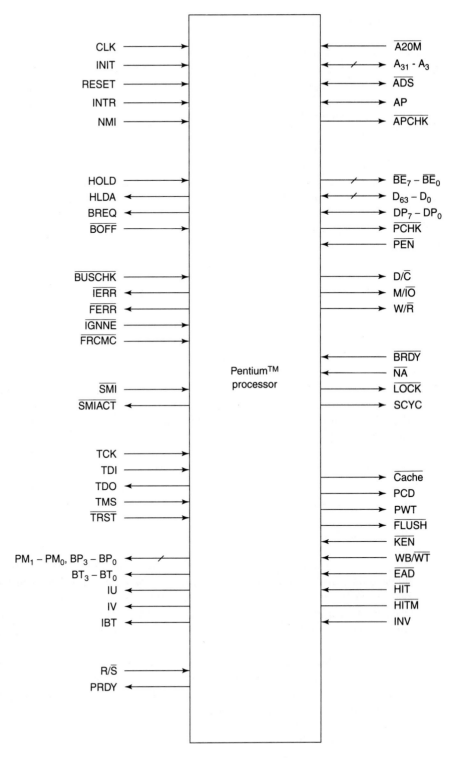

Figure 14.56 Pentium™ processor block diagram.

increased to eight. They are labeled $\overline{BE_0}$ through $\overline{BE_8}$ and DP_0 through DP_7, respectively.

During all write cycles, the bus interface unit generates a code at DP_0 through DP_7 that produces even parity for each byte of data on D_0 through D_{63}. The *parity enable* ($\overline{PEN}$) input must be set to logic 0 to enable parity checking during data read bus cycles. When a read bus cycle takes place, the data on D_0 through D_{63} and DP_0 through DP_7 are tested for even parity on a byte wide basis. If a data parity error is detected, this fact is signaled to external circuitry with logic 0 at the $\overline{PCHK}$ output. The MPU can be configured to automatically initiate an exception whenever a parity error is detected.

In the Pentium™ processor, parity generation and checking has been added to the address bus. Before an address is output on A_3 through A_{31}, an even parity bit is generated and output at pin *address parity* (AP). In this way, the memory subsystem can perform parity checks on both the data and the address. This results in an increased level of data integrity.

The address bus is actually bidirectional. This is because the Pentium™ processor, like the 80486SX, permits external devices to examine the contents of its internal caches. The operation is enhanced on the Pentium™ processor with address parity checking. The external system applies what is known as an *inquire address* to the processor on A_5 through A_{31}. This is the address of the cache storage location to be accessed during the inquire cycle. Logic 0 at the valid external address ($\overline{EADS}$) input, signals the MPU that the address is available. As part of the read operation, a parity check operation is performed on the inquire address, and if a parity error is detected, it is identified by logic 0 at the address parity check ($\overline{APCHK}$) output.

The Pentium™ processor's memory/IO interface can detect whether or not a bus cycle has run to completion correctly. The *bus check* ($\overline{BUSCHK}$) input is used for this purpose. External circuitry must determine whether or not the current bus cycle is not successfully completed. If the bus cycle is not completed, it switches $\overline{BUSCHK}$ to logic 0. This input can be used to initiate an exception routine to service the problem.

Pipelined Bus Cycles

Similar to the 80486 family of MPUs, the Pentium™ processor can perform single data transfer and burst data transfers. These basic bus cycles are shown in Figs. 14.57 (a) and (b), respectively. Notice that a nonpipelined single data read or write takes a minimum of two clock cycles, while a burst read or write takes two clock cycles for the first data transfer and one additional cycle for each of the other three data transfers.

The Pentium™ processor is equipped with a *next address* ($\overline{NA}$) input to enable pipelined bus cycles. Figure 14.58 illustrates the bus activity for pipelined burst read and write cycles. First a burst read is initiated to address "a". When $\overline{BRDY}$ switches to logic 0, $\overline{NA}$ also becomes active. Logic 0 at $\overline{NA}$ signals the MPU that the next address, identified as address "b", can be output on the address bus. As expected in a pipelined bus cycle, this address is available to the external memory

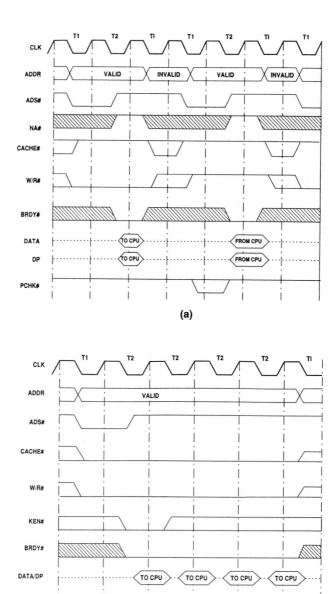

Figure 14.57 (a) Nonpipelined read and write bus cycle. (Reprinted by permission of Intel Corp., © Intel Corp. 1993) (b) Burst read bus cycle. (Reprinted by permission of Intel Corp., © Intel Corp. 1993)

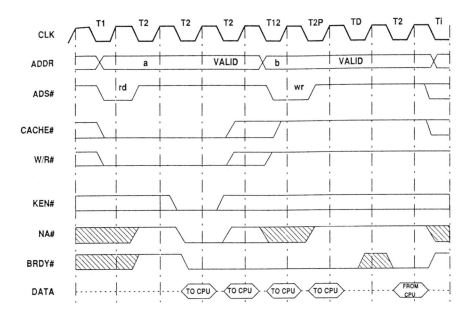

Figure 14.58 Pipelined back-to-back read/write bus cycle. (Reprinted by permission of Intel Corp., © Intel Corp. 1993)

subsystem prior to the completion of the burst read bus cycle. Therefore, the valid address is available for a longer period of time and the memory subsystem can be designed with slower access time memory devices.

Cache Memory Organization

The cache memory of the Pentium™ processor differs from that of the 80486SX in several ways. For instance, there are separate cache memories for storage of data and code; they employ a two-way set associative organization, and two write update methods, write-through and write-back, are supported. The separate caches and write-back capability leads to higher performance for the Pentium™ processor-based microcomputer system.

Let us examine the organization of the data and code caches. They both are 8KB in size. Since the two-way set associative organization is used, the storage array in each cache memory is organized into two separate 4KB areas. This organization is shown in Fig. 14.59. Line width is 32 bytes and updates to the cache are always done a line at a time. Therefore, the line fill cache read that occurs after a cache miss involves four quad-word (64-bit) data transfers. If an invalid line exists within the cache, this information is loaded into it; otherwise, the LRU algorithm decides which of the valid lines will get replaced.

As identified earlier, the Pentium™ processor's caches support both the write-through and write-back update methods. Different areas of the memory address space can be defined as either write-through or write-back and this can be done

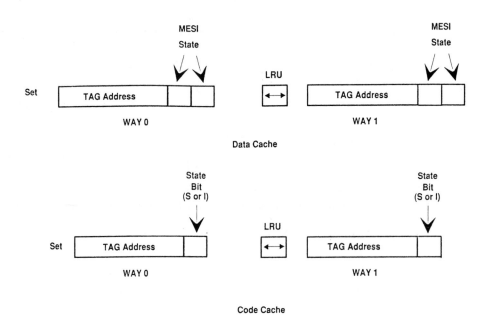

Figure 14.59 Organization of the on-chip cache of the Pentium™ processor. (Reprinted by permission of Intel Corp., © Intel Corp. 1993)

through software or hardware. For instance, the logic 1 at the write-back/write-through (WB/$\overline{\text{WT}}$) input selects write-back operation for the current write update. Remember that if a cache hit occurs during a write operation, the corresponding storage location in both the cache and the external memory must be updated. Unlike write-through operations, write-back updates of external memory are not performed at the same time the information is written into the cache. Instead, they are accumulated in the cache memory subsystem and written to memory at a later time. This reduces the bus activity and therefore enhances the microcomputer's performance.

ASSIGNMENTS

Section 14.2

1. Name the technology used to fabricate the 80386DX microprocessor.
2. What is the transistor count of the 80386DX?
3. Which signal is located at pin B7?

Section 14.3

4. How large is the real-address mode address bus and physical address space of the 80386DX MPU? How large is the protected-address mode address bus

and physical address space? How large is the protected-mode virtual address space?

5. If the byte enable code output during a data write bus cycle is $\overline{BE_3}\overline{BE_2}\overline{BE_1}\overline{BE_0} = 1110_2$, is a byte, word, or double-word data transfer taking place? Over which data bus lines are the data transferred? Does data duplication occur?

6. For which byte enable codes does data duplication take place?

7. What type of bus cycle is in progress when the bus status code $M/\overline{IO}$ $D/\overline{C}$ $W/\overline{R}$ equals 010?

8. Which signals implement the DMA interface?

9. What processor is most frequently attached to the processor extension interface?

Section 14.4

10. What speed 80386DX ICs are available from Intel Corporation? How are these speeds denoted in the part number?

11. At what pin is the CLK2 input applied?

12. What clock signal frequency must be applied to the CLK2 input of an 80386DX-25 to run it at full speed?

Section 14.5

13. What is the duration of PCLK for an 80386DX that is driven by CLK2 equals 50 MHz?

14. What two types of bus cycles can be performed by the 80386DX?

15. Explain what is meant by pipelining the 80386DX's bus.

16. What is an idle state?

17. What is a wait state?

18. What are the two T states of the 80386DX's bus cycle called?

19. If an 80386DX-25 is executing a nonpipelined write bus cycle that has no wait states, what would be the duration of this bus cycle if the 80386DX is operating at full speed?

20. If an 80386DX-25 that is running at full speed performs a bus cycle with two wait states, what is the duration of the bus cycle?

Section 14.6

21. How is memory organized from a hardware point of view in a protected-mode 80386DX microcomputer system? Real-mode 80386DX microcomputer system?

22. What are the five types of data transfers that can take place over the data bus? How many bus cycles are required for each type of data transfer?

23. If an 80386DX-25 is running at full speed and all memory accesses involve one wait state, how long will it take to fetch the word of data starting at address $0FF1A_{16}$? At address $0FF1F_{16}$?

24. During a bus cycle that involves a misaligned word transfer, which byte of data is transferred over the bus during the first bus cycle?

25. Give an overview of the function of each block in the memory interface diagram of Fig. 14.25.

26. When the instruction PUSH AX is executed, what bus status code is output by the 80386DX, which byte enable signals are active, and what read/write control signal is produced by the bus control logic?

Section 14.7

27. Which signal can be used to distinguish an I/O bus cycle and a memory bus cycle?

28. Which block produces the input (read), output (write), and bus control signals for the I/O interface?

29. Briefly describe the function of each block in the I/O interface circuit in Fig. 14.27.

30. If an 80386DX-25 running at full speed inserts two wait states into all I/O bus cycles, what is the duration of a nonpipelined bus cycle in which a byte of data is being output?

31. If the 80386DX in Problem 30 was outputting a word of data to a word-wide port at I/O address $1A3_{16}$, what would be the duration of the bus cycle?

32. What parameter identifies the beginning of the I/O permission bit map in a TSS? At what address of the TSS is this parameter held?

33. At what double-word address in the I/O permission bit map is the bit for I/O port 64 held? Which bit of this double word corresponds to port 64?

34. To what logic level should the bit in Problem 33 be set if I/O operations are to be inhibited to the port in protected mode?

Section 14.8

35. What is the real-mode interrupt address pointer table called? Protected-mode address pointer table?

36. What is the size of a real-mode interrupt vector? Protected-mode gate?

37. The contents of which register determine the location of the interrupt address pointer table? To what value is this register initialized at reset?

38. At what addresses is the protected-mode gate for type number 20 stored in memory?

39. Assume that gate 3 consists of the four words that follow:

$$(IDT + 8) = 1000_{16}$$

$$(IDT + A) = B000_{16}$$

$$(IDT + C) = AE00_{16}$$

$$(IDT + E) = 0000_{16}$$

(a) Is the gate descriptor active?
(b) What is the privilege level?
(c) Is the gate a trap gate or an interrupt gate?
(d) What is the starting address of the service routine?

40. If values stored in memory locations are as follows,

$$(IDT\_TABLE) = 01FF_{16}$$

$$(IDT\_TABLE + 2) = 0000_{16}$$

$$(IDT\_TABLE + 4) = 0001_{16}$$

what address is loaded into the interrupt descriptor table register when the instruction LIDT [IDT_TABLE] is executed? What is the maximum size of the table? How many gates are provided for in this table?

41. What is the key difference between the real-mode and protected-mode interrupt request/acknowledge handshake sequence for the 80386DX microprocessor?

42. List the real-mode internal interrupts serviced by the 80386DX.

43. Internal interrupts and exceptions are categorized into groups based on how the failing function is reported. List the three groups.

44. Which real-mode vector numbers are reserved for internal interrupts and exceptions?

45. Into which reporting group is the invalid opcode exception classified?

46. What is the cause of a stack fault exception?

47. Which exceptions take on a new meaning or are only active in the protected mode?

Section 14.9

48. What signal is located at pin A16 of the 80486SX's package?

49. Which lines of the 80486SX's memory/IO interface carry parity information?

50. What input signal and logic level does the external circuitry use to tell the 80486SX MPU that it can perform a burst bus cycle?

51. What does $\overline{KEN}$ stand for?

52. What signal permits an external device to take control of the 80486SX's bus interface at the completion of the current clock cycle?

53. What is the maximum number of bytes that can be transferred with a single burst bus cycle?

54. What is meant when a read cycle is said to be cacheable? How many bytes of data are transferred during a cacheable bus cycle?

55. What is the result of using a cache memory in a microcomputer system?

56. Is the internal cache of the 80486SX a first level or send level cache?

57. Define the term *cache hit*.

58. When an application program is tested on an 80486SX-based microcomputer system, it is found that 1340 instruction and data accesses are from the internal cache memory and 97 are from main memory. What is the hit rate?

59. If the microcomputer used for Problem 59 operates with 3 wait states for main memory accesses, what is the average number of wait states experienced executing the application?

60. What type of cache organization is used for the 80486SX's internal cache?

61. How large is the 80486SX's internal cache? What is the smallest element of data that can be loaded into the cache?

62. What write method is implemented for the internal cache of the 80486SX?

63. What happens when the $\overline{\text{FLUSH}}$ input of the 80486SX is switched to logic 0 by external circuitry?

64. What new internal exception is implemented in the 80486SX MPU?

Section 14.10

65. Approximately how many transistors are used to implement the Pentium™ processor?

66. At what pin of the Pentium™'s package is data bus line D_{45} located? Address line A_3?

67. What kind of parity is supported on the Pentium™ processor's bus interface? How are parity errors identified?

68. What does logic 0 at $\overline{\text{NA}}$ mean about the current bus cycle?

69. What type of organization is implemented with the Pentium™ processor's caches?

70. How much cache memory is provided on the Pentium™ processor?

71. How many bits are in the Pentium™ processor's cache line?

72. What does logic 0 on WB/$\overline{\text{WT}}$ mean about the current write bus cycle?

Answers to Selected Assignments

▲ CHAPTER 1

Section 1.2

1. Original IBM PC
3. I/O channel
5. Industry standard architecture
7. A reprogrammable microcomputer is a general-purpose computer designed to run programs for a wide variety of applications, for instance, accounting, word processing, and languages such as BASIC.
9. The microcomputer is similar to the minicomputer in that it is designed to perform general-purpose data processing; however, it is smaller in size, has reduced capabilities, and is lower in cost than a minicomputer.

Section 1.3

11. Input unit, output unit, microprocessing unit, and memory unit
13. 16-bit
15. Video display and printer
17. 360K bytes; 10M bytes
19. 48K bytes; 256K bytes

Section 1.4

21. 4-bit, 8-bit, 16-bit, 32-bit, and 64-bit

23. 8086, 8088, 80186, 80188, 80286

25. 27 MIPS

27. 30,000, 140,000, 275,000, 1,200,000

29. Event controller and data controller

31. 8088, 8086, 80286, 80386DX, 80486DX, and Pentium™ processor

33. *Upward software compatible* means that programs written for the 8088 or 8086 will run directly on the 80286, 80386DX, and 80486DX.

35. Floppy disk controller, communication controller, and local area network controller

▲ CHAPTER 2

Section 2.2

1. Software

3. 8088 machine code

5. Opcode is the mnemonic that identifies the operation to be performed by the instruction. ADD and MOV are the examples.

7. START

9. The assembly language or high-level language code that is input to a compiler is called *source code.* The machine code output of an assembler or compiler is called *object code.*

11. A real-time application is one in which the tasks required by the application must be completed before any other input to the program occurs to alter its operation.

Section 2.3

13. Bus interface unit and execution unit

15. 4 bytes; 6 bytes

Section 2.4

17. Aid to the assembly language programmer for understanding a microprocessor's software operation

19. 14

Section 2.5

21. $FFFFF_{16}$ and 00000_{16}

23. $00FF_{16}$

Section 2.6

25. Unsigned integer, signed integer, unpacked BCD, packed BCD, and ASCII

27. (0A000H) = F4H
(0A001H) = 01H

29. **(a)** 00000010, 00001001; 00101001
(b) 00001000, 00001000; 10001000

31. NEXT I

Section 2.7

33. Up to 256K bytes
35. Up to 128K bytes

Section 2.8

37. Pointers to interrupt service routines

Section 2.9

39. The instruction pointer is the offset address of the next instruction to be fetched by the 8088 relative to the current value in CS.

41. IP is incremented such that it points to the next sequential word of instruction code.

Section 2.10

43. With a postscript X to form AX, BX, CX, and DX
45. Count for string and multi-bit shift and rotate instructions

Section 2.11

47. Base pointer (BP) and stack pointer (SP)
49. DS

Section 2.12

51. *Flag*   *Type*

CF	Status
PF	Status
AF	Status
ZF	Status
SF	Status
OF	Status

TF Control
IF Control
DF Control

53. Instructions can be used to test the state of these flags and, based on their setting, modify the sequence in which instructions of the program are executed.

55. Instructions are provided that can load the complete register or modify specific flag bits.

Section 2.13

57. Offset and segment base
59. (a) ? = 0123H
  (b) ? = 2210H
  (c) ? = 3570H
  (d) ? = 2600H
61. $A000_{16}$

Section 2.14

63. The stack is the area of memory used to temporarily store information (parameters) to be passed to subroutines and other information such as the contents of IP and CS that is needed to return from a called subroutine to the main part of the program.

65. 128 words

Section 2.15

67. Separate
69. Page 0

Section 2.16

71. Register operand addressing mode
  Immediate operand addressing mode
  Direct addressing mode
  Register indirect addressing mode
  Based addressing mode
  Indexed addressing mode
  Based indexed addressing mode
73. (a) PA = $0B200_{16}$
  (b) PA = $0B100_{16}$
  (c) PA = $0B700_{16}$
  (d) PA = $0B600_{16}$
  (e) PA = $0B900_{16}$

▲ CHAPTER 3

Section 3.2

1. $0000001111000010_2 = 03C2H$

3. (a) $00011110_2 = 1EH$; (b) $1101001011000011_2 = D2C3H$; (c) $10010001_2 = 91H$

Section 3.3

5. 24 bytes

Section 3.4

7. Yes

9. -R CX   (↵)
CX XXXX
:0010   (↵)

11. -R   (↵)

Section 3.5

13. -E CS:0   (↵)
1342:0000 CD. 20. 00. 40. 00. 9A. EE. FE.
1342:0008 1D. F0. F5. 02. A7. 0A. 2E. 03.   (↵)

After a byte of data is displayed, the space bar is depressed to display the next byte. The values displayed may not be those shown, but will be identical to those displayed with the DUMP command.

15. -E SS:(SP) 0 ....0 (32 zeros)   (↵)
-

Section 3.6

17. Input command and output command

19. O 124 5A   (↵)

Section 3.7

21. 4 digits

Section 3.8

23. -E CS:100 32 0E 34 12   (↵)
-U CS:100 103   (↵)

```
     1342:100 320E3412      XOR CL,[1234]
     -W CS:100 1 50 1           (↵)
```

Section 3.9

25. -A CS:100   (↵)
   1342:0100 MOV [DI],DX   (↵)
   1342:0102   (↵)

Section 3.10

27. -L CS:300 1 50 1   (↵)
   -U CS:300 303   (↵)
   -R CX   (↵)
   CX XXXX
   :000F   (↵)
   -E DS:1234 FF   (↵)
   -T =CS:300   (↵)
   -D DS:1234 1235   (↵)

Section 3.11

29. A syntax error is an error in the rules of coding the program. On the other hand, an execution error is an error in the logic of the planned solution for the problem.

▲ CHAPTER 4

Section 4.2

1. Data transfer instructions, arithmetic instructions, logic instructions, shift instructions, and rotate instructions

Section 4.3

3. (a) Value 0110H is moved into AX.
   (b) 0110H is copied into DI.
   (c) 10H is copied into BL.
   (d) 0110H is copied into memory address DS:0100H.
   (e) 0110H is copied into memory address DS:0120H.
   (f) 0110H is copied into memory address DS:0114H.
   (g) 0110H is copied into memory address DS:0124H.

5. MOV [1010H],ES

7. (a) Contents of AX and BX are swapped.
   (b) Contents of BX and DI are swapped.

(c) Contents of memory location with offset DATA in the current data segment and register AX are swapped.

(d) Contents of the memory location pointed to by (DS)0 + (BX) + (DI) are swapped with those of register AX.

9. AL is loaded from the physical address $10000_{16} + 0100_{16} + 0010_{16} = 10110_{16}$.

11. MOV AX,DATA_SEG   ;Establish the data segment
    MOV DS,AX
    MOV AL,[MEM1]   ;Get the given code at MEM1
    MOV BX,TABL1
    XLAT   ;Translate
    MOV [MEM1],AL   ;Save new code at MEM1
    MOV AL,[MEM2]   ;Repeat for the second code at MEM2
    MOV BX,TABL2
    XLAT
    MOV [MEM2],AL

Section 4.4

13. **(a)** (AX) = 010FH
   (b) (SI) = 0110H
   (c) (DS:100H) = 11H
   (d) (DL) = 20H
   (e) (DL) = 0FH
   (f) (DS:220H) = 2FH
   (g) (DS:210H) = C0H
   (h) (AX) = 0400H
        (DX) = 0000H
   (i) (AL) = 0F0H
       (AH) = 0FFH
   (j) (AL) = 02H
       (AH) = 00H
   (k) (AL) = 08H
       (AH) = 00H

15. SBB AX,[BX]

17. (AH) = remainder = 3_{16}, (AL) = quotient = 12_{16}, therefore, (AX) = 0312_{16}

19. AAS

21. (AX) = 7FFFH, (DX) = 0000H

Section 4.5

23. **(a)** 0FH is ANDed with the contents of the byte-wide memory address DS:300H.
   (b) Contents of DX are ANDed with the contents of the word storage location pointed to by (DS)0 + (SI).

(c) Contents of AX are ORed with the word contents of the memory location pointed to by (DS)0 + (BX) + (DI).

(d) F0H is ORed with the contents of the byte-wide memory location pointed to by (DS)0 + (BX) + (DI) + 10H.

(e) Contents of the word-wide memory location pointed to by (DS)0 + (SI) + (BX) are exclusive-ORed with the contents of AX.

(f) The bits of the byte-wide memory location DS:300H are inverted.

(g) The bits of the word memory location pointed to by (DS)0 + (BX) + (DI) are inverted.

25. AND DX,0080H

27. The new contents of AX are the 2's complement of its old contents.

29. MOV AL,[CONTROL_FLAGS]
AND AL,81H
MOV [CONTROL_FLAGS],AL

Section 4.6

31. (a) Contents of DX are shifted left by a number of bit positions equal to the contents of CL. LSBs are filled with 0s, and CF equals the value of the last bit shifted out of the MSB position.

(b) Contents of the byte-wide memory location DS:400H are shifted left by a number of bit positions equal to the contents of CL. LSBs are filled with 0s, and CF equals the value of the last bit shifted out of the MSB position.

(c) Contents of the byte-wide memory location pointed to by (DS)0 + (DI) are shifted right by 1 bit position. MSB is filled with 0, and CF equals the value shifted out of the LSB position.

(d) Contents of the byte-wide memory location pointed to by (DS)0 + (DI) + (BX) are shifted right by a number of bit positions equal to the contents of CL. MSBs are filled with 0s, and CF equals the value of the last bit shifted out of the LSB position.

(e) Contents of the word-wide memory location pointed to by (DS)0 + (BX) + (DI) are shifted right by 1 bit position. MSB is filled with the value of the original MSB and CF equals the value shifted out of the LSB position.

(f) Contents of the word-wide memory location pointed to by (DS)0 + (BX) + (DI) + 10H are shifted right by a number of bit positions equal to the contents of CL. MSBs are filled with the value of the original MSB, and CF equals the value of the last bit shifted out of the LSB position.

33. SHL CX,1

35. The original contents of AX must have the four most significant bits equal to 0.

37. The first instruction reads the byte of control flags into AL. Then all but the flag in the most significant bit location B_7 are masked off. Finally, the flag in B_7 is shifted to the left and into the carry flag.

When the shift takes place, B7 is shifted into CF; all other bits in AL move one bit position to the left, and the LSB locations are filled with 0s. Therefore, the contents of AL become 00H.

Section 4.7

39. **(a)** Contents of DX are rotated left by a number of bit positions equal to the contents of CL. As each bit is rotated out of the MSB position, the LSB position and CF are filled with this value.

(b) Contents of the byte-wide memory location DS:400H are rotated left by a number of bit positions equal to the contents of CL. As each bit is rotated out of the MSB position, it is loaded into CF, and the prior contents of CF are loaded into the LSB position.

(c) Contents of the byte-wide memory location pointed to by (DS)0 + (DI) are rotated right by 1 bit position. As the bit is rotated out of the LSB position, the MSB position and CF are filled with this value.

(d) Contents of the byte-wide memory location pointed to by (DS)0 + (DI) + (BX) are rotated right by a number of bit positions equal to the contents of CL. As each bit is rotated out of the LSB position, the MSB position and CF are filled with this value.

(e) Contents of the word-wide memory location pointed to by (DS)0 + (BX) + (DI) are rotated right by 1 bit position. As the bit is rotated out of the LSB location, it is loaded into CF, and the prior contents of CF are loaded into the MSB position.

(f) Contents of the word-wide memory location pointed to by (DS)0 + (BX) + (DI) + 10H is rotated right by a number of bit positions equal to the contents of CL. As each bit is rotated out of the LSB position, it is loaded into CF, and the prior contents of CF are loaded into the MSB position.

41. RCL WORD PTR [BX],1

43. MOV AX, [ASCII_DATA]
MOV BX, AX
MOV CL, 08H
ROR BX, CL
AND AX, 00FFH
AND BX, 00FFH
MOV [ASCII_CHAR_L], AX
MOV [ASCII_CHAR_H], BX

▲ CHAPTER 5

Section 5.2

1. Executing the first instruction causes the contents of the status register to be copied into AH. The second instruction causes the value of the flags to be saved in memory location (DS)0 + (BX) + (DI).

3. STC; CLC

5. CLI
    MOV AX,0H
    MOV DS,AX
    MOV BX,0A000H
    LAHF
    MOV [BX],AH
    CLC

Section 5.3

7. (a) The byte of data in AL is compared with the byte of data in memory at address DS:100H by subtraction, and the status flags are set or reset to reflect the result.
   (b) The word contents of the data storage memory location pointed to by (DS)0 + (SI) are compared with the contents of AX by subtraction, and the status flags are set or reset to reflect the results.
   (c) The immediate data 1234H are compared with the word contents of the memory location pointed to by (DS)0 + (DI) by subtraction, and the status flags are set or reset to reflect the results.

9.

	(ZF)	(CF)
Initial state	0	0
After MOV BX,1111H	0	0
After MOV AX,0BBBBH	0	0
After CMP BX,AX	0	1

Section 5.4

11. IP; CS and IP

13. Intersegment

15. (a) 1075H:10H
   (b) 1075H:1000H
   (c) 1075H:1000H

17. (SF) = 0

19. (a) Intrasegment; short-label; if the carry flag is set, a jump is performed by loading IP with 10H.
   (b) Intrasegment; near-label; if PF is not set, a jump is performed by loading IP with 1000_{16}.
   (c) Intersegment; memptr32; if the overflow flag is set, a jump is performed by loading the two words of the 32-bit pointer addressed by the value (DS)0 + (BX) into IP and CS, respectively.

21. (a) $1000_{16} = 2^{12} = 4096$ times.
   (b) ;Set up the counter = 17

```
                MOV  CX,11H
DLY:            DEC  CX
                JNZ  DLY
NXT:            —    —
```

(c) ;Set up a nested loop with 16-bit inner and 16-bit outer
;counters. Load these counters so that the JNZ
;instruction is encountered 2^{32} times

```
                MOV  AX,0FFFFH
DLY1:           MOV  CX,0H
DLY2:           DEC  CX
                JNZ  DLY2
                DEC  AX
                JNZ  DLY1
NXT:            —
```

23.

```
                MOV  CX,64H          ;Set up array counter
                MOV  SI,0A000H       ;Set up source array pointer
                MOV  DI,0B000H       ;Set up destination array
                                     ;pointer
GO_ON:          MOV  AX,[SI]
                CMP  AX,[DI]         ;Compare the next element
                JNE  MIS_MATCH       ;Skip on a mismatch
                ADD  SI,2            ;Update pointers and counter
                ADD  DI,2
                DEC  CX
                JNZ  GO_ON           ;Repeat for the next element
                MOV  [FOUND],0H      ;If arrays are identical, save
                                     ;a zero
                JMP  DONE
MIS_MATCH:      MOV  [FOUND],SI      ;Else, save the mismatch address
DONE:           —    —
```

25. ;For the given binary number B, the BCD number's digits are given by
;D0 = R(B/10)
;D1 = R(Q(B/10)/10)
;D2 = R(Q(Q(B/10)/10)/10)
;D3 = R(Q(Q(Q(B/10)/10)/10)/10)
;where R and Q stand for the remainder and the quotient.

```
                MOV  SI,0            ;Result = 0
                MOV  CH,4            ;Counter
                MOV  BX,10           ;Divisor
                MOV  AX,DX           ;Get the binary number
NEXTDIGIT:      MOV  DX,0            ;For division make (DX) = 0
                DIV  BX              ;Compute the next BCD digit
```

```
        CMP    DX,9          ;Invalid if > 9
        JG     INVALID
        MOV    CL,12         ;Position as most significant digit
        SHL    DX,CL
        OR     SI,DX
        DEC    CH            ;Repeat for all four digits
        JZ     DONE
        MOV    CL,4          ;Prepare for next digit
        SHR    SI,CL
        JMP    NEXTDIGIT
INVALID: MOV   DX,FFFFH      ;Invalid code
        JMP    DONE1
  DONE: MOV    DX,SI
 DONE1:  —      —
```

Section 5.5

27. The call instruction saves the value in the instruction pointer, or in both the instruction pointer and code segment register, in addition to performing the jump operation.

29. IP; IP and CS

31. (a) 1075H:1000H
    (b) 1075H:0100H
    (c) 1000H:0100H

33. (a) The value in the DS register is pushed onto the top of the stack and the stack pointer is decremented by 2.
    (b) The word of data in memory location (DS)0 + (SI) is pushed onto the top of the stack and SP is decremented by 2.
    (c) The word at the top of the stack is popped into the DI register and SP is incremented by 2.
    (d) The word at the top of the stack is popped into the memory location pointed to by (DS)0 + (BX) + (DI) and SP is incremented by 2.
    (e) The word at the top of the stack is popped into the status register and SP is incremented by 2.

35. ;For the decimal number = D3D2D1D0,
    ;the binary number = 10(10(10(0+D3)+D2)+D1)+D0

```
            MOV    BX,0          ;Result = 0
            MOV    SI,0AH        ;Multiplier = 10
            MOV    CH,4          ;Number of digits = 4
            MOV    CL,4          ;Rotate counter = 4
            MOV    DI,DX
NXTDIGIT:   MOV    AX,DI         ;Get the decimal number
            ROL    AX,CL         ;Rotate to extract the digit
            MOV    DI,AX         ;Save the rotated decimal number
            AND    AX,0FH        ;Extract the digit
```

```
                ADD     AX,BX           ;Add to the last result
                DEC     CH
                JZ      DONE            ;Skip if this is the last digit
                MUL     SI              ;Multiply by 10
                MOV     BX,AX           ;and save
                JMP     NXTDIGIT        ;Repeat for the next digit
        DONE:   MOV     DX,AX           ;Result = (AX)
```

37. ;Assume that the offset of A[I] is AI1ADDR
;and the offset of B[I] is BI1ADDR

```
                MOV     AX,DATA_SEG     ;Initialize data segment
                MOV     DS,AX
                MOV     CX,62H
                MOV     SI,AI1ADDR      ;Source array pointer
                MOV     DI,BI1ADDR      ;Destination array pointer
                MOV     AX,[SI]
                MOV     [DI],AX         ;B[1] = A[1]
        MORE:   MOV     AX,[SI]         ;Store A[I] into AX
                ADD     SI,2            ;Increment pointer
                MOV     BX,[SI]         ;Store A[I+1] into BX
                ADD     SI,2
                MOV     CX,[SI]         ;Store A[I+2] into CX
                ADD     SI,2
                CALL    ARITH           ;Call arithmetic subroutine
                MOV     [DI],AX
                SUB     SI,4
                ADD     DI,2
                LOOP    MORE            ;Loop back for next element
                ADD     SI,4
        DONE:   MOV     AX,[SI]         ;B[100] = A[100]
                MOV     [DI],AX
                HLT
```

;Subroutine for arithmetic

$$;(AX) \leftarrow [(AX) - 5(BX) + 9(CX)]/4$$

```
        ARITH:  PUSHF                   ;Save flags and registers in stack
                PUSH    BX
                PUSH    CX
                PUSH    DX
                PUSH    DI
                MOV     DX,CX           ;(DX) ← (CX)
                MOV     DI,CX
                MOV     CL,3
```

```
        SAL     DX,CL
        ADD     DX,DI
        MOV     CL,2                    ;(AX) ← 5(BX)
        MOV     DI,BX
        SAL     BX,CL
        ADD     BX,DI
        SUB     AX,BX                   ;(AX) ← [(AX) − 5(BX) + 9(CX)]/4

        ADD     AX,DX
        SAR     AX,CL
        POP     DI                      ;Restore flags and registers
        POP     DX
        POP     CX
        POP     BX
        POPF
        RET                             ;Return
```

Section 5.6

39. ZF

41. Jump size = −126 to +129.

43.
```
                MOV     AL,1H
                MOV     CL,N
                JCXZ    DONE            ;N = 0 case
                LOOPZ   DONE            ;N = 1 case
                INC     CL              ;Restore N
        AGAIN:  MUL     CL
                LOOP    AGAIN
        DONE:   MOV     [FACT],AL
```

Section 5.7

45. DF

47. (a) CLD
       MOV ES,DS
       MOVSB
   (b) CLD
       LODSW
   (c) STD
       CMPSB

49. MOV   SI,OFFSET DATASEG1_ASCII_CHAR   ;ASCII offset
      MOV   DI,OFFSET DATASEG2_EBCDIC_CHAR   ;EBCDIC offset

```
        MOV     BX,OFFSET DATASEG3_ASCII_TO_EBCDIC    ;Translation
                                                      ;table offset
        CLD                         ;Select autoincrement mode
        MOV     CL,64H              ;Byte count
        MOV     AX,DATASEG1         ;ASCII segment
        MOV     DS,AX
        MOV     AX,DATASEG2         ;EBCDIC segment
        MOV     ES,AX
NEXTBYTE:
        LODSB                       ;Get the ASCII
        MOV     DX,DATASEG3         ;Translation table segment
        MOV     DS,DX
        XLAT                        ;Translate
        STOSB                       ;Save EBCDIC
        MOV     DX,DATASEG1         ;ASCII segment for next ASCII
        MOV     DS,AX               ;element
        LOOP    NEXTBYTE
DONE:   —       —
```

▲ CHAPTER 6

Section 6.2

1. **(a)** Describe the problem
   (b) Plan the steps of the solution
   (c) Implement a flowchart and assembly language program for the solution
   (d) Create a source file
   (e) Assemble the source file
   (f) Link the program into a run module
   (g) Execute and/or debug the program

3. Algorithm; software specification

7. Assembler

9. Linker

11. **(a)** PROG_A.ASM
    (b) PROG_A.LST, PROG_A.OBJ, and PROG_A.CRF
    (c) PROG_A.EXE and PROG_A.MAP

Section 6.3

13. Assembly language instructions tell the MPU what operations to perform.

15. Label, opcode, operand(s), and comment(s)

17. **(a)** Fields must be separated by at least one blank space.
    (b) Statements that do not have a label must have at least one blank space before the opcode.

19. 31

21. Operands tell where the data to be processed resides and how it is to be accessed.

23. Document what is done by the instruction or a group of instructions; comments are ignored by the assembler.

25. MOV AX,[0111111111011000B]; MOV AX,[7FD8H]

27. MOV AX,0

Section 6.4

29. Data pseudo-ops, conditional pseudo-ops, macro pseudo-ops, listing pseudo-ops

31. The symbol SRC_BLOCK is given 0100H as its value and symbol DEST_BLOCK is given 0120H as its value.

33. The variable SEG_ADDR is allocated word size memory and is assigned the value 1234_{16}.

35. INIT_COUNT DW 0F000H

37. SOURCE_BLOCK DW 0000H,1000H,2000H,3000H,4000H,5000H, 6000H,7000H,8000H,9000H,A000H,B000H,C000H,D000H,E000H,F000H

39. DATA_SEG SEGMENT   WORD   COMMON 'DATA'

DATA_SEG ENDS

41. A section of program that performs a specific function and can be called for execution from other modules.

43. An ORG statement specifies where the machine code generated by the assembler for subsequent instructions will reside in memory.

45. PAGE 55 80
TITLE BLOCK-MOVE PROGRAM

Section 6.5

47. *20 (ENTER)

49. Lines 10 through 12 are copied into lines 15 through 17, respectively

51. File, Edit, Search, and Options

Section 6. 6

53. Source module

55. Source module file = BLOCK.ASM
Object module file = BLOCK.OBJ
Source listing file = BLOCK.LST
Cross reference file = BLOCK.CRF

57. N is defined in line 13 and referenced in line 49.

Section 6.7

59. **(a)** Since separate programmers can work on the individual modules, the complete program can be written in a shorter period of time.
  (b) Because of the smaller size of modules, they can be edited and assembled in less time.
  (c) It is easier to reuse old software.
61. Run module: executable machine code version of the source program
  Link map: table showing the start address, stop address, and length of each memory segment employed by the program that was linked.

Section 6.8

63. C:\DOS>DEBUG A:LAB.EXE

▲ CHAPTER 7

Section 7.2

1. HMOS
3. 17
5. 1M byte

Section 7.3

7. The logic level of input $MN/\overline{MX}$ determines the mode. A logic 1 puts the MPU in minimum mode, and a logic 0 puts it in maximum mode.
9. $\overline{WR}$, $\overline{LOCK}$
11. $\overline{SSO}$.

Section 7.4

13. 20-bit, 8-bit; 20-bit, 16-bit
17. $\overline{BHE}$
19. $\overline{WR}$
21. HOLD, HLDA

Section 7.5

23. HOLD, HLDA, $\overline{WR}$, $IO/\overline{M}$, $DT/\overline{R}$, $\overline{DEN}$, ALE, and $\overline{INTA}$ in minimum mode are $\overline{RQ}/\overline{GT}_{1,0}$, $\overline{LOCK}$, $\overline{S}_2$-$\overline{S}_0$, QS_1, and QS_0, respectively, in the maximum mode.
25. $\overline{MRDC}$, $\overline{MWTC}$, $\overline{AMWC}$, $\overline{IORC}$, $\overline{IOWC}$, $\overline{AIORC}$, $\overline{INTA}$, MCE/PDEN, DEN, $DT/\overline{R}$, and ALE

27. $\overline{S_2}\overline{S_1}\overline{S_0} = 101_2$

29. $QS_1QS_0 = 10_2$.

Section 7.6

31. +4.5 V to +5.5 V

33. +2.0 V

Section 7.7

35. 5 MHz and 8 MHz

37. CLK, PCLK, and OSC; 10 MHz, 5 MHz, and 30 MHz

Section 7.8

39. 4; T_1, T_2, T_3, and T_4

41. An idle state is a period of no bus activity that occurs because the prefetch queue is full and the instruction currently being executed does not require bus activity.

43. 600 ns

Section 7.9

45. Address $B0003_{16}$ is applied over the lines A_0-A_{19} of the address bus, and a byte of data is fetched over data bus lines D_0-D_7. Only one bus cycle is required to read a byte from memory. Control signals in minimum mode at the time of the read are: $A_0 = 1$, $\overline{WR} = 1$, $\overline{RD} = 0$, $IO/\overline{M} = 0$, $DT/\overline{R} = 0$, and $\overline{DEN} = 0$.

47. High bank, $\overline{BHE}$

49. $\overline{BHE} = 0$, $A_0 = 0$, $\overline{WR} = 0$, $M/\overline{IO} = 1$, $DT/\overline{R} = 1$, and $\overline{DEN} = 0$

Section 7.10

51. $S_4S_3 = 10$

Section 7.11

53. $IO/\overline{M}$

55. $\overline{S_2}\overline{S_1}\overline{S_0} = 100$; $\overline{MRDC}$

57. $S_4S_3 = 01$ and $\overline{S_2}\overline{S_1}\overline{S_0} = 110$; $\overline{MWTC}$ and $\overline{AMWC}$

Section 7.12

59. Address is output on A_0 through A_{19}, ALE pulse is output, and $IO/\overline{M}$, $\overline{DEN}$ and $DT/\overline{R}$ are set to the appropriate logic levels.

61. $\overline{WR}$, $DT/\overline{R}$

Section 7.13

63. The 8288 bus controller produces the appropriately timed command and control signals needed to control transfers over the data bus.
The address bus latch is used to latch and buffer the address bits.
The address decoder decodes the higher order address bits to produce chip enable signals.
The bank write control logic determines which memory bank is selected during a write bus cycle.
The bank read control determines which memory bank is selected during a read bus cycle.
The data bus transceiver/buffer controls the direction of data transfers between the MPU and memory subsystem and supplies buffering for the data bus lines.

65. D-type latches

69. $\overline{DEN} = 0$, $DT/\overline{R} = 0$

71. $\overline{G} = 0$, $DIR = 1$, $CAB = X$, $CBA = X$, $SAB = 1$, and $SBA = X$

73. $\overline{Y_5}$

Section 7.14

75. Programmable logic array

77. Fuse links

81. 20 inputs; 8 outputs

Section 7.15

85. Programmable read only memory; erasable programmable read only memory

87. $131,072 \times 8$ bits $= 128K$ bytes

89. 27512

91. 6 V, 12.5 V

Section 7.16

93. Static random access read/write memory and dynamic random access read/write memory

95. Maintain the power supply and refresh the data periodically

97. $t_{WC} = 100$ ns, $t_{CW1} = 80$ ns, $t_{CW2} = 80$ ns, $t_{WP} = 60$ ns, $t_{DW} = 40$ ns, and $t_{WR} = 5$ ns

99. Row address and column address

101. Cost and board space required for the additional circuitry needed to perform row and column address multiplexing and periodic refreshing of the memory cells

103. $\Sigma_{\text{EVEN}} = 0$; $\Sigma_{\text{ODD}} = 1$

Section 7.17

107. Byte addresses 00000H through 03FFFH; word addresses 00000H through 03FFEH

109. 6; 3

▲ CHAPTER 8

Section 8.2

1. Isolated I/O and memory-mapped I/O

3. Memory-mapped I/O

Section 8.3

5. Address lines A_0 through A_{15} carry the address of the I/O port to be accessed; address lines A_{16} through A_{19} are held at the 0 logic level. Data bus lines D_0 through D_7 carry the data that are transferred between the MPU and I/O port.

7. In the 8086's I/O interface, the 8-bit data bus is replaced by a 16-bit data bus AD_0 through AD_{15}; control signal $IO/\overline{M}$ is replaced by $M/\overline{IO}$; and status signal $\overline{SSO}$ is replaced by $\overline{BHE}$.

9. 8288

11. $\overline{S_2 S_1 S_0} = 001$

Section 8.4

13. 16 bits

15. 32K word-wide I/O ports

17. 2; 1

Section 8.5

19. MOV DX, 1AH
   IN DX, AX

21. MOV AL,0FH
   MOV DX, 1000H
   OUT DX, AL

23. IN   AL, B0H   ;Read the input port
     AND AL,01H   ;Check the LSB
     SHR AL,1
     JC   ACTIVE_INPUT ;Branch to ACTIVE_INPUT if the LSB = 1

Section 8.6

25. Address is output in T_1; data are read (input) in T_3.

27. With two wait states, the 8086 requires 6 T-states for an output bus cycle. At 10M Hz clock, it therefore takes 600 ns for the output operation.

Section 8.7

29. $A_{15L}A_{14L} ...... A_{4L}A_{3L}A_{2L}A_{1L}A_{0L} = 1X.....X1110_2 = 800E_{16}$ with $X = 0$

31. Sets all outputs at Port 2 (O_{16}-O_{23}) to logic 1

Section 8.8

33. Port 4

35. MOV AX, 0A000H   ;Set up the segment start at A0000H
     MOV DS, AX
     MOV DX, 8002H   ;Input from port 1
     IN   AL, DX
     MOV [0000H],AL   ;Save the input at A0000H
     MOV DX,8004H   ;Input from port 2
     IN   AL, DX
     MOV [0001H], AL   ;Save the input at A0001H

Section 8.9

37. Handshaking

39. First, the address is clocked into the address latch. Address bits $A_{3L}A_{2L}A_{1L} = 000$, $A_{0L} = 0$, and $A_{15L} = 1$ enable the decoder and switch the P_0 output to 0. This output activates one input of the gate that drives the CLK input of the Port 0 latch. Later in the bus cycle, the byte of data is output on data bus lines D_0 through D_7. DT/$\overline{R}$ is logic 1 and $\overline{DEN}$ equals 0. Therefore, the transceiver is set for transmit (output) mode of operation and the byte of data is passed to the data inputs of all ports. Finally, the write pulse at $\overline{WR}$ supplies the second input of the gate for the CLK input of Port 0. Since both inputs of the gate are now logic 0, the output switches to 0. As $\overline{WR}$ returns to logic 1, the positive clock edge is presented to the latch, which enables the data to be latched and made available at outputs O_0 through O_7 of Port 0.

Section 8.10

41. Parallel I/O; 24 lines

43. Port A = mode 1 output; port B = mode 1 output

45. MODE 0 selects simple I/O operation. This means that the lines of the port can be configured as level-sensitive inputs or latched outputs. Port A and port B can be configured as 8-bit input or output ports, and port C can be configured for operation as two independent 4-bit input or output ports.

MODE 1 operation represents what is known as strobed I/O. In this mode, ports A and B are configured as two independent byte-wide I/O ports, each of which has a 3-bit control port associated with it. The control ports are formed from port C's lower and upper nibbles, respectively. When configured in this way, data applied to an input port must be strobed in with a signal produced in external hardware. An output port is provided with handshake signals that indicate when new data are available at its outputs and when an external device has read these values.

MODE 2 represents strobed bidirectional I/O. The key difference is that now the port works as either input or output and control signals are provided for both functions. Only Port A can be configured to work in this way.

47.
```
MOV   AX, 0H        ;Set up the data segment
MOV   DS, AX
MOV   AL, 92H       ;Write the control byte
MOV   [100H],AL
```

49.
```
MOV   AL, 03H       ;(AL) = control byte
MOV   DX, 100H      ;(DX) = control register address
OUT   DX, AL        ;Output the control byte to the control register
```

Section 8.11

51. The value at the inputs of port A of PPI 2 is read into AL.

53.
```
IN    AL, 08H       ;Read port A
MOV   BL, AL        ;Save in BL
IN    AL, 0AH       ;Read port B
ADD   AL, BL        ;Add the two numbers
OUT   0CH,AL        ;Output to port C
```

Section 8.12

55. To access port B on PPI 4

$A_0 = 0$, $A_2A_1 = 01$, and $A_5A_4A_3 = 010$

This gives the address = $XXXXXXXXXX010010_2 = 00012_{16}$ with Xs = 0

57.
```
MOV   BL,[0408H]    ;Read port A
MOV   AL,[040AH]    ;Read port B
```

```
ADD    AL,BL          ;Add the two readings
MOV    [040CH],AL     ;Write to port C
```

Section 8.13

59. Control word $D_7D_6D_5D_4D_3D_2D_1D_0 = 01011010_2 = 5AH$

61.
```
MOV    DX,1003H       ;Select the I/O location
MOV    AL,5AH         ;Get the control word
MOV    [DX],AL        ;Write it
```

63.
```
MOV    AL,10000000B   ;Latch counter 2
MOV    DX,1003H
MOV    [DX],AL
MOV    DX,1002H       ;Read the least significant byte
MOV    AL,[DX]
```

65. 838 ns, 500 ns

67. $N = 48_{10} = 30_{16}$

Section 8.14

69. No

71. 27

73.
```
MOV    DX,100DH
OUT    DX,AL
```

75.
```
MOV    AL, 56H
OUT    0FBH, AL
```

77.
```
MOV    DX,5008H
IN     AL,DX
```

Section 8.15

79. The system 2 activates its $\overline{RTS}$ line, which is applied to $\overline{DSR}$ of system 1. System 1 responds by activating its $\overline{DTR}$ line, which is returned to the $\overline{CTS}$ input of system 2. Then system 2 sends character bits along with the start bit and stop bits on the TX_D line. These bits are received by the terminal on its RX_D line.

Section 8.16

81. $C/\overline{D} = 0$, $\overline{RD} = 1$, $\overline{WR} = 0$, and $\overline{CS} = 0$

83.
```
MOV    AL,0FFH
MOV    MODE,AL
```

Section 8.17

85. 12 rows $\times$ 12 columns = 144 keys

87. P = 30

CLK = (100 kHz) (30) = 3 MHz

▲ CHAPTER 9

Section 9.2

1. External hardware interrupts, software interrupts, internal interrupts, nonmaskable interrupt, and reset

3. Software interrupts, external hardware interrupts, nonmaskable interrupt, and internal interrupts

5. Higher priority

Section 9.3

7. 4 bytes

9. Overflow

11. (IP_{40}) = (Location A0H), and (CS_{40}) = (Location A2H)

Section 9.4

13. Arithmetic; overflow flag

Section 9.5

15. ;This is an uninterruptible subroutine

    CLI   ;Disable interrupts at entry point

    .

    .   ;Body of subroutine

    .

    .

    STI   ;Enable interrupts

    RET   ;Return to calling program

Section 9.6

17. INTR is the interrupt request signal that must be applied to the 8088 MPU by external interrupt interface circuitry to request service for an interrupt-driven device. When this request is acknowledged by the MPU, it outputs an interrupt acknowledge bus status code on $\overline{S_2}\overline{S_1}\overline{S_0}$, and this code is decoded by the 8288 bus controller to produce the $\overline{INTA}$ signal. $\overline{INTA}$ is the signal that is used to tell the external device that its request for service has been granted.

19. D_0 through D_7

Section 9.7

21. When the 8088 microprocessor recognizes an interrupt request, it checks whether the interrupts are enabled. It does this by checking the IF. If IF is set, an interrupt acknowledge cycle is initiated. During this cycle, the $\overline{\text{INTA}}$ and $\overline{\text{LOCK}}$ signals are asserted. This tells the external interrupt hardware that the interrupt request has been accepted. Following the acknowledge bus cycle, the 8088 initiates a cycle to read the interrupt vector type. During this cycle the $\overline{\text{INTA}}$ signal is again asserted to get the vector type presented by the external interrupt hardware. Finally, the interrupt vector words corresponding to the type number are fetched from memory and loaded into IP and CS.

23. $1.8\mu s$ for three write cycles; 6 bytes

Section 9.8

25. $D_0 = 0$ ICW_4 not needed
$D_1 = 1$ Single-device
$D_3 = 0$ Edge-triggered
and assuming that all other bits are logic 0 gives
$ICW_1 = 00000010_2 = 02_{16}$

27. $D_0 = 1$ Use with the 8086/8088
$D_1 = 0$ Normal end of interrupt
$D_3 D_2 = 11$ Buffered mode master
$D_4 = 0$ Disable special fully nested mode
and assuming that the rest of the bits are logic 0, we get
$ICW_4 = 00001101_2 = 0D_{16}$

29. MOV AL, [0A001H]

31.
```
MOV  AL, [0A001H]    ;Read OCW3
MOV  [OCW3],AL       ;Copy in memory
NOT  AL              ;Extract RR bit
AND  AL,2H           ;Toggle RR bit
OR   [OCW3],AL       ;New OCW3
MOV  AL,[OCW3]       ;Prepare to output OCW3
MOV  [0A001H],AL     ;Update OCW3
```

Section 9.9

33. 22

Section 9.10

35. Vectored subroutine call

37. $CS_{80} \rightarrow$ (Location 142H) and $IP_{80} \rightarrow$ (Location 140H)

Section 9.11

39. NMI is different from the external hardware interrupts in three ways:
   (a) NMI is not masked out by IF
   (b) NMI is initiated from the NMI input lead instead of from the INTR input
   (c) The NMI input is edge-triggered instead of level sensitive like INTR. Therefore, its occurrence is latched inside the 8088 or 8086 as it switches to its active 1 logic level.

Section 9.12

41. 8284

43. FFFF0H

Section 9.13

45. Divide error, single step, breakpoint, and overflow error

47. Single step mode; $CS_1{:}IP_1$

▲ CHAPTER 10

Section 10.2

1. System address bus, system data bus, and system control bus

3. 060H, 061H, 062H, and 063H

5. Timer 0—to keep track of the time of the day, generate an interrupt to the microprocessor every 55 ms

Timer 1—to produce a DMA request every 15.12 us to initiate a refresh cycle of DRAM

Timer 2—has multiple functions, such as to generate programmable tones for the speaker and a record tone for the cassette

7. PA_0-PA_7 and PC_0-PC_3

9. Port B (PB_1)

11. Printer

13. 384K bytes

Section 10.3

15. 4.77 MHz

17. Pin 21

19. Logic 0 at $\overline{\text{DMA WAIT}}$ means wait states are required. Logic 0 at $\overline{\text{RDY}}$/ WAIT means data is ready and CPU can complete the cycle, thus wait states are not required.

21. 74LS373 latches and 74LS245 bus transceiver

23. $\overline{\text{MEMR}}$ = pin 7 and $\overline{\text{MEMW}}$ = pin 8

Section 10.4

25. I/O channel cards; 0

27. When a DMA request (DRQ_0-DRQ_3) goes active (logic 1), 8237A outputs logic 0 at HRQ $\overline{\text{DMA}}$. This signal is input to NAND gate U_{52} in the wait state logic circuit and causes logic 1 at its output. This output drives the CLR input of 74LS74 flip-flop U_{67}, which produces HOLDA, and releases the cleared flip-flop for operation. The output of NAND gate U_{52} is also used as an input to NAND gate U_5. When the 8088 outputs the status code $\overline{S_2 S_1 S_0}$ = 111 (passive state) and $\overline{\text{LOCK}}$ = 1, the output of U_5 switches to 0. This output is inverted to logic 1 at pin 8 of U_{83}.

On the next pulse at CLK, the logic 1 applied to input D_3 of flip-flop U_{98} is latched at output Q_3. Next, this output is latched into the 74LS74 flip-flop U_{67} synchronously with a pulse at CLK88 to make HOLDA logic 1. HOLDA is sent to the HLDA input of 8237A and signals that the 8088 has given up control of the system bus.

29. MOV AL,80H
OUT 0A0H,AL

31. Since the signal PCK and I/O CH CK are connected to PC_7 and PC_6 of the 8255A, respectively, the 8088 can read port C to determine which NMI source is requesting service.

PC_7	PC_6	NMI source
0	0	NP NPI
0	1	I/O CH CK
1	0	PCK

Section 10.5

33. DMA controller chip select ($\overline{\text{DMA CS}}$), interrupt controller chip select ($\overline{\text{INTR CS}}$), interval timer chip select ($\overline{\text{T/C CS}}$), and parallel peripheral interface chip select ($\overline{\text{PPI CS}}$)

35. Expressing the address in binary form, we get

$$A_{19}A_{18}A_{17}A_{16}A_{15}A_{14}A_{13}A_{12}A_{11}A_{10}A_9A_8A_7A_6A_5A_4A_3A_2A_1A_0$$
$$= 11111010000000000000$$

As the address FA000H is applied at the input of the ROM address decoder circuitry, address bits A_{16}-A_{19}, which are all 1, drive the inputs of NAND gate U_{64}. This input condition makes the $\overline{\text{ROM ADDR SEL}}$ output at pin 6 become logic 0. This signal along with $\overline{\text{XMEMR}}$ (logic 0) and $\overline{\text{RESET DRV}}$ (logic 1) enables the 74LS138 3 line-to-8 line decoder U_{46}. The inputs of this decoder are $A_{15}A_{14}A_{13} = 101$. Therefore, output $\overline{\text{CS}}_5$ switches to its active 0 level. $\overline{\text{CS}}_5$ enables EPROM XU_{31} in the ROM array and the signal $\overline{\text{ROM ADDR SEL}}$ controls the data direction through the 74LS245 bus transceiver U_{13}.

37. $\overline{\text{RAS}}_1$

Section 10.6

39. For the address $F4000_{16}$ we have A_{16}-$A_{19} = 1111$, $A_{14} = 1$, and the rest of the address bits are 0. Since A_{16}-$A_{19} = 1111$, $\overline{\text{ROM ADDR SEL}}$ is at its active 0 logic level. This output enables the 74LS138 decoder, U_{46}. Since $A_{15}A_{14}A_{13} = 010$, $\overline{\text{CS}}_2$ is active. $\overline{\text{CS}}_2$ selects XU_{28} in the ROM array and data is read from the first storage location of the EPROM chip. Also, $\overline{\text{ROM ADDR SEL}}$ directs the data from ROM to the 8088 via the 74LS245 bus transceiver U_{13}.

Section 10.7

41. DMA requests for channels 1, 2, and 3 are the I/O channel devices (boards plugged into the I/O channel).

43. *DMA page register*   *Contents*

1	A16
2	B16
3	C16

Instruction sequence:

```
MOV  AL,0AH
OUT  81H,AL
MOV  AL,0BH
OUT  82H,AL
MOV  AL,0CH
OUT  83H,AL
```

Section 10.8

45. Counter 1 divisor = 1.1 M/18.2 = 60440

Section 10.9

49. KBD IRQ is an output that is used as an interrupt to the MPU and, when active, it signals that a keyscan code needs to be read.

Section 10.10

51. I/O channel slots provide the system interface to add-on cards. Five 62-pin card slots are provided on the system board.

▲ CHAPTER 11

Section 11.2

1. Prototype circuit
3. Solderless breadboard
5. Bus interface module
I/O expansion bus cables
Breadboard unit

Section 11.3

7. The INT/EXT switch must be set to the EXT position.
9. 26 AWG
11. A_{31} through A_{12}
13. Logic 0 lights the green LED; logic 1 lights the red LED; and the high-Z level lights the amber LED.

Section 11.4

15. 74LS688, 74LS138, and 74LS32
17. A_{10} through A_{15}
19. The select outputs of the 74LS138 are gated with either $\overline{\text{IOR}}$ or $\overline{\text{IOW}}$ in 74LS32 OR gates. These signals are active only during an I/O cycle.
21. Yes
23. The setting of switch 7 is polled waiting for it to close.
25. Lights LEDs 0 through 3
27. The LEDs are lit in a binary counting pattern.
29. Change MOV CX,0FFFFH to MOV CX,7FFFH.

Section 11.5

33. IC test clip

35. Whether the test point is at the 0, 1, or high-Z logic state, or if it is pulsating

37. Amount of voltage, duration of the signal, and the signal waveshape

39. Troubleshooting

41. Hardware troubleshooting

43. **i)** Check to verify that correct pin numbers are marked into the schematic diagram.

   ii) Verify that the circuit layout diagram correctly implements the schematic.

   iii) Check that the ICs and jumpers are correctly installed to implement the circuit.

45.

Test point	Switch open	Switch closed
1	1	0
2	1	0
3	Pulse	Pulse

Section 11.6

47. Address bus, data bus, and control bus signals

49.

Oscilloscope	Logic analyzer
i) Requires periodic signal to display	**i)** Can display periodic or aperiodic signals
ii) Small number of channels	**ii)** Large number of channels
iii) Displays actual voltage values	**iii)** Displays logic values
iv) Generally does not store the signals for display	**iv)** Stores signals for display
v) Simple trigger condition using a single signal	**v)** Trigger signal can be a combination of a number of signals

▲ CHAPTER 12

Section 12.2

1. HMOSIII

3. PLCC, LCC, and PGA

Section 12.3

5. 24 bits, 16 bits

7. 6 bytes

9. The queue holds the fetched instructions for the execution unit to decode and perform the operations that they specify.

Section 12.4

11. That an 8086 object code program can run on the 80286

Section 12.5

13. Saves the contents of various registers of the processor such as AX, SP, etc., on the stack

15. Data area on the stack for a subroutine to provide space for the storage of local variables, linkage to the calling subroutine, and the return address.

17. A word of data from the word size port at address 1000H is input to the memory address 1075H:100H. The SI register is incremented to 102H, and CX is decremented by 2.

19. The instruction tests if VALUE DI lies between 0000H and 00FFH. If it is outside these bounds, interrupt 5 will occur.

Section 12.6

21. I/O write (output bus cycle)

23. No, it is one bit of a status code that must be decoded to produce an interrupt acknowledge signal.

25. 80287

Section 12.7

27. $\overline{\text{IOWC}}$

29. 1

Section 12.8

31. 25 MHz

Section 12.9

33. Four clocks; 400 ns

35. Perform-command state; external devices accept write data from the bus or, in the case of a read cycle, place data on the bus.

37. An idle state is a period of no bus activity that occurs because the prefetch queue is already full and the instruction currently being executed requires no bus activity.

Section 12.10

39. The bus controller produces the appropriately timed command and control signals needed to control transfers over the data bus. The decoder decodes the higher-order address bits to produce chip enable signals. The address latch is used to latch and buffer the lower bits of the address and chip enable signals. The data bus buffer/transceiver controls the direction of data transfers between the MPU and memory subsystem.

41. Odd-addressed byte, even-addressed byte, even-addressed word, and odd-addressed word. One bus cycle is required for any type of cycle, except the odd-addressed word cycle, which requires two bus cycles.

43. Odd-addressed byte

45. 320 ns

Section 12.11

47. M/$\overline{\text{IO}}$

49. The decoder is used to decode several of the upper I/O address bits to produce the $\overline{\text{I/OCE}}$ signals. The latch is used to latch the lower-order address bits and $\overline{\text{I/OCE}}$ outputs of the decoder. The bus controller decodes the I/O bus commands to produce the I/O and bus control signals for the I/O interface. The bus transceivers control the direction of data transfer over the bus.

51. 1.2s

Section 12.12

53. Hardware interrupts, software interrupts, internal interrupts and exceptions, software interrupts, and reset

55. Interrupt vector table; interrupt descriptor table

57. Interrupt descriptor table register, 0

59. INTR is the interrupt request signal that must be applied to the 80286 MPU by the external interrupt interface circuitry to request service for an interrupt-driven device. When this request is acknowledged by the MPU, it outputs an interrupt acknowledge bus status code on M/$\overline{\text{IO}}$ $\overline{\text{S}}_1\overline{\text{S}}_0$, and this code is decoded by the 82C288 bus controller to produce the $\overline{\text{INTA}}$ signal. $\overline{\text{INTA}}$ is the signal that is used to tell the external device that its request for service has been granted.

61. 22

63. Vectors 0 through 16

▲ CHAPTER 13

Section 13.2

1. 80386DX and 80386SX

3. 39; 49

Section 13.3

5. Bus unit, prefetch unit, decode unit, execution unit, segment unit, and page unit

7. Separate address and data buses

9. Prefetch unit

11. Translation lookaside buffer

Section 13.4

13. *Object code compatible* means that programs and operating systems written for the 8086 will run directly on the 80386DX in real-address mode.

15. FS, GS, and CR_0 registers

Section 13.5

17. DI, SI, BP, SP, BX, DX, CX, and AX

19. 1FH = 32 bytes; 4

21. The 16 bytes of data in the range 1075H:100H through 1075H:0F0H are output one after the other to the byte-wide output port at I/O address 2000H. Each time a byte is output, the count in the CX register and the pointer in SI are decremented by 1. The output sequence is repeated until the count in CX is zero.

23. MOV EBX,CR1

25. The byte of data in BL is sign-extended to 32 bits and copied into register EAX.

27. The first 32 bits of the 48-bit pointer starting at memory address DATA_F_ADDRESS are loaded into EDI and the next 16 bits are loaded into the FS register.

29. Set byte if not carry; (CF) = 0

Section 13.6

31. LIMIT and BASE

33. GTD_{START} = 210000H, GDT_{END} = 2101FFH; SIZE = 512 bytes; DESCRIPTORS = 64

35. Interrupt descriptor table register and interrupt descriptor table

37. Interrupt gates

39. Selector; the LDT descriptor pointed to by the selector is cached into the LDT cache.

41. PE

43. Task switched

45. CR$_3$

47. Page frame addresses

49. The selected task state segment descriptor is loaded into this register for on-chip access.

51. Code segment selector register; data segment selector register

53. Access the local descriptor table.

55. NT = nested task; RF = resume flag

57. 48 bits

59. 4 GB, 1 byte

61. 32 TB, 8192

63. Memory management unit

65. 00200100H

67. Offset field = 20 bit; page field = 10 bit; directory field = 10 bit

69. 4K bytes; offset of the linear address

Section 13.7

71. CS, DS, ES, FS, GS, or SS; GDTR or LDTR

73. ACCESS RIGHTS BYTE = 1AH
P = 0 = Not in physical memory
E = 1, R = 1 = Readable code segment
A = 0 = Descriptor is not cached

75. 20 most significant bits of the base address of a page table or a page frame

77. Page fault

Section 13.8

79. (INIT_GDTR) = FFFFH
(INIT_GDTR + 2) = 0000H
(INIT_GDTR + 4) = 0030H

81. MOV   BX, 2F0H
LLDT   BX

Section 13.9

83. A collection of program routines that perform a specific function

85. The descriptor is not loaded; instead, an error condition is signaled.

87. Level 3

89. Use of a separate LDT for each task

91. Current privilege level, requested privilege level

93. Level 3

95. Level 0, level 1, and level 2

97. Execution of this instruction initiates a call to a routine at a higher privilege level through the call gate pointed to by address NEW_ROUTINE.

99. Defines the state of the task that is to be initiated

101. TR

Section 13.10

103. Bit 17

105. Yes

Section 13.11

107. Floating-point math coprocessor and code and data cache memory

109. 136; 249

111. Complex instruction set computer; reduced instruction set computer, complex reduced instruction set computer

113. CRISC

115. Little endian

117.

```
                MOV   CX, COUNT
                MOV   SI, BIG_E_TABLE
                MOV   DI, LIT_E_TABLE
       NXTDW:   MOV   EAX, [SI]
                SWAP  EAX
                MOV   [DI], EAX
                ADD   SI, 04H
                ADD   DI, 04H
                LOOP  NXTDW
```

119. Since the contents of the destination operand, memory location SUM, and register AL are the same, ZF is set to 1 and the value of the source operand, 22_{16} is copied into destination SUM.

121. Cache disable (CD) and not write-through (NW)

123. WBINVD initiates a write back bus cycle instead of a flush bus cycle.

Section 13.12

125. 64 bits
127. ID, VIP, and VIF
129. 2

▲ CHAPTER 14

Section 14.2

1. CHMOSIII
3. INTR

Section 14.3

5. Byte, D_0-D_7, no
7. I/O data read
9. 80387 numeric coprocessor

Section 14.4

11. F12

Section 14.5

13. 40 ns
15. In Fig. 14.12, address n becomes valid in the T_2 state of the prior bus cycle and then the data transfer takes place in the next T_2 state. Also, at the same time that data transfer n occurs, the address n+1 is output on the address bus. This shows that during pipelining, the 80386DX starts to address the next storage location to be accessed while still reading or writing data for the previously addressed storage location.
17. An extension of the current bus cycle by a period equal to one or more T states because the $\overline{\text{READY}}$ input was tested and found to be logic 1.
19. 80 ns

Section 14.6

21. Four independent banks, each organized as 1 G $\times$ 8 bits; four banks each organized as 256 K $\times$ 8 bits
23. 120 ns; 240 ns
25. The bus control logic produces the appropriately timed command and control signals needed to control transfers over the data bus.

The address decoder decodes the higher order address bits to produce chip enable signals.

The address bus latch is used to latch and buffer the lower bits of the address and chip enable signals.

The bank write control logic determines to which memory bank $\overline{MWTC}$ is applied during write bus cycles.

The data bus transceiver/buffer controls the direction of data transfers between the MPU and memory subsystem and supplies buffering for the data bus lines.

Section 14.7

27. M/$\overline{IO}$

29. The I/O address decoder is used to decode several of the upper I/O address bits to produce the $\overline{I/O\ CE}$ signals.

The I/O address bus latch is used to latch lower order address bits and I/O $\overline{CE}$ outputs of the decoder.

The bus control logic decodes I/O bus commands to produce the input/output and bus control signals for the I/O interface.

The data bus transceivers control the direction of data transfer over the bus, multiplexes data between the 32-bit microprocessor data bus and the 8-bit I/O data bus, and supplies buffering for the data bus lines.

The I/O bank select decoder controls the enabling and multiplexing of the data bus transceivers.

31. 320 ns

33. BASE+8; LSB (bit 0)

Section 14.8

35. Interrupt vector table; interrupt descriptor table

37. Interrupt descriptor table register; 0000000003FF

39. (a) Active; (b) privilege level 2; (c) interrupt gate; (d) B000:1000

41. In the protected mode, the 80386DX's protection mechanism comes into play and checks are made to confirm that the gate is present; the offset is within the limit of the interrupt descriptor table; access byte of the descriptor for the type number is for a trap, interrupt, or task gate; and to assure that a privilege level violation will not occur.

43. Faults, traps, and aborts

45. Fault

47. Double fault, invalid task state segment, segment not present, and general protection fault

Section 14.9

49. DP_0, DP_1, DP_2, DP_3, and $\overline{PCHK}$

51. Cache enable

53. 4 double words = 16 bytes

55. Close to zero-wait-state operation, even though the system employs a main memory subsystem that operates with one or more wait states.

57. A bus cycle that reads code or data from the cache memory is called a cache hit.

59. .203 wait states/bus cycle

61. 8K bytes; line of data = 128 bits (16 bytes)

63. The contents of the internal cache are cleared. That is, the tag for each of the lines of information in the cache is marked as invalid.

Section 14.10

65. 3 million transistors

67. Data parity and address parity; $\overline{APCHK}$ = 0 address parity error and $\overline{PCHK}$ = 0 data parity error

69. Two-way set associative

71. 256 bits

Bibliography

Bradley, David J. *Assembly Language Programming for the IBM Personal Computer*. Englewood Cliffs, N.J.: Prentice-Hall, 1984.

Ciarcia, Steven. "The Intel 8086," *Byte,* November 1979.

Coffron, James W. *Programming the 8086/8088*. Berkeley, Calif.: Sybex, 1983.

Intel Corporation. *Components Data Catalog*. Santa Clara, Calif.: Intel Corporation, 1980.

————. *80286 Hardware Reference Manual*. Santa Clara, Calif.: Intel Corporation, 1987.

————. *80286 Operating Systems Writer's Guide*. Santa Clara, Calif.: Intel Corporation, 1986.

————. *80286 and 80287 Programmer's Reference Manual*. Santa Clara, Calif.: Intel Corporation, 1987.

————. *80386 Microprocessor Hardware Reference Manual*. Santa Clara, Calif.: Intel Corporation, 1987.

————. *80386 Programmer's Reference Manual*. Santa Clara, Calif.: Intel Corporation, 1987.

————. *80386 System Software Writer's Guide*. Santa Clara, Calif.: Intel Corporation, 1987.

————. *Introduction to the 80386*. Santa Clara, Calif.: Intel Corporation, September 1985.

————. *Memory*. Santa Clara, Calif.: Intel Corporation, 1989.

————. *i486™ Microprocessor Family Programmer's Reference Manual*. Santa Clara, Calif.: Intel Corporation, 1992.

————. *i486™ Microprocessor Hardware Reference Manual*. Santa Clara, Calif.: Intel Corporation, 1990.

———. *iAPX86,88 User's Manual.* Santa Clara, Calif.: Intel Corporation, July 1981.

———. *Intel486™ SX Microprocessor Data Book.* Santa Clara, Calif.: Intel Corporation, 1992.

———. *MCS-86™ User's Manual.* Santa Clara, Calif.: Intel Corporation, February 1979.

———. *Microprocessor.* Santa Clara, Calif.: Intel Corporation, 1989.

———. *Microprocessor and Peripheral Handbook,* vols. 1 and 2. Santa Clara, Calif.: Intel Corporation, 1989.

———. *Pentium™ Processors and Related Products.* Santa Clara, Calif.: Intel Corporation, 1995.

———. *Pentium™ Processor User's Manual,* vols. 1, 2, and 3. Santa Clara, Calif.: Intel Corporation, 1993.

———. *Peripheral.* Santa Clara, Calif.: Intel Corporation, 1989.

———. *Peripheral Design Handbook.* Santa Clara, Calif.: Intel Corporation, April 1978.

Morse, Stephen P. *The 8086 Primer.* Rochelle Park, N.J.: Hayden Book Company, 1978.

National Semiconductor Corporation, *Series 32000 Databook.* Santa Clara, Calif.: National Semiconductor Corporation, 1986.

Norton, Peter. *Inside the IBM PC.* Bowie, Md.: Robert J. Brady, 1983.

Rector, Russell, and George Alexy. *The 8086 Book.* Berkeley, Calif.: Osborne/McGraw-Hill, 1980.

Scanlon, Leo J. *IBM PC Assembly Language.* Bowie, Md.: Robert J. Brady, 1983.

Schneider, Al. *Fundamentals of IBM PC Assembly Language.* Blue Ridge Summit, Pa.: Tab Books, 1984.

Singh, Avtar, and Walter A. Triebel. *IBM PC/8088 Assembly Language Programming.* Englewood Cliffs, N.J.: Prentice-Hall, 1985.

Singh, Avtar, and Walter A. Triebel. *The 8088 Microprocessor: Programming, Interfacing, Software, Hardware, and Applications.* Englewood Cliffs, N.J.: Prentice-Hall, 1989.

Singh, Avtar, and Walter A. Triebel. *The 8086 and 80286 Microprocessors: Hardware, Software, and Interfacing.* Englewood Cliffs, N.J.: Prentice-Hall, 1990.

Strauss, Ed. *Inside the 80286.* New York: Brady Books, 1986.

Texas Instruments Incorporated. *Programmable Logic Data Book.* Dallas, Tex: Texas Instruments Incorporated, 1990.

Triebel, Walter A. *Integrated Digital Electronics.* Englewood Cliffs, N.J.: Prentice-Hall, 1979.

Triebel, Walter A. *The 80386DX Microprocessor: Hardware, Software, and Interfacing.* Englewood Cliffs, N.J.: Prentice-Hall, 1992.

Triebel, Walter A., and Alfred E. Chu. *Handbook of Semiconductor and Bubble Memories.* Englewood Cliffs, N.J.: Prentice-Hall, 1982.

Triebel, Walter A., and Avtar Singh. *The 8086 Microprocessor: Architecture, Software, and Interface Techniques.* Englewood Cliffs, N.J.: Prentice-Hall, 1985.

Willen, David C., and Jeffrey I. Krantz. *8088 Assembly Language Programming: the IBM PC.* Indianapolis, Ind.: Howard W. Sams, 1983.

Index